DRUGS AND CONTROLLED SUBSTANCES

Information
for Students

DRUGS AND CONTROLLED SUBSTANCES

Information *for Students*

STACEY L. BLACHFORD AND KRISTINE KRAPP, EDITORS

GALE®

Detroit • New York • San Diego • San Francisco • Cleveland • New Haven, Conn. • Waterville, Maine • London • Munich

Drugs and Controlled Substances: Information for Students

Project Editors
Stacey L. Blachford, Kristine Krapp

Editorial
Chris Jeryan, Kimberley McGrath,
Mark Springer

Permissions
Shalice Shaw

Imaging and Multimedia
Robert Duncan, Mary Grimes, Lezlie Light,
Dan Newell, David Oblender,
Christine O'Bryan, Kelly A. Quin

Product Design
Michelle Dimercurio, Tracey Rowens,
Kate Scheible

Manufacturing
Evi Seoud

Indexing
Linda Mamassian

LIBRARY OF CONGRESS CATALOG-IN-PUBLICATION DATA

Drugs and controlled substances : information for students / Stacey Blachford, Kristine Krapp, editors.
     p. cm
        Summary: Provides detailed information about the composition, history, effect, uses and abuses of common drugs, including illegal drugs and addictive substances, as well as commonly abused classes of prescription drugs.
        Includes bibliographical references and index.
        ISBN 0-7876-6264-X (hardcover : alk. paper)
        1. Drug abuse-Juvenile literature. [1. Drugs. 2. Drug abuse.] I.

HV5809.5.D784 2002
613.8—dc21
2002010925

ISBN 0-7876-6264-X
Printed in the United States of America
10 9 8 7 6 5

CONTENTS

PLEASE READ— IMPORTANT INFORMATION

Drugs and Controlled Substances: Information for Students is a medical reference product designed to inform and educate readers about a wide variety of drugs and controlled substances. The Gale Group believes the product to be comprehensive, but not necessarily definitive. It is intended to supplement, not replace, consultation with a physician or other health care practitioner. While the Gale Group has made substantial efforts to provide information that is accurate, comprehensive, and up-to-date, the Gale Group makes no representations or warranties of any kind, including without limitation, warranties of merchantability or fitness for a particular purpose, nor does it guarantee the accuracy, comprehensiveness, or timeliness of the information contained in this product. Readers should be aware that the universe of medical knowledge is constantly growing and changing, and that differences of medical opinion exist among authorities. Readers are also advised to seek professional diagnosis and treatment of any possible substance abuse problem, and to discuss information obtained from this book with their health care provider.

ADVISORY BOARD

CONTRIBUTORS

Laurie Barclay, MD: Neurologist, Neurological Consulting Services, Tampa, Florida

Christopher Barillas: Senior Editor, GayHealth.com, New York, New York

Maria Basile-Folkerts, Ph.D. candidate: Medical Writer, Hershey, Pennsylvania

Maury M. Breecher, Ph.D., M.P.H.: Health and Medical Writer, Feature Enterprises, Tarzana, California

Louise C. Chut, Ph.D., M.P.H.: Retired Professor of Public Health and Health Education, Pittsboro, North Carolina

Janet Filips: Health and Medical Writer, FilipsWrite, Inc., Eugene, Oregon

Paula Ford-Martin, MA: Principal Writer/Editor, Wordcrafts, Warwick, Rhode Island

Lisa Fratt: Medical Writer, Ashland, Wisconsin

Roberta Friedman: Freelance Science Writer, Santa Cruz, California

Candace Hoffmann: Freelance Writer and Editor, Lake Worth, Florida

Anne Jacobson, MPH: Freelance Medical Writer, Chicago, Illinois

Richard M. Kapit, M.D.: Freelance Medical and Science Writer, Garrett Park, Maryland

Marsha Lopez, Ph.D.: Faculty Research Associate, University of Maryland, Center for Substance Abuse Research, Baltimore, Maryland

L.A. McKeown: Freelance Medical Writer and Editor, Spring Lake, New Jersey

E.C. Meszaros: Freelance Clinical Writer and Editor, Cleveland, Ohio

Mark Mitchell, MD: Medical Writer, Seattle, Washington

Marianne O'Connor, MT, MPH: Medical Writer, Farmington Hills, Michigan

Alison Palkhivala: Medical Writer, Montreal, Canada

Scott Polzin, MS, CGC: Medical Writer, Buffalo Grove, Illinois

Linda Richards, RD, MS, CHES: Medical Writer, Alpine, California

Edward R. Rosick, DO, MPH: University Physician, Clinical Assistant Professor of Medicine, The Pennsylvania State University, State College, Pennsylvania

Patty Jo Sawvel: Journalist, Wake Forest University Addiction Studies Program for Journalists, Kernersville, North Carolina

Brian Sine: Freelance Writer, Kernersville, North Carolina

Genevieve Slomski, PhD: Freelance Medical Writer, New Britain, Connecticut

Barbara Sullivan Smith, M.Ed.: Family and Consumer Sciences Teacher, Bidderford Middle School, Bidderford, Maine

Kathy Stolley, Ph.D.: Senior Facilitator, Collaborative Technologies Consultant, Logicon Information Solutions, Virginia Beach, Virginia

Amy Loerch Strumolo: Freelance Writer and Editor, Beverly Hills, Michigan

Liz Swain: Freelance Writer and Editor, San Diego, California

Sue Wallace: Medical Writer, Santa Rosa, California

Ken Wells: Freelance Writer, Laguna Hills, California

Jennifer Wilson: Science Writer, Haddonfield, New Jersey

Drugs and Controlled Substances: Information for Students is a valuable source of information for students who want to learn more about commonly abused drugs and addictive substances. The book is especially appropriate for investigative assignments, as the entries include hard-to-find information on the physiological effects of these substances. The scope of this one-volume text covers illegal drugs, legal addictive drugs and other substances, and commonly abused classes of prescription and over-the-counter drugs.

Drugs and Controlled Substances: Information for Students (DCSIS) includes information that is accurate, unbiased, and highlighted by statistics. Sidebars provide additional information on the legal, historical, or social aspects of a particular drug or controlled substance. Definitions for medical or drug-related terminology are given, and variant names for drugs are featured.

How Each Entry is Organized

Entries are arranged alphabetically and follow a standardized format that allows students to easily find information, and also facilitates comparisons of different drugs. Rubrics include:

- **Official names, Street names**: This section lists the alternate names for a substance, including brand names, generic names, and chemical names for drugs, as well as common "street" names for drugs and other substances.

- **Drug classification**: This section lists the type of drug and its classification and schedule by the U.S. Drug Enforcement Administration, if applicable.

- **Overview**: Historical background is included here, including the drug's origin, development, and introduction to society. The current impact of the drug is discussed.

- **Chemical/organic composition**: This section includes discussion on the various compositions of the drug, if it is found in pure or altered forms, and whether or not it is often mixed with other substances or drugs.

- **Ingestion methods**: Availability of the drug or substance in different forms, for example, pill or powder, is discussed.

- **Therapeutic use**: This section describes the legitimate uses of the drug, including dosage information and conditions for which the drug is prescribed.

- **Usage trends:** Statistical data is provided on the national averages of usage and recent increases or declines in use. Information is broken down for age, ethnicity, and gender when available.

- **Mental effects**: The immediate, short-term, and long-term psychological effects of ingestion are discussed here.

- **Physiological effects**: This section summarizes the physical sensations found with drug use. Severe complications, overdose reactions, and special risk groups are included. Long-term physiological problems associated with drug use are discussed.

- **Reactions with other drugs or substances**: Substances or drugs that are frequently combined with the topic drug are listed, and the interaction of the two or more substances in the body are discussed.

- **Treatment and rehabilitation**: Different types of treatment and success rates are included here.

- **Personal and social consequences**: This section describes the impact of drug use on the user's personal life, including friendships, family relationships, and job performance. Also included are discussions of the drug's use on society as a whole, such as associated crime and violence.

- **Legal consequences**: Legal issues, including historical legality of the substance, are discussed here. Federal guidelines, regulations, and penalties are included.

- **See also**: This section lists other entries within the book that are related to the topic drug and may be of interest to the reader.

- **Sources**: Provided here are bibliographic citations of books, periodical content, and websites the reader can go to for more information. Also lists contact information for relevant organizations.

- **Key terms**: This is a mini-glossary of terms in the entry that may be unfamiliar to students.

In addition, a *DCSIS* entry may contain one or more of the following supplementary sidebars.

- **Law and order**: Briefly describes current or historical legal issues and rulings.

- **Fact or fiction?**: Addresses common misconceptions about drug use.

- **History notes**: Mentions historical anecdotes relevant to the topic drug.

- **In the news**: Discusses the social implications and current debate over drug use.

Additional Features

In addition to general entry information, the reader may also benefit from these features:

- Photos, illustrations, and charts within the entries that give the reader more information on the topic drug.

- A chronology of key events in the history of drug and controlled substance use and abuse.

- An insert of color photographs, making it easier for the reader to identify particular drugs.

- A glossary of drug-related terms used in the main body.

- An appendix detailing the contents of the Controlled Substances Act.

- A variant name index of chemical and "street" names that direct the reader to the main entry on the drug.

- A general index allowing easy access to entry information.

Acknowledgments

Special thanks are due to our advisory board members. The members of the advisory board performed a myriad of duties, from defining the scope of coverage to reviewing individual entries for accuracy and accessibility. The editors would like to express appreciation to them for their time and for their contributions. The contributors were skilled experts in their right, and their efforts were also invaluable in the creation of this book.

We Welcome Your Suggestions

The editors of *Drugs and Controlled Substances: Information for Students* welcome your comments and suggestions. Please direct all correspondence to:

Editor, *Drugs and Controlled Substances: Information for Students*
The Gale Group
72500 Drake Rd.
Farmington Hills, MI 48331-3535

CHRONOLOGY

c. 5000 B.C.: Dried peyote buttons, subsequently found in Shumla Cave, Texas, provide evidence of peyote use.

3500 B.C.: Jugs crafted by ancient civilizations to hold beer and wine. Alcohol used as disinfectant, medicinal remedy, and to reward soldiers.

c. 3400 B.C.: Opium is first cultivated in lower Mesopotamia. The Sumerians called the poppy Hul Gil or the "joy plant." The art of poppy cultivation subsequently spreads from the Sumerians to the Assyrians, and from the Assyrians to the Babylonians and Egyptians.

c. 2250 B.C.: World's oldest-known pharmacopeia, a Sumerian clay tablet, dated from the third century B.C., recognizes opium's psychoactive qualities and recommends its use as a painkiller, antidepressant, and sedative. It was also recommended, although with dubious efficacy, to treat gout, constipation, and forgetfulness.

c. 1300 B.C.: Peruvian carving depicts San Pedro cactus, a source of mescaline, on stone tablets.

c. 1000 B.C.: Marijuana used in Indian Hindu religious rituals and meditation. The Artharvaveda, one of the four Vedas, or sacred Hindu texts, portrays cannabis as a divine elixir that eases anxiety. Ancient Indian physicians prescribed marijuana for malaria and rheumatism, presumably for its analgesic qualities.

c. 700 B.C.: Archaeological tablets record that Persians and Assyrians also used cannabis as a drug.

c. 500 B.C.: Greek priests control the use of opium and ascribe supernatural powers to the drug.

c. 400 B.C.: Ancient Greek physician Hippocrates dismisses the supernatural attributes of opium. Hippocrates asserts opium has cathartic, narcotic, hypnotic, and styptic properties.

c. 4: Central American carvings and paintings depict the practice of extracting and ingesting the psychoactive psilocybin liquid from pulverized *Psilocybe* mushrooms.

c. 200: Chinese surgeons boil hemp in wine to produce an anesthetic called *ma fei san*.

c. 200: Galen (129–c. 199), the preeminent medical authority of late Antiquity and the Middle Ages, creates a philosophy of medicine, anatomy, and physiology that remains virtually unchallenged until the sixteenth and seventeenth centuries.

c. 250: Hua To, Chinese surgeon of the Three Kingdoms (A.D. 220–264) records widespread use of opium.

c. 300: Zosimus of Panopolis, Greek alchemist, founds a school in Alexandria where pupils are taught the basic chemical operations of filtration, fusion, sublimation, and distillation.

c. 400: Hemp cultivated in Europe and in England.

c. 900: Rhazes (845–930), Persian physician and alchemist, uses his knowledge of chemistry in the practice of medicine.

1000: In Coahuila, Mexico, corpses are buried with beaded necklaces of dried peyote buttons.

c. 1100: Updated version of *Mappae clavicula* contains the first description of a liquid, distilled from wine, that will catch fire. It is named "alcohol" in the sixteenth century.

c. 1150: Hildegard of Bingen (1098–1179) publishes *The Book of Simple Medicine*, a treatise on the medicinal qualities of plants and minerals.

c. 1200: Peoples of pre-Hispanic America throughout the Inca Empire (1200–1553) chew coca leaves for their stimulating effects and view the plant as a divine gift of the Sun God.

1202: English law, the Assize of Bread, prohibits adulteration of bread.

c. 1275: Arnold of Villanova (1235–1311), Spanish alchemist, first prepares pure alcohol.

c. 1300: Arabs develop the technique of roasting coffee beans (native to the Kaffa region of Ethiopia), and cultivation for medicinal purposes begins.

1348: The beginning of a three-year epidemic caused by *Yersinia pestis* that kills almost one-third of the population of urban Europe. In the aftermath of the epidemic, measures are introduced by the Italian government to improve public sanitation, marking the origin of public health.

c. 1350: Germany bans the sale of alcohol on Sundays and other religious holidays.

c. 1350: John of Rupescissa writes his *Liber lucis* in which he extols the therapeutic value of the quintessence of wine (alcohol). He also describes how to build an alchemical furnace.

c. 1500: Following the Spanish conquest of the Aztecs, unsuccessfully attempts are made to eradicate the use of the "magic mushroom" (*Psilocybe* mushrooms) in Central America.

1500: Hieronymus Brunschwig (c. 1450–c. 1512) of Germany writes his *Kleines Distillierbuch*. This copiously illustrated work remained the most important book on distilling for decades.

c. 1500: With the rise of the national navies during the sixteenth century, hemp farming is encouraged in England and continental Europe to meet the demand for rope and naval rigging.

c. 1525: Paracelsus (1493–1541), Swiss physician and alchemist, uses mineral substances as medicines. Denying Galen's authority, Paracelsus teaches that life is a chemical process.

1540: Valerius Cordus (1515–1544), German physician, provides the first written description of how to prepare ether.

1543: Andreas Vesalius (1514–1564) publishes his epoch-making treatise *The Fabric of the Human Body*. He generally accepted Galenic physiological doctrines.

c. 1550: Fray Bernardino Sahagun (1499–1590), a Spanish missionary who lived with and studied the Indians of Mexico, provides the earliest documented information about peyote. He writes that the Chichimecas and the Toltec Indians probably used peyote as early as 300 B.C.

1556: Andre Thevet brings tobacco seeds to France from Brazil, thus introducing tobacco to western Europe. Jean Nico ascribed medicinal properties to tobacco in 1559 at the French court, and the plant was renamed nicotina in his honor. By 1565, tobacco seeds were brought to England, where smoking was later made popular by Sir Walter Raleigh.

1568: Italian physician Constanzo Varolio (1543–1575) makes available to other scholars his independent studies of the structure of the human brain.

1583: Andreas Cesalpino (Cesalpinus) writes *On Plants*, a landmark in the development of botanical taxonomy.

1610: First chemistry textbook, *Tyrocinium chymicum*, is written by French chemist Jean Béguin (c. 1550–c. 1620) and published in Paris.

1612: Tobacco cultivation begins in America and soon becomes a major New World crop. Exports to England begin in 1613, with the first shipment by John Rolfe.

1614: Italian physician Santorio Santorio (1561–1636) publishes studies on metabolism.

1640: First distillery established in United States.

1665: Robert Hooke (1635–1703) publishes *Micrographia*, an account of observations made with the new instrument known as the microscope. Hooke presents his drawings of the tiny box-like structures found in cork and calls these tiny structures "cells." Although the cells he observes are not living, the name is retained. He also describes the streaming juices of live plant cells.

1709: John Freind (1675–1728), English physician and chemist, publishes *Praelectiones Chemicae*, one of the earliest attempts to use Newtonian principles to explain chemical phenomena.

1732: Herman Boerhaave (1668–1738), Dutch physician, publishes his *Elementa Chemicae*, whose comprehensiveness makes it the most popular chemical textbook for many decades. It serves chemistry as a great teaching book and presents a concise outline of all chemical knowledge.

1735: Carl Linnaeus (1707–1778) publishes his *Systema Naturae, or The Three Kingdoms of Nature Systematically Proposed in Classes, Orders, Genera, and Species*, a methodical and hierarchical classification of all living beings. He develops the binomial nomenclature for the classification of plants and animals. In this system, each type of living being is classified in terms of genus (denoting the group to which it belongs) and species (its particular, individual name). His classification of plants is primarily based on the characteristics of their reproductive organs.

1757: Albrecht von Haller (1757–1766), publishes the first volume of his eight-volume *Elements of Physiology of the Human Body*, which subsequently became a landmark in the history of modern physiology.

1772: Nitrous oxide is discovered by English scientist, theologian, and philosopher Joseph Priestly (1733–1804).

1775: William Withering, an English physician with a strong interest in botany, was the first to introduce the cardiotonic drug digitalis (from the foxglove plant *Digitalis purpurea*) into common medical practice for the treatment of dropsy. Dropsy is a now-obsolete term for edema (fluid retention or swelling) due to heart failure.

1798: Government legislation is passed to establish hospitals in the United States devoted to the care of ill mariners. This initiative leads to the establishment of a Hygenic Laboratory that eventually grows to become the National Institutes of Health.

1799: Chinese emperor Kia King's ban on opium fails to stop lucrative British monopoly over the opium trade.

1799: English scientist Humphrey Davy (1778–1829) suggests nitrous oxide can be used to reduce pain during surgery.

c. 1800: Records indicate use of chloral hydrate in the "Mickey Finn," an anesthetic cocktail used to abduct or lure sailors to serve on ships bound for sea.

1802: John Dalton (1766–1844) introduces modern atomic theory into the science of chemistry.

1804: German pharmacist F. W. Serturner discovers how to isolate the chemical morphine from the poppy plant (*Papaver somniferum*).

1820: First United States *Pharmacopoeia* is published.

1820: Methylxanthine crystals are isolated from coffee beans.

1823: Justus von Liebig (1803–1873) and Friedrich Wöhler (1800–1882), both German chemists, make a simultaneous discovery of isomerism. In this intriguing concept, two or more compounds can have the same chemical formula and yet have different structures and properties.

1824: Performances at London's West End Aldelphi Theatre entitled "M. Henry's Mechanical and Chemical Demonstrations" showed the effects of nitrous oxide on audience volunteers.

1826: René-Joachim-Henri Dutrochet (1776–1847), French physiologist, conducts the first quantitative experiments on osmosis. He determines that the pressures involved during the diffusion of solutions are proportional to the solution concentrations. He is also the first to observe the motion of particles suspended in a liquid, later called Brownian motion.

1827: Caffeine from tea, originally named "theine," is isolated.

1828: Friedrich Wöhler synthesizes urea. This is generally regarded as the first organic chemical produced in the laboratory, and an important step in disproving the idea that only living organisms can produce organic compounds. Work by Wöhler and others establish the foundations of organic chemistry and biochemistry.

1828: Luigi Rolando (1773–1831), Italian anatomist, achieves the first synthetic electrical stimulation of the brain.

1828: Nicotine ($C_{10}H_{14}N_2$, beta-pyridyl-alpha-N methylpyrrolidine), a highly poisonous alkaloid, is first isolated from tobacco.

1829: Salicin, the precursor of aspirin, is purified from the bark of the willow tree.

1831: Charles Robert Darwin (1809–1882) begins his historic voyage on the H.M.S. *Beagle* (1831–1836). His observations during the voyage lead to his theory of evolution by means of natural selection.

1832: French chemist Michel Chevreul (1786–1889) isolates creatine from muscle tissue.

1832: Heinrich Wilhelm Ferdinand Wackenroder (1798–1854), German chemist, discovers carotene (carotin) in carrots. This organic compound is usually found as pigment in plants, giving them a yellow, red, or orange color, and is converted in the liver into vitamin A.

1832: Pierre-Jean Robiquet (1780–1840), French apothecary, discovers codeine. Codeine is an alkaloid found in opium that is now used in prescription pain relievers and cough medicines.

1832: The French physiologist Anselme Payen (1795–1871) isolates diastase from barley. Diastase catalyzes the conversion of starch into sugar, and is an example of the organic catalysts within living tissue that eventually come to be called enzymes.

1837: Endinburgh chemist and physician William Gregory discovers a more efficient method to isolate and purify morphine.

1839: First Opium War begins between Britain and China. The conflict lasts until 1842. Imperial Chinese commissioner Lin Tse-Hsu seized or destroyed vast amounts of opium, including stocks owned by British traders. The result was a Chinese payment of an indemnity of more than 21 million silver dollars, and Hong Kong was ceded to Britain under the Treaty of Nanking.

1839: Theodore Schwann (1810–1882) extends the theory of cells to include animals and helps establish the basic unity of the two great kingdoms of life. He publishes *Microscopical Researches into the Accordance in the Structure and Growth of Animals and Plants*, in which he asserts that all living things are made up of cells, and that each cell contains certain essential components. He also coins the term "metabolism" to describe the overall chemical changes that take place in living tissues.

1841: Anesthetic properties of ether were first used by Dr. Crawford W. Long as he surgically removed two tumors from the neck of an anesthetized patient.

1844: First recorded use of nitrous oxide in United States dental practice by Gardner Quincy Colton, a former medical student, and dentist Horace Wells at Hartford, Connecticut.

1846: Louis Pasteur (1822–1895), French chemist, discovers molecular asymmetry and demonstrates the existence of isomers, becoming one of the earliest scientists to deal with the three-dimensional structure of molecules.

1848: Unites States Congress passes Drug Importation Act that allows United States Customs Service inspection to stop entry of foreign drugs.

1856: Second Opium War begins between Britain and China. The conflict lasts until 1860. Also known as the Arrow War, or the Anglo-French War in China, the war broke out after a British-flagged ship, the *Arrow*, is impounded by China. France joins Britain in the war after the murder of a French missionary. China is again defeated, resulting in another large indemnity and the legalization of opium under the Treaty of Tientsin.

1857: Louis Pasteur demonstrates that lactic acid fermentation is caused by a living organism. Between 1857 and 1880, he performs a series of experiments that refute the doctrine of spontaneous generation. He also introduces vaccines for fowl cholera, anthrax, and rabies, based on attenuated strains of viruses and bacteria.

1860: First use of sedative-hypnotic, or minor tranquilizer, bromide.

1860: German chemist, Albert Niemann, separates cocaine from the coca leaf.

1861: Alexander Mikhailovich Butlerov (1828–1886), Russian chemist, introduces the term "chemical structure" to mean that the chemical nature of a molecule is determined not only by the number and type of a atoms but also by their arrangement.

1861: Morphine gains wide medical use during United States Civil War.

1862: Department of Agriculture establishes the Bureau of Chemistry, the organizational forerunner of the Food and Drug Administration.

1863: German chemist Adolf von Baeyer (1835–1917) discovers barbituric acid.

1864: Amyl nitrite is first synthesized. During the last decades of the twentieth century, amyl nitrite and similar compounds (e.g., butyl, isobutyl, isoamyl, isopropyl, and cyclohexyl nitrates and nitrites) become the chemical basis of "poppers."

1864: German scientists von Mering and Fischer synthesize the first barbiturate.

1865: Gregor Mendel (1822–1884) presents his work on hybridization of peas to the Natural History Society of Brno, Czechoslovakia. The paper is published in the 1866 issue of the Society's *Proceedings*. Mendel presents statistical evidence that hereditary factors are inherited from both parents in a series of papers

on "Experiments on Plant Hybridization," published between 1866 and 1869. His experiments provide evidence of dominance, the laws of segregation, and independent assortment, although the work is generally ignored until 1900.

1867: Thomas Lauder Brunton (1844–1916), a medical student in Scotland, discovers that amyl nitrite relieves angina by increasing blood flow to the heart. A few years later, nitroglycerine is discovered to have similar dilating effect. Although both can still be prescribed for angina, nitroglycerine became more commonly prescribed because it is more easily administered and has fewer side effects.

1870: French researcher C. A. Natvelle purifies a substance he called digitalin from the foxglove leaf. This purified substance ultimately led to the formulation of the conventional cardiac drugs digoxin and digitoxin.

1871: Companies in both America and the United Kingdom succeed in producing compressed and liquid nitrous oxide in cylinders.

1879: Memphis, Tennessee, public health agency targets opium dens by making it illegal to sell, own, or borrow "opium or any deleterious drug" or the related paraphernalia. Critics point to a hypocrisy in denying the Chinese their accustomed comfort while white citizens could freely purchase morphine—indeed, could inhale, drink, or inject it. Not until 1909 did federal law outlaw smoking or possessing opium.

1880: David Ferrier (1843–1928), Scottish scientist, maps the region of the brain called the motor cortex and discovers the sensory strip.

1880: First attempt at passage of a nationwide food and drug law. Although defeated in Congress, United States Department of Agriculture's findings of widespread food adulteration spur continued interest in food and drug legislation.

1882: Production of the drug barbital begins, and doctors begin using the barbiturate in treatment protocols.

1887: Amphetamines are first synthesized.

1891: *British Medical Journal* reports that Indian hemp was frequently prescribed for "a form of insanity peculiar to women."

1891: Charles-Edouard Brown-Sequard suggests the concept of internal secretions (hormones).

1893: The first diet pills (e.g., thyroid extracts) are marketed in United States.

1895: Heinrich Dreser, working for the Bayer Company in Germany, produces a drug he thought was as effective an analgesic as morphine, but without its harmful side effects. Bayer began mass production of diacetylmorphine, and in 1898 began marketing the new drug under the brand name "Heroin" as a cough sedative.

1897: German chemist Arthur Heffter identifies mescaline as the chemical responsible for peyote's hallucinogenic effects.

1897: United States passes Tea Importation Act, allowing inspection of all foreign tea.

1898: Association of Official Agricultural Chemists (now AOAC International) establishes Committee on Food Standards.

1898: *King's American Dispensatory* called *Cannabis indica* "one of the most important of our remedies," particularly for "marked nervous depression..."

1898: German chemical company Bayer aggressively markets heroin as a cough cure for the rampant disease of the time, tuberculosis.

1901: Jokichi Takamine (1854–1922), Japanese-American chemist, and T. B. Aldrich first isolate epinephrine from the adrenal gland. Later known by the trade name Adrenalin, it is eventually identified as a neurotransmitter.

1902: Biologics Control Act is passed to ensure the safety of vaccines and serum used in clinical medicine.

1902: Carl Neuberg (1877–1956) introduces the term biochemistry.

1902: Ernest H. Starling (1866–1927) and William H. Bayliss (1860–1924), both English physiologists, discover and isolate the hormone "secretin," found in the duodenum.

1902: Santiago Ramon y Cajal (1852–1911), Spanish histologist, first discovers the nature of the connection between nerves, showing that the nervous system consists of a maze of individual cells. He demonstrates that neurons do not touch, but that the signal somehow crosses a gap (now termed a synapse.)

1902: United States Bureau of Chemistry expands studies of effects of chemical preservatives.

1902: United States law contains first regulations regarding artificial colors suitable for use in foods.

1903: Barbiturate-containing Veronal is marketed as a sleeping pill.

1903: Barbiturates (a class of drugs with more effective sedative-hypnotic effects) replace most use of sedative bromides.

1903: To determine the safety of additives and preservatives in foods and medicines, the United States government established a "poison squad," a group of young men who volunteered to eat foods treated with chemicals such as borax, formaldehyde, and benzoic acid. The poison squad was established by Dr. Harvey W. Wiley (1844–1930), head of the United States Bureau of Chemistry, the precursor to the FDA.

1906: Japan begins the production of monosodium glutamate as a flavor enhancer for foods. By 1926, production reaches industrial proportions.

1906: United States Congress passes Pure Food and Drug Act.

1909: Congressional legislation stopped U.S. imports of smokable opium or opium derivatives except for medicinal purposes.

1909: Jean Mayer (1920–1993), French physiologist, first suggests the name "insulin" for the hormone of the islet cells.

1909: Korbinian Bordmann (1868–1918), German neurologist, publishes a "map" of the cerebral cortex, assigning numbers to particular regions.

1910: Britain signs an agreement with China to dismantle the opium trade. However, the profits made from its cultivation, manufacture, and sale were so enormous that no serious interruption was felt until World War II closed supply routes throughout Asia.

1912: Casimir Funk (1884–1967), Polish-American biochemist, coins the term "vitamine." Because the dietary substances he discovers are in the amine group, he calls all of them "life-amines" (using the Latin word *vita* for "life").

1912: Ecstasy, 3,4-Methylenedioxymethamphetamine (MDMA), is developed in Germany.

1912: Phenobarbital is introduced under the trade name Luminal.

1912: The United States Public Health Service is established.

1912: United States Congress enacts the Shirley Amendment that prohibits false therapeutic claims in advertising or labeling medicines.

1913: United States Congress passes the Gould Amendment requiring accurate and clear labeling of weights, measures, and numbers on food packages.

1914: Harrison Narcotic Act bans opiates and cocaine in the United States. Only their use as a local anesthetic is legally retained.

1916: Oxycodone is first developed in Germany and marketed under the brand name Eukodal.

1918: Native American Church (NAC) is founded and formalizes the ritual use of peyote. Ultimately the United States government exempts the NAC from the ban on peyote if it is used as part of a bona fide religious ceremony. This point remains a center of legal controversy in states that want to limit its use or outlaw it completely.

1919: *The American Materia Medica, Therapeutics and Pharmacognosy* lists piperazines as a therapeutic agent able "soothing to the irritated (renal) passages."

1919: Eighteenth Amendment to the Constitution of the United States (ratified on January 29, 1919) ushers in prohibition laws prohibiting the sale and consumption of alcohol in United States.

1919: Methamphetamine is first manufactured in Japan.

1919: Volstead Act, passed by the U.S. Congress, defines "intoxicating liquor" as any beverage that contained as much as 0.5% alcohol (thus including beer as well as hard liquor).

1922: *The Eclectic Materia Medica, Pharmacology and Therapeutics*, recommends cannabis for: "marked nervous depression ... wakefulness in fevers; insomnia..."

1925: Johannes Hans Berger (1873–1941), German neurologist, records the first human electroencephalogram (EEG).

1925: League of Nations adopts strict rules governing international heroin trade.

1926: Phencyclidine (PCP) is first synthesized.

1927: Albert Szent-Györgyi (1893–1986), Hungarian-American physicist, discovers ascorbic acid, or vitamin C, while studying oxidation in plants.

1928: Adolf Windaus (1867–1959), German chemist, receives the Nobel Prize in chemistry for his research of the sterols and their connection with vitamins.

1929: Scottish biochemist Alexander Fleming (1881–1955) discovers penicillin. He observes that the mold *Penicillium notatum* inhibits the growth of some bacteria. This is the first antibiotic, and it opens a new era of "wonder drugs" to combat infection and disease.

1929: Willard Myron Allen, American physician, and George W. Corner (1889–1981), American anatomist, discover progesterone. They demonstrate that it is necessary for the maintenance of pregnancy.

1930: United States Food, Drug, and Insecticide Administration is renamed Food and Drug Administration (FDA).

1931: Amphetamine-based inhaler marketed to relieve the discomfort of nasal congestion due to colds, hay fever, and asthma.

1932: Pharmaceutical manufacturer Smith, Kline and French introduced Benzedrine, an over-the-counter amphetamine based inhaler for relieving nasal congestion.

1933: Twenty-first Amendment to the Constitution repeals Eighteenth Amendment and makes it legal to sell and consume alcohol in United States.

1935: Federal Bureau of Narcotics, forerunner of the modern Drug Enforcement Administration (DEA), begins a campaign that portrayed marijuana as a drug that led users to drug addiction, violence, and insanity. The government produced films such as *Marihuana* (1935), *Reefer Madness* (1936), and *Assassin of Youth* (1937).

1935: First Alcoholics Anonymous (AA) group is formed in Akron, Ohio.

1935: Testosterone is first isolated in the laboratory.

1936: Sulphonamides, a class of antibacterial drugs, is introduced.

1936: United States government begins to open a series of facilities to help deal with a rising number of opiate addicts in the United States.

1937: Amphetamine is used to treat a condition known as minimal brain dysfunction, a disorder later renamed attention deficit hyperactivity disorder (ADHD).

1937: Diethylene glycol, in elixir of sulfanilamide, kills 107 people, including many children. The mass poisoning highlights the need for additional legislation regarding drug safety.

1937: Marijuana Tax Act effectively criminalized its use and possession, even for medical reasons.

1938: Federal Food, Drug, and Cosmetics Act gives regulatory powers to the Food and Drug Administration (FDA).

1938: Federal Food, Drug, and Cosmetics Act stipulates that new drugs be clinically tested and safe.

1938: Meperidine synthesis initiates a string of synthetic opioids.

1938: Swiss chemist Albert Hofmann at Sandoz Laboratories synthesizes LSD. After initial testing on animals, Hoffman's subsequent accidental ingestion of the drug in 1943 reveals LSD's hallucinogenic properties.

1938: The Wheeler-Lea Act empowers U.S. Federal Trade Commission with the oversight of non-prescription drug advertising otherwise regulated by FDA.

1939: Ernest Chain (1906–1979) and H. W. Florey (1898–1968) refine the purification of penicillin, allowing the mass production of the antibiotic.

1939: Methadone, a synthetic opioid narcotic, is discovered in Germany. Originally named Amidon, methadone was used mainly as a pain reliever.

1940: Ernest Chain and E. P. Abraham detail the inactivation of penicillin by a substance produced by *Escherichia coli*. This is the first bacterial compound known to produce resistance to an antibacterial agent.

1940: FDA shifts to Federal Security Agency from the Department of Agriculture.

1941: FDA is required to test and establish purity and effectiveness of insulin.

1942: Opium Poppy Control Act outlaws possession of opium poppies in United States.

1942: Selman Waksman (1888–1973) suggests that the word "antibiotics" be used to identify antimicrobial compounds that are made by bacteria.

1944: New techniques and instruments, such as partition chromatography on paper strips and the photoelectric ultraviolet spectrophotometer, stimulate the development of biochemistry after World War II. New methodologies make it possible to isolate, purify, and identify many important biochemical substances, including the purines, pyrimidines, nucleosides, and nucleotides derived from nucleic acids.

1944: To combat battle fatigue during World War II, nearly 200 million amphetamine tablets are issued to American soldiers stationed in Great Britain during the war.

1944: United States Public Health Service Act is passed.

1945: After World War II, anabolic-androgenic steroids (AASs) are given to many starving concentration camp survivors to help them add skeletal muscle and build up body weight.

1945: FDA is required to test and certify the safety and effectiveness of penicillin and penicillin derivatives. Obsolete by the early 1980s, this mandate was discontinued in 1983.

1945: New techniques and instruments, such as partition chromatography on paper strips and the photoelectric ultraviolet spectrophotometer, stimulate the development of biochemistry after World War II. New methodologies make it possible to isolate, purify, and identify many important biochemical substances.

1948: Australian psychiatrist John Cade finds that lithium has a controlling effect on mania.

1948: Supreme Court ruling allows the Food and Drug Administration (FDA) to investigate drugs sales at the pharmacy level.

1948: World Health Organization is formed. The WHO subsequently became the principle international organization managing public health-related issues on a global scale. Headquartered in Geneva, the WHO became, by 2002, an organization of more than 190 member countries. The organization contributes to international public health in areas including disease prevention and control, promotion of good health, addressing diseases outbreaks, initiatives to eliminate diseases (e.g., vaccination programs), and development of treatment and prevention standards.

1949: FDA publishes "black book" guide to toxicity of chemicals in food.

1949: John F. Ender (1897–1985), Thomas H. Weller (1915–), and Frederick C. Robbins (1916–) publish "Cultivation of Polio Viruses in Cultures of Human Embryonic Tissues." The report by Enders and coworkers is a landmark in establishing techniques for the cultivation of poliovirus in cultures on non-neural tissue and for further virus research. The technique leads to the polio vaccine and other advances in virology.

1950: A United States Court of Appeals rules that drug labels must include intended regular uses of the drug.

1950: The artificial sweetener cyclamate is first introduced to the market by Abbot Laboratories under the name Sucaryl. It does not have saccharin's aftertaste and becomes essential to the low-calorie soft drink industry.

1951: U.S. Durham-Humphrey Amendment defines conditions under which drugs require medical supervision and further requires that prescriptions be written only by a licensed practitioner.

1952: Alan L. Hodgkin (1914–1998) and Andrew F. Huxley (1917–), both English physiologists, first work out the mechanism of nerve-impulse transmission, showing that a "sodium pump" system works to carry impulses.

1952: Clinical effectiveness allows Reserpine to rapidly replace induced insulin shock therapy (injecting patients with insulin until their blood sugar levels fall so low that they become comatose); electroconvulsive (ECT) therapy (inducing seizures by passing an electric current through the brain); and lobotomy (making an incision in the lobe of the brain) as treatments for certain types of mental illness. Moreover, knowledge about the chemistry of this natural plant stimulated the synthesis of other similar alkaloids that were later used as major tranquilizers.

1952: James T. Park (1922–) and Jack L. Strominger (1925–) demonstrate that penicillin blocks the synthesis of the peptidoglycan of bacteria. This represents the first demonstration of the action of a natural antibiotic.

1953: English novelist Aldous Huxley (1894–1963) publishes *The Doors of Perception*, a book in which he recounts his experiences with peyote.

1953: FDA is required to provide notice of finding in factory inspections and analyses of samples.

1953: James D. Watson (1928–) and Francis H. C. Crick (1916–) publish two landmark papers in the journal *Nature*. The papers are entitled *Molecular structure of nucleic acids: a structure for deoxyribose nucleic acid* and *Genetic implications of the structure of deoxyribonucleic acid*. Watson and Crick propose a double helical model for DNA and call attention to the genetic implications of their model. Their model is based, in part, on the x-ray crystallographic work of Rosalind Franklin (1920–1958) and the biochemical work of Erwin Chargaff (1905–). Their model explains how the genetic material is transmitted.

1953: Jonas Salk (1915–1995) begins testing a polio vaccine comprised of a mixture of killed viruses.

1953: Narcotics Anonymous (NA) is founded.

1953: United States Federal Security Agency becomes the Department of Health, Education, and Welfare (HEW).

1954: Frederick Sanger (1918–) determines the entire sequence of the amino acids in insulin.

1954: Piperazines find established use in veterinary medicine as anthelminthic drugs, designed to rid the lower intestinal tract of parasitic worms.

1955: National Institutes of Health organizes a Division of Biologics Control within FDA, following death from faulty polio vaccine.

1955: Scientists in India first synthesize methaqualone.

1955: Vincent Du Vigneaud (1901–1978), American biochemist, receives the Nobel Prize in Chemistry for his work on biochemically important sulfur compounds, especially for the first synthesis of a polypeptide hormone.

1956: American Medical Association defines alcoholism as a disease.

1956: Dimethyltriptamine (DMT) is demonstrated to be hallucinogenic.

1957: Alick Isaacs (1921–1967) and Jean Lindenmann (1924–) publish their pioneering report on the drug interferon, a protein produced by interaction between a virus and an infected cell that can interfere with the multiplication of viruses.

1957: Researchers John Baer, Karl Beyer (1914–1996), James Sprague (1916–), and Frederick Novello formulate the drug chlorothiazide, the first of the thiazide diuretics. This groundbreaking discovery marked a new era in medicine as the first safe and effective long-term treatment for chronic hypertension and heart failure.

1957: The World Health Organization advances the oral polio vaccine developed by Albert Sabin (1906–1993) as a safer alternative to the Salk vaccine.

1958: Aaron B. Lerner (1920–) isolates melatonin from the pineal gland.

1958: FDA publishes list of substances generally recognized as safe.

1958: The Parke-Davis pharmaceutical company synthesizes and patents PCP. After testing, Parke-Davis sells the drug as a general anesthetic called Sernyl.

1958: United States government passes food additives amendments that require manufacturers to establish safety and to eliminate additives demonstrated to cause cancer.

1959: Fentanyl, is first synthesized in Belgium by Janssen Parmaceutica, and used as a pain management drug.

1960: FDA requires warnings on labels of potentially hazardous household chemicals.

1960: Gamma butyrolactone (GBL) is first synthesized.

1960: GHB, a fast-acting central nervous system depressant, is developed as an alternative anesthetic (painkiller) for use in surgery because of its ability to induce sleep and reversible coma.

1961: Commencing a two year study, Harvard professor Timothy Leary attempts to reform criminals at the Massachusetts Correctional Institute. The inmates were given doses of psilocybin and psychological therapy. Ultimately, the psilocybin-subjected inmates

had the same rate of return to prison as the inmates who were not part of the study. In addition to this, they had more parole violations than the general parolees.

1961: Ketamine (originally CI581) is discovered by Calvin Stevens of Wayne State University.

1962: American Medical Association published a public warning in its journal *JAMA* regarding the increasingly widespread use of LSD for recreational purposes.

1962: Thalidomide, a sleeping pill, is discovered to be the cause of widespread and similar birth defects in babies born in England and western Europe. The FDA bans the drug in the United States.

1962: United States Congress passes Kefauver-Harris Drug Amendments that shift the burden of proof of clinical safety to drug manufacturers. For the first time, drug manufacturers had to prove their products were safe and effective before they could be sold.

1963: John Carew Eccles (1903–1997), Australian neurophysiologist, shares a Nobel Prize for his work on the mechanisms of nerve-impulse transmission. He also suggests that the mind is separate from the brain. The mind, he affirms, acts upon the brain by effecting subtle changes in the chemical signals that flow among brain cells.

1964: The first Surgeon General's Report on Smoking and Health is released, and the U.S. government first acknowledges and publicizes that cigarette smoking is a leading cause of cancer, bronchitis, and emphysema.

1965: At the height of tobacco use in America, surveys show 52% of adult men and 32% of adult women use tobacco products.

1965: Because of disturbing side effects including horrible nightmares, delusions, hallucinations, agitation, delirium, disorientation, and difficulty speaking, PCP use on humans is stopped in the United States. PCP continues to be sold as a veterinary anesthetic under the brand name Sernylan.

1965: James M. Schlatter, American chemist, combines two amino acids and obtains a sweet-tasting substance. This chemical is about 200 times sweeter than sugar and is named aspartame. In 1983, it is approved for use in carbonated beverages. It becomes the most widely used artificial sweetener.

1965: Manufacture of LSD becomes illegal in the United States. A year later is made illegal in the United Kingdom. The FDA subsequently classifies LSD as a Schedule I drug in 1970.

1965: United States Congress passes Drug Abuse Control Amendments—legislation that forms the FDA Bureau of Drug Abuse Control and gives the FDA tighter regulatory control over amphetamines, barbiturates, and other prescription drugs with high abuse potential.

1966: FDA and the National Academy of Sciences begin investigation of the effectiveness of drugs previously approved because they were thought safe.

1966: United States passes Fair Packaging and Labeling Act.

1966: United States Narcotic Addiction Rehabilitation Act authorizes the civil commitment of narcotic addicts, and gives federal financial assistance to states and local authorities to develop a local system of drug treatment programs. Methadone clinic treatment programs begin to dramatically rise.

1967: Love-In in honor of LSD was staged at Golden Gate Park in San Francisco, California. Prior to being made illegal, more than 40,000 patients had been treated with LSD as part of psychiatric therapy.

1967: News accounts depict illicit use of PCP, then sometimes known as the "Peace Pill," in the Haight-Ashbury district of San Francisco during the "Summer of Love." PCP reemerges in the early 1970s as a liquid, crystalline powder, and tablet.

1968: FDA administratively moves to Public Health Service.

1968: Psilocybin and *Psilocybe* mushrooms are made illegal in United States.

1968: United States Bureau of Narcotics and Dangerous Drugs (BNDD) is formed to coordinate efforts against abused drugs.

1969: FDA bans artificial sweetener cyclamate.

1969: FDA reinstates the prescription requirement for amyl nitrite.

1970: A United States Court of Appeals upholds prior rulings that widespread commercial use does not constitute substantial evidence of drug safety or effectiveness.

1970: United States Congress passes Controlled Substance Act (CSA). CSA puts strict controls on the production, import, and prescription of amphetamines. Many amphetamine forms, particularly diet pills, are removed from the over-the-counter market.

1970: FDA requires a patient information package insert in oral contraceptives. The insert must contain information regarding specific risks and benefits.

1970: Ketamine is used as battlefield anesthetic agent during Vietnam War.

1970: United States Comprehensive Drug Abuse Prevention and Control Act classifies drugs in five categories based on the effect of the drug, its medical use, and potential for abuse. Schedule I contains drugs such as heroin, which have no medical use but may be used in research. Schedule II drugs have a high potential for abuse. They are accepted for medical use with restrictions. These drugs may lead to severe psychological or physical dependence. Schedule III drugs have a medical use and less of a potential for abuse than drugs in Schedules I and II. Abuse of these drugs

may lead to "moderate or low psychological dependence or high psychological dependence." Schedule IV drugs have a low abuse potential as compared to Schedule III drugs. Although these substances have an accepted medical use, they can lead to limited psychological or physical dependence. Schedule V drugs have a low potential for abuse compared to Schedule IV drugs, an accepted medical use in the United States, and the likelihood of limited physical or psychological dependence if abused.

1970: Widespread use of peyote is halted by the Comprehensive Drug Abuse Prevention and Control Act of 1970. During the 1950s and 1960s, peyote was legal throughout most of the United States. During the peak of the psychedelic era, dried peyote cactus buttons were readily available through mail-order catalogs.

1971: Cigarette advertising is banned from television and radio. Nonsmokers' rights movement begins.

1971: United Kingdom passes the Misuse of Drugs Act.

1972: Recombinant technology emerges as one of the most powerful techniques of molecular biology. Scientists are able to splice together pieces of DNA to form recombinant genes. As the potential uses, therapeutic and industrial, became increasingly clear, scientists and venture capitalists establish biotechnology companies.

1973: United States Supreme Court upholds the 1962 drug effectiveness law. FDA is permitted to continue to regulate classes of drugs.

1974: 4-bromo-2,5-dimethoxyphenethylamine (2C-B, also known as Nexus) is first produced by American chemist and pharmacologist Alexander Shulgin.

1974: United States Narcotic Addict Treatment Act establishes minimum standards for all methadone treatment facilities, as well as setting standard definitions for addicts.

1975: Anabolic-androgenic steroids (AASs) are added to the International Olympic Committee's list of banned substances.

1975: John Warcup Cornforth (1917–), Australian-English chemist, receives the Nobel Prize for his work on the stereochemistry of enzyme-catalyzed reaction. Vladimir Prelog (1906–), Croatian-Swiss chemist, also receives the Nobel Prize in chemistry for his research into the stereochemistry of organic molecules and reactions.

1975: Rohypnol, developed by the pharmaceutical firm of Hoffmann-La Roche, is first sold in Switzerland as a sleeping aid for the treatment of insomnia. Reports begin surfacing that Rohypnol is abused as a recreational or "party" drug, often in combination with alcohol and/or other drugs.

1976: FBI warns "crack" cocaine use and cocaine addiction are on the rise in the Untied States.

1976: Oxycodone is approved by the Food and Drug Administration (FDA). Various formulations follow, including drugs that combine oxycodone with either aspirin or acetaminophen.

1976: United States Congress passes the Proxmire Amendments to stop the FDA from regulating vitamin and mineral supplements as drugs based on their potency. This legislation also prohibited the FDA from regulating the potency of vitamin and mineral supplements.

1978: American Indian Religious Freedom Act is passed and protects the religious traditions of Native Americans, including the use of peyote.

1978: Because of escalating reports of abuse, PCP is withdrawn completely from the United States market. Since 1978, there has been no legal therapeutic use of PCP. During the 1950s and 1960s, PCP was used as a intravenous anesthetic.

1979: Swiss company developed a distillation method to remove the caffeine from coffee, creating decaffeinated coffee without use of methylene chloride.

1980: Food and Drug Administration (FDA) proposes to remove caffeine from its Generally Recognized As Safe list. Subsequently, the FDA concluded in 1992 that, after reviewing the scientific literature, no harm is posed by a person's intake of up to 100 milligrams (mg) of caffeine per day.

1980: World Health Organization (WHO) classifies khat as a drug of abuse that may produce mild to moderate psychological dependency.

1981: Alprazolam (Xanax) is introduced and subsequently becomes the most widely prescribed benzodiazepine.

1982: The FDA issues regulations for tamper-resistant packaging after seven people died in Chicago from ingesting Tylenol capsules laced with cyanide. The following year, the federal Anti-Tampering Act was passed, making it a crime to tamper with packaged consumer products.

1982: The United States Food and Drug Administration approves the first genetically engineered drug, a form of human insulin produced by bacteria.

1982: *Toxicological Principles for the Safety Assessment of Direct Food Additives and Color Additives Used in Food* is published by the FDA and is known as the "Red Book."

1983: FDA bans products containing both PPA and caffeine.

1983: The United States Congress passes the Orphan Drug Act, which allowed the FDA to research and market drugs necessary for treating rare diseases.

1984: Marketing of less-costly generic drugs is expedited with congressional passage of the Drug Price Competition and Patent Term Restoration Act. Under the new regulations, the FDA could approve applications for generic drugs without requiring repeated research, when data had already demonstrated the brand-name drug as safe and effective. Additionally, manufacturers of new brand-name drugs could apply for up to five years additional protection for their patents as compensation for time spent during the approval process.

1984: Methaqualone (Quaalude, Sopor), a nonbarbiturate hypnotic that is said to give a heroin-like high without drowsiness, is banned in the United States.

1984: Nicotine gum is introduced.

1985: FDA approves synthetic THC, or dronabinol (Marinol) as an anti-emetic for cancer patients undergoing chemotherapy.

1985: Ecstasy, 3,4-Methylenedioxymethamphetamine (MDMA) becomes illegal in the United States.

1985: United Kingdom passes Intoxicating Substances (Supply) Act, making it an offense to supply a product that will be abused. Subsequent legislation, the Cigarette Lighter Refill (safety) Regulations, passed in 1999 regulated the sale of purified liquefied petroleum gas, mainly butane, the substance most often involved in inhalant fatalities in the United Kingdom.

1986: Congress passes the National Childhood Vaccine Injury Act, requiring patient information on vaccines and reporting of adverse events after vaccination.

1986: The United States Food and Drug Administration approves the first genetically engineered human vaccine for hepatitis B.

1986: United Kingdom passes Medicines Act.

1986: United States Congress passes Anti-Drug Abuse Act. This federal law includes mandatory minimum sentences for first-time offenders with harsher penalties for possession of crack cocaine than powder cocaine.

1986: United States Surgeon General's report focuses on the hazards of environmental tobacco smoke to nonsmokers.

1987: Legal drinking age is raised to 21 years in United States.

1987: New protocols are established by the FDA that permit the use of promising investigational drugs in treating patients with life-threatening or severely debilitating diseases and with no alternative therapies.

1988: Anti-Drug Abuse Act allows for the imposition of a civil penalty (fine) for persons possessing a small quantity of an illegal controlled substance.

1988: Canadian sprinter Ben Johnson (1961–) tests positive for anabolic-androgenic steroids (AASs) at the Seoul Olympic games and forfeits his gold medal to the second-place finisher, American Carl Lewis (1961–).

1988: Congress passes the Prescription Drug Marketing Act designed to maintain the sale and distribution of prescription drugs through legitimate commercial channels. The new law requires state-level licensing for drug wholesalers, restricts drug reimportation from other countries, institutes regulations regarding drug samples, and prohibits the traffic or counterfeiting of redeemable drug coupons.

1988: Food and Drug Administration Act officially establishes the FDA as an agency of the Department of Health and Human Services. The act provides for a Commissioner of Food and Drugs appointed by the President, and outlines the responsibilities of the Secretary and the Commissioner for research, enforcement, education, and information.

1988: U.S. Consumer Products Safety Commission bans the sale of butyl nitrite.

1990: GHB, a fast-acting central nervous system depressant, is made a Schedule I drug. In accord with the Controlled Substances Act (CSA), GHB is declared illegal in United States.

1990: National Council on Alcoholism and Drug Dependence and the American Society of Addictive Medicine defines alcoholism as a chronic disease influenced by genetic, psychological, and environmental factors. Alcoholism is described as a loss of control over drinking—a preoccupation with drinking despite negative consequences to one's physical, mental, and emotional makeup as well as one's work and family life.

1990: Supreme Court decision in *Employment Division v. Smith* said that the religious use of peyote by Native Americans is not protected by the First Amendment.

1990: United States Congress passes Nutrition Labeling and Education Act, which permitted manufacturers to make some health claims for foods, including dietary supplements.

1991: Anabolic-androgenic steroids (AASs) are listed as a Schedule III drugs in accord with the United States Controlled Substances Act (CSA).

1991: Nicotine skin patches are introduced.

1991: The FDA publishes regulations designed to accelerate the drug review process for new drugs developed to treat life-threatening diseases.

1992: Congress passes the Prescription Drug User Fee Act, which requires the FDA to use product application fees collected from drug manufacturers to hire more reviewers to assess applications.

1992: The Karolinska Institute publishes a study that asserts subjects who take creatine supplements can experience a significant increase in total muscle creatine content. Creatine is thrust onto the global athletic scene as British sprinters Linford Christie and Sally Gunnel win Olympic gold in Barcelona after reportedly training with the aid of creatine supplementation. Subsequently, a lack of well-designed clinical studies of creatine's long-term effects combined with loose regulatory standards for creatine supplement products causes some athletic associations, including

the United States Olympic Committee (USOC), to caution against its use without banning it outright.

1993: 4-bromo-2,5-dimethoxyphenethylamine (2C-B, also known as Nexus) becomes widely known as a "rave" drug in United States.

1993: The first news accounts that cite use of Rohypnol as a "date rape" drug are published. Rohypnol becomes one of more than 20 drugs that law enforcement officials assert are used in committing sexual assaults.

1993: United States Congress passes the Domestic Chemical Diversion Control Act (DCDCA), aiming to stop the conversion of legal substances into illegal substances.

1993: United States Religious Freedom Restoration Act and the American Indian Religious Freedom Act Amendments (AIRFA) restore right of Native Americans to use peyote in religious ceremonies.

1994: In response to a citizen's petition by the Coalition on Smoking or Health, the FDA announces that nicotine could receive scrutiny for regulation as a drug.

1994: Patent terms for drugs in the United States are extended from 17 to 20 years by the Uruguay Round Agreements Act.

1994: Previously industry secrets, public access to lists of cigarette additives reveals the use of 700 potential additives, of which 13 are not allowed in food.

1994: United States Congress passes Dietary Supplement Health and Education Act, which expressly defines a dietary supplement as a vitamin, a mineral, an herb or other botanical, an amino acid, or any other "dietary substance." This law prohibits claims that herbs can treat diseases or disorders, but it allows more general health claims about the effect of herbs on the "structure or function" of the body or about the "well-being" they induce. Under this law, the FDA bears the burden of having to prove an herbal is unsafe before restricting its use. This law also establishes the Office of Dietary Supplements within the National Institutes of Health to promote and compile research on dietary supplements.

1995: 4-bromo-2,5-dimethoxyphenethylamine (2C-B, also known as Nexus) hallucinogen classified as a Schedule I drug under the United States Controlled Substances Act (CSA).

1995: A study published by the *British Journal of Urology* asserts that khat (*Catha edulis*) chewing inhibits urine flow, constricts blood vessels, and promotes erectile dysfunction.

1995: Combinatorial chemistry, a technique which quickly surveys huge numbers of chemical combinations in order to select the most desirable molecular configurations, attracts the attention of chemical companies. Scientists predict the possibility of creating numerous new chemicals to serve the needs of industrial and pharmaceutical development.

1995: OxyContin is approved by the FDA for use in United States.

1995: Study by the Rand Corporation found that every dollar spent in drug treatment saves society seven dollars in crime, policing, incarceration, and health services.

1995: The National Household Survey on Drug Abuse found inhalants to be the second most commonly abused illicit drug by American youth ages 12–17 years, after marijuana.

1995: United States Food and Drug Administrations (FDA) declares tobacco cigarettes and cigars to be drug delivery devices and proposed extensive additional restrictions on sales and advertising to minors.

1996: Anabolic-androgenic steroids (AASs) and other performance-enhancing drugs are added to the United Kingdom Misuse of Drugs Act.

1996: FDA approves the antidepressant buproprion (Zyban) for the treatment of nicotine dependence.

1996: Nicotine nasal spray is introduced.

1996: Researchers find that abuse and violence can alter a child's brain chemistry, placing him or her at risk for various problems, including drug abuse, cognitive disabilities, and mental illness later in life.

1996: South Carolina Supreme Court decided in favor of the Medical University of South Carolina (MUSC) policy to secretly test pregnant patients for cocaine use. The court upheld MUSC's drug testing in an effort to protect the unborn. Cocaine greatly increases the chances of a miscarriage. Low birth weight "crack babies" have 20 times as great a risk of dying in their first month of life than normal-weight babies. Those who survive are at increased risk for birth defects. Subsequently, in 2001 the United States Supreme Court ruled that based on the Fourth Amendment, hospitals cannot test pregnant women for drugs without their consent and then inform the police.

1996: United States Comprehensive Methamphetamine Control Act increases penalties for the manufacture, distribution, and possession of methamphetamine, as well as the reagents and chemicals needed to make it.

1996: United States Drug-Induced Rape Prevention and Punishment Act makes it a felony to give an unsuspecting person a drug with the intent of committing violence, including rape. The law also imposes penalties of large fines and prison sentences of up to 20 years for importing or distributing more than one gram of date-rape drugs.

1997: 4-bromo-2,5-dimethoxyphenethylamine (2C-B, also known as Nexus) is banned in Great Britain.

1997: FDA proposes new rules regarding ephedra, which would have considered some products containing ephedra as adulterated supplements, making them subject to FDA regulation. The FDA based its adulterated claim on the fact that ephedrine alkaloids resemble amphetamine and, like amphetamine, stimulate the heart and nervous system. Congress rejects the FDA attempt to subject ephedra products to regulation. Subsequently, in 2000, an ephedra study published in the *New England Journal of Medicine* correlates heart attacks, strokes, seizures, and mental side effects (including anxiety, tremulousness, and personality changes) with ephedra intake. Other possible mental side effects associated with ephedra are depression and paranoid psychosis.

1997: FDA investigates correlation of heart valve disease in patients using fen-phen drug combination for weight loss. Similar reports were reported for patients using only dexfenluramine or fenfluramine. The FDA noted that the combination fen-phen treatment had not received FDA approval.

1997: Institute of Medicine (IOM), a branch of the National Academy of Sciences, publishes the report *Marijuana: Assessing the Science Base*, which concluded that cannabinoids showed significant promise as analgesics, appetite stimulants, and anti-emetics, and that further research into producing these medicines was warranted.

1997: Oregon voters approve Death with Dignity Act, allowing terminally ill people to receive prescriptions for lethal dosages of drugs to end their lives.

1997: Rohypnol is banned in the United States.

1997: The *Journal of the American Medical Association (JAMA)* published a study indicating ginkgo dietary supplements might be useful in treating Alzheimer's disease, sparking additional research interest.

1997: The National Institutes of Health (NIH) estimate that approximately 600,000 people in the United States are opiate-dependent, meaning they use an opiate drug daily or on a frequent basis.

1997: United States passes Food and Drug Administration Modernization Act and reauthorizes the Prescription Drug User Fee Act of 1992. The changes in policy allow for a more rapid review of drugs and delivery devices. The Act also expands FDA regulatory powers over advertising, especially with regard to health claims.

1998: A study at the Psychiatric University Hospital in Zurich, Switzerland, demonstrates that psilocybin produces a psychosis-like syndrome in healthy humans that is similar to early schizophrenia.

1998: Amendments made to the United States Higher Education Act make anyone convicted of a drug offense ineligible for federal student loans for anywhere from one year to an indefinite period of time. They may also render students ineligible for state aid.

1998: National Household Survey on Drug Abuse, estimates 9.7 million Americans are dependent on alcohol. This figure includes the 915,000 young people ages 12–17 years who have a drinking problem.

1998: Nicotine inhaler (Nicotrol Inhaler) is introduced.

1998: Researchers determine that one half of every dose of Ritalin, the widely prescribed drug for ADHD (attention-deficit/hyperactivity disorder), has no therapeutic effect. Ritalin, as do many drugs, consists of two molecular forms of a compound, each structurally mirroring the other. Yu-Shin Ding, Joanna S. Fowler (1942–), and Nora Volkow (1956–), of the Brookhaven National Laboratory in Upton, New York, find that only one form of the pair is therapeutically significant, suggesting the desirability of using the drug in a purer form.

1998: Sibutramine (Meridia) is introduced as a weight-loss drug. Sibutramine inhibits the reuptake of the brain chemicals norepinephrine, dopamine, and serotonin, but does not promote monoamine release like the amphetamines.

1998: The tobacco industry settled lengthy lawsuits by making a historic agreement with the States' Attorneys General called the Master Settlement Agreement (MSA). In exchange for protection from further lawsuits, the industry agreed to additional advertising restrictions and to reimburse the states billions of dollars over 25 years to pay for smoking-related illnesses.

1998: United States Drug Free Communities Act offers federal money to communities to help educate citizens on the dangers on methamphetamine use and production.

1998: United States Speed Trafficking Life in Prison Act increases penalties for the production, distribution, and use of methamphetamine.

1999: Drug Enforcement Administration (DEA) lists GBL as a scheduled (controlled) substance.

1999: FDA lists ketamine as a Schedule III drug. Schedule III drugs are approved for medical use, though their recreational use or abuse "may lead to moderate or low physical dependence or high psychological dependence." Possession of ketamine in the United States is illegal without a prescription or license to distribute.

1999: National Household Survey on Drug Abuse (NHSDA) estimates that a third of the American population (then an estimated 72 million people) had tried marijuana at least once.

1999: Pharmaceutical researchers in Japan find that an N-benzylpiperazine derivative stimulates acetylcholine neurotransmitter. This discovery subsequently leads to the discovery of donepezil (Aricept), which helps ward off memory loss in Alzheimer's disease and age-related dementias.

1999: U.S. Drug Enforcement Administration (DEA) seizes 30 gal (113.5 l) of a dimethyltriptamine (DMT, a hallucinogen) containing tea called "hoasca" from the office of the O Centro Espirita Beneficente Uniao do Vegetal (UDV), a New Mexico-based religious

organization with approximately 500 members. The organization subsequently sued the United States Government, alleging a violation of their constitutional right of freedom of religion. As of 2002 the case remained pending.

2000: *Journal of Pharmacy and Pharmacology* concludes that khat (*Catha edulis*), like amphetamines and ibuprofen, can relieve pain.

2000: National Collegiate Athletic Association (NCAA) releases a list of permissible and nonpermissible nutritional supplements that institutions and coaching staffs may provide their athletes. Under the NCAA policy, only those supplements that are considered non-muscle building substances can be provided to an NCAA athlete by a coach or institution. Under the NCAA rules, creatine is considered a nonpermissible substance.

2000: The National Cancer Institute (NCI) estimates that 3,000 lung cancer deaths and as many as 40,000 cardiac deaths per year among adult nonsmokers in the United States can be attributed to passive smoke or environmental tobacco smoke (ETS).

2000: Unapproved piperazine products become subject to FDA regulatory action.

2000: United States Congress considers but does not pass the Pain Relief Promotion Act, which would have amended the Controlled Substances Act to say that relieving pain or discomfort—within the context of professional medicine—is a legitimate use of controlled substances. The bill died in the Senate.

2000: United States Congress Ecstasy Anti-Proliferation Act increases federal sentencing guidelines for trafficking and possessing with intent to sell ecstasy, or 3,4-methylenedioxymethamphetamine (MDMA), and drastically increases jail terms for fewer numbers of pills in personal possession.

2000: United States Congress passes transportation spending bill including establishment of a national standard for drunk driving for adults at a 0.08% blood alcohol level (BAL). States are required to adopt this stricter standard by 2004 or face penalties. By 2001, more than half the states adopt this stricter standard.

2000: United States Drug Addiction Treatment Act allows opioids to be distributed to physicians for the treatment of opioid dependence.

2000: United States President William J. Clinton (1946–) signs the Hillary J. Farias and Samantha Reid Date Rape Drug Prohibition Act into law.

2001: *American Journal of Psychiatry* publishes studies providing evidence that methamphetamine can cause brain damage that results in slower motor and cognitive functioning—even in users who take the drug for less than a year.

2001: *International Journal of Cancer*, researchers assert that khat (*Catha edulis*) chewing, especially when accompanied by alcohol and tobacco consumption, may cause oral malignancy.

2001: Food and Drug Administration (FDA) approved the first clinical trial of MDMA (ecstasy) as a treatment for post-traumatic stress disorder (PTSD) in the United States. As of 2002 the proposed research waited for additional approvals.

2001: In February 2001, the complete draft sequence of the human genome is published. The public sequence data is published in the British journal *Nature*, and the Celera sequence is published in the American journal *Science*. Increased knowledge of the human genome allows greater specificity in pharmacological research and drug interaction studies.

2001: International Olympic Committee (IOC) announces that 15–20% of the approximately 600 nutritional supplements the agency tested were adulterated with substances that could lead to positive doping tests.

2001: National Football League (NFL) joins the National College Athletic Association (NCAA) and the International Olympic Committee (IOC) in issuing a ban on ephedrine use. The NFL ban on ephedrine prohibits NFL players and teams from endorsing products containing ephedrine or companies that sell or distribute those products.

2001: National Institute of Drug Abuse (NIDA) research asserts that children exposed to cocaine prior to birth sustained long-lasting brain changes. Eight years after birth, children exposed to cocaine prior to birth had detectable brain chemistry differences.

2001: Office of National Drug Control Policy annual report asserts that that about 80% of Americans abusing illegal drugs used marijuana.

2001: Study entitled *Global Illicit Drug Trends* conducted by the United Nations Office for Drug Control and Crime Prevention (ODCCP), estimates that 14 million people use cocaine worldwide. Although cocaine use leveled off, the United States still maintains the highest levels of cocaine abuse.

2001: The annual Monitoring the Future study (MTF), conducted by the University of Michigan and funded by the National Institute on Drug Abuse, found that 17.1% of eighth graders had abused inhalants at some point in their lives.

2001: Thoroughbred race horse wins a race at Suffolk Downs in Massachusetts but then tests positive for BZP (also known as Equine Ecstasy).

2001: To combat psilocybin use, a DNA test is devised to help identify *Psilocybe* mushrooms.

2001: U.S. military endorsed the situational temporary usefulness of caffeine, recommending it as a safe and effective stimulant for its soldiers in good health.

2001: U.S. Supreme Court ruled (unanimously) in *United States vs. Oakland Cannabis Buyers' Cooperative* that the cooperatives permitted under California law to sell marijuana to medical patients who had a physician's approval to use the drug were unconstitutional under federal law.

2002: A company called DrinkSafe Technology announces the invention of a coaster that can be used to test whether a drink has been drugged. If Rohypnol, GHB, or ketamine has been added, the coaster will change color when a drop of the tampered drink is placed on it.

2002: A Florida physician is convicted of manslaughter for prescribing OxyContin to four patients who died after overdosing on the powerful drug. News reports assert that he is the first doctor ever convicted in the death of patients whose deaths were related to OxyContin use.

2002: Health Canada, the Canadian health regulatory agency, requested a voluntary recall of products containing both natural and chemical ephedra.

2002: In the aftermath of the September 11, 2001, terrorist attacks on the United States, by the first few months of 2002 the U.S. government dramatically increases funding to stockpile drugs and other agents that could be used to counter a bioterrorist attack.

2002: Italy's Health Ministry announces the immediate withdrawal of all sibutramine (Meridia) products from the market due to health-related problems.

2002: Several states, including Connecticut and Minnesota, pass laws that ban teachers from recommending psychotropic drugs, especially Ritalin, to parents.

2002: The planned destruction of stocks of smallpox-causing variola virus at the two remaining depositories in the United States and Russia is delayed over fears that large-scale production of vaccine might be needed in the event of a bioterrorist action.

2002: U.S. federal district court judge rejects a U.S. Justice Department attempt to overturn Oregon's physician-assisted suicide law. The Justice Department claimed that the state law violated the federal Controlled Substances Act.

ALCOHOL

OFFICIAL NAMES: Ethyl alcohol, ethanol, grain alcohol
STREET NAMES: Booze, hooch, juice, sauce, spirits
DRUG CLASSIFICATIONS: Not classified, depressant

OVERVIEW

Jugs that held beer and wine have been found dating back to 3500 B.C. It was easy enough for prehistoric peoples to make alcohol. Mixtures of water and berries left alone in the sun turned into alcohol. Alcohol had its medicinal qualities as well. It was used as a disinfectant, to stimulate the flow of milk in nursing mothers, and to remedy a variety of illnesses.

By the Middle Ages, the upper classes consumed alcohol in abundance, while the peasant population made beer at home. In Italy and France, wine became an important product in commercial markets and continued to be an integral part of the European economy throughout the Renaissance period. Home brewing was largely replaced by the commercial manufacture of beer and wine in Europe by the early eighteenth century.

The first distillery in the United States opened in New York in 1640. Mass production, international trade, and expanding commercialism facilitated an increase in alcohol use into the twentieth century and brought with it concern over alcohol abuse.

In the United States there have been historical increases and decreases in alcohol use. There were high periods of alcohol consumption during the Civil War, World War I, and World War II. Low periods occurred during Prohibition and the Depression. Alcohol consumption rose in the 1980s, when many states in the United States lowered the drinking age to 18. Because of the number of teen deaths due to drinking and driving, the legal age of drinking was raised to 21 in 1987. Coincidentally, the rate of alcohol consumption decreased in the 1990s, but alcohol remains the most commonly used legal drug, and consumption of alcohol by young people is very high.

CHEMICAL/ORGANIC COMPOSITION

The chemical composition for ethanol or ethyl alcohol, otherwise known as alcohol, is C_2H_5OH. This means it is composed of two atoms of carbon, six atoms of hydrogen, and one oxygen atom. Ethanol is colorless and highly flammable. Alcohol is too strong to drink by itself, so it is mixed with water and other substances to create alcoholic beverages. Ethyl alcohol is the only safe alcohol to drink. Other alcohols like methanol (wood alcohol; CH_3OH) and isopropyl alcohol [rubbing alcohol; $(CH_3)_2CHOH$] are highly toxic and poisonous to the body.

Alcohol is produced by fermenting fruits, vegetables, and grains. Fermentation occurs when sugar in berries or grains is combined with yeast. An enzyme is released that changes the sugar into carbon dioxide and alcohol. When the combination of sugar, yeast, and berries reaches an alcohol concentration point of 14%, fermentation is complete and wine is formed. Similarly, when sugar, yeast, and grains such as barley, corn, or rice

KEY TERMS

ALCOHOLISM: A disease that results in chronic alcohol abuse. Alcoholism can cause early death from complications to the brain, liver, and heart.

DETOX: An abbreviation for detoxification, it refers to ridding the body of the toxic effects of regular, excessive alcohol consumption. During detox, alcoholics often experience severe withdrawal symptoms including acute cravings for alcohol, delirium tremens, and convulsions.

DISTILLATION: A heat-dependent process used to produce alcoholic beverages, such as whiskey, rum, and vodka. In this process, a fermented mash (of grains, vegetables, or fruits) is heated in a boiler, causing the alcohol to evaporate. The alcohol vapors are then collected and cooled in a condenser to produce the beverage.

DUI: Driving under the influence of alcohol.

ETHYL ALCOHOL: C_2H_5OH; also called grain alcohol or ethanol. This is the only type of alcohol that is safe to drink. Other alcohols like methyl alcohol and isopropyl alcohol are highly toxic and poisonous.

FETAL ALCOHOL SYNDROME: A pattern of birth defects, and learning and behavioral problems affecting individuals whose mothers consumed alcohol during pregnancy.

PROOF: A measure of the strength of an alcoholic beverage. The proof of an alcoholic beverage is twice the amount of its alcohol content. For example, 100 proof whiskey is 50% alcohol.

---

are combined and reach an alcohol concentration of about 6%, beer is made and fermentation stops.

Hard liquor is produced by a process called distillation. In distillation, liquids that have been fermented are boiled and the alcohol is extracted. At the boiling point, the alcohol separates from the fermented liquid to create a vapor. The vapor is held in a cooling tube until it turns into a liquid once again. The alcohol is then mixed with water. Hard liquor is about 60% water. Whiskey, rum, vodka, scotch, and gin are distilled liquors. These alcoholic beverages contain about 50% alcohol. The percentage of alcohol in hard liquor is called "proof." Proof is double the amount of pure alcohol, which means that a 100 proof whiskey contains 50% alcohol. A 4-ounce glass of wine, a 12-ounce beer, and a 1-ounce shot glass of hard liquor all have the same amount of alcohol or alcohol content. Cordials like brandy, port, and liqueurs are made from wine and have pure alcohol added to them. Sugar is added to make them sweet, thus hiding the taste of alcohol and making these drinks seem less potent than they really are.

INGESTION METHODS

When a person drinks alcohol, it immediately travels from the stomach to the small intestine and then into the bloodstream. When alcohol enters the bloodstream, a person begins to feel its effects. Because alcohol is absorbed faster than it is metabolized, the alcohol level in a person's blood rises quickly. Drinking alcohol on an empty stomach also causes blood alcohol levels (BAL) to rise quickly. High-protein foods in the body can slow down the absorption of alcohol, whereas carbonated alcoholic beverages such as champagne, rum and coke, and whiskey and ginger ale speed up the absorption of alcohol into the bloodstream. A smaller person will begin to feel the effects of alcohol sooner than a larger person because the larger person has more blood and body fluids.

Alcohol leaves the body through a process of elimination and oxidation. The liver removes alcohol from the blood and causes the alcohol to break down into water and carbon dioxide gas. The carbon dioxide gas leaves the body through the lungs, and the water is eliminated in urine. It takes the liver about one hour to process a glass of wine, one to two hours to process hard liquor, and about two hours to process a glass of beer. If large quantities of alcohol are present in the body, the liver has to work overtime to break it down and eliminate it from the body.

Alcohol is carried to the brain through the bloodstream. Because alcohol is a depressant, it has immediate effects on the brain's ability to function effectively. Alcohol can impair judgement, affect behavior and coordination, and cause nausea, slurred speech, and dehydration. Gail Gleason Milgram, Professor and Director of Education and Training at the Center of Alcohol Studies, offers a profile of behavior that can follow a rise in blood alcohol levels (BAL) due to drinking. She explains that when a person has a BAL of 0.03%, which is approximately one drink, "the drinker will feel relaxed and experience a slight feeling of exhilaration." After two drinks and a BAL of 0.06%, "the drinker will experience a feeling of warmth and relaxation" as well as a decline in coordination. After three drinks, speech can be slurred and muscle control can be affected. When a drinker has had five or six drinks, he or she can have difficulty walking and staying awake. At this point a person's BAL could reach 0.30%. Milgram further explains that when the BAL reaches 0.50%, "the drinker is in a deep coma or in danger of death." Many states use a BAL of 0.1% as a measure for drunk driving.

THERAPEUTIC USE

In the past, alcohol has been used as a treatment for infection, as an anesthetic, and as a sedative. Alcohol is

HISTORY NOTES

Prohibition in the United States

By the late nineteenth century the campaign for temperance had shifted to a drive for Prohibition—or, as H. L. Mencken put it, anti-alcohol groups shifted from the "hair-shirt" to the "flaming sword." Backed by the evangelical Protestant movement, the Women's Christian Temperance Union, and the Anti-Saloon League, a constitutional amendment to prohibit intoxicating drink was proposed in 1913. On December 22, 1917, Congress passed the Eighteenth Amendment, which was declared ratified on January 29, 1919. Section one read: "After one year from the ratification of this article the manufacture, sale, or transportation of intoxicating liquors within, the importation thereof into, or the exportation thereof from the United States and all territory subject to the jurisdiction thereof for beverage purposes is hereby prohibited." The Volstead Act, passed by Congress in September 1919 to codify the newly ratified constitutional amendment, defined "intoxicating liquor" as any beverage that contained as much as 0.5% alcohol (thus including beer as well as hard liquor in the forbidden category).

Alcohol consumption declined during Prohibition, but it was by no means eliminated. Creating and supplying bootleg liquor for Americans who would not relinquish lifelong drinking habits was a multimillion-dollar business. Because the business was illegal, the entrepreneurs who ran it were criminals. Thus, Prohibition had the unintended consequences of lining the pockets of organized crime and giving rise to notorious gangsters such as Al Capone, who made a fortune by providing illegal liquor to the hard-drinking city of Chicago and nearby areas. Crime associated with the underground liquor trade ballooned as federal, state, and local governments committed woefully inadequate resources to the enforcement of Prohibition.

On December 5, 1933, the "noble experiment" called Prohibition came to an end when the state of Utah became the thirty-sixth state to ratify the Twenty-first Amendment to the Constitution. The amendment, which had been passing feverishly through state legislatures across the country since April 10, repealed the Eighteenth Amendment. That Prohibition would end was a foregone conclusion. The rapidity with which the Eighteenth Amendment was repealed only emphasized its unpopularity. Enforcement of the law was Prohibition's greatest problem, and the federal war to support Prohibition had cost a lot of money and many law officers' lives. After the stock market crash of 1929 and the Depression that set in, repealing Prohibition became important to stimulate the economy. By the end of 1933 the noble experiment was over, a victim of economic and political forces, but also of simple public demand for the freedom to drink alcohol.

---

known as a pain suppressant and was used for hundreds of years for treating people with injuries and for those needing surgery. Alcohol was used to treat typhus as recently as the 1920s. Research in the 1990s showed that moderate amounts of alcohol could help reduce the risk of heart attacks but, conversely, alcohol abuse has been connected to heart disease. Today, there are no known therapeutic uses for alcohol.

USAGE TRENDS

According to the National Council on Alcoholism and Drug Dependence (NCADD), close to 14 million Americans use and abuse alcohol. One third are women and the rest are men. Fifty percent of adults in the United States admit to having alcoholism in their family. One out of every four children come from families where alcohol abuse is a problem.

Adult women drink less than men overall, but are more likely to damage their hearts, livers, and brains due to drinking. The death rate for women who drink large amounts of alcohol frequently is 50% to 100% higher than it is for male alcoholics. Young people who begin drinking before their teenage years are four times more likely to develop an addiction to alcohol than people who begin drinking at age 21. Data taken from *The 2000 Monitoring the Future Survey* indicate that:

- 22% of middle school students and close to 50% of high school students admit to having tried alcohol.

- 8% of middle school students and close to 30% of high school students report having been drunk from alcohol use.

- 14% of teens from ages 13 to 14 admitted to binge drinking as compared to 30% of high school teens.

The National Council on Alcoholism and Drug Dependence (NCADD) claims that in 1999 "44% of college students reported binge drinking (five or more drinks in a row for males or four or more drinks in a row for females)." The NCADD also reported that binge drinking among college fraternity and sorority students can be higher.

Alcohol and Calorie Content of Common Beverages			
Beverage	**Amount (ounces)**	**Alcohol (grams)**	**Energy (kilcalories)**
Beer			
Regular	12	12	140
Light	12	10	90
Distilled			
Gin, rum, vodka, whiskey, tequila	1.5	15	105
Brandy, cognac	1.0	9	65
Wine			
Red	4	11	80
Dry white	4	10	75
Sweet	4	12	105
Manhattan	3	21	165
Martini	3	19	180
Bourbon and soda	4	15	102
Whiskey sour	3	15	122
Margarita	4	18	168

SOURCE: Adapted from Gordon Wardlaw and Paul Insel. *Perspectives in Nutrition. 3rd ed.*

Chart by Argosy.

Alcohol Concentration and Effect Relationship	
BAC (%)	**Effects**
0.02–0.03	Mood elevation; slight muscle relaxation
0.05–0.06	Relaxation and warmth; increased reaction time; decreased fine muscle coordination
0.08–0.09	Impaired balance, speech, vision, hearing, and muscle coordination; euphoria
0.14–0.15	Gross impairment of physical and mental control
0.20–0.30	Severely intoxicated; very little control of mind or body
0.40–0.50	Unconscious; deep coma; death from respiratory depression

SOURCE: Vijay A. Ramchandani. Pharmacology and Neurobiology slide presentation. Alcohol Medical Scholars Program. <http://www.alcoholmedicalscholars.org/Pharmacology.ppt>

Chart by Argosy.

Scope and severity

Over 50% of Americans who currently drink report having a close relative who abuses alcohol; 25% are children of an alcoholic parent. Alcohol abuse can devastate families by causing separation, divorce, and domestic violence, as well child abuse and neglect. Six million children live with an alcohol-abusing parent, and this can result in problems at school such as low attendance, academic difficulties, attention deficit disorders, and behavioral problems. Each year in America, more than 100,000 people die from alcohol-related accidents (cars, falls, fires, drownings, burns), cancer, liver disease, and stroke.

Age, ethnic, and gender trends

According to the National Household Survey on Drug Abuse (NHSDA), "male and female rates of alcohol use among 12–17 year olds were similar in the 1990s for the first time." Peer pressure, incidence of teenage depression, and a need to fit in are all factors leading to alcohol use by teens. According to the U.S. Department of Health and Human Services, women drink most heavily when they are between the ages of 26 and 34. As women and men get older, there is evidence that drinking among men is greater than that of women. College-bound students are reported to drink less than those students not headed for college.

The biochemical reaction of alcohol in the body explains the differences in ethnic susceptibility to alcohol. Dr. Bert Vallee from Harvard Medical School has determined that the enzymes involved in the metabolism of alcohol can vary from ethnic group to ethnic group, and this variation influences the way in which individual members of these groups are affected by alcohol. These enzymes appear to be genetically inherited. For example, alcoholism among Jews and Italians is low compared to the levels seen among Scandinavians, Irish, and French. The ethnic groups with the highest susceptibility to alcohol are the Native Americans and Eskimos. These two groups have difficulty oxidizing and eliminating alcohol from the body. Asian populations show a physical reaction to alcohol sooner than Americans and Europeans because of the genetic makeup in their enzyme groupings that react with alcohol.

MENTAL EFFECTS

Alcohol acts as a depressant on the brain. Blood carries alcohol to the brain, where it acts on the body's central nervous system to slow a person's mental responses. There are a variety of mental effects associated with alcohol consumption. The more immediate are: a lessening of inhibitions, mental relaxation, exaggerated emotional response to people and situations, extreme changes in behavior, and impaired judgment. Low doses of alcohol can cause the release of certain chemicals in the brain that can cause a sense of euphoria—a "high" that makes alcohol seem like a stimulant. Memory is sharpened and the ability to think creatively is strengthened, but when alcohol consumption increases, its sedative effects cause a loss of self-control and inhibition. A self-conscious individual becomes more confident; a shy person becomes more talkative. Alcohol also can cause people to become argumentative or emotionally withdrawn. Relationship problems can develop. Judgment is affected and risk-taking behaviors can result. People are known to do things under the influence of alcohol that they would never consider doing when sober. As alcohol consumption increases and levels of alcohol in the blood rise, the reflexes are slowed; memory loss and a sense of confusion can occur. Committing crimes or being the victim of a crime, domestic violence, child abuse, automobile accidents, homicide, and suicide are among the events related to the consumption of alcohol.

The effects of alcohol are related to the size of the person and the amount of alcohol in the blood, as well as to the rate of consumption. After one drink a person weighing about 150 lb (68 kg) will feel relaxed and happy. After two drinks in an hour a person will fell less inhibited. Three drinks will affect a person's muscle control. Speech can become slurred and walking may be difficult. After four drinks judgment is affected and the ability to reason becomes impaired. Five drinks will make speech patterns difficult to understand and impair vision. After six drinks a person may begin to lose consciousness and fall asleep. Ten or more drinks can cause a person to fall into a deep sleep also known as "passing out." Long-term alcohol use can result in serious neurological disorders in the brain such as confusion, coordination problems, short-term memory loss, and emotional as well as psychological problems.

PHYSIOLOGICAL EFFECTS

The physical effects of alcohol on the body depend on the person's size, weight, sex, and age. Additionally, the amount of food present in the body and the amount of alcohol consumed determine one's physical response to alcohol. The immediate physical effects of alcohol consumption are slurred speech, nausea, lack of coordination, dizziness, and dehydration. Alcohol has no nutritional value, but it can have an effect on a person's weight. It decreases one's appetite by filling the body with empty calories and convinces the body it has had enough to eat. People who abuse alcohol run the risk of becoming malnourished.

Harmful side effects

Alcohol can suppress the immune system, making people more susceptible to infections. Because alcohol reduces inhibitions and impairs judgment, those under its influence may be prone to engage in unsafe sexual activity, raising the risks of HIV infection and sexually transmitted diseases. Alcohol use can interfere with a woman's ability to become pregnant. It can lower a man's sperm count and reduce his sexual drive.

Deaths Caused by Injuries Related to Alcohol, 1992	
Motor vehicle accidents	17,196
Pedal cycle, other road accidents	45
Water transport accidents	167
Air and space transport accidents	175
Accidental falls	4,372
Accidents caused by fire/flames	1,831
Accidental drowning, submersion	1,339
Suicide and self-inflicted injury	8,476
Homicide and injury purposely inflicted by other persons	11,609
Total Deaths	**45,210**

SOURCES: Analysis by the Lewin Group based on data from the National Institute of Alcohol Abuse and Alcoholism (1993), Stinson, et al. (1993), National Center for Health Statistics (1996), and Rice, et al. (1990).

Chart by Argosy.

There is no safe level of alcohol consumption for a woman at any time during a pregnancy. Every bottle of alcohol bears a warning label that reads: "According to the Surgeon General, women should not drink alcoholic beverages during pregnancy because of the risk of birth defects." If a pregnant woman drinks alcohol, her baby is drinking alcohol. If she becomes drunk, her baby is drunk.

Drinking alcohol during pregnancy can cause miscarriages, stillbirths, and serious birth defects such as fetal alcohol syndrome (FAS) and fetal alcohol effect (FAE). FAS is one of the leading causes of birth defects in children and the most preventable cause of mental retardation in the United States. Over 8,000 babies are born each year with fetal alcohol syndrome. It wasn't until 1973 that FAS was defined. FAS babies have lower birthweight, slower mental and physical growth rates, and abnormal facial features such as droopy eyelids, broad noses, large nostrils, and possible cleft palates. Additionally they can have deformed sex organs, internal problems, skeletal abnormalities, brain damage, and mental retardation. FAS is hard to diagnose because the symptoms can mimic those of other birth defects. Thirty thousand babies are born each year with fetal alcohol effect. FAE babies do not have the obvious facial and/or skeletal abnormalities, nor do they have the same level of brain damage as FAS babies, but FAE babies can have physical and behavioral problems such as learning disabilities, attention deficit disorders, and hyperactivity.

Drinking alcohol during pregnancy can result in birth defects including these abnormal facial features typical of fetal alcohol syndrome. AP/ World Wide Photos. Reproduced by permission.

Both the mother and father can be responsible for birth defects by drinking alcohol. Miscarriages can be a result of sperm damaged by alcohol. A man's sperm count can be lowered by alcohol consumption. A breast-feeding mother needs to know that any alcohol she consumes passes from her breast milk into her baby. The simplest way to prevent alcohol problems during pregnancy is not to drink while pregnant and to avoid any alcohol consumption when planning a pregnancy.

Long-term health effects

Prolonged use of alcohol can have serious negative effects on the body. It causes vitamin deficiencies. Alcohol can reduce iron levels, causing anemia, and deplete the body of niacin, causing skin damage. Internally, alcohol can cause inflammation of the stomach, liver, pancreas, and esophagus, causing ulcers, hepatitis, cirrhosis, pancreatitis, and several forms of cancer. The National Institute on Alcohol Abuse and Alcoholism (NIAAA) reports that "alcohol-induced liver disease is a major cause of illness and death in the United States." Long-term alcohol use is associated with high blood pressure, heart disease, stroke, and death.

REACTIONS WITH OTHER DRUGS OR SUBSTANCES

Alcohol should not be consumed while taking medications. Drinking alcohol along with antihistamines will increase the drowsiness that can occur with cold medicines. Alcohol can cause liver damage when taken in combination with acetaminophen. It has additional adverse effects when taken with other drugs. For example, when taken with aspirin alcohol can cause inflammation of the stomach and increase gastrointestinal bleeding. Alcohol combined with antidepressants slows down psychomotor performance. Alcohol taken with barbiturates (Nembutal, Seconal, Amytal, Tuinal, etc.) can increase depression. Tranquilizers that depress the central nervous system like Valium and Librium taken along with alcohol can cause high blood pressure, drowsiness, depression, and confusion in elderly people. Elderly people should avoid alcohol when taking antidepressants, muscle relaxants, sleeping aids, or cold medicines. Those people taking prescription or over-the-counter medicines should check with a physician about alcohol use.

Polysubstance use refers to combining one drug with another drug or drugs. It often involves the use of a legal drug like alcohol with an illegal drug such as marijuana, cocaine, heroin, and/or pills. Polysubstance use is common among young people. The user may get high on a stimulant like speed or cocaine and then use a depressant like alcohol to come down from the high. Alcohol is considered by many to be a gateway drug, as are nicotine and marijuana. Individuals who use one or more of these gateway drugs are believed to go on to deeper and more severe drug involvement. Jeanne Nagel in her book *Polysubstance Abuse* says "statistics reveal that alcoholics are 35 times more likely than non-alcoholics to use cocaine." She goes on to say that alcoholics are "17 times more likely to abuse sedatives, 13 times more likely to take opiates, 12 times more likely to ingest hallucinogens, and 11 times more likely to abuse stimulants." Furthermore, Nagel reports 90% of alcoholics smoke cigarettes, and alcohol abusers are six times more likely to abuse marijuana. When someone develops an addiction to more than one drug, the person is said to be cross-addicted.

TREATMENT AND REHABILITATION

There is no cure for alcoholism, but the progression of the disease can be arrested by total abstinence from alcohol. According to the 1998 National Household Survey on Drug Abuse, an estimated 9.7 million Americans are dependent on alcohol. This figure includes the 915,000 young people ages 12 to 17 who have a drinking problem. Public and private treatment facilities in the United States are capable of treating about 1.7 million people each year, a far cry from the number needing help.

There are several types of inpatient and outpatient treatment options available in this country. Inpatient programs are often found in hospital settings such as a hospital detox unit or a psychiatric unit. Detox is a short-term solution because it only addresses the physical aspect of drying out the drinker. It should be followed up with individual and/or family counseling and an understanding of the disease concept of alcoholism through a program like Alcoholics Anonymous. Psychiatric hospitals address both the problem of alcohol abuse and the emotional problems that accompany it. Treatment includes individual, group, and/or family counseling, drugs to treat psychiatric illnesses, and the additional support of a twelve-step program. Another type of inpatient program can be found at a 28-day rehabilitation facility. This type of treatment program offers detox from alcohol as well as support from substance abuse counselors; education on the disease concept of alcoholism; and individual, group, and family therapy. In addition, it utilizes support group meetings both on and offsite.

Outpatient programs can be connected to a hospital or a public or private treatment facility. These programs are often short term and require the patient to complete a series of daily or weekly visits for a period of several months. Like inpatient treatment, outpatient programs include individual and/or group therapy, trained substance abuse counselors, education on the disease of alcoholism, and a recommendation to attend a support group.

Another type of treatment program is a residential program in which the patient stays at a home for recovering alcoholics—a sober house where several alcoholics are working to stay sober with the help of counseling, job assistance, and regular attendance at support group meetings. There are residential programs specific to men, women, and young people trying to recover from alcohol addiction. The criminal justice system currently helps offenders get alcohol abuse treatment, and many prisons offer weekly Alcoholics Anonymous meetings for prison inmates trying to stay sober. There is no definitive evidence as to what treatment works best for which patient. Due to the lack of data on the effectiveness of individual programs, it is important for treatment facilities to offer a variety of options to meet the needs of their patients.

Treatment programs based on the twelve steps of Alcoholics Anonymous and that encourage attendance at Alcoholics Anonymous meetings have been the most common approach used in the United States. The first Alcoholics Anonymous group was formed in Akron, Ohio in 1935 by Bill Wilson and Dr. Bob Smith. Today there are approximately 99,000 groups in existence across America.

PERSONAL AND SOCIAL CONSEQUENCES

Alcoholism is a chronic, progressive disease that can be fatal. An Edinburgh physician described the disease concept of alcoholism as far back as 1804, but it wasn't until 1956 that the American Medical Association defined alcoholism as a disease. In 1990, the National Council on Alcoholism and Drug Dependence along with the American Society of Addictive Medicine defined alcoholism as a chronic disease that has genetic, psychological, and environmental factors that influence it. Alcoholism is described as a loss of control over drinking—a preoccupation with drinking despite negative consequences to one's physical, mental, and emotional makeup as well as one's work and family life. Alcoholics can be rich or poor, young or old, male or female, white or black. Anyone can become an alcoholic, but children of an alcoholic parent are four times more likely to develop the disease of alcoholism than children of non-alcoholic parents.

People who drink develop a tolerance to alcohol. Tolerance is the result of the way in which the body handles alcohol as well as alcohol's effect on the central nervous system. A non-alcoholic will have a consistent level of tolerance for alcohol, but an alcoholic's tolerance for alcohol will constantly change, requiring him or her to drink more to get the desired result that lower doses of alcohol had once produced. Tolerance changes the alcoholic's brain impulses, hormone levels, and the chemical make-up of cell membranes.

The alcoholic goes through several stages as the disease progresses. The stages of alcoholism were documented by E.M. Jellinek in 1952. The four stages are: the prealcoholic stage, the prodromal stage, the crucial stage, and the chronic or final stage.

The prealcoholic stage refers to that period of time when the individual has every intention of drinking socially but begins to use alcohol as a relief from stress and tension. This stage can last for several months to two years. During the prodromal stage the alcoholic continues to drink when others have stopped. He or she experiences blackouts—periods during which the individual continues to function (walking and talking) but has no memory of things that have been said or done. This stage can go on for four or five years.

The crucial stage is when the individual has lost control over the drinking—perhaps promising to stop, but unable to do so. The alcoholic may become defensive when confronted, looks for excuses to drink, blames others for his or her problems, and looks for relief in what is called "the geographic cure"—a new job, moving to a new location, or a change in marital status. At this stage the alcoholic's moods change from being pleasant and understanding to becoming irritable and unreasonable without warning. The alcoholic may experience job loss or the loss of family and friends. Legal problems may arise.

The final stage of alcoholism is the chronic stage. The alcoholic begins to suffer physical decline as a result of drinking, and may develop illnesses like liver disease or heart failure. There is the risk of overdose or possible suicide as the individual sees no way out of this malady.

The personal consequences of alcoholism reach far beyond the alcoholic. An alcoholic's drinking affects many people, especially the members of his or her family. Alcoholism is a family disease, and the members of an alcoholic family system develop roles that are unconsciously played out to draw attention away from the alcoholic. The spouse or partner of the alcoholic is called the enabler. The enabler's role is to protect the alcoholic from the negative consequences of drinking. The enabler works hard to control life in an alcoholic family.

Children tend to take on one of the following roles:

- The oldest child in an alcoholic family most commonly assumes the hero role. The hero brings honor and respect to the family by being a good student, an accomplished athlete, being involved in school activities, and caretaking younger children at home as a substitute parent. The hero is a perfectionist who hopes that by doing everything well the family's problem with alcohol will go away.

- The scapegoat tries to win the alcoholic's attention by engaging in negative behavior. This child often does poorly in school, can have behavioral problems or attention deficit disorders that affect learn-

IN THE NEWS

Alateen is a world-wide organization for the teens who are the relatives and friends of a problem drinker. Alateen is based on the twelve steps of Alcoholics Anonymous (Al-Anon). Each Alateen group is sponsored by an active, adult member of Al-Anon. Participation is voluntary, confidential, and free of charge. Information regarding Alateen meetings is available from each local Al-Anon Chapter.

As noted above, the basis of the Alateen program is the following twelve steps that members discuss and apply to their own lives.

- We admitted we were powerless over alcohol—that our lives had become unmanageable.

- We came to believe that a Power greater than ourselves could restore us to sanity.

- We made a decision to turn our will and our lives over to the care of God as we understood Him.

- We made a searching and fearless moral inventory of ourselves.

- We admitted to God, to ourselves, and to another human being the exact nature of our wrongs.

- We were entirely ready to have God remove all these defects of character.

- We humbly asked Him to remove our shortcomings.

- We made a list of all persons we had harmed, and became willing to make amends to them all.

- We made direct amends to such people wherever possible, except when to do so would injure them or others.

- We continued to take a personal inventory and when we were wrong promptly admitted it.

- We sought through prayer and meditation to improve our conscious contact with God as we understood Him, praying only for knowledge of His will for us and the power to carry that out.

- Having had a spiritual awakening as the result of these steps, we tried to carry this message to others, and to practice these principles in all our affairs.

---

ing, and emotional problems that may lead to alcohol and drug use.

- The lost child in an alcoholic family system withdraws into the isolation of his or her own world. This child has difficulty making friends, lacks the ability to develop intimate relationships, and often turns to food for comfort from the loneliness.

- The mascot is the family member who uses humor to mask pain. This child feels a responsibility to lighten the family tension by being funny and quick-witted. This behavior becomes a handicap in the development of the child's emotional maturity.

Without an understanding of the alcoholic family system, these children will often grow up and continue the cycle of alcoholic behavior. Through counseling and the help of support networks, these children can learn to break the cycle of family addiction and go on to lead healthy lives in adulthood.

Alcohol abuse in the United States costs an estimated $170 billion each year. Close to half of this figure is due to a loss in workplace productivity resulting from illness and work-related injury. Other contributing factors are alcohol-related health care expenses costing society over $26 million and automobile accidents estimated at $15 million. Fifty percent of the adults in prison are incarcerated for crimes that are alcohol related. Alco-

hol is involved in one-third of all suicides, one-half of all homicides, and one-third of all reported child abuse cases. Drinking can lead to physical injury. People who drink are four times more likely to be hospitalized than nondrinkers. Alcoholism can lead to family violence and physical abuse of children.

LEGAL CONSEQUENCES

In October 2000, the U.S. Congress passed a transportation spending bill that included the establishment of a national standard for drunk driving for adults at a 0.08% blood alcohol level (BAL). States are required to adopt this stricter standard by 2004 or face penalties. As of 2001, more than half the states had adopted this stricter standard, while most other states have a BAL limit of 0.1% in place. Penalties for DUI (driving under the influence of alcohol) offenses vary from state to state and can include fines, jail sentences, driver license supension or revokation, driving record points, community service, mandatory participation in a drug/alcohol program, and/or probation.

In 1999, according to the FBI's Uniform Crime Reports, the number of people arrested for DUI was 1,511,300. Alcohol is a factor in close to two-thirds of the homicides and assaults committed in this country. It is known to be connected to rape in both the offender and the victim. Sixty percent of sexual offenders have committed the offense under the influence of alcohol. Studies of prison inmates show that men are more likely to be drinking at the time of the offense than female offenders.

Dram Shop laws hold bar and restaurant owners responsible for the harm that intoxicated customers cause to other people or, in some cases, to themselves. As a result, college campuses and business organizations are placing greater emphasis on providing alcohol-free organizations and activities. Some colleges have established alcohol-free fraternities, sports events have instituted seating sections where no alcohol is allowed, and many bar owners provide taxi service for patrons who are too intoxicated to drive safely.

Legal history

Laws banning the sale of alcoholic beverages date back to the fourteenth century, when Germany banned the sale of alcohol on Sundays and other religious holidays. Even earlier Switzerland instituted laws requiring drinking establishments to close at certain times to combat public drunkenness. The first formal temperance movement began in Germany but movements promoting drinking in moderation became popular in other countries. In the middle of the seventeenth century, England imposed high taxes on alcoholic beverages. In America, taxes on whiskey brought about resistance by the distillers resulting in the Whiskey Rebellion of 1794.

Temperance movements began to spring up in America largely supported by religious groups. By the eighteenth century the American Temperance Society promoted the concept of total abstinence from alcohol. In 1919 laws prohibiting the sale and consumption of alcohol nationwide were enacted, but these laws were repealed in 1933 by the Twenty-first Amendment to the Constitution.

Federal guidelines, regulations, and penalties

Alcoholic beverage control laws (ABC laws) were developed to prevent the illegal sale of alcohol, to control the sale of alcohol, and to collect revenue for each state selling alcoholic beverages. The laws vary from state to state and are enforced by federal, state, and local law enforcement agencies. Restaurants, convenience stores, grocery stores, and bars selling alcohol must have special licensing. The licensing differs for the type of establishment selling alcohol or alcoholic beverages. Each state regulates where alcohol can be sold and where it can be consumed. A person must be 21 years old to purchase alcohol. Warning labels are required on all alcoholic beverages sold in the United States. These labels alert consumers to the possible dangers of alcohol use when pregnant, driving an automobile, or operating machinery.

RESOURCES

Books

Alcoholics Anonymous. *The Big Book.* 3rd ed. New York: Alcoholics Anonymous World Service, 1976.

Berkow, Robert, ed. *The Merck Manual of Medical Information.* Home ed. Whitehouse Station, NJ: Merck Research Laboratories, 1997.

Carson-Dewitt, Rosalyn, ed. *Encyclopedia of Drugs, Alcohol & Addictive Behavior.* 2nd ed. Vol.1-4. New York: Macmillan Reference USA, 2001.

Kinney, Jean, and Gwen Leaton. *Loosening the Grip.* 4th ed. Boston: Mosby-Year Book, Inc., 1991.

Milam, James R., and Katherine Ketcham. *Under The Influence.* New York: Bantam Books, 1981.

Nagle, Jeanne. *Polysubstance Abuse.* New York: Rosen Publishing Group, Inc., 2000.

National Institute on Alcohol Abuse and Alcoholism. *Tenth Special Report to the U.S. Congress on Alcohol and Health.* Bethesda, MD: NIAAA, 2000.

Schneider Institute for Health Policy at Brandeis University. *Substance Abuse, The Nation's Number One Health Problem.* Princeton, NJ: The Robert Wood Johnson Foundation, 2001.

Wegscheider, Sharon. *Another Chance, Hope & Health for the Alcoholic Family.* Palo Alto, CA: Science and Behavior Books, Inc., 1981.

Periodicals

Brink, Susan. "Your Brain On Alcohol." *U.S. News & World Report* (May 7, 2001): 50–57.

Johnston, L. D., P. M. O'Malley, and J.G. Bachman. *National Survey Results on Drug Use from The Monitoring the Future Study.* Rockville, Maryland: National Institute on Drug Abuse, 1975–1998.

U.S. Department of Health and Human Services (DHHS). Office of Applied Studies. *National Household Survey on Drug Abuse: Main Findings* (1997): 106–111.

Other

CNN.Com-Health. "Alcohol Named Europe's Youth Killer." February 20,2001. <http://www.cnn.com/2001/health/02/19/deaths.alcohol/index.html>.

National Council on Alcoholism and Drug Dependence, Inc. (NCADD). <http://www.ncadd.org>.

National Institute on Alcohol Abuse and Alcoholism (NIAAA). <http://www.niaaa.nih.gov>.

The Cool Spot. National Institute on Alcohol Abuse and Alcoholism (NIAAA) Web Site for Kids. <http://www.thecoolspot.org>.

ONDCP Teens Page. Office of Drug Control Policy. <http://www.mediacampaign.org/kidsteens/teens.html>.

Prevline (Prevention Online). National Clearinghouse for Alcohol and Drug Information(NCADI). <http://www.health.org/>.

Organizations

Al-Anon Family Group Headquarters, 1600 Corporate Landing Parkway, Virginia Beach, VA, USA, 23454-5617, <http://www.al-anon.alateen.org>.

Alcoholics Anonymous (AA) World Services, 475 Riverside Drive, 11th Floor, New York, NY, USA, 10115, (212) 870-3400, <http://www.alcoholics-anonymous.org>.

Barbara Sullivan Smith

AMPHETAMINES

OFFICIAL NAMES: Amphetamine (Adderall), laevoamphetamine (Benzedrine), dextroamphetamine (Dexedrine), methamphetamine (Methedrine)

STREET NAMES: Black dex, bens, bennies, benz, black and white, blackbirds, black bombers, black Cadillacs, black mollies, blacks, blue boys, blue mollies, brain pills, brain ticklers, brownies, browns, bumblebees, chicken powder, co-pilot, coasts-to-coasts, crisscross, cross tops, dex, dexies, diamonds, diet pills, dominoes, double cross, drivers, eye openers, fives, footballs, forwards, french blues, go, greenies, head drugs, hearts, horse heads, ice, jelly baby, jugs, leapers, lid poppers, lid poppers, lightning, MAP, minibennies, morning shot, nugget, oranges, peaches, pep pills, pink hearts, pixies, rhythm, rippers, road dope, rosa, roses, snap, snow pallets, sparkle plenty, sparklers, speed, spivias, splash, splivins, sweeties, sweets, tens, thrusters, truck drivers, turnabout, uppers, uppies, wake ups, West Coast turnarounds, whiffledust

DRUG CLASSIFICATIONS: Schedule II, stimulant

OVERVIEW

Amphetamine was first synthesized in 1886 by a German chemist, though it was not used for medical purposes until the early 1930s. Amphetamine dilates the small sacs of the lungs, providing relief to patients with breathing disorders. In 1931, the pharmaceutical company Smith, Kline, and French introduced the Benzedrine Inhaler to relieve the discomfort of nasal congestion due to colds, hay fever, and asthma. Soon after, the sulfate form of amphetamine was also aggressively marketed. Amphetamine was promoted as a sort of "wonder drug" without knowledge of its potentially addictive properties.

Because users complained of sleeplessness, druggists started compounding tablets for the treatment of a sleeping disorder known as narcolepsy in 1935. Amphetamine then became popular because it delayed fatigue. "Pep pills" soon became available over-the-counter. Truckers were quick to use the pills to keep awake during long-haul deliveries. The first reports of college students using amphetamines to beat fatigue while studying surfaced in 1936. Businessmen and their secretaries also began using amphetamines to induce increased alertness.

By 1937 amphetamine was being used to treat a condition known as minimal brain dysfunction, a disorder later renamed attention deficit hyperactivity disorder (ADHD). The use of amphetamine for that disorder continues into the twenty-first century.

During World War II, soldiers on both sides of the war used amphetamines to maintain alertness and increase stamina. Historians speculate that overuse produced states of uncontrolled aggression that may have contributed to "berserker" charges by soldiers on both sides during many battles. Historians have said that from 1942 until his suicide, Hitler received daily methamphetamine (MAP), a kind of amphetamine, injections from his doctor. Many historians believe that the amphetamine abuse corrupted Hitler's judgement, undermined his health, and probably influenced the course of the war.

Unfortunately, as the use of amphetamine spread, so did its abuse. The first major epidemic of modern times occurred in Japan after the end of World War II. Much of the country was devastated during the war, and the Japanese had to work long hours to rebuild their country. Japanese men who had been soldiers recalled how amphetamine kept them going during the war and sought to acquire the drug. As a result of that demand, inventories of amphetamines were released for sale without prescription. This led to a national epidemic that only ended in the mid-1950s after the Japanese government restricted access to amphetamines and passed stricter laws against illegal amphetamine use.

Major epidemics of amphetamine abuse and dependence occurred in the 1950s, 1960s, and again in the 1990s in the United States and western Europe, particularly in Denmark, Finland, Sweden, and the United Kingdom. In the United States during the 1950s, the availability of over-the-counter amphetamine "diet" pills fueled the epidemic. Amphetamines were even given to race horses during that time since it was believed the drug made them run faster.

In the 1960s, public health authorities noted the first epidemic of intravenous drug use centered around the Haight-Asbury district of San Francisco, California. Individuals, soon to be known as "speed freaks," had learned how to melt amphetamine down and inject the liquefied substance into their veins.

The new drug counterculture of the early 1960s prompted increased control measures. Countries throughout the world passed new laws and regulations in the 1960s and 1970s. In the United States, Congress passed the Controlled Substance Act (CSA) of 1970. The CSA included amendments to the federal food and drug laws that put strict controls on the production, import, and prescription of amphetamines. Many amphetamine forms, particularly diet pills, were removed from the over-the-counter market though they remain available by prescription.

As a result of those laws and regulations, and similar laws in other nations, a black market for amphetamines emerged in many countries. In the 1990s, illicit amphetamine production was increasingly reported in the western United States and eastern Europe, particularly in Poland and Hungary.

CHEMICAL/ORGANIC COMPOSITION

All amphetamines are synthetic, or manufactured, substances derived from alpha-methyl-beta-phenyl-ethyl-amine, a colorless liquid consisting of carbon, hydrogen, and nitrogen. In terms of their chemical structures, amphetamines are related to two natural substances known to boost energy within the human body. Those substances are ephedrine and adrenaline. Ephedrine is a natural stimulant found in plants of the genus *Ephedra*. It

KEY TERMS

ADDICTION: Physical dependence on a drug characterized by tolerance and withdrawal.

APHASIA: Partial or total loss of the ability to explain ideas or understand spoken or written language, resulting from damage to the brain caused by injury or disease.

ATTENTION DEFICIT HYPERACTIVITY DISORDER (ADHD): A mental disorder characterized by persistent impulsive behavior, difficulty concentrating, and hyperactivity that causes lowered social, academic, or occupational functioning.

CENTRAL NERVOUS SYSTEM (CNS): The part of the nervous system consisting of the brain and spinal cord to which sensory and motor information is transmitted, coordinating activity of the entire nervous system.

CRAVING: A powerful, often uncontrollable desire.

NARCOLEPSY: A rare, chronic sleep disorder characterized by constant daytime fatigue and sudden attacks of sleep.

PSYCHOSIS: A severe mental disorder characterized by the loss of the ability to distinguish what is objectively real from what is imaginary, frequently including hallucinations.

RUSH: A surge of pleasure that rapidly follows administration of a drug.

TOLERANCE: A condition in which higher and higher doses of a drug are needed to produce the original effect or high experienced.

WITHDRAWAL: A group of symptoms that may occur from suddenly stopping the use of a substance such as alcohol or other drugs after chronic or prolonged ingestion.

is the active ingredient in the Chinese herbal drug ma huang. Adrenaline is the body's "fight or flight" hormone.

According to the U.S. Department of Justice's Drug Enforcement Administration (DEA), amphetamine, dextroamphetamine, laevoamphetamine, and methamphetamine (MAP) are all referred to as amphetamines because their chemical properties and actions are "so similar" that "even experienced users have difficulty knowing which drug they have taken." Consequently, it doesn't matter what an amphetamine pill or capsule is called. The only difference between amphetamine and dextroamphetamine, for instance, is a few molecules of dextrose, a type of sugar.

The composition of amphetamine or dexamphetamine pills or capsules actually is a combination of the various types of amphetamine "salts." For instance, the

Amphetamine Combinations	
Streetname	**Drug combination**
Aimies	Amphetamine + amyl nitrite
Beans or Chalk	Amphetamine + crack cocaine
Bombido	Amphetamine + heroin
Amp	Amphetamine + marijuana dipped in formaldehyde
Chocolate	Amphetamine + marijuana + opium
Hammerheading	Amphetamine + Ecstasy + Viagra
H-Bomb	Amphetamine + heroin + Ecstasy
Hippieflip	Amphetamine + mushrooms
Purple hearts	Amphetamine + LSD + depressants

Chart by Argosy.

5 mg amphetamine tablet known as Adderall contains 1.25 mg of dextroamphetamine saccharate, 1.25 mg of amphetamine aspartate, 1.25 mg of dextroamphetamine sulfate, and 1.25 mg of amphetamine sulfate.

Methamphetamine is composed of the above named forms of amphetamine with the addition of ephedrine or pseudoephedrine. Many users consider MAP to have more of a "kick," which is why many who abuse amphetamines prefer methamphetamine. The legal form of methamphetamine is the prescription pill Methedrine. Most illegal forms of MAP come from illegal laboratories. MAP is relatively easy to manufacture and does not require sophisticated equipment. Illicit production has occurred in home kitchens, trailers, recreational vehicles, and rural cabins. It is often converted to its water-soluble form, a salt-like substance. However, MAP manufacturing can be dangerous. Combined in the wrong ways, the chemicals used in the process can explode. Illegal "chemists" and innocent victims have been maimed and killed by explosions and resulting fires.

In an attempt to limit the illegal manufacture of MAP in the latter part of the twentieth century, many governments, including the U.S. government, passed laws limiting the sale of ephedrine. Those laws were ineffective because the illicit drug makers learned how to use a chemical called pseudoephedrine to make methamphetamine. Pseudoephedrine is an ingredient found in many over-the-counter medicines used for colds, allergies, and the flu. Since it is readily available, the illegal drug makers have been able to continue to manufacture illicit MAP.

INGESTION METHODS

Prescription amphetamines come in tablet or capsule form. The most common way amphetamines are ingested is by swallowing amphetamine pills or capsules. However, drug abusers also crack open the capsules for the amphetamine powder or grind the tablets into a powder. That powder can then be inhaled or "snorted." Mixed with tobacco or marijuana, it can be smoked. The "ice" form of methamphetamine looks like shaved glass slivers or rock salt and can be smoked in a glass pipe.

Some hardcore drug abusers liquify the powder and the "ice" forms of MAP and inject the solution directly into their bloodstreams. When injected, the "high" or "rush" occurs almost immediately, increasing the danger of addiction to amphetamines, which experts compare to that of heroin or cocaine. An additional concern is the tendency for drug users to reuse and share syringes, dramatically increasing the risks of blood poisoning and contracting HIV/AIDS, hepatitis, or other diseases.

THERAPEUTIC USE

Amphetamines, in prescription form, have been found to be helpful in treating narcolepsy, a condition in which a person suffers from excessive or sudden, recurrent daytime sleepiness. However, narcolepsy is a fairly rare disease.

They have also sometimes been found useful for the treatment of ADHD, a condition that interferes with the learning ability of affected individuals. Millions of children have been diagnosed as having ADHD. Many of those children and increasing numbers of adults are treated with amphetamine-like drugs such as Ritalin and Cylert. The generic name for those amphetamine-like drugs is methylphenidate. Some children with ADHD do not respond to the various forms of methylphenidate and are placed on amphetamines instead.

Amphetamines have also been used and often misused for the treatment of obesity. Medical studies show that dieters who use prescription amphetamines usually do quite well at losing weight initially. However, when those dieters are taken off of amphetamines almost all regain their lost weight and become even heavier over a five-year period. Although the use of amphetamines for weight loss was popular in the 1950s and again in the 1980s and part of the 1990s, most medical doctors do not prescribe amphetamines for weight loss. Non-amphetamine weight-loss drugs are used instead. It remains uncertain as to whether those drugs will be any more effective over the long term in helping people keep off excess weight.

A 2001 study demonstrated a potential new therapeutic role for dextroamphetamine. The study indicated that it may help some stroke survivors recover faster from the stroke-caused speech disorder known as aphasia. Officially, however, amphetamine has been approved only for the treatment of narcolepsy, attention deficit hyperactivity disorder (ADHD), and obesity.

USAGE TRENDS

The use and abuse of amphetamine-like stimulants is a growing global problem, according to the World Health Organization (WHO). The United Nations estimated that in the year 2000, 29 million people around the world abused various types of amphetamine stimulants in the previous decade. That figure was larger than the number of people consuming cocaine and opiates combined. According to the 1999 National Household Survey on Drug Abuse, 9.4 million Americans had tried the MAP form of amphetamine during their lifetimes.

Scope and severity

No specific total amphetamine-use statistics are available. However, according to the year 2000 report of the Drug Abuse Warning Network, there was a 35% increase from 1999 to 2000 in the number of hospital emergency department (ED) cases in which amphetamines were mentioned. DAWN is a national surveillance system that collects data on drug-related emergency department visits.

Age, ethnic, and gender trends

There are few studies revealing age, ethnic, and gender trends in amphetamine abuse. According to a 1998 article in *Journal of Psychology*, the demographic characteristics of amphetamine/methamphetamine abusers changed in the mid-1990s compared to a period only five years previously. Young Caucasian white men who are unemployed and single have been especially likely to be amphetamine users, according to researcher John B. Murray. However, "more married, widowed, and divorced people" and fewer Caucasians were reported in outpatient and inpatient populations studied in 1994–1995 compared to a previous 1989–1994 study.

MENTAL EFFECTS

Amphetamines stimulate the central nervous system (CNS), producing feelings of euphoria, providing relief from fatigue, and increasing alertness. CNS stimulation provoked by amphetamines can also intensify emotions, increase aggression, and alter self-esteem.

As a prescription drug for the treatment of ADHD, amphetamines have been shown to increase performance accuracy, improve short-term memory, improve reaction time, aid in mathematical computation, increase problem-solving abilities in games, and help individuals concentrate.

Unfortunately, chronic amphetamine use can result in a psychological addiction, the belief that a person needs the drug in order to function. Psychological dependence can develop quickly, especially in people who already have clinical depression.

PHYSIOLOGICAL EFFECTS

Increased pulse rate and increased blood pressure are normal with amphetamine use. But even short-term use can cause adverse physical effects, including intoxication, irregular heartbeats (tachycardia), and excessive body warmth, a dangerous and sometimes deadly condition known as hyperthermia.

Prolonged abuse of amphetamine can lead to tolerance, making it necessary to take higher doses of the drug to get the effect or high originally experienced. Taking greater quantities of the drug increases the chance of an overdose. An overdose can increase blood sugar, cause an irregular heartbeat, and cause circulatory collapse. In other words, an overdose can kill. Fatal overdose reactions are usually preceded by convulsions, then coma. Death may occur due to burst blood vessels in the brain, heart attacks, or very high fever.

Chronic use can lead to dangerous changes within the body which cause cravings for the drug, agitation, decreased energy, increased appetite, insomnia, and a craving for sleep. Once the drug taking is temporarily stopped, abusers have been known to drop into deep sleeps that last up to 48 hours. Drivers of cars and trucks coming down from an amphetamine high have been known to fall asleep behind the wheel and cause deadly crashes.

Harmful side effects

Side effects include delayed and impaired judgment, sleep onset, reduced appetite, weight loss, tics, stomachache, headache, and jitteriness. Convulsions and coma may occur. Individuals who ingest amphetamine by dissolving the tablets in water and injecting the mixture risk complications due to the insoluble fillers used in the tablets. When injected, those materials block small blood vessels and can cause serious damage to the lungs and retina of the eye.

Chronic amphetamine users can demonstrate compulsive behavior and talk excessively and disjointedly. Affected individuals can become exhausted and lose insight into their actions, often insulting or otherwise alienating friends and family without obvious cause. High-dose amphetamine consumption causes abusers to become paranoid, or unrealistically suspicious of everyone, and experience hallucinations. Most high-dose amphetamine abusers become psychotic, or mentally deranged, within a week after continuous use. They experience delusions of being persecuted and auditory and visual hallucinations. Chronic amphetamine abuse is also associated with violence, criminal assault, homicides, suicides, and traffic accidents.

Infants born to mothers dependent on amphetamines have an increased risk of premature delivery and low birth weight. The infants may experience symptoms of drug withdrawal. Mothers taking the drug should refrain from nursing, since amphetamine is excreted in human milk. A number of studies using rodents as test animals indicate that women should not take amphetamines when pregnant.

Long-term health effects

Since amphetamines increase blood pressure, the chances for a stroke increases in users. Abusers of amphetamine may also be prone to degenerative disorders of the nervous system such as Parkinson's disease. Research published in the March 2001 issue of *American Journal of Psychiatry* indicates that MAP abuse leads to long-lasting changes in the human brain that are linked to impaired coordination and memory.

Medical studies indicate that five to 15% of the amphetamine users who become psychotic fail to recover completely even after physical withdrawal symptoms pass. Psychiatrists in Japan did a study demonstrating that amphetamine psychosis can persist for several years.

REACTIONS WITH OTHER DRUGS OR SUBSTANCES

Amphetamines are frequently combined with other drugs to prolong the "rush" or "high" or to add a psychedelic, or hallucinogenic, component to the experience. Despite the number of years that amphetamines have been abused, there are relatively few studies about their abuse potential and effects, and apparently there are no studies about the effects of amphetamine when combined with other drugs of abuse.

It is known that amphetamines may counter the sedative effect of antihistamines and other sedating agents. Amphetamines raise blood pressure, so abusers who take prescription anti-hypertension pills do not get the full benefit from those anti-hypertensives.

Amphetamines do not mix well with a class of antidepressant medication known as MAO inhibitors. Mixing the two types of drugs can cause headaches, increase blood pressure, and even result in death.

TREATMENT AND REHABILITATION

Withdrawal can be unpleasant, and feelings of cravings and depression can return long after the withdrawal period. During the withdrawal period, individuals may experience abdominal pain, increased fatigue, fever, infection, loss of appetite, diarrhea, shortness of breath, nausea, vomiting, dizziness, emotional upset, insomnia, nervousness, and weight loss. Amphetamine withdrawal brings on intense cravings for the drug, which often leads to relapse. Intense craving is experienced by 87% of all amphetamine abusers who attempt to abstain from the drug.

Current research has demonstrated that there are no medical treatments effective for treating amphetamine abuse. This means that other drugs cannot be substituted to assist in the weaning process. However, thousands of individuals have successfully gone through withdrawal and continue to abstain from amphetamine use despite the long and uncomfortable process. Twelve-step programs are helpful for many substance abusers in recovery.

Besides intense amphetamine cravings, other unpleasant withdrawal side affects include agitation, anxiety, vivid or unpleasant dreams, decreased energy, increased appetite, lethargy, and increased sleep. People in withdrawal lose interest in the pleasure of other activities. Their physical movements are slowed, and clinical depression is prevalent. Although symptoms may lessen after just four or five days, some symptoms can continue for weeks or even months.

While medical literature indicates that other drugs have limited benefits during the recovery process, the psychological/behavioral literature on addiction rehabilitation reveals that although relapse rates are high, rehabilitation is possible. Addiction experts say that amphetamine withdrawal and treatment is a time-consuming process, and behavioral and emotional support is essential for success. Organizations such Phoenix House, Freedom House, and SAFE (Substance Abuse Family Education) run withdrawal treatment and rehabilitation programs for teens that last for as long as a year at live-in residence centers.

PERSONAL AND SOCIAL CONSEQUENCES

Authorities point out that few people are capable of questioning the value of a drug that makes them feel good and is considered to have beneficial effects. However, occasional experimentation can easily become compulsive drug use and abuse. Abusers frequently do not recognize the effects amphetamines have on their failures and also often do not see how that "upper" has negative effects on their relationships with others.

Early onset of drug abuse is associated with early sexual activity, crime, and educational failure. Young amphetamine users risk exploitation by adults and are more likely to become involved in criminal or violent behavior and prostitution—having to resort to sex for survival. Consequently, they are also more likely to become infected with HIV or other sexually transmitted diseases and by tuberculosis or other bacterial, fungal, or viral infections. Chronic amphetamine abusers are also more at risk for mental and emotional disorders including anxiety, phobias, and depression. They are at higher risk of suicide.

Amphetamines have the potential to produce "unprovoked, random, and often senseless violence," according to the World Health Organization (WHO). They are likely to demonstrate paranoia, antisocial behavior, become overly verbally and physically aggressive, and start fights over literally nothing.

The social consequences of amphetamine abuse include higher rates of accidents, violence, and crime. This is a worldwide phenomenon, says WHO. According to the National Institute on Drug Abuse (NIDA), drug abuse cost American society $97.7 billion during 1992. That estimate included costs for substance abuse treatment and prevention, related health care, reduced job productivity, lost earnings, and other costs to society such as crime and social welfare. How much of that is due to amphetamine misuse is unknown, but the study estimated that the costs were borne almost equally by governments (46%) and by those who abuse drugs and members of their families (44%). More than half of the estimated costs of drug abuse were associated with drug-related crime.

 **IN THE NEWS**

Amphetamine abuse among teenagers is not just a problem faced by the United States and western countries. In Thailand, every day more teenagers become addicted to amphetamines. The number of youths arrested on drug-related charges sharply escalated in 1996, reportedly the year that the popularity of amphetamines among young people surpassed that of heroin.

In Thailand, amphetamine is called *ya maa*, "the horse drug—since it lets you work like a horse," report two Thai writers. It is also known as *ya baa*, the "crazy drug." Thai truck drivers discovered amphetamines first, and then others working long hours embraced the drug. Amphetamines became so popular on Thai highways that some gas stations started offering it along with fuel. The Inter Press Service quotes unnamed Thai government sources as saying that as many as one million Thais may be addicted to amphetamines. Many of the addicts are college and high school teens who were attracted to the drug's promise of increased energy and used it to study before tests.

As one of three countries known as the "Golden Triangle" (Thailand, Burma, and Laos), Thailand's drugs of choice historically have been opium, cocaine, or heroin. Nevertheless, the use of amphetamines and other synthetic drugs is rising in Thailand because synthetic drugs are easier and cheaper to produce. Traditional drugs need expensive natural materials—opium resin for heroin and cocaine leaves for cocaine—whereas the chemicals necessary to make amphetamines are available legally and are cheaper than the illegal, natural, opium-based products.

LEGAL CONSEQUENCES

Individuals who buy, sell, or transport illegal amphetamines, or those who buy, sell, or otherwise traffic in the equipment to manufacture illegal amphetamines risk hefty fines and imprisonment. In the United States, the consequences of illegal possession, sale, or even freely sharing amphetamines without a medical doctor's prescription can be severe under terms of the Controlled Substance Act (CSA) of 1970.

A first offense of simple possession of amphetamine without a doctor's prescription can result in imprisonment for not more than one year and a fine of $1,000 or both. A second offense can result in imprisonment for up to two years and a fine of $2,500. A third illegal possession offense can result in up to three years of prison time and a fine of $5,000.

Distribution, which includes selling or giving away more than 100 grams of amphetamine is illegal under CSA section 841. It is an offense punishable by prison terms of a minimum of five years and up to 40 years with fines of up to $2 million. If death or injury results from illegal distribution, the penalties become imprisonment for a minimum of 20 years to more than life and a fine of $2 million. A person convicted of selling amphetamines to someone under 21 years of age is subject to twice the maximum punishment.

Legal history

Before 1970, amphetamines were subject to numerous and sometimes confusing laws regulating their manufacture and distribution. In 1970, the U.S. Congress passed the Comprehensive Drug Abuse Prevention and

Control Act, which has been the legal foundation of the U.S. government's fight against the abuse of amphetamines and other drugs since its passage. The Controlled Substances Act (CSA) is title II of that legislation. The CSA placed all drug substances that had been regulated under existing federal laws into one of five schedules based on the substance's medicinal value, harmfulness, and potential for abuse and addiction. Schedule I is reserved for the most dangerous drugs that have no recognized medical use. Amphetamines fall under Schedule II, dangerous drugs with useful and legitimate medical uses that also have a high potential for abuse and addiction.

See also Designer drugs; Ecstasy (MDMA); Methamphetamine; Methylphenidate

RESOURCES

Books

Bayer, Linda. *Amphetamines and Other Uppers*. Broomall, PA., Chelsea House Publishers, 2000.

Cobb, Alice B. *Speed and Your Brain: The Incredibly Disgusting Story*. New York: Rosen Publishing group, 2000.

Kuhn, Cynthia. *Buzzed: The Straight Facts About the Most Used and Abused Drugs from Alcohol to Ecstacy*. New York: W.W. Norton & Company, Inc., 1998.

Littell, Mary Ann. *Speed and Methamphetamine Drug Dangers*. Berkeley Heights, NJ: Enslow Publishers, Inc., 1999.

Pellowski, Michael J. *Amphetamine Drug Dangers*. Berkeley Heights, NJ: Enslow Publishers, Inc., 2001.

Periodicals

"All They Need is the Love Clinic: A Dallas Program Helps Kids to Say No to Sex and Drugs." *Christianity Today* 45, no. 15 (December 3, 2001): 62-65.

Gilbert, Laura. "Just Say Know: The Truth About Drugs." *Teen Magazine* 45, no. 7 (July 2001): 90.

"Kicking Drugs: A Recovery Diary: Stacia Litchfield Had It All-Including A Hardcore Drug Addiction That Drove Her To Trade Sex For A High. Now, After A Grueling Three Years In Rehab, She's Emerged-Clean And Ready For A New Life." *Teen People* 4, no. 16 (August 1, 2001): 138+.

Other

"Confessions of a Teenage Drug Addict." May 2001. <http://www.thailandlife.com/drugs/index.html>.

Stocker, Steven. "Overall Teen Drug Use Stays Level, Use of MDMA and Steroids Increases." *NIDA Notes* 15, no. 1 (March 2000). <www.nida.gov>.

Organizations

American Council for Drug Education (ACDE), 204 Monroe Street, Rockville, MD, USA, 20852, (301) 294-0600, mail@add.org.

Narcotic Educational Foundation of America (NEFA), 28245 Avenue Crocker, Suite 230, Santa Clarita, CA, USA, 91355-1201, (661) 775-6968, mail@add.org, <http://www.cnoa.org/NEFA.htm>.

National Clearinghouse for Alcohol & Drug Information (NCADI), P.O. Box 2345, Rockville, MD, USA, 20852, (800) 729-6686, mail@add.org, <http://www.samhsa.gov/centers/clearinghouse/clearinghouses.html>.

National Families in Action, 2957 Clairmont Road, Suite 150, Atlanta, GA, USA, 30329, (404) 248-9676, mail@add.org, <http://www.emory.edu/NFIA/>.

Substance Abuse and Mental Health Services Administration (SAMHSA), U.S. Dept. of Health and Human Services, 5600 Fishers Lane, Rockville, MD, USA, 20857, (301)443-6239, (800) 622-Help, mail@add.org, <http://www.samhsa.gov/centers/clearinghouse/clearinghouses.html>.

University of Kentucky Center for Prevention Research, 1151 Red Mile Rd. Ste.1-A, Lexington, KY, USA, 40504, (606) 257-5588, <http://www.uky.edu/RGS/PreventionResearch/welcome.html>.

Maury M. Breecher, PhD, MPH

AMYL NITRITE

OVERVIEW

Amyl nitrite was discovered in England in the 1840s and used to treat angina pectoris, a heart condition marked by severe chest pains and shortness of breath. Until then, physicians had treated the condition by using leeches to "bleed" the body of impurities. Amyl nitrite was used to treat angina pectoris because it dilated blood vessels, causing the heart to get more oxygen and thereby relieving the pain. However, one of the side effects was that it caused the patient to experience a short but dizzying burst of euphoria.

The drug was packaged in small, mesh-covered glass vials, which could be crushed with the thumb and fingers and the vapors inhaled. (The vials of amyl nitrite became known as "poppers" because of the sound they made when crushed.) The drug triggered an almost immediate jump in the heart rate and a corresponding drop in blood pressure, causing smooth muscle tissue to relax. At the same time, it cuts the amount of oxygen to the brain, causing a sudden, intense weakness and dizziness that lasts two or three minutes.

Over time, amyl nitrite was used less and less to treat angina, but it grew in popularity with rumors that it allegedly intensified sexual orgasm. Although there is no research that suggests amyl nitrite is an effective aphrodisiac, by the 1950s it had gained a reputation in the British show business industry for enhancing sexual orgasm. In the 1960s, it found particular acceptance among gay men in the United States, especially in urban areas like New York, Los Angeles, and San Francisco.

In the 1970s, the drug became popular among young gay males in both the United States and Britain.

OFFICIAL NAMES: Amyl nitrate, amyl nitrite
STREET NAMES: Amy, high-tech, kix, liquid gold, locker room, poppers, ram, rave, rush, snappers, thrust, TNT
DRUG CLASSIFICATIONS: Not scheduled, inhalant

It was widely used in discos and dance clubs to get a momentary "rush" while dancing. The sudden usage increase coincided with the Food and Drug Administration's (FDA) decision to eliminate the need for a prescription to obtain the drug in the early 1960s. When the FDA reinstated the prescription requirement in 1969, manufacturers got around it by using slightly altered formulas. The alterations were minor and the effects of the drugs were the same.

The modified formulas, called butyl nitrite and isobutyl nitrite, did not require FDA approval because they were not marketed as either a drug or food product. They were marketed heavily in the gay community under the general name of "poppers." By 1974, poppers were in full swing within the gay community, and large advertising campaigns were mounted in gay publications, according to Randy Viele, outreach coordinator for Project H.O.P.E. (HIV Outreach Prevention Education) in northeast New York.

During the 1960s, amyl nitrite, along with a variety of other drugs, including marijuana, heroin, opium, LSD, and amphetamines, made its way to U.S. soldiers fighting in Vietnam. When the soldiers returned to the U.S. after their tour of duty, many continued their poppers habit. The FDA reinstated its ban on amyl nitrite without

KEY TERMS

AMPHETAMINES: A class of drugs frequently abused as a stimulant. Used medically to treat narcolepsy (a condition characterized by brief attacks of deep sleep) and as an appetite suppressant.

ANGINA PECTORIS: A disease marked by spasmodic attacks of intense, suffocating chest pain due to insufficient blood flow to the heart.

APHRODISIAC: A substance or drug that increases sexual desire.

BRONCHITIS: An acute inflammation of the bronchial tubes in the lungs.

CARCINOGENS: Substances or agents that cause cancer.

CARDIOPULMONARY RESUSCITATION: A procedure designed to restore normal breathing after the heart stops. It includes clearing air passages to the lungs, mouth-to-mouth artificial respiration, and heart massage by exerting pressure on the chest.

CEREBELLUM: A large part of the brain that helps with muscle coordination and balance.

CEREBRAL CORTEX: The surface layer of gray matter in the front part of the brain that helps in coordinating the senses and motor functions.

CYANIDE: Any of several chemical compounds that acts on the respiratory system and can quickly cause death.

ECSTASY: The street name for MDMA, an illegal club drug that is mildly hallucinogenic.

GHB (GAMMA HYDROXYBUTYRATE): Originally sold in health food stores as a growth hormone, a liquid nervous depressant touted for its ecstasy-like qualities. Banned by the FDA in 1990, the respiratory depression it can cause makes it among the most dangerous club drugs in circulation.

GLAUCOMA: A disease of the eye that can lead to blindness.

HALLUCINOGENS: A group of drugs that induces sensory distortions and hallucinations.

IMPOTENCE: The inability to achieve or maintain an erection.

KETAMINE: An anesthetic abused for its mind-altering effects that is popular as an illicit club drug. It is sometimes used to facilitate sexual assault, or date rape.

NITROGLYCERINE: A heavy, oily, explosive liquid used in medically in tiny amounts to dilate blood vessels in treating angina pectoris.

ROHYPNOL (FLUNTRAZEPAM): An overseas prescription sleeping aid that, in lower doses, gives users a feeling similar to alcohol intoxication; also used as a date rape drug.

---

a prescription in 1969, following reports from soldiers and former soldiers in the United States of serious problems caused by the drug. These problems included skin burns, fainting, dizziness, breathing difficulties, and blood anomalies.

In 1988, the U.S. Consumer Products Safety Commission banned the sale of butyl nitrite. But manufacturers kept one step ahead of federal regulatory agencies. Each time a specific formula was banned, the manufacturers would adjust by altering the chemical composition slightly. As of 2002, the newest popper was cyclohexyl nitrite, commonly sold in drug paraphernalia or "head" shops and adult bookstores as a head cleaner for VCRs. Cyclohexyl is chemically similar to amyl nitrite and butyl nitrite and produces the same effect when inhaled.

CHEMICAL/ORGANIC COMPOSITION

Amyl nitrite is generally sold in small glass bottles or, in rare cases, small vials or ampoules. It is chemically related to nitroglycerine. It is part of a group of closely related chemicals known as alkyl nitrites. In street terminology, amyl, butyl, isobutyl, isoamyl, isopropyl, and cyclohexyl nitrates and nitrites are collectively referred to as amyl nitrite or poppers. Depending on he specific molecule, it is the nitrite or nitrate portion of the molecule that causes the muscles to relax and blood vessels to dilate. This effect is achieved regardless of what organic molecule, such as amyl or butyl, to which it is attached.

INGESTION METHODS

Amyl nitrite vapor is usually inhaled through the nose and more rarely inhaled through the mouth. It can be fatal if swallowed and can cause burns if it comes in contact with the skin.

THERAPEUTIC USE

Amyl nitrite was originally manufactured and prescribed to treat angina pectoris, a heart condition marked by severe chest pains and shortness of breath. More effective treatments now exist, and it is rarely prescribed for this purpose.

Amyl nitrite is also considered an antidote for cyanide poisoning and is usually one of three medications found in cyanide poisoning kits used by the militaries of some countries, some emergency medical services, and at plants where cyanide is used. Cyanide is used by industry in many chemical syntheses, electroplating, plastics processing, gold and silver extraction, tanning, metallurgy, and as a fumigant against rodents. The most extreme use of cyanide is as a chemical weapon, since high doses can kill large groups of people almost instantly. This application, especially by terrorists, has become of increasing concern since the September 11, 2001, terrorist attacks on the United States and the subsequent anthrax attacks.

The North Atlantic Treaty Organization (NATO) and the U.S. military consider cyanide a possible weapon of so-called rogue nations such as Iraq, Iran, and North Korea, and terrorist groups. Iraq is believed to have used cyanide to kill thousands in the 1980s during its war with Iran and against Kurds in northern Iraq. With this in mind, the possibility of an antidote takes on added importance. However, the effectiveness of amyl nitrite as an antidote for cyanide poisoning has come under question by some medical authorities. The U.S. military removed amyl nitrite from its cyanide antidote kits, because of adverse side effects (low blood pressure, dizziness, and headaches) and other concerns.

USAGE TRENDS

The use of amyl nitrite as a prescription drug for angina pectoris has dropped considerably from a few decades ago and since the early 1960s has been prescribed rarely in the United States. Because a prescription is required to obtain amyl nitrite in the United States, two variants of the drug, butyl nitrate and isobutyl nitrate, became popular in the 1970s. After falling out of favor in the 1980s and 1990s, there again appears to be a slight surge in the drugs' usage. The primary users today are teenagers and young adults who attend raves and all-night dance parties. Poppers are often used in conjunction with other so-called rave or club drugs, such as 3, 4-methylenedioxymethamphetamine (MDMA or ecstasy), ketamine, 2C-B, and gamma hydroxybutyrate (GHB).

Scope and severity

There are few studies or research data that tracks the scope and severity of amyl nitrite usage, particularly among adults. It is usually lumped in the general category of inhalants. However, it is generally believed the problem is not as severe as with other, more readily available inhalants, such as solvents, aerosol propellants, and aliphatic nitrites, such as cyclohexyl nitrite.

HISTORY NOTES

Amyl nitrite was discovered in 1844 and was found to relax the tiny blood vessels known as capillaries that connect arteries and veins. In 1867, Thomas Lauder Brunton, a medical student in Scotland, found the drug helped relieve angina by increasing blood flow to the heart. A few years later, nitroglycerine was found to have a similar dilating effect. Although both can still be prescribed for angina, nitroglycerine is much more commonly prescribed because it is more easily administered and has fewer side effects. A prescription was required for amyl nitrite until the early 1960s when the FDA approved it for over-the-counter sale. That approval was withdrawn in 1969 when the FDA found the chemical was being used as a recreational drug.

Inhalant abuse is found in both urban and rural areas of the United States and Canada. Research indicates social and economic rather than racial and cultural factors in general impact the rate of inhalant abuse. Poverty, physical or mental abuse as a child, poor grades in school, and dropping out of school are all associated with increased inhalant abuse. At particularly high risk are Native American youths who live on reservations where poverty and school dropout rates are high.

According to *Alcoholism & Addiction Magazine,* researchers have put together a "user profile" of inhalant abusers. Almost all of the profile indicators relate to social and economic conditions. The profile of a typical inhalant abuser is: poor academic achievement in junior high or middle school, no father living at home, poor coping skills, insecurity and low self-esteem, low I.Q., depression, an alcoholic living in the home, family problems, and low family income.

Age, ethnic, and gender trends

Amyl nitrite abuse can be found in all ethnic groups, age levels, and genders. However, the predominance seems to be among older adolescents, white, from families with low to average incomes, male, and those who frequent dance clubs and raves. Most abusers use amyl nitrite in combination with other drugs.

The University of Michigan has conducted the Monitoring the Future (MTF) study, sponsored by the National Institute on Drug Abuse (NIDA), each year since 1991. It tracks drug use among students in the eighth, tenth, and twelfth grades. While inhalant use has

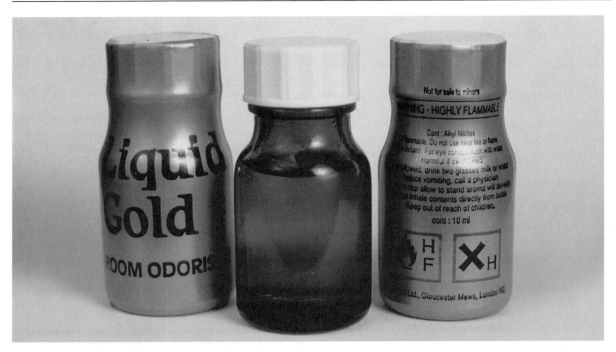

Small bottles of liquid drugs, such as those shown above, are known as poppers. Liquid Gold is one type of popper containing amyl nitrite, an intoxicating vapor that causes muscle relaxation and blood vessel dilation. The drugs in poppers can cause headache, nausea, and vomiting, and can dramatically decrease blood pressure, which may be fatal. Photo Researchers Inc., Science Photo Library. Reproduced by permission.

been tracked for all three grade levels, amyl nitrite use has been tracked only for twelfth grade students.

In 1991, 1.6% of the nation's high school seniors reported using amyl nitrite at least once during their lifetime. For the next five years, the survey found the rate relatively consistent, between 1.5% and 1.8%. In 1997, the rate rose to 2% and jumped to 2.7% the following year. It dropped to 1.7% in 1999 and plunged to less than 1% in 2000, the lowest level in 10 years. But in 2001, the rate jumped again, to 1.9%, a 1.1% increase over the previous year. It was the largest percentage increase between 2000 and 2001 of any of the 20 drugs or drug groups tracked by the study (which includes alcohol and tobacco), with the exception of steroids, which showed a 1.2% increase among twelfth-graders.

Researchers involved in the study were unsure what caused the increase. The only other drugs that showed usage gains among twelfth-graders between 2000 and 2001 were marijuana and hashish (0.2%), hallucinogens other than LSD (0.1%), PCP (0.2%), MDMA or ecstasy (0.7%), amphetamines (0.6%), tranquilizers (0.4%), and Rohypnol (0.3%). Since most of the increases were in the so-called club drugs, it is likely that amyl nitrite is being used in conjunction with these drugs.

Amyl nitrite was not tracked among eighth- and tenth-graders in the MTF study, but was included in the general category of inhalants. Data from national and state surveys have found that inhalant abuse is most commonly found in junior and senior high school students, reaching a peak in seventh through ninth grades. In the MTF survey, about 20% of eighth grade students said they have sniffed inhalants. This compared to about 16% of tenth-graders and 15% of high school seniors.

One obvious question then is how can fewer tenth and twelfth grade students than eighth grade students report they have ever used inhalants? There are two possible answers, according to NIDA. First, older students may not remember their earlier use of inhalants. Second, and more troubling to researchers, is that many eighth grade inhalant abusers may have dropped out of school before they reached the twelfth grade.

Gender differences in inhalant abuse have been identified at different age levels, according to NIDA studies. One study showed inhalant abuse is higher for boys than girls in the fourth through sixth grades, occurs at similar rates in the seventh through ninth grades when overall use is highest, and is higher for boys in the tenth through twelfth grades. The National Household Survey on Drug Abuse (NHSDA) among Americans found that in 1998, the use of inhalants among 12- to 17-year-olds was evenly divided among boys and girls. The same study found that among 18– to 25-year-olds, the rate of inhalant abuse was twice as high among males compared to females. This suggest the long-term use of inhalants is much more common among males.

Inhalant abuse among eighth, tenth, and twelfth grade students gradually declined between 1996 and 1999, according to MTF surveys. However, the rates are still higher than they were in the late 1980s, according NHSDA data. Usage seems to vary from state to state. Few states track the use of amyl nitrite among students. One that does is Maryland, which reports one of the lowest rates of inhalant abuse among students.

In the rural state of West Virginia, 28.4% of high school students reported they had used an inhalant to get high in 1997, according to the Office of National Drug Control Policy (ONDCP). Among female students, the rate was 26.4% and among males, 30.6%. In neighboring Kentucky, the rate was 18.2% for 1999. In Ohio, which has both large urban and rural areas, 17.1% of high school students said they had used an inhalant, according to a 1999 ONDCP report. In Texas, a 1996 survey found that 20% of seventh and eighth grade students had used an inhalant to get high at least once.

In Britain, the trend is taking amyl nitrite into the general youth and adolescent population. A 2000 survey of 16-year-olds in northwest England found that more than 20% said they have used inhalants at least once. The number of Canadian youths between 12 and 17 years of age who have tried inhalants is between 3% and 5%, according to the Canadian Medical Association (CMA). However, the percentage is much higher among certain impoverished populations, such as the Inuit and Aboriginal communities, where the CMA stated the problem is widespread and epidemic.

MENTAL EFFECTS

Inhalants in general can, and often do, cause serious impairment of mental functions. They also can cause irreversible brain damage, particularly to the cerebral cortex and the cerebellum. This can result in personality changes, memory impairment, hallucinations, loss of coordination, and slurred speech, according to the ONDCP.

Amyl nitrite and other poppers can cause confusion, dizziness, drowsiness, and a slowed perception of time, even with only limited use. For these reasons driving, operating machinery, or any other work that requires being alert or responsive, is not recommended while under the influence of amyl nitrite. Amyl nitrite can also cause people to feel less inhibited, relaxed, and give them a sense of well-being and intensified emotions. This can impair judgment, especially when it comes to sexual behavior.

PHYSIOLOGICAL EFFECTS

Amyl nitrite is rapidly absorbed into the blood stream and quickly reaches the brain, with effects usually beginning five to 10 seconds after inhaling. The initial effects are often referred to as a "rush" or "head rush" and last from two to five minutes. It causes the walls of blood vessels to relax, resulting in lowered blood pressure. This increases pulse rate because the heart is beating faster than usual to restore normal blood pressure. It also causes facial flushing and dizziness. The dilation of blood vessels in the brain appears to trigger an increase in pressure in the brain, which may give rise to the euphoria reportedly experienced by users. Amyl nitrite also causes muscles to involuntarily relax. Adverse reactions include skin and throat irritation, nausea, and headache.

Harmful side effects

Poppers have the ability to cause asphyxia, which can cause a person to stop breathing and become unconscious, resulting in a lack of oxygen or excess carbon dioxide in the body. They can also cause a short-term deficiency of oxygen reaching the tissues of the body, a condition called hypoxia. When inhaled, amyl nitrite ions can burn sensitive mucous membranes in the throat, nose, and lungs, causing irritation, pain, coughing, bronchitis, and difficulty breathing.

Excessive use of amyl nitrite can be dangerous to anyone. However, people with anemia, diabetes, glaucoma, an overactive thyroid, or high blood pressure, or who have had a recent head injury or heart attack, are at greater risk for encountering severe health problems, according to the NIDA. Pregnant women should not use amyl nitrite or any inhalant since the chemical can cross the placenta into the fetus, causing damage. Adverse reactions and side effects may be more frequent and severe in persons over the age of 60.

Many nitrates and nitrites increase pressure in the nerves and blood vessels of the eyes, which can cause a feeling of pressure behind the eyes and a severe headache. This can lead to glaucoma, a potentially blinding eye disorder.

Amyl nitrite, as with other inhalants, have the potential to cause sudden sniffing death (SSD) syndrome. The condition is brought on by unexpected disturbances in the heart's rhythm, causing heart failure and death. SSD syndrome can result when a user deeply inhales a chemical for its intoxicating effect. This causes a decrease in available oxygen to the body. If the user becomes startled or engages in sudden physical activity, the flow of adrenaline increases from the brain to the heart, inducing cardiac arrest. Death occurs within minutes.

Overdose symptoms include nausea, vomiting, dangerously low blood pressure, difficulty breathing, fainting, cold skin, blue lips or fingernails, rapid heartbeat, and headache or a strong feeling of pressure in the head.

Long-term health effects

The nitrite ions generated by amyl nitrite inhalation increase the body's production of certain carcinogens, which increases the risk for cancer. They can also damage red blood cells by interfering with oxygen supply to vital tissues that can cause an often-fatal anemia. This type of poisoning happens most frequently to users who swallow rather than inhale the chemical. It requires immediate medical attention.

The National Institute on Drug Abuse reports that recent research conducted on laboratory animals shows a possible link between the abuse of amyl nitrite and the development and progression of infectious diseases and tumors. The research indicates that inhaling nitrites and nitrates depletes many cells in the immune system and impairs the way the immune system fights infectious diseases, such as HIV, gonorrhea, syphilis, hepatitis A, and chicken pox. This also means that in people with HIV, using amyl nitrite can increase the speed at which the virus replicates. The higher a person's viral load, the greater the risk for developing AIDS.

One problem with long-term inhalant abuse is that it can break down myelin in the body, according to a NIDA report. Myelin is a fatty tissue that surrounds many of the body's nerve cells called neurons. The nerve cells in the brain and spinal cord are like a "command central" for the body. They transmit messages that control just about everything the body does. If the myelin breaks down, the nerve cells may not be able to transmit messages.

This could happen in the frontal cortex, the area of the brain that solves complex problems and plans for the future. If inhalants make their way into the brain's cerebellum, which controls movement and coordination, they can make a person move more slowly or clumsily. Studies also show that nerve cells in the brain's hippocampus can be damaged by inhalants. Since the hippocampus controls memory, a person who repeatedly uses inhalants may lose the ability to learn new things, or may have a hard time keeping track of simple conversations.

Many persons who have abused inhalants, especially for prolonged periods of several days, find they have a strong need to continue using them. Compulsive use and a mild withdrawal syndrome can occur with long-term inhalant abuse.

Other long-term effects of amyl nitrite use are unclear. Mood swings and personality changes have been reported but have not been studied. Tolerance to poppers develops on repeated exposure. Chemical dependence does not occur, and the drugs have a low potential for psychological dependence.

REACTIONS WITH OTHER DRUGS OR SUBSTANCES

Amyl nitrite is commonly used in conjunction with other illicit drugs, including marijuana, cocaine, methamphetamines, and hallucinogens, to enhance the high. Doing so increases the risk of adverse reactions. A British survey published in 2000 found that a majority of young people at dance clubs and raves regularly used more than one drug at a time, with amyl nitrite often part of the mix. For example, 49% of those surveyed said they regularly used amyl nitrite in conjunction with ecstasy. The use of amyl nitrite with these and other so-called club drugs can lead to psychiatric problems and physiological conditions such as overheating, dehydration, and heart strain.

Amyl nitrite is particularly dangerous when combined with the prescription drug Viagra, used to treat impotence. Since both act to dilate blood vessels, taking the two together can cause blood pressure to drop to dangerous levels. This can lead to heart attack and stroke. Amyl nitrite also should not be taken by men using minoxidil (Rogaine) to treat hair loss, since it has the potential to reduce blood pressure.

Amyl nitrite can also be dangerous for people who take prescription medications to treat hypertension or high blood pressure. These include:

- Diuretics, such as hydrochlorothiazide and hydrochlorothiazide combinations (Aldoril, Capozide, Dyazide, HydroDiuril, Maxzide, and Lopressor HCT).

- Beta-blockers, including carvedilol (Coreg), atenolol (Tenormin), betaxolol (Kerlone), metoprolol (Lopressor, Toprol XL), penbutolol (Levatol), and propranolol (Inderal).

- Angiotensin-converting enzyme (ACE) inhibitors, such as benazepril (Lotensin), enalapril (Vasotec), fosinopril (Monopril), lisinopril (Prinivil, Zestril), quinapril (Accupril), and ramipril (Altace).

- Calcium channel blockers, including diltiazem (Cardizem SR, Dilacor XR, Tiazac), nicardipine (Cardene), amlodipine (Norvasc), felodipine (Plendil), and enalapril maleate-felodipine ER (Lexxel).

- Angiotensin II receptor antagonists, such as losartan (Cozaar, Hyzaar), valsartan (Diovan), irbesartan (Avapro), and candesartan cilexetil (Atacand).

- Vasodilators, including guanfacine (Tenex), methyldopa (Aldomet), prazosin (Minipress), terazosin (Hytrin), hydralazine (Apresoline), and minoxidil (Loniten).

Amyl nitrite can also act adversely or unpredictably in people taking heart medications such as nitroglycerine, or anti-depression medications. There is also new research that suggests amyl nitrite can interfere with and reduce the effectiveness of HIV medications. Of particular concern are protease inhibitors, such as indinavir (Crixivan), saquinavir mesylate (Invirase), nelfinavir mesylate (Viracept), and ritonavir (Norvir).

TREATMENT AND REHABILITATION

There are no withdrawal symptoms for amyl nitrite commonly associated with other inhalants. Since amyl nitrite is not addictive, there is no suggested treatment or rehabilitation regimen that is specific to the drug. However, since amyl nitrite is often used in combination with other drugs, abusers are likely to benefit from drug dependency treatment programs, including counseling.

As with all abused drugs, education and knowledge regarding the dangers of sniffing amyl nitrite is a key to preventing use and in getting help when abuse occurs. Studies show that peer pressure is the number one reason young people try drugs. Therefore, it is important that young people not only resist the pressure, but try to persuade friends who are using amyl nitrite or abusing any drug to get help.

PERSONAL AND SOCIAL CONSEQUENCES

Amyl nitrite, unlike other inhalants, are abused primarily because they are believed to enhance sexual pleasure and performance through loss of inhibition. However, abandoning inhibition leads to unsafe sex and a much greater risk for sexually transmitted diseases, including HIV, hepatitis A, gonorrhea, and syphilis.

Studies and surveys in the United States and Great Britain show that people who use poppers generally tend to do worse in school and are more likely to drop out. Drop-outs are more likely to end up in low-paying jobs or become part of the welfare system. A number of studies show that people who abuse drugs are much more prone to illness, particularly viruses and other infections.

Students who are convicted of using or possessing amyl nitrite can be denied federal scholarships and loan guarantees, which may affect their ability to get a college education. In 2001, about 14,000 high school graduates were denied federal aid, at least temporarily, because of prior drug convictions.

LEGAL CONSEQUENCES

The FDA made the possession, use, or sale of amyl nitrite without a prescription illegal in the United States in 1969. In 1988, the U.S. Consumer Products Safety

IN THE NEWS

During the first few years of the AIDS epidemic in the early 1980s, poppers were suspected as being a contributing factor to the disease. Some researchers and many activists in the gay community thought the drug might be the cause of the virus. While it has been proven that poppers do not cause human immunodeficiency virus (HIV), the virus that leads to AIDS, there is substantial research evidence that links it to immune system problems in people with HIV, including increasing the risk for Kaposi's sarcoma (KS), a deadly cancer often found in people in the advanced stages of AIDS.

In a study conducted in the early 1980s, soon after HIV was identified as the cause of AIDS, the Centers for Disease Control (CDC) found that of 87 patients studied with KS, 84 reported regularly using poppers. Although there is no conclusive proof, later studies have also linked the use of amyl nitrite to immune system suppression and to the development of KS. In the 1980s, San Francisco banned the use of poppers in public places and required merchants to post warning about the drugs' health hazards. The city's health department cited the possible link between amyl nitrite use and HIV and KS as the reason for the actions. After a few years, the warnings disappeared from places where amyl nitrite was sold. The city revived the ban and warning requirement in 2001.

Commission banned the sale of butyl nitrite. However, the most commonly found poppers today contain cyclohexyl nitrite, which has a similar effect as amyl butyl nitrite. With cyclohexyl nitrite legal and readily available in the United States, the illegal use and sale of amyl and butyl nitrite is limited. Researchers point out that regardless of the legal status, the dangers of using any nitrite or nitrate are similar.

The laws and punishment regarding possession of poppers in the United States vary from state to state. In some states, it is illegal to inhale any type of fumes for the purpose of intoxication. For example, in New York, possession or use of any alkyl nitrite, including amyl, butyl, and isobutyl, is a Class A misdemeanor, which carries a jail term of up to one year. The judge also has other punishment options, including imposing a fine and driver's license suspension or revocation. In Connecticut, conviction for possession of amyl nitrite without a prescription carries a penalty for a first offense of up to seven years in prison and a fine of up to $50,000. The maximum penalty for a second conviction is 15 years in prison and a fine of $100,000.

Possession of amyl nitrite without a prescription in Pennsylvania is a misdemeanor under the state's Controlled Substances, Drugs, Devices, and Cosmetics Act. A first-time conviction carries a penalty of up to three years in state prison and a fine of up to $5,000. A second offense conviction carries a penalty of up to three years in prison and a fine of up to $25,000. In Georgia, amyl nitrite is considered a "dangerous drug." A conviction for possession without a prescription carries a penalty of up to a year in jail and a fine of up to $5,000. A conviction of amyl nitrite possession in South Dakota is a Class One misdemeanor. It carries a maximum penalty of one year in county jail and a fine of $1,000 for the first offense.

Several states have made it a crime to drive while under the influence of poppers, regardless of the formula. New Jersey adopted a law in 1995 that specifically bans driving while under the influence of amyl, butyl, ethyl, or propyl nitrates or nitrites. It further bans driving while under the influence of any inhalant or other substance that releases a toxic vapor or fumes capable of causing intoxication, inebriation, excitement, stupefaction, or the dulling of the brain or nervous system.

Conviction under the New Jersey law carries a fine of between $250 and $400 and up to 30 days in jail for a first offense. The offender can also lose their driver's license for six months to a year. For a second conviction, the penalty is a $500 to $1,000 fine and up to 90 days in jail. Offenders must also perform 30 days of community service work and lose their driver's license for two years. A third or subsequent conviction carries a $1,000 fine and up to six months in jail. Offenders also forfeit their driver's license for 10 years. In West Virginia, the minimum penalty for conviction of driving under the influence of amyl nitrite is one day in county jail and a $100 fine. The maximum sentence is six months in jail and a $500 fine.

California's Proposition 36

In 2000, California voters approved a ballot measure that allows state courts to sentence first- and second-time drug use offenders to rehabilitative treatment rather than jail or prison. The measure, Proposition 36 (Prop. 36), also known as the Substance Abuse and Crime Prevention Act, took effect July 1, 2001. As of March 1, 2002, more than 15,000 individuals had been referred to treatment under Prop. 36. The law mandates probation and drug abuse treatment for offenders instead of jail time. Persons sentenced under Prop. 36 are required to spend up to a year in a state-approved treatment regimen. Treatment can include outpatient care, inpatient treatment at a halfway house, psychotherapy, and drug education and prevention classes. The law applies to persons convicted of possession of amyl nitrite without a prescription.

The philosophy behind the law is two-fold. First, it frees up jail and prison space for persons convicted of violent offenses. Second, it mandates treatment and education that a drug user may not get in jail. The goal of Prop. 36 is to reduce repeat drug use and lower crime rates. Drug policy officials say it is too early to determine if the California program is successful in achieving either of these goals. A similar measure, Proposition 200, was approved by voters in Arizona in 1996.

International penalties

The sale of amyl nitrite is illegal in Great Britain without a prescription. But the possession or use without a prescription is not illegal. In New Zealand, amyl and butyl nitrites are controlled under the Medicines Act of 1981. This Act limits the availability of substances that can be used as medicines and imposes penalties for misuse of these drugs. Penalties can be up to three months in jail, a fine of $500, or both. Police also can hold people under the influence of the drug for detoxification under the Alcoholism and Drug Addiction Act 1966. This is rarely done, since the visible effects of amyl nitrite use usually wear off after a few minutes.

Legal history

Federal law required a prescription for the sale, use, or possession of amyl nitrite until 1960, when the FDA lifted the requirement. The FDA reinstated the prescription requirement in 1969. Other poppers were banned in 1988, and the law was amended in 1990 to include a broader range of nitrites.

In Great Britain, the Medicines Act deems it illegal to sell amyl nitrite without a prescription. However, possession or use without a prescription is not a crime. Most other nitrates sold as poppers have escaped prosecution under the Medicines Act since distributors claimed they were room deodorizers and not marketed as medicine. However, the European Union (EU), of which Great Britain is a member, has issued a directive that any substance for sale that has a mood-altering or psychoactive effect can be classified as a medicine even if it is not labeled or marketed as such. The Medicines Control Agency, which administers the Medicines Act, has concurred with the EU directive, although as of early 2002, there was no move to control or ban poppers.

Federal guidelines, regulations, and penalties

The federal Food, Drug, and Cosmetic Act bans the sale, possession, or use of amyl nitrite without a prescription. The law is usually enforced for trafficking in the drug. Federal charges of sale or possession brought in a federal court usually constitute a misdemeanor. Conviction carries a penalty of one year in prison and/or a $1,000 fine per count for a first offense. A second offense is usually a felony. Conviction carries a penalty of up to three years in federal prison and up to a $250,000. Most enforcement is left to state and local law enforcement agencies. Penalties and enforcement vary from state to state.

See also Inhalants

RESOURCES

Books

Monroe, Judy. *Inhalant Drug Dangers.* Berkeley Heights, NJ: Enslow Publishers, Inc., 2002.

Young, Ian. *The Stonewall Experiment: A Gay Psychohistory.* New York: Cassell, 1999.

Periodicals

Bradberry, S.M. "Volatile Nitrite Abuse: Mechanisms of Toxicity, Features, and Management." *Journal of Toxicology: Clinical Toxicology* (March 2000): 178.

Heredia, Christopher. "'Poppers' Link to HIV Prompts Call For Warnings in S.F." *San Francisco Chronicle* (Oct. 25, 2001): A22.

Lyttle, John. "Try and Ban Them If You Like. But You Won't Change the Undeniable Fact: Poppers Rule." *The Independent (London, England).* (Jan. 17, 1997): 4.

McGarvey, E.L., et al. "Adolescent Inhalant Abuse: Environments of Use." *American Journal of Drug and Alcohol Abuse.* (Nov. 1999): 731-741.

Meyerhoff, Michael K. "Facts About Inhalant Abuse." *Pediatrics for Parents* (July 2001): 9.

Scheller, Melanie. "Inhalants—Don't Let Them Take Your Breath Away." *Current Health 2 (A Weekly Reader Publication).* (Sept. 2000): 16.

Stapleton, Stephanie. "'Household High' Found to be Growing Threat to Teen Health." *American Medical News* (April 10, 2000): 32.

Organizations

National Institute on Drug Abuse (NIDA), National Institutes of Health, 6001 Executive Boulevard, Room 5213., Bethesda, MD, USA, 20892-9561, (301) 443-1124, (888) 644-6432, information@lists.nida.nih.gov, <http://www.drugabuse.gov>.

Ken R. Wells

ANTIDEPRESSANTS

OFFICIAL NAMES: Amitriptyline (Elavil), amoxapine (Asendin), bupropion (Wellbutrin), citalopram (Celexa), clomipramine (Anafranil), desipramine (Norpramin), doxepin (Sinequan), fluoxetine (Prozac), imipramine (Norfranil, Tofranil), isocarboxazid (Marplan), maprotiline (Ludiomil), mirtazapine (Remeron), nefazodone (Serzone), nortriptyline (Aventyl, Pamelor), paroxetine (Paxil), phenelzine (Nardil), protriptyline (Vivactil), sertraline (Zoloft), thioridazine (Mellaril), tranylcypromine (Parnate), trazodone (Desyrel), trimipramine (Surmontil), venlafaxine (Effexor); the herb St. John's wort (*Hypericum perforatum*) is sold over-the-counter without prescription
STREET NAMES: Happy pills
DRUG CLASSIFICATIONS: Not scheduled, psychotherapeutic drugs

OVERVIEW

Depression is an illness that affects the body, moods, and thoughts. It affects how people eat, sleep, take care of themselves, and how they think of themselves. It is an illness that requires medical assistance. It may originate with a stressful situation, a medication, or another illness.

Scientists were looking for drugs to treat different medical problems when their observations almost accidentally led them to the study of depression and its treatment. Many scientists continued in this new direction to the discovery of the current three classifications of antidepressant drugs used today: monamine oxidase inhibitors (MAOIs), tricyclic drugs (TCAs), and selective serotonin reuptake inhibitors (SSRIs).

One such accident occurred in the 1950s, when scientists searching for a tuberculosis treatment observed that the drug iproniazid caused mood elevation. Since there were few treatments for depression, the findings were exciting.

Reserpine, a drug used for the treatment of high blood pressure, was known to have the side effect of depression. Upon studying this effect, scientists observed that this drug caused a depletion of the amine neurotransmitters serotonin and norepinephrine. Neurotransmitters transmit "information" from one nerve to another across a "synapse." The neurotransmitters are than reabsorbed by the first nerve in the process called reuptake.

The depletion of the neurotransmitters—as observed with reserpine—came under study as the possible cause of depression and became known as the "amine hypothesis of depression." The drug iproniazid reversed some of these negative side effects, confirming the usefulness of drugs in the treatment of depression.

When used with psychiatric patients, iproniazid showed mood elevation and heralded the first class of antidepressants—the monoamine oxidase inhibitors (MAOIs)—into psychiatric practice.

Names associated in these discoveries include Roland Kuhn and John Cade. While looking for a treatment for depression, Kuhn worked with thorazine, the newly found drug effective with schizophrenia. He progressed to find the second classification of antidepressants, the tricyclic drug (TCA) imipramine, a close chemical relative of thorazine.

In the 1950s Marsilid (the brand name of iproniazid) and Tofranil (imipramine) were manufactured and sold as antidepressant drugs.

When studying manic patients, who have a form of depression with periods of abnormal excitability and excessive activity, Australian psychiatrist John Cade found that lithium had a controlling effect on the patient's mania. He used lithium as a solvent when he attempted to inject the urine of manic patients into guinea pigs and found it made the urine less toxic. It was this finding that sparked his interest in lithium. In 1948 he injected lithium into ten patients and observed that lithium controlled their mania.

As a result of these findings, the emphasis in the study of depression from the 1950s to the present has centered on the study of the brain and the chemical actions occurring there. Research emphasis in the 1980s moved to serotonin, a neurotransmitter in the brain. Through the 1990s into the 2000s, the newer and third classification of antidepressants became the serotonin reuptake inhibitors (SSRIs). Prozac is among this group of drugs. They interfere with the reabsorption of serotonin in the brain and have fewer side effects than the earlier classes of antidepressant drugs.

Extensive media coverage in the 1990s made the public aware of Prozac and greatly increased the demand for the drug. Some people got the impression that it had no side effects, helped in weight loss, and was a sort of "happy pill" that everyone should take. But neither this nor the other SSRI drugs improve mood or make healthy people high or happier if they are not clinically (observed symptoms) depressed.

Knowledge of these drugs has increased the public's demand for them at times of personal or societal tragedies and crises. In 1999, as many as 135 million prescriptions for antidepressants were filled in the United States.

As far back in history as the Greek physicians Hippocrates, Pliny, and Galen, through to present time, the herb St. John's wort has been used for its antidepressant effect. It is believed to influence the neurotransmitters in the brain. Although some research has shown it to be effective in cases of mild to moderate depression, many questions remain as to its safety and effectiveness.

In Germany, St. John's wort is approved for use in depression and anxiety. It is the most common antidepressant used and is usually sold by prescription. However, in the United States it is sold only as an herb and without prescription. It is frequently used by people with self-diagnosed depression. Preparations of St. John's wort will vary in potency according to manufacturer. Although extensive studies have been conducted on the

KEY TERMS

DEPRESSION: A feeling of sadness and helplessness with little drive for communication or socialization with others.

HERB: Any such plant used as a medicine, seasoning, or food. Mint, thyme, basil, St. John's wort, and sage are herbs.

NEUROTRANSMITTER: A chemical produced by one nerve cell that stimulates another nerve cell in the process of sending messages along the nerves.

POST-TRAUMATIC STRESS DISORDER: A mental disorder that can occur in those who have experienced a life threatening-situation. PTSD is characterized by nightmares and flashbacks, among other symptoms.

PSYCHOTHERAPEUTIC DRUGS: Drugs used to relieve the symptoms of mental illness, such as depression, anxiety, and psychosis.

PSYCHOTHERAPY: The non-drug treatment of psychological disorders. It can be in the form of behavioral therapy (where the person is gradually exposed to their fears) or cognitive therapy (where people learn to control their unrealistic or negative thinking.

REUPTAKE: The process by which a nerve cell reabsorbs the chemical it had used to send a message to another nerve cell.

STRESS: A disturbance in the body's physiological equibrium, resulting from psychological or physical forces on a person.

usefulness of St John's wort, the evidence has not been conclusive. More recent studies raise even more questions about its effectiveness.

By the end of 2002 the National Institutes of Health (NIH) will make their large study of the herb available. This should clear up the confusions concerning its effectiveness.

CHEMICAL/ORGANIC COMPOSITION

The antidepressants available in the United States are classified by either their chemical structure (e.g., the tricyclics, TCAs) or their actions on neurotransmitters (e.g., SSRIs and MAOIs) or simply as "other" (e.g., Wellbutrin). In the future, the classification of the antidepressants may become more confusing as new drugs are developed that are neither TCAs, SSRIs, or MAOIs.

A variety of substances (and more are being found each day) with differing chemical structures have antidepressant abilities. However, no group is known to be more effective than the others.

The tricyclic antidepressants have a three-ring nucleus and are norepinephrine and serotonin reuptake inhibitors. They have been used for decades. Trade names included in this group of drugs as of 2002 are: Etrafon, Limbitrol, Norpramin, Sinequan, Surmontil, and Vivactil.

The heterocyclic antidepressants were introduced between 1980 and 1996. They consist of an intertwined circular structure called benzene rings. Included among these are amoxapine and maprotiline, which have a similar structure to the tricyclics. Trazodone and bupropion are in this group but do not have this similar structure. These drugs do not have stronger potency than the earlier drugs. Newer drugs introduced since the 1990s include venlafaxine and mirtazapine.

The older generation of drugs are less desirable than the new selective serotonin reuptake inhibitors, because they have many actions in the body other than their antidepressant effect. Prozac (fluoxetine hydrochloride) is among this group. Other trade names in this group are Celexa, Paxil, and Zoloft.

The herb St. John's wort (*Hypericum perforatum*) has a number of constituent parts, including hyperforin, which is currently being studied as the responsible constituent for the antidepressant action. The herb contains at least ten compounds that can have an unpredictable effect on the consumer.

INGESTION METHODS

The prescription antidepressants are taken orally, once a day, either in capsules, tablets, oral suspensions, or solutions. In early 2002, a once-a-week dose in capsule and liquid forms became available for Prozac and some other antidepressants.

The leaves and tops of St. John's wort are taken as a tea, or as an olive oil extract taken internally or applied externally.

THERAPEUTIC USE

The antidepressants are used to relieve the symptoms of depression, which may include feelings of sadness, helplessness, loss of interest in usual activities, insomnia, loss of energy, problems concentrating, weight loss or gain, and decreased desire to socialize or communicate with others.

The three most common types of depression are major depression, dysthymia, and bipolar disorder. Major depression, which may occur once but usually occurs several times in a person's life, will interfere with the ability to work, eat, sleep, study, and take pleasure in formerly enjoyed activities. Dysthymia is less severe than major depression but will interfere with feeling good and functioning well. Bipolar disorder (formerly called manic-depression) can be more serious than the other forms of depression. In this illness the person's mood swings from symptoms of depression to extreme excitement with over-activity and feelings of elation. This type of depression can progress to serious mental illness if not treated.

Depression is twice as common in women than men and may occur with premenstrual syndrome or after childbirth as postpartum depression. Studies have not found any negative effects on the unborn child when the mother takes an antidepressant during the pregnancy, but this is a serious question that needs to be discussed with the physician. Antidepressants are very effective in the treatment of postpartum depression, but because they are secreted in the mother's milk, the option of breastfeeding is another essential area for discussion and decision. Usually, women are recommended to avoid drug use during pregnancy, including the use of St. John's wort.

Although less common than in women, about three to four million men have depression, and their rate of suicide is four times that of women. Men's symptoms of depression may be anger and irritability and be masked by alcohol and drug use.

In addition to the treatment of depression, the Food and Drug Administration (FDA) has approved the (on-label) use of the antidepressants for treatment of panic disorders, obsessive-compulsive disorders, bulimia nervosa, social phobia, and generalized anxiety disorder. And although not the treatment of choice, the tricyclics are sometimes used for enuresis—bed wetting.

A physician may prescribe an antidepressant for an off-label use. These are a variety of problems not specifically mentioned on the drug label. Among these are pain, anxiety, attention deficit hyperactivity disorder, post traumatic stress disorder, premenstrual exaggerated feelings of depression, social phobia, and obsessive-compulsive-related disorders such as compulsive hair pulling, compulsive gambling, compulsive buying, sexual addictions, and kleptomania (compulsive stealing).

Studies show that the SSRIs may help alcoholics reduce the amount of alcohol they consume and also increase the number of days they can abstain from alcohol. Patients with anorexia nervosa may also be helped by antidepressants. No other treatment has been approved by the FDA for this eating disorder, but the antidepressants are helping patients maintain their weight and avoid relapse.

 **IN THE NEWS**

Prozac is the most commonly prescribed antidepressant in the United States. In 1999, 135 million prescriptions were written for antidepressants, with Prozac (fluoxetine) the most commonly used.

Among the newer drugs, Prozac and other serotonin reuptake inhibitors (SSRIs) are as effective as the drugs formerly used for depression, but have fewer serious side effects. Another advantage is their effectiveness with other psychiatric conditions, such as post-traumatic stress disorder, anxiety, panic disorder, and eating disorders. In 2002, the U.S. Food and Drug Administration approve Prozac for bulimia nervosa, a disorder characterized by binge eating followed by purging or other efforts to lose weight.

Prozac blocks the reuptake of the chemical serotonin, which is believed to be plentiful in the areas of the brain controlling emotion. However, the brain's biochemical pathways, and serotonin's effect on emotion and mood, are not quite so simply understood. Scientists do not exactly know how the serotonin works in the brain and on mood.

Some psychiatrists warn that Prozac is not the cure-all for emotional problems, which are usually brought on by crisis situations and not necessarily by chemical imbalances in the brain. Although Prozac is widely used, some warn that the long-term effects on the brain are not yet known. The drug should always be used under close medical supervision.

Crisis use of antidepressants

Anticipating "Y2K" (year 2000) switch-over in computers, Americans increased their purchases of drugs, along with other supplies. The recent anthrax scare in America also resulted in people stockpiling Cipro, the antibiotic effective against the disease.

The attack on the World Trade Center resulted in a similar reaction from the public in New York City. After about three weeks, pharmacies and physicians received many calls for sedatives and antidepressants, with some requesting these drugs for the first time. While it is not uncommon for some people to use a sedative or antidepressant at the time of traumatic stress and anxiety, the demand was clearly much higher after September 11, 2001.

Two specific groups sought relief: those closely affected by the loss of a loved one, and others who became anxious with the threat to their security. As a temporary means of coping, the sedatives helped some people sleep, and the antidepressants helped in dealing with stress. However, psychotherapists cautioned that these drugs are only a temporary relief, and that people may want to get to the underlying feelings through psychotherapy.

This reaction to an extremely threatening or frightening experience is called post-traumatic stress disorder. It is characterized by general anxiety, nightmares or haunting recollections, and emotional detachment. Psychiatry has only accepted the existence of this specific disorder for the past 20 years, although it used to be known under different names. For example, during World War I, the term used for post-traumatic stress disorder was shell shock; in World War II, it was called combat fatigue; and after the Vietnam War, it was post-Vietnam syndrome.

Because each patient will respond differently to the various antidepressants, the physician may try several—or even combine them—in the search for the most effective treatment for a particular patient.

Although the tricyclic and MAOI antidepressants cause an immediate pharmacologic action (drug reaction in the body), their clinical action (observable reaction) is delayed. This delay can last weeks or even months. This makes it difficult to use these antidepressants to treat severe depression when an immediate response is desired. The more severe cases of depression and other psychiatric and emotional problems may require other treatments in addition to the drug therapy.

The antidepressants have been found effective in post-stroke patients when a positive attitude is needed for recovery. Treating post-stroke depression improves the chances of the patient regaining mental acuity.

USAGE TRENDS

An increasing demand for antidepressants is resulting from increased media coverage on television and in magazines. Also, antidepressants are frequently prescribed by physicians for patients they diagnose as having difficulty handling some personal problem or crisis. The 135 million prescriptions sold in 1999 is an indication of the popularity of these drugs, especially Prozac. Awareness of the availability of the drugs has also resulted in large numbers of people seeking the drugs at times of tragedy and crisis (as evidenced by the increased demand after the September 11, 2001 attack).

In addition to the demand for antidepressants as discussed above, their use has increased as their effectiveness and relative safety in the treatment of depression and other problems have been shown.

Some people will refuse antidepressants when their doctors offer to prescribe them, because they fear that taking the drug is an admission of a serious disease or problem. The very nature of depression may also leave the patient without hope of relief and discourage them from seeking help or accepting the antidepressants.

Falsely believing that a herb is safer than a prescribed drug, many people either take St. John's wort in place of, or in addition to, their prescription antidepressants. These are dangerous practices because of the serious side effects of the combinations and the serious consequences that may result when someone stops taking their antidepressant without the guidance of a physician.

Scope and severity

With an addiction, larger doses of the drug must be consumed to achieve the original high or "buzz." This build-up of tolerance does not occur with antidepressants. In those cases where an increase in drug dose is required, usually it is because the illness is no longer responding to the original dose. Another criteria of addiction not met by antidepressants is that they do not cause an artificial high but only help those depressed to reach a normal level of functioning.

Some patients may have to take the drug long-term to control their illness, and in some cases the illness will return after the medication is discontinued. However, the antidepressants have not been found to be addicting themselves. Actually, they may be useful in the treatment of patients undergoing treatment of addiction who are also depressed. Research shows that these patients may need specific antidepressants considering their state of addiction and depression.

The antidepressant therapy should not be stopped abruptly, but tapered off. The symptoms some may experience when stopping abruptly is not withdrawal as witnessed with addictions, but just the need of the body to adjust without the effect of the antidepressants on the neurotransmitters of the brain.

The inability of the antidepressants to make healthy people "high" prevents an illegal market for these drugs from developing.

Age, ethnic, and gender trends

Women are more prone to depression than men. They also differ in their reaction to SSRI and tetracycline antidepressants. It is interesting to note that women less than 44 years of age respond more effectively to the SSRIs than do women older than 44.

All age groups from children to the elderly that suffer from depression respond well to the antidepressants. Also, those elderly individuals with some loss of cognitive ability have shown some improvement in their skills, although the antidepressants do not return them to their former intellectual ability.

MENTAL EFFECTS

The antidepressants have not been found to effect judgment and thinking as some psychoactive drugs may. The antidepressants will relieve the symptoms of depression and those of the other psychological problems as mentioned above. The antidepressants will make it possible for people with depression to resume a normal life, such as returning to work and school. They will help people get over their feelings of worthlessness and assist them in social functioning.

The misuse of antidepressants may occur when patients diagnose themselves for depression, and their request for a prescription is honored by their physician. In such cases a placebo (sugar pill) might be just as effective. This person is not addicted to the drug, but may be overly concerned with his or her own personal health.

PHYSIOLOGICAL EFFECTS

The physiological action of antidepressants is not fully understood. However, they are thought to influence the metabolism, reuptake, or selective receptor antagonism of the neurotransmitters serotonin and norepinephrine. The MAOIs cause an increase of the neurotransmitters norepinephrine, serotonin, and dopamine in the brain by inhibiting their breakdown. The SSRIs prevent the reabsorbtion of serotonin, one of the 50-odd neurotransmitters in the brain.

Studies show little difference in the effects of the various antidepressants, but some individual patients appear to do better on one drug than another. In the search for the most effective drug for a particular patient, the physician may try various antidepressant drugs or even try some in combination.

Antidepressants do not cause addiction, which is usually evident by the build-up of tolerance (needing increasing amounts of a drug to achieve the initial effect). Withdrawal symptoms do not occur when the drug is discontinued. However, gradually decreasing the dosage will give the brain a chance to take over or function on its own without the drug, and help avoid some physiological symptoms such as the flu, headache, or nausea that sometimes occur. This gradual cutting back on the amount of drug can assist the physician in prescribing if the patient's symptoms return.

Harmful side effects

Patients are cautioned not to operate machinery until they know how the drug affects them personally (although antidepressants are not known to cause impairment in this way). Side effects can include agitation, insomnia or drowsiness, and thirst. Serious side effects are not expected with these drugs.

Because of their selective action on serotonin, the manufacturer of SSRIs claim there are fewer side effects from this class of drug than those of the tricyclics and MAOIs. These other drugs affect many neurotransmitters in the brain and therefore result in many side effects. However, the SSRIs can cause stomach upset, insomnia, and anxiety.

For the most part, antidepressants are considered safe. However, they may interact with other drugs taken by the patient—and the physician prescribing one of these drugs must take this into consideration. Additionally, some medical problems already under treatment may increase in severity in the presence of an antidepressant.

Patients suffering from bipolar disorder whose high periods exhibit anger, paranoia, or irritability may exhibit these symptoms when taking Prozac if they have not been first stabilized with another medication such as lithium.

The adverse effects of antidepressants will vary by drug and may include some or several of the following: insomnia, tremor, gastrointestinal symptoms, rashes, sexual dysfunction, anxiety, dizziness, dry mouth, sweating, sleepiness, blurred vision, constipation, aggravation of psychosis, weight gain, increased appetite, arrhythmias (disturbed rhythm of the heartbeat), hypertension or postural hypotension, nausea, and, with high doses, seizures.

It is unusual for the MAOIs to have a toxic effect. However, when it does occur the symptoms are severe and include dulled consciousness, seizures, shock, and hyperthermia (elevated temperature). Although some reactions with SSRIs—and even some fatalities—have occurred with overdoses, they are extremely rare. A reaction may be due to the combining of the SSRIs with other drugs.

Side effects of St. John's wort include headache, gastrointestinal discomfort, sun sensitivity, and dry mouth. Some of the effects of combining the herb with other drugs are very serious. For example, St. John's wort lessens the effectiveness of HIV drugs, as well as some drugs that are essential after a transplant operation and heart drugs (such as digoxin). It is essential that anyone desiring to take the herb consult with their doctor.

Overdoses of the antidepressants can result in death. However, the effects of overdosing will vary according to which drug is taken.

Long-term health effects

Long-term health effects from antidepressants include the increased risk of deliberate self-harm (DSH), which may occur more with the SRRIs than the tricyclic antidepressants. The self-harm may occur by overdosing with the prescribed drug, but is more frequently by other means.

Long-term use of the SSRIs has been found to increase the risk of gastrointestinal (GI) bleeding, especially in the elderly and in those who have previously experienced bleeding. In addition, although preliminary studies showed a decreased risk of heart attack for those using SSRIs, an increased risk for arrhythmias (irregular heart beats) and heart attacks has been observed in those taking the tricyclics. These older tricyclic antidepressants may disrupt the heartbeat, possibly resulting in death. Therefore, it is essential that physicians test patients prior to and during treatment with tricyclics.

Tricyclics may also pose a threat to vision by causing dry eyes, blurred vision, and even vision loss when narrow-angle glaucoma is present. Also, tricyclics may result in dry mouth that can lead to dental cavities, reduced urine output, and constipation. Although not fully understood, weight gain is also an effect. Whether a result of the drug or of the illness, sexual drive is decreased.

MAOIs frequently are not the first choice when an antidepressant is needed. This is because their side effects include sedation, dizziness, insomnia, sexual dysfunction, rapid heartbeat, constipation, and agitation. Severe sudden elevation of blood pressure, especially when the patient eats aged meats and cheeses, or takes some over-the-counter cold medications, poses a serious threat of a stroke or other symptoms including headache, vomiting, and palpitations.

Studies of the long term-health effects of St. John's wort are in progress. Avoidance of the herb by pregnant and lactating women is strongly recommended.

REACTIONS WITH OTHER DRUGS OR SUBSTANCES

Anyone prescribed an antidepressant should not take other medications without consulting with a physician. This warning of possible negative effects can also occur with over-the-counter-drugs that patients take themselves. A prescription for an antidepressant should include a list of foods to avoid, because some antidepressants can have dangerous reactions with foods.

Alcohol's ability to impair motor operation and driving skills will be increased if combined with an antidepressant. A few drinks taken by a person who has an antidepressant in their system is like having many more drinks.

The symptoms of jitters, insomnia, tremors, and agitation are common in those consuming caffeine and in those with depression or the other illnesses for which these drugs are prescribed. Combining caffeine with antidepressants may exaggerate the symptoms and make it difficult for the physician to arrive at an accurate diagnosis or evaluate the drug's effectiveness.

The reactions of recreational drugs with antidepressants are unpredictable and possibly very dangerous. The illness being treated with the antidepressants may also react negatively to recreational drugs.

In February, 2002, the Food and Drug Administration issued a Public Health Advisory warning physicians of the dangers of patients taking St. John's wort (as well as other herbs) in combination with prescription drugs. For one thing, the effects of combining St. John's wort with other drugs is practically impossible to predict. This is because people take varying amounts of the herb, and the potency of the herb's active compounds also varies from brand to brand.

To help avoid problems, it is important that the patient take the prescribed dosage. Physicians will have difficulty measuring the effectiveness of a drug when the prescription is not followed accurately.

TREATMENT AND REHABILITATION

Since antidepressants are not addictive, there is no need for treatment when the drugs are discontinued. However, when the drug is abruptly stopped, some users may experience discomfort—such as irritability, depressed mood, anxiety, and sleep disturbance—but these are not as severe as those of drugs that cause addiction. An ideal way of discontinuing the antidepressants is the "step-down method," a gradual lowering of the dose until the patient is weaned off the drug. This way, the physician can observe whether the patient's symptoms of depression return.

PERSONAL AND SOCIAL CONSEQUENCES

If depression has interfered with happiness or success, its treatment can have many positive consequences and result in a fuller and happier social life. Treatment may be long term, and may require psychotherapy in addition to the antidepressant drugs.

LEGAL CONSEQUENCES

Antidepressants are only available by prescription, and since individuals do not achieve a high with these drugs (as may occur with the drugs of abuse), there is not likely to be an illegal market for them.

RESOURCES

Books

Appleton, William S. *Prozac and the New Antidepressants.* New York: Plume, 2000.

Ernst, Edzard, Julia Rand, and Clare Stevinson. "Complementary Therapies for Depression," In *Alternative Medicine, An Objective Assessment.* Washington, DC: JAMA and Archives Journals, 2000.

Foster, Steven, and Varro E. Tyler. *Tyler's Honest Herbal.* New York: Haworth Herbal Press, 2000.

Katzung, Bertrum G. *Basic and Clinical Pharmacology.* New York: Lange Medical Books/McGraw-Hill, 2001.

Morrison, Andrew L. *The Antidepressant Sourcebook.* New York: Broadway Books, 1999.

O'Hara, Mary Ann, et al. "A Review of 12 Commonly Used Medicinal Herbs." *Alternative Medicine, An Objective Assessment.* Washington, DC: JAMA and Archives Journal, 2000.

Physicians Desk Reference. 56th ed. Montvale, NJ: Medical Economics, 2002.

Schlaadt, Ricahrd G. *Drugs, Society, & Behavior.* New York: Dushkin Publishing Group, Inc., 1992.

Wong, Albert H. C., Michael Smith, and Heather Boon. "Herbal Remedies in Psychiatric Practice," In *Alternative Medicine, An Objective Assessment.* Washington, DC: JAMA and Archives Journals, 2000.

Periodicals

"Another Look at St. John's Wort and Depression." *University of California, Berkley, Wellness Letter* 17, no. 11 (August 2001).

The New England Journal of Medicine. "Post-Stroke Depression Impedes Recovery." *Health News* September 2000.

"9/11/01 Post-Traumatic Stress Disorder." *Harvard Health Letter* 27, no. 1 (November 2001).

Schuster, Mark A., et al. "A National Survey of Stress Reactions after the September 11, 2001, Terrorist Attacks." *The New England Journal of Medicine* 345, no. 20 (November 15, 2001).

Other

Headline News. "New Yorkers are Increasingly Turning to Sedation." September 8, 2001. <http://www.drugawareness.org>.

National Center for Complementary and Alternative Medicine. <www.nccam.nih.gov>.

National Institute of Mental Health. *Depression.* May 31, 2002. <http://www.nimh.nih.gov>.

Louise Catherine Chut, PhD, MPH

BARBITURATES

OVERVIEW

Barbiturates are among the drugs classified as central nervous system (CNS) depressants. These drugs depress or slow down the activity of nerves that control emotions and bodily functions such as breathing. Barbiturates are prescribed as a sedative that calms the patient or as a hypnotic that helps a person sleep. Other uses include epilepsy treatment and anesthesia before surgery.

Barbiturates are compounds derived from barbituric acid, a substance discovered in 1863 by German chemist Adolf von Baeyer. The year after von Baeyer's discovery, German scientists von Mering and Fischer synthesized the first barbiturate. Production began on the drug called barbital, and medical practices began using it in treatment in 1882.

In 1903, barbital with the brand name of Veronal was marketed as a sleeping pill. Before that time, remedies for insomnia included drinking alcohol or taking bromides, chloral hydrate, or opiates.

In 1912, phenobarbital was introduced under the trade name Luminal. Since 1912, several thousand barbituric acid derivatives have been synthesized. At the beginning of the twenty-first century, only about 12 were on the market.

During the 1930s, many Americans received barbiturate prescriptions to help them sleep or relax. However, people discovered that barbiturates produced an intoxicating effect similar to that produced by drinking alcohol. People took barbiturates to get drunk. They combined the pills with alcohol to become more intoxicated.

OFFICIAL NAMES: Methohexital (Brevital), thiamylal (Surital), thiopental (Pentothal), pentobarbital (Nembutal), secobarbital (Seconal), amobarbital (Amytal), bubalbital (Florinal, Fioricet), butabarbital (Butisol), talbutal (Lotusate), aprobarbital (Alurate), amobarbital and secobarbital (Tuinal), phenobarbital (Luminal), mephobarbital (Mebaral)

STREET NAMES: Barbs, downers, red devils, Mexican reds, red birds, blue devils, blue heavens, goof balls, yellow jackets, block busters, reds, blues, pinks, Christmas trees, Amys, rainbows, purple hearts

DRUG CLASSIFICATIONS: Schedule II, III, IV; depressant

The sedative becomes a "thrill pill"

German chemists knew in the 1900s that barbiturates could be addictive. However, people who took barbiturates did not always exhibit symptoms of drug dependence or withdrawal. By the 1940s, the addictive nature of barbiturates alarmed groups ranging from the American Medical Association (AMA) to the United States Food and Drug Administration (FDA).

The 1938 Food, Drug, and Cosmetic Act gave regulatory powers to the FDA. The federal agency used those powers to restrict access to drugs that had a potential for abuse or misuse. The FDA placed barbiturates and amphetamines in that category of drugs that could only be obtained with a prescription from a doctor or dentist. In several decades, the federal government would classify barbiturates and amphetamines as the most abused prescription drugs in the country.

KEY TERMS

BROMIDE: A sedative compound made from the chemical element bromine.

CHLORAL HYDRATE: A colorless compound used as a sedative.

OPIATE: Drug derived directly from opium and used in its natural state, without chemical modification. Opiates include morphine, codeine, thebaine, noscapine, and papaverine.

POLYDRUG USE: Use of more than one drug.

During the 1940s, research indicated that barbiturates produced intoxication and were addictive. People showed signs of withdrawal when they stopped taking barbiturates.

The AMA began warning people about barbiturate abuse in articles with titles like "1,250,000 Doses A Year." That article appeared in a 1942 issue of *Hygeia*, an AMA magazine published for a general audience.

Warnings about the dangers of nonprescription use of barbiturates did not have the intended effect. Instead of taking precautions about barbiturates, people wanted to try the drug that some called a "thrill pill."

A popular drug combination

The barbiturate became one half of a polydrug habit that became acceptable throughout America. People took barbiturates to sleep at night. In the morning, the barbiturate might make them feel sleepy, so they took an amphetamine.

Amphetamines are central nervous system stimulants. People called them "uppers" because amphetamines gave them energy. Amphetamines cut a person's appetite, so people also used them as diet pills. In the evening a person still "up" from an amphetamine took a "downer" (barbiturate) to sleep at night. In the morning, the drug-taking cycle would start again.

Polydrug use was so widespread by the 1950s that the federal government classified barbiturates and amphetamines as the most abused drugs in the country. The abuse problem grew even though barbiturates were prescription drugs.

Prescription abuse

The FDA discovered the scope of the abuse problem after a 1948 Supreme Court ruling gave the agency the authority to investigate drug sales at the pharmacy level. According to an FDA report, barbiturate transactions included:

- A prescription refilled 61 times, with three refills after the patient died from barbiturate intoxication.

- A Kansas City woman obtained 40 refills for a prescription. Her doctor prescribed refills. Other refills came by mail order. The woman died from barbiturate intoxication.

- The staff at a Tennessee drug store could not explain what happened to more than 180,000 barbiturates sent to the store by manufacturers and wholesalers.

According to the FDA report, enforcement action during the 1940s and 1950s centered primarily on pharmacies. Those involved in the illegal sales of barbiturates included pharmacists as well as drug store owners and employees.

As pharmacies complied with the law, the FDA targeted black market sales of barbiturates from 1960 through 1965. Meanwhile, a new generation discovered barbiturates.

Drug use during the 1960s

During the 1960s, youths began to experiment with drugs on a wider scope. Middle-class and upper-class youths discovered that it was easy to obtain barbiturates; they often found them in their parents' medicine chests.

A United States Senate Subcommittee heard about the severity of the problem from a Dr. Sidney Cohen. He said that 10 billion barbiturate doses would be produced in 1969. That figure represented an 800% increase in the amount produced in 1942, according to the 1972 *Consumers Union Report on Licit and Illicit Drugs*.

The 1970s bring restricted access to barbiturates

According to the FDA, barbiturate abuse continued during the 1970s and 1980s. However, the adoption of the federal Comprehensive Drug Abuse Prevention and Control Act in 1970 would limit access to highly addictive drugs like barbiturates. The act placed barbiturates on a list of controlled substances that were subject to abuse. The act limited the number of prescriptions a person could receive. It also set annual quotas for the amount of drugs that pharmaceutical companies could manufacture.

As access to barbiturates was limited, benzodiazepines were promoted as a safer alternative. Benzodiazepines went on the market during the 1960s and were thought to be less addictive than barbiturates.

With barbiturates less available, drug abusers turned to other illegal substances during the 1970s and 1980s. One indication of drug demand was the record of

LAW AND ORDER

Controlled Substances Act used to challenge assisted-suicide law

A federal district court judge on April 17, 2002 rejected the United States Justice Department's attempt to overturn Oregon's physician-assisted suicide law. The Justice Department had claimed that the state law violated the federal Controlled Substances Act. Oregon was the first state to approve a law that allowed doctors to prescribe lethal dosages of medications like barbiturates to terminally ill patients.

Oregon voters in 1994 approved the "Death with Dignity Act." Opponents filed a legal challenge, and the act was put back on the ballot in 1997. Voters again approved the act that supporters say helps terminally ill people end their suffering. Foes of the law say that assisting with suicide is murder, and that it conflicts with the healing nature of medicine.

Under Oregon law, a terminally ill person can request a lethal dosage of medications if he or she has less than six months to live. Two doctors must confirm that diagnosis. They must also verify that the patient was mentally competent when making the request for the prescriptions. The patient then decides if and when to take the drugs.

Gov. John Kitzhaber, a physician, signed the act into law in 1998. From 1998 trough 2001, 91 people died after receiving the lethal prescriptions, according to the Oregon Public Health Services Department's 2001 annual report on the act.

The federal challenge to the law came in the form of a Nov. 6, 2001 directive from Attorney General John Ashcroft. That directive banned the prescription of what the Oregon law calls "Death with Dignity" drugs. Ashcroft said in the directive that a lethal prescription did not meet the "legitimate medical purpose" standard in the Controlled Substances Act.

Federal Judge Robert E. Jones in April of 2002 upheld Oregon's law and criticized the attorney general for attempting to "stifle" debate on the issue. Justice Department representatives said were considering an appeal. No appeal had been filed as of late April 2002.

---

drugs seized by the United States Customs Service. Customs confiscated greater quantities of marijuana, heroin, and cocaine. As a result, Customs recorded seizures of each drug separately.

Barbiturates in the late twentieth century

At the close of the twentieth century, the DEA reported that barbiturates represented about 20% of all depressant prescriptions in the United States. Uses ranged from epilepsy treatment to assisted suicide in Oregon. In 1997, Oregon voters approved the Death with Dignity Act, which allows doctors to prescribe lethal dosages of barbiturates to terminally ill people.

Furthermore, the late 1990s brought concerns about benzodiazepines, the drugs thought to be a safe alternative to barbiturates. Benzodiazepines produced side effects similar to those produced by barbiturates. These included the risk of addiction when high doses were taken. Benzodiazepines accounted for 30% of all prescriptions for controlled substance, according to the DEA.

CHEMICAL/ORGANIC COMPOSITION

Barbiturates are compounds derived from barbituric acid. These drugs are classified in four categories that are defined by the amount of time that it takes for barbiturate to produce results and how long those results last.

The ultrashort-acting barbiturates methohexital, thiamylal, and thiopental produce unconsciousness within several minutes. These drugs are used for anesthesia before surgery.

Short and intermediate-acting barbiturates take effect within 15 to 40 minutes. The effects of these barbiturates last from five to six hours. These medications are prescribed for sedation or to help people sleep. The barbiturates in this category are amobarbital, pentobarbital, secobarbital, bubalbital, butabarbital, talbutal, and aprobarbital.

Mephobarbital and phenobarbital are long-acting barbiturates that take effect within approximately one to two hours. These effects last approximately 12 hours.

According to the United States Drug Enforcement Agency (DEA), drug abusers favor short and intermediate-acting barbiturates. Barbiturate users often refer to the pills they take in terms of the color of the capsule. These street names include blues or blue devils for Amytal; reds, red birds; and red devils for Seconal; yellow jackets for Nembutal; purple hearts for Luminal; and rainbows and Christmas trees for Tuinal.

INGESTION METHODS

In the United States, barbiturates are manufactured in various forms. Most barbiturates come in pills and capsules that patients swallow. Some barbiturates are manufactured as an elixir, a liquid form of the drug that patients swallow.

Other barbiturates are manufactured as a powder that is injected into the patient's vein. In addition, pentobarbital is manufactured as a suppository that is inserted in the rectum. Pentobarbital is also available in capsule, tablet, elixir, and injection dosages. Phenobarbital is produced in capsule, tablet, injection, and elixir dosages.

Amobarbital is manufactured in pill, capsule, and injection dosages. Butabarbital is manufactured in capsule, tablet, and elixir dosages. Secobarbital is produced in capsule and injection dosages.

Aprobarbital is an elixir, mephobarbital is a tablet, and the drug containing secobarbital and amobarbital is a capsule. Legally prescribed barbiturates and those used in medical procedures are used in the form that the drug is produced. Some drug abusers will inject powder from capsules or ground-up tablets.

THERAPEUTIC USE

Barbiturates produce forms of central nervous system depression. Reactions to these drugs range from mild sedation (producing sleep) to a coma. Doctors may prescribe barbiturates as sedatives to calm patients' nerves, reduce tension or help them sleep. The drugs are also used as an anticonvulsant to control epileptic seizures.

In addition, the sleep-producing action of barbiturates is used to relax and partially anesthetize patients before some surgical procedures. Before some major brain surgeries, barbiturates (usually pentobarbital or thiopental) are used to temporarily induce coma in an effort to protect the brain; these drugs can reduce the metabolic rate of brain tissue and control cerebral blood flow.

Ultrashort-acting barbiturates

The ultrashort-acting barbiturates methohexital (Brevital), thiamylal (Surital), and thiopental (Pentothal) are administered as an anesthetic before surgery. The barbiturate is injected into the patient's vein to induce anesthesia. The patient then receives a longer-acting anesthetic like nitrous oxide. The drugs are used in hospital settings and are not subject to abuse, according to the DEA.

Short-acting and intermediate-acting barbiturates

The barbiturates in these categories are pentobarbital (Nembutal), secobarbital (Seconal, Amatyl), a combination of amobarbital and secobarbital (Tuinal), bubalbital (Florinal, Fioricet), butabarbital (Butisol), talbutal (Lotusate), and aprobarbital (Alurate).

Short-acting and intermediate barbiturates are prescribed as sedatives and sleeping pills. In addition, veterinarians use pentobarbital to anesthetize animals. This barbiturate is also used to euthanize or put animals to sleep.

Long-acting barbiturates

The long-acting barbiturates phenobarbital (Luminal) and mephobarbital (Mebaral) are used medically to help a patient sleep. Another use is day-long sedation, a procedure that treats tension and anxiety. Furthermore, long-acting barbiturates are used with other drugs in the treatment of convulsive conditions like epilepsy.

Phenobarbital is the oldest antiepileptic drug in common use and has a solid efficiency record for the control of seizure. However, due to some side effects (hypertension, depression, dizziness, rash, memory lapses) and drug interactions (primarily other anticonvulsants), phenobarbital is now generally used as a second-line treatment.

Assisted suicide

After Oregon voters in 1997 approved the Death with Dignity Act, terminally ill people could receive prescriptions for lethal dosages of drugs so that they could end their lives. To be eligible for the Death with Dignity drugs, the person needed a diagnosis of less than six months to live. That diagnosis would be verified by two physicians, who would also determine that the person was competent when the decision was made.

Secobarbital was prescribed to 67 out of 70 patients during 1998 through 2000, according to an Oregon Public Health Services report.

USAGE TRENDS

Passage of the federal Controlled Substances Act in 1970 restricted access to barbiturates. That action led to an eventual decline in the use and abuse of one of the most widely prescribed drugs of the twentieth century.

Scope and severity

In 1977, pharmacists filled approximately 7.9 million prescriptions for Luminal (phenobarbital), according to the National Institute of Drug Abuse (NIDA). NIDA estimated that approximately 1.7 million Nembutal prescriptions were filled, along with an estimated 1.5 million Seconal prescriptions, and 375,000 Amytal prescriptions.

NIDA research included estimates of deaths linked to use of a barbiturate. The federal agency estimated that 250 deaths were related to secobarbital, the same number for pentobarbital, 110 phenobarbital fatalities, and 30 deaths were connected to amobarbital.

At the start of the twenty-first century, the United States Drug Enforcement Agency said that barbiturates accounted for 20% of depressant prescriptions. Barbiturate use had declined so much that researchers no longer compiled separate statistics about the drug. Instead, barbiturates were placed in the sedative category that included tranquilizers.

Age, ethnic, and gender trends

During the 1950s, barbiturates were popular with the middle and upper classes. By the 1960s, barbiturate users spanned the generations from youths to older adults. However, recent surveys of illicit drug abuse illustrated the sharp decline in barbiturate abuse. In the National Household Survey on Drug Abuse for 2000, sedatives were placed in a category of psychotherapeutic drugs. This category included pain relievers, tranquilizers, stimulants, and pain relievers.

The survey conducted by the Substance Abuse and Mental Health Services Administration (SAMHSA) focused on the 14 million Americans who were current illicit drug users. Current use was defined as having used the drug the month before the survey. Those surveyed were age 12 and older.

Of that total, 1.8% of men and 1.7% of women had taken a psychotherapeutic drug for nonmedical reasons during the month before the survey. Of youths between the ages of 12 and 17, 7.7% of girls and 3.3% of girls were "likely" to use a illicit psychotherapeutic drugs.

Typically, women are more likely then men to receive barbiturate prescriptions because they are more likely to seek help for anxiety, depression, and insomnia. Barbiturates are also widely prescribed to older adults. Elderly persons use these drugs as sedatives, and again women receive the majority of the prescriptions.

MENTAL EFFECTS

The mental effects of barbiturates depend on the amount of the drug taken and the strength of the dosage. Generally, a person falls asleep when taking a prescribed dosage at bedtime.

Intoxication

A person experiences intoxication after taking a larger dose of a barbiturate. A mild state of intoxication brings a feeling of euphoria (happiness) that frequently leads to increased self-esteem and a lowering of inhibitions.

As intoxication increases, the person exhibits behavior similar to that displayed by a person intoxicated by alcohol. The person may be short-tempered, aggressive, and possibly violent. Other possible symptoms are impaired judgement and mood swings.

Upon waking, the person may experience "hangover" sensations that include dizziness. The person may still be sleepy and behave in a clumsy manner. Depression may be experienced.

Dependence

Barbiturate use can lead to both psychological and physical dependence. Psychological addiction can occur quickly. Signs of drug dependence include relying on the drug for a desired effect. The addicted abuser believes he or she must take a barbiturate to sleep, relax, or have a feeling of well-being. As the person relies emotionally on the drug, continued use of barbiturates leads to physical dependence.

As people develop tolerance for barbiturates, they may think they need more of the drug or a higher dosage to get the desired effect. This can lead to an overdose, which results from a person taking a larger than prescribed dose of a drug. Psychological symptoms of a barbiturate overdose include extreme drowsiness, intense confusion, and impaired judgement.

PHYSIOLOGICAL EFFECTS

Barbiturates act on the central nervous system, and use of these drugs can bring about changes ranging from mild sedation to a coma. Furthermore, an overdose or an attempt to withdraw abruptly from barbiturates can be fatal.

Short-term effects

Barbiturates help a person to sleep. However, this slumber differs from normal sleep. Barbiturate use decreases the amount of the dream phase of sleep known as the rapid eye movement (REM) stage. This phase of sleep is necessary for maintaining good health.

Barbiturates produce reactions similar to those of alcohol. A person may experience "hangover" symptoms including headache and dizziness. They may still feel tired and less alert as well. A person experiencing these symptoms should not drive or operate machinery. These hangover symptoms may last for hours.

Like alcohol, barbiturates are intoxicating. During the stage after mild intoxication, the person's speech may be slurred. The person may stagger and lose muscular control. Other symptoms of intoxication include irritability, shallow breathing, and fatigue.

Movie actress and sex symbol of the 1950s, Marilyn Monroe died of an overdose of barbiturates in 1962.

Hulton Archive. Reproduced by permission.

At-risk groups

Older adults and pregnant women should consider the risks associated with barbiturate use. When a person ages, the metabolization rate for drugs decreases. As a result, people over age 65 are at higher risk of the harmful effects of barbiturates. There is also greater risk for drug dependence.

When barbiturates are taken during pregnancy, the drug passes through the mother's bloodstream and through the placenta into the fetus. After the baby is born, it may experience withdrawal symptoms and have

trouble breathing. Other withdrawal symptoms include troubled sleep patterns, fever, and irritability. Furthermore, nursing mothers who take barbiturates may transmit the drug in their breast milk.

Harmful side effects

An individual using CNS depressants like barbiturates can develop a tolerance for the drugs. Over time, the body becomes used to the presence of barbiturates in the system. When this happens, the prescribed dose of the drug does not produce a desired result and the individual may take more pills or stronger dosages of barbiturates. A tolerance to that level can develop, requiring even more barbiturates or a stronger dosage. As tolerance continues to increase, the individual may take a fatal dose in their attempt to get the desired effect.

Overdose occurs when a drug is consumed in a dose that is greater than the body can handle. Symptoms of an overdose include intense tiredness, confusion, irritability, and fever or a low body temperature. The person may experience shortness of breath, sleepiness or difficulty getting to sleep, and weakness. Other signs of overdose are slurred speech, a slow heartbeat, and uncommon eye movements.

An overdose may be triggered by drinking alcohol or taking a drug like an amphetamine while using barbiturates. In an effect called synergy, the two drugs intensify the effects of each other. As a result, the prescribed dose of one drug could be fatal if taken with another drug.

The amount of a fatal dosage of barbiturate will vary with the individual. However, the lethal dose is usually 10 to 15 times as large as a usual dose. A fatal overdose starts with cardiovascular collapse followed by respiratory depression. The person then falls into a coma and dies.

Long-term health effects

Barbiturates are addictive. A person may develop a physical dependency after taking more than 400 mg of pentobarbital or secobarbital a day over an approximately 90-day period.

Long-term use of other barbiturates can also lead to physical and psychological dependence. Symptoms of dependence include the feeling that a person cannot relax or sleep without taking a barbiturate. Another sign of addiction is a tendency to increase the dosage.

People at risk of barbiturate abuse and addiction include alcoholics and abusers of opiates, sedative-hypnotics, and amphetamines.

Withdrawal

When a person stops taking barbiturates, the body begins to adapt to the lack of drugs in the system. If a person has used barbiturates in large doses or for an extended period of time, a physician should be consulted about the withdrawal process.

Onset of withdrawal symptoms usually begin eight to 16 hours after the last pill was taken. Symptoms may last up to 15 days if the person was a long-term barbiturate user or took large doses of the drug.

During this time, the person feels weak, dizzy, and anxious. Withdrawal brings tremors and shakes. The person may hallucinate, experience delusions, or become violent and hostile. Withdrawal symptoms generally diminish over time.

In some cases, withdrawal symptoms can be fatal, so a person cannot just stop taking barbiturates. The physician will establish a plan of gradual withdrawal from barbiturates.

REACTIONS WITH OTHER DRUGS OR SUBSTANCES

From the 1940s on, people took amphetamines, the highly addictive drugs referred to as "uppers," during the day. They used amphetamines to increase their energy and to relieve the effects of barbiturates. Those effects could include sleepiness and hangover symptoms.

By evening, people who still experienced the effects of the amphetamines turned to "downers," the street name for barbiturates. People took downers to slow down and sleep. In the morning, the drug-taking cycle started again. The person took an upper to counteract the effects of the downer.

Barbiturates are frequently taken in combination with amphetamines. Amphetamines are highly addictive drugs known as "uppers" since they increase energy. They are used to counteract the "downer" effect of barbiturates that induce sleep. This cycle is very dangerous. Both types of drug are addictive and can lead to tolerance. The combination of amphetamine use during the day and barbiturate use as night results in a synergy of the two drugs, which lowers the amount of the drug that is fatal. There is also synergy when a person uses barbiturates and consumes alcohol.

The person combining drugs does not know what dosage of the combination will be lethal. As a result, someone using a barbiturate could die after taking a prescribed dose of an amphetamine.

Barbiturates and other medications

Medications can cause adverse reactions for the person taking barbiturates. Tranquilizers and antihistamines depress the brain's control over breathing. This could increase the chance of respiratory failure when someone uses barbiturates.

Barbiturates may counteract the effects of birth control pills that contain estrogen. A woman taking those oral contraceptives may become pregnant after taking barbiturates.

TREATMENT AND REHABILITATION

Barbiturates act so powerfully on the nervous system that a person must gradually withdraw from these drugs. To suddenly stop taking barbiturates could result in serious medical complications or death. This withdrawal process, known as detoxification, is part of the treatment process for people dependent on barbiturates.

Medically supervised detoxification reduces the risk of death as the person's body adapts to reduced amounts of barbiturates. This treatment starts with the person receiving the usual amount of the barbiturate and then less and less of the drug over time. The person still endures withdrawal symptoms. However, the more serious symptoms may be less severe.

To lessen the REM rebound effect, it is recommended that a person reduce barbiturate consumption by one therapeutic dosage over a period of five or six days, according to *Physicians' Desk Reference*. Another method is to take two doses instead of three for a week.

Detoxification may occur in a hospital, or treatment may be given on an outpatient basis. Counseling is also part of the treatment regimen. After the person is successfully treated for physical addiction, he or she must follow through with psychological rehabilitation.

Behavioral treatment helps a person avoid barbiturates by providing guidance about how to function without drugs and how to cope with cravings. The behavior-modification treatments can be set up as one-on-one counseling sessions, group therapy, family counseling, or other types of therapies. For the person wanting to remain drug-free, ongoing support can be found in 12-step programs and other groups that meet regularly.

PERSONAL AND SOCIAL CONSEQUENCES

Barbiturates harm more people than those who take them. People who drive while intoxicated by barbiturates risk the lives of others. A pregnant woman who takes barbiturates passes the drugs along to her unborn baby. After the baby is born, the infant will have to undergo withdrawal from the barbiturate.

Barbiturates can also affect relationships. The drugs have been compared to alcohol in terms of the intoxicating effects. Both drugs produce a euphoric feeling during

???? FACT OR FICTION

The truth about truth serum

After the September 11, 2001, terrorist attacks in the United States, federal investigators discussed the use of truth serum to obtain information from jailed terrorism suspects. The serum is the barbiturate thiopental, which is also known as pentothal sodium. The use of this drug to make a reluctant person talk has been portrayed in movies, books, and on television.

As of April 2002, the federal suspects had not been drugged to obtain information. Pentothal sodium cannot force people to be honest. However, an injection of this barbiturate produces a semiconscious state that is like a hypnotic trance. In that state, people's inhibitions are lowered. In that relaxed state, people talk more and could reveal something that they wanted to keep secret.

---

the mild intoxication stage. People may enjoy being around the person at that point.

As the intoxication increases, the person may become belligerent. He or she may provoke an argument. There is a possibility of violence. Judgement is impaired, so the person might make an unsafe decision like trying to drive home.

Some people who abuse barbiturates do not worry about driving under the influence. The reason is not because they are confident about their ability to drive, but because they know that police will not smell alcohol on their breath.

In some ways, the effects of barbiturates are predictable. Prolonged barbiturate use can shorten a person's attention span. The person may suffer memory loss. Both conditions would make it difficult for a person to do well in school or perform on a job.

In addition, barbiturates make a person tired, anxious, and depressed. The person who took barbiturates to feel better finds that the drugs only deepen the depression.

As a person takes more or higher doses of a barbiturate, he or she does not know if that dose will be fatal. And with increased tolerance, the difference diminishes between an intoxicating dose and a fatal dose.

Furthermore, the method of withdrawing from barbiturates is not as simple as stopping completely. Barbiturates slow the brain's activity, so there could be a rebound when a person stops taking the drug. This rebound activity could lead to seizures and other harmful consequences.

LEGAL CONSEQUENCES

When barbiturates first went on the market during the 1930s, people in the United States did not need a prescription to buy them. Lawmakers soon realized that barbiturates were addictive. Some states adopted laws that banned the sale of nonprescription barbiturates. The federal government took similar action after the Food and Drug Administration gained regulatory power in 1938. That set the stage for a 40-year battle against barbiturate abuse.

Legal history

The federal Food, Drug, and Cosmetics Act of 1938 gave regulatory powers to the Food and Drug Administration (FDA). Pharmaceutical companies apply to the FDA for approval to manufacture a new drugs. The approval process includes research, testing, and hearings. Once a drug is approved, the FDA determines whether a prescription is required.

FDA regulations about prescription drugs apply to how the manufacturer promotes or advertises the medications. Unless specified by other regulations such as the Controlled Substances Act (CSA), there are no restrictions on the condition for which the doctor prescribes the pill, the dosage prescribed, or the amount of time that the patient will take the pill.

Federal guidelines, regulations, and penalties

The Controlled Substances Act (CSA) portion of the 1970 Comprehensive Drug Abuse Prevention and Control Act classified drugs in five categories based on the effect of the drug, its medical use, and potential for abuse. Schedule I contains drugs like heroin, which have no medical use but may be used in research. It is the most tightly controlled category.

Schedule II drugs have a high potential for abuse. They are accepted for medical use with restrictions. These drugs may lead to severe psychological or physical dependence. Barbiturates in this category are amobarbital (Amytal), pentobarbital (Nembutal), and secobarbital (Seconal, Tuinal).

Schedule III drugs have less of a potential for abuse than drugs in Schedules I and II. The drugs have a medical use. Abuse of these drugs may lead to "moderate or low psychological dependence or high psychological dependence," according to the CSA. Barbiturates in this category are aprobarbital (Alurate) butabarbital (Busitol, Bubatel), and butibal (Fiorinal). A prescription may be filled up to five times during the six months after the first prescription was written.

Schedule IV drugs have a low abuse potential as compared to Schedule III drugs. These substances have an accepted medical use. They could lead to limited psychological or physical dependence, according to the CSA. The Schedule IV barbiturates are barbital (Veronel), mephobarbital (Mebaral), and phenobarbital (Luminal). Five prescription refills are allowed during the six months after the patient received the first prescription.

Penalties. Federal law prohibits the possession, use, and distribution of illegal drugs. The Controlled Substances Act established tighter controls on the manufacture and distribution of drugs like diet pills. Limits were set on the amounts of Schedule II pills that could be manufactured.

Procedure for the legal distribution of pills included the requirement of a written prescription for Schedule II drugs. An exception is made in emergencies.

For Schedule III and IV drugs, the prescription may be written or called into the pharmacy. Both the health care practitioner and pharmacist are required to keep records when prescriptions are filled for controlled drugs.

Trafficking. Trafficking is the illegal distribution of controlled drugs. Federal penalties for this crime can include fines and imprisonment. Sentencing is based on factors such as whether the trafficker is a first-time offender. Penalties are higher for a second offense. In addition, if the illegal distribution of a Schedule II drug results in death or serious injury, the convicted offender faces a prison term of from 20 years to life.

In cases where there is no serious injury or death, the penalties for a first-time offense are:

- Schedule II: Trafficking 100 grams or more of methamphetamine carries a prison term of from 10 years to life and a fine of up to $4 million.

- Schedule III drugs: Trafficking any quantity of these drugs is punishable by up to five years in prison and a maximum fine of $250,000.

- Schedule IV drugs: Illegally distributing any quantity of these drugs carries a prison term of up to three years and a fine of up to $250,000.

Penalties for drug abusers. The federal penalty for the first-time offense of illegally possessing a controlled substance is up to one year in prison and a fine of from $1,000 to $100,000. Penalties are generally doubled for a second offense.

In some cases, a person may not receive a prison sentence. The Anti-Drug Abuse Act of 1988 imposes a civil penalty on the minor drug offender, the person pos-sessing a small quantity of an illegal controlled substance. Possession of this quantity known as a "personal use amount" carries a fine of up to $10,000.

Drug laws in the United Kingdom. In the United Kingdom, substances are regulated by the 1971 Misuse of Drugs Act and the 1986 Medicines Act. The 1971 act placed drugs in categories of A, B, or C. The A category contains the most dangerous drugs. The least dangerous drugs are in Category C.

The 1986 act established five medical schedules that are based on factors such as the therapeutic value of the drug. Another consideration is whether a prescription is required. Schedule 1 is the most strictly controlled category.

Barbiturates are a Class B drug unless the barbiturate is used in an injectable form. It then becomes a Class A drug.

The maximum penalty for possession of a Class B drug is five years of prison, an unlimited fine (of any amount), or prison and a fine. The maximum fine for supply (trafficking) is a 14-year prison term, an unlimited fine, or both penalties.

For Class A drugs, the penalty for possession is seven years in prison, an unlimited fine, or both. The supply penalty for this class, which includes cocaine and heroin, is life imprisonment, an unlimited fine, or both penalties.

See also Amphetamines; Antidepressants; Benzodiazepine; Diet pills; Tranquilizers

RESOURCES

Books

Breacher, Edward M., et al. *The Consumers Union Report on Licit and Illicit Drugs.* Boston: Little Brown & Co., 1972.

Dorsman, Jerry. *How to Quit Drugs for Good.* Rocklin, CA: Prima Publishing, 1998.

Hughes, Richard and Robert Brewin. *The Tranquilizing of America.* New York: Harcourt Brace Jovanovich, 1979.

Medical Economics. *Physicians' Desk Reference 2001.* Montvale, NJ: Medical Economics, 2001.

Wolfe, Sidney. *Worst Pills, Best Pills.* New York: Pocket Books, 1999.

Organizations

National Institute on Drug Abuse (NIDA), National Institutes of Health, 6001 Executive Blvd., Room 5213, Bethesda, MD, USA, 20892-9561, (301) 443-1124, (888) 644-6432, <http://www.nida.nih.gov>.

U.S. Drug Enforcement Administration, 2401 Jefferson Davis Highway, Alexandria, VA, USA, 22201, (800) 882-9539, <http://www.dea.gov>.

U.S. Food and Drug Administration (FDA), 560 Fishers Lane, Rockville, MD, USA, 20857-0001, (888) 463-6332, <http://www.fda.gov>.

Liz Swain

BENZODIAZEPINE

Although they have been used for over 30 years, benzodiazepines are still widely prescribed in the treatment of anxiety disorders and other medical conditions. These drugs are classified as sedative-hypnotic agents, which depress or slow down the body. In the past 15 years, the development of the newer selective serotonin reuptake inhibitors (SSRIs) for the treatment of depression and anxiety have pushed benzodiazepines aside as the first treatment choice because the SSRIs as a class of drugs have not yet been found to be addictive.

Benzodiazepines are used to treat a wide range of psychiatric and medical conditions. Because they work so quickly, benzodiazepines are often the first drugs chosen by physicians in treating new or suspected anxiety or psychiatric disorders. Compared to the newer SSRIs, which can often take weeks to have an effect, benzodiazepines can be felt to work within hours. This quick onset of action has both positive and negative sides. On the one hand, people feel better faster. On the other hand, this speediness of effect also makes benzodiazepines more likely to cause addiction than other medications prescribed by psychiatrists and psychologists. Physical and/or psychological dependence may occur within a matter of weeks, depending upon the individual taking them.

When taken alone, benzodiazepines have a relatively good safety record. Even when taken in overdose quantities alone these drugs rarely cause serious consequences. Unfortunately, however, when benzodiazepines are being abused, they may be used in combination with other drugs or alcohol, and it is these combinations that

OFFICIAL NAMES: Alprazolam (Xanax), chlorazepate (Tranxene) chlordiazepoxide (Librium, Novopoxide), clonazepam (Klonopin), clorazepate (Tranxene), diazepam (Valium, Vivol), estazolam (ProSom), flurazepam (Dalmane, Novoflupam, Somnol), flunitrazepam (Rohypnol), halazepam (Paxipam), lorazepam (Ativan), nitrazepam (Mogadon), oxazepam (Serax), prazepam (Centrax), quazepam (Doral), temazepam (Restoril), triazolam (Halcion)
STREET NAMES: Roofies, tranks, downers, benzos, goofballs, Mexican, roach, heavenly blues, valo, stupefy, date rape, anxiety
DRUG CLASSIFICATIONS: Schedule IV, depressant

can lead to serious physical consequences, including depressed respiration, coma, and even death.

Historical background

Benzodiazepines were developed in the 1950s as a safer alternative to barbiturates. Currently, about 2,000 different kinds of benzodiazepines are made. In the United States, only about 15 of these are approved by the FDA.

Some of the more commonly prescribed benzodiazepines include the following, which are ranked here approximately according to frequency of use:

• alprazolam (Xanax)

• clonazepam (Klonopin)

 **KEY TERMS**

ANXIETY DISORDERS: A group of mental disorders or conditions characterized in part by chronic feelings of fear, excessive and obsessive worrying, restlessness, and panic attacks. Anxiety disorders include panic disorder, agoraphobia, obsessive-compulsive disorder, Post-traumatic stress disorder, and others.

DOCTOR SHOPPING: A practice in which an individual continually switches physicians so that he or she can get enough of a prescription drug to feed an addiction. This practice makes it difficult for physicians to track whether the patient has already been prescribed the same drug by another physician.

PANIC ATTACKS: Sudden, repeated, paralyzing bouts of extreme fear and anxiety.

PHOBIA: The irrational fear of a specific object or situation that limits normal functioning.

REBOUND: Also known as discontinuation symptoms, these occur when the benzodiazepines are withdrawn. These symptoms are an aspect of withdrawal in which the patient develops anxiety, insomnia, or other serious emotional reactions that are more intense than before treatment with the drug was begun.

- diazepam (Valium)

- lorazepam (Ativan)

- clorazepate (Tranxene)

- oxazepam (Serax)

- prazepam (Centrax)

- clordiazepoxide (Librium)

- halazepam (Paxipam)

The top four—alprazolam, clonazepam, diazepam, and lorazepam—are consistently listed among the top 100 most commonly prescribed medications. Flunitrazepam (Rohypnol) has recently received a lot of attention, especially on college campuses, where its use as a "date rape" drug has placed it on the watch list of students and police. Flunitrazepam is one of the drugs, along with MDMA (ecstasy), used by teenagers and young adults as part of the nightclub, bar, "rave," or "trance" scene.

Flunitrazepam, also known by the brand name Rohypnol, and by the street names roofies, R2, Roche, roofinol, rope, rophies, forget-me pill, and Mexican valium, has received more press recently than most of the

other benzodiazepines. It comes as a small, white tablet, with "Roche" on one side, and an encircled "1" or "2" on the other side, which indicats the 1-mg or 2-mg dose. It is usually consumed orally, often combined with alcohol, and can also be snorted after crushing the tablets.

This drug is produced legally in countries such as Brazil, Colombia, Ecuador, Mexico, and Peru. It is frequently smuggled into the country disguised as vitamins or in its original packaging as cold medicine. Flunitrazepam is not approved in the United States, but is has been used widely in Texas, and is readily available in Miami, Florida, where it is a growing problem.

The pharmacologic effects of Rohypnol include sedation, muscle relaxation, and anxiety reduction. The sedative effects are said to be seven to 10 times that of diazepam (Valium). In high doses, flunitrazepam can cause malignant hyperthermia, or a sharp increase in body temperature that can cause muscle breakdown and failure of the kidneys and cardiovascular system.

Because it is colorless, tasteless, and odorless, flunitrazepam can be added to beverages and taken unknowingly. After taking this drug, the user can feel intoxicated, then sleepy, for up to eight hours. Speech may become slurred, and judgment impaired. Partial amnesia is a common effect, and for this reason, flunitrazepam has been used in committing date rape or sexual assault. Victims are usually unable to remember the assault, or identify who assaulted them while they were under the effects of flunitrazepam. These effects occur roughly 15–20 minutes after taking the drug, and last for four to eight hours. Deep sedation and respiratory distress are some of the more serious possible effects of Rohypnol, as are blackouts that can last up to 24 hours.

In 1996, Congress passed the Drug-Induced Rape Prevention and Punishment Act of 1996, which increased the federal penalties for those who used any controlled substance to aid them in sexual assault. This law makes it a punishable crime to give someone a controlled substance without that person's knowledge of it and with the intent to commit a violent crime against that person. It also includes stiffer penalties for those who possess or distribute this drug.

Other benzodiazepines

Benzodiazepines are classified according to how long their effects last and by their potency. The ultrashort acting benzodiazepines include midazolam (Versed) and triazolam (Halcion); the short-acting benzodiazepines include alprazolam (Xanax) and lorazepam (Ativan); the long-acting include chlordiazepoxide (Librium) and diazepam (Valium). High potency benzodiazepines include alprazolam, lorazepam, triazolam, and clonazepam (Klonopin). Low-potency benzodiazepines include chlordiazepoxide, clorazepate (Tranxene), diazepam, and flurazepam (Dalmane).

Because benzodiazepines, as a class, are usually equally effective in treating anxiety (in combination with cognitive-behavioral theraphy), psychiatrists usually select which of these drugs to prescribe based on its side effect profile. This means that the physician will weigh all the individual factors of each patient, and decide which drug is best suited for the patient's individual needs based on which side effects that person can or cannot tolerate. For example, some of the benzodiazepines are more easily processed by the liver. This may be particularly useful in patients taking birth control pills, propranolol, disulfuram, ulcer medications, and other drugs that may affect liver function. In such cases, lorazepam (Ativan) may be chosen because it has less of an effect on the liver.

Alprazolam (Xanax), lorazepam (Ativan), and oxazepam (Serax) are metabolized and cleared from the body more quickly than the other members of this family, and are therefore more likely to produce withdrawal symptoms when they are discontinued. These three drugs, however, are less likely to produce side effects such as impaired coordination, concentration, and memory; and muscular weakness or sedation.

Benzodiazepines do not depress breathing, blood pressure, or other vital functions, like many of the drugs used to treat psychiatric disorders. They are also less likely to cause damage to the body systems or death in cases of overdose.

Despite this, these agents still present a number of problems for many individuals, including the need for higher doses and addiction. Tolerance and physical and psychological dependence are common with continued treatment with all of these drugs.

When used for a longer period of time, a number of the benzodiazepines will slowly lose their effectiveness, and higher doses may be needed to achieve the desired effects. Further, if any of these medications are discontinued abruptly, withdrawal symptoms can occur, and these can be quite serious. These symptoms can include seizures, insomnia, nervousness, irritability, diarrhea, abdominal cramps, muscle aches, and memory impairment.

Several types of people should not take any of the benzodiazepines, because of the possibility of unwanted side effects. These include the following:

- People who have had previous negative reactions or serious side effects with any benzodiazepine.

- People who fly aircraft, drive, or operate heavy machinery.

- People with a history of drug or alcohol dependence.

- People with Alzheimer's disease, stroke, multiple sclerosis, or other brain disorders.

- People with anxiety that recurs after benzodiazepines are discontinued.

- People who are seriously depressed.

- Women who are pregnant.

- Women who are breastfeeding.

CHEMICAL/ORGANIC COMPOSITION

Benzodiazepines produce mild sedation when taken by slowing down activity in the central nervous system (CNS). These drugs act on the limbic system, the area of the brain that controls emotions. Specifically, they enhance the effects of a natural chemical neurotransmitter called gamma-aminobutyric acid (GABA), and heightens GABA's ability to block feelings of tension and anxiety by inhibiting neurons from firing and thereby dampening the transmission of nerve signals. The result is a calming effect.

Some of the benzodiazepines, such as alprazolam (Xanax) and triazolam (Halcion), bind especially tightly to the GABA receptors. This causes more intense sedation and hypnosis, as well as more severe rebound and withdrawal symptoms.

INGESTION METHODS

Benzodiazepines are usually taken in their pill form, although some people dissolve and inject them. Some of these drugs are also available in an injectable solution, including chlordiazepoxide, diazepam, and lorazepam. Diazepam is also available in a rectal solution. The onset of effect is roughly 30 minutes, and can last up to 48 hours.

THERAPEUTIC USE

Physicians use benzodiazepines to treat many disorders, including a number of anxiety disorders. These include acute anxiety, panic disorder, post-traumatic stress disorder, and obsessive-compulsive disorder. In addition, benzodiazepines can be used to treat agitation or anxiety that is caused by other psychiatric conditions such as acute mania, psychotic illness, depression, impulse control disorders, and catatonia or mutism.

Involuntary movement disorders also respond well to this class of drugs. These include restless leg syndrome, akathisia associated with neuroleptic use, choreiform disorders, and myoclonus.

Benzodiazepines are used to treat insomnia and for the acute treatment of epileptic seizures, convulsive disorders, and spastic disorders such as cerebral palsy, multiple sclerosis, and paraplegia caused by trauma to the spine.

Benzodiazepines can be used during detoxification from alcohol and other substances, as well as in surgery, dentistry, diagnostic studies (computed tomography, MRI, and endoscopy), cardioversion, and chemotherapy. They help reduce fear and anxiety, and in cases of detoxification, can actually lessen the symptoms of alcohol withdrawal.

USAGE TRENDS

Benzodiazepines are very commonly prescribed, and have consistently made the annual list of drugs most prescribed by physicians for many years. According to *Pharmacy Times*, the category of benzodiazepines ranked seventh in the list of the "Top 20 Product Categories," according to the total number of new prescriptions of benzodiazepines that were dispensed that year, which was 39,322,000. They ranked ninth on *Pharmacy Times* list of the "Top 20 Leading Product Categories for 2000," according to the total prescriptions dispensed, which were 66,564,000 for that year.

Alprazolam (Xanax), which was developed and introduced in 1981, is still the most prescribed benzodiazepine. It causes fewer side effects, because the body can eliminate it in less than 12 hours. Chlordiazepoxide (Klonopin) is the second most commonly prescribed benzodiazepine.

Benzodiazepines are most commonly prescribed for women and elderly patients. This may be partially due to the fact that women, in general, seem to be more willing to seek psychological help than men. In addition, four out of five people who experience panic attacks are women. Elderly patients are commonly afflicted with other conditions, such as insomnia and depression, which respond well to treatment with benzodiazepines.

Although benzodiazepines are the most commonly prescribed psychoactive drugs in the world, they are rarely used as recreational drugs because they have only mild to moderate euphoriant effects. According to reports from the United States Drug Enforcement Agency, these drugs are not valued on the street in the same way cocaine, heroin, or even alcohol is; therefore they are relatively inexpensive. Abuse of benzodiazepines is high among heroin and cocaine abusers. Abuse is found among adolescents and young adults as well, who may take these drugs to get buzzed. According to an in-depth review of the benzodiazepines in *American Family Physician* in 2000, about 80% of benzodiazepine abuse is in those who use other drugs, opioid users being the most common.

The dark side to benzodiazepines is that they are the most commonly implicated substances in drug overdoses, many of which are a result of combining benzodiazepines with other drugs, including alcohol. Two of the benzodiazepines commonly prescribed for sleep—flurazepam (Dalmane) and temazepam (Restoril)—were associated with the most deaths per million prescriptions.

Hospital admissions due to benzodiazepine abuse have been studied as well. According to the Treatment Episode Data Set (TEDS) from the Substance Abuse and Mental Health Services Administration (SAMHSA) of the United States Department of Health and Human Services, tranquilizers such as the benzodiazepines were the primary substance of 0.3% of TEDS admissions in 1998. In addition, 39% of patients admitted for tranquilizer use reported abuse of alcohol as well as tranquilizers. Admissions for tranquilizer abuse were mostly female (48%) and white (90%).

A full 61% of the hospital admissions were aged 35 and older. Interestingly, the data also show that 32% of tranquilizer admissions patients first used tranquilizers after the age of 30. This is consistent with other data and surveys, which also show that the use of tranquilizers, including benzodiazepines, increases with age.

Patterns of benzodiazepine use in young adults can be found in a survey entitled *Monitoring the Future: National Survey Results on Drug Use, 1975-2000. Volume II: College Students and Adults Ages 19-40*. This is a compilation of data from a long-term research program conducted by the University of Michigan's Institute for Social Research, with funding from the National Institute on Drug Abuse.

The survey consists of a series of ongoing national annual surveys of high school seniors (begun in 1975) and of eighth and tenth grade students (begun in 1991). Follow-up surveys of the previous participants from each high school senior class were also conducted, starting with the class of 1976. Volume 2 of the survey is a compilation of the resulting surveys from graduating high school seniors (from the classes of 1976 through 1999) as they moved into adulthood through age 40. These data were used to determine the most updated prevalence rates of benzodiazepine use in young adults.

Overall, the survey found that there were steady increases in the use of all agents that were CNS depressants, such as benzodiazepines among high school seniors, college students, and young adults. From the 1970s through the early 1990s, usage of these drugs declined. A small increase in the use of these drug, however, has become evident from the early 1990s through 2000.

According to the survey data, the annual prevalence of the use of benzodiazepines among college students dropped by 50% between the years of 1980 to 1984 (6.9% to 3.5%, respectively), and then dropped by another 50% between 1984 and 1994 (to 1.8%). Then, usage rates began a steady increase, reaching 4.2% by 2000. In young adults not considered to be college students, these rates dropped more sharply during the early 1980s. Similarly, in high school seniors, the use of benzodiazepines also dropped from 1977 to 1992 (from 10.8% to 2.8%, respectively), and then rose to a total of 5.7% in 2000.

According to this same survey, the lifetime prevalence of use of tranquilizers in the year 2000 for full-time college students was low, at 8.8%, as compared to young adults who were one to four years beyond high school in the same age group, which was 12.7%. This was higher among full-time college students who were male than in those who were female (10.0% vs. 7.9%, respectively). These drugs were most likely to be used by non-collegiate males (14.5%), and to a lesser degree, females (11.3%).

In this survey, college students were defined as high school graduates who were one to four years past high school and who were enrolled full-time in a two-year or four-year college at the beginning of March of the year reported on. For each year of the survey, roughly 1,100 to 1,500 respondents comprised the college student sample, and about 1,000 to 1,700 respondents comprised the group of young adults not considered college students.

Young men not enrolled in college were the most common users of benzodiazepines in the year 2000. Young adults who were not in college were also more likely than college students to use these drugs. Annual use of benzodiazepines was again most likely in young adult men who were not full-time college students (7.6%), followed by women who were not students (6.3%), compared with only 4.8% of full-time college males and only 3.8% of full-time college female students. Overall, the annual prevalence of the use of benzodiazepines in all young adults enrolled full-time in college was 4.2%, compared with 6.8% in young adults not enrolled in full-time college.

In this same survey, many young adults reported that benzodiazepines were readily available to them (37–38%). This availability was decreased in the long term among young adults aged 19–22 years, with 36.5% saying that these drugs were "fairly easy" or "very easy" to get in 2000. This was a decrease from the 37.1% who reported this availability in 1999, and a decrease from the 67.4% who reported this in 1980.

Among 19–22 year olds, the percentage of youths reporting that most or all of their friends used benzodiazepine increased, from 1.9% in 1980 to 2.1% in 2000. There was also an increase of 0.9% in the number of 19 to 22 year olds who reported that most or all of their friends used benzodiazepines from 1999 to 2000.

The percentage of young adults aged 19–22 years who reported that they had any exposure to benzodiazepines also increased from 14.3% in 1999 to 18.5% in 2000, an increase of 4.3%. This was decreased, however, from responses in 1980, when a full 29.6% of young

HISTORY NOTES

Historically, tranquilizers were not one of the drugs made famous in the drug culture of the 1960s. Yet these drugs, including benzodiazepines and minor tranquilizers, were becoming a mainstay of treatment for many middle-class housewives throughout the United States at that time. These women were far from the college campus, hippie love-ins, and concert-going youths that made the decade famous for its experimentations in free love and hallucinogenic drugs.

The practice of taking minor tranquilizers was so widespread during this time that they were made famous in the song by the Rolling Stones called "Mother's Little Helper." It is estimated that in the 1970s, as many as 30 million women were taking minor tranquilizers. This made up almost 50% of the female population at that time. Psychiatrists were freely prescribing these minor tranquilizers to unhappy housewives, with no thought of their addictive properties, and many housewives became unknowingly and undeniably addicted to these drugs.

adults in this age group reported having any exposure to benzodiazepines. In those saying they were often exposed to benzodiazepine use, the percentage again increased, from 1.5% in 1999 to 1.7% in 2000, an increase of 0.2%.

Lifetime use of benzodiazepines has decreased slighty over the years, but this reduction has been minimal. According to the results from an annual survey done by SAMSHA (Substance Abuse and Mental Health Services Administration, of the United States Department of Health), use of tranquilizers or benzodiazepines has decreased. Data from SAMSHA's 2000 National Household Survey on Drug Abuse shows that in persons aged 18–25, lifetime use of tranquilizers decreased from 7.9% in 1999 to 7.4% in 2000. Past year usage of tranquilizers in this age group also decreased, from 3.1% in 1999, to 3.0% in 2000. Finally, past month usage of tranquilizers in the 18 to 25-year-old respondents to the survey decreased, from 1.1% in 1999, to 1.0% in 2000.

MENTAL EFFECTS

Benzodiazepines work to reduce inhibition and anxiety. They depress the central nervous system. This in turn reduces emotional reactions, mental alertness, attention span, and feelings of anxiety, bringing a sense of relaxation and well being. In addition, benzodi-

IN THE NEWS

A recent and well-publicized example of prescription fraud occurred in Florida. In February 2002, Governor Jeb Bush's daughter, Noelle Bush, was arrested on charges of prescription fraud in Tallahassee. Ms. Bush, aged 24, was trying to buy Xanax, after allegedly having used the name of a retired doctor to call in a false prescription. If convicted, Ms. Bush will be guilty of a third degree felony, according to Florida law, and face a sentence of up to five years in prison and a $5,000 fine.

azepines can cause drowsiness and mental confusion. These effects are immediate and can last hours or days. When taken long-term, benzodiazepines can cause increased aggressiveness and severe depression.

Several studies have shown that impairment of a person's cognitive or mental function can occur in people taking benzodiazepines. These effects can include problems such as lapses of memory, and confusion. For example, college students who take benzodiazepines before exams to help them relax or sleep may not remember some of what they have been studying.

Common side effects of benzodiazepines include drowsiness, loss of coordination, unsteady gait, dizziness, lightheadedness, and slurred speech. Some of the less common side effects include changes in sexual desire or ability, constipation, a false sense of well being, nausea and vomiting, urinary problems, and fatigue. Euphoria, restlessness, hallucinations, and hypomanic behavior have been reported, as have uninhibited bizarre behaviors, hostility, rage, paranoia, depression, and suicidal thoughts.

Serious side effects with these drugs are rare, but can include behavior problems such as outbursts of anger, depression, hallucinations, low blood pressure, muscle weakness, skin rash or itching, sore throat, fever and chills, sores in the throat or mouth, unusual bruising or bleeding, extreme fatigue, yellowish tinge to the eyes or skin, and difficulty concentrating. If any of these side effects occurs, a doctor should be contacted immediately.

In particular, individuals taking nitrazepam (Mogadon) often report an increase in the incidence of nightmares, especially during the first week of use. Flurazepam (Dalmane, Novoflupam, Somnol) also occasionally causes an increase in nightmares, as well as anxiety, irritability, tachycardia, sweating, and garrulousness.

PHYSIOLOGICAL EFFECTS

Benzodiazepines act on the central nervous system by slowing it down, thereby causing sedation and muscle relaxation. Immediate physiologic effects include depressed heartbeat and breathing, and physical unsteadiness. Side effects include skin rashes, nausea, and dizziness.

Regular use of any benzodiazepine can lead to physical and psychological dependence in as little as four to six weeks. Cravings for the drug, increased tolerance and the need for higher and higher doses, and withdrawal symptoms are all signs of dependence on the benzodiazepines. When stopped abruptly, individuals who are dependent on these agents can experience serious withdrawal symptoms and even seizures. Symptoms of withdrawal include anxiety, headache, dizziness, shakiness, loss of appetite, insomnia, and sometimes, fever, seizures, and even psychosis. People who are long-term addicts of the benzodiazepines may need to be hospitalized for withdrawal.

Harmful side effects

When taken in high doses, these drugs can produce some serious side effects. These side effects, which can be a signal that there is too much medication in the body or that toxic effects are being felt by the body, include drowsiness, confusion, dizziness, blurred vision, weakness, slurred speech, lack of coordination, difficulty breathing, and coma.

Driving and hazardous work should not be performed while taking benzodiazepines because they can impair mental alertness and coordination. Persons taking any of the benzodiazepine medications should never drink alcohol. Use during pregnancy and nursing should be avoided as well.

Benzodiazepines can have particularly potent effects when taken during pregnancy, and can cause congenital defects such as cleft lip or cleft palate. In addition, infants born to a mother addicted to the benzodiazepines can also experience withdrawal symptoms including respiratory distress, difficulty feeding, disruption of sleep patterns, decreased responsiveness, sweating, irritability, and fever. In addition, some benzodiazepines can accumulate in higher concentrations in the bloodstream and organs of an infant than in the mother. Also important to note is that these drugs may be present in higher concentrations in the breast milk of addicted mothers than in the bloodstream.

Long-term health effects

Use of any of benzodiazepines for as little as four to six weeks can lead to psychological or physical dependence. Dependence can develop sooner in patients taking short-acting, high-potency benzodiazepines like alprazolam (Xanax), as compared with someone taking a longer acting, low-potency agent such as chlordiazepoxide.

Benzodiazepines also should not be taken by people who have a history of alcohol or drug abuse, stroke or other brain disorder, chronic lung disease, hyperactivity, depression or other mental illness, myasthenia gravis, sleep apnea, epilepsy, porphyria, kidney disease, or liver disease.

REACTIONS WITH OTHER DRUGS OR SUBSTANCES

Benzodiazepines have an extremely low risk of acute toxicity when they are used alone. Unfortunately, these drugs are often used with other medications such as other CNS depressants, which can include commonly used antihistamines and alcohol, causing toxicity.

Drinking alcoholic beverages while taking any of the benzodiazepine medications will increase all the side effects of the benzodiazepine, especially the sedative effects and the tendency for slowed breathing. Concurrent use of alcohol and these drugs can also increase the memory lapses that occur with benzodiazepines. High doses of benzodiazepines and alcohol can impair an individual's ability to breathe and dangerously lower blood pressures. This could result in coma and death. Alcohol and benzodiazepines should never be taken together.

Use of benzodiazepines with narcotics, such as meperidine (Demerol), oxycodone (Percodan), codeine, morphine, or pentazocine (Talwin), increase their sedative effects. Combining these agents can lead to serious reductions in breathing rate, and even death. These two types of drugs should never be taken together.

Benzodiazepines should not be used with other drugs that inhibit the CNS, including hypnotic agents, sedating antidepressants, neuroleptic agents, anticonvulsants, and even antihistamines. Combined use with the barbiturates and other sedatives, such as phenobarbitol (Luminal), pentobarbital (Nembutal), secobarbitol (Seconal), and amobarbital/secobarbital (Tuinal), can also increase sedation and depress breathing to dangerous levels.

Combined use of more than one benzodiazepine is unnecessary and unsafe, as is combined use of benzodiazepines and sleeping pills.

Certain drugs can reduce the ability of the liver to clear benzodiazepines from the body. These include ulcer drugs, such as cimetidine (Tagamet), birth control pills, propranolol (used to treat hypertension, heart disorders, and migraines), and disulfuram (Antabuse), which is used for the treatment of alcoholism.

Finally, benzodiazepines should not be used to treat anxiety that is associated with depression because some-times these drugs can actually make the depression worse. Instead, the choice for treatment in such cases should be one of the antidepressant medications.

TREATMENT AND REHABILITATION

Signs of addiction to benzodiazepines can be both specific and nonspecific. Chronic abuse can be signaled by the return of anxiety, insomnia, anorexia, headaches, and weakness in muscles. Changes in appearance and behavior that affect relationships and performance at work can be some of the nonspecific signs. Abrupt mood changes can also be a nonspecific sign. Addicted individuals will feel an intense craving for the drug, and then become ill if it is not obtained. Higher and higher doses are usually needed to achieve the same effects. Sudden cessation of the drug may cause withdrawal symptoms including shaking, nervousness, vomiting, fast heartbeat, sweating, and insomnia. Seizures or hallucinations can occur, but rarely.

Individuals who are addicted to benzodiazepines should not try to quit "cold turkey" on their own. Often, individuals addicted to a benzodiazepine have an addiction to another substance or drug, such as cocaine or alcohol. These multiple addictions are complicated. Recovery from these addictions should not be attempted alone. Withdrawal from abuse of benzodiazepines may cause life-threatening complications.

Withdrawal symptoms resulting from use of very high doses of benzodiazepines are comparable to those experienced by alcoholics when they stop drinking alcohol. The first signs of withdrawal develop two to 20 days after stopping the drug, and can initially include insomnia, irritability, and nervousness. This may progress to include abdominal and muscle cramps, nausea and vomiting, trembling, sweating, hyperarousal, and sensitivity to environmental stimuli. More severe withdrawal symptoms can include confusion, depersonalization, anxiety and obsession, psychosis, organic brain syndrome, and even seizures. Symptoms can takes weeks or even months to subside.

The first step in overcoming an addiction to any benzodiazepine is to undergo detoxification under strict medical supervision. The dosage of benzodiazepine must be gradually lowered over time. During this time, psychological counseling may be helpful, as well as cognitive-behavioral therapy, which focuses on changing a patient's thinking, expectations, and behavior and increasing his or her skills for coping with the everyday stresses in life.

PERSONAL AND SOCIAL CONSEQUENCES

The personal and social consequences of benzodiazepine abuse have not, to date, been extensively studied. A few seminal studies have shown, however, that use and abuse of the benzodiazepines carry the possibilities of impaired decision-making, decreased learning skills, released aggression, and an impaired ability to empathize, all of which can have profound effects on an individual's educational, social, and workplace environments.

LEGAL CONSEQUENCES

Medical prescriptions are the primary source of benzodiazepines for those who abuse these drugs, although prescriptions can be rerouted illegally. Some people addicted to benzodiazepines also use a practice known as "doctor shopping," where the patients obtain several prescriptions by continuously switching doctors. In this way, they can get enough of their drug, via a doctor, to keep up with their addiction. The doctors used by the patient are usually unaware that the patient has already been prescribed the same drug by another doctor.

Writing fraudulent prescriptions on stolen prescription pads is a common practice used to obtain prescription drugs. Another means of getting prescription drugs such as benzodiazepines is by buying the drug from a patient who was legitimately prescribed the medication. These "legitimate" patients can be friends, parents, relatives, or even people on the street offering their prescriptions in exchange for money.

The legal consequences for the possession of a controlled substance such as a benzodiazepine without a prescription can be a felony conviction at the state or federal level.

Laws vary by state, but many have specific laws against the trafficking, possession, and use of drugs that are controlled substances, such as benzodiazepines. In addition, many other states have recently included laws against "doctor shopping" in attempts to stop prescription drug fraud.

Physicians who write prescriptions fraudulently are also subject to various legal consequences including felony convictions and the revocation of their license to practice medicine. However, the legal consequences tend to be less serious for the physicians involved as compared with lay persons. Many states now require the automatic suspension of medical, dental, and pharmacy licenses when these health-care professionals are convicted. However, many medical professionals convicted of prescription drug crimes have been able to keep their licenses. Unfortunately, the way current laws are written, most physicians avoid facing serious drug-trafficking charges after writing a prescription, even if it is fraudulent.

See also Ecstasy (MDMA); Ketamine; Rohypnol

RESOURCES

Books

American Psychiatric Association. *Benzodiazepine Dependence, Toxicity, and Abuse: A Task Force Report of the American Psychiatric Association.* Washington, DC: American Psychiatric Association, 1990.

Breggin, P.R. "Review of Behavioral Effects of Benzodiazepines with an Appendix on Drawing Scientific Conclusions from the FDA's Spontaneous Reporting System (MedWatch)." In *Brain Disabling Treatments in Psychiatry: Drugs, Electroshock and the Role of the FDA.* New York: Springer Publishing, 1997.

Drummond, Edward H. *The Complete Guide to Psychiatric Drugs: Straight Talk for Best Results.* New York: John Wiley & Sons, Inc., 2000.

Preston, John D., John H. O'Neal, and Mary C. Talaga. *Consumer Guide to Psychiatric Drugs.* New York: New Harbinger Publishers, 1998.

Periodicals

Longo, L.P., and B. Johnson. "Addiction: Part I. Benzodiazepines-Side Effects, Abuse Risk, and Alternatives." *American Family Physician* (April 1, 2000): 2121-31.

Other

"Common Questions About Benzodiazepine Risks." Web page. *The Journal of Addiction and Mental Health.* (March/April 2001). <http://www.camh.net/journal/journalv4no2/questions.html>.

"Monitoring the Future: National Survey Results on Drug Use, 1975-2000. Volume II: College College Students and Adults Ages 19-40." Report from the University of Michigan Institute for Social Research.

U.S. Department of Justice Drug Enforcement Administration. "Flunitrazepam (Rohypnol)." <http://www.usdoj.gov/dea/concern/flunitrazepam.html>.

Organizations

National Institute on Drug Abuse (NIDA), National Institutes of Health, 6001 Executive Boulevard, Room 5213, Bethesda, MD, USA, 20892-9561, (301) 443-1124, (888) 644-6432, information@lists.nida.nih.gov,<http://www.drugabuse.gov/Infofax/marijuana.html>.

Elizabeth C. Meszaros

BENZYLPIPERAZINE/ TRIFLUOROMETHYL- PHENYLPIPERAZINE

OVERVIEW

Chemicals known as piperazines have industrial applications worldwide, and it is legal to purchase bulk quantities of these chemicals on the Internet for this purpose. By changing chemical groups added to the basic piperazine skeletal structure, different chemicals can be formed that vary considerably in their industrial, medical, and mind-altering properties. Piperazine citrate and related compounds destroy intestinal worms, making these chemicals useful in both medical and veterinary preparations. Other medicinal and mind-altering qualities of piperazines are being exploited as possible treatments of depression, psychosis, Alzheimer's disease, and tumors.

The piperazines influence brain function through their effects on brain chemistry at different receptors, or specialized locations within nerves allowing them to communicate with each other through chemical messengers called neurotransmitters. By stimulating different groups and locations of nerve cells that contain a specific neurotransmitter called serotonin, piperazine derivatives can have varied, profound effects on mood, learning, perceptions, and movement.

Benzylpiperazine (BZP) is one of the more commonly used piperazines on the club scene because it stimulates the brain and central nervous system, to the point of creating hallucinogenic experiences in some users. Although many describe its stimulant effects as noticeably different from those of "speed," or amphetamines, it is not particularly popular because of its many side effects.

Like BZP, 3-trifluoromethylphenylpiperazine monohydrochloride (TFMPP) is a piperazine stimulant. Most

OFFICIAL NAMES: Benzylpiperazine (BZP), trifluoromethylphenylpiperazine (TFMPP), 1-benzyl-1,4-diazacyclohexane dihydrochloride
STREET NAMES: Legal E, legal X, A2, the substance, piperazine, 2C-T-Z
DRUG CLASSIFICATIONS: Not scheduled, stimulant, hallucinogen

users prefer to combine TFMPP with ecstasy (MDMA). Some users report decreased anxiety, increased closeness with others, and feelings of unexplained happiness, but others describe their experiences with these drugs as frightening and extremely unpleasant.

Piperazines are not currently scheduled or classified in the United States, making possession legal. As of August 2001, these chemicals were not controlled under the Controlled Substances Act (CSA). In the United States, some samples of ecstasy pills seized by authorities contain TFMPP. Piperazines sold in bulk over the Internet have made their way to the club and rave scene and are increasingly sold as club drugs to adolescents and young adults, sometimes as ecstasy, but usually as "BZP," "legal E," "legal X," or "A2." A BZP variant known as 2C-T-Z can be snorted or taken by mouth. Toxic reactions to BZP and TFMPP include their stimulant effects such as dangerously rapid heart rhythms and seizures. As of September 2000, there were two reported deaths from BZP/TFMPP.

CHEMICAL/ORGANIC COMPOSITION

Substituting different chemical groups onto the basic piperazine structure creates piperazine derivatives

KEY TERMS

ANTHELMINTHIC DRUGS: Drugs that rid the lower intestinal tract of parasitic worms.

DEMENTIA: A type of disease characterized by progressive loss of memory, learning, and thinking ability.

EUPHORIA: An exaggerated feeling of well being.

NEUROTRANSMITTER: Chemical messengers used by nerve cells to communicate with each other.

RECEPTOR: A specialized part of a nerve cell that recognizes neurotransmitters and communicates with other nerve cells.

like benzylpiperazine (BZP), also known as N-benzylpiperazine or 1-benzylpiperazine, and trifluoromethylphenylpiperazine (TFMPP). BZP is a benzyl amine, while TFMPP is a phenyl amine.

BZP is an odorless, colorless, or faint yellow oily liquid at room temperature, and freezes at 32°F (0°C). As it is a strong base, meaning that it has a high pH, it can cause burns to the skin, lungs, or intestinal tract if consumed in this form. For human or animal consumption, it must be converted to a monohydrochloride or dihydrochloride salt. Most industrial sources supply a BZP preparation that is 97% pure, but they do not disclose what the impurities consist of, and many impurities in industrial chemicals may be toxic or even fatal if consumed.

INGESTION METHODS

Most piperazines seized at raves have been in tablet form, containing both BZP and TFMPP, ranging in color from pink to yellow or tan, and marked with different symbols including a spider, fly, "A," or a simple straight line. While there is no way of knowing the dose of BZP and/or TFMPP in these tablets, most users prefer doses ranging 35–150 mg. Some users have reported snorting or smoking BZP preparations.

THERAPEUTIC USE

Since the early 1950s, piperazines have been widely used in veterinary medicine as anthelminthic drugs, which rid the lower intestinal tract of parasitic worms. In humans, diethylcarbamazine and piperazine citrate serve a similar function and are used to treat pinworm and roundworm infestations in adults and children. While

these drugs have little effect on immature worms, or larvae, which nest in muscles, skin, and other body tissues, they paralyze the muscles of mature worms, dislodging them from the wall of the intestinal tract so that they are eliminated with waves of intestinal movement.

In 1999, pharmaceutical researchers in Japan found that an N-benzylpiperazine derivative stimulates a brain chemical called acetylcholine, which is involved in learning and memory. This eventually led to the discovery of donepezil (Aricept), which helps ward off memory loss in Alzheimer's disease and other age-related dementias, or brain diseases associated with progressive loss of memory, learning, and thinking ability.

Other BZP derivatives are being investigated for possible therapeutic uses in depression, other psychiatric illnesses, epilepsy or seizure disorders, pain, and inflammatory diseases. Phenylpiperazine derivatives were developed to target specific tumors known as neuroblastomas. As of April 2002, no piperazines were being used for these conditions.

USAGE TRENDS

BZP abuse was first reported in the United States and Switzerland in 2000. Because piperazine abuse is relatively recent, there are as of yet no statistics available concerning the scope of the problem. Like ecstasy, BZP and TFMPP have made their way to the club and rave scene, but are also increasingly reported in U.S. high schools and colleges. As piperazine sales target mostly young adults and school children, these groups are believed to account for most illegal use.

The Drug Enforcement Administration (DEA) started seeing small amounts of BZP and TFMPP in 2000; they continued to increase in 2001 and 2002. The DEA has seized several hundred pounds/kilograms of powdered BZP from India. Most of the seizures have taken place in the South, Southwest, Chicago, and Connecticut. The DEA has applied to have BZP and TFMPP emergency scheduled. Emergency scheduling is the authority given by Congress to the administrator of the DEA to temporarily place new drugs that are considered dangerous into Schedule I until they can be properly reviewed and scheduled through normal channels.

MENTAL EFFECTS

Piperazines like BZP and TFMPP stimulate the brain, resulting in sensations and experiences which may be pleasant or unpleasant, frightening, dangerous, or lethal. Animal research has shown that BZP triggers the release of neurotransmitters called dopamine and norepinephrine, while TFMPP acts by stimulating nerve receptors sensitive to serotonin, another neurotransmitter.

At doses of 20–100 mg, both BZP and TFMPP may produce a range of mental experiences lasting six to eight hours. Sought-after effects may include euphoria, alertness, reduced need for sleep, heightened sense of touch and other pleasurable sensations, and a sense of emotional bonding to others that is not necessarily based on shared experiences, common interests, or other reasons for close relationships.

Both drugs can produce significant increases in heart rate and blood pressure. Like speed or amphetamine, the stimulant effects of BZP on the brain are mirrored in the body, and may have equally disastrous results. Animal experiments suggest that piperazines such as TFMPP can actually inhibit learning rather than enhancing it.

PHYSIOLOGICAL EFFECTS

Contact of BZP with the eyes or skin may cause severe irritation and possible burns. If it is inhaled, it may cause severe irritation of the respiratory tract with sore throat, coughing, and shortness of breath, or even chemical burns. Prolonged respiratory exposure may cause delayed lung effects, including fluid in the lungs with breathing difficulty.

When swallowed, piperazines are readily absorbed from the gastrointestinal tract. They are partially broken down or metabolized by the liver and kidney, and the remainder is excreted in the urine. Because there is a wide variability in the rates of piperazine breakdown and excretion by different individuals, there is also a wide range of toxic effects and doses causing toxicity. Physical effects reported by piperazine users include nausea, vomiting, body flushing, stomach pains, frequent urination, bladder infection or irritation, thirst, dry mouth, severe migraine headache, sensations of skin crawling, dilated pupils, and "hangover" feelings lasting up to two days.

Effects on brain centers controlling movement may be experienced as muscle stiffness, tremor or uncontrollable shaking, jaw clenching, and nervous tics. Like amphetamine, piperazines produce increases in heart rate, blood pressure, and body temperature, which can be dangerous or even fatal. At high doses, piperazines may produce hallucinations, seizures or convulsions, and respiratory depression that can cause death.

People who use BZP or TFMPP lose interest in food and may stop eating altogether. After about two weeks on the drug, the effects on food intake and weight loss decrease, and after stopping the drug, there may be a rebound increase in excessive eating and weight gain.

HISTORY NOTES

Piperazines have an interesting history in medical therapeutics, although they often failed to deliver the effects originally promised. As far back as 1919, Finley Ellingwood, M.D., touted their uses as "renal sedatives and correctives" in *The American Materia Medica, Therapeutics and Pharmacognosy*. Indications for use included "persistent, excessive excretion of uric acid and the urates with constant backache, dry skin and scanty urine, or where there is a brick dust sediment in the urine...It acts more rapidly than other better known agents, and is direct and positive. It is soothing to the irritated passages." Other conditions said to respond to the piperazines included chronic rheumatic arthritis, gout, acute rheumatism, and rheumatic pericarditis, or inflammation of the coverings of the heart. Although the author claimed that "further experience should broaden its field of usefulness," none of the indications cited in this treatise have withstood the test of time.

Since the early 1950s, piperazines have been widely used in veterinary medicine and in humans as anthelminthic drugs to rid the lower intestinal tract of parasitic worms. In 1999, Japanese researchers found that an N-benzylpiperidine derivative chemically related to the piperazines improved learning in rats. This eventually led to the discovery of donepezil (Aricept) used to slow down progressive memory loss in Alzheimer's disease and related conditions. Although other BZP derivatives are being investigated for possible therapeutic uses in depression, other psychiatric illnesses, epilepsy or seizure disorders, pain, inflammatory diseases, and certain tumors, none were being used for these conditions as of April 2002.

Harmful side effects

Because piperazine abuse is such a recent phenomenon, harmful effects of BZP and TFMPP are not yet well-described, and selective effects in children and women and during pregnancy are still unknown. However, two deaths have already been reported.

Long-term health effects

Government agencies have no well-documented information on the long-term health effects of BZP and TFMPP. According to the Health and Safety Executive of the United Kingdom, piperazines are thought to have significant potential to cause asthma, most likely related to their effects on the immune system, although the mechanism is unclear.

IN THE NEWS

October 6, 2001: Equine Ecstasy?

BZP made thoroughbred racing history when a horse winning a race at Suffolk Downs in Massachusetts tested positive for the drug. "[BZP] is found on the street and popular with some young adults, but we have never seen it in a horse. We spoke to several other states, and this drug is new to the horse industry," said William Keen, chief steward for the Massachusetts Racing Commission (MRC), according to a story in Standardbred Canada on November 29, 2001. The MRC imposed the maximum penalty under Racing Commissioners International guidelines, which was a $500 fine, loss of purse monies, and 60-day suspension, and notified the state racing commission, which could impose additional penalties. At the hearing, the suspended trainer, Tammi Piermarini, pleaded ignorance. Her husband testified that he bought the drug through a Canadian Web site that claimed it was a bronchodilator, which would open the airways and allow the horse to breathe more easily. "What this means and what this has always meant is that people, wittingly or unwittingly, are trying to get horses to run faster basically by any means necessary," Brian Mulligan wrote in the December 13, 2001, issue of *Buzz Daly: Sportsbook Scene.*

January 10, 2002: In a series of ecstasy-related arrests in Washington County in northwest Arkansas, Timothy Paul Moldenhauer, age 23, was convicted of delivery of a counterfeit substance. Police said that he claimed he had ecstasy pills, when he actually had benzylpiperazine pills, a legal drug. Moldenhauer was sentenced to five years for the counterfeit drug in Washington County Circuit Court, according to a story by Julie Allison in *The Morning News*, Fort Smith, Arkansas, on January 22, 2002.

Similar effects of BZP and speed in former addicts, including increased blood pressure and similar short-term mental experiences induced by the drugs, suggest that BZP can be addictive and liable to abuse, especially by former or current addicts of other substances.

REACTIONS WITH OTHER DRUGS OR SUBSTANCES

BZP and TFMPP may contaminate ecstasy tablets, and users hoping for an extended or intensified "high" from ecstasy sometimes deliberately combine these drugs. A 2001 report in the medical literature from Zurich, Switzerland, describes a 23-year-old woman who died after consuming both BZP and ecstasy. When she was admitted to the hospital 11 hours after taking the drug combination, she experienced high blood pressure, coma, decreased reflexes, and non-reacting pupils. Excess drinking of water before coming to the hospital had caused extremely low levels of sodium in the blood, brain swelling, and ultimately, death.

Users have reported combining BZP with alcohol, Xanax, dextromethorphan, marijuana, and hydrocodone, and have described most of the experiences as frightening or unpleasant.

Warnings are given against combining piperazines, used to treat parasitic infections, with psychiatric medications known as phenothiazines, as piperazines can dramatically worsen the stiffness, tremor, and other movement abnormalities caused by phenothiazines. The combination may even cause violent seizures or convulsions.

TREATMENT AND REHABILITATION

Emergency treatment depends on the immediate toxic effects of BZP and TFMPP. High blood pressure, abnormal heart rate or rhythm, seizures or convulsions, fever, and abnormal movements all have specific treatments and may require hospitalization for intravenous medications and general supportive care. Coma or decreased level of consciousness, respiratory depression, difficulty breathing, and severe allergic reaction may require treatment in an intensive care unit and assisted respiration. If a user experiences any untoward effects, or if someone inadvertently takes a much larger dose of medicinal piperazines than prescribed, it is prudent to contact a doctor, emergency medical services, or poison control.

As piperazine abuse has been recognized only recently, specific detoxification, addiction, and rehabilitation programs have not yet been developed, nor are success rates known for specific treatments. Presumably, treatment protocols will follow general principles of other substance abuse programs and will include psychological counseling.

PERSONAL AND SOCIAL CONSEQUENCES

As with other mind-altering substances, use of BZP or TFMPP may give rise to hallucinations, anxiety, panic attacks, confusion, impaired judgment, or other psychological symptoms that may jeopardize work or school performance, relationships, or personal safety or that of others. Loss of control or inappropriate behavior may cause others to view the user as untrustworthy, immature, or even crazy. Physical side effects can have temporary or permanent health consequences. Addiction can cause the user to abandon life goals and incur debt, which may lead to loss of employment, theft, or other criminal activity.

LEGAL CONSEQUENCES

BZP and TFMPP are not scheduled, classified, or controlled, nor are they approved drugs. They can legally be purchased from chemical supply houses, but are not intended for human consumption. Using the drugs in race horses may lead to fines, loss of winnings, and suspension of racing privileges. Misrepresenting the drugs as ecstasy can lead to conviction for delivery of a counterfeit substance, which may incur a prison sentence of five years.

A Federal Register document April 29, 1999, was intended to provide guidance on the manufacture and distribution of unapproved piperazine products in food-producing animals. On August 27, 1999, the U.S. Department of Health and Human Services approved a supplemental new animal drug application filed by Fleming Laboratories, Inc., for the use of piperazine in chickens, turkeys, and swine for treatment of certain parasitic infections. The Food and Drug Administration (FDA) provided that firms without approved new drug applications for piperazine for use in food-producing animals could continue to manufacture and distribute piperazine only until August 27, 1999. However, the FDA agreed to distribution of these products until December 31, 1999. After that date, unapproved piperazine products could be subject to regulatory action.

See also Designer drugs; Ecstasy (MDMA)

RESOURCES

Periodicals

Balmelli, C., H. Kupferschmidt, K. Rentsch, and M. Schneemann. "[Fatal Brain Edema after Ingestion of Ecstasy and Benzylpiperazine]." [Article in German]. *Dtsch. Med. Wochenschr.* 126, no. 28-29 (July 13, 2001): 809-11.

de Boer, D., I. J. Bosman, E. Hidvegi, C. Manzoni, A. A. Benko, L. J. dos Reys, and R. A. Maes. "Piperazine-Like Compounds: A New Group of Designer Drugs-of-Abuse on the European Market." *Forensic Science International* 121, no. 1-2 (September 2001): 47-56.

O'Dell. L. E., M. J. Kreifeldt, F. R. George, and M. C. Ritz. "The Role of Serotonin(2) Receptors in Mediating Cocaine-Induced Convulsions." *Pharmacology Biochemistry and Behavior* 65, no. 4 (April 2000): 677-81.

Paredes, R. G., J. L. Contreras, and A. Agmo. "Serotonin and Sexual Behavior in the Male Rabbit." *Journal of Neural Transmission* 170, no. 7 (2000): 767-77.

Tohyama, Y., F. Yamane, M. Fikre-Merid, P. Blier, and M. Diksic. "Effects of Serotine Receptors Agonists, TFMPP and CGS12066B, on Regional Serotonin Synthesis in the Rat Brain: An Autoradiographic Study." *Journal of Neurochemistry* 80, no. 5 (March 2002): 788-98.

Other

Health & Safety Executive Regulatory Impact Assessments: Proposed Maximum Exposure Limit for Piperazine and Piperazine Dihydrochloride. Jan. 2001. Accessed 4/17/02. <http://www.hse.gov.uk/ria/chemical/piperaz.htm>.

Pendleton, Robert *BZP (1 Benzylpiperazine): Frequently Asked Questions.* Accessed 4/8/02. <http://www.lycaeum.org/drugs.old/bzp.shtml>.

Piperazine Citrate. Accessed 4/17/02. <http://www.nursespdr.com/members/database/ndrhtml/piperazinecitrate.html>.

U.S. Department Of Justice DEA Diversion Control Program *Drugs and Chemicals of Concern.* August, 2001. Accessed 4/8/02. <http://www.deadiversion.usdoj.gov/drugs_concern/bzp_tmp/summary.htm>.

Laurie L. Barclay, M.D.

CAFFEINE

OFFICIAL NAMES: Caffeine
STREET NAMES: None
DRUG CLASSIFICATIONS: Not scheduled, stimulant

OVERVIEW

Doubtlessly the most widely used drug today, caffeine is consumed daily by 90% of the world's people. Evidence of its use exists as far back as the Stone Age, and today, children, teens, and adults everywhere ingest it in coffee, tea, and soft drinks.

Legend has it that the stimulant effect of the coffee bean was first noted by an Ethiopian shepherd guarding his flock, a thousand years ago. Sufi monks steeped the berries in hot water and found that the brew helped them stay awake for long nights of prayer. Meanwhile, written records show that, during the Tang dynasty, which lasted from the seventh to the tenth century, the Chinese were already steeping and consuming tea as a drink believed to lengthen life.

By the Middle Ages, coffee was a popular drink of Muslims. In fact, the word coffee is derived from the Arabic, *qahweh* (pronounced kahveh). It was the Turks, however, who controlled much of the world's trade in coffee by the Middle Ages. The Turkish Empire, attempting to expand into Europe, laid siege to Vienna in 1683. The war failed, but the retreating Turks left behind 500 sacks of coffee beans, which an entrepreneur used to open the first coffeehouse in Vienna. Coffee use spread throughout Europe.

In 1675, King Charles II issued an order to close the coffeehouses that were already widespread throughout England, citing idleness as the chief complaint. Two days before the proclamation was to take effect, however, Charles backed down, fearing massive protests by coffee drinkers. Ironically, in the ensuing decades, the British came to prefer tea, probably due to the acquisition of its colony in India and the establishment of the tea trade there.

The social use of coffee then spread to America. By the eighteenth century, plantations devoted to the coffee plant were actively producing the bean in Indonesia and the West Indies.

Later, during the Vietnam War, coffee also played a part in the protest movement growing at home. Coffee bars flourished near military bases across the United States, where discussions flowed, along with the coffee, over strategies to aid war protestors.

Both health claims and controversies have followed caffeine through the centuries. By the 1960s, health concerns over coffee use were raised in the medical literature as well as the popular press. Research linked coffee consumption to medical conditions such as pancreatic cancer, breast lumps, and elevated levels of cholesterol.

In 1979, a Swiss company developed a distillation method to remove the caffeine from coffee, creating decaffeinated coffee. The Swiss water process proved popular among young urban professionals as it was considered to make a more "natural" product in comparison to the earlier method of making decaffeinated coffee, which used chemicals such as methylene chloride. The Swiss method also retained more of the flavorful oils residing in the coffee bean. Caffeine-free versions of colas soon followed.

Most follow-ups to earlier studies warning of the adverse effects of caffeine have failed to duplicate the initial findings, especially for the moderate use of caffeine. However, at the start of the new millennium, youth culture thrived on the excessive use of caffeine. New drinks were purposely formulated to contain large amounts of the mild stimulant, increasing the risk of possible adverse effects.

Critics of popular beverages such as Red Bull and Adrenaline Rush suggest that the high caffeine and sugar content pose a potential risk of dehydration for athletes, and that they could also pose a significant danger for adverse effects on the heart. In addition, these high-caffeine drinks are used as mixer beverages for alcohol, a potentially dangerous combination.

Some body builders tout the combination of caffeine with the herbal stimulant ephedra as harmless, and suggest the combination helps turn fat into muscle. A study published in 2001 does support the claim that caffeine and ephedrine can boost results in laboratory attempts to mimic the tasks of competing athletes. However, ephedra, the herbal drug containing the chemical ephedrine, has been linked to several deaths.

In 1980, the Food and Drug Administration (FDA) proposed to remove caffeine from its Generally Recognized As Safe list. But the FDA concluded in 1992 that, after reviewing the scientific literature, no harm is posed by a person's intake of up to 100 mg per day. As of 2001, the FDA recognized caffeine as a substance that is a food additive with a provisional listing status.

CHEMICAL/ORGANIC COMPOSITION

Caffeine, the active substance responsible for the stimulant effect of the coffee plant's berry, is a methylxanthine, one of the family of stimulants present in more than 60 species of plants. The pure chemical forms white, bitter-tasting crystals, which were first isolated from coffee in 1820. Other family members are theophylline, found in tea leaves, and theobromine, found in the cacao pods that are ground to make chocolate. The most potent component in the coffee family by unit weight is theophylline, while theobromine, the weakest component by unit weight, stays in the body longer than does caffeine.

Caffeine is also a trimethylxanthine, which is made up of three methyl groups. Efforts by the liver to deactivate caffeine at first appear counterproductive. Liver enzymes usually detoxify potentially harmful chemicals obtained through food, or those naturally present in the

KEY TERMS

BODY MASS INDEX (BMI): A measurement of body fat based on a person's height and weight.

ELECTROLYTE: The salts that the body requires in its fluids to function properly.

HYPERTENSION: Long-term elevation of blood pressure; defined by two readings, systolic and diastolic blood pressure, respectively, that are above the normal of 140 and 90 mm Hg. Hypertension risks damage to the blood vessels, and complications, including stroke, heart attack, and kidney failure.

OSTEOPOROSIS: A loss in total bone density that may be the result of a chronic calcium deficiency, early menopause, certain endocrine diseases, advanced age, endocrine diseases, certain medications, or other risk factors.

URINARY INCONTINENCE: Inability to retain urine in the bladder until the person chooses to empty it.

body. But what is left after the liver initially removes a methyl from caffeine are theophylline and paraxanthine, both of which are still active. Only when the final methyl is stripped away is the chemical inert. This production of active metabolites is why the stimulant lasts a relatively long time. It is also why people with liver disease, or those who consume other drugs that engage the liver enzymes, cannot efficiently clear caffeine from their body. Impaired caffeine metabolism is also evident in women taking estrogen for birth control or who are at the high estrogen phase of their monthly cycle. Newborn babies whose livers are not yet fully developed also break down caffeine more slowly until the enzymes are fully activated.

The methylxanthine molecule is built on a foundation common to many biologic compounds, the xanthine double ring of carbons. The three methylxanthines, caffeine, theophylline, and theobromine, all block the action of the body's adenosine molecule, sending a signal that helps slow the chemical buildup inside cells. Because the methylxanthines closely resemble adenosine at the molecular level, they can occupy the molecular sites on cells that normally recognize, and react to, adenosine. Caffeine prevents the normal slowing action of adenosine at the cellular level, in both nerves and muscle.

Scientists working with cell and tissue preparations recognized that caffeine and the other methylxanthines can block an enzyme called phosphodiesterase. It seems now, however, that this action is carried out at caffeine doses that are much higher than what people normally

Popular drinks are purposely formulated to contain large doses of caffeine, a mild stimulant. The drinks are designed for people who do not like coffee but want a caffeine jolt. Photo by Charles Bennett, AP/Wide World Photos.

Reproduced by permission.

consume. A similar caveat goes for the supposed action of caffeine on calcium stores in muscle. It is an effect only evident at high doses.

Caffeine is present in coffee, tea, and chocolate. These plant-derived beverages and foods also contain the other methylxanthines, which some scientists say serve as defense chemicals for leaves and berries produced in climates where there is no winter to kill off chewing bugs. Tea contains mostly caffeine, with small amounts of theophylline and theobromine, but tea is a weaker plant extract than the stronger brew, coffee. Theobromine is the primary methylxanthine found in cocoa, which also contains a small amount of caffeine per cup. Caffeine content ranges from as little as 5 mg in a cup of hot cocoa to 300 mg in 6 oz (177 ml) of espresso. Colas have about 50 mg per 12 fl oz (355 ml).

The robusta strain of coffee plant cultivated in Indonesia and Africa contains about 2.2% caffeine, while the arabica variety, grown in Central and South America, contains half that concentration. The caffeine in tea was purified in 1827, and was initially given its own name of "theine," as chemists of the day thought it different from the caffeine in coffee.

The kola nut, source of some of the flavoring of cola drinks, also has a bit of caffeine. About 5% of the 35 mg in a standard 9.5 oz (280 ml) serving of cola is naturally present from the kola nuts. The caffeine in sodas is added by the manufacturer.

Caffeine is available by prescription as a solution of caffeine citrate. Caffeine is also an active ingredient in many headache medicines, both by prescription and sold over the counter, as well as in nonprescription aids and herbal preparations for alertness and dieting. Body builders may readily buy and use a "stack," a pill comprising of ephedra, caffeine, and aspirin. Often caffeine is added intentionally to the mixes in today's energy drinks. Many abused illegal drugs, as well as some drugs sold legally, contain caffeine, either for added effect, or as a "filler," used in powder form to cut the potency of street drugs.

INGESTION METHODS

The vast majority of caffeine is ingested in a beverage such as coffee, tea, or soda. Beyond beverages, caffeine is also consumed in snacks such as chocolate candy bars, or as a component in drug medications.

THERAPEUTIC USES

Caffeine is approved as a prescription drug for treating premature infants who are born before their lungs and brain are mature enough for automatic breathing. These babies may have a condition called apnea, in which they cease breathing, which could cause damage to the brain and other organs. Caffeine has been demonstrated to aid in keeping premature babies breathing regularly. But a study published in 2001 found that very-low-birth-weight preemies also failed to gain weight when treated for their apnea with caffeine. Apparently the caffeine raised the babies' metabolic rate, causing them to burn more calories.

Many headache medications also contain caffeine, which can increase the effectiveness of the other drugs that alleviate both tension and migraine headaches. People who get migraines can have their headaches controlled by pills that combine caffeine with aspirin or acetaminophen. A study in 2000 showed that the effect of caffeine also increases the effectiveness of ibuprofen.

A study in 1999 confirmed that rebound headaches will occur if regular caffeine users suddenly cease taking the stimulant. To cut down on heavy caffeine use, it was recommended that all forms of caffeine (including caffeine-containing medications) be temporarily eliminated.

In 1999, it was reported that caffeine combined with alcohol could prevent damage from strokes. However, the doses that provide the benefit are quite specific, and the treatment has to be given at a time quite close to the stroke. Another study casts doubt on these findings, and indeed suggests that caffeine cuts blood flow in the brain, an action that would be harmful in people suffering strokes. Then, a report published in 2001 concluded that caffeine could have adverse consequences for patients trying to recover from stroke. By slowing blood flow through the brain, caffeine could starve already struggling nerve cells.

A functional magnetic resonance imaging (fMRI) study of the brain can actually determine between the regular and the occasional coffee drinker. Caffeine consistently slows blood flow by 25% to the gray matter of the brain, which contains the cells, and by 20% to the white matter, which contains the connecting nerve fibers. Heavy users of caffeine show more blood flow in the gray matter in the front of the brain when they had abstained for 30 hours, compared to those who infrequently ingest caffeine. With fMRI, the doctor can look inside the brain and observe the phenomenon of caffeine withdrawal in action.

The therapeutic treatment of obesity with caffeine is another controversial area of interest. Many over-the-counter diet aids contain caffeine, but it has not yet been determined whether there is a medically safe way to use caffeine as a fat fighter. A 2000 study showed that a combination of herbal ephedra and caffeine lowered participants' body weight by both decreasing fat and decreasing the body mass index (BMI). Losses were 15 and 7 pounds for those taking the herbal supplement and a placebo, respectively.

???? FACT OR FICTION

The idea that caffeine is added to soft drinks to addict consumers is actually a claim by researchers at Johns Hopkins University, in a study published in 2000. Although most would suggest it is a bit reactive to compare caffeine to nicotine, the soft drink industry is somewhat defensive about the subject.

The Johns Hopkins study had 25 adults attempt to choose, from paired soda samples, which one contained caffeine. Until the caffeine level exceeded that limit allowed by the FDA (6 mg per ounce), only 8% of the volunteers could tell the difference. A spokesperson for the soft drink industry suggested that the study was poorly designed and carried out, and called the conclusions "irresponsible."

Meanwhile, it has been pointed out that soft drink companies plaster their logos everywhere, sponsor giveaways designed to serve as ads, and spend tens of millions of dollars where kids are a captive audience, such as in school cafeterias, where vending machines selling sodas are often installed to produce school revenue. A maker of caffeinated water says, "The only market available is to start them out younger and younger."

Green tea with caffeine also seeks to weigh in as an herbal fat fighter. The thermogenic effect of tea is carried out at various control points in the adrenergic pathway. Caffeine, through the action of phosphodiesterase enzymes, indirectly boosts the adrenergic signals. However, there is no direct evidence that green tea successfully allows people to lose weight and keep it off.

USAGE TRENDS

Caffeine is widely used due to its relative safety as compared to other stimulants. In fact, in 2001 the U.S. military endorsed the usefulness of caffeine, recommending it as a safe and effective stimulant for its soldiers.

Scope and severity

Ninety-five percent of all caffeine is consumed in the form of tea and coffee. Following water, tea is the most popular beverage in the world. About 1.5 billion cups of coffee are consumed every day throughout the world.

Since water that is not boiled is unsafe to drink in many areas of the world, travelers are advised to drink coffee and tea instead. However, the diuretic effect of caffeine can cause dehydration.

Age, ethnic, and gender trends

The average daily consumption of caffeine for adults in the United States is about 210 mg. Coffee accounts for 60% of the total caffeine consumed in the United States, while soft drinks and tea each represent 16% of the total. In the United Kingdom, by comparison, caffeine intake is twice the American rate, and tea accounts for 72% of the British total. In Scandinavian countries, coffee is the preferred beverage. For instance, in Sweden, coffee makes up 85% of the total per capita of caffeine consumption. Finland is renowned for the practice of brewing particularly potent coffee, boiled and decanted directly from ground beans.

MENTAL EFFECTS

Within minutes of consumption, a caffeinated beverage will cause the drinker to feel more alert. Simple intellectual tasks are performed more readily, as are physical jobs that require endurance. However, while reaction time is shortened by caffeine, fine motor control suffers, perhaps due to the slight tremor that becomes more pronounced with higher doses of caffeine. The larger doses of caffeine, especially for people who do not use it regularly, cause headache and nervousness.

Caffeine decreases the duration of slow waves in the electroencephalogram (EEG) for about five hours after it is ingested. Taken near bedtime, caffeine will delay the time it takes for the consumer to fall asleep, and will reduce the depth and quality of sleep. Sleepers will also move more and waken more easily. These effects are evident with the amount of caffeine present in a cup or two of coffee, approximately 75–150 mg.

PHYSIOLOGICAL EFFECTS

Caffeine, by blocking the action of the body's adenosine, affects a wide variety of organs, as well as the brain, the gut, and basic metabolism. Theophylline works more actively on respiration and the heart. Caffeine is more active in the gut and in the central nervous system. Theobromine has very weak, if any, effect on the brain, but it retains the methylxanthine effect on the kidneys, increasing urination.

Caffeine dissolves easily in fats, so it encounters no barrier as it spreads in the body when taken by mouth. It rapidly crosses the mucosa of the stomach and soaks through the blood-brain barrier. In the bloodstream, the peak level of caffeine is achieved within half an hour. It takes four hours for the body to clear half a dose of the drug. This rate of metabolism of caffeine is slower in newborns and in women late in pregnancy. Smokers, though, rid caffeine more rapidly. Children also rid their bodies of caffeine more readily than adults.

Metabolic processes speed up appreciably under the influence of caffeine. Fatty acids are released into the blood, and a general increase in metabolism is evident as there is increased muscle activity, raised temperature, or both. More calcium is made available through caffeine's action in the muscles for contraction, but this effect is evident only at caffeine doses higher than people commonly use. Gut motility and secretion increase with a release of stomach acid and digestive enzymes. Urination is also stimulated; caffeine directly affects the kidneys, cutting into their ability to reabsorb electrolytes and water. For every cup of coffee or two to three cans of caffeinated soft drink consumed, about 5 mg of calcium is lost in the urine.

Breathing rate increases in response to caffeine. The effect on respiration occurs at the level of the brain stem's respiration control center. Theophylline has the most potent action of all the methylxanthines, affecting the smooth muscle of the bronchial tree in the lungs. This is why theophylline is a treatment for asthma. Doctors may recommend weak tea for their asthmatic patients with colds; this bronchodilating action of the theophylline in the tea will aid in clearing mucus.

Caffeine temporarily increases blood pressure, but the body readily compensates and adjusts back to its normal blood pressure. However, people with hypertension may have a more sensitive response to the drug, as caffeine may raise the blood pressure to a higher level in those with chronic high blood pressure.

For migraine patients, the effect of caffeine on the blood vessels around the brain is beneficial; it constricts both the inner and outer vessels, relieving pain. Also, because caffeine increases the acidity in the stomach, it speeds the absorption of pain medications.

Sports competitors recognize that caffeine can boost performance. Large amounts of caffeine release free fatty acids into the bloodstream, reserving the stores of glycogen in muscle for later use. Two to four cups of coffee contain the amount of caffeine that can enhance exercise performance in the average man weighing about 165 lb (75 kg), and it is two to three cups for a 130-lb (59 kg) woman. A down side to caffeine use during a sporting event is the need to urinate, caused by caffeine's diuretic effect on the kidneys.

Harmful side effects

Some people find that caffeine irritates their gastrointestinal tract. It is still unclear if the effect is from caffeine itself, or from another as-yet-undetermined substance that could be in coffee. Regardless, people with stomach ulcers or irritation may not find relief by switching from caffeinated to decaffeinated coffee.

Caffeine content of common dietary and medicinal sources	
Source	**Standard amount (in milligrams)**
Bottled beverages (12 oz)	
Red bull	115.5
Jolt	72
Mountain Dew	55
Diet Coke	45
Dr. Pepper	41
Coca-Cola Classic	34
Coffee (8 oz)	
Brewed	80–135
Instant	65–100
Decaf brew	3–4
Tea (8 oz)	
Ice tea	47
Brewed	40–60
Instant	30
Green tea	15
Chocolate	
Hot cocoa (8 oz)	14
Chocolate milk (6 oz)	4
Chocolate bar (1 oz)	3–6
Medications (per tablet)	
Vivarin	200
No-doz	100
Midol, Maximum Strength	65
Anacin	32
Dristan	30

SOURCE: Center for Science in the Public Interest. <http://cspinet.org/new/cafchart.htm>

Chart by Argosy.

Effects of caffeine on the heart can be considerable. Rapid or irregular heartbeats can result from ingesting large amounts of caffeine. People at risk for heart attacks might be ill advised to drink coffee or indulge in other sources of caffeine. Caffeine intake exceeding the amount found in five or more cups of drip coffee a day results in a statistically increased risk of cardiac arrest.

Frankly toxic effects, such as persistent insomnia and anxiety, only become evident when people drink more than eight or nine cups of coffee or tea a day. Convulsions and delirium can follow enormous doses, and a near-fatal dose can induce a state similar to that of a diabetic lacking insulin. Blood sugar surges, and ketones appear in the urine. The lowest recorded fatal dose of caffeine was 3200 mg, which was given by accident directly into the bloodstream. It takes the equivalent of 40 cups of coffee consumed by mouth in a short interval for caffeine to kill a person.

Long-term health effects

When studies in the 1980s raised concern about possible adverse effects, including miscarriage, birth defects, and infertility, doctors advised pregnant women to cut out caffeine entirely. Most of these studies have not been confirmed. Certainly, the amounts of caffeine

IN THE NEWS

Modern genetic research has already raised the possibility that gene-altered plants could be crafted to make decaffeinated beans. In 2000, an international team of scientists published their successful cloning of a gene responsible for caffeine in tea. The gene, TCS1, is the blueprint for the enzyme that controls the final two steps in the tea plant's four-step synthesis of caffeine. Another gene in coffee had been announced and patented earlier that year. Both tea and coffee plants use the same enzymatic steps for creating caffeine. The two genes characterized so far are for different steps in making caffeine.

To back up their findings, the TCS1 researchers inserted the DNA sequence into the genes of a bacteria. When supplied with the precursors to caffeine, only the engineered bacteria produced caffeine.

One potential problem is that plants with the key gene inactivated might build up appreciable amounts of the xanthine precursors to caffeine. These would have to be tested to ensure that they are not themselves able to mimic caffeine's effects on the body.

used to cause birth defects in rodents exceed the usual amounts consumed by people. By the year 2000, doctors simply told women who were pregnant or planning pregnancy, to keep caffeine consumption within the bounds of a cup or two of coffee a day.

Most studies find that moderate use of caffeine does not impair fertility, risk miscarriage, or increase the chance of having a baby with birth defects. The March of Dimes has concluded that moderate caffeine is of low risk to pregnant and nursing women.

A study in the early 1990s compared more than 2,800 women who had recently given birth to 1,800 women diagnosed as infertile. Caffeine habits had little or no impact on the reported time it took to conceive in those who had given birth, and was not a risk factor in the infertile. A similar study in Denmark only pointed to smoking as a factor in delayed conception.

Babies born to women who consumed large amounts of caffeine during pregnancy might demonstrate delayed growth or delayed mental or physical development. However, caffeine consumption equivalent to about a cup and a half of coffee a day had no effect on a child's birth weight, length, and head circumference; nor did it have an effect on follow-up exams of the children at eight months of age and at

seven years. In a study of 1,500 women, neither the motor skills nor the intelligence of these children was affected by their mother's caffeine consumption. Review of more than 20 studies since the 1980s show no evidence that caffeine causes either low birth weight babies, or early birth.

One study carried out between 1959 and 1966 found that very high levels of a caffeine metabolite is a marker for spontaneous abortion. Measured at 11 weeks gestation, the amount of the metabolite, paraxanthine, in blood serum was higher in women who had lost a pregnancy than in women in the control group. The risk of spontaneous abortion in women with the very highest level of paraxanthine was twice that than for the women with the lowest recorded levels. The levels were measured more than 30 years later, and the findings reported in 2000.

Caffeine can enter the milk of breastfeeding mothers. Babies younger than six months cannot metabolize caffeine as well as do adults. Mothers are advised, however, that up to three cups of coffee, or several cans of soda, can be consumed without passing caffeine on to their nursing infants.

The American Cancer Society states that there does not seem to be any relationship between caffeine and cancer. However, other adverse effects for women remain a concern, such as the possibility that large amounts of caffeine could contribute to osteoporosis (thinned and fragile bones), particularly in elderly women. As caffeine is a diuretic, which increases loss of fluids and electrolytes in the urine, it could rob the body of calcium. Nevertheless, a study published in 2001 concluded that the net effect of carbonated sodas on the body's calcium is negligible, and that the loss of calcium in urine due to carbonated drinks is too small to affect calcium balance.

REACTIONS WITH OTHER DRUGS OR SUBSTANCES

Caffeine cannot sober a drunk or save someone who is lethargic or unconscious from an overdose of a sedating drug. However, because caffeine lowers stomach pH, it can affect the absorption of other substances. Other drugs such as oral contraceptives, cimetidine, disulfiram, and alcohol can delay the body's ability to rid itself of caffeine.

TREATMENT AND REHABILITATION

Legally, caffeine is not regulated as a dangerously addictive substance. Yet, withdrawal from caffeine is documented as a recognized set of symptoms in the medical literature. Many people who regularly consume caffeine and then suddenly stop will experience headache, irritability, muscle aches, and lethargy, including impaired concentration.

As with any active agent that produces a withdrawal syndrome, the common-sense approach is to gradually wean oneself from caffeine in order to minimize any symptoms. Those wishing to decrease their use should taper off slowly and perhaps substitute cups of caffeinated drinks with decaffeinated varieties or other caffeine-free beverages.

The extent to which people suffer withdrawal from caffeine use remains controversial. However, a study reported that 11,000 subjects were interviewed about their daily consumption of caffeine, among a host of other questions about lifestyle. Only 11% reported withdrawal symptoms from stopping caffeine intake, and only 3% said their symptoms interfered with daily living. Notably, that figure breaks down differently for the genders: 5.5% of women, but only 0.9% of men, reported symptoms from stopping caffeine intake that affected daily activities. Nevertheless, the study concluded that caffeine withdrawal remains a well-documented phenomenon. A major symptom of abrupt cessation of caffeine use is a headache of moderate to severe intensity that generally begins within 18 hours of the last dose. It peaks at about three to six hours of onset. The feeling is of fullness in the head that continues to a diffuse, throbbing pain, and is worsened by physical activity. Sadness and mild nausea are also reported by a quarter of those who show the withdrawal headache. Those who chronically consume 500 to 600 mg of caffeine per day are more likely to experience withdrawal if they suddenly cease their habit.

PERSONAL AND SOCIAL CONSEQUENCES

A caffeine roundtable discussion by experts concluded that there is no evidence that caffeine is linked to the socially damaging behaviors that characterize drugs of abuse.

LEGAL CONSEQUENCES

There are no legal consequences since caffeine is not a scheduled substance.

Legal history

In 1909, the federal government seized a shipment of Coca-Cola syrup, citing the added caffeine as a poisonous and deleterious substance. In 1959, caffeine was listed in the Code of Federal Regulations as generally recognized as safe, when used in cola type drinks at a level set at 0.02%, based on industry standards at that time. In 1997, the FDA required labeling of the caffeine content of foods and drinks.

Federal guidelines, regulations, and penalties

The FDA allows soft drink manufacturers to add caffeine to a limit of 72 mg per 12-ounce (355 ml) serving. Coffee and tea, containing caffeine naturally rather than as an additive, are not regulated for caffeine content.

See also Ephedra; Herbal drugs

RESOURCES

Books

Braun, Stephen. *Buzz*. New York: Oxford University Press, 1996.

Pendergrast, Mark. *Uncommon Grounds*. New York: Basic Books, 1999.

Periodicals

Bell, Douglas. "Effect of Caffeine and Ephedrine Ingestion on Anaerobic Exercise and Performance." *Medicine and Science in Sports and Exercise* 33 (August 2001): 1399-1403.

Cordes, Helen. "Generation Wired." *The Nation* (April 27,1998) On-line edition. <http://past.thenation.com/1998/980427.htm>.

Sparano, Nicole. "Is the Combination of Ibuprofen Plus Caffeine Effective for the Treatment of Tension-type Headache?" *Journal of Family Practice* 50 (January 2001): 312-319.

Other

Center for the Evaluation of Risks to Human Reproduction Web site. <http://cerhr.niehs.nih.gov/genpub/topics/caffeine-ccae.html>.

Cohen, Elizabeth. "Energy Drinks Pack a Punch, But Is It Too Much?" CNN.com. <http://www.cnn.com/2001/HEALTH/diet.fitness/05/29/energy.drinks.02/>. May 29, 2001 (January 30, 2002).

Organizations

American College of Sports Medicine, 401 Michigan Street, Indianapolis, IN, USA, 46202-3233, (317) 637-9200, (317) 634-7817, mkeckhaver@acsm.org, <http://www.acsm.org>.

National Headache Foundation, 428 W. St. James Place, 2nd Floor, Chicago, IL, USA, 60614-2750, (888) 643-5552, (773) 525-7357, (888) 643-5552, info@headaches.org, <http://www.headaches.org>.

Roberta L. Friedman, Ph.D.

CATHA EDULIS

OFFICIAL NAMES: *Catha edulis* or *Catha edulis* Forssk
STREET NAMES: Khat, *qat* in Yemen, *tschat* in Ethiopia; *miraa* in Kenya; Abyssinian tea, African salad, African tea, Arabian tea, Bushman's tea, chafta, chat, ciat, crafta, djimma, flower of paradise, ikwa, ischott, iubulu, kaad, kafta, kat, la salade, liss, liruti, mairongi, mandoma, maonj, marongi, mbugula mabwe, mhulu, miungi, mlonge, msabukinga, masbukinja, msuruti, msuvuti, msekera, muholo, muhulu, muirungi, mulungi, muraa, musitate, mutsawari, mwandama, mzengo, nangungwe, ol meraa, ol nerra, quat, salahin, seri, Somali tea, tohai, tohat, tsad, tschad, tschat, tshut, tumayot, waifo, warfi, warfo
DRUG CLASSIFICATIONS: Cathinone: Schedule I, stimulant; cathine: Schedule IV, stimulant

OVERVIEW

The *Catha edulis* (khat) plant is a flowering evergreen shrub or tree with a slender trunk and thin bark. Khat is a central nervous system (CNS) stimulant that contains the psychoactive ingredients cathinone, which is structurally and chemically similar to the d-amphetamines (drugs like cocaine); and cathine, a milder form of cathinone; as well as cahine and norephedrine. Khat, which is believed to have originated in Ethiopia, is native to the eastern and southern regions of Africa and the southern Arab peninsula. However, the plant was later cultivated in Kenya, Malawi (formerly Nyasaland), Uganda, Tanzania (formerly Tanganyika), Arabia, Zimbabwe (formerly the Congo), Zambia (formerly Rhodesia), and South Africa. In those countries, khat trees are sometimes planted between coffee trees.

The plant grows best at elevations of 4,500–6,500 ft (1,370–1,980 m). In areas with frost, the shrub grows no higher than 5 ft (1.5 m). However, in areas where the rainfall is heavy, such as the highlands of Ethiopia and regions near the equator, khat trees can reach 20 ft (6 m). Although khat thrives in areas of plentiful rainfall, the plant also grows during periods of drought when other crops fail.

Khat's elliptical leaves, which resemble basil in size and shape, are reddish-green and glossy but become yellow-green and leathery as they age. The plant's flowers are small and white. The most prized parts of the plants are the young shoots, buds, and leaves near the top of the plant. Although the older leaves near the middle and lower sections of the plant are also used, as are the stems, these portions of the plant are considered inferior and less potent.

The leaves are not picked until the plant is four years old; harvest occurs during the dry season. The first harvest is considered inferior to later ones. Leaves gathered from plants over six years of age are most valued, possibly due to greater alkaloid accumulation. In addition, the foliage of cultivated plants is preferred over wild plants.

The production and consumption of khat occupy a prominent position in Yemeni culture. The increased affluence of that country in the 1980s and 1990s allowed an increasing percentage of the population to indulge in the habit, which the government has attempted through various measures to discourage. Greater demand, however, has fueled a substantial increase in khat acreage. As productivity declines, older coffee plantations are often converted to khat fields. Much of the land devoted to khat was formerly considered marginal for commercial agricultural purposes and later benefited from regular soil-enhancement programs. A portion of Yemen's khat crop is exported to Ethiopia and Kenya.

Stimulant properties

Khat leaves left unrefrigerated beyond 48 hours contain only cathine, which explains users' preference for fresh leaves. The young leaves and buds are chewed as a mild stimulant; the chewing produces a strong aroma and generates intense thirst.

The amphetamine class of stimulants are potent, indirect-acting agents that cause a release of the neurotransmitters dopamine and norepinephrine from storage areas in the CNS. The mildest CNS stimulant is phenethylamine (PEA), a component of cheese and chocolate, while cocaine is considered a potent CNS stimulant.

The neurons activated by amphetamines are dense in the pleasure center of the brain; and the depletion of the stores sets up a demand for progressively higher doses to achieve the same "high," and accounts for the sometimes profound depression, or "crash," that follows a drug binge.

In experiments with such animals as rats and monkeys, which were trained to self-administer amphetamines, researchers observed a pattern that they described as "spree-type." The animals took the drug frequently day and night, stopping only after becoming exhausted, and beginning again after recovery. This pattern is similar to that seen in amphetamine-dependent humans. Thus, in terms of pharmacology, chewing khat leaves produces the same amphetamine effect.

Stimulants first may cause exhilaration and hyperactivity, dilated pupils, then produce irritability, anxiety, apprehension, and insomnia. Large doses of stimulants can cause repetitive teeth grinding, weight loss, and paranoia. An overdose can result in dizziness, tremors, agitation, panic, hostility, abdominal cramps, chest pains, and palpitations. Extreme overdoses can result in cardiac arrest, stroke, or death.

In the 1990s, methcathinone—called by various street names such as cat, goob, Jeff, speed, bathtub speed, mulka, gaggers, the C, wild cat, Cadillac express, and ephedrine—appeared as a drug of abuse on the black market. Methcathinone, a synthetic form of cathinone, is an even more potent stimulant than its natural counterpart and is illegal in the United States.

Although methcathinone was studied in the 1950s to determine its potential for medical use, the study was abandoned due to the safety risks and side effects. Then

KEY TERMS

ALKALOID: Any organic agent isolated from plants that contains nitrogen and reacts with an acid to form a salt.

AMPHETAMINES: A class of drugs frequently abused as a stimulant. Used medically to treat narcolepsy (a condition characterized by brief attacks of deep sleep) and as an appetite suppressant.

DOPAMINE: Neurotransmitter associated with the regulation of movement, emotional response, pleasure, and pain.

---

in 1989, a University of Michigan student stole the old drug samples and documentation and began to manufacture and sell the drug throughout the United States.

Traditional use

The ancient Egyptians considered khat to be a sacred plant, a "divine food." The Egyptians did not use khat merely for its stimulant properties but rather to unlock what they considered to be the divine aspect of their human nature.

Khat is believed to have been traded as a commodity even before coffee and is used throughout the Middle East countries in much the same way as coffee is used in Western culture. In addition to its use as a mild stimulant, khat use in Africa and the Middle East is more of a social phenomenon. Its intake occurs in moderation, for the most part, and often takes place in special rooms designed for that purpose.

Since antiquity, khat has also been used in religious contexts by natives of Eastern Africa and the Arab peninsula. For example, khat was used, in moderation, as a stimulant to alleviate feelings of hunger (some members of the Islamic faith use khat during Ramadan, the ninth month of the Moslem year, which is spent fasting from sunrise to sunset) and fatigue.

In Yemen, khat has played a pivotal role in poetry, music, architecture, family relations, wedding and funerary rites, home furnishings, clothes, what people eat, when restaurants open and close, where roads go to and where not, who owns a car and who does not, office hours, television schedules, and even sexual relations. However, there has been a decreased productivity and a diversion of income attributed to its use as well.

Modern use

Conservative estimates state that khat accounts for one third of the gross national product of Yemen. In

LAW AND ORDER

In 2001, it was estimated that about a ton (907 kg) of khat was shipped into Great Britain every day. Concerned about khat abuse in the United Kingdom, some people within the Somali and Yemeni communities called for the UK to align itself with most other Western countries and ban khat. In 2001, a petition urging the government to outlaw the plant circulated in the northwest of England. As of early 2002, however, khat was still legal and available at some grocery and general stores, where it is sold alongside the vegetables and herbs.

Ethiopia, khat is also a major cash crop. In the United States, khat use is most popular among immigrants from Yemen and the East African nations of Somalia and Ethiopia. The U.S. public became more aware of this exotic drug through media reports pertaining to the United Nations' mission in Somalia, where khat use is endemic, and the drug's role in the Persian Gulf War.

Khat can be purchased in the United States in various ethnic bars, restaurants, grocery stores, and smoke shops. Once imported and available on the streets of the United States, khat found its way into the hands of a broader population of users than ever before. Its use has been linked to the dance/rave scene in the United States as well as in countries around the world.

Fresh khat leaves are most often prepared for shipment in bouquet-sized bundles, wrapped in plastic bags or banana leaves, then tied together. The bundles are sprayed with water to keep the leaves fresh and moist, especially important when the leaves are shipped outside of the country of origin.

CHEMICAL/ORGANIC COMPOSITION

Although the *Catha edulis* plant contains a number of chemicals, vitamins, and minerals, its main active ingredient is cathinone, an alkaloid with a chemical structure similar to ephedrine and d-amphetamine. Like amphetamine, it increases the levels of dopamine in the brain and acts as a mild stimulant. For this reason, khat is sometimes referred to as a natural amphetamine.

Within two days of harvest, cathonine levels in the plant's leaves diminish, and the substance that remains is a milder form of cathonine called cathine.

INGESTION METHODS

Khat leaves are typically chewed like tobacco. Users fill the mouth with fresh leaves that they chew to release the active ingredients. Khat is also sold as dried or crushed leaves, frozen leaves, or in powdered form.

Another method of ingesting khat is by chewing a paste made of khat leaves, water, and sugar or honey, sometimes flavored with herbs. A tea made from the flowers of the khat plant—"flower of paradise" in Yemen—is considered restorative. In addition, the leaves are sometimes added to plain tea, or smoked in combination with tobacco. Ethiopians often drink a juice extract made from khat leaves.

THERAPEUTIC USE

In the United States, khat is not approved for medical use. However, a study in the January 2000 issue of *Journal of Pharmacy and Pharmacology* concluded that khat, like amphetamines and ibuprofen, can relieve pain.

Although it is mainly used in social situations throughout Africa and the Middle East, khat is sometimes used by farmers and laborers to alleviate fatigue, by students to improve concentration before exams, and by the elderly to improve cognitive function. In Ethiopia, khat advocates claim that the plant eases symptoms of diabetes, asthma, and intestinal tract disorders. The processed leaves and roots are used to treat influenza, cough, other respiratory ailments, and gonorrhea.

Amphetamines were first marketed in the United States in 1932 as a treatment for asthma, and subsequently were used to treat narcolepsy. Gaining popularity as a defense against battle fatigue in World War II, nearly 200 million amphetamine tablets were issued to American soldiers stationed in Great Britain during the war. By the 1950s, stimulants were used to treat depression. But often amphetamines were used by people who just needed a lift, or who needed to stay alert, such as workers on the night shift, students, and truck drivers. However, by 1970, the Controlled Substances Act (CSA) severely restricted the use of amphetamines, which were classified as Schedule II drugs.

As of 2001, the U.S. Food and Drug Administration (FDA) approved the use of stimulants for treating attention-deficit/hyperactivity disorder (ADHD), narcolepsy, and Parkinson's disease. These drugs are also used in combination with other medications to manage pain, and to treat depression and other psychiatric disorders.

Because amphetamines are anorectics (appetite suppressants), these drugs were formerly the treatment of choice for obesity. Due to the potential for abuse and for adverse side effects such as increased heart and respiratory rate, and increased blood pressure, these drugs

Two men buy khat, a popular stimulant, in Yemen. AP/Wide World Photos. Reproduced by permission.

were eventually replaced by safer weight-loss medications. However, khat, an amphetamine-like substance, is used to counter obesity in countries such as Germany.

The amphetamines were replaced by amphetamine analogs—substances somewhat less potent than amphetamines. Fen-Phen, the combination of fenfluramine and phentermine, was a popular appetite suppressant in the 1990s, but was associated with severe health problems such as pulmonary hypertension, heart valve dysfunction, and nerve damage. As a result, both drugs were withdrawn from the market.

Sibutramine (Meridia), a weight-loss drug introduced in 1998, inhibits the reuptake of the brain chemicals norepinephrine, dopamine, and serotonin, but does not promote monoamine release like the amphetamines. Yet the drug has been linked to serious side effects, including rapid heart rate, increased blood pressure, heart disease, stroke, seizure, and mental impairments. In March 2002, Italy's Health Ministry announced that it was immediately withdrawing all sibutramine products from the market due to health-related problems. Also, Meridia was the subject of a class action lawsuit filed in the United States.

USAGE TRENDS

For centuries, khat use was long confined to its native growing regions because the leaves needed to reach their destination within 48 hours of harvesting to retain their potency. However, with improved roads and air transportation, khat use spread to many other parts of the globe. During the 1980s, a flood of refugees from sub-Saharan Africa entered the United States, Canada, Australia, and various West European countries, bringing their habit of khat chewing with them.

Scope and severity

Worldwide, it is estimated that from five to 10 million people use khat on a daily basis. Many of the users originate from countries between Sudan and Madagascar and in the southwestern part of the Arab peninsula, especially Yemen.

In Yemen, khat use is so widespread (about 80% of the adult population) that even government officials use the drug openly. Also, visitors are encouraged to try it. However, in 1999, concerned that too many khat-chewing government workers were neglecting their jobs and whiling away their income, President Ali Abdullah Saleh attempted to set an example by announcing that he would limit his chewing to weekends.

Although statistics vary from country to country, estimates suggest that khat users spend from $6 to $20 per day on their habit. Growing and selling khat is also big business. The Yemeni production and distribution of khat traded to Somalia alone brings in an estimated $100 million annually. Khat must be imported because the Somalis only produce enough khat for local use. Within

???? FACT OR FICTION

A number of sources contend that the khat tree originated in Harar, an Arab town in the Ethiopian hills. The Ethiopians are believed to have brought the tree to the Yemeni city of Ta'izz in 1222, but precise documentation is unavailable. Exactly when khat began its long journey from an innocuous and unnoticed tree to today's cultural mainstay is a mystery, but it seems likely that religious men first discovered its properties, using it to ward off sleep during long, nighttime meditations, and carrying it with them on missionary journeys.

Somalia, 61% of the population use khat, with 18% reporting habitual use and 21% occasional use. Somalian warlords have been known to ration it out to soldiers on a daily basis. And in Djibouti, the United Nations estimates that approximately 98% of the men use khat, which is flown in from Ethiopia.

Khat use has also spread into Europe. In the United Kingdom (where khat is legal), it is occasionally imported in twig-like bunches for sale in some grocery stores and specialty health food stores.

Since the 1990s, news reports and statistics suggest that the U.S. market for khat, although more limited than other illegal drugs, has increased. Khat is smuggled into the United States and commonly sold in restaurants, bars, grocery stores, and smoke shops that cater to East Africans and Yemeni immigrants. It is also bought and sold by soldiers who encountered it during foreign service.

In 2000, U.S. Customs seized 70,008 lbs (31,755 kg) of khat on its way from East Africa and Yemen, up from 48,938 lbs (22,197 kg) in 1999. Marijuana seizures, by comparison, totaled 1.2 million lbs (544,310 kg) in 2000.

Age, ethnic, and gender trends

Traditionally, the bitter leaf of the khat plant was chewed primarily in social situations by older men in Yemen and throughout Saharan and sub-Saharan Africa. However, in the early 1990s, a growing number of men began chewing khat for up to 12 hours a day. The reasons for this increase in khat use has been attributed to feelings of hopelessness and boredom in the face of rising poverty and joblessness in many Middle Eastern and African countries.

Khat use also began spreading to an even greater number of women and children. In 2000, it was reported that 80% of Yemeni males, 60% of females, and an increasing number of children under the age of 10 had chewed khat daily for long periods of their life.

In Saudi Arabia, although the cultivation and consumption of khat are forbidden, and the ban is strictly enforced, khat chewing continues. Furthermore, the ban on khat is also supported by the Saudi clergy on the grounds that the Koran forbids anything that harms the body. However, this perspective on khat is not maintained by the Yemeni religious authorities.

During the 1990s, khat was introduced on college campuses in the United States and elsewhere, and a growing number of students began using the stimulant to stay up later at night. Khat was labeled the "poor man's ecstasy."

MENTAL EFFECTS

Although the main effects of chewing khat are a moderate degree of euphoria and excitation, users also report increased levels of:

- concentration
- loquaciousness
- confidence
- friendliness
- contentment

High doses or prolonged use, however, may induce sleeplessness, hyperactivity, and aggression. In addition, according to the Drug Enforcement Administration (DEA), compulsive use "may result in manic behavior with grandiose delusions or in a paranoid-type of illness, sometimes accompanied by hallucinations." Although psychosis has been reported, the phenomenon is rare. Khat has also been known to cause cognitive impairment.

International organizations have been confronting problems associated with khat since 1935. The World Health Organization (WHO) played a pivotal role in encouraging and funding scientific studies designed to understand not only khat's active ingredients but also the physical, psychological, and social problems associated with its use. In 1980, the WHO classified khat as a drug of abuse that may produce mild to moderate psychological dependency.

PHYSIOLOGICAL EFFECTS

In one study on a group of 80 healthy volunteers, researchers found that during a three-hour period of chewing fresh khat leaves, there was a significant progressive rise in blood pressure and heart rate even one hour after chewing had ceased. These reactions were due to the stimulant effects of the drug.

Additional physiologic effects reported with khat use include:

- dizziness
- lassitude
- stomach pain
- thirst
- dilated pupils (mydriasis)
- anorexia
- constipation
- impotence
- insomnia
- thirst

The unpleasant side effects of khat, especially the insomnia, have led some users to seek counteracting agents such as tranquilizers and alcohol—substances that are particularly hazardous in combination with khat.

Harmful side effects

In one study, 44 species of fungus were isolated from 30 samples of khat leaves gathered in Yemen. Researchers considered the toxins found in some of these species a threat to public health.

In addition, to ward off a wide range of insects, diseases, and weeds—and to preserve an important cash crop—toxic chemicals are often used to spray the plants. When the leaves are chewed, these toxins enter the bloodstream, causing potential health problems, including chemical hepatitis.

The overall effect of khat on patients with diabetes is harmful. The anorectic effect of khat leads to skipping meals; also, users are less likely to follow dietary advice, and consuming sweet beverages with khat aggravates hyperglycemia (high blood sugar levels). The anorectic nature of khat largely explains the malnutrition often seen in habitual khat users.

Some researchers believe that there is not a high potential for khat abuse because the volume of leaves required limits the ingestion and absorption of a large amount of the active ingredients. Yet the effects of khat have been difficult to quantify. The leaves are a non-standardized material, and their potency depends on freshness and place of origin. Yet although there is no known record of khat resulting in overdose, adverse side effects are somewhat greater in children, in those over 55 years of age, and in those who use large quantities of the substance for extended periods of time.

Long-term health effects

Because khat is chewed for the most part, medical problems associated with the oral cavity and digestive tract are common and may lead to inflammation and secondary infections. There is also some evidence of increased risk of oral cancer.

In a 1995 study published by the *British Journal of Urology*, researchers found that khat chewing inhibits urine flow, an effect caused by blood vessel constriction, which also causes erectile dysfunction. This constriction also affects blood pressure and heart rate; however, further studies are needed to determine the possible long-term cardiovascular damage associated with regular khat use.

Several studies suggest that long-term khat use causes reproductive toxicity. In addition to neurological effects—damage to the nervous and respiratory system have been documented—khat consumption is also associated with reproductive problems in men and women. Heavy use of khat is associated with decreased semen volume, sperm count, and sperm motility, and with an increased number of sperm appearing microscopically abnormal.

Women who chewed khat gained less weight during their pregnancies, and blood flow to the uterus was decreased, retarding fetal development and resulting in low-birth weight babies with a greater potential for medical problems. Mothers also produced less milk. These adverse effects are considered a serous public health concern by some researchers.

REACTIONS WITH OTHER DRUGS OR SUBSTANCES

Khat may interact with drugs used in treatment of other diseases and produce emotional and mental disorders. For example, when combined with niridazole—a drug used in treating schistosomiasis (a parasitic disease endemic throughout Asia, Africa, and tropical America)—severe anxiety reactions, insomnia, and even psychoses may develop. Also, khat would be likely to react with other stimulants such as alcohol, coffee, or cigarettes, causing palpitations and agitation.

Similarly, in a study published in the May 2001 issue of *International Journal of Cancer*, researchers found that khat chewing, especially when accompanied by alcohol and tobacco consumption, may cause oral malignancy.

Monoamine oxidase inhibitors (used in the treatment of bipolar disorder) should not be used with khat, as the combination may cause a potentially dangerous increase in blood pressure.

IN THE NEWS

The social aspect of khat chewing is as important, if not more important, than the physical high it creates. In Yemen, for example, khat sessions are a major part of life; participants regard the time spent chewing as productive time, such as when business deals are arranged, and communication is enhanced.

In Yemen, work days end between 2 P.M. and 3 P.M., at which time groups of 10–50 people convene in a home to dine and chew. In almost every house there is a *mafraj*, the most pleasant room in the house; it is in this room that khat sessions are held. No food is served with khat; only water is available to help wash the leaves' juices into the system. Between 3.5 and 7 oz (100 and 200 g) of leaves are chewed over three or four hours.

Stimulation can occur within the first 15 minutes of chewing, although the peak "high" is reached in the third hour. Effects from the chewing can remain in the system up to 24 hours. Following a high, a slight depression sets in and remains for a few hours. Tea with milk is often served at the end of a khat session.

Fewer women than men chew khat, and the sexes hold khat sessions separately. Reports indicate that women's khat sessions, with dancing and music, are often more lively than men's.

TREATMENT AND REHABILITATION

Because the psychiatric manifestations induced by khat are similar to the effects of other known stimulants, treatment of khat dependency is similar to that of dependency on amphetamines.

Reportedly, there are no physical symptoms of khat withdrawal of the type associated with other stimulants such as alcohol, morphine, or the barbiturates. Abandoning the habit, however, is frequently followed by depression, loss of energy, and an increased desire to sleep. The severity of depression varies and may lead to agitation and sometimes sleep disturbances. For the most part, former users are less prone to constipation and smoke less. If they consume alcohol, they usually drink less, and their appetite increases.

In a study published in the July 1995 issue of *American Journal of Therapy*, researchers described a successful attempt to treat a case of khat dependency using protocols similar to those developed for cocaine. Specific procedures for treatment entailed an outpatient detoxification with bromocriptine mesylate 1.25 mg every six

hours. The dosage was gradually tapered downward over four weeks. Previous attempts to treat khat-induced psychosis have employed thioridazine (300 mg a day) for one week without symptom recurrence.

PERSONAL AND SOCIAL CONSEQUENCES

Although immediate and severe medical problems are thought to be infrequent, khat use often leads to health problems. Reducing khat consumption, according to researchers, would relieve several million people, mostly men, of a costly and potentially addictive habit. It would also make available scarce arable land and irrigation water for other crops. Government figures show that khat consumes 75% of Yemen's irrigation capabilities.

Khat chewers may cause harm to their families due to negligence, dissipation of the family income, and inappropriate behavior. In Yemen, even poor families admit to spending at least 50% of their income on khat.

Overall, women and children seem to be suffering most from khat consumption. Many men spend so much money on khat that their families go hungry and remain in poverty. Several countries concerned by the khat problem, such as Yemen, have taken steps to restrict its use.

LEGAL CONSEQUENCES

Cathinone and cathine are controlled under the United Nations' Convention on Psychotropic Substances. In the United States, Canada, Switzerland, Scandinavia, and most of the Middle East, excluding Yemen, the leaf itself is banned. The khat plant is not controlled under domestic law in the United Kingdom.

From the standpoint of their cultural norms, however, African/Arab sellers and users living outside of their country of origin do not consider khat to be illegal and often openly advertise its availability on signs in restaurants and grocery stores much as they would any other food product.

Legal history

Khat was freely available in Saudi Arabia prior to 1971, when it was classified as a narcotic and declared illegal. Further cultivation, commercial activity, and personal khat use was banned. The basis for this legal change was the local religious teaching of Islam, which strongly recommends preventing harm to the individual or society. The Saudi government applied very severe punishments against users and smugglers, including the death penalty. However, in some areas bordering Yemen, many have continued to use khat.

Khat leaves have been illicitly bundled and shipped into the United States in increasing amounts since the

1990s. According to the Federal Drug Information Network database, more than 57,000 lbs (25,850 kg) of khat leaves were seized in 1998.

Nevertheless, law enforcement efforts directed against khat use in the United States have been minimal as there is some doubt about whether khat will ever become as popular a street drug as marijuana, crack cocaine, and other drugs. However, illegal laboratories have been discovered manufacturing a synthetic form or khat's most active ingredient (cathinone), which is called "methcathinone" and known on the street as "cat."

Federal guidelines, regulations, and penalties

In the United States, the Federal Controlled Substances Act (CSA), Title II of the Comprehensive Drug Abuse Prevention and Control Act of 1970, consolidates a number of laws regulating the manufacture and distribution of drugs and chemicals used in the illegal production of controlled substances.

The CSA classifies cathinone is a Schedule I substance, the same category as heroin and cocaine, and cathine as Schedule IV, which carries no mandatory prison penalties.

Federal trafficking penalties for Schedule I and II drugs range from a minimum of five years to a maximum of life in prison. Penalties for trafficking Schedule III and IV drugs range from three to five years in prison and a fine of $25,000. However, in the case of khat, drug enforcement in the United States appears to be random and not a high priority.

Until the late 1990s, authorities had been foregoing prosecutions of khat smugglers. According to officials, khat presents some unusual problems for prosecutors, particularly the short shelf-life of the drug. In addition, because of the bulk of the product, the amount carried by a single person is under the level to trigger federal prosecution. As a result, most air shipments are merely seized and shipped to government incinerators for destruction, while the couriers are deported.

See also Amphetamines; Ecstasy; Ephedra; Herbal drugs; Methamphetamines

RESOURCES

Books

Gorman, Jack M. *The Essential Guide to Psychotropic Drugs.* New York: St. Martin's Press, 1998.

Keltner, Norman L., and David G. Folks. *Psychotropic Drugs.* Philadelphia: Mosby, 2001.

Rushby, Kevin. *Eating the Flowers of Paradise: A Journey Through the Drug Fields of Ethiopia and Yemen.* New York: St. Martin's Press, 1999.

Periodicals

Bures, Frank. "From Civil War to Drug War." *MotherJones.com* (November/December 2001).

Kandela, P. "Women's Rights, a Tourist Boom, and the Power of Khat in Yemen." *Lancet* (April 22, 2000): 1437.

Robinson, Simon. "The Cost of Catha Edulis." *Time Europe* (December 20, 1999).

Organizations

National Clearinghouse for Alcohol and Drug Information (NCADI), P.O. Box 2345, Rockville, MD, USA, 20847-2345, (800) 729-6686, webmaster@health.org, <http://www.health.org>.

National Council on Alcohol and Drug Depenedence, 12 West 21st Street, New York, NY, USA, 10010, (800) 622-2255 or (800) 475-4673, <http://www.ncadd.org>.

National Institute on Drug Abuse (NIDA), National Institutes of Health, 6001 Executive Boulevard, Room 5213, Bethesda, MD, USA, 20892-9561, (301) 443-1124, (888) 644-6432, information@lists.nida.nih.gov, <http://www.drugabuse.gov>.

Substance Abuse and Mental Health Services Administration (SAMSHA)/Center for Substance Abuse Treatment (CSAT), 5600 Fishers Lane, Rockville, MD, USA, 20857, (301) 443-8956, info@samsha.gov, <http://www.samhsa.gov>.

Genevieve T. Slomski, Ph.D.

COCAINE

OFFICIAL NAMES: Powder cocaine, crack cocaine
STREET NAMES: Base, Bernice, blow, "C", coke, dream, dust, flakes, nose candy, Peruvian marching powder, powder, rock, stardust, snow, sugar, the devil's dandruff, white lady
DRUG CLASSIFICATIONS: Schedule II, stimulant

OVERVIEW

South Americans in the Andes Mountains legally and liberally chew coca leaves. By adding a little lime or plant ash, the naturally occurring cocaine alkaloid is released and absorbed into the cheek. This has a mild stimulating effect similar to drinking several cups of strong coffee. In this way, the mountain people have combated heat, cold, hunger, and fatigue for over 4,000 years. The leaves are used medicinally to alleviate problems of the digestive system, altitude sickness, and psychological ills. Used in the whole-leaf form, cocaine does not produce a "high" and is not addictive.

Coca leaves were not used in Europe or the United States because coca leaves do not travel well. But in 1860, a German chemist, Albert Niemann, separated cocaine from the leaf. In doing so, he unleashed the most powerful naturally occurring stimulant. In the salt form (cocaine hydrochloride), which is commonly known as powder cocaine, it travels very well. Soon, large quantities were being consumed abroad.

Initially, cocaine was thought to be a "cure-all," and, like the whole-leaf form, powder cocaine was believed to be non-addictive. Due to this misinforma-

tion, from the 1860s until the early 1900s, the use of cocaine was unregulated. It was used widely in Europe and in the United States. People could buy anything from cocaine-laced beverages, such as Vin Mariani coca wine and Coca-Cola, to 99.9% pure powder cocaine. Vin Mariani was a wine and cocaine concoction endorsed by Pope Leo XVIII and by over 7,000 physicians. In the 1880s, John Pemberton created Coca-Cola—the non-alcoholic "health drink" containing 60 mg of cocaine. (It should be noted that Coca-Cola no longer uses cocaine in its products.) Cocaine was believed to remedy many conditions, including fatigue, toothache, hay fever, asthma, seasickness, and vomiting during pregnancy. No prescription was necessary, and cocaine could easily be purchased at grocery stores, drug stores, and through mail-order catalogues.

Bona fide scientific and medical research lagged behind the commercial marketing of cocaine. It was not until the 1880s that cocaine was seriously studied. A German physician did a study on the effects of cocaine on the Bavarian army. He wrote a paper on the endurance-enhancing qualities of cocaine. This paper was read by Dr. Sigmund Freud, who then experimented on himself. Freud discovered that cocaine affects the heart and produces a powerful "high." He later prescribed cocaine for heart disease, psychiatry, and morphine addiction. He wrote his own paper, "On Coca," extolling the virtues of the drug, which he claimed was non-addictive. In 1884, Karl Koller started using cocaine as a topical anesthetic for eye surgery and it was soon used in dentistry. In 1885, cocaine was used as a spinal anesthetic for dogs. William S. Halsted, considered to be the father of modern surgery, discovered that cocaine injected under the skin makes an effective local anesthetic for surgery.

It was not until the 1890s that public opinion began to shift against cocaine use. By then, reports of nasal damage, addiction, and cocaine-related deaths had begun to circulate. The toxic and addictive nature of cocaine became public knowledge. By the time the government stepped in to ban cocaine in 1914, most people were already shunning it.

In the 1970s there was a resurgence of powder cocaine use. This preceded the epidemic of crack cocaine in the 1980s. Because crack cocaine is cheaper than powder, it became more readily available to the young and the poor. Crack addiction and crime began to increase rapidly and this increase was publicized in the media. In response to public concern, the Anti-Drug Abuse Act of 1986 and 1988 was passed. Known sometimes as the 100:1 law, this federal law includes mandatory minimum sentences for first-time offenders. The penalties are much harsher for possession of crack cocaine than powder cocaine.

In a 2001 study entitled *Global Illicit Drug Trends* conducted by the United Nations Office for Drug Control and Crime Prevention (ODCCP), it was estimated that 14 million people used cocaine worldwide. Though cocaine use has leveled off in the United States, it still leads the world in cocaine abuse. In 1999, cocaine use was stable in the United States, but increased in Western Europe and in several South American countries. Because of the addictive and destructive nature of cocaine, there is a concerted worldwide effort to reduce the production and illicit use of cocaine.

CHEMICAL/ORGANIC COMPOSITION

Cocaine is the most potent naturally occurring stimulant. It is found as an alkaloid (nitrogen-containing organic base) in the leaves of the *Erythroxylon coca* trees in the Andes Mountains. Coca leaves contain 0.5–1.8% cocaine (benzoylmethylecgonine or BZ) that can be refined to nearly 100% purity. Research indicates that the plant produces cocaine to kill insects that prey on it. In humans, it is a central nervous system (CNS) stimulant.

TYPES OF COCAINE

Anesthetic

Cocaine was the first local anesthetic to be discovered and this is its only legal use in the United States. Cocaine is particularly effective as a local anesthetic because it numbs the site of application almost immediately and it minimizes bleeding. Typically a 1–4% solution is used clinically. This highly diluted solution does not have a psychoactive or changing effect on the brain.

KEY TERMS

ANESTHETIC: An agent that causes loss of sensation or unconsciousness.

COCA PASTE: An impure free base made from coca leaves. It is used mainly in South America. Coca paste is smoked and is highly addictive.

COCAETHYLENE: A substance formed by the body when cocaine and alcohol are consumed together. Cocaethylene increases the chances of serious adverse reaction or sudden death from cocaine.

COCAINE BUGS: Hallucinations that feel like bugs crawling under the skin, occurring in heavy or binge users of cocaine. This sensation can be so intense that users will scratch their skin or use a knife to attempt to remove the bugs.

COCAINE PSYCHOSIS: A mental illness characterized by paranoia, disorientation, and severe depression. It is often the result of long-term cocaine abuse.

CRACK COCAINE: A highly addictive free-base cocaine that is smoked. Crack is made by combining powder cocaine and sodium bicarbonate.

FREE BASE: The form of cocaine that can be smoked. There are three free-base forms of cocaine: coca paste made from processed coca leaves; crack (which is made with powder cocaine and sodium bicarbonate); and "free base" (which is made with powder cocaine, ammonia and ether. This form is rarely used since crack was discovered). All free base is highly addictive.

POWDER COCAINE (COCAINE HYDROCHLORIDE): A psychoactive substance derived from coca leaves. Powder cocaine is either snorted into the nose or mixed with water and injected into the veins. It is addictive when snorted and more so if injected.

SPEEDBALL: Also called "dynamite" or "whiz-bang," a speedball is a combination of cocaine or methampetamine (stimulants) and heroin (a depressant). This combination increases the chances of serious adverse reactions and can be more toxic than either drug alone.

While cocaine is still used for ear, nose, and throat surgery, Lidocaine, a synthetic derivative of cocaine, is the most widely used local anesthetic.

Coca leaves

Cocaine is ingested in its mildest form by chewing coca leaves. Alkalines such as lime or ash are added to the leaves to release the cocaine alkaloid. In addition to cocaine, the leaves contain protein, minerals, vitamins, and over 14 alkaloids. Instead of experiencing a "rush"

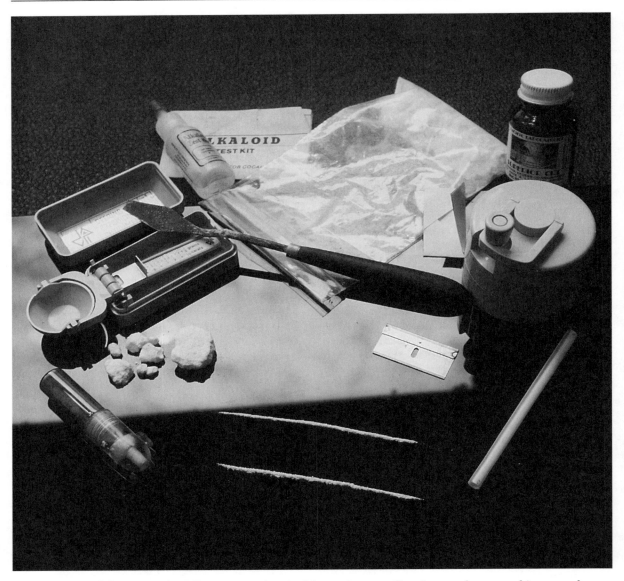

Various types of drug paraphanalia are associated with cocaine use. Cocaine can be snorted in a powder form; its use usually involves a mirror, straight edge razor, and a straw. It may be melted into a liquid form for intravenous injection with a syringe, or it may be smoked in a pipe-like apparatus. Other devices can be found with cocaine, such as those used to cut, measure, and test the puritiy of the product, are seen above.

Photo by Nick Ut, AP/World Wide Photo. Reproduced by permission.

or a "high," chewers first notice numbness of the mouth followed by alertness and a sense of well-being. The stimulant effect is about as potent as the caffeine in several cups of strong coffee. Regular coffee breaks in the United States is the social equivalent of regular coca leaf breaks in the mountains of South America. Chewing coca leaves is also part of the religious tradition. In addition to chewing coca leaves, the people also make the leaves into tea. Coca leaves are not smoked because the temperature needed to burn the leaves destroys the cocaine alkaloid before it can be inhaled.

Coca paste

Sometimes called "bazooka," coca paste is an impure free-base form of cocaine that is smoked. It contains 20–90% cocaine and it is psychoactive. Smokers experience a "rush" or a "spike" similar to the effects of smoking crack or injecting powder cocaine. This is followed by a "high." Coca paste is highly addictive. To make the paste, lime water, kerosene, and sulfuric acid are added to coca leaves. By removing the bulky leaf matter, 250 lbs (114 kg) of coca leaves are converted into 22 lbs (10 kg) of coca paste. Solvent residues give the paste an unpleasant taste and odor. It is usually added to tobacco or marijuana cigarettes. Use of coca paste is restricted mainly to South America as it is bulky and difficult to ship. With additional processing, coca paste can be converted into powder cocaine, which is easier to smuggle and is much more profitable for South American cartels.

Powder cocaine

Powder cocaine (cocaine hydrochloride) can be over 100 times more potent than coca leaves. By adding acids and purifying agents, 22 lbs (10 kg) of coca paste can be refined to 2.2 lbs (1 kg) of powder. This powder approaches 100% purity, but it is diluted with fillers before it is sold on the streets in the United States. Common fillers are cheaper drugs such as amphetamines or sugars such as lactose or inositol. Average street powder purity is 60%. The most common way to use powder is to snort it into the nose, but it can also be dissolved in water and injected into the veins. Powder cocaine cannot be smoked. Powder cocaine is addictive when snorted and highly addictive when injected.

Free base

Free base is a form of cocaine that can be smoked. There are three free-base forms of cocaine: coca paste, free base, and crack. Coca paste is made directly from coca leaves with solvents and acids. It is not available in the United States. Another form called "free base" was developed in the mid-1970s. In this process, powder cocaine is changed into free base by using water, ammonia, and highly flammable ether. It is a dangerous process because the volatile chemicals sometimes explode or ignite. Comedian Richard Pryor was badly burned while "freebasing." By far, the most common free base is crack. In a very stable process, cocaine and sodium bicarbonate are combined. The precipitate, crack, is nearly 100% pure cocaine. All three forms of free base are highly addictive.

Crack cocaine

Crack is free-base cocaine extracted from powder cocaine using water and sodium bicarbonate. The resulting precipitate is dried and cut into "rocks" weighing between one-tenth to one-half a gram. Ten grams of powder cocaine will convert to 8.9 grams of nearly pure crack. A rock is placed into a glass pipe, heated, and the vapors are inhaled. It is called "crack" because when it is heated, the sodium bicarbonate makes a crackling sound. Because crack is inexpensive and delivers large amounts of cocaine to the lungs, it has become the most popular form of cocaine. Crack is highly addictive.

INGESTION METHODS

The way cocaine is ingested greatly determines the intensity of the effect it will have on the brain and the body. As ingestion methods increase the speed at which cocaine reaches the brain, it also increases the "high" and the risk of addiction.

Mouth and stomach

South American natives chew coca leaves mixed with lime or plant ash to gradually release small amounts of cocaine alkaloid. Some of the cocaine is absorbed by the mucous membranes of the mouth and the intestines absorb some of the juice as it is swallowed. The small amount of cocaine entering the bloodstream numbs the mouth, decreases the feeling of hunger, and has a stimulant effect similar to drinking several cups of strong coffee. It does not cause a "high," but the feeling of well-being can last one to two hours.

Snorting

Typically, a line of 20–30 mg of powder cocaine is placed on a mirror or glass and is snuffed into the nose. In less than one minute, this blood-vessel-rich nasal area transports the cocaine to the brain, resulting in a "high" or "euphoria." Because of the constricting effect cocaine has on the blood vessels, absorption is slower than when cocaine is smoked or used intravenously. The "high" from snorting is less intense, but it lasts longer. Snorting cocaine is addictive.

Injecting

Powder cocaine can be dissolved in water and injected into the veins. In less than 16 seconds, the cocaine is mixed with the blood, sent to the lungs, returned to the heart and received by the brain. The intense euphoria is greater than a "high" and is referred to as a "rush." The "rush" generally lasts only a few minutes and the remaining "high" drops off quickly. This is the least socially acceptable way to ingest cocaine. Injecting cocaine is highly addictive.

Smoking

Powder cocaine and coca leaves cannot be smoked. The heat required to smoke these forms of cocaine destroys its psychoactive properties. In order to smoke cocaine, it must be changed to a free-base form. In South America, the most common free base is coca paste. In the West, people smoke crack, and to a much lesser extent, free base made with ether. The free base or crack is put into a glass pipe, heated, and the vapors are inhaled.

If it is inhaled deeply into the lungs, the vapors will come in contact with over 300 million alveolar sacs representing 171 yd^2 (143 m^2) of surface area. Within three seconds, cocaine is absorbed into the blood and pumped directly to the brain. This immediate brain "rush" or "spike" is slightly faster than the injection method and is achieved without the use of needles. Smoking cocaine by inhaling free-base vapors creates the fastest and most intense "rush" and subsequent "high." This is highly addictive.

THERAPEUTIC USE

The medicinal and ceremonial uses of cocaine via coca leaves can be traced back over 4,000 years to pre-Columbian times. It continues to be used legally and is part of the daily culture of South American Indians. Coca leaves are chewed to combat fatigue and to ward off hunger. They are also used to alleviate problems of the larynx, digestive system, metabolism of carbohydrates, vertigo, altitude sickness, and for psychological ills.

After 1860, cocaine was being processed into powder and shipped to the United States and Europe. As described, in the 1880s, people could buy 99.9% pure powder cocaine at the grocery store and in mail-order catalogs, and could drink cocaine-laced "health" drinks. It was a common nonprescription remedy for hay fever, children's toothaches, asthma, mountain sickness, seasickness, vomiting during pregnancy, and cramps. Snorting also became popular and some people began injecting cocaine. One company, Parke-Davis, not only sold cocaine—it offered needle and syringe kits.

As use proliferated, the toxic effects of cocaine became apparent. People were getting addicted. In 1914, the Harrison Narcotic Act banned cocaine in the United States. Only use as a local anesthetic was legally retained. It is still used today in nasal, mouth, and throat surgery. Anesthetic solutions contain 1–4% cocaine.

A need was seen for a synthetic and less toxic anesthetic. In 1905, Procaine was synthesized and became the prototype for synthesized anesthetics for the next 50 years. In 1948, Lidocaine was developed and is now the most commonly used local anesthetic. Other synthesized local anesthetics include bupivacaine and tetracaine.

USAGE TRENDS

Americans' attitude toward cocaine has run the gamut from acceptance to ambivalence to outrage. In the late 1870s, soon after cocaine was first introduced as a non-addictive "cure-all," the drug was found in family medicine cabinets for dozens of applications. Also, in keeping with the spirit of the American Industrial Revolution, cocaine was touted as a tonic to energize workers and ensure peak efficiency. By the 1890s, cocaine had gone beyond medical application and began to contribute to the pleasure-centered Gay Nineties. During

this time of widespread use, medical journals began to report on the toxic and addictive properties of cocaine.

Public support turned against cocaine and it became a focal point of the temperance crusade in 1903. The Harrison Act of 1914 classified cocaine as a narcotic and prohibited its use in the United States except as a local anesthetic. During that same year, all 48 states passed similar laws. The 1930s through the 1960s became a time of intolerance as exemplified by the tough drug laws that were passed. Then ambivalence set in. People forgot the reason for the outrage. In the 1960s, few people personally knew a cocaine user or addict.

By the 1970s, another epidemic of cocaine use was underway. Cocaine became part of the disco scene with bright lights, glittery clothes, and the energy to dance the night away. Cocaine, generally snorted, gained a reputation as being a drug for the affluent. In the 1980s, a new form of cocaine known as crack became available. Crack could be smoked, delivered a more intense high, and cost about one-tenth as much as powdered cocaine. Cocaine use peaked in 1985 when the number of Americans who had ever used cocaine soared to 25 million.

As cocaine-related hospital emergency visits increased and negative media stories began to proliferate, public opinion once again moved against recreational cocaine use. Crack especially was singled out as being extremely addictive and destructive. Amid this outcry, the Anti-Drug Abuse Act of 1986 was passed and crack possession now carried much heavier penalties than its counterpart, powder cocaine.

By the time the law was passed, cocaine use was already on its way down. It declined steeply until 1992 when the trend once again reversed. According to the National Household Survey on Drug Abuse (NHSDA), the cocaine-using population had crept back up to about three million people by 1993. The gradual increase continued. By 1999, the NHSDA reported cocaine use by 3.7 million or 1.7% of Americans. The Community Epidemiology Work Group (CEWG), which follows drug abuse trends in 21 major U.S. metropolitan areas showed a slight downward trend in crack/cocaine use in their 2000 report.

Scope and severity

The fact that less than 2% of the American population uses cocaine is not cause to minimize its scope and severity. These three million or so Americans consume about 50% of the world's cocaine production. According to the Drug Abuse Warning Network (DAWN) for 2000, cocaine was the second most frequently mentioned drug that caused people to be admitted to hospital emergency rooms. Also, of the 32,288 suspects referred to federal prosecutors for drug charges during 1999, 43% were charged with offenses relating to powder cocaine or crack. The Office of National Drug Control Policy (ONDCP) reports in the November 2001 *Pulse Check*,

An advertisement for cocaine toothache drops, circa 1885. Copyright CORBIS. Reproduced by permission.

that over half the Pulse Check communities listed crack as the drug with the most severe or second-most severe consequences, whether medically, legally, or otherwise. The same report listed powder cocaine as widely available in 85% of the 21 Pulse Check cities. Crack was listed as widely available by 75% of the Pulse Check sources.

As of 2002, about 14 million people worldwide use cocaine. According to the ONDCP, the United States leads the world in cocaine abuse. While U.S. cocaine use has remained relatively stable over the last decade, the United Nations Commission on Narcotic Drugs reported in March 2000 that 34 countries out of 112 reported an increase in cocaine use from 1997 to 1998. In the European Union, the increase in cocaine use was mainly in the group of people aged 16 to 29 years.

Age, ethnic, and gender trends

In 2000, according to the NHSDA, cocaine use dropped over the course of the year from 0.2% to 0.1% in youths aged 12 and 13. Youths aged 14 and 15 had no change for the same time period with 0.5% using cocaine. Cocaine use increased in youths aged 16 and 17, from 0.9% to 1.1%. Crack use declined in young adults aged 18 to 25 and went from 0.3% to 0.1%. Adults aged 26 and older had no change in cocaine use, but there was a decline in crack use for adults 26 to 34 years. This study also indicated that 43% of cocaine users were under the age of 26. The ONDCP reports in November 2001 that nine Pulse Check cities considered

young adults (18–30 years) to be the primary crack user group, while eight cities cited adults older than 30 years.

Though crack and powder cocaine are different forms of the same drug, clearly divided ethnic preferences exist. The NHSDA reported in 2000, African Americans are the predominant users of crack, whereas whites are the predominant users of powder cocaine. Socioeconomic status may contribute to this trend. The Hispanic population uses more powder cocaine than crack, but figures overall remain low.

Regarding gender differences, again the NHSDA separates the statistics for powder cocaine and crack. Males are more likely than females to use powder cocaine. However, males and females are equally likely to use crack in many surveyed cities. Studies indicate that female crack use has been increasing over the past five years.

No single risk factor predicts cocaine use. However, because cocaine use is approved of and practiced by such a small percentage of the population, a person's willingness to take risks is often a factor. Other factors include a person's level of impulsiveness, other available sources of attaining pleasure, the availability of cocaine, and the relationship of adolescents with their parents. Because recreational cocaine use is against the law, how people view breaking the law is also a factor. It is noteworthy that young people who illegally smoke are ten times as likely to use an illegal drug than their non-smoking peers.

LAW AND ORDER

Are cocaine sentencing laws unfair?

According to the Federal Trafficking Penalties, a first-time offender convicted of possessing five grams of crack cocaine, will receive a mandatory minimum sentence of five years in prison without parole. Five grams of crack cocaine, which can fit into a tablespoon, can be broken into 50–200 "rocks" to be smoked.

If that same first-time offender had been convicted of possessing powder cocaine—the offender would need 500 grams of powder to trigger the same mandatory sentence. In other words, the offender could possess 100 times as much powder cocaine as crack cocaine. Five hundred grams is over one pound and would fill a cereal bowl. It is the equivalent of 10,000 doses suitable for snorting or dissolving in water and injecting.

There is a relationship between crack and powder cocaine. Cocaine arrives in the United States from Columbia in the form of powder cocaine (cocaine hydrochloride). Crack is then made in the United States by mixing powder cocaine and sodium bicarbonate. The resulting precipitate is dried and cut into "rocks." Five

hundred grams of powder cocaine can be converted into 445 grams of crack or between 4,550–17,800 doses. Without powder cocaine, there would be no crack.

So why is there a disparity in the federal sentencing guidelines? In the 1980s, as the powder cocaine epidemic was drawing to a close, a new epidemic was emerging—crack cocaine. Crack sold for as cheaply as three to five dollars per rock. Suddenly, the market exploded and crack use spread to the young and the poor. Though cocaine powder is powerfully addictive, crack seems to be even more so.

Wanting to send a strong message that crack was intolerable, Congress passed the Anti-Drug Abuse Act of 1986 and 1988 with the 100:1 powder cocaine vs. crack ratio. Because more African Americans tend to use crack, whereas more Hispanics and whites tend to use powder cocaine, this law continues to result in harsher prison terms for blacks. In 1996, the American Medical Association published a study and recommended a revised powder cocaine/crack ratio of 2 or 3:1. In 1997 the Department of Justice recommended that the ratio be reduced to 10:1. The Drug Sentencing Reform Act of 2001 (S. 1874) has been introduced into the Senate and would increase the amount of crack necessary to trigger mandatory sentences while increasing the penalties for powder cocaine convictions, if it becomes law. This is one of numerous bills proposed since 1988, none of which have passed.

Students who use cocaine must be willing to deviate greatly from the norm. However, the trend of acceptance is changing. According to the "Monitoring the Future" study, in the decade of the 1990s, perceived risk and disapproval of powder cocaine and crack decreased in eighth, tenth, and twelfth grades.

MENTAL EFFECTS

Small doses of cocaine can cause users to feel both mentally and sexually excited, self-confident, uninhibited, talkative, clever, and in control. Larger doses and heavy use can cause the opposite effects. Heavy users can become confused mentally, uninterested in sex, paranoid (feeling everyone is against them), antisocial, aggressive, and are subject to cocaine psychosis (a mental illness whose symptoms include paranoia, disorientation, and severe depression).

The pleasurable feelings from cocaine use last only 15–30 minutes if it is snorted and only five to 10 minutes if cocaine is smoked or injected into the veins. When the "high" is over, the user feels tired, sluggish, and "low."

This cycle can precipitate repeated cocaine use to try to recapture the first high. Oddly, the more often cocaine is used, the less intense the pleasure. This is called tolerance. If use continues to the point of addiction, users take cocaine just to feel "normal."

Heavy users and binge users can experience visual and auditory hallucinations. A tactile hallucination (a hallucination involving the sense of touch) called "cocaine bugs" causes users to feel imaginary bugs crawling under their skin. Users can scratch or use a knife to try to remove the "bugs" in reaction to this sensation. In 1999, two NIDA-funded studies confirmed that heavy cocaine use can cause long-lasting brain impairment. In one study, it was found that the user's problem-solving skills and cognitive skills lagged behind that of moderate or non-users. In a second study, a month after last use, heavy users performed much worse than moderate or non-users in tasks involving planning and reasoning. Users can become psychologically dependent on cocaine, using the drug to take the place of real-life experiences and problem-solving strategies. People who become dependent and then quit using cocaine often experience an intense craving for the drug long after the last use.

PHYSIOLOGICAL EFFECTS

Cocaine is a central nervous system (CNS) stimulant that causes a significant increase in heart rate, respiration, blood pressure, and body temperature. According to DAWN, one in thirteen cocaine users go to the hospital to be treated for severe reactions that could be life-threatening. Sudden death can result from heart failure, respiratory failure, seizures, strokes, and cerebral hemorrhage. There is no antidote for cocaine overdose. Even if the adverse reactions do not result in death, they can do permanent damage to the body.

For years, scientists have known that cocaine interferes with the brain's dopamine system. Dopamine is a neurotransmitter—a chemical that passes nerve impulses from one nerve cell to another, and dopamine is associated with movement, emotional response, and the ability to experience pleasure. Research indicates that serotonin transporters are also inactivated with cocaine use. Serotonin is another neurotransmitter, and adequate levels are associated with well-being. Low levels of serotonin in the brain have been linked to depression. Inactivation of dopamine and serotonin transporters leads to receptor over-stimulation and the "high." Continued use of cocaine can result in long-term changes in the brain chemistry as receptors decrease in number. These changes can be persistent and even irreversible, and may be responsible for the feeling of depression that lasts long after withdrawal.

As late as the 1980s, there was a pervasive myth that cocaine is not addictive. This was because withdrawal symptoms were not thought to be physical. When a person addicted to a substance stops taking the substance, he or she experiences withdrawal symptoms. The withdrawal symptoms are unpleasant, and encourage the person to take the substance again in order to avoid the withdrawal. Cocaine withdrawal symptoms include an intense and irresistible craving for cocaine, depression or "crash," and sometimes paranoia. It is now known that cocaine is powerfully addictive. Research indicates that after repeated ingestion of cocaine, nearly 100% of monkeys and rats tested will self-administer the drug. Cocaine is one of the easiest drugs to get animals to take willingly.

Cocaine is metabolized very quickly by the body. Within minutes, enzymes in the blood and in the liver split the cocaine molecule into two halves, rendering it inactive. Cocaine and its metabolites are excreted in the urine. The body's efficient metabolism of cocaine causes the "high" to be relatively short-lived. This often causes cocaine users to take several doses of cocaine in a short time, which can increase the chances of an overdose.

Harmful side effects

The most serious effect of using cocaine is the possibility of sudden death. It can happen after the first use or anytime thereafter. Sudden death can occur with cocaine use alone, but it more commonly occurs when cocaine is combined with alcohol or other drugs. More common side effects include irreversible damage to the heart and liver, along with damage inflicted by strokes and seizures. Cocaine users are also at risk for addiction. Addiction is often viewed as a disease. It occurs when drug use is no longer a voluntary choice but an uncontrollable compulsion. Some crack users report addiction after just one use.

The point of ingestion determines the specific side effects. For instance, snorting powder cocaine over time will damage the septum and ulcerate the mucous membrane of the nose. Smoking crack cocaine can cause lung trauma and bleeding. Injecting cocaine into the veins often causes inflammation, infections, and carries a greater risk for contracting AIDS/HIV and hepatitis.

Cocaine use during pregnancy is especially dangerous. It can cause harm to both the mother and the baby. Cocaine causes spasms in the blood vessels, including those in the placenta. Sometimes placenta abruption (separation of the placenta from the wall of the uterus before the baby is born) and bleeding occurs, which can be fatal to the mother and baby. Children born to mothers who used cocaine during pregnancy are often termed "crack babies." These babies tend to be abnormally small. Because of their low birth weight, they are 20 times more likely to die in their first month of life than babies of normal weight. The babies have an increased risk of mental retardation, cerebral palsy, and vision and hearing disabilities. Cocaine-induced prenatal strokes can cause permanent brain damage. Another common abnormality of these babies is their unusually small head. While they seem to have normal intelligence, studies indicate more behavioral problems for exposed children than unexposed children.

Long-term health effects

Cocaine constricts blood vessels and decreases blood flow. Using imaging technology such as magnetic resonance angiography (MRA) and transcranial Doppler sonography (TDC), scientists can see both short-term and long-term blood flow deficits in the brains of cocaine users. Long-term cocaine use can also cause atherosclerosis, or thickening of the blood vessels. Because of this, cocaine abusers in their thirties can have arteries as constricted as non-abusers in their sixties. With reduced blood flow to the brain, some cocaine abusers have shown cognitive deficits in attention span, memory, and problem-solving. Other effects include serious damage to the heart, lungs, and liver.

Cocaine also has a reputation for being disinhibiting. Users may take unusual risks that can lead to long-term consequences. These risks can range from sexual encounters to automobile accidents caused by poor judgment or aggression.

REACTIONS WITH OTHER DRUGS OR SUBSTANCES

Cocaine is almost always used with other drugs, including alcohol, heroin, amphetamines, and marijuana. Combining drugs increases the chances of overdose and serious side effects. The most common drug to be combined with cocaine is alcohol. Alcoholic beverages prolong the cocaine "high" and reduce drug-induced paranoia. This combination creates a new substance, cocaethylene. Cocaethylene is as potent as cocaine and lasts longer. However, it can be more toxic to the heart. The combination of cocaine and alcohol results in more deaths than any other illegal drug combination.

Combining cocaine with heroin is called a "speedball," "dynamite," or "whiz-bang." It is a very dangerous combination because cocaine speeds up the respiratory system while heroin depresses it. However, at high doses, cocaine can begin to depress the respiratory system, as well. In speedballing, cocaine and heroin are typically ingested at the same time. However, some users ingest the drugs alternately to feel either more "energetic" or more "relaxed." This combination can be more toxic than using either drug alone. Comedian John Belushi died using this combination in 1982.

Amphetamines are often combined with cocaine to extend the "high." Cocaine creates a "rush" but it is short-lived. Adding amphetamines extends the "high" for up to ten hours. Using these drugs together increases the chances of an overdose and increases toxic effects.

Cocaine is also frequently combined with marijuana. Called a "diablito" or "turbo," a cigar is filled with marijuana and crack and then smoked. This increases the risk to the cardiovascular system as both drugs speed up the heart and increase blood pressure.

Brompton's mixture

In the 1970s, a combination of cocaine, methadone, and alcohol was given to terminal cancer patients. The methadone and alcohol relieved the pain but induced a lethargic and clouded state for the patients. Cocaine was added to make patients more alert. New medications are more effective and cocaine is no longer used for cancer patients.

TREATMENT AND REHABILITATION

According to the 1997 National Association of State Alcohol and Drug Abuse Directors (NASADAD), excepting alcohol, the largest number of publicly funded drug treatment admissions were for cocaine. The biggest challenge to cocaine treatment and rehabilitation is preventing relapse (the return to using drugs) caused by a persistent and intense craving for cocaine. To this end, after detoxification, which can take less than a week,

treatment programs often include deconditioning. Deconditioning exposes abstinent users to cues that produce powerful and pleasurable memories of cocaine use. By keeping the patients from reinforcing the memories with cocaine use, the cues eventually lose their power to produce a craving.

While cocaine addiction can be treated successfully, there is no one program that is effective for everyone. *Principles of Effective Drug Treatment*, published by NIDA, recommends a multi-faceted approach to treatment. It suggests behavioral therapies, medications, rehabilitation and social services. The idea is to treat the whole person.

Regarding medication, NIDA research reports that medications that act on both the dopamine and serotonin receptors might reduce the intense craving and depression. Behavior therapies can include group and/or individual counseling, popular 12-Step programs, therapeutic communities, and chemical dependency inpatient and outpatient programs. Rehabilitative treatment includes training focused on resolving problems related to jobs, home life, and the criminal justice system.

PERSONAL AND SOCIAL CONSEQUENCES

When cocaine use progresses to a point of dependence it can be devastating. At this stage, drug seeking often becomes the first priority. Suddenly, values such as love of family and commitment to work can take second place to finding, buying, and using cocaine.

Habitual users can lose the trust and respect of the people important to them. Lying, stealing, and isolating oneself all take a heavy toll on family, friends, and employment relationships.

Aside from theft, NIDA funded research shows that drug abusers cost employers about twice as much in medical and worker's compensation claims than drug-free workers. As a result, more and more businesses are requiring drug screening before hiring and are employing periodic drug-testing thereafter.

While a single dose of cocaine may cost as little as five or ten dollars, an addiction can cost hundreds of dollars a week. This can lead to financial ruin and often progresses to criminal activity. (Users desperate for more drugs may turn to illegal activity, including robbery or prostitution, in order to finance their habit.) Conviction of an illegal drug offense can trigger minimum mandatory prison sentences. Also, students convicted of cocaine possession can be disqualified from obtaining federal college grants and loans.

Though less than 2% of Americans use cocaine, it has profound national consequences. Health and human services related to drug and alcohol abuse cost taxpayers

LAW AND ORDER

Women's rights vs. safety of unborn

Do hospitals have the right to secretly test pregnant patients for cocaine and to inform the police if the test is positive? The Medical University of South Carolina (MUSC) thought so. In 1989, MUSC began giving urine tests to women suspected of cocaine use. If the test was positive, sometimes the police were called. Later, MUSC gave women who tested positive a choice—treatment or arrest.

In 1993, 10 women who tested positive at MUSC filed a suit based on the Fourth Amendment. They held that drug tests without consent was tantamount to unreasonable search and seizure. It was also argued that pregnant women might avoid prenatal care if such care could result in going to jail.

In 1996, the South Carolina Supreme Court decided in favor of the city. Its ruling was based on protecting the child. A fetus, in the last trimester, is a person. A preg-

nant woman is liable if she uses cocaine, thereby passing it on to her unborn child. The court upheld MUSC's drug testing in an effort to protect the unborn.

Indeed, there is no shortage of evidence that cocaine is harmful to the unborn child. Cocaine greatly increases the chances of a miscarriage. Low birth weight "crack babies" have 20 times as great a risk of dying in their first month of life than normal-weight babies. Those who survive are at increased risk for birth defects, including a five-fold greater chance of having an abnormal urinary tract. According to the National Institute of Drug Abuse (NIDA) research released October 2001, these children sustained long-lasting brain changes. Eight years after birth, children exposed to cocaine prior to birth had detectable brain chemistry differences. The study concluded that this finding might be a biological explanation as to why some cocaine-exposed children are more impulsive and easily distractible than unexposed children.

The case ultimately went to the United States Supreme Court. On March 21, 2001, after hearing arguments for both sides, the U.S. Supreme Court ruled in favor of the women based on the Fourth Amendment. Hospitals cannot test pregnant women for drugs without their consent and then inform the police.

---

more than $294 billion dollars annually. This cost rose 50% from 1985 to 1992. A NIDA-funded study showed that cocaine use was the primary factor contributing to this increase.

LEGAL CONSEQUENCES

Under the Controlled Substance Act, cocaine is a Schedule II drug. This means that cocaine has a high potential for abuse and that abuse may lead to severe physical and psychological dependence. It also means that cocaine has accepted medical uses with severe restrictions. The only legal use of cocaine in the United States is as a local anesthetic.

The Anti-Drug Abuse Act of 1986 and 1988 established federal mandatory minimum drug sentencing guidelines. The punishment exacted by the federal law is substantially greater than the punishment imposed by most state laws. For example, someone convicted of cocaine possession that receives a 12-year sentence in the state system may be liable for a mandatory life term if tried in the federal system. Also, most state laws do not differentiate between powder cocaine and crack cocaine. Federal law carries a much harsher penalty for crack than for powder. Possession of five grams of crack or 500

grams of powder carries a mandatory first-offense penalty of not less than five years in prison.

Legal history

Cocaine accessed by chewing coca leaves has been a legal and common tradition in South America for over 4,000 years. It continues to be legal.

Purified powder cocaine was legal in Europe and the United States from its introduction in the 1860s until 1914. During that time, cocaine use reached epidemic proportions. Medical reports of addiction and sudden death caused public opinion to move against cocaine use. In 1906, the Pure Food and Drug Act mandated that cocaine be listed as an ingredient in all medicines whether they were sold by individuals or drug companies. President William Taft declared cocaine as Public Enemy No. 1, and in 1914 Congress passed the Harrison Narcotics Act. Cocaine thus became one of the first drugs to be banned in the United States. That same year, all 48 states had laws banning cocaine. The only legal use for cocaine was as a local anesthetic.

While laws continued to be passed over the next seven decades, none proved to be as controversial as the Anti-Drug Abuse Act of 1986 and 1988. Like the Harrison Act, this law arose during an epidemic of cocaine use.

???? FACT OR FICTION

Coca-Cola once contained cocaine

It is true that when Coca-Cola was first produced in the mid-1880s it contained cocaine. In fact, the drink derives its name from its two "medicinal ingredients"— coca leaves and kola nuts. No one really knows how much cocaine Coca-Cola originally contained, but it certainly contained some. By 1902, the amount of cocaine in an ounce of Coca-Cola syrup was as little as 1/400 of a grain, and by 1905 all cocaine was eliminated from the beverage.

This time, it was the 1980s epidemic fueled by crack. In 1986, the death of two promising young athletes, Len Bias and Don Rogers, added to public outrage. The new laws differentiated between powder cocaine and crack and were much harsher on the latter. These laws require 100 times as much powder cocaine possession as crack to trigger an identical minimum mandatory prison sentence. Ongoing controversy surrounds this law. Several bills have been introduced to reduce the disparity, but none have been passed into law as of early 2002.

Drug trafficking organizations in Columbia control the world's cocaine supply. The United States is actively engaged in fighting Columbia-based drug cartels. The U.S. Drug Enforcement Administration Congressional testimony of March 2, 2001 stated that targeting organized crime groups in Columbia will continue to be a priority and a matter of national security.

Federal guidelines, regulations, and penalties

Federal Trafficking Penalties, which are outlined in the Anti-Drug Abuse Act of 1986 and 1988, make a significant distinction between powder cocaine and crack cocaine. A first-time offender convicted for possession of 5–49 grams of crack cocaine will receive a mandatory minimum sentence of five years and not more than 40 years. Fines for individuals can be up to $2 million. The federal mandatory minimum sentences for powder cocaine begin at 500–4,999 grams and trigger the same sentence. Penalties for convicted second-time offenders are a minimum mandatory sentence of 10 years to life, with fines up to $4 million. This law is often referred to

as the 100:1 law and has been challenged and reviewed several times.

RESOURCES

Books

Berger, Gilda. *Crack, The New Drug Epidemic*. Franklin Watts, 1987.

Carroll, Marilyn. *Cocaine and Crack*. Enslow Publishers Inc., 1994.

Friedman, David P., and Sue Rusche. *False Messengers: How Addictive Drugs Change the Brain*. Harwood Academic Publishers, 1999.

Goldstein, Avram. *Addiction: From Biology to Drug Policy*. Oxford University Press, 2001.

Other

Center for Education and Information on Drugs and Alcohol. NSW+Health. *Cocaine* <http://www.ceida.net.au/tools_for_workers/drugs/cocaine.html>.

National Institute on Drug Abuse. National Institutes of Health. "Cocaine Abuse May Lead to Strokes and Mental Deficits." *NIDA Notes* 13, no. 3 (July 1998). <http://www.nida.nih.gov/NIDA_Notes/NNVol12N3/Cocaine.html>.

National Institute on Drug Abuse. National Institutes of Health. "Oops: How Casual Drug Use Leads to Addiction." *NIDA NOTES* <http://www.nida.nih.gov/Published_Articles/Oops.html>.

United States Department of Justice. Drug Enforcement Administration. *Cocaine*. <http://usdoj.gov/dea/concern/cocaine.html>.

United States Office of National Drug Control Policy. "Crack: The Perception." *Pulse Check: Trends in Drug Abuse* (November 2001). <http://www.whitehousedrugpolicy.gov/publications/drugfact/pulsechk/fall2001/crack.html>.

United States Office of National Drug Control Policy. "Powder Cocaine: The Perception." *Pulse Check: Trends in Drug Abuse* (November 2001). <http://www.whitehousedrugpolicy.gov/publications/drugfact/pulsechk/fall2001/powder.html>.

Organizations

Cocaine Anonymous World Services, P.O. Box 2000, Los Angeles, CA, USA, 90049-8000, (310) 559-5833, cawso@ca.org, <http://www.ca.org>.

Cocaine Helpline, 1-800-662-HELP.

National Institute on Drug Abuse (NIDA), National Institutes of Health, 6001 Executive Boulevard, Room 5213, Bethesda, MD, USA, 20892-9561, (301) 443-1124, (888) 644-6432, information@lists.gov/Inforfax/cocaine.html, <http://www.drugabuse.gov/Inforfax/cocaine.html>.

Patty Jo Sawvel

CODEINE

Codeine is classified as an opiate analgesic. Analgesics are substances that, when ingested or injected, diminish or relieve pain; opiates are drugs that can be derived from opium. Opiates, along with opioids, the broader group to which opiates belong, are the most effective of all analgesics. All opioids are analgesics, but most analgesics are not opioids.

Many different drugs act as analgesics. One method of classifying these drugs is to separate them into two groups—those that require a doctor's prescription and those that do not. Medications that do not require a doctor's prescription are called over-the-counter (OTC) drugs. OTC analgesics include acetaminophen (Tylenol), aspirin, and ibuprofen. Codeine, a prescription analgesic, is one of the most frequently prescribed medications used worldwide to treat pain.

Pain is universal; everyone experiences different kinds of acute (short-term) pain during their life. However, too much pain for too long, (moderate to severe chronic pain), can be harmful, both physically and psychologically. Approximately one-third of all people in the United States experience moderate to severe chronic pain during their life. Half of all individuals who seek medical attention report pain as their primary complaint.

Codeine and other opioid medications are used medically because of their ability to relieve physical pain—in fact, it is the only reason for their medical use as a group. A broader view of opioids reveals that they also can have profound effects on emotional pain—which is perhaps a frequent, if unconscious, reason for their non-medical use/abuse. Physical and emotional

OFFICIAL NAMES: Codeine, codeine phosphate, codeine sulfate, methylmorphine
STREET NAMES: T–threes, schoolboy, coties, dors and fours, cough syrup, barr (codeine cough syrup), down (codeine cough syrup), karo (codeine cough syrup), lean (codeine cough syrup), nods (codeine cough syrup)
DRUG CLASSIFICATIONS: Schedule II, III, or V, narcotic

pain often have an inseparable connection between them. Even something as simple as stubbing a toe usually elicits a short, but dramatic, emotional response. However, the primary medical use for codeine is only in the treatment of physical pain.

In considering the analgesic effects of opioids such as codeine, it is important to know that the body has two connected systems, one that signals pain and another that responds to it. Both systems have interacting physical and chemical components. The physical portion includes neurons of the central (brain and spinal cord) and peripheral nervous systems. The chemical portion includes substances that aid in the transmission of signals between nerve cells (neurotransmitters), along with chemicals and proteins that have specific roles in normal nerve cell function. The most important group of neurochemicals in the pain killing system is the endogenous opioids. An "endogenous" substance is something that is naturally produced by the body. Endogenous opioids function as the body's own analgesics.

KEY TERMS

ANALGESIC: A type of drug that alleviates pain without loss of consciousness.

ENDOGENOUS OPIOIDS: Naturally occurring opioids in the body; includes three classes of neurotransmitters—the endorphins, enkephalins, and dynorphins.

OPIATE: Drug derived directly from opium and used in its natural state, without chemical modification. Opiates include morphine, codeine, thebaine, noscapine, and papaverine.

OPIOID: A drug, hormone, or other chemical substance having sedative or narcotic effects similar to those containing opium or its derivatives; a natural brain opiate.

OPIOID RECEPTORS: A class of proteins on the surface of cells that bind with opioids, either endogenous or drugs. An opioid either activates (agonist) or prevents activation by another opioid (antagonist).

The body's natural painkilling system, then, involves the interaction of endogenous opioids with neurons that transmit and process pain signals. Opioid medications such as codeine mimic the effects of certain endogenous opioids. However, ingested/injected opioids tend to produce much stronger effects than those of the endogenous variety.

Opioid receptors are the cell-surface proteins which all opioids interact with to produce their effects. An opioid, whether endogenous or in drug form, fits into a receptor somewhat like a key in a lock. Opioid attachment activates the receptor and initiates complex changes in the nerve cell. Activated opioid receptors produce chemical changes that reduce the ability of a nerve cell to transmit pain signals. They also decrease the "perception" of pain by neurons in the brain. In the absence of pain, those same chemical changes can produce euphoria. Loosely translated from Greek, euphoria means "good feeling."

Codeine is extracted from opium. Opium is a chemically complex drug derived from a flowering plant, the opium poppy. The scientific name for the opium poppy is *Papaver somniferum*, which translated from Greek means "poppy that causes sleep." Opium is produced by drying the thick liquid harvested from the unripe seed capsule of the flower. It contains several different medically important chemicals known as "alkaloids" (nonacidic chemicals), the most important being morphine and codeine.

Societies have used the medicinal properties of opium for several thousand years. Even up to the early part of the twentieth century, opium was used as a medicine to treat a large variety of conditions. For some of those conditions, particularly those involving pain and/or diarrhea, it was a highly effective treatment. However, by modern standards, most of opium's historical uses for illness would be considered medically useless or unsound because of the dangers of opium use.

Two of the most important effects of opium are its abilities to relieve pain and produce euphoria. Euphoria is best described as an exaggerated sense of well-being, possibly with mild elation or a sense of calmness. Opium's ability to produce euphoria may be what prompted its use by so many throughout history as a cure-all. After all, while it may not have had the curative effect on a person's illness that was suspected or promised, it usually made them *feel* better.

Achieving consistent results with opium has always been difficult. Different methods of production and naturally varying concentrations of morphine and codeine produce widely varying results from one batch to the next. Once the chemical methods became available, scientists were eager to isolate the active ingredient(s), hoping to produce a "pure" analgesic.

Morphine was isolated from opium in 1806, which was a significant step in scientific pharmacology. For the first time, a powerful, pain-relieving medicine was available whose effects were predictable. However, it eventually became clear that the addictive potential of morphine is equal to that of opium, with many of the same side effects. Undaunted, scientists began the quest, which is ongoing, for the "perfect" opioid—a drug with the analgesic power of morphine, but with much milder side effects and little or no addictive potential.

Codeine was extracted from opium in 1832, and was the first partial success in the attempt to discover a safer and less addictive drug. However, with fewer side effects came a less potent analgesic. About 100 mg of codeine are needed to produce the same effect as 10 mg of morphine. It was believed at the time (and it is still debated) that codeine's milder effects on a per weight basis actually result in fewer side effects when equally effective dosages are given (i.e., 100 mg of codeine produces fewer side effects than 10 mg of morphine). For the most part, standard medical practice has been to prescribe codeine for moderate pain, and reserve morphine for more severe pain.

Semi-synthetic and synthetic opioids (meperidine, hydrocodone, fentanyl, etc.) are the result of many attempts to produce effective yet safer analgesics. The fact that both morphine and codeine are still widely used indicates that the newer opioids have been only moderately successful. However, current knowledge of the opioid system makes the goal of producing the perfect (or near-perfect) opioid analgesic a more realistic possibility in the future.

Since the middle of the nineteenth century, most social attention to opium has focused on its use as an illicit drug. In fact, in many ways it has come to symbolize the worst aspects of illegal drugs. This negative social stigma has carried over to the derivatives of opium—the opioid drugs. While there is some basis for this perception, it has unfortunately generated undue fear, even within the medical professions, that anyone using an opioid drug, even someone in pain, is at great risk of becoming addicted.

CHEMICAL/ORGANIC COMPOSITION

Opium typically contains between 0.5% and 3.0% codeine by weight. Chemically, codeine is nearly identical in structure to morphine. The only difference between the two is that codeine contains an extra methyl group (two hydrogen atoms bound to a carbon atom) at one end of the molecule. In fact, once absorbed in the body, an enzyme removes the methyl group (demethylation) from codeine to produce morphine. Thus, codeine itself is not an analgesic.

The enzyme responsible for converting codeine to morphine is known as cytochrome P450 2D6, abbreviated CYP2D6. About 8% of people in the Caucasian population, 6% in the black population, and 1% of Asians have a genetic trait that results in a deficiency of CYP2D6. This means that codeine has little or no effect on them. A large number of other genetic variants of the CYP2D6 enzyme result in a wide variation in how well people metabolize codeine.

INGESTION METHODS

Codeine-containing medications are most often taken orally, either in tablet form or as syrup (also called "elixir"). Codeine may also be given by intramuscular (IM) injection. Intravenous codeine administration is not used because of the risk of causing dangerously low blood pressure (hypotension). Codeine suppositories are given rectally, but usually only in infants and children who have had surgery.

It is difficult, but possible, to extract the codeine from tablet and syrup preparations. This is usually done by people who wish to abuse codeine and need higher doses than could be safely taken when it is combined with other medications. Once extracted, the codeine powder is typically mixed with a liquid of some kind and drunk. Since OTC medicines with codeine contain very small amounts of the drug, large quantities must be purchased in order to be able to extract enough codeine to

abuse. This can be expensive and cause suspicion in a single pharmacy.

Codeine is not routinely sold in the United States as an individual drug. It is combined instead with one or more other OTC analgesics or cough suppressants into a single compound medication. Codeine is familiar to most people as an ingredient in a series of analgesic preparations in combination with Tylenol-brand acetaminophen. The number after "Tylenol" designates the amount of codeine in each tablet:

- Tylenol #1 — 8 mg codeine (not marketed in the United States)
- Tylenol #2 — 15 mg codeine
- Tylenol #3 — 30 mg codeine
- Tylenol #4 — 60 mg codeine

All combinations contain 300 mg acetaminophen per tablet. Other pharmaceutical companies produce similar preparations that may have slightly different amounts of acetaminophen, but the number designation and codeine quantity stay constant across brands. Some preparations also include up to 30 mg of caffeine to help counteract drowsiness from the codeine.

THERAPEUTIC USE

Codeine is most often used in the treatment of mild to moderate pain that does not respond fully to OTC analgesics. A number of different cough-suppressant (antitussives) medications contain low concentrations of codeine. The effects of codeine on the nerves and muscles of the intestines make it an effective treatment for diarrhea. However, since equally effective OTC medications are available, codeine is now rarely used for this purpose.

For some time, the medical community has debated whether codeine is truly effective in relieving pain and suppressing coughs. Several studies have shown that codeine alone is not significantly more effective than maximum doses of nonprescription analgesics such as acetaminophen or ibuprofen. Most research has shown, however, that codeine added to nonprescription analgesics provides a small but significant benefit. Still, some studies have shown that certain cough medicines are equally effective with or without codeine. More research is needed to resolve this issue.

Even if the physical benefits from codeine were truly minimal, the classification of codeine as a narcotic (implication: "powerful") analgesic might provide a significant placebo effect in some individuals.

Codeine is a common ingredient in cough syrup. Photo by Ford Smith/CORBIS. Reproduced by permission.

USAGE TRENDS

The United States imports about 70% of the world's opium. About 95% of that opium is consumed in the form of schedule III preparations, of which codeine is the most common. Until the mid-1970s, opium had been the main raw material used for the production of morphine and codeine. Since 1978, however, concentrate of poppy straw has been used with increasing frequency for that purpose. "Poppy straw" is a term used for the remainder of the poppy plant—but primarily refers to the seed capsule itself—once the seeds and opium-producing fluid have been removed. The majority of morphine and codeine production now comes from concentrate of poppy straw.

The concentrations of morphine and codeine in both raw opium and poppy straw vary greatly, but morphine concentrations as a percentage of total weight are typically about 10 times greater than are those of codeine. Therefore, processing of opium and poppy straw produces much more morphine than codeine. However, greater quantities of codeine than morphine are required for medical purposes. Based on the discrepancies between production and use of the two drugs, about 80% of morphine is converted into codeine.

The global manufacture of codeine underwent a 22% increase in the 1980s, from 162 tons (147,000 kg) in 1980, to 197 tons (180,000 kg) in 1989. The rate of production increased during the 1990s, with total codeine production reaching 280 tons (255,000 kg) in 1999. Overall, a 65% increase in global codeine production occurred in the 20 years between 1980 and 1999. Most codeine goes directly into medications, but some is also used to produce other opioid medications such as dihydrocodeine and hydrocodone. Actual figures for the number of codeine prescriptions written in the United States in any particular year are difficult to obtain, since less than half of all states track these numbers. Of all prescriptions written for opioid analgesics, about 15% are for codeine.

Scope and severity

Just as the medical use of codeine has increased, its misuse and abuse have also increased, although not in proportion. The issue of drug abuse can be analyzed from many different perspectives and categorized in a number of ways. One method is to compare and contrast the abuse of illegal drugs (marijuana, cocaine, etc.) with that of legal drugs (OTC and prescription medications). The majority of national and international attention and resources go toward illegal drug abuse. However, prescription drug abuse is a large and growing proportion of the complete drug abuse picture.

Each year, the National Household Survey on Drug Abuse (NHSDA), conducted by the Substance Abuse and Mental Health Services Administration (SAMHSA) of the United States Department of Health and Human Services, collects statistical data on five drug groups, including marijuana/hashish, psychotherapeutic drugs, cocaine/crack, hallucinogens, and inhalants. The medications included in the psychotherapeutic drug group are stimulants, sedatives, tranquilizers, and pain relievers. Codeine and other opioids constitute the majority of the pain relievers in the group.

In 2000, the NHSDA found 1.7% of all people 12 years and older reported nonmedical use of a psychotherapeutic medication during the previous month. More than 9 million Americans over age 12 reported use at any time during the year. Those in the 18- to 25-year-old age group have the highest rates of drug abuse. In 2000, 3.6% of individuals in that age group reported nonmedical use of prescription drugs in the month prior to when they were surveyed, but less than half that many, 1.6%, reported the same type of drug abuse in 1994. An estimated 1.6 million Americans used prescription pain relievers nonmedically for the first time in 1998. During the 1980s, there were generally fewer than 500,000 first-time users per year.

The Drug Abuse Warning Network (DAWN) is an ongoing program sponsored by SAMHSA. Approximately 500 hospital emergency rooms throughout the United States gather data from admitted patients on drugs of abuse (i.e., the number of times a specific drug is mentioned by ER patients). A study published in the *Journal of the American Medical Association* in 2000 compared the increase in legitimate medical use of opioids with one indicator of the increase in abuse of those same drugs. Specifically, five opioid drugs—morphine, fentanyl, oxycodone, hydromorphone, and meperidine—as a group showed a cumulative increase in medical use of nearly 250% from 1990 to 1996. Data collected from DAWN for the same time period showed a 7% increase in emergency room mentions of abuse of these drugs. As a proportion of all opioid drugs mentioned, the five drugs studied decreased from 23% in 1990 to 16% in 1996. This means that mentions of other opioid analgesics, including codeine (although raw numbers for codeine were not analyzed), increased during that time period by 16%. By comparison, the reports of abuse of illicit drugs increased 110%. Admittedly, the data collected by DAWN evaluates only one facet of the drug abuse problem—drug abuse contributing to emergency room visits. However, from these data at least, it does not appear that a significant increase in medical use of opioid drugs resulted in a proportionate increase in abuse. More studies looking at a broader picture of opioid analgesic abuse are needed.

Age, ethnic, and gender trends

Between 1990 and 1998, abuse of some illegal drugs among teens and young adults leveled off or decreased slightly. However, increases in new users of prescription pain relievers were reported in young teens, age 12–17, as well as in young adults age 18–25. In 2000, the NHSDA found that the youngest teens, age 12–14, reported psychotherapeutic medications as the most frequent drugs of abuse, with that group alone making up 53% of the total of all drug abuse reports. Teens and young adults in the

18–25 age group reported prescription drug abuse at a rate of 36%, while 28% of those over age 26 reported that type of abuse. Most teenagers begin prescription drug abuse by taking someone else's medication, usually someone from their family. Teens are also more likely than adults to be acquainted with someone who sells prescription drugs like codeine illegally.

On the other end of the age spectrum, prescription drug abuse among older adults is also a growing concern. Persons 65 and older comprise 13% of the United States population, but consume about 33% of all prescription drugs. A study of 1,500 elderly patients found that 3% were abusing prescription drugs. Unlike people in younger age groups, however, the elderly are more likely to misuse prescription drugs than abuse them. If abuse does occur, it may begin with misuse due to inappropriate prescribing or the patient not following instructions correctly. Continued misuse may then progress to dependence and abuse, especially with medications such as codeine. Other factors may influence codeine misuse and abuse in older adults. There may be age-related physical changes that influence codeine metabolism, or confusion about the effects codeine can produce. The elderly also have a higher likelihood of other undiagnosed medical conditions, such as depression, that increase the risk for codeine abuse. Finally, a survey of elderly persons admitted to a treatment program found that 70% were female and of the various drugs of abuse in that group, 70% were opioids.

The NHSDA study showed that boys in the youngest age group (12–17) are more likely to experiment with illegal drugs, but girls of that age have a 20% higher rate of prescription drug abuse. In addition, for all teens of that age that abuse prescription drugs, girls are twice as likely to become addicted as boys are. Women are also more likely to abuse and become addicted to prescription drugs in the young- and middle- adult age groups. Part of this may be that women are prescribed potential drugs of abuse more often than men are.

At all age groups, whites are more likely than other racial or ethnic groups to abuse prescription drugs, and many people who abuse these drugs have psychiatric disorders. In 2000, the *New England Journal of Medicine* published a report on a survey of pharmacies in New York. The data showed that pharmacies in predominantly minority neighborhoods (greater than 60% nonwhite population) were three times less likely to stock enough opioid drugs to fill prescriptions on demand than were pharmacies in predominantly white neighborhoods. This may be due to financial constraints in trying to maintain inventories of drugs in those minority neighborhood pharmacies. However, it may also be from fear of crime. A number of pharmacies in the United States were burglarized for their opioid drugs, especially the drug OxyContin, in the late 1990s. The events made national headlines, and intensified the debate over the benefits and drawbacks of opioid drugs.

LAW AND ORDER

Law enforcement groups at both state and national levels agree that crime related to prescription drug abuse is a serious problem. Despite this, very little attention and few resources are allocated to address the issue. According to a 1996 article in the *Los Angeles Times*, just 0.5% of all federal money spent on the war on drugs at that time went toward investigating and prosecuting prescription drug offenses. One example from the *Los Angeles Times* clearly illustrates the discrepancy that also exists in how perpetrators of prescription drug and illegal drug crimes are punished. Eric Tucker, a physician in California, pleaded guilty to issuing fraudulent prescriptions for the opioid drug Dilaudid, also known as "drugstore heroin." At the time of his arrest, the number of prescribed doses for Dilaudid that had come out of Tucker's office each year exceeded that of County-USC Medical Center, the largest public hospital on the west coast. He also issued more than 7,000 bogus prescriptions for the powerful stimulant Preludin. In total, Tucker was thought to have put millions of doses of powerfully addictive narcotic drugs on the illegal prescription drug market. At about the same time, a man from Los Angeles, Daniel Siemianowski, was convicted of possession of 4 oz (113 g) of crack and powder cocaine—his first offense. A comparison by weight would show that the amount of drugs in Siemianowski's possession was about the same as just 12 prescriptions written for 30 Dilaudid tablets each by Tucker. Siemianowski was sentenced to a year in jail, while Tucker lost his medical license and spent just eight days in jail. Most other cases in which a physician or dentist is convicted of a prescription drug crime also involve comparatively lenient sentences.

Health professionals (doctors, nurses, dentists, veterinarians, etc.) and their staff may be at risk for codeine abuse because of their ready access to the drug. On the other hand, one would expect health care workers to be at less risk due to their training and knowledge of the effects of drug abuse. In fact, health care workers do not appear to have rates of codeine or other opioid abuse much different from the rest of the population.

MENTAL EFFECTS

Most people describe the euphoria produced by codeine as a pronounced feeling of well-being and calmness. A few people may get a mild stimulant effect and a feeling of elation. Evidence indicates that the euphoria produced by codeine and other opioids is similar to, but stronger than, the perceived feeling from high levels of endogenous opioids in the body—the so-called endorphin rush experienced by some athletes after heavy exercise. Instead of euphoria after a codeine dose, some people report a feeling of dysphoria—a general feeling of discomfort and restlessness. Still other people may just feel drowsy, with no noticeable positive or negative effect on their mood.

It remains a misconception that opioids offer no true analgesic effect, but instead produce a type of euphoria that simply results in one not caring about their pain. With the discovery of opioid receptors in the central nervous system, along with an understanding of how opioids such as codeine affect nerve cells, no dispute remains that opioids are indeed potent pain relievers. Up to a certain limit (usually an amount great enough to produce serious side effects), the more codeine ingested in a single dose, the greater the analgesia and the more pronounced the mental effects would be.

People with moderate or severe pain who take prescribed doses of codeine usually obtain at least some relief from their pain, but generally do not report feelings of euphoria. Those with mild pain who take one of the higher doses of codeine (e.g., Tylenol #4) may experience pain relief along with some euphoria. People who abuse codeine are most likely to experience euphoric feelings, and are at the greatest risk of becoming addicted.

PHYSIOLOGICAL EFFECTS

Other than analgesia, the most common physiological effects produced by medicinal quantities of codeine are nausea, vomiting, constipation, and itching of the skin (pruritis). These symptoms would be considered relatively harmless (benign) side effects. They typically disappear in most people after taking the drug for several days, or by reducing the dosage. If someone has diarrhea prior to using codeine, the physiological side effect of constipation then becomes a medicinal effect for that symptom. For most people, the higher the codeine dose, the more likely side effects will be present or the more severe the side effects will be.

Harmful side effects

Overall, codeine's lower potency results in fewer side effects compared to other drugs in the class. The complication of greatest concern is respiratory depression. Opioids affect the area of the brain that controls breathing. A large enough single dose of any opioid, including codeine, can stop breathing completely, resulting in death. Combining codeine with another central nervous system depressant, such as alcohol or sedatives, is especially risky. Unfortunately, people who abuse codeine often abuse other drugs as well. While drowsiness itself is not a harmful side effect, it can be dangerous when driving or engaging in other activities that require concentration and alertness.

Since most codeine is dispensed as part of a compound preparation, potential side effects of the other drug(s) must also be considered. For instance, someone with stomach ulcers should not take codeine that is combined with a nonsteroidal anti-inflammatory drug (NSAID) such as aspirin or ibuprofen. Another type of risk from a compound preparation relates to codeine abuse. For instance, a person who abuses codeine might routinely take a dose of 100–200 mg of codeine to produce noticeable euphoria. Using Tylenol #3 to obtain this dose would also mean ingesting 1,000–2,000 mg of acetaminophen. Taking that amount of acetaminophen for any extended period presents a risk for liver damage, especially in combination with alcohol.

Long-term health effects

There are very few adverse health effects as far as organ or tissue damage from long-term (years) use of codeine. This is in contrast to most other abused drugs, with alcohol and tobacco being the obvious examples.

The relative lack of any known serious organ or tissue damage produced by codeine use is counterbalanced, however, by its high risk for abuse and addiction. Even though codeine may be the least addictive of the group, opioids are arguably the most addictive drugs known. Drugs with a high risk of addiction also present a high risk for long-term use, which can include either years of continual use or a repeated cycle of use and abstinence. The latter can be especially difficult with codeine given the potentially serious withdrawal symptoms associated with stopping the drug suddenly. Most people with codeine addiction do not seek professional help, and self-treating an addiction usually involves stopping the drug suddenly.

A sudden withdrawal from codeine after a long period of use always results in some withdrawal symptoms. The longer and more serious the abuse, and the more suddenly the drug is stopped, the more difficult and painful the withdrawal symptoms will be. Chronic use of codeine can result in some tolerance to the drug so that higher doses must be taken to obtain the same initial effects. However, the level of tolerance seems to be less in people using codeine legitimately for pain. Long-term use also can lead to physical dependence, a process in which the body adapts to the presence of the drug, resulting in withdrawal symptoms if its use is abruptly stopped. Symptoms of withdrawal can include restlessness, muscle and bone pain, insomnia, diarrhea, runny nose, chills with goose bumps, and involuntary leg movements. The involuntary leg movements associated with opioid withdrawal are what originally lead to the phrase "kicking the habit." The phrase "quitting cold turkey" originated because the goose bumps on a person's skin that often occur during withdrawal resemble cold turkey skin.

REACTIONS WITH OTHER DRUGS OR SUBSTANCES

Using alcohol while taking codeine poses a serious risk. Like codeine, alcohol is a CNS depressant, and the two drugs combined increase the risk of heavy sedation and respiratory depression. Other drugs that should be avoided or used only under a doctor's supervision while taking codeine include benzodiazepines (tranquilizers in the same class as Valium), most antihistamines, and sedatives/hypnotics (sleep medications). Certain types of antidepressants should be used with caution when taking codeine, especially monoamine oxidase (MAO) inhibitors and those in the selective serotonin reuptake inhibitor (SSRI) class. Some codeine abusers use glutethimide (Doriden), a potent tranquilizer, to produce effects similar to heroin increasing the risks for serious side effects and addiction.

TREATMENT AND REHABILITATION

Serious addiction to codeine is not as common as it once was, possibly due to the availability of greater numbers of competing, more potent opioids. The perception by some that addiction to a "weak" opioid like codeine is not serious results in fewer individuals seeking treatment for their codeine addiction. However, in those cases where treatment is needed, codeine addiction should be approached in the same manner as addiction to other opioids, such as heroin or morphine.

Codeine overdose can be treated with the opioid antagonist, Narcan (naloxone). The goal of treating codeine addiction is for the addicted person to stop taking the drug completely and permanently. Most people who overcome codeine addiction do so by themselves, but some may need professional assistance. In either case, it is invaluable for someone to have help and support from friends and family. For chronic addiction (addiction lasting more than one year), codeine may be replaced by methadone, another opioid medication. Methadone is provided to the patient either through a physician or through a qualified drug treatment program. In a structured setting, the patient and health care professionals have a much better chance of controlling drug use with methadone, and eventually may achieve complete abstinence. The benefits of methadone over codeine are that it only needs to be taken once a day, it reduces or eliminates withdrawal symptoms and the craving for codeine, and it has fewer side effects.

???? FACT OR FICTION

Many commonly held assumptions about codeine and other opioid use need to be modified, according to a consensus statement issued by the American Academy of Pain Medicine and the American Pain Society.

Fiction—Opioids are always addictive. Patients who use them regularly will become drug addicts.

Fact—Studies show that very few chronic pain patients become addicted to their opioid pain relievers. What's more, even known addicts can benefit from carefully supervised, judiciously prescribed opioids for treating pain due to serious medical conditions.

Fiction—Over time, chronic pain patients will develop a tolerance to opioids, making it necessary to continually increase the dosage.

Fact—Tolerance does not appear to be prevalent among long-term opioid users. In some cases, what appears to be a decrease in pain relief over time is actually a progression of the disease being treated.

Fiction—Opioids often cause prohibitive side effects, like depressed respiration, sedation, and nausea.

Fact—Respiratory depression tends to be short-lived and generally occurs only in patients who have just started taking a medication. Likewise, sedation and nausea usually decrease with continued use. (Adapted from Johns Hopkins Magazine, June 1999.)

PERSONAL AND SOCIAL CONSEQUENCES

Illicit drug use provides little or no personal and social benefits, though codeine and other opioids do offer personal and social medical benefits. However these benefits must be weighed against the potential costs of abuse and addiction for individuals and society.

Most codeine prescriptions are written for Schedule III preparations. These medications provide an important middle ground between two drug groups—less effective OTC and nonnarcotic prescription analgesics on one side, and Schedule II analgesics on the other. Distribution and prescriptions are more tightly regulated for Schedule II than for Schedule III drugs. Consequently, for a patient whose pain level is not severe enough to require a Schedule II drug, yet is too severe for or does not respond well to OTC or other prescription analgesics, codeine can provide an effective compromise.

The social consequences of having a broad range of analgesics to treat chronic pain are significant. Conditions associated with chronic pain are the largest contributors to lost work time and productivity. In addition, home and family life may be disrupted for those whose pain is not effectively treated. Therefore, while a doctor must weigh the risks and benefits of treating with codeine on an individual basis, judicious use of codeine and other opioids would seem to present much greater social benefits than costs.

Personal costs—financial, physical, and emotional—can be significant for those individuals who abuse codeine and become addicted. An established addiction can be expensive to maintain, even with a relatively inexpensive medication (through legal purchase) such as codeine. Many people describe a serious opioid addiction as "all consuming"; everything in their life eventually revolves around obtaining more of the drug. With the drug as their focus, they lose friends, alienate family members, and they may be unable to hold a job. With a lower cost and greater availability compared to other opioids, codeine may serve as a starting point for a progression to more powerful, costly, and addictive Schedule II drugs, not to mention illicit drugs.

It might seem logical that anyone who goes to great lengths to obtain codeine is addicted, abusing it recreationally, or selling it for profit, but this is not always the case. While the situation is improving, many people with chronic pain still find it difficult to locate a doctor who will prescribe opioid analgesics. A person with chronic pain may show drug-seeking behavior if they find it difficult to obtain prescriptions for the medication. In fact, a doctor treating such a person might mistake the behavior for psychological addiction rather than somewhat desperate attempts to obtain relief for an ineffectively treated condition.

Codeine plays a relatively minor role in the overall picture of opioid prescription drug abuse. Evidence indicates that proper prescribing of codeine for legitimate medical concerns does not greatly increase the risk of addiction and abuse. Those in the medical community agree that more education is needed on both sides to help prevent the potential for abuse and addiction, so that patients truly in need are not denied access to codeine based on misperceptions and fear. The benefits for individuals and society are great when chronic pain is treated safely and effectively.

LEGAL CONSEQUENCES

Whether requiring a written order in a hospital chart (or other inpatient health care institution) or a prescription written on a special form, hospital and community pharmacies exercise special caution when dispensing codeine and other controlled substances. In some cases, a doctor may choose to telephone the patient's pharmacy with the prescription. However, for medication such as codeine, they must provide their DEA number and some relevant medical information. This helps to prevent someone from calling a pharmacy to obtain codeine by impersonating a physician. It is unlikely that anyone other than a physician or dentist would have access to both a valid DEA number and the medical knowledge necessary to sound credible to pharmacy staff when ordering such a medication.

It is illegal to write a prescription or an order for codeine without a valid medical license. Those professionals that may legally write prescriptions or orders for codeine include medical doctors (MD), doctors of osteopathy (DO), podiatrists (PO), dentists (DDS), and veterinarians (DVM). Physicians or dentists who knowingly write multiple prescriptions for patients without a valid medical reason are subject to possible disciplinary action and criminal prosecution. Writing and filling fake prescriptions for profit is a more serious offense. Likewise, it is illegal to obtain, or try to obtain, prescriptions for codeine under false pretenses (fabricated symptoms and scenarios). Nineteen states have a law (a felony in some) prohibiting a patient from obtaining the same controlled substance from multiple prescribers within a limited time period (doctor shopping). Unlike the illegal activities associated with most other drugs, the perpetrators of crimes involving prescription drugs are most often white, middle-class women. Their crimes usually involve doctor shopping and/or prescription forgery.

Many people in the government and medical community fear that increased production of opioid drugs correlates with increased rates of abuse and addiction. Pharmacies were increasingly burglarized for their opioid drugs, which seemed to bolster this argument. However, the newsworthiness of those crimes serves to overemphasize one side of the debate. Studies have consistently shown that patients with chronic pain who use opioids appropriately rarely become addicted. In 2001 and 2002, a number of groups advocating for effective pain management joined with government agencies, including the Drug Enforcement Administration (DEA), to begin a long-term effort to increase the availability of effective pain management drugs for patients, while decreasing the illegal use and abuse of these drugs.

Legal history

In the United States, the Harrison Narcotics Act of 1914 provided the first real regulation of the general sale of opiates. The exceptions were sales to licensed physicians for use on their own patients, and sales to those people who could provide a written prescription from a doctor. The adoption of laws controlling the production and distribution of all prescription medications occurred primarily because of morphine and codeine.

Codeine is a controlled substance in the United States. Its manufacture and distribution are controlled by the Food and Drug Administration (FDA) and the DEA. The majority of other countries have controls similar to those of the United States. International control is overseen by the International Narcotic Control Board (INCB).

Several foreign countries and some states continue to sell medications with small amounts of codeine over the counter. In the United States, though, even OTC codeine medications have restrictions. A person purchasing codeine must be at least 18 years of age and provide valid identification. In addition, their name may be entered in a special logbook maintained by the pharmacy.

Federal guidelines, regulations, and penalties

Injectable forms of codeine are classified under the Controlled Substances Act (CSA) as Schedule II, even though they do not typically contain more than 60 mg per dose. Analgesics containing 15–60 mg of codeine per single dose carry a Schedule III classification (although the upper single dose limit in many states is 90 mg). Schedule III drugs have a lower potential for abuse than drugs in Schedule II, and abuse of the drug may lead to moderate or low physical dependence and/or high psychological dependence.

Medications containing less than 15 mg of codeine per single dose (most contain either 8 mg or 12 mg) are classified as Schedule V. Cough suppressants with codeine make up the majority of this category. Drugs in Schedule V have a low potential for abuse, but abuse may lead to limited physical dependence and/or psychological dependence compared to drugs in Schedule IV.

See also Fentanyl; Heroin; Meperidine; Morphine; Opium; Oxycodone

RESOURCES

Books

American Cancer Society. *American Cancer Society's Guide to Pain Control.* Atlanta: American Cancer Society Health Content Products, 2001.

Andrews, Tom. *Codeine Diary: A Memoir.* Toronto: Little, Brown and Company Limited, 1998.

Booth, Martin. *Opium: A History.* New York: St. Martin's Press, 1996.

Courtwright, David T. *Forces of Habit: Drugs and the Making of the Modern World.* Cambridge: Harvard University Press, 2001.

Kuhn, Cynthia, et al. *Buzzed: The Straight Facts About the Most Used and Abused Drugs from Alcohol to Ecstasy.* New York: W.W. Norton and Company, Inc., 1998.

Rudgley, Richard. *Essential Substances: A Cultural History of Intoxicants in Society.* New York: Kodansha America, Inc., 1994.

Periodicals

Brookoff, Daniel. "Chronic Pain: 1. A New Disease?" *Hospital Practice* 35 (July 15, 2000): 45-59.

Brookoff, Daniel. "Chronic Pain: 2. The Case for Opioids." *Hospital Practice* 35 (September 15, 2000): 69-84.

Demott, Kathryn. "Opioids Still Worthwhile Despite Street-drug Taint." *Clinical Psychiatry News* 29 (June 2001): 46.

Joranson, David E., et al. "Trends in Medical Use and Abuse of Opioid Analgesics." *The Journal of the American Medical Association* 282 (April 5, 2000): 1710-4.

Mitka, Mike. "Abuse of Prescription Drugs: Is a Patient Ailing or Addicted?" *The Journal of the American Medical Association* 283 (March 1, 2000): 1126.

Potter, Michael, et al. "Opioids for Chronic Nonmalignant Pain." *Journal of Family Practice* 50 (February 2001): 145.

Rich, Ben A. "Physicians' Legal Duty to Relieve Suffering." *The Western Journal of Medicine* 175 (September 2001): 151.

Walling, Anne D. "Codeine Plus Acetaminophen: Benefits and Side Effects." *American Family Physician* 54 (November 15, 1996): 2302.

Weikel, Dan. "Rx for an Epidemic: Prescription Fraud—Abusing the System. Token Enforcement Allows Pill Peddlers to Flourish." *Los Angeles Times* (August 18, 1996): A1.

Other

Codeine Information. (March 29, 2002). <http://codeine.50g.com>.

Purdue Pharma L.P. "Painfully Obvious: The Effects of Abusing Prescription Drugs." (March 29, 2002). <http://www.painfullyobvious.com>.

United Nations Office for Drug Control and Crime Prevention. <http://www.undcp.org>.

"The Vaults of Erowid: Documenting the Complex Relationship between Humans and Psychoactives." (March 29, 2002). <http://www.erowid.org>.

Organizations

Drug Enforcement Administration (DEA), Information Services Section (CPI), 2401 Jefferson Davis Highway, Alexandria,, VA, USA, 22301, <http://www.usdoj.gov/dea>.

National Institute on Drug Abuse (NIDA), National Institutes of Health, 6001 Executive Boulevard, Room 5213, Bethesda, MD, USA, 20892-9561, (301) 443-1124, (888) 644-6432, Information@lists.nida.nih.gov, <http://www.drugabuse.gov/NIDAHome.html>.

Office of Disease Prevention and Health Promotion, U.S. Department of Health and Human Services, 200 Independence Avenue SW., Room 738G, Washington, DC, USA, 20201, (202) 401-6295, <http://odphp.osophs.dhhs.gov>.

Office of FirstGov c/o GSA, 750 17th Street, NW, Suite 200, Washington, DC, USA, 20006-4634, <http://www.whitehousedrugpolicy.gov>.

SAMHSA-Center for Substance Abuse Prevention (CSAP), (301) 443-0365.

Substance Abuse and Mental Health Services Administration (SAMHSA), U.S. Dept. of Health and Human Services, 5600 Fishers Lane, Rockville,, MD, USA, 20857, (301) 443-6239, info@samhsa.gov, <http://www.samhsa.gov>.

Substance Abuse and Mental Health Services Administration (SAMHSA)/Center for Substance Abuse Treatment (CSAT), 5600 Fishers Lane, Rockville, MD, USA, 20857, (301) 443-5700, info@samsha.gov, <http://www.samhsa.gov>.

U.S. Food and Drug Administration (FDA), 5600 Fishers Lane, Rockville, MD, USA, 20857-0001, (888) 463-6332, <http://www.fda.gov>.

Scott J. Polzin, MS

CREATINE

OVERVIEW

Creatine was first discovered and isolated in muscle tissue in 1832 by French chemist Michel Chevreul. The compound is a naturally occurring, non-essential amino acid found in red meat, pork, dairy products, and fish. Most people take in approximately 1–2 grams (g) of dietary creatine from these sources daily (vegetarians somewhat less). Together, the kidneys, liver, and pancreas produce an additional 1–2 g of creatine daily, synthesized from the amino acids L-arginine, glycine, and L-methionine. Both creatine and phosphocreatine (which is creatine bound to phosphate; PCr, Crphos) are stored in skeletal muscle, organs, and body tissues. Phosphocreatine helps to power muscle contractions and decrease the amount of time the muscle takes to recover and "refuel."

Oral creatine supplements first gained popularity among athletes in the early 1990s following the publication of a Karolinska Institute study that found that subjects who took creatine supplements experienced a significant increase in total muscle creatine content. In theory, increased creatine stores would increase PCr stored in the muscles, which would in turn provide a larger power supply for anaerobic muscle activity and exercise (short bursts of exercise which don't require oxygen).

Creatine was thrust onto the global athletic scene in 1992 when British sprinters Linford Christie and Sally Gunnel won Olympic gold in Barcelona after reportedly training with the aid of creatine supplementation. Since that time, a number of clinical studies have looked at both the ergogenic (output enhancing effect) and therapeutic benefits of creatine.

OFFICIAL NAMES: Creatine monohydrate, creatine phosphate
STREET NAMES: Legal steroid, muscle candy, ergogenic aid, performance-enhancing substance
DRUG CLASSIFICATIONS: Not scheduled, dietary supplement

Because creatine is considered a nutritional supplement, it is available legally and without a prescription in the United States. As of early 2002, creatine supplementation was not explicitly prohibited by the U.S. Olympic Committee (USOC), the National Collegiate Athletic Association (NCAA), the Major League Baseball (MLB), the National Football League (NFL), and other major national athletic organizations. However, a lack of well-designed clinical studies of creatine's long-term effects combined with loose regulatory standards for creatine supplement products manufactured in the United States has caused some athletic associations, including the USOC, to caution against its use without banning it outright.

Despite these issues, creatine remains well-known as a nutritional, performance-enhancing supplement used by athletes to improve high-intensity muscle endurance and performance. Bodybuilders and weightlifters supplement with creatine to bulk up muscles, and athletes involved in team sports train with creatine to increase their energy for sprints and other short and intense muscular tasks. Statistics show that the use of creatine by adolescent and adult athletes is growing. Yet research is still largely inconclusive on exactly how

KEY TERMS

AMINO ACIDS: Organic molecules that make up proteins. The human body requires 20 amino acids to function properly. Essential amino acids are supplied by food and non-essential amino acids (including creatine) are produced within the body.

ANAEROBIC EXERCISE: Exercise that isn't fueled by oxygen intake (as aerobic exercise is). Anaerobic exercise is defined by short, vigorous, and frequent muscle contractions, and includes activities like sprinting and weight lifting.

ANTIOXIDANT: A substance that prevents oxidation and protects cells from free radicals. Free radicals are molecules that contain an odd number of electrons. They can cause tissue death and damage.

ATHEROSCLEROSIS: A cardiovascular condition which causes arteries to narrow, or clog, with plaque build-up from excess blood cholesterol.

CONGESTIVE HEART FAILURE: A potentially fatal condition in which the heart loses its ability to pump an adequate volume of blood. As blood flow slows, fluid builds up in tissues throughout the body.

DIETARY SUPPLEMENT HEALTH AND EDUCATION ACT (DSHEA): Passed in 1994, this law allows manufacturers to sell dietary and nutritional supplements without federal regulation. According to this act, supplements can be regulated only after they are proven to be harmful to users.

ERGOGENIC: Something that increases work output.

INBORN ERROR OF METABOLISM: An inherited genetic defect present from birth that causes a deficiency in the body's essential enzymes and impairs metabolism.

U.S. PHARMACOPEIA (USP): A non-profit organization that provides standards for prescription and over-the-counter drugs, nutritional and dietary supplements, and health care products. USP publishes its standards in the United States Pharmacopeia and the National Formulary (USP-NF), which are officially recognized by the U.S. Food and Drug Administration (FDA). USP also has a dietary supplement verification program (DSVP).

and in what situations supplements help athletes out of the laboratory and on the field.

CHEMICAL/ORGANIC COMPOSITION

Endogenous creatine is creatine that is synthesized, or manufactured, within the body by the liver, kidneys, and pancreas. It is produced from the amino acids arginine and glycine, and methionine, and is then transported throughout the body where it is stored in the organs, tissues, and muscles. The body can biosynthesize, or manufacture, up to 2 g of creatine daily. However, animal studies have shown that when supplemental creatine is taken regularly, the amount of endogenous creatine produced by the body is reduced. This tendency is thought to reverse itself once creatine supplementation stops.

The majority of creatine in the body (over 95%) is stored in skeletal muscle. About two-thirds of this is bound with phosphates, forming the compound creatine phosphate (PCr).

PCr acts on anaerobic adenosine triphosphate (ATP), the substance that powers muscle contractions. When ATP powers a muscle contraction, it loses one of its three phosphate molecules, changing from a triphosphate to a diphospate. The phosphate loss converts ATP to ADP (or adenosine diphosphate). Creatine phosphate provides an extra phosphate molecule for the ADP to convert or regenerate quickly back to ATP again and refuel muscle performance. Storing extra creatine in the skeletal muscles theoretically will provide for faster, more frequent ATP conversion.

Creatine monohydrate, the most popular form of off-the-shelf creatine supplementation, is an odorless, white, water-soluble powder. Its chemical name is N-(aminoiminomethyl)-N-methylglycine monohydrate.

In addition to unadulterated creatine monohydrate, special formulations of the supplement are available in the U.S. market which may include supplemental phosphates, amino acids, carbohydrates, and other dietary additives. There have also been laboratory reports of creatine that has been altered during the manufacturing process with other unlabeled and potentially harmful substances.

INGESTION METHODS

Creatine is sold in powdered, liquid, tablet, capsule, and chewing-gum formulations. The most popular formulation of creatine is creatine monohydrate, which is also the creatine formula that has been most extensively tested in clinical studies. Pure creatine monohydrate is a white, odorless, crystal powder with a faintly sweet taste. Other variations of creatine supplements are available, including creatine citrate and creatine phosphate. However, the clinical data on the effectiveness of these formulas is limited.

There are two types of dosing techniques commonly used. The first is to start with a large loading dose of 20 g, taken in 5-g increments four times a day, for 2–5 days. This is followed by a lower daily maintenance dose of 2 g or less for up to six weeks. The second method is to forgo the loading dose and simply use the smaller daily dose. The latter method may avoid some of the gastrointestinal distress and cramping that has been occasionally reported with loading doses.

Oversupplementation with creatine is common, and can be harmful to individuals with existing kidney problems or to athletes who don't properly hydrate themselves during workouts. Human skeletal muscle can only store up to 160 millimoles (mmol)/kg per day. After this limit is reached, any excess dietary or supplemental creatine will be excreted in the urine. When the body is already demanding fluids to replace those naturally lost during physical activity, severe dehydration can be a very real danger. For this reason, anyone taking creatine should always maintain adequate fluid intake of at least six to eight glasses of water daily.

Creatine is sometimes mixed or taken with sports drinks or other carbohydrate-heavy beverages. This practice is based on results of a 1996 clinical study published in the *American Journal of Physiology*, which reported that carbohydrate solutions increased uptake of creatine by skeletal muscle in study subjects. The *American College of Sports Medicine* recommends against regular heavy carbohydrate loading of 100 g or more along with creatine dosing because of the potential negative health affects of high sugar intake over time.

Some creatine products currently on the market are also "enriched" with other nutrients, including protein, glucose, vitamins, herbal ingredients, and other amino acids. Again, no hard data exists on the effectiveness of taking creatine in combination with other dietary supplements or herbals.

THERAPEUTIC USE

Children with guanidinoacetate methyltransferase (GAMT) deficiency require long-term treatment with creatine supplementation. GAMT deficiency is a rare inborn error of metabolism caused by an insufficient amount of stored creatine along with an excessive accumulation of guanidinoacetate (GAA) in the brain. GAA is one of the building blocks of creatine formed through a chemical reaction of the amino acid arginine. GAMT deficiency, which is typically diagnosed in infancy, causes seizures and developmental delays that can be at least partially reversed with high doses of supplemental creatine.

Creatine has also been shown to be of some benefit in neurological and musculoskeletal diseases and conditions that involve muscle wasting or deterioration of muscle function, such as amyotrophic lateral sclerosis (ALS), myasthenia gravis, muscular dystrophy, Huntington's disease, Parkinson's disease, and McArdle's disease.

Several studies have demonstrated that creatine may improve muscle function and increase exercise capacity in older adults experiencing age-related strength and exercise capacity loss. As of early 2002, only a handful of clinical studies had explored this phenomenon, and further research is needed to confirm and explain this finding. It should be noted, however, that there is some research that suggests creatine may not be as effective in older users as it is in younger individuals.

Individuals who face extended bedrest or immobilization in order to recover from surgery may also benefit from creatine supplementation. One study, which looked at knee surgery patients in rehabilitation, found that subjects who received creatine intravenously during their recovery gained leg strength faster than those who did not. Further research published in the *Archives of Physical Medicine and Rehabilitation* in 2002 found that creatine supplementation improved upper body exercise capacity in patients with cervical spinal cord injuries.

Creatine may also be a promising treatment for other types of physical rehabilitation. Research conducted at Catholic University Leuven (Belgium) looked at the role of creatine in the recovery of university students who had been immobilized in full leg casts for two weeks. The students who received creatine monohydrate supplements had greater muscle function and mass than the students who received a placebo at both three weeks and 10 weeks of physical rehabilitation.

New research on the antioxidative properties of creatine shows that the supplement may have even therapeutic properties beyond the treatment of musculoskeletal disease and injury. A 2000 study in *Annals of Neurology* reported that creatine had a protective effect against traumatic brain injury (TBI) in animal studies, reducing brain damage in mice and rats by up to 50%.

In other animal research, clinical studies have demonstrated that creatine inhibits the growth of solid tumors in rats. No data on the effects of creatine supplementation on cancer in humans had been published as of early 2002.

Finally, creatine supplements may be useful in the treatment of heart problems. Creatine has improved exercise capacity in patients suffering from congestive heart failure, and lowered blood cholesterol in animal studies. Limited study of creatine's effect on blood cholesterol levels in healthy humans has had mixed results, with one study reporting a positive impact and another reporting no effect at all. Further research is needed to determine if creatine is beneficial in improving blood cholesterol and preventing atherosclerosis.

???? FACT OR FICTION

Does creatine cause cancer? In early 2001, the media was abuzz with reports that creatine had been linked to cancer. The story stemmed from a report issued by France's Agency of Medical Security for Food (AFSSA), which claimed that creatine posed a "potential carcinogenic risk" for users and urged all sports governing bodies to institute a ban of the substance. The report was allegedly based on a review of the available scientific research on creatine supplementation. But was the real science lost in translation?

Several U.S. researchers speculate that the authors of the French report mistakenly drew their conclusion from published studies analyzing naturally occurring creatine found in protein-rich animal products such as beef and pork. When these creatine-containing foods are heated and cooked, the creatine and amino acids interact to form compounds known as heterocyclic amines (HCAs), which have been shown to cause cancer in animal studies. The level of HCAs can vary with cooking method and other factors. Creatine monohydrate does not contain HCAs, and as of early 2002, no published or reported clinical research existed to demonstrate that creatine monohydrate taken in supplement form causes cancer.

USAGE TRENDS

Worldwide demand for nutritional supplements is projected to reach $162 billion by 2004. Sports supplements in particular are a rapidly-growing market in the United States. According to *Nutrition Business Journal*, a dietary supplement trade group publication, Americans spent $1.6 billion on creatine and other performance-enhancing dietary products in 2000.

Scope and severity

Market research analysts Frost & Sullivan report that the U.S. creatine market is growing an estimated 15–20% each year, and sales of the product are projected to exceed $350 million by 2006. The American College of Sports Medicine has estimated the national consumption of creatine in 1999 was 2,755 tons (2,500 metric tons).

Age, ethnic, and gender trends

Several studies and surveys have found that creatine use is on the rise among adolescent athletes in middle and high schools, with use of the supplement being reported in every grade from the sixth through the twelfth. Creatine use and awareness of use by peers was more common among boys, and at least one study published in the *Southern Medical Journal* (2001) found that the majority of student athletes were misinformed about the proper dosing or "loading method" of the supplement and consumed excessive amounts of creatine.

The University of Wisconsin's Department of Sports Medicine found that 30% of high school football players surveyed in that state used or had used creatine, and the use of the supplement tended to increase with age. Similarly, a survey of high school and middle school athletes in Westchester County, New York, reported creatine use among 44% of high school seniors surveyed.

Another large-scale national survey conducted by the Blue Cross and Blue Shield Association's Healthy Competition Foundation in 2001 found that an estimated one million adolescents surveyed (12–17 years of age) had tried performance-enhancing substances such as creatine. In addition, 55% of those surveyed knew someone who took supplements to improve sports performance.

A 2001 National Collegiate Athletic Association report entitled "NCAA Study of Substance Use Habits of College Student-Athletes" revealed that among the 29.8% of NCAA athletes who admitted using dietary supplements in the past 12 months, creatine was taken by 25.8% (second only to protein supplements). Fifty-seven percent of these athletes first used nutritional supplements in high school.

The Third National Health and Nutrition Examination Survey (NHANES III), a national study conducted by the National Center for Health Statistics (NCHS) and the U.S. Centers for Disease Control (CDC) reported that 40% of Americans had used a dietary supplement in the month before they were interviewed for the study. Although NHANES did not break down supplement use into specific subtypes, the data gives some interesting insights into the growing acceptance of dietary supplement products in America.

Thirty percent of African Americans surveyed in NHANES III reported supplement use, as did 29% of Mexican Americans. Supplement use was highest among Caucasians (43%), and women were more likely to take them than men (44% vs. 35%). Interestingly, this gender gap appears to be reversed in the use of creatine and other performance-enhancing sports supplements, where males have a higher incidence of use. This is likely attributable to the fact that overall, U.S. high school and collegiate athletic programs have a larger population of male athletes than female. In 2001, there were 232,000 male athletes playing at the college level compared to 163,000 female. Similarly, 2.7 million girls took part in high school athletic programs during the 1998-99 school year, compared to 3.8 million boys.

MENTAL EFFECTS

There are no known long-term psychological effects from creatine supplementation. However, at least one study has linked the use of performance-enhancing supplements to an increased incidence of health risk behaviors. The 2001 study, which surveyed approximately 500 men and women between the ages of 17 and 35, found that study participants who took ergogenic nutritional supplements such as creatine were more likely to get drunk, drink and drive, and become involved in physical confrontations. However, since the research was limited by the fact that it involved a very specific population (subjects were new recruits entering military service), further study is needed to determine if ergogenic aids such as creatine are directly linked to an increase in these behaviors.

PHYSIOLOGICAL EFFECTS

Creatine is an ergogenic aid, increasing energy output for short, rapid bursts of muscle contractions (anaerobic exercise). More simply put, creatine recharges the muscles for activities requiring short, strong, and repetitive bursts of activity, such as sprints or weight lifting. It also minimizes muscle fatigue during contractions.

However, study results have been mixed as to exactly for which activities creatine has an ergogenic effect. For example, studies involving stationary cycle sprints have demonstrated positive performance enhancing results for creatine, but it is still unknown whether these results can be consistently reproduced in actual competition outside of the laboratory. In addition, some cycling studies have not shown any significant benefit to creatine supplementation.

The literature does reach a consensus on one point—creatine does not enhance aerobic activity, which is required in endurance sports such as cross-country running, basketball, or long-distance cycling. However, to the extent that these sports may require short bursts of activity, such as sprints at the end of a cycling or running race, creatine may offer athletes some performance gains.

Creatine supplementation causes rapid weight gain, mostly likely via water retention by skeletal muscles. The typical weight gain during the loading period of creatine supplementation is 1–4 lb (0.45–1.8 kg). Whether this weight gain comes from water retention, an increase of lean body mass, or a combination of both has not been conclusively established. Research has shown that individuals taking creatine urinate less during the first several days of the loading dose period, which may support the water retention theory. Further studies are again needed to determine the exact mechanisms by which creatine increases overall weight.

Once creatine phosphate is metabolized, it is converted to creatinine, a waste product, which is cleared

Creatine was thrust into the global athletic scene in 1992 when British sprinter Linford Christie won a gold medal after reportedly training with the aid of creatine supplements. Photo by Mark Duncan, AP/Wide World Photos. *Reproduced by permission.*

from the bloodstream by the kidneys. Excess free creatine (or creatine unbound to phosphate) is also cleared from the body this way. Elevated serum (or blood) creatinine levels of over 1.2 mg/dL for women and 1.4 mg/dL for men may indicate the onset of kidney disease. Anyone taking creatine supplements for therapeutic or athletic purposes should do so under a doctor's care. Regular serum creatinine tests may be recommended for these individuals to monitor their kidney function.

IN THE NEWS

What do home run king Mark McGwire, French tennis champ Mary Pierce, international soccer star Zinedine Zidane, British sprinter Linford Christie, and NFL tight end Shannon Sharpe all have in common? All have spoken openly to the media about their use of creatine supplements in athletic training.

According to *Nutrition Business Journal*, a trade publication of the dietary supplement industry, sales of performance-enhancing nutritional supplements skyrocketed when McGwire spoke publicly of his creatine and androstenedione (andro) use during the media blitz surrounding his 70 single-season home-run hitting streak in the 1998 major league baseball season. The professional athlete as role model is a time-honored tradition in the U.S., and corporations such as McDonald's and General Mills scrambled to sign up McGwire to endorse Wheaties and Big Macs following his record-breaking season.

The full impact that the well-publicized use of supplements by sports icons has had on young athletes worldwide is difficult to determine. A 2000 survey by the Kaiser Family Foundation found that 73% of 10–17 year olds surveyed cited a famous athlete as someone they looked up to or wanted to be like. And while 55% were aware of Mark McGwire's use of andro, only 5% reported ever having purchased a dietary supplement because of a famous athlete. Yet the fact remains that performance-enhancing supplement use is at an all-time high among America's youth.

Anyone with existing kidney disease, or with health conditions that put them at high risk for kidney problems (such as diabetes) should avoid creatine supplements.

Pregnant women, women who breastfeed, and children and adolescents under 18 years of age should avoid creatine use, as its long-term effect on these populations has not been adequately studied. Individuals with chronic medical conditions should consult with their healthcare professional before taking creatine or any other dietary supplement.

Harmful side effects

Some athletes using creatine supplements for training have reported muscle cramping and gastrointestinal distress (i.e., diarrhea, stomach cramps, vomiting), particularly with loading doses. At this time, all reports are anecdotal, which means that they are reported by individual users or healthcare providers but have not been conclusively proven through clinical research or controlled studies.

Creatine supplementation causes water retention by muscle tissue, which may be the source of muscle cramps. It has also been theorized that athletes who experience this side effect have a fluid or electrolyte imbalance due to dehydration. In some cases, adequate water intake may eliminate the muscle cramping.

As of early 2002, controlled clinical studies had not discovered any direct link between creatine use and muscle pain or strains when supplements are taken according to generally accepted guidelines. In fact, preliminary results from an Arkansas State University study of college baseball players found that those who used creatine did not have any more cramping or muscle injuries than non-supplementing players.

Gastrointestinal side effects, such as nausea, vomiting, diarrhea, and stomach cramps, have also not been conclusively linked to creatine supplements that are taken following generally accepted guidelines. The practice of taking creatine during or immediately prior to a workout has been found to cause gastrointestinal distress after exercise, as has taking creatine with large amounts of sugar or glucose, which has a tendency to slow digestion. Neither of these ingestion methods is recommended by the American College of Sports Medicine. Further controlled clinical studies are needed to determine the mechanisms and prevalence of these side effects.

The Special Nutritionals Adverse Event Monitoring System (SN/AEMS) of the U.S. Food and Drug Administration (FDA), a database of consumer reactions to nutritional supplements and substances, has had 31 reports of adverse reactions to products containing creatine between 1993–1998. Reported symptoms include (but were not limited to):

- seizures
- headache
- shortness of breath
- nausea
- rash
- irregular heartbeat
- fatigue

Some of the SN/AEMS incidents involved creatine monohydrate that was mixed with or taken with other supplements and substances, so it is difficult to determine to what extent creatine played a role in these reactions. There have also been anecdotal case reports of hypertension (high blood pressure) and elevated liver enzymes in athletes taking creatine supplements.

Dehydration may also be a risk for creatine users. Creatine causes skeletal muscle to absorb intercellular fluid from bodily tissues and into the muscle where it is retained. For this reason, athletes who are already losing fluid during physical activity may be further dehydrated by creatine supplementation.

In addition, muscle can only absorb up to 160 mmol/kg of creatine. All excess dietary and supplemental creatine must be excreted out of the body, which can increase urinary output and put undue stress on the kidneys.

There have also been published reports of fatalities in individuals using creatine monohydrate. During November and December of 1997, three collegiate wrestlers in three different states died during training to "make weight" for upcoming wrestling meets. Although there was initially widespread media speculation that creatine played a major role in their sudden deaths, it was later determined by the U.S. Centers for Disease Control (CDC) that the fatalities were directly attributable to severe hyperthermia (overheating, or heat exhaustion) and dehydration. All three had been attempting rapid weight loss by "sweating off" the pounds, wearing rubber suits to undertake a strenuous workout regimen, and refusing adequate fluid intake.

Although the CDC did not cite creatine use as a factor in these dehydration-related deaths, the American College of Sports Medicine (ACSM) notes that preliminary clinical evidence indicates that creatine does appear to affect fluid balance in athletes. In a consensus statement on the use of creatine supplementation, the ACSM has said that "The potential acute effects of high-dose creatine supplementation on body fluid balance has not been fully investigated, and ingestion of creatine before or during exercise is not recommended." The ACSM also recommends that creatine supplementation should be avoided by anyone exercising or participating in sports in extremely high temperatures due to the dehydration risk.

Because creatine is regulated by the FDA as a dietary supplement and not a drug, the purity of the product is a concern. A test of 100 popular nutritional supplements conducted by the International Olympic Committee (IOC) at the German Sports University in Cologne found that 16 were adulterated with nandrolone, a steroid. Nandrolone was not a listed ingredient on the product label, and most of the creatine products tested originated in the United States.

In other independent tests, ConsumerLab.com, a privately held U.S. company that specializes in laboratory analysis of nutritional and herbal supplements for purity, strength, and truth in labeling, found that 15% of creatine supplements tested did not meet industry standards for creatine content, purity, and label claims.

Long-term health effects

The data on the long-term health effects of creatine supplementation is extremely limited. However, at least one animal study has found that creatine caused a decline in kidney function in rats with existing renal (kidney) disease. In addition, published case reports have indicated that creatine can cause further renal impairment in people with pre-existing kidney disease. However, several studies of healthy athletes have shown that both short-term and extended creatine supplementation had no effect on kidney function.

Creatine is not recommended for use by individuals with kidney problems, or by anyone at risk for kidney disease (such as those with a family history of kidney problems or diabetes). Again, further controlled clinical studies are needed to determine the long-term impact and safety of creatine supplement use on human renal function.

REACTIONS WITH OTHER DRUGS OR SUBSTANCES

According to the *Physician's Desk Reference (PDR) for Nutritional Supplements*, there are no known adverse interactions between creatine monohydrate supplements and prescription drugs, herbs, and/or other dietary supplements. However, the effects of creatine may be decreased or altered by the use of other drugs or supplements, so anyone considering taking the supplement should consult a physician first.

Creatine has a dehydrating affect, and ingestion of other diuretic substances such as caffeine may increase the chance of rapid and dangerous fluid loss. In addition to enhancing this diuretic affect, caffeine may also interfere with the ergogenic activity of creatine. A small Belgian study published in the *Journal of Applied Physiology* in early 2002 found that caffeine ingestion of three or more days interfered with the ability of creatine supplementation to shorten muscle relaxation time between isometric muscle contractions. Caffeine is a common ingredient in soft drinks, coffee, tea, chocolate, and other foods and beverages, and is used by some endurance athletes as a training aid.

There are reports of illness and adverse reactions arising in individuals taking creatine in conjunction with other supplement products. One such case study involved a man suffering a stroke after consuming both ma huang extract and creatine monohydrate. It is difficult to determine the exact role creatine plays in cases involving the use of more than one supplement product, but these incidents emphasize the need for anyone taking dietary or nutritional supplements to do so with extreme caution and consult their doctor or pharmacist about possible interactions. Just like prescription drugs, "natural" and herbal products can trigger dangerous interactions with other supplements and with prescription or over-the-counter medications.

TREATMENT AND REHABILITATION

None.

PERSONAL AND SOCIAL CONSEQUENCES

Because creatine is a legal dietary supplement and a non-addictive substance, the social pressures accompanying its use are not as intense as those that surround controlled substances and illicit drugs. And since the major professional U.S. sporting organizations allow its use in training, it does not have the stigma that steroids and other banned substances have. In addition, since the creatine use of a number of famous and talented professional athletes has been well-publicized by the media, many amateur athletes view the supplement as a miracle-drug of sorts.

The use of creatine by high-profile athletes around the world has also increased its popularity among youth and adolescents, who are taking the supplement in record numbers. A recent survey by the Healthy Competition Foundation found that 390,000 children between 10 and 14 years of age had taken performance-enhancing supplements of some type, and 57% of all respondents had used creatine. Unfortunately, there has not been a similar rise in education efforts about the supplement, and many who supplement with creatine do so in a manner that is inconsistent with the current clinical research (i.e., over-supplementation, use for non-anaerobic activities, etc.), possibly endangering their health.

In recent years, there has been a trend against the use of creatine and other performance-enhancing supplements among high school and collegiate athletic organizations. The National Federation of State High School Associations developed a position statement that states that "coaches should never supply, recommend or permit the use of any drug, medication, or food supplement solely for performance-enhancing purposes."

And in August 2000, the National Collegiate Athletic Association (NCAA) released a list of permissible and nonpermissible nutritional supplements that institutions and coaching staffs may provide their athletes. Under the NCAA policy, only those supplements that are considered non-muscle building substances can be provided to an NCAA athlete by a coach or institution. Creatine is considered a nonpermissible substance, however, athletes may still purchase and take the supplement on their own initiative and at their own risk.

LEGAL CONSEQUENCES

As previously stated, creatine is not a controlled substance and is available for over-the-counter retail purchase in the United States.

Legal history

As of early 2002, creatine supplementation was not on the list of banned or prohibited supplements of the International Olympic Committee, the United States Olympic Committee, or the NCAA. However, since nutritional supplements are not closely regulated by the FDA, the United States Anti-Doping Agency (the USADA, which oversees drug testing for the USOC) warns that ingestion of any nutritional supplement is at the athlete's own risk.

A number of prominent international sports and sports medicine organizations—including the International Olympic Committee, the Federation Internationale de Nation Amateur (FINA, the world governing body of swimming), the Sport Nutrition Advisory Committee of the Coaching Association of Canada, the U.S. Anti-Doping Agency, and the UK Sports Council—also maintain a "take at your own risk" policy for the use of creatine and other nutritional supplements by athletes. Some associations such as the Irish Sports Council have taken a stronger stance, advising athletes against creatine and performance supplement use of any kind. The French Rugby Federation (FFR) has an outright ban on creatine. In addition, France has classified creatine as a performance-enhancing drug, and its sale is banned in that country.

There have been cases of Olympic athletes taking adulterated supplement products they assumed were pure and later testing positive for steroids and other banned substances not listed on the product label. American bobsledder Pavle Jovanovic and Norweigan Greco-Roman wrestler Fritz Aanes are just two of the dozens of Olympic athletes banned in recent years for positive steroid drug tests. Both Jovanovic and Aanes claimed they took the banned substance unintentionally when they ingested contaminated dietary supplements. Subsequent testing of Aanes's dietary supplement did indeed find the banned steroid precursor nandrolone. However, even if steroid ingestion is unintentional, the athlete is still assumed to be responsible for its use, and Jovanovic and Aanes were banned from competition for two years as a result.

In 2001 the International Olympic Committee announced that 15–20% of the approximately 600 nutritional supplements the agency tested were adulterated with substances that could lead to positive doping tests. The IOC and the World Anti-Doping Agency (WADA), called upon the U.S. government for stricter regulation and labeling of supplements.

Federal guidelines, regulations, and penalties

Creatine is classified as a nutritional or dietary supplement, and as such it is regulated by the United States Food and Drug Administration (FDA) as a dietary supplement. Dietary supplements do not have to meet the same stringent manufacturing and clinical testing and approval requirements that are required of drugs before reaching the U.S. consumer market. Federal legislation known as the Dietary Supplement Health and Education Act (DSHEA) was passed in 1994 in an effort to standardize the manufacture, labeling, composition, and safety of botanicals, herbs, and nutritional supplements. In January 2000, the FDA's Center for Food Safety and Applied Nutrition (CFSAN) announced a 10-year plan for establishing and fully implementing these regulations by the year 2010.

But DSHEA is very different then the standard approval process for drugs and medical devices, and emphasizes the regulatory enforcement of label claims and advertising and marketing issues rather than the efficacy and quality of the supplements themselves. Unlike new drug and medical device applications, controlled clinical trials aren't part of the supplement review process, nor is any FDA inspection of a company's manufacturing facilities or quality control systems.

Under the act, a dietary supplement manufacturer is required to make certain submissions or notifications to the FDA only when specific health claims are made for the product. And the primary responsibility for the safety of the supplement rests with the product manufacturer; any required regulatory submissions can be made up to 30 days after the supplements are already available for sale to the general public. There are also no regulatory restrictions on the serving size a manufacturer chooses for the supplement, nor on the amount of included active ingredients. As such, the potency and dosage of creatine supplements may vary widely from manufacturer to manufacturer.

Anyone deciding to take creatine monohydrate should obtain the supplement from a reputable manufacturer that observes stringent quality control procedures and industry-accepted good manufacturing practices

(GMPs). A good way to determine the quality of a supplement is to look for the designations "USP" or "USP Verified" on the product label. This designation indicates that the supplement meets the guidelines of the U.S. Pharmacopeia dietary supplement verification program (DSVP). Dietary supplements prepared under USP guidelines meet nationally recognized strength, quality, purity, packaging, and labeling standards as recommended by the FDA. The USP seal also tells the consumer that the supplement manufacturer is in compliance with FDA-prescribed GMPs.

See also Steroids

RESOURCES

Books

Burke, Edmund R. *Creatine: What You Need to Know.* New York: Avery Penguin Putnam, 1999.

Hendler, Sheldon, and David Rorvik, eds. *PDR for Nutritional Supplements.* Montvale, NJ: Medical Economics/Thomson Healthcare, 2001.

Periodicals

Murphy, Dee. "What You Should Know About Creatine." *Current Health* 26, no. 6 (Feb 2000): 13.

"Sports Supplement Dangers." *Consumer Reports* 66, no. 6 (June 2001): 40.

Other

U.S. Food and Drug Administration. Center for Food Safety & Applied Nutrition. Office of Nutritional Products, Labeling, and Dietary Supplements (ONPLDS). <http://www.cfsan.fda.gov/~dms/supplmnt.html>. (April 1, 2002).

U.S. Anti-Doping Agency (USADA): The Independent Anti-doping Agency for Olympic Sports in the U.S. <http://www.usantidoping.org/>. (April 1, 2002).

Organizations

Healthy Competition Foundation, PO Box 81289, Chicago, IL, USA, 60681-0289, (312) 297-5824, healthycompetition@bcbsa.com, <http://www.healthycompetition.org>.

Paula Anne Ford-Martin

DESIGNER DRUGS

OFFICIAL NAMES: 2C-B (4-bromo-2,5 dimethoxyphenethy-lamine)
STREET NAMES: Nexus, 2C-B, bromo, toonies, performax 2's, spectrum, synergy, venus, Eve, erox, zenith, cloud nine, utopia, cee-beetje, afterburner, bromo mescaline
DRUG CLASSIFICATIONS: Schedule I, synthetic hallucinogen
OFFICIAL NAMES: 3, 4-Methylenedioxymethamphetamine (MDMA)
STREET NAMES: Ecstasy, E, X, XTC, Adam, Eve, hug, beans, love drug
DRUG CLASSIFICATIONS: Schedule I, hallucinogen
OFFICIAL NAMES: Gamma hydroxybutyrate (GHB)
STREET NAMES: Liquid x, Georgia home boy, goop, gamma-oh, grievous bodily harm
DRUG CLASSIFICATIONS: Schedule I, hallucinogen
OFFICIAL NAMES: Ketamine hydrochloride (brand names include Ketaject, Ketaset and Ketalar)
STREET NAMES: K, ket, quick, lady K, special K, vitamin K
DRUG CLASSIFICATIONS: Schedule III, dissociative anesthetic
OFFICIAL NAMES: Methamphetamine
STREET NAMES: Crystal, speed, meth, chalk, ice, glass
DRUG CLASSIFICATIONS: Schedule II, stimulant
OFFICIAL NAMES: Phencyclidine (PCP)
STREET NAMES: Angel dust, ozone, wack, rocket fuel, embalming fluid, fry, formaldehyde, wet, water, amp, hog
DRUG CLASSIFICATIONS: Schedule II, hallucinogen

OVERVIEW

Illicit drugs that fall under the heading of designer drugs encompass substances originally manufactured to have the same or more potent effects of illegal drugs, but which were chemically distinctive and, thus, not technically illegal. Their creation, traffic, and use were designed to sidestep the Controlled Substances Act (CSA) that banned the illegal sale of narcotics, stimulants, depressants, and hallucinogens.

Before the advent of so-called designer drugs, substances were explicitly banned by law or not technically illegal. The underground chemists knew that, by changing base ingredients or otherwise modulating the chemical structure of drugs, they could create completely new compounds called analogs that are different enough from controlled substances that they would not violate the law, yet close enough to produce many of the same effects.

Finally, in the mid-1980s, the U.S. government added designer drugs to the Drug Enforcement Administration's (DEA) list of controlled substances. The DEA also took exception to the phrase "designer drug," suggesting the use of the technically more precise phrase of "controlled substance analogs" (CsA).

The surge in CsA use in the United States, particularly among teens, is tied by many experts to the growth and influence of "raves" or "trances," large, all-night dance parties that cater to young audiences. Rave society is richly developed with dominant and reinforcing styles of music, dance, cultural mood, and expression. It also supports a social environment that encourages the liberal experimentation of drugs to heighten or deepen the event experience.

It is important to note from the outset that not all "club drugs" or "rave drugs" are designer drugs, although the terms are often used synonymously. Though the use of Rohypnol at raves is well document-

KEY TERMS

2C-B (NEXUS): A synthetic hallucinogenic gaining wider illicit use as a stronger but shorter-lasting alternative to MDMA.

DXM (DEXTROMETHORPHAN): Easily synthesized dissociative psychedelic found in some cough medicines, used illicitly for numbing and hallucinogenic properties.

GHB (GAMMA HYDROXYBUTYRATE): Originally sold in health food stores as a growth hormone, a liquid nervous depressant touted for its ecstasy-like qualities. Banned by the FDA in 1990, the respiratory depression it can cause makes it among the most dangerous club drugs in circulation.

KETAMINE: An anesthetic abused for its mind-altering effects that is popular as an illicit club drug. It is sometimes used to facilitate sexual assault, or date rape.

LSD (D-LYSERGIC ACID DIETHYLAMIDE): A powerful chemical compound renowned for its hallucinogenic properties.

MDMA (3,4-METHYLENEDIOXYMETHAMPHETAMINE): Known as ecstasy, E and X, MDMA is the most popular of the "club drugs," a synthetic stimulant with mild hallucinogenic properties.

METHAMPHETAMINE (CRYSTAL): An amine derivative of amphetamine, used in the form of its crystalline hydrochloride as a central nervous system stimulant. It is often illicitly produced in secret labs.

PCC (1-PIPERIDINOCYCLOHEXANECARBONITRILE): An unstable by-product common to PCP's illicit manufacture; when smoked, PCC releases hydrogen cyanide, which is inhaled by the user.

PCP (PHENCYCLIDINE): Also known as angel dust, a powerful and toxic synthetic chemical developed in home laboratories.

PMA (PARAMETHOXYAMPHETAMINE): Highly toxic hallucinogenic compound linked to sudden collapse and seizures, structurally similar to MDMA and occasionally substituted as such.

ROHYPNOL (FLUNTRAZEPAM): An overseas prescription sleeping aid that, in lower doses, gives users a feeling similar to alcohol intoxication; also used as a date rape drug.

---

ed, for example, it is a prescription sleeping aid sold overseas, and the cultural histories and usage patterns of drugs such as LSD and mescaline are quite distinct from the designer drug phenomenon.

This overview will therefore focus on the following substances and narrow discussion of their use primarily to the club environments where they are most used and abused. These drugs include: ecstasy (MDMA), gamma hydroxybutyrate (GHB), ketamine (special K), methamphetamine (crystal), 2C-B (nexus), and phencyclidine (PCP).

CHEMICAL/ORGANIC COMPOSITION

The composition of the six controlled substance analogs listed above often stimulate the same areas of the brain, but are chemically quite distinct from one another. MDMA (3, 4-methylenedioxymethamphetamine) is a complex drug that makes simple classification difficult. Its chemical structure is related both to the stimulant methamphetamine and the hallucinogen mescaline. Methamphetamine bears a close resemblance to two powerful chemicals in the body, dopamine and norepinephrine, which regulate mood, memory, and movement.

2C-B (sometimes called bromomescaline) is a hallucinogenic phenethylamine, related structurally to mescaline and the lesser known phenethylamine analogs

DOB (2, 5-dimethoxy-4 bromoamphetamine) and DOM (2, 5-dimethoxy-4-methylamphetamine). DOM, also known as STP, gained a considerable following in the 1960s, despite its association with violent behavior. 2-CB is distantly related to MDMA (ecstasy).

GHB is readily manufactured from its precursor, gamma-butyrolactone (also known as 2(3h)-furanone dihydro, or GBL). GHB is relatively easy to synthesize in household laboratories, mixing ingredients such as floor cleaning products, nail polish, and super glue removers with sodium hydroxide in the form of lye. Unintentional poisonings from bad homemade batches are not uncommon.

Phencyclidine (PCP) is a synthetic chemical that can be derived from an essential oil of the sassafras tree and is the best-known representative of the class of drugs collectively known as arylcyclohexylamines. As a chemical, PCP was first synthesized in 1926 and was briefly used in the 1950s as a dissociative anaesthetic. The chemicals needed to manufacture PCP are also readily available and inexpensive, and the production process requires little formal chemical knowledge or laboratory equipment.

Other precursor analogs chemically related to PCP include N-ethyl-1 phenylcyclohexylamine (PCE), 1-(1-phenyl-cyclohexyl)-pyrrolidine (PCP or PHP), and 1-(1-(2 thienyl-cyclohexyl)-piperdine (TPCP or TCP). PCC (1-iperidinocyclohexanecarbonitrile) is particularly

This poster advertises the stiffer penalties for the use of ecstasy. Photo by AP/Wide World Photos. Reproduced by permission.

common and particularly dangerous. It appears as a chemical by-product in poorly synthesized batches of PCP, and its ingestion may have serious health consequences.

Another member of the arylcyclohexylamine structural class is ketamine, which is a noncompetitive N-methyl-D-aspartate (NMDA) receptor antagonist, meaning it disables certain higher-function signaling mechanisms in the brain (consciousness, memory, perception, and motor activity) from lower functions (breathing and heart rate). Ketamine is manufactured commercially for use as a surgical anesthetic for both humans and animals.

Ketamine is chemically related to other dissociative anesthetics, including dextromethorphan (DXM), found in some over-the-counter cough syrups, and nitrous oxide (often called "whippets"). Ketamine also shares a close chemical kinship to the prescriptives tiletamine and memantine. Tiletamine is used in combination with zolazepam as a veterinary anesthetic under the brand names Zoletic and Telazol.

INGESTION METHODS

Though regular drug users will frequently modify their ingestion methods to hasten the impact of the drug's effects, such as grinding MDMA tablets into

powder and snorting it rather than swallowing the pill), this overview will focus on the most common means of delivery and usage.

Of all the designer drugs, ecstasy is by far the most commonly used drug, and is sold and distributed in pressed tablets or capsules and ingested orally. Users have also been known to snort it.

2C-B, or bromomescaline, is also sold and taken in capsules or tablets. There are also reports of Nexus being snorted, although unlike ecstasy, snorting 2C-B is said to be excruciatingly painful.

GHB is sometimes sold as a powder in a bag or capsules, but is most commonly sold and consumed as a liquid in small (30 ml) glass or plastic bottles, enough for three moderate doses. Dosing of GHB is extremely variable. Quantities used with ecstasy or other stimulants to modulate the highs of both drugs.

PCP is available in the form of tablets, capsules, liquid, and powder. In its base form, PCP is a white crystalline powder that is snorted, pressed into tablets, or mixed together with water or alcohol. More commonly, it is sprayed in its liquid form on leafy material such as oregano, mint, or marijuana, and sold to end users in the form of joints to be smoked.

THERAPEUTIC USE

Research into the benefits of drug therapy in clinical settings for the treatment of psychosis, schizophrenia, and other mental ailments was in large part responsible for the widespread use of MDMA during its introduction. The empathic properties associated with MDMA, giving users a sense of heightened emotional attachment and connectedness, made its use very intriguing for psychotherapists.

Studies are currently underway in Spain and Israel to assess MDMA's effectiveness in the treatment of post traumatic stress disorder (PTSD). On November 2, 2001, the Food and Drug Administration (FDA) approved the first clinical trial of MDMA as a treatment for PTSD in the United States. The study is currently awaiting approval from the research review board at the Medical University of South Carolina.

Following the drug scheduling of MDMA in the mid-1980s, 2C-B was marketed as a legal substitute for use by American psychotherapists. In clinical settings, it was used as a mood-altering agent, capable of creating a warm, empathetic bond between doctors and patients. Also, the drug's action was said to dissolve the patient's ego-defenses and inner resistances, thus enabling the person to get in touch with suppressed emotions and repressed memories.

Ketamine, like MDMA, was once thought to hold great promise for use in the field of experimental psychotherapy, although its use has been sidelined for this purpose in the United States.

In the early years following the introduction of ketamine and other antagonists into clinical settings, doctors and researchers thought they held great promise. They were not only considered excellent anesthetics, they appeared to assist brain function and recovery after damage from strokes, head injuries, hypoxia, polio, and a variety of other conditions. Evidence of brain damage where NMDA antagonists are most active did not surface until later.

PCP (phencyclidine) was developed in the 1950s as an intravenous anesthetic. Use of PCP in humans was discontinued in 1965, because it was found that patients often became agitated, delusional, and irrational while recovering from its anesthetic effects. Commercial production of PCP ended in 1978.

GHB (gamma hydroxybutyrate) was originally developed as an anesthetic, but was withdrawn due to unwanted side effects. GHB holds several U.S. patents for use in the treatment of sleep disorders such as narcolepsy and insomnia, and as a muscle relaxant. GHB is used as a fast-acting anesthetic in small animals. The compounds and compositions made from GHB are useful in the treatment of Parkinson's disease, schizophrenia, and other dopamine-related disorders.

Amphetamine attracted a widespread audience in 1932, when it was marketed as the nasal inhaler Benzedrine by the pharmaceutical company Smith Kline & French. Amphetamine is still widely used as a bronchio dilator, allowing asthmatics to breathe more freely.

Methamphetamines are still legally produced in the United States for attention-deficit disorder (ADD) under the trade names Desoxyn or Ritalin (methylphenidate). As the street name "speed" suggests, amphetamines elevate mood, heighten endurance, and eliminate fatigue.

USAGE TRENDS

Designer drug use is most common among young adults and is most commonly associated with large-scale dance events, nightclubs, and raves. The 1999 National Household Survey on Drug Abuse found an estimated 1.5% (3.4 million) of Americans had used MDMA at least once during their lifetime. The heaviest use (5% or 1.4 million people) was reported for those between 18 and 25 years old.

During 2000, 4% of the U.S. population (8.8 million people) said they had tried methamphetamine in their lifetime. The age demographic skews slightly older, with highest rate of methamphetamine use reported by adults 26 or older (4.3% of these adults report at least trying

methamphetamine in 2000). Of those between the ages of 18 to 25, 4.1% reported lifetime use and, for those between the ages of 12 and 17, 1.3% reported lifetime use of methamphetamine. The number of methamphetamine emergency room treatment admissions in the United States has been climbing steadily and alarmingly, from 14,496 admissions in 1992 to 53,560 in 1997 and 57,834 in 1999.

GHB use appears to be increasing alongside its wider availability, according to the Drug Abuse Warning Network (DAWN). Emergency room admissions tracked by the organization find mentions of GHB have risen dramatically since the mid-1990s from just 56 in 1994 to 4,969 in 2000. Although ketamine use has remained steady over the same period, hospital data collected by the U.S. Department of Health and Human Services suggest the 18–25 age group still accounts for 58% of all ketamine-related incidents.

Use of PCP increased between 1991 and 1996, at which time levels began to drop. Although levels of use remain relatively low, they are higher than in the early 1990s. DAWN estimates 6,510 emergency room visits in 1995 secondary to PCP use (or PCP in combination with another chemical/drug), up from 3,470 in 1991. As of 2000, approximately 5.8 million individuals aged 12 and older had used PCP at least once in their lifetime; most of these users were adults over 18 years of age.

From 1999 to 2000, the use of MDMA among high school-aged teens increased in every measured grade—eighth, tenth, and twelfth. For tenth and twelfth graders, this is the second consecutive year MDMA use has increased. Past year use of MDMA increased among eighth graders from 1.7% in 1999 to 3.1% in 2000; from 4.4% to 5.4% among tenth graders; and from 5.6% to 8.2% among high school seniors. The perceived availability of MDMA also rose sharply, from 40.1% in 1999 to 51.4% in 2000.

Reports on the use of 2C-B are sporadic, but growing in number, leading law enforcement to believe that it could emerge as a significant drug in rave culture. The DEA reports a number of significant arrests throughout the United States. Information compiled by the National Institute on Drug Abuse indicates that 2C-B has become popular for recreational use in Germany and Switzerland. Clandestine manufacture has been reported in the Netherlands. The drug is reportedly making an appearance at dance clubs in the Washington, D.C. area.

MENTAL EFFECTS

Known to many as the "hug drug" or the "feel good" drug, MDMA reduces inhibitions while enhancing sensitivity to sound, light, and touch. The mixed effects of stimulant and psychedelic peak after approximately two hours and may continue for up to six hours. The drug lowers inhibitions, increases mood sensitivity, and gives club-goers energy to dance well into the morning hours. People say they are friendlier, happier, and "more connected" to music and to other people when on the drug.

Like MDMA, recreational users of 2C-B say the drug greatly heightens their appreciation of and sensitivity to music and say that it greatly enhances the enjoyment of dancing. At higher doses (15–20 mg), recreational users report heightened tactile sensations and profoundly altered states of consciousness.

GHB is another drug reported to have MDMA-like effects. Some people report positive mood changes and an increased appreciation for music, dancing, and talking while on the drug. Slurring of speech, giddiness, and mild incoherency are also common. Some users of GHB report heightened tactile sensitivity, relaxation, and sexual arousal.

Users of ketamine report the immediate effect as a non-localized numbness all over the body, altered vision, muffled hearing, and a floating sensation. Many people, after using the drug once, will not knowingly use it again. At higher doses, ketamine leads to out-of-body experiences with a pronounced hallucinatory state. Users liken the effects to an intense religious experience and an out-of-body sensation. Visions of angels and empathic beings are not uncommon.

Stimulants such as methamphetamine give users an intense sensation, called a rush or flash, that lasts only a few minutes and is described as extremely pleasurable. Oral or intranasal use produces a euphoric high, but not a rush. Some report that they feel "superhuman" after losing a night or two of sleep while binging on the drug. People also report feeling unusually sharp or in control. Wanting to prolong the high and delay the inevitable crash is emblematic of the drug's addictive character.

Individual responses to PCP at low and moderate doses are varied. Many people, after using the drug once, will not knowingly use it again. Others seek it because they claim the drug makes them funnier, more insightful, and gives them feelings of invulnerability. Users generally progress from feeling detached, distant, and removed from their immediate surroundings to a surging sense of power and strength. Others report prominent body-image distortions (enlarged or detached head and limbs) against a background of depersonalizing numbness and a sense of profound isolation.

The mental state considered by many to be the hallmark of PCP intoxication, the recurring delusion of superhuman strength, has prompted people to snap handcuffs and, unarmed, attack large groups of people or the police. The pronounced analgesic effects of the drug have fed delusions of immortality, causing people to jump from windows or cliffs. Such extreme and bizarre behavior is often accompanied by gruesome self-mutilation or violence against innocent bystanders. Hospitals have recorded nonviolent people pulling out teeth and attacking family members in reaction to paranoid delusions.

Recent experiences can have a substantial effect on the mental effect of 2C-B use on the user. Physically or psychologically unsettling events in the days before a "trip" can blossom into more serious distress and trauma while using the drug. Some users have described hallucinations that are debilitating in their intensity and that are looked back upon as the most terrifying drug-related experiences of their lives.

PHYSIOLOGICAL EFFECTS

Many designer drugs share a steep dose-response curve, meaning its effects can triple or quadruple with only minor increases in consumption. A 150 mg dose of MDMA, for example, can produce double the effects of a 120 mg dose. As many of the designer analogs are manufactured in underground laboratories, unknowns about the concentration of active ingredients have the potential to cause life-threatening situations.

Even experienced users of ketamine can miscalculate the dosage and find themselves on the verge of slipping into unconsciousness. In non-clinical settings, this potentially life-threatening state is called a "K-hole" and may be accompanied by convulsions, vomiting, and respiratory depression. Researchers report that while most users recover within 72 hours after ketamine usage, language and some aspects of memory impairment linger. Visual flashbacks have been reported days or weeks after use. Amnesia, aggressive behavior, and paranoid or delusional thinking have been reported after high recreational ingestion of ketamine.

The central nervous system actions that result from taking even small amounts of methamphetamine, on the other hand, include extreme alertness, increased energy, decreased appetite, increased respiration, hyperthermia, and euphoria—generally the effects sought by users. But over time, side effects such as irritability, insomnia, confusion, tremors, convulsions, anxiety, paranoia, and aggressiveness begin to intrude. These symptoms are magnified by lack of sleep. Withdrawal often produces severe depression.

The impact of MDMA use on the body includes muscle tension, involuntary teeth clenching, nausea, blurred vision, rapid eye movement, faintness, and chills or sweating. Immediate side effects may include nausea, dizziness, disorientation, anxiety, and panic attacks. 2C-B, a close cousin to MDMA, has a stimulating effect on the central nervous system, usually causing a slight rise in blood pressure and a quickening of the heart rate. As a result, 2C-B could pose a danger to those suffering from diabetes, epilepsy, or cardiac problems.

Because of high demand, ecstasy pills are frequently mixed with fillers and other active substances, most commonly amphetamines (speed), caffeine, and ephedrine (a natural amphetamine-like substance). Some pills have been found to contain DXM (dextromethorphan), a dissociative psychedelic found in some cough medicine, and PMA (paramethoxyamphetamine), a highly toxic hallucinogenic stimulant.

Because 2C-B is clandestinely produced, users are unaware of the dose they are ingesting and may be overwhelmed by the drug's effects. Users seeking MDMA-like effects do not expect or enjoy the unpleasant physical side effects on the body, including acute nausea, diarrhea, cramps, and gas. There are also several reports of allergic-type reactions causing increased mucus production concentrated in the windpipe and lungs.

2C-B is not physically addictive, as is the case with methamphetamine or GHB. However, if used very regularly, there is the possibility that psychological dependence could develop. When used at dance clubs or large indoor events, there are dangers associated with overexertion as a common reaction to drug's stimulatory effect, thereby causing dehydration and possible collapse. Nevertheless, to date, no deaths have been attributed to this drug.

GHB temporarily inhibits the release of dopamine in the brain. This may cause increased dopamine storage, which is followed by increased dopamine release when the GHB influence wears off. This effect could account for the middle-of-the-night awakenings common with use of higher GHB doses, and the general feelings of increased well-being, alertness, and arousal the next day.

There is much debate and considerable conflicting evidence regarding the mechanism of action of PCP. It is thought to stimulate alpha-adrenergic receptors in the brain and to elevate epinephrine, norepinephrine, and serotonin levels. PCP is also thought to inhibit communication along certain central nervous system pathways. Still others think that PCP acts on opiate receptors.

The physical effects of PCP on the user can be as varied and unpredictable as the psychological reactions. At low to moderate doses, PCP produces a slight increase in breathing rate and a more pronounced rise in blood pressure and pulse rate. Respiration becomes shallow, and flushing and profuse sweating occur. Generalized numbness of the extremities and loss of muscular coordination may also occur.

Harmful side effects

Most of the pleasing physical sensations and mental effects of drugs covered in this section come from the forced release of serotonin and dopamine in the brain. Over the medium and long term, repeated abuse has been shown to damage dopamine transporters by shriveling the nerve endings of these crucial cells.

Methamphetamine and MDMA have been shown to cause damage to dopamine transporters. Anecdotally, users of both these drugs refer to the hardships of "coming down" and the "hangover" typified by fatigue and depression that typically lasts several days.

Methamphetamine use causes a sharp spike in blood pressure, dangerously irregular heartbeats, chest pain, shortness of breath, diarrhea, nausea, and vomiting. The drug can increase body temperature to critical levels, provoking cascading failures in vital systems. Brain hemorrhage is perhaps the biggest risk associated with abuse of the drug, which, if not fatal, can cause permanent paralysis and speech loss.

Ketamine toxicity is less of a concern than the accidents caused by the suddenness and duration of the dissociative state. Sudden collapse can lead to accident or injury, and loss of consciousness coupled with vomiting can lead to a blockage of the airway that could cause the user to choke to death.

At high doses, PCP prompts a drop in blood pressure, pulse rate, and respiration. These reactions may be accompanied by nausea, vomiting, blurred vision, uncontrolled eye movement, drooling, loss of balance, an exaggerated gait, seizures, convulsions, coma, and death.

PCC, a common by-product of PCP's illicit manufacture (sometimes accounting for 10–25% of the mixture), causes abdominal cramps, diarrhea, and in sufficient doses, coma. PCC is an unstable compound, degrading to piperidine. Contaminated batches of PCP can sometimes be recognized by a strong fishy odor. When heated, as when it is smoked and inhaled, PCC liberates hydrogen cyanide, so cyanide poisoning in PCP smokers is also a strong possibility.

Long-term health effects

Some of the popularity associated with so-called designer drugs comes from the belief that these drugs are "safe" and not addictive. Both assumptions are wrong.

Methamphetamine is highly addictive. Users trying to abstain from use may suffer withdrawal symptoms that include depression, anxiety, fatigue, paranoia, aggression, and intense drug cravings. Chronic abuse of methamphetamine produces a psychosis similar to schizophrenia and may include violent behavior, anxiety, confusion, and insomnia. Users can also exhibit psychotic behavior, including auditory hallucinations, mood disturbances, delusions, and paranoia, possibly resulting in homicidal or suicidal thoughts.

Methamphetamine can cause brain damage that results in slower motor and cognitive functioning—even in users who take the drug for less than a year—according to two studies published in the March 2001 issue of the *American Journal of Psychiatry*. Over time, the damage that meth use does to dopamine receptors appears to seriously reduce the overall level of dopamine in the brain. This can result in symptoms like those of Parkinson's disease, Alzheimer's disease, stroke, and epilepsy, characterized by shaking and difficulty with walking, movement, coordination, and memory.

GHB is also addictive. Regular, daily use of GHB can cause physical dependency with harsh withdrawal symptoms. At four to six average doses per week, people report finding that they need to increase their dose to get the same level of intoxication. Many subsequently report that they need a little GHB just to feel normal. With very heavy use (one or more doses per day), many people report very serious physical addiction. Stopping "cold turkey" results in anxiety, inability to sleep, and feeling like the heart is arrhythmic (irregular).

More people are overdosing on GHB than ecstasy. In 2000, 2,482 GHB users visited the emergency room for an overdose, compared with 1,742 ecstasy users. There also are more deaths from GHB. According to the DEA, 73 people have died from taking GHB since 1995, compared to 27 ecstasy-related deaths from 1994 to 1998.

Although not thought to incite physical dependency, MDMA should not be considered risk-free. Recent studies confirm that MDMA is neurotoxic. A report published in June 1999 by researchers at Johns Hopkins University confirmed that the forced release of serotonin damages serotonin receptors in the brain. The serotonin system plays a direct role in regulating mood, aggression, sexual activity, sleep, and sensitivity to pain. The study, conducted on primates, showed that exposure to MDMA for four days caused brain damage that was evident six to seven years later. It was the first study to demonstrate MDMA's potential for causing permanent brain damage.

Recent studies suggest all N-methyl-D-aspartate (NMDA) antagonists cause brain damage to the portions of the brain responsible for higher cognitive functions like memory and speech. These are the areas most affected by dissociative anesthetics and include ketamine, dextromethorphan (DXM), phencyclidine (PCP or angel dust), nitrous oxide (whippets), and dizocilpine (MK-801).

The long-term impact of 2C-B use is unknown. The September 1998 *Journal of Analytical Toxicology* reported that very little data exist about the pharmacological properties, metabolism, and toxicity of 2C-B. The relationship between its use and disease and death are unknown.

Given the similarity of its chemical structure to MDMA and the relatedness of effects on the user, it seems reasonable to infer that 2C-B may possess similar neurotoxic qualities, but more research is needed before any such conclusions can be drawn.

REACTIONS WITH OTHER DRUGS OR SUBSTANCES

According to the ONDCP, MDMA is frequently used in combination with other so-called club drugs, greatly increasing risks to the user. These other drugs include LSD, psilocybin mushrooms, GHB, ketamine, and nitrous oxide. MDMA and marijuana is a common combination in the South and West of the United States; MDMA and methamphetamine combinations are found in the West. "Candy flipping," the use of ecstasy and LSD, was mentioned in several areas, including Chicago, Denver, Honolulu, Memphis, Miami, Philadelphia, Washington, D.C., and Los Angeles.

Users of GHB are warned that it should never, under any circumstances, be mixed with alcohol or other nervous system depressants. Combining even a low GHB dose with alcohol can trigger the overdose reaction and a state of unresponsive unconsciousness and depressed breathing. GHB has been linked to 70 deaths in the United States, most often attributed to its ingestion with alcohol. About a third of those deaths have been tied to GHB overdose alone.

Other nervous system depressants that could trigger a GHB overdose reaction are benzodiazepines (mild tranquilizers such as Valium and Xanax), phenothiazines (potent tranquilizers like Thorazine and Stellazine), various painkillers (barbiturates and opiates), anticonvulsants (Dilantin and phenobarbital), and even many over-the-counter allergy and sleep remedies.

GHB taken in combination with ecstasy or methamphetamine can lead to the impression in users that their tolerance for the drug has increased far beyond what it actually has. Individuals who report consuming up to five times the normal dose when on speed or ecstasy acknowledge that their "average" high dose landed them in the hospital when taken alone.

Combining the use of ketamine with drugs that suppress respiratory function, including alcohol, barbiturates, or Valium, is dangerous and potentially life threatening. Users mixing these drugs risk slowing their breathing and heart rates to dangerously low levels that starve the brain of oxygen, which increases risks of permanent brain damage, coma, and death.

Ketamine is almost never taken alone in a club environment. It is frequently mixed with a stimulant like cocaine or methamphetamine and taken simultaneously (commonly called "trail mix"). Because its effects are relatively short-lived compared with drugs like MDMA, it is often used as a "booster," or a secondary substance, that draws out desired pleasurable effects of the primary drug.

Because of its easy synthesis, PCP is frequently used as either an additive in drugs such as MDMA, cocaine, and methamphetamine, or substituted for and sold on the street as THC (active ingredient in marijuana), cannabinol, mescaline, psilocybin, LSD, amphetamine, and other psychedelics.

PCP has a sedative effect on certain systems in the body and interactions with other central nervous system depressants such as alcohol and benzodiazepines may lead to coma or accidental overdose.

The trend of selling marijuana with drug treatments that have been sprayed on marijuana, mint, or oregano leaves is gaining popularity in the United States, and federal, state, and local authorities believe that PCP is playing a major role in the resurgence of a trend originally popular in the 1970s. Hospitals report that the physical effects of highs associated with "wet" or dipsticks (joints presumably dipped in embalming fluid) are nearly identical to those long associated with PCP use.

Anecdotal evidence lends support to these claims. "Embalming fluid" is a common street slang term for PCP. Confusion about the origin of the term is thought by many to have influenced the trend whereby PCP is actually mixed with formaldehyde (or other embalming chemicals) and used as a recreational psychoactive.

The spiked joints are called "squares" and the wet marijuana is called "fry"; adolescents are congregating in "fry houses." A sample joint obtained by Houston law enforcement and submitted to spectral analysis revealed PCP and byproducts of its home-lab manufacture, PCC and PCH.

Health officials describe "burn-out" (also called amotivational syndrome), a state long associated with prolonged abuse of PCP, that results from recreational exposure to fry. These symptoms include memory dysfunction, lethargy, lack of interest or motivation, and decreased spontaneous speech and blank staring.

Because of neurotoxicity and overdose concerns, 2C-B may have potentially dangerous interactions with users taking monoamine oxidase inhibitors (MAOIs). MAOIs are most commonly found in the prescription antidepressants Nardil (phenelzine), Parnate (tranylcypromine), Marplan (isocarboxazid), Eldepryl (l-deprenyl), and Aurorex or Manerix (moclobemide). Ayahuasca also contains MAOIs (harmine and harmaline).

TREATMENT AND REHABILITATION

Generous funding of drug treatment programs is costly and politically challenging but absolutely essential. A 1995 study by the Rand Corporation found that every dollar spent in drug treatment saves society seven dollars in crime, policing, incarceration, and health services.

The National Institute on Drug Abuse (NIDA) confirms that the most successful drug rehabilitation programs are those that tailor treatment to the user, not the other way around. While there is no single treatment program that works successfully in every circumstance, programs that have the highest success rates are those that take into consideration differences in age, nationality, race, sexual orientation, gender, economic status, and education level.

Once these are factored in, therapeutic efforts can target the needs, problems, and pressures unique to that individual's life experience. As any recovering addict will attest, getting over the attachment to the drug is only the beginning of a much longer journey.

People turn to drugs to escape, fit in, feel better about themselves, or just to feel better—ending that dependency often means replacing the place drugs used to occupy with something stronger. The goal of every successful drug treatment program is to identify what that something is, and to give individuals the tools they need to achieve it.

Therapies help users devise their own coping strategies for confronting temptation and opportunity and preventing relapse. Even if relapse does occur, people may be taught how to tap into a network of support that will help them out of that situation as well.

With these difficulties in mind, drug treatment programs do surprisingly well at keeping people on the road to recovery. The NIDA says the treatment of addiction is as successful in 2002 as the treatment of other chronic diseases such as diabetes, hypertension, and asthma.

PERSONAL AND SOCIAL CONSEQUENCES

So-called designer drugs have a particularly glamorous appeal, marketed by dealers as safe, non-addictive, fun drugs that carry minimal risks to the user. This is not now, nor has it ever been, the case.

All drug use has built-in disadvantages that handicap the user. Drugs have a way of reshaping lives to accommodate their use. People who decide they want to experiment or "have a little fun" with any of the drugs covered in this overview may discover somewhere down the line that their relationships, particularly with non-drug users, have changed—some irrevocably. Academic or work-related pursuits may seem less important, and may suffer as a result. Family members may be neglected.

With addictive substances such as methamphetamine, the dangers of use are more pronounced. Even those who claim not to have a problem with recreational, or what might be termed occasional, use of drugs might be kidding themselves. The low that follows a euphoric high can make the rest of the user's life seem dull and depressing when compared to a drug-enhanced state. The allure of recapturing a feeling of euphoria that has suddenly deserted other aspects of their "real" lives may be prove too enticing to pass by, and result in dependence or addiction.

Repeated use of certain drugs brings about dramatic changes in both the structure and function of the brain. The euphoric effect derived from their use is itself a sign that the drug or drugs are changing the chemical wiring in the brain. As it adjusts to the imbalances being inflicted upon it, the user needs more of the drug to recapture the high. In a shorter span of time than many realize, this change becomes more pronounced and indelible, until finally the individual has become addicted to the drug.

The hallucinatory potential of many controlled substance analogs (MDMA, GHB, ketamine, PCP) may trigger traumatic emotional episodes in many users. While there is little evidence to support the claim that drug use can cause long-term psychotic or schizophrenic behaviors, individuals with an underlying mental condition may find their experimentation with so-called designer drugs triggers an outbreak of symptoms associated with mental illness. Anecdotal evidence suggests that psychotic breaks and schizophrenia-like symptoms are far more frequent with heavy or regular dissociative anesthetic use (including ketamine and PCP).

LEGAL CONSEQUENCES

In 1970, amphetamines constituted 14% of all psychoactive drugs prescribed by physicians in the United States. The passage of the Controlled Substances Act (CSA) abruptly changed the availability of amphetamines by imposing severe manufacturing quotas and by establishing strict guidelines for their use.

The passage of the CSA pushed the manufacture of banned substances into illicit laboratories and promoted experimentation with substances that were similar to, but distinct from, controlled substances. The federal government responded by modifying the Controlled Substances Act in 1986, banning all designer drugs and all possible variations of controlled substances.

The amendment states that any new drug that is substantially similar to a controlled substance currently listed under the Code of Federal Regulations (CFR), Schedule I or II, and has either pharmacological properties similar to a Schedule I or II substance or is represented as having those properties, will be considered a controlled substance and duly categorized as Schedule I.

In case there be any doubt about the government's intent to prosecute and jail people charged with drug offenses, it is worth noting that between 1980 and 1997, drug arrests tripled in the United States. In 1997, four out of five drug arrests (79.5%) were for possession.

In the country's largest state, California, the number of people locked up for drug offenses has increased 25-fold since 1980. Nearly half of all drug offenders imprisoned in the state in 2000 were imprisoned on possession charges alone.

See also Ecstasy (MDMA); GHB; Ketamine; Methamphetamine; PCP (phencyclidine); 2C-B

RESOURCES

Books

Holland, Julie, M.D. *Ecstasy: The Complete Guide, A Comprehensive Look at the Risks and Benefits of MDMA.* Rochester, VT: Inner Traditions. 2001.

Periodicals

De Boer, D., et al. "More Data About the New Psychoactive Drug 2C-B." *Journal of Analytical Toxicology* 23 (May/June 1999): 227-228.

European Monitoring Center for Drugs and Drug Addiction. *Report on the Risk Assessment of Ketamine in the Framework of the Joint Action on New Synthetic Drugs.* September 2000.

European Monitoring Center For Drugs And Drug Addiction. *Risk-Assessment Report.* October 1999.

Groombridge, Christopher. "The Identification of 4 Methylthioamphetamine in a Drug Seizure." *Microgram* 31 (May 1998): 150-159.

MacKeen, Dawn. "Kicking the PCP Habit." *Salon* Health & Body Sec. August 24, 1999.

Poortman-van der Meer, Anneke J. "The Identification of 4 Methylthioamphetamine." *Microgram* 31 (June 1998): 174-179.

U.N. World Health Organization. *Guide to Drug Use Epidemiology.* March 2000.

U.N. World Health Organization. United Nations International Drug Control Program. *Evaluation of Psychoactive Substance Use.* February 2000.

U.S. Department of Health and Human Services. *2001 Monitoring the Future, National Results of Adolescent Drug Use.* January 2002.

U.S. Department of Health and Human Services. Community Epidemiology Work Group. National Institutes of Health *Epidemiologic Trends in Drug Abuse, Advance Report.* June 2000.

U.S. Department of Health and Human Services. Substance Abuse and Mental Health Services Administration. *2000 National Household Survey on Drug Abuse.* October 2001.

U.S. Department of Health and Human Services. Substance Abuse and Mental Health Services Administration. Drug Abuse Warning Network. *The DAWN Report: Club Drugs.* December 2000.

U.S. Department of Health and Human Services. Substance Abuse and Mental Health Services Administration. Drug Abuse Warning Network. *Year-End 2000 Emergency Department Data.* July 2001.

U.S. Department of Justice. National Drug Intelligence Center. *National Drug Threat Assessment 2002.* December 2001.

U.S. Office of National Drug Control Policy. *Pulse Check: Trends in Drug Abuse.* 2000.

Other

U.S. Department of Health and Human Services. Substance Abuse and Mental Health Services Administration. <http://www.samhsa.gov>.

U.S. Department of Justice. Drug Enforcement Administration. <http://www.usdoj.gov/dea>.

U.S. National Institute on Drug Abuse. <http://www.nida.nih.gov>.

U.S. Office of National Drug Control Policy. <http://www.whitehousedrugpolicy.org>.

Christopher V.G. Barillas

DEXTROAMPHETAMINE

OFFICIAL NAMES: Dextroamphetamine, D-amphetamine, dextroamphetamine sulfate (Dexedrine)
STREET NAMES: Speed, uppers, bennies, beans, dexies, black beauties, go pills, L.A. turnarounds, West Coast turnarounds, pep pills
DRUG CLASSIFICATIONS: Schedule II, stimulant

OVERVIEW

Dextroamphetamines are a part of the amphetamine class of drugs, central nervous system (CNS) stimulants that are used in the treatment of certain brain-based disorders. Because of their long-lasting and potent stimulant effects, they are also highly physically and psychologically addictive and have a high rate of abuse.

Amphetamines were first synthesized in 1887 by the German chemist L. Edeleano. However, they were not generally used until 1932, when pharmaceutical manufacturer Smith, Kline and French introduced Benzedrine, an over-the-counter inhaler for relieving nasal congestion. By the late '30s, the drug was available in tablet form for the treatment of several neurological disorders, including narcolepsy (a sleeping disorder), Parkinson's disease, and minimal brain dysfunction (now called attention deficit hyperactivity disorder, or ADHD).

During World War II, dextroamphetamines and methamphetamines were widely distributed among Allied, German, and Japanese soldiers to keep them awake and alert on the battlefield. Beyond the front, civilians who worked in factories manufacturing goods for the war effort were also using the drug to boost pro-

ductivity. After the war, use escalated abroad. Abuse of amphetamines became a widespread problem in Japan, until legislation known as the "Amphetamine Control Law" was passed in 1951.

In 1952, Smith, Kline and French introduced the stimulant Dexedrine (dextroamphetamine sulfate) for narcolepsy in the United States. It was manufactured as a Spansule, the first time-release capsule, which gradually released the drug over a period of time.

In the United States, amphetamines were prescribed for many reasons, from the treatment of depression to weight loss. The drug was being used by long-distance truckers, who dubbed the drug "West Coast turnaround" because of its ability to help them stay awake during long-haul and coast-to-coast runs. Athletes used the stimulant to enhance performance, and the military continued its use through the Korean conflict and into Vietnam.

In the 1960s the abuse of the drug became more widespread. A new method of using—injecting liquid methampetamine—gained popularity after doctors in San Francisco began prescribing the treatment for heroin addicts. As massive prescription fraud and drug abuse mounted, calls for stricter legislation of amphetamines were becoming louder.

Senate testimony given in the late 60s in support of passage of the Controlled Substances Act (CSA) reported that 50% of the amphetamines being produced annually in the U.S. were ending up in the illegal drug market. In order to stop rising abuse, the amphetamines were changed to a Schedule II drug with passage of the CSA in 1970. According to the U.S. Drug Enforcement Administration (DEA), over two billion units of amphetamine and methamphetamine were legally manufactured in the United States in 1970, enough for ten doses for every person in the United States at the time. Stricter limits would be established to slow production of the drug.

Stimulants like amphetamines may look attractive to athletes for their ability to slow appetite and raise energy levels and mood. They may be attracted to amphetamine use by the belief that a lower weight will improve athletic performance. However, the negative side effects experienced from long-term abuse of amphetamines are greater than any temporary gains in ability. Amphetamines are considered a banned substance by the International Olympic Committee (IOC), the United States Anti-Doping Agency (USADA), the World Anti-Doping Agency (WADA), and a number of other national and international sporting authorities. Amphetamines are also banned by the National Collegiate Athletic Association (NCAA); however, the NCAA does make exceptions for players with a documented medical need for stimulant drugs (i.e., ADHD).

CHEMICAL/ORGANIC COMPOSITION

The molecular formula for dextroamphetamine is $C_9H_{13}N$. The full chemical name for dextroamphetamine sulfate, the formulation used in the medication Dexedrine, is d-alpha-methylphenethylamine.

INGESTION METHODS

Dextroamphetamines come in capsule and tablet form. For the treatment of narcolepsy, patients are typically prescribed 5–60 mg per day. Patients with ADHD usually take anywhere from 3 to 60 mg depending on age and response to the drug.

Illicit methods of taking amphetamines include smoking (in combination with marijuana or tobacco) or injecting it alone or with other drugs. The tablet form of the drug is sometimes crushed and snorted. Dextroamphetamine pills and capsules may also be taken orally by individuals who have no clinical need for the drug.

THERAPEUTIC USE

Amphetamines such as dextroamphetamine sulfate (Dexedrine), amphetamine and dextroamphetamine sulfate combinations (Adderall), and methamphetamine hydrochloride (Desoxyl) are standard therapies in the treatment of ADHD. Although it's not completely understood how it works, when used as part of a comprehensive treatment program, the stimulant can help improve symptoms of poor concentration, hyperactivity, and distractibility for many children with ADHD. Other com-

KEY TERMS

AMPHETAMINE PSYCHOSIS: A delusional state of mind caused by severe amphetamine abuse. Paranoia, hallucinations, and unfounded feelings of persecution are common features.

ATTENTION DEFICIT HYPERACTIVITY DISORDER (ADHD): A mental disorder characterized by persistent impulsive behavior, difficulty concentrating, and hyperactivity that causes lowered social, academic, or occupational functioning.

CATAPLEXY: An abrupt, total loss of muscle control spurred by an emotional event. Cataplexy frequently occurs along with narcolepsy.

METHAMPHETAMINE (CRYSTAL): An amine derivative of amphetamine, used in the form of its crystalline hydrochloride as a central nervous system stimulant. It is often illicitly produced in secret labs.

METHYLPHENIDATE: Ritalin; a stimulant drug choice for the treatment of attention deficit hyperactivity disorder (ADHD).

NARCOLEPSY: A rare, chronic sleep disorder characterized by constant daytime fatigue and sudden attacks of sleep.

TIC: A repetitive, involuntary spasm that increases in severity when it is purposefully surpressed. Tics may be motor (such as muscle contractions or eye blinking) or vocal.

TOURETTE'S SYNDROME: A chronic tic disorder involving multiple motor and/or vocal tics that cause distress or significant impairment in social, occupational, or other important areas of functioning.

ponents of an effective treatment program for ADHD include family counseling, behavioral therapy, and a customized educational curriculum.

One of the oldest uses for dextroamphetamines is in the treatment of narcolepsy, a sleep disorder characterized by constant daytime fatigue and sleepiness, with a disturbance in nighttime REM sleep (the period of sleep when dreams occur). During the day or other periods of time when they would normaly be awake, people with narcolepsy often experience sudden episodes of REM sleep. They may also suffer from sleep paralysis and/or cataplexy, an abrupt, total loss of muscle control. Central nervous system stimulants like dextroamphetamine help to relieve these symptoms.

In the 1970s, both Dexedrine and another dextroamphetamine sulfate formula called Obetrol were

HISTORY NOTES

Dextroamphetamine has flown with the Mercury Missions, *Apollo 11,* and the first 24 space shuttle missions. Combined with scopolamine, an alkaloid of belladonna (*Atropos belladonna*, or deadly nightshade), the drug was the sole remedy for one of the biggest early challenges of space flight—motion sickness. It was also used to battle fatigue on some flights. For example, in 1963, *Mercury 7* astronaut Gordon Cooper took the drug before re-entering Earth's atmosphere.

However, this oral remedy was not always completely effective for nausea, because weightlessness of space made its absorption in the digestive tract unpredictable. According to NASA reports, during the first 24 missions of the Space Shuttle program, 67% of crew members on their first flight reported symptoms of space motion sickness. While the majority recovered from symptoms by the third day in space using the dextroamphetamine and scopolamine combination, the 72-hour wait ate up a considerable portion of the mission. In 1988, intramuscular injections of the more effective drug promethazine replaced dextroamphetamine/scopolamine as the space-sickness drug of choice.

approved for use as anti-obesity drugs. However, the manufacturer (Rexar) was bought by a new company (Richwood pharmaceuticals) who resubmitted the drug to the Food and Drug Administration (FDA). It was relabeled as a treatment for ADHD only and reintroduced in 1996 as Adderall. As of 2002, none of the dextroamphetamine drugs on the U.S. market were labeled for use as an appetite suppressant or weight loss aid (although Desoxyl, or methamphetamine hydrochloride, is approved for the treatment of obesity).

USAGE TRENDS

The National Institute on Drug Abuse (NIDA) estimates that there were approximately 900,000 Americans age 12 and older misusing prescription stimulants in 1999. Because of its popularity as a treatment for ADHD, adolescents are at a special risk for misusing dextroamphetamine drugs.

According to the U.S. Centers for Disease Control (CDC) the number of prescriptions written for ADHD medications quadrupled between 1989 and 1998. And in 1999, both Adderall and Dexedrine were ranked among the top 200 for number of new drug prescriptions, rank-

ing 59 (4,140 new prescriptions) and 169 (1,735 new prescriptions), respectively. Adderall accounted for $155.7 million in U.S. pharmaceutical sales in 1999.

Scope and severity

Amphetamine abuse is one of the most significant global drug problems. According to the United Nations Office for Drug Control and Crime Prevention (UNDC-CP), by the late 1990s, an estimated 29 million people worldwide were taking amphetamines—a larger group than cocaine and all opiate drugs combined.

In 2000, 922 emergency room visits related to dextroamphetamine use were reported to the Drug Abuse Warning Network (DAWN). Amphetamines in general (excluding methamphetamines) were the seventh most reported drug for emergency room visits among children aged 6 to 17, and eighth most reported among patients aged 18 to 34. Amphetamines were also among the top 15 most-reported drugs for emergency department visits among women, accounting for 2.43% of the total female admissions.

Age, ethnic, and gender trends

There have been a number of anecdotal reports of illicit use of Dexedrine, Adderall, Ritalin (methylphenidate), and other ADHD stimulants among college students in recent years. In 2000, University of Wisconsin health officials estimated that one in five of their students were using ADHD stimulant medications without a doctor's prescription.

Although a slight rise in the popularity of amphetamines occured in the 1990s in the United States, amphetamine use (excluding methamphetamines) in the United States seems to have leveled off in recent years. The 2001 "Monitoring the Future" study, an annual survey of drug use among adolescents and young adults performed by the University of Michigan and the NIDA, reports that between 1991 and 2000, overall amphetamine use among high school students, college students, and young adults has declined.

Stimulant "sharing" of prescription dextroamphetamines and other ADHD medications is also a problem among adolescents. A Canadian study published in 2001 found that 15% of children who used stimulants for medical purposes reported giving these drugs to peers, while 7% had sold their stimulants at some point. Theft of medication was also a problem, with 4.3% having ADHD drugs stolen, and another 3% reporting being coerced out of medication at some point.

In the United States, a 1998 study of Wisconsin children who were prescribed Ritalin for the treatment of ADHD reported that 16% of the children in the study had been asked to sell or share their medication. Security was also an issue, with 37% of schools reporting that stimulants were stored in an unlocked space and 10% of children being allowed to carry and administer their own medication.

The 2000 "Monitoring the Future" report found that 10% of eighth graders have tried prescription amphetamines, with 3.4% reporting use of the drugs in the prior month. Amphetamine use was highest among white high school students in comparison to African-American and Hispanic high school students. Adolescent girls were also more likely to abuse amphetamines than boys. This trend reversed in the older subjects surveyed, with males aged 19 to 32 reporting slightly higher use of amphetamines than females of the same age group.

Among 40-year-olds included in a follow-up of the study, 53% had tried amphetamines at some point in their lifetime. However, only 1% reported use of the drugs in the past year.

MENTAL EFFECTS

Dextroamphetamine stimulates the production of the neurotransmitters dopamine and norepinephrine. Neurotransmitters are the brain chemicals responsible for transporting electrical impulses from nerve cell to nerve cell. Dopamine, the neurotransmitter associated with feelings of pleasure, triggers the euphoria that is related to dextroamphetamine use. Norepinephrine is a neurotransmitter thought to be responsible for the adrenaline-like effects of the drug.

Because it stimulates the central nervous system, dextroamphetamine fights mental fatigue. The drug can also improve mood and give users a sense of power, euphoria, and well-being. With chronic use, however, it may cause obsessive thoughts and feelings of paranoia, anxiety, hypersensitivity—and, in extreme cases, psychosis.

Amphetamine psychosis causes feelings of severe paranoia and auditory and visual hallucinations. The amphetamine addict who is psychotic typically experiences delusions of persecution, believing someone, or everyone, is "out to get" them. Because of these paranoid delusions, violence can frequently occur during amphetamine psychosis. Once the amphetamine abuser is free of the drug, psychosis fades quickly. However, symptoms such as mental confusion, memory problems, and delusional thoughts may last up to several months or longer.

PHYSIOLOGICAL EFFECTS

In addition to their trademark effects on mood and mental status, dextroamphetamines significantly influence the cardiovascular system. They increase the heart rate and boost blood pressure. They are also weak bronchodilators—meaning they open the bronchial tubes (air passages) of the lungs. In fact, one of the early uses for dextroamphetamines was asthma treatment.

Dextroamphetamine also acts as an anoretic agent, suppressing appetite. Formulas popular in the 1970s, such as Obetrol, were marketed as weight loss drugs.

Harmful side effects

Common side effects of dextroamphetamine include, but are not limited to:

- difficulty sleeping
- dry mouth
- unintentional weight loss
- headache
- nausea
- nervousness
- rash
- picking at the skin
- rise in blood pressure and pulse
- diarrhea or constipation

When used for medical purposes, dextroamphetamines are prescribed at the lowest possible dosage. The dosage is then raised gradually until the desired therapeutic effect is achieved. All amphetamines are highly addictive. Tolerance to the drug builds slowly but steadily. Tolerance occurs when it takes more and more of the drug to produce the same physiological effects. With amphetamines, it may also develop unevenly, with some effects of the drug weakening before others.

Symptoms of overdose may include panic or anxiety attacks, hallucinations, confusion, tremor or shaking, arrhythmia (irregular heartbeat), vomiting, collapse of the circulatory system, stomach cramps, convulsions, and coma. Overdose can be fatal.

Dextroamphetamine can make tics worse, so its use may not be recommended for someone with Tourette's syndome or another tic disorder. Anyone who suffers from hypertension, arteriosclerosis, hyperthyroidism, or glaucoma should also not take dextroamphetamines.

Animal studies show that amphetamine abuse may cause birth defects. There are no controlled studies of this effect in humans; however it is known that pregnant women who are amphetamine-dependent may give birth prematurely and are more likely to have infants with a low birth weight. Amphetamines cross the placenta, so a baby born to an amphetamine abuser may experience withdrawal symptoms once the drug begins to leave the infant's system.

Amphetamines also pass into a nursing mother's milk. For this reason, women taking amphetamines should avoid breastfeeding. Dextroamphetamines are not recommended for the treatment of ADHD in children under the age of 3, as the drugs have not been sufficiently tested in this age group. In addition, there are few long-term follow-up studies on the long-term effects of extended dextroamphetamine use by pediatric ADHD patients.

Long-term health effects

Chronic dextroamphetamine use and abuse can cause sexual dysfunction (impotence). Because of the stress amphetamines place on the cardiovascular system, heart attack, cardiovascular shock, and cerebral hemorrhage may also occur with chronic use.

Symptoms of dextroamphetamine abuse include insomnia, irritability, hyperactivity, and psychosis. Psychosis is characterized by radical changes in personality, impaired functioning, and a distorted sense of reality. Hallucinations, delusions, and feelings of paranoia are also common features of psychosis.

Withdrawal from chronic amphetamine abuse can be long and difficult. Also, it results in depression and at least two of the following symptoms: fatigue, vivid dreams, irregular sleep patterns, increased appetite, and psychomotor problems.

REACTIONS WITH OTHER DRUGS OR SUBSTANCES

Dextroamphetamines interact with a number of drugs and other substances. These include:

- Hypertension drugs. Because amphetamines stimulate the circulatory system and raise blood pressure, they can inhibit the effect of drugs used to lower blood pressure.

- MAOIs. MAO inhibitors, a class of antidepressant drugs, can slow the metabolism of amphetamines. This mix of drugs may result in skyrocketing blood pressure, severe headaches, and potentially fatal neurological damage.

- Tricyclic antidepressants. When taken with dextroamphetamine, the effects of tricyclic antidepressants (such as desipramine) may increase.

- Meperidine (Demerol). Amphetamines can increase the analgesic (pain killing) effect of meperidine.

- Ethosuximide (Zerontin). The intestinal absorption of this anti-epileptic drug is effected by dextroamphetamine, which may delay or decrease its effectiveness.

The drug chlorpromazine (Thorazine) blocks the effects amphetamines have on the central nervous system, and is sometimes used to treat cases of amphetamine overdose or intoxication. Additional drugs, foods, and substances that may also counteract dextroamphetamines and make them less effective include antihistamines, lithium carbonate, haloperidol, and any acidic agent such as fruit juice or ascorbic acid.

Other drugs may increase the effects of dextroamphetamine. For example, bicarbonate and other alkalinizing agents increase the amount of amphetamines absorbed in the digestive system. Thiazides (potassium-depleting diuretics) decrease the amount of amphetamines that leave the body in urine. Also, other central nervous system stimulants, such as cocaine and nicotine, can amplify the stimulating effects of dextroamphetamines.

TREATMENT AND REHABILITATION

Treatment for amphetamine dependence may be either "inpatient" or "outpatient." Inpatient, or residential, drug programs require a patient to live at the hospital or rehab facility for a period of several weeks to several months. Outpatient programs allow patients to spend part of their day at the treatment facility, and return home at night.

For amphetamine addicts and drug abusers, the controlled, therapeutic environment of residential rehab provides a safe place to learn new behaviors and explore the emotional issues behind their drug use. And for patients experiencing amphetamine or other drug withdrawal symptoms, an inpatient facility is the best option for a safe and gradual detoxification from the drug.

Once an amphetamine abuser stops taking the drug, withdrawal symptoms begin as the body tries to adjust to the absence of the stimulant. This results in very uncomfortable and potentially life-threatening physical symptoms, called withdrawal syndrome. According to the World Health Organization (WHO), withdrawal is experienced by 87% of amphetamine users who stop the drug.

Frequent symptoms of amphetamine withdrawal include excessive fatigue and depression. These may also occur: nausea, vomiting, chills, cramps, headaches, and arrhythmia (a change in the rhythm of the heartbeat). A physician may prescribe antidepressants to help alleviate depression during amphetamine withdrawal. Also during withdrawal, if psychosis and/or hallucinations are experienced, treatment with chlorpromazine (Thorazine) or haloperidol (Haldol) may be necessary. Finally, ammonium chloride may be prescribed to more quickly remove amphetamines through the urine.

Once detoxification is complete, the drug abuser can start the rehabilitation and long-term recovery process with a clear head. Research shows that detoxification alone is not an effective treatment. Addicts who leave rehab immediately after detox with no further counseling or interventions will likely soon be abusing stimulants or another mind-altering substance again.

Recovery refers to the life-long process of avoiding drug use, as well as the mental and physical rehabilitation of the damage done by drug abuse. An individual in recovery from drug addiction must avoid all psychoactive drugs, including alcohol. Amphetamine cravings can be extremely powerful, and may last indefinitely. Anything can "trigger" a relapse.

An effective drug rehabilitation program changes patterns of behavior and deals with the underlying emotional issues surrounding drug use. Education about the long-term physical and psychological effects of substance abuse is also typically part of a rehab program.

Therapy and/or counseling is also very important. Different therapy approaches used in substance abuse treatment include: individual psychotherapy, behavioral therapy, cognitive-behavioral therapy, group therapy, and family therapy. Often, more than one therapeutic approach is used during drug rehabilitation.

Individual psychotherapy

One-on-one counseling explores the emotional issues underlying a patient's drug dependence and abuse. Individual psychotherapy is particularly useful when there is also some type of mental disorder, such as depression or an anxiety disorder, along with the drug abuse.

Behavioral therapy

Behavioral therapy focuses on replacing unhealthy behaviors with healthier ones. It uses tools such as rewards (positive reinforcement for healthy behavior) and rehearsal (practicing the new behavior) to achieve a drug-free life.

Cognitive-behavioral therapy

Like behavioral therapy, cognitive-behavioral therapy (CBT) also tries teaching new behavioral patterns. However, the primary difference is CBT assumes that thinking is behind behavior and emotions. Therefore, CBT also focuses on—and tries to change—the thoughts that led to the drug abuse.

Family therapy

Family members often develop habits and ways of coping (called "enabling") that accidentally help the addict continue their substance abuse. Group counseling sessions with a licensed counselor or therapist can help family members build healthy relationships and relearn old behaviors. This is particularly important for adolescents in drug treatment, who should be able to rely on the support of family.

HISTORY NOTES

Dextroamphetamine has a long history of use by the military. After distribution of the drug in the fields and foxholes of World War II, the American Armed Forces started zealously testing the drug on their pilots and other personnel. One study of amphetamine use in the military reported that between 1966 and 1969, the U.S. military consumed more amphetamines than the British and American armed forces combined during World War II.

Amphetamine research continued into the twenty-first century. A study performed by the United States Army Aeromedical Research Laboratory and published in 2000 describes the use of Dexedrine in a pilot kept awake for 64 hours. Other research has reported dextroamphetamine's success in improving alertness and flight performance by fighting fatigue, confusion, and air sickness in the cockpit without the presence of detrimental side effects. A 1995 report from Langley Air Force Base revealed widespread amphetamine use in Operation Desert Storm. Sixty-five percent of U.S. Air Force Tactical Air Command pilots surveyed reported taking amphetamines during their missions, with 58–61% of users considering amphetamine use essential to the operation. Indications for use of the drug included "aircrew fatigue" and "mission type."

Group therapy

Group therapy offers recovering drug abusers a safe and comfortable place to work out problems with peers and a group leader (typically a therapist or counselor). It also provides drug abusers insight into their thoughts and behaviors through the eyes and experiences of others. Substance abusers who have difficulty building healthy relationships can benefit from the interactions in group therapy. Offering suggestions and emotional support to other members of the group can help improve their self-esteem and social skills.

Self-help and 12-step groups

Self-help organizations offer recovering drug abusers and addicts important support groups to replace their former drug-using social circle. They also help create an important sense of identity and belonging to a new, recovery-focused group.

Twelve-step groups, one of the most popular types of self-help organizations, have been active in the United States since the founding of Alcoholics Anonymous (AA) in 1935. Narcotics Anonymous (NA), a group that serves recovering drug addicts, was founded in 1953. Like AA and other 12-step programs, NA is based on the spiritual philosophy that turning one's will and life over to "a higher power" (i.e., God, another spiritual entity, or the group itself) for guidance and self-evaluation is the key to lasting recovery.

The accessibility of self-help groups is one of their most attractive features. No dues or fees are required for AA and NA, so they're a good option for the uninsured and underinsured. Meetings are held in public places like local hospitals, healthcare centers, churches, and other community organizations, and frequent and regular attendance is encouraged.

In addition, 12-step groups work to empower members and promote self-esteem and self-reliance. NA meetings are not run by a counselor or therapist, but by the group or a member of the group. And the organization encourages sponsorship (mentoring another member), speaking at meetings, and other positive peer-to-peer interactions that can help reinforce healthy social behaviors. Today, the internet and on-line support communities has added a further degree of accessibility to those who live in rural or remote areas.

PERSONAL AND SOCIAL CONSEQUENCES

Criminal drug charges may harm future employment, career advancement, and educational opportunities. Amendments made to the Higher Education Act in 1998 make anyone convicted of a drug offense ineligible for federal student loans for anywhere from one year to indefinitely. They may also be ineligible for state aid. An individual convicted of a drug offense may also be denied employment based on his or her criminal history.

Amphetamine abusers and addicts become preoccupied with when and where they will be able to get their next dose. Relationships with family and friends frequently deteriorate as the drug takes center stage in the addict's life. Money problems may began to surface as the addict funds his growing habit. Substance abuse also contributes to crime, domestic violence, sexual assault, drop-out rates, unemployment, and homelessness. It is also a factor in the spread of sexually transmitted diseases (STDs) and unwanted pregnancy.

The financial toll is enormous as well. The Office of National Drug Control Policy estimated an economic loss due to illicit drugs of over $160 billion from the U.S. economy for the year 2000. This figure represented an increase of 5.8% annually between 1998 and 2000, and included $14.8 billion in healthcare costs and $110.4 billion in lost productivity from drug-related illness, incarceration, and death.

LEGAL CONSEQUENCES

Abuse of any amphetamine can have serious legal consequences. A conviction of illegal possession of amphetamines in the United States carries fines of up to $10,000 and possible jail time. A felony may also result in the loss of one's driver's license and right to vote, depending on the state where the conviction occurred.

Under the Controlled Substances Act of 1988, being arrested for use or possession of a small amount of dextroamphetamine in the United States is classified by the U.S. Drug Enforcement Administration (DEA) as a "personal use amount." Anyone charged with an offense of possessing a personal use amount faces a civil fine of up to $10,000. The fine amount is based on the offender's income and assets, as well as the circumstances surrounding the case. With first offenses, jail time is typically not involved, and the proceedings are civil rather than criminal. This means that if the offender pays the fine, stays out of trouble for three years, and passes a subsequent drug test, the case is dismissed and no criminal or civil record of it is made.

Olympic athletes who test positive for amphetamines are suspended from participation in the Games. They may also be stripped of any medals they have won in competition.

Legal history

The Drug Abuse Control Amendments of 1965—the legislation that formed the FDA Bureau of Drug Abuse Control—gave the FDA tighter regulatory control over amphetamines, barbiturates, and other prescription drugs with high abuse potential. By 1970, legal control of amphetamines was even stricter, with the drug being placed in Schedule II of the new Controlled Substances Act (CSA).

Schedule II drugs are prescription medications that have a legitimate medical use, but are recognized as having a high potential for abuse that may lead to severe psychological and/or physical dependence. To prevent abuse and diversion, schedule II drugs (like dextroamphetamine) require a written doctor's prescription, do not allow automatic refills, and require special security precautions. Pharmacies and hospitals that dispense schedule II drugs must register with the DEA. In addition, limits are placed on the amount of dextroamphetamine produced by manufacturers for the U.S. each year.

Federal guidelines, regulations, and penalties

While dextroamphetamine's more potent cousin, methamphetamine, is frequently made in secret labs with potentially dangerous substances, the majority of illicit dextroamphetamine drug supply comes actual prescription drugs obtained illegally, either through fraud or theft.

Anyone convicted of transporting or dealing dextroamphetamine faces stiff penalties. Federal guidelines mandate that a first-time trafficking offender face up to 20 years in prison and a $1 million fine. If death or serious injury is involved with the trafficking charge, the sentence must be at least 20 years with a maximum sentence of life in prison.

Amphetamines are designated a class B drug in the United Kingdom under the Misuse of Drugs Act 1971. Possession carries a penalty of imprisonment for three months to five years, and trafficking carries a sentence of six months to 14 years. A fine may also be imposed.

See also Amphetamines; Methamphetamine; Methylphenidate

RESOURCES

Books

American Psychiatric Association. *Diagnostic and Statistical Manual of Mental Disorders.* 4th ed. Washington, DC: American Psychiatric Press, Inc., 1994.

Physicians' Desk Reference. 56th ed. Montvale, NJ: Medical Economics, 2002.

Periodicals

Emonson, D., and R. Vanderbeek. "The Use of Amphetamines in U.S. Air Force Tactical Operations during Desert Shield and Storm." *Aviation Space and Environmental Medicine* 66, 3 (1995): 802.

Johnston, Lloyd D., et al. *Monitoring the Future: National Survey Results on Drug Use, 1975-2000.* Vols. I and II. Bethesda, MD: National Institute on Drug Abuse, 2001.

Other

Drugs of Abuse. U.S. Drug Enforcement Administration. March 20, 2002 (April 1, 2002). <http://www.usdoj.gov/dea/concern/abuse/contents.htm>.

U.S. Anti-Doping Agency. 2001 (April 1, 2002). <http://www.usantidoping.org/>.

Organizations

National Institute on Drug Abuse (NIDA); part of the National Institutes of Health (NIH), 6001 Executive Boulevard, Room 5213, Bethesda, MD, USA, 20892-9561, (301) 443-1124, (888) 644-6432, Information@lists.nida.nih.gov, <http://www.nida.nih.gov/>.

Paula Anne Ford-Martin

DEXTROMETHORPHAN

OFFICIAL NAMES: Benylin Adult Formula Cough Syrup, Benylin Pediatric Cough Suppressant, Benylin Expectorant, Cheracol-D, Cough-X, Creo-Terpin, Delsym Cough Formula, Diabe-TUSS DM Syrup, Duratuss DM, Fenesin DM, GG-DM SR, Glycotuss-DM, Guaibid DM, Guaifenex DM, Halotussin DM, Hold DM, Humibid DM, Iophen DM NR, Mucobid DM, Naldecon DX Liquigel, Pertussin CS Children's Strength, Pertussin DM Extra Strength, Respa-DM, Robitussin Maximum Strength Cough Suppressant, Robitussin Pediatric Cough Suppressant, Safe Tussin 30, Scot-Tussin DM, Sucrets 4-Hour Cough Suppressant, T-Tusin DM, Touro DM, Trocal, Tuss-DM, Tussi-Organidin DM NR, Vicks 44 Cough Relief

STREET NAMES: Roboing, DXM, robo, skittles, vitamin D, dex, tussin

DRUG CLASSIFICATIONS: Not scheduled, antitussive

OVERVIEW

Dextromethorphan is an agent used to help control coughs that are associated with influenza or colds. It has the cough-suppressing effects of its distantly related family, the opiates, but does not produce the significant effects on the central nervous system as they do. When used at therapeutic, or recommended, doses, dextromethorphan does not produce respiratory depression properties or other significant side effects that are common in most opiates. Cough syrups sold over the counter often have dextromethorphan as one of the key ingredients.

Dextromethorphan is not used to treat coughs that are chronic in nature, such as those associated with asthma, smoking, or emphysema, nor is it used in cases where there is a significant amount of mucous or phlegm associated with the cough. Dextromethorphan produces its cough-suppressing effects by depressing the cough center in the medulla region of the brain.

Dextromethorphan is available without a prescription in the United States. However, most patients receive special instructions from their physician on how to use this medication properly.

There is increasing concern over the street abuse of dextromethorphan, which is available in a variety of products. There have been a few reports of abuse and a handful of case reports of overdose and death. Nevertheless, dextromethorphan was specifically left out of the Controlled Substances Act (CSA) of 1970 and has not been added to the Drug Enforcement Administration (DEA) scheduling process despite these reports. This decision was made because dextromethorphan is not considered a narcotic and is generally thought to have a low addiction potential. However, the DEA is monitoring dextromethorphan and may add it to its list of controlled substances at some point in the future.

Abusers of dextromethorphan are sometimes referred to as "syrup heads." When large amounts of dextromethorphan-containing solution are ingested, it is often referred to as "robodosing" or "robo-tripping." Heavy ingestion of dextromethorphan may cause abusers to stagger, sometimes referred to as the "robo-walk." The decreased cognitive function associated with abuse is sometimes referred to as "drippy."

CHEMICAL/ORGANIC COMPOSITION

Dextromethorphan (d-3-methoxy-N-methylmorphinan), a chemical relative of levomethorphan, was developed by modifying levomethorphan. However, unlike levomethorphan, dextromethorphan officially has no addictive or analgesic properties.

INGESTION METHODS

Dextromethorphan is administered by the oral route only in the forms of syrup, lozenges, extended-release oral suspension, chewable tablets, and capsules.

Extra fluid should be ingested when taking dextromethorphan for therapeutic purposes, which helps relieve congestion associated with colds or influenza. Dextromethorphan should also be taken with food if it upsets the patient's stomach. The liquid form of dextromethorphan should be measured carefully with a special spoon or cup and not with a standard tablespoon to accurately measure the correct amount; pharmacists can often provide these accurate measuring devices. Dextromethorphan should be used only as directed by a physician. If the instructions are unclear, the patient can usually receive reliable information about dextromethorphan from a pharmacist or nurse.

There have been reports that dextromethorphan is sometimes sniffed when used in a recreational abusive situation.

THERAPEUTIC USE

Dextromethorphan is generally used in the relief of cough associated with colds or influenza, but is not associated with any chronic conditions such as asthma, smoking, and emphysema. Dextromethorphan is combined with different compounds to produce varying effects. One such combination is with guaifenesin and pseudoephedrine. Guaifenesin is a drug called an expectorant, which means that it helps expel bronchial secretions from the respiratory tract. Pseudoephedrine hydrochloride is a decongestant that helps clear the nasal passages.

Iodinated glycerol, another agent that is often combined with dextromethorphan, functions as an expectorant. Promethazine hydrochloride is an antihistamine agent sometimes combined with dextromethorphan.

Precautions

Dextromethorphan should be used with caution in individuals who are debilitated or under sedation. Individuals who are prescribed bed rest should also use the drug with great caution. If the symptoms of the condi-

KEY TERMS

ANTICONVULSANTS: Drugs that relieve or prevent seizures.

ECSTASY: The street name for MDMA, an illegal club drug that is mildly hallucinogenic.

HYPERSENSITIVITY: An unusual response to a given stimulus.

MEDULLA: The lower portion of the brain stem.

RESPIRATORY DEPRESSION: The slowing of a person's breathing rate. Severe respiratory depression can cause a person to go into a coma or even stop breathing.

tion are not completely resolved with the use of dextromethorphan, then a physician should be consulted about performing additional diagnostic tests or alternative treatment plans. Those with a history of hypersensitivity to dextromethorphan with side effects such as heart rhythm changes, tremor, insomnia, dizziness, and weakness should not use it.

Dextromethorphan should be used with great caution in individuals who have a history of chronic or persistent cough, persistent headache, nausea, vomiting, or fever.

USAGE TRENDS

Dextromethorphan abuse has increased in recent years. This has also coincided with an increase in the reports of adverse effects, including rare case reports of overdose and death. Many users have switched to a concentrated, powdered form of the drug instead of the significant volumes of cough syrup that need to be ingested to become intoxicated. This powdered form, called dextromethorphan hydrobromide, is being sold at an increased rate. Furthermore, a relatively simple step-by-step method for obtaining dextromethorphan from cough syrup has been published on the Internet.

Contrary to the effects associated with the therapeutic use of dextromethorphan, those who abuse the drug report a variety of mind-altering effects such as visual hallucinations, changes in time perception, and an increased sense of perceptual awareness. It has been determined that a small amount of Robitussin can produce intoxication in most persons. Abusers have been found to use anywhere from one-half bottle to three or four bottles of Robitussin every day. Drinking large amounts of Robitussin or other cough syrups tends to cause vomiting.

LAW AND ORDER

While the DEA is keeping a watchful eye on the abuse trends of dextromethorphan, many states are starting to take notice of the drug and its abuse. Still, most states have little or no legal guidelines regulating or restricting the use of the drug. One state that has done something is Utah, which passed a law that required pharmacies and other cough syrup vendors to place medications containing dextromethorphan behind the counter so that greater control could be placed over their sale. The passage of this law in the 1980s followed a significant increase in abuse of the drug by adolescents in the state.

Pennsylvania's drug and cosmetics-regulating body also began to have concerns about dextromethorphan and its potential for abuse in 1990. This body organized an investigation of the drug following a rash of reports in the media as well as reports from government entities in other states that indicated dextromethorphan was becoming a significant abuse problem. The investigation eventually found insufficient data to justify a change in the over-the-counter status of the drug.

Dextromethorphan is sold alone or, when mixed with other drugs such as phenylpropanolamine or ephedrine, is marketed as "ecstasy," after the widely abused street drug. Of course, this formulation is not the same compound as ecstasy. It has also been used to deceive persons who are seeking to buy narcotics such as heroin. The greatest amount of dextromethorphan abuse so far has occurred with the over-the-counter cough formulas. Reportedly, dextromethorphan is also being sold on the Internet in pill and capsule forms as well as the powder.

A recent survey of 315 students in the fourth through twelfth grades who used over-the-counter medications to become intoxicated found that a majority used a medication that contained dextromethorphan. The study found that the risk of abusing dextromethorphan increased with age, and that dextromethorphan has a greater abuse potential than previously identified in scientific literature.

Age, ethnic, and gender trends

Nearly all of the abusers have been reported to be teenagers and young adults. There is no current information on abuse trends among different ethnic groups or among males and females.

MENTAL EFFECTS

Dizziness may occur in a small proportion of cases when dextromethorphan is used therapeutically. Mental confusion and central nervous system overstimulation may occur when there is an overdose of the drug. When dextromethorphan is abused, there is an increased risk of motor impairment that could affect activities that require quick judgment and reaction, such as operating heavy machinery.

PHYSIOLOGICAL EFFECTS

Dextromethorphan produces effects centrally at the cough center to raise the threshold for coughing. Researchers have also proposed that dextromethorphan has important interactions with compounds in the brain that have excitatory effects. Some researchers believe that dextromethorphan may eventually be used as a drug to protect the brain against strokes and bacterial meningitis. However, the Food and Drug Administration (FDA) has not yet approved dextromethorphan for these uses.

Researchers have determined that dextromethorphan is approximately equal to codeine in cough-suppressing ability. Dextromethorphan is rapidly absorbed from the gastrointestinal tract of the body where it is metabolized by the liver and then mostly excreted in the urine. Dextromethorphan begins to exert its effects within 15 to 30 minutes. The duration of the drug's action is about three to six hours.

Dextromethorphan has been placed in the FDA pregnancy category C, meaning that it has yet to be determined whether this drug can harm an unborn baby. Pregnant women should not take this drug without first consulting their physician. Researchers do not yet know if dextromethorphan passes into the breast milk in the nursing mother. Dextromethorphan cannot be detected by using any currently available urine screening techniques or during a standard clinical examination.

Harmful side effects

Significant side effects are extremely uncommon with dextromethorphan when it is taken at therapeutic levels. However, dizziness and nausea can occur in a small proportion of cases. Like most drugs, dextromethorphan can be dangerous when taken at levels above the therapeutic range. In such cases, central nervous system over-stimulation can occur. Conversely, mental confusion can occur in these cases. Extremely high doses can lead to respiratory depression. Young people are increasingly abusing dextromethorphan at nightclubs or "raves." It is here where the drug is either mixed with, or substituted for, ecstasy. The combination of drug use and vigorous dancing has led to an increased number of reports of users developing heatstroke-like symptoms.

The intoxication syndrome associated with dextromethorphan tends to produce the following symptoms in the abuser: high blood pressure, clumsiness, disrupted speech, increased sweating, increased excitability, changes in eye movement, and fatigue. More general symptoms of overdose can include muscle spasticity in the body as a whole, slow and labored breathing, shallow breathing, pinpoint pupils, bluish tint to fingernails and lips, spasms in the gastrointestinal tract, low blood pressure, weak pulse, hallucinations, and drowsiness.

Emergency medical personnel should be contacted immediately if an overdose is suspected. If a poison control center suspects a dextromethorphan overdose, induced vomiting may be recommended. The usual home treatment involves the administration of ipecac syrup to induce vomiting.

Long-term health effects

No serious long-term effects are associated with the therapeutic use of dextromethorphan. However, information has not been adequately collected on the health effects associated with the long-term abuse of dextromethorphan.

REACTIONS WITH OTHER DRUGS OR SUBSTANCES

Patients should not use dextromethorphan if they are taking any drug in the class known as monoamine oxidase inhibitors (MAOI), including phenelzine (Nardil), isocarboxazid (Marplan), and tranylcypromine (Parnate), which are used in the treatment of depression. The combination of MAOIs with dextromethorphan can lead to toxic levels of dextromethorphan in the blood.

Dextromethorphan is known to interact with quinidine and terbinafine. In both cases, there is a reduction in the metabolism of dextromethorphan by the liver. Terbinafine is a drug used to treat fungal infections. Quinidine is used for the treatment of malarial infections and heart rhythm problems. There has been a case report of a drug interaction between the use of fluoxetine (Prozac) and dextromethorphan. Fluoxetine is an antidepressant in the class of drugs called serotonin reuptake inhibitors.

TREATMENT AND REHABILITATION

While there is a general belief that dextromethorphan is not addictive, there is an increasing amount of information that suggests otherwise. The fact that many abusers repeatedly abuse the drug makes it a strong possibility that dextromethorphan is an addictive drug.

???? FACT OR FICTION

The World Health Organization classified dextromethorphan as a non-analgesic, non-addictive substance in the late 1960s. In 1970, the Controlled Substance Act further added weight to this notion that dextromethorphan is not in the same class of drugs as its opiate forbearers in its abuse potential. This led to the decision of the DEA to leave dextromethorphan off its schedules of controlled substances.

However, in the period since this decision, it has become increasingly clear that dextromethorphan is an abused drug. The degree to which it is abused is not really known, and this explains why the DEA is carefully monitoring this over-the-counter drug and its increasing availability on the Internet. State drug enforcement agencies are also keeping a watchful eye on dextromethorphan and its abuse, especially among adolescents. Both the DEA and the states may move the drug to the list of controlled substances in the coming years. Such a move would likely deal a severe blow to the abuse of dextromethorphan.

Despite the undoubted increase in the abuse of dextromethorphan, it is not scientifically known how addictive the substance is. Officially, it is not considered a strongly addictive substance. However, the pattern of abuse would suggest that its addictive potential is greatly underrated.

Conventional treatment programs can help those who abuse dextromethorphan, but they must become informed about the specific features of the drug. These programs must also test for the drug using a less familiar test.

There are two types of dependence when addictive drugs are used for a significant period of time. Physical dependence is when the body becomes physiologically adapted to having the drugs in the body; it is not the same as being addicted. Physical dependence does not usually develop to a clinically obvious degree until after the drug has been used for several weeks. Physical dependence occurs when withdrawal symptoms develop after the drug is no longer being used. There is no known withdrawal syndrome associated with the cessation of dextromethorphan use. It is unlikely that dextromethorphan causes physical dependence.

Psychological dependence is synonymous with addiction. Persons with a psychological dependence on a drug generally have a history of compulsive behaviors and a propensity to become involved with drugs for non-

HISTORY NOTES

While it is true that dextromethorphan is not technically a member of the opiate family, it is distantly related in its chemical composition. Dextromethorphan is created by from levomethorphan, which is classified as an opioid, the synthetic or semi-synthetic relatives of the natural chemical family called the opiates. Levomethorphan has most of the same qualities of all drugs in the opiate and opioid classes. This includes strong suppressive effects on the respiratory system. It is these strong effects on the respiratory system that make dextromethorphan an effective anti-cough agent. Opiate and opioid compounds have anti-cough properties but produce greater overall respiratory depression than dextromethorphan.

It was initially believed that dextromethorphan preserved the anti-cough properties of the opioid drugs but not many of the other therapeutic and harmful effects of the opioid class. This is why dextromethorphan was not included in the list of drugs comprising the Controlled Substances Act of 1970. It is certainly true that dextromethorphan taken at recommended therapeutic levels has anti-cough properties and virtually no analgesic or harmful side effects. However, new evidence suggests that when this drug is taken in extremely high doses, analgesic- and narcotic-like effects occur.

medical reasons. Addiction may or may not occur with physical dependence or tolerance. Patients with legitimate medical needs for a drug usually do not become addicted and can receive increased doses over time without becoming addicted. Of the two types of dependence, dextromethorphan is more likely to cause some type of psychological dependence. However, there is no scientific confirmation of this yet.

The general treatment program for dextromethorphan abuse and potential dependence should be similar to other drug treatment regimens. The patient should receive extensive counseling, education, and monitoring to end the cycle of abuse and dependence. However, dextromethorphan use probably does not need to be gradually tapered down to prevent or reduce withdrawal symptoms as there is no current evidence that dextromethorphan is physically addictive. Dextromethorphan urinalysis testing requires a special test that is typically not used for other types of abused substances.

PERSONAL AND SOCIAL CONSEQUENCES

Currently, there is no evidence that the abuse of over-the-counter medications necessarily leads to a progression of addiction to illicit substances such as opiates, cocaine, or amphetamines. However, evidence gathered from many research studies suggests some association between the abuse of drugs and the progression of abuse to stronger and more dangerous drugs.

LEGAL CONSEQUENCES

With the exception of some restrictions on product placement in states such as Utah, there are no significant legal consequences for using, abusing, producing, and selling dextromethorphan.

Legal history

Opiates were legal in the United States until a federal law was enacted in 1914. Until then, it was legal to put opiates into patent medicines, for example, that were sold over-the-counter. The 1914 law was the first to regulate the sale and distribution of controlled substances. This law was not enacted to benefit public health, however, but to generate tax revenue.

Federal guidelines, regulations, and penalties

Dextromethorphan is not classified as a controlled substance under the Controlled Substances Act (CSA) of 1970. The CSA was created as a means to regulate the distribution and use of prescription drugs that are highly addictive, such as codeine, oxycodone, morphine, and hydromorphone.

The Drug Enforcement Administration (DEA) and Food and Drug Administration (FDA) are aggressively monitoring the use and abuse of dextromethorphan. It is conceivable that dextromethorphan could be first classified as a drug obtainable only with a prescription. Furthermore, the DEA could place dextromethorphan on one of its schedules of controlled substances, which would force physicians, pharmacists, nurses, and hospitals to record the administration of the drug. At this stage, the former is far more likely than the latter since it has not been proven that dextromethorphan is an addictive substance.

See also Ecstasy (MDMA)

RESOURCES

Books

Booth, Martin. *Opium: A History.* New York: St. Martin's Press, 1996.

 **IN THE NEWS**

There is evidence that most abusers keep abusing dextromethorphan because it is legal and readily available. In addition, the pattern of abuse spreads from one person to another within a social group and from one social group to another as young people gather at venues where other drugs such as ecstasy are being used.

An entire subculture is beginning to develop around the abuse of dextromethorphan. This subculture tends to encourage the use and abuse of the drug. Musical groups such as Oedipus Complex, Dr. Max, and Nightchild devote songs to the drug and reportedly write some of their songs while under the influence of the drug. There are now several Web sites on the Internet that encourage the use of dextromethorphan.

Many of these sites have graphics that are purportedly similar visually to the mental images that are sometimes generated when abusing the drug. These Web sites also contain information about how to purchase, produce, and take the drug. Some of the more responsible sites offer information about risks and side effects. Other sites contain information about how to obtain bulk quantities of dextromethorphan powder that enables individ-uals to package the drug into capsules or tablets to be sold or given away at raves or dance clubs. Often, the formulations are designed in an attractive manner with varying colors and shapes. This type of production and distribution is especially dangerous since there is no quality control as in over-the-counter cough formulations, and doses can be wildly variable.

Many of those concerned with the problem of dextromethorphan abuse are pointing to education as the best solution to the problem, at least in the short term. Prevention is an approach that is more effective when a drug is illegal or available only through prescription. Dextromethorphan will likely be legal and available over the counter for some time. Another unusual feature of dextromethorphan is that it is not detectable with standard drug testing, so most drug treatment programs, organizations, and corporations do not test for it. Testing plays a large role in the control of illicit drugs.

Dextromethorphan is a relatively inexpensive drug for individuals to abuse due to its legal status and an abundant supply of the substance as an over-the-counter drug. These factors are the primary reason for the increasing abuse of the drug. It is one of the easiest ways for adolescents to become intoxicated without breaking the law, as is the case for illegal drugs such as marijuana, prescription drugs such as oxycodone, and legal but restricted substances such as alcohol.

Consumer Reports Complete Drug Reference, 2002 Edition. Denver: Micromedex Thomson Healthcare, 2001.

Ellsworth, Allan J., et al. *Mosby's Medical Drug Reference, 2001-2002.* St. Louis: Mosby, 2001.

Hardman, Joel G., and Lee E. Limbird, ed. *Goodman & Gilman's: The Pharmacological Basis of Therapeutics.* 10th Edition. New York: McGraw-Hill, 2001.

Mosby's GenRx. 9th Edition. St. Louis: Mosby, 1999.

Tierney, Lawrence M., et al, eds. *Current Medical Diagnosis & Treatment.* 39th Edition. New York: McGraw-Hill, 2000.

Venes, Donald, et al, eds. *Taber's Cyclopedic Medical Dictionary.* 19th Edition. Philadelphia: F.A. Davis, 2001.

Periodicals

Noonan, Craig, et al. "Dextromethorphan Abuse Among Youth." *Archives of Family Medicine* 9 (2000): 791.

Other

Burcham, Lee. "Convenience-Store High: How Ordinary Cough Medicine is Being Abused for its Mind-Altering Effects." *The National Clearinghouse for Alcohol and Drug Information Reporter* June 12, 2001.

"Dextromethorphan." International Programme on Chemical Safety Poisons Information Monograph 179. <http://www.inchem.org>.

"Dextromethorphan." United States Department of Justice Drug Enforcement Administration Diversion Control Program. <http://www.deadiversion.usdoj.gov>.

"Dextromethorphan Overdose." MEDLINEplus Medical Encyclopedia. <http://www.nlm.nih.gov>.

Factline on Non-Medical Use of Dextromethorphan. Indiana Prevention Resource Center. <http://www.drugs.indiana.edu>.

"Hallucinogens and Dissociative Drugs." National Institute on Drug Abuse. <http://www.nida.nih.gov>.

Organizations

National Clearinghouse for Alcohol and Drug Information (NCADI), P.O. Box 2345, Rockville, MD, USA, 20847-2345, (800) 729-6686, webmaster@health.org, <http://www.health.org>.

National Drug Intelligence Center (NDIC), 319 Washington Street, 5th Floor, Johnstown, PA, USA, 15901-1622, (814) 532-4601, (814) 532-4690, cmbwebmgr@ndic.osis.gov, <http://www.usdoj.gov/ndic/>.

National Institute on Drug Abuse (NIDA), National Institutes of Health, 6001 Executive Boulevard, Room 5213, Bethesda, MD, USA, 20892-9561, (301) 443-1124, (888) 644-6432, information@lists.nida.nih.gov, <http://www.nida.nih.gov>.

Substance Abuse and Mental Health Services Administration (SAMHSA)/Center for Substance Abuse Treatment (CSAT), 5600 Fishers Lane, Rockville, MD, USA, 20857, (301) 443-8956, info@samhsa.gov, <http://www.samhsa.gov>.

Mark A. Mitchell, M.D.

DIET PILLS

The use of diet pills to lose weight is a twentieth-century phenomenon that carried over into the twenty-first century. During earlier centuries, society regarded plumpness as a sign of good health. Up until the late nineteenth century, a full figure indicated financial status, because a plump person could afford to eat.

An 1880s American drawing portrayed a woman asking her doctor for advice about a "fattening cure" to help her gain weight. A sign on the doctor's wall showed a list of "Flesh Forming Ingredients" that include cocoa extract and French chocolates.

The first diet pill

Attitudes about weight had changed somewhat by 1893 when the first diet pill was marketed. The pill was a thyroid extract sold under names like "Frank J. Kellogg's Safe Fat Reducer." People lost weight. However, there were dangerous side effects for people who did not have a hypothyroid condition. Hypothyroidism is a glandular condition characterized by an impaired rate of metabolism.

People who did not have the glandular condition and took the extract could experience chest pains, an increased heart rate, and higher blood pressure. Some died suddenly.

People used the thyroid hormone as a weight loss remedy until the 1950s. At the start of the twenty-first century, only hypothyroid patients received thyroid hormones as a weight-loss treatment.

OFFICIAL NAMES: Benzphetamine (Didrex), dexfenlu-ramine (Redux), diethylpropion (Tenuate, Tenuate dospan, Tepanil), fenfluramine (Pondimin), mazindol (Sanorex, Mazanor), methamphetamine (Desoxyn), orlistat (Xenical), phendimetrazine (Bontril, Plegine, Prelu-2, X-Trozine), phentermine (Adipex-P, Fastin, Ionamin, Oby-trim), sibutramine (Meridia)
STREET NAMES: Methamphetamine: Speed, crank
DRUG CLASSIFICATIONS: Schedule II, III, and IV, stimulant

Diet remedies of the 1920s

The 1920s were a time of change. During the decade known as the "Roaring '20s," women smoked cigarettes in public and shortened their hemlines to reveal their legs. While both activities were considered shocking, they reflected a new freedom for women.

Attitudes also changed about weight. People, especially women, regarded a thin body as the ideal figure. That attitude continued into the twenty-first century. Excess weight was seen as a sign of character flaws such as a lack of self-control, laziness, or poor self-image.

During the 1920s, people trying to lose weight took laxatives—medicines that relieve constipation by loosening the bowels. Through the decades, people continued to use laxatives to lose weight.

Also in the 1920s, weight loss products included La-Mar Reducing Soap. This product promised to "wash

KEY TERMS

ANORECTICS: Diet pills developed to replace amphetamines.

ESOPHAGUS: The tube in the throat that carries food to the stomach.

LIPIDS: A group of organic compounds consisting of fats and other substances.

METABOLISM: The body's ability to break down and process substances taken into the body.

SCHIZOPHRENIA: A medical condition that falls under the category of psychotic disorders. People with schizophrenia suffer from a variety of symptoms, including confusion, disordered thinking, paranoia, hallucinations, emotional numbness, and speech problems.

SYMPATHOMIMETIC: A medication similar to amphetamine, but is less powerful and has less potential for addiction than amphetamine.

---

away fat and years of age," according to an advertisement from the London, England soap manufacturer.

Soap and other weight-loss gimmicks were put aside in 1933 when dinitrophenol went on the marketed as a weight loss drug. People began taking this drug after learning about the weight lost by textile factory workers exposed to dinitrophenol during the 1900s.

Thousands take dinitrophenol

Dinitrophenol was used in explosives during World War I. It was used as an insecticide and an herbicide. It was also a popular weight loss remedy; 100,000 people took dinitrophenol in 1936.

This diet pill increased a person's metabolic rate, but it had dangerous side effects. At least 12 women who took it lost their eyesight. Other people lost their sense of taste; dinitrophenol caused skin rashes. People died from hyperpyrexia, an abnormally high fever brought on by increased metabolism.

Those dangerous and sometimes fatal side effects led the United States Congress to enact the Food, Drug, and Cosmetics Act in 1938. The act gave the Food and Drug Administration (FDA) powers to regulate substances marketed as drugs.

Some people still purchased dinitrophenol through mail-order businesses during the 1940s. Use of this drug declined until the late twentieth century, when bodybuilders took dinitrophenol as a weight loss remedy. The

FDA and law enforcement officials were again investigating the sales and misuse of the drug linked to the death of a New York man in September 2001.

In earlier decades, use of dinitrophenol dropped as dieters discovered amphetamine, a medication developed in 1887. Amphetamine stimulates the central nervous system, which can reduce a person's appetite. Caffeine, which is found in beverages like coffee, is a weak stimulant. During the twentieth century, dieters would drink coffee and take amphetamines to lose weight.

Medical uses of amphetamines

During the 1930s, European doctors prescribed amphetamines to treat respiratory conditions such as colds, hay fever, and asthma. The medications were also used to treat narcolepsy, a condition in which a patient experiences uncontrollable attacks of sleep. In addition, amphetamines were used to calm hyperactive children.

While the drugs soothed children with the condition now known as attention deficit hyperactivity disorder (ADHD), most people experienced a completely different reaction to amphetamines. The drugs gave them more energy and helped them to stay awake.

Those effects led to another use of amphetamines during World War II. Soldiers from America, Britain, Japan, and Germany took amphetamines to combat the weariness of battle fatigue.

The immediate effects of using amphetamines are additional energy, an exhilarated feeling of happiness known as euphoria, and increases in activity and concentration levels. The drugs also reduce the sensation of being hungry.

Dieters discover amphetamines

In 1937, the amphetamine dextroamphetamine was sold as a diet pill under the trade name Dexedrine. This medication was twice as potent as other amphetamines. It was also regarded as having the least amount of side effects. However, amphetamines were highly addictive.

People called amphetamines "uppers" because the drugs gave them energy. Sometimes that side effect meant that people could not sleep at night. As a result, they took sleeping pills. Referred to as "downers," these drugs were extremely addictive barbiturates that some users called liquid alcohol.

Taking barbiturates helped people sleep, but the drugs interfered with the dream patterns that come with restful sleep. People woke up feeling tired and took an amphetamine so they would be "up" again.

The FDA in 1938 realized that amphetamines and barbiturates had a strong potential for "misuse and abuse." The federal agency used its new regulatory powers and declared that prescriptions were required for both drugs. Physicians or dentists could write those prescriptions.

Widespread drug abuse

During the 1940s and 1950s, amphetamines and barbiturates were the most widely abused drugs in the United States, according to an FDA report.

A prescription was needed for amphetamines, but people who were dependent on these drugs found ways to get them legally. They went to doctors who would continue to write refill prescriptions for amphetamine diet pills. Another option was to go to more than one doctor. People also went to diet clinics or found pharmacists who did not ask for a prescription.

For people who acted in movies, studio doctors supplied medications that helped them lose weight and work 18-hour days. Although Hollywood and celebrities had a different lifestyle than most Americans, their experiences mirrored the belief of the time that amphetamines and barbiturates were an accepted part of American life.

When actress Sheree North filmed the 1956 movie *How to Be Very, Very Popular,* she received methamphetamine shots, bottles of Benzedrine (another amphetamine) for daytime use and the barbiturate Nembutal to sleep at night. The actress described that situation in the book *Marilyn: The Last Take.* In the 1993 book written by Peter Harry Brown and Patte Barham about the late actress Marilyn Monroe, North said that people did not know the drugs were harmful. She became addicted to the drugs, as did Monroe.

Amphetamine and barbiturate abuse was so widespread that the FDA worked from the 1940s through the 1960s on that problem. The FDA prosecuted doctors and pharmacies, while other federal agencies combatted illegal sales of prescription drugs.

The government also realized that the legal sale of amphetamines was a problem. During the 1960s, youths curious about drugs could find amphetamines in their parents' medicine cabinets.

Access to amphetamines restricted

In 1970, pharmaceutical companies in the United States produced 12 million amphetamine tablets. That same year, the Senate and House of Representatives ratified the Comprehensive Drug Abuse Prevention and Control Act. The law restricted the access to highly addictive drugs like amphetamines.

During the 1970s, amphetamines accounted for 8% of prescriptions in the United States. In addition to dieters, other amphetamine users included long-distance truck drivers and college students. Both groups took the pills to stay awake.

In the 1920s, weight loss products included La-Mar Reducing Soap. This product promised to "wash away fat and years of age," according to an advertisement from the London, England soap manufacturer. Bettmann/CORBIS. Reproduced by permission.

With the nation aware of the dangers of amphetamines, pharmaceutical companies worked to produce diet pills with less potential for misuse or abuse.

Alternates to amphetamines

Pharmaceutical companies developed diet pills with amphetamine congeners, chemicals that were similar to amphetamines. Although not as potent as amphetamines, these pills had more of an appetite-reducing effect than caffeine.

The diet pills developed to replace amphetamines became known as anorectics or appetite suppressants and are central nervous system stimulants. The FDA approved phentermine in 1959, fenfluramine in 1973, and dexfenfluramine in 1996.

The FDA approved the appetite suppressants for the short-term treatment of obesity. The FDA does not place restrictions on what conditions a physician prescribes the pills for, the dosage, or the amount of time that the patient takes the pills.

Prescribing medications for times or conditions not approved by the FDA is called "off-label" use. Examples of off-label use include prescribing a short-term drug for

LAW AND ORDER

Fighting to stop illegal Internet drug sales

Toward the end of the twentieth century, the United States and Thailand tackled the international problem of illegal Internet drug sales. A United Nations (U.N.) board also called for action.

The federal Drug Enforcement Agency (DEA) worked with officials in Thailand to shut down three online pharmacies that illegally sold substances containing controlled drugs such as phentermine, a diet pill. Internet shopping is legal. However, under federal law, a prescription is needed to buy controlled drugs.

The Internet pharmacies sold drugs without a prescription and sent most of their products to the United States. Authorities in the United States became aware of the trafficking because packages and letters containing illegal drugs constantly arrived from Thailand. Drug addicts accounted for many of the customers.

With authorities from both countries working together, Thai officials shut down three Internet pharmacies during November of 1999 through January of 2000.

That effort succeeded. However, the U.N. in February of 2001 warned that not all countries had laws that could be used to stop Internet drug trafficking. The U.N.'s International Narcotics Control Board called on countries to adopt laws to halt Internet abuse such as the sale of illegal drugs by online pharmacies and drug stores.

In its annual report, the board said that "a limited number of countries" had taken legal action to stop Internet misuse. The U.N. board estimated that approximately 600 million people used the Internet in 2001.

Another warning about online pharmacies came from the United States Food and Drug Administration (FDA). The FDA cautioned the public against buying medical products from a foreign country. In most cases, it would be illegal to import those drugs, the FDA said. Consumers faced the risk of being swindled. If that happened, the government could do "very little" to help get the money back.

---

a longer period or time and prescribing a combination of two weight loss medications.

Off-label use

Off-label use during the 1990s became an issue after doctors in the United States and other countries began prescribing fenfluramine (Pondimin) or dexfenfluramine (Redux) in combination with phentermine. The combinations known informally as "fen-phen" (sometimes also written as "phen-fen") or "fen-dex" had not been approved by the FDA, a process that involves research and hearings.

Media reports about the diet pill combinations focused on the promise of weight loss. The public embraced the message, ignoring the fact that these pills were anti-obesity drugs to be used for only several weeks.

Millions of prescriptions

People clamored for the pill combination that helped them take off the pounds. More than 18 million prescriptions were written for fen-phen in 1996, according to *Time* magazine.

The diet pill combination posed a health risk. Side effects from long-term use included primary pulmonary

hypertension (PPH). This is a rare condition that affects blood vessels in the lungs. The disease is potentially fatal, with death occurring within four years in 45% of its victims.

Most PPH deaths occurred to people taking fenfluramine or dexfenfluramine separately or in combination, according to a 2001 report from the National Institutes of Health (NIH). In 1996, there was also concern that long-term use of those drugs could damage brain cells.

The diet pill combination posed another risk. The Mayo Clinic announced that 24 patients who used the combination were diagnosed with valvular heart disease. In these cases, the condition caused leakiness (regurgitation) in the valves, according to an FDA report.

The federal agency issued a July 8, 1997 health advisory that stated that the FDA had received 100 reports of heart valve disease. The condition was diagnosed in people who took fen-phen as well as those who used only dexfenluramine or fenfluramine. The FDA noted that the combination treatment had not received FDA approval. In addition, FDA approval was based on short-term use for obesity treatment.

The FDA had also received requests to take the drugs off the market. The requests based on health concerns came from organizations including the National

Association for the Advancement of Fat Acceptance, and Public Citizen, the advocacy group founded by consumer advocate Ralph Nader.

Available anorectics

In 1997, the manufacturers withdrew fenfluramine and dexfenfluramine from the market. Phentermine is still sold because no cases of heart valve disease were reported when that drug was taken alone, according to the FDA report.

Also on the market were anorectic diet pills including benzphetamine, diethylpropion, mazindol, and phendimetrazine. Another anorectic, methamphetamine, was sold under the trade name Desoxyn. It was also prescribed for the treatment of ADHD.

Methamphetamine is highly addictive and rarely prescribed for the short-term treatment of obesity. It is abused by addicts who may inject the drug.

Long-term diet pills

In 1997, the FDA approved sibutramine, a medication sold under the brand name Meridia. Sibutramine is an appetite suppressant prescribed for long-term treatment of severely obese patients. However, safety and effectiveness had not been determined when the sibutramine was taken for more than one year.

Another type of diet pill received FDA approval in 1999. Orlistat, sold under the name of Xenical, was a lipase inhibitor. It affects the body's lipase enzyme and blocks about 30% of fat absorbed by the body.

Diet pill concerns in the twenty-first century

In March of 2002, Public Citizen filed a petition calling for the FDA to ban Meridia. Public Citizen quoted from FDA documents that showed that use of sibutramine was allegedly associated with 29 deaths and 400 adverse medical reactions. Those incidents occurred throughout the world, and Italy had banned the drug. The issue was also being studied by the United Kingdom, which banned phentermine in 2000. The ban was prompted by concern that it could cause heart disease.

A spokesman for Abbott Labs, which manufactures Meridia, said that Abbott had not seen evidence of a connection between use of sibutramine and the deaths and medical reactions. As of April of 2002, the FDA had not taken action to ban the drug.

Twenty-first century diet remedies

By the start of the twenty-first century, research was underway on at least 20 different diet pills. While some twentieth-century diet pills like Dexedrine were no longer prescribed for weight loss, people attempting to lose weight used methods tried by other generations.

People with eating disorders took laxatives. Some dieters drank coffee to suppress their hunger cravings, or they tried nonprescription remedies. Caffeine is an ingredient in many over-the-counter diet remedies.

Some dieters tried herbal remedies. These are not regulated by the FDA, and patients should check with a medical professional before taking herbal medications.

CHEMICAL/ORGANIC COMPOSITION

Amphetamine stimulates the central nervous system, which suppresses the appetite. Most diet pills are sympathomimetics. They are similar to amphetamines, but are less powerful and have less potential for addiction. The sympathomimetics are benzphetamine, diethylpropion, mazindol, methamphetamine, phendimetrazine, phentermine, and sibutramine.

Orlistat is a gastrointestinal lipase inhibitor that blocks fat absorbtion in the intestine.

INGESTION METHODS

Weight loss medications are manufactured in pill and capsule form. A doctor's prescription is required, and the medications are taken by mouth. The patient follows a dosage schedule set by the physician.

Illegal amphetamines and methamphetamine may be taken in liquid form. Addicts inject these drugs because the effect is stronger than when the drug is taken in pill form. In addition, some abusers snort (sniff) methamphetamine.

THERAPEUTIC USE

While many people think that diet pills are used to slim down and improve their appearance, weight loss medications are not a cosmetic remedy. These drugs are used to treat obesity, a medical condition characterized by excess fat stored on the body. People who are overweight or obese weigh more than is considered healthy for their heights and ages. Obese people are at risk for conditions including non-insulin-dependent diabetes, stroke, and heart disease. Obesity contributes to the deaths of about 300,000 Americans annually, according to the FDA.

In general, people are considered obese if they weigh more than 20% over the amount that is considered healthy based on factors such as age, height, and weight.

Body mass index

A more specific standard is used for treating obesity with diet pills. These drugs are prescribed to a person with a body mass index (BMI) of at least 30 and no medical conditions related to obesity. Body mass index is a relationship between weight and height, and it is used as an indicator of health risk due to excess weight. The BMI is determined by measuring the person's height and weight, converting those measurements into metric measurements, and plugging those figures into an equation. A BMI of 30 is assigned to a 5-foot-5-inch person weighing 170 pounds, a 5-foot-7-inch person weighing 180 pounds, and a 6-foot person weighing 220 pounds.

Furthermore, diet drugs may also be prescribed for someone with a BMI of 27 or higher if that person has other health conditions such as hypertension or diabetes. A BMI of 27 is assigned to a 5-foot-5-inch person weighing 160 pounds, a 5-foot-7-inch person weighing 170 pounds, and a 6-foot person weighing 200 pounds.

Prescription diet pills are not recommended for people who are slightly overweight.

Short-term treatment

Most diet pills are prescribed for short-term use that ranges from a few weeks to several months. The goal of this treatment is for the patient to lose weight or not gain additional weight. Furthermore, diet pills are only part of the treatment that focuses on modifying the patient's behavior. These modifications generally consist of exercising more and following a low-calorie, low-fat diet.

Most appetite suppressants are prescribed for short-term use. While a physician may prescribe a different dose, the general daily dose for an adult is:

- Benzphetamine is taken from one to three times and is taken before a meal.

- Diethylpropion in 25-mg tablet form is used from one to three times. It is taken one hour before eating. The time-release, 75-mg tablet is taken in the middle of the morning.

- Mazindol is taken once, but the dose may be adjusted.

- Phendimetrazine in 35-mg tablet form is taken one hour before breakfast. Some patients may be prescribed a half-tablet (18.5-mg) that is taken twice during the day. The time-release, 105-mg tablet is taken 30 to 60 minutes before breakfast.

- Phentermine comes in tablet and capsule forms. It is used before breakfast or taken one to two hours afterward.

Methamphetamine

Methamphetamine has a high potential for abuse, and is only prescribed if the patient has not lost weight after trying other treatments. The dose is one 5-mg tablet, and it is taken a half-hour before each meal. Use of this drug should stop after several weeks.

Long-term diet pill treatment

Most prescription diet pills are prescribed for short-term use of not more than several months. Sibutramine and orlistat have been prescribed for longer use in the treatment of significantly obese people. For both medications, this treatment ranged from six months to one year. The safety and effectiveness of use for longer than one year have not been determined.

Sibutramine comes in capsule form and is used once daily. Patients can take sibutramine with food or without it. Orlistat is taken three times daily with a meal that contains fat. It may be taken an hour before the meal.

USAGE TRENDS

Diet pill usage trends must be examined both in terms of legally prescribed medications and those obtained through illegal means. Prescription diet pills are manufactured for the treatment of obesity, an increasingly common medical problem. However, not just obese or overweight people use diet pills. Some people take diet pills to lose a few pounds quickly; others have eating disorders. Furthermore, people who lose weight using methods like diet pills tend to regain it once they stop dieting. They may start taking pills again to lose the new weight.

Scope and severity

According to a 2001 report from the United States Department of Agriculture (USDA), about half of American adults are overweight or obese. That same trend was found in Australia, according to a 2001 report from Euromonitor International, a market research business.

American spending trends. Americans spend approximately $33 billion annually on weight loss remedies such as diet pills, books, and weight reduction programs, according to the USDA report.

Spending for prescription diet pills reached a record of approximately $467 million in 1996, according to the American Society of Bariatric Physicians, an association focused on weight loss. Fen-phen sales accounted for much of that record. After the withdrawal of dexfenluramine and fenfluramine from the market, diet pill sales dropped.

In 1998, prescription diet pill sales totaled $169.2 million for January through November. IMS Health Inc. charted sales trends that showed 1.1 million prescriptions filled for Meridia, 351,000 prescriptions for Ionamin, and 341,000 Adipex-P prescriptions. Prescriptions for other diet pills totaled 4.5 million.

Australian trends. Australians spend more than $500 million on dieting efforts, according to Euromonitor. However, not all dieters needed to lose weight. Underweight Australian girls used legal diet pills and amphetamines, as well as caffeine and tobacco, to lose weight, according to "Drug Use by Young Females," a 1998 University of Sydney study.

The study noted that some Australian researchers found a double standard in 1982 and 1996. Both years, it appeared acceptable for girls to take diet pills and other drugs to slim down. That was regarded as a medical condition. On the other hand, boys took stimulant drugs for the intoxicating effect.

Age, ethnic, and gender trends

Passage of the 1970 Controlled Substances Act restricted Americans' access to amphetamines. Before that, amphetamine users included dieters who were primarily women, truck drivers who were usually men, and college students of both genders.

The federal government classifies most diet pills as stimulants. Trends related to the illegal use of drugs like stimulants can be seen in the National Household Survey on Drug Abuse. The federal Substance and Mental Health Services Administration (SAMHSA) coordinates the survey.

In 2000, approximately 14 million Americans—6.3% of the population—used an illicit drug during the month before the survey. Those surveyed were 12 and older. In the survey, stimulants were included in the category of psychotherapeutic drugs that included pain relievers, sedatives, and tranquilizers.

Of the 14 million Americans surveyed in 2000, psychotherapeutic drugs were taken for a "nonmedical reason" by 1.8% of men, 1.7% of women, 3.3% of girls aged 12 to 17, and 2.7% of boys in that age group.

MENTAL EFFECTS

A person takes diet pills to slim down. As the person loses weight, she or he will feel happy about these accomplishments. Self-confidence will rise as the person works towards a weight goal. However, use of diet pills may produce other psychological effects.

Possible effects range from a feeling of well-being to psychological addiction. Furthermore, these pills may be abused by people with an eating disorder like anorexia. If anorexia is not treated, the affected person may experience mood changes and have problems remembering or concentrating. Eventually, untreated anorexia can be fatal.

HISTORY NOTES

Popular 1960s book carried an anti-drug message

Four years before the approval of the 1970 Comprehensive Drug Abuse Prevention and Control Act, a nonfiction book with pills on the cover stayed on the *New York Times* bestseller list for 28 weeks.

Author Jacqueline Susann said that she wrote *Valley of the Dolls* to warn people against taking drugs and drinking alcohol. Her book told the story of three women who used diet pills, barbiturates, and alcohol.

The book set in the entertainment world reflected society's acceptance of those drugs. Susann wrote about what led the women to take drugs and the effects of drug abuse, including overdose. Drugs changed one character's personality, and she was hospitalized to withdraw from drugs.

While the book set a sales record, some in the literary world looked down on Susann's writing. It may not have been great literature, but the book described a world Susann knew well, according to *Lovely Me*, the 1987 biography about her by Barbara Seaman. Susann took Dexedrine to lose weight and barbiturates to sleep at night. She nearly overdosed twice.

While promoting her book, Susann spoke about the hazards of drugs. She talked about how continued use of pills and alcohol could lead a person to consume more of each. The person could become confused about the amount consumed. In that confusion, the person would take another drink or pill and could die.

Sympathomimetic drugs

Taking anorectics may cause a feeling of well-being. The drugs could also make a person feel light-headed or dizzy. Anorectics are related in composition to amphetamines and may lead to psychological abuse and addiction. Symptoms of dependence include the need to continue taking the diet pill or to increase the dosage. These drugs should not be taken by people who abused drugs in the past.

When people stop taking anorectic drugs, they may experience withdrawal symptoms. These may include depression, apathy, confusion, and irritability.

Sympathomimetic drug overdose. A person who abuses drugs is at risk of an overdose. Symptoms include irritability, personality changes, and a mental condition that resembles schizophrenia.

Furthermore, a drug overdose can cause the person to see, hear, or experience feelings that are not real. These sensations are known as hallucinations.

Long-term diet pills

Although sibutramine is prescribed for long-term use, the drug is a sympathomimetic. A patient taking it may feel more energetic. However, there is a potential for misuse.

As of 2002, orlistat produced no known psychological effects.

PHYSIOLOGICAL EFFECTS

A person who takes diet pills expects to lose weight. These drugs help with weight reduction by suppressing the appetite and increasing the sensation of feeling full. People who take diet pills and follow a weight-management plan of diet and exercise should lose weight. However, diet pills also produce other possible physiological changes that range from dizziness to an increased number of bowel movements.

Sympathomimetic diet pills. Taking anorectics can impair a person's ability to drive, operate heavy equipment, or perform other potentially hazardous activities. In addition, taking sympathomimetics late in the day can cause insomnia.

Other side effects include dizziness, dryness in the mouth, a false feeling of well-being, nausea, irritability, and nervousness. A person taking these drugs may tremble or shake. Other symptoms occur less frequently. These include blurred vision and a lessening of the sex drive or decreased ability to experience an erection. The person may sweat more and need to urinate more frequently.

Orlistat. Orlistat can cause temporary symptoms such as an increased number of bowel movements, gas with discharge, oily or fatty stools, and the inability to control bowel movement. The person taking orlistat may feel an urgent need to go to the bathroom. These symptoms are generally mild and short-term in nature. However, the symptoms can be aggravated if a person eats high-fat foods.

In addition, orlistat reduces the body's ability to absorb some vitamins. To compensate for that, person taking orlistat must take a multivitamin two hours before or after taking the drug.

Pregnancy and motherhood. Women who are pregnant or nursing their babies should consult with their physician about diet pill use. Orlistat is not recommended for use by pregnant women. Factors to consider about other diet pills are:

- The effects of methamphetamine on pregnant women are not known, so expectant mothers are advised against taking this drug unless health benefits outweigh risk factors.

- Pregnant mothers who are dependent on amphetamines risk giving birth prematurely. The baby may have a low birth weight and could experience withdrawal symptoms.

- The FDA placed benzphetamine in its pregnancy category X because the drug causes birth defects.

- The effects of phendimetrazine on an unborn baby are unknown.

- Nursing mothers should check with their doctors about use of sympathomimetics. It is not known if the mother transmits the drug to the baby through breast milk.

Harmful side effects

Anorectics. Taking anorectics can produce dizziness, restlessness, or blurred vision. People using these drugs may not realize they are extremely tired. Long-term use can lead to addiction.

Sympathomimetics can be physically addictive and should not be prescribed to people with a history of drug abuse. A person may develop a tolerance to the drug and attempt to increase the dosage. The person may develop intoxication symptoms such as insomnia and severe skin diseases.

Withdrawal symptoms. When people stop taking anorectics, their bodies need to adapt to the lack of drugs in their systems. The amount of withdrawal time will vary, depending on the strength of the dosage and how long the patient used it. Withdrawal symptoms could include insomnia, nightmares, nausea, vomiting, and stomach cramps. The person may also experience strong hunger pangs.

Sympathomimetic drug overdose. Some overdose symptoms are similar to those experienced during withdrawal. These include cramps, nightmares, nausea, and trembling. Vomiting will be more intense. The person may be dizzy and blood pressure may drop or rise. Respiration (breathing) is rapid, and the person may faint.

The final signs of a fatal overdose are generally convulsions and coma.

Sibutramine. Sibutramine can cause mild increases in blood pressure and pulse rates. The FDA advised people taking sibutramine to have their blood pressure evaluated regularly.

As of 2002, it was not known whether sibutramine caused primary pulmonary hypertension. However, sibutramine was not recommended for people with conditions including heart disease, irregular heartbeat, or a history of stroke.

Long-term health effects

Only two diet pills on the market in 2002 were recommended for long-term use, orlistat and sibutramine. Long-term effects of sibutramine were not known in 2000.

Use of orlistat could interfere with the body's absorption of fat-soluble vitamins and beta carotene. Long-term use could result in deficiencies of vitamins A, D, E, and K, and beta carotene. Patients are advised to take supplements. Another possible side effect is calcium deficiency.

Long-term use of sympathomimetic diet pills. A patient generally develops a tolerance to the effects of an anorectic drug within several weeks, and the pill is no longer effective as an appetite suppressant. Use of the drug should then be discontinued because of the risk of addiction.

REACTIONS WITH OTHER DRUGS OR SUBSTANCES

Before taking diet pills, patients need to discuss the medications that they take with their health care providers. Physicians may adjust the dosage or advise patients to discontinue medications.

Drug interactions

Monamine oxidase (MAO) inhibitors are antidepressants that can interact with sympathomimetic appetite depressants. Patients must discontinue using MAO inhibitors two weeks before taking these diet pills. Use of MAO inhibitors while taking anorectics will cause a sharp rise in blood pressure.

Furthermore, taking some other antidepressants and diet pills may cause high blood pressure or an irregular heartbeat.

TREATMENT AND REHABILITATION

When a person abuses diet pills, the type of treatment needed will be based on several factors. The person may need to be treated for psychological and physical dependency. If the person has an eating disorder, that condition needs to be treated. If the person is overweight, he or she may need help learning to lose weight without pills.

Drug dependency

Treatment of drug dependency may start with detoxification, during which the person withdraws the physical effects of diet pills. In severe cases, a person may be hospitalized. Otherwise, the person will work with a doctor or other health care provider to end the physical craving for a drug.

Counseling is recommended after detoxification to help the person fight the psychological craving for drugs. A person may meet individually with a counselor or participate in group sessions.

Eating disorders

Psychological counseling is an important component of the treatment of eating disorders. The National Eating Disorders Association recommends treatment that is adapted to the individual. In that way, the person can address the causes and symptoms of the eating disorder.

Medical treatment focuses on helping the patient return to a healthy weight. In severe cases, a patient may be hospitalized.

Support groups and success

The success rate of treatment depends on factors such as the type of drug used, and the severity of the addiction or eating disorder. Since recovery is an ongoing process, support groups can help a person with post-treatment goals.

People recovering from diet pill addiction may find additional support in 12-step programs, similar to the Narcotics Anonymous or Alcoholics Anonymous programs. There are also support groups and programs for people with eating disorders, people who are compulsive eaters, and those trying to lose weight.

PERSONAL AND SOCIAL CONSEQUENCES

In a society where people are often judged by their appearance and the ideal body is thin, taking diet pills is often considered acceptable behavior. However, diet pills are a temporary solution to a long-term problem.

Maintaining a healthy weight is a ongoing process that involves eating healthy meals and exercising regularly, according to organizations ranging from the United States National Institutes of Health (NIH) to the American Medical Association. According to the NIH, treating obesity with diet pills for a few months does not work over the long term. To be effective, a person would need to take pills for years, possibly for a lifetime.

At the start of the twenty-first century, there were no lifelong diet pill remedies. People who use diet pills often gain weight when they stop taking weight-loss drugs. They put on the weight they lost and sometimes gain more weight. This process is called the "yo-yo syndrome" because a person's weight goes up and down like a yo-yo.

With repeated dieting, a person may lose muscle and gain back fat. The person who regains weight may also feel like a failure. While the yo-yo syndrome is not limited to people who take diet pills, a 1996 NIH report showed that nearly 100% of people who took fen-phen gained weight after they stopped taking the diet pill combination.

Misuse of diet pills can cause medical problems. In addition, there is a potential for addiction to some diet pills. Overuse of pills can affect concentration so that a person's grades or work performance suffers. Mental and physical health are also affected by eating disorders.

Diet pills and eating disorders

Although excessive weight and obesity are problems in the United States and other countries, there is also a concern about people who diet to an unhealthy low weight. These people have an unrealistic image of themselves, so they continuously try to lose weight. They look in the mirror and see a heavy person. In reality, they may be extremely underweight.

These people have eating disorders. The condition primarily affects young women of high school and college ages. However, men were increasingly diagnosed with eating disorders by the end of the twentieth century.

People with anorexia nervosa starve themselves. People with bulimia eat and purge their food by vomiting or by some other means. People with both conditions may take diet pills, as well as laxatives, diuretics, and caffeine beverages.

Causes of eating disorders are varied. People may be perfectionists. They may feel they will gain control of their lives if they lose weight. Some male anorexics said they felt the pressure to be in shape for activities like sports. For teenage girls, their role models were the thin women in television programs, movies, and advertisements.

While people with these disorders think they gained control of their lives, they instead can become seriously ill. Anorexics can experience shortness of breath, chest pains, and stomachaches or nausea. Bulimics can experience dehydration and hormonal imbalances. Their esophagus and other internal organs may be damaged.

If not treated, eating disorders can be fatal. For someone with an eating disorder, taking diet pills can aggravate an unhealthy condition.

LEGAL CONSEQUENCES

The federal government regulates prescription diet pills in several ways. Some drugs are classified as controlled substances; all drugs are regulated by the Food and Drug Administration (FDA). The FDA determines whether a new drug can be manufactured or if production should be halted on a drug currently on the market.

Legal history

The federal Food, Drug, and Cosmetics Act of 1938 gave regulatory powers to the FDA. Pharmaceutical companies apply to the FDA for approval to manufacture a new drug. The approval process includes research, testing, and hearings. Once a drug is approved, the FDA determines whether a prescription is required.

FDA regulations about prescription drugs also apply to how the manufacturer promotes or advertises the medications. Unless specified by other regulations such as the Controlled Substances Act (CSA), there are no restrictions on what condition the doctor prescribes the pill for, the dosage, or the amount of time that the patient will take the pill.

Controlled substances. The Controlled Substances Act (CSA) portion of the 1970 Comprehensive Drug Abuse Prevention and Control Act classified drugs in five categories based on the effect of the drug, its medical use, and potential for abuse. Schedule I contains drugs like heroin, which have no medical use but may be used in research. It is the most tightly controlled category.

Federal guidelines, regulations, and penalties

The CSA classifies the methamphetamine Desoxyn as a stimulant. Anorectic drugs, the diet pills developed to replace amphetamines, are regarded by the government as controlled substances. While these drugs are not as powerful as amphetamines, their effects are similar.

Schedule II drugs. Schedule II drugs have a high potential for abuse. They are accepted for medical use with restrictions. These drugs may lead to severe psychological or physical dependence, according to the CSA. Desoxyn is a Schedule II drug. Dexedrine, the popular diet pill of the 1950s, is also in this category. It is no longer prescribed for weight loss. A prescription is required for these drugs, and it cannot be refilled.

Schedule III drugs. Schedule III drugs have less of a potential for abuse than drugs in Schedules I and II. The drugs have a medical use. Abuse of these drugs may lead to "moderate or low psychological dependence or high psychological dependence," according to the CSA. Anorectics in this category are benzphetamine (Didrex) and phendimetrazine (Bontril, Plegine, and Prelu-2). A prescription may be filled up to five times during the six months after the first prescription was written.

Schedule IV drugs. Schedule IV drugs have a low abuse potential as compared to Schedule III drugs. These substances have an accepted medical use. They could lead to limited psychological or physical dependence, according to the CSA.

The anorectic drugs in this category are phentermine (Ionamin, ApidexP), diethylpropion (Tenuate, Tepanil), and mazindol (Mazanor, Sanorex). Sibutramine (Meridia) is also in this category. The withdrawn drugs dexfenluramine (Redux) and fenfluramine (Pondimin) were also in this category.

In Schedule IV, five prescription refills are allowed during the six months after the patient received the first prescription.

Other diet pills. Other diet pills are classified in various ways. Orlistat (Xenical) is not classified as a controlled substance. A prescription is required.

Over-the-counter diet pills are classified as Schedule V drugs. Medications in this category have the lowest potential for abuse, have an accepted medical use, and a limited potential for physical or psychological dependence.

Penalties. Federal law prohibits the possession, use, and distribution of illegal drugs. This law applies to diet pills obtained without a prescription. The Controlled Substances Act established tighter controls on the manufacture and distribution of drugs like diet pills. Limits were set on the amounts of Schedule II pills that could be manufactured.

Procedure for the legal distribution of pills includes the requirement of a written prescription for Schedule II drugs. An exception is made in emergencies.

For Schedule III and IV drugs, the prescription may be written or called into the pharmacy. Both the health care practitioner and pharmacist are required to keep records when prescriptions are filled for controlled drugs.

Trafficking. Trafficking is the illegal distribution of controlled drugs. Federal penalties for this crime can include fines and imprisonment. Sentencing is based on factors such as whether the trafficker is a first-time offender. Penalties are higher for a second offense. In addition, if the illegal distribution of a Schedule II drug results in death or serious injury, the convicted offender faces a prison term of from 20 years to life.

In cases where there is no serious injury or death, the penalties for a first-time offense are:

- Schedule II: Trafficking 100 grams or more of methamphetamine carries a prison term of from 10 years to life and a fine of up to $4 million.

- Schedule III drugs: Trafficking any quantity of these drugs is punishable by up to five years in prison and a maximum fine of $250,000.

- Schedule IV drugs: Illegally distributing any quantity of these drugs carries a prison term of up to three years and a fine of up to $250,000.

Penalties for drug abusers. The federal penalty for the first-time offense of illegally possessing a controlled substance is up to one year in prison and a fine of from $1,000 to $100,000. Penalties are generally doubled for a second offense.

In some cases, a person may not receive a prison sentence. The Anti-Drug Abuse Act of 1988 imposes a civil penalty on the minor drug offender, the person possessing a small quantity of an illegal controlled substance. Possession of this quantity known as a "personal use amount" carries a fine of up to $10,000.

See also Amphetamines; Antidepressants; Barbiturates; Caffeine; Herbal drugs; Methamphetamine

RESOURCES

Books

Brown, Peter H., and Patte B. Barham. *Marilyn: The Last Take.* New York: Signet Books, 1993.

Clayton, Lawrence. *Diet Pill Dangers.* Springfield, NJ: Enslow Publishers, Inc., 1999.

Dorsman, Jerry. *How to Quit Drugs for Good.* Rocklin, CA: Prima Publishing, 1998.

Seaman, Barbara. *Lovely Me.* New York: William and Morrow and Company, 1987.

Yancy, Diane. *Eating Disorders.* Brookfield, CT: Twenty-First Century Medical Library, 1999.

Periodicals

Gorman, Christine. "Danger in the diet pills?" *Time* 150 (July 21, 1997): 58.

Organizations

Compulsive Eaters Anonymous, 5500 E. Atherton Street, Suite 22715, Long Beach, CA, USA, 90815-4017, (562) 342-9344.

Food Addicts Anonymous World Service Office, 4623 Forest Hill Blvd, Suite 109-4, West Palm Beach, FL, USA, 33415-9120, (561) 967-3871, info@foodaddictsanonymous.org, <http://www.foodaddictsanonymous.org>.

National Association to Advance Fat Acceptance, P.O. Box 188620, Sacramento, CA, USA, 95818, (916) 558-6880, (916) 558-6881, <http://www.naafa.org>.

National Eating Disorders Association, 603 Stewart St., Suite 803, Seattle, WA, USA, 98101, (206) 382-3587, info@NationalEatingDisorders.org, <http://www.nationaleatingdisorders.org>.

National Institute on Drug Abuse (NIDA), National Institutes of Health, 6001 Executive Blvd., Room 5213, Bethesda, MD, USA,

20892-9561, (301) 443-1124, (888) 644-6432, <http://www.nida.nih.gov>.

U.S. Drug Enforcement Administration, 2401 Jefferson Davis Highway, Alexandria, VA, USA, 22201, (800) 882-9539, <http://www.dea.gov>.

U.S. Food and Drug Administration (FDA), 560 Fishers Lane, Rockville, MD, USA, 20857-0001, (888) 463-6332, <http://www.fda.gov>.

Liz Swain

DIMETHYLTRYPTAMINE (DMT)

OVERVIEW

Dimethyltryptamine (DMT) is a hallucinogen, a broad group of drugs defined more by the effects they produce than by any common chemical structure. As a group, hallucinogens produce varying levels of visual, auditory, and tactile distortions and so-called "out-of-body" sensations. As with all drugs, the intensity of effect depends not only on ingestion of a specific drug and dose but also on the user's perception or expectation of the experience. Although persons with psychotic disturbances may hallucinate without an external stimulus, normal individuals can induce the same (but temporary) effect using hallucinogenic drugs.

DMT, or N,N-dimethyltryptamine, is a hallucinogenic chemical found in a variety of natural and synthetic compounds. It is present in many plant genera (*Acacia, Anadenanthera, Mimosa, Piptadenia, Virola*) and is a major component of several hallucinogenic snuffs (cohoba, parica, yopo). DMT is also present in the intoxicating beverage ayahuasca, which is made from *Banisteriopsis caapi* plants.

Like many hallucinogens, DMT has been used for hundreds of years. The oldest known record of DMT use comes from an eighth century burial site in northern Chile, where bags of snuff remnants containing DMT, 5-MeO-DMT, and bufotenine were found. Through the sixteenth to nineteenth centuries, natives of Columbia and surrounding areas used several DMT-containing concoctions, including snuff from the yopo tree and brews made with *Anadenanthera columbrina*. In the early 1950s, DMT and 5-MeO-DMT were identified as the main psy-

OFFICIAL NAMES: N,N-dimethyltryptamine, Nigerine, desoxybufotenine, 3-(2-dimethylaminoethyl)-indole
STREET NAMES: 45-minute psychosis, AMT, businessman's LSD, businessman's special, businessman's trip, DET, fantasia
DRUG CLASSIFICATIONS: Schedule I, hallucinogen

choactive ingredients of cohoba snuff. DMT was isolated as the active ingredient in *A. peregrina* in 1954.

CHEMICAL/ORGANIC COMPOSITION

Purified dimethyltryptamine is a white, pungent-smelling, crystalline solid. It is insoluble in water, but soluble in organic solvents and aqueous acids. DMT is a hallucinogenic chemical found in a variety of natural and synthetic compounds. Specifically, DMT can be found in the leaves, seeds, or roots of the following plant genera and species:

- *Acacia* genus, including *A. maidenii* (also called maiden's wattle) and *A. phlebophylla* (also called buffalo sallow wattle)

- *Anadenanthera* genus, including *A. peregrina* (also called yopo), *A. columbrina*, *A. excelsa*, and *A. macrocarpa*

- *Arundo donax* (giant river reed)

- *Banisteriopsis rusbyana*, which is added to the harmaline drinks derived from other plants of the *Banisteriopsis* genus to make "oco-yage"

KEY TERMS

ACTIVE INGREDIENT: The chemical or substance in a compound known or believed to have a therapeutic effect.

AYAHUASCA: An intoxicating beverage made from *Banisteriopsis caapi* plants, which contain DMT.

HALLUCINOGENS: A group of drugs that induces sensory distortions and hallucinations.

SNUFF: A preparation of DMT-containing plants that is smoked; also traditionally called cohoba, parica, and yopo.

- *Desmanthus* genus, including *D. illinoensis* and *D. leptolobus*; also called the bundle flower, Illinois bundle flower, Illinois bundle weed, prairie *Mimosa*, pezhe gasatho (rattle plant), atikatsatsiks (spider-bean), kitsitsaris (bad plant), and the narrow-pod bundle flower

- *Diploterys cabrerana* (Chagro-panga)

- *Phalaris* genus, including *P. aquatica*, *P. arundinacea*, *P. canariensis*, and *P. tuberosa*

- *Psychotria viridis*, which is also added to the *Banisteriopsis* drinks

- *Mimosa* genus, including *M. hostilis* and *M. verrucosa*; also called jurema preta (*hostilis*), jurema branca (*verrucosa*), mimosa, caatinga, white jurema, and black jurema

- *Virola* genus, including *V. theiodora*, *V. calophylla*, *V. calophylloidea*, *V. surinamensis*, *V. cuspidata*, *V. elongata*, *V. lorentensis*, *V. peruviana*, *V. rufula*, and *V. sebifera*

In addition to plant sources of hallucinogenic chemicals, several species of toads produce venom that has psychoactive properties. Members of the genus *Bufo*, particularly *Bufo marinus* and *Bufo alvarius*, contain bufotenine and 5-MeO-DMT. Typically toads are either licked or milked for their venom, which is then smoked or ingested. Alternatively, their dried skin may be smoked.

INGESTION METHODS

DMT is used in both its natural and synthetic forms. Natural DMT can be taken orally as an herbal tea or other beverage. If prepared this way, it is combined with another substance in order to maintain its effect. For example, certain religious groups concoct a beverage from plants that contain DMT and use this drink in sacred rituals. The drink, called ayahuasca, is usually made from two plants: chacruna, which contains DMT; and yag, which contains a substance called harmaline that allows DMT to pass through the stomach. The taste of ayahuasca is reportedly so foul that some people cannot bring themselves to drink it.

DMT usually has no effect when taken orally because it is inactivated in the stomach by an enzyme called monoamine oxidase. Adding harmaline blocks the effects of this enzyme and allows the drug to enter the user's system. To become active orally, DMT must be combined with monoamine oxidase inhibitors (MAOIs), a highly potent and potentially dangerous medication.

Synthetic DMT is usually smoked, injected, or sniffed. The drug sometimes comes in the form of a crystal ready-made for smoking. Alternatively, some users will soak parsley in a liquid form of the drug and then smoke the dried leaves. When smoked or injected, DMT acts quickly. Its effects begin in five minutes or less, peak in about 20 minutes, and are usually over in an hour. The brevity of the DMT experience has earned it the nickname "businessman's trip." When sniffed, the effects of synthetic DMT begin and end even more rapidly. The intoxication begins in about 10 seconds, lasts for two or three minutes, and is over within 10 minutes.

THERAPEUTIC USE

Scientists in the United States and other countries are exploring the use of hallucinogens such as DMT to treat drug and alcohol addiction. It is still too early, however, to say whether this unusual treatment approach works. For example, scientists at the Orenda Institute in Baltimore are examining LSD as a possible treatment for heroin, opium, and alcohol addiction. Researchers at the University of Miami are studying the psychedelic drug ibogaine as a treatment for cocaine addiction. Other scientists are exploring the use of hallucinogenic drugs to help ease the pain of cancer patients.

According to a 1992 report by Richard Yensen, Ph.D., and Donna Dryer, M.D., director and medical director at the Orenda Institute, a 1960s study of 135 alcoholics found that six months after treatment with LSD, 53% of a high-dose group were still not drinking compared with 33% of a low-dose group. Alcoholics receiving conventional therapy had a 12% improvement rate.

In a study of 31 cancer patients experiencing anxiety, depression, and uncontrollable pain, 71% showed improvement in their physical and emotional status after each LSD session. According to Yensen, researchers also observed that many cancer patients receiving LSD reported that their desire for addictive pain medicines, such as morphine, had diminished or vanished, along with the pain.

The National Institute on Drug Abuse (NIDA) funds some of these studies, and the FDA has allowed them because of the possible medical benefit. "These are very small studies, mostly with fewer than 10 patients," comments Dr. Curtis Wright, an M.D. with the addiction medicine staff in the FDA's Center for Drug Evaluation and Research. "It's far too early to tell whether these drugs work or not to provide any therapeutic benefit."

The medicinal use of ayahuasca, a plant beverage with psychotropic effects, has been proposed as a possible treatment for cocaine addiction. Proponents of this approach argue that DMT and other hallucinogens allow the substance abuser to modify his state of consciousness. In this altered state, the substance abuser looks for a meaning in his life.

USAGE TRENDS

Scope and severity

Though little is known about the trends of DMT in particular, several studies have tracked the use of hallucinogens in the United States.

Between 1991 and 1996, the percentage of Americans who had used hallucinogens at least once in their lives grew from 6% to 14%. In 2000, approximately one million Americans—representing 0.4% of the population aged 12 and older—were current users of hallucinogens. Current users are those individuals who have used the substance at least once in the previous 30 days.

Age, ethnic, and gender trends

In the 1990s, the rise in hallucinogen use coincided with the growth of "raves," underground dance parties that cater to those under age 21. A rave is a large party where participants often dance all night to very loud "house music," which is characterized by technically synthesized rhythms of 120-180 beats per minute. Raves primarily attract a middle-income audience, often high school and college students.

In a survey of drug treatment programs across the United States, counselors reported that hallucinogen consumption is part of an extensive drug use history for most youths in treatment. Rarely do counselors see adolescents who abuse only hallucinogens such as DMT. Instead, adolescents use a variety of drugs, although alcohol, marijuana, and hallucinogens (particularly LSD) are the most frequently abused substances.

The systemic violence often associated with the trafficking of heroin and cocaine has not been found with hallucinogen trafficking. This may be due in part to the observation that hallucinogens are relatively inexpensive, domestically produced, and not part of a network of distributors battling over territory or markets.

MENTAL EFFECTS

DMT is reported to have mental effects similar to those of LSD, but often more intense. When smoked or injected, the effects come on suddenly and can be overwhelming. DMT users report a sense of leaving or transcending time. They also note a feeling that objects lose form and dissolve into a mix of vibrations. Thoughts and visions rush by at great speed. Users also describe feeling like they are transported to another universe. Finally, DMT users report feeling like they are being visited from non-human beings, often described as "elves" or "fairies." Often people taking DMT report unpleasant experiences on these drugs, or "bad trips," that may cause paranoia, panic, and the feeling of being out of control.

PHYSIOLOGICAL EFFECTS

Following injection with DMT, users experience dilated pupils, rapid heartbeat, and an increase in blood pressure. Several minutes later, when full intoxication is induced, users have difficulty concentrating. Typically, there is a mood change that includes euphoria and unmotivated laughter. Finally, users experience paranoia, anxiety, a sense of foreboding, and panic.

DMT may cause unpredictable behavior depending on the amount taken, where the drug is used, and the user's personality. Common unpredictable effects include:

- distortion of sensory perceptions
- difficulty speaking or communicating
- sense of suspended time
- alternating feelings of motor paralysis and motor hyperactivity
- depressed appetite
- loss of sexual desire

Similar to other hallucinogens, repeated use of DMT does not appear to lead to either physical or psychological dependency.

Harmful side effects

DMT is a Schedule I hallucinogen, meaning it has no acceptable medical use, presents an unacceptable safety risk, and has a high potential for abuse.

Hallucinogens may cause unpredictable behavior depending on the amount taken, where the drug is used, and on the user's personality. Common side effects

IN THE NEWS

DMT has been the focus of a controversial court case in Santa Fe, New Mexico that began in late 2000. In the case, members of the O Centro Espirita Beneficiente Uniao do Vegetal (UDV), a religious organization with approximately 500 members in the U.S., are alleging that the United States government violated their constitutional right of freedom of religion.

The allegation stems from an incident on May 21, 1999, when the U.S. Drug Enforcement Administration (DEA) seized 30 gallons of a DMT-containing tea called hoasca from the office of the church president. UDV church members claim hoasca is an essential sacrament, like peyote is to the Native American church. At the time, no church members were arrested or charged with any crime.

On November 1, 2000, UDV members sued the DEA. Nancy Hollander, the attorney representing UDV, tried to get a preliminary injunction blocking the federal government from interfering with the group's practice of drinking hoasca.

To help argue the point that the confiscation of the DMT-containing tea was arbitrary, Hollander brought in to court plants from two Albuquerque nurseries that were freely available to the public. The plants—phalaris grass and San Pedro cactus—contain DMT and mescaline, respectively. Hollander questioned a DEA agent why no effort has been made to confiscate these plants as well. As of early 2002, the case had not been settled.

include dizziness, nausea, hallucinations, sweating, runny nose, excessive salivation, and other symptoms associated with psychedelic drugs.

DMT can cause neuronal damage in the brain. It causes impaired judgment that often leads to rash decisions and accidents. It can cause extremely frightening trips or flashbacks. Some people have become frightened and paranoid after taking DMT. Its effects can be disorientating, resulting in panic and confusion.

Although most hallucinogens do not normally cause addiction, they do build tolerance quickly, requiring larger amounts of the drug to achieve the same effect, or "high." The risks of adverse reactions and overdose increase as users take larger amounts of the drug to get high. Repeated doses of DMT or ingestion of multiple DMT-containing substances, such as a plant brew or combination of snuffs, can produce highly adverse effects that can be fatal.

Finally, visual and auditory distortions resulting from DMT use can last 10 to 12 hours, endangering users who drive. Public safety—for example, the safety of other drivers and pedestrians—may also be compromised.

Long-term health effects

The long-term effects of heavy hallucinogen use include impaired mental function and distorted abstract reasoning. In addition, hallucinogen users are susceptible to flashbacks of the drug experience for a long time afterward. Many users can also experience spontaneous recurrence of visual or sensory distortions.

Some studies have documented changes in the mental functions of some chronic hallucinogen users. For example, some users develop signs of brain damage affecting memory, attention span, mental confusion, and difficulty thinking. Long-term PCP users report memory and speech difficulties, as well as hearing unreal sounds and voices. In addition, ecstasy may cause long-term brain damage because it is toxic to neurons.

Though it is clear that hallucinogen use alters mental function, is not known whether the changes are permanent or if they will disappear after use is stopped. After long-term hallucinogen use, some individuals may experience prolonged psychosis and may require therapy or institutionalization. It is not known whether these drugs cause this condition or merely expose a previous tendency to psychosis.

REACTIONS WITH OTHER DRUGS OR SUBSTANCES

When ingested by mouth, DMT and 5-MeO-DMT have no effect. A naturally occurring stomach enzyme blocks the uptake of DMT into the system. To become active orally, DMT must be combined with monoamine oxydase inhibitors (MAOIs), a highly potent and potentially dangerous medication.

There are significant dangers in using MAOIs. Most MAOIs potentiate the cardiovascular effects of chemicals called tyramines, which are found in a variety of foods. Taken with beans, beer, aged cheese, chicken liver, chocolate, citrus fruits, coffee, cream, figs, pickled herring, wine, or yeast, MAOIs can cause a hypertensive crisis, including a dangerous rise in blood pressure.

Under the influence of DMT, the effects of amphetamines, general anesthetics, sedatives, antihistamines, alcohol, potent analgesics, and anticholinergic and antidepressant agents are prolonged and intensified.

If used with DMT, certain antipsychotic medications called phenothiazines can be fatal, especially if they are combined with strychnine or belladonna alkaloids.

TREATMENT AND REHABILITATION

As mentioned previously, most DMT abusers use a variety of drugs. Treatment and rehabilitation programs are therefore comprehensive and include users of several types of drugs.

Basic principles

Intoxicated or "high" patients can be "talked down" from frightening experiences related to recent DMT use. This should ideally be done in a quiet environment with few stimuli. Because DMT's effects are short-lived, intoxicated individuals should feel better within an hour of taking the drug.

Once a user is sober, a plan for rehabilitation should be formed. If a user is to remain drug-free, follow-up treatment, usually with psychiatric help and access to community resources, is vital. In addition, lifestyle changes such as avoiding people, places, and things related to hallucinogen use should be encouraged. During the rehabilitation period, drug urine tests can be used to ensure compliance.

Psychotherapy

Some heavy hallucinogen drug users, like other heavy drug users, have pre-existing mental problems, such as chronic anxiety, depression, or feelings of inadequacy. In these cases, the drug abuse is a visible symptom rather than the primary problem. Such persons can benefit from psychotherapy as part of a comprehensive rehabilitation program.

Psychotherapy is particularly useful when it focuses on the reasons for the patient's drug abuse. In addition, the drug abuse itself—including its past, present, and future consequences—must be considered carefully in psychotherapy.

Initial psychosocial treatment should focus on confronting denial and teaching the disease concept of addictions. Additional sessions will allow the substance abuser to cultivate an understanding of him or herself as a recovering person. Finally, in psychotherapy patients can learn to recognize the negative consequences of hallucinogen abuse, avoid situational cues that stimulate craving, and formulate plans for ongoing sobriety.

Medications

As part of a comprehensive rehabilitation program, prescription medications may help recovering substance abusers with persistent mental health needs. For example, anti-anxiety medications such as diazepam (Valium) and antipsychotic drugs such as haloperidol (Haldol) may address acute needs.

Many substance abusers turn to drugs as a form of self-medication for conditions such as depression. Thus, long-term treatment with antidepressants may prove useful to recovering substance abusers. It is important to note that phenothiazines, a type of antipsychotic medication, can be fatal when used with hallucinogens including DMT. This is especially true if the phenothiazines are mixed with strychnine or belladonna alkaloids.

Support groups

Hallucinogen abusers may benefit from support groups such as Narcotics Anonymous. Support group meetings provide members with acceptance, understanding, forgiveness, confrontation, and a means for positive identification. New group members are typically asked to admit to a problem, give up a sense of personal control over the disease, do a personal assessment, make amends, and help others. Finally, members pick sponsors—more experienced members who guide them through their recovery.

PERSONAL AND SOCIAL CONSEQUENCES

Threats to the safety of users and those with whom they come in contact are major problems associated with hallucinogen use. Any of the club drugs taken alone can impair motor skills; in combination they can produce deadly synergistic effects. The enduring effects of drugs such as LSD or MDMA (ecstasy) can pose special problems. For example, ingestion of a drug with the potential to cause visual and auditory distortion lasting 10–12 hours may mean that the user will drive home from a party while still under its influence.

The systemic violence connected to heroin and cocaine trafficking has not been found with hallucinogen trafficking. Despite law enforcement efforts to disrupt the production and distribution of hallucinogens, a small number of manufacturers and distributors primarily located in northern California have provided a relatively steady supply, distributed through local user networks, for more than 20 years. Although rising use may not pose severe threats to law enforcement, it does present problems for public health officials in terms of the health and safety of young users who are rediscovering this family of drugs.

Hallucinogens appear to be a popular drug among today's young, more affluent users. Several sources have reported their popularity among nonminority high school and college users who often reside outside the inner cities. The drugs are relatively inexpensive, domestically produced, and part of a stable, noncompetitive distribution network.

LEGAL CONSEQUENCES

Legal history

DMT was demonstrated to be hallucinogenic in 1956. The drug is explicitly named as a Schedule I drug in the federal Controlled Substances Act. DMT is also illegal in the United Kingdom, where it is classified as a Class A drug.

Federal guidelines, regulations, and penalties

The most common plant constituents of ayahuasca (*Banisteriopsis caapi* and *Psychotria viridis*) are not specifically scheduled in the United States. Neither is the ayahuasca brew specifically named as a scheduled substance. However, *P. viridis* contains DMT. Under the DEA's guidelines, a plant or brew is illegal if it contains DMT or any other controlled substance.

See also Hallucinogens; LSD; PCP (phencyclidine)

RESOURCES

Books

Hoffer, A., and H. Osmond. *The Hallucinogens.* New York: Academic Press, 1967.

Hollister, Lee E. *Chemical Psychoses: LSD and Related Drugs.* Springfield: Charles C. Thomas Publisher 1968.

Niesink, R. J. M., et al, eds. *Drugs of Abuse and Addiction: Neurobehavioral Toxicology.* New York: CRC Press, 1999.

Schultes, Robert E., and Albert Hofmann. *The Botany and Chemistry of Hallucinogens.* Springfield: Charles C. Thomas Publisher, 1980.

Periodicals

Callaway J. C., and C. S. Grob. "Ayahuasca Preparation and Serotonin Reuptake Inhibitors: A Potential Combination for Severe Adverse Reactions." *Journal of Psychoactive Drugs* 4 (1998): 367-369.

Freedland, C. S., and Robert S. Mansbach. "Behavioral Profile of Consituents in Ayahuasca, an Amazonian Psychoactive Plant Mixture." *Drug and Alcohol Dependence* 54 (1999): 183-194.

Kurtzweil, P. "Medical Possibilities for Psychedelic Drugs." *U.S. Food and Drug Association Consumer Magazine* (1995).

Mabit, M. "Takiwasi: Ayahuasca and Shamanism in Addiction Therapy." *MAPS Newsletter* 6 (1996): 24-27.

Riba, J., Antoni Rodgriquez-Fornells, Rick J. Strassman, and Manel J. Barbanoj. "Psychometric Assessment of the Hallucinogen Rating Scale." *Drug and Alcohol Dependence* 62 (2001): 215-223.

Riba, J., et al. "Subjective Effects and Tolerability of the South American Psychoactive Beverage Ayahuasca in Health Volunteers." *Psychopharmacology* 154 (2001): 85-95.

Sharpe, Tom. "Hallucinogenic Tea Case Starts in Albuquerque." *The New Mexican* (October 28, 2001).

Sharpe, Tom. "Attorney: Tea's drug found in many plants." *The New Mexican* (November 1, 2001).

Strassman, Rick. *Behavioral Brain Research* 73 (1996): 121-124.

———. *Biological Psychiatry* 39 (1996): 784-795.

———. "Contact Through the Veil." *The Entheogen Review.* 1 (2000): 1-9.

United States Substance Abuse and Mental Health Services Administration. "Hallucinogen Use." *National Household Survey on Drug Abuse* (1997).

———. "Illicit Drug Use." *National Household Survey on Drug Abuse* (2000).

Organizations

Center for Substance Abuse Research (CESAR), 4321 Hartwick Road, Suite 501, College Park, MD, USA, 20740, (301) 403-8329, (301) 403-8342, cesar@cesar.umd.edu, <http://www.cesar.umd.edu/>.

National Institute on Drug Abuse (NIDA), National Institutes of Health, 6001 Executive Boulevard, Room 5213, Bethesda, MD, USA, 20892-9561, (301) 443-1124, (888) 644-6432, <http://www.nida.nih.gov>.

Partnership For A Drug-Free America, 405 Lexington Avenue, Suite 1601, New York, NY, USA, 10174, (212) 922-1560, (212) 922-1570, <http://drugfreeamerica.org/>.

Substance Abuse and Mental Health Services Administration (SAMHSA), U.S. Dept. of Health and Human Services, 5600 Fishers Lane, Rockville, MD, USA, 20857, (301)443-6239, info@samhsa.gov, <http://www.samhsa.gov>.

Anne Jacobson

DIURETICS

Diuretics are a class of drugs that increase urine output. In healthcare, they are used to treat conditions that cause edema, or water retention. They are also prescribed for several chronic conditions, including asthma, heart disease, and hypertension (high blood pressure).

Because diuretics cause an overall water weight loss, they are often abused by individuals with eating disorders such as anorexia and bulimia. They may also be misused (and sometimes abused) by athletes to "make weight" for certain classes of competition (i.e., wrestling).

Diuretic use in sports may also be prompted by the belief that a lower weight will improve athletic performance. However, the side effects experienced from long-term diuretic abuse typically offset any temporary gains in ability. Diuretics are considered a banned substance by the International Olympic Committee (IOC), the United States Anti-Doping Agency (USADA), the World Anti-Doping Agency (WADA), the National Collegiate Athletic Association (NCAA), and a number of other national and international sporting authorities.

The term diuretics comes from the Greek *diuresis*, meaning "to urinate." In medieval medicine, diuretics were used to restore the body's humors (blood, bile, and phlegm) to balance, along with other "therapeutic" methods such as blood-letting and induced vomiting.

William Withering, an English physician with a strong interest in botany, was the first to introduce the diuretic digitalis (from the foxglove plant *Digitalis purpurea*) into common medical practice for the treatment

OFFICIAL NAMES: Acetazolamide, amiloride, bendroflumethiazide, benzthiazide, bumetanide, chlorothiazide, chlorthalidone, dichlorphenamide, dorzolamide, ethacrynic acid, flumethiazide, furosemide, glycerin, isosorbide, hydrochlorothiazide (HCT), hydroflumethiazide, mannitol, methyclothiazide, metolazone, polythiazide, quinethazone, spironolactone, torsemide, triamterene, trichlormethiazide
STREET NAMES: Water pills
DRUG CLASSIFICATIONS: Not scheduled

of dropsy. Dropsy, a now-obsolete term for edema (fluid retention or swelling), was frequently related to congestive heart failure and was a common cause of death at the time for lack of an effective treatment.

Although there had been accounts of the use of foxglove in medicine since classical times, Withering was the first to standardize its use and establish digitalis as a legitimate medical therapy. He learned of the botanical therapy from local folk medicine, and began treating patients with it. Ten years after Withering began using the drug, he published *An Account of the Foxglove and Some of Its Medical Uses; With Practical Remarks on Dropsy and Other Diseases* (1785), in which he described his experiences with the drug and experiments with different preparations and dosages. Digitalis remains a treatment for heart failure today.

In the 1920s, researchers discovered the diuretic effects of substances known as organic mercurials that were used to treat a heart disorder related to syphilis. They

KEY TERMS

ANOREXIA: An eating disorder characterized by a refusal to maintain body weight at a minimal normal weight for age and height, an intense fear of gaining weight, and a distorted sense of self-image.

BULIMIA: An eating disorder characterized by binge eating and then excessive behavior (such as vomiting, laxative or diuretic abuse, or exercising excessively) to rid the body of the food and/eaten.

CIRRHOSIS: A chronic liver disease that is caused by alcohol abuse, toxins, nutritional deficiency, or infection. A main symptom of cirrhosis is portal hypertension.

EDEMA: Water retention in the tissues that causes swelling.

ELECTROLYTE IMBALANCE: Improper proportions of acids, bases, salts, and fluids in the body. Electrolytes include the salts sodium, potassium, magnesium, chloride chlorine. They can conduct electricity, and therefore are essential in nerve, muscle, and heart function.

NEUROTRANSMITTER: Chemical in the brain that transmits messages between neurons, or nerve cells.

OSTEOPOROSIS: A loss in total bone density that may be the result of a chronic calcium deficiency, early menopause, certain endocrine diseases, advanced age, endocrine diseases, certain medications, or other risk factors.

PANCREATITIS: Inflammation of the pancreas, an essential part of both the endocrine and the digestive systems. The pancreas secretes juices that aid in digestion, and a number of hormones (including insulin).

PELVIC TONING EXERCISES: Exercises that focus on tightening the muscles of the pelvic floor to relieve urinary stress incontinence. Also known as Kegel or PC muscle exercises.

were quickly employed as a treatment for congestive heart failure (CHF). While they helped edema, their long-term usefulness was limited since they became ineffective with regular use and, more importantly, they could be highly toxic to the heart and nervous system over time.

The antibiotic class of sulfonamides was introduced in 1936. Although not designed as a diuretic, the drug caused increased urinary output in patients who used it. Over a decade later, Dr. William Schwartz tried the drug on three heart patients and found it was effective for lowering blood pressure and relieving the symptoms of congestive heart failure, but also concluded that the drug could not be safely used for any length of time.

In 1957, researchers John Baer, Karl Beyer, James Sprague, and Frederick Novello formulated the drug chlorothiazide, the first of the thiazide diuretics. This groundbreaking discovery marked a new era in medicine as the first safe and effective long-term treatment for chronic hypertension and heart failure.

Loop diuretics, the next class of diuretic drugs to be developed, are also the most potent. Their introduction was a major advance in the treatment of congestive heart failure. Furosemide (Lasix), the first of the loop diuretics, debuted in 1965.

Over-the-counter diuretic formulations became available around this time as well. Pamabrom, a medication that relieves the fluid retention and bloating associated with a woman's menstrual cycle, is still the active ingredient in a number of over-the-counter preparations (e.g., Aqua-Ban, Pamprin).

There are also many drugs and dietary supplements that may have diuretic action as a side effect, but have a different primary purpose. For example, the supplement creatine is an ergogenic (energy-enhancer), but it also promotes fluid loss with regular use.

CHEMICAL/ORGANIC COMPOSITION

Diuretics work by increasing the amount of sodium and fluids excreted by the kidneys. Less fluid means less total blood volume and improved circulation and blood pressure. There are five main classes of the drug: loop diuretics, thiazide diuretics, potassium-sparing diuretics, osmotic diuretics, and carbonic anhydrase inhibitors.

Loop diuretics

The most potent type of diuretic, loop diuretics are named after the loop of Henle, a component of a nephron. The nephrons are the filtering units of the kidney, and are responsible for moving fluids and waste out of the bloodstream, resulting in urine formation. The loop of Henle is a branch within each nephron where sodium and potassium are reabsorbed back into the bloodstream instead of being filtered into the urine. Loop diuretics inhibit this action and promote excretion of the sodium and potassium instead, along with calcium and magnesium. Since excess sodium causes excess fluid build-up, this results in fluid loss. Furosemide (Lasix), bumetanide (Bumex), torsemide (Demadex), and ethacryinic acid (Edecrin) are all loop diuretics.

Thiazide diuretics

Thiazide diuretics such as chlorothiazide (Diuril) and hydrochlorothiazide (HCTZ) work by blocking the action of aldosterone, a hormone that promotes sodium reabsorption by the kidneys. They are potassium-deplet-

The International Olympic Committee stripped Bulgaria's Ivan Ivanov of his silver medal for weightlifting in the 2000 Olympics when he tested positive for furosemide, a diuretic. Photo by David Guttenfelder, AP/Wide World Photos. Reproduced by permission.

ing diuretics, meaning that they cause a loss of potassium, known as hypokalemia.

Potassium-sparing diuretics

Potassium-sparing diuretics include amiloride (Midamor) and triamterene (Dyrenium). They are used in the treatment of cirrhosis and congestive heart failure. They may be used in conjunction with thiazide diuretics to offset the potassium loss associated with those medications.

Osmotic diuretics

As their name suggests, osmotic diuretics such as mannitol (Osmitrol), isosorbide (Ismotic), and glycerin (Osmoglyn) draw fluid from the tissues of the body through principles of osmosis. Osmotic diuretics are typically given to treat or prevent acute renal failure (kidney failure). They may also be used to relieve intracranial pressure (swelling of the brain) in cases of head injury or hydrocephalus.

Carbonic anhydrase inhibitors

Carbonic anhydrase inhibitors such as dorzolamide (Trusopt) and dichlorphenamide (Daranide) are used to treat glaucoma patients and altitude sickness. Acetazolamide (Diamox), a carbonic anhydrase inhibitor, is also used to treat seizures related to epilepsy. CA inhibitors work by promoting the excretion of sodium and bicarbonate.

INGESTION METHODS

Diuretics are most commonly available in pill form. In a hospital setting, they may be administered intravenously or injected. Carbonic anhydrase inhibitors may be administered in eye drop form [dorzolamide (Trusopt)] to glaucoma patients.

THERAPEUTIC USE

Diuretics are prescribed in cases where excess fluids in bodily tissues (edema) cause illness, discomfort, or medical complications.

Medical conditions that may warrant the use of diuretics include:

Hypertension (high blood pressure)

A standard treatment for hypertension, diuretics flush excess water and sodium from the body. They also lower blood pressure by reducing the total volume of

HISTORY NOTES

Diuretics and doping

The first Olympic games of the new millennium were marred by a doping scandal when three Bulgarian weightlifters tested positive for diuretics. Izabela Dragneva, Ivan Ivanov, and Sevdalin Minchev, who had won gold, silver, and bronze, respectively, were stripped of their medals after drug testing revealed the presence of furosemide, a banned substance. After the third suspension, the Bulgarian Weightlifting Federation was sanctioned and suspended from participation in the rest of the 2000 Summer Games in Sydney, Australia. However, the Court of Arbitration for Sport overturned the ban after Bulgaria agreed to pay a $50,000 fine. Alan Tsagaev, a Bulgarian lifter whose test was clean, went on to win the silver in his weight class.

Diuretics are used by athletes to lose weight quickly in order to compete in lower weight classes for sports like wrestling, boxing, and weightlifting. In addition, they are sometimes taken as "masking" drugs to speed the elimination of banned performance-enhancing substances such as steroids from the body. Bulgarian coach Ivan Abadjiev blamed the positive drug tests at the Sydney games on an herbal tonic he had given the athletes before competition.

---

fluid in the bloodstream. A reduced total volume of blood means that the heart does not have to work as hard to circulate it through the body.

Often, diuretics are used in combination with other drugs to relieve hypertension. Types of diuretics used to treat hypertension include thiazides, such as chlorothiazide (Diuril) and hydrochlorothiazide (Esidrex); potassium-sparing diuretics, such as spironolactone (Aldactone); and loop diuretics, such as furosemide (Lasix).

Congestive heart failure (CHF)

Congestive heart failure occurs when the pumping ability of the heart is impaired, and the heart itself becomes enlarged. This may be due to coronary artery disease, chronic hypertension, diabetes, arrhythmia (irregular heartbeat), infection, or a heart valve disorder. The result is edema, or swelling caused by fluid retention, a major symptom of congestive heart failure. Patients with CHF experience swollen legs, ankles, feet, and/or fluid in the lungs (pulmonary edema). Sometimes fluid builds up around other organs, such as the liver, as well. Loop diuretics such as furosemide (Lasix) are fre-

quently prescribed to alleviate edema from congestive heart failure. Thiazide and potassium-sparing diuretics may also be prescribed.

Other drugs that may be prescribed in conjunction with diuretics for the treatment of CHF include vasodilators (drugs that dilate blood vessels, such as ACE inhibitors); inotropics (drugs that increase the heart's ability to contract, such as digoxin); and beta blockers (drugs that inhibit the action of epinephrine, such as carvedilol).

Diabetes insipidus

Also known as water diabetes, diabetes insipidus (DI) is a rare chronic disease that causes excessive urination. If not properly treated, it can result in electrolyte imbalance and dehydration. It may be caused by a number of factors, including lithium use (a psychiatric drug used for bipolar disorder), neurological disease, or an inadequate amount of ADH (anti-diuretic hormone, or vasopressin, which is produced by the pituitary gland). DI caused by insufficient ADH is called central diabetes insipidus.

Nephrogenic diabetes insipidus, which occurs less often than central diabetes insipidus, is characterized by the inability of the kidneys to reabsorb water into the bloodstream. Treatment with thiazide or potassium-sparing diuretics can help maintain a fluid and electrolyte balance in some individuals with diabetes insipidus.

Other

Diuretics may also be prescribed for a number of other disorders and conditions that trigger fluid retention, including:

- Nephrotic syndrome. Thiazide or loop diuretics are used in the treatment of this kidney disorder that causes increased protein in the urine.

- Cirrhosis. Potassium-sparing diuretics are frequently prescribed for the patients with this liver disease.

- Renal hypercalciuria (kidney stones). Thiazide diuretics such as metolazone (Zaroxolyn) that increase calcium levels in the body are used in the treatment of kidney stones.

- Water retention related to menstruation. Pamabrom, an ingredient in over-the-counter diuretic preparations, can relieve bloating related to a woman's menstrual cycle.

Several studies have shown that thiazide diuretics prevent calcium loss in bones, which may improve bone density and protect against osteoporosis. Preliminary research also suggests that diuretics are helpful in preventing stroke. Further studies are needed to confirm these findings.

USAGE TRENDS

The U.S. Centers for Disease Control (CDC) and the National Center for Health Statistics (NCHS) report that cardiovascular-renal drugs (including diuretics, beta blockers, and calcium channel blockers) were the most frequently prescribed medications in the United States in 1999 (the most recent year for which data was available). In fact, the loop diuretic Lasix was the second most frequently prescribed medication overall, with more than 12.9 million prescriptions written. It was second only to the allergy drug Claritin.

Scope and severity

Statistics on the misuse of diuretic drugs are more difficult to determine. Estimates vary as to the number of people currently suffering from eating disorders, and not all individuals with an eating disorder abuse diuretics. In addition, the sense of shame and emotional turmoil associated with the disease make the unreported incidence of eating disorders high. Federal and institutional estimates put the number at approximately 5–8 million Americans.

Age, ethnic, and gender trends

According to the National Institutes of Mental Health (NIMH), up to 3.7% of females suffer from anorexia, and up to 4.2% of females suffer from bulimia at some point in their lives. Males develop eating disorders much less frequently, representing only 5–15% of all U.S. cases of anorexia or bulimia.

The 1999 text *Mental Health: A Report of the Surgeon General,* states that the mortality, or death rate, among females age 15–24 with anorexia is an estimated 0.56% per year, approximately 12 times higher than that of girls of the same age in the general population. In addition to medical problems related to eating disorders, anorexia and bulimia are frequently accompanied by other psychiatric disturbances, including mood disorders (depression, anxiety) and substance abuse. Depression is the third leading cause of death for adolescents ages 15–24, and the eleventh leading cause of death for Americans of all ages.

In a Wesleyan University study of binge eating disorder (BED) published in 2000, researchers found that African-American women with the disorder reported laxative and diuretic abuse more frequently than white women. However, BED was considered a significant health problem in both racial groups.

Diuretic use and eating disorders in sports and professional athletics are growing concerns both in the United States and abroad. Sports that require weigh-ins, from wrestling to regatta sailing, can put the pressure on athletes to take extreme measures to lose weight quickly. Often, those measures include diuretic abuse, rubber suits, starvation diets, exposure to high temperatures, and other unsafe practices that can put athletes at risk for severe dehydration and even death.

A 1996 report in the journal *Pediatrics* that looked at a variety of studies and surveys of athletic weight-control practices reported that up to 52% of female collegiate athletes had engaged in unhealthy weight-control behaviors including diuretic use.

Weight loss in athletes is sometimes encouraged by coaching staff, as well. In sports such as gymnastics, swimming, and track—where "smaller is better"—female athletes in particular often develop eating disorders and unhealthy weight loss practices, including diuretic abuse. A 1999 NCAA-sponsored study of college athletes found that 13% of female athletes surveyed showed signs of bulimia or anorexia, and an additional 36% were considered at risk for developing an eating disorder. In addition, 3.89% of female and 3.65% of male athletes surveyed reported diuretic use for the purpose of purging at least once in their lifetime. In addition, one-fourth of the males surveyed used saunas or steam baths to lose weight at least once a week and 4.4% of females vomited for weight loss. Female athletes who develop eating disorders or eating disordered behavior are at a higher risk for osteoporosis and amenorrhea (interruption of the menstrual cycle).

MENTAL EFFECTS

Diuretics are not a psychoactive drug and have no direct mental effects. However, abuse and misuse of this medication can lead to severe dehydration, which may lead to headaches and mental confusion.

Because they affect sodium, potassium, and chloride levels in the body, diuretics can trigger electrolyte imbalances. An electrolyte imbalance can cause a variety of neurological symptoms, including confusion, fainting, dizziness, and headache.

PHYSIOLOGICAL EFFECTS

Diuretics increase urine and sodium output, and in some cases they may also increase urinary output of potassium, calcium, and magnesium. In large quantities, they can affect electrolyte balance.

Harmful side effects

The main risk of diuretic abuse is severe dehydration. This is of special concern to athletes who might take the drug to make weight for sporting events or to improve performance. Anyone exercising or participating in athletic competition is already at risk for dehydration from the fluids they are losing from sweating; diuretics can accelerate the process.

 **IN THE NEWS**

Boosting: the anti-diuretic

The Paralympics are also not immune to cases of doping. The IPC, the International Paralympic Committee that oversees the event, uses the same list of banned substances as the International Olympic Committee (IOC) and the World Anti-Doping Agency (WADA). In fact, two powerlifters tested positive for diuretics in out-of-competition tests before the 2000 Sydney Paralympics, and were banned from those games. However, depending on their medical needs, disabled athletes may successfully apply to therapeutically use certain listed drugs, including diuretics.

A type of doping that is unique to the Paralympics is a practice known as boosting. Boosting is the act of deliberating triggering autonomic dysreflexia, a "fight or flight" reaction that occurs in individuals with spinal cord injuries and is characterized by a rise in blood pressure. How is it achieved? Athletes block their catheters so that their bladders overfill and distend. The pain nerve impulses can't reach the brain, and over-stimulate the autonomic nervous system instead. As a result, the blood vessels dilate and the pressure rises. The brain is unable to regulate blood pressure below the level of the injury, so autonomic dysreflexia results. A "boost" is estimated to improve performance by as much as 15%, but the practice is extremely dangerous to an athlete's health.

In addition to blocking catheter flow, some athletes use pins, wires, tourniquets, and other irritants to achieve this response. Other signs of boosting include pale skin, sweating, gooseflesh, and tremors. The IPC Sport Science and Medical Committee has established testing procedures for boosting in an effort to end this dangerous practice.

Anyone who must take diuretics for therapeutic purposes should take the proper precautions when exercising. This includes adequate and regular intake of water, sports drinks, or other non-caffeinated fluids; loose and comfortable clothing; adequate rest periods; and awareness of the signs of heat exhaustion (clammy and cool skin, fatigue, nausea, weakness, confusion, vision disturbances, and a possible loss of consciousness).

Other common side effects of diuretic use may include:

- rash

- nausea

- dizziness

- urinary incontinence

- photosensitivity (a sensitivity to sunlight)

- high blood glucose levels (blood sugars)

Other side effects that have been reported with diuretic use, but are not considered common, include:

- hearing loss

- pancreatitis

- anemia

- leukopenia (depletion of white blood cells)

Potassium-sparing diuretics (e.g., spironolactone, amiloride, triamterene) may cause a dangerous build-up of excessive potassium in the body. Signs of hyperkalemia, or excess potassium, include:

- arrhythmia (irregular heartbeat)

- breathing difficulties

- numbness or tingling sensation in the hands or feet

- fatigue

- weakness

- anxiety and/or difficulty concentrating

The potassium-depleting diuretics (e.g., hydrochlorothiazide, chlorthalidone, metolazone) cause potassium loss that may be reversed by supplementation and/or dietary adjustments. As previously stated, potassium can be harmful in high amounts, so any supplementation should be recommended and supervised by a doctor.

- fast or irregular heartbeat

- muscle cramps

- nausea and/or vomiting

- dry mouth and persistent thirst

- fatigue

- weakness

- mood swings

Although diuretics may sometimes be given to pregnant women suffering from preeclampsia, in general, diuretic use is usually not recommended in pregnancy because of the potential risk to the developing fetus. In addition, some diuretics may pass through into breast milk and can cause lactation problems. Therefore, women who are pregnant or breastfeeding should always check with their doctor before taking diuretics.

Certain types of diuretics may be contraindicated (not recommended) for use by people with chronic medical conditions, including diabetes, pancreatitis, and lupus erythematosus. Anyone with a known allergy to diuretics or to sulfa drugs should alert their doctor before taking a diuretic.

Long-term health effects

Anyone taking diuretics for longer than six months may experience a folate, or folic acid, deficiency. Folic acid plays a part in the health and reproduction of virtually every cell in the body. It is responsible for protein metabolism, the prevention of neural tube defects in pregnancy, blood cell production, and the synthesis of neurotransmitters. Individuals with folate deficiencies may suffer from anemia, depression and other mood disorders, and may give birth to babies with neural tube defects. Supplementation with folic acid may be useful in reversing these effects.

Individuals on long-term diuretic therapy may also experience elevated levels of homocysteine, an amino acid regulated by folate. High homocysteine levels increase the risk of heart disease. Thiamin, or vitamin B_1, depletion is another possible side effect of loop diuretics. Individuals with thiamin deficiencies are at risk for fatigue, heart enlargement, muscle cramps, heart rate irregularities, and impaired mental function.

Insufficient zinc intake is another possible side effect of diuretic use. Individuals with zinc deficiency may experience hair loss, problems with night vision, slow wound healing, dermatitis, and a predisposition to infection and illness due to lowered immune function.

Because diuretics affect electrolyte balance, they can cause deficiencies in magnesium and calcium as well as the previously mentioned potassium. Magnesium deficiency may occur with chronic use of the loop and thiazide diuretics. Symptoms include nausea and vomiting, muscle cramps and weakness, insomnia, arrhythmia (irregular heartbeat), difficulty sleeping, and a loss of exercise tolerance. Calcium deficiency is a possible side effect of both loop and potassium-sparing diuretics. Signs of insufficient calcium in the body include muscle cramps, low bone density (which may be indicated by bones that break easily), tooth decay, heart palpitations, and difficulty sleeping.

REACTIONS WITH OTHER DRUGS OR SUBSTANCES

Although over-the-counter diuretic preparations are available without a prescription, because of the risk for serious and potentially fatal complications and side effects, diuretics should always be taken under the recommendation and guidance of a trained healthcare professional.

Certain medications may impair or enhance the therapeutic effects of diuretic drugs. Anyone prescribed a diuretic should inform their physician of all other drugs and supplements they are taking in case of a possible interaction.

Drugs that are also known to decrease potassium levels, such as glucocorticoids and digoxin, should be avoided by anyone taking potassium-depleting diuretics. If they are prescribed, a physician should closely monitor the potassium levels of the patient. Potassium deficiency, or hypokalemia, can cause serious and potentially dangerous side effects (see Harmful side effects section).

Potassium-sparing diuretics, such as amiloride (Midamor), spironolactone (Aldactone), and triamterene (Dyrenium), impair the ability of the kidneys to filter potassium from the body. This can result in a condition called hyperkalemia, or excessive potassium, a potentially dangerous situation (see Harmful side effects section). Anyone taking potassium-sparing diuretics should avoid excessive dietary intake of foods high in the mineral. Bananas, tomatoes, sweet potatoes, and oranges are some of the foods that are rich in potassium.

Diuretics may also interact with herbs and dietary supplements. Licorice (*Glycyrrhiza glabra*) can lower potassium levels, and should be avoided with potassium-sparing diuretics. In addition, herbal diuretics can amplify, or increase, the effect of prescription diuretics. Some of the more well-known diuretic herbs include bilberry (*Vaccinium myrtillus*), celery seed (*Apium graveolens*), dandelion leaf (*Taraxacum officinale*), and elder flower (*Sambucus nigra, S. canadensis*), goldenrod (*Solidago virgaurea*), horse chestnut seeds (*Aesculus hippocastanum*), horsetail (*Equisetum arvense*), juniper (*Juniperus communis*), parsley (*Petroselinum sativum*), St. John's wort (*Hypericum perforatum*), and uva ursi (bearberry; *Arctostaphylos uva ursi*). Just because a preparation is labeled natural does not mean it cannot cause harmful interactions with other medications and substances. Individuals should always check with their physician or healthcare professional before taking herbal and supplement products with diuretics.

Foods and beverages rich in caffeine, such as coffee, tea, and chocolate, can also have a diuretic effect at high doses, and should not be taken in excess with prescription diuretics. Alcohol has a diuretic effect as well, and should be avoided in individuals taking a diuretic medication.

TREATMENT AND REHABILITATION

Treatment for diuretic abuse starts with addressing the roots of the physical or psychological problems. There are a number of rehabilitation programs available for the treatment of eating disorders such as bulimia, anorexia, and binge eating disorder (BED). Programs are usually residential, or inpatient, meaning that the patient lives in the hospital or other rehabilitation facility for the length of treatment (several weeks to several months).

The first goal of rehabilitation from any eating disorder is to stabilize both weight and self-destructive behavior such as diuretic abuse and binge eating. Patients with anorexia may be severely malnourished, and could have additional related health problems such as impaired kidney function and dehydration that need immediate medical attention. They may also require intravenous feeding.

Patients need to relearn healthy nutrition, meal management, and exercise patterns. Taking regularly scheduled meals, meeting with a registered dietitian, and participating in classes on appropriate nutrition and fitness will help to establish good habits. Overweight individuals being treated for binge eating disorder may also learn new healthy and realistic strategies for weight loss in this environment.

Equally important is the effective treatment of eating disorders and associated diuretic abuse is to address the emotional motives and distorted thinking behind the patient's behavior. Individual or group psychotherapy or cognitive-behavioral therapy can help the patient work through self-esteem and self-image problems. Studies show that cognitive behavioral therapy has a 40-50% success rate with bulimia nervosa and BED patients. Family therapy may also be part of the treatment program.

The goal of cognitive-behavioral therapy (CBT) is to teach the patient new behaviors by exposing the irrational thoughts that trigger the old, self-destructive behaviors of anorexia or bulimia. Once the disordered thinking is changed, the behavior will follow. Learning how to recognize the thoughts and emotions surrounding eating disordered behavior, and rehearsing the new and desirable behaviors (such as avoiding situations and places that trigger the old behavior), is a key part of long-term recovery and relapse prevention with CBT.

If the patient has a pre-existing mood disorder, such as depression or anxiety disorder, antidepressant medication may also be prescribed. Studies have shown that the selective serotonin reuptake inhibitors (SSRIs) such as fluoxetine (Prozac) and sertraline (Zoloft) are effective in people with bulimia and anorexia. These medications reduce depression by increasing levels of serotonin, a neurotransmitter.

Eating disorders can be chronic conditions that need life-long vigilance and attention. A 1999 Harvard Medical School study of 246 women with eating disorders found that one-third of patients relapsed, or returned to eating disordered behaviors, following initial full recovery from both bulimia and anorexia.

Athletes who abuse or misuse diuretics for purposes of performance enhancement or making weight face special treatment challenges. Weight loss and an excessively low percentage of body fat may be praised by coaches, trainers, and teammates, making behavioral changes even more difficult. In addition, obsessive exercise and workout routines may be rewarded in sports and competition rather than questioned. A treatment strategy that includes education of not just the athlete, but also the people around him or her, is essential.

PERSONAL AND SOCIAL CONSEQUENCES

Urinary incontinence, or leakage, that may be associated with diuretic use can cause social embarrassment, self-esteem issues, depression, and anxiety. A person suffering from incontinence may stop participating in social activities, sports, and other activities they once enjoyed because of the risk of embarrassing "accidents." Bladder training, biofeedback, pelvic toning exercises, or special urethral or vaginal inserts may help to treat urinary incontinence problems related to diuretics.

While uncomplicated diuretic use itself has little impact on personal and social well-being, the conditions associated with misuse of the medication can have serious consequences. Aside from the physical problems associated with eating disorders, the dysfunctional behavior itself can greatly affect relationships with friends and family and basic social functioning. Individuals with eating disorders may avoid going out with friends to eat or drink socially. Their rigid schedules of bingeing and purging and/or exercise may take over their life to the extent that they withdraw socially.

Competitive athletes who misuse diuretics, either due to an eating disorder or for performance-enhancing purposes, may be suspended or banned from competition. In addition, if diuretic use becomes chronic and spirals into other eating disordered behaviors, athletic performance will ultimately suffer, and the athlete may face added pressures from coaching staff and teammates.

LEGAL CONSEQUENCES

Diuretics are not a controlled substance, and over-the-counter brands are easily and legally accessible in the United States and throughout the world.

Professional athletes who test positive for diuretics in the Olympics are suspended from participation in the games. They may also be stripped of any medals they have won in competition. Testing for banned substances may be conducted in competition or out of competition.

Federal guidelines, regulations, and penalties

The U.S. Food and Drug Administration (FDA) is the federal authority that oversees the regulation of non-controlled drugs such as diuretics. Any legal penalties for trafficking (illegally selling or distributing) prescription diuretics would typically be determined at the state level unless the charges involved theft from a federal facility such as a VA (Veterans Administration) hospital.

See also Caffeine

RESOURCES

Books

Medical Economics Corporation. *Physicians' Desk Reference (PDR). 56th Edition.* Montvale, NJ: Medical Economics, 2002.

Otis, Carol and Roger Goldingay. *The Athletic Woman's Survival Guide: How to Win the Battle Against Eating Disorders, Amenorrhea, and Osteoporosis.* Champaign, IL: Human Kinetics, 2000.

Periodicals

Anderson, Kelli. "Losing to Win." *Sports Illustrated for Women* 3, no. 3 (May/June 2001): 88+.

Hoel, Donna, and Robert Howard. "Hypertension: Stalking the Silent Killer." *Postgraduate Medicine* 101, no. 2 (February 1997). Available at: <http://www.postgradmed.com/issues/1997/02_97/hoel.htm>. Accessed April 1, 2002.

Other

National Institute of Mental Health. <http://www.nimh.nih.gov/publicat/eatingdisordersmenu.cfm>. *Facts About Eating Disorders.* Accessed April 1, 2002.

U.S. Anti-Doping Agency (USADA). <http://www.usantidoping.org/>. Accessed April 1, 2002. Drug reference line: 1-800-233-0393.

Organizations

National Eating Disorders Association, 603 Stewart St., Suite 803, Seattle, WA, USA, 98101, (206) 382-3587, info@NationalEatingDisorders.org, <http://www.nationaleatingdisorders.org/>.

Paula Anne Ford-Martin

ECSTASY (MDMA)

OFFICIAL NAMES: Ecstasy, 3,4-Methylenedioxymetham-
phetamine (MDMA)
STREET NAMES: E, XTC, X, Adam, lover's speed, hug drug,
roll, bean, M, clarity, disco biscuits, Scooby snacks, bibs
DRUG CLASSIFICATIONS: Schedule I, stimulant with hallucinogenic properties

OVERVIEW

MDMA was developed in Germany in 1912 and
patented in 1914 by the German pharmaceutical company Merck. It does not appear to have been specifically
created for any particular use, but rather, resulted from
another drug development procedure. There is practically no historical mention of the drug again until the
1950s, when the United States army experimented with
it as an agent of psychological warfare. As a result of
therapeutic drug experiments in the late 1960s and early
1970s, people began to use MDMA recreationally
because they liked the feelings of well being and openness it produced, and by psychotherapists who gave the
drug to their patients to enhance therapy as a "penicillin
for the soul." Presumably it was around this time
MDMA picked up the name ecstasy, which comes from
the Greek *ekstasis* meaning "flight of soul from body."
Ecstasy production and use was not regulated in any way
until 1985, when concerns about widespread use prompted the U.S. Drug Enforcement Administration (DEA) to
initiate medical reviews of the drug. The drug was given
Schedule I status, meaning it has no accepted medical
utility. Its use is now illegal in the United States.

Despite the restriction, ecstasy use has continued
and dramatically increased at the turn of the millenium.
In fact, ecstasy is one of the few drugs whose use is
increasing among 12- to 25-year-olds. Ecstasy is most
often used by young people at parties or in dance clubs,
because users find that feelings of extreme happiness
and uninhibited confidence produced by the drug
encourage socializing, and that the drug's stimulant
properties are ideal for prolonged periods of dancing.
For some time the perception was that ecstasy was not
harmful, but as its use has spread exponentially, reports
of death as a result of ecstasy use have become increasingly common. Researchers have also discovered that
the chemical is a neurotoxin and that ecstasy users may
risk depression as a result of continued use.

CHEMICAL/ORGANIC COMPOSITION

Unlike drugs such as cocaine, marijuana, tobacco,
and heroin, ecstasy is not derived from a naturally occurring plant; rather it is a synthetic drug created in a laboratory. An average ecstasy tablet contains between 75 mg
and 150 mg of MDMA, along with some inactive filler
compounds, but they can range anywhere from 0 mg to
400 mg MDMA. Due to its synthetic nature, ecstasy is
frequently cut with other drugs, and some recent drug
busts have found tablets sold as ecstasy to contain less
than 30% actual MDMA. Some other drugs often sold as
or in combination with MDMA as ecstasy are methyl-
enedioxyamphetamine (MDA), dimethyltrypatamine
(DMT), dipropyltryptamine (DPT), paramethoxyamphetamine (PMA), and numerous other stimulants and
hallucinogens including PCP, cocaine, ketamine (special
k), methamphetamine, gamma hydroxybutyrate (GHB),

lysergic acid (LSD), pseudoephedrine, and dextromethorphan (cough medicine). Like most drug users, ecstasy users rarely use just ecstasy. Other drugs commonly taken in combination with ecstasy are alcohol, marijuana, heroin, cocaine, LSD, other "club drugs," and sometimes antidepressants or benzodiazepines to counteract the feeling of "coming down" off ecstasy.

INGESTION METHODS

Ecstasy is generally illegally sold in tablet or capsule form and is consumed orally, although it can be snorted in powder form, injected, or inserted anally as a suppository. The most common form of ecstasy is a small pill, colored and stamped with a logo of some sort. These characteristics can identify a particular batch or manufacturer of ecstasy, and some have nicknames based on the logo that appears on the tablet. After a good experience with a particular dose of ecstasy, the user might search out a pill with the same appearance in hopes that it will generate the same effect. Similarly, ecstasy users disseminate information through web sites and chat-rooms about certain tablets or doses that are known not to contain ecstasy or are known to produce negative effects. However, all ecstasy use is unsafe.

THERAPEUTIC USE

Ecstasy has not been proven safe or effective for any medical use, and it is not available by prescription. In the 1970s, ecstasy was used as an aid in psychotherapy because the drug reportedly could intensify the patient's feelings of openness and intimacy in revealing deeply personal feelings; however it was declared illegal a decade later. There continue to be supporters of ecstasy use in psychotherapy and for treatment of stress and anxiety disorders.

USAGE TRENDS

Until relatively recently, researchers had little data on usage trends of ecstasy because it was not included in national surveys of drug use. The most comprehensive and up-to-date information on usage trends among young people in the United States comes from just a few sources, including *The National Household Survey on Drug Abuse* and the *Monitoring the Future* surveys. The *National Household Survey on Drug Abuse* is an annual survey conducted by the Substance Abuse and Mental Health Services Administration that estimates the incidence and prevalence of drug use in the general population ages 12 and over. In 2000, nearly 3% of the population ages 12 and over reported at least one lifetime use of ecstasy, showing a substantial increase from 1999 and years prior. The majority of users were in younger age

KEY TERMS

DOPAMINE: Neurotransmitter associated with the regulation of movement, emotional response, pleasure, and pain.

METABOLISM: The body's ability to break down and process substances taken into the body.

NEURONS: Nerve cells found throughout the central nervous system. Neurons release neurotransmitters.

NEUROTRANSMITTER: Chemical in the brain that transmits messages between neurons, or nerve cells.

RECEPTOR: A specialized part of a nerve cell that recognizes neurotransmitters and communicates with other nerve cells.

SEROTONIN: An important neurotransmitter in the brain that regulates mood, appetite, sensory perception, and other central nervous system functions.

SYNAPSE: The gap between communicating nerve cells.

SYNERGY: The effect from a combination of drugs that is greater than the sum of their individual effects.

groups, with 9.7% of young adults aged 18–25 reporting at least one lifetime use of ecstasy, an increase of more than 2% from the previous year.

Because ecstasy is primarily used by adolescents and young adults, a survey focusing on this area of the population should provide the most accurate assessment of patterns and trends of ecstasy use. The *Monitoring the Future* survey, supported by the National Institute on Drug Abuse, was designed to track drug use patterns and attitudes of secondary school and college students in the United States since 1975. The *Monitoring the Future* survey started incorporating questions on ecstasy in the 1989 survey for young adults and the 1996 survey for younger students. Results from this survey have shown a trend of increasing use across all age ranges. The study found 3.4% of eighth graders had used ecstasy in 1996. Numbers dropped slightly for the next couple of years, but have shown a sharp increase to 5.2% of eighth graders in 2001. Among tenth graders the prevalence of ecstasy use went from 5.6% to 8.0% in the same time period, again with a slight dip in 1998. Just over 6% of twelfth graders reported ecstasy use 1996, an estimate that has jumped to 11.7% by 2001. College students have shown a similar trend. Around 2% of college students reported use in 1991, a number that slowly increased until 1996, when it sharply increased to more than 13% in 2000.

Ecstasy tablets. Photo by Andrew Brookes/CORBIS. Reproduced by permission.

Scope and severity

Usage and research of ecstasy in the United States appears to be at least five years behind that in European countries. Some reports suggest 80% of all ecstasy in circulation comes from the Netherlands. By the end of 2001, much of the research on the health effects of ecstasy has come from outside the United States, from places such as Australia, Ireland, Great Britain, and Germany, among others. The ecstasy users studied also differ somewhat; to qualify as an ecstasy user in many of the European studies, a higher number of total uses is required than in U.S. studies.

Ecstasy use originally was associated with certain subcultures, such as people involved in New Age spirituality, the dance club scene, gay men, followers of the Grateful Dead, and college students. This is no longer the case, as ecstasy use has become more mainstream in popular culture.

Age, ethnic, and gender trends

The majority of ecstasy users are Caucasian, educated, and are concentrated in the adolescent to young adult age groups. In addition, many studies have not shown the differences in ecstasy use between males and females usually seen with other drugs. Although drug use tends to start among people in younger age groups, ecstasy is rarely found to continue into older ages as is the case with many other drugs. As the availability of

ecstasy has become more widespread, the drug is branching out to different age and ethnic groups, which will be reflected in the results of future national surveys.

MENTAL EFFECTS

Both desirable and undesirable mental effects are experienced as a result of ecstasy use. Naturally, someone taking ecstasy is looking for the desirable effects, which include feelings of elation, openness, comfort, affection or arousal, self-confidence, and seemingly endless energy and endurance to dance the night away. There have also been reports of sharpened senses and mental clarity, feelings of floating, and hallucinations (which for some is an undesirable effect). However, the same mechanism associated with the desirable effects of ecstasy use is also associated with the undesirable effects.

Some of the negative effects of ecstasy use can be thought of as a distortion of the effects others view as positive. For example, feelings of awareness and energy are replaced by feelings of anxiety, agitation, confusion, and fear, potentially leading to irrational or erratic behavior, panic attacks, or even psychotic episodes. Both these desirable and undesirable effects are short-term and can last anywhere from three to eight hours. Another short-term effect is hyperthermia, or overheating, which can result in death.

Upon taking a dose of ecstasy the user feels a rush, sometimes within the first 20 minutes, followed by a peak high that levels off before a period of "coming down." For some, the "coming down" is better described as a "crash" that involves the negative mental effects associated with ecstasy use. Many of the negative effects continue beyond the period of actively using the drug. In the days following an episode of ecstasy use, the user often experiences depression, difficulty concentrating, and disturbances in mood, sleep, and appetite. Also common are paranoia, confusion, and impulsive or irrational behavior, in addition to muscle aches and stiffness from excessive activity usually associated with its use. Although the majority of ecstasy users consider the experience a positive one, with repeated use the initial euphoria felt with ecstasy use becomes less intense, and the undesired effects eventually tend to outweigh the desired ones.

PHYSIOLOGICAL EFFECTS

Ecstasy affects a number of body systems. The effects of ecstasy on the brain system are what lead to both the desired and undesired mental effects of the drug. Within the brain, there are different groups of chemical messengers called neurotransmitters that are responsible for the communication within the brain and between the brain and the body. Neurotransmitters flow

Image of front side of pill	ADAM (White)	EVA (Yellow)	Amor (White)	Love (Pink)	Heart (White)	Drops (Yellow)	Sun (Yellow)	Half moon (White)	Heart & Arrow (Pink)	VW (Yellow)
	Beetle (Beige)	Mercedes (White)	Triple Five (White)	V.I.P. (Yellow)	Cal (White)	PT (Beige)	Slit-eye (White)	ANADIN (Beige)	Boomerang (Yellow)	Bulls (White)	Dolphin (Yellow)
	Elephant (Yellow)	Dog (Yellow)	Pigs (White)	Pelican (White)	Pigeon (White)	Dove (White)	Sparrow (Yellow)	Bird (White)	Kermit (Yellow)	Flintstone (Yellow)	Batman (White)
	Superman (Yellow)	Popeye (Yellow)	Chiemsee (Yellow)	Fido (White)	Indian chief (White)	Sonic (White)	Smiley (White)	Playboy (White)	Swallow (Orange)	Dinosaur (Red)	Anchor (Blue)
	Mushroom (White)	Olympics (White)	Hammer & Sickle (Yellow)	Hammer & Sickle (Red)	Trefoil (Blue)	Trefoil (White)	Love symbol (White)	Yellow Sunshine (Yellow)	Pink Panther (Pink)	Snowball (White)	Ying-Yang (Beige)

Various types of ecstasy pills. Illustration by Argosy.

from one neuron (nerve cell) to another, where they individually attach to sites called receptors, and trigger a signal or message from the sending neuron. Pumps, called transporters, then return neurotransmitters to the neuron that released them to be stored for future use.

Ecstasy is suspected to interfere with a number of different neurotransmitter systems, primarily serotonin and dopamine. Serotonin is involved in the regulation of mood, appetite, emotion, sleep, perception, anxiety, aggression, and memory; dopamine is involved in the regulation of movement, emotional response, and ability to feel pleasure and pain. Ecstasy stimulates an excess release of these neurotransmitters, while at the same time blocking the transporters that pump them back to the releasing neuron, which creates a high concentration of neurotransmitters in the space between the cells, called the synapse. This overabundance of serotonin and dopamine is what causes the feelings of elation, altered perception, and high energy.

During this time the neurons are unable to replace all the neurotransmitters that are being released and not returned, so in the days following ecstasy use fewer neurotransmitters are released, and the number of transporters is reduced. This diminished function, primarily serotonin function, explains the depressed mood and other disturbances previously described as occurring in the days following an episode of ecstasy use. Regular ecstasy use destroys a neuron's ability to release serotonin, an effect that is long-lasting and may or may not be permanent.

Noradrenaline is another neurotransmitter similarly influenced by ecstasy use, and is involved in the regulation of blood pressure and heart rate. The effects produced by this system are undesirable and potentially harmful.

Other physical reactions that might be experienced during ecstasy use include muscle tension, jaw clenching, nausea and vomiting, excessive sweating, involuntary movements, chills, blurred vision, and feeling faint. Some of these reactions are associated with a sharp rise in body temperature induced by the drug itself and the increase in physical activity that often goes along with ecstasy use. Reactions such as jaw clenching and muscle tension and aches frequently continue after the period of drug use. Teenagers may use pacifiers to modify the jaw clenching associated with ecstasy use.

Overdose is usually characterized by an extremely elevated body temperature, heart rate, and blood pressure. Combining ecstasy with other drugs may or may not be intentional, since the true contents of an ecstasy tablet or capsule are rarely known to the user. For example, PMA, sold with or in place of MDMA as ecstasy, takes nearly four times longer than MDMA to take effect; therefore the user might take extra doses thinking the original was not adequate. Multiple doses, coupled

LAW AND ORDER

In November 2001, the United States Food and Drug Administration (FDA) approved the first study aimed at developing ecstasy as a prescription treatment for post-traumatic stress disorder (PTSD). As of 2002, the researchers conducting the study, whose work was spearheaded by the Multidisciplinary Association for Psychedelic Studies (MAPS) were still awaiting approval from the university review board where the study is expected to take place. The investigators expect the feelings of trust and openness associated with ecstasy to help people who have experienced traumatic events work through their emotions and recover more quickly by reducing fear, depression, and anxiety. This is one of the first studies of its kind since ecstasy was placed on Schedule I by the Drug Enforcement Administration in

1985. Schedule I drugs are illegal to possess, except in research performed under highly regulated conditions designed to protect patients. Other Schedule I drugs include heroin, marijuana, and LSD.

Before ecstasy was made illegal, the drug was used by a few therapists as an aid in psychotherapy for the same reasons proposed by this new study. Therapists who encouraged ecstasy use for their patients claimed that it helped them to be less inhibited, more honest and open when expressing their feelings, and to place past and current experiences in a new perspective. A former director of the National Institute on Drug Abuse, among others, has criticized the study proposed by MAPS, suggesting there is no appropriate medical use for ecstasy, and disagrees with introducing ecstasy to an otherwise drug-free person. Presumably, the therapists encouraging ecstasy-assisted psychotherapy expect close monitoring during periods of ecstasy use will cut down on any harmful effects, and that the benefits to the patients' treatment will outweigh any negative long-term effects of ecstasy. Results and analysis of the study will give more insight into the therapeutic use of ecstasy.

---

with the toxic effects PMA has on the heart, can have tragic consequences.

Ecstasy is toxic to the body, and the extent to which a person is affected depends on many factors, including the body chemistry of the user, the dose consumed, additional drugs also consumed, and the chemical composition and quantity of the drug or drugs taken as ecstasy.

Harmful side effects

Ecstasy use is associated with physiological damage to a number of body systems. These include the heart, brain, liver, kidneys, and the body's ability to regulate temperature. Ecstasy increases heart rate and blood pressure, which is especially dangerous for someone with a known or unknown heart condition, but can also cause an irregular heartbeat in an ordinarily healthy person. An irregular heartbeat means the heart pumps less effectively; therefore the blood flow to the brain and other organs is not adequate. This condition increases the risk for heart attack, stroke, and other types of heart failure.

The intense activity by ecstasy users at dance parties and raves contributes to the effect of the drug and results in profuse sweating and dehydration. A loss of bodily salt combined with rapidly drinking large quantities of water can result in a fluid imbalance that leads to epilepsy-like seizures or a compression of a part of the brain that regulates breathing or circulation. Salt and fluid depletion in combination with the intense activity and elevated body temperature often associated with

ecstasy use can break down skeletal muscle cells, eventually leading to kidney damage and failure.

Elevated body temperature is one of the most toxic effects of ecstasy, and this risk is augmented by its use at dance parties and raves. The lack of air circulation in a crowded environment creates an elevated room temperature, which, together with increases in body temperature can cause brain toxicity similar to heat stroke. High body temperature can also lead to severe liver inflammation or damage, abnormal blood clotting, and death.

Long-term health effects

Animal studies on ecstasy have found that the effects of the drug on the brain appear to be associated with long-term impairments in memory, learning, impulse control, mood, and sleep. These studies have guided human research into the long-term effects of ecstasy to focus on the drug's toxic effects on serotonin in the brain. As of 2001, clear evidence of long-term damage in humans is limited but suggests that excessive neurotransmitter activity induced by ecstasy use damages the neurons that release serotonin, which is thought to impair learning and memory. Researchers from Johns Hopkins University have demonstrated that this type of damage, in conjunction with verbal and visual memory impairment, persists for at least seven years in monkeys. Similar results were seen in humans who had not used ecstasy for at least two weeks, leading the investigators to declare that one instance of ecstasy use puts the user at risk for brain damage and long-term impairment in learning and memory. The period of no drug use prior to the learning and memory test suggests that the impairment cannot be attributed to any withdrawal effects.

Researchers at the National Institute on Drug Abuse, University College London, and University of Technology in Germany have found that ecstasy users and past-users perform worse than non-users on tasks associated with the serotonin system in the brain, such as learning, memory, and attention. This research also suggests that ecstasy use is associated with long-term depression and anxiety, even among people who had not used for more than six months.

Another study showed ecstasy users to have decreased blood flow to the brain (thought to be regulated by serotonin), and that the reduction in blood flow depended on dose, meaning there was a greater decrease among participants who had used ecstasy more often. Similarly, memory and learning impairment was more profound among people who had used ecstasy more often.

One difficulty with studying the long-term effects of ecstasy is that ecstasy users rarely use just one drug; therefore the deficits in learning, memory, and impulsivity cannot be linked exclusively to ecstasy. In addition, research in humans is too preliminary to be entirely sure that ecstasy use is causing these deficits. As of 2002, more studies are focusing on humans, and within the next couple of years research is expected to provide more definitive evidence of ecstasy's long-term effects, the mechanisms of action, and whether the deficits presented in this section are irreversible.

REACTIONS WITH OTHER DRUGS OR SUBSTANCES

Ecstasy is most often taken in combination with other drugs, intentionally or unintentionally. A person taking ecstasy might also drink alcohol; smoke marijuana; or take cocaine, methamphetamine, PCP, ketamine or additional "club drugs," among others. In different regions of the country, users have nicknames for particular drug combinations with ecstasy. For example, "candy-flipping" is a name for mixing LSD with ecstasy.

The Substance Abuse and Mental Health Administration sponsors a system called the Drug Abuse Warning Network (DAWN), which tracks drug-related visits to emergency rooms in the United States. The number of ecstasy-related emergency room visits reported to this network jumped from 250 in 1994 to nearly 3,000 visits in 1999. Almost 80% of these episodes involve the use of another drug in addition to ecstasy, and for nearly half of these, the other drug was alcohol. About one quarter of ecstasy-related emergency room visits also show marijuana use; nearly 20% show cocaine use; and close to 40% involve combinations with ketamine.

The ways in which these drugs react with ecstasy is still unclear, partly due to a phenomenon called synergy. Synergy refers to a reaction that magnifies the effects of drugs when they are combined. The effect of one dose of drug plus another dose of drug might add up to two, or because of synergy this combination of one plus one might add up to three or four or ten. Although alcohol is a depressant and ecstasy has stimulant properties, they both dehydrate the user, possibly in a synergistic fashion. Many of the other drugs taken at the same time as ecstasy produce similar physical reactions, such as modifications in heart rate, blood pressure, and body temperature. Therefore the health effects described in the previous section could be magnified many times over, explaining why most emergency room visits involve multiple drugs.

At times, the use of other drugs in addition to ecstasy might be part of the social scene in which ecstasy is taken, especially as particular drugs are combined or taken with ecstasy to achieve a specific effect. However, sometimes the drug combinations are unknown because they are part of the tablet or substance being sold as ecstasy. Many of the reported ecstasy overdose reactions have been attributed to substances other than MDMA, including PMA, which are much more toxic than MDMA. There is also evidence that some of these substances can have a harmful reaction with certain antidepressants or other prescription medication. Besides taking the drug to a laboratory for analysis, there is no way for the user to know what combinations of drugs are contained in the substance assumed to be ecstasy. Ecstasy testing kits provide a false sense of security because although they might identify the presence of an ecstasy-like substance, the kit doesn't differentiate between MDMA-like substances, tell how much of it is actual MDMA, or reveal what other potentially harmful substances are combined with it. An ecstasy-like substance could be any number of compounds, either more or less harmful than MDMA, including dextromethorphan (DXM), which is the active ingredient in cough medicine.

It is difficult to identify specific reactions ecstasy has with other drugs because most of the time it is unknown what drugs are being combined with each other. Some harmful effects might be due to synergy; others could be related to metabolism. Metabolism is the process that breaks down substances that are taken into the body and eliminates them. Some drugs, both legal and illegal, modify how the body would normally metabolize ecstasy, which could lead to a toxic buildup of very high concentrations of the drug in the system. However, because of the uncertainty of drug combinations and reactions with ecstasy, it is difficult to predict when a harmful reaction could occur.

TREATMENT AND REHABILITATION

Although ecstasy use is more widespread than other drugs of abuse seen in treatment centers, as of 2001 there were few data on the addictive properties and subsequent treatment of ecstasy abuse. Behavioral therapy, counseling, and psychotherapy used for other drugs of abuse, more specifically cocaine or amphetamine, apply similarly to ecstasy use. There is some evidence that after prolonged ecstasy use, the negative effects become more prominent than the positive and users stop on their own. This may explain why ecstasy users do not exhibit the same patterns of dependence shown by other drugs whose users end up in treatment. Some negative effects that might encourage the user to stop are anxiety, depression, panic, and paranoia; however, the user with these symptoms could already be left with long-term damage. Treatment of ecstasy use often refers to treatment of the symptoms associated with use. Doctors can usually remedy these symptoms with both behavioral and prescription drug therapies, as if they were disorders not induced by drug use. The sharp increase in the reported number of users over the past few years leads researchers to expect a similar increase in users seeking traditional drug treatment in the near future.

PERSONAL AND SOCIAL CONSEQUENCES

The consumption of ecstasy generally takes place in social settings, such as parties, and users enjoy the drug for its effects of sociability and extroversion. Some ecstasy users report welcoming people from different religious backgrounds and lifestyles, with whom they otherwise would not associate, while others report feeling as if they love and are loved by everyone around them. In this sense, ecstasy users see the social consequences of drug use to be extremely positive and part of the reason for taking the drug in the first place. This drug-induced arousal can lead to unintended sexual encounters and unsafe sex practices that the user not engage in if not under the influence of ecstasy.

The social nature of ecstasy use and feelings of safety and comfort associated with the drug contribute to the consumption of other drugs as well. When a group of peers takes ecstasy together and part of the group decides to take either more ecstasy or some other drug, there is a very good chance that everyone in the group will do the same, trusting their peers not to steer them wrong.

Among ecstasy users there is a perception of approval and safety associated with their drug use. Outside this group, the majority of their peers feel differently. The *Monitoring the Future* survey asked eighth through twelfth graders their feelings regarding ecstasy's harmfulness, availability, and whether they approve of others using ecstasy. In 2001, between 35% and 46% of students felt that even one or two instances of ecstasy use placed the user at great risk, more than a 10% increase from twelfth graders five years before. In contrast, 69% to more than 79% of eighth through twelfth graders disapprove of even one or two instances of ecstasy use, showing no change in the perception of twelfth graders from five years prior. Nearly 62% of twelfth graders reported that ecstasy was easy to get, an increase of 200% in the past ten years. So although a high percentage of adolescents do not approve of ecstasy use, many do not believe it to be harmful and could find it if they decided they wanted to use it.

The mental effects associated with ecstasy, such as mood disorders, learning and memory impairment, paranoia, irrational behavior, and inattention, potentially could interfere with a person's duties at school or work, although reports of this type of impact are sparse. The culture surrounding ecstasy use is associated with the taking of other drugs; therefore those drugs introduced while on ecstasy have the potential to persist as drug problems beyond the period of ecstasy use. Multiple drug users might experience difficulties with social and occupational functioning, but these effects could not be clearly attributed to ecstasy use. Similarly, crime and violence has been associated much more often with other drugs than with ecstasy (aside from illegal possession of the drug). However, "club drugs" as a group have been associated with sexual offenses, and all drug users are more likely to be involved in traffic accidents while under the influence. Again, as tracking of ecstasy use patterns and trends becomes more widespread, clearer information on the social consequences of ecstasy use will become available.

LEGAL CONSEQUENCES

Legal history

The penalties for ecstasy use and possession are complicated and rapidly changing. As lawmakers become aware of the availability and potential harmfulness of ecstasy, state and federal regulations are requiring more severe penalties than originally suggested when ecstasy became illegal in 1985. When ecstasy was originally moved to Schedule I in 1985, it was under a provision that allowed "emergency scheduling," which could take place without a hearing. Ecstasy's Schedule I status was made permanent a couple of years later. The Ecstasy Anti-Proliferation Act of 2000 was passed by legislators who saw that the rate of ecstasy use was growing faster than any other drug in the United States, and who believed the levels of punishment for trafficking were too low. This act prompted a change in the federal sentencing guidelines for trafficking and possessing with intent to sell, drastically increasing jail terms for fewer numbers of pills in possession.

Federal guidelines, regulations, and penalties

Rather than having separate regulations for possession for every illegal drug, legislators have outlined sentencing regulations for different amounts of marijuana possession, and then created a marijuana equivalency table in which different amounts of other drugs are said to be equal to specific amounts of marijuana. For example, one gram of cocaine is equivalent to 200 grams of marijuana, and one gram of heroin is equivalent to 1,000 grams of marijuana. Base offense levels, which guide sentencing, are determined according to this equivalency scale. Prior to the Ecstasy Anti-Proliferation Act of 2000, one gram of ecstasy (about three pills) was equivalent to 35 grams of marijuana. However, in response to the Act, legislators proposed drastic changes for trafficking penalties. The change proposed was to increase the equivalency of one gram of ecstasy be the same as 1,000 grams of marijuana, the same as heroin. There was outspoken disagreement from the scientific community, many of whom felt that if ecstasy's equivalency were to be changed it should be lowered, based on comparison of ecstasy with more harmful drugs. Unlike heroin, ecstasy was not associated with non-drug crime; the ecstasy market was not associated with violence; there were very few reports of ecstasy users needing drug treatment; and the number of ecstasy-associated emergency room visits was not near the number associated with heroin.

As a result of the protests, a slightly different sentencing regulation was proposed and went into effect in May 2001. Instead, one gram of ecstasy is now equivalent to 500 grams of marijuana, making one dose of ecstasy five times more legally damaging, in terms of jail time, to possess than one dose of heroin. Possession of at least 800 pills or 200 grams of ecstasy carries a minimum sentence of up to six years for a first offense. Before the change, the minimum for a first offense was 15–21 months, and 11,000 pills were needed for a sentence of six years.

Although there are federal guidelines for sentencing of drug possession, the penalties imposed are a bit more subjective. There is a particular offense level based on the amount of ecstasy or number of pills in possession, and a penalty associated with that offense level. The penalty for first offense possession of a small (personal) amount of ecstasy is a maximum of one year in prison and a fine. Someone with one prior conviction is subject to a term of 15 days to two years in prison, and two or more prior convictions to a term of 90 days to three years, both with increasing fines. Along with the base offense level, courts also take into account the offender's history of drug offenses, whether another crime was committed, and circumstances at the time of the arrest.

Federal guidelines are a springboard for state sentencing guidelines, which are different for each state in

HISTORY NOTES

Ecstasy was created accidentally by a German pharmaceutical company in 1912 and was patented in 1914. Some reports state its intended use as an appetite suppressant, although such reports appear unfounded. Ecstasy was used in the 1950s in experiments being performed by the United States Army, which considered using the drug as a truth serum in psychological warfare. A decade later ecstasy use became recreational, as people used the drug to feel good and open their minds while some psychotherapists recommended it to their patients as "penicillin for the soul" to aid therapy. It was not until recreational use began that the drug MDMA, now know as ecstasy, got its name from the Greek *ekstasis*, meaning "flight of soul from body." Recreational use continued within certain subcultures of the population, and as it became apparent that availability was more widespread, the Drug Enforcement Agency made ecstasy illegal by placing it in Schedule I of the Controlled Substances Act of 1970. In 1985 ecstasy was placed in Schedule I on an emergency basis, meaning without any hearings on the topic. After hearing evidence for and against scheduling ecstasy, it was declared to be permanently on Schedule I in 1988. All ecstasy use since that time is therefore illegal in the United States.

---

the country. Some states are much harsher than others in how they treat ecstasy-related offenses, and since the passage of the Ecstasy Anti-Proliferation Act of 2000, state laws are being proposed and changed quite rapidly. For example, in many instances, offenders in California with no prior possession charges, parole violations, or felonies, and who were not involved in other criminal activity at the time of arrest can plead guilty to a "diversion program" that will send them to drug treatment or subscribe community service rather than sending them to prison. If successfully completed, the plea of guilty will be set aside, and the criminal record cleared.

In Texas, on the other hand, possession of less than one gram (about three pills) carries a sentence of 18 days to two years with a very hefty fine. Possession of one to four grams carries a sentence of two to 20 years, four to 400 grams a minimum of five years, and more than 400 grams carries a sentence of 10 years to life in prison. New Jersey recently changed their sentencing regulations for ecstasy to five years in prison for up to 50 pills, five to 10 years for between 50 and 500 pills, and 20 years in prison for more than 500 pills. Illinois also recently changed its sentencing regulations in response to a widely reported ecstasy-related death, to four to 15 years in prison for possession of 15 doses of ecstasy.

See also Designer drugs; GHB; Ketamine; LSD; PCP

RESOURCES

Books

Kuhn, Cynthia, Scott Swartzwelder, and Wilkie Wilson. "Entactogens." *Buzzed: The Straight Facts about the Most Used and Abused Drugs from Alcohol to Ecstasy.* New York: W.W. Norton & Company, Inc., 1998, pp.70-76.

Other

Clubdrugs.org. A service of the National Institute on Drug Abuse. (March 5, 2002). <http://www.clubdrugs.org>.

Johnston, L.D., P.M. O'Malley, and J.G. Bachman. (December 19, 2001). *Rise in Ecstasy Use Among American Teens Begins to Slow.* University of Michigan News and Information Services: Ann Arbor, MI. [On-line]. Available: <http://www.monitoringthefuture.org>; accessed 03/05/2002.

Mathias, Robert, and Patrick Zickler. "NIDA Conference Highlights Scientific Findings on MDMA/Ecstasy." *NIDA Notes. Update on Ecstasy Research.* 16, no. 5 (December 2001). [On-line]. Available: <http://www.nida.nih.gov/NIDA_Notes/NNVol16N5/Conference.html>; accessed 03/05/2002.

MDMA (Ecstasy). (January 23, 2002). National Institute on Drug Abuse: Bethesda, MD. [On-line]. Available: <http://www.drugabuse.gov/drugpages/mdma.html>; accessed 03/05/2002.

Substance Abuse and Mental Health Services Administration. (February 28, 2002). Office of Applied Studies. Department of Health and Human Services. Available: <http://www.drugabusestatistics.samhsa.gov>; accessed 03/05/2002.

Organizations

Center for Substance Abuse Research, 4321 Hartwick Road, Suite 501, College Park, MD, USA, 20740, (301) 403-8329, (301) 403-8342, cesar@cesar.umd.edu, <http://www.cesar.umd.edu/>.

National Institute on Drug Abuse (NIDA), National Institutes of Health, 6001 Executive Boulevard, Room 5213, Bethesda, MD, USA, 20892-9561, (301) 443-1124, (888) 644-6432, Information@lists.nida.nih.gov, <http://www.drugabuse.gov>.

Substance Abuse and Mental Health Services Administration (SAMHSA), U.S. Dept. of Health and Human Services, 5600 Fishers Lane, Rockville, MD, USA, 20857, (301) 443-6239, (301) 443-9847, info@samhsa.gov, <http://www.samhsa.gov>.

Marsha F. Lopez, Ph.D.

EPHEDRA

OFFICIAL NAMES: Ephedra, *Ephedra sinica*
STREET NAMES: Mahuang, ma huang, desert tea, Mormon tea, American ephedra, European ephedra, Pakistani ephedra, ephedrine, ephedrine alkaloids, pseudoephedrine
DRUG CLASSIFICATIONS: Not scheduled, dietary supplement

OVERVIEW

Ephedra has a long, varied, and global history. Most varieties of the drug or herb are legal as of 2002. Despite its legal status, however, ephedra is not safe in large quantities. In fact, some non-profit groups, lawyers, and even some physicians and state and federal health agencies claim that ephedra can be harmful. They have sought to ban or at least more strictly regulate products containing ephedra, because these supplements have been associated with some very serious side effects, including strokes and heart attacks.

The earliest known use of ephedra was in ancient China, where it was used as an herbal remedy to treat a variety of ailments. Physicians in the United States began prescribing ephedra in the early part of the twentieth century as a decongestant for stuffy noses and a bronchodilator to open blocked airways.

Today, products containing ephedra and its synthetic or chemical equivalent are primarily used for two purposes in the United States. Ephedra is found in many dietary supplements and energy bars for weight loss and body builders. Ma huang, or ephedra, may also be found in so-called energy-boosting drinks. Both health food stores and supermarkets sell products containing ephedra, such as Easy Trim, Diet Max, Metabolife, Ripped Fuel, and Quick Shot. Some ephedrine supplements such as Ecstasy and Black Beauties have the same name as illegal street drugs. The labels of products containing ephedra may claim that the product will fight fat, build lean muscle mass, curb appetite, boost energy, increase metabolism, and help lose weight. Such claims, however, are not necessarily true.

Ephedra is subject to the Dietary Supplement Health and Education Act (DSHEA), which was passed in 1994. The act essentially protects dietary supplements like ephedra. That is, while U.S. federal agencies can regulate prescription drug and food additives, DSHEA exempts herbal products and supplements from federal regulation. The law states that the United States Food and Drug Administration (FDA) cannot regulate dietary supplements unless, or until, they are proven to be unsafe and pose a risk to users. The United States Drug Enforcement Administration (DEA) monitors ephedrine because it can be used to make methamphetamine.

Today, supplements containing ephedra are at the center of a controversy, with opponents claiming that they are dangerous and should be banned. Supplement makers and the herbal products industry, however, maintain that ephedra is safe and reports of adverse effects are overblown, exaggerated, and inaccurate. The Food and Drug Administration (FDA) has received hundreds of reports of adverse effects of ephedra, including strokes,

KEY TERMS

ADVERSE EVENT: Term used to denote a side effect, or negative health consequence, reported after taking a certain substance. The event may or may not be linked to the substance.

CARDIOVASCULAR SYSTEM: The body system composed of the heart and blood vessels.

DIETARY SUPPLEMENT: A substance sold and marketed under the protection of the DSHEA. These substances are available without a prescription and are not subject to rigorous clinical testing.

DIETARY SUPPLEMENT HEALTH AND EDUCATION ACT (DSHEA): Passed in 1994, this law allows manufacturers to sell dietary and nutrition supplements without federal regulation. According to this act, supplements can be regulated only after they are proven to be harmful to users.

FOOD AND DRUG ADMINISTRATION (FDA): The federal agency responsible for reviewing and regulating drugs and supplements.

heart attacks, heart rate irregularities, seizures, psychoses, and death. Dating back to the early 1990s, reports of ephedra-related adverse events raised concern among physicians and legislators. In 1997, the FDA proposed a new rule about ephedra, which would have considered some products containing ephedra as adulterated supplements, making them subject to FDA regulation. The FDA based its adulterated claim on the fact that ephedrine alkaloids resemble amphetamine and, like amphetamine, stimulate the heart and nervous system. However, this attempt to subject ephedra products to regulation failed.

Since 1997, a number of groups have lined up on each side of the ephedra battle. A non-profit group called Halt Ephedrine Abuse Today has spoken out about the dangers of ephedra. On the other side of the battle is the Ephedra Education Council, a group backed and supported by the herbal products industry and supplement manufacturers. Many of the companies that sell products containing ephedra do not want any further restrictions on the products.

A big concern about ephedra is that drug traffickers and laboratory operators are using ephedrine to make methamphetamines (speed). Consequently, in the United States, ephedrine is subject to regulatory laws. The Drug Enforcement Administration (DEA) carefully monitors medications containing ephedrine.

The United States is not the only country concerned about the safety of ephedra. Health Canada, the Canadian health regulatory agency, requested a voluntary recall of products containing both natural and chemical ephedra in 2002, because it received 60 reports of adverse events related to ephedra use.

CHEMICAL/ORGANIC COMPOSITION

Ephedra is available in both natural and synthetic forms. The Asian version of natural ephedra comes from a 1.5–4 ft (0.45–1.2 m) high shrub-like plant that grows in desert regions of Asia from northern China to Inner Mongolia. There are three Asian species of ephedra—*Ephedra sinica*, *E. intermedia*, and *E. equisetina*. Chinese and other early users of ephedra dried the green stems of the plants and ground them into a powder for medicinal use. The Asian version of the plant generally has the highest concentration of ephedrine. The ephedra plant is also grown in North America and other parts of the world, but some of these ephedra species have no alkaloid content, and it is the alkaloid content of the plant that causes its medicinal effects.

In the United States, ephedrine alkaloids are derived from the *Ephedra sinica*, or ma huang plant. Most ephedra supplements contain a standard extract of 6–8% ephedrine alkaloids. Other herbs and ingredients, including caffeine, may also be added to ephedra supplements.

The molecular structure of ephedra resembles that of amphetamine, a stimulant. Dietary supplement product manufacturers often mixed caffeine with ephedra. Some experts believe that caffeine probably enhances or heightens ephedra's stimulant effects. Ephedra may also be combined with other herbs in supplements, depending on the desired effects.

INGESTION METHODS

Ephedra is available in multiple forms. It is a common ingredient in energy boosting bars, sold as "Herbal Ecstasy" in some health food stores, and is also available as powder that can be mixed with water. Health food stores may sell powdered ephedrine stems, which can be used in a tea, or they may sell infusion, extracts, tinctures, or tablets of ephedra. Health food stores may also sell ephedra as the ma huang herb. Many manufacturers tend to advertise or market ephedra supplements as natural or as a botanical herb, because some consumers equate natural with safe. In China, ephedra may be boiled with cinnamon twig, licorice root, and almond to treat the common cold.

THERAPEUTIC USE

Ephedra has been used to treat a variety of ailments for thousands of years. Five thousand years ago the Chinese used ephedra as a medication to treat sweating, lung and bronchial constriction, water retention, coughing, shortness of breath, the common cold, and fevers.

Ephedra was introduced in the United States in the earlier part of the twentieth century when physicians began prescribing it for its bronchodilating and decongesting properties. Ephedra alkaloids stimulate certain receptors in the body, such as the airways in the lungs. By stimulating the airways, ephedra may open the blocked airways or nasal passages that occur with the common cold and asthma. This may help alleviate symptoms of the common cold. Ephedra can also affect other parts of the body. It also stimulates other receptors in the body, including receptors in the heart. This can increase the heart rate of ephedra users, and it may also increase blood pressure and decrease circulation. The end result may be very serious health consequences for some ephedra users.

Today, ephedra is primarily used in the United States for two purposes. It is used as a weight-loss aid or body-building product and as a nasal decongestant. As a relative of methamphetamine, ephedra can affect the body in many of the same ways. Ephedra can stimulate the nervous system, dilate bronchial tubes, elevate blood pressure, and increase heart rate. Manufacturers of weight-loss products containing ephedra claim that it suppresses the appetite and increases metabolism. Because ephedra can dilate bronchial tubes and decongest the nasal passages, it is also used an ingredient in some over-the-counter decongestants and cough and cold products.

As of January 2002, the maximum allowable dosage of ephedra is 8 mg per dose, or 32 mg per day. Most ephedra supplement products advise users to take two or three doses per day. What the product label says and what the actual content of the product is may be different. A research study published in 2000 tested the amount of ephedra alkaloids in dietary supplements and compared the results to the product label. The researchers found that more than half of the supplements did not list the ephedra alkaloid content or had a significant difference between the amounts listed on the label and the actual ephedra alkaloid content. The labels of most ephedra supplements state that the product is not intended for users less than 18 years old.

USAGE TRENDS

Despite the growing health concerns about ephedra, products containing ephedra remain popular in the United States. Studies indicate that use of ephedra may begin in the high school years. High school and college ath-

 **IN THE NEWS**

In August 2001, at least 10 members of the Northwestern University football team collapsed during training. The training consisted of a routine sprinting drill. The drill proved to be deadly for Rashidi Wheeler, a 22-year-old safety.

Despite suffering from asthma, Wheeler had succeeded in the tough world of college football. After Wheeler collapsed, he was taken away in an ambulance, and another player informed coaches that Wheeler had taken Ultimate Orange, an ephedra supplement. Trainers and paramedics tried to help Wheeler catch his breath with his inhaler. Unfortunately, the inhaler did not help and Wheeler died.

A former Northwestern University football player claimed that Ultimate Orange, a powdered performance-enhancing dietary supplement, was popular among football players. Ultimate Orange was marketed as a strength-building supplement. Next Nutrition, the company that manufactured Ultimate Orange, had discontinued the product and all other ephedra supplements prior to the Northwestern incident.

Although toxicology reports showed ephedrine in Wheeler's system at the time of his death, the Cook County coroner claimed ephedrine did not cause Wheeler's death. The Northwestern incident is not the first time that a college football player who was using ephedra supplements died. In February 2001, Florida State University football player Devaugn Darling collapsed and died after a workout. Darling's autopsy also showed that he had taken an ephedrine supplement prior to his death. The presence of ephedrine in his system, however, does not prove that it caused his death.

---

letes may purchase products containing ephedra because they believe that the supplements can build muscle mass and enhance performance, while teenaged and adult weight-conscious consumers may purchase supplements as a diet aid. And finally, some users may turn to ephedra products as a legal high.

Scope and severity

Exact data about the scope of ephedra use is unavailable, but the Ephedra Education Council estimates that more than three billion servings of ephedra products are consumed each year, and it claims that use increased dramatically between 1997 and 2002. But a *New England Journal Medicine* article about ephedra

The earliest known use of ephedra was in ancient China, where it was used as an herbal remedy to treat a variety of ailments. Plantaphile, Germany. Reproduced by permission.

points out that actual consumption may be higher. That is, if ephedra supplements were used as directed, at three doses a day for 12 weeks, 12 million Americans used ephedra supplements in 1999. These figures refer only to ephedra supplements, not over-the-counter nasal decongestants and cough and cold remedies.

Age, ethnic, and gender trends

Because ephedra manufacturers claim that the product enhances athletic performance and builds lean muscle mass, ephedrine supplements are especially popular among both male and female athletes. A 2001 survey of National College Athletic Association (NCAA) student athletes revealed that 42% of college athletes use nutritional supplements. Not all of these supplements contain ephedrine, but many do. According to the survey, 3.9% of NCAA student athletes use ephedrine. This is an increase from a similar survey completed in 1997, which showed that 3.5% of athletes used ephedrine. Products containing ephedrine are particularly popular among women gymnasts. In 2001, 8.3% of NCAA women gymnasts used ephedrine products. In 1997, 1.1% of women gymnasts used ephedrine. On the other hand, ephedrine use among NCAA wrestlers fell from 10.4% in 1997 to 4.3% in 2001.

The NCAA survey also revealed that most drug use, including ephedrine use, begins in high school. In fact, 62% of student athletes in the NCAA survey reported that they had started using nutritional supplements in junior or senior high school.

MENTAL EFFECTS

Opponents of ephedra claim that the product is legal methamphetamine, or speed. In February 2000, medical experts raised concerns about mental side effects of ephedrine such as nervousness and irritability. The group Halt Ephedrine Abuse Today completed an on-line survey of 355 people who had taken ephedra products; more than 60% of respondents reported feeling mental side effects such as nervousness, headaches, insomnia, and paranoia. The 2000 ephedra study published in the *New England Journal of Medicine* also listed mental side effects, including anxiety, tremulousness, and personality changes. Other possible mental side effects associated with ephedra are depression and paranoid psychosis. Lawyers representing clients who have been allegedly harmed by ephedra have reported that the victims suffer from depression and paranoid psychosis. These types of side effects, as well as some of the other physiological side effects reported by ephedra users, commonly occur with illicit stimulant drugs.

PHYSIOLOGICAL EFFECTS

There are a number of physiological effects related to ephedra consumption, and it is these side effects and reports of adverse events that are causing both the FDA and several state regulatory bodies to consider regulating it.

Some medical experts have testified about ephedrine's physiological side effects, which include hypertension and an increased risk of heart attack or stroke. The Halt Ephedrine Abuse Today survey found that more than 60% of respondents reported feeling physiological side effects such as a rapid heartbeat, nervousness, headaches, insomnia, shortness of breath, and chest pain. Physiological effects reported in the *New England Journal of Medicine* include palpitations and insomnia.

At higher doses, ephedra may be toxic. An overdose of ephedra can cause nausea, vomiting, fever, palpitations, tachycardia, hypertension, psychosis, respiratory depression, convulsions, and coma.

The FDA has been receiving reports of adverse effects related to ephedra use since the early 1990s. Many of the initial concerns were linked to one ephedra product—Formula One. However, when state and federal agencies investigated the product, they could not prove that it contained ephedra, and after the manufacturer of Formula One reformulated the product, reports of adverse events linked with the product ceased. But there have been many reports of adverse events associated with ephedra since 1994. The severity of those events spurred the FDA to action, which sought an independent review in an attempt to determine if ephedra had been the cause. Another purpose of the independent review was to determine the risks of consuming ephedra.

The researchers determined that ephedra posed serious risks to users. In addition, the ephedra research study published in 2000 in the *New England Journal of Medicine* claimed that ephedra could cause heart attacks, strokes, seizures, and death.

According to the researchers, nearly half of the adverse events definitely, probably, or possibly caused by ephedra were cardiovascular side effects. The most common cardiovascular side effect was hypertension, or high blood pressure. Other reported cardiovascular events were palpitations, tachycardia (an abnormally fast heartbeat), stroke, and seizures. The researchers stated that 10 of the adverse events definitely, probably, or possibly caused by ephedra resulted in death, and 13 of the events caused permanent disability. In one-fifth of the cases, there was not enough evidence or information about the incident, and the remaining complications were not related to ephedra.

Researchers found that the majority of the complications in the study occurred in young, healthy ephedra users. Victims did not need to be long-time users of ephedra to experience complications; some adverse events occurred in people who took ephedra for days or weeks. Two women who became pregnant while using ephedra had miscarriages. It was concluded that supplements containing ephedra might pose a serious health risk to some users. Moreover, it was suggested that a better understanding of the risks of ephedra use is required. With a better understanding of the incidence of adverse events and the at-risk population, the FDA can recommend appropriate dosing guidelines, and it can warn users about the potentially serious side effects of ephedra.

IN THE NEWS

Manufacturers of nutritional supplements containing ephedrine claim that the products can enhance athletic performance and improve physical fitness. Indeed, ephedrine supplements are popular among all sorts of athletes. As health concerns about ephedra grow, however, many professional and amateur athletes will find that they may have to choose between the sport they love and a questionable supplement.

In September 2001, the National Football League (NFL) joined the National College Athletic Association (NCAA) and the International Olympic Committee (IOC) and banned its players from using ephedrine. The ephedrine ban means that NFL players can be randomly tested throughout the year for ephedrine use.

The NFL instituted the ephedrine ban partly in response to health concerns. NFL doctors warned players about the growing body of evidence linking ephedrine use with strokes, seizures, and fatal heart rhythm.

Endorsements from popular athletes often spell success for a product. Companies like to have the support of famous athletes because consumers, especially teenagers, often want to emulate their favorite athletes. They want to buy the shoes that Michael Jordan wears or drink the energy drink Brett Favre likes. The NFL ban on ephedrine means that NFL players and teams cannot endorse products containing ephedrine or companies that sell or distribute those products. Many hope this ban will stop some teens from buying ephedra products.

Adverse event reporting

It is important to note that the FDA's MedWatch reports, or reports of adverse events, do not include all adverse events associated with ephedra. Some studies indicate that less than 15% of adverse events are reported to the FDA. Furthermore, the rate of adverse event reporting for herbal products or supplements may be even lower than 15%, as people do not make the connection between an herbal product they believe is safe and an adverse event. As a result, there may be more adverse events linked with ephedra use than the FDA or medical experts are aware of. Consequently, users may actually run a greater risk of adverse events.

Manufacturers of dietary supplements take a different stance when it comes to adverse events reporting. They claim that adverse events are anecdotal records and do not prove that ephedra caused the side effect or adverse event. The ephedra manufacturers' trade group also contends that victims may not recall which product they took or when. While these points are worth considering, they are made by companies and groups that have a vested interest in keeping ephedra on the market with as few regulations as possible.

Harmful side effects

Potential harmful side effects associated with ephedra include nervousness, irritability, headaches, insomnia, palpitations, depression, and paranoia. Other possible side effects are hypertension and rapid heartbeat. Ephedra users also face an increased risk of seizures, heart attack, and stroke. A heart attack or stroke caused by ephedra can result in death.

Long-term health effects

The long-term health effects of ephedra use are unknown; however, users who suffer a heart attack or stroke face the long-term health consequences of those ailments.

REACTIONS WITH OTHER DRUGS OR SUBSTANCES

Ephedra supplements typically contain caffeine, and users may consume caffeine in carbonated beverages, coffee, or tea. Researchers suspect that caffeine may enhance ephedra's stimulant effects on cardiovascular and/or central nervous system responses. This may account for the types of adverse events that have been reported by ephedra users.

When ephedra is used in combination with decongestants or other nervous system stimulants, the effect on the nervous system may be increased.

Ephedra has negative interactions with cardiac heart glycosides, halothene, guanethidine, MAO inhibitors, and secale alkaloid derivatives or oxytocin.

TREATMENT AND REHABILITATION

Although the FDA, some medical authorities, and some states recognize that ephedra and its relative, phenylpropanolamine (PPA), may cause adverse health events or serious side effects, ephedra is not considered an addictive, habit-forming drug. Drug treatment and rehabilitation programs, therefore, do not address ephedra or PPA use.

PERSONAL AND SOCIAL CONSEQUENCES

Statistics and research do not yet connect ephedra use with adverse personal or social consequences. However, if an ephedra user does suffer a serious adverse effect after taking ephedra, there may be personal and social consequences with which to contend.

Even if serious health consequences do not follow ephedra use, users may experience other personal consequences. College athletes may incur a doping suspension if they test positive for ephedra, because the National College Athletic Association (NCAA) bans ephedrine.

LEGAL CONSEQUENCES

Like most herbal supplements, the federal regulation that applies to ephedra is the Dietary Supplement Health and Education Act (DSHEA). This law was first passed in 1994 and allows supplement manufacturers to market and sell products without federal regulation. The FDA can only step in to regulate ephedra or other herbal supplements when they are proven to be unsafe or pose a risk to users.

Although DSHEA essentially tied the FDA's hands with regard to ephedra, individual state governments do have the power to enact laws about it. In the 1990s, there were reports of potential problems and serious ephedra-related health consequences such as heart attacks and strokes. Some states decided to pass their own legislation. In 1994, Ohio became one of the first states to pass a law restricting ephedra, which in fact banned the sale of products containing ephedrine. Texas also passed a similar ban in 1994, although the law was overturned a few weeks after it was passed.

More and more states are passing laws to regulate ephedra sales and labeling. By 2001, nearly half of the states in the United States had passed laws to regulate sales or labeling of ephedra products. Essentially, legal restrictions on ephedra fall into a few categories. A state may regulate how a product is formulated. This type of law might mandate that ephedra must occur naturally, that is, it is not produced synthetically in a laboratory. Another type of restriction is a dosage restriction.

States may also restrict labeling and marketing of ephedra products. In a few states, the law requires that labels of ephedra products comply with DSHEA or federal laws. Other states prohibit the term ephedrine on the label. Some states require exact dosing information on the product label, while other states require that the label inform users of potential risk and adverse health consequences, particularly with improper use. In New York, the Department of Health forbids manufacturers to market ephedra as a legal stimulant or legal alternative to illegal drugs. The FDA's Medwatch phone number must be printed on the label of any product containing ephedra that is sold in Texas. A few states prohibit the sales of ephedra to consumers under the age of 18. Finally, in some states if a product indicates the term ephedrine (vs.

 **IN THE NEWS**

Phenylpropanolamine (PPA), a chemical cousin of ephedra, has garnered its fair share of negative publicity. PPA, a common ingredient in over-the-counter cold remedies and diet pills, appears to be linked with an increased risk of stroke. The first reports linking PPA with intracranial hemorrhage, or stroke, involved diet pills formulated with both PPA and caffeine. The FDA banned products containing both PPA and caffeine in 1983. However, doctors continued to report some cases of stroke, which occurred after patients had taken products containing PPA. In fact, more than 30 strokes were reported in persons taking PPA since 1979. The majority of these reports involved PPA in diet pills, but a few reports involved PPA in cough and cold medicines. Many of the affected persons were young women between the ages of 17 and 45.

In 1992, both the FDA and manufacturers of products containing PPA recommended an epidemiological study of the link between PPA and stroke. Investigators at the Yale University School of Medicine designed a Hemorrhagic Stroke Project. Their goal was to find the link, if any, between PPA and stroke among men and women ages 18 to 49. They also wanted to determine the link between PPA and stroke by type of exposure (cough and cold medication or appetite suppressant). Finally, they wanted to find the link between first use of PPA and stroke and PPA in appetite suppressants and stroke in women ages 18 to 49.

The researchers at the Yale University School of Medicine studied more than 700 persons between the ages of 18 and 49 who had had a stroke. The Hemorrhagic Stroke Project was completed in 2000. When the investigators released results of the study, the report linked PPA with an increased risk of hemorrhagic stroke, or bleeding into the brain or into the tissue surrounding the brain, among women using products containing PPA for weight control or nasal decongestion. Researchers found that women taking weight-loss aids containing PPA, such as Dexatrim and Acutrim, had a 16-fold increase in their risk for hemorrhagic stroke. Many of the female study participants had the stroke after taking just one dose of the product containing PPA. The Yale physicians also concluded that men as well as women may also be at risk for hemorrhagic stroke when they take products containing PPA.

The researchers determined that people using cough and cold products containing PPA had a slightly increased risk for stroke. After the FDA's Nonprescription Drug Advisory Committee reviewed the results of the study, the FDA asked drug manufacturers to stop selling products containing PPA and worked to remove PPA from all over-the-counter drug products. Many manufacturers of cough and cold remedies and nasal decongestants containing PPA have voluntarily reformulated their products and eliminated PPA as an ingredient. Nevertheless, the FDA urged all consumers to carefully read the labels of cold remedies to insure that they do not contain PPA. As of 2002, some manufacturers of cold products had started to advertise their products as PPA-free.

---

ephedra) on the label, it must be sold as prescription instead of an over-the-counter supplement.

Ephedra has been the subject of a number of lawsuits in the United States. As users report adverse events, lawyers have started to champion their causes and sue product manufacturers. Some lawyers advertise on the Internet and seek clients who believe that they have been harmed by ephedra. An ephedra lawsuit can garner a lot of money for a lawyer and a client.

Legal history

Ephedra has a long history of legal use in the United States and around the world. Today, the laws that apply to ephedra cover sales, formulation, and labeling by manufacturers; they do not outlaw its use by consumers as with street drugs such as marijuana and cocaine. Because ephedrine can be used to manufacture methamphetamine, companies that sell bulk ephedrine and ephedrine tablets are subject to laws designed to halt the conversion of ephedrine into methamphetamine.

Federal guidelines, regulations, and penalties

Since clandestine lab operators use ephedra to make methamphetamine, the DEA monitors supplements containing ephedrine. One kilogram of ephedrine, the equivalent of 48,000 25-mg ephedrine tablets, can be used to produce anywhere from 1.1 to 1.6 lbs (.5 to 0.75 kg) of methamphetamine in a drug lab. Pseudoephedrine can be used for the same purpose.

In the late 1980s, drug traffickers and clandestine laboratory operators began to purchase bulk ephedrine powder to make methamphetamine. The government responded in 1988 and passed the Chemical Diversion and Trafficking Act (CDTA) to control the import, export, and distribution of bulk ephedrine powder. The drug traffickers then turned to ephedrine tablets to make methamphetamine, which were exempt from the CDTA. Drug traffickers and lab operators found that they could buy large quantities of ephedrine tablets and convert them to methamphetamine. A number of mail-order companies even advertised 1,000-count bottles of ephedrine tablets in national magazines. Although the CDTA allowed for criminal prosecution of companies selling tablets if they knew the tablets were being used to make an illegal substance, the companies were able to claim they had no knowledge of their products' ultimate use.

In 1993, Congress passed a new law, the Domestic Chemical Diversion Control Act (DCDCA), to include ephedrine tablets in the first law. According to the law, all distributors, importers, and exporters who sell List 1 chemicals, such as ephedrine, must register with the DEA. The DEA can deny registration or revoke registration to companies whose actions threaten public health and safety. Thus, if the company sells ephedrine tablets that are then converted into illegal substances, its registration may be denied. By 1994, lab operators responded by using pseudoephedrine to make methamphetamine.

See also Methamphetamine

RESOURCES

Books

Kee, Chang Huang. *The Pharmacology of Chinese Herbs.* Boca Raton, FL: CRC Press, 1992.

Scanlon, William, and Nye Stevens. *Dietary Supplements: Uncertainties in Analyses Underlying FDA's Proposed Rule on Ephedrine Alkaloids.* Collingdale, PA: DIANE Publishing Company, 1999.

Periodicals

Cho, Arthur K. "Ice: A New Dosage Form of an Old Drug." *Science* 249 (August 10, 1990): 631-634.

Sager, Mike. "The Ice Age." *Rolling Stone* (February 8, 1990): 53-116.

Organizations

Ephedra Educational Council, 2000 K St., NW, Suite 801, Washington, DC, USA, 20006, <http://www.ephedrafacts.com>.

Halt Ephedrine Abuse Today, P.O. Box 1103, Novi, MI, USA, 48376-1103.

Healthcare Reality Check, <http://www.hcrc.org>.

Institute of Traditional Medicine, 2127 SE Hawthorne Blvd., Portland, OR, USA, 97214, (503) 233-4907, <http://www.itmonline.org>.

National Center for Drug Free Sport, 810 Baltimore, Suite 200, Kansas City, MO, USA, 64105, (816) 474-8655, <http://www.drugfreesport.com>.

Lisa A. Fratt

FENTANYL

OVERVIEW

Fentanyl is a very powerful synthetic opioid analgesic routinely used legally for anesthesia. The amount of fentanyl that could fit on the head of a pin is enough to kill ten people. It is a member of the narcotic analgesic class of drugs that reduce pain. Today it is used in 70% of the surgeries performed in the United States. It has been administered since the early 1970s for prenatal use. Since 1991 it has also been used to treat chronic pain associated with cancer or other terminal diseases. Because it takes effect quickly and has few undesirable side effects when controlled by a physician, it is revered by the medical community. Fentanyl is used in the treatment of all ages, from children to the elderly.

Fentanyl was first abused by medical professionals who were able to obtain the legally produced opioid from drug companies. Today, it is a designer drug that black market chemists in clandestine laboratories with high levels of expertise and equipment manufacture in home labs. As a street drug, it can be several hundred to three thousand times more potent than morphine. Sometimes it is sold as heroin to unsuspecting users.

Fentanyl and its derivatives are opioid narcotics similar to heroin and are consumed on the street in many of the same ways. These opioids work through receptors in the brain and spine, mimicking naturally present peptides commonly known as endorphins, enkephalins, and dynorphins. The type of receptor that fentanyl predominately bonds with is the mu receptor.

The number of synthetic drugs that can be derived from the fentanyl molecule is almost limitless. Variations of fentanyl devised in street labs continue to appear,

OFFICIAL NAMES: Fentanyl
STREET NAMES: Brand names include Actiq, Alfenta, Duragesic, Oralet, Sublimaze, and Sufenta. Street terms include Apache, China girl, China town, China white, dance fever, friend, goodfellas, great bear, He-man, jackpot, king ivory, Mexican brown, murder 8, P-dope, Persian white, P-funk, poison, synthetic heroin, Tango & Cash, TNT, tombstone
DRUG CLASSIFICATIONS: Schedule I or II, narcotic analgesic

making it even more difficult to track the drug. Adding to the difficulty of tracking fentanyl is the fact that it takes multiple tests to recognize it in a user's system. It does not appear in common urine analysis, so most users are not detected until they overdose.

History

Fentanyl is a relatively new drug and still under testing. It is a completely synthetic drug first made in Belgium in the late 1950s. Fentanyl is the name given to the synthetic molecule by its creators, Janssen Parmaceutica, of Belgium. It was originally marketed by Janssen under the trade name Sublimaze. Sublimaze was introduced into clinical practice in the 1960s as an intravenous anesthetic.

According to *Newsweek*, the pharmaceutical market doubled between 1996 and 2000. As a whole, it generates $45 billion annually. Painkillers such as the legally produced fentanyl account for $1.8 billion of this figure.

KEY TERMS

ANALGESIC: A type of drug that alleviates pain without loss of consciousness.

ANALOG: Different forms of a chemical or drug structurally related to the parent chemical or drug.

ANTAGONIST: A drug that counteracts or blocks the effects of another drug.

CLANDESTINE LABORATORY: An illegal laboratory used to make designer drugs.

DESIGNER DRUGS: Drugs that are produced in an illegal laboratory that are chemically similar to pharmaceutical drugs.

INTRAVENOUS DRUG: Any drug that is injected via a needle into the bloodstream.

OPIATE: Drug derived directly from opium and used in its natural state, without chemical modification. Opiates include morphine, codeine, thebaine, noscapine, and papaverine.

According to the National Institute on Drug Abuse (NIDA), 1.6 million people abused prescription drugs in 1998. These figures represent only the legally produced drugs and do not include designer drugs sold on the street.

Fentanyls first appeared on the streets under the name China white in the late 1970s. It was viewed as a "safe" alternative to heroin because it was a derivative of a prescription drug. Furthermore, fentanyl is virtually undetectable in a person's system by a drug screening urinalysis. Users were thus attracted to it as a way to get around the law. However, analogs, drugs that differ slightly in chemical structure but are similar to other drugs, were added to the list of controlled substances by the United States Drug Enforcement Administration (DEA) in 1984 and 1986. This meant that the street variations of fentanyl were made illegal to possess or produce.

China white was popular on the West Coast of the United States in the early 1980s and was estimated at 6,000 times the potency of morphine. In the late 1980s, fentanyl was introduced into the club scene in New York, and designer variations were spawned. In the 1990s fentanyl was introduced as a lollipop for young cancer patients to treat their pain and suffering. In this form it entered into all-night raves and club parties.

CHEMICAL/ORGANIC COMPOSITION

Fentanyl is a completely synthetic molecule. Its actual chemical name is N-(1-phenethyl-4-piperidyl) propionanilide. Most of the derivatives of fentanyl are more powerful than the molecule itself. To date there have been dozens of fentanyl derivatives designed. Today, any derivative of fentanyl is commonly referred to as fentanyl, though each is given its own chemical name. For example, the drug that was sold under the name of China white in the 1980s was given the name alpha-methylfentanyl. Other common medical derivatives are fenzylfentanyl, fluorofentanyl, thiofentanyl, carfentanil, and sufentanil.

Because fentanyl is so much more potent than heroin or other opioids, it must be diluted before it can be consumed. Clandestine chemists often use powdered sugar, baby powder, baby laxative, or antihistamines to dilute the street drug. Because the designer drugs can contain a variety of different diluting materials and are many times more powerful, these drugs are more dangerous than legally produced opioids.

INGESTION METHODS

Fentanyl is administered by medical personnel in several ways. Originally it was developed and used primarily as an anesthesia administered through an intravenous (IV) hookup. It is still used in this form during surgery, it is not used in this way for chronic pain because it entails either having a constant IV drip or repeated shots throughout the day. Today it is also administered by epidural, which is a shot administered directly into the spine. For a local anesthetic during surgery, fentanyl is administered via needle directly into a muscle.

Oral ingestion of fentanyl is the most common way it is used to relieve chronic pain today. This is achieved primarily in a lollipop or lozenge that allows for a slow ingestion into the body. Most of the lollipops and lozenges are cherry flavored; for children in cancer wards, this is the preferred method of administration because they seldom view the "treats" as medication. Rectal administration is sometimes used as well if the patient cannot receive oral medication or if they have a strong nausea reaction to the fentanyl. This method is used only as a last resort, and few patients opt for it.

Fentanyl is also available in a patch form (much like a nicotine patch used for smoking cessation) that can also be used for long-term treatment. This form of administration is referred to as transdermal fentanyl and is sold under the trade name Duregasic. The fentanyl is absorbed directly into the skin from the patch and enters the bloodstream, which carries it to the mu receptors. This form of administration appears much easier than it is. When applying the patch, much caution is needed in making sure that the side with the fentanyl does not come in contact with the applier's hands. The sweat on our palms speeds the absorbtion of fentanyl into the bloodstream, and more of the drug is taken in than is desired at one time.

The street versions of fentanyl are ingested in the same ways as heroin. It is usually sold in a powder form and either smoked, snorted, or injected into a vein. Since fentanyl is water-soluble, the powder form can be cold-stirred into a solution and does not need to be boiled like other opioids. However, injection is the most common method used for ingestion on the street. It is so much more potent than heroin that in many of the overdose deaths, the user is found with the needle still in an arm, in some instances with plunger not fully compressed. Some of the designer fentanyl today is made into pill form, but in this form of ingestion, more time elapses before the user feels its effects.

The transdermal patches and lollipops are also stolen and sold on the streets. Instead of wearing the patch as intended, users will get the fentanyl out to either inject or inhale the drug. Lollipops and lozenges are used on the street in high dosages and generally in connection with other drugs. Rather than letting the lozenges dissolve in the mouth, street users may crunch several at a time.

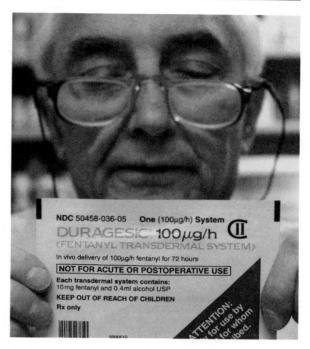

A pharmacist holds a pain patch containing the powerful painkiller fentanyl. Photo by Dan Loh, AP/Wide World Photos. Reproduced by permission.

THERAPEUTIC USE

Fentanyl is still a new drug. Research is ongoing on its applications and benefits. It is expected that future fentanyl derivatives will be of even greater therapeutic use and importance. Fentanyl is used in 70% of surgeries today. Many anesthesiologists view fentanyl as a superior anesthetic because it acts only on specific nerve receptors that are primarily in the central nervous system. These sites are primarily linked with pain sensation, respiration control, and physical dependence. In contrast, general anesthetics affect the whole body and render the patient unconscious. Because fentanyl acts primarily on the central nervous system, the patient is able to remain awake throughout surgery.

Fentanyl is primarily used alone, but sometimes it is combined with other opiates such as Licodaine, Bupivacaine, or morphine in epidural administration or in some IVs. However, one of the more appealing virtues of fentanyl is that, unlike other opioids, it has a very mild effect on the emetic trigger zone of the medulla. For this reason, patients have less nausea and no vomiting when fentanyl is used. With other drugs, such as morphine, this unwanted side effect can be intense. Fentanyl also does not cause the release of histamine, which makes it safer for the cardiovascular system than morphine.

Fentanyl is widely used in epidurals for women in delivery. This is called a continuous infusion epidural analgesia (CIEA). In this method, a needle is inserted into a woman's spinal cavity, where it offers a continuous drip of the drug throughout the birthing process. The benefit is that it lessens the pain associated with delivering a baby while still allowing the woman to have an active role in the birthing process. When administered in the lower spinal area, it is very short-acting and does not completely numb the lower body. Morphine and Demerol, which have been used more frequently in the past, render the lower extremities completely numb, making it more difficult for the patient to participate in the delivery. Thus, because the woman is able to be more active when using fentanyl, the delivery process is quicker.

Fentanyl is also used in treating people who suffer from pain associated with long-term illnesses such as cancer. It is not, however, the most inexpensive method. Transdermal fentanyl costs roughly three times what an equivalent amount of sustained-release morphine sulfate, which has similar effects on the patient, would cost. For this reason it is not used as often as other forms of pain relief unless other avenues have failed. However, some health professionals believe fentanyl offers greater benefits in helping people cope with pain. Transdermal fentanyl is faster acting than other options and lasts up to 72 hours per application. Transdermal fentanyl is considered most beneficial for people who have a consistent pain with few momentary increases in the pain. This is because there is a steady release of fentanyl into the body with no variation. It is also suitable for people who cannot swallow or open their mouths for oral medication. However, it is recommended that patients on transdermal fentanyl be given a prescription for another opiate such as morphine, hydromorphine, or oxycodone for temporary pain relief when there is a temporary increase in their suffering.

For people with ongoing pain who desire oral doses, who cannot wear a patch, or who have moments of higher pain, fentanyl is given in a lozenge or lollipop. The raspberry-colored lozenges are quickly absorbed through the buccal mucosa in the mouth and more slowly through the gastrointestinal tract. The onset of analgesia is usually within 15 minutes by this method, and one dosage lasts one to two hours. After a patient begins feeling the effects of the fentanyl and the pain is subsiding, he or she should remove the lozenge from the mouth. This reduces the intake of the drug and slows the rate at which the patient becomes tolerant of the drug

Recently fentanyl has been tested on AIDS patients. The drug is useful in blocking pain receptors, which helps patients cope with their pain. It also helps AZT to cross the blood-brain barrier. When used alone, AZT also has several side effects that early testing has shown to be reduced when fentanyl is added to the treatment.

USAGE TRENDS

Scope and severity

Fentanyl abuse among non-medical personnel has come in waves as new derivatives are discovered. However, the problem is growing in the United States. The Substance Abuse and Mental Health Services Administration (SAMHSA) states that 576 people were treated in emergency rooms for fentanyl abuse in 2000. This is higher than the 337 recorded instances in 1999. Figures from 2001 are incomplete, but at least 512 people were treated in emergency rooms in the first six months of the year. Since fentanyl is difficult to detect, these figures are believed to be lower than actual cases.

It is known that the abuse of prescription fentanyl is on the rise, but the degree of increase is difficult to distinguish. Doctors are increasingly wary of turning down requests for pain medication for fear of lawsuits if the patient truly is in a lot of pain. Determining how much pain a patient feels is nearly impossible for the doctor, so they must rely on what the patient tells them. This has led to an increase of people illicitly getting pain relievers for personal use or distribution. Some patients lie to their doctors about their conditions in order to get painkillers; others have gone to several doctors to get several prescriptions.

There are also a growing number of doctors wanting to supplement their income and do so by writing prescriptions for people who do not need them. Doctors who do this are referred to as "script writers." These script writers can generally double their salary by selling the prescriptions for large sums of money. Middle-class drug users are increasingly viewing this route of acquisition as preferable because there are fewer stigmas attached to buying from a doctor and there is less risk of a drug deal turning violent. As demand for the pharmaceutical versions of designer drugs increases, the business of dispensing bogus prescriptions becomes even more profitable.

Age, ethnic, and gender trends

According to the American Society of Anesthesiologists, it is rare for an anesthesiology department not to have someone, at some point, need treatment for a chemical dependency. Anesthesiology has the highest incidence of chemical dependency among medical specialists. It is hypothesized that this is because they daily administer these drugs to others and are lulled into believing that they are less dangerous than they are. These professionals also have a high amount of accessibility to addictive drugs and seem to have a greater curiosity of the effects of drugs than other doctors. Due to its ready accessibility and difficulty of detection, fentanyl has long been the drug of choice to abuse by anesthesiologists.

Other than anesthesiologists, many professionals within the medical community abuse fentanyl. However, the majority of these are considered to be less skilled healthcare workers, rather than the pharmacists or doctors who abuse other drugs. Namely, abusers who steal fentanyl from hospitals are usually nursing aides and uncertified healthcare providers.

On the street, users tend to fall into one of three categories. The first group are those that view fentanyl as safer than heroin. Users in this category tend to be white, upper-middle class, male, educated at or above the college level, and ignorant to drug use. This group generally involves novice drug users who often are the ones who die from overdoses. There is not the same stigma attached to designer drugs as there seems to be with heroin, so people in this group view them as social drugs. Fentanyl is also attractive to this group because it is soluble through the skin. When ingested by directly absorbing the drug through the skin, users do not require a needle which can leave "track marks."

The second group of people consists of addicts of other opiates who use fentanyl predominately only when their personal drug of choice is unavailable. Those in this group will generally choose other opiates because they tend to "shoot" the drug and many have complained of a burning sensation after injecting fentanyl. In a survey among opiate users in a Contra Costa County, California, treatment clinic, users in this category do not like to use fentanyl as much as heroin. These users felt that heroin gave them a more euphoric feeling.

The third group of people includes those at raves who experiment with a wide variety of designer drugs. The fentanyl used by this group is manufactured in clandestine laboratories. Users in this group are generally white, middle class, and in their teens or twenties. For the most part, users in this group are female. However, males in this group frequently take whatever drug the females are using.

MENTAL EFFECTS

Generally speaking, fentanyl acts on the central nervous system and the gastrointestinal tract. Because of this, most of the effects of the drug are physical. It also causes many of the same effects as heroin, including euphoria and drowsiness. However, some research shows that the effects of heroin are more euphoric, and fentanyl is more analgesic.

During surgery fentanyl is used as an analgesic. Analgesia by definition is an absence of pain. Therefore, fentanyl causes the brain to not feel pain. Or, clinically speaking, analgesia refers to a reduction in the intensity of pain perceived. It is the goal of the anesthesiologist to make the pain as tolerable as possible without undue respiratory depression of the patient. Analgesia may be induced by interrupting the nociceptive process at one or more points between the peripheral nociceptor and the cerebral cortex. In this respect, fentanyl tricks the mind. It imitates natural peptides found in the body (such as endorphins) and stimulates a cellular response.

The receptor most affected by fentanyl is the mu receptor in the brain, which is substantially involved with addiction potential. This is why fentanyl can be so addictive to some people.

Rarely, high amounts of fentanyl have also been known to cause hallucinations. This does not happen in prescribed doses. However, people who misapply the transdermal patch and get large amounts of the drug on their hands without immediately washing them can have hallucinations. The patch can also sometimes release erratic levels of the drug into the system due to poor adhesion of the patch or exposure to too much of the drug in one location. For this reason, wearers of the patch need to rotate the patch often, but the patch can be difficult to accurately affix due to sweating and hair follicles.

Hallucinations often occur from street forms of the drug. This is because users usually take larger dosages and have less tolerance. Also, users of the designer drugs generally inhale or inject the drug, so larger quantities hit the receptors at one time.

IN THE NEWS

DEA efforts increase fentanyl use

Illegal use of fentanyl in the United States is linked to the availability of heroin. The majority of the users of the designer analogs of fentanyl prefer heroin and will use it instead when available. Due to the United States' War on Drugs, the availability of fentanyl substitutes is being limited.

Those who argue that the War on Drugs is failing point to a rise in use of synthetic drugs. They contend that, in fighting the drug trafficking from other countries, the DEA is actually increasing the market for synthetic drugs like fentanyl. An escalation of the destruction of opium fields in countries such as Mexico, Afghanistan, and Pakistan has lowered the amount of heroin smuggled into the United States. While this is applauded by some, detractors believe that since the War on Drugs does not result in fewer drug users it is not effective.

This is an ongoing debate with valid points by both sides. Those on one side maintain that any reduction of illegal use is advantageous to the United States. They also argue that destroying opium fields is only one avenue being used, and that it is useful in connection with other methods. Detractors generally believe that helping addicts quit using and teaching potential users to never start is the only effective method. They argue that with no market in which to sell, there will be none wanting to buy the drugs.

PHYSIOLOGICAL EFFECTS

The major physiological effects of fentanyl are euphoria, drowsiness, respiratory depression, decreased gastrointestinal mobility, nausea, and muscular rigidity. People build up a tolerance to fentanyl the more they use it, causing them to need more to obtain the same effects they once received from a smaller dose. The "high" of fentanyl can last 10–72 hours, depending on the ingestion method, the fentanyl derivative used, and the amount taken.

Harmful side effects

Fentanyl acts on the heart rate, blood pressure, and respiratory system. It can decrease the heart rate by as much as 25% in a controlled setting and even more if too much is ingested too quickly. In a clinical setting, this is

???? FACT OR FICTION

"Fentanyl was designed for animal use."

This is not true. Fentanyl was designed for use in humans and only later used in connection with animals. It is true that fentanyl is widely distributed by veterinarians for use with animals, and that it has similar effects on animals as on people. Because of this similarity, veterinarians may administer fentanyl because human reports of drug effects can be helpful in dealing with animal patients, who cannot tell doctors when they are in pain.

Veterinarians do have a dilemma in prescribing fentanyl or other analgesics because they must register with the DEA just as other medical professionals, and are under the same scrutiny. However, they do not have the luxury of providing social security numbers or medical history on their patients. This makes it easier for them to illegally obtain the drug. It also puts them under more scrutiny from the federal government.

less dangerous due to monitors that can alert staff to these changes and machines that control breathing and heart rate. However, in the streets, these side effects can quickly cause death. Experienced drug users who use fentanyl often have a supply of cocaine or methamphetamine with them, thinking that if they experience the respiratory failure sometimes associated with fentanyl, they can then use the stimulant to keep from dying. It is possible for just one patch combined with other depressants to kill a user.

Designer heroin, or street-made fentanyl, adds many side effects due to the impurities added to the drug. Aside from allergic reactions from additives unknown to the user, street chemists are often unaware of the potency of the drug they are creating. Clandestine laboratories may not dilute the drug enough, causing too much of the drug to be ingested. This can cause immediate death. Reports have also shown that irreparable harm can be done to the receptors of a user's brain from a single use of "designer heroin."

The effects that the drug has on the gastrointestinal tract are quite severe. Fentanyl use, whether clinical or recreational, will cause constipation in the user. It is recommended that patients always take laxatives or stool softeners when using fentanyl. At least one bowel movement every two to three days is recommended. Longer periods of time between movements can result in damage to the colon, intestines, and stomach. If it has been longer than three days since the last bowel movement, patients are instructed to contact their physician,

who may suggest an enema or suppository to encourage bowel release.

In regular users of fentanyl, dry mouth is common. It is suggested that patients chew sugarless gum, suck on hard candy, and most importantly, drink plenty of water. Dehydration can occur if fentanyl users fail to consume more water than they normally do. A regular user of fentanyl must make sure to tell their doctor if they are having surgery. The added fentanyl in their system from the anesthesia can cause death.

Some other rare side effects from fentanyl include breathing difficulties, wheezing, cold and clammy skin, seizures, slow or fast heartbeat, severe rash, and unusual weakness. A physician should be notified immediately if any of these symptoms occur. It is more common for patients to experience confusion, fainting spells, and nervousness or restlessness; any of these also need medical attention. Some side effects that do not require immediate medical attention but can be reported if bothersome include itching, blurred vision, clumsiness, difficulty urinating, headache, and nausea.

According to the American Association of Pediatrics, clinical use of fentanyl is considered safe for pregnant and nursing mothers. Other organizations have deemed the results of studies to be inconclusive. Some of the drug will pass into the baby from a nursing mother, so constipation, dry mouth, and drowsiness can be expected. Babies born to mothers who abused fentanyl during pregnancy can be expected to have an addiction to fentanyl at birth.

Long-term health effects

As with any narcotic, fentanyl is addictive. Because it interacts with the mu receptor, which has an effect on addiction, it is highly addictive. Fentanyl users also build a tolerance to the drug's effects, thus needing more of the drug to reach the same euphoric experiences. Building up a tolerance to the drug can be harmful to the user. As the user continues to consume more and more of the drug to achieve the same effects, an overdose becomes likely.

Even though fentanyl is habit-forming, addiction can only be experienced by those using the drug for recreational or pleasure purposes. According to the SAMSHA, users who are being treated for extreme pain cannot be addicted to their medication because they have a physical, not psychological, need for the medication. They may become tolerant to the drug, though, and should not stop treatment without a doctor's supervision.

The more of the drug that is used, the more dangerous the effects of the constipation can be. Long-term constipation left untreated can be very dangerous to the user, so doctors may suggest a change of diet. Patients are encouraged to include more fiber and bran in their diets to help offset the consequences of the constipation.

This is especially important in elderly patients, who often have problems with constipation that are unrelated to fentanyl use.

REACTIONS WITH OTHER DRUGS OR SUBSTANCES

One of the side effects of fentanyl is drowsiness, so any other medication that causes drowsiness can greatly increase this effect in a user. For this reason, users of fentanyl must not consume alcoholic beverages, because a user can fall asleep quickly and possibly depress the user's respiratory system even more. Some medications to be avoided include barbiturates, antidepressants, tranquilizers, muscle relaxants, and antihistamines used in some cold medicines.

It is very important that anyone using fentanyl, either pharmaceutical or clandestine, let their health care professional know of their use prior to surgery or when being prescribed other medications. As was discussed earlier, high dosages of fentanyl are deadly. Because it is used in 70% of surgeries today, any additional use of fentanyl during surgery can lead to complications or death.

According to the makers of Duragesic, it is important not to also use slow-release forms of morphine or oxycodone while using the patch. This would include switching between the two forms of medication or using both at the same time. Other medications that can react negatively with fentanyl use include medicines for high blood pressure and seizures.

Patients taking naltrexone (trade name Trexan) must tell their health care professional because the two drugs will cancel any effects that the other has. Some other medications that reduce the effects of fentanyl are buprenorphine, dezocine, nalbuphine, and pentazoncine. These medications also can cause side effects in people who have become physically dependent on fentanyl.

TREATMENT AND REHABILITATION

Most hospitals in the United States today are aware of the trend of abuse among anesthesiologists. In recent years, hospitals have stepped up efforts to help personnel realize when coworkers might be abusing various drugs, including fentanyl. Due to necessity, anesthesiology staffers have become especially adept at observing signs of addiction in their coworkers. Assistance is covered under most hospital healthcare insurance plans. This is due to the high number of addicts within the hospital community and the harm that can come to patients if a doctor's addiction is left untreated.

Addiction requires a user to get help from professionals. A person is considered an addict if they continue using a drug despite adverse consequences or if they can-

not go without the drug. There are numerous opiate detoxification programs in the United States that can treat abusers, though their methods vary. The traditional method for treating opiate addiction is by detoxification. This means clearing the body of the drug and giving small amounts of methadone to help curb some of the desire for the drug. When the desire is diminished to abuse drugs and the withdrawal symptoms have subsided, the person can be released. This is a very long and tenuous process. Some have questioned its success rate as many "rehabilitated users" return to abuse.

There are a small but growing number of institutions that are beginning to use an ultra-rapid opiate detoxification program. It is still considered an experimental practice with techniques varying from site to site. However, there are three main differences between traditional and ultra-rapid opiate detoxification. In traditional programs, a patient attempts to function normally while fighting the heavy withdrawal symptoms. In ultra-rapid detoxification, the user is put under anesthesia and is thus able to sleep through the pains of withdrawal. The amount of time varies between institutions, but usually lasts a day or two. A drug called naltrexone is given, which accelerates the onset of withdrawal. Some doctors believe that naltrexone only be given to a patient who has been free of opiates for seven days, which means that a user still must face severe withdrawals. Opiate blockers are given upon release of the program, which has been found to suppress both desire for the drug as well as some lingering withdrawal symptoms.

The first three days of the treatment are the most difficult for the abuser due to the highly intensive withdrawal pains. During this time approximately 30% of opiate-dependent abusers in a traditional detoxification program quit the program. Some of the withdrawal symptoms the user faces include runny nose, tearing, sneezing, insomnia, loss of appetite, depression, irritability, severe abdominal cramps, pain in the muscles and bones of the back, sweating, nausea, tremors, increased heart rate and blood pressure, and weight loss due to dehydration.

Removing the drug from the user's system is only the first step in an ongoing process regardless of which technique is used. For an addict, the drug has become a part of his or her lifestyle. That lifestyle must change in order for that person to remain clean. Twelve-step programs such as Narcotics Anonymous have proven very helpful to many in the everyday battle to avoid relapse.

This creates a very difficult situation for anesthesiologists who are recovering from an addiction to fentanyl. Since it is used so often in their work, they must handle and administer the drug that they have abused. This is why the risk of relapse is especially high among opiate-addicted anesthesiologists who decide to return to their profession. Among those who do have a relapse, the incidence of death from overdose is high.

In a May 2001 newsletter, the American Society of Anesthesiologists offers seven questions that an anesthesiologist who is a recovering fentanyl addict should ask themselves before trying to return to their jobs. An abbreviated list follows: If you were a freshman in college and could choose any profession with the wisdom you have now, what would you consider pursuing? If you could not be in anesthesiology, what other possibilities would you consider? What are some positives and negatives of practicing anesthesia? What is stressful for you in the practice of anesthesia? Since the relapse rate is so high, why would you put yourself and your patients at risk? How does your significant other feel about the risk you would be talking returning to anesthesiology? What safeguards would you put in place to avoid a relapse?

Depending on recovering addict's honest answers to these questions, it is often suggested that they find a different field. However, former abusers are allowed to return as long as they are not currently using.

PERSONAL AND SOCIAL CONSEQUENCES

Teenagers and young adults are often introduced to designer drugs through peer pressure and their social environment. They often segregate themselves from non-users and surround themselves with those who view their choice as acceptable. This limits their exposure to those who scorn their lifestyle. However, society in general views designer drugs and their users negatively, so someone who abuses can face difficulty finding a job or keeping non-abusing friends.

As discussed earlier, anesthesiologists who abuse fentanyl often have difficulty keeping the job for which they have trained and studied for years to obtain. Even those who undergo treatment can have a hard time finding a new position in a different field because they will have to be retrained. Other white-collar workers in the middle to upper-middle class who abuse fentanyl can also lose their jobs, families, and friends when their addiction comes to light.

People who use fentanyl for chronic pain often try to hide their use. They often believe that others will think less of them for needing something to help them deal with their pain. Since fentanyl is only prescribed to those who are in extreme pain and need to block the receptors in their brain that signals pain, patients should not be viewed as drug "users" who are trying to get high. This constitutes the difference between medicinal and recreational uses of fentanyl.

LEGAL CONSEQUENCES

According to the DEA, fentanyl and its analogs are Schedule I and II narcotics. This means that anyone who possesses fentanyl without a legal prescription can face criminal charges. Whether the drug is Schedule I or II depends on how much of the drug is possessed or sold. It is important to remember that when the weight of the drug is determined, anything that is part of the substance is included. This means that an entire fentanyl lollipop is weighed, not just the amount of fentanyl in the lollipop. This is especially of concern to street users who buy the designer drug already dissolved in water, because water is much heavier than the drug.

Anyone who sells or distributes fentanyl or one of its analogs, regardless of whether it is pharmaceutically or clandestinely created, can face criminal charges. This includes giving someone else some of a legally prescribed dosage. Any doctor who falsely prescribes fentanyl to someone can face criminal charges.

Anyone possessing more than 40 g of fentanyl can be prosecuted for a Schedule I offense. Possession of more than 10 g of a fentanyl analog is also a Schedule I offense. The harsher penalties for fentanyl analogs are because all analogs are illegally produced in clandestine laboratories. Possessing less than 40 g of fentanyl or less than 10 g of an analog is a Schedule II offense.

Legal history

The Controlled Substances Act of 1970 was an attempt to tightly control all potentially harmful substances. It was designed to limit the use of drugs such as fentanyl and codeine to clinical use only. Drug users found a way around this law. By designing the drug in clandestine labs, they would alter the chemical makeup just enough so that prosecutors could not charge users. However, the law was altered in 1984 to include analogs of illegal drugs. The wording was cleaned up even more in 1986, and since then, any analog of an illegal drug is also considered illegal. In fact, analogs are viewed in an inceasingly negative light; as of 2002, analogs are considered more dangerous and thus demand stiffer penalties for violators of the law.

Federal guidelines, regulations, and penalties

Fentanyl is used throughout the world. In most countries, few can legally possess the drug. However, 11 countries—including the United States—use fentanyl not only for pain associated with the effects of cancer but also for those with general chronic pain.

In the United States, fentanyl and its analogs can be considered either a Schedule I or II drug depending on the amount involved. The DEA is pushing to remove all designer drugs from the street, so makers are being targeted. Doctors who write false prescriptions are increasingly under scrutiny as well.

First-time offense violators who possess 40–399 g of fentanyl mixture can receive not less than five years or more than 40 years in prison; if death or serious injury is involved, then not less than 20 years or more than life in prison. This is in addition to a fine of not more than $2 million for an individual. The same penalties apply to 10–99 g of fentanyl analog. For a second offense, the violator can receive not less than 10 years or more than life unless serious injury or death is involved. In this case, the term becomes not less than life in prison. The fine doubles to not more than $4 million for the second offense.

First-time offenders who possess 400 g or more of fentanyl or 100 g or more of an analog can receive not less than 10 years or more than life in prison unless there is a death or serious injury. This is in addition to a maximum $4 million fine. A second offense brings a mandatory 20-year prison sentence with a maximum of life. If death or serious injury occurs in a second offense, a life sentence in prison is the minimum. A fine of not more than $8 million can accompany the prison sentence.

RESOURCES

Books

Ottomanelli, Gennaro. *Assessment and Treatment of Chemical Dependency.* Westport, CT: Praeger, 2001.

Polishuk, Paul V. and Henry C. Nipper. "The Neurobiology of Fentanyl and its Derivatives," edited by Ronald R. Watson. *Drugs of Abuse and Neurobiology* Boca Raton, FL: 2000.

Periodicals

"Anesthesiologists: Addicted to the Drugs They Administer." *American Society of Anesthesiologists: Newsletter* (May 2001).

"Just the Facts: Designer Drugs." Florida Alcohol and Drug Abuse Association (2000).

Oncology Nursing Forum. "A Research-Based Guideline for Appropriate Use of Transdermal Fentanyl to Treat Chronic Pain." 25, 9 (1998).

"What You Can Do About Drug Use In America." National Clearinghouse for Alcohol and Drug Information. (1991).

Other

Addiction Recovery Institute. <http://www.detox24.com> Accessed 17 July 2002.

Office of National Drug Control Policy. <http://www.whitehousedrugpolicy.gov> Accessed 17 July 2002.

United States Department of Justice Drug Enforcement Agency. <http://www.usdoj.gov/dea> Accessed 17 July 2002.

United States Food and Drug Administration. *Warning against misusing of Fentanyl Analgesic Skin Patch.* <http://www.fda.gov:80/bbs/topics/NEWS/NEW00459.html.> Accessed 17 July 2002.

Organizations

Narcotics Anonymous (NA), PO Box 9999, Van Nuys, CA, USA, 91409, (818) 773-9999, (818) 700-0700, <http://www.na.org>.

National Federation of Parents for Drug-Free Youth, 9551 Big Bend, St. Louis, MO, USA, 63122, (314) 968-1322.

National Institute on Drug Abuse (NIDA), National Institutes of Health, 6001 Executive Boulevard, Room 5213, Bethesda, MD, USA, 20892-9561, (301) 443-1124, (888) 644-6432, information@lists.nida.nih.gov, <http://www.drugabuse.gov/Infofax/marijuana.html>.

Brian Clifford Sine

GBL

OFFICIAL NAMES: Gamma butyrolactone (GBL), dihydro-2(3H)-furanone, 4-butanolide, 2(3H)-furanone dihydro, tetrahydro-2-furanone, butyrolactone gamma, gamma hydroxybutyric acid (GHB), 1,4 butanediol (BD; tetramethylene glycol; Sucol B), sodium oxybate (Xyrem)
STREET NAMES: Renewtrient, revivarant, revivarant G, blue nitro, blue nitro vitality, blue moon, BLO, blow, gamma G, remforce, longevity, GH revitalizer, insom-X, firewater, invigorate, G3, GH-gold (GHG), genx (genex), jolt, verve (verv), liquid gold, N-force, pure raine, reactive, rejoov, rejuv+nite, regenerize, remedy GH, thunder, X-12
DRUG CLASSIFICATIONS: Schedule I, depressant

OVERVIEW

GBL and related chemicals, GHB and BD, are used to make floor stripper, paint thinner, and other industrial products. All three substances are central nervous system depressants with sedative-hypnotic and hallucinogenic properties. Health food stores sold GHB as a dietary supplement after it was synthesized in 1960, before its dangerous, addictive, and even lethal effects came to light. In the 1980s, GHB was popular among body builders, who believed it could release a growth hormone that would stimulate muscle growth. In 1990, after more than 30 reports of GHB-linked illness, the Food and Drug Administration (FDA) declared that GHB was unsafe and illegal except in the carefully controlled environment of agency-approved drug studies. Despite these warnings, GHB continues to be illegally promoted for muscle building, for releasing inhibitions and feeling high, and for combating depression, sleep problems, and weight gain.

After the FDA banned the use of GHB in 1990, some supplement manufacturers switched ingredients to either GBL or BD, similar chemicals that the body converts to GHB, and which have the same potentially deadly effects. GBL-related products are illegally marketed and promoted with false claims to build muscles, improve physical and athletic performance, enhance sex, reduce stress, induce sleep, release growth hormone, relieve depression, and prolong life. They have been sold in health food stores as dietary supplements, advertised in muscle-building magazines, and listed as "party drugs" on Internet sites. Their most notorious use is as "date rape" drugs, as they are odorless and colorless, induce loss of consciousness, and cause memory loss in the victim, preventing identification of the attacker.

The FDA has determined that dietary supplements containing these chemicals are actually unapproved drugs because of their harmful and life-threatening effects, including breathing problems, unconsciousness or coma, vomiting, epileptic fits or seizures, and death. It is now illegal to sell anything for human consumption that contains GBL, GHB, or BD. In an attempt to avoid legal consequences, manufacturers of many of the products formerly sold as dietary supplements have changed the name or the intended use of the product, such as calling it a cleaning solution. However, information provided about the products continues to promote many of the former claims that these substances are performance boosters or sexual enhancers.

Because the public ignored these warnings and laws, causing a serious health hazard, the FDA had to re-issue warnings on GHB in 1997 and 1998, and extended its warnings to include GBL and BD. On January 21, 1999, the FDA asked manufacturers to recall their GBL-containing products and issued press releases warning consumers not to take them. The Trimfast Group, Inc. agreed to recall its products, Revivarant and Revivarant G, and most other companies followed suit. The Drug Enforcement Administration (DEA) listed GBL as a scheduled substance in January 1999. On February 18, 2000, GBL became a List I chemical, subject to the criminal, civil, and administrative sanctions of the Controlled Substances Act (CSA).

To protect the public health, the FDA threatened to use all potential regulatory actions against manufacturers that did not voluntarily recall products containing GBL and related drugs, GHB and BD. In 1999, the FDA declared BD a Class I health hazard, a potentially life-threatening substance, and the DEA made BD a scheduled substance in April 2000. The DEA is continuing to crack down on sales of BD, which should decrease the legally available supply, but which could increase the number of addicts going through withdrawal.

Only public education can help stop illegal use of GBL and its deadly chemical cousins. The National Institute on Drug Abuse (NIDA) is donating $54 million to warn teens, young adults, parents, educators, and public officials about the dangers of GBL and other club drugs, in partnership with Join Together, National Families in Action, the American Academy of Child and Adolescent Psychiatry, and the Community Anti-Drug Coalitions of America.

Part of the reason use of GBL and similar products have gone unchecked is that the FDA has less authority to control dietary supplements, which are not subject to the same strict review procedures as are drugs. Consumers should be aware that products available in health food stores or even on supermarket shelves can be just as dangerous as prescription drugs. Just because a product is labeled "natural" does not mean it is safe, and "natural" poisons like wild mushrooms cause many emergency room visits, cases of brain damage, and even deaths each year.

CHEMICAL/ORGANIC COMPOSITION

Gamma butyrolactone (GBL) is also known by other chemical names, including dihydro-2(3H)-furanone, 4-butanolide, 2(3H)-furanone dihydro, tetrahydro-2-furanone, and butyrolactone gamma. When GBL enters the body, it is broken down to gamma hydroxybutyric acid (GHB), an equally dangerous chemical that is also sold illegally. Because the body absorbs GBL better than it does GHB, any given amount of GBL is more potent than the same amount of GHB. Dietary supplements, which are now illegal because they contain GBL, GHB, or the related chemical 1,4 butanediol (BD), could list these ingredients on the label, or they might list tetramethylene glycol or 2(3H)-furanone dihydro. However, some of these products have no label at all. Now

KEY TERMS

ANALOGS: Different forms of a chemical or drug structurally related to the parent chemical or drug.

DELUSIONS: False beliefs.

HALLUCINATION: The experience of seeing, feeling, hearing, smelling, or tasting something that is not really there.

INTUBATION: Putting a plastic tube into the lungs through the nose and throat to allow artificial respiration in a person unable to breathe independently.

RESPIRATORY DEPRESSION: The slowing of a person's breathing rate. Severe respiratory depression can cause a person to go into a coma or even stop breathing.

SEIZURES (EPILEPTIC FITS): Bursts of abnormal electrical activity in the brain causing episodic symptoms, including coma or reduced level of awareness, flailing movements of arms and legs, and loss of control of bowels and bladder. Prolonged, untreated seizures may cause brain damage or even death.

that GBL is illegal, it is sometimes made in secret laboratories. As a result, the purity, potency, and contaminants of the drug are completely unpredictable, adding to the dangers involved in using it.

INGESTION METHODS

As GBL is an industrial and household solvent, there have been unintentional poisonings. The clear liquid or light-colored powder can be mixed with water, alcohol, or soda, allowing the unwary to drink it accidentally or be tricked into drinking it when someone secretly laces the drink. At night clubs and "raves," partygoers often carry the drug around in eye-drop bottles, water bottles, or disguised as mouthwash with added food coloring and flavorings.

The typical dose is 1–2 tsp to 5 g of powder mixed in a beverage, depending on the purity, which can vary considerably. Renewtrient and other products containing GBL or related chemicals are sometimes sold in capsules.

THERAPEUTIC USE

GBL and related drugs, GHB and BD, are illegal substances and currently have no approved medical indications in the United States.

LAW AND ORDER

March 15, 2000: The largest GBL distribution arrest in the United States to date was made when Michael Brian Hall, a former Honeywell computer engineer and Mensa member, was arrested on charges he sold GBL through his Inova Products website. Cash-only bail was set at $5 million. The Phoenix Division of the DEA, the U.S. Department of Justice Bureau of Narcotics Enforcement, and the Santa Clara County District Attorney's Office claimed that Hall purchased GBL in 55-gallon drums from a distributor, and then resold it to hundreds of dealers nationwide. His illegal income of about $25,000 per week came from selling the contents of each drum, or about 180,000 doses of GBL, for $3,200, about three times the original price. Hall was caught while en route to the post office with 2.5-gallon containers of GBL. While imprisoned in Phoenix, he was beaten by another inmate who thought he was a rapist because he sold a date-rape drug.

October 1, 1999: John Keith Dilg, a 23-year-old former student at Southern Illinois University, was accused of running one of the largest GHB production operations discovered to date. He was the first person to face federal charges in Chicago for making more than 1,100 pounds of liquid GHB in clandestine labs, including one in his parents' home, and was charged with three federal felonies: conspiracy to violate FDA laws, operating an unregistered drug-manufacturing facility, and mislabeling drugs.

March 1999: Four males, ages 17 to 25, were arraigned on charges of manslaughter and poisoning in the death of Michigan ninth-grader Samantha Reid. They were charged with slipping the "date-rape" drug GBL or GHB into her soft drink at a party in Grosse Isle, causing her to vomit, lapse into a coma, and then die. Two other girls survived being drugged at the party. At trial in February 2000, the three younger males were found guilty of involuntary manslaughter and lesser charges of poisoning, and the oldest was convicted of being an accessory to manslaughter, poisoning, and possession of marijuana and GHB. Poisoning carries a maximum sentence of life in prison, and manslaughter a maximum of 15 years.

February 2, 1998: California chiropractor Daniel Bricker, age 30, was fined $2,000 and imprisoned for illegally distributing and mislabeling liquids containing GBL at a 1996 New Year's Eve "rave" party. More than 100 party guests fell ill, including 30 taken to local hospitals with complaints of dizziness, nausea, and difficulty breathing. Special agents from the FDA's Office of Criminal Investigations seized more than 10,000 vials of Cherry fX Bombs, Lemon fX Drops, and Orange fX Rush, along with documents containing results of laboratory tests on these products that proved that Bricker knew they were harmful. An FDA agent revealed that Bricker had planned to spike the party punch with kava-kava, but when he could not get it in time, he substituted the industrial solvent. "He knew in advance that these people would get sick from it, and he distributed it anyway in the hopes of making some money. It was an extremely dangerous thing to do," an FDA agent was quoted as saying in the July–August 1998 FDA Investigators' Reports. Bricker's sentence included three months in prison and three months in a rehabilitation halfway house.

USAGE TRENDS

According to NIDA, young people are freely experimenting with GBL despite the grave legal and health consequences, and GBL abuse has increased substantially in recent years. GBL and related drugs are popular on the club scene, especially with the college crowd, as an alternative to drinking alcohol, because they are relatively inexpensive compared with other drugs and because they have no calories.

Scope and severity

Since 1990, the DEA has documented more than 15,600 overdoses and law enforcement encounters related to GHB, as well as 72 deaths. As of 2000, the FDA has investigated 124 cases involving large-scale interstate manufacture and distribution of GHB. Law enforcement agencies have investigated 850 incidents involving GHB, including 150 home laboratories and 500 seized and analyzed drug supplies. As of December 1999, the FDA's Office of Criminal Investigations had recorded 116 arrests, 55 convictions, and 38 indictments related to GBL.

The DEA has documented at least 15 sexual assault cases involving 30 victims under the influence of GHB. In a study of urine samples from victims of alleged sexual assault, 711 urine samples were positive for drugs, including 48 that tested positive for GHB. In response to a 1999 Glamour magazine survey, 19% of female college students questioned said they knew someone who was the victim of date-rape related to GHB.

More than half of GHB-related emergency room visits are for unexpected reaction and overdose following recreational use. The U.S. government's Drug Abuse Warning Network (DAWN) reported an alarming rise in

GHB-related emergency room visits, from 20 in 1992, 55 in 1994, 764 in 1997, 2,973 in 1999, to 4,969 in 2000.

However, this is probably a gross underestimate of the actual scope of the problem. Laboratories often fail to detect or identify GHB because it leaves the body in about 12 hours, and many doctors who are unfamiliar with this relatively new drug of abuse fail to recognize the signs and symptoms of GBL-related poisoning. A Los Angeles Police Department agent cited his personal knowledge of more than 200 deaths, 300 addicts, hundreds of rape victims, and thousands of overdoses, all related to GHB and related products.

In 1999, GHB accounted for 32 percent of calls to Boston poison centers involving illegal drugs. In Chicago and San Francisco, GHB use is lower than that of the club drug MDMA (ecstasy), but GHB accounts for a disproportionately large share of club drug overdoses.

From October 1998 through January 1999, poison control centers identified 34 emergency room visits in New Mexico and Texas following the use of products containing GBL, including Firewater, Blue Nitro Vitality, RenewTrient, Revivarant, and Revivarant-G. Symptoms requiring urgent care included cardiac arrest, respiratory depression, coma or decreased level of consciousness, dangerously slow or rapid heart rhythm, fainting, seizures, confusion, combative behavior, memory loss, anxiety and nervousness, nausea and vomiting, tremors and twitching, and inappropriately elevated mood. In 13 patients, symptoms were severe enough to warrant hospitalization.

From January 1999 to August 2000, the FDA received 48 reports of acute BD intoxication, including loss of consciousness, dangerously low respiratory rates, vomiting, and slowed heartbeat. In a series of nine toxic reactions to BD reported in the *New England Journal of Medicine* in early 2001, the effects of BD were similar to those of GBL and GHB, and included addiction, withdrawal, and death.

Age, ethnic, and gender trends

GHB and related products are popular with high school and college students. More than 60% of GHB abusers are between the ages of 18 and 25 years. Of the 72 individuals known to have died from GHB since 1995, 40% were between the ages of 15 and 24 years, and 27% were between the ages of 25 and 29 years. According to DAWN statistics, 60% of GHB-related emergency room visits are in patients age 25 and under.

In a 2001 study of 295 gay and bisexual men, 29% reported using GBL or GHB during their most recent circuit party weekend.

MENTAL EFFECTS

Like alcohol and barbiturates, GBL and related drugs, GHB and BD, powerfully and rapidly depress brain function. These drugs easily enter the brain, where they have a devastating effect on brain chemistry. Mild effects could include enhanced sensations of pleasure, sleepiness, depression, feelings of intoxication, loosened inhibitions, aggressive or combative behavior, or poor judgment. More serious and frightening effects include out-of-body experiences, uncontrolled body movements, and vertigo, a sensation of dizziness.

Psychiatric symptoms include hallucinations (seeing or hearing things that are not there) or delusions (false beliefs). Very few users remember their experience because of the associated memory loss. Individual variability in how the body handles these drugs, and an even greater variability in the composition of illegally produced drugs, makes it virtually impossible to control or anticipate how much brain function will shut down, and increases the risk of deadly overdose.

PHYSIOLOGICAL EFFECTS

When swallowed, GBL is converted in the body to GHB, causing psychological symptoms and brain depression as indicated above, as well as other symptoms that include low blood pressure or heart rate, low body temperature, and nausea and vomiting. As GBL and related drugs shut down vital brain functions, breathing slows down and may even stop. If emergency treatment is not available, respiratory depression or dangerous slowing of heart rate can cause death.

Physical effects begin within 15–30 minutes of taking the drug and last three to six hours. The sometimes deadly effects of GBL and related drugs appear to be dose-related, so that the larger the dose, the more frequent and severe the ill effects. At GHB doses of 0.5–1.5 grams, the user may feel relaxed or drunk; doses of 1.0–2.5 grams increase muscle relaxation and impair coordination; and doses over 2.5 grams can cause nausea, vomiting, drowsiness, breathing difficulty, slow heart rate, coma, and death.

Harmful side effects

Overall, the DEA has reported more than 72 deaths and 5,500 emergency room overdoses associated with GHB, and serious ill effects related to GBL and related drugs, GHB and BD, in at least five children under 18 years of age. All five children had vomiting and became unconscious, and most had respiratory depression and dangerous slowing of heart rate. As GBL crosses the placenta, a pregnant woman exposes her unborn baby to its dangerous effects.

Slow, shallow breathing, and irregular or slow heart rhythms related to use of these drugs can deprive the brain of oxygen and blood flow, causing unconsciousness, coma, epileptic fits or seizures, loss of muscle tone, and permanent brain damage. Lack of oxygen and blood flow to other vital organs can cause other serious complications such as kidney failure, requiring dialysis; or pulmonary edema associated with fluid collection in the lungs; shortness of breath; coughing up blood; and heart failure. The combination of unconsciousness, difficulty breathing, and vomiting can cause aspiration, or choking to death on vomit.

From October 1998 through January 1999, poison control centers in New Mexico identified 14 patients seen in emergency rooms for symptoms related to use of products containing GBL. Five of these patients had also consumed alcohol and/or other drugs. The most common symptoms and signs were nausea and vomiting in 10 (71%), decreased level of consciousness in nine (64%), slow heart rate in seven (50%), prolonged unconsciousness in six (43%), fainting in six (43%), seizures in four (29%), confusion in four (29%), combative behavior in four (29%), respiratory depression in three (21%), memory loss in two (14%), and inappropriately elevated mood in two (14%). Three were hospitalized, one with cardiac arrest, one with respiratory arrest, and one after a car crash associated with the effects resulting from use of GBL.

During the same timeframe, there were 20 emergency room visits for complications of GBL use reported in Texas. These patients ranged in age from 11 to 41 years, and 10 had also consumed alcohol and/or other drugs. Ten had to be hospitalized, including one with respiratory arrest. The most common symptoms and signs were decreased level of consciousness in 13 (65%), prolonged unconsciousness in nine (45%), respiratory depression in nine (45%), anxiety and nervousness in seven (35%), nausea and vomiting in six (30%), confusion in six (30%), tremors and twitching in four (20%), rapid heart rate in three (15%), and combative behavior in three (15%).

In a series of nine toxic reactions to BD reported in the *New England Journal of Medicine* in early 2001, the effects of BD were similar to those of GBL and GHB, and included addiction, withdrawal, and death. The eight patients seen at Hennepin County Medical Center, Minneapolis, Minnesota, had used BD recreationally, to enhance bodybuilding, or to treat depression or sleep problems. One patient was seen twice with toxic effects and had withdrawal symptoms after her second episode, including hallucinations, sleeplessness, fear, agitation, and uncontrollable body movements. Reactions in most patients included vomiting, loss of bowel and bladder control, agitation, striking out at others, fading in and out of consciousness, respiratory depression, and death. Six patients, including two who died, had not used alcohol or any other drugs with BD. Those who died had taken

5.4–20 g of BD, and the others took doses ranging from 1 to 14 g.

Long-term health effects

GBL and related drugs can cause physical and psychological dependence and addiction with sustained use. Withdrawal symptoms in users of high doses, especially when used for longer than four months, can include sleeplessness, muscle cramps, tremor, anxiety, hallucinations, and delusions lasting from 48 hours to 12 days after last use.

In a series reported in 2001 of five patients seen for abrupt withdrawal from GBL, symptoms included rapid heart rate, high blood pressure, delusions of being persecuted or harmed, hallucinations, and fluctuating states of consciousness. Most of the patients were body builders, and ranged in age from 23 to 33 years. Patients had been taking GBL for two to nine months, and developed withdrawal symptoms one to six hours after their last dose, with symptoms lasting up to 14 days.

In testimony before the FDA, drug researcher Deborah Zvorsec reported that GHB users need increasing amounts of the substance to feel good. By the time they realize they have become tolerant or even addicted, they develop severe anxiety, sleeplessness, panic attacks, and hallucinations when they try to stop. Detoxification, even with medical supervision, resembles the terrifying state of hallucinations and extreme anxiety called "DTs," or delirium tremens, that accompany alcohol withdrawal. After detoxification most patients suffer from severe depression and anxiety lasting weeks to months, and some also have muscle twitching and tremors, or uncontrolled shaking. Very few are able to refrain from using GHB again. "GHB is perhaps the most addictive drug ever abused," Zvorsec testified.

While some users may recover completely and rapidly from intoxication with GBL or related drugs, previous exposure does not predict future response. These users may be lulled into a false sense of security, thinking they are immune to any toxic reactions, only to suffer serious reaction or even death the next time.

REACTIONS WITH OTHER DRUGS OR SUBSTANCES

As GBL and related drugs are powerful sedatives that depress brain function and respiration, they are especially dangerous when mixed with alcohol or other drugs with similar effects. They can cause seizures and are more deadly when mixed with ecstasy or other club drugs that excite the nervous system. On the club scene or at raves, combining these drugs is unfortunately a common practice.

 **IN THE NEWS**

December 17, 1999: Phoenix Suns forward Tom Gugliotta suffered a nearly-fatal seizure on the team bus after a game in Portland and was hospitalized in serious condition. The Suns' team doctor said Gugliotta told him he had taken a supplement containing GBL because he had been having trouble sleeping. The FDA's Office of Criminal Investigations had already recorded 116 arrests, 55 convictions, and 38 indictments related to GBL and was actively scanning the Internet and searching retail shelves to close down sales by "opportunists."

October 3, 1999: Nicole Pekarick died from regular use of Renewtrient, according to testimony of her mother before an FDA panel. In October of 1998, the honors college student and varsity athletic team captain began using this "muscle supplement" at her boyfriend's recommondation. Information on the Internet suggested she could drink it before bedtime and wake up in only four hours, feeling refreshed, rested, and ready for another workout. By April of 1999, she had stopped attending

classes and paying bills, was constantly losing things, and had bruises all over her arms and legs. By May she had dropped out of school, and by June she would sleep for three hours in the middle of the day. Although she kept using Renewtrient despite her mother's protests, she abused no other drugs. Her younger sister reported that she often "embarrassed herself" and "acted weird" without even remembering her own behavior, and added, "It disgusts me to see her out of control."

In August of 1999, Nicole soiled herself while having a seizure in a public bathroom. She had to be intubated for artificial respiration and strapped to the hospital bed for uncontrollable thrashing. When she regained consciousness, her mother begged her to enter treatment for chemical dependency, but she was "clueless" about her own condition and refused. Although she eventually acknowledged she had a problem and seemed to do better after treatment, she never woke up from a nap on October 3, 1999. The autopsy showed that she had GBL and GHL in her system, but no other drugs. Her mother lamented her death, noting that this loving, caring, health-conscious, intelligent woman never realized her dream of becoming a biomedical engineer and helping the handicapped by designing artificial body parts.

TREATMENT AND REHABILITATION

After a single episode of intoxication with GBL or related drugs, symptoms usually resolve with supportive care within 2–96 hours, provided users get emergency treatment before permanent complications develop. There is no antidote for these poisons. Treatment consists of careful medical observation and supportive therapy until symptoms of toxicity subside.

Repeated users of GBL or related drugs should have intensive monitoring and medical intervention for withdrawal symptoms when discontinuing use. Withdrawal can take 10–14 days even with medical assistance, and should be followed by counseling for anxiety, depression, and substance abuse for as long as is needed. Attempting withdrawal without medical assistance is dangerous, and can result in suicide from intense depression or accidental overdose if the user tries to taper off the drug. Even with medical help, very few who go through withdrawal are cured of their addiction and, instead, continue to use the drug.

Patients undergoing abrupt withdrawal from GBL are monitored in the intensive care unit and are typically hospitalized for about five days for supportive care and treatment with pentobarbital, a strong sedative sometimes used for anesthesia. Withdrawal symptoms are so severe that benzodiazepines, which are milder tranquilizers than pentobarbital and which are typically the first line of treatment

for drug withdrawal, were not effective. After discharge, patients received gradually decreasing doses of pentobarbital or benzodiazepines to control their symptoms of anxiety, delusions, and hallucinations.

PERSONAL AND SOCIAL CONSEQUENCES

Users of GBL or related drugs may experience memory loss, lapses in judgment, aggressive outbursts, embarrassing or strange behavior, confusion, anxiety, or depression. Any or all of these symptoms affect the individual both directly and by influencing how others perceive the user, causing loss of friendship, trust, and respect. Users who suffer from delusions or hallucinations may even be perceived as being mentally ill.

Erratic behavior associated with psychiatric symptoms like these can cause violence, accidents, suicide, or harm to self or others with permanent physical and legal consequences and irreversible damage to relationships, school work, and employment prospects. Hallucinations and delusions can be terrifying, leave permanent psychological damage, and even endanger life.

Addicted users who need increasing amounts of the drug to prevent withdrawal symptoms may end up spending up to $200 per day, or $70,000 per year, according to Dr. Zvorsec, causing significant problems with debt or even turning to crime to support the habit.

Those who trick others into using GBL or related drugs by slipping it into their drink are viewed as rapists. Offering the drug to others with or without their knowledge or consent may result in criminal charges of sexual assault, rape, manslaughter, or poisoning, punishable by fines and imprisonment.

LEGAL CONSEQUENCES

In California, a chiropractor who distributed liquids containing GHB at a party, causing other partygoers to get sick, was punished with a $2,000 fine and imprisonment. In Michigan, four men were accused of manslaughter and poisoning when they slipped GHB or GBL into a ninth-grader's drink, causing her to vomit, go into a coma, and die. Manslaughter carries a maximum sentence of 15 years in prison, and poisoning carries a maximum sentence of life imprisonment.

Both the FDA and the U.S. Department of Justice have ongoing criminal enforcement actions against GHB. As of 2000, the government had investigated 850 incidents involving GHB, including 124 cases of large-scale interstate manufacture and distribution of GHB, 150 clandestine laboratories, and 500 seized and analyzed laboratory exhibits. There have been more than 33 GHB-related convictions.

Legal history

In 1990, based on more than 30 reports of illness linked to GHB, the FDA banned its use except in the carefully controlled environment of agency-approved drug studies. In January 1999, the FDA requested a voluntary recall of all GBL-containing products sold in health food stores and warned the public of its abuse potential and danger to public health. It is now illegal to sell anything for human consumption that contains GBL, GHB, or BD.

Federal guidelines, regulations, and penalties

GHB is already classified as a controlled substance by more than 20 states, and some other states also impose criminal penalties for possession of GHB. If Congress classifies GHB as a controlled substance, marketing the drug illegally would subject the offender to federal penalties, including imprisonment and fines.

GBL became a Schedule II substance in California effective January 1, 2000. In that state, possession of GBL or GHB is an alternate felony/misdemeanor, punishable by 16 months or two or three years in the state prison, or up to one year in the county jail. Possession for sale is a felony, punishable by 16 months, two years, or three years in state prison. Sale or transportation is a felony punishable by a state prison term of two, three, or four years. Transportation between non-neighboring counties is a felony punishable by incarceration in state prison for three, six, or nine years.

On February 18, 2000, GBL became a List I chemical, subject to the criminal, civil, and administrative sanctions of the CSA. This legislation, Public Law 106-172, was named the Hillary Farias and Samantha Reid Date-Rape Prohibition Act of 1999 for the two Michigan girls poisoned with GBL, one fatally.

See also Alcohol; Ecstasy (MDMA); GHB; Rohypnol

RESOURCES

Periodicals

"Adverse Events Associated with Ingestion of Gamma-Butyrolactone Minnesota, New Mexico, and Texas, 1998-1999." *Morbidity and Mortality Weekly Report* 48 (February 26, 1999): 137-140.

Catalano, Maria C., et al. "GBL Withdrawal Syndromes." *Psychosomatics* 42 (February 2001): 83-88.

Nordenberg, Tamar. "California Man Imprisoned after fX Drinks Injure Partygoers." *FDA Investigators' Reports—FDA Consumer Magazine* (July–August 1998).

Nordenberg, Tamar. "The Death of the Party: All the Rave, GHB's Hazards Go Unnoticed." *FDA Consumer Magazine* (March–April 2000).

Winickoff, J. P., et al. "Verve and Jolt: Deadly New Internet Drugs." *Pediatrics* 106, no. 4 (October 2000): 829-830.

Other

Food and Drug Administration website. <http://www.fda.gov>. July 5, 2002 (July 8, 2002).

FDA Talk Paper T99-5: FDA Warns about Products Containing Gamma Butyrolactone or GBL and Asks Companies to Issue a Recall (January 21, 1999). <http:www.fda.gov/bbs/topics/ANSWERS/ANS00937.html>. Accessed 3/25/02.

FDA Talk Paper T99-21: U.S. FDA Warns about GBL-Related Products (May 11, 1999). <http://old.healthnet.org/programs/e-drug-hma/e-drug.199905/msg00021.html. Accessed 3/25/02>.

Neuroscience for Kids: 1,4-Butanediol (BD): Danger! <http://faculty.washington.edu/chudler/14b.html>. April 17, 2001 (March 30, 2002).

Neuroscience for Kids: Gamma hydroxybutyrate (GHB) = Bad News. <http://faculty.washington.edu/chudler/ghb.html>. April 16, 2001 (March 30, 2002).

Project GHB website. <http://www.projectghb.org>. Accessed March 29, 2002.

Supplement Watch: GBL. <http://www.supplementwatch.com/supatoz/supplement.asp?supplementId=137>. July 8, 2002 (July 8, 2002).

U.S. Department of Justice, DEA Diversion Control Program. *Drugs and Chemicals of Concern: Gamma Hydroxybutyric Acid.* (August 2001). <http://www.deadiversion.usdoj.gov/drugs_concern/ghb/summary.htm>. Accessed March 30, 2002.

Organizations

National Institute on Drug Abuse (NIDA), National Institutes of Health, 6001 Executive Boulevard, Room 5213, Bethesda, MD, USA, 20892-9561, (301) 443-1124, (888) 644-6432, Information@lists.nida.nih.gov, <http://www.nida.nih.gov/AboutNIDA.html>.

Laurie L. Barclay, MD

GHB

OFFICIAL NAMES: Gamma-hydroxybutyrate (GHB), 4-hydroxy butyrate, gamma hydrate, gamma-hydroxybutyrate sodium, gamma hydroxybutyric acid, gamma-OH, sodium oxybate, sodium oxybutyrate

STREET NAMES: Blue Nitro, cherry meth, easy lay, energy drink, everclear, firewater, G, gamma-oh, Georgia home boy, g-juice, goop, grievous bodily harm, growth hormone booster, insom-X, invigorate, lemon fX drops, liquid ecstasy, liquid E, liquid X, longevity, nature's Quaalude, orange fX rush, oxy-sleep, poor man's heroin, remforce, Revivarant, salty dog, salty water, scoop, soap, somatomax, vita-G, water, wolfies, zonked

DRUG CLASSIFICATIONS: Schedule I, depressant

OVERVIEW

An odorless, colorless substance, GHB is a fast-acting central nervous system depressant. Sometimes it has a salty taste, while at other times it may be perceived as having no taste at all. Depending on the dose, effects of GHB can range from euphoria (feeling of well being; giddiness), intoxication, muscle relaxation, and hallucinations, to dizziness, nausea, vomiting, respiratory depression (slowed breathing), seizures, confusion, drowsiness, unconsciousness, coma, and even death. GHB may also cause memory loss of events that follow ingestion. The effects of GHB can be felt within 15 to 30 minutes after ingestion and typically last three to six hours.

GHB was first developed in 1960 as an alternative anesthetic (painkiller) for use in surgery because of its ability to induce sleep and reversible coma. But it had little effectiveness as a painkiller, and the coma that it caused was often associated with seizure activity, including jerking movements of the limbs or face.

Then, in the 1980s, GHB was endorsed by the health food industry as a growth hormone stimulator, and was marketed and sold to help body builders increase muscle mass and maintain weight. But, also, GHB was embraced as an aid in weight loss and as an over-the-counter sleep agent because of its sedative side effects.

In response to several accounts of adverse reactions in people taking nutritional and weight loss supplements containing GHB, the Food and Drug Administration (FDA) banned the drug in 1990. In doing so, the agency declared GHB unsafe and illegal for use except under FDA-approved, physician-supervised treatment protocols. In 1997, the FDA reissued its warning on GHB as an unapproved and potentially dangerous, illegal drug in the United States. In March 2000, GHB was placed in Schedule I of the Controlled Substances Act (CSA). This designation labeled GHB as having a high potential for abuse and raised the issue that the drug was potentially unsafe for use even under medical supervision.

Despite these actions, however, GHB continues to be illegally manufactured and sold. GHB, and kits for making GHB, are available on the Internet and on the steroid black market. It is possible to make the drug without sophisticated laboratory equipment. Because of such ease of access, GHB is usually made in a home kitchen and sold locally on the street. The product may be disguised by adding food coloring or flavorings, or by storing it in bottles labeled as other products such as mouthwash or spring water. Storage in water bottles is especially dangerous, because someone might assume the content is plain water and instead drink a large dose of GHB.

Because production is not regulated, the amount of GHB in a dose—typically one level teaspoon—can vary dramatically from 0.5 to 5 grams. Users may ingest many doses while attempting to attain desired effects.

The risk of overdose with GHB is high as the drug is unpredictable; individual reaction to GHB is also highly varied. At higher doses, GHB has become the most deadly of the club drugs, according to government statistics. Overdoses usually require emergency room treatment, sometimes including intensive care for respiratory depression and coma.

Use as a club drug

Despite the fact that it was made illegal in 1990, GHB became a common club drug (drugs used at late-night dance parties or so-called raves or trances, concerts, nightclubs, and bars). In these settings, GHB became commonly known as a euphoriant, and its popularity grew, especially in light of its easy access and low cost. When actor River Phoenix died outside a nightclub in Los Angeles in October 1993, it was suggested that he had overdosed on GHB. While the rumor was never confirmed, it further stimulated interest in GHB.

Common club drugs include other synthetic drugs: MDMA (ecstasy), ketamine (Special K, vitamin K, Kit Kat, Keller, super acid, and super C), and Rohypnol (chemical name is flunitrazepam; also known as roofies, forget pills, the drop drug, rope, LaRocha, ropies, Mexican valium, roachies, ruffles, wolfies, and rophies).

Recreational users of GHB claim that inhibitions are lowered, sex drive increases, and a euphoric, out-of-body high is experienced. Some people who use GHB consider it a weaker alternative to hallucinogens, LSD, and PCP. Others use GHB after taking ecstasy to counteract the stimulant effect. But even those who use GHB recreationally say that its unpredictable effects can sometimes overwhelm them and cause negative reactions, especially when taken at higher doses.

GHB is usually sold by the capful, or "swig," for $5 to $25. It is generally found in liquid form, but may be found in a highly soluble powder form. Either way, it is typically added to a liquid such as water, sports drinks like Gatorade, or soft drinks. Mixing the drug with a sweetened drink can mask GHB's salty taste. GHB is also mixed into an alcoholic drink, which enhances its effects but increases the potential for adverse reaction, particularly respiratory distress. The use of alcohol is typical if date rape is intended, as the victim is usually unaware that GHB has been added to the drink.

KEY TERMS

ADDICTION: Physical dependence on a drug characterized by tolerance and withdrawal.

COMA: An abnormal state of depressed responsiveness with absence of response to stimuli.

NARCOLEPSY: A rare, chronic sleep disorder characterized by constant daytime fatigue and sudden attacks of sleep.

OVERDOSE: The result of ingesting too much of a substance such as a drug either in one dose or over the course of time. Symptoms of drug overdose vary with the type of drug taken, and may include severe drowsiness or unconsciousness.

RESPIRATORY DEPRESSION: The slowing of a person's breathing rate. Severe respiratory depression can cause a person to go into a coma or even stop breathing.

WITHDRAWAL: A group of symptoms that may occur from suddenly stopping the use of a substance such as alcohol or other drugs after chronic or prolonged ingestion.

Use as a date rape drug

Several cases have documented the use of GHB to incapacitate victims of sexual assault. Along with another club drug, Rohypnol (known most commonly as roofies), GHB is often called a date rape drug. Both Rohypnol and GHB have been implicated in date rape cases.

In higher doses, GHB has powerful tranquilizing effects that can cause a person to pass out. It makes that person more vulnerable to attack by incapacitating him or her. Even though GHB has a slightly salty taste, it can go undetected when mixed into a drink.

Between 1996 and 2001, the U.S. Drug Enforcement Administration (DEA) received reports of at least 15 sexual assault cases believed to involve GHB. Prosecuting rape cases that may involve GHB are particularly difficult because the drug causes memory loss in the victim, an effect called retrograde amnesia. GHB also moves so quickly through the body that it often is not detectable in blood or urine tests by the time the person arrives at a hospital.

In 1996, the Drug-Induced Rape Prevention and Punishment Act made it a felony to give an unsuspecting person a date rape drug with the intent of committing violence, including rape. There are penalties of large fines and up to 20 years in prison for importing or distributing these drugs. Regardless of this law, however, GHB continues to be favored as a date rape drug. As

LAW AND ORDER

On Saturday, January 16, 1999, two high school girls, Samantha Reid and Melanie Sindone, joined three male seniors for a night out. After finding nothing to do, the seniors drove the girls to the apartment of an older friend in Grosse Isle, Michigan.

There, in what they say was an attempt to liven the party, the young men slipped either GHB or the chemically related GBL into Reid's soft drink and Sindone's alcoholic drink without their knowledge. Within minutes of consuming their drinks, the drug caused both girls to vomit and go into a coma. It wasn't until hours later that they were taken to the hospital. Sindone survived, but her best friend did not. Reid died as a result of vomit blocking air from entering her lungs.

A little more than a year later, the four men were prosecuted in the nation's first GHB-related homicide lawsuit. The three younger men from suburban Detroit, Michigan, Joshua Cole, 19, Daniel Brayman, 19, and Nicholas Holtschlag, 18, were convicted of involuntary manslaughter and two counts each of mixing a harmful substance in a drink. Erick Limmer, 26, was convicted of being an accessory to manslaughter after the fact, mixing a harmful substance in a drink, delivery of marijuana, and possession of GHB.

In March 2000, the three younger men were sentenced to up to 15 years in prison and Limmer was sentenced to up to five years in prison. It is possible that they will all be released within about five years.

The case was watched closely by authorities, and in response to public outcry over Samantha Reid's death, Congress banned the substance in April 2000. At the same time, President Clinton signed the Hillary J. Farias and Samantha Reid Date Rape Drug Prohibition Act into law. The law also commemorates Farias, a 17-year-old high-school senior from La Porte, Texas, who died from a GHB overdose after someone slipped it into her soda.

reported by authorities, date rape cases involving GHB are on the rise.

It is possible to reduce the risk of being a victim of date rape drugs like GHB. Protective measures include:

• Never put a drink down and leave it unattended.

• Never drink from a container opened by someone else.

• Do not drink from a communal container such as a punch bowl.

• Do not accept a drink of any sort from someone else.

• Attend parties with friends and watch out for one another.

Additionally, authorities suggest avoiding parties where people are drinking alcohol since GHB and other date rape drugs may be more likely to be available at these events.

CHEMICAL/ORGANIC COMPOSITION

GHB is a natural substance produced in small amounts in the human body. The active ingredient in GHB is a sodium salt known as sodium oxybate, which has a number of other chemical names.

GHB is believed to be a weak partial activator of gamma-aminobutyric acid (GABA-A) receptor (a specialized cell or group of nerve endings that responds to sensory stimuli). The receptor has binding sites present in areas of the brain, including the cortex, hypothalamus, midbrain, basal ganglia, substantia nigra, and the hippocampus.

It may not be possible to detect GHB and related compounds with common urine or serum (body fluid) tests. In cases where an unused portion of the drug cannot be recovered, gas chromatography-mass spectrometry (a high-technology instrument that separates a chemical mixture and identifies its composition) can be used to detect GHB and related compounds from a sample of serum, plasma, blood, or urine.

In its naturally occurring, biological composition, GHB is not readily available. However, GHB can be made in unsophisticated home laboratories from easily obtained materials. By combining gamma butyrolactone (GBL) with either sodium hydroxide or potassium hydroxide, the chemicals give off heat as they react, creating the final product. GHB is a clear liquid that does not have to be isolated or separated from the solution. Some companies sell kits over the Internet that provide the customer with everything needed to manufacture GHB, and include how-to instructions. Selling kits created for the purpose of producing recreational GHB is illegal, however, as is purchasing such kits.

Precursors of GHB

GHB precursors, or analogs (similar chemical compounds also known as "chemical cousins"), were the legal way for users to achieve effects physiologically equivalent to GHB. Then, in February 2000, federal legislation made the GHB precursors controlled substances.

Jennifer Granholm, Michigan Attorney General, holds up a GHB processing kit that may be obtained over the Internet. It contains sodium hydroxide or potassium hydroxide, GBL, and litmus paper. Photo by AP/Wide World Photos. Reproduced by permission.

However, ready availability of the precursors has made it very difficult to enforce the law.

Chemicals related to GHB may be listed as party drugs on the Internet, advertised in muscle-building magazines, or sold as dietary supplements in health food stores. A number of chemicals that convert to GHB after ingestion has been identified in scientific papers.

Two of the most potentially deadly precursors of GHB, both of which are converted into GHB in the body, have been identified by the FDA. One is gamma butyrolactone (GBL), which is marketed under brand names such as Renewtrient, Revivarant or Revivarant G, Blue Nitro or Blue Nitro Vitality, GH Revitalizer, Gamma G, and Reinforce. The other is 1,4 butanediol (BD), a chemical in products sold under brand names like Revitalize Plus, Serenity, Enliven, GHRE, Somato-Pro, NRG3, Thunder Nectar, and Weight Belt Cleaner.

Gamma butyrolactone (GBL). GBL is a widely used chemical solvent, and one of the more readily available analogues of GHB because it is used in many industrial cleaners. While GBL is not intended for use as a drug, because it converts into GHB inside the body when ingested, it is commonly sold illegally as GHB.

Some partygoers purposely drink small quantities of GBL straight since it is converted into GHB in the stomach. This can cause a severe physical reaction, usually violent vomiting of the fluid. But, as with GHB, GBL can be added to water and is nearly undetectable.

GBL has been marketed as a health supplement as well. However, these products, including Renewtrient, Longevity, Revivarant, Blue Nitro, Insom-X, Remforce, Firewater, and Invigorate, were removed from the market. Many, though, have been re-introduced under new names, utilizing 1,4 butanediol (BD) as a replacement for GBL, which became a List I chemical in February 2000.

1,4 butanediol (BD). The chemical BD has also become part of the recreational drug scene. BD, which is related to both GHB and GBL, also converts to GHB when ingested. BD is also widely available since it is used in making plastics and as an industrial degreaser. As of 2001, BD was not scheduled under federal guidelines, though it has been declared a Class I health hazard.

Potency

The purity and strength of GHB are difficult to determine because the drug can be made from a number of chemical formulas that produce different amounts of GHB when the user's body metabolizes it. The fact that the drug is typically made in home laboratories increases its unpredictability, according to the DEA. A teaspoon of the drug may contain between 0.5 g and 5 g of GHB.

The dose response curve for GHB is varied. A small increase in dose can push the sedative effects to a lethal level. A high dose of GHB can inhibit the body's ability to eliminate the drug, leading to greater effects or longer duration than expected.

As little as one teaspoon of GHB can result in an overdose, which can cause slowed heart rate, confusion, agitation, respiratory depression, seizures, loss of peripheral (outer) vision, agitation, hallucinations, hypothermia (low body temperature), nausea, vomiting, coma, and unconsciousness. The risk of a deadly overdose is increased if both coma and vomiting or coma and a blocked airway occur.

The Drug Enforcement Administration (DEA) warns that GHB is unpredictable, making it a particularly dangerous drug to consume. A dose that might make a small woman high could kill a large man. Or, a person can get high one day while an equal dose another day might prove fatal for that same person.

Effects of long-term GHB use are largely unknown. Individuals who use GHB, however, have reported that they must increase dosage in order to maintain the desired euphoric and relaxing effects.

INGESTION METHODS

GHB is produced in either a liquid form or as a white powdered material. It is taken orally, typically combined with a liquid mixer such as a soft drink, water, or sports drink. It is sometimes mixed with alcohol. It may be sold in small vials at club parties.

GHB usually has a salty taste, but this saltiness can go unrecognized, especially if it is mixed with a sweet drink. Because the taste can be masked, and it is colorless, the risk for accidental ingestion of GHB increases. The drug can be slipped into a drink without the recipient's knowledge.

THERAPEUTIC USE

Although GHB was initially developed as an anesthetic, it was never ultimately used in the United States for that purpose. Outside of the United States, however, GHB is still occasionally used for anesthesia, resuscitation, and addiction therapy.

During the 1990s, a U.S. pharmaceutical company Orphan Medical, Inc. began exploring the use of GHB as a therapeutic solution for narcolepsy, a chronic condition that causes excessive daytime sleepiness.

When President Clinton signed the Hillary J. Farias and Samantha Reid Date Rape Drug Prohibition Act into law in 2000, he ordered the DEA to categorize GHB as a dangerous drug with no medical benefits. However, he also allowed Orphan Medical an exemption to continue its research on therapeutic uses for the compound and to market it for narcolepsy if it was approved by the FDA.

Preliminary studies suggest that GHB-based drugs may also be useful in treating Alzheimer's disease or Parkinson's disease, but it is still too early to tell. Two European studies found GHB effective in relieving alcohol craving and alcohol withdrawal symptoms. In one study, alcoholics took a moderated daily dose for three months. Participants reduced their drinking by half, and their days of abstinence tripled. Another study found that GHB relieved opiate withdrawal symptoms.

USAGE TRENDS

Scope and severity

Little data is available on the relatively new issue of GHB abuse. The government has only been tracking GHB use since it was declared illegal in March 2000. Additionally, GHB abuse is difficult to monitor because the drug is usually clandestinely manufactured. Also, GHB use often goes undetected since there is no simple diagnostic test that can be used by hospital emergency departments.

IN THE NEWS

While GHB is generally viewed as a dangerous drug, under controlled circumstances it may have therapeutic effects for people with specific disorders. In recent years, one U.S. pharmaceutical company has pursued GHB as a possible treatment for the severe, chronic sleep disorder called narcolepsy.

The company, Orphan Medical Inc., began exploring the use of GHB as a solution for narcolepsy in the 1990s. When GHB was classified in 2000 as a dangerous drug with no medical benefits, Orphan Medical received an exemption to pursue research on its use for treating narcolepsy.

With no effective treatment for narcolepsy currently available, the approximately 100,000 to 125,000 people in the United States afflicted with the often debilitating disease are eager for this research to yield a therapeutic drug. Narcolepsy causes excessive daytime sleepiness often accompanied by cataplexy, a sudden loss of muscle tone in response to strong emotions. Cataplexy can cause a person to collapse unexpectedly during waking hours.

In 2001, Orphan Medical filed a new drug application with the FDA for a drug called Xyrem (sodium oxybate, oral solution), which uses GHB as the active ingredient. In clinical trials, Xyrem has been shown to reduce cataplexy and restore normal sleep patterns. If approved, Xyrem would be the only treatment approved by the FDA as effective in managing cataplexy in people with narcolepsy.

An FDA Advisory Committee gave majority approval of Xyrem's ability to treat cataplexy in late 2001, although the committee was split regarding the drug's safety. It voted overwhelmingly in support of the need for a risk management plan for the safe use of Xyrem, as Orphan Medical had recommended.

Some fear exists regarding the abuse of Xyrem, and about how to control distribution in the age of the Internet and on-line pharmacies. Orphan Medical is working with the government to develop a distribution scheme to control prescriptions of Xyrem and limit its use to treat narcolepsy.

However, it has been reported that abuse of GHB has increased substantially since the late 1980s. Young people often abuse GHB and other club drugs in club settings such as raves, nightclubs, bars, and parties. Companies have marketed GHB as a strength-training aid and antidepressant. Body builders claim they use GHB because it stimulates the release of growth hormones and builds muscle. Individuals who have trouble sleeping may take it as a sedative. Alcoholics may take GHB in an attempt to eliminate alcohol cravings; this use is not medically approved in the United States.

There are no definitive numbers available on GHB abuse and overdoses, but various agencies have started tracking this information. The DEA reports more than 7,100 GHB overdoses and encounters with law enforcement between 1990 and 2001. Over that same time period, 65 GHB-related deaths, mainly from respiratory depression, have been documented. The Drug Abuse Warning Network (DAWN) listed 20 emergency room episodes in 1992, and the number of episodes has climbed steadily since then to 2,973 in 1999. That number leaped to 4,969 in 2000.

Official reports are believed to under-represent problems associated with GHB use because many doctors are not yet familiar with it and may not know to test for it. Also, emergency rooms are often unable to detect or identify the drug because it leaves the body within 12 hours. In 2001, the National Institute on Drug Abuse (NIDA) announced that, through its GHB Antidote Initiative, it was beginning the process of developing a treatment for GHB poisoning.

GHB use is particularly high in urban areas, although its use is growing in suburban settings throughout the country as well. GHB is mainly known today as a club drug, but is gaining a reputation as a date rape drug. As of 2001, the DEA documented 15 sexual assault cases involving 30 victims under the influence of GHB. Of urine samples submitted from 711 victims of alleged sexual assault, 48 tested positive for GHB.

Additionally, GHB and its precursors are used by body builders as an alternative to anabolic steroids. The drug has been marketed for its alleged ability to release large amounts of "natural" human growth hormone during sleep, build muscle, and reduce fat.

Age, ethnic, and gender trends

GHB is most popular with high school and college students, as it is found most frequently at late-night dance parties, college parties, and nightclubs where attendees are typically between the ages of 18 and 29. But GHB use cuts across all boundaries.

More than 60% of people hospitalized for GHB use were between the ages of 18 and 25 years old. Of the 63 documented deaths attributed to GHB since 1995, 40%

Defendants, from left, Nicholas Holtschlag, Erick Limmer, Daniel Brayman, and Joshua Cole stand trial in a Detroit courtroom for the January 1999 poisoning death of Samantha Reid. Reid died after a soft drink she was consuming at a party was apparently spiked with the drug GHB. AP Photo/Paul Warner. Reproduced by permission.

were between the ages of 15 and 24 years old and an additional 29% were between 25 and 29 years old.

A 1999 DAWN report lists 267 emergency department mentions of GHB in patients aged 17 years old and younger, 1,498 mentions of use by patients aged 18–25, 905 mentions by patients aged 26–34, and 299 mentions by patients aged 35 and older.

GHB seems to be most popular among whites; however data show that its use expands to other races and ethnicities. In 1999, the number of emergency department mentions of GHB use included those by 2,297 white patients, 76 mentions by black patients, 52 mentions by Hispanic patients, and 548 mentions by other or unknown ethnicities of patients.

Gender does not seem to play a role in GHB use.

MENTAL EFFECTS

GHB can significantly affect the behavior of a person under the influence of the drug. It can cause confusion, aggressive behavior, and impaired judgment. People under the influence of GHB may be less aware of their surroundings, and they may be unable to fully control or protect themselves.

At lower doses, GHB may cause headache, euphoria, an out-of-body high, sleepiness, increased sex drive, hallucinations, and short-term amnesia (loss of memory). In higher doses, it can induce a coma and seizure-like episodes.

PHYSIOLOGICAL EFFECTS

Besides the mental effects, GHB affects the body in a wide range of other ways, including:

- Neurological system: nystagmus (involuntary, rapid eye movement); vertigo (a false sensation of motion or spinning); dizziness; ataxia (poor muscle coordination); weakness; and sedation.

- Respiratory system: respiratory depression; hypothermia; bradycardia with increases or decreases in blood pressure; apnea (cessation of breathing that is usually temporary).

- Gastrointestinal system: vomiting.

- Endocrine system: mild hyperglycemia (abnormally high concentration of sugar in the blood).

Harmful side effects

GHB can be harmful and even deadly to people who use it. But it may mistakenly be perceived as a safe drug because it was only recently made illegal. Also, it was previously available in health food stores as a dietary supplement, is marketed over the Internet, and is prescribed for limited medical use.

For those who take GHB deliberately, the objective is to take the right amount to achieve the desired high. But the drug is unpredictable and users risk deadly overdose, which can occur within 15 minutes of ingestion. An overdose can result in such severe adverse effects as vomiting, difficulty breathing, seizures (especially when GHB is combined with methamphetamine), unconsciousness, coma (especially when combined with alcohol), and death.

The danger of a fatal overdose is increased when GHB is combined with alcohol or opiates.

Long-term health effects

The long-term effects of GHB use are largely unknown. Recent research shows that some club drugs can have lasting effects on the brain, resulting in memory loss, impaired motor skills, and distorted sensations. It is possible that GHB may cause these long-term effects as well.

Repeated GHB use is associated with mood swings, liver tumors, violent behavior, and dependence. If the drug is discontinued, the user can experience withdrawal. Severe withdrawal symptoms include extreme agitation, delirium, insomnia, tremor, rapid heart rate, and anxiety.

REACTIONS WITH OTHER DRUGS OR SUBSTANCES

The danger of taking GHB is increased when the user also takes other drugs. Taking any combination of drugs is always risky because the effect of each drug is amplified and unpredictable. This is particularly true with GHB. Combining GHB with another drug may increase the chance of fatality. Many of the deaths associated with GHB use occurred in individuals who also consumed alcohol or other drugs that depress the central nervous system, such as codeine, heroin, methadone, morphine, barbiturates, nicotine, tranquilizers, and some sleeping pills. Mixing GHB with a central nervous system depressant increases the risk of unconsciousness and coma.

GHB is also sometimes combined with a stimulant drug such as methamphetamine or ecstasy. This combination increases the risk of seizure.

TREATMENT AND REHABILITATION

Overdose treatment

When an overdose is suspected, immediate hospitalization is recommended. If rescue therapy is delayed, incorrectly administered, or is not available, the result may be anoxic injury (lack of oxygen to the brain, which can cause brain damage) or death.

For simple GHB ingestion in a spontaneously breathing patient, intubation (insertion of tube into the trachea) may not be necessary. In these cases, management may include positioning the body to reduce the risk of choking, oxygen supplementation, monitoring, stimulation, treatment for persistent bradycardia (abnormal slowness of the heart), and admission to the hospital for observation.

Intubation is only recommended for severe respiratory depression, hypoxia, or a combination toxic exposure. Coma reversal agents are considered to be of little or no use. Recovery of consciousness generally takes two to six hours.

There is no definitive treatment to counteract the effects of GHB, although two drugs, neostigmine and physostigmine, have shown promise as potential reversal agents. If supportive medical care is delivered in a timely manner, the patient will usually recover several hours post-ingestion.

If evidence of GHB ingestion cannot be confirmed, other causes for the patient's altered mental status must be ruled out. Physicians or others providing care in a medical setting should be aware of the possibility that GHB was co-ingested with other drugs, and treat the patient accordingly.

If it is suspected that GHB intake was combined with another drug, the stomach should be pumped (gastric lavage), and activated charcoal may be considered. In the case of isolated GHB ingestion, however, these interventions are of limited value because GBH is absorbed quite rapidly and only small amounts of the drug are usually involved.

Withdrawal treatment

While the addictive potential of GHB is not yet known, individuals who use GHB have reported that they must steadily increase dosage to achieve the desired effects. Some people who abuse GHB have reported difficulty reducing or discontinuing use.

But since GHB is rapidly absorbed by the body and eliminated within 12 hours, GHB dependence is rare. Frequent dosing every one to three hours is required to maintain levels sufficient for dependence, according to a report in the medical journal *American Family Physician*. The report concludes that GHB withdrawal syndrome is becoming increasingly common as the accessibility and use of GHB-related products increases. Discontinuation of GHB after long-term use can cause prolonged illness, typically lasting three to 12 days.

The withdrawal syndrome occurs over several days, starting with mild effects that may include tachycardia (rapid heart beat), hypertension (high blood pressure), tremor, and diaphoresis (heavy perspiration). Additional symptoms may include hallucinations and anxiety, as well as confusion, insomnia, disorientation, delirium with agitation, and combative behavior, which often requires restraints and sedation.

As the withdrawal progresses, symptoms can become episodic, ranging unpredictably from mild to severe. Treatment typically focuses on providing support and managing symptoms, such as sedation with benzodiazepines and barbituates. In-patient hospitalization is recommended for detoxification.

The diagnosis of GHB withdrawal may be difficult because it is similar to sedative or alcohol withdrawal syndromes, as well as to withdrawal from sympathomimetic agents such as cocaine, methamphetamine, and ecstasy. GHB withdrawal may also be confused with serotonin syndrome (a reaction caused by a combination of drugs, one of which increases serotonin levels in the body, such as Prozac) and neuroleptic malignant syndrome (a rare reaction to an antiseizure medication).

PERSONAL AND SOCIAL CONSEQUENCES

Use of GHB can impair judgment and cause short-term (retrograde) amnesia, increasing the possibility for risky behavior and sexual assault. It also impairs ability to drive, increasing the risk for a car accident. If use is long term, the abuser risks unknown health consequences and, if use is discontinued, the abuser is subject to potential withdrawal illness.

When GHB use is suspected or discovered, physicians and other hospital staff may counsel patients about the dangers of GHB use. They may make a referral to a rehabilitation program. As with any other drug, the physician should inquire about the possibility of the abuse of multiple drugs.

To truly restrict GHB use, experts emphasize that public education is needed to supplement legal actions. In an effort to teach people the dangers of GHB and other club drugs, the NIDA has launched a national educational campaign with partner organizations Join Together, National Families in Action, the American Academy of Child and Adolescent Psychiatry, and the Community Anti-Drug Coalitions of America.

LEGAL CONSEQUENCES

Legislation

On February 18, 2000, the Hillary Farias and Samantha Reed Date-Rape Prohibition Act (Public Law 106-172) made the GHB precursor GBL a List I chemical, subject to the criminal, civil, and administrative sanctions of the Controlled Substances Act. On March 13, 2000, GHB became a Schedule I controlled substance (65 FR 13235-13238), subject to the regulatory controls and the criminal, civil, and administrative sanctions of the Controlled Substances Act. Schedule I, which is the same as for heroin, LSD, and marijuana, states that the drug has no medical use and cannot be prescribed, and that the drug has a high potential for abuse.

Previously, the Drug-Induced Rape Prevention and Punishment Act of 1996 had made it a felony to give an unsuspecting person a date rape drug—a category that includes GHB—with the intent of committing violence, including rape. In February 2001, legislators in Pennsylvania strengthened analog statutes to include chemicals substantially similar in substance or effect. The action is intended to further combat the use of GHB precursors like GBL and BD.

GHB was first made illegal in 1990, when several reports of adverse reactions in individuals using nutritional and weight loss supplements containing GHB led the FDA to ban the drug. This ban made GHB use illicit except under FDA-approved, physician-supervised protocols.

GHB remains legal in many countries in Europe, Central, and South America, and elsewhere.

Legal history

Until 1990, when it was declared illegal except for approved medical use, GHB use was legal in the United States, and it was typically sold at health food stores. Numerous cases of illness related to GHB led the federal government to declare its use, manufacture, and distribution illegal.

The first known court case involving GHB use occurred in May 1990, after a teenager in Duluth, Georgia, drank a mixture of water and two teaspoons of Somatomax PM obtained from a health food store. Within 20 minutes, the teen was in a coma; his parents took him to the hospital for emergency treatment, where he recovered. Hospital physicians told the parents that if their son had been found a half hour later, he might have died. When the parents reported the incident to the FDA, the agency launched an investigation that uncovered 57 more cases of GHB-related illness and prompted wide-scale prosecution of GHB sale and misuse.

In March 1991, the FDA and the U.S. Department of Justice indicted the operators of Amino Discounters Ltd. on criminal charges of making, distributing, and promoting GHB. Amino Discounters manufactured and distributed the drug, sold under the brand name Somatomax PM. The indictment charged the firm and the individuals involved with counts of operating an unregistered drug firm, selling misbranded drugs in interstate commerce, and manufacturing misbranded drugs. The individuals pleaded guilty and were convicted.

In a separate indictment in San Francisco, a grand jury named the operators of a company called California Body Club, in San Leandro and Carmel, California, with illegal distribution of GHB obtained from Amino Discounters. The indictment charged the company with promoting, selling, and shipping GHB, and also with distributing drugs with false and misleading labels. The operators pleaded guilty and were sentenced to in-home detention, probation, and community service.

Since these initial cases, laws against GHB have been tightened and the government has increased efforts to prosecute illegal distributors and users of GHB and its precursors.

Federal guidelines, regulations, and penalties

GHB is a Schedule I controlled substance according to the Controlled Substances Act. As such, it is unlawful for any person knowingly or intentionally to manufacture, distribute, or dispense GHB, or to possess with intent to manufacture, distribute, or dispense GHB. The penalty for manufacturing or distribution of GHB includes sentencing individuals to 20 or more years in jail and a large fine.

It is also unlawful for any person to knowingly or intentionally possess GHB. Any person who violates this law may be sentenced to not more than one year in jail, fined a minimum of $1,000, or both. Repeated offenses may result in greater penalties.

GHB is also officially classified as a date rape drug, a classification intended to establish the basis for harsher penalties under federal law if the distribution facilitates a violent crime. The Drug-Induced Rape Prevention and Punishment Act of 1996 makes it a felony to give an unsuspecting person a date rape drug with the intent of committing violence, including rape. The law also imposes penalties of large fines and up to 20 years in prison for importing or distributing more than one gram of these drugs, which include GHB.

See also Ecstasy (MDMA); GBL; Rohypnol

RESOURCES

Books

National Institutes of Health. National Institute on Drug Abuse. "Epidemiologic Trends in Drug Abuse Advance Report." December 2000.

Periodicals

Cohen, J. S. "Lethal Cocktail: The Tragedy and the Aftermath of GHB (Special Report)." *Detroit News.* <http://www.detnews.com/specialreports/1999/ghb>.

"GHB: Its Use and Misuse." *Harvard Mental Health Letter* 17 (March 2001): 7-8.

Li, J., S. A. Stokes, and A. Woeckener. "A Tale of Novel Intoxication: A Review of the Effects of Gamma-Hydroxybutyric Acid with Recommendations for Management." *Annals of Emergency Medicine* 31 (1998): 729-36.

Nicholson, K. L., and R. L. Balster. "GHB: A New and Novel Drug of Abuse (Review)." *Drug and Alcohol Dependence* 63 (June 1, 2001): 1-22.

Nordenberg, T. "The Death of the Party." *FDA Consumer* 34 (March-April 2000): 14-22.

O'Connell, T. "Gamma-Hydroxybutyrate (GHB): A Newer Drug of Abuse." *American Family Physician* 62 (December 1, 2000): 2478-83.

Sadovsky, R. "Gamma-Hydroxybutyrate and Withdrawal Syndrome." *American Family Physician* 64 (September, 15, 2001): 1059-60.

Taylor, C. "Turning a Bad Drug Good." *New York Times Magazine* 151 (December 9, 2001): 105+.

Winickoff, J. P., et al. "Verve and Jolt: Deadly New Internet Drugs." *Pediatrics* 106 (October 2000): 829-30.

Zvosec, D. L., et al. "Adverse Events, including Death, Associated with the Use of 1, 4-Butanediol." *New England Journal of Medicine* 344 (January 11, 2001): 87-95.

Other

U.S. Department of Health and Human Services. National Institute on Drug Abuse. *Club Drugs: Community Drug Alert Bulletin.* December 1999.

U.S. Department of Health and Human Services. Substance Abuse and Mental Health Statistics. Drug Alert Warning Network. "The DAWN Report: Club Drugs (December 2000)." <http://www.samhsa.gov/oas/dawn.htm>.

U.S. Department of Justice. Drug Enforcement Agency. "Drugs of Concern: Gamma Hydroxybutyrate (GHB)." <http://www.usdoj.gov:80/dea/concern/ghb.htm>.

U.S. Drug Enforcement Administration. "DEA Press Release Fact Sheet: Gamma Hydroxybutyric Acid, March 13, 2000." <http://www.usdoj.gov/dea/pubs/pressrel/pr031300_01.htm>.

White House Office of National Drug Control Policy. "Drug Facts: Club Drugs, 2001." <http://whitehousedrugpolicy.gov/drugfact/club>.

Whitten, L. "Conference Highlights Increasing GHB Abuse." *NIDA Notes* 16 (May 2001). <http://165.112.78.61/NIDA_Notes/NNVol16N2/Conference.html>.

Organizations

National Institute on Drug Abuse (NIDA), National Institutes of Health, 6001 Executive Boulevard, Room 5213, Bethesda, MD, USA, 20892-9561, (301) 443-1124, (888) 644-6432, information@lists.nida.nih.gov, <http://www.nida.nih.gov>.

U.S. Drug Enforcement Administration, 2401 Jefferson Davis Highway, Alexandria, VA, USA, 22301, (800) 882-9539, <http://www.usdoj.gov/dea>.

U.S. Food and Drug Administration (FDA), 5600 Fishers Lane, Rockville, MD, USA, 20857-0001, (888) 463-6332, <http://www.fda.gov>.

Jennifer F. Wilson

HERBAL DRUGS

OFFICIAL NAMES: Botanicals, nutraceuticals, phytophar-maceuticals, dietary supplements, natural supplements
STREET NAMES: Ginseng (*Panax ginseng*), echinacea (*Echinacea purpurea*), ginkgo (*Ginkgo biloba*), garlic (*Allium sativum*), saw palmetto (*Serenoa repens*), St. John's wort (*Hypericum perforatum*). St. John's wort is also known as hard-hay, amber, goatweed, Klamath weed, and Tipton weed. Garlic supplements are Garlix, Gar-Pure, and Cardiomax.
DRUG CLASSIFICATIONS: Not scheduled, dietary supplements

OVERVIEW

Herbal drugs are made from the roots, stems, leaves, bark, fruit, seeds, or flowers of various plants known or believed to have medicinal properties. Many conventional drugs are also derived from plants. In fact, the word "drug" comes from the French word *drogue*, meaning "dried herb."

Herbal and conventional drugs differ significantly, however. When a conventional drug is derived from a plant, this drug is a purified form of the specific substance in the plant that is proven to have a beneficial medical effect. This substance, called the active ingredient, is delivered to the patient in a precise amount, or dose. Herbal drugs, in contrast, are made up of all the other substances and chemicals in the plant, in addition to any active ingredient they might contain. Sometimes, manufacturers of an herbal drug aren't sure which substance in the plant is the active ingredient, or how much active ingredient their herbal product delivers. Even when the active ingredient is known, the amount of it can vary widely—as much as 10,000-fold—between products made by different manufacturers.

Because herbal drugs are not regulated as drugs by the FDA, they don't have to undergo the rigorous testing that conventional drugs must undergo before they are marketed. The manufacturers of conventional drugs must prove the safety and efficacy of their products to the FDA before the FDA approves their use. This proof comes in the form of extensive scientific studies of the drug in animals and in people. With herbal drugs, the situation is reversed: Because herbals are classified as foods, the FDA bears the burden of having to prove an herbal product is unsafe before the agency can take it off the market or restrict its use.

The controversy over herbals

The increasing use of herbal drugs in the United States and Europe during the last decades of the twentieth century has generated considerable controversy. Opponents of herbal drugs point to the lack of conclusive scientific evidence that these substances are safe and effective. They warn about the lack of standards in manufacturing that have led to toxic and sometimes fatal side effects and adverse reactions, and they call for more strict regulation of their sale and use. Proponents argue that herbal remedies have been around for thousands of years and so have stood the test of time, and they point to the growing number of scientific studies that seem to indicate that some herbal medicines work. Both sides call for more research to determine which herbal drugs

KEY TERMS

ACTIVE INGREDIENT: The chemical or substance in a compound known or believed to have a therapeutic effect.

CLINICAL TRIAL: A scientific experiment that tests the effect of a drug in humans.

DECOCTION: A tea or soup made from boiling herbs in water.

FLAVONOIDS: Chemical compounds found in many herbal drugs. Flavonoids may help fight off infections and clear the body of harmful free radical molecules.

PATENT MEDICINES: Medical remedies of doubtful value commonly sold in the 1800s and 1900s. Many patent medicines were herb-based, although they were often laced with alcohol, narcotics, and other drugs.

PLACEBO EFFECT: A psychological phenomenon noted by researchers in which patients who receive a phony medication feel better and report improvements in subjective symptoms such as pain or depression.

TINCTURE: An extract of an herb made by soaking it in glycerine, alcohol, or vinegar for several weeks, then straining the liquid.

---

are actually effective and which may be ineffective or even dangerous.

A brief history of herbal medicines

People have long recognized the healing properties of certain plants. Herbal drugs have likely been around as long as humans have. Medicinal herbs were found on the body of an "ice man" frozen in the Swiss Alps for more than 5,000 years. Scientists think the man used these herbs to treat an intestinal disorder.

Many herbal medicines have an ancient history. The ginkgo tree has long been cultivated for medical use in China and Japan, where some of these hardy trees are over 1,000 years old. Chinese herbalists made tea from ginkgo seeds and prescribed the drink for many problems, including memory loss and asthma. In the 1700s, the tree was brought to Europe from China. In the 1950s, the Dr. Willmar Schwabe Company of Germany investigated the properties of the ginkgo leaf for possible medical use, and by 1970, ginkgo became one of the most widely prescribed herbals for dementia and for a type of weakness and pain in the limbs called intermittent claudication. In 1997, the *Journal of the American Medical Association* (JAMA) published a study indicating ginkgo might be useful in treating Alzheimer's disease, sparking interest in the United States.

Before Europeans arrived in America, echinacea was a popular herbal drug among Native Americans, who used it to treat respiratory infections, inflammation of the eyes, toothache, and snakebite. European colonists quickly adopted the herb. In the nineteenth century, European Americans used echinacea as a "blood purifier," believing that it cleared the blood of disease-causing toxins. Europeans used echinacea to treat diseases such as eczema, veneral diseases, lymphangitis (swelling of the lymph vessels), and sepsis (infection of the blood with microorganisms).

Many of the herbal drugs used in the United Sates and Europe are derived from traditional Chinese medicine and Ayurvedic medicine in India. These traditions are thousands of years old, and they rely heavily on plant-based prescriptions to treat various illnesses. Many other herbal drugs are folk remedies from other cultures. Historians of medicine note that every culture has its own tradition of folk medicine: treatments or cures widely believed to be effective, based on information gathered from trial and error on the curative properties of plants and passed down through generations.

Before the advent of modern and synthetic drugs in the nineteenth century, the United States had its own folk medicine tradition. In colonial times, people often relied on homemade botanical remedies based on the folk traditions of their original countries. People also learned about the healing properties of local plants from Native Americans.

As more Europeans came to the Americas and settlements grew into cities, some herbal remedies transformed into "patent medicines," which people could buy at the local store or from traveling salesmen. Packaged in fancy bottles and laced with generous amounts of alcohol, these medicines were of doubtful value, although their labels claimed they could cure everything from the common cold to cancer. One manufacturer of such medicines was H. C. F. Meyer, who in the late 1800s sold combinations of echinacea and other herbs. His outlandish, exaggerated, and poorly written labels helped define the "snake oil salesman" as an American icon.

From herbs to conventional drugs

In the 1800s, doctors, pharmacists, and scientists began to examine herbal remedies more closely. They began to identify the active ingredients in medicinal plants and to isolate and purify those substances. For example, the French pharmacist H. Leroux purified the drug salicin, the precursor of aspirin, from the bark of the willow tree in 1829.

The 1800s saw the transformation of many herbal remedies into conventional drugs. The story about how one herb, foxglove (*Digitalis purpurea*), was transformed into the modern-day cardiac drug digoxin, provides a good example.

In the 1700s, the condition known as dropsy was a common cause of death. (In the twenty-first century, doctors call dropsy congestive heart failure.) Dropsy occurs when the heart is too weak to keep all of the blood moving through the body. The blood accumulates in blood vessels and eventually seeps into surrounding tissues. Dropsy sufferers begin to swell with the excess fluid, and their arms and legs puff up so that they cannot move. Oftentimes, fluid fills the lung cavities and makes it impossible to breathe. Dropsy victims actually drown in their own bodily fluid.

In England, the folk remedy for dropsy was an herbal decoction, or "soup," made from boiling about 20 different plants, including the herb foxglove. In the late 1700s, the English doctor and botanist William Withering, practicing in Stafford, examined this herbal remedy more closely. He recognized that the folk remedy worked, and he systematically tested each plant ingredient on his dropsy patients until he found the one that improved heart function—the leaf of the foxglove plant, also known as digitalis leaf.

Although he had discovered the medicinal properties of foxglove, Withering ran into a big problem: dosage. As he began to treat patients with a decoction of foxglove, he found that the boundary between an effective dose and a fatally poisonous one was dangerously slim. One of Withering's first patients recovered after just a few doses. But another of Withering's patients almost died from the effects of foxglove overdose—continuous vomiting and diarrhea. The dosage problem was complicated by the fact that the foxglove plant varied in potency from plant to plant and in different seasons. Withering would have to use three times as many leaves for his decoction in winter than in summer, when the plant bloomed.

In 1775, Withering began 10 years of experiments with foxglove. He gave dropsy patients small doses of the herb to start with, then gradually increased the dosage until the vomiting and diarrhea started. When that happened, he decreased the dose a little until the side effects disappeared but the beneficial effect on the heart remained. In this way, he was able to roughly determine the correct dosage. In 1785, he published a famous book on the properties of the foxglove plant, *An Account of the Foxglove and Some of Its Medical Uses*. The medical community recognized foxglove as a remedy for congestive heart failure until well into the twentieth century.

However, in the 1800s efforts were under way to purify the active ingredients from herbs and do away with the plant altogether. In 1804, the German pharmacist F.W. Serturner discovered how to isolate the chemical morphine from the poppy plant (*Papaver somniferum*). In 1870, the French researcher C.A. Natvelle used a similar process to purify a substance he called digitalin from the foxglove leaf. This purified substance became the conventional cardiac drugs digoxin and digitoxin.

In the late 1800s and early 1900s, advances in chemistry allowed scientists to further modify the drugs derived from plants to reduce their side effects. Chemists were also able to synthesize in the laboratory entirely new drugs with new beneficial properties. Eventually, it became cheaper and easier to synthesize the substances once derived from plants, rather than extract them from herbs themselves.

As modern, scientific medicine offered a growing number of effective drugs, interest in herbal remedies declined. The first edition of the *United States Pharmacopoeia*, a drug compendium published in 1820, listed about 200 plants recognized as drugs. These included hops (*Humulus lupulus*), licorice (*Glycyrrhiza glabra*), peppermint (*Mentha piperita*), senna (*Cassia senna*), and valerian root (*Valeriana officinalis*). But by 1936, the *Pharmacopoeia* listed on only 79 herbal drugs.

In the 1960s, however, a popular interest in alternative and complementary medicine sprang up in the United States and Europe. This growing interest in alternative medicine, which includes use of herbal drugs, has continued into the twenty-first century. Historians, public health experts, and cultural commentators are not sure why alternative medicine has become so popular, but they point to several factors that likely influenced this cultural shift.

First, the cost of health care has been rising, and people have grown dissatisfied with managed care, which has resulted in people spending less time with their doctors. Second, people have been concerned about the safety of synthetic drugs, especially after the tragedy, beginning in Europe, of birth defects caused by the drug thalidomide. Third, many people have conditions for which conventional medicine has produced no satisfactory cure, such as certain cancers, back pain, and arthritis. Disillusioned with scientific medicine and desperate for relief, these people have turned to alternative therapies such as herbal drugs. Finally, the cultural emphasis on health and wellness, self-reliance, and a renewed focus on all things "natural," has probably led to the increased use of herbal drugs. Kenneth Shine, president of the U.S. Institute of Medicine, has commented that the easy availability of information about herbal drugs on the Internet probably has contributed their increased use.

CHEMICAL/ORGANIC COMPOSITION

The chemical composition of herbal drugs is highly complex and uncertain, especially when compared with conventional drugs. Herbal drugs contain all the chemicals inherent in the plant. Even when the active ingredient in an herbal product is known (or suspected), it is difficult for manufacturers to standardize how much active ingredient their product contains. The potency of herbal drugs is affected by growing conditions, storage, handling, and the manufacturing process used. For example, one manufacturer might grind plants up and put them into pill form, while another might prepare an extract from the plant. The consumer protection-focused magazine *Consumer Reports* examined the composition of herbals and found that the potency of products based on the same plant varied as much as 10,000 fold.

Herbal products do not always contain the plant they are supposed to contain. In an apparent case of mistaken identity, the Chinese herbal slimming aid *"Fangji"* was replaced by *"Guang fangji"* and distributed in Germany and France. The highly toxic *Guang fangji* caused several cases of a kidney disease known as fibrosing interstitial nephritis. Producers of herbals have also cut costs by padding their product with related but cheaper plants. Because of the high cost of pure ginseng, some products labeled as ginseng are supplemented with mandrake or snakeroot.

Herbal drugs may contain additives not listed on the label, and these additives are sometimes the source of the "herbal" medicine's effect. Investigations by *Consumer Reports* and others have shown herbal products to contain aspirin, caffeine, steroids, non-steroidal anti-inflammatory drugs, antibiotics, sedatives, and even narcotics.

Finally, herbal products imported from China may be contaminated with pesticides or with heavy metals added during the manufacturing process. Contaminated Chinese herbals have led to cases of arsenic, lead, mercury, thallium, and cadmium poisoning. Similarly, investigations of traditional Indian Ayurvedic remedies have shown them to sometimes contain dangerous levels of lead, zinc, mercury, arsenic, aluminum, and tin.

Flavonoids: an active ingredient in many herbals

Many medicinal plants contain chemical compounds called flavonoids. Some evidence suggests that flavonoids, also called bioflavonoids, can have beneficial effects on the body. Flavonoids may be able to help ward off bacteria and viruses and reduce inflammation. They may also be antioxidants, which are molecules that clear the body of harmful chemicals called oxygen free radicals. (Oxygen free radicals are highly reactive molecules that damage cells and have been associated with diseases such as cancer, diabetes, and cardiovascular disease.)

Flavonoids concentrate in the seeds, bark, flowers, or fruit of most plants. The herbal remedy green tea (*Camellia sinensis*), which is used for stomach disorders, contains about 30% flavonoids by weight. Apples and onions, which are listed in the *Physicians' Desk Reference for Herbal Medicines* (*PDR-HM*), also contain high amounts of flavonoids.

Flavonoids are divided into many classes and subclasses, each with a slightly different chemical structure and function. Classes of flavonoids include flavanols, flavanones, catechins, anthocyanins, and isoflavones.

Subclasses of flavonoids include genistein, found in soy, and quercetin, found in onions.

INGESTION METHODS

Herbal drugs are taken in a variety of ways. A person looking for ginseng in a health foods store would find ginseng tablets, ginseng capsules, a liquid ginseng extract, dried ginseng root, ginseng gum, and possibly even ginseng cigarettes. Another popular way to take herbal drugs is to make a tea from the dried leaves, roots, or flowers of the plant. Many herbals come in an ointment form, which people apply topically (to the skin) to treat wounds, burns, or skin conditions such as eczema. Following are come common ways herbal medicines are prepared and taken:

A *decoction* is a tea made from boiling the bark, roots, or other woody parts of the plant in water.

An *infusion* is a tea made by pouring hot water over the dried leaves, flowers, or fruit of the plant and allowing it to steep. The water is usually boiling, but some infusions use cold water.

A *tincture* is an extract of the plant made by soaking herbs in glycerine, alcohol, or vinegar for several weeks. The liquid is strained from the plant and can be used therapeutically by adding it to hot water or other beverages. Tinctures can also be taken by the spoonful like other medicines.

A *liniment* is an extract of an herb added to either alcohol or vinegar and applied to the skin.

A *poultice* is a soft, moist mass of plant material, often crushed or bruised, which has been wrapped in a fine woven cloth. People apply poultices to burns, wounds, or other skin damage or disease.

THERAPEUTIC USE

The potential therapeutic effects of herbal drugs have not been extensively tested or conclusively proven. However, scientific study of herbals is under way in the United States and abroad, and many herbs may well prove to be useful. The results of initial studies on many herbals, such as saw palmetto and St. John's wort, are promising.

Because herbal medicines are not classified as drugs by the FDA, the manufacturers of herbals cannot make claims that their product is effective at treating any disease or disorder. They can, however, make more general health claims. For example, companies that sell St. John's wort cannot say their product is useful for treating depression or anxiety, but they can say St. John's wort "helps support a healthy emotional balance" or "helps maintain a positive attitude."

Despite the lack of conclusive evidence on their effectiveness, herbal drugs are widely believed to be useful in treating a variety of conditions, both common and unusual, and mild and serious. Common conditions for which people take herbal drugs include colds and flu, muscular aches and pains, acne, indigestion, constipation, coughs, corns, menstrual cramps, dandruff, diarrhea, fatigue, flatulence, frostbite, warts, hair loss, headaches, heartburn, insect bites, lice, motion sickness, nausea, insomnia, dizziness, and warts. (The *PDR-HM* lists 25 herbal medicines used to relieve flatulence.)

More serious conditions for which people take herbal drugs include depression, irregular heartbeat and other heart problems, arthritis, arteriosclerosis (hardening of the arteries), asthma, high blood pressure, various cancers, diabetes, epilepsy, gallstones, sexually transmitted diseases, hepatitis, jaundice, malaria, measles, obesity, tetanus, tuberculosis, and ulcers.

As popular interest in herbal medicines grows, scientists have been conducting more clinical trials (studies in people) to evaluate herbals' effectiveness at treating particular disorders. One source of reliable, scientific knowledge on herbal drugs is the reports from the German government's herbal watchdog agency, the so-called "Commission E." After reviewing the scientific literature on more than 300 herbals, this commission approved more than 200 and disapproved about 100 for use in Germany. Building upon the work of Commission E, the *PDR-HM*, published in the United States, lists about 600 herbal medicines, and gives an evaluation of the usefulness of each. Another good source is the *Clinical Evaluation of Medicinal Herbs and Other Therapeutic Natural Products,* also published in the United States. This book evaluates and reports on the clinical trials performed on a wide variety of herbs.

Following is a list of popular herbal drugs in the United States, the therapeutic use or uses for which people take them, and what scientists have learned so far about their effectiveness:

- Echinacea. The several varieties of this plant, also called the purple coneflower, are used to strengthen the body's immune system and for both prevention and treatment of colds and flu. Sixteen clinical trials involving over 3,000 patients have produced mixed results. In some of the studies, echinacea reduced the severity and duration of colds and flu. However, the evidence that this herb can actually *prevent* colds and flu is weak at best.

- Garlic. Fresh and dried garlic are used to lower cholesterol and to treat the common cold, coughs, bronchitis, fever, and inflammation of the mouth. Garlic appears to be effective for these uses. Twenty-five clinical trials involving more than 1,000 patients

As popular interest in herbal medicine grows, more food items such as these bags of herbal snacks will be available to consumers. Photo by Ruth Fremson, AP/Wide World Photos. Reproduced by permission.

have tested garlic's cholesterol-lowering properties. Although these studies produced mixed results, they indicate overall that garlic can reduce cholesterol by about 10%. Other uses for which garlic has not been proven effective include treatment of menstrual pain and diabetes.

- Ginkgo. The leaves and seeds of this plant, native to China, Japan, and Korea, are used to improve age-related loss of memory, including the dementia associated with Alzheimer's disease, and to relieve ringing of the ears and a type of pain and weakness in the limbs called intermittent claudication. More than 40 studies involving more than 1,000 patients show that ginkgo has a modest effect on dementia and intermittent claudication, but does not seem to help with memory loss or ringing of the ears.

- Ginseng. The dried roots of this plant, which is native to China, are believed to increase stamina and concentration. Few well-designed, rigorous studies of ginseng have been conducted, and those that have been done found no evidence for ginseng's effectiveness.

- Saw palmetto. The fruit of this plant, indigenous to the southern coastal regions of the United States, is used to relieve urination problems caused by an enlarged prostate gland. Sixteen short-term clinical trials involving approximately 3,000 men indicate that saw palmetto is effective for this use, although long-term trials need to be done to confirm the herb's effectiveness. The herb improves urine flow, although it does not seem to reduce the size of the prostate. In some European countries, saw palmetto is commonly prescribed for men with an enlarged prostate.

- St. John's wort. The dried buds and flowers of this plant are used to treat mild to moderate depression and anxiety. More than 30 well-designed studies involving thousands of patients show the herb works about as well as conventional antidepressants for treating mild to moderate depression.

USAGE TRENDS

Scope and severity

Estimates of herbal drug use in the United States vary, depending on how the researchers define herbal drugs and what types of questions they ask in their surveys. However, all research indicates that the use of herbal drugs grew substantially during the 1980s and 1990s. Sales of herbal drugs increased by as much as 20% per year during these decades, far outpacing sales of conventional drugs. By most estimates, Americans spend more than $1 billion each year on herbal medicines. A report prepared by the *Nutrition Business Journal* estimates that Americans spent more than $4 billion on herbal drugs in 2000.

About 14% of the U.S. population uses herbal drugs or other dietary supplements, according to a telephone survey conducted by the Slone Epidemiology Unit of Boston University. The results of this survey, which asked participants if they had taken an herbal remedy during the past week, were published in a 2002 issue of JAMA.

Another survey published in 2000 yielded a much higher figure for herbal drug use. Forty percent of patients at a health maintenance organization (an HMO) took herbal drugs, according to a survey published in the *Journal of the American Pharmacists Association*. The herbals most frequently used were garlic, aloe, cranberry, and echinacea.

Age, ethnic, and gender trends

According to the Slone survey, middle-aged men and women tend to be the most frequent users of herbal drugs or dietary supplements. However, researchers found that it is mostly young men who take the supplement creatine, which is promoted as a muscle builder. Older men most often took saw palmetto and also the dietary supplement glucosamine, which is believed to

combat arthritis. Older women most commonly took ginkgo.

A survey of 272 college students found that almost half, or 48.5%, reported taking an herbal drug within the past year, according to a study published in the *Journal of American College Health*. Echinacea, ginseng, and St. John's wort were the most popular herbals among these college students, and the study found no significant difference in herbal drug use between males or females, or among students of different ethnic backgrounds.

Elderly Americans take their share of herbal medications, according to a study conducted by the University of Michigan and presented at the 2002 annual meeting of the American Association for Geriatric Psychiatry. This survey of elderly veterans with depression or dementia found that 20% of them were treating themselves with herbal drugs. Of the elderly patients using herbals, 33.3% used ginkgo, 26.7% used St. John's wort, and 20% took other herbs.

Ethnic trends

Because herbal drugs are a relatively new phenomenon, little data exist on differences among ethnic groups in herbal drug use. However, a study published in the *Journal of the American Pharmacists Association* in 2000 concluded that Hispanics used herbal drugs more often than whites, and that Hispanics and whites preferred different methods of taking herbal drugs. After administering a questionnaire to patients age 65 and older at a senior health center, the study's authors determined that 77% of the Hispanics used herbal remedies, as opposed to 47% of the whites. (The overall usage rate was 61%.) In addition, Hispanics preferred herbal teas, while whites most often took their herbals in a capsule or tablet form.

Herbals around the world

Europeans are even more enthusiastic than Americans are about herbals. Europeans spend three times as much on herbal drugs as Americans do. In Germany, two-thirds of the population uses herbal drugs, according to one poll. Herbal medicines make up about 30% of all drugs sold in German pharmacies, and German physicians routinely prescribe these medicines. Part of the reason for the greater acceptance of herbals in Germany is that the German equivalent of the FDA strictly evaluates and regulates herbal products, so consumers feel more confident about using them.

Worldwide, more than 80% of the population uses herbal and folk remedies. In developing countries where many people do not have access to modern health care, traditional folk medicine is the only option.

MENTAL EFFECTS

Many herbal drugs are believed to reduce anxiety and depression The *PDR-HM* lists 47 herbals used to manage anxiety disorders. Of these, St. John's wort and kava (*Piper methysticum*) are popular in the United States, and although they are not proven medicines, preliminary evidence suggests they may be effective.

The active ingredient of St. John's wort is a substance called hyperforin. Like other antidepressants, hyperforin appears to work by helping to restore the proper balance to brain chemistry. In particular, hyperforin helps restore the balance of certain neurotransmitters, or chemical messengers, in the brain. These neurotransmitters include serotonin, norepinephrine, and dopamine.

Kava contains a substance called dihydrokavain, which is a mild sedative and pain reliever. Preliminary research shows that kava reduces nervous anxiety, tension, and agitation, although these effects usually take at least a week, and often a month or more, to set in. Although other anti-anxiety drugs such as benzodiazepines are more effective than kava, the herb does not seem to impair mental functioning or reaction times the way benzodiazepines do.

Some researchers suggest that perhaps the biggest mental effect induced by those herbals that are untested and unproven is the placebo effect: If people believe they are taking an effective medication, their attitude about their illness improves and they feel better, at least initially. In particular, the placebo effect can cause patients to report improvements in subjectively measured symptoms such as pain or depression. That is why many drug studies include a placebo group—patients who receive a dummy pill instead of the drug being tested. That way, researchers can compare the placebo group with the group receiving the drug and determine if the drug in question induces more than the placebo effect.

PHYSIOLOGICAL EFFECTS

Herbal drugs act on the body in a variety of ways. Echinacea may boost the body's immune system and help fight off bacterial and viral infections. Garlic appears to lower levels of cholesterol in the blood. Ginkgo may improve circulation by thinning the blood. The chemical compounds called flavonoids found in many herbal medications may help clear the body of harmful molecules called oxygen free radicals. However, exactly how echinacea, garlic, ginkgo, and other herbal drugs affect the body is still being studied.

Harmful side effects

All drugs, even conventional drugs, may cause toxic side effects in some people, and herbal drugs are no exception. Critics of herbal drugs believe that they carry a greater risk of harmful side effects than conventional drugs do because the lack of manufacturing standards and quality control for herbal drugs leads to uncertainty about their potency. The skeptics cite a long list of documented toxic side effects and even fatalities caused by herbals, and they point to a list of herbal drugs known to cause serious side effects.

Proponents of herbal drugs argue that these medications must be safe because they have been used by countless people for thousands of years. They cite preliminary studies that show that some herbal remedies work as well as conventional drugs and produce fewer side effects. For example, an herbal mixture of fennel, peppermint, and wormwood improved symptoms of abdominal pain more effectively and with fewer side effects than the conventional drug metoclopramide, according to a study published in *Phytomedicine*. And many studies have shown that St. John's wort seems to be as effective as standard antidepressants for mild to moderate depression while carrying a lower risk of side effects.

Following are some herbals known to cause serious side effects:

- Comfrey (*Symphytum officionale*). Ointments made from comfrey are used topically for wound and bone healing. Comfrey tea and pills have been prescribed by herbalists to treat gastrointestinal ulcers and diarrhea. However, the FDA advised dietary supplement manufacturers to take comfrey off the market in 2001 because of the gathering evidence that comfrey taken internally causes severe liver toxicity. The FDA also noted the lack of evidence for comfrey's effectiveness. Comfrey should not be used by pregnant women or breastfeeding mothers.

- Ephedra (*Ephedra sinica*), also called *ma huang*. This herb contains amphetamine-like substances called ephedrine alkaloids that can powerfully stimulate the heart and central nervous system. Ephedra is most often taken by young and middle-aged adults for weight loss, increased energy, and body building. The FDA has received and investigated hundreds of reports of serious side effects associated with ephedra, including high blood pressure, irregular heart rate, seizures, heart attacks, strokes, and death. People with high blood pressure, heart conditions, and neurologic disorders should not take ephedra. Pregnant woman should also avoid this herb.

- Kava. This herb has been promoted for a variety of uses, including relief of stress, anxiety, insomnia, and premenstrual syndrome. However, in 2001 the FDA wrote a letter to health care professionals advising them that kava had been implicated in 25 cases of severe liver toxicity in Germany and Switzerland. The FDA has also received several reports of serious injuries associated with kava in the United States, including one report of a previously healthy woman who required a liver transplant. Kava should not be used by pregnant women or breastfeeding mothers.

- Licorice (*Glycyrrhiza glabra*). Herbalists use licorice root and licorice juice to treat gastritis and stomach ulcers. However, licorice can cause significant sodium retention and high blood pressure in people who consume more than 3 grams per day for more than six weeks. Licorice should not be used by pregnant women or by patients with liver diseases such as chronic hepatitis or cirrhosis of the liver.

- Pennyroyal (*Mentha pulegium*). This widely available herb, drunk as an infusion, is used for digestive disorders, colds, and skin diseases. It is also used to induce abortions. However, pennyroyal is known to be toxic to the liver. One published report documented more than 20 cases of severe toxic reactions caused by this herb, including two fatalities. The *PDR-HM* recommends against using pennyroyal. Because pennyroyal can cause abortions at high doses, pregnant women especially should not use it.

- Finally, initial studies indicate that the following herbals are likely free of serious side effects: chamomile, garlic, ginkgo, peppermint, sabal (*Sabal serrulata*), saw palmetto, and St. John's wort.

Long-term health effects

No one knows what the long-term health effects of taking herbal drugs might be. Long-term studies to assess the delayed effects or rare adverse effects of herbals have not been conducted.

REACTIONS WITH OTHER DRUGS OR SUBSTANCES

One in six patients taking prescription drugs is also taking one or more herbal drugs, according the Slone survey published in *JAMA*. The study's authors concluded that this situation creates a high potential for adverse drug-herb interactions. Although most herbals have not been studied for possible interactions with prescription drugs, a few researchers are beginning to explore this potential problem. Following is a list of some herbal drugs commonly used in the United States and what is known about their interaction with conventional drugs.

Cranberry (*Vaccinium macrocarpon*). Excessive intake of cranberry juice, used to treat urinary tract infections, may reduce the blood levels of certain drugs, including some antidepressants, antipsychotics, and morphine-based painkillers.

Dong quai (*Angelica sinensis*). One study in rabbits suggests that this herb can enhance the blood-thinning effect of the drug warfarin, although dong quai does not appear to have any blood-thinning ability on its own. (Herbalists believe dong quai relieves menstrual cramps, pre-menstrual syndrome, and many symptoms of menopause.)

Echinacea. Studies have so far found no drug interactions for this herb. In Germany, echinacea is often combined with antibiotics to treat bacterial infections, although no studies have evaluated the safety or effectiveness of this combination.

Garlic. According to a study from the National Institutes of Health, garlic supplements sharply decrease the amount of the anti-HIV drug saquinavir in the body, presumably reducing the drug's effectiveness. In addition, because of garlic's apparent blood-thinning properties, it should be used with caution by patients who are already on blood-thinning drugs such as warfarin. One study indicated that patients taking both warfarin and garlic took longer to stop bleeding.

Ginkgo. Because this herb can inhibit blood platelet activity, it should be used cautiously with blood-thinning drugs such as warfarin, heparin, or even aspirin.

Ginseng. This herb may react with the drug phenelzine, causing headaches, tremors, and manic-like symptoms, according to reports. However, it is possible that the ginseng in these cases may have been contaminated with caffeine. Ginseng also lowers blood concentrations of alcohol and warfarin.

Kava. This anti-anxiety herb may react synergistically with (enhancing the effect of) drugs that affect the central nervous system, such as alcohol, barbiturates, or prescribed anti-anxiety drugs. One patient was hospitalized from a reaction between Xanax and kava extract. Herbalists often recommend combinations of kava and St. John's wort to treat anxiety, but the safety of this combination has not been established.

St. John's wort. Preliminary reports indicate that St. John's wort may interfere with the anti-tumor drugs etoposide (VePesid), teniposide (Vumon), mitoxantrone (Novantrone), and doxorubicin (Adriamycin). This herb also lowers the amount of indinavir, an anti-retroviral drug used to treat HIV/AIDS, in the blood. Because St. John's wort likely reduces the effect of other anti-retroviral drugs as well, people being treated for AIDS should avoid this herb.

Valerian (*Valerian officinalis*). No drug interactions have been reported, but animal studies suggest that valerian, used as a sedative and sleep aid, might increase the effects of barbiturates such as pentobarbital, hexobarbital, and thiopental.

PERSONAL AND SOCIAL CONSEQUENCES

Doctors and public health advocates repeatedly warn about one negative consequence of using herbal remedies: Patients who use herbs and other alternative treatments are more likely not to take advantage of conventional treatments, and the results of this decision can be disastrous. Many doctors have seen patients with early-stage cancer who decided to treat themselves with herbal drugs rather than undergo conventional cancer treatment such as chemotherapy. When the herbal treatments failed, the patients returned to their doctors, but by that time their cancers had progressed to the stage where they were incurable.

Doctors warn that people who take herbals may also be more likely to continue unhealthy behavior, such as smoking or drinking large amounts of alcohol, with the mistaken belief that their herbal remedies will protect them from the negative consequences.

A person is probably more likely to accidentally overdose on an herbal drug than on a prescribed drug. Because the potency of herbal drugs can vary so widely from manufacturer to manufacturer and even from batch to batch, users never know how much of what substances they are ingesting when they take herbal drugs. Also, many people assume that because herbals are "natural," they are safe. Additionally, they might assume that "if a small amount is good, more must be better." People who continue to feel sick after they have started taking an herbal may end up increasing the dose to dangerous levels.

LEGAL CONSEQUENCES

Legal history

For decades, the FDA and the herbal products industry have engaged in disputes over the proper way to regulate herbal drugs. The FDA has tried to protect consumers from ineffective or unsafe products. The herbal manufacturers, who have grown more influential as their products have increased in popularity, have argued that consumers should have access to information about herbal drugs and be allowed to make their own choices. Following are some of the important laws passed in the United States affecting herbal drugs that highlight the history of this conflict.

The 1938 Federal Food, Drug, and Cosmetic Act mandated that all new drugs, including herbals, be proved safe before they could be sold. This legislation was prompted when a sulfa drug containing an unsafe additive killed more than 100 people in 1937. However, this law said that it was up to the FDA to prove a drug was unsafe. Drug manufacturers did not have to explicitly prove their products were safe.

The Kefauver-Harris Drug Amendments of 1962 shifted the burden of proof to drug manufacturers. For the first time, drug manufacturers had to prove their products were safe and effective before they could be sold. The tragedy in Europe of birth defects caused by the sedative thalidomide spurred U.S. public concern about drug safety and public support for this legislation. (It should be noted that the FDA did not allow thalidomide in the United States because of safety concerns.) In response to this new legislation, many manufacturers of herbal drugs began marketing them as "dietary supplements." This shift allowed them to bypass the new law, but they could no longer make any therapeutic claims about their products.

Congress passed the 1976 Proxmire Amendments to stop the FDA from regulating vitamin and mineral supplements as drugs based on their potency. This legislation also prohibited the FDA from regulating the potency of vitamin and mineral supplements. Although the language of this law did not expressly state that herbal products were also protected from regulation as drugs, it was assumed that herbals were covered as well.

The 1990 Nutrition Labeling and Education Act permitted manufacturers to make some health claims for foods, including dietary supplements, if the claims were approved by the FDA. This law stipulated stringent requirements for claims made on behalf of herbal and dietary supplements. The law also required standardized nutrition labels for all packaged foods.

Federal guidelines, regulations, and penalties

The 1994 Dietary Supplement Health and Education Act expressly defines a dietary supplement as a vitamin, a mineral, an herb or other botanical, an amino acid, or any other "dietary substance." This law prohibits claims that herbs can treat diseases or disorders, but it allows more general health claims about the effect of herbs on the "structure or function" of the body or about the "well-being" they induce. Under this law, the FDA bears the burden of having to prove an herbal is unsafe before restricting its use. This law also established the Office of Dietary Supplements within the National Institutes of Health to promote and compile research on dietary supplements.

The poison squad of 1903

To determine the safety of additives and preservatives in foods and medicines, the U.S. government established a "poison squad" in 1903. This group of young men volunteered to eat foods treated with chemicals such as borax, formaldehyde, and benzoic acid. The principles of the federal laws that arose from this experiment still govern herbal dietary supplements in 2002.

Although establishing the "poison squad" might seem a drastic measure, at the time the U.S. food and drug industry operated virtually without control. Although many manufacturers provided wholesome products, many others used chemical preservatives and toxic coloring agents in foods, and did so with very little regulation or oversight. The government desperately needed knowledge about these additives in order to properly regulate them.

In addition, the purveyors of thousands of patent medicines—containing drugs such as opium, morphine, heroin, and cocaine—sold them without restriction. The makers of these medicines, who regularly made false claims about their therapeutic value, did not even list ingredients or warnings on the labels.

The poison squad was established by Dr. Harvey W. Wiley, head of the U.S. Bureau of Chemistry, the precursor to the FDA. Wiley campaigned for more stringent food and drug laws, sharing his findings with the public through speaking at women's clubs and civic and business organizations.

Patent medicine firms and whiskey distilleries opposed Wiley's campaign, believing new federal regulations would put them out of business. But Wiley's efforts were instrumental in influencing Congress to pass the Food and Drug Act of 1906, which prohibited interstate commerce in misbranded or adulterated foods and drugs. In 1912, Congress passed the Sherley Amendment, which prohibited manufacturers from making fraudulent therapeutic claims when labeling their medicines.

See also Ephedra

RESOURCES

Books

Bratman, Steven, and David J. Kroll. *Clinical Evaluation of Medicinal Herbs and Other Therapeutic Natural Products.* Roseville, CA: Prima Publishing, 1999.

Ernst, Edzard, ed. *Herbal Medicine: A Concise Overview for Professionals.* Oxford: Butterworth-Heinemann, 2000.

Fleming, Thomas, ed. *Physicians' Desk Reference for Herbal Medicines.* Montvale, NJ: Medical Economics Company, 1998.

Klein, Siegrid, and Chance Riggins. *The Complete German Commission E Monographs: Therapeutic Guide to Herbal Medicines.* Boston: Integrative Medicine Communications, 1998.

Miller, Lucinda G., and Wallace J. Murray, eds. *Herbal Medicinals: A Clinician's Guide.* Binghampton, NY: Pharmaceutical Products Press, 1998.

Periodicals

Dodes, Rachel. "Alternative Medicine from an Ethnobiological Perspective." *For Health Priorities* 11 no. 3 (1999).

Ernst, Edzard. "Harmless Herbs? A Review of the Recent Literature." *The American Journal of Medicine* 104 (February 1998): 170-178.

Goldman, Peter. "Herbal Medicines Today and the Roots of Modern Pharmacology." *Annals of Internal Medicine* 135 no. 8 (October 2000): 594-600.

Hatcher, Tiffani. "The Proverbial Herb." *American Journal of Nursing* 101 no. 2 (February 2001).

Mitka, Mike. "FDA Never Promised an Herb Garden-But Sellers and Buyers Eager to See One Grow." *Journal of the American Medical Association* 280 no. 18 (November 11, 1998).

Shine, Kenneth I. "A Critique on Complementary and Alternative Medicine." *The Journal of Alternative and Complementary Medicine* 7 supplement 1 (2001): S-145-S-152.

Winslow, Lisa Corbin, and David J. Kroll. "Herbs as Medicines." *Archives of Internal Medicine* 158 no. 20 (November 9, 1998): 2192-2199.

Organizations

American Botanical Council, P.O. Box 144345, Austin, TX, USA, 78714-4345, (512) 926-4900, <http://www.herbalgram.org>.

Food and Drug Administration, Center for Food Safety and Applied Nutrition, 200 C Street, SW, Washington, DC, USA, 20204, (888) 723-3366, <http://www.cfsan.fda.gov>.

National Center for Complementary and Alternative Medicine, National Institutes of Health (NIH), P.O. Box 8218, Silver Spring, MD, USA, 20907-8218, (888) 644-6226, <http://nccam.nih.gov/nccam>.

Office of Dietary Supplements, NIH, 31 Center Drive, Room 1B29, Bethesda, MD, USA, 20892-2086, (301) 435-2920, <http://odp.od.nih.gov/ods>.

Anne Jacobson

HEROIN

OVERVIEW

According to the U.S. Central Intelligence Agency, worldwide production of opium has doubled since the mid-1980s. The result has been easier and cheaper access to the drug and worsening social problems, such as crime, associated with its abuse. Derived from opium, heroin is a highly addictive drug, and its use is a serious and growing problem. Rising purity levels and lower prices have fueled heroin's popularity.

The widely held misconception that snorting or smoking it is "less addictive" than intravenous injection lures new young users. Any ingestion of heroin promotes tolerance and drug cravings that can, and frequently do, lead to addiction. Teens and young adults across the country are learning the hard way that heroin addiction can come just as easily in a pipe as a needle.

Opium production occurs in three source regions—Southeast Asia, Southwest Asia, and Latin America. While an undetermined amount of the opium is consumed in the producing regions, a significant amount of the drug is converted to heroin and sent to its major markets in Europe and North America.

Origin and production

Heroin is a narcotic derived from the opium poppy plant (*Papaver somniferum*). Opium poppy is grown primarily by destitute farmers in what is known as the Golden Crescent in Southwest Asia (encompassing Turkey, Iran, Afghanistan, and Pakistan) and the Golden Triangle in Southeast Asia (Burma, Thailand, Laos, and Vietnam). In the Americas, Columbia and Mexico are chief producers.

The poppy plant produces raw opium. Crude refineries modify the opium into a brown paste that is molded and dried into bricks. More sophisticated laboratories are found in Bangkok, Karachi, and Hong Kong. These labs change opium into what is known as number three heroin, a smokeable form. Purification of heroin to the "injectable" fourth stage (number four heroin) involves a volatile chemical combination that can result in catastrophic explosions.

History

The history of opium usage stretches back to 3400 B. C., where it was first cultivated in lower Mesopotamia. The Sumerians called the poppy Hul Gil or the "joy plant." The art of poppy cultivation spread from the Sumerians to the Assyrians, and from the Assyrians to the Babylonians and Egyptians.

The Egyptians applied proven agricultural methods to growing opium poppies, and the trade flourished throughout the ancient world. For the next 3,000 years, opium was an important trade item among civilizations

 # KEY TERMS

BUPRENORPHINE: (Also known as Temgesic and Subutex.) New substances that have proven to reduce cravings associated with heroin withdrawal. May also be helpful in treating cocaine addiction.

ENDORPHINS: Naturally produced chemicals in the brain that create feelings of happiness, euphoria, serenity and fearlessness.

LAAM (LEVO-ALPHA-ACETYLMETHADOL): Like methadone, LAAM is a synthetic opiate used to treat heroin addiction, blunting withdrawal for up to 72 hours.

MDMA (3,4-METHYLENEDIOXYMETHAMPHETA-MINE): Known as ecstasy, E, and X, MDMA is the most popular of the "club drugs," a synthetic stimulant with mild hallucinogenic properties.

METHADONE (METHADONE HYDROCHLORIDE): Like LAAM, a synthetic opiate used to treat heroin addiction. Methadone is non-intoxicating and blunts symptoms of withdrawal.

NALOXONE: A short-acting narcotic antagonist that binds to opiate receptors and blocks them. Used to treat opiate overdose.

NALTREXONE: A long-lasting narcotic antagonist that blocks opiate receptors. Used to treat heroin addiction.

OPIOID: A drug, hormone, or other chemical substance having sedative or narcotic effects similar to those containing opium or its derivatives; a natural brain opiate.

SPEEDBALL: Also called "dynamite" or "whiz-bang," a speedball is a combination of cocaine or methampetamine (stimulants) and heroin (a depressant). This combination increases the chances of serious adverse reactions and can be more toxic than either drug alone.

---

clustered around the Mediterranean. Prized by merchants and traders, opium would find its way into markets in Greece, Carthage, India, Persia, and China.

As Europe began its slow emergence from the Dark Ages in the sixteenth century, opium began to reappear in medical journals on the continent. A century later, an English apothecary named Thomas Sydenham introduced "Sydenham's Laudanum," pills made from opium, sherry, and herbs. They were popular remedies for a variety of ills.

Portugese traders with routes to the East China Sea smoked opium with tobacco in long-stemmed pipes. They reintroduced the practice to the Chinese who had frowned on its use. The British East India Company

assumed control of poppy-producing fields in India and dominated the opium trade. By the late 1700s, the East India Company had established a monopoly on its import into China, Europe, and the United States.

Opium had long been used by the Chinese to stop diarrhea, but in the seventeenth and eighteenth centuries, its recreational use exploded. In 1800, the Imperial government of Kia King banned its import and trade completely, but could not effectively enforce the ban. Opium dens flourished in the port cities and spread inward.

With its officials routinely bribed, China quickly became a haven for corruption, lawlessness, and addiction. In desperation, the imperial government made opium illegal in 1836 and took action against Chinese merchants and Western traders who continued to traffic in the drug. This and other trade disputes with the British led to the first of two Opium Wars.

By the time opium was banned by the U.S. Congress in 1905, the abuse of black market heroin had already taken hold. In 1910, Britain signed an agreement with China to dismantle the opium trade. But the profits made from its cultivation, manufacture, and sale were so enormous that no serious interruption would be felt until World War II closed supply routes throughout Asia. And although Bayer ended the manufacture of heroin for medicinal use in 1913, illicit importation and distribution networks in New York and San Francisco were already well established.

U.S. military involvement in Vietnam was credited with the next major surge in heroin smuggling into the United States. Political and economic turmoil in the region led to a surge in production from Southeast Asia's Golden Triangle. By the end of the U.S. war in Vietnam, there were some 750,000 heroin addicts on American streets.

Despite the billions of dollars spent to keep heroin off its streets, America's efforts have been unsuccessful. Heroin is not only more plentiful in the United States than it was 30 years ago, but it is also cheaper and at its point of sale almost 10 times as pure.

CHEMICAL/ORGANIC COMPOSITION

All drugs derived from opium poppy are called opiates. Of the opiates, heroin (diacetylmorphine) is the most potent and fast-acting. Though heroin is no longer used in medical settings, its less potent cousins—codeine, liquid morphine, pethidine, and methadone—are found in clinics and hospitals all over the world. But it wasn't until the early 1970s that scientists began to understand the real reasons behind heroin's propensity for abuse and addiction.

The chemical composition of opiates are remarkably similar to endorphins, chemicals produced by the brain in times of distress or injury to relieve pain or ease fear. There are three major types of endorphins: beta endorphins, located in the brain; and enkephalins and dynorphin, which are distributed throughout the brain and body.

These natural chemicals are small chain peptides that bind to opiate receptors distributed throughout the brain—including the limbic system, where their activation produces feelings of happiness, euphoria, serenity, and fearlessness.

The endorphins enkephalin and dynorphin possess natural analgesic (pain-relieving) qualities. When they bind to opiate receptors in the spinal cord, they suppress the ability of the brain to register pain. Heroin binds to these same opiate receptors in the brain and body.

Types of heroin

Most heroin is packaged and shipped in bricks of powder. Pure heroin is white, but the color when it reaches the user can vary from yellow to dark brown, owing either to impurities during the manufacturing process, the presence of powdered additives, or both.

Heroin is usually cut with baking soda, powdered milk, baby powder, sugar, starch, or quinine, but has also known to be cut with lidocaine, curry powder, strychinine, and even laundry detergent. Law enforcement officials in New York report the existence of heroin cut with a rat poison from Santa Domingo called *Tres Pasos* (meaning "three steps"). Three is the number of steps the mice take before dying after exposure to the poison.

Another form of heroin commonly distributed in the western and southwestern regions of the United States is called Black Tar or Mexican Brown. These varieties are produced in Mexico and—because they're manufactured crudely—have an either hard black coal or sticky, tar-like consistency. Purity rates range from 20–80%.

In 1980, the purity of heroin was somewhere in the 4% range. In 2002, the average bag sold by dealers in the United States was almost 40% pure, and sold for less than one-fifth the 1980 price.

INGESTION METHODS

Until very recently, the most common means of administering heroin was injection with a hypodermic needle, either intravenously (into a vein; called "mainlining"), subcutaneously (just under the skin; called "skin-popping") or intramuscularly (injected into muscle rather than a vein). Injection by regular users and addicts was preferred because the street drug was so diluted with fillers that injection was the most efficient way to get high.

LAW AND ORDER

According to the Centers for Disease Control, injection drug use directly and indirectly accounts for more than 36% of all AIDS cases in the United States.

For decades, HIV prevention advocates have been campaigning for funding of needle-exchange programs to reduce HIV transmission rates, but have run into a wall of opposition from conservative politicians who claim needle exchange programs were unproven and, worse, that they "encouraged" drug use.

Following through on these assertions, in 1998 the U.S. Congress imposed a federal ban on funding for any program or agency that incorporated needle exchange into its AIDS prevention efforts. Republican leaders said that if researchers and advocates could prove needle exchange programs were effective and did not contribute to increased use, they would consider lifting the ban.

A survey of 81 cities around the world compared rates of HIV infection rates among injection drug users in cities that had needle exchange programs with those cities that did not. In the 52 cities lacking needle exchange, HIV infection rates increased an average of 5.9% per year. In the 29 cities with needle exchange programs, HIV infection rates actually fell and by almost the same percentage—5.8% per year.

Data from hundreds of such studies were compiled, summarized, and included in eight federally funded reports presented to Congress. All confirmed that needle exchange programs reduced rates of HIV infection among drug users and did not encourage wider use in the communities they served—a degree of unanimity in research data highly unusual in science.

Even so, Congressional leaders decided to make the federal ban on needle exchange programs permanent.

Many first-time intravenous users of heroin have intensely negative reactions to the drug, including nausea and vomiting. For many, this is enough to turn them off heroin for good, but for others, social pressures and other factors compel them to keep trying until they find the high they anticipated.

With purity levels of packaged heroin increasing, the drug can now be snorted or smoked, severing for many people the negative associations heroin has with intravenous drug use. This has greatly expanded heroin's

Colombian anti-narcotic police officer walks through a field of opium poppies, the raw material for heroin. Columbia is the source of 80% of the processed cocaine and a growing percentage of the heroin that reaches the United States. Photo by Ricardo Mazalan, AP/World Wide Photos. Reproduced by permission.

pool of potential users and addicts, especially among young people.

According to a recent study by the National Institute on Drug Abuse (NIDA), smoking produces lower levels of heroin in the blood than injection, but the effects on the user are roughly similar. Smoking heroin also gives users more control over their intake of the drug without the burden of preparing another intravenous dose.

Snorting heroin is probably the least efficient means of taking the drug and has several immediate drawbacks, including strong stomach cramps and a constantly running nose. Many regular users of heroin began by snorting the drug on occasion. This kind of early heroin use is called "chipping." A high percentage of chippers eventually turn to injection of the drug before realizing they are hooked.

THERAPEUTIC USE

Because of its analgesic (painkilling) properties, opium and its derivatives have long been used for the treatment of ailments. Throughout the nineteenth century in England and the United States, opium was administered in plasters, pills, cough drops, lozenges, and many other applications dispensed by physicians and pharmacists.

In 1895, while working for the Bayer Company in Germany, Heinrich Dreser produced a drug he thought was as effective an analgesic as morphine, but without its harmful side effects. Bayer began mass production of diacetylmorphine, and in 1898 began marketing the new drug under the brand name "heroin" as a cough sedative.

Pharmacists in France, England, and the United States regularly marketed heroin as an excellent pain killer and a cure for disease, including respiratory ailments and diarrhea.

Several medical societies in the United States at that time offered heroin as a safe means of treating morphine addiction. Articles appearing in American medical journals early in the twentieth century spoke highly of heroin's ability to soothe the painful aches, shakes, and vomiting experienced by recovering morphine addicts, and it was widely used as a "step down" cure.

Within a decade, doctors realized they were merely substituting one opiate addiction for an even more powerful one.

Internationally, heroin's use as a medicine wasn't regulated until 1925 when the League of Nations adopted strict rules governing international heroin trade. The same body later stipulated that heroin producers could only manufacture quantities sufficient for medical use, though these guidelines were unenforceable and largely ignored.

USAGE TRENDS

Every government agency that has sought to quantify usage trends of heroin in the United States over the last several years has come to one inescapable conclusion: heroin use across the country is climbing dramatically, especially among young people.

In 2000, heroin was second only to cocaine in the number of drug-related emergency room episodes reported to a national registry run by the Drug Abuse Warning Network. Heroin, listed as a principal agent in respiratory and cardiac emergencies, went from 33,884 episodes nationwide in 1990 to 94,804 in 2000—an increase of nearly 180%.

Locally the numbers are even more dramatic. In a similar eight-year period (between 1991 and 1998), the rate of heroin-related incidents at area hospitals increased by 413% in Miami, 288% in Chicago, and 238% in St. Louis.

Scope and severity

The Office of National Drug Control Policy's (ONDCP) study of 21 major metropolitan areas in the United States revealed that the most likely user of heroin is over 30 years old. However, younger adults (18–30) comprise a substantial portion of those believed to be experimenting with heroin use. In the South, younger adults are more likely than adults over 30 to be regular users of the drug.

Figures compiled by the U.S. Department of Health and Human Services National Household Survey on Drug Abuse (NHSDA) estimate that there were approximately 104,000 new heroin users in 1999. Among these new users, 87,000 were between the ages of 12 and 25 and 34,000 of them were under age 18. The average age at first use among these new heroin users was 19.8 years.

The same study found that the number of people who had used heroin in the last month, an indication of more regular use, had climbed from 68,000 in 1993 to 208,000 in 1999.

Nationwide, the NHSDA released estimates in 1999 that said approximately 2.7 million Americans (1.2% of the population) are thought to have used heroin at least once in their lifetimes.

Age, ethnic, and gender trends

According to the National Institute on Drug Abuse (NIDA), among high-school-age teens, rates of heroin use remained relatively stable and low from the late 1970s until the start of 1990s.

After 1991, however, use began to rise among tenth- and twelfth-graders, and after 1993, among eighth-graders as well. In 1999, prevalence of heroin use was roughly the same for all three grade levels. Although the number of students who reported using heroin in the last year remain under 2% in 1999, the rates are about two to three times higher than those reported in 1991.

The NIDA released figures showing 1.7% of eighth graders, 1.7% of tenth graders, and 1.8% of high school seniors (twelfth graders) reported using heroin at least once. The results are remarkably static as respondents leave school and enter college, suggesting a strong adolescent culture of drug experimentation. Among college students, 1.7% reported using heroin at least once in their lifetime, while 1.8% of young adults aged 19–28 reported lifetime heroin use.

When asked about heroin use in the last 30 days, 0.6% of eighth graders, 0.3% of tenth graders, and 0.4% of twelfth graders reported using heroin at least once, compared to 0.2% of college students and 0.1% of young adults.

In a separate report issued by the Centers for Disease Control (CDC), the indications of heroin experimentation among teens in high school were even higher. In the CDC report, 2.4% of sampled high school students reported having tried heroin at least once.

Drawing on data supplied by individual states, estimates of teen use varied between a low of 1.7% to a high of 5.2%. The CDC report also looked at specific metropolitan areas and these estimates mirrored state data; surveys pegged teen prevalence with a low of 1.0% and a high of 5.3%.

In a 2001 study entitled *Epidemiologic Trends in Drug Abuse* conducted by the Community Epidemiology Work Group (CEWG), a branch of NIDA, the number of men who abused heroin strongly outweighed the number of female users.

These trends appear to be established early on. Male high school students who report trying heroin, for example, outnumber female students in the CDC study by a ratio of almost three to one.

According to the ONDCP, which conducts in-depth drug usage profiles in 21 American cities, heroin users are most likely to be white and male. Whites and blacks are equally represented among heroin users in Birmingham, Alabama, and Columbia, South Carolina; and Hispanics are the dominant user group in El Paso, Texas, and Los Angeles, California. In Denver and Philadelphia, white users predominate, but Hispanics are overrepresented relative to their percentage of the general population. Similarly, in Boston, whites are more numerous among heroin users, but blacks are overrepresented.

MENTAL EFFECTS

The force of heroin's initial impact on the user, and the duration and intensity of the high, depends on the method of ingestion. If injected directly into the bloodstream, the euphoric "rush" hits the user in less than 10 seconds. Intramuscular or subcutaneous injection produces a much more gradual response as the drug takes longer (six to eight minutes) to filter into the bloodstream. Smoking heroin also produces less of an initial rush and a more gradual response to the dose, anywhere from 10 to 15 minutes.

It is the drug's sudden entry into the brain that accounts for the initial surge of energy. The rush is thought to last as long as it takes the brain and body to break heroin down into morphine, which is then absorbed by the body's opioid receptors. This stage finds the user going "on the nod," an alternatively wakeful and pleasurably drowsy state that lasts four to six hours.

Given that the morphine is artificially dosing the brain's opiate receptors, it is not surprising to hear users describe a powerful state of complete fulfillment and a tremendous sense of self-satisfaction while under the influence of the drug. Over time, because of the development of tolerance (needing higher doses more frequently to achieve the same effects felt at first use), heavy users and addicts lose the ability to get high and use the drug solely to counteract the effects of withdrawal.

PHYSIOLOGICAL EFFECTS

Heroin is a central nervous system depressant. The drug slows heart and breathing rates dramatically. During the "nod off" phase, consciousness may be lost. Any one of these effects is dangerous to the user; in combination, they are potentially life-threatening. Given the high incidence of nausea and vomiting associated with heroin use, for example, users who lose consciousness and then become sick are at risk of choking to death.

As is the case with other opiates, regular ingestion of heroin creates rapid tolerance in the user. Even over a relatively short period, weekend users may find themselves taking larger doses of the drug to achieve the same high. As many recovering addicts will attest, this is the often the first addictive hook heroin gets into recreational users.

The mechanics of tolerance are still not fully understood. One hypothesis suggests that when habitual heroin ingestion upsets the body's natural chemical equilibrium, the body attempts to compensate for it. More of the drug is then needed to overwhelm the body's attempt to suppress the drug's influence. This kind of tolerance is found with regular use of nearly all psychoactive substances.

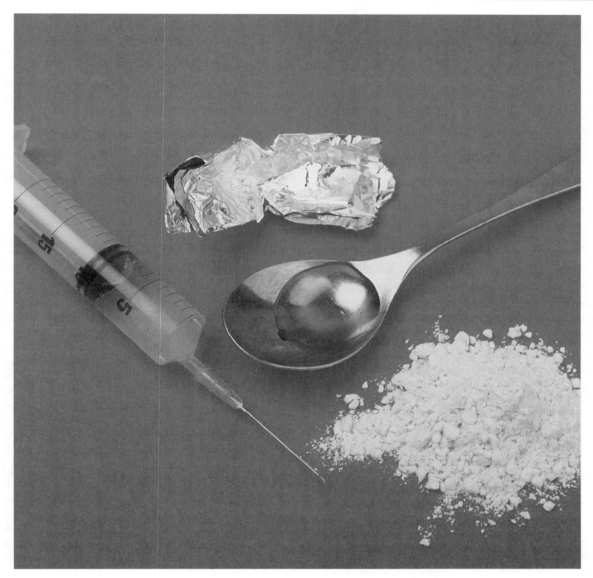

Heroin appears in various forms. It usually begins as a powder that is dissolved in water prior to intravenous injection with a syringe. Photo by Garry Watson, Photo Researchers, Inc./Science Photo Library. Reproduced by permission.

Tolerance to heroin can vary greatly among individuals. A "regular" or "safe" dose for an experienced user can kill someone who has never tried it before. Even occasional users who build up some tolerance and take several weeks off from the drug can suffer an overdose from their "usual" dose.

Depending on tolerance, and the amount and purity of the drug consumed, a lethal dose of heroin can range anywhere from 200 to 500 mg. Hardened addicts have survived doses three times that high.

The growing purity level of street heroin sold in American cities and suburbs is one of the most worrisome aspects of the drug's resurgence. Users accus-tomed to 25% purity can easily overdose if they use the same amount of the drug that is 50% or 70% pure.

A 2001 study conducted by the ONDCP found that Colombian heroin purity ranges from as low as 7% to as high as 95%. Purity of Mexican black heroin sold in South and West ranged from 14% to 58%—with both extremes reported in Seattle. These kinds of fluctuations can have deadly consequences for the user.

Harmful side effects

Heroin use can cause tragic complications during pregnancy, greatly increasing the chances of spontaneous miscarriage, breech deliveries, premature birth, or

IN THE NEWS

Apart from infectious bloodborne diseases, reactions associated with toxic and semi-toxic additives, unknown purity levels, and the possibility of overdose, intravenous drug users also have to weigh the possibility of fatal bacterial infections.

In April of 2000, a contaminated batch of heroin began a deadly march across Great Britain. By August, more than 40 people in England, Wales, Scotland, and Ireland died. Researchers eventually identified *Clostridium vovyi* type A, a highly toxic bacterium that grows in soil and animals. *Clostridium* itself is harmless, but its dormant spores produce deadly toxins when released.

Health officials said that bacterial infections are rather common in people who ingest drugs intravenously, but such deadly outbreaks are unusual.

Apparently all those who died had injected the drug intramuscularly rather than directly into the bloodstream. Oxygen in the blood usually kills any stray bacterium in the heroin, but there is no oxygen in muscles, and the bacterium were able to grow and release their cargo of toxic spores.

In all, 109 addicts across Ireland and the U.K. fell ill between April and August. Some users felt no ill effects at all, while others experienced swelling and abscesses. For 43 users, the reaction was followed by the rapid onset of toxic shock. Some of them died within hours.

Antibiotics effectively kill the bacteria, but nothing in modern medicine could combat the toxicity of the *Clostridium* spores. The *Clostridium* infection caused massive inflammation of vital organs, internal hemorrhaging, and death. Experts say there is no telling when or where it may strike again.

---

stillbirth. Research conducted by NIDA suggests that babies born to heroin-addicted mothers are at higher risk for sudden infant death syndrome (SIDS). Infants who do survive the pregnancy are often born addicted to heroin and exhibit severe withdrawal symptoms for a period of weeks and even months.

Heroin addicts are at a much higher risk for contracting HIV, hepatitis C, and bloodborne pathogens through the sharing and reuse of hypodermic syringes and other "works" associated with injection drug use. Government studies suggest that one-third of all HIV and more than half of all hepatitis C cases are the result of injection drug use.

Long-term health effects

Of course, one of the most debilitating effects of heroin use is dependence and addiction. Dependence follows the same trajectory as tolerance.

Eight to twelve hours after the addict's last dose, the user begins to experience the onset of flu-like symptoms: watery eyes, sneezing, muscle aches, weakness, and vomiting. The symptoms increase in severity over the next two to three days and include shivering, muscle spasms, paranoia, fear, hallucinations, and debilitating cramps in the stomach and extremities. Within a week, the body has corrected the imbalance created by the regular ingestion of heroin, and the symptoms subside. However, intense cravings for the drug last for a much longer period of time and often contribute to relapse.

Health consequences of chronic heroin abuse include scarred and collapsed veins, bacterial infections of the blood vessels and heart valves, boils, a variety of soft-tissue infections, kidney problems, and liver disease. Pneumonia, tuberculosis, and other lung diseases are also common among long-term users, which can be attributed to either poor nutrition and depressed respiratory function or both. Many of the additives heroin is cut with do not dissolve in the body and can block blood vessels, translating into higher risk of sudden death from stroke or heart attack.

Recovering heroin addicts often endure years of corrective dental work due to neglect and the side effects of regular drug use. Heroin addicts often have cavities along the gum-line and gum disease, because the drug causes a marked decrease in the production of saliva. Saliva protects the mouth by neutralizing acids that cause cavities and providing lubrication that reduces the retention of food debris.

A NIDA-supported study conducted by the University of Southern California Los Angeles examined the lives of some 587 heroin addicts admitted to criminals' addiction programs in the early 1960s. The researchers found their lives were marked by cycles of abstinence, relapse, crime, incarceration, chronic disease, and early death. By 1997, nearly half of the group had died. A full 40% of the survivors were still struggling with their addiction and reported using heroin in the last year. Fewer then 10% were in a working addiction program.

REACTIONS WITH OTHER DRUGS OR SUBSTANCES

Even experienced users caution mixing heroin with anything else: alcohol, amphetamines, and especially cocaine all greatly increase the dangers of using heroin by itself.

Ingesting heroin along while consuming alcohol is considered especially dangerous. Drinking alcohol increases the likelihood of vomiting and the dangers of choking. Also, both heroin and alcohol are central nervous system depressants and could slow the heart rate and breathing to dangerously low levels.

Combining cocaine and heroin, regardless of the ingestion method, is called "speedballing." Speedballing is extremely dangerous. For reasons that are not completely understood, the drugs enhance each other's effectiveness. Heroin enhances the electric high produced by cocaine, while cocaine elevates the mellowing aspects of heroin.

Physiologically, cocaine is a powerful stimulant that quickens the heartbeat, but it wears off much faster than heroin, which works to depress the heart rate. The stimulant effect of the cocaine and the depressant effect of heroin wreak havoc on the heart, which can lose its rhythm. Cocaine frequently masks how much heroin has been consumed, and when the cocaine's effects dissipate, heart failure can result. John Belushi and River Pheonix both died this way after taking speedballs.

In some parts of the western United States, particularly California where methamphetamine (crystal) is plentiful, speedballing a mix of heroin and methamphetamine, whether they are inhaled or injected, is increasing in popularity. In addition to methamphetamine, some heroin users take benzodiazepines—types of tranquilizers—to increase the effect of the opiate. Sources report that the use of MDMA (ecstasy) is increasing among heroin users, and that Rohypnol, a sleeping aid, is being taken to "soften the fall" when the effects of the drug combination begin to wear off.

TREATMENT AND REHABILITATION

A variety of treatments and treatment programs that are available to people addicted to heroin, though the treatment options available and the quality of the care provided greatly increase with the ability to pay. In a recent *Rolling Stone* interview, one anonymous addict said it cost his parents $150,000 for his two-year stay in a drug treatment center. Publicly subsidized treatment programs frequently have waiting lists and are forced to turn people away. The cold realities of drug treatment are even more troubling.

Despite progress, most studies post the failure rate of most treatment programs at or near 80%. Most addicts who try to abstain relapse at least once, and often several times before successfully kicking their drug addiction.

A common first step of treating heroin addiction is detoxification. The objective is to relieve withdrawal symptoms while allowing patients to adjust to life without heroin. "Detox," as it is sometimes called, is not an end in itself but a beginning that must also include broad therapeutic programs. Most successful programs of this type are in-patient residential regimens lasting three to six months.

Because any opiate derivative will suffice to soothe heroin cravings associated with withdrawal, methadone, a synthetic opiate that has no sedating side effects, has been an effective treatment for heroin and morphine addiction for more than 30 years. The medication is taken orally and suppresses narcotic withdrawal for a period of 24 to 36 hours. Methadone can be taken continuously for 10 years or longer with no harmful side effects.

Like methadone, LAAM (levo-alpha-acetyl-methadol) is a synthetic opiate used to treat heroin addiction. LAAM can block the effects of heroin for up to 72 hours. This makes outpatient treatment much more convenient, given that patients need to dose only two to three times a week. Naloxone and naltrexone are new medications that are also effective at blocking the pleasurable effects of heroin, helping motivated individuals to abstain.

Buprenorphine (Temgesic, Subutex) is a new medication that has been shown to be even more effective in blocking the effects of heroin than methadone. Recent preclinical studies have shown that buprenorphine may also significantly reduce cravings associated with cocaine addiction.

Though drug-based treatment regimens can be helpful in conquering heroin addiction, integrating them with behavioral and therapeutic programs (both individual and group counseling) have consistently proven more effective at preventing relapse over the long term.

PERSONAL AND SOCIAL CONSEQUENCES

There is nothing glamorous, cool, or chic about heroin use. It is a personally and socially destructive compound that in imperceptible stages can reorient the user's priorities around its consumption.

Few, if any, heroin addicts set out to sacrifice their families, friends, and futures in service of their next fix, but that is what often happens. Heroin gradually sinks its hooks deeper into the user's psyche. What starts out as very occasional use can evolve in small steps to more frequent use. Monthly use can soon become weekly use. Before long, it is the drug that is dictating when it is consumed.

Heroin addiction is not easy or cheap to overcome. Many heroin addicts face a life of continual relapse, declining economic opportunity, broken families, and failing health. In a *Rolling Stone* interview, one user who failed in her attempt to stay clean likened the experience of sobriety to wanting to tear the muscle off her bones.

Heroin abuse has repercussions that extend far beyond the individual user and his or her family. The consequences of drug abuse and addiction carry a social price in festering criminality, violence, and disruptions to the workplace and educational environments that cost billions of dollars each year.

LEGAL CONSEQUENCES

Strict penalties are provided for drug convictions, including mandatory prison terms for many offenses. Federal law states that any conviction for possession, use, or distribution of illicit substances can result in loss of federal benefits, confiscation of property, fines, and jail sentences.

Persons convicted on federal charges of possessing any controlled substance face penalties of up to one year in prison and a mandatory fine of no less than $1,000 up to a maximum of $100,000. Second convictions are punishable by not less than 15 days but not more than two years in prison and a minimum fine of $2,500. Subsequent convictions are punishable by not less than 90 days but not more than three years in prison and a minimum fine of $5,000.

If death or serious bodily injury results from the use of an illegally distributed controlled substance, the person convicted of distributing that substance faces a mandatory life sentence and fines of up to $8 million.

Persons convicted on federal charges of drug trafficking within 1,000 feet of a university face penalties of prison terms and fines that are twice as high as the regular penalties for the offense, with a mandatory prison sentence of at least one year.

See also Cocaine; Methadone; Opium

RESOURCES

Books

Berridge, Virginia, and Griffith Edwards. *Heroin, Opium and the People: Opiate Use in Nineteenth-Century England.* New York: St. Martins Press, 1981.

Fernandez, Humberto. *Heroin.* Center City, NY: Hazelden Information Education, 1998.

Inciardi, James. *The War on Drugs II: The Continuing Epic of Heroin, Cocaine, Crack, Crime, AIDS and Public Policy.* Mountain View, CA: Mayfield Publishing Company, 1991.

Periodicals

European Union. European Monitoring Center for Drugs and Drug Addiction. *Report on the Risk Assessment of Ketamine in the Framework of the Joint Action on New Synthetic Drugs.* September 25, 2000.

U.S. Department of Health and Human Services. *2001 Monitoring the Future: National Results of Adolescent Drug Use.* Washington, DC: U.S. Dept. of Health and Human Services, January 2002.

U.S. Department of Health and Human Services. National Institute on Drug Abuse. "Buprenorphine Proves Effective, Expands Options For Treatment of Heroin Addiction." *NIDA Notes* (May 2001).

U.S. Department of Health and Human Services. National Institute on Drug Abuse. "Heroin Snorters Risk Transition To Injection Drug Use And Infectious Disease." *NIDA Notes* (August 1999).

U.S. Department of Health and Human Services. National Institute on Drug Abuse. *Heroin Update: Smoking, Injecting Cause Similar Effects; Usage Patterns May be Shifting.* Washington, DC: U.S. Dept. of Health and Human Services, July/August 1995.

U.S. Department of Health and Human Services. National Institute on Drug Abuse. "33-Year Study Finds Lifelong Lethal Consequences of Heroin Addiction." *NIDA Notes* (October 2001).

U.S. Department of Health and Human Services. Substance Abuse and Mental Health Services Administration. National Clearinghouse for Alcohol and Drug Information. *Heroin Treatment Admissions Increase: 1993-1999.* Washington, DC: U.S. Dept. of Health and Human Services, January 2002.

U.S. Department of Justice. National Drug Intelligence Center. *National Drug Threat Assessment 2002.* Washington, DC: U.S. Dept. of Justice, December 2001.

U.S. Office of National Drug Control Policy. "Pulse Check: Trends in Drug Abuse: Heroin." November 2001.

Other

U. S. Department of Health and Human Services. Substance Abuse and Mental Health Services Administration. July 8, 2002. <http://www.samhsa.gov>. Accessed July 8, 2002.

U.S. Department of Justice. Drug Enforcement Administration. <http://www.usdoj.gov/dea>. Accessed July 8, 2002.

U.S. National Institute on Drug Abuse. June 27, 2002. <http://www.nida.nih.gov>. Accessed July 8, 2002.

U.S. Office of the National Drug Control Policy. July 5, 2002. <http://www.whitehousedrugpolicy.org>. Accessed July 8, 2002.

Christopher V.G. Barillas

HYDROMORPHONE

OVERVIEW

Hydromorphone is a semi-synthetic prescription drug that has similar pain-relieving properties to that of morphine and codeine. It is classified as an opioid or narcotic analgesic. It is an effective treatment for moderate-to-severe pain and is sometimes used in patients with a non-productive cough. It is used to treat several types of pain, including headache, cancer pain, and back pain.

Hydromorphone is formed by making a slight alteration to the morphine molecule. The primary active ingredient in hydromorphone is thebaine. Thebaine is one of several compounds called alkaloids that are found in all narcotic analgesics. Thebaine is a word based on the name of the ancient Egyptian city of Thebes. The residents of Thebes are known to have harvested significant amounts of opium from the poppy plant variety known as *Papaver somniferum*. Hydromorphone provides pain relief by bonding with specific pain receptors in the body. The pain-relieving effects of hydromorphone are very similar to those provided by morphine, but hydromorphone is actually more potent.

Hydromorphone is in the opiate family of drugs. The opiates and their semi-synthetic and synthetic descendants are big business for legal and illegal entities. Some 30 million prescriptions and orders are written annually in the United States alone for controlled substances, many of these for narcotic analgesics. A large part of the international illicit drug trade involves the sale of drugs in the opiate family. A substantial amount of crime committed in the world is linked with this drug trade and with illicit drug use.

History

Hydromorphone and its natural opioid relatives have been used to relieve pain, treat a variety of ailments, and create euphoric feelings at least as far back as the time of the ancient Greeks. In early Greek history, the priests controlled the use of opium and ascribed to it supernatural powers. In the fifth century BC, Hippocrates, the "father of medicine," dismissed the supernatural attributes of opium. Hippocrates believed opium had cathartic, narcotic, hypnotic, and styptic properties. He believed that all diseases had a natural origin and could be cured by natural therapies. All of the natural opiates historically were derived from opium poppy plants. The liquid extracted from the poppy seeds was typically dried to create a concentrated powder. These extracts were then smoked, eaten, or drunk.

From the world of the ancient Greeks, word of the powerful properties of opium spread quickly to the Romans. The Romans not only used opium as a painkiller and for religious rites, but also considered it an excellent poison. In the case of suicide, it was considered a pleasant means to exit this world. Somnus, the Roman god of sleep, was often depicted as a small boy who carried around poppy flowers and an opium horn. After the collapse of the Roman Empire, the use and knowledge of

KEY TERMS

ANALGESIC: A type of drug that alleviates pain without loss of consciousness.

HYPNOTIC: A drug that induces sleep by depressing the central nervous system.

NARCOTIC: A natural or synthetic drug that has properties similar to opium or opium derivatives.

NEUROPATHIC: Relating to a disease of the nerves.

OPIATE: Drug derived directly from opium and used in its natural state, without chemical modification. Opiates include morphine, codeine, thebaine, noscapine, and papaverine.

PHYSICAL DEPENDENCE: A condition that may occur after prolonged use of an opiate, but differing from addiction because the user is dependent on the drug for pain relief, rather than emotional or psychological relief.

PSYCHOSIS: A severe mental disorder characterized by the loss of the ability to distinguish what is objectively real from what is imaginary, frequently including hallucinations.

STYPTIC: The contraction of a blood vessel or the containment of a hemorrhage.

WITHDRAWAL: A group of symptoms that may occur from suddenly stopping the use of a substance such as alcohol or other drugs after chronic or prolonged ingestion.

---

opium spread to the Islamic world, where considerable study of the drug was performed.

After many centuries of declining use, opium began to reappear in Europe around the beginning of the Renaissance. Opiate use steadily increased over the next few centuries, reaching a new high in the nineteenth century. It was widely used by artists and writers during the Romantic Era.

Opium was first cultivated and processed in England during the ninteenth century. It was commonly used as a sedative and painkiller. However, it was also used to treat fever and diarrhea. At this time in history, diarrhea was a major killer. Opium, with its constipating effects, proved to be effective in treating various types of serious diarrhea, especially that associated with cholera. The problem of addiction to opiates, long recognized even at this time, was largely ignored.

The active components of opium were not isolated until the first half of the nineteenth century. The first of these components to be isolated was morphine, named for Morpheus, the Greek god of dreams. Soon after, other alkaloids in the poppy were isolated, such as codeine in 1832, narceine in 1832, thebaine in 1835, and papaverine in 1848. The later invention of the hypodermic needle allowed opium to be delivered in greater concentrations and with greater rapidity to patients in severe pain. Morphine injections were used to treat a variety of complaints, including menstrual pain, eye inflammation, and rheumatism. Unfortunately, it also led to greater abuse of the drug for non-medicinal uses.

Heroin was first created in 1874 by boiling a solution of morphine and acetic anhydride. Heroin is an extremely concentrated form of opiate that was initially hailed as a miracle drug. Heroin acts quickly in the body, where it is immediately converted into morphine. Heroin is more fat-soluble and, because of this, can enter the central nervous system much more readily than morphine. It has five to eight times the analgesic power of morphine, but it was originally sold as a cough suppressant and treatment for respiratory ailments. Heroin was widely used in the United States and Europe in small quantities in cough lozenges and elixirs.

All of the opiates were legal and freely-available drugs in the United States and most other countries until the early part of the twentieth century. It was at this point that opiates began to be taxed and regulated not only in the United States but also throughout the world. The twentieth century was characterized by a division of the opiate family into the legal production of compounds, such as morphine, codeine, and hydromorphone for legitimate medical purposes and, on the other hand, the illegal production and distribution of heroin and other illicit narcotics for recreational purposes. The legitimate production of narcotic analgesics has led to innovative and effective means to alleviate pain as well as to ensure the purity and safety of the given drug. The legitimate pharmaceutical industry has also developed drugs to help treat various types of opiate addiction.

Most of the illegal opiates, especially heroin, enter the United States through the Mexican border. According to some law enforcement officials, heroin use may be supplanted in future years by increased use of prescription narcotics, provided that they continue to be available. As a result, the distribution and use of prescription narcotics is closely monitored by state and federal law enforcement agencies. Illicit hydromorphone abuse has not reached the same epidemic levels as OxyContin but remains a problem and a concern for drug enforcement authorities.

CHEMICAL/ORGANIC COMPOSITION

Structurally, hydromorphone is similar to morphine and has similar painkilling and other effects in the body. Hydromorphone by weight is actually a stronger painkiller than morphine. Hydromorphone is combined with a substance called guaifenesin in cough syrup formulations.

INGESTION METHODS

Hydromorphone is available through injections, tablets, oral solution, and suppositories. The usual route of administration is by way of swallowing tablets. For patients who have difficulty swallowing tablets, a flavored oral solution is available. This liquid form of the drug can be poured into a medicine dropper for measurement by the patient or a nurse. The liquid can also be added to soft foods to make it easier for the patient to ingest. Some of these liquid formulations may contain alcohol.

THERAPEUTIC USE

Hydromorphone is primarily used to treat patients who are experiencing moderate-to-severe back pain, cancer pain, and headache. In addition, hydromorphone is used before and during a variety of surgical dental procedures. Hydromorphone is also available as a cough syrup for the control of dry, non-productive cough or persistent, exhausting cough.

Chronic pain, especially back pain, is one of the most common maladies treated with hydromorphone and other narcotic analgesics. This type of pain can often be alleviated to the point where the person can function to some degree. Hydromorphone is also effectively used to treat cancer pain. Much of the pain associated with cancer involves what is called neuropathic pain. This is pain caused by interference or disruption of nerve cells and nerve transmission in the body.

Hydromorphone is also used to treat chronic pain syndromes. These pain syndromes can develop from a variety of injuries and can affect muscles, joints, and other parts of the body. In such cases, patients often take the drug on an "as needed" basis. Hydromorphone is frequently prescribed to treat pain associated with moderate-to-severe osteoarthritis. Narcotic analgesics are generally prescribed for these patients when other painkilling drugs are not effective.

Patients who have neuropathic pain also use hydromorphone. This includes AIDS and diabetes patients who often develop peripheral neuropathy as their conditions progress. This complication produces a tingling or burning sensation in the hands or feet. If untreated, the pain can progress to the point where normal activities, such as walking, can be severely impaired.

Hydromorphone is also indicated for use during surgical procedures, and pain associated with trauma to bone and tissue, biliary colic, myocardial infarction, severe burns, and renal colic.

Hydromorphone is more potent than morphine by weight and is believed to produce analgesic effects four to eight times greater than morphine. Side effects are comparable to morphine with the exception of vomiting, which tends to be less frequent with hydromorphone use.

USAGE TRENDS

Scope and severity

Despite worry over the potential for addiction, opioid use for medical purposes has been increasing in recent years for most narcotic analgesics. However, despite the overall increase in the use of opioids for legitimate medical reasons, drug abuse among legitimate users has fallen during this period of time.

Evidence gathered from surveys in the United States suggest prescription drug abuse is increasing. In these surveys, prescription drug abuse in the 1980s was compared with trends in the 1990s. During the 1980s, researchers estimated that less than one-half million persons abused prescription drugs. However, this number increased by 181% between 1990 and 1998 among pain-relieving drugs.

Evidence collected by the National Institute on Drug Abuse (NIDA) during 1999 suggests more than four million persons in the United States over the age of 12 years were using a variety of prescription drugs for nonmedical purposes. Many of these individuals were first-time users of these drugs. Most of the first-time users were between 12 and 25 years of age.

Statistics gathered by NIDA indicate that prescription drug abuse among girls is significantly increasing. Overall, girls are using illicit drugs at a higher rate than boys in the same age groups. The prescription drugs most likely to be abused by young people of both sexes are opioids. Tranquilizers and stimulants are also highly abused by many young people.

Women are more likely than men to receive prescribed drugs that are abused among adult populations. These prescribed drugs are most often antidepressants and pain relievers. Evidence indicates that men and women are at similar risk for becoming addicted to opioids. However, women are far more likely to become addicted to other types of prescription drugs than men.

The use of pain relievers is also significant in the elderly; it is well-known that pain is a widespread problem in this age group. Up to one-half of the elderly not living in nursing homes are affected by pain on a regular basis. The American Geriatrics Society also reports that as many as 20% of those over the age of 65 years use prescription pain relievers at least once per week. Furthermore, about 60% of the elderly have taken some type of prescription pain reliever for a minimum of six months. In nursing homes, these rates are even higher.

LAW AND ORDER

About 30 million prescriptions and orders are written each year for controlled substances. It is not precisely known how many of these prescriptions and orders are diverted illegally, but it is known that these controlled substances account for more than 30% of all deaths and injuries associated with drug abuse. Hydromorphone is in this group of controlled substances, a group that also includes codeine, methadone, hydrocodone, oxycodone, and amphetamine. The profitability of selling these prescription drugs is high. Even at market value, most of these drugs only cost pennies per unit to buy but are sold for several times that value on the street.

The DEA currently believes that physicians and pharmacists are the primary forces that allow this criminal behavior to occur. It is their easy access to these controlled substances that creates a pipeline of drug distribution to criminals who sell them on the street.

The DEA investigated a physician in Texas over a four-year-period to uncover the astonishing fact that this man had written 7% of all hydromorphone prescriptions in the state of Texas between 1988 and 1990. This doctor had written more than 500 prescriptions that totaled more than 54,000 dosage units of hydromorphone during this two-year period. The man sold the prescriptions for $500 each, and had his receptionist create fictitious patient records to help disguise the criminal activity. The man received 33 months in prison for drug trafficking and was ordered to pay $80,000 restitution to the Texas Medicaid program.

The success of legal prohibition of opiates and related compounds can be considered mixed at best. Most economists and legal scholars believe the prohibition of drug trade and use increases the price of the drugs on the black market. Strong penalties for using drugs, such as illicit opiates, discourages addicts from receiving treatment, and leads many to commit crimes to pay for the high price of drugs. Economists point to the relatively inexpensive price of legal but prescribed narcotics compared to the price on the streets, where both legally and illegally produced narcotics are sold at exorbitant prices. Still, evidence gathered from countries where narcotic use is decriminalized or has less serious penalties suggests addiction rates are as high or higher, and crime rates are still relatively high.

The elderly need greater attention when they receive strong pain-relieving drugs, such as opioids. This is based on the fact that elderly patients are more likely to accidentally misuse prescription drugs than the general population. They are more likely to inaccurately read drug labels and to not follow health-care provider instructions. Generally, the elderly need lower doses of drugs, especially potent drugs, than the general population.

Another area of concern in prescription drug abuse is with health-care providers, such as nurses, doctors, pharmacists, dentists, and others. These persons have ready access to highly addictive drugs, such as the opioids, and are more vulnerable to such abuse. In addition, these professions are more stressful than average, and this may be a factor in the higher-than-normal rates of abuse in this group.

Many drug abusers have developed elaborate schemes for obtaining prescription drugs for nonmedical purposes. They are often able to successfully dupe physicians into prescribing drugs, such as opioids, for recreational drug use. Many physicians believe these individuals are in pain and need relief. Organizations such as the Substance Abuse and Mental Health Services Administration are attempting to educate physicians about the warning sign behaviors associated with these abusers.

Age, ethnic, and gender trends

According to a report commissioned by the Texas Commission on Alcohol and Drug Abuse, adult clients who were admitted to a heroin inhalation addiction treatment program in 1998 tended to be male (65%), African-American (36%), and low-income (average yearly income $6,784). This fits with data collected from opiate addicts from other parts of the country. Researchers also know that hydromorphone, when available on the street, is commonly substituted for heroin. However, it is also known that women are much more likely to abuse prescription drugs than men, but men are much more likely to abuse the illicit forms of drugs, including opiates. Abuse of opiates, like abuse of most all other drugs, is mostly carried out by younger persons, but this is not always the case.

MENTAL EFFECTS

Hydromorphone, as with other narcotic analgesics, should be used with great caution when performing acts that require alertness, such as driving or operating heavy machinery. The most common side effects on the brain from taking hydromorphone are sedation and drowsiness. Dizziness and agitation also are known to occur when taking this drug. Like many drugs, hydromorphone should not be discontinued suddenly. Doses should be gradually tapered and then stopped.

Hydromorphone is highly addictive. Its use needs to be carefully monitored by the treating physician. Long-term use of the drug can lead to physical and psychological dependency. Mood can also be affected by hydromorphone and other narcotic analgesics. Infrequently, hallucinations and disorientation can develop. Insomnia develops in a minority of cases.

PHYSIOLOGICAL EFFECTS

Hydromorphone and other narcotic analgesics have specific effects on the central nervous system in the body. These effects are produced through the binding of opioid-specific receptors in the brain. Hydromorphone also produces similar effects in organs in the body that contain smooth muscle. The primary therapeutic effects of hydromorphone are analgesia and sedation. One of the most important aspects of narcotic analgesics, such as hydromorphone, is that they produce significant analgesia without causing a loss of consciousness.

Hydromorphone affects the respiratory center in the brain, and this is why it suppresses the cough reflex. Hydromorphone is partially broken down, or metabolized, by the liver and is absorbed by a variety of tissues and organs, including the gastrointestinal tract, smooth muscle, skeletal muscle, pancreas, lungs, cardiovascular system, and central nervous system. Once metabolized by the liver, hydromorphone moves out of the body by way of the kidneys and into the urine. The precise mechanisms by which hydromorphone and the other narcotic analgesics work are not entirely known.

The levels of hydromorphone usually peak in the body about 45 minutes after oral administration of the drug. Injections into muscle produce effects within 15 to 30 minutes and reach peak levels between one-half to one and one-half hours later. The duration of effect usually lasts four to five hours. The actual amount of hydromorphone prescribed or administered depends on a variety of factors, including age, the degree of pain, the amount of opioid tolerance, and the body mass of the patient.

Hydromorphone produces pain-relieving qualities in the central nervous system. It also tends to produce a euphoric feeling in the user. Negative effects by way of the central nervous system include decreased blood pressure and slowed breathing. Hydromorphone slows down the processes of the gastrointestinal tract and commonly causes constipation. Patients taking hydromorphone need to increase water and fiber intake to prevent and treat constipation.

 **IN THE NEWS**

Researchers at the National Institute on Drug Abuse have formed a group called the Community Epidemiology Work Group (CEWG) to monitor drug abuse trends in 21 major cities in the United States. Investigators found that in 1999, the most recent year fully analyzed, heroin and morphine abuse is on the increase in 15 of these cities. Overall, emergency room visits associated with heroin use increased 51.4% in the 18- to 25-year-old category between 1997 and 1999. It is known that hydromorphone and oxycodone are commonly substituted for heroin and morphine by many drug abusers.

A study in the April 5, 2000 issue of the *Journal of the American Medical Association* found that hydromorphone use for medical indications increased by 19% from 1990 to 1996. This increase coincided with an decrease in the number of hydromorphone drug abuse mentions during this period. The decrease in hydromorphone drug abuse (15%) suggests a low risk of addiction associated with the medical use of hydromorphone in the treatment of severe pain.

The most common side effects associated with the use of hydromorphone are increased sweating, light-headedness, dizziness, sedation, mental depression, nausea, and vomiting. Less commonly seen side effects include weakness, headache, muscle rigidity, decreased feeling in the extremities, double vision, hallucinations, disorientation, muscle coordination problems, muscle tremor, hearing loss, agitation, euphoric feelings, blurred vision, and insomnia. Additional side effects can include changes in heart rhythm, chills, decreased blood pressure, increased blood pressure, diarrhea, cramps, itching, dry mouth, skin flushing, breathing alterations, constipation, anorexia, cramps, alterations in taste, skin rashes, and urinary difficulties.

Patients with a history of cardiovascular, respiratory, or intestinal problems should use hydromorphone with great caution. One of the most serious and overlooked side effects that develops from the long-term use of opioids is the potential for serious dehydration.

Hydromorphone has comparable side effects to those produced by morphine use. This is true for sedation, respiratory depression, and constipation, but hydromorphone is associated with less vomiting than morphine. Nausea caused by hydromorphone and other opioids can be minimized by administering the drug along with food and having the patient lie down following administration.

???? FACT OR FICTION

One of the prevailing views about opioid use is that it is common for persons using the drug for medical purposes to become addicted. While this does occur, it is not common among those who legitimately need the drug for pain and who have no history of substance abuse or addiction. Addiction is sometimes confused with tolerance in cases where patients are receiving opioids for serious pain. Tolerance to opioids happens when the drug dose has to be increased to produce a similar pharmacological effect. When tolerance develops, there is also a decrease in the length of time that the opioid produces its effect. In patients with intractable cancer pain, doses can usually be increased carefully over time without serious risk to the patient.

Extra caution should be taken when hydromorphone is prescribed to the elderly, those with significant physical impairment, and those with a history of liver, lung, or kidney disease. In addition, those with thyroid problems, Addison's disease, central nervous system depression, coma, psychosis caused by toxic agents, and those with a history of gallbladder disease should receive hydromorphone only with great caution. The same is true for persons with a history of prostate enlargement, a narrowing of the urethra, severe alcoholism, delirium tremens, recent gastrointestinal surgery, or severe scoliosis.

Harmful side effects

Using more than the recommended dose of hydromorphone can cause a variety of serious health complications, such as convulsions, coma, and death. Early symptoms of overdose include confusion, nervousness, dizziness, low blood pressure, severe weakness, decreased pupil size, drowsiness, and slowed breathing. Later manifestations of serious overdose include significant changes in heart rate, low blood pressure, coma, and cardiac arrest. Persons who overdose on hydromorphone are usually treated with narcotic antagonists, such as naloxone. It is vital for the attending emergency physician to maintain respiratory function in these patients. Naloxone not only helps reduce the effects of hydromorphone throughout the body but also has specific respiratory-protecting effects.

Individuals who have developed tolerance to opioids and who have overdosed on hydromorphone are not likely to develop the serious depression of the respiratory system that occurs in individuals with no such tolerance who have overdosed on hydromorphone. The typical treatment of narcotic overdoses with narcotic antagonists can lead to a severe withdrawal reaction in those who have developed tolerance to opioids.

The Food and Health Administration has placed hydromorphone in the pregnancy category C. This means that pregnant women should receive hydromorphone only with great caution and should receive a high-potency formulation only when it is absolutely necessary. This classification is based on animal studies that suggest birth defects are more likely in animals receiving high doses of the drug. There have been no strictly controlled scientific studies in humans.

Women who are breastfeeding should likewise use caution before taking hydromorphone. This caution is based on the fact that low levels of narcotic drugs have been found in the milk of mothers who use these drugs. Therefore, *Mosby's Medical Drug Reference* recommends that nursing mothers not use hydromorphone. Women who are breastfeeding should inform their doctor or dentist that they are nursing if they require a strong prescription pain medication.

Persons with a history of acute bronchial asthma should not receive hydromorphone. Persons with a history of head injury, increased pressure within the brain, seizures, serious abdominal problems, liver disease, kidney disease, thyroid disease, prostate disease, and low blood pressure should use hydromorphone with great caution. Also, the elderly should receive hydromorphone with great caution.

Long-term health effects

The primary long-term concern of those who use hydromorphone is the risk of addiction. The National Institute on Drug Abuse has determined that persons who become addicted to hydromorphone and other narcotic analgesics are at increased risk of convulsion, overdose, and death.

Persons with a history of drug abuse of any kind should not receive hydromorphone unless absolutely necessary because of the great potential for addiction. Hydromorphone can become addictive for anyone who has received doses higher than those prescribed by a doctor and in those who use the drug for recreational purposes. In addition, those who receive the drug at prescribed levels for a lengthy period are at a relatively slight increased risk of addiction.

REACTIONS WITH OTHER DRUGS OR SUBSTANCES

Hydromorphone should never be combined with other drugs that depress the central nervous system. Such drugs include sedatives, tranquilizers, alcohol, and anesthetics. In addition, other types of drugs, such as antidepressants, antihistamines, anticonvulsants, and muscle relaxants should not be combined with hydromorphone. All of these combinations can produce excessive drowsiness. Patients should inform their doctor or dentist if they are currently taking any of these medications or have taken them in the last two weeks.

Hydromorphone should not be combined with other pain medications. This includes over-the-counter medications that are commonly used to treat pain, such as Nuprin or Tylenol. If the prescribed dose of hydromorphone does not sufficiently alleviate the pain, then the treating doctor can adjust the dose. The patient should not make adjustments of hydromorphone dose on his or her own or add pain medications to the regimen.

Patients who have received hydromorphone for long periods of time or those with confirmed opioid dependency should not receive the so-called agonist/antagonist analgesics, such as nalbuphine, pentazocine, butorphanol, dezocine, and buprenorphine. The use of these drugs in these patients can intensify withdrawal symptoms.

TREATMENT AND REHABILITATION

Addiction to hydromorphone and other prescription painkillers is one of the major reasons behind admittance to drug rehabilitation clinics. Treatment for opiate addiction has been occurring in the United States since the early part of the twentieth century. In these early days of treatment, doctors in private practice prescribed narcotics to those addicted to opiate drugs. Later, governments outlawed this practice and began operating clinics where morphine could be obtained by addicts. Eventually, these clinics were also closed. At that point in time, addicts began to be treated in public health hospitals or placed in jail.

The problem of opiate drug abuse both with illegal and prescription narcotics increased during the 1960s. In the years that followed, researchers and clinicians looked to new methods to treat the growing problem. Genetic factors have gained importance as one of the major underlying factors in narcotic and other types of dependence. The idea is that addicts have a stronger vulnerability to substance-abuse behaviors than those with no such inclination. Mental illness, previous history of substance abuse, and other environmental factors are undoubtedly important in the development of narcotic addiction.

It is important that patients who use hydromorphone and other narcotic analgesics not stop taking these drugs suddenly. Doses should be gradually tapered down with the help of the prescribing physician. Rapid cessation of these drugs can produce withdrawal symptoms. Although these withdrawal symptoms are not life threatening, they can cause significant discomfort. These symptoms begin with insomnia, restlessness, anxiety,

IN THE NEWS

Hydromorphone has long been a highly used painkilling drug in the United States. It is more potent by weight than morphine, and this makes it an attractive treatment for those with intractable pain, such as terminal cancer patients. Abuse among those with legitimate medical needs is low, but there is evidence that abuse of hydromorphone on the street by opioid addicts is on the rise. Like OxyContin (oxycodone), though not to the same degree, hydromorphone is being diverted to the street for illicit purposes, primarily by pharmacists and physicians.

The markup street price of hydromorphone is significant though not as great as that of oxycodone. Typically, the drug sells for $6 to $8 for tablets ranging from 2 mg to 8 mg. While much of the illicit hydromorphone distribution channel can be blamed on criminal activity by pharmacists and physicians, there is a considerable amount of criminal behavior being committed by patients. One of the most common tactics used by addicts and those who are misappropriating opioid prescription drugs is to visit multiple doctors and attempt to obtain multiple prescriptions for a made-up condition. This is referred to as "doctor shopping."

The fear of opioids falling into the wrong hands has prompted some pharmacies not to stock narcotic analgesics, and some hospitals have limited the use of opioids to cancer patients only. There have even been reports of patients keeping their prescriptions secret out of fear of having their pills stolen.

and yawning and progress to more serious symptoms, such as vomiting, fever, sweating, abdominal pain, nausea, diarrhea, muscle aches, and other body pain.

Symptoms begin about 72 hours after the last dose and include anxiety, weakness, increased irritability, muscle twitching, kicking movements, significant backache, hot and cold flashes, anorexia, insomnia, muscle spasm, and intestinal spasm. Additional symptoms can include repetitive sneezing, increased body temperature, increased blood pressure, diarrhea, vomiting, increased respiratory rate, and increased heart rate.

If withdrawal symptoms do develop, some medical approaches can be used to treat symptoms. One approach uses the drug clonidine, which is typically used to treat patients with high blood pressure. Clonidine has been found to lessen some of the withdrawal symptoms. Tranquilizers can be used to treat symptoms such as insomnia and anxiety. Ibuprofen or naproxen can treat symptoms such as muscle ache, headache, or joint pain. Another approach is to replace hydromorphone, or any other narcotic analgesic, with methadone, a narcotic that has long been used to help treat heroin addicts.

The Drug Addiction Treatment Act of 2000 allows opioids to be distributed to physicians for the treatment of opioid dependence. This allows physicians to treat opioid-addicted patients on an individual basis and eliminates the need for the patient to attend a methadone clinic. Patients receiving this treatment should have been opioid-dependent for more than one year, had at least two previously unsuccessful opioid treatment episodes during a calendar year, and had a relapse to opioid dependence after previous opioid treatment. The only currently approved drugs under this act are methadone and levo-alpha-acetylmethadol. The treatment program not only involves drug therapy with these agents but also provides a combination of counseling and rehabilitation activities.

PERSONAL AND SOCIAL CONSEQUENCES

The opiates and their semi-synthetic and synthetic relatives have long been among the most important drugs in the world because of their ability to alleviate the most severe forms of pain. Often, this pain is derived from invasive surgical procedures or from advanced cancer pain that is virtually untreatable without this family of drugs. A clear majority of persons who use opiates and their relatives never develop an addiction problem. However, addiction can develop quickly in those with a propensity for these drugs. This can occur in those who are using them for medical reasons as well as in those who use them recreationally.

A drawback to physicians' increased caution for prescription drug abuse has been the reluctance by some medical providers to prescribe opioids for persons having a legitimate medical need for the drugs. This has led to the under-prescribing of opioids and the under-treatment of patients with significant pain. Many in the medical community have held the view that increased opioid prescription rates would necessarily increase the rate of opioid abuse. This is not the case, according to a study published in the April 2000 issue of the *Journal of the American Medical Association*. This study showed that even though the rate of oxycodone use had increased by 23% in a recent period of time, the reported rate of abuse did not significantly change.

The increased vigilance of legal authorities to crack down on prescription drug abuse has led to situations where patients are afraid to ask for sufficient pain medication for fear of being seen as an "addict" or someone with a low pain threshold. Many physicians are afraid to prescribe opioids because they are required by law to record and justify all narcotic analgesic prescriptions.

This fear of prescribing opioids even when the patient is obviously suffering has been labeled *opiophobia*. They face potential criminal prosecution if these records do not conform to federal law. Many physicians are also wary of getting their patients "hooked" on these narcotics.

Those patients who do become addicted to opioids as well as those who become addicted for nonmedical reasons typically have a difficult time getting off the drugs. These individuals usually face a variety of problems along the way. They often have a difficult time holding a job, and their family life tends to be unstable. If untreated for addiction, many of these individuals eventually resort to living off welfare programs.

Opiate addiction has also helped spread diseases, such as the human immunodeficiency virus, hepatitis B virus, hepatitis C virus, and tuberculosis among addicts who inject the opiate drugs and share dirty needles. The rate of opiate-associated emergency hospital visits in recent years has significantly increased. Furthermore, the number of deaths related to those opiate overdoses has almost doubled in this period. All of these trends point to the significant social costs associated with opiate abuse in the United States.

LEGAL CONSEQUENCES

Researchers long ago found an association between narcotics addiction and increased levels of crime. Significant numbers of prisoners incarcerated in the United States have been imprisoned because of crimes involving drugs and drug abuse. A report by a conference at the National Institutes of Health found that more than one-fourth of all prisoners at all state and federal prisons were convicted of drug-related crimes.

Researchers have found strong associations between opiate addiction and theft. Opiate addicts steal to obtain greater amounts and quality of drug. The goal of many researchers and drug treatment programs is to not only to treat the opiate addiction problem of the individual but also to reduce the amount of theft and other crimes associated with this problem.

Legal history

Until 1914, it was legal to put opiates into patent medicines, for example, that were sold over-the-counter. A 1914 law was the first to regulate the sale and distribution of controlled substances. At the time, this law was not enacted to benefit public health, but rather to generate tax revenue.

Federal guidelines, regulations, and penalties

Hydromorphone is classified as a Schedule II controlled substance under the Controlled Substances Act

(CSA) of 1970. This act of the United States Congress placed enforcement of the CSA on the shoulders of the Drug Enforcement Administration (DEA). The CSA was created as a means to regulate the distribution and use of prescription drugs that are highly addictive, such as codeine, oxycodone, morphine, and hydromorphone. The CSA was not enacted to limit or disrupt the practice of medicine and the legitimate use of narcotic analgesics in patients with significant pain.

Under the CSA, a Schedule II drug is one that has a high potential for abuse and whose use may lead to significant psychological or physical dependence. Prescriptions for these drugs must be typewritten or written in ink and signed by the practitioner, or verbal prescriptions must be confirmed in writing within 72 hours and may be given only in a genuine emergency. No renewals are allowed without a new prescription.

Despite the significant power bestowed by Congress on the DEA to enforce the CSA, the actual power of the DEA to regulate and control physician practice is not unlimited. This provision allows physicians some leeway when treating terminal cancer patients with intractable pain, for instance. Such patients often receive significant amounts of opioids, and this could raise the eyebrows of the DEA. All physicians who prescribe drugs classified under the CSA are registered with the DEA for monitoring reasons. Likewise, other components of the health care system, such as hospitals and pharmacies, must also register with the DEA. All of the individuals and entities that dispense drugs covered under the CSA receive a number issued by the DEA. This number can be tracked every time one of these controlled substances is prescribed. All of these entities must also keep very accurate records that document all of the information associated with the prescription.

The primary aim of the CSA and the DEA's implementation of the law is to find those physicians who are prescribing opioids and other controlled substances for nonmedical purposes. All of the entities included in the chain of the production and distribution of the controlled substance are carefully watched by the DEA for signs of irregularities. Violators of the CSA can be charged with a felony and are subject to fines and imprisonment.

In addition to federal laws enforced by the DEA, many states have supplemental laws that cover controlled substances. These state laws have even more detailed guidelines on dosage limits and the total number of pills that can be prescribed. One of the oddities present in the CSA and the DEA guidelines is that there are no limitations on the amount of drug prescribed at one time or on the length of treatment for the patient. This is surprising because the guidelines for dispensing Schedule II drugs are so precise in some areas, such as the inability to renew prescriptions. The laws generated by some states attempt to eliminate some of the loopholes created by the CSA and the DEA guidelines.

See also Cocaine; Heroin; Morphine; Opium

RESOURCES

Books

Booth, Martin. *Opium: A History.* New York: St. Martin's Press, 1996.

Consumer Reports Complete Drug Reference, 2002 ed. Edited by Consumer Reports Staff. Denver: Micromedex Thomson Healthcare, 2001.

Ellsworth, Allan J., et al. *Mosby's Medical Drug Reference 2001-2002.* St. Louis: Mosby, 2001.

Hardman, Joel G., and Lee E. Limbird, ed. *Goodman & Gilman's The Pharmacological Basis of Therapeutics,* tenth ed. New York: McGraw-Hill, 2001.

Mosby's GenRx, 9th ed. St. Louis: Mosby, 1999.

Periodicals

Chernin, Tammy. "Painkillers and Pill Popping." *Drug Topics* (August 6, 2001).

Joranson, David E., et al. "Trends in Medical Use and Abuse of Opioid Analgesics." *Journal of the American Medical Association* (April 5, 2000).

Kalb, Claudia. "Playing With Painkillers." *Newsweek* (April 9, 2001).

Other

Congressional Testimony. Statement of Asa Hutchinson, Administrator, Drug Enforcement Administration before the House Committee on Appropriations. December 11, 2001. <http://www.usdoj.gov/dea/pubs/testimony.htm>.

Center for Drug Evaluation and Research. U.S. Food and Drug Administration. 18 July 2002. <http://www.fda.gov/cder/index.html>.

Haddox, J. David. "Legal and Clinical Issues In Prescribing Controlled Substance." 18 July 2002. <http://www.moffitt.usf.edu/pubs/ccj/v6ns/article7.htm>.

Maxwell, Jane C. "Substance Abuse Trends in Texas: December 1998." 18 July 2002. <http://www.tcada.state.tx.us/research/trends/dec98>.

Nationwide Trends. National Institute on Drug Abuse. 18 July 2002. <http://www.nida.nih.gov/infofax/nationtrends.html>.

Organizations

National Clearinghouse for Alcohol and Drug Information (NCADI), P.O. Box 2345, Rockville, MD, USA, 20847-2345, (800) 729-6686, webmaster@health.org, <http://www.health.org>.

National Drug Intelligence Center (NDIC), 319 Washington Street, 5th Floor, Johnstown, PA, USA, 15901-1622, (814) 532-4601, (814) 532-4690, cmbwebmgr@ndic.osis.gov, <http://www.usdoj.gov/ndic/>.

National Institute on Drug Abuse (NIDA), National Institutes of Health, 6001 Executive Boulevard, Room 5213, Bethesda, MD, USA, 20892-9561, (301) 443-1124, (888) 644-6432, information@lists.nida.nih.gov, <http://www.nida.nih.gov>.

Substance Abuse and Mental Health Services Administration (SAMHSA)/Center for Substance Abuse Treatment (CSAT)., 5600 Fishers Lane, Rockville, MD, USA, 20857, (301) 443-8956, info@samhsa.gov, <http://www.samhsa.gov>.

Mark Mitchell, MD

INHALANTS

OFFICIAL NAMES: Aerosol propellants, medical anesthetic gases, amyl nitrite, butane, chlorofluorocarbons, chloroform, ether, halothane, isobutyl nitrite, nitrous oxide, toluene, organic solvents, refrigerant gases, volatile solvents
STREET NAMES: Aimies, air blast, ames, amys, aroma of men, bolt, boppers, bullet, bullet bolt, buzz bomb, climax, discorama, hardware, heart-on, highball, hippie crack, honey oil, huff, kick, laughing gas, lightning bolt, locker room, Medusa, moon gas, Oz, pearls, poor man's pot, poppers, quicksilver, rush, rush snappers, Satan's secret, shoot the breeze, snappers, sniff, snotballs, spray, Texas shoe-shine, thrust, toilet water, tolly, toncho, whippets or whippits, whiteout
DRUG CLASSIFICATIONS: Not scheduled

OVERVIEW

Inhalant is a term applied to an estimated 1,000 to 1,400 legal products used in households, industry, businesses, and medical settings. These products are as common as a felt-tip marker, a bottle of correction fluid or nail polish remover, a tank of gasoline, a tube of model airplane glue, air freshener or vegetable cooking spray, or a can of silver spray paint.

Inhalants contain chemicals that are volatile, meaning they evaporate or vaporize quickly. When someone inhales a concentrated amount of these vapors, the vapors affect his or her normal mental functioning.

Inhalant abuse refers to the intentional inhalation of such products to experience a carefree, euphoric high. The exact mind-altering effects of inhalants vary, depending on the product involved, but they are generally similar to those produced by alcohol intoxication or anesthesia. The health ramifications can be serious, in both the short and long term, because most inhalants are highly toxic.

Hundreds of thousands of Americans experiment with inhalants for the first time each year, according to results of the 2000 National Household Survey from the Substance Abuse and Mental Health Services Administration (SAMHSA), an agency of the U.S. Department of Health & Human Services. The survey found that in 1999, one million Americans tried inhalants for the first time—the highest annual number of inhalant initiates since 1965. The 1998 estimate of new inhalant abusers was 918,000; in 1997 it reached 975,000.

Volatile solvents are useful in industry and in homes because of their ability to dissolve fat. When inhaled, however, this property poses problems to the brain and the network of nerves that connect the brain and spinal cord to the rest of the body. "...thus, because the brain is a lipid-rich organ, chronic solvent abuse dissolves brain cells," the American Academy of Pediatrics wrote in a 1996 policy paper about inhalants. The chemical vapors also damage the myelin sheath, the fatty wrapper that insulates the fibers of many nerve cells that carry signals.

Solvent abusers can die, sometimes after a single prolonged episode of sniffing, from either physical effects of the chemicals or dangerous behavior related to the user's impaired state of mind. The National Inhalant Prevention Coalition, a nonprofit organization based in Austin, Texas, records 100 to 125 deaths from inhalants

KEY TERMS

ANESTHETIC: An agent that causes loss of sensation or unconsciousness.

BAGGING: Breathing mind-altering fumes from a substance sprayed or placed inside a plastic or paper bag, with the bag held tightly around the mouth.

HUFFING: Breathing mind-altering fumes from a cloth that has been soaked in a volatile substance then stuffed into the mouth.

INHALANTS: Legal household, industrial, medical, and office products that are volatile (vaporize or evaporate easily), producing chemical vapors. Abusers inhale concentrated amounts of these vapors, by various means, to alter their consciousness.

SNIFFING OR SNORTING: Inhaling intoxicating vapors, through the nose, from a volatile substance such as an anesthetic gas, industrial or household solvent, art supply, or aerosol propellant.

SUDDEN SNIFFING DEATH (SSD) SYNDROME: Fatal cardiac arrest that results, under certain conditions, after someone deeply inhales a volatile chemical for its intoxicating effects. Death occurs within minutes.

a year, a number it considers a partial measure. The United States has no central system for logging deaths and injuries from inhalant use.

Though inhalants are legitimate, legal products, the consequences of their misuse have led 38 state legislatures in the United States to enact laws governing their sale and possession to minors. In the United Kingdom as well, prevention efforts include legislation that makes possession of volatile substances more difficult for youth.

Scientists differ in their exact definition of inhalants. However, inhalants generally meet three criteria: they are volatile at room temperature; they are not already part of a distinct class of inhaled drugs, such as nicotine or cocaine; and they are inhaled, by various means, to alter the user's consciousness.

In 2001, the annual Monitoring the Future study (MTF), conducted by the University of Michigan and funded by the National Institute on Drug Abuse, found that 17.1% of eighth graders had abused inhalants at some point in their lives. In 1995, the National Household Survey on Drug Abuse found inhalants to be the second most commonly abused illicit drug by American youth ages 12 years to 17 years, after marijuana.

History

The intoxicating action of certain chemical vapors is not a new discovery. Some researchers have claimed that Pythoness, a mystic in ancient Delphi, delivered her famous oracles while under the influence of heady fumes escaping from an underground cavern.

In the 1770s, Sir Joseph Priestly, an English chemist, discovered nitrous oxide (laughing gas). In 1799, Sir Humphrey Davy suggested it could be used to reduce pain during surgery. In nineteenth-century North America, Europe, and Great Britain, anesthetics (nitrous oxide and ether) and volatile hydrocarbons were inhaled for recreation. In the early twentieth century, the fashion turned to inhaling ether and chloroform, a toxic, volatile liquid then being used as a general anesthetic.

In the 1940s and 1950s, abusers began inhaling gasoline. A report of a youth's addiction to gasoline was printed in the scientific literature in the early 1960s, and gasoline remains a dangerous and widely abused inhalant around the world. Also in the 1960s, sniffing glue—such as the type used in building model airplanes—became popular among some youths, and glue sniffing remains popular today.

Inhalant abuse can also be a hazard in some occupations. People who work in the refrigeration industry may abuse Freon, hydrocarbons used in refrigerants; and people working in medical fields may abuse nitrous oxide. A 1979 study, "Abuse of Nitrous Oxide," published in *Anesthesia & Analgesia,* found that 20% of dental and medical students had abused nitrous oxide.

Most abusers are drawn to inhalants for their psychoactive, or mind-altering, effects. Users of nitrites are the exception. The nitrites make up an inhalant subcategory that includes amyl, butyl, and cyclohexyl nitrites. These substances were nicknamed poppers because in the past, they were packaged in ampules. Users cracked the ampules to release the vapors. Nitrites are abused, internationally, because they produce a sexual rush, accompanied by a sense of power and exhilaration.

Nitrites were highly popular in the United States in 1970s, particularly in the gay community. One study, published in 1988 in the National Institute of Drug Abuse Research Monograph Series, reported that by 1979 up to five million people used nitrites weekly. By the early 1980s, however, nitrite use dropped dramatically. In the United States, amyl nitrite became available solely by prescription in 1979. Also, nitrite use was associated with Kaposi's sarcoma, the most common cancer affecting people with AIDS.

Amyl nitrite's place on the streets has largely been taken by butyl nitrite, a similar chemical with milder effects. These products, sold as "room odorizers" under such brand names as Locker Room and Rush, are often available at head shops, concerts, raves, and dance clubs.

Materials used for sniffing, including two aerosol cans and a small tube of glue. Medical Stock Photo, Inc. Reproduced by permission.

Legal, accessible, dangerous

Re-Solv, a nonprofit group in the United Kingdom that works against solvent abuse, claims that the average home contains about 30 abusable products.

Because they are readily available, inhalants may be the first drug with which children and adolescents experiment—preceding cigarettes. The products are inexpensive or can be easily shoplifted, and many are as close as a kitchen cupboard or utility closet. In addition, inhalants can be easily hidden and are sold legally, factors that contribute to their widespread use. Inhalants are also popular because they produce a high that, in general, hits fast and wears off quickly.

Inhalants' everyday nature may lead some young people to think that the substances are harmless. In addition, risk-taking adolescents may believe they are different and immune to damage, and thus dismiss health warnings about inhalants.

In fact, inhalants can kill, either from accidental causes related to their use, side effects, or a syndrome called sudden sniffing death. Even when inhalant use is not fatal, it can cripple users' bodies and minds. Research has shown that even short-term inhalant use can damage brain functioning over the long term. It also can trip up different parts of the nervous system, including nerve pathways and the brain's cerebral cortex, cerebellum, and hippocampus. Depending on the chemicals involved, inhalants damage the heart, liver, kidneys, bone marrow, and lungs, and also reduce the blood's ability to carry oxygen. Inhalant users may also develop hearing, vision, immune system, and muscle damage over the long term.

In the 1960s, people talked of glue sniffing as "melting your brain." Indeed, brain scans of long-term heavy toluene abusers (an industrial solvent common in many inhaled substances, including glue) show visible shrinkage of brain tissue.

USAGE TRENDS

Much inhalant use is confined to early adolescence. But some users become dependent, and they continue abusing inhalants into adulthood. For other users, inhalants may be the first stop on a long path of misusing dangerous substances.

A study published in 2000 in the *Journal of Substance Abuse* compared three groups of college students at a university in New Mexico: Those who had used inhalants before age 18; those who smoked marijuana before age 18 (but did not use inhalants); and those who used neither marijuana nor inhalants before age 18. Researchers reported that early use of inhalants greatly increased college students' risk of frequent drinking, binge drinking, smoking, and illicit-drug use. Compared with early marijuana use alone, early inhalant use was associated with twice the rate of binge and frequent drinking, and significantly greater rates of tobacco and drug use. The researchers suggested that universities identify early inhalant users and target them for special intervention and prevention efforts.

In a study of imprisoned youth in Canada, published in the October 1999 issue of the *American Journal of Drug and Alcohol Abuse,* many participants cited inhalants as their first substance of abuse, preceding cigarettes, marijuana, illegal hallucinogens, and opiates.

Age, gender, and ethnic trends

The authors of the two studies mentioned above emphasized that this progression does not necessarily mean that young people who use inhalants will later move on to other drugs. Instead, the factors that make youths vulnerable to inhalant use—social and environmental influences, parents, biology and genetics, emotional and learning disorders, attitudes, personality, and behavior—may also increase the likelihood of their turning to other mood-changing substances. Regardless of why inhalant use begins, early inhalant use has been found to increase users' risk of developing drinking and drug problems later in life.

Some researchers have identified adolescent depression as playing an important role in predicting who begins to use, or continues to use, illicit substances. In studies, inhalant users were found to suffer more emotional problems—particularly depression, anxiety, and anger—than those who used other drugs or did not use drugs at all. Inhalant abusers who seek treatment have high rates of psychological illnesses, especially conduct and personality disorders, and typically are dependent on another drug.

Considering the widespread abuse of inhalants, little scientific research has been done on the subject. Conducting research is complicated because inhalants are not limited to one basic compound but include a wide range of chemicals and products.

In 2002, the National Institute on Drug Abuse (NIDA) dedicated about $2 million to fund studies on the nature and extent of inhalant abuse. NIDA sought proposals for research in the following areas: different types of abused substances; socio-cultural, socioeconomic, gender, and regional differences in use; and factors associated with individuals' risk of, vulnerability to, protection against, and resistance to inhalant abuse.

Many research questions remain about the role that factors such as family, role models, existing health problems (such as mental illness, HIV/AIDS, or alcohol abuse), and peer influences play in a young person's decision to start, continue, increase, or stop abusing inhalants.

Categorizing inhalants

The general category of inhalants is broken into smaller categories for purposes of research and discussion. Researchers and organizations working in drug abuse do not use a uniform set of subcategories, however. Common broad subcategories include three or four of the following: nitrous oxide (a gas used in anesthetic and aerosols), volatile nitrites, petroleum distillates, volatile solvents, gases, anesthetics, and aerosols.

Others place them in more specific, descriptive subcategories. The National Institute on Drug Abuse identifies six:

- industrial or household products (paint thinners or solvents, degreasers or cleaning fluids, gasoline, and volatile substances in glues)

- art and office supply solvents (correction fluids, glues, and solvents in markers)

- gases such as butane and chlorofluorocarbons used in household or commercial products (butane lighters, whipped cream dispensers, electronic contact cleaners, and refrigerant gases)

- household aerosol propellants (hair, cooking, lubricant, and fabric protector sprays)

- medical anesthetic gases (ether, chloroform, halothane, and nitrous oxide)

- aliphatic nitrites

However inhalants are categorized, the two most commonly abused types are solvents and gases.

A solvent is a substance that can dissolve another substance, and a volatile solvent is a liquid that vaporizes at room temperature. Volatile solvents include adhesives such as airplane glue and rubber cement; aerosols such as spray paint, hair spray, and air freshener; solvents such as nail polish remover, paint remover, and lighter fluid; and cleaners such as dry cleaning fluid, spot remover, and degreasers.

Gases include anesthesia used in medical procedures, as well as gases used in household or commercial products, such as butane lighters, propane tanks, whipped cream dispensers, and refrigerants.

CHEMICAL/ORGANIC COMPOSITION

No single chemical structure defines inhalants, because the term itself describes any vapor-producing volatile chemical that abusers sniff, huff, spray, or inhale to achieve intoxication. By nature, inhalants come in many forms—about 1,000 to 1,400 different products, according to different U.S. authorities. Also, some products are a mix of chemicals that, when combined, multiply and heighten the toxic impact.

LAW AND ORDER

Massachusetts considers inhalant abuse to be a crime against public health. As an example, following is the text of the pertinent Massachusetts General Law:

Section 18. Substance having property of releasing toxic vapors.

No person shall intentionally smell or inhale the fumes of any substance having the property of releasing toxic vapors, for the purpose of causing a condition of intoxication, euphoria, excitement, exhilaration, stupefaction, or dulled senses or nervous system, nor possess, buy or sell any such substance for the purpose of violating or aiding another to violate this section.

This section shall not apply to the inhalation of anesthesia for medical or dental purposes.

Whoever violates the provisions of this section shall be punished by a fine of not more than two hundred dollars or imprisonment for not more than six months, or both.

Consequences also vary from state to state. They can include fines, jail time, and, less often, treatment.

Following are examples of such chemicals, by category, listed by the National Inhalant Prevention Coalition and Kaiser Permanente:

- Aerosols: Sprays containing propellants and solvents. In the United States, spray paints contain butane and propane (aliphatic hydrocarbons), fluorocarbon, hydrocarbons, and toluene; hair sprays and air fresheners contain butane, propane, and fluorocarbon; aerosol spray topical pain relievers and asthma sprays contain fluorocarbon.

- Anesthetics: Nitrous oxide (N_2O) or laughing gas, the most abused of the gases. Liquid anesthetic contains halothane and enflurane; local anesthetic contains ethyl chloride. Vegetable oil cooking spray and whipping cream cartridges also contain nitrous oxide.

- Cleaning agents: Dry cleaning fluid and spot removers contain tetrachloroethylene and trichloroethane; degreasers contain those ingredients as well as trichloroethylene and methylene chloride. Trichlorethylene and trichlorethane are

???? FACT OR FICTION

Are inhalants dangerous only after long-time use? No. Some damage done by inhalants occurs after many uses over a period of time. But time is not a factor in a syndrome called sudden sniffing death. An otherwise healthy, first-time abuser is as vulnerable as a long-time user to this fatal effect. Victims of sudden sniffing death die within several minutes after inhaling, usually too quickly to reach a hospital.

According to the Cincinnati Drug and Poison Information Center, sudden sniffing death is due to several factors. Because of the way inhalants affect the brain, the blood carries lower levels of oxygen to the brain and rest of the body. The amount of oxygen is decreased even further because the abuser is inhaling chemicals, bringing them into the lungs instead of air.

Inhalants make the heart extra sensitive to adrenaline, a hormone secreted in reaction to stresses. Adrenaline can trigger an irregular heartbeat, which disrupts the body's ability to ship oxygen-rich blood to the brain. Lastly, if an abuser is startled or sent into a fight-or-flight reaction, the body will release extra adrenaline. The extra-sensitivity can disturb the heart rhythm to the point of fatal cardiac arrest.

also found in antifreeze, caulking compounds, and in some paints, glues, adhesives, and sealants.

- Solvents: Polish remover contains acetone; paint remover, paint thinner, and correction fluids contain toluene (an aromatic hydrocarbon), methylene chloride, and methanol; fuel gas contains butane; lighter fluid contains butane and isopropane; fire extinguishers contain bromochlorodifluoromethane.

- Nitrites: Room odorizers such as Locker Room, Rush, Poppers, Bolt, and Climax (also marketed as video head cleaner) contain amyl nitrite, butyl nitrite, and propyl nitrite.

- Freons: Halogenated hydrocarbons, refrigerants.

- Gasoline: A mixture of toluene and benzene and C6-C8 aliphatic.

INGESTION METHODS

Inhalants are so called because, almost exclusively, abusers breathe them into the nose or mouth. Some of the methods for accomplishing this pose additional dangers, such as unconsciousness, suffocation, and freezing of mouth or throat tissue, or vocal chords. Users may also incur injuries from falling, and may suffer sudden cardiac arrest. (Rarely, abusers mix inhalants into soft drinks and drink them.)

NIDA and the Partnership for a Drug-Free America describe several methods by which inhalants area consumed:

- Sniffing or snorting fumes from a container.

- Spraying aerosols directly into the nose or mouth.

- Bagging, which involves sniffing or inhaling fumes from substances sprayed or deposited inside a plastic or paper bag.

- Huffing, which involves soaking a cloth, sock, or roll of toilet paper with an inhalant, then stuffing that in the mouth.

- Inhaling from balloons filled with nitrous oxide.

Once inhaled, the chemicals move into the lungs; from there, they enter the bloodstream. The blood quickly carries the toxins to organs throughout the body, including the brain.

THERAPEUTIC USE

Most inhalants have no medical use. Exceptions are the anesthetic gases and amyl nitrite. Anesthetic gases slow the heart's pumping action, resulting in a drop in blood pressure. They also deaden pain and put surgery patients into an unconscious state. Amyl nitrite, a clear, yellowish liquid, relaxes the smooth muscle in the walls of the arteries. That relaxation dilates the blood vessels, reduces blood pressure, and increases the heart rate.

USAGE TRENDS

The Monitoring the Future study (MTF), funded by the National Institutes of Health's National Institute on Drug Abuse and conducted by the University of Michigan's Institute for Social Research since 1975, looks at lifetime, annual, and 30-day use of 13 categories of drugs, including inhalants. For the 2001 survey, more than 44,000 students filled out questionnaires in a nationally representative sample of eighth, tenth, and twelfth graders at private and public schools.

The 2001 MTF study found a continuation of the gradual decline in inhalant abuse that began in 1996 and 1997 among U.S. middle school and high school students. The study found a peak in inhalant use, for all grades, in 1995.

In the spring 2001 MTF study, 9.1% of eighth graders, 6.6% of tenth graders and 4.5% of twelfth graders reported using inhalants the previous year. In contrast, in 1997 11.8% of eighth graders, 8.7% of tenth graders, and 6.7% of twelfth graders reported using inhalants the previous year. In general, the appeal of inhalants appears to peak in middle school.

Lifetime use of inhalants, defined as whether U.S. students had used them at least once at some point in their lives, dropped from 21% of eighth graders in 1997 to 17.1% in 2001.

Paradoxically, fewer twelfth graders reported that they had used inhalants in the past than did eighth graders. Researchers are puzzled by the fact that, over the years, a lower percentage of high school seniors report that they've ever used inhalants than do middle-school students. The researcher say the conflicting information may be caused by the fact that older students do not recall everything they did when they were younger; and/or that chronic inhalant abusers drop out of school and thus no longer participate in the survey.

The Partnership for a Drug-Free America sponsored a smaller national survey, the 2000 Partnership Attitude Tracking Study, that included 7,290 teenagers in grades seven through 12. In the survey, 13% of students reported using inhalants in the previous year, compared with 11% in 1999. Twenty-one percent said they had tried inhalants at some point in their lives, and 78% percent of the teens said they recognized the deadly consequences of using inhalants. Earlier studies by the same organization found that teens saw dangers in regular use of inhalants, but not in occasional use.

Scope and severity

In looking at how inhalant abuse compares to other drug use, the MTF study found that among eighth graders, 9.1% reported they had used inhalant the previous year, while 41.9% used alcohol, 15.4% reported marijuana/hashish use; and 12.2% used cigarettes.

In its National Drug Threat Assessment 2002, the National Drug Intelligence Center reported that adolescents tend to initially experiment with four substances: alcohol, tobacco, inhalants, and marijuana.

The 2000 National Household Survey on Drug Abuse, a SAMHSA project, found that 8.9% of youths aged 12 to 17—about 2.1 million adolescents—had used inhalants at some time in their lives. In this same age group, 3.9% had used glue, shoe polish, or toluene; and 3.3% reported using gasoline or lighter fluid.

Solvent abuse—particularly toluene-containing products such as gasoline and glue—is common around the world. NIDA considers it "an international public health concern," and notes that the problem is particularly severe in poor nations with high populations of homeless children. Some researchers have attributed the prevalence of glue sniffing in poverty-stricken countries

to the fact that it offers children an escape from hunger pains and their desperate circumstances.

Glue sniffing exploded in Singapore between 1980 and 1991. The Central Narcotics Bureau of Singapore reported 24 cases of inhalent abuse in 1980. In 1985 the reported cases rose to 1,005. Recently, in South America, researchers found that almost a quarter of children of low-income families in Sao Paulo, Brazil, had inhaled a volatile substance at some time in their lives, and 4.9% had done so within the previous month. In Mexico, researchers who conducted a survey of street children found that 12% had started using glue regularly by the age of nine.

Researchers have found high inhalant use in other countries as well. An estimated 3.5% to 10% of children age 12 and under in the United Kingdom have abused volatile substances; and between 0.5% and 1% have become long-term users. In 1999, Australia's National Drug & Alcohol Centre secondary school survey of 25,480 students found that 32% of 12-year-old boys and 37% of 12-year-old girls reported that they had used an inhalant at some point.

Sniffing gasoline is also a serious problem among Native Americans in Canada, among young Aborigines in some rural desert communities in Australia, and among street children in Tanzania and Uganda.

The 1999 European School Survey Project on Alcohol and Other Drugs found the following rates of lifetime inhalant use reported by graduating high school students: Ireland, 22%; Greenland, 19%; Malta, 16%; United Kingdom, 15%; Slovenia, 14%; Greece, 14%; Croatia, 13%; Iceland, 11%; France, 11%; Lithuania, 10%; Hungary, 4%; Portugal, 3%; Bulgaria, 3%; and Romania, 2%.

Age, ethnic, and gender trends

Inhalant users typically fall into one of three groups: young experimenters who may use a variety of inhalants and some marijuana and alcohol; abusers who use multiple drugs, with inhalants as a backup to their drug of choice; and chronic adult users. While inhalant use tends to be at its highest during adolescence, some early abusers move from experimentation into regular, long-term use, and some continue to abuse the substances into their 50s and 60s. Those who continue using inhalants at later ages develop more severe social and psychological problems than do those who discontinue use after adolescence.

In a three-year study of inhalant abuse data from poison centers in 45 states, researchers found that inhalant abuse can begin early in childhood—in some reported cases, before the age of six—and peaks in early adolescence. The study, published in the August 2000 issue of the *Journal of Toxicology*, found that children under age 18 made up 47% of all inhalant abuse patients;

and that 31% of all deaths related to inhalant use occurred in youths between the ages of 13 and 19.

Research on gender differences in use of inhalants have produced varying findings. In 1998, the National Household Survey on Drug Abuse found an even gender split in adolescents (ages 12–17) who experimented with inhalants. However, continued use was more common among older males; the rate of inhalant abuse by males 18 years to 25 years was twice that of their female peers.

Another study, reported by NIDA, found that boys abused inhalants more often than girls in grades four through six. Use evened out in the peak-use years of grades seven through nine; and returned to higher rates for males in grades 10 through 12.

Other researchers have found gender differences in the type of inhalant preferred. For instance, in a Virginia study published in the *American Journal of Drug and Alcohol Abuse* (October 1999), males were significantly more likely than females to abuse gasoline; and females were significantly more likely to abuse hair spray than their male age peers.

Some studies in North America have found the highest rate of inhalant abuse among white and Latino youths, and among Native American youths who live on reservations. The lowest rate of inhalant use is among African-American youths.

In two 1990s studies of high schools in Illinois, published in the November 2000 issue of the *American Journal of Drug and Alcohol Abuse*, researchers found that white and Hispanic teens from strong, two-parent families were less likely to abuse inhalants than those from single-parent families; and that Asian students whose academic performance was poor were more likely to use inhalants than "high-achievers" were.

Death resulting from inhalant use is more common in males. The Drug Abuse Warning Network (DAWN) monitors drug-related deaths as reported by medical examiners in 40 metropolitan areas. In 1999, medical examiners in these cities recorded 129 deaths from inhalants, a 25% increase over the 103 inhalant deaths recorded in 1998. Those who died in 1999 from inhalant use ranged from adolescents to adults age 55 and older, and were predominantly white.

From an socioeconomic perspective, inhalant abuse is most often associated with poverty, but there are abusers in all classes. Older inhalant users may develop abuse problems because they have access to volatile chemicals and anesthetics at the workplace.

The role of community and cultural influences on inhalant use remains uncertain. Some researchers attribute higher use rates among Latinos to poverty, lack of opportunity, and social problems, rather than ethnicity. Others have found traits that distinguish families with greater rates of inhalant abuse, regardless of economic status. Such families may have chaotic lifestyles and with multiple relationship difficulties and other problems. In other cases, the parents may have their own problems with drug and alcohol abuse, or may have either abused their children or lacked strong influence over them. Some parents do not discourage their children from using inhalants or do not disapprove of their children's peers who abuse the substances.

MENTAL EFFECTS

Inhalants deliver their mind-altering effects very quickly, satisfying the desires of users looking for instant gratification. The effects, depending on the inhalant, last from several seconds to several hours.

Abusers initially feel happy, giddy, excited, and uninhibited. After these immediate effects wear off, they may feel lightheaded, dizzy, drowsy, or agitated. They may hallucinate, have delusions, and/or experience a loss of sensation or of "feeling no pain." Concentrated doses can cause confusion and delirium.

Some users try to extend the brief high by sniffing repeatedly over a few hours, a practice that increases the risks of unconsciousness and death.

With time, regular abusers may experience personality and mental changes, including loss of short-term memory and difficulties with attention and learning. They can become apathetic and belligerent, and exhibit poor judgment in personal and work situations. Over the long term, inhalant abusers may display disorientation, inattentiveness, and irritability. They may also suffer from depression.

PHYSIOLOGICAL EFFECTS

The physical effects of inhalants vary because different inhalants combine different chemicals, and they produce different effects during and shortly after use.

Based on their studies of animals, scientists believe that, in general, when toxic vapors circulate to the brain, they depress the central nervous system. The action is similar to that of alcohol, sedatives, and anesthetics. Thus, many of the immediate physical changes inhalant users experience are similar to those caused by alcohol or anesthetics, including relaxation, slurred speech, slowed reflexes, lack of coordination, sleepiness, dizziness, headache, nausea, and vomiting. Abusers might also sneeze, cough, and drool.

Overdose can lead to a fast, irregular heartbeat, which can be fatal—a syndrome called sudden sniffing death.

Toluene, an ingredient in many abused inhalants, possibly works on dopamine, a brain chemical involved in the pleasure-producing effects of other abused substances. More research is needed to understand how inhalants produce their physiological effects.

Nitrites, used to enhance sexual experiences, are in a different category in terms of their effects. When inhaled, nitrates dilate the blood vessels and speed the heartbeat. As a result, abusers feel warm and excited for several minutes. They may also become flushed and dizzy, and may develop a headache.

Harmful side effects

The toxic chemicals in inhalants are capable of damaging many different organs and body systems, including the nervous system (brain, spinal cord, and nerves), heart, lungs, circulatory system, liver, kidneys, and the senses of smell, sight, and hearing. The young age of most abusers increases the potential for damage, because their bodies have not fully matured.

Trichloroethylene, an ingredient in spray paints and correction fluid, can damage the liver. Nitrites and methylene chloride (in paint thinner) reduce the blood's ability to carry proper amounts of oxygen. Inhaled spray paint can damage the lungs. Regular users of nitrous oxide and hexane (an ingredient in some glues and fuels) damage their nervous systems, resulting in numbness, tingling, or paralysis. Toluene hinders the kidneys' ability to regulate the amount of acid in the blood. (When the abuse stops, the kidneys go back to properly controlling acid levels, but the user may later develop kidney stones.) Trichloroethylene, a chemical in spot removers and degreasers, can damage hearing, vision, and the liver. Toluene affects reproduction, and may cause changes in chromosomes, abnormalities during pregnancy, and premature births. An overdose of amyl nitrite can be fatal.

Other side effects of inhalant use include persistent headaches, appetite loss, nosebleeds (sometimes severe enough to require hospitalization), and skin rashes (from contact with glue). Long-term inhalant abusers may lose weight, muscle tone and strength, and coordination.

Inhalants cross the placenta and are dangerous to the developing fetus. Infants born to solvent abusers suffer neonatal (newborn) inhalant withdrawal: high-pitched, extreme crying; poor sleeping and eating; quivering and trembling; and rigid, tense muscles. Researchers do not know if abnormalities that these infants develop are due to inhalants or another cause, such as alcohol. Studies of animals indicate that toluene causes low birth weight, skeletal abnormalities, and development delays.

IN THE NEWS

While ecstasy and OxyContin make headlines as the latest dangerous drugs, news coverage of inhalants is much more subdued. When surveyed, 40% of parents were unaware that sniffing inhalants is extremely dangerous, according to the Partnership for a Drug-Free America. Yet in 2000, 16.7 million youths reported having used inhalants at some point, according to the Substance Abuse and Mental Health Services Administration's Household Survey on Drug Abuse. That contrasts with the 6.4 million ecstasy users and 400,000 OxyContin users the survey identified.

Inhalant use has been called a silent epidemic, the breath of death, and the drug problem most resistant to prevention efforts. Huffing and sniffing are potentially deadly for both new and experienced users, yet the issue has escaped the attention of many parents, teachers, physicians, and law enforcement officers. National surveys variously show that only 3% to 10% of parents believe their children have abused inhalants. Others see it as a harmless passing phase.

How does an overlooked health risk break into the news? The National Inhalant Prevention Coalition, with the support of the Mental Health Services Administration Center for Substance Abuse Treatment, publicizes the subject each March, during National Inhalants and Poison Awareness Week. In 1999, the American Academy of Pediatrics commissioned an inhalant abuse survey, which received a great deal of national news coverage.

Long-term health effects

Long-term, heavy use of inhalants damages the brain and the network of nerves that connects the brain and spinal cord to other organs. Research already conducted is inadequate, however, to determine the level of damage caused by relatively low levels of inhalant use. There also is insufficient information on the extent to which damage is reversible once a person stops using the substances.

Most damage to the nervous system develops after the abuse has continued two or three times a week for at least six months; but any amount of solvent abuse can break down nerve fibers.

Because different inhalants damage different parts of the brain and nervous system, the resulting problems depend on which areas were affected. If the frontal cortex is affected, problem-solving and advance-planning skills are impaired. The abuser may lose physical coordination and speed if the cerebellum is damaged. Oxygen deprivation in the hippocampus causes problems with learning new information or remembering familiar things. Damage to the myelin sheath (a protective coating on nerve cells) disrupts the nerves' ability to send and receive the messages that enable the body to think and act.

Health effects from inhalants range from mild to severe. A distinction between harmful side effects and long-term effects has not been fully determined. "Although some inhalant-induced damage to the nervous and other organ systems may be at least partially reversible when inhalant abuse is stopped, many syndromes caused by repeated or prolonged abuse are irreversible," according to the NIDA research report on inhalants, which was updated in February 2002.

NIDA's list of irreversible effects include hearing loss, limb spasms, brain damage, and bone marrow damage. Serious but potentially reversible effects include liver and kidney damage, and depletion of oxygen from the blood.

Nitrites carry special risks, even with modest use. Based on their research with animals, scientists suspect that nitrite abuse reduces the number of cells in the immune system. This possibly hinders the body's efforts to fight infectious diseases and resist the growth of tumors.

Death is also a possible consequence of inhalant abuse, because the chemicals displace oxygen, leading to an increased risk of sudden sniffing death. Users also die from asphyxiation (from inhaling repeatedly, which leaves the lungs full of chemicals instead of oxygen), suffocation (from blocking air to the lungs while inhaling fumes from a plastic bag over the head), choking (from inhaling and choking on vomit), and from a variety of accidental injuries caused by mental and physical effects of inhalants (car wrecks, drowning, falls, burns).

REACTIONS WITH OTHER DRUGS OR SUBSTANCES

Inhalants are not usually used with another illicit substance, though early users of inhalants have, on later surveys, reported early use (before age 18) of other drugs as well: marijuana, cocaine, amphetamines, and hallucinogens. Because some inhalants are flammable, this adds the additional health danger of fire and burns if someone near the abuser lights up to smoke tobacco or marijuana.

When users do combine inhalants with other drugs, the effects increase the health risks. Alcohol slows down the metabolism of toluene, thus raising its concentration in the blood. Cocaine can boost the chance of fatal irregular heart rhythms. Use of all of these substances, alone or in combination, increases the risk of dangerous behaviors.

TREATMENT AND REHABILITATION

Despite the extent of inhalant abuse and its potential for destroying mental and physical functions, little is known about effective behavior modification or drug-abuse prevention approaches to treating inhalant abusers. Inhalant abusers are often excluded from more general studies on drug abuse.

Relapse and treatment failure rates are high among inhalant abusers. Some professionals believe that programs specific to inhalant abuse, perhaps led by recovering abusers, are critical to improving treatment success. Few such programs exist. Indeed, some general treatment programs exclude inhalant abusers because of the difficulties in successfully treating them. The National Inhalant Prevention Coalition helps callers find centers that treat inhalant abuse.

As of 2002, inhalant abusers are mostly treated in the same programs that address addiction to other substances. The programs use the same approaches that are effective with other drug problems. Clinicians start by taking a history of the patient. That includes conducting a physical exam, screening for organ damage, and taking a detailed history of the length, type, and frequency of abuse. Building self-esteem and self-confidence, and strengthening ethnic identity, appear to help inhalant abusers recover, according to studies published in the 1970s.

When the patient is a teenager or younger, the treatment center conducts a family assessment. Treatment counselors attempt to assess parents' problems with drugs or their general mental health. The goals are to spot problems within the family and begin addressing them. The process includes identifying what is stressing users and teaching them better coping skills; treating any accompanying psychiatric conditions or additional addictions; and encouraging the child to engage in healthy friendships and stay away from peers who abuse inhalants.

Inhalants take a toll on the users' thinking skills, which can complicate treatment. Some patients need extra neurological and cognitive testing so that treatment can be properly tailored to their needs.

The toxic chemicals in inhalants are stored in fatty tissue in the body for weeks. Thus, when long-term abusers attempt to quit, they may develop withdrawal symptoms several hours to a few days afterward. The Office of National Drug Control Policy and the American Academy of Pediatrics list these common withdrawal symptoms: hand tremors, excessive sweating, constant headache, rapid pulse, insomnia, nausea, vomiting, physical agitation, anxiety, hallucinations, and grand mal seizures.

Much remains unknown about the physiology of withdrawal from various subcategories of inhalants and the best ways to address withdrawal symptoms. In early 2002, the National Institute on Drug Abuse, which had not funded a study specifically looking at treatment for inhalant abusers, was actively encouraging researchers to submit proposals in this area.

Long-term treatment, as long as two years, has yielded the best results for inhalant abusers. The aftercare must continue outside the facility and into the community to be effective. Research shows that recovery is helped by factors such as parent groups who patrol inhalant abuse hot spots, and communities that offer structured recreational or other programs for youths to fill the time they previously spent sniffing or huffing.

PERSONAL AND SOCIAL CONSEQUENCES

Because many abusers begin using inhalants when they are young, they do not engage in the normal process of social, personal, and physical development during adolescence. This handicaps their physical and emotional maturity.

Moreover, the side effects of inhalants are a bad match for driving a vehicle, operating machinery, absorbing information in a classroom, offering stable friendship, participating positively in a family, or tackling any task with energy, focus, and efficiency.

Regular inhalant abusers perform poorly in school. In general, they earn low grades, score poorly on intelligence tests, experience problems with short-term memory, and have a weak ability to form abstract thoughts and exercise sound judgment. They also have a greater likelihood of developing attention deficit disorder. They tend to be absent from school a great deal, and drop out of school more often than nonusers do.

Psychological studies have shown that inhalant abusers are generally apathetic and have a negative view of the future. They have a greater likelihood of developing emotional problems, particularly anxiety, depression, and anger. They are more likely to break the law, particularly by engaging in theft and burglary, than do users of other drugs. They also tend to be disruptive, deviant, or delinquent.

Some of these problems may spring from the inhalant abuse; others may have developed before the abuse began, inclining the users to seek an escape from reality or their problems.

LEGAL CONSEQUENCES

The estimated 1,000 to 1,400 products considered to be inhalants are legal products and are not regulated under the federal Controlled Substances Act. However, the National Conference on State Legislatures reports that, as of June 2000, 38 states had enacted laws to address the issues of minors' use of inhalants. In various ways, the laws attempt to prevent the sale, use, and distribution to minors of certain products that are commonly abused.

California, for instance, prohibits the sale, distribution, or dispensation to a minor of toluene, materials containing toluene, and nitrous oxide. Minors are also forbidden to possess these substances. Louisiana prohibits the sale, transfer, or possession of model glue and inhalable toluene substances to minors. In Ohio, it is illegal to inhale certain compounds for intoxication—a common, general prohibition other states have enacted.

Some states draw their prohibitions more narrowly. New Jersey, for instance, prohibits selling or offering to sell minors products containing chlorofluorocarbon that is used in refrigerant.

Some states regulate inhalant sales tightly at the retail level. Minnesota, for instance, requires businesses to post signs stating the illegality of selling butane or butane lighters to minors. Minnesota also prohibits selling general inhalable compounds to minors, and it prohibits minors' use and possession of them for intoxification.

In Massachusetts, retailers must ask minors for identification before selling them glue or cement that contains a solvent that can release toxic vapors. Also, the products must contain oil of mustard or a similar deterrent against inhalation. Young Massachusetts inhalant purchasers must also legibly write their name and address in a bound register, which the retailer must make available to police and keep for at least six months after the final entry.

Some other governments take a similar approach to controlling access. Great Britain's Intoxicating Substances (Supply) Act of 1985 made it an offense to supply a product that will be abused. The Cigarette Lighter Refill (safety) Regulations of 1999 govern sale of purified liquefied petroleum gas, mainly butane, the substance most often involved in inhalant fatalities in the United Kingdom. It is illegal to sell this type of cigarette lighter refill to anyone under age 18.

Despite the laws, inhalant abuse remains a major health problem. As the American Academy of Pediatrics stated in a 2000 paper on preventing inhalant abuse, "... since inhalants are legal and kids can get them from so many different ways, it is not possible to make inhalants entirely off limits."

See also Amyl nitrite; Nitrous oxide

RESOURCES

Books

Glowa, John A., and Solomon H. Snyder. *Inhalants: The Toxic Fumes.* Broomall, PA: Chelsea House Publishers, 1991.

Periodicals

Bykowski, Mike. "Sniff Out Inhalant Abuse Among Young Patients." *Family Practice News* (November 1, 1999).

Meyerhoff, Michael. "Facts About Inhalant Abuse." *Pediatrics for Parents* (July 2001).

Stapleton, Stephanie. "Is Your Patient (or Child) Abusing Inhalants?" *American Medical News* (April 9, 2001).

Other

"Common Inhalants." American Academy of Pediatrics Medical Library. 2000 (April 6, 2002). <http://www.medem.com/search/article_display.cfm?path=n:&mstr=/ZZZDARS2B7C.html&soc=AAP&srch_typ=NAV_SERCH>.

"Effects of Inhalants." American Academy of Pediatrics Medical Library. 2000 (April 6, 2002). <http://www.medem.com/search/article_display.cfm?path=n:&mstr=/ZZZ5B6O2B7C.html&soc=AAP&srch_typ=NAV_SERCH>.

"Mind Over Matter: The Brain's Response to Inhalants." <http://165.112.78.61/MOM/IN/MOMIN1.html>.

"Preventing Inhalant Abuse." American Academy of Pediatrics Medical Library. 2000 (April 6, 2002). <http://www.medem.com/search/article_display.cfm?path=n:&mstr=/ZZZ2TQUQA7C.html&soc=AAP&srch_typ=NAV_SERCH>.

U.S. Department of Health and Human Services. National Institutes of Health. *Inhalant Abuse.* National Institute on Drug Abuse Research Report Series. Revised July 2000. NIH Publication Number 00-3818.

Organizations

Monitoring the Future Study, Survey Research Center, Institute for Social Research at the University of Michigan, P.O. Box 1248, Ann Arbor, MI, USA, 48106, (734) 764-8365, (734) 647-4575, MTFinfo@isr.umich.edu.webmaster@health.org, <http://www.monitoringthefuture.org>.

National Clearinghouse for Alcohol and Drug Information (NCADI), P.O. Box 2345, Rockville, MD, USA, 20847-2345, (800) 729-6686, webmaster@health.org, <http://www.health.org>.

National Drug Intelligence Center (NDIC), 319 Washington Street, 5th Floor, Johnstown, PA, USA, 15901-1622, (814) 532-4601, (814) 532-4690, cmbwebmgr@ndic.osis.gov, <http://www.usdoj.gov/ndic/>.

National Inhalant Prevention Coalition, 2904 Kerbey Lane, Austin, TX, USA, 78703, (512) 480-8953, (512) 477-3932, (800) 269-4237, nipc@io.com, <http://www.inhalants.org>.

National Institute on Drug Abuse, National Institutes of Health (NIH), 6001 Executive Boulevard, Room 5213, Bethesda, MD, USA, 20892-9561, (301) 443-1124, (888) 644-6432, information@lists.nida.nih.gov, <http://www.nida.nih.gov>.

Substance Abuse and Mental Health Services Administration (SAMSHA)/Center for Substance Abuse Treatment (CSAT), 5600 Fishers Lane, Rockville, MD, USA, 20857, (301) 443-8956, info@samhsa.gov, <http://www.samhsa.gov>.

Janet D. Filips

KETAMINE

OFFICIAL NAMES: Ketamine hydrochloride, Ketaject, Ketaset, and Ketalar.
STREET NAMES: K, ket, quick, Lady K, special K, vitamin K, Kit-Kat, green, blind squid, jet, super acid, honey oil, cat valium, super C
DRUG CLASSIFICATIONS: Schedule III, dissociative anesthetic

OVERVIEW

The original name for ketamine was CI581. Its discovery is credited to Dr. Calvin Stevens of Wayne State University who isolated the compound in 1961. The pharmaceutical giant Parke-Davis funded its development as an alternative to the anesthetic phencyclidine or PCP.

Ketamine is a fast-acting intravenous or intramuscular anesthetic used primarily by veterinarians. It has unique hypnotic (sleep-producing), analgesic (pain-relieving) and amnesic (inducing short term memory loss) properties that in proper doses does not depress breathing, making it highly prized by surgeons. No other drug in clinical use combines these three important features.

Ketamine was first used clinically in 1970, and was thought to be an ideal anesthetic agent. The U.S. military put it to use in Vietnam as an easily administered battlefield drug. It had a wide safety margin in terms of its dosage, making it ideally suited to the chaotic atmosphere of the battlefield.

But as its use increased, so did reports of its hallucinatory side effects. Significant numbers of patients who were given the anesthetic, whether on the battlefield or in hospitals, reported visions of interactions with dead friends and relatives, angels, and other religious figures when they began regaining consciousness.

Physicians began administering tranquilizers to block the hallucinations associated with ketamine's "emergent state," a condition that refers to the patient's return to consciousness. By both official and unofficial channels, word of the drug's intense hallucinogenic effect spread among doctors, scientists, veterinarians, and academics and found fertile ground in an emerging subculture rapidly becoming dominated by psychedelic drug use.

Given the popularity of marijuana, LSD, mescaline, cocaine, and heroin, the use of ketamine in the 1970s and 1980s remained largely confined to either experimental therapeutic use, or what has been described by author Jay Stevens as "the neuro-consciousness frontier," a small group of accredited and unaccredited individuals who experimented with the effects of hallucinogenic substances.

The man most closely associated with early ketamine experimentation and research was John C. Lilly, M.D., an accomplished researcher made famous by his groundbreaking early work in the early neurosciences. (Lilly died in 2001.)

Lilly's research, which electronically mapped the brain's pain and pleasure pathways, opened the door to decades of neural imaging advances. He invented the isolation tank and explored the effects of sensory depri-

KEY TERMS

CRYSTAL METH (METHAMPHETAMINE): A central nervous system stimulant that has emerged as a readily available alternative to MDMA at clubs and raves. Also known as "speed."

DISSOCIATIVE ANESTHETIC: An anesthetic that produces an unresponsive state by chemically muting the ability of N-methyl-D-aspartate (NMDA) receptors in the brain to process signals.

DXM (DEXTROMETHORPHAN): Easily synthesized dissociative psychedelic found in some cough medicines, used illicitly for numbing and hallucinogenic properties.

GHB (GAMMA HYDROXYBUTYRATE): Originally sold in health food stores as a growth hormone, a liquid nervous depressant touted for its ecstasy-like qualities. Banned by the FDA in 1990, the respiratory depression it can cause makes it among the most dangerous club drugs in circulation.

LSD (D-LYSERGIC ACID DIETHYLAMIDE): A powerful chemical compound renowned for its hallucinogenic properties.

MDMA (3,4-METHYLENEDIOXYMETHAMPHETA-MINE): Known as ecstasy, E and X, MDMA is the most popular of the "club drugs," a synthetic stimulant with mild hallucinogenic properties.

NMDA RECEPTOR ANTAGONIST: A class of anesthetics that block particular neurotransmitters located in the brain's cerebral cortex and hippocampus—regions responsible for memory, language, and motor control.

PCP (PHENCYCLIDINE): Also known as angel dust, a powerful and toxic synthetic chemical developed in home laboratories.

ROHYPNOL (FLUNTRAZEPAM): An overseas prescription sleeping aid that, in lower doses, gives users a feeling similar to alcohol intoxication; also used as a date rape drug.

vation; he was also responsible for trail-blazing work in human-dolphin communication—efforts that were later popularized in the films *Altered States* and *The Day of the Dolphin*.

What is not as well known is that Lilly also had a chronic problem with ketamine abuse. In his disturbing 1978 autobiography *The Scientist*, Lilly relates that in taking ketamine for his migraines, he felt transformed by the drug's hallucinogenic effects. In his words, ketamine gave him the ability to "look across the border into other realities."

His tolerance and dependence built up quickly. Within several months, Lilly was injecting the drug several times a day and reaching dosages of 50 mg an hour for stretches lasting up to 20 hours. His case is exceptional, but it is often cited to counter claims that ketamine is not addictive.

With law enforcement officials tightening their grip on the distribution of marijuana, heroin, cocaine, LSD, and other high traffic drugs throughout the late 1970s and early 1980s, interest in what came to be known as designer drugs and later club drugs greatly increased. Ecstasy (MDMA) made its debut in New York and London's gay club scenes in the late 1980s and early 1990s and spread rapidly into the club-going mainstream.

The combination of a large and growing youth market for ecstasy in the United States and Britain, coupled with higher rates of intervention by police, led to a search for new experiences and cheaper alternatives, and ketamine, not yet illegal, quickly filled the void.

In 1995 ketamine was added to the Drug Enforcement Administration's (DEA) Emerging Drugs List. Four years later, in August of 1999, ketamine became a federally illegal (Schedule III) drug in the United States.

Ketamine, though used with much less frequency than MDMA and methamphetamine, is increasingly popular among young people. References to its use are abundant in rave and dance culture. Popular musicians such as Madonna and the Chemical Brothers have also incorporated mention of ketamine usage into their music.

CHEMICAL/ORGANIC COMPOSITION

The chemical composition of ketamine hydrochloride is $C_{13}H_{16}ClNO$. The formal name for the chemical is 2-(2-chlorophenyl)-(methylamino)-cyclohexanone hydrochloride. The chemical structure and effects of ketamine are similar to those of PCP, which it was developed to replace, but ketamine is much less potent and its effects are of much shorter duration.

Ketamine is characterized as a dissociative anesthetic. The term "dissociative" refers to the severing of normal thought processes from consciousness, making the user feel removed from the physical body. Ketamine chemically interferes with the brain's ability to monitor and regulate higher functions, such as memory, perception, and motor activity. The drug has little impact, meanwhile, on lower functions that regulate the heart rate and breathing, which is why it is such an effective surgical anesthetic.

Ketamine is a non-competitive N-methyl-D-aspartate (NMDA) receptor antagonist, meaning that it interferes with the brain's ability to receive, process, and broadcast certain signals. Specifically, ketamine interferes with the ability of the receptors to receive escitatory amino acids or EAAs, the chemical neurotransmitters in the brain that make brain cells fire in tandem with millions of others. The simultaneous firing of cells along established pathways are what allows the brain to regulate movement, register pain, recall a memory, or initiate any multitude of the brain's higher functions.

Scientists are only now beginning to discover why ketamine works the way it does. NDMA receptors in the human brain are densely localized in the cerebral cortex and hippocampus, areas that are important for higher functions like memory creation and retrieval. Ketamine, by blocking NDMA receptors, effectively disables the normal functioning of the hippocampus, accounting for short-term disorientation and memory loss.

A 1998 study using data from positron emission tomography or PET scans on humans also demonstrated that ketamine stimulates the release of dopamine, the brain's pleasure chemical. Most drugs of abuse spur the forced release of dopamine, reinforcing pleasurable associations in the user.

Ketamine belongs to the same family of drugs as dextromethorphan (DXM), which is found in some brands of over-the-counter cough syrup; nitrous oxide, better known as "whippets," so named because of the metal whipped cream chargers the gas is commonly packaged in; and phencyclidine (PCP), also known as angel dust.

Ketamine also shares a close chemical kinship to prescription drugs Tiletamine and Memantine. Tiletamine is used in combination with zolazepam as a veterinary anesthetic under the brand names Zoletic and Telazol. Memantine is derived from the anti-influenza drug amantadine, and also works to block NDMA receptors. Memantine has been approved for use in Parkinson's disease and dementia in the elderly. It is also being used experimentally with AIDS patients for the treatment of HIV encephalopathy.

INGESTION METHODS

Ketamine is sold to veterinary offices and hospitals in liquid form under the brand names Ketaject, Ketaset, and Ketalar. When properly administered as an anesthetic in a clinical setting, it is usually delivered by intramuscular injection, though small children and the elderly may receive oral doses.

Ketamine may be procured illegally in its original clear liquid state, and can either be injected, mixed with another liquid and drank, or dribbled over cigarettes and tobacco and smoked. It is far more common, however, for users and dealers to evaporate or "bake" ketamine into a powder.

In economic terms, dealers and middlemen have ample incentive to dilute or "cut" other substances into

Tweezers holding an ampoule containing a solution of ketamine, a drug that is used legally as an anesthetic in children and the elderly; it is also tied to illegal use at dance parties. Photo Researchers, Inc. Reproduced by permission.

the ketamine to stretch a limited supply. Frequently, ketamine is cut with other stimulants, additives, or opiates, compressed into pills or loaded into capsules, and sold as something else entirely.

A study conducted in Australia, which analyzed the purity of ecstasy tablets seized by police, for example, found on average the MDMA content to be a little more than a third of the total—the rest being a mix of heroin, PCP, speed, caffeine, ketamine, and other fillers.

Nasal ingestion

Ketamine is usually snorted as a powder, either cut into lines or delivered in small "hits" or "bumps" of varying size. Thumb-sized plastic "bullet" dispensers are in common use, and deliver pre-set 30–50 mg doses per nasal hit. Larger bullets most likely contain larger intake chambers.

The impact of ketamine on the user at a low dosage differs dramatically from its impact at a higher dosage. This gives ketamine what is known as a steep dose response curve. Ketamine also differs from other inhalants in that the onset of its effects can take anywhere from five to 15 minutes, depending on the person's height, weight, tolerance, and other factors. Keta-

HISTORY NOTES

Surveys conducted in dance or rave settings across Europe found a significant number of people tried ketamine, but that the degree of regular use varies widely by geography and within groups of club goers. A survey conducted in London found that some 40% of the club goers surveyed planned on using ketamine that evening.

A survey conducted in Austria at the same time found that regular users of MDMA and amphetamines thought there were significant psychological risks associated with ketamine use. The authors also mentioned that the drug is perceived as being "high status."

In Belgium, 89 kilos (about 200 lbs) of pure ketamine powder were seized in September 1999 along with a series of smaller busts made in January 2000. Belgium, Ireland, the Netherlands, and the UK have reported the seizure of significant amounts of ketamine. Ketamine seizures are nevertheless small when compared to seizures of methamphetamine and ecstasy (MDMA).

The European Monitoring Centre for Drugs and Drug Addiction (EMCDDA) reports that while club drug use is predominant in the under 25 demographic, it cites surveys and anecdotal reports that indicate there is a group of users who are "older, highly educated, experienced, MDMA users, particularly in the free party/new age travellers scene, in the gay club scene, and among small groups of self-exploratory individuals."

The report says that the most vulnerable group of users to ketamine overdose are those who take it under the illusion they are taking MDMA or some other stimulant drug. Someone expecting to take MDMA, cocaine, or amphetamine, for instance, may find themselves on a roadway behind the wheel of a car being affected instead by sudden physical incapacity.

mine also lingers in the system for up to an hour, and its effects are cumulative.

Even experienced users, not mindful of the response lag or other variables, frequently ingest more than they intend and end up in what is commonly referred to as a "K-hole"—a state of near paralysis if not complete unconsciousness.

The low-dose threshold, the amount by which most users will begin to feel the effect of the drug, begins with ketamine at about 10 mg. A 10–30 mg nasal dose of ket-

amine will render most users light-headed, with mildly altered visual and tactile senses.

The medium-dose threshold is anywhere between 30 and 70 mg (a single inhaled hit for many) and results in pronounced disorientation, audio and visual distortion, and a loss of muscle coordination.

The high-dose threshold is the maximum dosage a person can tolerate before losing consciousness entirely. Most users will lapse into a dissociative state at dosages of between 100 and 150 mg, with the rest succumbing at 150–225 mg. Vomiting is not uncommon at high doses. Doses at or near 250 mg will render most users unconscious from 30 minutes to three hours or more.

Oral ingestion

Mixed with water or another liquid, the oral ingestion of ketamine differs from nasal ingestion in several important respects. First, it takes longer for the drug to take effect (up to 20 minutes on a medium-full stomach) and the effect of the drug lasts much longer, from three to six hours or more depending on the dose. The threshold tolerances between light, moderate, strong, and anesthetic doses are also somewhat higher when ingested orally.

Increasingly, ketamine is being sold in press-pill or capsule form. There is no way to accurately gauge how much pure ketamine is being consumed when purchased in this form or with which other drugs (heroin, caffeine, methamphetamine, etc.) it has been combined.

Intramuscular injection

When injected intramuscularly (into muscle as opposed to a vein), ketamine's impact is more immediate (about 90 seconds) and the tolerance threshold is much, much lower. Very small differences in the amount of the drug entering the system have profoundly different effects on the user.

Taking ketamine by injection is dangerous. The risks of accidental death or permanent injury from overdose by injection are greater than with any other method.

THERAPEUTIC USE

Ketamine has been approved for both human and animal use as an injectable anesthetic in medical settings since 1970. About 90% of the ketamine legally sold in the United States in 2001 was intended for veterinary use, and over the past several years medical usage of ketamine has remained fairly constant. Production of ketamine, however, has increased almost 40% over the last six years, indicating a great deal of the substance is being diverted for illegal use.

Ketamine and other NMDA antagonists were first thought to be wonder drugs. Not only were they excellent anesthetics, but they appeared to offset brain damage from strokes, head injuries, hypoxia, polio, and a variety of other conditions. Euphoria over their potential was eventually dampened by reports of their hallucinatory side effects and brain damage where the drugs were most active.

Ketamine, like MDMA, was once thought to hold great promise for use in the field of experimental psychotherapy. Though the drug has been sidelined for this purpose in the United States, its use in Russia's reformed psychiatric establishment is yielding some interesting results.

Russian studies conducted in the early- to mid-1990s suggests ketamine can contribute to stabilizing positive psychological changes reached in therapy and enhance personal growth. Another author suggested that it may enhance the creative activities of patients and harmonize their relationships with other people. In 1997, a ten-year review of ketamine-assisted treatment of alcoholism in Russia resulted in the publication of several controversial abstracts. One clinical trial comparing ketamine psychedelic therapy (KPT) and conventional treatment found that 73 out of 111, or 66%, of patients who received ketamine-assisted therapy remained alcohol free after one year compared to just 24% (24 out of 100 patients) who were counseled by conventional methods. Changes in brain metabolism were also cited, which may have reinforced the patients' desire to stay sober.

Research continues to illuminate different aspects of ketamine pharmacology, some of it promising enough to indicate that new clinical uses (principally in the field of anesthesiology) for the drug will be approved. It is still used as a general anesthetic for children and geriatric patients because it is well tolerated. Benzodiazepine-based tranquilizers are used to keep the auditory and visual hallucinations to a minimum.

USAGE TRENDS

Before the late 1980s, ketamine was not widely abused. In 1984, the Department of Health and Human Services recommended the DEA classify ketamine and products containing it under Schedule III of the Controlled Substances Act (CSA). But citing too few reports of a problem, the DEA postponed action.

Indications of ketamine's growing popularity as an illicit drug soon emerged, however. Veterinary clinics and animal hospitals were broken into with increasing frequency and reporting their stocks of ketamine stolen. In 1997, an advisory from the American Veterinary Medical Association urged its members to install burglar alarms and to keep ketamine under lock and key. By that time the agency had documented hundreds of such burglaries.

Closer monitoring of ketamine supplies has made it more difficult to obtain. Traffickers are still able to maintain their supplies of the substance, but the impact of the supply squeeze occasionally puts the price of the drug beyond the reach of many. Anti-theft measures and the attention of law enforcement have restricted access to the drug so much that doses that sold for $25–$30 in the mid-1990s are now selling for up to $75–$100 in areas of high demand.

The clandestine manufacture of ketamine has not been noted by authorities. In contrast to its chemical cousin PCP, synthesizing ketamine outside of a major laboratory is very difficult. If the supply situation remains unchanged or worsens (from the point of view of the illegal user) ketamine use will likely decline in favor of cheaper and more readily available alternatives.

Club drugs and raves

The increase in drug use among adolescents is tied by many experts to the growth of "raves" or "trances," all-night dance parties that cater to young audiences. Rave culture is well-advanced and international in scope. It has its own dominant fashions, its own style of music (hypnotic and psychedelic electronica), a preferred style of dance, and its own ethos (peace, love, unity, and respect). It also harbors a dominant social environment that encourages the liberal use of drugs such as MDMA (ecstasy), GHB, LSD, methamphetamine, rohypnol, and ketamine. These "club drugs" or "designer drugs" have surged in popularity over the last decade because of their association with these large-scale events. However, ketamine is not as regularly used as other club drugs because of its unpleasant side effects.

The increase in drug use over the last ten years among adolescents has led some health officials to argue that recreational drug use (meaning drug use on which the user is not dependent) is becoming normalized within youth culture. These officials say the social costs and constraints associated with drug use, for example, being labeled as "druggies" by their peers, are breaking down and that the implications for future usage trends are ominous.

Whether this argument proves to be accurate or not, it is certainly true that there is a strong correlation between attending these rave events and drug use. A 1998 British Crime Survey reported that 80% of club goers used drugs at some point in their lives compared to 52% of the general population. A 1999 report found that while 10% of the British population reported using illegal drugs in the last year, some 55% of club goers said they planned to use ecstasy or an amphetamine on that particular night.

Because alcohol is often not available at raves, there is usually no age restriction to admission. Rave attendees are generally between the ages of 15 and 25, and this data is remarkably uniform internationally. In Australia,

???? FACT OR FICTION

Ketamine is not a tranquilizer for horses or any other animal. Ketamine is a surgical anesthetic. It is still in standard use on children and the very old because of its wide safety margin *when used by professionals in clinical settings.* Any drug that renders its user unconscious carries with it dangers that should not be trivialized.

A K-hole is a condition of near or complete immobility and unconsciousness, frequently preceded by vomiting. For obvious reasons, it is a phrase sometimes used derisively by people in club settings to describe the condition of a soiled and immobile patron.

Ketamine shares some chemical properties with PCP (phencyclidine) but they are not the same. Ketamine is far less toxic and its effects are not as long-lasting. Though PCP was also developed for use as an anesthetic, it was discontinued because it provoked psychotic episodes in some patients.

Is regular use of ketamine harmful? The short answer is maybe. Ketamine was never designed for long-term, regular use. Its impact on particular areas of the brain involving memory and language are only now being explored. Regular users who stop using the drug report slurred speech, difficulty concentrating, and loss of some memory function.

---

the mean age of surveyed club goers was 18.9 years. An analysis of club drug use demographics in Britain showed a decrease in the age of users, from the mid to late 20s to the early 20s and late teen years. The same holds true in the United States.

Age, ethnic, and gender trends

Hospital data collected by the Substance Abuse and Mental Health Services Administration, a division of the U.S. Department of Health and Human Services, suggests the age of the typical American club drug user is between 18 and 25. Whereas only 20% of all drug-related emergency room visits involved patients 25 and under, this age group accounts for 58% of ketamine incidents, 67% of all recorded MDMA incidents, 50% of recorded GHB incidents, and 46% of all LSD incidents.

Traditionally, males predominate in drug usage; that pattern is also shifting. Young women are partaking in club drugs as never before. In Britain, the male to female ratio of 2:1 has eroded. In the United States, differences in gender regarding club drug use have all but disappeared.

Racially, white patients account for 61% of all drug-related hospital visits in the United States, followed by black (26%) and Hispanics (11%). With the exception of rohypnol, the 69–80% of all club drug incidents recorded by Drug Abuse Warning Network (DAWN) involve white, non-Hispanic patients—a fairly typical reflection of the U.S. population. A far larger share (56%) of rohypnol mentions are attributed to Hispanic patients, but this may have to do with the small sample size available to researchers.

DAWN says emergency room visits associated with club drug use of ecstasy increased 58% between 1999 and 2000 (from 2,850 to 4,511). The report offers no evidence of a similar surge over the same period for GHB, ketamine or rohypnol, though it should be noted that ecstasy tablets sold anywhere in the world are routinely cut with other drugs, ketamine included.

In its review of emergency room data, DAWN found 263 mentions of ketamine between 1999 and 2000. The study also reported that more than 70% of drug-related emergency room visits resulted from simultaneous use. Though alcohol was most frequently mentioned as being used in conjunction with other drugs, 37% of emergency room episodes involving ketamine and 15% involving GHB also included concurrent use of ecstasy.

The gay community

Though data on the regular party-going subset of the gay community is comparatively sparse, the research that has been conducted indicates gay men of a much broader age demographic are users of ketamine and other club drugs.

Dr. Grant N. Colfax of the San Francisco Department of Public Health surveyed nearly 300 gay and bisexual men in the San Francisco area attending what are known as circuit parties—large scale gay dance parties, predominantly male and similar in scope and attendance to rave events.

Most of the men surveyed by Colfax reported using at least one recreational drug when attending an out-of-town circuit event, and though these results are not typical of gay men in general, within this subset of the community, recreational drug use appears to be the norm.

A full 80% of those surveyed by Colfax reported taking ecstasy; 66% took ketamine; 43% took crystal methamphetamines; and 29% took so-called "liquid ecstasy" or GHB.

Some of ketamine's dangers are behavioral. Many users say that in low doses ketamine acts as an aphrodisiac and that it lowers sexual inhibitions. In the age of HIV and AIDS, the use of ketamine in sexual situations can lead to uncharacteristic recklessness.

Researchers and social workers in the AIDS field say the use of ketamine and other inhibition-relaxing drugs during sex may push sexual partners to do things they would not otherwise do. Use of the drug is worsening already complacent attitudes, especially among young gay men, about the need to protect themselves from HIV infection.

MENTAL EFFECTS

Within five minutes of taking ketamine, users generally feel a non-localized numbness, a heaviness in the limbs, blurred vision, muffled or distorted hearing, and a floating sensation. Users say the drug creates feelings of detachment and introversion.

At higher doses, ketamine leads to pronounced changes in judgment, distorted vision, auditory hallucinations, such as humming or buzzing, and marked disorientation. Some users report a profound impact on the perception of time, which appears to slow to a complete halt in the emergent, or heavily hallucinatory state.

Visions of life and death, some calming, others frightening, have been reported. Religious hallucinations, out-of-body experiences, and a pronounced dissociative state that some have called another plane of consciousness are also credited to ketamine. While in what is referred to as K-land or the K-state, users claim to gain insights into their personalities, the people they know, and the workings of the universe.

Even experienced users misjudge the dosing and land in a life-threatening K-hole. In addition to vivid hallucinations, this state may be punctuated by convulsions, respiratory depression, and loss of consciousness. Memory is also acutely affected. Users may not remember taking the drug, or who or where they are. Users may experience bouts of paranoia or anger.

The ketamine "high" usually can last anywhere from 45 minutes to an hour. However, depending on the dosage, tolerance, and method of ingestion, the drug's effects can linger for four hours or more. Like most anesthetic agents, it may take the user 24–48 hours before they feel "normal" again.

PHYSIOLOGICAL EFFECTS

Reported physical effects of ketamine use include an initial energy rush, numbness, and irregular muscle coordination. Large amounts can cause anesthesia and muscle spasm. Eating and drinking alcohol before taking ketamine (as with other anesthetics) may cause vomiting. If this is combined with unconsciousness, there is an acute danger of choking or death.

As an anesthetic, ketamine increases sympathetic nervous activity, which results in an increased heart rate, increased blood pressure, some dilation of bronchial tubes, pupil dilation, and related secondary effects.

Specifically, blood pressure rises by about 25%, and the heart rate is increased in the area of 20%. There is wide variation in the kinds of responses individuals can have to the drug, and occasionally, alarming increases in blood pressure can occur.

At low and moderate (subanesthetic) doses, users have difficulty walking; balance and muscle control are compromised. Vision is blurred and distorted, which can worsen a user's disorientation. Speech is slurred, and there is numbness in the extremities. At higher dosages, standing becomes difficult or impossible. Users are prone to collapse and may lapse in and out of consciousness.

Harmful side effects

Multiple, repeated dosing of ketamine is common by most users, as is its combination with other drugs. Too many "bumps" in a row or within a small window of time frequently knocks users out cold, putting them into the anesthetic condition for which the drug was manufactured. This K-hole can last up to two hours or more, depending on the dose. The K-hole is frequently preceded by nausea or vomiting.

Adverse effects noted with the anesthetic use of ketamine include the sudden loss of respiratory function, spasms of the trachea or larynx, and vomiting. Literature on the emergency treatment of ketamine overdose is rare. Clinical recommendations advise making sure the airway is clear, that breathing is continually monitored, and that the heart rate remains steady.

On its own, ketamine toxicity is less of a concern than accidents caused by the intensity of the dissociative state and loss of muscle coordination and control. However, given that ketamine is frequently taken with other drugs such as alcohol or ecstasy, clinical reports on the dangers of its recreational use are probably inadequate.

A study conducted in Britain reported that ketamine's impact on short- and long-term memory can linger for up to three days after a dose. Researchers looked at a broad array of memory functions, word association and language tests, attention span, and other factors related to mood. Though some recovery was noted 72 hours after ketamine usage, the researchers noted lasting impairments related to language and some aspects of memory.

Injecting ketamine intramuscularly carries with it risks common to cocaine and heroin addicts and other injection-drug users. Sharing needles can lead to the transmission of blood-borne viral infections such as HIV and hepatitis B and C, as well as increased risk of escalation of drug use and overdose.

Long-term health effects

A review of current data suggests all dissociative anesthetics cause brain damage if used heavily. Dissociatives include ketamine, dextromethorphan (or DXM), phencyclidine (PCP or angel dust), nitrous oxide (whippets) and dizocilpine (MK-801). All are N-methyl-D-aspartate (NMDA) antagonists, meaning they temporarily block a crucial neurotransmitter in the brain.

Research conducted by Dr. J.W. Olney revealed the existence of small vacuoles (essentially, very tiny holes) in the brains of mice given high doses of dizocilpine or MK-801. The tiny holes are now called Olney's lesions and the condition is formally referenced in the medical community as NMDA antagonist neurotoxicity or NAN. NAN has also been tied to ketamine and PCP use, even in commonly-used doses.

Though more study is needed, reports of ketamine-related brain damage are growing more numerous, and the types of impairment people report experiencing (slurred speech, memory loss, difficulty concentrating) are directly tied to the centers of the brain most affected by the drug.

All dissociative anesthetics are extremely toxic to developing fetuses and should never be used during pregnancy. Severe brain damage and mental retardation may result.

REACTIONS WITH OTHER DRUGS OR SUBSTANCES

The consumption of more than one drug over a small window of time and mixing two or more drugs together for a blending of effects is characteristic of club-drug use. As discussed above, ketamine is often mixed with alcohol, GHB, MDMA (ecstasy), rohypnol, and methamphetamine. Some 37% of reported ketamine combination episodes are linked with ecstasy.

Each drug affects the body in a characteristic way. MDMA and methamphetamine for example, are vasoconstrictors, which decrease blood flow to certain parts of the body. Ketamine is a vasodilator, a drug that increases blood flow. Mixing a vasoconstrictor with a vasodilator (combining ecstasy and ketamine, for example) can dramatically increase blood pressure in the user and boost the risk of sudden cardiac arrest or stroke.

Ketamine should never be used with other drugs that decrease breathing; these include alcohol, barbiturates, or Valium. Users mixing these drugs risk slowing their breathing and heart rates to dangerously low levels—starving their brains of oxygen and risking permanent brain damage if not death.

TREATMENT AND REHABILITATION

Though ketamine is still not thought to be physically addictive, dependence on the drug can be developed quickly in some people. Individuals can be so

drawn to the feeling of detachment it provides and the emotional insights the drug is said to give to some users that walking away from repeated use may prove impossible for some.

Tolerance, dependence, and withdrawal indicators have been observed in a number of studies. Users who are fond of its escapist qualities say it has a high potential for psychological dependence and that tolerance to the drug develops fairly quickly.

Symptoms reported by ketamine users who have stopped using the drug include drug craving, persistent amnesia, slurred speech, and difficulty concentrating. Frequent and persistent use of ketamine over extended periods of time have led to reports of marked personality changes in the user and evidence of brain damage.

Treatment for ketamine dependence may involve psychotherapy or a 12-step program. Antidepressants may be used to treat depression that resulted in the drug use.

PERSONAL AND SOCIAL CONSEQUENCES

Because of its hallucinatory qualities, ketamine is sometimes compared with other psychedelics, including LSD, mescaline, and psilocybin. There is no evidence to support that these types of drugs "cause" long-term psychotic or schizophrenic behaviors, but individuals with an underlying mental condition may find the drug experience triggers an outbreak of the disease.

Anecdotal evidence suggests that psychotic breaks and schizophrenia-like symptoms are far more frequent with heavy or regular dissociative anesthetic use than any other type of psychedelic.

Because of its pain-killing properties, ketamine can expose its users to grievous injury that may not become apparent until hours later. The sudden loss of consciousness associated with higher doses of ketamine can become life-threatening if the user is driving a car or swimming. Professionals caution that ketamine impairs judgement, mental sharpness, and muscle coordination for up to 24 hours after it is taken, long after the immediate effects of the drug have worn off. As discussed earlier, ketamine is also associated with the relaxation of sexual inhibitions, which can be dangerous if one of the partners has HIV.

LEGAL CONSEQUENCES

On August 12, 1999, the U.S. Drug Enforcement Administration made ketamine a Schedule III drug. Schedule III drugs are approved for medical use, though their recreational use or abuse "may lead to moderate or low physical dependence or high psychological dependence." Possession of ketamine in the United States is illegal without a prescription or license to distribute.

Penalties for possession of Schedule I and II drugs (methamphetamine, heroin, cocaine, PCP, LSD, and marijuana among others) are far more severe than are the penalties for possession of Schedule III drugs, but they should not be dismissed entirely. Federal sentencing guidelines for possession of ketamine, regardless of the quantity, stipulate prison terms of not more than five years and individual fines of not more than $250,000. Second time offenders will almost certainly earn jail time, with a sentence determined by the judge but not to exceed 10 years. The fine is also doubled, to $500,000.

When ketamine is used by an individual in the commission of another crime, such as rape, the penalties are particularly severe. Rape of a victim who is "physically incapable of declining participation" in the sex act is punishable by fines and imprisonment up to 20 years. Moreover, the rapist does not necessarily have to be the one who drugged the victim; he could be just taking advantage of an existing situation.

A rapist who "renders another person unconscious" or "substantially impairs the ability of that other person to appraise or control conduct" could be sentenced to life in prison.

See also Ecstasy (MDMA); GHB; PCP; Rohypnol

RESOURCES

Books

Jansen, Karl. *Ketamine: Dreams & Realities*. Sarasota, FL: Multidisciplinary Association for Psychedelic Studies, 2001.

Rudgley, Richard. *The Encyclopedia of Psychoactive Substances*. New York: Little, Brown and Company, 1998.

Stafford, Peter. *Psychedelics Encyclopedia*. Berkeley, CA: Ronin Publishing, 1992.

Stevens, Jay. *Storming Heaven: LSD and the American Dream*. Berkeley, CA: Atlantic Monthly Press, 1987.

Periodicals

Cloud, John. "Is Your Kid On K?" *TIME Magazine* 150, no. 16 (October 20, 1997).

Curran, Valerie H., and Lisa Monaghan. "In and out of the K-hole: A comparison of the acute and resudual effects of ketamine in frequent and infrequent users." *Addiction* 96, no. 5 (May 2001): 749-760.

Curran, Valerie H., and Celia Morgan. "Cognitive, dissociative, and psychotogenic effects of ketamine in recreational users on the night of drug use and 3 days later." *Addiction* 95, no. 4 (April 2000): 575-591.

European Union. European Monitoring Center for Drugs and Drug Addiction. "Report on the Risk Assessment of ketamine in the Framework of the Joint Action on New Synthetic Drugs." (September 25, 2000).

Krupitsky, E.M., and A.Y. Grinenko. "Ketamine Psychadelic Therapy (KPT): A Review of the Results of Ten Years of Research." *Journal of Psychoactive Drugs* 29, no. 2 (April-June 1997): 165-183.

Lenton, Simon, Annabel Boys, and Kathy Norcross. "Raves, Drugs and Experience: Drug use by a sample of people who attend raves in Western Australia." *Addiction* 92, no. 10 (April 1997): 1327-1337.

McKinney, Merritt. "Gay Men May Take Health Risks at 'Circuit Parties.'" *Journal of Acquired Immune Deficiency Syndromes* 28 (2001): 373-379.

Quittner, Jeremy. "All mixed up." *The Advocate* (May 22, 2001).

Riley, Sarah J., G. Charlotte, D. H. Danielle, and M. Cadger. "Patterns of Recreational Drug Use at Dance Events in Edinburgh, Scotland." *Addiction* 96, no. 7 (July 2001): 1035-1047.

Sack, Kevin. "For Gay Men, HIV Peril and Rising Drug Use." *The New York Times* January 29, 1999.

United States Department of Health and Human Services. Substance Abuse and Mental Health Services Administration. Drug Abuse Warning Network. "The DAWN Report: Club Drugs." (December 2000).

United States Office of National Drug Policy. "Pulse Check: Trends in Drug Abuse." (Mid-Year 2000).

University of Oxford. "Administering a Ketamine Anesthetic." *Practical Procedures* 4, Article 5 (1994).

Weir, Erica. "Raves: A Review of the Culture, the Drugs and the Prevention of Harm." *Canadian Medical Association Journal* 162, no. 13 (June 2000): 1843-1849.

Other

United States Department of Health and Human Services. Substance Abuse and Mental Health Services Administration. <http://www.samhsa.gov>.

United States Department of Justice. Drug Enforcement Administration. <http://www.usdoj.gov/dea>.

United States. National Institute on Drug Abuse. <http://www.nida.nih.gov>.

United States. Office of National Drug Control Policy. <http://www.whitehousedrugpolicy.org>.

Christopher V.G. Barillas

LSD (LYSERGIC ACID DIETHYLAMIDE)

OFFICIAL NAMES: LSD (lysergic acid diethylamide), LSD25
STREET NAMES: Acid, zen, sugar, tabs, blotter, cid, doses, trips, boomers, lightning flash, hawk, cheer, liquid acid, L, microdot, dot, paper mushrooms, tab, hits, tripper, yellow sunshines, rainbows, smilies, stars, strawberries
DRUG CLASSIFICATIONS: Schedule I, hallucinogen

OVERVIEW

Lysergic acid diethylamide, or LSD, is the most potent and widely used of the category of drugs known as hallucinogenics. Hallucinogenic drugs, also called psychedelics, distort and confuse the senses, making people see, hear, feel, smell, or taste things that are not really there. The word hallucinate comes from a Latin word meaning "to wander in the mind." LSD falls into the category of hallucinogenic drugs called indole hallucinogens. This means it is derived from ergot, which is a fungus that grows on grains, particularly rye.

With respect to its hallucinogenic properties, LSD affects vision most strongly, although it can distort or enhance all the senses. The drug also produces intense, unstable emotions. It can make people feel deeply connected with others and with the universe, and can even elicit deeply spiritual experiences. In some people, LSD promotes a sense of deep understanding that forever changes their patterns of thinking or outlook (called a mind-expanding or consciousness-expanding experience). On the negative side, LSD can induce panic, anxiety, or paranoia, and can even disconnect people from reality to such an extent that they become a danger to themselves or others.

LSD is quickly absorbed throughout the body and affects the nervous system at many sites. It is the most powerful known hallucinogenic substance. As little as 30 to 50 micrograms (millionths of a gram) is required to produce effects that last six to 12 hours, sometimes longer. The effects usually start about 30 to 90 minutes after taking the drug; a faster response time may occur at higher doses.

LSD has a fascinating social history. It was initially synthesized in 1938 by Swiss chemist Dr. Albert Hofmann during experiments he performed for Sandoz Laboratories with chemicals called ergot derivates. Other drugs produced from these naturally occurring substances were useful for treating migraine headaches and gynecological problems. It was hoped that additional therapeutic uses could be found from similar compounds.

The testing of LSD on animals in the late 1930s did not identify any useful purpose, but when Dr. Hofmann accidentally ingested the drug in 1943 its hallucinogenic properties were revealed. The drug initially attracted the attention of psychiatrists, who hoped that taking the drug would give them a better understanding of their severely ill patients. Doctors also gave LSD to psychiatric patients to help reduce their inhibitions and enhance psychotherapy. The United States Army and the Central Intelligence Agency (CIA) were interested in LSD as a potential truth serum or brainwashing tool. They also investigated its use as a form of "nonviolent warfare," since LSD can be very incapacitating.

Probably the most important role LSD has played historically is in the hippie movement of the 1960s. LSD use was central to the rebellious movement that encouraged love and peace over war. To the hippie generation

KEY TERMS

BAD TRIP: A negative LSD experience, characterized by anxiety, panic, and despair, which can be extremely traumatic.

CANDY FLIPPING: The practice of combining ecstasy with LSD, which is popular among young people who attend raves and dance clubs.

CLUB DRUGS: Mostly synthetic, illicit substances found at raves and nightclubs. This group includes LSD, ecstasy, GHB, Rohypnol, ketamine, and methamphetamine.

COMING DOWN: The experience of a drug wearing off.

DROP: A common term used to describe the taking of LSD, as in "dropping acid."

EMPATHY: A feeling of connectedness and understanding with another person or people.

ERGOT: A fungus that grows on grains, particularly rye, that contains lysergic acid, a chemical used to make LSD.

FLASHBACK: The re-experiencing of a drug high without actually taking the drug. A flashback is usually limited to visual hallucinations and disturbances and can occur weeks, months, or years after taking the drug.

HALLUCINATION: The experience of seeing, feeling, hearing, smelling, or tasting something that is not really there.

HALLUCINOGENS: A group of drugs that induces sensory distortions and hallucinations.

HIT: A common term for a dose of LSD.

HPPD: Short for "hallucinogen persisting perception disorder," which is the medical term for flashbacks.

LYSERGIC ACID: A naturally occurring chemical that is used to make LSD.

NEUROTRANSMITTER: Chemical in the brain that transmits messages between neurons, or nerve cells.

PSYCHEDELIC: A term given to hallucinogenic drugs, like LSD, which implies that these drugs have the ability to access as yet untapped potential of the mind.

PSYCHOSIS: A severe mental disorder characterized by the loss of the ability to distinguish what is objectively real from what is imaginary, frequently including hallucinations.

RAVE: An all-night dance party that includes loud, pulsing "house" music and flashing lights. Many participants take hallucinogenic and other mind-altering drugs.

SEROTONIN: An important neurotransmitter in the brain that regulates mood, appetite, sensory perception and other central nervous system functions.

SYNESTHESIA: A chemical "cross-wiring" of the brain circuits often due to the use of hallucinogens that results in colors being felt or heard and sound being tasted or seen.

TALK DOWN: The process in which someone helps a person on drugs reconnect with reality by talking in soothing tones and helping distinguish reality from fantasy.

TRIP: A common term for a drug experience.

---

of the '60s, LSD was believed to help people develop a peaceful outlook and have profound mystical experiences. It was also popular among artists, particularly musicians, as a means of stimulating creativity.

Sandoz believed that LSD had great potential as a therapeutic drug. However, its increasing street use and association with the counterculture of the sixties made it fall out of favor with most legitimate researchers as well as drug enforcement agencies in various countries, particularly the United States and Britain. As a result, the company stopped producing LSD in 1968.

In 1979, Hofmann wrote an essay entitled *LSD: My Problem Child*. In it, he described how he first synthesized LSD, his early experiments with the drug, related hallucinogenic drugs found in nature, and the events that led Sandoz Laboratories to abandon the drug.

Traditionally, LSD has been most popular among white, middle-class high school and college students. It is used more in America than anywhere else, although it has enjoyed some popularly in Western Europe, particularly

Britain. LSD use was highest in the 1960s, and by 1970 an estimated one million to two million Americans had tried the drug. Use of LSD dropped off somewhat in the 1970s and 1980s, but it resurfaced in the 1990s and early twenty-first century, particularly among young adults who attend dance clubs and all-night dance parties called raves.

CHEMICAL/ORGANIC COMPOSITION

LSD is a semisynthetic drug. That means that it is made up of a natural substance, called lysergic acid, which is altered artificially in the laboratory. Lysergic acid is present in a group of substances called ergot alkaloids that are found in nature. These include ergot (*Claviceps purpurea*), a fungus that grows on rye and other grains. It also includes certain types of morning glory flowers, such as the heavenly blue, pearly gates, wedding bells, flying saucers, and the Hawaiian baby woodrose.

Doses of LSD have been found to be contaminated with other hallucinogen drugs, particularly PCP or mesca-

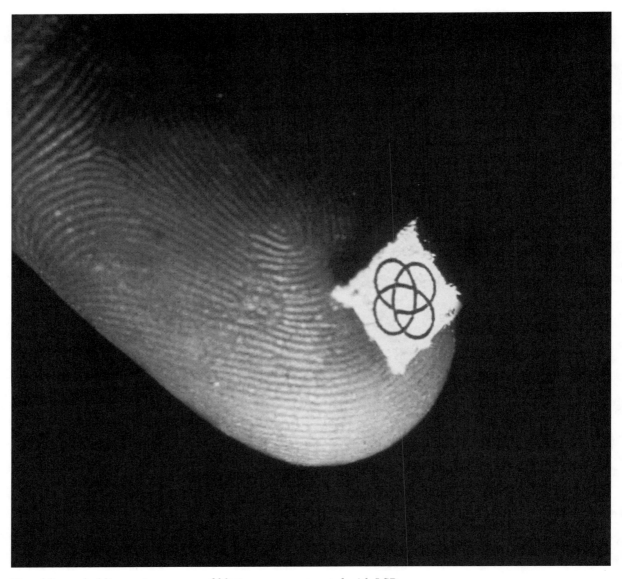

Tip of finger holding a tiny square of blotter paper saturated with LSD. Custom Medical Stock Photos. Reproduced by permission.

line. LSD is also commonly sold as another hallucinogenic drug, since it is relatively inexpensive to produce.

INGESTION METHODS

LSD is almost always taken by mouth. The white, odorless, slightly bitter-tasting crystalline powder is usually dissolved into a liquid form and soaked into blotter paper. The paper is then cut into quarter-inch-square-sized individual doses, called tabs, trips, hits, or doses. The paper is usually decorated with specific designs, such as dolphins, strawberries, or mushrooms, which help identify the manufacturer. Such designs also help to conceal how old the LSD is, as the drug tends to turn yellowish with age.

Less commonly, white LSD powder is squeezed into tiny pills (called microdots) or placed in capsules. It can also be formed into clear gelatin squares called window panes. In the 1990s, LSD has turned up at raves in blue-colored gel wraps that look like bubble-wrap packing material and in small breath freshener-type spray bottles. LSD has also been found on or in postage stamps, cookies, drinks, sugar cubes, and commercially produced candies.

More than 200 types of LSD tablets and more than 350 LSD blotting paper designs have been found. A dose of LSD typically costs about $2 to $5 (U.S.).

In rare cases, people soak tobacco leaves in LSD and smoke it, but this is generally considered to produce a poor-quality high. Even more rarely, some people inject the drug directly into their muscles to produce a more intense experience.

THERAPEUTIC USE

LSD has no officially recognized therapeutic value. However, its use as a therapeutic drug has a rich history. Early research with LSD suggested that it produces states similar to those experienced by people experiencing a type of severe psychiatric disturbance called psychosis, in which patients often hear voices that aren't there, lose touch with reality, have disordered thinking, and experience paranoid thoughts. Mental health experts therefore tried taking LSD to see if it could help them understand their patients' problems.

Soon after, it was also discovered that LSD appears to lower people's inhibitions, making it easier for them to remember and talk about repressed thoughts and experiences. Under positive circumstances, it also promotes empathy among those present who are also taking the drug. These discoveries led mental health experts to give LSD to people with milder mental illnesses, such as depression, to see if it could speed up or improve the effects of psychotherapy. LSD was also used experimentally to help people recover from addiction to other drugs, particularly alcohol.

Despite early positive findings, it was concluded that an LSD high is actually quite different from a psychotic state and that the therapeutic effects as well as the safety of LSD are not certain. Of particular concern was the patient's risk of having "bad trips," which could be so severe as to cause lasting trauma, particularly in those with a history of psychiatric illness. The drug also developed a bad reputation in the 1960s as it gained popularity as a street drug of abuse. For these reasons and others, research into the therapeutic use of LSD dropped off in the 1970s.

USAGE TRENDS

Hallucinogenic drugs have been used by different cultures, often in religious ceremonies, for thousands of years. Before LSD, however, this use was limited by the fact that hallucinogenic plants only grow in certain climates and certain areas. When LSD became available on the street in the 1960s, hallucinogen usage soared across the United States and, later, in Western Europe.

Age, ethnic, and gender trends

LSD is the most widely used hallucinogenic drug. Traditionally it has been favored by middle- to upper-middle-class white, educated people in high school or college. It is also popular among artists and musicians because it is believed that LSD experiences can enhance the creative process. It is integrated into the lifestyle of people who follow certain rock groups, such as the Grateful Dead. Historically, LSD has also been a common drug of abuse among mental health professionals. In general, LSD has enjoyed far more popularity in the United States than in any other country.

Patterns of LSD use can best be explained through the drug's history. In the 1940s and 1950s, the drug was tested for various therapeutic uses. At this time, LSD became popular among mental health professionals.

In the 1960s, LSD research was undertaken on college campuses to examine the drug's ability to help change undesirable outlook and behavior patterns as well as elicit profound spiritual experiences. Psychologist Timothy Leary, Ph.D., spearheaded this research. At Harvard University, Leary gave the hallucinogen psilocybin, a drug very similar to LSD, and later, actual LSD, to college professors, graduate students, and other intellectuals in controlled, positive environments to study the experience and its later impact on behavior and outlook. Although Leary was fired from Harvard in 1963, he used his position as a scholar to educate other researchers, and interested individuals about what he believed were the important positive effects of LSD. He was instrumental in promoting the use of LSD across college campuses in the United States, although he never advocated taking the drug for purely recreational purposes.

By 1962, LSD was widely available on the streets of America, and the American Medical Association published a public warning in its journal regarding the increasingly widespread use of LSD for recreational purposes. The drug was most popular in New York and California.

In 1965, street use of LSD in the United States surged, and it peaked from 1967 to 1969. By one estimate, 40% or more of students at Stanford University were using hallucinogenic drugs in 1967. LSD use was high on many other American college campuses as well. Leary himself estimated approximately one million Americans had used LSD at least once by 1967.

The popularity of LSD in the 1960s was at least partially spurred by the political situation at the time. Increasing numbers of young people were seeking higher education, and there was heightened interest in social issues and the workings of the mind. As young people became disenchanted with government decisions, such as the American participation in the Vietnam War, the rebellious "turn on, tune in, and drop out" mentality took hold. LSD was an integral part of that development.

LSD has also experienced some popularity in Britain and other European countries, starting a few years after its use began in the United States. However, LSD has never been used as much in Europe as in America.

As LSD's popularity soared, stories started appearing in the media about crazy things people did while on the drug, such as staring into the sun until they went blind, committing suicide, or committing murder. These stories tended to be wildly exaggerated and, in some cases, simply untrue. However, this negative publicity, combined with stiffer and stiffer legal penalties for manufacture or possession of the drug, eventually helped decrease its popularity. LSD use dropped off in the 1970s and 1980s, while other drugs, particularly crack, cocaine, and heroin, became more common. LSD was still used during these decades, however, mainly by white, middle-class high school and college students.

In the early 1990s, there was a resurgence of LSD popularity. Experts disagree somewhat on why the resurgence occurred, but it seems to be at least partially related to emergence of the rave and club culture. Ravers and clubbers enjoy dancing all night under the influence of drugs that give them more energy (e.g., amphetamines or "speed") as well as hallucinogenic drugs, including LSD and ecstasy (MDMA).

In the 1990s and since the early twenty-first century, LSD has rarely been bought "on the street" from strangers. Most often, it is sold at concerts and raves, and people usually buy it through friends and acquaintances. The typical LSD user is a white, middle-class high school or college student who tends to be a risk taker. Men are slightly more likely to take LSD than are women. In the United States, most illegal LSD is produced in Northern California and distributed through San Francisco to the rest of the country.

Scope and severity

The Monitoring the Future Study (MTF) is a survey performed every year since 1975 by the University of Michigan Institute for Social Research on nearly 17,000 American high school students about their drug use. The survey is funded by the National Institute on Drug Abuse (NIDA). According to this survey, recent LSD use has remained below 10% among high school seniors since 1975. The lowest use of LSD was in 1986, when 7.2% reported using LSD at least once, and 4.4% reporting use in the last year. By 1997, 13.6% of seniors said they had used LSD at least once, and 8.4% reported using it in the previous year. From 1996 to 2000, LSD use dropped off slightly among high school students.

Another study, the National Household Survey on Drug Abuse (NHSDA), tracks drug, alcohol, and tobacco use in a sample of 13,000 Americans aged 12 and over. According to this survey, 6% of respondents had used LSD in 1988. The number increased to 7.7% in 1996, and most users were in the 18-to-25 age group.

According to a special analysis of NHSDA and MTF data, the United States experienced a hallucinogen use epidemic in the '90s that peaked in 1996 among predominantly white youths aged 14 to 24. Use remained approximately stable until 1999, then dropped off slightly in 2000 and 2001. This renewal of interest in LSD spurred reports on the drug in major newspapers such as the *New York Times* and *Washington Post*, as well as on TV news programs.

According to the Drug Abuse Warning Network, LSD-related emergency room admissions have shown an up-and-down pattern since 1993. In 2000, 4,106 LSD-related admissions were reported.

NIDA reports that 13 million to 17 million Americans have used a hallucinogen at least once. In 1999, 8.1% of high school seniors had used LSD in the previous year. One study identified LSD as the third most common drug of abuse among college students, after alcohol and marijuana.

In Britain, LSD usage patterns are similar to those in the United States. The drug became popular in Britain in the mid-1960s, use declined in 1970s and 1980s but picked up again in the 1990s with the rave and club scene. A 1998 study in England and Wales revealed that 11% of respondents aged 16 to 29 said they had tried LSD at least once, and 2% said they had tried it in the previous year.

Patterns of LSD use have changed since the 1960s. According to the United States Drug Enforcement Administration (DEA), typical doses of LSD obtained from illegal sources in the 1990s ranged from 20 to 80 micrograms (mcg), which produces a high that can last 12 hours or longer. In the 1960s and 1970s, a typical dose was closer to 100 to 200 mcg. The LSD available today is produced by about 10 laboratories, all located in or near San Francisco. At the doses used today, 1 gram of crystal LSD produces about 20,000 individual doses.

In the 1960s LSD was often used as a mind-opening or consciousness-expanding experience that encouraged deep understanding or empathy between people. In the 1990s and early twenty-first century, the appeal of LSD appears to be the enjoyment of the intense experience, as users claim it makes everyday life more exciting, unpredictable, and interesting. LSD use is closely tied to attending raves, clubs, and concerts and is often combined with ecstasy by ravers in a practice called "candy flipping."

People who take LSD most often schedule the experience for a special occasion, such as a rave or concert. Even those termed "acid heads" by their friends because of their high use of LSD rarely take the drug more than once or twice a week. Use of LSD is limited by the fact that tolerance to the drug develops very quickly. After someone takes three or four doses close together, a few days must pass without taking the drug

HISTORY NOTES

LSD was first developed in Switzerland by chemist Albert Hofmann in 1938. He was working on chemicals derived from lysergic acid for Sandoz Laboratories because similar agents had known therapeutic uses, including the treatment of migraine headaches and gynecological problems. Hofmann did not learn about LSD's hallucinogenic properties until he accidentally ingested some in 1943. Here is an excerpt from Hofmann's report to the head of the laboratory's pharmaceutical department describing his first, accidental LSD experience:

"... I was seized by a peculiar restlessness associated with the sensation of mild dizziness. On arriving home, I lay down and sank into a kind of drunkenness, which was not unpleasant and which was characterized by extreme activity of the imagination. As I lay in a dazed condition with my eyes closed, (I experienced daylight as disagreeably bright) there surged upon me an uninterrupted stream of fantastic images of extraordinary plasticity and vividness and accompanied by an intense, kaleidoscopic-like play of colors."

After Hofmann's discovery, the psychiatric profession took great interest in LSD as a possible therapeutic drug because it was believed that an LSD high closely mimicked psychosis. Mental health experts who were treating psychotic patients took the drug to help them understand what their patients were experiencing. It turned out that an LSD high was, in fact, quite different from a psychotic experience, so the professionals treating patients switched to using the drug with less severely ill patients.

LSD can dramatically reduce people's inhibitions, making it easier for them to talk about their problems and remember past traumatic events. The drug was therefore tested as a possible way of enhancing psychotherapy in people with conditions such as anxiety, depression, and alcohol dependence. It was also used to help alleviate the fear of death in people dying of cancer and other incurable diseases. By 1965, more than 40,000 patients had been treated with LSD as part of psychiatric therapy.

Use of LSD for therapy fell out of favor for several reasons, but the primary one was that it developed a bad reputation as a recreational drug of abuse in the 1960s. Wild stories about people injuring themselves or others while on LSD began to circulate. Research into LSD as a therapeutic drug dropped off in the 1970s.

---

for it to be effective again. Also, LSD separates the user so much from reality that he or she cannot function normally while taking it. It is virtually impossible to effectively work, attend classes, drive a car, or even have a normal conversation while on LSD. As a result, people generally don't take the drug if they need to be doing something else.

A few people, usually high school-aged individuals, take LSD on a regular basis to the point that it interferes with their everyday lives, dramatically disrupting sleep, eating, and personal hygiene habits. These heavy users usually notice that their lives are affected by heavy LSD use, but they first attribute this feeling to the effects of the drug itself. In other words, they think the LSD is making them believe that their lives are affected, when, in fact, everything is fine. Fortunately, even these users eventually realize the effect LSD is having on their lives and stop taking the drug. The vast majority of people who use LSD in their youth stop of their own accord as they get older.

MENTAL EFFECTS

LSD is very similar in its chemical composition to serotonin, a chemical found in the brain. Serotonin is a neurotransmitter, which means it is responsible for

some of the communication that goes on between brain cells. Serotonin is known to be responsible for behavioral, perceptual, and regulatory systems in the brain, including mood, hunger, body temperature, sex drive, muscle control, and sensory perception. It also helps control mood, thinking, and the identification of new experiences.

It is believed that LSD works by stimulating the effects of serotonin in the brain. This would help explain why all of the senses are usually enhanced or distorted (synesthesia) in people taking LSD and why the drug has a profound effect on mood, thinking, and some basic bodily functions such as temperature control and muscle movement.

Early mental effects

LSD produces profound mental effects that increase with higher doses. Starting about 30 to 90 minutes after taking LSD, depending on the dose, a user will start to notice the following mental effects:

- Distortion and intensification of all the senses, especially vision. The shapes of objects may appear to blend together or melt, and colors may appear brighter or changed. Depth perception might also become distorted, and objects might have halos or leave trails when they move.

IN THE NEWS

In the 1960s, LSD and related hallucinogens captured the attention of college professors in psychology, religion, and other disciplines because of the drugs' potential to "expand" the mind, thereby helping to improve mental health, encourage empathy, change unhealthy behavior patterns (such as criminal behavior), improve outlook, and produce profoundly religious or spiritual experiences. Many artists, particularly musicians, also used LSD to stimulate the creative process. LSD was central to the hippie movement of the 1960s that focused on peace, love, and individual freedom.

Spearheading the research into LSD as a consciousness-expanding drug was Timothy Leary, Ph.D., a psychologist at Harvard University. With his partner, Richard Alpert Ph.D, Leary led studies at Harvard from 1960 to 1963 on the effects of taking LSD and similar drugs. Their research took them to local prisons, where the pair attempted to use hallucinogens to change criminal behavior, and to a local church, where they found that giving hallucinogens to religious people induced profound spiritual experiences. Leary and his followers believed that LSD could save the world by encouraging empathy and expanding the minds of world leaders.

Leary's research soon lost favor with the authorities, and he and Alpert were eventually fired by Harvard. In 1970, Leary was jailed for drug possession. After his release in 1975, he continued to publicly advocate using mind-expanding drugs under appropriate conditions.

Despite the negative publicity that dogged Leary and the fact that he never encouraged used of the hallucinogens for purely recreational purposes, his work was extremely influential in popularizing LSD and in bringing about the hippie revolution of the 1960s. This revolution peaked in 1967, when a "Love In" in honor of LSD was staged at Golden Gate Park in San Francisco.

A few famous proponents of LSD during this time period included author Ken Kesey, author and philosopher Aldous Huxley, poet Allen Ginsberg, and The Beatles, a famous musical group.

- Distortions in time and space, in which time seems to flow more slowly and the sense of the shape or position of the body is altered.

- Synesthesia, or the blending or crossing over of senses, so that people might feel they can see sounds or hear colors.

- A feeling that everything is very real and familiar.

- A strong sense of connection with other people (empathy) or connectedness to the universe.

- A sense of heightened understanding.

- Impaired judgment, which can make everyday tasks like driving a car dangerous.

- A feeling of being rooted to the spot, even when moving.

- Intensification of and rapid changes in mood.

- The turning inward of attention, often with the sense of being a passive observer of oneself.

- Uncontrolled laughing or a sense of inner tension relieved by laughing or crying.

- Euphoria, a feeling of well-being or elation.

- A sense of being out of the body.

Late mental effects

Starting about one to two hours after taking the drug and usually continuing for eight to 12 hours (depending on the dose) LSD produces the following effects:

- Vivid hallucinations, or the sensing of things that are not there. Hallucinations produced by LSD are usually visual and are often related to what is really there. So, a person on LSD might see the furniture moving around the room or see people appear unrecognizably different.

- Extreme emotional instability, to the point of feeling intense fear and panic one second, despair another, and pure joy the next. Some people who have taken LSD say they feel like they are experiencing several intense emotions at once.

- Difficulty communicating, especially with people who are not also on LSD.

- Difficulty concentrating.

- Difficulty distinguishing reality from illusion.

- A heightened sense of clarity combined with a reduced ability to control what is being experienced.

As the effects of LSD start to wear off, a period called "coming down," occurs. Many people experience some anxiety, depression, and/or fatigue during this time. Unlike what occurs after use of many other drugs, including marijuana and alcohol, people tend to remember their LSD experience.

Negative mental effects

Many people find LSD to be a positive experience, one that makes them feel more connected to the people they get high with as well as with the universe as a whole. When an LSD trip goes badly, however, it can be a very distressing experience. In fact, a bad trip can be so traumatic for some people that they never fully recover. Someone experiencing a bad trip on LSD often feels:

- extreme anxiety or panic

- fear of losing control, going insane, or dying

- fear that their sense of self is fragmenting or disintegrating

- vivid and sudden thoughts and memories of previous traumatic experiences

- despair

- perception of rapid aging in oneself or in others

- desire to commit suicide (which, in a few rare cases, has actually been successfully carried out)

- extreme confusion

- paranoia

- aggression

Factors affecting mental effects

It is impossible to predict who will have a positive experience with LSD and who will have a negative one. The same person might enjoy an LSD experience one day and have a devastatingly bad trip another day. Early studies with LSD revealed, however, that a number of factors play a crucial role in how an LSD trip is experienced. These include:

- The setting in which the drug is taken. A comfortable, safe setting in which the user is surrounded by supportive, trusted people increases the chances that an LSD trip will be positive.

- Dose. The higher the dose, the more intense the experience and the greater the risk that it will be too much for the drug taker to handle.

- Personality of the drug taker. People who can easily relax and let go are more likely to experience LSD positively than are people who are uncomfortable when they lose control of a situation.

- Mood of drug taker. LSD tends to intensify the mood a person was in before taking the drug.

- Expectations of drug taker. To a certain degree, the LSD experience will mimic what the drug taker expects it to be.

- Reason for taking the drug. People who take the drug of their own accord are more likely to have a positive experience than those who take it for self-therapy or because of peer pressure.

- Mental health of the drug taker. People with a history of mental health problems are more likely to have bad trips, although negative experiences also occur in people with no such history.

Tolerance to LSD builds up very quickly. After three or four doses are taken over a short period of time, the drug stops having an effect. It only takes a few days off the drug for it to start working again, however. Interestingly, tolerance to LSD also leads to tolerance of other hallucinogenic drugs, even ones that are not chemically related to LSD.

PHYSIOLOGICAL EFFECTS

LSD has such powerful mental effects that people do not always notice its physical effects. However, the drug is a powerful stimulant and, as such, has a dramatic effect on the body. Physiological effects people experience with LSD, starting very soon after taking the drug, include:

- dilated pupils

- changes in body temperature

- nausea

- vomiting

- headache

- goose bumps

- hair standing on end

- profuse sweating

- increased blood sugar

- rapid heart rate

- increased blood pressure

- loss of appetite

- inability to sleep

- dry mouth

- tremors

- dizziness

- numbness

• weakness

• seizures (rare, and only with very high doses)

Harmful side effects

Despite frightening rumors that circulated in the 1960s and 1970s, there is no evidence that taking LSD, even regularly and in high doses, causes damage to the brain, genes, or developing fetuses. Massive overdoses of the drug can, in rare cases, lead to coma, respiratory arrest, overheating of the body, and problems with blood clotting.

Pregnant women should not take LSD because it is known to cause contractions of the uterus. This can bring on a miscarriage.

An LSD trip, especially a bad trip, can make people lose touch with reality to the point that they are a danger to themselves and others. People have been known to have fatal accidents while on LSD because they lost touch with their surroundings. Some people have even purposely harmed themselves or committed suicide during LSD-induced despair. A bad trip can also bring on paranoid thoughts and aggressive tendencies that have led people to harm or even murder others. While these extreme reactions to LSD are rare, they do occur.

Long-term health effects

There are two major long-term risks of taking LSD—flash backs and LSD psychosis.

Flashbacks are known as hallucinogen persisting perception disorder, or HPPD. This is a spontaneous re-experiencing of the effects of LSD that occur without taking the drug. Usually, a flashback does not produce the full effects of an LSD trip. The most common experience is visual hallucinations or disturbances, such as seeing motion at the edges of one's field of vision when nothing has actually moved, or seeing halos around objects or trails behind moving objects. They can occur in people who have been heavy users of LSD or in someone who has taken the drug only once, and they may happen weeks, months, or even years after taking LSD. Most people find flashbacks to be unpleasant and often frightening, particularly because they can mimic the symptoms of serious neurological disorders or brain tumors.

It is not known how common flashbacks are. Estimates of the proportion of LSD users who later experience flashbacks range from 15% to 77%. Flashbacks are more likely to occur in people who regularly took LSD for a long time and in those with other mental health problems. They can also be brought on by taking SSRI (selective serotonin reuptake inhibitor) antidepressant drugs, alcohol, marijuana, or phenothiazines, which are drugs used to treat psychosis. Other flashback triggers are movement in a darkened area, fatigue, hunger, and anxiety.

A very small number of people who take LSD never seem to fully recover from the experience, especially if they had a bad trip. LSD psychosis causes an individual to continue experiencing symptoms related to LSD use including dramatic mood swings, hallucinations, visual disturbances, or severe depression and anxiety. This disorder is most likely to occur in people who had an unstable mental state before taking the drug, who took the drug for the wrong reasons (e.g., to try to treat themselves or because of peer pressure), or who took the drug in a stressful setting. However, well-adjusted people who took LSD in a safe setting also have been known to develop LSD psychosis after only one dose.

There is considerable controversy among experts as to what causes LSD psychosis. Various theories are that the LSD itself somehow damages the brain (although there are no physical signs of brain damage in people who have taken LSD); that a bad trip (like any traumatic experience) brings out mental illness in people who were already susceptible; and/or that LSD breaks down the barriers between the conscious and unconscious mind at the same time that it blocks people's normal inhibitions, thus creating a very vulnerable state.

Regardless of the cause of LSD psychosis, people with this condition usually respond to treatments for the mental illnesses their condition resembles. So, if their symptoms resemble psychosis, they generally respond to antipsychotic drugs.

REACTIONS WITH OTHER DRUGS OR SUBSTANCES

Little research has been conducted on how LSD interacts with other drugs. The most complete research is with antidepressant drugs because these commonly prescribed medications affect the same brain chemical, serotonin, that LSD does. There are three types of antidepressants, and each interacts differently with LSD:

1. SSRI antidepressants, which include Prozac (fluoxetine), Zoloft (sertraline), and Paxil (paroxetine), usually decrease the effects of LSD when they are taken together. However, taking an SSRI antidepressant can bring on disturbing flashbacks in someone who has taken LSD in the past.

2. Tricyclic antidepressants, including Tofranil (imipramine) and Anafranil (clomipramine), usually intensify the effects of LSD.

3. MAOI antidepressants, such as Nardil (phenelzine), usually decrease the effects of LSD.

Interactions with other drugs have been less closely studied, but anecdotal reports suggest that lithium, a drug used to stabilize mood in people with manic depression or bipolar disorder, increases the response to LSD.

Alcohol can make the visual hallucinations associated with LSD decrease, and people taking LSD often feel they can drink more without getting drunk (a sensation that may not reflect reality).

Ecstasy is another hallucinogen and, like LSD, is popular in club settings. These two drugs are often combined at raves and concerts in a practice called "candy flipping." Some people say that the good mood induced by taking ecstasy can decrease the risk of having a bad trip on LSD. On the other hand, both drugs are powerful hallucinogens and taking them together can create a very intense experience indeed. Often, the more intense the experience, the greater the risk of having a bad trip.

Marijuana can cause paranoia in many people. As a result, it is not considered a good mix with LSD because paranoia can bring on a bad trip. According to research conducted by the NIDA, the combination of LSD and marijuana may bring on psychosis in teenagers.

TREATMENT AND REHABILITATION

Fortunately, LSD is not a drug typically associated with long-term abuse. It does not cause physical dependence or addiction, and even psychological dependence appears to be short-lived in most people. Among users, the drug is usually saved for special occasions because taking it more than three or four times over a few days can lead to a tolerance that stops the drug from having any effect. Even those who take LSD regularly usually stop on their own after a few months or years. LSD is rarely taken by anyone after their high school or college years. People usually stop taking LSD because of bad trips or because they have simply had enough of the very intense experience.

Treatment for LSD is sometimes required for its negative short- and long-term effects, however. The most common reason for requiring medical attention after taking LSD is for a bad trip. People having a bad LSD trip can usually be talked down by a trusted person, who calmly explains that the drug taker is safe, that the hallucinations are not real, and that the effects are temporary.

In general, medical personnel avoid giving people on LSD any medication because they cannot be sure what the person has taken, and some of the drugs that might be helpful interact dangerously with street drugs. Left in a quiet room with as little stimulation as possible and with a trusted person to watch over them, people having a bad trip usually settle down and experience lessening of negative effects. However, people who are out of control on high doses of LSD may, in rare cases, require a tranquilizer, such as Valium (diazepam) to calm down. In very rare cases, doctors may give such a person an antipsychotic medication, which is the type of drug given to people with psychosis. Some antipsychotics block the effect of LSD on the brain.

Another reason LSD users sometimes require medical attention is because of flashbacks. There is no way to block flashbacks, so the best way to treat them is to help teach the individual how to cope with them. This involves explaining that the flashbacks are not dangerous or a sign of brain damage, and that the effects usually go away on their own quite quickly. Sometimes, people require psychotherapy to help them overcome the fear associated with flashbacks.

A third reason LSD users might require medical attention is when they develop LSD psychosis. As mentioned earlier, regardless of the underlying cause of psychosis, the best treatment appears to be the same as that used for people who have similar mental health problems not related to taking LSD. So, a person with psychosis following an LSD trip generally responds as well to antipsychotic therapy as a person who develops psychosis without taking LSD does.

PERSONAL AND SOCIAL CONSEQUENCES

Fortunately, most people who try LSD reserve the drug's use for special occasions. However, some heavy users take LSD long enough and frequently enough for it to interfere significantly with their lives. This kind of chronic LSD use can completely disconnect a person from everyday reality, leading to poor performance at school and work, as well as poor or chaotic sleeping, eating, and personal hygiene habits. Although LSD has been touted as a drug that improves connectedness and understanding among users, most heavy LSD users actually stop being able to communicate normally with the people in their lives, especially those who have not shared the LSD experience. They essentially withdraw into an illusory world created by regular LSD use.

Heavy LSD users often notice that their lives are falling apart, but they often initially believe that everything is really the same, and that it is the LSD itself that is making them think their lives are in chaos. This is an example of the extent to which heavy LSD use can disconnect a person from reality. Fortunately, heavy users usually do eventually realize the effect LSD is having on their lives and stop taking the drug on their own. It is rare for people beyond college age to keep taking LSD.

Taking LSD can disconnect people from reality so much that they might do crazy things while they are high, including harming themselves or others. Once a person comes down from an LSD trip, he or she must face the consequences of his or her actions while under the drug's influence. Unlike many drugs that affect memory, LSD enables people to remember everything they did while under the drug's influence.

As with all illegal drugs, taking LSD puts people at risk of getting in trouble with the law. A conviction for drug possession or manufacture can have a substantial negative impact on later efforts to get into college or find a job.

Drugs bought illegally off the street are often not what their sellers claim them to be. This is also true for LSD. Whenever people take LSD, they are risking that they might actually be taking another drug (or combination of drugs), such as mescaline or PCP (angel dust) or that they are taking a much higher dose of LSD than expected.

LEGAL CONSEQUENCES

In the United States, there is no legal use for LSD. As a Schedule I drug, it is considered by the U. S. government to have a high abuse potential, no known medical application, and questionable safety.

Legal history

In the United States, manufacture of LSD first became illegal in 1965. Over the next few years, individual states enacted increasingly stiffer penalties for the manufacture and sale of the drug. In 1968, LSD possession was declared a misdemeanor and its sale a felony. It became a Schedule I drug in 1970. Chemicals used to make LSD, including lysergic acid, ergotamine, and ergonovine, are also controlled substances.

In the United Kingdom, LSD was made illegal in 1966, and medical research with the drug was prohibited in 1973 with passage of the Misuse of Drugs Act. This act listed LSD as a Class A drug, meaning it is not legally available for medical use, and it is illegal to possess or supply it.

Federal guidelines, regulations and penalties

The legal penalties for LSD possession in the United States are severe. Possession of 1 to 9 grams (a dollar bill weighs approximately 1 gram) can lead to a mandatory sentence of five to 40 years in jail and a fine up to $2 million. Sentences are even stiffer for possession of higher doses, for repeated offenses, or for providing LSD that leads to serious injury or death. The most severe LSD-related penalty for an individual is life in prison and up to $8 million in fines.

In the United Kingdom, maximum penalties for LSD-related violations range from seven years imprisonment and a fine for possession, to life imprisonment and a fine for supplying the drug.

See also Designer drugs; DMT (dimethyltryptamine); Ecstasy (MDMA); GHB; Mescaline; PCP (phencyclidine); Psilocybin

RESOURCES

Books

Belenko, Steven R., ed. *Drugs and Drug Policy in America: A Documentary History.* Westport, CT: Greenwood Press, 2000.

Bray, Robert M., and Mary E. Marsden, eds. *Drug Use in Metropolitan America.* Thousand Oaks, CA: Sage Publications Inc., 1999.

Henderson, Leigh A., and William J. Glass, eds. *LSD: Still With Us After All These Years.* New York: Lexington Books, 1994.

Leary, Timothy. *Flashbacks: A Personal and Cultural History of an Era.* New York: G.P. Putnam's Sons, 1990.

Lee, Martin A., and Bruce Shlain. *Acid Dreams: The Complete Social History of LSD: The CIA, the Sixties, and Beyond.* New York: Grove Press, 1985.

Slack, Charles, W. *Timothy Leary, the Madness of the Sixties and Me.* New York: Peter H. Wyden Publisher, 1974.

Weil, Andrew, and Winifred Rosen. *From Chocolate to Morphine: Everything You Need to Know about Mind-Altering Drugs.* Boston: Houghton Mifflin Company, 1998.

Periodicals

Carter, M. "Flying High for the U.S. Army." *New Scientist* 71, no. 1015 (August 1976): 451.

Labreche, J. "The CIA Affair: A Bad Trip Revisited." *Maclean's* 92, no. 7 (February 1979): 18-20.

U.S. Department of Health and Human Services. "Hallucinogenic and Dissociative Drugs." National Institute on Drug Abuse Research Report Series. March 2001.

Other

Bonson, Kit. "National Institute of Mental Health: Interactions Between Hallucinogens and Antidepressants." *The Vaults of Erowid.* June 7, 2001 (February 15, 2002). <http://erowid.org/chemicals/maois/maois_info4.html>.

"LSD." *Drugscope.* 2000 (February 15, 2002). <http://www.drugscope.org.uk/st_info.asp?file=\wip\11\1\1\lsd.html>.

Machem, C. Crawford, and Alan H. Hall. "CBRNE–Incapacitating Agents, LSD." *EMedicine Journal* 2, no. 10 (October 2001). <http://www.emedicine.com/emerg/topic911.htm>.

Monitoring the Future Study (MTF). Monitoring the Future Study home page. July 2, 2002 (July 8, 2002). <http://www.monitoringthefuture.org>.

National Institute on Drug Abuse. *Club Drugs: Community Alert Bulletin.* February 21, 2002 (July 8, 2002). <http://www.drugabuse.gov/clubalert/clubdrugalert.html>.

National Institute on Drug Abuse. *InfoFax: Science Based Facts on Drug Abuse and Addiction.* October 25, 2001 (February 15, 2002). <http://www.nida.nih.gov/Infofax/Infofaxindex.html>.

National Institute on Drug Abuse. *Mind Over Matter: The Brain's Response to Hallucinogens.* (January 24, 2002). <http://www.drugabuse.gov/mom/hall/momhall1.html>.

Perry, Paul. "LSD Psychosis." *University of Iowa Health Care Virtual Hospital.* 1996. (February 15, 2002). <http://www.vh.org/Providers/Conferences/CPS/28.html>.

U.S. Department of Justice. Drug Enforcement Administration. *LSD in the United States.* (July 8, 2002). <http://www. usdoj.gov/dea/pubs/lsd/toc.htm>.

U.S. Department of Justice. Drug Enforcement Administration. Diversion Control Program. *Drugs and Chemicals of Concern: d-Lysergic Acid Diethylamide (LSD, acid, cid, blotter acid).* August 2001 (January 24, 2002). <http://www.deadiversion.usdoj.gov/ drugs_concern/lsd/summary.htm>.

Organizations

National Institute on Drug Abuse (NIDA), National Institutes of Health, 6001 Executive Boulevard, Room 5213, Bethesda, MD, USA, 20892-9561, (301) 443-1124, (888) 644-6432, information@lists.nida.nih.gov, <http://www.drugabuse.gov/ Infofax/marijuana.html>.

Alison Farah Palkhivala, B.A.

MARIJUANA

OFFICIAL NAMES: Marijuana, hashish, hashish oil
STREET NAMES: There are more than 200 slang terms for marijuana, including: A-bomb, Acapulco gold, ace, African black, Aunt Mary, bhang, blanche, boo, boom, bush, charas, chronic, dagga, dope, gangster, ganja, grass, hash, hash oil, herb, kef, kief, kif, marihuana, Mary Jane, nickel, oil, old man, pot, reefer, sinsemilla, sensi, skunk, smoke, tar, weed
DRUG CLASSIFICATIONS: Schedule I, hallucinogen

OVERVIEW

Marijuana is derived from the Indian hemp plant, *Cannabis sativa*, a member of the Cannabaceae family and the Urticales (nettle) order. Some botanists claim that this genus contains as many as three other species: *C. indica*, *C. ruderalis*, and even *Humulus lupulus*, the hops plant. Other botanists insist that the differences between plants reflect simple variations, not different species.

Cannabis sativa is dioecious, which means that it produces both male and female plants. All types of cannabis strains—both male and female plants—produce THC, the active ingredient that, when smoked or ingested, intoxicates the user. This substance can be detected in every part of the plant, including the stems. The highest concentration of THC, however, is found in the resin, which is most abundant in the flowers of female plants.

Several hemp plant types have sturdy stems that can grow to heights of 20 ft (6 m). These stems contain a strong and durable fiber that can be processed to make rope, cloth, and paper. Other hemp plant types produce oil- and protein-rich seeds that are used in some industrial applications and a few types of animal feed. By far the hemp plant most frequently cultivated, however, is the short bushy strain whose leaves and flowers contain high concentrations of THC.

Marijuana defies easy classification as a drug. It is described as a psychogenic (a cannabinoid), a narcotic (although it does not contain opium), and a hallucinogen (the government's designation). Each of these definitions, however, is at best a compromise. Opinion is further divided on whether the drug is a stimulant or a depressant. Controversy also rages over marijuana's medicinal properties, which are alleged and denied fiercely by proponents and detractors, respectively. One fact remains indisputable: Marijuana is the most abused illegal drug in the world.

History

The use of marijuana for both medicinal purposes and relaxation has a history almost as long as its other applications, such as paper or cloth. The world's oldest-known pharmacopeia, dated from the third century B.C., recognized the drug's psychoactive qualities and recommended its use as a painkiller, antidepressant, and sedative. It was also recommended, although with dubious efficacy, to treat gout, constipation, and forgetfulness. Three thousand years later, during the second century A.D., a Chinese surgeon boiled hemp in wine to produce an anaesthetic he called *ma fei san*. Interestingly, aside from its medicinal uses, marijuana never became the popular recreational drug in China that it has in other parts of the world.

From China, marijuana spread eastward. In India, its use as a drug began around 1,000 B.C., and it soon became an important part of Hindu religious rituals and meditation. The Artharvaveda, one of the four Vedas, or sacred Hindu texts, portrays cannabis as a divine elixir that eases anxiety. Ancient Indian physicians prescribed marijuana for malaria and rheumatism, presumably for its analgesic qualities. Other early medical indications—for "blood clearing" and to encourage the formation of pus (thought to be a sign of healing)—say more about the state of medicine during those centuries than cannabis's therapeutic value. The Persians and Assyrians also used cannabis as a drug, as reflected in tablets from the eighth and seventh centuries B.C., respectively.

However practical its uses, though, cannabis was always consumed recreationally. Marijuana became popular in the Moslem world, partly because the Islamic faith forbade the use of alcohol. The Sufis, a mystical Islamic sect, used marijuana as part of their religious rituals. Over the centuries, Arab traders brought cannabis to east Africa, and from there it spread throughout the continent.

By 400 A.D., hemp was being cultivated in Europe and in England. With the rise of the national navies during the sixteenth century, hemp farming was encouraged to meet the demand for rope and naval rigging. After Napoleon's Egyptian campaign brought hashish to Europe, nineteenth-century French writers, artists, and intellectuals took up its use. When some of their surreal experiences with hashish were publicized, the shocked reaction by the public established drug use as a lower-class, disreputable pursuit.

Hemp farming became an important crop in America as well. In fact, the Virginia Assembly required every farmer in the colony to grow it, and imposed penalties on those who did not. By the middle of the nineteenth century, hempen cloth was a staple of American life; it was turned into everything from garments to the covers on Conestoga wagons. The advent of steam power for ships and railroads reduced demand for hemp considerably. Today, superior manmade alternatives have all but eliminated the profitability of hemp as a crop.

In the early part of the twentieth century, American soldiers fighting Pancho Villa in Mexico and civilians stationed in Panama during the construction of the canal discovered the intoxicating power of marijuana and brought it back to the States. The influx of nearly a million Mexican laborers between 1900 and 1930 also brought marijuana smoking into the country. Port cities such as New York, Chicago, and New Orleans were points of entry for the drug as well.

In the 1930s, the Federal Bureau of Narcotics, forerunner of today's Drug Enforcement Administration (DEA), began a propaganda campaign that portrayed marijuana as a drug that led users to drug addiction, vio-

KEY TERMS

ADDICTION: Physical dependence on a drug characterized by tolerance and withdrawal.

BHANG: The mildest form of cannabis used in India.

CANNABINOID: One of the approximately 60 chemical compounds found in *Cannabis sativa*.

CANNABIS: Refers to all plant and/or drug forms of the Indian hemp plant, *Cannabis sativa*.

CHARAS: Concentrated cannabis resin, similar to hashish.

DEPENDENCE: A psychological compulsion to use a drug that is not linked to physical addiction.

GANJA: A moderately potent form of Indian cannabis, marked by a greater THC content than bhang.

HASHISH: Concentrated cannabis resin, similar to charas.

HASHISH OIL: The most potent form of cannabis resin, extracted by chemical solvent.

HEMP: Cannabis plants that are grown for fiber; in nineteenth-century medicine, also referred to cannabis used medicinally.

MARIJUANA: The dried leaves and flowers of female *Cannabis sativa* plants.

TETRAHYDROCANNABINOLS (THC): A group of cannabinoid compounds thought to cause most of the psychoactive reactions to marijuana use.

lence, and insanity. The government produced films such as *Marihuana* (1935), *Reefer Madness* (1936), and *Assassin of Youth* (1937) in its attempts scare people straight. At that point, however, cannabis was not only legal, it was an approved medication frequently prescribed by doctors. Marijuana's status changed drastically in 1937, when the Marijuana Tax Act effectively criminalized its use and possession, even for medical reasons.

The Beat Generation of the 1950s began the counterculture movement, and icons like Kerouac and Ginsberg glamorized the use of marijuana as part of their rebellion against the mainstream. The revolution continued in the 1960s, when flower children and hippies promoted marijuana as a harmless drug, a view that acquired particular resonance among the young. The pendulum swung back toward the center in the 1980s, after drug abuse reached its zenith in 1979 and people began to assess its true toll. As scientific research progressed, the dangers that marijuana posed—and the possible therapeutic benefits it possessed—came to light.

Hashish is a highly potent, concentrated cannabis resin that has been collected, dried, and pressed into bricks. Photo by Owen Franken/CORBIS. Reproduced by permission.

CHEMICAL/ORGANIC COMPOSITION

More than 400 chemical compounds have been identified in marijuana. Approximately 60 of these are unique to the cannabis plant, substances called cannabinoids. Of the cannabinoids, a group of isomers (chemically similar substances) called tetrahydrocannabinols (THC) are thought to be the most psychoactive. These are Δ^1–THC (also called Δ^9–THC) and Δ^6–THC (also called Δ^8–THC). Other cannabinoids include cannabidiolic acid (CBDA), cannabidiol (CBD), and cannabinol (CBN). Their role in marijuana intoxication is less well understood. The amount of THC produced depends on the strain of cannabis and on environmental factors such as growth, harvest, and storage conditions.

Because marijuana is a natural product it can also harbor bacteria and fungi, some of which can be harmful if inhaled. Scientists have found bacteria such as *Aspergillus, Salmonella, Klebsiella, Enterobacter*, and *Streptococcus* on marijuana samples. This is especially significant for people with compromised immune systems, such as cancer or AIDS patients, many of whom may consider marijuana to counter some of the effects of their disease or treatments.

Not all chemicals found in marijuana occur naturally. When the plant is burned for smoking, hundreds of additional chemicals are produced in the process.

Among them are carbon monoxide, cyanide, benzopyrene, and tar, the same toxic chemicals present in cigarette smoke. (Some researchers feel that any beneficial effects that may be found in the medicinal use of marijuana are actually negated by the current lack of a suitable alternative delivery method.) Additionally, any pesticides sprayed on the plant by the grower are present in the smoke, and are inhaled along with the THC.

Types of cannabis

Indian cannabis. In India, where cannabis has been part of the culture for centuries, three types of cannabis are used.

Bhang is the mildest of India's cannabis concoctions, and is usually eaten as a sweetmeat or consumed as a beverage. It consists of dried cannabis leaves that are ground to a fine paste, mixed with a combination of sugar, spices, and fruit. Because the cannabis is ingested orally, the drug's effects are felt more slowly than when it is smoked. In India, bhang is a poor man's drug and is used the way beer and wine are in the West. Like alcohol, bhang is often a part of social and religious occasions. Bhang is the weakest of all cannabis preparations and generally has a low THC concentration.

Ganja, like marijuana, is made from THC-rich cannabis flowers and resin. It is smoked (sometimes mixed with tobacco) in a pipe, a cigarette, or in bidis, small Indian cigars. Like bhang, ganja is favored by the

LAW AND ORDER

On May 14, 2001, the U.S. Supreme Court ruled 8 to 0 in *United States vs. Oakland Cannabis Buyers' Cooperative* that the cooperatives permitted under California law to sell marijuana to medical patients who had a physician's approval to use the drug were unconstitutional under federal law.

One of the justices, Stephen G. Breyer, declined to rule on the case because his brother, a U.S. district judge, had issued two of the original rulings that barred California cannabis buyers' cooperatives from distributing marijuana. These rulings started the chain of events that brought the case to the Supreme Court.

The justices engaged in an often-spirited debate about whether or not marijuana was an effective treatment for certain diseases and conditions. They declined, however, to consider the validity of "medical marijuana" arguments, deciding instead to interpret the narrow question they had been given: Does the Controlled Substances Act, as written, allow a medical exception to its prohibition on growing, possessing, and/or selling marijuana?

The answer, according to the court, is no, since the Controlled Substance Act defines Schedule I drugs as those with "no currently accepted medical use in treatment in the United States." The ruling allows state laws permitting the personal use and cultivation of medical marijuana to stand, but prohibits the kind of organized distribution that the cooperatives had engaged in, since, the court reasoned, these organizations cannot claim a medical necessity for marijuana use.

The court's ruling passes the question of marijuana's medical future to Congress, which would have to rewrite current laws to allow it to be used therapeutically. In response, Rep. Barney Frank (D-Mass.) introduced a bill to reclassify marijuana as a Schedule II drug, which would permit physicians to prescribe it for their patients if state law permitted its use.

---

lower classes of Indian society. It is usually at least twice as potent as bhang, with a higher THC concentration.

Charas is the nearly pure concentrated resin of the cannabis plant. Like ganja, it is smoked, but its THC concentration is far higher.

Marijuana. Marijuana is the dried tobacco-like leaves and flowers of the cannabis plant and is the most common form of the drug in the United States. Marijuana is usually smoked, although it is occasionally baked into foods such as brownies or brewed as tea for drinking. Different grades of marijuana have different levels of THC. Sinsemilla (Spanish for "seedless"), which contains mostly flowers and buds with few or no seeds, is considered the most potent form of marijuana.

Hashish. Like charas, hashish is a highly potent, concentrated cannabis resin that has been collected, dried, and pressed into bricks. It is sometimes mixed with tobacco or marijuana and is usually ingested by smoking.

Hashish oil. Also known as hash oil, this substance is cannabis resin that has been extracted from the plant with a chemical solvent such as alcohol or butane. Like hashish, it contains very high concentrations of THC. Hash oil is usually added to tobacco or marijuana cigarettes and is ingested by smoking.

Drug combinations. Marijuana is frequently combined with other drugs, including heroin, cocaine, crack cocaine, LSD, and ecstasy. One particularly dangerous drug combination, called "wet sticks" or "dip sticks," appeared in the 1990s. These are marijuana joints that have been soaked in embalming fluid, then dried. They are frequently laced with PCP (phencyclidine) as well, although users may not be aware of this. Embalming fluid is extremely poisonous as it contains both formaldehyde, which can cause brain damage and lung failure, and methanol, which can lead to convulsions, coma, and death. PCP is a notoriously unpredictable drug that can lead its users to violent and self-destructive acts. Newer varieties of wet sticks have been discovered to contain both PCP and ether. All are extremely dangerous.

Taking any combination of drugs is always risky because the effect of each drug is amplified and unpredictable. When ingested with alcohol, marijuana's antiemetic (antivomiting) properties can suppress the gag reflex. This may prevent the body from purging toxic amounts of alcohol, which could lead to alcohol poisoning. People on antidepressant medication such as tricyclics who also use marijuana can develop an accelerated heartbeat and high blood pressure, both of which can be dangerous over the long term. Patients who take selective serotonin reuptake inhibitors (SSRIs) such as Paxil and Prozac, and also use marijuana, are at greater risk for severe psychotic episodes. When marijuana is combined with cocaine, the body's drug absorption rate doubles and the stress on the cardiovascular system can rise to dangerous levels since both drugs speed up the heart and raise blood pressure.

Although cannabis is illegal in the United States, in other parts of the world it is used recreationally and in religious practices. Photo by Daniel Lainé/CORBIS. Reproduced by permission.

Dronabinol. Dronabinol is a synthetic form of THC that was approved for medical use by the FDA in 1985. Sold under the trade name Marinol, it is prescribed as an antiemitic for cancer patients undergoing chemotherapy and as an appetite stimulant for AIDS patients who become anorexic. Marinol is manufactured in 2.5-, 5-, and 10-mg capsules, which are taken orally. Critics argue that suppositories would be more useful than capsules since cancer and AIDS patients are often unable to keep food down.

Potency

Marijuana's potency depends on the amount of THC it contains. This is determined by many factors, among them the type of drug (marijuana, hashish, hash oil) and the strain of cannabis from which it came. In the decades since the 1960s, the potency of marijuana has increased markedly, from 10 to 25 times the average THC content, according to the United States government. Other sources give different figures, but few dispute that cultivation, especially hydroponics, has dramatically increased the THC content of marijuana over the years.

INGESTION METHODS

Marijuana is usually ingested by smoking, often in joints, which are loosely rolled cigarettes, or blunts, which are hollowed-out cigars in which the tobacco filler has been replaced with marijuana. A water pipe, or bong, which filters the smoke through water, can also be used, and is frequently employed when smoking hashish or charas. Marijuana can also be ingested orally, either mixed with other foods or brewed as a tea.

THERAPEUTIC USE

Perhaps no other aspect of marijuana use causes so emotional a response as the question of its medical value. Long before government mandates dictated medical policy, ancient physicians and healers used cannabis to try to relax muscle spasms, ease anxiety, and relieve pain. In the West, cannabis entered the medical lexicon only in the 1800s. As in the ancient world, the list of conditions it was thought to treat was extensive, including rabies, cholera, tetanus, gonorrhea, and angina, along with nausea, menstrual cramps, and depression. As the century progressed and medicine advanced from art to science, articles were published in medical journals touting the drug's effectiveness. Cannabis appeared in both the United States Dispensatory and the United States Pharmacopeia (where it was listed until 1942) as an approved medicament. It was also a frequent component of patent medicines, many of them produced by well-known pharmaceutical companies. These patent medicines were freely available and could be purchased with or without a doctor's prescription.

During the twentieth century, the Pure Food and Drug Act of 1906 and the Marijuana Tax Act of 1937 removed cannabis from pharmacy shelves and medicine bottles, turning marijuana into an illegal substance and an underground drug. In 1985, the FDA approved synthetic THC, or dronabinol (Marinol) as an antiemetic for cancer patients undergoing chemotherapy. Seven years later it was approved as an appetite stimulant for AIDS patients. Originally released as a tightly controlled Schedule II drug (the same class as morphine), in 1999 the DEA reclassified Marinol as a Schedule III drug, giving it the same restrictions as codeine and making it far easier for patients to fill their prescriptions.

Natural marijuana (as distinct from the synthetic THC in Marinol) may indeed have medical uses, and research, both private and federally sponsored, is underway to determine its effectiveness. Proponents claim it may help reduce elevated eye pressure in glaucoma, soothe the muscle spasms that accompany diseases like multiple sclerosis, prevent epileptic seizures, reduce inflammation, and relieve pain, especially that of migraine headaches and arthritis. Studies suggest possible benefits as an anti-asthmatic and anxiolytic/antidepressant. In 1997, the Institute of Medicine (IOM), a branch of the National Academy of Sciences, published the report, *Marijuana: Assessing the Science Base*, which concluded that cannabinoids showed significant promise as analgesics, appetite stimulants, and antiemetics, and that further research into producing these medicines was warranted. Evidence supporting their therapeutic potential for glaucoma, epilepsy, and other neurological/movement disorders was less encouraging, however.

Medically, the problem with marijuana is that currently the most effective way to deliver the drug is through smoking, which brings with it a host of cautions and health concerns. To counter this, at least one pharmaceutical company is investigating alternative delivery systems for the active compounds found in marijuana, such as a sublingual spray of THC and CBD that began clinical trials in Great Britain and Canada in 2001. Other companies have developed a vaporizer that heats marijuana to a temperature below its burning point but still high enough to release the drug's active chemicals, which are then breathed in via an inhaler.

USAGE TRENDS

Scope and severity

Marijuana is by far the most frequently abused illegal drug worldwide. The Office of National Drug Control Policy stated in its 2001 Annual Report that about 80% of Americans abusing illegal drugs used marijuana. The National Institute of Drug Abuse (NIDA), a branch of the National Institutes of Health (NIH), indicated in

2000 that marijuana is also more likely than other illegal drugs to be combined with other controlled substances.

Nationally, the National Household Survey on Drug Abuse (NHSDA) estimated in 1999 that a third of the American population (72 million people) have tried marijuana at least once, but only 8.6% had used it during the past year. Figures decline even further when respondents were asked about more frequent use: Only about 5.1% (11.2 million) of the American population aged 12 and older were monthly marijuana or hashish users. This is roughly the same as in 1991, but less than half the rate of 13.2% reported in 1979.

Age, ethnic, and gender trends

The age group least likely to have tried marijuana were those over 70, according to a poll conducted in 2001. Of that group, only 2% said they had ever tried the drug. Of those aged 60–70 years old, only 15% had done so. These were followed by 51–59-year-olds (35%), 35–50-year-olds (53%), 26–34-year-olds (40%), and 18–25-year-olds, the youngest population segment surveyed, who were the most likely of all the groups to have used marijuana—55% of them said they had tried the drug.

A concurrence among different studies is that the use of marijuana, at least among young people, is on a decline. However, a National Center on Addiction and Substance Abuse (CASA) study showed that eighth graders in rural areas are more likely (11.6%) than their urban counterparts (8.6%) to have used marijuana. Usage by older teens has been consistent, while 19.4% of tenth graders and a sobering 23.1% of high school seniors had reported using marijuana. A 1999 study showed that 49.7% of high school seniors surveyed admitted using marijuana, many starting at 13 or younger.

In a 2001 study, the number of men who abused marijuana consistently outnumbered women, and by a large margin. Males comprised anywhere from 60–72% of marijuana users, and men were also far more likely than women to be admitted to treatment centers for marijuana abuse.

Marijuana use also varies by racial and ethnic groups. American Indians/Alaskan Natives of all ages were the most likely of any racial/ethnic category to have used marijuana. Use among whites and blacks was roughly equivalent, while figures for Hispanics were lower, although the numbers varied depending on their subgroup (e.g., Puerto Rican, Mexican, Cuban, etc.). Asians/Pacific Islanders were the least likely to have used marijuana, though 18–25-year-olds reported statistically significant usage, and even that was the lowest of any group studied.

Marijuana is the most abused drug in the European Union. As in the United States, young people were much more likely than other age groups to have used marijuana. Reflecting their national trends, about 15% of the youth surveyed in Finland and Sweden had tried the drug, compared with highs of 28–40% in Denmark, France, Ireland, Netherlands, Spain, and the United Kingdom.

One group that is highly likely to use marijuana, however, cuts across racial, ethnic, and demographic lines: arrestees. The U.S. Department of Justice (DOJ) found that those arrested for crimes were more likely to test positive for marijuana than any other drug.

MENTAL EFFECTS

Users often experience a mellow sense of well-being and relaxation that makes them feel expansive, creative, and more sensitive to all types of stimuli. Perception of time slows, and ability to gauge distance, depth, and speed accurately is distorted. Users can also spiral downward into anxiety, paranoia, panic attacks, and hallucinations. This effect is more pronounced when larger doses of THC are ingested, such as when hashish or other more concentrated forms of marijuana are used. Higher doses are also possible when marijuana is eaten rather than smoked; this occurs when more of the drug is ingested before it can be metabolized.

Within seconds of entering the bloodstream, the cannabinoids in marijuana bind to special areas in the brain called THC receptors. These regions, located throughout the brain, are heavily concentrated in the hippocampus, which controls learning and memory. This means that one of marijuana's most pronounced effects is its interference with the ability to form short-term memories. A 1996 study published in the *Journal of the American Medical Association* showed that heavy marijuana users, defined as those who ingest the drug on a daily or nearly daily basis, scored significantly lower on learning and other tests.

Other studies of heavy marijuana users show that the drug inhibits the ability to focus attention, learn new information, and solve problems as long as two days after taking it. This most likely occurs because THC changes the way the brain processes new information; THC stifles neural activity in the hippocampus by suppressing acetylcholine release. Long-term use can cause changes in users' brains that are similar to those caused by other controlled substances.

PHYSIOLOGICAL EFFECTS

While it is true that most people smoke marijuana precisely for its mental effects, they may not be aware of the physical changes that accompany the high. One of the drug's first effects is to raise the heart rate and blood pressure. The eyes become bloodshot and the pupils

dilate; the mouth and throat also become dry. The appetite is stimulated, and users often become unusually hungry.

At the same time, the cannabinoids in marijuana, already at work in the hippocampus, bind to THC receptors in other parts of the brain, including the basal ganglia, which govern the body's involuntary muscles, and the cerebellum, which controls coordination and sense of balance. These changes relax muscles all over the body, slowing reaction time and impairing the body's ability to move efficiently. When the high wears off, fatigue and torpor replace the creativity and hyperawareness users may experience initially.

As the drug is broken down by the body, fat-soluble THC metabolites accumulate in the liver and other organs. Thirty percent of any one dose of THC is still in the body a week later, and smaller but still-detectable amounts are present two weeks after that. The more often marijuana is used, the greater the buildup in the body; heavy users' urine may show traces of the drug more than a month after the last dose.

Harmful side effects

Despite a popular myth that cannabis use is harmless, marijuana smoke, like cigarette smoke, contains cyanide, as well as higher levels of benzopyrene and carbon monoxide. Marijuana joints the same size as a cigarette produce five times the carbon monoxide in subjects' blood. Smoking marijuana produces three to four times the tar of tobacco, and more of it stays in the lungs. Because marijuana smoke is inhaled more deeply and held far longer in the lungs than tobacco smoke, damage to the delicate pleural tissues is as or more pronounced. Some researchers equate one joint to five cigarettes; others contend that three to four joints are as damaging as a pack of cigarettes.

Women who smoke marijuana during pregnancy may have low birth-weight babies who are at risk for developmental difficulties and are more susceptible to disease. Like other drugs, THC also crosses the placental barrier and affects the embryo as it grows; some studies indicate that this may increase a baby's risk of developing leukemia. THC also passes into breast milk, where research has shown that it can affect a child's motor development. Toddlers whose parents smoke marijuana have been found to be angrier and to have more behavioral problems than children whose parents do not use marijuana.

Long-term health effects

Marijuana smokers are at higher risk than nonusers for chronic lung diseases such as bronchitis, asthma, lung infections, and emphysema. Research also indicates that heavy marijuana use can lead to the DNA damage and cellular changes that produce lung cancer; these changes appeared to occur in marijuana smokers at an

HISTORY NOTES

Until 1937, when the United States ruled that marijuana was an illegal substance, cannabis was an accepted, if often ineffective, medication. The following are excerpts from medical journals and pharmacopoeias that show some of the far-fetched afflictions for which cannabis was prescribed—and also how much medical progress has been made in the last century.

The July 4, 1891, *British Medical Journal* reports that Indian hemp was frequently prescribed for "a form of insanity peculiar to women, caused by mental worry of moral shock, in which it clearly acts as a psychic anodyne [tranquilizer]—[it] seems to remove the mental distress and unrest."

In 1898, *King's American Dispensatory* called *Cannabis indica* "one of the most important of our remedies," particularly for "marked nervous depression. ... [I]t has been efficient in delirium tremens, wakefulness in fevers, neuralgia, gout, rheumatism, infantile

convulsions, low mental conditions, insanity ... [a]cute mania and dementia, epilepsy, hysterical catalepsy, cerebral softening (with potassium bromide), anemia of the cerebral cortex, paralysis agitans and senile tremors... [I]n mental disturbances the guides to its use are mental oppression, a dull, drowsy, or stupid countenance (a dreamy condition), with dizziness and violent throbbings in the head, and a morbid fear of becoming insane."

In 1902, *A Compend of Materia Medica, Therapeutics, and Prescription Writing* prescribed "*Cannabis indica*—Indian hemp" for a variety of colorful conditions: Uterine affections, as chronic metritis [inflammation of the womb], subinvolution, menorrhagia, dysmenorrhoea [painful menstruation], etc.,—its powers as an anodyne and stimulant of the uterine muscular fibre render it a very efficient agent."

The Eclectic Materia Medica, Pharmacology and Therapeutics, 1922, recommended cannabis for: "Marked nervous depression ... wakefulness in fevers; insomnia, with brief periods of sleep, disturbed by unpleasant dreams; ... mental illusions; hallucinations; cerebral anemia from spasm of cerebral vessels; palpitation of the heart, with sharp, stitching pain; and menstrual headache, with great nervous depression."

---

earlier age than in tobacco smokers. Cancers of the head and neck are also more common in marijuana smokers. People who smoke both marijuana and tobacco are at an even higher risk of serious disease.

In men, heavy long-term marijuana use can lead to lowered sperm counts and even impotence. It can also cause a hormone imbalance that leads to gynecomastia, the development of feminine breasts. Women who abuse marijuana may experience menstrual cycles that are off balance.

REACTIONS WITH OTHER DRUGS OR SUBSTANCES

As noted above, marijuana is frequently combined with other drugs. Sometimes joints or blunts are laced with PCP, crack, heroin, or other controlled substances; at other times, marijuana is used along with drugs like alcohol or cocaine. Any such drug combination amplifies the effect of both substances, sometimes dangerously. The National Highway Transportation Safety Administration showed that a combined dose of alcohol and marijuana was far more debilitating than either one alone. Using marijuana with LSD or other hallucinogens increases the psychotropic effect, sometimes adversely. Combining marijuana with cocaine increases the already

measurable stress that each drug independently exerts on the cardiovascular system.

TREATMENT AND REHABILITATION

Experts are divided on whether or not heavy, long-term marijuana use causes the same kind of addiction that opium or crack does. Evidence shows that daily marijuana use over time can lead to withdrawal symptoms such as aggression, irritability, and stomach pains; these are hallmarks of addiction. Also, long-term use can cause some of the same destructive brain changes as those found in other types of drug addictions. Studies in 1997 showed that THC causes a dopamine release in the brains of rats equivalent to that seen with heroin. It is estimated that more than 120,000 people seek treatment for marijuana dependence each year, indicating that at the very least marijuana use can become an overwhelming compulsion that is extremely difficult to break.

After alcohol and nicotine, marijuana is the drug on which more people become dependent than any other. Dependence is greatly increased by the additional abuse of another drug (particularly alcohol) and the presence of psychiatric disorders. In addition, young people seem especially vulnerable to marijuana dependence. In a 1998 study, out of a group of 229 adolescents already dependent on one substance (usually alcohol), 83% of those who tried marijuana six or more times became dependent on it as well. Most of these young people also showed symptoms of antisocial/behavioral problems.

The first step in treating marijuana dependence is detoxification. This is a series of medical and nutritional therapies designed to help the patient through withdrawal symptoms by eliminating drugs from the body. Once detox has been accomplished, psychological counseling and education programs help users face life without depending on drugs. However, success is not guaranteed. Users relapse frequently, sometimes merely shifting their dependence from marijuana to alcohol or another drug.

PERSONAL AND SOCIAL CONSEQUENCES

Heavy users with an average daily intake of three to five joints are likely to have problems in all aspects of their lives, both at home and at work, ranging from strained familial relationships to job loss. They are also more likely to exhibit neurotic or even psychotic behavior. Research shows that marijuana users, especially heavy users, end up in the hospital more frequently than nonusers, often from injuries.

One of the worst aspects of heavy marijuana use may be what researchers call the "amotivational syndrome" that robs people of their ambition, drive, and energy. A 2000 study showed that teenagers who use marijuana drop out of high school at more than twice the rate of nonusers; those who also abuse other drugs have even higher dropout rates.

Teenagers who face legal consequences because of their marijuana use may jeopardize their chance of getting financial aid for college. Applications for students requesting federal college loans ask whether or not they have ever been convicted on state or federal drug charges. An affirmative answer—or none at all—will hold up the application and may well cause the application to be rejected.

Marijuana users will find that many employers weed out substance abusers, because they are much more likely to be absent or have on-the-job accidents. In 1996, about a third of all potential hires were screened for drug use. At major corporations, the figure was 81%, and in the top-ranked Fortune 200 companies, it rose to 98%. Standards at many federal agencies are even more stringent: The Federal Bureau of Investigation (FBI) will disqualify applicants who had used marijuana within the past three years or a total of 15 times altogether.

LEGAL CONSEQUENCES

Marijuana is a Schedule I drug under the Controlled Substances Act whose possession and distribution is for-bidden by law in the United States. Alaska, California, Colorado, Maine, Massachusetts, Minnesota, Mississippi, Nebraska, New York, North Carolina, Ohio, and Oregon have all but eliminated criminal penalties for possessing small amounts—up to roughly 1 oz (28 g). Many other states allow first-time offenders to be sentenced to treatment instead of jail, or to receive a conditional discharge requiring them to fulfill provisions established by the court (such as pleading guilty) to have the charges dismissed. Other states are less tolerant, but most have listed possession of small amounts as misdemeanors punishable by fines.

Since 1996, eight states—Alaska, California, Colorado, Hawaii, Maine, Nevada, Oregon, and Washington—have allowed patients with certain diseases and a doctor's prescription to grow and use their own marijuana.

It is important to note, however, that neither medical provisions nor lightened penalties for first-time drug offenders legalizes the use or possession of marijuana, and that comparatively light sentences usually apply only to first-time offenders. Those who get caught more than once or who are carrying more than very small amounts of the drug face significant legal consequences. In addition, the federal government maintains that state laws do not supersede its regulations, and that prosecution for marijuana possession is still possible under the U.S. Code. The FBI, in fact, makes more drug arrests for marijuana than for any other kind of drug.

Only one country, the Netherlands, allows small amounts of marijuana to be sold openly in state-controlled "coffee shops." Cannabis, like other drugs, remains illegal, but the Dutch make a clear distinction between "hard" drugs like heroin and "soft" drugs like marijuana, agreeing to tolerate sales of less than 5 g (0.18 oz) to adults over 18 in a controlled environment. Liberal Dutch drug policies, however, have made the country a mecca for drug addicts from other countries, many of them indigent. This influx has increased property crime rates in the Netherlands; consequently, the government has reduced the number of coffee shops allowed to operate. Neighboring countries also charge that marijuana's easy availability in the Netherlands gives both hard and soft drug traffickers a base in Europe, and contributes to the importation of illegal substances into other countries. Despite these concerns, in January 2001, Belgium decriminalized personal possession and sale of unspecified small amounts of marijuana, but will continue to focus prosecution efforts on the production and sale of large quantities. Unlike the Dutch, the Belgians will not sanction commercial sales of marijuana in any quantities.

Only two countries, the Netherlands and Canada, allow patients with certain medical conditions and a physician's approval to grow and use their own marijuana. In the United States, however, the drug remains illegal; possession and sale over certain amounts are prosecutable offenses.

Legal history

Until the twentieth century, cannabis was a legal product in every state. It was an accepted medication for a variety of conditions, and a frequent ingredient in patent medicines. In 1906, the Pure Food and Drug Act forbade "the manufacture, sale, or transportation of adulterated or misbranded or poisonous or deleterious foods, drugs, medicines, and liquors," including those containing cannabis. The law put most patent medicine manufacturers out of business.

By 1931, 29 states had outlawed marijuana. In 1937, Congress passed the Marijuana Tax Act, which effectively criminalized marijuana possession anywhere in the United States, even for ostensibly medicinal use. In the 1950s, federal penalties increased further; a first-time marijuana conviction could mean as much as 10 years in jail and up to $20,000 in fines. Beginning in the 1960s, however, the perception of marijuana as a relatively harmless drug gained popular acceptance, particularly among the young. In 1970, Congress lifted many mandatory sentences for drug crimes. The Comprehensive Drug Abuse Prevention and Control Act allowed possession of small amounts of marijuana, although the drug remained a controlled substance, and large-scale trafficking was heavily penalized. After years of relative tolerance, however, mandatory sentences for drug-related crimes were reinstated in 1986 by the Anti-Drug Abuse Act, which tied criminal penalties to the quantities of drugs involved. Later amendments to the act further tightened the judicial noose with a "three-strikes" clause and capital punishment for high-level criminals.

Federal guidelines, regulations, and penalties

Marijuana trafficking is vigorously prosecuted in the United States, with the FBI reporting that nearly half of its 1.5 million drug arrests in 2000 were for marijuana. More than 87% of these arrests were for possession. First-offense convictions for possession of less than 110 lbs (50 kg) of marijuana are punishable by up to five years in prison and fines of up to $250,000 for an individual. Those convicted of possessing more than 2,205 lbs (1,000 kg) of marijuana face up to life in prison and fines of up to $4,000,000.

RESOURCES

Books

Hermes, William J., and Anne Galperin. *Marijuana: Its Effects on Mind and Body.* New York: Chelsea House, 1992.

Joy, Janet E., Stanley J. Watson Jr., and John A. Benson Jr., eds. *Marijuana and Medicine: Assessing the Science Base.* Washington, DC: National Academy Press, 1999.

Rudgley, Richard. "Cannabis." In *The Encyclopedia of Psychoactive Substances.* Boston: Little, Brown and Company, 1998.

United States Commission on Marihuana and Drug Abuse. *Drug Use in America. Marihuana and Drug Abuse Commission: Problem in Perspective, Second Report.* Washington, DC: U.S. Government Printing Office, 1973.

Periodicals

Klug, Elizabeth A. "Young Adult Arrestees Use Marijuana More Than Any Other Drug, Reports the Department of Justice." *Corrections Compendium* 26, no. 8 (August 2001): 22.

National Highway Transportation Safety Administration. "Marijuana & Alcohol Combined Increase Impairment." *Technology Transfer Series* no. 201. (June 1999).

National Institutes of Health. National Institute on Drug Abuse. "Epidemiologic Trends in Drug Abuse Advance Report." (December 2000).

Other

Bonsor, Kevin. "How Marijuana Works: Potency." *Marshall Brain's How Stuff Works.* <http://www.howstuffworks.com/marijuana5.htm>. (April 7, 2002).

Bonsor, Kevin. "How Marijuana Works: Marijuana and the Brain." *Marshall Brain's How Stuff Works.* http://www.howstuffworks.com/marijuana3.htm. (April 7, 2002).

U.S. Department of Health and Human Services. Substance Abuse and Mental Health Services Administration. Center for Substance Abuse Prevention. "Know the Facts: Marijuana and the Brain." <http://www.forreal.org/know/mjbrain.asp>. (April 7, 2002).

U.S. Department of Justice. Drug Enforcement Agency. <http://www.usdoj.gov/dea/>.

Organizations

Marijuana Anonymous World Services, P.O. Box 2912, Van Nuys, CA, USA, 91404, (800)766-6779, office@marijuana-anonymous.org, <http://www.marijuana-anonymous.org/index.shtml>.

National Institute on Drug Abuse (NIDA), National Institutes of Health, 6001 Executive Boulevard, Room 5213, Bethesda, MD, USA, 20892-9561, (301) 443-1124, (888) 644-6432, information@lists.nida.nih.gov, <http://www.drugabuse.gov/Infofax/marijuana.html>.

Amy Loerch Strumolo

MELATONIN

OFFICIAL NAMES: Melatonin, 5-methoxy-N-acetyltrypt-amine
STREET NAMES: Melliquid, mellow tonin, somniset
DRUG CLASSIFICATIONS: Not scheduled

OVERVIEW

Melatonin is a natural hormone produced by many animals. In humans, it is produced in several parts of the body, including the pineal gland, which is a small organ located at the base of the brain. Historically, the pineal gland was thought to have some sort of metaphysical function. It was often called the "third eye" and was said to be "the seat of the soul" by Descartes. It is now known to be involved in the neuroendocrine system, which involves the interaction of the nervous and endocrine systems (organs that produce hormones). This interaction results in the regulation of essential body functions. The neuroendocrine system is responsible for the fight or flight response, as well as many other processes that keep people alive and healthy. Melatonin is thought to be important in maintaining certain essential physiological functions such as sleep.

There are many nerve fibers in the pineal gland. Some of these fibers release noradrenalin, a chemical messenger produced by the nervous system. Noradrenalin stimulates certain cells in the pineal gland, called pinealocytes, to produce and release melatonin.

Some parts of the brain, like the cerebral cortex, are much more highly evolved in humans than in other animals. The pineal gland, however, is a very basic organ that first evolved in primitive species. It is found in lampreys, fish, amphibians, and reptiles, as well as in mammals. The hormone melatonin has also been found in insects and plants.

Researchers first hypothesized the existence of melatonin almost 100 years ago. Back in 1917, scientists noticed that an unknown substance from the pineal gland affected melanophores, a kind of pigment cell found in frog skin. More than 40 years later, a dermatologist, Dr. Aaron Lerner, finally isolated this substance from the pineal gland and named it melatonin.

Over the next few decades, researchers learned that melatonin had many other effects in addition to influencing pigmentation in amphibians. Most current research has studied its influence on promoting sleep. Other studies have linked this hormone to other processes such as reducing jet lag, boosting the immune system, and fighting cancer.

Scientists have learned that the retina of the eye and parts of the gastrointestinal tract also produce melatonin. It is not known if the function of melatonin produced by these parts of the body differs from that made by the pineal gland.

The production of melatonin varies over the course of a day. Darkness stimulates the pineal gland to produce melatonin, while the presence of light inhibits the release of this hormone. Melatonin levels are so low during the daytime that they are almost immeasurable. The amount of melatonin starts to increase around 9 P.M. or 10 P.M.

Levels continue to increase during the early part of the night and peak at about 2 A.M. to 4 A.M. and thereafter start to decrease through the rest of the morning.

While everyone follows this general pattern of diurnal melatonin secretion, each individual has his or her own unique pattern. Melatonin peaks and valleys can occur at different times in different people and may explain why some individuals are "morning" people, while others are "night owls."

This circadian rhythm of melatonin production is not limited to humans and animals. Certain types of alga show a daily variability in their synthesis of melatonin. Darkness stimulates melatonin production by these one-celled creatures.

The presence of light influences the pattern of melatonin release. In some people, melatonin is secreted for a shorter period during the shorter nights of summer. But in winter, melatonin release lasts longer during the prolonged darkness in these susceptible individuals. Some scientists hypothesize that this variation in melatonin production may be responsible for seasonal affective disorder (SAD). SAD is a form of depression that occurs during the winter. It is frequently successfully treated by exposure to artificial light.

Artificial light, like natural light, influences the synthesis of melatonin by the pineal gland. Exposure to light during the night will inhibit melatonin production. Research results show that women who work night shifts have an increased risk of getting breast cancer; scientists are investigating whether this alteration in melatonin production may be linked to the development of cancer.

Melatonin secretion also varies over the course of a lifetime. Newborn babies produce very little of this hormone, but after the first few months of life the pineal gland increases its production of melatonin. Very small babies produce a relatively constant amount of melatonin throughout the day and night. They do not have any diurnal variation in the production or release of melatonin. It is not until infants are between nine and 12 weeks old that the pineal gland starts to shift towards a nocturnal production of this hormone. Highest levels occur in children who are about four to seven years old. Older children and adults produce smaller amounts, as production gradually decreases during puberty. The typical adult male produces about 30 micrograms of melatonin during a typical day.

Because melatonin production goes down during puberty, some researchers suspect that the decreasing levels of this hormone are somehow linked to sexual maturation. Melatonin also influences the levels of certain reproductive hormones such as prolactin and luteinizing hormone. Due to these effects, many experts recommend that children, teenagers, pregnant women, and breastfeeding mothers do not take melatonin.

KEY TERMS

ENDOCRINE SYSTEM: Organs that produce hormones.

ENDOGENOUS: Produced within the body.

EXOGENOUS: Produced by a source outside of the body.

HORMONE: Substance secreted by a gland into the bloodstream and carried to another part of the body, where it causes a physiological change.

JET LAG: Condition caused by traveling over several time zones in a short period of time.

NORADRENALINE: Chemical produced by the nervous system.

SEASONAL AFFECTIVE DISORDER (SAD): Type of depression that occurs during the fall and winter months.

Researchers used to think that older adults produced very little melatonin. Since the elderly tend to have more problems with insomnia and other sleeping disorders, scientists hypothesized that these lower levels of melatonin were the cause of sleeping problems in this population.

However, a study published in the January 2001 issue of the *American Journal of Physiology* showed that melatonin levels are just as high in older adults as they are in younger individuals. Dr. J. B. Fourtillan measured melatonin levels in 34 healthy adults who were over 65 years of age and in 101 healthy adults who were under 30 years of age. The levels of this hormone did not differ between the two age groups.

Researchers still need to learn a lot about what melatonin does and how it can be safely used. Scientists have not completed enough studies to know exactly what functions melatonin carries out in the human body. Similarly, physicians do not understand at what time during the day or night melatonin should be taken or what dose is most effective. Nor do physicians know enough about the long-term effects of taking melatonin since it has only became popular in the 1990s.

In spite of this lack of information, several popular books came out during the 1990s advocating the supposed usefulness of melatonin as a treatment for everything from insomnia to jet lag to aging. Consumer interest in melatonin increased dramatically. It is estimated that millions of Americans take melatonin supplements as a "natural" remedy.

Although melatonin is a hormone and a drug, it is not regulated by the Food and Drug Administration (FDA). That is because melatonin is naturally found in certain foods. However, the amount of melatonin in over-the-counter medications is a great deal higher than what is found in food, or is produced by the human body. A typical supplement may contain anywhere from 500 micrograms to 5 mg. A supplement containing 500 micrograms will produce blood concentrations similar to those normally found in the human body. Doses of 1–5 mg will result in blood levels anywhere from 10 to 100 times higher than normal.

Melatonin can have different effects depending on when it is taken. If taken slightly before bedtime, it may be useful in adjusting a person's sleep schedule following a long flight. Taken during the day, however, it will not change the sleeping pattern; it will just make the person sleepy. Similarly, some cancer research suggests that melatonin may be helpful as a cancer therapy if given at the correct time of day. If it is given at the wrong time, it may end up having no effect or may actually increase the risk of developing cancer.

Because melatonin is not regulated by the FDA, commercially available preparations are not subject to the same scrutiny as medications under the direction of this federal agency. Melatonin supplements do not have to be extensively tested in animals and humans before being sold in over-the-counter preparations. Manufacturers do not have to maintain high production standards, nor do they have to be as concerned with instituting FDA-required safety checks. Manufacturers are, however, limited by law in one way: They cannot claim that their product will cure or treat anything. They can only make general statements. While they can say that melatonin helps people sleep, they cannot say that it treats insomnia.

CHEMICAL/ORGANIC COMPOSITION

Melatonin is made from tryptophan, a type of amino acid. Pinealocytes absorb tryptophan from the blood. Through a series of chemical reactions, the pinealocytes then convert the amino acid into melatonin.

Melatonin is a relatively simple type of chemical compound. It is rapidly absorbed and will reach its peak concentration within about an hour after it is swallowed. Melatonin is fat soluable, which means it is able to enter all the cells of the body, including brain cells. So melatonin can easily leave the bloodstream and enter brain cells. But melatonin does not remain in the bloodstream for very long as it is quickly broken down by the liver. It takes about 30 to 40 minutes for the liver to remove one half of the melatonin that is present in the blood.

Many over-the-counter drugs contain melatonin. Some of these products are made from animal sources. However, most commercially available melatonin is synthetic.

Since melatonin is naturally found in some foods, it is legal to sell it as a dietary supplement in the United States under the U.S. Dietary Supplement Health and Education Act (DSHEA) of 1994. Dietary supplements like multivitamins are not as carefully regulated by the federal government as are prescription medications. However, the amount of melatonin in food is very low. A person would have to eat 120 bananas or 30 large bowls of rice to get the same amount of melatonin that is contained in a 3-mg capsule. The amount of melatonin contained in dietary supplements is much, much higher than that produced by the pineal gland or obtained through food.

Since commercially available drugs containing melatonin are not regulated, they are not held to the same high standards of purity and efficacy as are other medications. Melatonin, being a hormone, is just as potentially dangerous as other naturally occurring substances such as estrogens and androgens.

Drugs that are not regulated by the FDA are more likely to be contaminated with impurities. They may also be inaccurately labeled and not contain the amount of melatonin listed on the label. According to the National Sleep Foundation, a batch of melatonin was examined and found to contain much more of the hormone than was listed on the label. According to another study, one third of the medications that supposedly contained melatonin did not contain any melatonin, while an additional 40% contained much less than was stated on the label.

While many commercially available preparations contain only melatonin, many others contain a combination of this hormone with other active ingredients. Some of these other ingredients may be vitamins such as pyridoxine, while others are natural remedies such as kava root and valerian. It is even available combined with acetaminophen, a common over-the-counter pain reliever. Frequently, the long-term effects and safety of these other ingredients are not known. Even less is known about any possible interactions between these substances and melatonin, because melatonin has been available and used commercially for only a short period of time. Many experts have suggested that it would be preferable to test melatonin in controlled studies to determine if it is effective and safe before it was released on the market and used by millions of people.

INGESTION METHODS

Melatonin is usually taken orally. It is available in pills, capsules, and liquids. It also can be absorbed from under the tongue. It is sometimes injected when it is used as a treatment for cancer.

Most commercial preparations contain much higher doses than the 30 micrograms typically produced by an average adult male. While researchers do not know what dose may be optimal for therapeutic use, several studies indicate that between 0.5 to 5.0 mg is sufficient for treating jet lag. Some studies suggest that time-release forms, however, may be ineffective.

The natural production of melatonin by the pineal gland varies during the course of a day. Melatonin levels are very low during the daylight hours and increase when it is dark. The time a person swallows an over-the-counter formulation of melatonin is just as important as the amount ingested. Taking melatonin during the middle of the day may not help people to sleep better at night and, instead, may make them tired and decrease their alertness.

Slow-release capsules are also available. However, the results of a review of 10 studies that investigated the effectiveness of melatonin for treating jet lag indicated that time-release capsules are not effective for treating jet lag.

THERAPEUTIC USE

Melatonin may be an effective treatment for several conditions. Studies suggest that it may be helpful in treating sleep disorders, jet lag, and even cancer. However, research on this topic is still very limited and experts have warned consumers that very little is known about the effectiveness or long-term safety of taking melatonin supplements.

Sleep disorders

While the popular press has publicized the usefulness of melatonin as a natural sleeping aid, the results of studies are often contradictory. Some studies suggest that melatonin is helpful in treating insomnia, while others have shown that it is absolutely useless.

Researchers still have not investigated melatonin's effectiveness in treating insomnia in most age groups. As of 2000, only three studies had investigated the usefulness of melatonin in treating insomnia in people younger than 65 years of age.

While the effectiveness of melatonin in treating sleep disorders in most people remains unclear, research shows that it can be helpful for certain individuals. For example, many blind people have sleep disorders, and melatonin has been shown to help promote sleep in this population. Studies have also shown that it is helpful in treating sleep disorders in disabled children.

Jet lag/shift work

People and animals follow a natural circadian rhythm. Humans and many animals tend to be diurnal. They get up in the morning, are active during the day, and sleep at night. Disruptions in this natural cycle can be difficult. With the advent of air travel, people could

???? # FACT OR FICTION

Over-the-counter medications must be safe, right? And since melatonin can be bought at any pharmacy or natural food store in the United States, it must be safe, too? It would seem logical that anything that is legal and easy to buy would be healthy, but that is not necessarily true.

Because melatonin is found in certain foods, the Food and Drug Administration considers it to be a dietary supplement instead of a drug. However, since melatonin has not been studied very extensively, it is still unknown if it causes long-term side effects.

While legally speaking melatonin is a dietary supplement, biologically speaking it is a hormone. Other types of hormones include estrogen and testosterone. Hormones are known to have major effects on the human body. Only one other hormone can be sold over the counter in the United States. All other hormones require a doctor's prescription. Many other countries do not allow over-the-counter sales of melatonin because it is a hormone and has not been studied well enough to know if it is safe to take.

travel halfway around the world, passing through several time zones. Their circadian rhythm can be very disrupted by the time differences. Besides having difficulties sleeping at the appropriate time, people with jet lag may also experience constipation and other digestive difficulties.

Shift workers have a similar difficulty in trying to stay awake at a time when they would normally be asleep. Nurses working an evening shift may start to get sleepy while they are still at work, while those on the morning shift may have a great deal of difficulty getting up well before dawn.

Melatonin may be helpful for both shift workers and air travelers trying to adjust to the local time. According to a paper published in 2002, nine out of 10 studies that investigated the effectiveness of melatonin in treating jet lag demonstrated that melatonin did help ease this condition. Individuals who had traveled across five or more time zones and then took melatonin close to the time they wanted to fall asleep were more easily able to make the adjustment to local time. Doses between 0.5 mg and 5 mg were effective, although the larger dose helped a bit more in promoting sleep. Larger doses did not provide any additional benefits. Reviewers suggested that melatonin was more effective when crossing more time zones and for eastbound travelers. The study review also indicated that time-release preparations or

Scientists have discovered the chemical structure of melatonin so that it can be manufactured commercially.

Photo by Bryn Colton/CORBIS. Reproduced by permission.

taking any form of melatonin earlier in the day was ineffective. Not only was it not helpful, but taking melatonin during the middle of day just made people sleepy and delayed their adjustment to the local time.

While more research is needed, a few studies indicate that melatonin can help people adjust to working the night shift. It can also help people readjust back to sleeping during the night and staying awake during the day when they discontinue working the night shift. In one study of 32 night workers published in 2002, those taking 0.5–3.0 mg of melatonin during the afternoon helped them sleep during the day before leaving for work.

In addition to questions concerning the effectiveness of melatonin for any condition, researchers still do not know enough about the long-term consequences of taking melatonin on a regular basis. Many experts caution that until melatonin has been proven to be safe and not cause serious side effects, using it as a therapeutic agent is too risky.

Cancer

In the 1970s, researchers noticed that the amount of melatonin found in the blood of certain cancer patients was lower than in healthy individuals. Soon afterwards, other studies showed that the nighttime increase in melatonin, which occurs naturally in most humans, was markedly decreased in some cancer patients.

Experts are not sure how melatonin influences the development of cancer. A recent study published in 1999 in *Cancer Research* suggests that melatonin may help to starve cancer cells. Tumors use a type of fat called linoleic acid as a food source. Melatonin prevented the tumor cells in rats from being able to metabolize linoleic, but only when it was given to rats during the late afternoon. When it was given to the rats earlier in the day it did not have any effect.

Most of the research investigating the effectiveness of melatonin in treating cancer have been conducted in rats and mice, or in test tube samples of human cells. However, there have been several clinical trials that show that melatonin may be helpful as a therapy for different types of cancer. Again, timing of the dose is very important. Several other studies have shown that melatonin is not effective, or even promotes tumor growth, depending on when during the day it is given.

Other conditions

While melatonin is not currently being used to treat these conditions, research is currently underway investigating its role in preventing Alzheimer's disease. A study published in *Biochemistry* in 2001 showed that melatonin can inhibit the development of amyloid beta, a toxic substance that has been linked to the development of Alzheimer's. Other studies suggest that melatonin may be helpful in reducing the side effects caused by medications that are used to treat schizophrenia.

USAGE TRENDS

No one knows the exact number of people who use melatonin. According to a CNN report, 20 million Americans have taken melatonin to treat jet lag or sleeping disorders. It is legal and therefore easy to buy this hormone in over-the-counter medication in the United States. Several other countries have had a different attitude towards such widespread use of a potentially dangerous hormone; several European countries and Canada restrict the sale of melatonin.

Scope and severity

While it is estimated that millions of Americans have taken melatonin, the scope and severity of its use in the United States is unknown. Regardless, the use of this hormone is probably much higher in the United States where it is legal than in Canada or Europe where it is not.

Age, ethnic, and gender trends

Since the elderly tend to have more problems with insomnia than do younger individuals, it is thought that this age group is more likely to use melatonin. Howev-

HISTORY NOTES

Scientists first realized that melatonin existed and was produced by the pineal gland back in 1917. Yet researchers were not able to isolate this hormone until the 1950s.

Why did it take them so long to discover melatonin? The pineal gland is very small. It weighs only about 100 mg in humans. And it does not produce very much melatonin. The typical adult male makes only 30 micrograms during an entire day. Also, the techniques available for isolating chemical compounds that were available during the early and mid-twentieth century were not very precise. It took a considerable amount of work for researchers to actually find melatonin.

Dr. Alan Lerner and his coworkers required pineal glands from 250,000 cows in order to come up with enough melatonin to be able to isolate and identify this hormone. Fortunately, modern researchers have much more precise technology. Nowadays, researchers can easily measure and compare the amount of melatonin produced by a single individual instead of combining samples from one quarter of a million people. Current technology can easily measure the amount of melatonin present in the blood, urine, or saliva.

er, there is no proof that this is true. Research studies investigating which groups use melatonin are needed before it is possible to definitively state who is more likely to use this hormone.

MENTAL EFFECTS

Very little is known about what types of long-term psychological effects can be caused by the use of melatonin.

It is clear, however, that melatonin has short-term mental effects. It definitely can cause drowsiness when taken during the day. Melatonin taken at night, however, will not cause daytime sleepiness. People who take melatonin are also less likely to respond correctly to visual and auditory signals. They are more likely to make mistakes and their reaction time decreases when they take this hormone. Several studies have shown that taking melatonin inhibits a person's ability to concentrate and can cause confusion. People should therefore not take it when they need to stay alert, such as when they will be driving a car. The effects begin within approximately an hour of taking melatonin and last for about two hours.

Some experts are concerned that melatonin may worsen depression and recommend that people who have a mental illness not take this hormone.

Paradoxically, when taken with other drugs, melatonin may have very different mental effects. It tends to stimulate some of the biochemical effects caused by methamphetamines; it can end up aggravating insomnia, instead of causing sleepiness, when taken with these drugs. Taking melatonin with benzodiazepines has been reported to cause anxiety.

PHYSIOLOGICAL EFFECTS

Melatonin causes general effects that are felt throughout the body and specific effects on certain organs. Melatonin reduces body temperature so people may feel slightly cooler after they take a supplement containing this substance in addition to becoming sleepy. Melatonin produced by the pineal gland also has this effect. However, there is a slight variation in the ability of melatonin to reduce body temperature. Melatonin is not as effective at lowering body temperature during the luteal phase of the menstrual cycle, which is just before ovulation. Physicians and many women have long known that a woman's body temperature increases slightly just before ovulation.

Melatonin also causes vasoconstriction, which is the narrowing of the blood vessels.

Sleep/circadian sleep rhythms

The most well-known effect of melatonin is that it regulates the sleep cycle. Production of melatonin by the pineal gland increases with darkness. Increased melatonin levels, in turn, promote sleep.

Melatonin is not essential for sleep to occur. Many people take naps during the daylight hours and can stay awake into the early hours of the morning, although melatonin levels are very low at this time. Still, most people find it very difficult to stay awake all night and sleep during the day. Melatonin does, somehow, make sleeping easier. The abnormal production of melatonin has been linked to sleeping difficulties. Many blind people who do not have any perception of light also have an abnormal pattern of melatonin production. They may not have higher levels during the night or their highest levels of melatonin can actually occur during the day. These individuals tend to have sleeping disorders. They may have difficulty sleeping at night and take naps during the daytime. Exactly how melatonin is related to the maintenance of a normal sleep cycle is not yet understood.

Reproductive effects

Melatonin influences the level of other hormones in the body. It has been shown to have a particularly strong effect on prolactin and luteinizing hormone, both of which are major reproductive hormones. Some authorities caution that it may reduce the sexual drive in men.

The natural production of melatonin by the pineal gland peaks at the age of only four or five years of age. Since a decrease in its production occurs during sexual maturation, researchers warn that taking it during adolescence may have a detrimental effect on puberty.

Immune effects

Melatonin has been shown to boost certain parts of the immune system. It boosts the activity of natural killer cells, a type of immune cell. It also prevents apoptosis, a type of destruction of T-lymphocytes, which are other important immune cells found in the bloodstream. Melatonin also limits the effect of corticosteroids on the immune system. Corticosteroids are very potent drugs that are sometimes used to inhibit the immune system. Some people have autoimmune diseases in which their immune system attacks the cells of their own bodies. Physicians frequently prescribe corticosteroids for these individuals.

Harmful side effects

As there has been very little research studying the safety of taking melatonin, most experts caution people against using it, or to limit their intake of it. However, it is known that melatonin may be particularly dangerous for certain people. People should not take melatonin if they:

- Have not finished, or even started, puberty. The decreased production of melatonin by the pineal gland that occurs during late childhood and early adolescence may be linked to sexual maturation.

- Are breast-feeding. Melatonin affects the level of prolactin, a hormone that controls the production of breast milk.

- Are pregnant. Melatonin influences the levels of various sex hormones.

- Have a history of stroke or other cerebrovascular disease. Melatonin causes vasoconstriction, which, under certain circumstances, can be a risk factor for cerebrovascular disease.

- Have a history of liver disease. Melatonin is metabolized in the liver. Melatonin may remain within the body for a longer time and in larger amounts if the liver is not able to break down this hormone so that it can be excreted.

- Have an autoimmune disease. Melatonin has been shown to boost some processes of the immune system. People who have an autoimmune disease already have an overactive immune system, which is attacking their own body. Taking a substance such as melatonin, which further stimulates immune activity, may make their symptoms much more severe.

- Are depressed or have a neurological disorder. Although melatonin may be linked to the development of seasonal affective disorder (SAD), its exact role in emotional and neurological illnesses remains unclear.

- Take certain medications such as benzodiazepines, methamphetamines, dehydroepiandrosterone, magnesium, zinc, corticosteroids, and succinylcholine.

Melatonin can cause some adverse effects. People should contact their health care provider if they have difficulty sleeping or feel too sleepy, develop a headache, chills, or itching, feel confused, or have a fast pulse after taking melatonin. Individuals who will be undergoing surgery should tell the anesthesiologist that they have been taking melatonin.

Long-term health effects

No one knows what kind of effects may result after taking melatonin for a long period time. It has not been studied and its widespread use only started during the 1990s. Many experts strongly warn people not to take melatonin, or to at least limit their use to a short period of time such as for a few days after taking a long trip as a short-term treatment for jet lag. But some experts caution that withdrawal may occur after taking very high doses of melatonin.

REACTIONS WITH OTHER DRUGS OR SUBSTANCES

Much remains unknown about melatonin's interaction with many other drugs and substances. However, it is known that melatonin does interact with, and may limit the effectiveness of, benzodiazepines, methamphetamines, dehydroepiandrosterone, magnesium, zinc, corticosteroids, and succinylcholine. People who are being treated with these drugs should not take melatonin.

Interactions between drugs or substances and endogenous melatonin

Selective serotonin reuptake inhibitors (SSRIs) are a type of antidepressant that stimulates the pineal gland's ability to produce melatonin. Antipsychotic drugs also have this effect. Other medicines have the opposite effect. Certain types of medicines used to treat cardiovascular disease called beta blockers reduce the production of melatonin by the pineal gland. Nonsteroidal antiinflammatories, which are used to treat pain and/or fever,

benzodiazepines, and caffeine also inhibit the production of melatonin.

Interactions between drugs or substances and exogenous melatonin

Individuals who take melatonin supplements and benzodiazepines may feel very anxious and unsettled. Instead of causing sleepiness, melatonin can aggravate insomnia when taken with metamphetamines.

TREATMENT AND REHABILITATION

Currently, there are no treatment or rehabilitation options for people who use melatonin. It is not known if long-term users may have difficulty with sleeping or other side effects when they quit taking melatonin supplements. Discontinuing the use of melatonin after short-term use, such as for adjusting to jet lag, has not proved to be difficult or to cause any side effects.

Some experts, however, are concerned that abruptly discontinuing the use of melatonin after taking very high doses may result in withdrawal. Whether or not this is truly the case, or how it is best to deal with any symptoms of withdrawal, is not known.

PERSONAL AND SOCIAL CONSEQUENCES

The long-term personal and social consequences of routinely using melatonin are not known. It is known, however, that millions of people take over-the-counter melatonin preparations containing very large doses of melatonin relative to the amount produced by the human body or contained in foods. Even less is known about its interaction with other drugs or "natural remedies." Many experts are concerned that such large-scale use of a hormone may not be safe. Serious health implications of using melatonin may not be discovered until many people have placed themselves at risk.

Melatonin can cause unpleasant side effects, even when taken for a short period of time. The use of melatonin has been linked to sleepiness, confused thinking, rapid heartbeat, chills, headache, inability to sleep, and itching. People who experience these symptoms when using melatonin should contact their health care provider.

LEGAL CONSEQUENCES

It is legal to possess and use melatonin in the United States. However, it is illegal to use melatonin without a prescription in other countries.

RESOURCES

Books

Shneerson, John. *Handbook of Sleep Medicine.* Oxford, UK: Blackwell Science Inc., 2000.

Smokensky, Michael, and Lynne Lamberg. *The Body Clock Guide to Better Health.* New York: Henry Holt & Company, Inc., 2000.

Periodicals

Pray, W. Steven. "Consult Your Pharmacist—The Sleep-Wake Cycle and Jet Lag." *U.S. Pharmacist* 24 no. 3 (1999): 10.

"What About Melatonin?" *Nursing* (May 2001).

Other

"Melatonin." May 2002 (July 8, 2002). <http://www.familydoc-tor.org/handouts/258.html>.

"Proper Dose of Melatonin Curbs Insomnia in Older Adults." 2002 (July 8, 2002). <http://www.endo-society.org/pubrelations/pressReleases/melatonin.cfm>.

Organizations

National Sleep Foundation, 1522 K Street, NW, Suite 500, Washington, DC, USA, 20005, (202) 347-3471, (202) 347-3472, nsf@sleepfoundation.org, <http://www.sleepfoundation.org>.

Sue Wallace

MEPERIDINE

OVERVIEW

Meperidine is a synthetic, opioid analgesic. An analgesic is any drug or substance that, when ingested or injected, diminishes or relieves pain. Another word for analgesic is "painkiller." Many different drugs act as analgesics. One method of classifying analgesics is to distinguish between those that require a doctor's prescription and those that do not. Medications obtainable without a doctor's prescription are known as over-the-counter (OTC) drugs. OTC analgesics are the most familiar, and include such medications as acetaminophen (Tylenol), aspirin, and ibuprofen (Advil; Midol).

The most effective and widely used prescription analgesics belong to a class of drugs known as opioids. Opioid drugs can be classified as natural, semi-synthetic, or synthetic. Natural opioids are also frequently referred to as opiates. Both terms, opiate and opioid, are derivations of opium. The drug groups were so-named because they produce effects similar to opium, which itself is a plant-based, chemically complex drug. Opium has been used throughout recorded history for both medicinal and recreational purposes.

Opium is made by drying the liquid that comes from the unripe seed capsule of the opium poppy, a flowering plant common to certain parts of the world. References to opium and its medicinal value have been found in writings dating from several thousand years ago. Up until the twentieth century, opium was prized for its ability to alleviate pain, treat diarrhea, and elevate mood. In addition to its well-established use as a treatment for pain and diarrhea, opium was touted and used as a cure for a wide range of other medical problems. In truth,

however, opium had little or no real medical effects on the majority of those conditions. Instead, its ability to produce euphoria, a profound sense of well-being and calmness (elevated mood), made opium appear to be a highly effective medicine. After all, regardless of the illness or condition, a person who used opium nearly always *felt* better, whether or not they were truly getting better. In higher quantities, opium is also effective at inducing sleep. In fact, the scientific name for the opium poppy is *Papaver somniferum*, Greek for "poppy that causes sleep." In even greater quantities, opium can induce coma and death.

Although opium has genuine medical benefits, it also poses significant risks. Perhaps most important is the inherent difficulty in predicting how weak or strong opium's effects will be on any particular occasion. The concentrations of the primary active chemicals, morphine and codeine, can vary significantly from one batch of opium to the next. One reason a drug abuser might prefer prescription over illegal drugs is that they always know how much of a prescription drug they are taking. Someone who buys heroin, for instance, could be getting a nearly pure drug, or could be purchasing mostly cornstarch. Used as a medicine, opium was a risky proposition. Once the technologies in chemistry were devel-

KEY TERMS

ANALGESIC: A type of drug that alleviates pain without loss of consciousness.

MORPHINE: The primary alkaloid chemical in opium, used as a drug to treat severe acute and chronic pain.

NEUROTRANSMITTER: A substance released by one nerve cell that activates or inhibits a neighboring nerve cell.

OPIATE: Drug derived directly from opium and used in its natural state, without chemical modification. Opiates include morphine, codeine, thebaine, noscapine, and papaverine.

OPIOID: A drug, hormone, or other chemical substance having sedative or narcotic effects similar to those containing opium or its derivatives; a natural brain opiate.

SYNTHETIC OPIOID: An opioid drug produced from chemicals that are created in a laboratory.

---

oped, researchers in medicine and pharmacology were eager to purify the active chemicals in opium.

Along with knowledge of its desirable effects, people in ancient times were no doubt also aware of opium's undesirable effects. Serious forms of psychological and physical addiction can develop after even short-term opium use. The highly addictive nature of opium, and by extension the opioids, tends to overshadow all other issues related to the drugs. Aside from developing predictable drugs, the primary reason for previous and ongoing research in this area is to develop a powerful analgesic with as few of the harmful side effects of opium and the current opioids as possible. Addictive potential is the side effect researchers would most like to eliminate.

It was not until 1806 that a German chemist was able to isolate morphine from opium. This was a major breakthrough in pharmacology; a pure, highly effective analgesic was finally available. Unlike opium, morphine's potency is always the same, which allows for accurate scientific study of its effects. Data from studies of morphine have provided specific information about the safest and most effective dosages to use.

Morphine was the first limited success of attempts to improve on opium. The medical community was initially hopeful that, in addition to its analgesic power, morphine would be the break-through drug for treating opium addiction. In fact, morphine was successful in that regard; opium addicts that were given morphine were often cured of their addiction. However, it became

painfully clear that those same patients developed an equally powerful addiction to morphine. The isolation of codeine in 1832 was also a limited success; it produces fewer side effects and is less addictive, but is much less potent than morphine.

Meperidine was first synthesized in the late 1930s, and was one of the first synthetic opioids. The fact that both morphine and codeine are still widely used, though, indicates that meperidine, along with all of the opioids produced since that time, have been only modest successes. Research continues with the hope of discovering the "perfect" opioid analgesic.

To understand the benefits and drawbacks of opioid drugs, one needs to understand their primary effects on the body; specifically, how they function as pain relievers. In the broadest sense, there are two types of pain—physical and emotional. Physical pain, while unpleasant, is necessary for survival. It serves as notification of the presence of injury or disease, which in turn prompts a person to take appropriate, possibly even life-saving action. Half of all individuals who seek medical attention report pain as their primary complaint.

Opioids produce their effects by interacting with cell-surface proteins known as opioid receptors. An opioid, whether endogenous (naturally produced by the body) or in drug form, fits into a receptor somewhat like a key in a lock. This activates the receptor and initiates complex changes in the nerve cell. Activated opioid receptors produce chemical changes that reduce the ability of a nerve cell to transmit pain signals. They also decrease the "perception" of pain by neurons in the brain. If opioids are used when one is not in pain, those same chemical changes in the brain's nerve cells can produce feelings of euphoria.

In a basic sense, both the good (analgesia) and bad (addiction) effects of opioids are caused by the same process: the interaction of drugs with nerve cells, especially those in the brain. As a neuron transmits or processes pain signals, it is functioning in an abnormal, hyperactive state. Opioids work to reduce that activity and bring the neuron back toward a more normal state. Applying the opioid effect to a neuron that is already in a normal state, however, tends to force the response of neurons in the opposite direction of pain, toward pleasure (euphoria). If neurons remain in this artificially produced state for any length of time, they become tolerant of the effect. Once the opioid is removed, the affected neurons move back toward the pain end of the spectrum, something known as the "rebound effect."

People that use meperidine for acute pain, such as after an injury, typically do not have long enough exposure to develop tolerance and addiction. People with chronic pain, however, may develop some tolerance and physical addiction in the sense that, if they stop the drug, their pain returns. Only rarely, though, do people using opioids long-term for legitimate medical reasons develop psychological addiction. A person who begins abusing an opioid drug to get high, and continues using the drug, will develop both physical and psychological tolerance and addiction. Eventually, they will need the drug not to get high, but to keep from having the pain of withdrawal. These scenarios also apply to endogenous opioids, although to a much lesser extent. For instance, athletes that produce high levels of endorphins—one of the endogenous opioids—after exercise often report that they feel depressed if they stop exercising.

CHEMICAL/ORGANIC COMPOSITION

Meperidine hydrochloride (the full name) is a synthetic opioid. It is synthesized by the reaction of chemicals not found in opium. Specifically, meperidine hydrochloride is produced by the reaction of dichlorodiethyl methylamine with benzyl cyanide, to produce ethyl 1-methyl-4-phenyl-isonipecotate hydrochloride (meperidine's chemical name). Some references to meperidine classify it as a totally synthetic opioid. Semi-synthetic opioids are produced by using one of the opiates as a starting material. Two examples of semi-synthetic opioids are hydrocodone and heroin. Hydrocodone is produced by the chemical modification of codeine, while heroin is made by chemically altering morphine.

Although morphine and meperidine are quite similar in their clinical effects, they are not that similar in chemical composition. The important chemical determinant of an opioid analgesic, however, is not its structural resemblance to morphine, but its ability to bind with and activate an opioid receptor.

INGESTION METHODS

Meperidine can be taken orally or injected. Oral forms include tablets and syrup. Dosages of tablets range from 25 mg to 100 mg meperidine per tablet. The syrup form contains 50 mg meperidine per 5 ml. The typical dosage is from 50 mg to 150 mg every three to four hours.

Injections of meperidine can be given intramuscularly (in the muscle), subcutaneously (under the skin), and intravenously (directly into the bloodstream). The body responds more readily to meperidine when it is injected, so dosages are usually about half that of the oral form, again every three to four hours. As with other opioids, intravenous administration of meperidine is often given at a low, continual dose.

Patients recovering from surgery can request that meperidine be administered through a system known as patient controlled anesthesia (PCA). This system allows a patient to administer his or her own medication in small doses. The machine has an electronic control mechanism that allows only a specific amount of meperidine to be administered by the patient each hour. PCA alleviates the need for a nurse to give the patient an intramuscular injection every three to four hours, and keeps meperidine in the body at a more constant level.

THERAPEUTIC USE

Meperidine is used for the treatment of moderate-to-severe pain, most commonly following surgery. It is sometimes given as an adjunct to anesthesia just before and during surgery. Meperidine also remains one of the more frequently used opioid analgesics in obstetric departments for severe pain during labor and delivery. Meperidine may be preferred over morphine after surgery because it produces less nausea and constipation in most people.

Meperidine is generally not recommended for use in infants and small children. Likewise, the elderly may have underlying medical conditions that present special risks with meperidine use.

Meperidine is occasionally used in outpatients for the treatment of acute pain, especially if other opioids prove ineffective. Its use for chronic pain is less accepted. Meperidine is eliminated from the body more quickly than other opioids, which means it must be taken more frequently, and its analgesic effects fluctuate more rapidly.

USAGE TRENDS

A study published in the *Journal of the American Medical Association* in 2000, obtained Drug Enforcement Administration (DEA) data on trends in legitimate medical use of several opioid medications, including meperidine, for the period of 1990 to 1996. In that seven-year span, meperidine use in the United States decreased by 35% (5,200 kg to 3,400 kg).

In the early 1980s, approximately 15,400 kg of meperidine were consumed worldwide each year. By 1999, that figure decreased to 12,200 kg, a 20% drop. Most of the decrease in the use of meperidine may be due to the ongoing development of other safer, longer lasting Schedule II opioids.

Scope and severity

One method of analyzing the issue of drug abuse is to compare and contrast the abuse of illegal drugs (marijuana, cocaine, etc.) with that of legal drugs (OTC and prescription medications). The majority of national and international attention and resources go toward illicit drug abuse. However, prescription drug abuse is a large and growing proportion of the complete drug abuse picture.

HISTORY NOTES

In the early 1980s, a form of designer meperidine, known as MPPP, was being illegally manufactured. MPPP was also referred to as "synthetic heroin." In some cases, the chemical technique was not precise, and a toxic chemical byproduct, MPTP, was produced. MPTP is a known industrial toxin that can destroy nerve cells in certain portions of the brain

People ingesting this contaminated form of MPPP began exhibiting symptoms of Parkinson disease—rigidity of the muscles with uncontrollable twitching. The neurological damage caused by MPTP appears to be permanent. These cases were instrumental in initiating passage of the so-called Analogue Drug Laws. Prior to that time, someone who manufactured a novel (new) drug in an illegal lab could possibly evade some DEA regulations if the drug's specific chemical formula was not listed under the Schedule of Controlled Substances.

The Analogue Drug Laws were passed to cover drugs created with the intent of producing effects similar to a drug already listed under the Schedule of Controlled Substances. The "designer meperidine" cases provided a good example of why designer drugs can be the most dangerous.

Each year, the National Household Survey on Drug Abuse (NHSDA)—the United States Department of Health and Human Services—collects statistical data on five drug groups: marijuana and hashish; psychotherapeutic drugs; cocaine and crack; hallucinogens; and inhalants. Psychotherapeutic drugs include stimulants, sedatives, tranquilizers, and pain relievers. Meperidine and other opioids constitute the majority of the pain relievers in that group.

In 2000, the NHSDA found 1.7% of all people 12 years and older reported nonmedical use of any psychotherapeutic medication during the previous month. More than nine million Americans over age 12 reported use at any time during the year. Those in the 18 to 25-year-old age group have the highest rates of drug abuse. In 2000, 3.6% of individuals in that age group reported nonmedical use of prescription drugs in the month prior to the date on which they were surveyed, but less than half that many, 1.6%, reported the same type of drug abuse in 1994. An estimated 1.6 million Americans used prescription pain relievers nonmedically for the first time in 1998. During the 1980s, there were generally fewer than 500,000 first-time users per year.

The study in the *Journal of the American Medical Association* mentioned previously also analyzed data from The Drug Abuse Warning Network (DAWN). As mentioned, the study showed a 35% decrease in the medical use of meperidine. However, use of the other four opioid drugs studied (morphine, fentanyl, oxycodone, and hydromorphone) increased, such that the group as a whole showed a cumulative increase of nearly 250%. Data collected from DAWN for the same time-period showed a 7% increase in emergency room mentions of abuse of these drugs. By comparison, the reports of abuse of illicit drugs increased 110%. Admittedly, the data collected by DAWN evaluates only one facet of the drug abuse problem—drug abuse that contributes to emergency room visits. However, from these data at least, it does not appear that a significant increase in medical use of opioid drugs resulted in a proportionate increase in abuse. Further studies looking at a broader picture of opioid analgesic abuse are needed.

Age, ethnic, and gender trends

Between 1990 and 1998, abuse of some illegal drugs among teens and young adults leveled off or decreased slightly. However, increases in new users of prescription pain relievers were reported in young teens, age 12–17, as well as in young adults age 18–25. In 2000, the NHSDA found that the youngest teens, age 12–14, reported psychotherapeutic medications as the most frequent drugs of abuse, making up 53% of the total of all drug abuse reports. Teens and young adults in the 18–25 age group reported prescription drug abuse at a rate of 36%, while 28% of those over age 26 reported that type of abuse. Most teenagers begin prescription drug abuse by taking another person's medication, usually someone from their family. Teens are also more likely than adults to be acquainted with someone illegally who sells prescription drugs like meperidine.

On the other end of the age spectrum, prescription drug abuse among older adults is also a growing concern. Persons 65 and older comprise 13% of the United States population, but consume about 33% of all prescription drugs. A study of 1,500 elderly patients found that 3% were abusing prescription drugs. Unlike people in younger age groups, however, the elderly are more likely to misuse prescription drugs than abuse them. If abuse does occur, it may begin with misuse due to inappropriate prescribing or the patient not following instructions correctly.

The NHSDA study showed that boys in the youngest age group (12–17) are more likely to experiment with illegal drugs, but girls of that age have a 20% higher rate of prescription drug abuse. In addition, for all teens of that age who abuse prescription drugs, girls are twice as likely to become addicted as boys are. Women are also more likely to abuse and become addicted to prescription drugs in the young- and middle-adult age groups. Part of this may be that women are prescribed potential drugs of abuse more often than men are. Finally, a survey of elderly persons admitted to a treatment program found that 70% were female. Of the various drugs of abuse in that group, 70% were opioids. At all age groups, whites are more likely than other racial or ethnic groups to abuse prescription drugs.

Health professionals (doctors, nurses, dentists, veterinarians, etc.) and their staff may be at risk for meperidine abuse because of their ready access to the drug. Several highly publicized cases involving health care workers who removed injectable meperidine from vials for their own use—and replaced it with some other (harmless) liquid to give to the patient—would seem to lend credence to that argument. On the other hand, one would expect health care workers to be at lesser risk due to their training and knowledge of the effects of drug abuse. In fact, the publicized cases of meperidine theft present an unbalanced picture, since health care workers do not appear to have rates of meperidine or other opioid abuse much different from the rest of the population.

MENTAL EFFECTS

As with all opioids, meperidine is capable of producing euphoria. A few people may get a mild stimulant effect and a feeling of elation. However, instead of euphoria after a meperidine dose, some people report a feeling of dysphoria—a general feeling of discomfort and restlessness—or even disorientation and confusion. Still other people may just feel drowsy, with no noticeable positive or negative effect on their mood.

It remains a misconception that opioids offer no true analgesic effect, but instead produce a type of euphoria that simply results in one not caring about one's pain. With the available detailed knowledge of the interaction between opioids and opioid receptors in the central nervous system, that myth has been dispelled. Up to a limit (usually an amount great enough to produce serious side effects), the more meperidine ingested in a single dose, the greater the analgesia and the more pronounced the mental effects.

PHYSIOLOGICAL EFFECTS

Other than analgesia, the most common physiological effects produced by medicinal quantities of meperidine are nausea, vomiting, dry mouth, dizziness, constipation, and itchy skin. These relatively harmless side effects typically disappear in most people after taking the drug for several days, or by reducing the dosage. For most people, higher doses of meperidine are more likely to produce side effects. For those who experience side effects at lower doses, any higher dose is likely to make them more pronounced.

Harmful side effects

The complication of greatest concern is respiratory depression. Opioids affect the area of the brain that controls breathing. A large enough single dose of any opioid, including meperidine, can stop breathing completely, resulting in death. Combining meperidine with another central nervous system depressant, such as alcohol or sedatives, is especially risky. While drowsiness itself is not a harmful side effect, it can be dangerous if someone drives or engages in some other activity that requires them to be alert.

Meperidine presents a higher risk for seizures than other opioids. Seizures induced by meperidine also tend to be resistant to treatment with opioid antagonists. Therefore, people with a history of seizures, and those at increased risk for first occurrence of a seizure (such as someone with head trauma) should avoid meperidine if possible. Other potential neurological side effects include tremors, delirium, and hallucinations. These side effects are uncommon, but serious. Some people may have an allergic reaction to meperidine, and severe cases can involve respiratory arrest; cold, clammy skin; generalized weakness; and unconsciousness or coma.

Patients with kidney or liver disease should exercise caution when using meperidine for any length of time. A by-product of meperidine, normeperidine, is broken down in the liver and excreted by the kidneys. Someone with impaired function of either organ may develop high levels of normeperidine, which can be toxic to the nervous system. Some people, especially the elderly, may have no history of kidney or liver disease, but can have reduced kidney and liver function following surgery. Therefore, if elderly patients must be given meperidine, the safest course may be to limit its length of use as much as possible.

Long-term health effects

Direct, negative effects on long-term health from chronic meperidine use are mostly limited to the slight possibility of central nervous system damage. There are surprisingly few other adverse health effects as far as organ or tissue damage is concerned. This is in contrast to most other abused drugs, with alcohol and tobacco being the obvious examples, and does not match the social stigma associated with opioid drugs.

Compared with other drugs, the relative lack of direct organ or tissue damage from meperidine use is counterbalanced by its high risk for abuse and addiction. High addiction potential in a drug typically means a high risk for long-term use. Long-term use can include either years of continual use or a repeated cycle of use and abstinence. The latter can be especially difficult with meperidine, given the potentially serious withdrawal symptoms associated with abruptly stopping the drug. People with meperidine or other prescription drug addiction are less likely to seek professional help than those who abuse illegal drugs. This may be due to a misperception that addiction to prescription drugs cannot or should not be as serious as illegal drug addiction. Unfortunately, self-treating an addiction usually involves abrupt cessation of the drug, with negative health effects.

The longer and more heavy the abuse, and the more suddenly the drug is ceased, the more serious and painful the withdrawal symptoms will be. Symptoms of withdrawal associated with physical addiction can include restlessness, muscle and bone pain, insomnia, diarrhea, runny nose, chills with goose bumps, and involuntary leg movements. The involuntary leg movements associated with opioid withdrawal are what originally led to the phrase "kicking the habit." In addition, the goose bumps that often occur during withdrawal originated the use of the phrase "quitting cold turkey," since the person's skin resembles that of cold turkey skin. Signs of withdrawal associated with psychological addiction include strong dysphoria (feeling badly) and a nearly uncontrollable craving for the drug.

REACTIONS WITH OTHER DRUGS OR SUBSTANCES

Some who abuse opioids are under the mistaken impression that using alcohol with the drug will enhance its effects. Like meperidine, alcohol is a cental nervous system depressant, so when both are used together, the risk for respiratory depression and death increases. Also, because alcohol impairs judgment, a drunk person is more likely to believe he can handle more of the drug than he truly can, just as many intoxicated people dangerously believe they are much better drivers than they are. Most people who end up in hospital emergency rooms after an opioid overdose were also using alcohol.

Other classes of drugs that should be avoided when using meperidine include benzodiazepines (drugs in the same class as Valium), most antihistamines, and sedatives/hypnotics (sleeping pills). Several types of antidepressants, including tricyclics, selective serotonin reuptake inhibitors (SSRIs, drugs in the same class as Prozac), and especially monoamine oxidase inhibitors (MAOIs), should be used with great caution or not at all in combination with meperidine. In general, any other central nervous system depressant should either be avoided or used under the guidance of a physician when taking meperidine.

TREATMENT AND REHABILITATION

As a Schedule II opioid narcotic, meperidine is highly addictive. Treatment for opioid overdose usually involves administration of an opioid antagonist such as Narcan (naloxone), which reverses or blocks the effects of the drug. However, in some cases, those who overdose on meperidine do not respond well to opioid antagonists.

Most people who overcome meperidine addiction do so by themselves, but some may need professional assistance. In either case, it is invaluable for someone to have the help and support of friends and family. For chronic addiction (drug use and addiction lasting more than one year), meperidine may be replaced by methadone, another opioid medication. The patient receives methadone either through a physician or through a qualified drug treatment program. In a structured setting, the patient and health care professionals have a much better chance of controlling drug use with methadone, and eventually may achieve complete abstinence. Methadone need only be taken once a day, it reduces or eliminates withdrawal symptoms and the craving for meperidine, and it has fewer side effects.

PERSONAL AND SOCIAL CONSEQUENCES

Meperidine and the other opioids do offer great personal and social medical benefits. However, these benefits must be weighed against the potential costs of abuse and addiction. The social consequences of having a broad range of effective analgesics to treat chronic pain are significant. Conditions associated with chronic pain are the largest contributors to lost work time and decreased productivity. In addition, in the long-term, many individuals with ineffectively treated pain only add to the medical costs society must bear. Therefore, doctors must weigh the risks and benefits of prescribing meperidine for each individual. Careful use of meperidine and other opioids would seem to present much greater social benefits than costs.

Personal costs—financial, physical, and emotional—can be huge for those individuals who abuse meperidine and become addicted. An established addiction can be expensive to maintain. Many people describe a serious opioid addiction as "all consuming"; everything in their lives eventually revolves around obtaining more of the drug. With the drug as their focus, they lose friends, alienate family members, and may be unable to hold a job. Those who are caught committing crimes to maintain their addiction may pay a very high price—loss of their freedom. Finally, whether through overdose or violence, those who abuse prescription or illicit drugs may pay the ultimate price—loss of their life.

Evidence indicates that proper meperidine prescription for legitimate medical concerns does not greatly increase the risk of addiction and abuse. Those in the medical community agree that more education is needed by both doctors and patients to help prevent the potential for abuse and addiction, so that patients truly in need are not denied access to meperidine based on misperceptions and fear. The benefits for individuals and society are great when pain is treated safely and effectively.

LEGAL CONSEQUENCES

As a Schedule II drug, meperidine is strictly controlled in the United States, as well as in other parts of the world. Its manufacture and distribution in the United States are controlled by the Food and Drug Administration (FDA) and the Drug Enforcement Administration (DEA). International control is overseen by the International Narcotic Control Board (INCB).

Hospital and community pharmacies exercise special caution when dispensing meperidine and other controlled substances. In an emergency, a doctor may choose to telephone the patient's pharmacy with the prescription. However, for medications such as meperidine, telephoned prescriptions can usually only provide a small amount of the drug, and the doctor must provide their DEA number and some relevant medical information. Refills for Schedule II medications are not allowed; a patient must obtain a new prescription from their doctor.

It is illegal to write a prescription or an order for meperidine without a valid medical license. Professionals who may legally write prescriptions or orders for meperidine include medical doctors, doctors of osteopathy, podiatrists, dentists, and veterinarians. Physicians or dentists who knowingly write multiple prescriptions for patients without a valid medical reason may end up in prison. Writing and filling bogus prescriptions for profit is an even more serious offense.

Likewise, it is illegal to obtain, or try to obtain, prescriptions for meperidine or other opioids under false pretenses (fabricated symptoms and scenarios). Nineteen states have a law (a felony in some) prohibiting patients from obtaining the same controlled substance from multiple prescribers within a limited time-period ("doctor-shopping"). The perpetrators of crimes involving prescription drugs are most often white, middle-class women. Their crimes usually involve doctor-shopping and/or prescription forgery.

Many people argue that increased production of opioid drugs leads to increased rates of abuse and addiction. The national attention on burglarized pharmacies, and drugs pilfered from hospitals, seem to bolster this argument. However, studies have consistently shown that patients with chronic pain who use opioids appropriately rarely become addicted. In 2001 and 2002, a number of groups that advocate for effective pain management joined with government agencies, including the DEA, to begin a long-term effort to increase the availability of effective pain-management drugs for patients, while decreasing the chances for illegal use and abuse.

See also Codeine; Designer drugs; Fentanyl; Heroin; Morphine; Opium; Oxycodone

RESOURCES

Books

American Cancer Society. *American Cancer Society's Guide to Pain Control.* Atlanta: American Cancer Society Health Content Products, 2001.

Booth, Martin. *Opium: A History.* New York: St. Martin's Press, 1996.

Courtwright, David T. *Forces of Habit: Drugs and the Making of the Modern World.* Cambridge, MA: Harvard University Press, 2001.

Kuhn, Cynthia, et al. *Buzzed: The Straight Facts about the Most Used and Abused Drugs from Alcohol to Ecstasy.* New York: W.W. Norton and Company, Inc., 1998.

Rudgley, Richard. *Essential Substances: A Cultural History of Intoxicants in Society.* New York: Kodansha America, Inc., 1994.

Periodicals

Brookoff, Daniel. "Chronic Pain: 1. A New Disease?" *Hospital Practice* 35 (July 15, 2000): 45-59.

Brookoff, Daniel. "Chronic Pain: 2. The Case for Opioids." *Hospital Practice* 35 (September 15, 2000): 69-84.

Carver, Alan. "Medical Use and Abuse of Opioid Analgesics." *Neurology Alert* 18 (June 2000): 77.

Demott, Kathryn. "Opioids Still Worthwhile Despite Street-Drug Taint." *Clinical Psychiatry News* 29 (June 2001): 46.

Foster, Roxie L. "Pain Management." *Journal of the Society of Pediatric Nurses* 1 (July-Sept. 1996): 93.

Joranson, David E., et al. "Trends in Medical Use and Abuse of Opioid Analgesics." *The Journal of the American Medical Association* 282 (April 5, 2000): 1710-4.

Kettelman, Karen. "What's So Bad About Meperidine?" *Nursing* 30 (October 2000):20.

Mitka, Mike. "Abuse of Prescription Drugs: Is a Patient Ailing or Addicted?" *The Journal of the American Medical Association* 283 (March 1, 2000): 1126.

Potter, Michael, et al. "Opioids for Chronic Nonmalignant Pain." *Journal of Family Practice* 50 (February 2001): 145.

Reidenberg, Marcus M. "Clinical Pharmacology." *The Journal of the American Medical Association* 273 (June 7, 1995): 1664-5.

Rich, Ben A. "Physicians' Legal Duty to Relieve Suffering." *The Western Journal of Medicine* 175 (September 2001): 151.

Rowbotham, David J. "Endogenous Opioids, Placebo Response, and Pain." *The Lancet* 357 (June 16, 2001): 1901.

Self, Timothy H. "Minimizing Risk of Meperidine Neurotoxicity." *The Journal of Critical Illness* 16 (May 2001): 237.

Sullivan, Louis W. "The Painkiller Prescription: Protect Use, Prevent Abuse." *The Journal of Musculoskeletal Medicine* 18 (September 2001): 438.

Other

Painfully Obvious: The Effects of Abusing Prescription Drugs. 2002. <http://www.painfullyobvious.com>.

United Nations Office for Drug Control and Crime Prevention. (April 4, 2002). <http://www.undcp.org>.

The Vaults of Erowid: Documenting the Complex Relationship between Humans and Psychoactives. 2002. <http://www.erowid.org>.

Organizations

Drug Enforcement Administration (DEA), Information Services Section (CPI), 2401 Jefferson Davis Highway, Alexandria, VA, USA, 22301, <http://www.usdoj.gov/dea>.

National Institute on Drug Abuse (NIDA), National Institutes of Health, 6001 Executive Boulevard, Room 5213, Bethesda, MD, USA, 20892-9561, (301) 443-1124, (888) 644-6432, Information@lists.nida.nih.gov, <http://www.drugabusegov/NIDAHome.html>.

Office of Disease Prevention and Health Promotion, U.S. Department of Health and Human Services, 200 Independence Avenue SW., Room 738G, Washington, DC, USA, 20201, (202) 401-6295, <http://odphp.osophs.dhhs.gov>.

Office of FirstGov c/o GSA, 750 17th Street, N.W., Suite 200, Washington, DC, USA, 20006-4634, <http://www.whitehousedrugpolicy.gov>.

Substance Abuse and Mental Health Services Administration (SAMHSA), U.S. Dept. of Health and Human Services, 5600 Fishers Lane, Rockville,, MD, USA, 20857, (301) 443-6239, info@samhsa.gov, <http://www.samhsa.gov>.

Substance Abuse and Mental Health Services Administration (SAMHSA)/Center for Substance Abuse Treatment (CSAT), 5600 Fishers Lane, Rockville, MD, USA, 20857, (301) 443-5700, info@samsha.gov, <http://www.samhsa.gov>.

U.S. Food and Drug Administration (FDA), 5600 Fishers Lane, Rockville, MD, USA, 20857-0001, (888) 463-6332, <http://www.fda.gov>.

Scott J. Polzin , MS

MESCALINE

OFFICIAL NAMES: Mescaline, peyote
STREET NAMES: Buttons, cactus buttons, cactus head, Aztec, chief, big chief, mesc, mescal, mezc, moon, topi, blue cap
DRUG CLASSIFICATIONS: Schedule I, hallucinogen

OVERVIEW

Mescaline is said to be the oldest known hallucinogenic drug. Before drugs were manufactured in a lab, cooked up in someone's basement, or stolen from a medicine cabinet for illegal and abusive use, they were found in plants. Often, drugs in plants were discovered quite accidentally.

Foraging for food, early humans used trial and error to determine which plants were edible and, unfortunately, which were deadly. However, some plants that were neither food nor poison had another entirely surprising effect. These plants produced an intoxicated, or drunken, state or caused the user to have visions or hear voices of people who were not there. To the ancients, these waking dreams (which are called hallucinations—distortions of perception that seem real but are not) were voices from their gods or the spirit world.

Such plants—now classified as psychoactive or hallucinogenic—became a centerpiece for sacred rituals, a means to explain the unexplainable, and a mainstay of medicine bags. How a primitive people or another culture might use a drug as part of their worship rituals differs greatly from its use as a recreational or street drug where very often it is misused and abused.

Mescaline (peyote) is one such drug that has a cultural history dating from before the time of Christ as well as a separate history as a street drug. It is derived mainly from two members of the Cactaceae family—the peyote cactus (*Lophophora williamsii*) and the San Pedro cactus (*Trichocereus pachanoi*).

L. williamsii is a gray-green or blue-green cactus that grows close to the ground. It looks like a small, segmented cushion. These cushion-like segments are called podarea and they surround a wooly center of tufted hairs called trichomes. *L. williamsii* does not have prickly spines as do other cacti. (Other genus and species names of the peyote cactus are *Lophophora echinata var. diffusa* and *Echinocactus williamsii*.) The peyote cactus is indigenous (grows naturally) to the area ranging from southern Texas to San Luis Potosi in southern Mexico. Another Lophophora species is *Lophophora difusa*. This yellow-green cactus is fleshier, without a well-defined podarea. It grows only in the dry, central area of Queretaro, Mexico.

The San Pedro cactus (*T. pachanoi*), unlike *L. williamsii*, has spines and grows in a large column, sometimes as high as 20 ft (12.5 m). This common cactus is often used as an ornamental plant, and originated in the mountains of Ecuador and Peru. Other cacti of the *Trichocereus* family also contain hallucinogenic compounds. The San Pedro cactus is also known as *Echinopsis pachanoi*, *Cereus pachanoi*, *Cereus rosei*, *Echinopsis peruvianus*, and *T. peruvianus*.

The derivation of the name peyote is uncertain. The Nahuatl word, *pi-youtl*, means "silk cocoon" or "cater-

KEY TERMS

ENTHEOGEN: A term from the Greek meaning "God-facilitating substance." Some scholars prefer this term to hallucinogenic when applied to plants such as the peyote cactus that are used in religious practices.

HALLUCINOGENS: A group of drugs that induces sensory distortions and hallucinations.

PEYOTE: A hallucinogenic cactus, usually *L. williamsii,* from which mescaline is derived.

PODAREA: Raised segmented cushion-part of the peyote cactus.

TOLERANCE: A condition in which higher and higher doses of a drug are needed to produce the original effect or high experienced.

TRICHOMES: Tuft of hairs in the center of the peyote cactus.

TRIP: A common term for a drug experience.

---

pillar cocoon," due to the plant's appearance. The Mexican word, *piule,* has a more simple meaning of "hallucinogenic plant." Both are generally regarded as its possible predecessor.

Today though, in academic literature as well as street usage, the drug is referred to as both mescaline and peyote (regardless from which cactus it is actually extracted), often with both words having the same meaning. However, in the strictest sense, mescaline refers to the hallucinogenic crystalline extract of the peyote cactus, a form that is rare.

Mescaline is one of 40–60 alkaloids (nitrogen-containing organic compounds) that are found in these psychoactive cacti. Depending on its maturity, the typical peyote cactus has about a 4% mescaline content. Extremely slow growing, a cactus can take more than four years to grow a dime-sized top section, or "button," the part that is cut off and eaten. A plant is not considered mature until it is 13 years old. A cactus that is the size of a baseball is estimated to be about 30 years old. Native American and Mexican Indians call these plants "Father or Grandfather Peyote," and they are highly revered.

History

Found only in the New World, there is evidence that peyote was used before the time of Christ. Some of the most solid archeological data suggest that the drug was taken by the Aztecs 3,000 years ago. An archeological find in Coahuila, Mexico, of a skeleton with a beaded necklace of dried peyote buttons is 1,000 years old. In Peru, a carving of a San Pedro cactus on a stone tablet dates back to 1300 B.C. Dried peyote buttons found in the Shumla Cave in Texas are said to date from 5000 B.C.

The writings of Fray Bernardino Sahagun (1499–1590), a Spanish missionary who lived with and studied the Indians of Mexico, provide the earliest documented information about peyote. He writes that the Chichimecas and the Toltec Indians probably used peyote as early as 300 B.C.

Dr. Francisco Hernandez, King Philip II's personal physician, gave the first physical description of the cactus plant. Along with describing its psychoactive qualities, he also wrote about its medicinal uses, namely, to relive painful joints.

However, the newcomers to the New World were not accepting of the well-established peyote cults. Campaigns were quickly undertaken to make peyote illegal. When Mexico outlawed it in 1720, the ritual was so entrenched that the practice continued in secret. In fact, the Huichol Indians of Mexico still perform a peyote ritual that is probably very similar to that performed in the days before colonization.

In the same century, there is evidence of peyote use in the United States. The first recorded use of peyote is 1760. By the time of the Civil War (1860–1864), Native Americans were familiar with the plant and had a strong ritual surrounding its use. It was about 1880 that the peyote ceremony of the Kiowa and Comanche tribes first drew public attention. These Plains Indian tribes incorporated aspects of the Mexican peyote worship into their vision-quest ritual. The Plains Indians probably learned about the hallucinogenic cactus when they crossed the border into northern Mexico during various raids on the Mescalero Indians.

Experts suggest that the peyote ritual was embraced by the Native Americans because they saw it as a way to preserve their cultural heritage at a time when their way of life was slipping away. It was during this time that they were relocated to reservations. Tribal missionaries spread word of the beneficial effects of the peyote ritual on moral. In 1918, the Native American Church (NAC) was founded and further formalized the ritual use of peyote. It also set off a long history of debate over First Amendment rights and the use of a controlled substance by members of a church. In 1920, the church had more than 13,000 members comprising 30 tribes. By 2002, there were more than 250,000 members.

But there is another side to peyote—its use as a recreational or street drug. In 1897, Arthur Heffter, a German chemist, was the first to identify mescaline as the chemical responsible for peyote's hallucinogenic effects. It was the first hallucinogenic compound synthesized. At the time, the science community wanted to know what chemical would cause hallucinations in otherwise normal individuals who were not suffering from a psychosis or brain disorder.

In the late nineteenth and twentieth centuries, hallucinogenic substances were viewed as possible tools for understanding and treating psychiatric and other mental disorders. Tribal medicine men, or shamans, have always maintained it was an effective medicine to treat a number of ailments including alcoholism. However, peyote did not really catch on as a drug to be explored in the recreational arena until 1953 when the English novelist Aldous Huxley (1894–1963) wrote *The Doors of Perception* where he recounted his experiences with the peyote.

In the 1960s and 1970s, serious research involving mescaline and LSD continued and it was hoped that their use in psychotherapy would be established. Timothy Leary (1920–96), a Harvard professor best known for his lifelong experiments with LSD, also studied mescaline. He is best known for giving the motto "Turn on, tune in, and drop out," to the hippie generation of the 1960s.

As academic interest in psychedelics flourished, street use became common, especially on college campuses. Opponents of psychedelic research said it failed to show that it had a viable use in psychotherapy, and growing street use demonstrated that the drugs had the potential for abuse and were dangerous. Users began reporting that some of their "trips," as the experience under the influence of the drug is called, were bad trips, causing them and the medical community concern. Flashbacks—recurrences of the trip even without the drug—were also reported. Organizations such as the National Clearinghouse or Alcohol and Drug Information cautions that using hallucinogens, including mescaline, in large quantities may cause convulsions, blood vessel damage in the brain, or even irreversible brain damage.

In 1929, New Mexico was the first state to outlaw peyote, and in 1967 the federal government banned it all together. In 1970, the Comprehensive Drug Abuse Prevention and Control Act made peyote, mescaline, and every other hallucinogen a Schedule I drug, defined as having no known medical use. Money for research dried up and the tide turned against hallucinogens' popularity as a street drug. Street use of peyote and mescaline was virtually nonexistent at the close of the twentieth century.

The federal government exempted the NAC from the ban on peyote if it is used as part of a bona fide religious ceremony. This point remains a center of legal controversy in states that want to limit its use or outlaw it completely.

CHEMICAL/ORGANIC COMPOSITION

Of the alkaloids so far identified in just *L. williamsii* alone, 15 are Beta-phenethylamine and simple isoquinoline alkaloids. Mescaline, N-methylmescaline, N-acetylemescaline, anhalamine, anhalonine, anhalidine, anhalinine, anhalonidine, lophophorine, O-methylanhalondedine, and pellotine have all been identified as the principal components of the plant. However, only mescaline has so far been determined to cause hallucinations.

Mescaline is chemically classified as a phenethylamine. Some of its identified chemical compounds are 3,4,5–trimethoxy-beta-phenethylamine, 3,4,5–trimethoxybenzeneethanamine, 3,4,5–trimethoxyphene-thylamine, and mescaline. This chemical classification makes the drug different from the other hallucinogens, specifically the more popular LSD, which is classified as an indole. Its chemical formula is $C_{11}H_{17}NO_3$.

Some designer drugs are mescaline analogs, meaning they are similar in chemical structure. The most popular mescaline analog is 3,4–methylenediozy-methamphetamine (MDMA or Ecstasy). Other analogs of mescaline include amphetamines and methamphetamines.

INGESTION METHODS

Dried peyote cactus buttons are chewed and swallowed or made into a powder and swallowed in tablet form. Peyote can also be brewed and drunk as a tea.

According to the Drug Enforcement Administration (DEA), the usual dose of mescaline that will produce hallucinations is about 0.3–0.5 g, which is the equivalent of about 5 g of dried peyote. The effect of the drug lasts about 12 hours. Mescaline can be extracted from peyote or produced synthetically.

Synthetic mescaline, however, is extremely rare. It is very expensive to produce and is therefore not in demand on the underground drug market. It takes about a half-gram of mescaline sulfate to produce a psychedelic trip. Synthetic mescaline is pricey at about $100 to $200 per gram.

Dried peyote buttons ground into a powdered form and made into tablets can be dangerous as the tablets can be adulterated, or mixed with other substances or drugs. In the United States, it has been reported that street samples of what are believed to be pure synthetic mescaline often have another substance added.

In Canada, Health Canada Online reports that 90% of what is supposed to be mescaline is actually phencyclidine (PCP), lysergic acid diethylamide (LSD), or another drug or substance. This can be dangerous

Peyote cactus. These plants contain mescaline, a chemical with hallucinogenic properties. Custom Medical Stock Photo, Inc. Reproduced by permission.

because some of these drugs can be much more harmful than mescaline or peyote. For instance, PCP or "Angel Dust" may cause severe paranoia or even convulsions and coma. These sorts of side effects are not usually associated with mescaline alone.

THERAPEUTIC USE

There is no recognized therapeutic use for peyote or mescaline. However, interest in mescaline as a medicine appeared almost as soon as it was discovered. A look through bibliographic citations and literature shows publications on peyote or mescaline dating from 1894 through nearly every decade to present day.

In the 1960s, interest in the therapeutic use of psychedelics was at its height. The experimental psychiatric community and others were looking at mescaline and other hallucinogens as possible ways to treat a wide array of psychiatric disorders such as depression, obsessive-compulsive behavior and autism. Once the drugs became illegal, legitimate study for all intents and purposes was halted. However, personal exploration and research continued illegally in some sectors.

In the 1990s there was a resurgence in interest in studying the effects of peyote, especially among the Native American population who have used it for so long. Testimony before the Congress of the United States and elsewhere that the use of peyote in the spiritual practices of the NAC has helped Native Americans combat the problems of alcoholism and that it appears relatively safe has revived the interest of the research community.

Outside of clinical research, use of peyote as a means to self-discovery is of great interest to both members of the NAC and lay people alike. A group in the San Francisco Bay area, the Council on Spiritual Practices (CSP), refers to peyote and other hallucinogenic plants as "entheogens" instead of hallucinogens. Entheogen comes from a Greek base meaning "God-facilitating substance."

Those who seek what they call a responsible religious use of entheogens are also trying to answer the questions about their inherent dangers. Researchers at Duke University are studying the PET scans of mescaline users to see what happens during spiritual use.

USAGE TRENDS

It is extremely difficult to determine the extent of peyote and mescaline use. After 1998, it seemed to disappear from the various governmental indicators for drug use. If it shows up at all, it is usually lumped under the heading of "other hallucinogens," not including LSD, which usually has its own category.

According to the DEA, as of October 2001, of the approximate 14 million Americans over age 12 who used illicit drugs, 22.3% used LSD. There is no mention of mescaline use in that survey.

The National Institute on Drug Abuse's (NIDA) Director's Report to the National Advisory Council on Drug Abuse in September 2000, did list mescaline use as being "common among adolescents and young adults in Boston. Peyote is readily available in Phoenix." However, there was no indication how many people this might involve or their ages or usage trends.

The Office of National Drug Control Policy (ONDCP) suggests that local DEA offices may have statistical breakdowns for mescaline and peyote use separate from other hallucinogens and LSD.

Scope and severity

Mescaline is not a very popular street drug as exemplified by a DEA report that shows that from 1980 to 1987, 19.4 lbs (9 kg) of peyote were confiscated in drug raids compared to more than 15 million lbs (7 million kg) of marijuana confiscated during the same time period. They report no trafficking of peyote.

In Texas, where the peyote cactus grows, its distribution to members of the NAC throughout the United States is controlled by Texas laws and regulations.

Age, ethnic, and gender trends

Again, there is no breakdown for mescaline use. A few interesting statistics from the National Institute of Justice (NIJ) show that about one-third of college campuses reported an increase in hallucinogen use in the mid-1990s—mostly LSD and psilocybin. According to the NIJ, "Campus sources identified hallucinogen users today as mainstream students, not the more marginal hippie students of the 1960s. Private and public campuses are equally likely to report hallucinogen use; religious schools are most likely to report little or no use. Larger campuses and institutions in urban areas report the widest range of drug use."

While use of hallucinogens appeared to increase during the early to mid-1990s, possibly due to the growth of "raves," NIDA reported a slight decline in their use among eighth, tenth, and twelfth graders from 1998 to 2000.

MENTAL EFFECTS

Most of what is known about the effects of hallucinogens is known from the widespread use and study of LSD during the 1960s and 1970s. According to NIDA, LSD is the most widely used drug of all the psychedelics and its affects are seen as typical of all drugs in this class. The way LSD works applies to other

LAW AND ORDER

Exempting peyote from the federal substance abuse schedule is not so easy. Consider how some states interpret this law. Arizona and Oregon contend that as long as peyote is used with "sincere religious intent," uses are exempt. In Colorado, Minnesota, Nevada, and New Mexico, users must be members of a "bona fide religious organization." Idaho, Iowa, Kansas, Oklahoma, South Dakota, and Wisconsin designate its use "only within an NAC ceremony." NAC membership is required in Idaho, Texas, and Wyoming, with Idaho and Texas further requiring that a person be of Native American descent. Kansas also states that incarcerated people are not exempt from the illegalities of using peyote regardless of any NAC affiliation.

Texas is often singled out as having laws closely aligned to old Jim Crow laws that determined whether someone was of African American descent by determining their percentage of African American blood. For the peyote exemption under Texas law, an NAC member must have at least 25% Native American blood.

Added to the confusion is the right of a church to determine its membership. Some chapters of the NAC say that anyone, even non-Indians, may be members of the church and participate in their ceremonies. Others restrict membership to Native Americans only. They may do this legally as the civil rights laws do not apply to churches.

All of these variations in interpretation of the law serve to keep it an ongoing and hot topic as the legalities and illegalities are interpreted according to state and federal law. Peyote remains a Schedule I, hallucinogen, and its use is punishable by law. The exemption for the NAC is subject to state interpretation and many cases often go all the way to the Supreme Court.

hallucinogens such as mescaline, psilocybin, and ibogaine.

Hallucinogens chemically affect the user's brain. Psychedelic drugs like mescaline have an emotional and sensory impact on the user. The user experiences rapid mood swings—feeling happy one minute and instantly fearful and paranoid in the next. This emotional up and down can be so rapid that the user may experience several emotions at the same time or in rapid-fire fashion one after the other.

HISTORY NOTES

After a Piute shaman named Wovoka had an apocalyptic vision about the Second Coming of an Indian Jesus who would save them from the white man, he formed the Ghost Dance religion in 1889. Other tribal leaders sent representatives to learn about this trance-inducing dancing that went on for five nights. The violent shaking described by one government agent as crazed and disgusting was enough for the Bureau of Indian Affairs to decide it could pose a threat to the white settlers, and outlawed it. The Sioux Indians of South Dakota had the last Ghost Dance. They took so seriously the precepts of the ritual that they wore "ghost shirts" into the battle of Wounded Knee, thinking the shirts and the dance would protect them from the soldiers' bullets. In one of the saddest tragedies of American history, more than 300 Indian men, women, and children were massacred.

In 1918, the Native American Church (NAC) was formed to provide a cohesion among Indian tribes as demoralization, alcoholism, and poverty threatened to undermine their ancient culture and traditions. The early founders of the NAC were considered prophets; they include John Wilson, John Rave, and the Comanche chief, Quanah Parker. James Mooney, an anthropologist from the Smithsonian Institute, was instrumental in helping get the church firmly established.

The church has incorporated formal laws to which they expect their members to adhere—they are to abstain from alcohol, be faithful to their spouses, not be sexually promiscuous, and be peaceful and free from deceit.

Peyote use in the ritual revolves around a person called the Roadman who is responsible for leading the ceremony. Drumming, singing, and dancing are all part of this carefully structured ritual that came to be known as The Peyote Road.

In 2002, there were more than 250,000 members of the NAC in the United States and Canada. As many as 24 states—Arizona, California, Colorado, Idaho, Illinois, Indiana, Iowa, Kansas, Maine, Michigan, Minnesota, Montana, Nebraska, Nevada, New Mexico, New York, North Carolina, North Dakota, Oklahoma, Oregon, South Dakota, Texas, Utah, Washington, Wisconsin, and Wyoming—have NAC member churches.

Users report a heightened awareness and intensity of color, sound, smells, and taste. Sometimes these sensations can appear mixed up and users report "hearing colors" or "seeing sounds." This blending of the sensual experience is a neurological phenomenon known as synesthesia.

The psychedelic drug-induced state of an hallucinogen is called a "trip." Trips can be good or bad. Many people say that under the influence of a hallucinogen, they feel very happy and interpret the experience as mentally stimulating or even enlightening in a spiritual sense. Some people say the experience helps them to better understand themselves, which is why throughout history the interest in using psychedelics as a therapeutic aid waxes and wanes in clinical interest.

However, the bad trips can be as equally terrifying as the good trips are stimulating. When a person has a bad trip, the individual often compares it to the most frightening nightmare. Often, those having a bad trip will be anxious, feel they are going insane, experience profound depression, and think they may be dying. Bad trips are also accompanied by a feeling of being out of control.

PHYSIOLOGICAL EFFECTS

Most people who take peyote report that their first reaction is to the taste; the buttons taste bad. Sometimes, the initial effects of eating them are nausea and vomiting, especially if many buttons are consumed. Some people report taking as many as 30 at a time. If taken in tablet form, more of the drug might be ingested at once and all of the drug's effects, good and bad, could be heightened.

About 30 minutes to over an hour after the buttons are eaten the drug's effects are felt. While the hallucinations may be two hours long, the drug's concentration in the brain and its other effects might last 10 to 12 hours.

As a result of the initial symptoms, it is rare for users to overdose on mescaline. However, this does not mean that mescaline is without other potentially dangerous physical effects. Mescaline can cause dilated pupils, high blood pressure, increased heart rate, dizziness, loss of appetite, dry mouth, sweating, numbness, anxiety, sleeplessness, uterine contractions, nausea, and tremors.

According to NIDA's Research Report Series on Hallucinogens and Dissociative Drugs, most likely the drug works by disrupting the interaction of nerve cells and the neurotransmitter, serotonin. Serotonin helps to regulate the areas in the brain that control behavior, perception, and the systems of the body that regulate such functions as hunger, body temperature, sexual behavior, muscle control, and the senses.

Not much is known about hallucinogens in general and mescaline in particular. While much of the research has pointed to the close ties with serotonin, others are now looking at the similarity between mescaline and amphetamine, with which it shares an even closer similar structure. This is especially evident in the mescaline analogs such as ecstasy, which has an extreme amphetamine-like effect on users. Amphetamines affect the adrenal system.

Harmful side effects

Because of peyote's bad taste, overdoses are rare. However, some of the drug's side effects such as nausea, sweating, and tremors are experienced when doses of 300–500 mg are taken. Other adverse side effects may include slowing heartbeat and breathing, and contractions of the intestines and the uterus, which could be dangerous for pregnant women taking the drug.

Another concern is the user's mental state. If a psychological disorder is already present, the user's condition could be worsened. Some people, even those without existing psychoses, report panic reactions when taking the drug.

Unlike other drugs, when a frequent user stops taking mescaline, there are no withdrawal symptoms. In other words, peyote does not cause an addiction, or physical dependence on a drug. However, while using mescaline, a tolerance to psychedelics in general will develop, meaning it will take a larger dose for the user to get the same effects. This tolerance carries over if the user switches to other psychedelics such as LSD or psilocybin, but does not last if mescaline use is discontinued.

Purity of the drug is always a concern. If mescaline is taken in its dried button form, users are fairly assured it is the real thing. In tablet form, there is always the possibility of adulteration. Possible harmful side effects from the unknown drug or additive always pose a danger.

Long-term health effects

Mescaline is not considered addictive the way drugs such as heroin or methamphetamines are. Nevertheless, this does not mean it is without possible health consequences. When the drug is discontinued, and there is a dip in serotonin activity, a condition called dysphoria may result. Dysphoria is an overall feeling of anxiety, depression, restlessness, and general dissatisfaction, for which fluoxetine (Prozac) is sometimes prescribed for three to six months.

Psychedelic use can carry with it two long-term mental health problems that can be quite disturbing. These conditions are hallucinogen-persisting perception disorder (HPPD), also known as flashbacks. HPPD may persist for years, long after a person stops taking mescaline. According the NIDA, "these episodes are spontaneous, repeated, sometimes continuous recurrences of some of the sensory distortions originally produced by LSD." This holds true for mescaline, the organization says, as well as other hallucinogens.

Another long-term health effect of psychedelic use is persistent or drug-induced psychosis, in which former users can fall into a "long-lasting psychotic-like state." They can appear severely depressed, have mood swings, and have hallucinations and visual disturbances. Like HPPD, persistent psychosis can last for years. Often it occurs in people who have no previous history of psychological problems.

REACTIONS WITH OTHER DRUGS OR SUBSTANCES

Often drug users combine drugs. "Love flipping," or "love trip," is the practice of taking mescaline at the same time as ecstasy. Because MDMA is a mescaline analog, and given the dangerous side effects known about MDMA, the addition of mescaline might further increase the overall harmful side effects of both drugs.

TREATMENT AND REHABILITATION

While there is no formal treatment for HPPD and drug-induced psychosis, those who have trouble coping with the symptoms are often treated with antidepressants to help reduce the symptoms. Former users who experience flashbacks are often fearful and confused by the inexplicable hallucinations, and it is reported that they think they may have suffered brain damage or are going insane. Psychotherapy may help them cope.

PERSONAL AND SOCIAL CONSEQUENCES

Because mescaline is so closely tied to its psychological effects, it can have profound effects on the user. The side effects of anxiety and depression after taking it can make social functioning difficult; flashbacks and drug-induced psychosis may require long-term care and can affect job performance and personal relationships. People with existing psychological problems might have them worsened. Functioning while under the influence of mescaline can lead to poor judgment or dangerous acts that could hurt the user or others.

LEGAL CONSEQUENCES

The DEA defines peyote as a Schedule I, hallucinogen, meaning that it has a "high potential for abuse, has no currently accepted medical use in treatment in the United States, and there is a lack of accepted safety for use of the drug or other substances under medical supervision."

Use of peyote or mescaline carries the same fines and punishments as any other Schedule I substance, which can include imprisonment. NAC members who use peyote outside the religious ceremony are not exempt from the consequences for illegal use. The federal guidelines refer specifically to the peyote cactus, *L. williamsii*. However, any other psychoactive cactus bought and used with the express intent of extracting the mescaline content will carry the same consequences under the law as using the more common form of the peyote cactus.

Traveling to other countries where peyote might be grown could result in legal consequences. Buying, selling, carrying, or using drugs, including mescaline, outside of the United States can result in interrogation and imprisonment for weeks, months, or life. Each country has its own legal guidelines and punishments for drug use and trafficking. Some countries make no distinctions for a person who has a small quantity of peyote for personal use; such a person could be tried with the same consequences as a full-fledged trafficker. Countries such as Malaysia, Pakistan, and Turkey use the death penalty for even the most minor drug offense.

Legal history

The legal history surrounding peyote use is ambivalent. On one hand, there is the straightforward ban on street usage and its consequences as a Schedule I, hallucinogen. On the other hand, there is the problematic usage by the federally recognized religion of the Native American Church that pits federal drug laws against First Amendment rights.

The legality-illegality considerations of peyote use by Native Americans has been on-again, off-again since the Civil War years. In 1920, New Mexico became the first state to outlaw its use. In 1959, the law was amended to allow Native Americans to use it during religious ceremonies.

In the 1950s and 1960s, peyote was legal throughout most of the United States. During the peak of the psychedelic era, dried peyote cactus buttons were readily available through mail-order catalogues.

When the Comprehensive Drug Abuse Prevention and Control Act (Public Law 91-513) made mescaline and peyote a Schedule I, hallucinogen, the free-flowing use of the cactus as a street drug slowed dramatically.

The law did allow an exemption for members of the NAC.

Nevertheless, states interpreted the law in their own way. A religion that used a controlled substance in its ceremony caused a lot of debate among lawyers and civil libertarians alike. It was the First Amendment of the U.S. Constitution, which provides for the right to worship without interference from federal or state governments, versus a church's right to use an illegal substance as part of its ceremony.

The American Indian Religious Freedom Act, adopted August 1978, protected the religious traditions of Native Americans, but this law was challenged almost from its inception.

The 1990 Supreme Court decision in *Employment Division v. Smith* said that the religious use of peyote by Native Americans is not protected by the First Amendment. This decision was met with the outcry of many religious and civil liberties groups, which led to two legislative acts: the Religious Freedom Restoration Act of 1993 and the American Indian Religious Freedom Act Amendments (AIRFA). Amended again in 1996, AIRFA allowed for the same protection for the traditional, ceremonial use of peyote by American Indians in all 50 states.

The law allows for the "use, possession, or transportation of peyote by an Indian for bona fide traditional ceremonial purposes in connection with the practice of a traditional Indian religion is lawful, and shall not be prohibited by the United States or any State." The law also protects peyoteros, those who harvest peyote.

Discretion, though, is left to the states to decide if the transportation, possession, or use of peyote is harmful to anyone and therefore allows states to make their own laws regulating use.

Federal guidelines, regulations, and penalties

Using, possessing, manufacturing, or distributing peyote could result in a prison sentence of not more than 15 years, a fine of not more than $25,000, or both.

In Canada, mescaline or peyote is a restricted drug, regulated by the Food and Drugs Act (FDA). A first offense is punishable by up to six months in jail and a fine of up to $1,000. Subsequent offenses are punishable by one year and up to $2,000; if convicted by indictment, individuals may be fined up to $4,000 and earn three years in jail. Penalties for trafficking and/or possession for the purpose of trafficking are punishable by up to 18 months in jail for summary conviction, and up to 10 years upon conviction by indictment.

See also Ecstasy (MDMA); LSD; PCP (phencyclidine); Psilocybin

RESOURCES

Books

Anderson, Edward F. "Botany of Peyote." In *Peyote, The Divine Cactus*. Tucson: University of Arizona Press, 1980.

Huxley, Aldous. *The Doors of Perception*. London: Chatto & Windus, 1954.

Jesse, Robert. "Testimony of the Council on Spiritual Practices." In *Entheogeons and the Future of Religion*. San Francisco: Council on Spiritual Practices, 1997.

Schultes, Richard Evans, and Albert Hoffmann. "The Tracks of the Little Deer." In *Plants of the Gods—Their Sacred, Healing and Hallucenogenic Powers*. Rochester, VT: Healing Arts Press, 1992.

Turner, D. M. *The Essential Pyschedelic Guide*. Ohio: Panther Press, 1994.

Periodicals

Patchelder, Tim. "Drug Addictions, Hallucinogens, and Shamanisms: The View from Anthropology." *Townsend Letter for Doctors and Patients* (July 2001).

Other

Bierma, Paige. "Hallucinogens (Psychedelics)." *Health Topics A-Z*. February 1, 2001 (July 8, 2002). <http://www.ahealthyme.com/topic/topic100586899;$sessionid$V3JQT1QAAABZFWCYSYTDEMQ#2>.

Council on Spiritual Practices. <http://www.csp.org/>.

The Multidisciplinary Association for Psychedelic Studies. <http://www.maps.org/>.

U.S. Department of Justice. Drug Enforcement Administration. <http://www.usdoj.gov/dea/>.

U.S. Department of Health and Human Services. National Institutes of Health. National Institute on Drug Abuse. <http://www.nida.nih.gov/>.

Organizations

National Institute on Drug Abuse (NIDA), National Institutes of Health, 6001 Executive Blvd., Bethesda, MD, USA, 20892-9561, (301) 443-1124, (888) 644-6432.

Candace A. Hoffmann

METHADONE

OFFICIAL NAMES: Methadone, Dolophine
STREET NAMES: Fizzies, dollies, dolls
DRUG CLASSIFICATIONS: Schedule II, opioid narcotic analgesic

OVERVIEW

Methadone is a synthetic opioid narcotic, discovered in Germany in 1939. Its original name was Amidon, and it was used mainly as a pain reliever. After the conclusion of World War II, Eli Lilly and other American pharmaceutical companies began clinical trials of the medication, renamed methadone, and also began commercial production. Its original uses in the United States were for pain control and as a component of cough medicine.

While methadone works well as a pain control medication, its main use today is in the treatment of heroin addiction. Methadone itself is an addicting drug; its effects are much longer acting than heroin. Easier to administer on a once-daily basis, it is effective orally, which protects addicts from acquiring diseases such as HIV/AIDS, hepatitis B, and hepatitis C, obtained when they use dirty needles. Tolerance and dependence on methadone may develop in long-term users, and withdrawal symptoms, while less severe than among heroin users, are generally longer lasting.

CHEMICAL/ORGANIC COMPOSITION

Methadone is an odorless, white powder that dissolves easily in water and alcohol. In methadone treatment programs, it is often mixed with an insoluble matrix to form what are known as methadone biscuits. These biscuits stay in the stomach longer because it takes awhile for the stomach acids to break down the matrix. This is important because it allows more of the methadone to be absorbed, rather than passing quickly through the stomach when in liquid form.

INGESTION METHODS

Methadone is manufactured as tablets, diskettes (also known as biscuits), and liquid. People who use the drug illegally often inject either the liquid form or crushed and dissolved tablets. Methadone is detectable in a person's bloodstream seven to 10 days after use.

When used as a cough suppressant, methadone is taken in a liquid or tablet form in very small (1–2 mg) doses every four to six hours. For relief of moderate to severe pain, it is generally given as a tablet or as an intramuscular injection, 2.5–20 mg every three to four hours. When used in heroin detoxification and methadone maintenance programs, it is given as oral tablets, biscuits, or liquid, 20–120 mg every 24–48 hours.

THERAPEUTIC USE

The most well-known use of methadone is for treating heroin addiction. It is calculated that between

500,000 and one million Americans are addicted to heroin. Along with the obvious infectious risks to heroin users such as HIV/AIDS and hepatitis, heroin addicts often engage in criminal activity to obtain heroin, an illegal drug, to support their addiction. Methadone is an agonist, which means it fits into the brain's opiate receptors and blocks heroin. It reduces the intense cravings addicts experience when they try to give up heroin and enables them to participate in therapy and other aspects of their treatment. Methadone also reduces the need for addicts to commit crimes to obtain heroin and protects them from disease. Recent studies have found that persons in a methadone maintenance program were three to six times less likely than heroin users to become infected with HIV, even if they continue to use illegal drugs.

Methadone generally lasts about one day in the body, meaning that a person in a maintenance program has to take methadone at least once a day. Federal regulations require that to be eligible for enrollment in a methadone maintenance program, potential patients must be at least 18 years of age and demonstrate that they have had at least a one-year history of heroin (or other opiate) addiction. An exception is made for patients between the ages of 16 and 18 who can document a history of at least two unsuccessful detoxification trials.

Methadone maintenance programs are generally managed through methadone clinics, which also provide counseling and rehabilitation services. There are currently 42 states that have methadone maintenance programs, along with the District of Columbia, Puerto Rico, and the U.S. Virgin Islands.

The goal of a methadone maintenance program for people who are just coming off heroin is to decrease their withdrawal symptoms and their desire to use heroin. Initially, people starting in a methadone maintenance program will be given 30–40 mg of methadone a day, although there are addiction specialists who recommend higher initial doses such as 60–80 mg a day. In fact, most programs today are switching to the larger dose because research shows the larger dose is required for methadone to work effectively. Further into a methadone maintenance program, the dosages of the drug will be adjusted so that a person will not have cravings for heroin but also will not have any side effects from the methadone, such as sedation or euphoria.

Besides its use in treating illegal opiate addiction, methadone is occasionally used in other areas of medicine. All of the opiates, including methadone, are powerful pain control medications. Since pain is one of the most frequent, and least well-managed, aspects of cancer care, physicians often use multiple medications to try to control cancer pain. Methadone can be given in 20 mg tablets or by intramuscular injection every four to six hours to control moderate to severe cancer pain. Methadone is often used when there is a desire to let the patient sleep because of its high sedating properties.

Methadone can also be used to treat a common condition called restless leg syndrome. This condition generally affects middle-aged to older adults, although it is occasionally seen in adolescents. In restless leg syndrome, people complain of a strong, almost uncontrollable desire to move their legs, especially at night. In people who are unable to sleep because of this disorder, 10 mg of methadone, given at bedtime, often is effective at slowing or stopping the leg movements.

USAGE TRENDS

Scope and severity

The number of people entering methadone treatment programs to help them fight their heroin habit has steadily increased since methadone was first approved to treat heroin addiction. The latest statistics show that there are 170,000 admissions to methadone treatment programs throughout the United States every year.

Several major studies have been undertaken to gather data on opiate drug abusers who enter methadone treatment programs. The first of these was the Drug Abuse Reporting Program (DARP), which gathered data between 1969 and 1973. The second study, which examined patient characteristics of heroin addicts entering a methadone maintenance program, was the Treatment Outcomes Prospective Study (TOPS), which ran from 1979 to 1981. The most recent nationwide research, known as the Drug Abuse Treatment Outcomes Study (DATOS), collected data from 1991 to 1993.

There were many significant changes noted between the studies. In DARP, the earliest study, the patients entering methadone treatment programs had been, on average, addicted to heroin for at least nine years. In the 1990s, that number had increased to 13 years. Furthermore, the number of patients who had received previous treatment for heroin addiction increased from 50% in the 1960s to 75% in the 1990s. The proportion of addicts that had at least three prior treatment attempts increased from 13% in the 1960s study to 40% for the 1990s study. Use of other drugs such as cocaine among people entering methadone treatment programs increased from approximately 30% in the 1960s to 50% in the 1990s.

Age, ethnic, and gender trends

Based on data from these studies, there has been a significant change in the past three decades in the age, ethnic, and gender composition of methadone users. The proportion of women entering methadone treatment programs increased from 22% in the early studies to 39% in the most recent studies. The proportion of African Americans entering methadone programs decreased from 58% in the 1960s to only 28% in the 1990s, while the per-

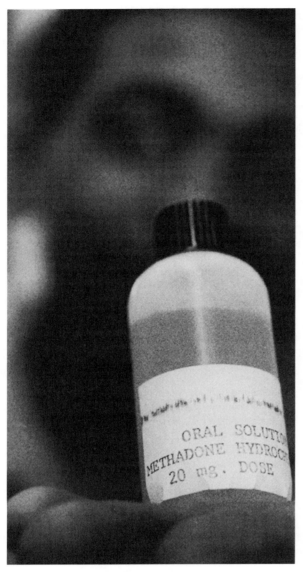

Methadone is used in the treatment of heroin addiction. AP/Wide World Photos. Reproduced by permission.

centage of Hispanics rose from 10% to 24% over that same time period. The percentage of whites entering methadone programs increased from 29% in the 1960s to 38% in the 1990s. Forty-six percent of the methadone program participants were between the ages of 35 and 44. Only 20% were below the age of 30.

MENTAL EFFECTS

Methadone and all other opiates produce multiple effects on a user's psychological and mental status. These effects are generally dose-related, with more powerful effects seen at higher doses.

In order to influence a person's mental state, methadone, along with any other drug or substance, must first be able to cross what is known as the blood-brain barrier. The blood-brain barrier is an actual physical barrier, made up of tightly interspaced blood vessels that protect the brain from substances that might be harmful. The more effective a substance is at getting through the blood-brain barrier, the greater the effect it has on the person's mental status. Methadone and other opiates cross the blood-brain barrier quite easily.

Most users of methadone, especially new users, report feelings of well being and tranquility after taking the drug. How methadone produces these feelings is still being researched. Some scientists think that methadone and other opiates cause these effects by acting on a part of the brain known as the locus cerulus. This area of the brain is known to play a major role in feelings of pain, panic, fear, and anxiety. It is thought that by dampening the action of the locus cerulus, methadone and other opiates cause thoughts and feelings of tranquility and ease.

Methadone and opiates were first used for pain relief, and are still chiefly used in that area of medicine. It is important to remember that methadone and other opiates do not exert their pain control by altering a person's sensitivity to pain. Rather, methadone and other opiates interfere with the transmission of pain impulses from the nervous system to the brain. They accomplish this by a variety of methods. First, they decrease the transmission of nerve signals that conduct pain messages from various parts of the body to the spine. Secondly, they prevent production of neurochemicals that transfer this pain information to the spine. Finally, they mimic the actions of endorphins, which are the body's own pain-controlling chemicals. While methadone and other opiates work quite well to control pain, they do not affect touch, vision, or hearing.

Methadone also produces clouding of thoughts, drowsiness, and sleep in people who use it. It is thought that psychological effects seen in people who use methadone, including the inability to concentrate, apathy, and lethargy are related to methadone's pro-drowsiness effects, although researchers have yet to pinpoint the way in which methadone causes these effects. Methadone is often used by clinicians who specialize in addictive disorders to help heroin addicts resume a normal sleep cycle, since it is a powerful trigger at inducing sleep.

There are some reports by users that methadone use may cause hallucinations. While it is well known that heroin users often describe a dream-like mental state when using heroin, this effect is rarely seen in people who use methadone. The reason behind this is probably due to methadone's slower onset of action and reduced level of intensity. Likewise, while users of heroin and other harder narcotics sometimes report feelings of acute anxiety, especially when first using the drug, users of methadone rarely report these psychological effects.

PHYSIOLOGICAL EFFECTS

Methadone, like all opiates, is a chemically simple compound that has a variety of effects on those who take it. But while other opiates exert powerful euphoric effects on a person by acting very much like chemicals called endorphins and enkephalins, methadone produces only a mild (or no) euphoria, to which patients quickly become tolerate. Endorphins and enkephalins are naturally produced inside the brain. When released in the brain's reward system, they produce a mind reward and users feel good as a result. Methadone and other opiates mimic these natural brain chemicals, which is why they are so addicting.

Scientific research has shown that methadone and other opiates have specific areas, or sites, that they attach to in order to exert their influence on the brain and body. These sites, called receptors, are classified as mu, delta, and kappa, depending on what body functions they influence. Opiate activation of mu and delta receptors seems to influence mood, respiration, pain, blood pressure, and gastrointestinal functions. Kappa receptors appear to be more involved in the perception and aversion to pain. The degree of methadone's effect on these receptors can vary widely between individuals, however, there are certain effects that are almost universal.

Nausea is a side effect of all opiates. People who take opiates, including methadone, for a long period of time generally develop a tolerance for its nauseating effects. Vomiting, while common with other opiates such as heroin, is actually a rare side effect of methadone. These side effects are due to the stimulation by opiates of the part of the brain called the medulla, which controls nausea and vomiting.

Another important side effect of all opiates on the central nervous system is respiratory depression. This is caused by an inhibitory effect on the brain stem, which is the part of the brain that controls breathing and other involuntary bodily systems such as heart beat, etc. Like nausea and vomiting, people who take methadone and other opiates normally develop a tolerance to this side effect. However, even people who have taken methadone for a long period of time can develop major respiratory depression.

Cough suppression is another side effect of opiates. In fact, some opiates such as codeine are specifically marketed as cough suppressants. Other less common side effects of methadone include convulsions with very high doses, and a heavy feeling in the arms and legs. While not fully understood, it is thought that this side effect is due to the methadone causing increased blood circulation to the peripheral blood vessels of the body, especially to the arms and legs.

???? FACT OR FICTION

Methadone was developed in Germany in the 1930s by scientists looking to develop synthetic pain medications. The supply of opium, the natural constituent of many pain medications, was cut off to Germany by the allies during World War II. There is a persistent fallacy, found even today in some textbooks, that purport methadone, or Dolophine, was named after Adolph Hitler. Actually, the "dol" in Dolophine comes from the Latin word *dolor*, meaning pain, and has nothing to do with Adolph Hitler.

One of the most annoying physiological side effect of methadone use is a feeling of dryness in the mucous membranes of the mouth, eyes, and nose. This is caused by methadone reducing the secretion of saliva, tears, and mucous. Regular users of methadone refer to the dryness of the mouth as "cotton mouth," since the feeling is akin to having one's mouth stuffed full of cotton.

Methadone and all other opiates also have the unwanted physiological side effect of producing constipation. Generally, involuntary movements, or waves, of the muscles in the small and large intestines propel fecal matter through the intestines and out of the body. However, methadone and other opiates significantly slow these involuntary movements, and result in constipation. Even after long usage, many users of methadone will continue to report continued constipation.

A very visible physiological effect of methadone and all other opiates is the constriction of a person's pupils. The pupils, which are the black center of the eye, can be likened to lens on a camera. When pupils are wide open, then more light can pass through. When the pupils are constricted, very little light can pass through. Persons who are on methadone often have pupils that are quite small, making it very difficult for the person to see in anything but bright light.

There are other physiological effects of methadone for which there is no known mechanism. In women who use methadone, there can be changes seen in their menstrual cycle. It has been hypothesized that these changes are due to methadone's effect on the hormones that regulate menstruation, but this has not yet been proven.

Another side effect of methadone is a change in a user's sexual desire and function. One theory is that opiates decrease testosterone levels in both men and women; one small study of 29 methadone users found testosterone levels to be decreased by 40%. Methadone also inhibits sexual function by increasing the tone in the muscles surrounding the urethra and therefore causing a delay in orgasm in men.

It is generally thought that methadone is extremely dangerous for women who are pregnant. The fact is that there are no well-researched studies showing any adverse physiological effects for pregnant women who are using methadone for heroin withdrawal. However, while the risk for pregnant women may be minimal, there are very real physiological risks for their babies.

The first problem for the baby of a woman who is using methadone is a higher risk of low birth rate. Most studies show that babies born to women who are using methadone for heroin detoxification have a 25% greater risk of low birth weights than babies whose mothers were not using methadone. It is thought by some researchers that methadone itself somehow causes babies to be born underweight, but the majority of drug addiction specialists feel that the higher incidence of low birth weight seen among methadone users is due in fact to social factors such as poor nutrition, smoking, and poverty.

Babies who are born to mothers who are using methadone are at high risk of experiencing a syndrome known as the methadone withdrawal syndrome. This syndrome usually occurs within 48 hours of birth, but can be seen anytime during the first two weeks of birth. Symptoms are quite variable, but generally include irritability and sleep disturbances; prolonged sneezing; loud, shrill cries; watery stools; hyperactivity; poor weight gain; and aversion to bright lights.

Besides the classical withdrawal signs, there are other reported physiological problems in babies born to mothers who are using methadone. Some studies have reported that there is a higher rate of infant mortality and SIDS (sudden infant death syndrome) in babies who are born to methadone-using mothers. However, these studies were done in the 1970s, when there was a generally higher rate of infant mortality. Subsequent studies have failed to prove a definitive relationship between methadone use by pregnant women and a subsequent increase in death rates in their infant offspring.

Many physicians who do not treat opiate addicts on a regular basis believe that methadone inhibits and interferes with the functioning of a person's immune system. While it is true that some of the shorter acting opiates like heroin do inhibit a person's immune system, and thus make them more prone to infections, methadone does not inhibit the immune system. This is an important fact, especially in light of the fact that many ex-heroin users have HIV and AIDS. There are even some researchers who believe that methadone, by ways still unknown, may even help restore the functioning of the immune system in patients with HIV.

Harmful side effects

The harmful side effects of methadone, if taken in controlled conditions of a heroin detoxification program, are actually very small. The three main side effects of methadone use are tooth decay, constipation, and accidental overdose. Over half the users of methadone report problems with their teeth related to their methadone usage. Methadone use makes users more prone to tooth decay because methadone in a treatment clinic is generally given as a syrup-based mixture that has a high-sugar content, and is also acidic. Also, methadone itself inhibits the production of saliva in the mouth, which indirectly promotes the production of plaque. To help prevent tooth decay in methadone users, researchers are formulating water-based, sugar-free solutions of methadone, and promoting a low-sugar diet along with regular dental checkups for long-term users of methadone.

Chronic constipation is also another troublesome side effect of prolonged methadone use. As discussed previously, methadone significantly slows the involuntary movements of the small and large intestines. By consuming a high-fiber diet and plenty of water, chronic users of methadone can reduce, but not eliminate, the occurrence of constipation.

The third and most serious side effect of long-term methadone use is the danger of an overdose. Methadone is one of the most powerful opiates, and with its slow onset of action and long half-life, that is, the time it stays active in the body, it can cause overdose, even in chronic users. Early signs of methadone overdose include nausea and vomiting, drowsiness, reduced heart rate, and pinpoint pupils. Signs of a more severe overdose include breathlessness and convulsions, which may result in death. To help prevent a methadone overdose, people should follow the advice of the physician or treatment specialist who provides methadone to them, and they should not mix methadone with other drugs, especially tranquilizers or alcohol. All suspected cases of methadone overdose should immediately be taken to the nearest hospital emergency room.

Long-term health effects

The long-term health effects of methadone, if taken in the controlled conditions of a methadone maintenance program, are minimal. Through the study of thousands of patients, researchers have shown that while some physiological changes do occur in people taking methadone, problematic long-term health effects during prolonged treatment are very rare. In fact, the most important long-term side effect seems to be that there are significant improvements in the general health of heroin addicts who enter a methadone maintenance program.

REACTIONS WITH OTHER DRUGS OR SUBSTANCES

Methadone is mainly broken down, or metabolized, in the liver. Therefore, any other medications or substances that affect the functioning of the liver can change the rate of metabolism of methadone, either increasing or decreasing the amount in a person's bloodstream.

There are many drugs that increase the rate of the liver's metabolism. More commonly used medications that fall into this category include rifampin, which is used to treat tuberculosis, and dilantin, phenytoin, and carbamazepine, which are medications commonly used to treat seizures and epilepsy. Chronic alcohol abuse also speeds up the metabolism of the liver. Since all of these substances cause the liver to break down methadone faster then it normally would, one way to correct the problem would be to increase the dose of methadone or break down the dose into several smaller doses given throughout the day. This should only be done on a physician's advice.

Other medications that can slow down the metabolism of the liver, thereby causing a person to get a higher dose of methadone than they normally would, include Cimetidine, commonly used for upset stomachs, diazepam, a commonly used anti-anxiety medication, and fluvoxamine, a recently introduced antidepressant medication. Interestingly, alcohol, when used only occasionally, increases methadone levels as compared to decreasing methadone levels when it is used and abused on a chronic basis.

There are other well-known medications that can increase the level of a methadone in a person's bloodstream. Medications, including the common antibiotics, erythromycin and clarithromycin, along with vitamin E and the pain reliever ibuprofen, can all cause an increase in methadone levels by affecting the way methadone is carried in the bloodstream by plasma proteins. All the mentioned medications cause methadone to be "knocked away" from its plasma protein carriers, causing a great surge of methadone in the bloodstream. As with medications and substances that slow the metabolism of the liver, patients who are taking any other medications should discuss this with all the specialists involved in treating them for various problems so that they do not overdose on methadone.

Besides being affected by medications and substances that affect the liver's metabolism, methadone itself affects the liver's metabolism of certain substances. A significant number of people who are taking methadone for heroin addiction also are HIV positive and are taking anti-HIV medications such as Desipramine (DMI) and zidovudine (AZT). Through its actions on the liver, methadone decreases the metabolism of these medications. Because of this, certain troublesome side effects of DMI and AZT, including nausea,

HISTORY NOTES

People have used opiate drugs for some 3,500 years. For most of that time, opiates consisted of crude opium cultivated from the poppy plant. In the early 1800s, morphine and codeine, more refined isolates of opium, were developed. These drugs were initially used for pain and cough control. In 1898, the Bayer Corporation further refined codeine into the drug we know as heroin. The initial thought was that by changing the chemical structure of codeine, a more powerful cough suppressant could be formed. In the last half of the twentieth century, further compounds were synthesized from the basic chemical structure of opium, including methadone.

---

vomiting, and fatigue, can increase when a person is on both methadone and these anti-HIV medications.

TREATMENT AND REHABILITATION

Getting people off methadone, referred to as methadone detoxification, is a complex process. People who are on methadone to combat their heroin addiction often decide to stop using methadone when they and their counselors have decided that they are ready to live without drugs. However, there are times when, even though the patient is not truly ready to stop methadone, they feel they must stop for a variety of reasons such as getting a new job, moving to a new area, the societal stigma of being on methadone, or an upcoming or actual prison sentence. Whatever the reason, methadone detoxification must be done carefully.

Almost all people on methadone who decide to go off of it will have withdrawal symptoms such as anxiety, depression, nausea/vomiting, and difficulty sleeping. To help minimize these effects of methadone detoxification, a gradual reduction in the dose of methadone is done over a long period of time to help the person adjust to not having methadone in their body.

For short-term detoxification, a person would decrease and stop methadone in less then a month. It should be noted that people in short-term detoxification programs have a higher likelihood of returning to heroin abuse than do people in a long-term methadone detoxification program.

In a long-term detoxification program, people on methadone may spend up to six months gradually cutting back on the amount of methadone that they use. The entire detoxification program would take four months.

PERSONAL AND SOCIAL CONSEQUENCES

The personal and social consequences of drug abuse are wide-reaching. Consequences of drug abuse affect all people and all ages. The impact of drug abuse is a complete societal problem that leaves no person in this country, either directly or indirectly, untouched.

Opiate abuse, mainly heroin abuse, is the main reason people turn to methadone treatment programs. The consequences of opiate abuse can be staggering. People who are addicted to opiates generally have a variety of psychiatric, medical, and social problems. As compared to other persons their own age and sex, opiate addicts have a significantly higher incidence of anxiety, depression, schizophrenic-like symptoms, and other serious psychiatric disorders. Opiate abusers frequently suffer from multiple medical problems. Due to their high rate of injecting heroin to get high, opiate addicts have a very high rate of hepatitis B, hepatitis C, and HIV/AIDS.

People who are addicted to opiates also have a number of societal problems. Maintaining meaningful employment is almost impossible for a person addicted to opiates. Likewise, maintaining stable relationships or marriage, making and keeping friends, and functioning as a caring and dependable parent are almost impossible tasks for someone whose life revolves around the next high. Most opiate addicts have to steal in order to maintain their habit, so they are at very high risk of being jailed for drug-related crimes.

LEGAL CONSEQUENCES

The penalties for illegally using and distributing methadone are severe. Methadone is classified as a Schedule II substance. For illegal possession of methadone, the penalty (for first offenders) for possession of greater than 100 g is a fine of not more than four million dollars. The penalty for a second offense is a fine of no more than eight million dollars.

The penalties for trafficking illegal methadone are even more severe. For a first offense, the penalty can be up to 20 years in prison. For a second offense, the penalty can be up to 30 years in prison.

Legal history

Methadone began to be used as a treatment for heroin addiction in the 1960s. In 1963, Dr. Vincent Dole, an expert in metabolic disorders, and Dr. Marie Nyswander, a psychiatrist who had worked in the U.S. Public Health facility for heroin addicts in Lexington, Kentucky, began

experimenting with several drugs to help addicts recover from their addiction. The doctors discovered that when heroin addicts were given methadone, their behavior radically changed. Suddenly, instead of focusing on getting more heroin, the focus of the addict's attention turned away from drugs and to pursuits in life they had had before they were addicted to heroin. Dr. Dole and Dr. Nyswander realized that once a heroin addict was given an adequate treatment dose of methadone, that person could remain on the same dose for a long period of time and function almost as well as they did when they were not addicts.

Within a year, Nyswander and Dole had developed a methadone maintenance treatment program. They based their program on the idea that heroin addicts suffer from a metabolic disorder much as a person with diabetes suffers from a metabolic disorder. They reasoned that just as insulin stabilizes a person with diabetes, methadone could stabilize a person with a heroin addiction. However, even though Nyswander and Dole viewed their program as a physical treatment for a physiological disorder, they also used intense psychological counseling services to help their patients get over their addiction. This new form of treatment for heroin addiction spread rapidly over the next few years, and by 1972 there were more than 800 methadone maintenance programs in the United States.

Federal guidelines, regulations, and penalties

Since the passage of the Harrison Narcotic Act in 1914 by the U.S. Congress, the federal government has been involved in the control of narcotics and the treatment of addicts. In terms of treatment of narcotic addicts, the federal government opened facilities in Lexington, Kentucky, and Fort Worth, Texas, between 1936 and 1939 to help deal with the rising number of opiate addicts in the United States.

After the development of methadone maintenance programs in the mid-1960s, the federal government, through the action of the 1966 Narcotic Addiction Rehabilitation Act, authorized the civil commitment of narcotic addicts, as well as giving federal finanical assistance to states and local authorities to develop a local system of drug treatment programs. The act required that these treatment programs include mandatory three-times-a-week counseling sessions; weekly urine tests; restorative dental services; and psychological counseling and vocational training.

In 1970, the Comprehensive Drug Abuse Prevention and Control Act was enacted into federal law. One purpose of the act was to clarify the ways in which medical personnel could legally dispense methadone to heroin addicts. In order to further clarify heroin treatment parameters, the Narcotic Addict Treatment Act of 1974 was passed, which set forth minimum standards for all methadone treatment facilities, as well as setting standard definitions for addicts. In the 1980s, these regulations were amended to allow younger patients (ages 16–18) to legally enter treatment programs. The regulations passed in the 1980s are still in effect today.

See also Heroin

RESOURCES

Books

Bray, R., and Mary Ellen Marsden. *Drug Use in Metropolitan America*. Thousand Oaks, CA: Sage Publications, 1997.

Lowinson, J., et al. *Substance Abuse: A Comprehensive Textbook*. Baltimore: Williams & Wilkins, 2001.

McDowell, D., and Henry Spitz. *Substance Abuse: From Principles to Practice*. Philadelphia: Taylor & Francis, 1999.

Smith, D., and Richard Seymour. *Clinician's Guide to Substance Abuse*. New York: McGraw Hill, 2000.

Other

"Drugs Used for the Treatment of Narcotic Addicts." Treatment Improvement Exchange. <www.treatment.org/taps/tap12/tap12part291.html>.

Federal Regulations of Drug Treatment. 1995. <http://books.nap.edu/books/0309052408/html/120.html>.

Edward R. Rosick, D.O., M.P.H.

METHAMPHETAMINE

OFFICIAL NAMES: Methampethamine
STREET NAMES: Meth, speed, crank, zip, chalk, ice, crystal
DRUG CLASSIFICATIONS: Schedule II, stimulant

OVERVIEW

Methamphetamine is a powerful stimulant of the central nervous system. Ordinarily it is a white, odorless powder that can be taken orally, smoked, or injected. It was developed early in the twentieth century from amphetamine, which was synthesized in 1887. Methamphetamine, which is more powerful than amphetamine, was first manufactured in Japan in 1919. It originally was used as a nasal decongestant and bronchial dilator for people with asthma.

Like its parent compound amphetamine, methamphetamine soon began to be used by people for its stimulating properties on the body and brain. During World War II, it was used extensively by both the Allied and Axis soldiers to fight fatigue on the battlefield.

After World War II, there was a huge increase in use of methamphetamines, when supplies of the drug for military use became available to the public. Initially, the use of methamphetamines for its stimulating properties was limited to college students, truck drivers, and athletes. However, in the 1960s, injectible methamphetamine was introduced into society, creating a large group of addicts. In 1970, the Controlled Substances Act

(CSA) severely restricted the legal production of methamphetamines, causing the illegal manufacturing and distribution of methamphetamine to increase. In the 1980s, a smokeable form of methamphetamine, known as ice or crank, came into widespread use.

Today, illegal use of methamphetamine is one of the United States' leading drug abuse problems. Methamphetamine is both highly addicting and highly destructive to its users. Methampethamine trafficking and abuse has been on the rise, causing a devastating impact on communities across the nation. Illegal production of methamphetamine accounts for almost all of the methamphetamine abused in the United States. Large-scale production of methamphetamine is centered in California; however, more and more methamphetamine is being manufactured in Mexico and smuggled into the United States by organized crime groups. Because they already have well-established distribution networks and operators for their cocaine, heroin, and marijuana trafficking, Mexican drug lords have found it easy to tap into, and increasingly control, the illegal methamphetamine market.

CHEMICAL/ORGANIC COMPOSITION

Methamphetamine is a white, odorless, bitter-tasting powder that dissolves easily in water or alcohol. Methamphetamine production begins with a common chemical known as ephedrine. After using several toxic chemicals, including hydriodic acid, chemical solvents, and heavy metals such as mercury and lead, methamphetamine is produced. Chronic users often combine methamphetamine with cocaine or heroin; this combination is known as a "speedball."

INGESTION METHODS

Methamphetamine, when used as a legal medication, is taken as tablets. When used illegally, it is taken in pill form orally, powered form for injection, or crystalline form to be smoked.

THERAPEUTIC USE

Until the 1970s, methamphetamines were used for a variety of medical conditions in the United States. However, with the growing abuse of these powerful drugs, the federal government imposed strict controls on their usage and prescription. Currently, the use of methamphetamines in medicine are restricted for only a few types of medical conditions, including weight reduction for obese patients, narcolepsy, and attention-deficit disorder (ADD).

Methamphetamines and amphetamines are both used for treatment of obesity since they decrease hunger in patients. It is thought that both methamphetamines and amphetamines decrease the urge to eat by affecting certain areas of the brain that are associated with appetite and eating behaviors. While methamphetamines work reasonably well in controlling hunger, they are not indicated for long-term control of obesity because tolerance to the drug develops rapidly. Therefore, more and more methamphetamine has to be taken in order to achieve appetite suppression. Patients usually take methamphetamines or amphetamines for a maximum of six to eight weeks at a time, during which period most people will lose 6–10 lbs (2.7–4.5 kg).

Narcolepsy is a rare condition in which people literally fall asleep, quite suddenly, with no conscious control. This may occur only once or twice a day, but may occur up to 100 times a day. Low doses of methamphetamine or amphetamine are given to these patients on a very controlled basis to help keep the multiple episodes of sleeping under reasonable control.

Attention-deficit disorder (ADD) is widely diagnosed in school-aged children, although the disorder is seen well into adulthood. It is characterized by impulsive behavior, inability to concentrate, and short attention span. Methamphetamines and amphetamines, when given to people with this disorder, have the paradoxical effect of increasing the attention span, decreasing hyperactive behavior, and increasing the ability to concentrate. There are several types of methamphetamine and amphetamine available to treat this condition, including long-lasting, once-a-day preparations.

 **KEY TERMS**

ANTISPASMODIC: A substance or drug that relieves muscle spasms and/or cramps.

ANXIETY DISORDERS: A group of mental disorders or conditions characterized in part by chronic feelings of fear, excessive and obsessive worrying, restlessness, and panic attacks. Anxiety disorders include panic disorder, agoraphobia, obsessive-compulsive disorder, post-traumatic stress disorder, and others.

APHRODISIAC: A substance or drug that increases sexual desire.

ATAXIA: Loss of control of muscle coordination.

BARBITURATES: Highly habit-forming (addictive) sedative drugs based on barbituric acid. Barbiturates are central nervous system depressants.

HYPNOTIC: A drug that induces sleep by depressing the central nervous system.

NEURONS: Nerve cells found throughout the central nervous system. Neurons release neurotransmitters.

PRECURSORS: A substance or compound from which another substance is synthesized, or made.

RECREATIONAL USE: The casual and infrequent use of a drug or substance, often in social situations, for its pleasurable effects.

RELAPSE: Term used in substance abuse treatment and recovery that refers to an addict's return to substance use and abuse following a period of abstinence or sobriety.

Methamphetamine is also used in other medical situations. People with severe depression are sometimes given short courses of a stimulant such as methamphetamine or amphetamine. However, physicians need to be cautious when giving a person with depression methamphetamine, since there can be a "let-down" period after stopping the drug that may cause the depression to actually worsen. Methamphetamines are also sometimes used to treat severe cases of epilepsy or Parkinson's disease in which the normally prescribed medications have failed.

USAGE TRENDS

Until approximately 10–15 years ago, illegal methamphetamine use was predominately a problem in California and surrounding western states. Outlaw motorcycle gangs significantly controlled methamphetamine manufacturing and distribution. However, drug lords from Mexico began to become involved. Through

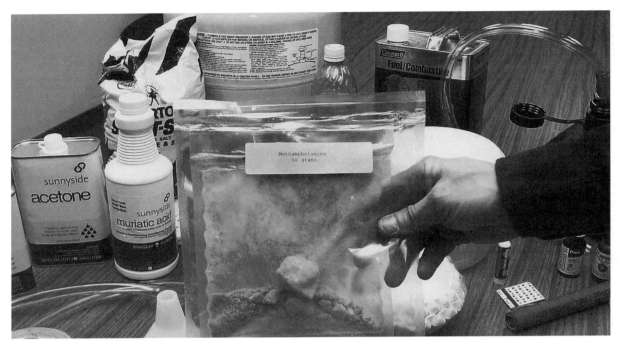

A law enforcement official holds a bag containing methamphetamine. Surrounding are some common household items used in the manufacture of the drug. Photo by Will Kincaid, AP/World Wide Photos. Reproduced by permission.

their nationwide distribution and transportation networks of other illegal drugs, the Mexican drug traffickers were easily able to expand methamphetamine to all corners of the United States.

There are a variety of reasons that people use and abuse methamphetamine. Various studies report that about 10% of methamphetamine users were first introduced to the drug by family members. Most users state that they began using the drug as an experiment, to get more energy, and to get high. Around half of methamphetamine users state they use the drug either by smoking it or snorting it, with people under the age of 18 preferring to smoke it. People who use other drugs such as cocaine generally (64% of the time) state a preference for methamphetamine, due to its long-lasting nature and powerful high.

A significant percentage of methamphetamine users have had legal trouble. From multiple studies, a full 40% of adult methamphetamine users have been charged with a drug or alcohol violation, while 25% have been booked for theft and 16% have been arrested for violent behavior. About one-third of methamphetamine users report to have been engaged in illegal drug activity besides use, with selling drugs the most common activity. Forty percent of juveniles who are methamphetmine users reported also being involved in drug dealing. Most methamphetamine users who are also dealers report they became dealers to support their own drug habit.

Scope and severity

Methamphetamine is a dangerous, highly addictive drug that can be manufactured with commonly available, inexpensive chemicals. With a street price of $3,000 per pound (per half kilogram), making and selling methamphetamine can be a lucrative, albeit deadly, industry. While methamphetamine abuse has been a problem in California for decades, it was not the 1990s that it began to be a nationwide problem.

There have been numerous studies over the past few years trying to gauge the extent of methamphetamine use. According to the 1998 National Household Survey on Drug Abuse, an estimated 4.7 million people had tried methamphetamine at some point in their lives. That same survey, done again in the year 2000, showed that the number of methamphetamine users had grown to 8.8 million.

The Drug Abuse Warning Network, which collects information on drug-related episodes from the nation's emergency rooms, showed that methamphetamine-related visits to emergency rooms more than tripled between 1991 and 1994, rising from 4,900 to more than 17,000. That number stayed the same until the late 1990s, and actually decreased somewhat (to 13,500) by 2000.

The Treatment Episode Data Set collects usage data from drug treatment centers around the country. Between 1993 and 1999, it was reported that methamphetamine addicts made up about 5% of the 1.6 million admissions to publicly funded substance abuse treatment center facilities. The survey also showed that in 1993, most methamphetmaine users were concentrated in three Western states—California, Oregon, and Nevada. By 1996, the treatment rate for methamphetamine abuse had increased 79%. By 1999, high methamphetamine admission rates to treatment centers were seen in most states west of the Mississippi River.

Age, ethnic, and gender trends

Methamphetamine use and abuse was traditionally believed to be one of white, blue-collar males. However, that has rapidly shifted in the past decade, with methamphetamine being used by a very diverse population.

A study of the ethnicity of methamphetamine users done between 1996 and 1997 shows that they are multicultural. In Los Angles, 30% of users were white, 5% were Hispanic, and only 2% were black. However, that same survey showed that in Portland, Oregon, whites made up 94% of all methamphetamine users; 54% of these were male, while 46% were female. In Los Angles, 88% of the methamphetamine users were male, with only 12% being female.

The 1999 Monitoring the Future study examined drug use among high-school students. This study found that the use of methamphetamines has been steadily increasing since 1990 in this age group. Almost 5% of high school seniors stated to being methamphetamine users, up from 2.7% in 1990. In high-use methamphetamine areas such as the Midwest, the use of methamphetamine among teenagers is even higher. A survey done in 1998 in Marshall County, Iowa, showed that almost one third of the 1,600 students in the county high school had tried methamphetamine.

MENTAL EFFECTS

When discussing the mental and psychological effects of methamphetamine, it is useful to examine the two main types of abuse patterns of this substance, since each pattern has distinct psychological consequences. The two main abuse patterns of methamphetamine are low-intensity use and binge, or high-intensity use.

Low-intensity users of methamphetamine are typically described as occasional users of the drug, and so are not classified as true methamphetamine addicts. Low-intensity users generally swallow or snort methamphetamine for the extra mental stimulation it provides and are not necessarily using the drug to get high. Low-intensity users include truck drivers, high school or college students, and other people who need to stay alert and be able to concentrate for long periods of time without sleep. When methamphetamine is used in this manner, most people will experience increased mental alertness, focus,

[???] **FACT OR FICTION**

Because they both seem to function as "uppers," some people think that cocaine and methamphetamine are essentially the same drug. While it is true that they both have similar mental and physiological effects, the two drugs do act quite differently. In contrast to cocaine, which is rapidly broken down in the body, methamphetamine tends to accumulate in both the body and brain, thereby leading to longer effects and more potential to cause long-term brain damage. Also, cocaine is derived from a natural substance, the coca plant, while methamphetamine is a totally synthetic chemical.

and concentration, enhanced self-confidence, and greater energy. Most low-intensity users will not experience the euphoria associated with binge or high-intensity users.

Binge users, or high-intensity users, of methamphetamine generally smoke or inject the drug for the express purpose of getting high. Almost immediately after injecting or smoking the drug, the user will experience what is called a "rush," a euphoria that quickly becomes psychologically addictive. During this rush, the user will have feelings that are similar to having a sexual orgasm, along with increased heart rate and blood pressure. This psychological and physiological rush is caused by methamphetamine's effect of causing a release of epinephrine into the body and brain. Epinephrine is one of the body's hormones that is released when someone is very excited or frightened. There is also a release of a chemical in the brain called dopamine, which is naturally released in the brain when a person feels great pleasure. All the feelings a user has during a rush will last anywhere from five to 30 minutes.

After the rush, a binge user of methamphetamine will experience a high lasting four to 16 hours. This high is also known as the "shoulder," during which time a methamphetamine user will feel aggressive, smarter, and can be quite argumentative. After the high, many users will continue to smoke or inject methamphetamine for days on end. As the binge continues, they generally become more argumentative, combative, and mentally hyperactive. A binge episode can last from three to 15 days.

After a long binge, a period known as "tweaking" can set in. Tweaking occurs at the end of the binge when no amount of methamphetamine can bring back the rush or high. The user generally experiences mental symptoms of emptiness, depression, and paranoia; they also often suffer a form of methamphetamine-induced schizophrenia. Users who experience this will have visual or

HISTORY NOTES

During World War II, there were massive amounts of methamphetamines produced by both the Allies and Axis powers. After the war ended, there were huge stockpiles of methamphetamines left in many countries, especially in Japan and throughout northern Europe. In the late 1940s and early 1950s, a huge surge in methamphetamine abuse was noted in Scandinavia and Japan following the dumping of these methamphetamine stocks onto the civilian market. It took these areas many years to get control of this drug epidemic.

auditory hallucinations as well as the feelings of bugs crawling underneath their skin. Often, methamphetamine users will take heroin or drink alcohol during this stage to try to combat the negative mental effects.

An episode known as "crashing" finally occurs when the methamphetamine user falls into a deep exhaustive sleep. Crashing happens when all the body's stores of epinephrine have been used up. A crash can last from one to three days.

PHYSIOLOGICAL EFFECTS

Methamphetamine is a very powerful stimulant that affects the central nervous system (CNS). The CNS is associated with thought and emotions, and movement, along with basic body functions such as heart rate and breathing rate. The brain and spinal cord are the major anatomical components of the CNS. Any substance, like methamphetamine, that can cause major changes in the CNS can most certainly have major and sometimes deadly consequences.

Two neurochemicals that are vitally important for the proper functioning of the CNS are dopamine and serotonin. By alternating the levels of both dopamine and serotonin in the CNS, methamphetamine is able to cause a wide range of physiological effects.

By directly affecting the central nervous system, methamphetamine initially causes a generalized feeling of energy, increased concentration, and lack of appetite. However, the initial feelings of mental enhancement soon give way to anxiety, depression, confusion, paranoia, and hallucinations. Seizures and convulsions are common side effects of methamphetamine use.

Methamphetamines indirectly cause side effects to many other areas of the body through their actions on the CNS. Concerning the heart, methamphetamine use can cause an increased and/or irregular heart rate; heart pains that a user may believe is a heart attack (and may actually be a heart attack); skipped heart beats, or palpitations; high or low blood pressure; and the bursting of blood vessels in the heart called an arterial aneurysm.

Methamphetamine can have damaging effects on the lungs. Its use can cause shortness of breath, wheezing, and asthma. There have been reports of a condition called pneumothorax among methamphetamine users that occurs when the lining of the lung actually rips away from the chest wall, causing a part of the lung to collapse.

Further into the body, methamphetamine has been implicated in damages to the kidney and liver. In the kidney, methamphetamine use has been shown to cause acute kidney failure by constriction of the blood vessels that nourish the kidney. In the liver, methamphetamines have been shown to cause direct liver damage both through the drug itself and through the many contaminants street methamphetamine often contains.

Harmful side effects

Through its action on the dopamine and serotonin neurons in the brain, methamphetamine can cause paranoia, hallucinations, and severe mood disturbances. Methampethamine can also cause stroke through an increase in blood pressure, along with seizures. Other commonly seen side effects include irregular heart rate, damage to small blood vessels in the brain and eyes, and hyperthermia, which is an unregulated increase in the body's temperature.

The effects of methamphetamine on unborn babies in pregnant women can be significant. Methamphetamine has been known to cause spontaneous abortions or severe birth defects. Babies born to mothers who use methamphetamine often have low birth weights, tremors, excessive crying spells, along with behavioral disorders that can last well into late childhood.

Long-term health effects

The most problematic long-term health effect of methamphetamine use is addiction, which can be considered a chronic, hard-to-treat disease characterized by chronic drug-seeking behavior and drug use. Methamphetamine is known to cause long-term changes to the brain, and scientists are just now beginning to understand how damaging these changes can be. Chronically addicted methamphetamine users can exhibit antisocial symptoms such as erratic violent behavior. Other long-term mental and behavioral changes that are seen include confusion, paranoia, auditory and visual hallucinations, and the sensation of insects crawling on the skin that is called "formica-

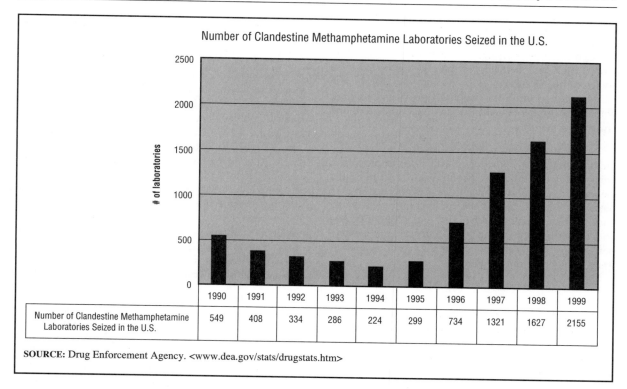

Number of Clandestine Methamphetamine Laboratories Seized in the U.S.

	1990	1991	1992	1993	1994	1995	1996	1997	1998	1999
Number of Clandestine Methamphetamine Laboratories Seized in the U.S.	549	408	334	286	224	299	734	1321	1627	2155

SOURCE: Drug Enforcement Agency. <www.dea.gov/stats/drugstats.htm>

Graph by Argosy.

tion." There can be such extensive damage to the brain from long-term use that it is often difficult to recognize a methamphetamine abuser from a person who has chronic schizophrenia.

Several recent studies have used brain-imaging studies to show the damaging effects of long-term methamphetamine use. In a study of 26 long-term metamphetamine users in California, magnetic resonance spectroscopy showed that the brains of these users had extensive damage as compared to people who were not long-term methamphetamine users. Another study in 2001 showed through the use of positron emission tomography (PET) scanning that the brains of long-term users of methamphetamine had significantly less neurons (brain cells) involved in the manufacture and transport of dopamine as compared to non-methamphetamine users.

In addition to brain damage, long-term methamphetamine users suffer from other health effects. Chronic users of methamphetamine can damage their heart, resulting in inflammation of the heart lining. Long-term methamphetamine users, especially those that inject the drug, are commonly seen with skin ulcers and skin infections. Also, by using needles to inject the drug, chronic methamphetamine abusers are at high risk of developing hepatitis B and C, along with HIV and AIDS.

REACTIONS WITH OTHER DRUGS OR SUBSTANCES

Methamphetamine is often combined with other illegal drugs. A common combination is mixing methamphetamine with heroin, either in an injection or in smoking. This mixture is called a speedball. Methamphetamine users will also mix in cocaine to increase the initial rush. Methamphetamine addicts are often alcoholics.

Methamphetamine also changes the level of some commonly used legal medications. With the high levels of HIV and AIDS that are seen in intravenous drug users, many will be on anti-HIV medication. Methamphetamine increases the blood level of some anti-HIV medications, which could cause serious side effects. Also, many users of methamphetamine suffer from psychiatric problems, including depression. Methamphetamine increases the blood levels of a class of commonly used antidepressants known as tricyclic antidepressants, which, when taken at high levels, can cause respiratory depression and even death.

TREATMENT AND REHABILITATION

Many addiction specialists believe that methamphetamine addiction is one of the hardest, if not the hardest, illegal drug addictions to treat. Methamphetamines affect the brain of addicts in many ways, and actually causes marked brain changes and damage. Because of its powerful effects, methamphetamine is one of the most addictive illegal substances on the streets today. It may take months to years for people to get over long-term withdrawal symptoms such as anxiety, depression, and craving for the drug.

Currently, the most effective form of treatment for methamphetamine addiction appears to be cognitive behavioral interventions in a controlled treatment center. Cognitive behavioral interventions are designed to help modify and change a person's thinking processes, along with their expectations, behaviors, and skills in coping with the various stresses of life. Methamphetamine support groups have also been useful in keeping people off drugs for long periods of time.

There are currently no medications that can be given to methamphetamine addicts to help them quit their habit. The National Institute of Drug Abuse (NIDA) is currently testing several medications and substances in hopes that they will provide some help in treating methamphetamine addiction, including selegiline, which is a medication that increases dopamine levels in the brain and is currently used in treating patients with Parkinson's disease. Another substance is hydergine, which increases blood flow to the brain and is used to help patients with Alzheimer's dementia and those recovering from strokes. Other, more experimental substances include DADLE (D-Ala2,D-Leu5), which is a synthetic brain chemical that has been shown to block and reverse methamphetamine-induced brain damage in mice; glial-derived neuro-trophic factor, which has been shown to decrease methamphetamine's neurotoxic effects in monkeys; and natural and/or synthetic antioxidants, which have been shown to decrease or prevent methamphetamine's neurotoxic effects in mice.

PERSONAL AND SOCIAL CONSEQUENCES

The personal and social consequences of drug abuse are wide-reaching. Consequences of drug abuse affect all ethnic groups and all ages. The impact of drug abuse is a complete societal problem that leaves no person in this country, either directly or indirectly, untouched.

Methamphetamine addiction is quickly reaching epidemic proportions in some areas of the country. The drug lends itself to addiction in many ways. First, it is cheap to manufacture and therefore is inexpensive on the street, especially when compared to other powerful drugs such as cocaine or heroin. Second, smoking or injecting methamphetamine brings on an almost instantaneous high that lasts much longer than an equivalent amount of cocaine. However, because tolerance to methamphetamine occurs quite rapidly, users typically indulge in what is referred to as a "binge and crash" pattern of use, that is, using methamphetamine over and over to try and recreate their original high.

The personal consequences of methamphetamine abuse can be staggering. People addicted to methamphetamine generally have a variety of psychiatric and medical problems. As compared to persons their own age, people who abuse methamphetamine have a significantly higher incidence of anxiety, depression, schizophrenic-like symptoms, paranoia, drastic mood swings, and other serious psychiatric disorders. Long-term users of methamphetamine often display very violent behaviors. Methamphetamine abusers also suffer from multiple medical problems. Due to their intravenous use, methamphetamine addicts have a very high rate of hepatitis B, hepatitis C, and HIV. People who abuse methamphetamines are also at higher risk of high blood pressure and irregular heart rates.

The effects of having a family member who is addicted to methamphetamine can be terrible for the user's spouse and children. Addicts often find that maintaining meaningful employment is almost impossible. Likewise, maintaining stable relationships or marriage and making and keeping friends are nearly impossible tasks for addicts. Most methamphetamine addicts have to steal in order to maintain their habit, so they are at very high risk of being jailed.

The children of methamphetamine addicts also suffer from the their parent's addiction. The risk of danger to them begins even before birth. Methamphetamine use during pregnancy decreases the life-sustaining blood flow to the unborn child, along with having a direct toxic effect on the developing baby's brain. After birth, infants born to mothers who are methamphetamine addicts may show classical withdrawal signs, including uncontrollable trembling, trouble making eye contact, trouble feeding, and sleeping excessively.

These children grow up and show higher levels of aggressive behavior, have greater difficulty adjusting to different social environments, and have a higher rate of difficulties at school when compared to children whose mothers were not methamphetamine users.

Methamphetamine users also pose a danger to the communities in which they reside. Many users of methamphetamine also manufacture the drug, since the precursor chemicals needed are cheap and easily available. However, these chemicals are highly toxic, and thus introduce the risk to the community of toxic gases, fires, and explosions.

Chemical residues and waste generated in the manufacturing of methamphetamine pose a serious danger to the environment. This waste is often poured down the drain, into storm sewers, or into crudely dug pits in the ground. These chemicals can leach into the soil and groundwater and cause contamination for many years.

LEGAL CONSEQUENCES

The federal penalties for methamphetamine use and trafficking are quite severe. The basic, mandatory minimum sentences under federal law are five years in prison for 10 grams of methamphetamine, and 10 years in prison for 100 grams of the drug. State penalties vary considerably. A methamphetamine user in Minnesota caught with 10 grams of the drug would face a $500,000 fine and 25 years in prison. However, the same offender in Virginia would face fines of only $1,000 and six months in prison.

Legal history

Methamphetamine was discovered and first produced in Japan in 1919. It was quickly introduced to the United States and was marketed initially as an over-the-counter remedy for congestion and asthma. In World War II, it was widely produced by the government and used by military personnel in the war effort. After World War II, it became a prescription drug and was used for weight loss and for its stimulating effects. In 1970, methamphetamine and amphetamine came under strict control of the U.S. government through the Comprehensive Drug Abuse Prevention and Control Act.

Federal guidelines, regulations, and penalties

Methamphetamine use is under strict governmental controls and laws. The Comprehensive Drug Abuse Prevention and Control Act of 1970 established five schedules, or lists, of controlled medications and substances, with substances in Schedule I having the highest abuse potential and substances in Schedule V having the lowest abuse potential. Methamphetamines are classified as a Schedule II drug. According to the government, all Schedule II drugs have a high potential for abuse, have the potential to lead to severe mental or physiological dependence, and have currently accepted medical uses.

Due to the destructive nature of methamphetamine on both its users and the community at large, the federal government has continued to play an increasing role in its control. The Comprehensive Methamphetamine Control Act of 1996 increased penalties for the manufacture, distribution, and possession of methamphetamine, as well as the reagents and chemicals needed to make it. The act also required that any products containing pseudoephedrine, a key ingredient in the manufacturing of methamphetamine, must be sold only in blister packs, with the intent of making it harder for methamphetamine makers to purchase large amounts. Stores that sell pseudoephedrine were also required to report any large-volume sales of the chemical.

Two more laws were passed in 1998 to control methamphetamine. While the Speed Trafficking Life in Prison Act increased penalties for the production, distri-bution, and use of methamphetamine, the Drug Free Communities Act offered federal money to communities to help educate citizens on the dangers on methamphetamine use and production.

In 1999, the DEFEAT Methamphetamine Bill authorized $30 million for the Drug Enforcement Administration (DEA) to develop a comprehensive, nationwide plan to target and control methamphetamine. It also added $25 million for methamphetamine prevention efforts, especially in rural and urban areas hard hit by methamphetamine use. This bill also added to the list of chemicals considered precursors to methamphetamine production that could result in criminal penalties. In the same year, the Comprehensive Methamphetamine Abuse Reduction Bill authorized more federal money for methamphetamine treatment and prevention programs, as well as targeting federal resources to high-use methamphetamine areas.

The federal Office of National Drug Trafficking Areas has identified multiple areas in the United States that have particularly high rates of methamphetamine use and manufacturing. These areas are known as High Intensity Drug Trafficking Areas (HIDTA), including Iowa, Kansas, Missouri, Nebraska, and South Dakota. Through the designation of these HIDTA areas, federal law enforcement agencies hope to promote a comprehensive, cooperative strategy with local and state law enforcement agencies to significantly reduce metamphetamine trafficking and use.

See also Amphetamines

RESOURCES

Books

Bray, R., and Mary Ellen Marsden. *Drug Use in Metropolitan America.* Thousand Oaks, CA: Sage Publications, 1997.

Lowinson, J., et al. *Substance Abuse: A Comprehensive Textbook.* Baltimore: Williams & Wilkins, 2001.

McDowell, D., and Henry Spitz. *Substance Abuse: From Principles to Practice.* Philadelphia: Taylor & Francis, 1999.

Pennell, S., et al. *Meth Matters: Report on Methamphetamine Users in Five Western Cities.* Washington, DC: U.S. Department of Justice, 1999.

Smith, D., and Richard Seymour. *Clinician's Guide to Substance Abuse.* New York: McGraw Hill, 2000.

Periodicals

Volkow, N., L. Chang, G. Wang, et al. "Association of Dopamine Transporter Reduction with Psychomotor Impairment in Methamphetamine Abusers." *The American Journal of Psychiatry* 3 (March 2001): 377-382.

Volkow, N., L. Chang, G. Wang, et al. "Higher Cortical and Lower Subcortical Metabolism in Detoxified Methamphetamine Abusers." *The American Journal of Psychiatry* 3 (March 2001): 383-389.

Other

Koch Crime Institute. <http://www.kci.org/meth>.

Narconon. <http://www.stopaddiction.com/meth_ice.html>.

National Institute on Drug Abuse. <http://www.drugabuse.gov>.

Edward R. Rosick, D.O., M.P.H.

METHAQUALONE

OFFICIAL NAMES: Methaqualone
STREET NAMES: Quaaludes, ludes, quads, quay, sopors, 714s, mandrax, mandrakes, mandies, buttons, disco biscuits, love drug
DRUG CLASSIFICATIONS: Schedule I, non-narcotic depressant

OVERVIEW

Methaqualone is an addictive, or habit-forming, synthetic drug that alters brain function. In their search for new medications to fight malaria, a potentially deadly tropical disease spread by mosquitoes, scientists in India first synthesized methaqualone in 1955. The drug was found to be hypnotic and a potent sedative, but it was then thought to be non-addictive.

Pharmaceutical manufacturers in the United Kingdom (UK) began marketing the drug in the 1960s. Despite emerging international medical reports of possible dependence and abuse problems, the U.S. Food and Drug Administration (FDA) also approved methaqualone use by prescription. In 1965 U.S. manufacturers introduced methaqualone to the medical community for the treatment of anxiety and sleep disorders. Although it was available under a number of trade names, the drug would be known by its most popular and notorious brand name, Quaalude.

Methaqualone enjoyed immense popularity as a prescription drug, with over four million prescriptions written in 1973 at the height of its popularity. Its rise as an illicit street drug was fast and furious as Quaaludes permeated popular culture. Their use was widespread on college campuses; many celebrities openly took them; and the media and word of mouth passed along the drug's erroneous reputation as an aphrodisiac (or "love drug"). In response to the growing abuse, the federal government took measures at the end of 1973 to tighten controls on its access.

In the 1970s and early 1980s, however, so-called "stress clinics" started to appear across America, providing an easy source of prescriptions for Quaaludes with just a cursory physical examination. In addition to the abuse of legal prescriptions, an estimated one billion tablets of counterfeit Quaaludes flowed into the United States each year.

The addictive quality and the speed with which tolerance to the drug developed was becoming apparent, and in the 1970s medical literature issued frequent reports of methaqualone abuse, dependence, and withdrawal. Hospital admissions and fatalities related to methaqualone grew exponentially. In 1982, there were a reported 2,764 emergency room visits attributed to Quaalude use.

In the 1980s, the FDA, attempting to curtail its use again, reclassified methaqualone as a Schedule I drug, a highly addictive substance with no current medical necessity in the United States. Its production as a legal medication was halted. The reclassification along with an aggressive campaign by the Drug Enforcement Agency (DEA) against illegal labs and overseas supplies finally slowed the Quaalude flood to a trickle.

Today, methaqualone use has dropped dramatically in the United States, and just a handful of cases are reported annually to the Drug Abuse Warning Network

KEY TERMS

ANTISPASMODIC: A substance or drug that relieves muscle spasms and/or cramps.

ANXIETY DISORDERS: A group of mental disorders or conditions characterized in part by chronic feelings of fear, excessive and obsessive worrying, restlessness, and panic attacks. Anxiety disorders include panic disorder, agoraphobia, obsessive-compulsive disorder, Post-traumatic stress disorder, and others.

APHRODISIAC: A substance or drug that increases sexual desire.

ATAXIA: Loss of control of muscle coordination.

BARBITURATES: Highly habit-forming (addictive) sedative drugs based on barbituric acid. Barbiturates are central nervous system depressants.

HYPNOTIC: A drug that induces sleep by depressing the central nervous system.

NEURONS: Nerve cells found throughout the central nervous system. Neurons release neurotransmitters.

PRECURSORS: A substance or compound from which another substance is synthesized, or made.

RECREATIONAL USE: The casual and infrequent use of a drug or substance, often in social situations, for its pleasurable effects.

RELAPSE: Term used in substance abuse treatment and recovery that refers to an addict's return to substance use and abuse following a period of abstinence or sobriety.

(DAWN) of the Substance Abuse Mental Health Services Administration (SAMHSA). Counterfeit Quaaludes sold on the street often contain sedatives other than methaqualone. However, methaqualone abuse and trafficking in South Africa is widespread.

CHEMICAL/ORGANIC COMPOSITION

The chemical name for methaqualone is 2-methyl-3-O-tolyl-4(3H)-quinazolinone ($C_{16}H_{14}N_2O$). It is a white, crystalline, odorless substance with a bitter taste.

The key precursors, or ingredients, in the manufacture of methaqualone are the chemicals N-acetylanthranilic acid and anthranilic acid. Because methaqualone is produced illegally, the drug is frequently cut, or adulterated, with other substances called fillers, ranging from talcum powder to heroin.

INGESTION METHODS

Before methaqualone's legal production and marketing was stopped worldwide, the drug was manufactured in both tablet and capsule form in various strengths.

Counterfeit versions of the drug are still produced in South Africa, India, and other parts of the world today. The drugs look remarkably similar to the original pharmaceutical tablet versions, including the manufacturer's markings. Methaqualone is also found in illicit capsule and powder forms.

During the 1970s, a popular method of recreational methaqualone use was to take the drug with a glass of wine. The practice was known as "luding out" (in reference to the brand name Quaalude). Taking methaqualone with alcohol, another depressant of the central nervous system (CNS), increased the sedative effect of the drug. It could also prove to be deadly if the potent depressant combination caused respiratory failure. Mandrax, also the brand name for the now-illegal UK version of methaqualone, is made by combining the drug with small amounts of antihistamine. In South Africa, where methaqualone abuse has become a serious public health problem, Mandrax is sometimes mixed marijuana.

THERAPEUTIC USE

Methaqualone was originally prescribed for the treatment of insomnia and anxiety disorders. It was also prescribed as an alleged "stress reducer."

Today, there are no recognized therapeutic uses for methaqualone. Because the drug is so highly physically and psychologically addictive, it has been given a Schedule I status by the United States Drug Enforcement Agency (DEA). Schedule I drugs are substances that have a high potential for abuse, have no current medical necessity in the United States, and are considered unsafe for use even under a physician's supervision. Other Schedule I drugs include heroin, mescaline, and LSD. Methaqualone is a banned substance internationally as well and is not used as a therapeutic prescription drug overseas.

USAGE TRENDS

Methaqualone use and abuse in the United States dropped significantly after its reclassification to an illicit Schedule I drug. Fatalities and injuries related to the drug's use have also declined accordingly. According to the National Narcotics Intelligence Consumers Committee, annual U.S. emergency room visits related to methaqualone fell from 2,764 in 1982 to just 163 in 1988.

Scope and severity

The DAWN survey shows a definite downward trend in the number of methaqualone-related emergency room visits in the United States, with a total of 574 incidents in 1998, 271 in 1999, and 127 in 2000.

Age, ethnic, and gender trends

When methaqualone was legal in the United States, its status as a prescription drug meant its abuse could and cross lines of race, culture, and class status.

Illicit Quaalude use and abuse on college campuses was widespread in the 1970s and rose dramatically between 1978 and 1981. The National Institute of Drug Abuse (NIDA) and the University of Michigan reported that by 1981, 6.5% of college students reported having used methaqualone without a prescription at least once in the previous year. By 1989, five years after the drug's reclassification as a Schedule I substance, only 0.2% of college students reported use of methaqualone within the previous year. Data also shows that in 1981, 10.4% of college students had tried methaqualone at least once in their lifetime compared to 8.7% of young adults (ages 19 to 28) in 1989.

Among American high school students, methaqualone use has dropped to record low levels. According to "Monitoring The Future: National Survey Results on Drug Use, 1975-2000," a U.S. survey of drug use patterns of secondary school students, use of the drug in 2000 was a mere 0.3% compared to 8% in 1981. Even for those adolescents who try Quaaludes, the drug may not have the allure it did in past decades. The "Monitoring the Future" survey reports that 63% of high school seniors who try methaqualone one or more times did not continue use of the drug (in the 12 months prior to the 2000 survey). Rates for methaqualone use were higher for whites than for any other racial or ethnic group among high school seniors.

MENTAL EFFECTS

Methaqualone grew in popularity due to its ability to lower inhibitions and heighten a sense of well-being. However, psychological addiction to methaqualone can occur quickly, even in what was once considered to be a therapeutic dose. When the drug was still available by prescription, pharmaceutical manuals discouraged its use for more than three months due to its addictive qualities. Psychological dependence on and abuse of the drug can lead to physical tolerance and the need to increase dosages. Common features of psychological dependence on methaqualone are memory loss; difficulties with work or school; cognitive impairment or learning problems; and preoccupation with obtaining the drug.

HISTORY NOTES

Pharmaceutical manufacturer William H. Rorer, Inc. introduced methaqualone to the American public as Quaalude in 1965. Rorer chose to exploit the brand recognition of their other top-selling product, Maalox, by incorporating the double a ("aa") into the Quaalude name. According to the *American Heritage Dictionary,* 4th edition, Quaalude is also thought to result from condensing the phrase "quiet interlude" in reference to the drug's sedative effect. Did the marketing strategy work? Quaaludes grew to become the sixth-most-popular prescription sedative before William H. Rorer, Inc. sold the trademark rights to the product and Quaalude name to pharmaceutical manufacturer Lemmon Company in 1978.

PHYSIOLOGICAL EFFECTS

Methaqualone is also classified as a sedative-hypnotic drug. It reaches peak levels in the bloodstream one to two hours after ingestion, and the user can feel its effects four to eight hours after taking the drug. Like alcohol, methaqualone is a CNS depressant. It is called a depressant because it decreases neurotransmitter levels in the brain and central nervous system. Neurotransmitters are CNS chemicals that allow signals to travel between neurons, or brain cells, and regulate thought processes, behavior, and emotion. Due to its depressant action on the central nervous system, methaqualone suppresses coughs and spasms.

Methaqualone also affects involuntary body functions that are controlled by the autonomic nervous system, lowering blood pressure, breathing rate, and pulse and bringing about a state of deep relaxation. Though thought to be an aphrodisiac because it lowers inhibitions, methaqualone, as a CNS depressant, usually impairs sexual performance, inhibiting arousal and climax.

Harmful side effects

Methaqualone abusers rapidly build up a tolerance to the drug, and need increasingly larger doses to achieve the same physical and mental effects. However, the user's body and nervous system do not build up a resistance to the drug at the same rate. For this reason, tolerance can easily lead to unintentional overdose as the central nervous system is overwhelmed and shut down by increased doses of the drug. Coma and death can result. Ingestion of more than 800 mg of methaqualone in an adult and 150 mg in a child is considered toxic. The average lethal oral dose is 8–20 grams (100–200 mg/kg),

 **IN THE NEWS**

In the late 1960s and 1970s, as methaqualone's reputation grew to mythic proportions in the media, America's Quaalude craze became apparent in the popular, and not-so-popular, music of the time. Syd Barrett, founding member and original guitarist and vocalist of Pink Floyd, was asked to leave the band shortly after appearing on stage heavily sedated and sporting a pomade of crushed Mandrax and Brylcream on his head. Fee Waybill of the lesser known The Tubes regularly performed as alter-ego Quay Lude in the band's glam rock opera, "White Punks on Dope." And in the song "Flakes" (1979), Frank Zappa takes a jab at Bob Dylan's alleged frequent use of Mandrax with the lyric, "Want to buy some Mandies, Bob?" Zappa, who was staunchly anti-drug, refers to Quaaludes in one interview as a "way to make people artificially stupid."

Methaqualone overdose also claimed a number of celebrity lives during this era. In 1972, Billy Murcia, drummer for the New York Dolls, overdosed on methaqualone during a concert and subsequently choked to death. In 1975, Anissa Jones, former child star of the television show "Family Affair," died of an overdose of barbiturates and Quaaludes. While under the influence of Quaaludes, comedian Freddie Prinze died of an accidental, self-inflicted gunshot wound to the head. Other methaqualone users who died in the 1970s in drug-related circumstances include Jimi Hendrix, Brian Jones, and Elvis Presley.

and coma can occur after ingestion of 2.4 grams, according to the National Library of Medicine (NLM) Hazardous Substance Database. However, methaqualone can cause coma or death at lower levels if it is taken with another CNS depressant such as alcohol. Because methaqualone is a street drug of varying quality, the rate at which tolerance progresses depends on the strength of the product. In addition, dangerous and even fatal delays in proper treatment can occur when health care personnel do not know what other substances to consider.

Reported side effects of methaqualone include gastrointestinal distress (nausea, vomiting, stomach cramps, diarrhea), headache, chills, sweating, irregular heartbeat, slurred speech, skin rash and itching, seizures, and fatigue. Because methaqualone induces sleep, there is a danger of users vomiting in their sleep and choking to death.

Methaqualone affects muscle movement and proper functioning of nerve sensation. Users experience paresthesia, which is a numb tingling, or "pins and needles" sensation, most commonly in the fingers and face. Individuals who take heavy doses of methaqualone also have a heightened pain threshold. The coordination of brain and body becomes disconnected, and nerve signals are slowed or stopped on their way to the brain's command center. While under the influence of methaqualone, users may hurt themselves without realizing it.

Methaqualone also causes ataxia, or uncontrolled muscle twitching and movement. Users are sometimes referred to as "wallbangers" because they can appear as though they have lost control of their bodies, and may also repeatedly run into things for lack of feeling the painful effects. This side effect, combined with the impaired judgment and lowered inhibitions that accompany with methaqualone use, can result in serious injury, accidents, and death.

Driving or operating heavy machinery is particularly dangerous for anyone under the influence of methaqualone due to ataxia and slowed reflexes. According to a study published in the *Journal of the American Medical Association*, of the 246 methaqualone-related deaths reported between 1971 and 1981, one-third of the deaths caused by trauma were associated with auto accidents.

Long-term health effects

Liver damage can result from long-term abuse of methaqualone or from ingestion of heavily adulterated methaqualone. The liver is responsible for metabolizing, or processing, drugs in the body, and impurities in the drug can cause irreversible damage to the organ.

Peripheral neuropathy, or damage to the nerves of the extremities (hands and feet) is also associated with methaqualone abuse. Typically this disorder, which is characterized by numbness in the hands and feet, reverses itself after abuse has stopped, but it has been reported to last up to five months in some long-term methaqualone abusers.

Methaqualone passes through to breast milk in lactating women. Animal studies have shown the drug to cause birth defects when used during pregnancy.

REACTIONS WITH OTHER DRUGS OR SUBSTANCES

The sedative and hypnotic effects of methaqualone are greatly increased when the drug is mixed with other CNS depressants such as alcohol or marijuana and can result in coma or death.

Because methaqualone is illegal in the United States and around the world, the only available supplies of the drug are illicitly produced. Bootleg methaqualone may contain a number of other substances, from harmless sugar fillers to potentially deadly chemicals. Talcum powder, flour, baking soda, heroin, decongestants, analgesics, diuretics, laxatives, and of other substances are commonly used to cut methaqualone. Depending on the filler used and impurities that can enter the drug in the manufacturing process, an array of damaging side effects can result. These range from mild gastrointestinal problems to a serious condition known as necrotizing cystitis that causes irreversible damage to the bladder.

TREATMENT AND REHABILITATION

When a depressant drug like methaqualone is stopped abruptly, the body responds by overreacting to the substance's absence. Functions such as heart rate that were slowed by the depressant will suddenly accelerate, often erratically. Conversely, withdrawal of a stimulant drug can cause an overall sluggishness that results in depression and extreme fatigue. These changes result in very uncomfortable and potentially life-threatening physical symptoms, called withdrawal syndrome.

The length of time detoxification takes depends on the patient and his or her pattern of methaqualone abuse. Seven to 10 days is an average detox time for someone dependent on methaqualone. Withdrawal symptoms usually begin approximately 12 to 24 hours after individuals have taken their last dose, and peak 24 to 72 hours after. Methaqualone abusers in withdrawal typically suffer from potentially serious symptoms, including nausea, vomiting, tremors, tachycardia (irregular heartbeat), excessive perspiration, anxiety, insomnia, delirium, convulsions, and grand mal seizures. For this reason, methaqualone detoxification should always take place under the supervision of a healthcare professional in a hospital or rehabilitation setting, so withdrawal symptoms can be treated appropriately.

A physician may also prescribe another sedative to ease the withdrawal symptoms during the initial detoxification period. Antidepressants are sometimes prescribed for patients with anxiety and sleep disorders.

In addition to providing a controlled environment for detoxification, inpatient treatment is helpful in cases where there is a risk that patients might harm themselves or others or if there is another physical or mental illness that requires a doctor's observation and care.

Outpatient, or ambulatory, treatment is another option for substance abusers. Patients in outpatient substance abuse treatment spend their days, or a portion of their days, in a rehab facility while returning home at night.

Once detoxification is complete, the drug abuser can start the rehabilitation and long-term recovery process with a clear head. Research shows that detoxification alone is not an effective treatment, and addicts who leave rehab immediately after detox with no further counseling or interventions soon abuse methaqualone or another mind-altering substance again.

An effective drug rehabilitation program removes the drug of choice from the abuser's body and surroundings. It also focuses on changing patterns of the abuser's behavior and dealing with the underlying emotional issues surrounding his or her drug use. Drug education on the long-term effects of substance abuse is also typically part of a rehab program.

Recovery refers to the life-long process of avoiding substance use and the mental and physical rehabilitation of the damage done during active substance abuse. An individual in recovery must avoid not just methaqualone or another drug of choice, but any mind- and mood-altering drug, including alcohol. Substance cravings can be strong, and may last indefinitely. Recovering addicts are always in danger of slipping back into substance use, and relapse can occur with a single dose or drink. Triggers, or common causes, for relapse include major life changes such as unemployment or career change, relationship and financial problems, and family stresses. Yet more subtle circumstances—seeing people or visiting places an addict associates with the drug use—can also prompt a relapse.

Therapy and individual or group counseling are key parts of rehabilitation as well. There are a number of different therapy approaches in substance abuse treatment, and often more than one therapeutic approach is used during the patient's stay in drug rehabilitation.

Individual psychotherapy

One-on-one counseling explores the emotional issues underlying a patient's drug dependence and abuse. Individual psychotherapy is particularly helpful when there is also some type of mental disorder, such as depression or an anxiety disorder, along with the drug abuse.

Behavioral therapy

Behavioral therapy focuses on replacing unhealthy behaviors with healthier ones. It uses tools such as rewards (positive reinforcement for healthy behavior) and rehearsal (practicing the new behavior) to achieve a drug-free life.

Cognitive-behavioral therapy

Like behavioral therapy, cognitive-behavioral therapy (CBT) also tries teaching new behavioral patterns. However, the primary difference is CBT assumes that thinking is behind behavior and emotions. Therefore,

CBT also focuses on—and tries to change—the thoughts that led to the drug abuse.

Family therapy

Family members often develop habits and ways of coping (called "enabling") that unintentionally help the addict continue their substance abuse. Group counseling sessions with a licensed counselor or therapist can help family members build healthy relationships and relearn old behaviors. This is particularly important for adolescents in drug treatment, who should be able to rely on the support of family.

Group therapy

Group therapy offers recovering drug abusers a safe and comfortable place to work out problems with peers and a group leader (typically a therapist or counselor). It also provides drug abusers insight into their thoughts and behaviors through the eyes and experiences of others. Substance abusers who have difficulty building healthy relationships can benefit from the social interactions in group therapy. Offering suggestions and emotional support to other members of the group can help improve their self-esteem and social skills.

Self-help and 12-step groups

Self-help organizations offer recovering drug abusers and addicts important support groups to replace their former drug-using social circle. They also help create an important sense of identity and belonging to a new, recovery-focused group.

Twelve-step groups, one of the most popular types of self-help organizations, have been active in the United States since the founding of Alcoholics Anonymous (AA) in 1935. Narcotics Anonymous (NA), a group that serves recovering drug addicts, was founded in 1953. Like AA and other 12-step programs, NA is based on the spiritual philosophy that turning one's will and life over to "a higher power" (i.e., God, another spiritual entity, or the group itself) for guidance and self-evaluation is the key to lasting recovery.

The accessibility of self-help groups is one of their most attractive features. No dues or fees are required for AA and NA, so they are a good option for the uninsured and underinsured. Meetings are held in public places like local hospitals, healthcare centers, churches, and other community organizations, and frequent and regular attendance is encouraged.

In addition, twelve-step groups work to empower members and promote self-esteem and self-reliance. NA meetings are not run by a counselor or therapist, but by the group or a member of the group. And the organization encourages sponsorship (mentoring another member), speaking at meetings, and other positive peer-to-peer interactions that can help reinforce healthy social behaviors. Today, the internet and on-line support communities have added a further degree of accessibility to those who live in rural or remote areas.

PERSONAL AND SOCIAL CONSEQUENCES

As an illegal, controlled substance, abuse of methaqualone can have serious social consequences for the user. Convictions carry heavy fines and possible jail time. Depending on the state, a conviction may also result in the suspension of the user's drivers license, and his or her constitutional right to vote may be revoked.

Criminal drug charges may have negative consequences for employment, career advancement, and educational opportunities as well. Amendments made to the Higher Education Act in 1998 require that anyone convicted of a drug offense be deemed ineligible for federal student loans from upwards of one year or even indefinitely. An individual convicted of a drug offense may also be denied access to state aid and employment based on his or her criminal history.

As with any highly addictive drug, methaqualone abusers become preoccupied with when and where they will be able to get their next dose. Interpersonal relationships with family and friends frequently deteriorate as drug use dominates the addict's life. Personal finances may also suffer as the drug user funnels more money towards his or her habit or becomes unemployed due to poor job performance resulting from drug impairment.

Substance abuse in general is a far-reaching societal problem, impacting personal relationships and health as well as crime, domestic violence, sexual assault, dropout rates, unemployment, and homelessness. It is also a factor in public health problems such as unwanted pregnancy, HIV/AIDS transmission, and the spread of sexually transmitted diseases (STDs).

Drug abuse takes a tremendous national financial toll as well. The Office of National Drug Control Policy estimates that illegal drugs will account for an economic loss of over $160 billion from the U.S. economy for the year 2000. This figure represents an increase of 5.8% annually between 1998 and 2000, and includes $14.8 billion in healthcare costs and $110.4 billion in lost productivity from drug-related illness, incarceration, and death.

LEGAL CONSEQUENCES

Legal history

When methaqualone first entered the U.S. market in the mid-sixties, it was classified as a Schedule V drug by the U.S. Drug Enforcement Agency (DEA). Schedule V drugs are considered the least dangerous and addictive of prescription medications and require only a doctor's prescription for access.

As the abuse of methaqualone increased, the DEA took action to limit access, changing the drug to a Schedule II substance in 1973. Schedule II drugs are those that are potentially dangerous with a high risk of psychological and physical addiction, but still can be medically beneficial if administered under a physician's care. They require a doctor's written prescription and cannot be refilled without additional prescriptions. Schedule II drugs also have stringent legal standards for manufacturer-to-pharmacy distribution, storage, and record-keeping.

Despite the reclassification of methaqualone to Schedule II, the use and abuse of the drug soared throughout the '70s and early '80s. Legitimate use for the drug rapidly decreased with the new classification. By 1982, Lemmon Company, the only remaining U.S. manufacturer of the drug, reported that prescriptions written for Quaaludes had dropped from a high of four million in 1973 to less than 300,000, a decline of over 90%.

In 1983, Congress began hearing testimony on a proposal to reclassify methaqualone to a Schedule I controlled substance. Schedule I drugs are those that are highly addictive and dangerous and have no recognized medical value. But because the drug was still manufactured and prescribed in the United States, which seemed to meet the Schedule II criteria of providing some therapeutic value, the FDA and DEA were reluctant to move the drug to Schedule I.

In the meantime, parts of the country such as Miami and Atlanta experienced an explosion of methaqualone abuse and began legislating against the drug on a state level. By 1984, nine states with growing methaqualone problems including Florida, Georgia, and Illinois had banned the sale of the drug.

Citing increasing political pressures and negative publicity surrounding Quaaludes, the Lemmon Company halted production and distribution of the drug as of January 31, 1984. With the final remaining obstacle to reclassification removed, Congress changed methaqualone to a Schedule I controlled substance in August of 1984, effectively outlawing the drug in the United States.

Statistically, however, legal sources of methaqualone had only been a fraction of the total Quaalude supply in the United States. In 2001, the DEA estimated the illicit, or counterfeit, production of the drug at 150 metric tons annually in the early 1980s, over 20 times the amount of legitimate methaqualone produced worldwide.

In the early 1980s, Colombia was a flourishing center of methaqualone counterfeiting. Operation Swordfish, a DEA investigation targeting organized drug crime in Miami, resulted in the seizure of 250,000 methaqualone pills in addition to large quantities of marijua-

na, cocaine, and cash and put a major dent into Miami's flourishing drug trade. After methaqualone was moved to Schedule I, the DEA, the Department of State, and U.S. Customs worked with agencies in foreign countries producing the drug to control the export of methaqualone and its precursor chemicals.

Today, South Africa is both the world's largest producer and consumer of methqualone in the form of counterfeit Mandrax. The country also serves as a drug gateway between southern Asia and the United States. A report by the United Nations Office for Drug Control and Crime Prevention (ODCCP) points out that part of the Mandrax problem is that vast quantities of the legal chemicals used to produce methaqualone are produced in southern Asia and are not adequately regulated. Illegal methaqualone production is also starting to spread to surrounding areas of Africa, including Kenya, Mozambique, Swaziland, Tanzania, and Zambia.

In 1999 and 2000, South Africa signed agreements with the United States that provided anti-drug crime assistance. The South African Narcotics Bureau (SANAB) has worked extensively with the United States DEA and the United Nations International Drug Control Program (UNDCP) to stop narcotics production and trafficking in the region. The relationship has meant an increase in methaqualone-related arrests. In November and December of 2001, 5.8 tons of methaqualone and Mandrax powder were seized from drug manufacturing operations in Johannesburg and Port Elizabeth. The December raid alone, which represented 3.3 tons, had a street value of 550 million rand ($49.05 million USD) and was the largest seizure to date by South African authorities. In January 2002, South African police confiscated 1.5 million Mandrax tablets worth an estimated 1.5 million rand ($133,779.00 USD).

Federal guidelines, regulations, and penalties

A conviction of methaqualone possession in the United States is a federal offense that can carry serious consequences. If the amount of methaqualone is small, it is classified by DEA as a "personal use amount" under the Controlled Substances Act of 1988. Anyone charged with his or her first offense of possessing a personal use amount faces a civil fine of up to $10,000. The fine amount is based on the offender's income and assets and the circumstances surrounding the case. With first offenses, jail time is typically not involved, and the proceedings are civil rather than criminal. This means that if the offender pays the fine, stays out of trouble for a three-year period, and passes a drug test, the case is dismissed and no criminal or civil record is made.

Anyone convicted of methaqualone trafficking (transporting or dealing the drug) faces significantly harsher penalties. Federal guidelines mandate that a first-time trafficking offender face up to 20 years in prison and a $1 million fine. If death or serious injury is involved with the trafficking charge, the sentence must be at least 20 years with a maximum sentence of life in prison.

Methaqualone was designated a Class B drug in the United Kingdom under the Misuse of Drugs Act of 1971. As such, possession carries a penalty of three months to five years imprisonment, and trafficking carries a sentence of six months to 14 years. A fine may also be imposed.

See also Rohypnol

RESOURCES

Books

Johnston, Lloyd D., et al. *Monitoring the Future: National Survey Results on Drug Use, 1975-2000.* Vols. I and II. Bethesda, MD: National Institute on Drug Abuse, 2001.

Ziemer, Maryann. *Quaaludes.* Berkeley Heights, NJ: Enslow Publishers, 1997.

Other

South Africa Health Info. <http://www.sahealthinfo.org/admodule/cannabis.htm>. April 17, 2002 (July 8, 2002.]

U.S. Department of Justice. Drug Enforcement Agency. February 2002 (April 1, 2002). <http://www.usdoj.gov/dea/concern/abuse/contents.htm>.

Organizations

National Institute on Drug Abuse (NIDA), National Institutes of Health, 6001 Executive Boulevard, Room 5213, Bethesda, MD, USA, 20892-9561, (301) 443-1124, (888) 644-6432, Information@lists.nida.nih.gov, <http://www.nida.nih.gov/>.

Paula Anne Ford-Martin

METHYLPHENIDATE

Methylphenidate (MPH), one of the most commonly prescribed psychoactive drugs in the United States, is the drug of choice for the treatment of attention deficit hyperactivity disorder (ADHD) in children, adolescents, and adults. It is also a drug of choice for thieves: MPH is on the U.S. Department of Justice's Drug Enforcement Administration's (DEA) list of the top 10 prescription drugs most often stolen.

According to *The Christian Science Monitor*, legal use of MPH in the 1990s increased by about 700% between 1990 and 2000. However, as the legal usage of MPH increased, so did its abuse. That abuse is well documented among high school and college students who use it to overcome fatigue and to enhance memory, without realizing the drug's dangers.

Children with ADHD are inattentive, impulsive, and hyperactive. The areas of their brains that control attention and restraint do not function properly. Stimulant drugs, specifically amphetamines, have been used in the United States to treat children with inattention and hyperactivity disorders since the 1930s. MPH was also discovered to have a calming effect on hyperactive children and a "focusing" effect on those with attention deficit disorder (ADD). However, it was not until the 1960s that the U.S. Food and Drug Administration (FDA) approved methylphenidate for the treatment of ADHD. At the turn of the twenty-first century, approximately 90% of all methylphenidate was prescribed for ADHD children. Most of the rest was prescribed to treat adults with a sleeping sickness known as narcolepsy.

OFFICIAL NAMES: Methylphenidate, Ritalin, Methylin, Metadate, Concerta
STREET NAMES: Vitamin R, West Coast
DRUG CLASSIFICATIONS: Schedule II, stimulant

Estimates suggest that 6–7% of all American school-age children were being prescribed MPH for behavior problems in 2002. Although the exact amount of MPH abuse is unknown, experts agree its prevalence is low compared to cocaine abuse, but warn that the number of new cases of methylphenidate abuse is growing. In 2001, Terrace Woodworth, DEA deputy director, told the U.S. Congress that the problem of MPH abuse is primarily a U.S. problem. The United States is the primary consumer of methylphenidate, producing and consuming about 85% of the entire world's supply.

Unlike other amphetamine stimulants, MPH has not been clandestinely manufactured in homemade laboratories. According to the DEA, legally manufactured MPH has been diverted for illegal, non-prescription use. Police authorities report rising rates of illegal sales, prescription forgery, scams involving doctor shopping, and outright thefts of the drug. In a one-year period from 1996 to 1997, the DEA reports that 700,000 pills were stolen.

Methylphenidate, a derivative of piperidine, a synthetic chemical that is used in the manufacture of rubber,

KEY TERMS

ATTENTION DEFICIT HYPERACTIVITY DISORDER (ADHD): A mental disorder characterized by persistent impulsive behavior, difficulty concentrating, and hyperactivity that causes lowered social, academic, or occupational functioning.

DRUG ABUSE RESISTANCE EDUCATION (D.A.R.E.): A national substance abuse education and prevention program.

NARCOLEPSY: A rare, chronic sleep disorder characterized by constant daytime fatigue and sudden attacks of sleep.

NEUROTRANSMITTER: Chemical in the brain that transmits messages between neurons, or nerve cells.

SYNAPSE: The gap between communicating nerve cells.

is structurally similar to amphetamine and cocaine. These three drugs are all central nervous system stimulants that act on a chemical within the human body known as dopamine, one of the substances within the human body that controls feelings of pleasure.

Unlike cocaine and amphetamine, however, MPH does not cause feelings of pleasure in the brains of individuals with ADHD. However, when healthy people unaffected by ADHD take methylphenidate illicitly, they get, at least initially, a sharp signal reception that the brain interprets as pleasure. Unfortunately, people without ADHD soon develop a tolerance to the drug and need increasing amounts of the drug to achieve the same effect, often leading to methylphenidate abuse.

INGESTION METHODS

MPH is most often taken in pill form. It is available in prescribed quantities of 5-, 10-, and 20-mg tablets. A sustained or delayed release 20-mg tablet is also available. In 2001, the FDA approved Concerta, a longer acting MPH tablet that is taken once a day. Besides its long lasting action, Concerta has another benefit: Abusers sometimes grind MPH tablets into a powder and snort it up their noses, but Concerta is formulated so that it cannot be ground into a powder. According to the DEA, methylphenidate abusers also dissolve the immediate-release MPH tablets in water and then inject the mixture.

THERAPEUTIC USE

Besides attention deficit hyperactivity disorder (ADHD), methylphenidate is used to treat narcolepsy, a

sleeping disorder. Occasionally, MPH has also been used to treat behavioral symptoms that result from traumatic brain injury (TBI), stroke, depression, and the pain experienced by people with cancer. Combined with pain relievers, MPH tends to produce significant reductions in pain intensity and sedation in cancer patients.

Individuals with narcolepsy suffer sudden onsets of deep sleep. Regular use of MPH on a twice-a-day dosage schedule (or a once-a-day schedule if the newer sustained release forms of MPH are used) allows those individuals to live relatively normal lives.

Individuals with TBI, which usually is caused by a blow to the head, a fall, or a car accident, often exhibit ADHD-like symptoms. MPH is sometimes used to treat those symptoms. Before the development of modern antidepressants, MPH was sometimes used for the treatment of depression. Any benefits seen in TBI treatment appear to be related to an improvement in symptoms of depression.

However, by far the largest group of users of methylphenidate are people who have ADHD. Children with ADHD often exhibit symptoms such as inattention, distractibility, impulsiveness, and hyperactivity. These symptoms interfere with the patient's ability to learn. MPH is used to modify brain chemistry and allows the individuals to better focus on tasks such as homework.

One unpredictable benefit of MPH treatment, according to a 1999 research paper, is that children with ADHD who receive MPH treatment may be less likely to develop substance abuse disorders.

USAGE TRENDS

While the prevalence of MPH abuse is low, at least compared to other forms of drug abuse, officials worry that the rate of MPH abuse is increasing, especially among high school and college students.

Scope and severity

In 1999, methylphenidate was the most widely dispensed stimulant medication used for treating ADHD. More of it was used than amphetamine, the next most frequently used stimulant that is used to treat ADHD.

Yearly, an estimated four to six million children in the United States take MPH on a daily basis as a treatment for ADHD. In comparison, only about 25,000 school-age youths were on the medication in England and Wales during 2000. Definitive statistics are not available for the drug's illegal use, and so the exact extent to which it is being abused in any country is unknown. However, it is known that abuse rates increase along with the number of legal prescriptions written. In a study of MPH abusers over a four-year period of 1992–1996, researchers found a significant

???? FACT OR FICTION

Do you have ADHD? U.S. medical doctors use a publication published by the American Psychiatric Association to guide them in their diagnosis of attention deficit and hyperactivity disorder (ADHD). That publication is the Diagnostic and Statistical Manual of Mental Disorders (DSM). To be diagnosed as ADHD, a person would have to have either six or more symptoms of inattention or six or more symptoms of hyperactivity-impulsivity "for at least six months to a degree that is maladaptive" and "inconsistent to the person's developmental level."

The symptoms of inattention include:

• Failure to give close attention to details or careless mistakes in schoolwork, work, or other activities.

• Difficulty maintaining attention in work tasks or play.

• Frequent incidents of failure to listen when directly spoken to.

• Frequent failure to follow through on instructions and tasks ranging from schoolwork to chores or workplace duties.

• Frequent difficulty in organizing tasks and activities.

• Avoiding tasks that require sustained mental effort.

• Frequent loss of objects such as tools, pencils, or books necessary for task or activity completion.

• Easily distracted by outside stimuli, and often forgetful in daily activities.

The symptoms of hyperactivity-impulsivity include:

• Fidgeting with hands or feet or squirming in one's seat.

• Frequently leaving one's seat in a classroom or in other situations in which remaining seated is expected.

• Running or climbing in inappropriate situations.

• Frequently having difficulty playing or engaging in leisure activities quietly.

• Often on the go or frequently acts as if driven.

• Talking excessively.

• Frequently blurting out answers before questions have been completed, difficulty awaiting one's turn, and often interrupting or intruding on others by butting into conversations or games.

---

increase in methylphenidate misuse, especially in white adolescents.

According to a 2001 published survey of cases reported to poison control centers, there was a sevenfold increase in the number of cases in which MPH was involved during the five-year period that ended in 1999. However, the total number of cases making up the sevenfold increase totaled only 530.

In 1990, there were 271 emergency room mentions for MPH in reports to the Drug Abuse Warning Network (DAWN). In 1999, that figure had grown to 1,478 mentions, but the good news is that the 1999 figure represented a slight decrease from 1998's all-time high of 1,728 mentions. To put those figures into context, in 1998 there were 168,763 cocaine-related visits to hospital emergency rooms.

Age, ethnic, and gender trends

According to the Woodworth congressional testimony, "Boys are four times more likely to receive a diagnosis of ADHD and be prescribed stimulant medication." Critics are also disturbed about a trend of prescribing the drug to ever-younger children. For instance, in 1998 a national auditing firm estimated that 4,000 MPH pre-

scriptions were written for children two years of age or less. Some experts, disturbed by this disquieting statistic, point out that MPH has not been approved for use in children under six years of age because safety and effectiveness in that age range has not been established.

MENTAL EFFECTS

Methylphenidate is considered a mild central nervous system stimulant that affects the brain and nerves, relieving fatigue, and inducing clearer thoughts for relatively short periods. According to the DEA, possible effects experienced by those who do not have ADHD or narcolepsy include increased alertness, excitation, and euphoria. Increased energy and increased mental clarity may be experienced for a short period.

PHYSIOLOGICAL EFFECTS

Physiological effects include increased pulse rate and blood pressure, which contribute to the feelings of increased energy and stamina.

Harmful side effects

Common harmful side effects include insomnia, nervousness, and loss of appetite. Other adverse reactions include skin rash, fever, anorexia, nausea, dizziness, headache, abdominal pain, irregular heartbeat and breathing, and generalized anxiety. The irregular breathing may come from an allergic reaction to the drug. The allergic reaction can also cause swelling of the lips, tongue, face, or throat.

Individuals who ingest methylphenidate by dissolving the tablets in water and injecting the mixture risk complications due to the insoluble fillers used in the tablets. When injected, these materials block small blood vessels and can cause serious damage to the lungs and retina of the eye.

Snorting the drug can also be dangerous. The delicate tissues that line the nasal cavities and air passages can be damaged by direct contact with MPH because the tablets contain hydrocholoride salt of methylphenidate, which yields dilute hydrochloric acid when it comes into contact with moisture within the nose. While this is not a problem in the stomach (because hydrochloric acid is one of the stomach acids used to digest foods), the acid can burn the delicate epithelial nasal tissues. This can result in open sores, nose bleeds, and with chronic use can lead to deterioration of the nasal cartilage.

"Shooting up," street parlance for dissolving the drug in water and using a syringe to inject it, can cause harmful side effects. Not only can dust, dirt, and other contaminants fall into the liquid mixture, but bacteria, talc, lint, and other particles are also injected with the drug. The inert ingredients that manufacturers include to increase the bulk of the tablets can create serious health problems when injected directly into veins or body tissues. Complications from injections include overdose, blood clots, infections such as blood poisoning, abscesses, hepatitis, AIDS from sharing needles, scars, and circulatory and pulmonary problems. The effects of overdose include agitation, increased body temperature, hallucinations, paranoia, convulsions, and possibly even death.

The FDA classifies methylphenidate as being in pregnancy category C, which means it is not known whether it would harm an unborn baby. Medical authorities advise pregnant women not to take MPH without consulting a doctor.

Other side effects of MPH include allergic reactions, extensive bruising, and abnormally low red and white blood cells counts. Individuals who abuse the drug suffer from loss of appetite so severe that they develop anorexia. They can also suffer abdominal pain, extreme weight loss, and skin rashes.

Long-term health effects

Chronic abuse of MPH can lead to marked tolerance and psychological dependence. According to the DEA, chronic MPH intoxication is identical to the paranoid psychosis of amphetamine intoxication. Studies indicate that 5–15% of the amphetamine users who become psychotic fail to make a complete recovery.

REACTIONS WITH OTHER DRUGS OR SUBSTANCES

Because of the dangerous adverse reactions (including the risk of death), individuals should not take methylphenidate if they have taken a class of drugs known as monamine oxidase (MAO) inhibitors within 14 days. Most MAO inhibitors are antidepressants, but some anti-tuberculosis drugs such as Ethambutol also have MAO effects. Since drug users are prone to many infectious diseases, it is not unheard of for drug abusers to come down with tuberculosis (TB).

TREATMENT AND REHABILITATION

Withdrawal from methylphenidate abuse can be both difficult and dangerous. Medical reference books warn that MPH withdrawal should be undertaken with careful supervision by slowly reducing dosages over time.

Individuals who go through MPH withdrawal experience intense cravings for the drug. Other expected unpleasant withdrawal side effects include agitation, anxiety, decreased energy, fatigue, increased appetite, lethargy, increased need for sleep, and vivid or unpleasant dreams. During withdrawal, individuals may also experience abdominal pain, fever, infection, loss of appetite, diarrhea, shortness of breath, nausea, vomiting, dizziness, emotional upset, insomnia, nervousness, and weight loss. MPH withdrawal can also cause depression and suicidal feelings. Psychosis and paranoia, though rare, can also be precipitated.

A review of the medical literature reveals no specific treatments or rehabilitation regimes for MPH withdrawal. However, drug rehabilitation organizations can help individuals go through MPH withdrawal.

PERSONAL AND SOCIAL CONSEQUENCES

Like its chemical cousins cocaine and amphetamine, MPH abuse can lead to tolerance and psychic dependence. Tolerance develops when the drug is used chronically and higher and higher dosages are needed to get the same effects. Frequent episodes of binge use can be followed by severe depression and an overpowering

IN THE NEWS

The number of children ages two to four years of age who are being prescribed stimulants such as Ritalin, antidepressants, and other psychiatric drugs soared by 50% from 1991 to 1995, according to a study of 200,000 preschoolers that appeared in the February 23, 2000, *Journal of the American Medical Association* (*JAMA*).

The authors of the report, Julie Magno Zito, an assistant professor of pharmacy and medicine at the University of Maryland, and her colleagues, studied the use of psychotropic medications in very young children enrolled in two state Medicaid program and a managed-care organization. The researchers examined data for three psychotropic medication classes: stimulants (methylphenidate, i.e., Ritalin), antidepressants, and neuroleptics (anti-epilepsy drugs). The researchers found that from 1 to 1.5% of all children ages two to four enrolled in those programs were receiving one or the other of those antipsychotic medications. Overwhelmingly, methylphenidate was the leading treatment.

Experts are troubled by the findings because the effects of such drugs on such young and growing children are still unknown. Dr. Joseph T. Coyle of Harvard Medical School's psychiatry department, in an accompanying *JAMA* editorial, pointed out that the brains of chil-

dren that young are still developing. "Early childhood is a time of tremendous change in the human brain," Coyle said.

Although the study did not examine reasons for the increased use of medications on the children, Zito speculated, in an interview with *Society* magazine (July 2000), that parents of the children may feel pressured "to have their children conform in their behavior."

In a commentary in the medical journal *Contemporary Pediatrics* (May 2000), Dr. Michael G. Burke, chairman of the department of pediatrics at St. Agnes Hospital, Baltimore, asked, "What is a three-year-old learning in preschool that demands enough attention to justify treatment for ADHD? Before playing hard ball with Ritalin, we can almost always hold off until the child enters big-league first and second grade."

In his *JAMA* editorial, Coyle offered another reason for the increase in prescription drug use in that age group. He explained that reduced financing for state Medicaid programs have caused those programs to limit what they pay for the evaluation of behavioral disorders in children.

"As a consequence, it appears that behaviorally disturbed children are now increasingly subjected to quick and inexpensive pharmacologic fixes" as opposed to "...(several combinations of) therapy associated with optimal outcomes," he continued. "These disturbing prescription practices suggest a growing crisis in mental health services to children..."

---

desire to continue using the drug despite the onset of serious negative medical and social consequences, including psychotic episodes, paranoid delusions, hallucinations, hospitalization, or incarceration.

LEGAL CONSEQUENCES

In the United States, the legal consequence of possession, illegal sale, or even giving away of MPH drugs can be severe under terms of the Controlled Substance Act (CSA), which is part of the Comprehensive Drug Abuse Prevention and Control Act of 1970, the legal foundation of the federal government's fight against the abuse of drugs and other substances. Because of the abuse potential of MPH, the DEA has placed stringent Schedule II controls and licensing requirements on the manufacture, distribution, and prescription of the substance. Breaking those rules can result in fines and imprisonment.

Under Section 844 of the CSA, simple possession of a controlled substance (including methylphenidate)

without a doctor's prescription can result in imprisonment for one year for a first offense and a fine of $1,000 or both. A second offense can result in imprisonment for up to two years and a fine of $2,500. A third offense can result in up to three years of prison time and a fine of $5,000.

Distribution, which includes selling or even giving any mixture or substance containing a detectable amount of methylphenidate is illegal under CSA Section 841. For a first offense, it is punishable by a prison term of not more than 20 years and fines up to $1 million for an individual or $5 million if not an individual. If death or serious bodily injury results, imprisonment terms not less than 20 years or more than life. A second offense is punishable by a prison term of not more than 30 years, and a fine of up to $2 million for an individual or up to $10 million if not an individual. If death or serious injury results, life imprisonment is the punishment. A person convicted of selling MPH to someone younger than 21 years of age is subject to "twice the maximum punishment authorized."

Legal history

The FDA approved Ritalin, the original brand name of methylphenidate, in 1961 as a Schedule II drug. When the U.S. Congress passed the CSA in 1970, MPH, as a controlled Schedule II substance, came under the regulation of that law.

In 2001, plaintiffs representing children treated with Ritalin filed a federal lawsuit against Novartis Pharmaceuticals Corp. (the manufacturers of Ritalin), the American Psychiatric Association (APA), and the Children and Adults with Attention Deficit Hyperactivity Disorder organization (CHADD). The lawsuit charged that the trio of organizations had conspired to increase the sales of MPH by broadening the definition of ADHD in the APA's Diagnostic and Statistical Manual of Mental Disorders (DSM). The plaintiffs also criticized CHADD for accepting grant money from Novartis.

However, senior U.S. District Judge Rudi Brewster ruled that the plaintiffs did not have enough evidence to support their claims. He gave them additional time to produce new evidence, but when they failed to do so he ultimately dismissed the case with prejudice, meaning the plaintiffs cannot re-file it.

In 2002, several states, including Connecticut and Minnesota, passed laws that ban teachers from recommending psychotropic drugs, especially Ritalin, to parents. The legislators were concerned that educators were pressuring parents to put their children on MPH so that it would be easier for teachers to deal with ADHD kids in classrooms. Legislators believe it should be up to parents and their doctors to decide whether their children should be put on the drug.

Federal guidelines, regulations, and penalties

Since methylphenidate is a Schedule II controlled substance, it is tightly regulated from manufacture to delivery to the doctor or pharmacy. Schedule II drugs require strict manufacturing quotas, careful inventory controls that require special order forms, and separate record-keeping requirements. Prescriptions may not be refilled—a new prescription is required for every new supply. Unlike less stringently regulated drugs, the methylphenidate prescriptions cannot be phoned in to the pharmacy; the prescriptions must be written. Some states such as California and Indiana require special numbered and triplicate prescription forms for tracking purposes. Breaking those regulations can result in jail time of up to one year and a fine of $25,000, according to CSA Section 842: Prohibited Acts B.

See also Amphetamines

RESOURCES

Books

Breggin, P. R. *Talking Back to Ritalin: What Doctors Aren't Telling You About Stimulants for Children*. Monroe, ME: Common Courage Press, 1998.

DeGrandpre, R. *Ritalin Nation: Rapid Fire Culture and the Transformation of Human Consciousness*. New York: W.W. Norton & Company, 1999.

Diller, L. H. *Running on Ritalin: A Physician Reflects on Children, Society and Performance in a Pill*. New York: Bantam Books, 1998.

Hallowell, E. M., and Ratey, J. J. *Driven to Distraction: Recognizing and Coping with Attention Deficit Disorder from Childhood to Adulthood*. New York: Pantheon Books, 1994.

Periodicals

"Abusing Ritalin: Dangers of Prescription Drug Abuse." *Scholastic Choices* v. 17 (September 2001).

"Frequently Asked Question About Ritalin." *Ritalin on College Campuses*. <http://pubweb.acns.nwu.edu/~cam717/faq.html>.

Marks, A. "Schoolyard Hustlers' New Drug: Ritalin." *The Christian Science Monitor's Electronic Edition* (October 31, 2000): pp. 4.

"Ritalin (Methylphenidate)." *Alberta Alcohol and Drug Abuse Commission (AADAC)*. <http://corp.aadac.com/drugs/factsheets/Ritalin.asp>.

Other

Ciampa, L. *Ritalin Abuse Scoring High on College Illegal Drug Circuit*. CNN.Com (January 8, 2001). <http://www.cnn.com/2001HEALTH/children/01/08/college.ritalin/>.

Organizations

Attention Deficit Information Network, 475 Hillside Ave., Needham, MA, USA, 02194, (617) 455-9895.

Children and Adults with Attention Deficit Disorders, 499 N.W. 70th Ave., Suite 101, Planation, FL, USA, 33317, (800) 233-4050, <http://www.chadd.org>.

Health Services Administration (SAMHSA), U.S. Dept. of Health and Human Services, 5600 Fishers Lane, Rockville, MD, USA, 20857, (301) 443-0001, (301) 443-1563, 1-800-622-Help, mail@add.org, <http://www.samhsa.gov/centers/cmhs/cmhs.html>.

National Attention Deficit Disorder Association, 1788 Second Street, Suite 200, Highland Park, IL, USA, 60035, (847) 432-3223, (847) 432-5874, mail@add.org, <http://www.add.org>.

University of Kentucky Center for Prevention Research, 1151 Red Mile Rd. Ste. 1-A, Lexington, KY, USA, 40507, (606) 257-5588, <http://www.uky.edu/RGS/PreventionResearch/welcome.html>.

Maury M. Breecher, PhD, MPH

MORPHINE

OFFICIAL NAMES: Morphine sulfate or morphine hydrochloride (solutions for injection), Duramorph (for spinal use), MS Contin and Oramorph SR (long-acting, controlled release oral form), Kadian (oral, sustained release), MSIR (instant release), Roxanol (liquid concentrate)
STREET NAMES: M, morph, Miss Emma, monkey, white stuff
DRUG CLASSIFICATIONS: Schedule II, opiate

OVERVIEW

Morphine is the most active part of opium, a pure chemical isolated from the dried sap of the unripe poppy pod. Even today, morphine is still made from poppies. It is the prototype opiate, the parent from which all the others sprang. But efforts over the past two centuries to separate the beneficial aspects of opiates from their social drawbacks have failed. Even totally synthetic drugs that mimic morphine and the other opiates remain utterly linked to addiction.

At the turn of the nineteenth century, opium was an important part of medical practice. By the time that Frederick Serturner, a young clerk in a small German pharmacy, extracted morphine from opium, the world was already experienced in both medicinal and recreational opium use. Serturner's extraction was the first alkaloid ever isolated, and he named it after the Greek god of dreams, Morpheus.

Morphine's discovery became well-known after Serturner published his findings in 1817. In 1837, an Endinburgh chemist and physician, William Gregory, found a cheaper way to isolate and purify it. But not until the 1850s, with the introduction of the hypodermic needle, would morphine gain wider use.

The Civil War was a ready stage for the entry of morphine into common medical practice. Medics from the North and the South used morphine for the massive practice of amputation. With no delicate, germ-free surgical technique available, any serious wound to a limb called for its swift and horrendously painful removal.

The Union army obtained 29,828 oz (846 kg) of morphine sulfate. And when Confederates realized that a blockade of their ports could part them from sources of opium, they tried getting Southern women to cultivate and produce opium from garden-grown poppies. On both sides, discharged soldiers went home as addicts after the hostilities ceased.

In the years after the war, however, women abused morphine even more than man. The spread of patent medicines and the unregulated sale of hypodermics brought opiate use into the parlors of the upper classes. Fashionable women could buy and wear syringes pinned to their clothing, as they did watches or brooches. Surveys by public health officials in Michigan and Iowa recorded that by the 1880s about 75% of all drug addicts were women seeking to ease neuralgia (sharp, severe nerve pain), cramps, and morning sickness. Meanwhile, babies and toddlers were soothed with various nostrums, or "quack medicines," containing opiates, with alcohol as another major constituent. "Mrs. Lambert's Ladies

KEY TERMS

ALKALOID: Any organic agent isolated from plants that contains nitrogen and reacts with an acid to form a salt.

DEPENDENCE: A psychological compulsion to use a drug that is not linked to physical addiction.

EUPHORIA: An exaggerated feeling of well being.

NARCOTIC: A natural or synthetic drug that has properties similar to opium or opium derivatives.

NEUROPATHIC: Relating to a disease of the nerves.

OPIATE: A drug originating in the opium poppy, such as codeine and morphine.

OPIOID: A drug, hormone, or other chemical substance having sedative or narcotic effects similar to those containing opium or its derivatives; a natural brain opiate.

SYNAPSE: The gap between communicating nerve cells.

THALAMUS: The central area of the brain below the cerebral lobes that relays messages from the spine to the forebrain.

TOLERANCE: A condition in which higher and higher doses of a drug are needed to produce the original effect or high experienced.

Elixir" is an example: 23% alcohol with 40 mg of morphine in every bottle. Also, "Mrs. Winslow's Soothing Syrup," with 0.05 g of morphine per bottle. Even patent medicines to cure morphine dependence were sold; inevitably they contained alcohol or opium. Thomas Edison patented and marketed his own nostrum, "Poly-Form." It contained morphine, chloroform, ether, chloral hydrate, alcohol, and spices.

By the late 1800s, one in 25 Americans used large amounts of opiates. No laws limited their use. People simply went to the local druggist for morphine, no prescription required. Abuse was considered a vice or a weakness, not a crime. But doctors did begin to recognize and criticize their own profession's ability to create a lifelong servitude to the drug. Newspapers recorded morphine as an agent for suicides and deaths by accidental overdose.

At the turn of the century, the German chemical company Bayer was capitalizing on a previously unnoticed chemical improvement on morphine. In 1898, Bayer began aggressively marketing heroin as a cough cure for the rampant disease of the time, tuberculosis. Heroin, a derivative of morphine, crosses directly into the brain, where it is converted immediately back to morphine. Unbelievably, it was said to be non-addictive.

Heroin was even proposed as a way to cure morphine addicts. This turns out to be a recurring theme in the story of narcotics: to hopeful physicians, a new version brought to market appeared to be free of abuse potential, until enough people used it to prove otherwise.

In medical practice today, morphine is regarded as the standard for pain relief by which all other drugs are measured. Still, doctors may be hesitant to use morphine. They must register with the federal Drug Enforcement Administration (DEA) to dispense the drug, and paper trails lead easily to doctors who prescribe it too freely. A current debate in medicine seeks to expand the medical use of the drug, and to change state laws to recognize the legitimate place for morphine in a physician's practice.

CHEMICAL/ORGANIC COMPOSITION

Morphine is an alkaloid, the chemical class to which many drugs belong. Pure morphine is a white powder, bitter to the taste. More than 1,000 tons of morphine are isolated from opium a year, although most of it is converted to codeine. Morphine comprises anywhere from 3% to 17%—usually about 10%—of the more than 20 alkaloids present in opium.

The many rings of the morphine molecule include a benzene ring that fits into the receptors for the brain's own opiates (the endorphins and enkephalins). The nerve cells studded with these receptors recognize the morphine molecule by the close fit of the benzene ring and the binding of a critical nitrogen atom. Many other opioids duplicate these molecular features.

In the 1970s, researchers were able to discover exactly how morphine works in the brain. When stimulated by tiny electric currents, certain nerve tracts within the core of the brain can produce a painkiller strong enough to allow abdominal surgery in lab rodents. The painkiller consists of simple amino acids that, in their naturally folded state, mimic the structure of the morphine molecule. They were named enkephalins, for "in the head," and endorphins, for "the morphine within."

INGESTION METHODS

Morphine is available by prescription in many forms. It can be taken orally as a liquid or as pills, and by injection under the skin, into the veins, or into the space surrounding the spinal cord. Rectal suppositories for pain control provide longer-lasting relief with less potential for nausea. As an abused drug, morphine can be smoked and sniffed as well as swallowed.

THERAPEUTIC USE

Morphine has a clear-cut place in medicine. For cancer, after surgeries, in childbirth, and even for chronic, daily headaches that resist all other treatments, morphine is effective in relieving symptoms. It is still the most widely prescribed drug for severe pain. Typical doses of morphine injected into muscle are 5–20 mg every four hours. Oral doses must be higher, between 8 and 20 mg.

Emergency use of morphine is by intravenous injection, avoiding any "first pass effect" (the "watering down" of drugs that occurs in the liver) or the time for passage through skin or muscle. This dosage is 4–10 mg, and the analgesia (pain relief) is nearly immediate.

Doctors may use morphine to ease childbirth. Women in early and middle labor can be given an opiate, including morphine, to be able to rest between contractions. However, giving an opioid too late into labor can make the baby sleepy on delivery. The baby may also not be able to breathe actively because morphine the morphine has slowed its respiration, but an opioid blocker, naloxone, can be given.

Patients recovering from surgery are able to control their pain by devices called patient-controlled analgesia (PCA). PCA works by way of a pump set up by a hospital technician. The pump is then operated by the patient, who presses a button to deliver doses on demand. Morphine is commonly given in these PCA devices. Pain after certain surgeries can be further lessened by injecting very low doses of morphine into the space around the spinal cord before surgery. This can reduce the severe pain after heart surgeries, for instance, which require the surgeon to separate the breast bone.

A survey of patients in hospices published in 1999 showed that none of the 55 patients receiving 300 or more milligrams of morphine a day for pain relief had difficulty breathing because of the drug. Survival times in hospice were not any different for those on these high morphine doses.

USAGE TRENDS

Morphine is infrequently found "on the street," yet it can get there by its widening use in legitimate medicine. Abuse also can appear in health professionals. Street use in combination with cocaine or methamphetamine has also been documented.

A study published in 2000 reviewed data obtained from 1990 to 1996 on the number of morphine prescriptions written, and the emergency room admissions related to its abuse. Doctors prescribed 59% more morphine in that time period. Yet the number of people seeking emergency aid for morphine abuse rose by just 3%. The

???? FACT OR FICTION

For the past century, scientists have struggled to create an opiate that stops pain without creating tolerance and addiction. Today, genetic engineering may provide some clues.

Recent experiments with rats suggest that, at least at the molecular level, tolerance to morphine can indeed be separated from the physical dependence on it. Specifically, tolerance is the need for larger and larger doses in order to maintain the effect of an initial dose. Dependence refers to the appearance of withdrawal symptoms once the drug is stopped. For years, tolerance and dependence have been thought to go hand-in-hand. Yet, rats missing a particular protein do not require increased doses of morphine to maintain its painkilling effect, but do develop withdrawal when chronic dosing is stopped. The National Institute on Drug Abuse says these experiments lend more hope for the eventual design of addiction-free pain medicines.

Drug companies are also still searching for the perfect pain pill. Naltrexone has typically been used to rehabilitate morphine addicts. Naltrexone is a long-acting blocker that stops opiates from occupying the places in the brain that absorb them. It is a paradox, then, that animal tests in 2001 showed the painkilling action of low doses of morphine was raised by adding naltrexone. The researcher was part of a company trying to develop the combination in order to prevent the development in patients of tolerance to opiates.

study concluded that legitimate use by medical professionals attempting to help patients does not necessarily lead to increased use on the street.

In medical school, doctors learn to treat morphine with suspicion. Even when the use of the drug is clinically called for, they may be hesitant to prescribe it. Many experts on pain say that prescribing morphine for surgical recovery, or even for chronic pain, will not turn most people into drug addicts. While the medical use of morphine does indirectly increase the potential supply to the street addict, restricting its medical use harms people in pain.

A survey published in 2001 shows that primary care physicians would much rather prescribe Schedule III pain relievers—such as acetaminophen with codeine—for chronic pain not due to cancers. Thirty-five percent of the 161 doctors responding to the mailed survey stated they would never prescribe Schedule II opioids to be used around-the-clock by patients in persistent pain. Those who would be willing to give the Schedule II drugs were those who also indicated a lower degree of concern about

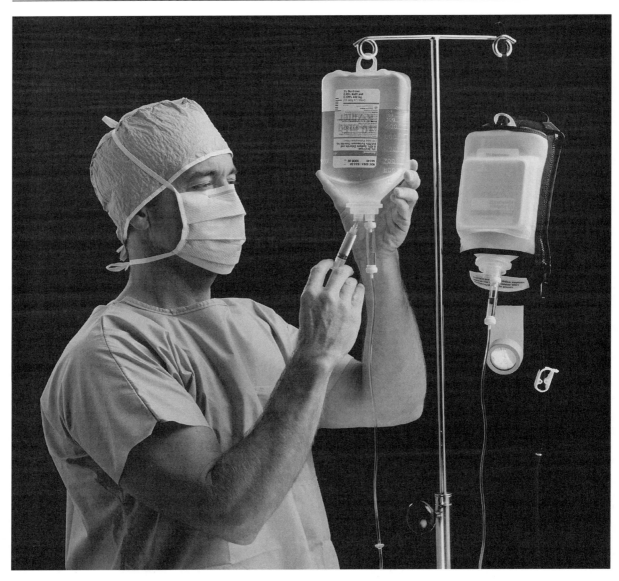

Morphine is usually given to patients via their IV bags. Photo by James W. Porter/CORBIS. Reproduced by permission.

physical dependence, tolerance, and addiction. The survey researchers noted that few carefully designed studies have been carried out to test morphine and similar opioids in relieving chronic pain other than that from malignancies (cancerous tumors that grow uncontrollably). In addition, doctors are often scrutinized by state medical boards for prescribing Schedule II drugs.

A joint statement issued by 21 health oganizations and the Drug Enforcement Administration acknowledges the balancing act that medical use of morphine engenders. "Preventing drug abuse is an important societal goal," the statement says, but "it should not hinder patients' ability to receive the health care they need and deserve."

Scope and severity

In 1999, four million people in the United States were using prescription drugs outside medical use. Of these, 2.6 million were misusing pain relievers, according to the National Institute on Drug Abuse (NIDA).

Doctors must be able to recognize the occasional patient who is seeking morphine to feed an addiction. Physicians must be wary of being manipulated. Allegations of overprescription of scheduled drugs is the leading reason physicians are investigated, as well as the leading reason for the suspenstion of a doctor's license.

Age, ethnic, and gender trends

Older people receive prescriptions at three times the rate of the rest of the population. But the National Household Survey on Drug Abuse recorded the sharpest increase in nonmedical use of prescription drugs in young adults and teens.

The sexes are known to react differently to opiates. In humans, women are more likely to misuse opiates. Research in animals shows that females require higher doses to relieve pain (the sex steroid hormones change the brain's organization early in life to create this difference). Female rats also appear to enjoy morphine more than males. The females continued to choose to receive the drug even at doses so high that their breathing was halted, doses that the males chose to avoid.

MENTAL EFFECTS

Morphine blocks the deep, aching perception of chronic pain, without interrupting the fast signals sent by an acute injury. As pain signals rise through the spinal cord to reach the brain, morphine interrupts them at a "relay station" within the core of the brain, called the thalamus. Morphine also blocks pain messages as they enter the spinal cord.

This interruption is not complete: the message of pain still reaches the brain. However, morphine blocks the emotions surrounding pain: people receiving the drug still know they are having pain, but it bothers them less.

Two views are offered to explain the action of morphine on pain. One says that the opiates work on all types of pain. The other says that opiates cannot work on a certain type of pain, called neuropathic, which is the pain created by damaged nerves themselves. When opiates do work in neuropathic pain, some experts say, it is only because the drugs improve the patient's mood. In the early 1990s, one research team found that half of pains judged as neuropathic did respond to morphine. The changes in mood reflected the relief of pain, the researchers noted, regardless of the type of pain.

Researchers say that the euphoria produced by morphine is due to its action on dopamine. Dopamine is a neurotransmitter—nerve messenger—in the brain that acts in those parts of the brain that register pleasure.

The other mental effects of morphine take place at the arousal centers of the brain, in the brainstem, to produce a sleepiness and relaxation. However, some patients experience restlessness instead of drowsiness, with increased limb movement rather than relaxation. Confusion and slurred speech almost always accompany morphine at higher doses. Meanwhile, the so-called "pinpoint pupils" of opiate overdose are created by morphine's action on the iris, resulting in blurred vision and impaired ability to see in the dark.

HISTORY NOTES

William Halstead was a founder of Johns Hopkins University, and the inventor of the radical mastectomy (removal of the breast). Halstead was also the first American surgeon to investigate cocaine as a local anaesthetic, a painkiller applied directly to the wound or other source of pain. Unfortunately, Halstead took his work home with him.

Cocaine addiction repeatedly interrupted his career, and he had to take leaves of absence and check in to hospitals to fight it. By the time he joined the faculty at Hopkins, in 1889, he had managed to overcome cocaine with the aid of morphine.

Halstead continued to abuse morphine until his death in 1922, yet managed to develop many new surgical techniques; advance the use of aseptic practice in surgery; and train a set of physician-scholars who in turn trained others.

Acting in the brainstem, as well as in the respiratory centers of the brain, morphine slows respiration and suppresses the cough reflex.

PHYSIOLOGICAL EFFECTS

In the gastrointestinal system, morphine slows the stomach and smooth muscle of the gut, causing constipation and loss of appetite. It slightly lowers body temperature, causing flushing and sweating. Morphine also causes sensations of itching or prickling of the skin, especially after intravenous use. Morphine can decrease libido and interfere with a woman's menstrual cycle.

Recent findings are leading researchers to try local applying opiates to joints affected by arthritis.

Harmful side effects

The slowed breathing caused by morphine is dangerous in those who already have trouble breathing. Indeed, the slowing of respiration is considered the most dangerous action of the opiate drugs. At high doses, the respiratory suppression caused by morphine and other potent opioids can lead, in extreme instances, to death.

Morphine's effects in the digestive tract can also be severe, especially for cancer patients already rendered nauseous by chemotherapy. Nausea and vomiting are commonly encountered at therapeutic doses of morphine (although there are medicines to counter this). Morphine may also cause constipation.

Long-term health effects

Morphine can be highly addictive. When an addict stops using, the signs of all opiate withdrawal include anxiety, restlessness, yawning, flu-like symptoms including muscle and bone pain, diarrhea, insomnia, vomiting, cold flashes, goose bumps, and involuntary movement of the legs. All aspects of withdrawal are physiologically opposite to the acute effects of the drug. It takes days or even weeks for the recovering addict to regain balance.

Steady or repeated use of morphine causes tolerance as well as withdrawal (also called physical dependence). More and more drug is needed to produce the same effect as the original dose. A tolerant morphine user can take massive doses that would kill a first timer. Compared to the therapeutic range of 5–20 mg, several hundred milligrams a day is not unusual in either cancer patients or street addicts. In extreme cases, four or five grams of morphine may be taken a day.

A newly discovered risk of opiate abuse relates to a role of endogenous opiates—opiates naturally produced by the body—as growth factors. External opiates like morphine will block such functioning, possibly harming a growing embryo as well as the mother's adaptation to pregnancy.

Endogenous opiates also help form new brains cells. Morphine abuse will interfere with this process, ultimately destroying the formation of new cells.

REACTIONS WITH OTHER DRUGS OR SUBSTANCES

The respiratory depression induced by morphine can add to that of alcohol, barbiturates, benzodiazepines (such as Valium), and even with antihistamines taken for allergies. Combined effects of these drugs with morphine can dangerously compromise breathing. Tricyclic antidepressants can hamper the metabolism of morphine.

TREATMENT AND REHABILITATION

Overdoses of morphine resulting in unconsciousness can be rapidly reversed with the opiate antagonist naloxone (Narcan). Given by intravenous injection, naloxone works in a minute or two by occupying the opiate receptors in the brain, without any action of its own other than to block morphine or other opioids. A dose of 0.4–0.8 mg (to a maximum of 10 mg) is given every three to five minutes to revive an overdosed person.

Abruptly stopping the abuse of morphine will result in withdrawal. While not life threatening, as are with-

drawal from alcohol or other depressants, going "cold turkey" is immensely unpleasant. The recovering addict may become suicidal from the suffering experienced.

Medical means of getting an addict off morphine allows withdrawal with less drastic symptoms. Methadone, legally administered through drug rehabilitation programs, can be substituted for morphine just as it is for heroin. A totally synthetic opioid, methadone lasts longer within the body than either morphine or heroin. Methadone closely mimics the basic opiate structure.

Methadone is given orally (different from the usual means of abuse), and thereby also substitutes for the paraphernalia that accompany illicit drug use. Methadone helps relieve the craving for more drug and delays the appearance of withdrawal symptoms as long as it is in the body. Doses are gradually decreased. If the dose of morphine that was abused is known, then 1 mg of methadone can substitute for 4 mg of morphine. Otherwise, a dose of 10–50 mg a day is generally used, and can be reduced by 20% per day.

Clonidine (Catapres) is another drug used to treat opiate addiction. It can relieve the anxiety, runny nose, salivation, sweating, abdominal cramps, and muscle aches of opiate withdrawal. Side effects are dry mouth, dizziness, and drowsiness. Clonidine is initially taken at 0.8–1.2 mg a day, maintained for a few days, and then gradually decreased. Combined with the opiate blocker naltrexone, clonidine can allow a more rapid detoxification (the removal of morphine from the body). Detox in a single day can be accomplished by heavy sedation or anesthesia while giving naltrexone to an unconscious addict. This controversial method has not been studied in controlled trials.

Recovering addicts who fear a moment of weakness can strenghten themselves with the long-acting opioid antagonist naltrexone. Using naltrexone makes it impossible to get high from taking other opioids. But naltrexone must be taken before any other opioids are used, or withdrawal will occur. The usual dose of naltrexone is 25–50 mg orally, in the morning. Depression has been reported with its use, and it also raises toxin levels in the liver. Headache and nausea are encountered with naltrexone use.

LAAM, the abbreviation of levo alpha acetyl methadol, is another opiate blocker that has been used to wean addicts. It persists up to 72 hours.

Getting past withdrawal is only the first step in confronting morphine abuse. The psychological need for the drug must be addressed as well. Narcotics Anonymous and other programs are devoted to this challenge. A peer group that replaces the one that encouraged the addiction is a key feature of successful rehabilitation.

For those who are taking morphine to control pain, the same principle of tapering off the dose applies, with gradual lowering of the dosage over a period of a few weeks. However, short-term use of morphine for acute pain in a medical setting rarely requires weaning.

PERSONAL AND SOCIAL CONSEQUENCES

Because addicts are so intent on finding their next fix, they often neglect basic aspects of hygiene and nutrition. Infections and illness often result. Skin infections as well as more serious bloodborne infections follow use of unsterile needles. Deadly viruses are also shared through dirty needles. Babies born to addicted mothers usually go through withdrawal that their immature systems cannot handle. Finally, risk of arrest or of death by violence usually goes along with a lifestyle that includes illegal drugs. The death rate of those abusing narcotics is estimated to increase by 2% for each year spent abusing the drug, with abuse of ten years carrying a 20% risk of death by overdose or drug-related crime.

LEGAL CONSEQUENCES

Under the Controlled Substances Act, morphine is a Schedule II drug. Doctors must be licensed by state medical authorities to prescribe it legally. They must also register with the Drug Enforcement Administration (DEA) and obtain a DEA number to use when writing the prescriptions. The DEA number helps keep track of how many prescriptions a doctor writes. Any trafficking in morphine—or any other Schedule II drug—results in federal penalties of up to 20 years. If death or serious injury results, the penalties for a first offense are 20 years to life and fines of up to $1 million. In 1988, the penalties were slightly changed: now those who are caught with only a small quantity of morphine face civil fines of up to $10,000.

Legal history

Opium smoking in the United States spread with the immigration of Chinese workers in the western frontier—they built most of the train tracks, for instance—but it still was perfectly legal. In 1879, the Memphis, Tennessee public health agency targeted opium dens by making it illegal to sell, own, or borrow "opium or any deleterious drug" or the paraphernalia related to smoking them. Critics writing at the time pointed to the hypocrisy in denying the Chinese their accustomed comfort while white citizens could freely purchase morphine—indeed, could inhale, drink, or inject it. Not until 1909 did federal law outlaw smoking opium, and the agent itself.

Federal guidelines, regulations, and penalties

In 1914, the Harrison Narcotic Act outlawed heroin in the United States. The federal Controlled Substances Act of 1970 classified morphine as a Schedule II drug, which means it has potential for abuse but also accepted medical uses.

In 2000, Congress considered the Pain Relief Promotion Act, which would have amended the Controlled Substances Act to say that relieving pain or discomfort—within the context of professional medicine—is a legitimate use of controlled substances. The bill died in in the Senate. Sponsors of the bill plan to reintroduce it.

In the medical community, there is a growing awareness of the legitimate use of opiates to reduce pain. State medical boards are adopting new guidelines to reflect this, as well as to urge aggressive treatment for pain. These new guidelines allow physicians to document their reasons for using opiates.

See also Codeine; Heroin; Meperidine; Opium; Oxycodone

RESOURCES

Books

Hodgson, Barbara. *Opium: A Portrait of the Heavenly Doom.* San Francisco: Chronicle Books, 1999.

Metzger, Thomas. *The Birth of Heroin and the Demonization of the Dope Fiend.* Port Townsend, WA: Loompanics Unlimited, 1998.

Periodicals

Giannini, A. James. "An Approach to Drug Abuse, Intoxication and Withdrawal." *American Family Physician* 61 (May 1, 2001): 2763-2774.

Gorman, Christine. "The Case for Morphine." *Time* online. 1997 (February 13, 2002). <www.time.com/time/magazine/1997/dom/970428/medicine.the_case_for.html>.

Kolata, Gina. "When Morphine Fails to Kill." *The New York Times* July 23, 1997.

Potter, Michael. "Opioids for Chronic Nonmalignant Pain." *The Journal of Family Practice* 50 (February 1, 2001): 145-151.

Other

Lane, Laura. "Benefits from Opioids Outweigh Risks, Study Says." CNN.com health. April 4, 2000 (February 12, 2002). <http://www.cnn.com/2000/HEALTH/04/04/pain.killer.wmd/>.

Medina, James L. "Narcotic Abuse." *eMedicine* Online Consumer Journal. March 4, 2001 (February 13, 2002). <http://www.emedicine.com/aaem/topic321.htm>.

Organizations

American Academy of Pain Medicine, 4700 W. Lake Avenue, Glenview, IL, USA, 60025, (847) 375-4731, (877) 734-8750, aapm@amctec.com, <http://www.painmed.org>.

Pain & Policy Studies Group, 406 Science Drive, Suite 202, Madison, WI, USA, 53711-1068, (608) 263-7662, (608) 263-0259, ppsg@med.wisc.edu, <hhttp://www.medsch.wisc.edu/painpolicy/about.htm>.

Roberta L. Friedman, Ph.D.

NICOTINE

OFFICIAL NAMES: Nicotine, tobacco
STREET NAMES: Cigarettes, pipes, cigars, bidis (beedies), kreteks (clove cigarettes), spit tobacco (spit), chewing tobacco (chew), snuff
DRUG CLASSIFICATIONS: Not scheduled, stimulant

OVERVIEW

Nicotine dependence is almost invariably caused by addiction to tobacco, because tobacco is the overwhelming source of nicotine. Nicotine present within tobacco products causes physical and mental effects rapidly leading to addiction, and the user continues using tobacco despite adverse health consequences and usually a desire to stop. The widespread use of tobacco, despite its known dangers, probably reflects its low cost and easy availability, its high level of social acceptance until recent years, and its seemingly mild immediate side effects.

Nicotine use often begins in adolescence in response to commercial and social pressures and continues because of the positively reinforcing effects of nicotine, which can include both relaxation and increased alertness. In later stages of use, smoking may be used mainly to relieve withdrawal symptoms such as irritability and discomfort.

Addictive characteristics of nicotine

Nicotine meets the criteria for causing chemical dependence with the following characteristics:

- Users can exhibit tolerance, which is when additional amounts of nicotine are required to produce an effect.

- A great deal of time may be spent using nicotine (such as leaving work for cigarette breaks), and it is usually taken in larger amounts or over longer periods of time than was intended.

- Users may have a persistent desire for nicotine (craving) and unsuccessful attempts to cut down or control its use.

- Nicotine causes withdrawal symptoms, and its ingestion may continue despite knowledge of the harm it causes.

- Daily tobacco use becomes compulsive, repetitive, and imperative.

- The user avoids withdrawal symptoms and experiences the rewards by repeated dosing, that is, by ingesting more nicotine from tobacco products.

- There is a high rate of relapse once use ceases.

Nicotine dependence resembles that of alcohol, heroin, and cocaine but appears to be more harmless to smokers for two reasons. First, there are usually several years or decades before signs of disease are detected. Second, smoking does not produce a disabling state of intoxication seen with the other drugs. On the contrary, nicotine may improve attention or decrease fatigue and therefore improve performance.

KEY TERMS

ACETYLCHOLINE: A chemical that transmits nerve impulses from one nerve fiber to another (neurotransmitter). The pleasurable effects of nicotine are a direct result of nicotine binding to acetylcholine receptors.

CARBON MONOXIDE (CO): A gaseous byproduct of incomplete burning of tobacco. It replaces necessary oxygen being carried by the hemoglobin in the blood and is thought to contribute to the development of cardiovascular disease.

CHRONIC OBSTRUCTIVE PULMONARY DISEASE (COPD): A general term to describe airflow obstruction due to emphysema and chronic bronchitis.

COMPENSATORY SMOKING: Smokers puff harder, deeper, and more frequently to obtain desired amounts of nicotine from fewer cigarettes or from low-nicotine cigarettes. Smokers may also hold the smoke in the lungs longer before exhaling and smoke the cigarette further down.

COTININE: A breakdown product of nicotine that stays much longer in the blood than nicotine, and so can be used as a measurement of nicotine exposure, ETS exposure, or even nonsmoking compliance.

DOPAMINE: Neurotransmitter associated with the regulation of movement, emotional response, pleasure, and pain.

EMPHYSEMA: An irreversible, smoking-related disease in which damage of the tiny air sacs (alveoli) in the lung results in air being trapped and a reduced exchange of gases. The result is shortness of breath, wheezing, coughing, and difficulty breathing.

ENVIRONMENTAL TOBACCO SMOKE (ETS): Also called passive or second hand smoke, ETS is the combination of the smoke arising from smoldering tobacco together with exhaled smoke and is responsible for extensive health problems in smokers and nonsmokers alike.

HALF-LIFE: The amount of time it takes for one half of a substance to be broken down or excreted. Nicotine has a short half-life, therefore, frequent tobacco intake is required to maintain desired nicotine levels in the blood.

MASTER SETTLEMENT AGREEMENT (MSA): A 1998 agreement between the States' Attorneys General and the tobacco industry. Tobacco companies agreed to several changes in advertising and promotion in exchange for protection from further lawsuits. Companies also agreed to pay billions of dollars over 25 years to reimburse states for the cost of treating smoking-related illnesses.

NICOTINE: An alkaloid derived from the tobacco plant that is responsible for smoking's addictive effects; it is toxic at high doses but can be effective as a medicine at lower doses.

SMOKER'S COUGH: Recurring cough experienced by smokers because damaged tiny hair-like structures (cilia) in airways can not move mucus and debris up and out efficiently.

TAR/TPM: Total particulate matter. An all-purpose term for particle-phase constituents of tobacco smoke, many of which are carcinogenic (cancer-causing) or otherwise toxic.

WITHDRAWAL: A group of symptoms that may occur from suddenly stopping the use of a substance such as alcohol or other drugs after chronic or prolonged ingestion.

Increased risk of developing dependence

Risk of dependence and disease increases with the number of cigarettes smoked and duration of smoking. There is a marked increase in dependence when use exceeds five cigarettes daily. The earlier individuals start to smoke, the more severe their addiction will be.

People with anxiety and depression are at greater risk of dependence as nicotine is used as a "self-medication" to enhance mood. Youths with adjustment problems, who are risk takers, or have extraverted (outgoing) personalities are at increased risk for smoking. Children whose parents are regular smokers are at high risk.

Genetic factors influence the risk of nicotine addiction, as with other addictive substances. Inheriting certain genes can either contribute to or help protect individuals from nicotine addiction. In some cases, the genetic vulnerability to nicotine addiction may be linked to a similar vulnerability to alcohol dependence. Genetic differences in dopamine receptors and rate of nicotine breakdown have been shown to effect the likelihood of nicotine dependence.

Introduction into society

Ingestion of nicotine is an ancient and widespread practice. Native North, Central, and South Americans have smoked, chewed, sniffed, and drank tobacco preparations for thousands of years. It was used in religious and ceremonial rituals, as a medication, and to suppress hunger. The word tobacco is derived from tobaga pipes used by Central American natives.

Christopher Columbus brought the practice back to Europe where it was first used for its medicinal properties. French diplomat Jean Nicot, for whom nicotine is

Smoking is increasingly common among teenage girls. AP/Wide World Photos. Reproduced by permission.

one of the most important national crops over the next 200 years. By the early 1960s pipe smoking and snuff gave way to cigars and cigarettes with the development of a cigarette-rolling machine and the safety match. Cigarette consumption increased during both World Wars, and mass marketing caused a dramatic jump in cigarette use during the next several decades.

The height of the smoking epidemic in the United States was in 1965 when 52% of adult men and 32% of adult women smoked. Attitudes of Americans had slowly begun to change by the 1950s when long-term studies clearly linked tobacco and disease. Progress was made nationwide to decrease smoking rates using public health announcements on television, education in schools, increases of federal excise taxes, and warning labels on cigarette packages. In 1971 cigarette advertising was banned from television and radio, and during that same year the nonsmokers' rights movement began. Social acceptability of smoking began to fall, reinforced by the 1986 Surgeon General's report focusing on the hazards of environmental tobacco smoke to nonsmokers. By the end of the century, less than 25% of adults smoked, but the rate of decline slowed dramatically in the 1980s and 1990s for both men and women.

General impact today

Tobacco use, particularly smoking, is the number one cause of preventable death in the United States, causing 20% of all deaths. Smoking is a major risk factor for heart disease, stroke, lung and other forms of cancer, and chronic lung diseases—all leading causes of death. It is a major risk factor for a variety of other medical conditions as well.

There are at least 434,000 deaths attributable to smoking per year in the United States, almost 1,200 per day, one every 73 seconds. This death rate is higher than the combined total of deaths due to AIDS, alcohol, cocaine, heroin, homicide, suicide, motor vehicle crashes, and fires. Approximately half of all continuing smokers die from diseases caused by smoking. Of these, approximately half die between the ages 35 and 69, losing an average of 20 to 25 years of life expectancy. Continued smoking throughout life doubles age-specific mortality rates, nearly tripling them in late middle age.

Estimates of disease due to smoking do not include the contribution of smoking to overall poor health status. Poor general health may decrease survival for many diseases, including those not caused by smoking, and may limit the treatment options available to the patient. For example, a smoker with emphysema may not be a safe candidate for a surgery needed to treat another medical problem.

Reducing tobacco use

Despite overwhelming evidence for the adverse health effects of tobacco use, smoking habits have been difficult to change. Nicotine addiction, along with heavy

named, helped popularize its use to treat a wide array of illnesses: upset stomachs, ulcers, headaches, toothaches, constipation, and asthma. It was also used as a poultice and antiseptic for cuts, burns, and sores.

Nonmedical pipe smoking, chewing, and snuff were initially limited to sailors who had adopted the Native American habit but spread rapidly from Europe to Africa and Asia in the early 16th century. At the same time, there was strong condemnation of tobacco use on both health and social grounds. Popes and kings banned its use, perhaps slowing its spread as its popularity increased.

The commercial tobacco industry in North America began in the Jamestown colony in 1612 and grew to be promotion by the tobacco industry, maintains high levels of use. The Centers for Disease Control and Prevention (CDC) estimates that the average 14-year-old has been exposed to more than $20 billion in advertising since age six, creating a "friendly familiarity" with tobacco products. In1999, total advertising and promotional spending by the tobacco companies rose to $8.24 billion, more than $22 million per day. However, education, combined with community-wide and media-based activities, can postpone or prevent smoking onset in 20% to 40% of adolescents.

Studies show that the best ways to reduce tobacco use combine:

- restrictions or outright bans on tobacco advertising and promotion

- raising excise taxes on tobacco products

- enforcement of smoke-free environments in public areas and worksites

- banning of tobacco sales in vending machines

- warning labels on tobacco products and advertisements

- continuous education, especially for minors, on health effects of smoking

- a minimum age of 18 for sellers of tobacco products

- citation of storeowners who sell tobacco to minors

- licensing of tobacco-selling establishments plus compliance checks

The FDA was unsuccessful in its attempt from 1995 to 2000 to have nicotine named as a drug and cigarettes named as a drug delivery device and thus subject to FDA control. Such control would have had the potential to severely restrict promotion and access to tobacco products.

CHEMICAL/ORGANIC COMPOSITION

Nicotine (C_{10} H_{14} N_2, beta-pyridyl-alpha-N methylpyrrolidine) is a very poisonous, water- and lipid-soluble, liquid alkaloid with a burning taste. It is colorless, but turns brown and takes on the odor of tobacco upon exposure to air. First isolated in 1828, it is used as an insecticide in agriculture, and as a killer of parasites in veterinary medicine.

Tobacco plant leaves of two species, *Nicotiana tobacum* and the milder flavored *Nicotiana rusticum*, generally contain 2–8% nicotine. The average cigarette contains between 8 and 10 mg. Some nicotine is lost from the tobacco leaf during the curing (slow drying in sun, hot air, or smoke), storing, and manufacturing processes. The NCI points out that each can of chewing tobacco holds a lethal dose of nicotine. Also, each tin of

[????] FACT OR FICTION

Adolescents have a clear idea of the risks of tobacco use.

Fiction. Studies indicate that adolescents underestimate the risks of tobacco use (including cigarettes, chewing tobacco, and cigars) and believe its practice to be more widespread and more socially accepted than it actually is. A study released in 2001 shows that 43% of eighth graders do not think there is a great risk associated with smoking one pack of cigarettes per day. This lack of awareness is due in part to the continuing efforts of the tobacco industry to convey an image that sophisticated, active, confident, sexy, athletic, beautiful people smoke. These characteristics were embodied in the macho "Marlboro Man" and attractive "Virginia Slims" models. When adolescents are informed of the common tactics used to induce them to buy certain products, they become very skilled at pinpointing advertisements that are targeted at them. They realize the attractive actors in tobacco advertisements more closely resemble people who do not smoke.

A 1993 study in the *Journal of the American Medical Association* stated that children as young as three years old recognized Old Joe Camel, a cartoon character used to promote Camel cigarettes. Even though tobacco advertisements have not been allowed on TV or radio since 1971, and even though these children could not read, they recognized the character from print media or billboards. The Joe Camel campaign was discontinued in 1997 following a complaint by the Federal Trade Commission that it was inducing minors to smoke.

snuff delivers as much nicotine as 30–40 cigarettes, with 4.5–6.5 mg nicotine per pinch. Holding a pinch of snuff in the mouth for 20–30 minutes yields nicotine levels two to three times the amount of nicotine delivered by a regular-size cigarette.

Burned tobacco contains some 4,800 distinct chemicals in either gas or particle phases. Many of the compounds in both phases are highly reactive, poisonous, and toxic. Harmful products include oxidants and poisons produced during burning, as well as radioactivity, heavy metals, and pesticides that may have accumulated within the tobacco leaf. Sixty-nine of these substances are known to cause cancer in humans and animals, and many others are known to be strong irritants.

The gaseous phase contains the harmful gases carbon monoxide (CO) and nitrogen oxide, along with carbon dioxide, ammonia, hydrogen cyanide, benzene,

Anti-tobacco ad citing the link between cigarette smoking and impotence. California Deparment of Health Services.

toluene, formaldehyde, acetone, acetaldehyde, methanol, and vinyl chloride. CO is a byproduct of the incomplete burning of tobacco and is thought to be a major culprit in causing cardiovascular (heart) disease.

The compounds of the particle phase are collectively called tar, or total particulate matter (TPM). Tar is the oily residue left behind when moisture evaporates from burned tobacco. It contains thousands of compounds, including cancer-causing aromatic amines, nitrosamines, and polycyclic aromatic hydrocarbons that are present in both smoking and smokeless tobacco. Other harmful constituents include radioactive lead and polonium as well as arsenic, among others.

Additives

The manufacturers of tobacco products add fillers, flavor enhancers, preservatives, and other additives to make the product more desirable to consumers, especially low-tar brands. Each company's list of additives was a closely guarded trade secret until 1984, when the lists were submitted to the government. The public was barred from seeing the lists until 1994. The initial list contained 700 potential additives, of which 13 are not allowed in food. One additive, ammonia, may be included to boost the absorption of nicotine and enhance the addictive "kick." Sweeteners and chocolate may help make cigarettes more attractive to children and first-time users.

Menthol is commonly added to certain brands as it numbs the throat to the irritating effects of smoke. Menthol opens up the lung passages and allows more smoke to be inhaled deeper into the lungs. It makes the lungs more permeable to tars and carcinogens (cancer-causing agents), causing greater disease. These cigarettes also boost nicotine and CO levels. Menthol cigarettes accounted for 26% of the market in 1999.

Low tar and nicotine cigarettes and compensatory smoking

In the 1950s tobacco companies introduced filters on cigarettes to try to remove some of the toxins in smoke. By 1999, 98% of United States smokers used filter-tipped cigarettes. The companies then made other changes to the cigarette to further reduce the amount of tar and nicotine delivered to the smoker. Such changes included altering the composition of the tobacco and adding ventilation holes in the filter to dilute smoke with air. The average tar yield has fallen from 37 mg to 12 mg since 1968. The average nicotine yield fell from 2.7 mg to 0.85 mg.

In theory, filters and other changes to decrease the amount of tar and nicotine in cigarettes should decrease the health hazards of smoking. In fact, the mortality risk among current smokers has risen in the last 40 years even though tar and nicotine levels have fallen. Many smokers of low-yield brands compensate by taking deeper, longer, or more frequent puffs from their cigarettes to get the nicotine their body desires. They may hold the smoke longer in their lungs before exhaling or smoke the cigarette further down. This is referred to as "compensatory smoking." They may also increase the amount of tar and nicotine taken into the lungs by unintentionally blocking tiny ventilation holes in the filter with their fingers or lips. The smoker may end up inhaling as much or more tar and nicotine as in regular brands. Additionally, low tar products may also have higher levels of CO, and a variety of other toxins.

Kreteks and bidis

Increasing numbers of teens are turning to alternative cigarettes called bidis, tiny flavored cigarettes from India, and kreteks or clove cigarettes from Indonesia. Bidis (or beedies) are small, unfiltered cigarettes, hand-rolled in leaves. Flavorings such as chocolate, strawberry, and vanilla are added to the American versions of bidis to make them more appealing to minors. Bidis contain more than three times the amount of nicotine and five times the amount of tar than regular cigarette smoke. They are also puffed more frequently than regular cigarettes to prevent them from going out.

Kreteks contain tobacco and 40% shredded clove buds. They have a pleasant, sweet aroma of cloves, but have such high levels of tar, nicotine, and CO, that smoking one is equivalent to smoking 20 light American cigarettes. Eugenol, the local anesthetic in cloves, permits the inhalation of the harsh smoke.

INGESTION METHODS

Nicotine is ingested by smoking shredded tobacco in cigarettes, cigars, and pipes, or through smokeless tobacco. Smokeless tobacco comes in two major forms: snuff and chewing tobacco. Snuff is cured, ground tobacco manufactured in three varieties: dry, moist, and fine cut. Chewing tobacco is coarser than snuff and is also produced in three forms: loose-leaf, plug, and twist.

Today, moist snuff is usually taken orally, similar to chewing tobacco. Usually a pinch of snuff or a plug of chewing tobacco is placed between the gum and cheek, or the leaves or plug are chewed. Saliva mixes with the tobacco, and nicotine is absorbed through the lining of the mouth. This moist tobacco is referred to as a "chaw" or "quid" of chewing tobacco or a "dip" or "pinch" of snuff. It may be kept in the mouth for hours, and the user expectorates (spits out) the saliva that mixes with the tobacco. Dry snuff, which is less commonly used, is usually inhaled through the nose.

Absorption and metabolism

Nicotine is easily absorbed through all body surfaces including the lungs, oral and nasal passages, skin, and gastrointestinal tract. Absorption is influenced by the pH (acidity) of the smoke or chew. Cigarette smoke is acidic, and therefore the nicotine is best absorbed through the alveoli (tiny air sacs) of the lungs during deep inhalation. Cigar and pipe smokers typically do not inhale the alkaline smoke, and nicotine absorption, like that of smokeless tobacco, occurs through the lining of the mouth. Inhalation provides the quickest route of nicotine delivery to the brain and is therefore the most addictive. Absorption through the mouth is slower and through the skin slower yet.

Nicotine in chewing tobacco is absorbed in the first 10 minutes, with peak levels occurring within 30 minutes. The nicotine from a puff of cigarette reaches the brain within 10 seconds. With approximately 10 puffs per cigarette, a pack per day delivers 200 doses (hits) of this potent drug to the brain. The repeated, frequent peaks in nicotine levels in the brain and blood contribute to its addictiveness.

The smoke is 1% to 2% nicotine and approximately 1–3 mg of the drug reaches the smoker's bloodstream per cigarette. Half of the nicotine is eliminated from the blood in 30 to 120 minutes. This short half-life is the result of a portion of nicotine in the blood being metabolized (broken down or changed into other substances) in the liver, lungs, and other organs. Primarily, it is oxidized into cotinine, a less active substance. The kidney then rapidly removes nicotine and cotinine from the body.

The short half-life of nicotine contributes to its abuse potential. The initial effects drop off after a few minutes, causing the user to continue self-administering nicotine throughout the day to maintain pleasurable effects and prevent withdrawal symptoms. Studies clearly show that animals will self-administer nicotine intermittently to avoid both very low and very high levels of nicotine.

THERAPEUTIC USE

Nicotine is most often used in replacement therapy for tobacco addiction, but also has some potential uses to treat other conditions. It has been helpful in stopping bleeding in ulcerative colitis. Nicotine gum is being tested in conjunction with Tourette syndrome where it has been seen to lessen the severity and frequency of tics. Nicotine may reduce tremors in Parkinson's patients because it increases dopamine levels, which are reduced in these patients. It also improves attention in Alzheimer's patients. Nicotine is being studied for its effect on dystonias (movement disorders), chronic pain syndrome, sleep apnea, ulcers, attention deficit disorder, obesity, and chronic inflammatory skin disorders as well.

USAGE TRENDS

Scope and severity

Cigarette smoking is the most common substance use disorder in the United States. A billion cigarettes were produced in the entire United States in 1885. Today over one billion are smoked daily. Nationally, there were 48 million adult (18 years and older) smokers in 2001. The average smoker smokes 20 cigarettes per day.

Low-income adults smoke more than high-income adults. People with less education smoke more than those with college degrees. Habitual users of alcohol, cocaine, and heroin are more likely to be smokers too. More than 80% of alcoholics are smokers, and alcoholic drinkers are at least twice as likely to be smokers than are nondrinkers. The highest prevalence rates are seen with psychiatric patients: up to 88% of schizophrenics smoke, and approximately 50% of patients with anxiety, personality disorders, and depression smoke. Forty percent of adults with attention deficit hyperactivity disorder (ADHD) smoke.

However, the 2001 smoking rate of 25% is markedly decreased from the height of the smoking epidemic in 1965, when 42% of adults over 18 years old smoked. More than half of the smokers in the United States since the mid-1960s have quit. However, following years of steady decline, rates showed only modest declines in the 1990s.

The consumption of cigars has been increasing since 1993 with growing popularity among younger, affluent people. In 1998, 5% of adults had smoked a cigar product in the last month. Pipe smoking is in decline, with only 2% of men in partaking in 1991, and very uncommon usage among women. Pipe smoking is mainly found in men over the age of 45, who are also likely to be users of other tobacco products, especially cigarettes. National data from 1999 shows 6% of adult men and 1% of women use chewing tobacco or snuff. But the popularity of smokeless tobacco is increasing, especially among younger white males.

Gender trends

Historically, smoking became prevalent among men before women, but the gap between male and female smoking rates narrowed in the mid-1980s and has remained constant. The American 2001 smoking rate of 28% men and 22% women decreased from the 1965 peak, when 52% of men and 32% of women smoked. In developing countries, 48% of males smoke. Rates among women are substantially lower (7%) but increasing.

The prevalence of smoking during pregnancy has declined steadily in recent years, although 13–22% of pregnant women continue to smoke. Only about one third of women who stop during pregnancy are still abstinent one year after the delivery.

Studies indicate that men and women differ in their smoking behavior. Women tend to smoke fewer cigarettes per day than men, are more likely to use filtered or low-tar and -nicotine cigarettes, and inhale less deeply. Women are less likely to use smokeless tobacco, cigars, or pipes than men are. Correspondingly, lung cancer rates are lower in women than men. However, in 2001, the United States Surgeon General noted a 600% increase since 1950 in women's death rate from lung cancer, primarily caused by previous decades of cigarette smoking.

Age trends

Most tobacco users begin the habit in their teens. Initiation and addiction to smoking occurs in 90% of tobacco users by their eighteenth birthday. Every day in the United States, more than 6,000 young people try a cigarette, and almost 3,000 become regular smokers. First-time cigarette use is most likely to occur between ages 11 and 15, in sixth through tenth grade. A long-term national study found that 70% of high-school seniors who smoked as few as one to five cigarettes a day were still smoking five years later, and most were smoking more cigarettes per day. Tobacco is often the first drug used by young people who go on to use alcohol, marijuana, and other drugs.

In 1999, 44% of male students and 37% of female students reported using some form of tobacco (cigarettes, cigars, or smokeless tobacco) in the past month. Thirty-five percent of high-school students were current smokers, including 39% of white students, 33% of Hispanic students, and 20% of African American students. The 2000 rate of high school use of bidis was 5% and 5.8% for kreteks.

Overall, the percentage of American high-school students who smoked increased through the mid-1990s after declining in the 1970s and 1980s. The CDC found that the sharpest rise in daily smoking rates began in 1988, the year the Joe Camel advertising campaign began. A study released in 2001 shows that high school smoking levels peaked in 1997 and have since made steady progress downward. The decline is attributed to several factors, including decreased advertising targeted at youth, increased anti-smoking advertising, and increased prices of cigarettes.

Adolescent boys are shifting from smoking to smokeless tobacco partly due to the mistaken belief that it is a safe substitute for smoking. Nationwide in 2000, 4% of middle school boys and 12% of high school boys used chewing tobacco or snuff. White male students were more likely than Hispanic or African American male students to use smokeless tobacco. The median age for first use of smokeless tobacco is 12, two years younger than the median age for first use of cigarettes.

An increasing number of boys and girls are experimenting with cigars, unaware that the risks are similar to cigarette smoking. In 1999, an alarming 25% of high school males, and 10% of high school females were using cigars. White students are more likely than African American students to smoke cigar products.

Ethnic trends

Multiple factors determine patterns of tobacco use among racial and ethnic minority groups in the United States: socioeconomic status, cultural characteristics, degree of assimilation into American culture, stress, biological elements, targeted advertising, price of tobacco products, and the varying capacity of communities to mount effective tobacco control initiatives.

Between 1983 and 1995, cigarette smoking declined for whites (34% to 26%), African Americans (37% to 27%), Hispanics (30% to 19%), and Asian and Pacific Islanders (24% to 15%). The prevalence of tobacco use among Native American and Alaskan Natives stayed at 41% between 1983 and 1995.

The American Heart Association smoking statistics for the year 2000 are as follows:

• Native American men: 38%; women: 31%

• African American men: 32%; women: 22%

• Caucasian American men: 27%; women: 23%

• Hispanic American men: 26%; women: 14%

• Asian and Pacific Islander American men: 22%; women: 12%

It is important to note that although African Americans do not have the highest smoking rates of racial groups in the United States, they appear to bear the greatest adverse health effects, particularly lung cancer in males. Some studies propose that the use of mentholated cigarettes by 80% of African Americans might be a cause.

Occupational and workplace trends

Professional, technical workers, and clergy have the lowest smoking rates whereas the military, law enforcement, and blue-collar workers have the highest rates. More adults are taking up the smokeless tobacco habit if they are no longer allowed to smoke on the job. Professional baseball players have an alarmingly high rate of 35% to 40% chewing tobacco use, and approximately half of those have pre-cancerous lesions of the mouth.

Larger employers with over 100 workers are more likely to adopt restrictive smoking policies, compared to smaller companies. Hospitality, service, and blue-collar workplaces in manufacturing and processing industries are less likely to be smoke-free environments.

Global trends

Tobacco use is one of the major causes of preventable death in the world. The estimated 1.2 billion smokers in the world consume an average of 14 cigarettes per day. In the year 2000, 4.2 million deaths were due to tobacco use, and the figure is expected to rise to 10 million deaths annually by the year 2030. Seven million of those deaths are expected to occur in developing countries. While smoking rates are slowly declining in developed nations, they are steadily growing in developing nations at a rate of 3.4% per year. Smoking will eventually kill about 500 million people alive in the world today. One billion people will die from tobacco in this century.

MENTAL EFFECTS

Nicotine has several effects that are due to its action on the brain. Beginning smokers may experience dizziness or lightheadedness and sometimes vertigo. At higher doses, nausea and vomiting may occur. These effects can also be elicited in chronic smokers with

 **IN THE NEWS**

In November of 2001 the World Health Organization (WHO) called on lawmakers around the world to take action against tobacco advertising. An international public opinion survey conducted on four continents showed overwhelming public support for stronger regulations to control tobacco. A study conducted by the World Bank and WHO found that comprehensive advertising bans and price increases do decrease tobacco use.

At the same time, tobacco companies were launching a massive public relations effort to persuade governments not to enact laws limiting tobacco promotion and advertising. As the industry faces efforts within the United States to decrease tobacco consumption, it has attempted to develop new and larger markets in other nations. These nations also face the threat of trade sanctions by the United States if they resist the tobacco industry's expansion.

The WHO, the World Bank, and the United Nations Foundation have created, with assistance from the CDC, new programs to confront this problem. A global tobacco surveillance system has been set up, and the Framework Convention on Tobacco Control (FCTC) will be a treaty that when signed by member nations, will set forth rules to contain the spread of tobacco use.

---

forced, rapid smoking. Most smokers learn to avoid such unpleasant effects by adjusting their inhalation patterns.

Studies have indicated that there are two major pleasurable effects of nicotine ingestion that reinforce the habit: stimulation (vigilance, wakefulness) and relaxation. Tobacco users may feel that smoking helps them concentrate and feel clear headed, and studies do show that nicotine causes an improvement in attention, recall, information processing, reaction time, and problem solving. Smokers may also feel that smoking helps them relax in stressful situations or that it lifts their mood. They may feel calm and experience less anger, tension, depression, and stress. Both stimulation and relaxation may be experienced at the same time, resulting in a state of relaxed wakefulness.

Nicotine is known to bind to acetylcholine receptors (the receiving areas on cells) that are located throughout the central nervous system as well as the peripheral nervous system. Acetylcholine is a neurotransmitter: it transmits nerve impulses from one nerve fiber to another. The pleasurable effects of nicotine are a

Number (in millions) of adults 18 years and older who were current, former, or never smokers, overall and by sex, race, Hispanic origin, age, and education.

	1965	1970	1974	1979	1983	1988	1992	1993	1994	1995	1997	1998
Smoking Status Total Population												
Current	50.1	48.1	48.9	51.1	53.5	49.4	48.4	46.4	48.0	47.0	48.0	47.2
Former	16.0	23.8	25.8	32.5	36.2	41.8	42.8	45.6	46.0	44.3	44.3	44.8
Never	52.0	56.8	57.3	68.9	76.8	84.5	91.6	93.7	93.9	98.8	101.6	103.8
Sex:												
Male												
Current	28.9	26.4	25.8	26.9	27.6	25.6	25.0	24.5	25.3	24.5	25.7	24.8
Former	11.0	15.8	16.6	20.4	22.2	24.6	25.1	26.5	26.3	25.0	25.1	25.7
Never	15.8	17.8	17.5	24.5	28.8	33.0	37.1	37.5	38.0	41.3	42.2	43.3
Female												
Current	21.1	21.6	23.1	24.1	25.9	23.7	23.5	21.9	22.7	22.4	22.3	22.4
Former	5.0	8.0	9.1	12.1	14.0	17.1	17.7	19.2	19.6	19.3	19.2	19.1
Never	36.2	39.0	39.8	44.4	48.0	51.5	54.5	56.2	55.9	57.5	59.4	60.4
Race:												
White												
Current	44.6	42.6	42.7	44.6	46.2	41.9	41.3	39.1	40.6	39.7	40.0	39.6
Former	15.0	22.3	24.1	29.9	33.1	38.1	38.6	41.0	41.6	40.0	39.7	40.0
Never	46.4	50.1	50.5	59.5	65.8	70.8	75.4	76.7	76.2	80.6	81.9	82.6
Black												
Current	5.0	5.1	5.8	5.8	6.4	6.1	5.7	5.5	5.8	5.5	5.9	5.4
Former	0.9	1.3	1.4	2.2	2.5	2.9	3.3	3.3	3.1	3.1	3.0	3.1
Never	5.0	5.9	6.0	7.8	8.9	10.3	11.6	12.2	12.5	12.8	13.0	13.6
Hispanic Origin												
Hispanic												
Current	NA	NA	NA	2.7	2.6	2.8	2.8	2.9	3.1	3.2	3.9	3.9
Former	NA	NA	NA	1.6	1.6	2.3	2.2	2.3	2.6	2.9	2.8	3.2
Never	NA	NA	NA	4.9	6.0	6.8	8.5	9.0	10.3	11.5	12.4	12.9
Non-Hispanic												
Current	NA	NA	NA	48.1	50.6	46.4	45.5	43.3	44.7	43.6	44.1	43.4
Former	NA	NA	NA	30.8	34.5	39.4	40.4	43.0	43.2	41.4	41.4	41.7
Never	NA	NA	NA	63.6	70.4	77.4	82.7	84.4	83.2	87.0	89.3	90.8
Age (years)												
18–24												
Current	8.0	8.3	8.8	9.6	9.8	6.6	6.4	6.2	6.9	6.2	7.1	7.0
Former	1.2	2.0	2.2	2.9	2.6	2.4	1.5	1.7	1.8	2.1	1.8	2.0
Never	8.4	11.6	12.3	15.3	16.1	16.5	16.3	16.0	16.3	16.5	15.9	16.1
25–44												
Current	23.1	20.8	21.5	22.7	24.7	25.3	24.8	23.7	24.7	23.6	23.7	22.6
Former	6.1	8.8	8.9	11.4	12.9	14.7	14.6	15.1	14.9	14.5	13.2	12.9
Never	15.9	17.1	17.9	24.2	30.4	36.7	41.2	42.3	42.6	44.5	45.9	46.8
45–64												
Current	15.9	15.9	15.2	15.0	14.7	13.3	13.1	12.9	12.7	13.1	13.3	14.1
Former	6.1	8.9	10.0	11.7	12.7	14.9	15.6	16.9	17.0	15.9	17.0	17.0
Never	16.1	16.3	15.1	16.4	16.7	17.0	19.2	19.9	20.2	22.4	24.2	25.2
>65												
Current	3.1	3.0	3.5	3.8	4.3	4.2	4.2	3.7	3.7	4.0	3.8	3.5
Former	2.6	4.0	4.7	6.4	7.9	9.8	11.1	11.9	12.3	11.8	12.3	12.9
Never	11.6	11.8	12.0	13.1	13.6	14.3	15.0	15.5	14.8	15.4	15.7	15.6
Education* (years)												
<12												
Current	NA	17.8	16.4	14.0	13.2	11.1	10.0	9.2	9.9	9.3	9.5	9.1
Former	NA	8.8	8.6	9.0	8.9	8.7	8.7	8.3	8.1	7.8	8.0	7.7
Never	NA	20.8	18.3	16.8	16.1	14.0	13.7	13.3	13.0	13.6	14.6	13.5
12												
Current	NA	13.7	14.3	16.0	17.8	18.5	18.4	17.6	17.5	17.6	15.1	14.9
Former	NA	6.9	7.7	10.3	12.0	14.2	14.8	16.2	15.4	14.8	12.6	12.8
Never	NA	14.3	14.9	19.0	21.1	24.0	25.6	26.7	25.7	27.4	23.0	24.0
13–15												
Current	NA	4.4	5.1	6.4	7.2	7.9	8.0	8.4	8.8	8.0	11.3	11.1
Former	NA	2.5	3.3	4.5	5.6	7.6	8.6	9.5	9.6	9.2	11.7	11.7
Never	NA	4.4	5.1	7.3	9.6	12.6	14.6	15.7	15.8	16.7	22.0	22.4
>16												
Current	NA	3.4	4.0	4.7	5.3	5.1	5.6	4.9	4.6	5.6	4.7	4.8
Former	NA	3.3	3.9	5.5	6.8	8.8	9.0	9.8	10.6	10.4	9.9	10.4
Never	NA	5.1	6.0	9.6	13.6	17.3	21.2	21.7	22.6	24.3	25.6	27.0

*Data on education are presented for persons greater than or equal to 25 years of age.
SOURCE: National Health Interview Surveys: 1965, 1970, 1974, 1979, 1983, 1988, 1992, 1993, 1994, 1995.
Centers for Disease Control. Tobacco Information and Prevention Source (TIPS).
<http://www.cdc.gov/tobacco/research_data/adults_prev/tab_3.html>

Chart by Argosy.

direct result of nicotine binding to these acetylcholine receptors, which then triggers the release of other neurotransmitters and hormones. Epinephrine, dopamine, norepinephrine, acetylcholine, serotonin, vasopressin, and beta-endorphin are all released. Epinephrine (adrenaline) release results in a "rush" or "kick" as it stimulates the body, increasing heart rate, blood pressure, breathing rate, and blood sugar. The wide variety of chemical messengers in the following list adapted from Neal L. Benowitz (1999) may explain the diverse, and sometimes seemingly opposite effects of nicotine (stimulation and relaxation) reported by smokers:

- Dopamine causes pleasure and appetite suppression.

- Norepinephrine causes mental stimulation and appetite suppression.

- Acetylcholine causes mental stimulation and cognitive (thinking) enhancement.

- Vasopressin causes memory improvement.

- Serotonin causes mood enhancement and appetite suppression.

- Beta-endorphin causes a reduction of anxiety and tension.

Furthermore, nicotine may have different effects at different doses. Rapidly delivered, increasing doses are likely to cause a stimulating reaction, whereas slower, chronic intake has a more calming, sedating effect.

Nicotine is thought to cause addiction primarily through its action to increase the levels of dopamine, which activates the brain circuitry that regulates feelings of pleasure and motivation, the so-called reward system. Increased dopamine in this system produces pleasurable sensations, as seen in other drugs of abuse such as cocaine and heroin.

Substances in smoke other than nicotine may also affect the brain. An unknown substance in smoke causes a decrease in the level of monoamine oxidase (MAO), an important enzyme responsible for breaking down dopamine. The decrease in MAO results in higher dopamine levels, which contributes to the desire to keep smoking.

The desire to smoke can also be brought on by reinforcing factors called "external stimuli" such as the sight, taste, and smell of tobacco smoke, as well as the social setting and rituals associated with smoking. These previously neutral stimuli in the environment, or certain events, can become associated with tobacco use and thus become triggers for a desire to smoke.

PHYSIOLOGICAL EFFECTS

Immediate effects

As with the mental effects of nicotine, the physiological effects are brought about by its actions on the nervous system, both peripheral and central. Nicotine changes the transmission of nerve impulses by binding to acetylcholine receptors, and induces the release of several chemical messengers, which in turn affect several body systems.

In the cardiovascular system, there is a 10 to 20 beat per minute increase in heart rate, a 5–10 mm increase in blood pressure, and an increase in the strength of heart contractions. Nicotine increases the incidence of cardiac arrhythmia (irregular heartbeat) in susceptible people. It causes constriction of blood vessels in the skin, and causes platelets to adhere together leading to an increased possibility of blood clots.

Nicotine is irritating to the digestive tract. Salivation increases, and the strength of stomach contractions decreases. Nausea and vomiting may occur. Appetite is suppressed, particularly in females for sweet food. Metabolism is increased and brown fat is stimulated, which along with appetite suppression can lead to weight loss.

Nicotine causes local irritation in the respiratory system, as well as decreased motion of the cilia, the tiny hairs that sweep debris and mucus upward, out of the respiratory tract. A recurrent "smoker's cough" results as the body tries to rid itself of accumulated mucus. Breathing is accelerated by nicotine.

In the endocrine (gland secretion) system, besides increased release of epinephrine and norepinephrine, there is increased release of the growth hormone, cortisol, and the antidiuretic hormone. The increased levels of circulating catecholamines (epinephrine, norepinephrine, and dopamine) play a role in causing cardiovascular diseases by changing the balance of lipoproteins circulating in the blood. They increase the harmful low-density lipoproteins (LDL) and decrease the protective high-density lipoproteins (HDL), increasing the risk of cardiovascular disease.

Nicotine toxicity

Ingestion of 60 mg of nicotine can be fatal to an adult. This is an amount that might be ingested with exposure to some insecticide sprays. A smaller amount is toxic to children and pets who accidentally ingest tobacco products. Tobacco pickers and patients on nicotine replacement therapy who continue to smoke have also experienced nicotine toxicity. Symptoms include salivation, dizziness, vomiting, tremors, convulsions, and severely low blood pressure. Death may result in a few minutes due to respiratory failure caused by lung paralysis.

Carbon monoxide and tar

It is important to emphasize that although nicotine causes a wide variety of physical and mental effects, the majority of health problems from smoking are due to carbon monoxide and tar, much more so than nicotine. CO decreases the ability of the blood to carry oxygen. This leads to an increased production of red blood cells to compensate for the loss of oxygen carrying capacity. Along with nicotine, CO contributes to lipoprotein changes and increased blood-clotting ability, leading to cardiovascular disease. Tar, with its many known carcinogens and other irritants, is largely responsible for various forms of cancer, especially lung cancer.

Withdrawal syndrome

An attempt to stop using tobacco products, or even decrease their consumption, often results in the user experiencing unpleasant withdrawal symptoms that are due specifically to nicotine. Symptoms may start within hours after cessation of use, peak usually at the second to fourth day and may last for weeks or months.

Withdrawal symptoms include:

- restlessness

- anxiety

- impatience

- irritability or anger

- difficulty concentrating

- excessive hunger

- depression

- disorientation

- loss of energy or fatigue

- decreased heart rate and blood pressure

- dizziness

- stomach or bowel problems

- headaches

- sweating

- insomnia

- heart palpitations

- tremors

- decreased motor performance

- increased muscle tension

- craving for tobacco products

The symptoms are often worse in the evening. Weight gain is common, 4–7 lb (2–3 kg) on average.

Among tobacco users with no history of depression, 20% experience depression during withdrawal. The rate jumps to 80% for those with a past history of depression. Women are more prone to depression during withdrawal than men.

Long-term health effects

Smoking causes one third of all cancers and 87% of lung cancer. Because of tobacco use, lung cancer is the number one cancer killer of both men and women. It is also associated with cancer of the mouth, throat, voice box, esophagus, stomach, bladder, kidney, pancreas, uterus, and cervix. Smoking is also possibly linked to leukemia, and cancer of the breast, prostate, and colon. The overall rates of death from cancer are twice as high among smokers as among nonsmokers, with heavy smokers having death rates that are four times greater than nonsmokers. The role of nicotine itself in causing cancer is controversial.

The majority of smoking-related illnesses are cardiovascular and respiratory. Nearly one fifth of heart disease deaths in the United States are related to smoking. It is a major cause of atherosclerosis (narrowing and hardening of the arteries) and high blood pressure and the resulting angina, heart attacks, and strokes due to both hemorrhage and blood clots. It also increases the risk of abdominal aortic aneurysm.

Smoking leads to respiratory problems other than lung cancer. It causes chronic bronchitis, emphysema, and lower resistance to flu and pneumonia. It worsens asthma symptoms in adults and children. As these problems persist, chronic obstructive pulmonary disease (COPD, airway obstruction) develops. Eighty to 85% of deaths due to COPD are from smoking. The role of nicotine in chronic lung diseases such as COPD, emphysema, and asthma is uncertain. However it is known that nicotine can cause an enzyme to be released which is able to destroy parts of the lungs as is seen in emphysema.

Smoking is especially harmful to diabetics who are already at an increased risk of cardiovascular disease, stroke, and kidney disease. The habit also negatively affects joints and interferes with the healing of wounds. Healing of fractures is delayed because smoking impairs the formation of new bone. Smokers are more likely to develop degenerative disorders and injuries of the spine. The risk for peptic ulcers is increased. Smoking also may upset thyroid function.

Heavy smoking is a contributory factor in male impotence due to a decreased amount of blood flowing into the penis. Smoking also increases the risk of infertility in men by decreasing sperm motility and density. A nearly twofold increase in hearing loss, cataracts, and macular degeneration of the eye has been observed in smokers. Smokers have a decreased sense of taste and smell and are prone to periodontal disease, such as receding gums, as well as increased dental cavities.

Women

Women face additional adverse health effects from smoking. About 30% of cancers of the cervix are attributable to both active and passive smoking. Women who smoke have a high risk for osteoporosis and hip fractures following menopause. They are likelier to have early onset of menopause due to nicotine's anti-estrogen effect. However, the decreased estrogen levels seen in female smokers appear to decrease their risk of endometrial cancer up to 50%. Women smokers have an increased risk of infertility, especially those women who started before age 18 or who smoke one or more packs per day. In 1987, lung cancer surpassed breast cancer as the leading cause of cancer death among women.

Pregnancy

Pregnant women who smoke create additional health concerns for their unborn child. Many substances in tobacco smoke, including nicotine, cross the placenta and are found in breast milk. Mothers who smoke heavily have almost a two-fold increase in miscarriage and birth defects and are more likely to deliver low-birth-weight babies. Smoking during pregnancy also causes ectopic pregnancy, premature births, and stillbirths. Infant mortality rates in pregnant smokers are increased 33%.

Sudden infant death syndrome (SIDS) is strongly linked to smoking in pregnant women and new mothers. Children of smoking mothers are more likely to have motor control problems, perception impairments, symptoms of hyperactivity, and conduct disorder in childhood. These children have a higher risk for cancer later in life.

Teens

The younger a person begins smoking, the greater the risk of developing serious illnesses. Smoking teens experience adverse health effects, including a general decrease in physical fitness, increased coughing and phlegm, greater susceptibility to respiratory illnesses, and early development of artery disease (a precursor to heart disease). They have a slower rate of lung growth, and by adulthood, possible reduced lung function.

Cigars and pipes

Cigars and pipes have health consequences similar to those of cigarettes, including nicotine dependence, heart disease, and cancer of the lung, mouth, throat, voice box, esophagus, prostate, bladder, and possibly the pancreas. Additionally, pipe smoking causes cancer of the lip. Inhaling cigar or pipe smoke significantly raises the risk of disease.

Smokeless tobacco

Smokeless tobacco causes cancer of the mouth, esophagus, and stomach. Users who swallow the tobacco or the saliva increase their risk of esophageal damage and stomach ulcers. Dentists report seeing users with

LAW AND ORDER

In 1998 the tobacco industry settled lengthy lawsuits by making a historic agreement with the States' Attorneys General called the Master Settlement Agreement (MSA). In exchange for protection from further lawsuits, the industry agreed to reimburse the states billions of dollars over 25 years to pay for smoking-related illnesses. The MSA immediately banned new billboard and public transit advertisements, prohibited distribution of free samples except at adult-only facilities, and disallowed cartoons and targeting of youth in advertising.

The agreement and the accompanying negative publicity for tobacco companies, along with increased anti-smoking advertising, had a significant effect on tobacco consumption. Cigarette sales fell 10% from 1998 to 1999, with per capita sales declining by 112 cigarettes per person. High-school smoking rates declined significantly between 1997 and 2001. The MSA energized the global tobacco control movement as many are worried that tobacco companies will dramatically boost advertising to youths abroad to make up for anticipated future losses.

leukoplakia (pre-cancerous lesions) in the mouth, receding gums, dental cavities, chronic mouth sores, with badly discolored teeth, and bad breath. Smokeless tobacco may also contain high levels of sodium, which may contribute to high blood pressure.

REACTIONS WITH OTHER DRUGS OR SUBSTANCES

Smoking causes the liver to produce more enzymes that break down a variety of drugs, resulting in lower than expected blood levels. It may be necessary to monitor smokers who take other drugs on a long-term basis, and adjust their doses during smoking cessation. These medications include asthma drugs such as theophylline (Slo-Bid, Theo-Dur), blood thinners such as warfarin (Coumadin), antipsychoitc drugs such as Clozapine (Clozaril), migraine drugs such as ergotamine, and some tricyclic antidepressants. Nicotine is also reported to decrease the blood-pressure-lowering effects of drugs such as nifedipine (Procardia), atenolol (Tenormin), and propanolol (Inderal).

Women who use birth control pills should not smoke as they are at increased risk for heart attacks, blood clots, stroke, liver cancer, and gallbladder disease. The risk increases with age (especially over the age of 35) and smoking more than 15 cigarettes per day.

TREATMENT AND REHABILITATION

Nicotine and tobacco dependence is best treated as a chronic condition with remission and relapse. Up to 80% of tobacco users say they would like to quit. About one third of smokers try to quit each year, 90% of these without treatment, but only 2.5–5% are successful. Of those who try to quit without treatment, more than 90% fail, with most relapsing within a week. Most people experience relapses and require repeated attempts before achieving long-term abstinence. However, effective treatments do exist, and eventually 50% of smokers succeed in permanently quitting.

Attempts to quit tobacco use should focus on small steps toward future abstinence. Cigarette smokers who try to change to other forms of tobacco, such as pipes or cigars, are still at significant risk of disease. All forms of tobacco use entail serious adverse health effects and continued nicotine dependence. Turning to low-yield or smaller cigarettes, or smoking only part of a cigarette rarely works due to compensatory smoking.

A comprehensive treatment approach ideally has two parts: handling symptoms of withdrawal, and changing habits and social settings associated with tobacco use. The various forms of treatment include drug therapy, behavioral therapies, and general support. Drug treatment of nicotine addiction, combined with behavioral support, will enable 20–25% of users to remain abstinent one year following treatment. Several effective over-the-counter (OTC) and prescription drugs are available. Some medications involve significant cost, especially if a prescription is required, but are less expensive than the cost of continuing tobacco use.

Nicotine replacement therapy

The greatest danger of nicotine dependency is related mostly to the tobacco rather than nicotine itself. Nicotine replacement therapy (NRT) is far safer than tobacco use. Although the ultimate goal is to stop ingestion of nicotine, temporary nicotine replacement therapy is useful in dealing with withdrawal symptoms. Each type of NRT helps to approximately double the achievement of abstinence when used properly but should be combined with behavioral therapy and support. These forms of nicotine have little abuse potential since they do not produce the pleasurable effects of tobacco products. Seriously ill people, pregnant women, and breastfeeding women should consult a physician when considering NRT. All tobacco use should be avoided during NRT to prevent nicotine toxicity.

Nicotine gum (Nicorette) was introduced in 1984 and is currently sold without prescription in two and four mg doses. The user chews the gum briefly and then "parks" it between the cheek and gum so that nicotine can be absorbed through the lining of the mouth. Normally nicotine gum is used two to three months. Optimal usage may involve 10–20 pieces per day. Heavier smokers should use the four mg dose.

Nicotine skin patches (NicoDerm CQ, Nicotrol, Habitrol, ProStep) were introduced in 1991 and 1992, and are sold OTC or by prescription. Nicotine in the patch is absorbed through the skin (transdermally) in different strengths, for 16 or 24 hours a day. The release of nicotine through the skin is continuous and thus provides steady concentrations of nicotine in the blood. The 16-hour patch is removed at night for those experiencing sleeping difficulty. Patches are easy to use and only applied once per day; but dosing is not flexible, onset of symptom relief is slow, and mild irritation can occur at the patch site. Recommended use is six weeks with either constant or decreasing strengths.

Nicotine nasal spray (Nicotrol NS) requires a prescription. Introduced in 1996, the nasal spray delivers nicotine through the lining of the nose when it is squirted into each nostril once or twice an hour. This method provides the fastest delivery of nicotine of the currently available products and reduces cravings within minutes. However, this form has a greater potential for inappropriate use. Nose and eye irritation is common, but usually stops within one week.

Nicotine inhaler (Nicotrol Inhaler) requires a prescription. Introduced in 1998 and designed to look like a cigarette, the inhaler is a plastic cylinder holding a cartridge containing nicotine. Nicotine is absorbed through the lining of the mouth when the user puffs on the inhaler. Each cartridge lasts for 80 long puffs and is designed for 20 minutes of use. A minimum of six cartridges per day is needed for three to six weeks, when usage begins to taper off. This product mimics the hand to mouth ritual of smoking and delivers nicotine faster than the patch, but frequent use during the day is required, and mouth or throat irritation may occur.

Non-nicotine medication

In 1996 the FDA approved the antidepressant buproprion (Zyban) for the treatment of nicotine dependence. This sustained-release pill blocks nicotine's pleasurable effects and helps to maintain abstinence whether the user has depression or not. The length of suggested use is for seven to 12 weeks, including one to two weeks before quitting tobacco. Buproprion doubles the quit rate and has been demonstrated to be safe when used jointly with NRT.

Clonidine (Catapres), a high blood pressure medication, can be prescribed orally or as a patch for nicotine addiction and doubles the quit rate. It appears to reduce craving for tobacco but does not consistently reduce other withdrawal symptoms. The antidepressant nortriptylene (Pamelor) triples the quit rate. However, both have greater side effects than those previously listed, and are considered second-line therapies.

Other medications that have been studied for nicotine addiction but were found to yield poor or variable results include naltrexone, naloxone, lobeline, mecamylamine, and buspirone. Hypnosis and herbal remedies have been reported to be of potential use but are not scientifically proven. A review of nine studies of acupuncture therapy for smoking cessation shows it to increase the quit rate a modest 1.5 times.

Education, counseling, and behavioral strategies

Knowledge of the seriousness of adverse health effects due to tobacco use is helpful in motivating a user to quit, as well as maintaining abstinence. Physicians who advise their patients to quit smoking can produce cessation rates of 5–10%. Thus, education plays a critical role in tobacco cessation for all ages. A variety of self-help materials (books, tapes, pamphlets, newsletters, software, and Internet sites) are available to inform and aid in quitting tobacco use.

Having a strong motivation to quit tobacco use is usually not sufficient motivation to quit. Other key factors to successful cessation include avoiding smokers and smoking environments and receiving support from family and friends. Even then, most users will require some further assistance beyond self-help materials to successfully quit.

Individual and group counseling by trained therapists is beneficial to those trying to quit tobacco. Over the past decade, this approach has spread from primarily clinic-based, formal smoking-cessation programs to numerous community and public health settings. Two of the most widely available offerings are the American Cancer Society Fresh Start program and the American Lung Association Freedom From Smoking program. These group programs consist of multiple sessions using behavior modification techniques. The goals of behavioral methods are to reduce the reinforcing value of smoking, discover high-risk relapse situations, create an aversion to smoking, develop self-monitoring of smoking behavior, learn coping strategies, and establish alternative rewards. Coping skills are essential for both short- and long-term prevention of relapse. A form of aversive conditioning, called rapid smoking, leads to good quit rates but dangerously high blood nicotine levels.

Groups with problems quitting

Women and African Americans have greater difficulty quitting tobacco use. NRT does not seem to reduce craving as effectively for women as it does for men. Women seem to be less sensitive to nicotine than men, but more sensitive to external stimuli—the sight, smell, and touch involved in smoking. Women have greater concerns about weight gain, restrictions on

medication during pregnancy, and influences of the menstrual cycle on mood. Cessation programs should be tailored for women to rely less on NRT and more on behavioral support.

African Americans are more likely than whites to try to quit smoking, but less likely to succeed. This group apparently metabolizes nicotine differently from other racial and ethnic groups. Nicotine uptake is almost 30% higher in African American smokers than white smokers, and elimination from the body is slower than with other groups. Higher nicotine blood levels over a longer period result in stronger nicotine dependence and more difficulty quitting.

Health benefits of smoking cessation

Immediate benefits of smoking cessation include a return to normal blood pressure and pulse rate. Levels of CO and oxygen in the blood return to normal within eight hours. Within 24 hours the chance of heart attack decreases, and within 48 hours nerve endings start to re-grow and the ability to taste and smell increases. In two to three weeks lung capacity has increased, and there is improved breathing and fewer respiratory ailments. In the next one to nine months, there is a decreased incidence of coughing, sinus infection, shortness of breath, and an increase in overall energy. Cilia re-grow in the airways, which increases the body's ability to handle mucus, clean the lungs, and reduce the chance of infection. There is reduced constriction of blood vessels in already diseased heart patients.

Heavy smokers and long-time smokers are at the greatest risk of disease, so they also have the most to gain from quitting. The decreased risk of disease varies with each disease state depending on how long the smoker has abstained. The risk of death from cardiovascular disease among former smokers approximates that of nonsmokers once the smoker has been tobacco-free for 15 years. The risk of death from lung cancer or COPD is essentially unchanged for the first five years following cessation but then declines steadily from five to 20 years. However, even beyond 20 years cessation, the risk of death due to lung cancer or COPD remains elevated above that of non-smokers. Quitting smoking substantially decreases the risk of esophageal, mouth, voice box, pancreatic, bladder, and cervical cancers. Smokers who quit before age 50 cut their risk of dying in the next 15 years in half.

Cost effectiveness of treatment

Treating nicotine and tobacco dependence can prevent a variety of costly chronic diseases, including heart disease, cancer, and chronic lung disease. It is estimated that smoking cessation efforts are more cost effective than other commonly provided preventive services such as screening for breast, colon, and cervical cancer, treatment of mildly elevated blood pressure, and treatment of high cholesterol.

PERSONAL AND SOCIAL CONSEQUENCES

The personal consequences of nicotine dependence are clearly the potentially life threatening illnesses that tobacco causes. Additional negative consequences become evident as tobacco use becomes less socially acceptable. Unlike the use of other recreational drugs or alcohol, tobacco use does not alter consciousness or cause escape from social responsibility. Therefore, until recently, smoking was regarded as a matter of personal choice. The links between second-hand smoke and disease in nonsmokers altered that view. Smokers often must face isolation and the outdoor elements to avoid exposing family, friends, and coworkers to second-hand smoke. Even then, they may face negative feedback from those around them.

Smoking causes several cosmetic changes too. Tobacco stains teeth and fingers. Smoke odor on breath, clothes, and hair may be offensive to others. Smokers are nearly five times more likely to develop more and deeper skin wrinkles, and have a higher risk for baldness and prematurely gray hair.

Environmental tobacco smoke

The smoke from smoldering tobacco together with exhaled smoke are called environmental tobacco smoke (ETS), second-hand smoke, or passive smoke. ETS is classified by the Environmental Protection Agency as a class A carcinogen (proven cancer-causing substance). The smoldering tobacco, called "sidestream smoke," contains more toxic byproducts than the inhaled/exhaled "mainstream smoke," which is burned more completely as it is drawn through the cigarette.

ETS increases the risk of heart disease and lung conditions, especially asthma and bronchitis in children. In 2000, the National Cancer Institute (NCI) estimated that 3,000 lung cancer deaths, and as many as 40,000 cardiac deaths per year among adult nonsmokers in the United States can be attributed to ETS. Passive smoke also causes increased angina symptoms, allergic attacks, eye irritation, headaches, cough, and nasal symptoms. ETS is linked with low birth weight babies, sudden infant death syndrome (SIDS), and increased pneumonia and middle ear infections in children. More than 88% of nonsmokers in the United States, aged four years and older, have detectable levels of serum cotinine, an indication of ETS exposure.

Costs

Tobacco use has the highest cost to society of any substance of abuse, with the possible exception of alcohol. The American Lung Association estimated in the year 2000 that direct medical costs of tobacco-caused illness were approximately $50 billion. However, this cost is well below the total medical costs to society because it does not include such costs as burn care from smoking-related fires, and hospital care for low birth-weight infants of mothers who smoke.

Additionally, tobacco use creates an estimated $47 billion in indirect costs such as lost productivity. Smokers of one pack of cigarettes per day have 50% greater illness, absenteeism, and rate of hospitalization than nonsmokers. In 1996 the United States Department of Health and Human Services estimated the total cost of tobacco use to businesses to be more than $5,000 per employee per year

LEGAL CONSEQUENCES

Tobacco is a legal substance when purchased and used by adults. Despite widespread efforts to prevent minors from purchasing tobacco, a high proportion continues to do so. All 50 states ban the sale of tobacco to anyone under the age of 18, but many of the laws are weak and enforcement is generally poor. Various studies demonstrated that 32% to 87% of underage youths were able to purchase cigarettes over the counter.

A growing number of states and localities are imposing penalties, usually in the form of citations, against minors who purchase tobacco products. Less frequently, when the store is cited, the penalty is usually directed against the sales clerk rather than the business owner. The result is that the business owner, who sets store policy and gains financially from the illegal sale, is free from penalty.

A working group of States' Attorneys General recommended in 1994 that enforcement focus on commercial sellers of tobacco products before targeting the youth users. Most states already require licensing of stores selling tobacco, but the group further recommended unannounced compliance checks and graduated fines and license suspension for repeated sales to minors.

RESOURCES

Books

Baer, Andrea. *Quit Smoking for Good*. Freedom, CA: The Crossing Press, 1998.

Brigham, Janet. *Dying To Quit, Why We Smoke and How We Stop*. Washington, DC: Joseph Henry Press, 1998.

Fisher, Edwin B., and Toni L. Goldfarb. *7 Steps to a Smoke-Free Life, American Lung Association*. New York: John Wiley & Sons, Inc., 1998.

Whelan, Elizabeth M. *Cigarettes: What the Warning Label Doesn't Tell You: The First Comprehensive Guide to the Health Consequences of Smoking*. Amherst, NY: Prometheus Books, 1997.

Periodicals

DeLucia, Anthony J. "Tobacco Abuse and Its Treatment." *American Association of Occupational Health Nurse Journal* 49, no.5 (May 2001): 243-259.

Lewis, C. "Every Breath You Take. Preventing and Treating Emphysema." *FDA Consumer* 33, no.2 (March-April): 9-13.

Other

Freedom From Smoking Online. American Lung Association online smoking cessation clinic. <www.lungusa.org/ffs/>.

TobaccoPedia: The Online Tobacco Encyclopedia. <http://tobaccopedia.org>.

U.S. Public Health Service. Centers for Disease Control and Prevention. *Tobacco Information and Prevention Source (TIPS).* <www.cdc.gov/tobacco/index.htm>.

U.S. Public Health Service. Reports of the Surgeon General. <www.surgeongeneral.gov/library/reports.htm>

World Health Organization. *Tobacco Free Initiative.* <http://tobacco.who.int/>.

Organizations

American Lung Association, 1740 Broadway, 14th Floor, New York, NY, USA, 10019, (212) 315-8700, (212)265-5642, (800) 586-4872, <http://www.lungusa.org/tobacco>.

Office on Smoking and Health National Center for Disease Prevention and Health Promotion Centers for Disease Control and Prevention, (770) 488-5705, (770) 488-5705, <http://www.cdc.gov/tobacco>.

Marianne F. O'Connor, MT, MPH

NITROUS OXIDE

OFFICIAL NAMES: Nitrous oxide
STREET NAMES: N$_2$O, nitrous, laughing gas, whippets, whip-its, hippie crack
DRUG CLASSIFICATIONS: Not scheduled

OVERVIEW

Nitrous oxide is a gas with anesthetic (numbness-causing) and (painkilling) analgesic properties. It was first discovered in 1772 by English scientist, theologian, and philosopher Joseph Priestly. Priestly was also the man who co-discovered oxygen (which he termed "phlogisticated air"). In 1776, he wrote about the discovery of N$_2$O, which he called "nitrous air."

The first scientist to discover the unique anesthetic and intoxicant effects of nitrous oxide was Sir Humphry Davy, an English physiologist whose self-experimentations with the gas became legendary. In Davy's book *Researches, Chemical and Philosophical: Chiefly concerning nitrous oxide, or dephiogisticated nitrous air, and its respiration* (1800) he suggests that nitrous may be a useful anesthetic in surgical situations, and "appears capable of destroying physical pain."

However, despite Davy's writings on the subject, nitrous oxide had no serious medical use for another four decades. Instead, nitrous, now nicknamed "laughing gas," enjoyed popularity as a way for the English upper classes to entertain themselves at social gatherings. Among those who regularly inhaled the gas for its pleasurable and uninhibiting properties were the poets Robert Southey and Samuel Taylor Coleridge, and the author Peter Roget (of *Roget's Thesaurus*). Laughing gas was also demonstrated in theaters and at festivals; in 1824, a run of performances at London's West End Aldelphi Theatre entitled "M. Henry's Mechanical and Chemical Demonstrations" showed the effects of nitrous oxide on audience volunteers to a disbelieving crowd.

Meanwhile in America, laughing gas was appearing in traveling medicine shows and carnivals. Gardner Quincy Colton, a former medical student, presided over one of these nitrous oxide demonstrations in Hartford, Connecticut, in December of 1844. One of the audience volunteers who had just inhaled the gas injured his leg without feeling any pain. In the audience was dentist Horace Wells, who took note of this and immediately seized on the idea that nitrous oxide might be a powerful anesthetic in the operating room.

Enlisting Colton to bring his nitrous oxide equipment to the dentist's office, Wells used himself as the test subject. Colton administered the gas while a dentist colleague and friend of Wells' pulled a tooth from his mouth. The experiment was successful; Wells woke up shortly after and reported feeling no pain from the procedure. Buoyed by this success, Wells began using nitrous oxide as an anesthetic in his dental practice.

In January 1845, at the Harvard Medical School and the Massachusetts General Hospital, Wells made a presentation in which he used a bag of nitrous oxide to sedate the patient before removing a tooth. Unfortunately, the bag was withdrawn too soon, and the patient complained of pain after the procedure, so the experiment was considered a failure. Nitrous would remain an entertaining oddity until Gardner Colton, the medical school dropout and traveling showman who first introduced the gas to Wells, returned it to medicine in the early 1860s. Starting his own business, Colton provided anesthetic services for dentists using 100% pure nitrous oxide gas. His business proved successful.

In 1868, Chicago dentist Dr. Edmund Andrews published a paper reporting his use of an 80%/20% mix of nitrous and oxygen on patients undergoing dental surgery. The mixture allowed for a longer period of unconsciousness for lengthy procedures. Later that same year, a UK company, Coxeter and Sons, developed a gas mask and tank system for the administration of nitrous oxide and other gases during surgery. Also that year, another English firm, Barth, compressed N_2O into cylinders. By 1871, companies in both America and the UK had succeeded in producing compressed and liquid nitrous oxide in cylinders.

By the end of the century, nitrous oxide had also gained popularity as a anesthesia for women in labor, remaining a standard anesthetic choice for that purpose in the United Kingdom.

Unfortunately, the laughing gas parties and parlor tricks of the early 1800s have evolved into abuse, and nitrous oxide is one of many commonly abused inhalants in the United States. The National Inhalant Prevention Coalition reports that one in five American children have used an inhalant by eighth grade.

CHEMICAL/ORGANIC COMPOSITION

The chemical symbol for nitrous oxide is N_2O (shorthand for two atoms of nitrogen joined with one atom of oxygen). The gas itself is clear and colorless, with a slightly sweet odor and taste.

Nitrous oxide is synthesized, or produced, by heating ammonium nitrate (NH_4NO_3) and then condensing out the water and filtering impurities. The gas is then compressed and turned into liquid for storage in tanks, cylinders, or cartridges.

Commercial grade nitrous oxide—such as that used in food and beverage dispensing, fuel injection, and chemical and semiconductor manufacturing—may contain a number of impurities, including the toxic chemicals sulphuric acid, ammonia, and nitric oxide.

Nitrous oxide should not be confused with nitric oxide, or NO, another gas that dilates the blood vessels (but is an air pollutant).

Ingestion methods

Depending on its intended use, nitrous oxide may be purchased in varying "grades," or degrees of purity.

KEY TERMS

ANALGESIC: A type of drug that alleviates pain without loss of consciousness.

HUFFING: Breathing mind-altering fumes from a cloth that has been soaked in a volatile substance and stuffed into the mouth.

HYPOXIA: A condition in which too little oxygen reaches body tissues.

NITRIC OXIDE: NO; a potentially toxic gas found both in the atmosphere and in the body in small amounts. In the body, nitric oxide helps to move oxygen to the tissues and transmit nerve impulses.

RECREATIONAL USE: The casual and infrequent use of a drug or substance, often in social situations, for its pleasurable effects.

RELAPSE: Term used in substance abuse treatment and recovery that refers to an addict's return to substance use and abuse following a period of abstinence or sobriety.

Medical grade nitrous oxide is a prescription drug sold as a compressed liquid in cylinder tanks. Its buyer requires appropriate credentials to obtain it (which are governed by state law). Nitrous oxide used for other legitimate applications, such as manufacturing and auto racing, is often sold in a "denatured" form. Denatured nitrous contains chemicals that render it unfit for human consumption.

N_2O is used as an aerosol propellant in cans of whipped cream and some other food and beverage products. These products are also a source of N_2O for some nitrous abusers.

A food-grade version of the gas is also sold in small metal cartridges as a propellant for whipped cream cans and dispensers (hence the name slang name "whippets"). These small, bullet-shaped charging cartridges are legal. Because of their accessibility, portability, and low-cost, whippets are the most common means of taking the drug among nitrous oxide abusers.

Sometimes, masks or plastic bags are filled with laughing gas and then placed over the mouth and/or head. This practice carries a particularly high risk for serious injury and possible death, because the user can lose consciousness and suffocate on the mask or bag. Suffocation can also occur when nitrous oxide is consumed in large quantities in a poorly ventilated space, such as a car or closet, or when the user doesn't breathe in a sufficient amount of oxygen during prolonged use.

An 1846 poster lists the effects of laughing gas. Photo
by Bettmann/CORBIS. Reproduced by permission.

THERAPEUTIC USES

As an anesthetic, nitrous oxide has many legitimate
uses. In dentistry it is used to calm patients and lower
their anxiety (a process known as conscious sedation).

American obstetricians used nitrous oxide as a
common pain management tool for women in labor
through the early 1970s. Today, the anesthetic has been
largely replaced in the United States, but a 50/50 mix of
nitrous oxide and oxygen is still the anesthetic of choice
for women in labor in the UK—over 60% use the gas for
pain relief.

Nitrous oxide's ability to reduce anxiety is useful
for uncomfortable or painful medical procedures. Some
studies have also shown that children over the age of six
experience less discomfort and mental distress when
given nitrous oxide during short but painful medical
procedures.

And somewhat ironically, nitrous oxide appears to
have some use as an treatment for withdrawal symptoms. Several South African studies have demonstrated
the usefulness of nitrous oxide in treating withdrawal
symptoms and reducing cravings during alcohol, marijuana, and nicotine detoxification. And in early 2002, a
small study published in *Clinical Psychiatry* found that
the gas may also be helpful in helping smokers kick the
habit. Researchers found that 92% of patients who
inhaled a 50%/50% mixture of nitrous oxide and oxygen

for 20 minutes on the day they quit smoking experienced
decreased cravings for cigarettes over the following
three days. Further studies are needed to determine the
role that nitrous oxide may have in smoking cessation
and substance abuse treatment.

USAGE TRENDS

Nitrous oxide is difficult to categorize. Technically,
it is an inhalant, yet there are several characteristics that
set the drug apart from the typical volatile substances
that inhalant abusers favor. First, N_2O is not as readily
accessible as hair spray, glue, household cleaners, and
other off-the-shelf huffing chemicals of choice. Secondly, since nitrous oxide is an actual prescription anesthetic, it may have more perceived prestige among users
who would look down at most volatile substance abuse
as "kid's stuff."

According to the National Institute on Drug Abuse
(NIDA), nitrous oxide is showing up more frequently at
raves, mixed-and-matched with other club drugs like
ketamine, ectasy/MDMA, GHB, and LSD. There have
also been cases of nitrous oxide abuse in healthcare professionals. Nurses, anesthesiologists, and other medical
personnel with easy access to the drug may be at risk of
developing dependence problems. According to the
American Association of Nurse Anesthetists (AANA),
over 15% of anesthesia providers (including anesthesiologists and certified registered nurse anesthetists, or
CRNAs) are substance abusers.

This abuse is not unique to the United States, either.
In late 2001, an investigation was launched into the
birthing unit staff at Australia's Wollongong Hospital.
Ten Australian midwives and a physician allegedly took
part in a series of "laughing gas parties," illicitly
indulging in the hospital's supply of nitrous oxide and
the sedative temazipan.

Dentists are also at risk. The Talbott Recovery Center, a nationally recognized drug treatment facility that
specializes in the rehabilitation of healthcare professionals, suggests that addiction may develop due to the
nature of a dentist's work (i.e., long and sometimes
tedious procedures, relative isolation, and the stress of
dealing with anxious patients), combined with open
access to anesthetic drugs. The *Journal of the California
Dental Association* reports that the most commonly
abused drugs among dentists are alcohol, hydrocodone,
and nitrous oxide.

Scope and severity

An annual survey conducted by the Substance
Abuse and Mental Health Services Administration
(SAMHSA) reports that 8.27 million Americans have
used nitrous oxide illicitly (not for medical purposes) at
least once in their lifetime.

Inhalant abuse as a whole is a growing crisis worldwide. An international study funded and published by NIDA in 1995 ("Epidemiology of Inhalant Abuse: An International Prospective"), reports increasing inhalant abuse in Mexico, Latin America, Nigeria, Asia, the United Kingdom, and Australia. In Latin America alone, over half of the estimated 40 million street children abuse inhalants (primarily glues and solvents).

Age, ethnic, and gender trends

Inhalant abuse starts early. As of 2000, approximately 2.1 million, or 8.9%, of American youths aged 12 to 17 had used some form of inhalant at some time in their lives. "Monitoring the Future," an annual survey of drug use among youth and young adults conducted by the NIDA and the University of Michigan, reports that one in five eighth graders surveyed in 2000 had used inhalants at least once in their lives, and one in 20 reported use in the prior month. Inhalants are the second most popular class of drugs for eighth graders (marijuana is first) and the third most popular (after marijuana and amphetamines) for tenth graders.

One-third of all inhalant abusers admitted to treatment programs in 1999 had first used inhalants by the age of 12, with an additional 24% reporting first use by age 14. Overall, the general use of inhalants decreases with age, with 9% of eighth graders reporting inhalant use in the past year compared to just 2% of young adults (in the "National Household Drug Use Survey 2000").

Nitrous oxide use, however, follows the opposite trend. In 2000, 456,000 children ages 12–17 reported use in the prior 12 months, in comparison to over 2.6 million between the ages of 18 and 25, and 5.1 million adults age 26 or older. This may be due to N_2O's growing status as a club drug.

MENTAL EFFECTS

Nitrous oxide depresses the central nervous system (CNS). It also affects the activity of neurotransmitters—the CNS chemicals that enable nerve impulses, or signals, to travel from neuron to neuron and regulate thought processes, behavior, and emotion. Once inhaled, it enters the lungs and is carried through the body via the bloodstream. Users experience an immediate feeling of giddiness (not unlike alcohol intoxication), a "floating" and disconnected sensation, dizziness, mental confusion, and slurred speech. In strong enough concentrations, N_2O can cause also short-term memory loss (dissociative amnesia).

Psychological dependence on nitrous oxide can lead users to try riskier and often fatal methods of increasing their intake of the drug, such as filling garbage bags with

IN THE NEWS

Internet sales of whippet cartridges are a growing problem that has resulted in the death of at least one nitrous user. Sold under the guise of whipped cream propellants and erotic aids, whippets are frequently sold alongside crackers, balloons, and other drug paraphernalia that make their intended use fairly clear.

In 1999, a 20-year-old Virginia Polytechnic Institute student suffocated to death after inhaling nitrous purchased through one of these online merchants, the now-defunct Bongmart.com. Although the web site marketed the nitrous "for food use only," investigators with the FDA's Office of Criminal Investigations (OCI) said it was clear that the intended use was for nitrous intoxication. The merchant was convicted of delivering a misbranded drug into interstate commerce.

the gas and putting them over their heads. Memory loss, difficulties with work or school, learning problems, and preoccupation with obtaining the drug are all common features of psychological dependence.

PHYSIOLOGICAL EFFECTS

In addition to the mental effects described above, nitrous oxide impairs motor control and causes a partial insensitivity to pain. Users may lose consciousness at high doses. The intoxication from nitrous is typically short-lived—sometimes lasting under a minute.

Harmful side effects

The biggest risk of nitrous oxide use and abuse is hypoxia, or insufficient oxygen intake. Most abusers take the gas at high concentrations without an oxygen mix. High levels of nitrous oxide in the body can make a person unconscious or even stop breathing. Nitrous oxide displaces oxygen (pushes it out), so there is less of it in the bloodstream. Because the blood carries oxygen throughout the body to "feed" tissues and organs, diminished oxygen capacity can result in brain damage. Lack of oxygen can also cause a loss of consciousness and death by suffocation.

It is this oxygen deprivation that sometimes causes a bluish tinge on the lips of chronic nitrous abusers. After the initial high of nitrous wears off, chronic users may also experience such varied side effects as nausea, visual disturbances (seeing spots), feelings of claustrophobia, fatigue, and difficulty concentrating.

In cases of severe abuse, published studies have described chronic symptoms such as impairment of the nervous system, tingling and/or numbness of the hands and feet, and uncontrolled muscle twitching and movement. These side effects may be related to the depletion of vitamin B_{12} and folate caused by nitrous oxide abuse. They are usually reversible if nitrous use is stopped.

Because of the extreme cold temperature of nitrous oxide, frostbite of the face, mouth, throat, and hands may occur. In many cases, the injury is made worse by the anesthetic affect of the drug; the nitrous user may do further damage to the skin because he or she does not initially feel the frostbite.

Anyone inhaling gas directly from a nitrous tank valve is vulnerable to frostbite and possible lung damage, in addition to the various side effects already mentioned.

Also, if nitrous users inhale the gas standing up, they will more likely than not fall down—hard—possibly breaking a limb or suffering a head injury.

Also, working with any compressed gas may be dangerous. Although nitrous oxide itself is not flammable, the pressurized contents can explode and cause serious injury if a gas tank or cylinder is improperly stored, or is dropped, knocked over, or punctured.

Long-term health effects

Chronic nitrous oxide abuse can remove a lot of vitamin B_{12} from the bloodstream. B_{12} (cobalamin) is necessary for the creation of blood cells and neurotransmitters, as well as the protective layers that cover nerves. This results in nerve damage and pain; balancing, walking, and concentration difficulties; mental impairment; mood disturbances (such as depression); and other physical problems. Chronic nitrous oxide use may also interfere with the production in bone marrow of white blood cells and red blood cells. Treatment with intramuscular injections of B_{12} may reverse these symptoms.

As a consequence of B_{12} depletion, levels of folic acid may also be reduced in chronic N_2O abusers. Again, supplements may help.

Nitrous oxide abuse may also lead to spontaneous abortion in pregnant women. It also interferes with DNA synthesis. For these reasons, it is not given to pregnant women, particularly in the first two trimesters. Heavy, ongoing nitrous oxide exposure during pregnancy has caused birth defects in animal studies, as well.

It is important to note that there have been no harmful physiological effects observed in infants born to mothers who are administered nitrous oxide and oxygen during labor itself, as the gas is quickly metabolized. However, a few long-term studies have shown a possible link between heavy nitrous oxide use during labor and the later development of opiate and methamphetamine addiction of offspring in adulthood.

Long-term nitrous oxide exposure may also cause infertility. Several studies of dental workers and midwives who had been exposed to low levels of the gas in the workplace found that their fertility was reduced in direct relation to the level and length of exposure. Equipment to limit nitrous oxide levels can be installed in a doctor's office to reduce this risk.

Individuals with certain chronic illnesses and medical conditions may also suffer severe and potentially fatal side effects from the use of nitrous oxide. For example, anyone with a history of pulmonary hypertension, asthma, airway obstruction, head injury, or chest infection should not take nitrous under any circumstances.

REACTIONS WITH OTHER DRUGS OR SUBSTANCES

When used along with other CNS depressants (such as alcohol) nitrous oxide can stop the user's breathing, which can be fatal.

Anyone with the condition phenylketonuria (PKU), a metabolic disorder, should be particularly careful about nitrous oxide use. Individuals with PKU require a diet that is high in protein in low in animal fats, which frequently results in a vitamin B_{12} deficiency. Nitrous oxide can remove even more B_{12} from these individuals' bloodstreams, possibly causing mental impairments, as well as severe nerve and brain damage.

TREATMENT AND REHABILITATION

In 1999, 7.8 million Americans reported the illicit use of nitrous oxide at least once in the prior 12 months. Yet according to SAMHSA, substance abuse treatment admissions for all inhalants accounted for only slightly over 1,300 of the almost 1.6 million substance abuse treatment admissions that same year.

Inhalant treatment numbers are low because inhalants are accessible and legal. They are easy to hide, use, and abuse in secrecy. And because they are legal, users often don't consider them a "real drug." Adults sometimes consider inhalant use a phase that adolescents will "grow out of" in time. Interestingly enough, the majority of inhalant users who reported illicit use of nitrous oxide are 18 and older—with most of them over the age of 25 (according to data in the "National Household Survey on Drug Abuse 2000").

Specialized treatment programs targeted at inhalant abusers are still rare in the United States, although many general drug treatment programs can

Nitrous oxide inhalation equipment. The Vaults of Erowid. http://www.erowid.org/chemicals/nitrous. Reproduced by permission.

and do successfully treat these patients. Unfortunately, inhalant abusers suffer a higher rate of "relapse" (a return to drug use) than abusers of other drugs, in part because legal inhalants are widely available in just about any store.

As of early 2002, there were only a handful of specialized inhalant abuse treatment centers in the United States, including programs in Texas, Wisconsin, South Dakota, and New Mexico.

Several treatment programs in the United States have been designed for healthcare professionals with substance abuse problems. Facilities like the Talbott Recovery Center in Atlanta, Georgia have customized rehab programs for physicians, pharmacists, dentists,

and nurses. These programs focus on long-term recovery, as well as on returning the patient to their healthcare career or a suitable alternative.

Drug rehabilitation programs may be either "inpatient" or "outpatient." Inpatient, or residential, drug programs require a patient to live at the hospital or rehab facility for a period of several weeks to several months. Outpatient programs allow patients to spend part of their day at the treatment facility, and return home at night. Nitrous oxide is rapidly eliminated from the body, and abuse of N_2O alone is not associated with withdrawal. This means that a lengthy detoxification period (removal of the drug from the body) is typically not required.

HISTORY NOTES

Samuel Colt is perhaps best known as the inventor of the Colt 45 revolver. But in the 1830s, at the tender age of 19, Colt was touring the United States and Canada as Doctor and/or Professor Coult, amazing onlookers with live demonstrations of laughing-gas inhalation. For $.25 ($.10 for children), audience members could watch Sam Colt administer the gas to volunteers, who would then entertain the crowd with their inebriated reactions. These money-making nitrous oxide demonstrations helped finance the prototype and production of Colt's first five-shot revolver.

Today, according to NIDA estimates, a single large compressed gas cylinder containing 14,000–16,000 liters of nitrous oxide could net a drug entrepreneur enough for one of Colt's originals. A 14,000 liter tank is enough to fill 4,700 balloons of nitrous, earning the seller between $14,100 and $23,500 (based on a street value of $3 to $5 for each balloon). However, a trafficking conviction can quickly erase any profit margin; in 2001 an Arizona man was fined $40,000 and sentenced to 15 months in prison for nitrous sales that resulted in the death of a Virginia college student.

However, if the patient has also been abusing other inhalants, the detoxification period could conceivably take up to 40 days, depending on the chemicals involved. Withdrawal symptoms in inhalant abusers may include nausea, vomiting, muscle pain and cramping, chills and sweats, irritability, tremors, headaches, and hallucinations. Depending on the severity of the symptoms and the patient's physical condition, the controlled environment of a residential setting may be preferred for the detox period.

After detox, the primary goals of treatment are abstinence (i.e., quitting the drug) and long-term recovery. Recovery is the life-long process of avoiding not just drug use, but the unhealthy behaviors and thought patterns that trigger it as well. An effective drug rehabilitation program focuses on changing these patterns of behavior and teaching recovering patients coping skills. Drug education on the long-term physical and mental effects of substance abuse is also part of a rehab program.

"Relapse"—using a drug again after a period of sobriety or abstinence—may occur if the emotional and behavioral issues surrounding drug use aren't understood. Some of the methods used to understand them

include individual psychotherapy, behavioral therapy, cognitive-behavioral therapy, group therapy, and family counseling.

Individual psychotherapy

One-on-one counseling that explores the emotional issues underlying a patient's drug dependence and abuse. Individual psychotherapy is particularly when there is also some type of mental disorder, such as depression or an anxiety disorder along with the drug abuse.

Behavioral therapy

Behavioral therapy focuses on replacing unhealthy behaviors with healthier ones. It uses tools such as rewards (positive reinforcement for healthy behavior) and rehearsal (practicing the new behavior) to achieve a drug-free life.

Cognitive-behavioral therapy

Like behavioral therapy, cognitive-behavioral therapy (CBT) also tries teaching new behavioral patterns. However, the primary difference is CBT assumes that thinking is behind behavior and emotions. Therefore, CBT also focuses on—and tries to change—the thoughts that led to the drug abuse.

Family therapy

Family members often develop habits and ways of coping (called "enabling") that unintentionally help the addict continue their substance abuse. Group counseling sessions with a licensed counselor or therapist can help family members build healthy relationships and relearn old behaviors. This is particularly important for adolescents in drug treatment, who should be able to rely on the support of family.

Group therapy

Group therapy offers recovering drug abusers a safe and comfortable place to work out problems with peers and a group leader (typically a therapist or counselor). It also provides drug abusers insight into their thoughts and behaviors through the eyes and experiences of others. Substance abusers who have difficulty building healthy relationships can benefit from the interactions in group therapy. Offering suggestions and emotional support to other members of the group can help improve their self-esteem and social skills.

Self-help and twelve-step groups

Self-help organizations offer recovering drug abusers and addicts important support groups to replace their former drug-using social circle. They also help create an important sense of identity and belonging to a new, recovery-focused group.

Twelve-step groups, one of the most popular types of self-help organizations, have been active in the United States since the founding of Alcoholics Anonymous (AA) in 1935. Narcotics Anonymous (NA), a group that serves recovering drug addicts, was founded in 1953. Like AA and other 12-step programs, NA is based on the spiritual philosophy that turning one's will and life over to "a higher power" (i.e., God, another spiritual entity, or the group itself) for guidance and self-evaluation is the key to lasting recovery.

The accessibility of self-help groups is one of their most attractive features. No dues or fees are required for AA and NA, so they are a good option for the uninsured and underinsured. Meetings are held in public places like local hospitals, healthcare centers, churches, and other community organizations, and frequent and regular attendance is encouraged.

In addition, 12-step groups work to empower members and promote self-esteem and self-reliance. NA meetings are not run by a counselor or therapist, but by the group or a member of the group. The organization encourages sponsorship (mentoring another member), speaking at meetings, and other positive peer-to-peer interactions that can help reinforce healthy social behaviors. Today, the internet and on-line support communities have added a further degree of accessibility to those who live in rural or remote areas.

PERSONAL AND SOCIAL CONSEQUENCES

Substance abusers become preoccupied with when and where they will be able to get their next dose. As drug use takes center stage in an abuse's life, relationships with family and friends frequently deteriorate. Although nitrous oxide and other inhalants are known for their relatively low cost, an N_2O abuser may suffer financial hardships as a result of unemployment, automobile accidents, or poor performance at school.

Chronic inhalant use is related to poor academic performance. According to the "National Household Survey on Drug Abuse 2000," kids with a D average in school were three times more likely to have used inhalants in the prior 12 months than the A-average students surveyed.

Substance abuse in general is a far-reaching societal problem, impacting not only personal relationships and health but also contributing to crime, domestic violence, sexual assault, drop-out rates, unemployment, and homelessness. It is also a factor in public health problems, like the spread of sexually transmitted diseases (STDs) and unwanted pregnancy. Chronic inhalant abuse can lead to serious birth defects.

Inhalant abuse is a financial drain on society as well. Indian Health Services estimates a cost of $1.6 million to treat a young adult with a history of inhalant abuse and all its associated physical, mental, legal, occupational, and social problems. The Office of National Drug Control Policy (ONDCP) estimates that illegal drugs cost the U.S. economy $160 billion in the year 2000, an annual increase of 5.8% between 1998 and 2000. That estimate includes $14.8 billion in healthcare costs and $110.4 billion in lost productivity from drug-related illness, incarceration, and death.

The perception of inhalants as dangerous, harmful substances has risen among young people. In 2001, 76.4% of tenth graders said they thought regular inhalant abuse a "great risk" to the user. And socially, inhalants are becoming risky as well, with 91.3% of tenth graders strongly disapproving of regular inhalant use among their peers. This may be due in part an to anti-inhalant advertising campaign launched in the mid-1990s by the Partnership for a Drug-Free America.

LEGAL CONSEQUENCES

Most states have laws regarding inhalant (or volatile substance) use and abuse on the books. In recent years, laws that are specific to nitrous oxide use and distribution have been written in many states. For example, in Connecticut, Arizona, Texas, and Michigan, it is illegal for anyone under the age of 18 to purchase nitrous oxide, even in food grade cartridges. In Arizona, anyone caught selling N_2O to minors faces up to 18 months in jail and a $150,000 fine.

In Wisconsin, the minimum age for purchasing nitrous oxide is 21. However, state legislation passed in 1998 makes it illegal for anyone to inhale or even intend to inhale nitrous outside of medical or dental settings. Anyone who distributes or delivers nitrous to someone with the knowledge that they are using it for illicit purposes can also be charged under Wisconsin law. A number of states, including Texas, California, Ohio, and Iowa, have variations on this law.

Illicit use, or possession with intent to use, is typically a misdemeanor in most states, and may be punishable by a small fine. Knowingly selling nitrous for illicit use carries a heftier price tag; it is a felony in many states and can involve significant jail time and cash fines.

Legal history

Nitrous oxide is not a U.S. Drug Enforcement Administration controlled substance. Nitrous oxide is regulated at the federal level by the United States Food and Drug Administration (FDA), as a food-grade propellant, medical grade gas, and prescription drug. In the

1990s, in an attempt to curb growing abuse of nitrous oxide, a number of states passed laws placing strong safeguards and stricter penalties on its illicit use.

Federal guidelines, regulations, and penalties

Use of the medical grade gas is by prescription only, and regulated by the FDA. Compressed medical gas suppliers must register with FDA, and are subjected to facility inspections from FDA at least once every two years. Licenses required to purchase and administer nitrous oxide in the healthcare setting is regulated on a state level.

Theft of nitrous oxide tanks from medical and other facilities is not uncommon. Some industry trade groups are working with state legislatures to pass stricter regulations on nitrous sales and theft-prevention guidelines in an effort to deter abuse.

See also Inhalants

RESOURCES

Books

Fenster, Julie M. *Ether Day: The Strange Tale of America's Greatest Medical Discovery and the Haunted Men Who Made It.* New York: HarperCollins, 2001.

Periodicals

Johnston, Lloyd D., et al. *Monitoring the Future: National Survey Results on Drug Use, 1975-2000.* Vols. I and II. Bethesda, MD: National Institute on Drug Abuse, 2001.

Organizations

National Inhalant Prevention Coalition, 2904 Kerbey Lane, Austin, TX, USA, 78703, (512) 480-8953, (512) 477-3932, (800) 269-4237, nipc@io.com, <http://www.inhalants.org/>.

National Institute on Drug Abuse (NIDA), National Institutes of Health, 6001 Executive Boulevard, Room 5213, Bethesda, MD, USA, 20892-9561, (301) 443-1124, (888) 644-6432, Information@lists.nida.nih.gov, <http://www.nida.nih.gov>.

Paula Anne Ford-Martin

OPIUM

OFFICIAL NAMES: Opium, laudanum, paregoric, Dover's powder
STREET NAMES: Big O, black stuff, block, gum, hop/hops, ah-pen-yen, Aunti, Aunti Emma, black, black pill, chandoo/chandu, Chinese molasses, Chinese tobacco, dopium, Dover's deck, dream gun, dream stick, dreams, easing powder, fi-do-nie, gee, God's medicine, gondola, goric, great tobacco, guma, joy plant, midnight oil, O, O.P., ope, pen yan, pin gon, pin yen, pox, skee, toxy, toys, when-shee, ze, zero
DRUG CLASSIFICATIONS: Schedule II, narcotic

OVERVIEW

Opium, the parent of heroin and a myriad of other addictive derivatives, has a long and fascinating history. Opium has been used for medical, religious, and recreational purposes, and has been featured in, and used to inspire, art, literature, and poetry. As an international commodity, it has been the focus of regulation, legislation, even war. Opium's addictive and detrimental effects have caused untold suffering throughout history. Its ability to relieve pain has brought untold relief to the injured, ill, and dying.

Opium is a naturally occurring narcotic derived from the annual plant *Papaver somniferum*, widely known as the opium poppy. Although readily recognized in many countries and even celebrated at various times and places in history, the opium poppy lives legally in the United States and many other countries today only in memory and myth. For example, these poppies are popularly recognized in the United States for their role in the children's story, *The Wizard of Oz*, as the flowers the Wicked Witch used to put Dorothy and her companions to sleep as they traveled to the Emerald City in the mythical land of Oz. However, the true history of the drug and the poppy flower tells an intriguing story in itself.

Scholars have suggested several origins for the opium poppy, including southern Europe, Turkey, and northwestern Africa. Exactly when opium came into medicinal and recreational use is also uncertain; however, it is clear that the cultivation of the plant and use of opium are ancient practices, dating to 4000 B.C. or even earlier. Poppy seeds and seed pods have been discovered in the remains of Neolithic lake villages in what is now Switzerland. The Sumerians referred to the opium poppy as Hul Gil, the "joy plant." The Assyrians, Babylonians, and Egyptians cultivated the opium poppy with trade routes extending into Greece and Europe. The opium derivative, thebaine, even takes its name from poppy fields in the ancient Egyptian city of Thebes. Poppies appeared in Homer's *Illiad* and *Odyssey* and Virgil's *Aeneid*. Several Roman gods were regularly depicted with poppies. It has even been suggested that the vinegar and gall offered to Jesus Christ during his crucifixion was an opium mixture.

Arab traders introduced the opium poppy east into China sometime between the fifth and the eighth century. It was later traded to Europe by the Venetians and then by the Portuguese. Well-known explorers Columbus, Magellan, and Vasco de Gama were all instructed to find opium.

KEY TERMS

ALKALOID: Any organic agent isolated from plants that contains nitrogen and reacts with an acid to form a salt.

ANALGESIC: A type of drug that alleviates pain without loss of consciousness.

DROSS: The residue remaining in the pipe after prepared opium has been smoked.

NARCOTIC: A natural or synthetic drug that has properties similar to opium or opium derivatives.

OPIATE: Drug derived directly from opium and used in its natural state, without chemical modification. Opiates include morphine, codeine, thebaine, noscapine, and papaverine.

OPIOID: A drug, hormone, or other chemical substance having sedative or narcotic effects similar to those containing opium or its derivatives; a natural brain opiate.

OPIOPHOBIA: The fear of patients becoming addicted to their narcotic pain medication.

Opium became very popular, especially in Southeast Asia. Among its attractions, opium provided medicine, cheap recreation, and an alternative to alcohol. It was also affordable to the poor and enabled them to do with less food.

Opium cultivation and use became especially prevalent in India and later in China where the Chinese smoked an opium-tobacco mixture (*madak* or *madhak*). Sometime during the mid-1700s, they began to smoke pure opium—a habit that spread from the wealthy to the common people. British merchants, in particular, capitalized on the Chinese demand for opium. By building on their already thriving colonial Indian tea trade, the merchants readily dominated opium trade with China. Tensions between Britain and China over the opium trade eventually resulted in the Opium Wars, two separate conflicts occurring during 1839–42 and 1856–60. A number of Westerners made great profits in the opium trade, reputedly including John Cushing, John Jacob Astor, and Warren Delano II (grandfather of U.S. President Franklin Delano Roosevelt).

In the 1800s, Chinese immigrants took their opium-smoking habit around the globe. Chinese laborers were kept impoverished by their habit when by their creditors would sell them high-priced opium. However, opium smoking and the medicinal use of opium increasingly gained popularity across all levels of society. A number of famous people used or became addicted to opium, including writers who used opium while seeking to enhance creativity, imagination, and spontaneity. Writers that embraced opium during this general period include Goethe, Samuel Taylor Coleridge, William Wordsworth, John Keats, Sir Walter Scott, Lord Byron, Elizabeth Barrett Browning, and Edgar Allen Poe. Thomas De Quincey even wrote an autobiographical book, *Confessions of an English Opium-Eater*.

By the late 1800s, an unregulated patent medicine trade was booming across the United States. These medicines were actually unpatented concoctions, many containing opium; patent medicines that followed contained morphine, heroin, or cocaine. Similar to today's over-the-counter medicines, these concoctions were readily available for purchase in pharmacies, grocery stores, bookstores, and even by mail order without a doctor's prescription. They were marketed as treatments for ailments ranging from athlete's foot to cancer and were frequently promoted for their painkilling and "soothing" properties. Dover's Powder (a mixture of ipecac and opium) and Mrs. Winslow's Soothing Syrup (a cough suppressant) were two popular products.

Use of opium-laced medicines was also widespread in Britain. Since there were no laws required labeling the content of these medicines until the Pure Food and Drug Act of 1906, many users were unaware of exactly what was in their medicine bottle.

Not fully understanding the processes or implications of addiction, physicians encouraged the use of these medicines, which resulted in a growing addiction problem in the United States. The development of opium derivatives compounded the problem. For example, the discovery of morphine, a powerful painkiller derived from opium, and the invention of the hypodermic needle combined to create a new and efficient way to administer drugs. For the first time in history, a powerful painkiller could be administered in a measurable dose. The method was readily embraced by the medical community and provided untold relief for those injured or suffering from dysentery during the Civil War. However, so many soldiers became addicted that morphine addiction came to be known as the "soldier's disease." Heroin, another opium derivative, was isolated in the late 1800s. Due to its depressant effects on the respiratory system, heroin was widely touted as a cough and lung medicine, a welcome intervention in an era before tuberculosis could be cured with antibiotics. Ironically, it was even hailed as a cure for opium addiction at one point.

Addiction was widespread by the turn of the twentieth century, especially among the middle and upper classes, and many addicts were young to middle-aged white women who had originally taken addictive substances under the advice of their physicians. Although there are no verifiable statistics from that time, estimates range from 100,000 to more than one million addicts in the United States. Unlike today, opium use was not associated with criminality but with illness.

An Afghan farmer scrapes sap from a poppy bulb to make opium or heroin. Photo by Amir Shah, AP World Wide Photos. Reproduced by permission.

As a result of various government efforts, many patent medicines were eliminated from the market. Legislative efforts continued throughout the century. The 1970 passage of the Controlled Substances Act (CSA), Title II of the Comprehensive Drug Abuse Prevention and Control Act, established comprehensive federal guidelines for controlling narcotics that consolidated previous laws.

CHEMICAL/ORGANIC COMPOSITION

Opium is classified as a narcotic. By definition, narcotics have analgesic (or painkilling) properties as well as effects beyond lessening pain, such as producing euphoria and addiction. Opium has long been valued for its analgesic effects. However, not all analgesics are narcotics, because they do not produce these side effects; aspirin and Tylenol are examples of non-narcotic analgesics.

Raw opium is harvested from the seed pod of the opium poppy. As many as 50 substances called alkaloids can then be derived from opium, and the opium can be further processed. Alkaloids are naturally occurring plant products that possess some pharmacological activity, and are found in other plants as well as opium poppies. Cocaine and nicotine are examples of alkaloids derived from the coca plant and the tobacco plant,

respectively. Because of their chemical composition, alkaloids are often used in producing medicines.

The alkaloids derived from opium are collectively known as opiates. Morphine, codeine, and thebaine are well-known opium derivatives. Paregoric is an opium tincture (opium in an alcohol mixture).

Semisynthetic and synthetic narcotics are also produced that have opiate-like effects; these narcotics are collectively known as opioids. They include methadone and the designer drug fentanyl, and a number of commonly prescribed medicines such as Darvon, Demerol, Dilaudid, Orlaam, OxyContin, Percodan, Talwin, and Vicodin.

Opium production

The poppies that produce opium grow to be 3–5 ft (1.5 m) tall, produce brightly colored flowers ranging from white, to pink, red, or purple, and do well in warm, dry climates. The plant is an annual, meaning it must be re-planted each season, and will flower and produce the seed pod from which opium is derived only once in its 120-day growth cycle. Many popular varieties of poppy produce three to five of these mature pods per plant.

After the poppies bloom, petals drop off and farmers are able to collect the opium from the unripe seed pod in the center of the flower. Illicitly harvesting opium is labor-intensive work that must be done by hand. The pod is slit with specially designed knives. Called taping,

LAW AND ORDER

Before the Pure Food and Drug Act of 1906, makers of patent medicines were not required to label the ingredients of their products. Treatments for babies' colic, "women's disorders," and almost any imaginable ailment were marketed to users who had no way of knowing their ingredients or the proportions of opium, cocaine, alcohol, or other drugs in those medicines. At best, many of these concoctions were worthless as medical treatments; at worst, they were addictive and even deadly.

Responding to a growing recognition of the problems and implications of addiction during the late 1800s, the media and medical groups began to speak out about the dangers of many of these substances. The public became interested in what their medicine bottles contained. Before that time, if consumers of these medicines had known the ingredients in their medicines, few of them or their physicians would have understood the dangers of these drugs anyway.

A seemingly unrelated event also demonstrated the need for product labeling. In 1906, Sinclair Lewis published *The Jungle*, a book exposing the filthy meat handling practices in the Chicago meat packing industry. Among the atrocities he documented were rat and human remains being mixed in with the meat and rampant mislabeling of products. The public and politicians were justifiably outraged.

The Pure Food and Drug Act was passed later that year, ensuring that all adulterated or mislabeled food and drugs could not be transported across state lines. It required dangerous ingredients to be noted on drug labels, called for illegal foods and drugs to be seized, and created the agency that later became the Food and Drug Administration (FDA). Since patent medicines were included in this Act, it ultimately resulted in the demise of the patent medicine industry since the public and physicians could know and assess the ingredients in their medicines.

---

scoring, or lancing, the slit is made just deep enough to get the white latex-like sap to ooze onto the outside of the pod where the farmer allows it to dry. After the sap darkens and thickens into a sticky gum, the farmer collects it by scraping it off with another specially designed tool. This sap is raw opium. High-quality opium will be brown and sticky.

The pods can continue to ooze their sap for several days, so the farmer may tap pods to collect the opium several times. Some of the most productive seed pods will also be harvested to provide seeds for the next year's crop. On average, a single pod produces less than 80 mg of raw opium, according to the United States Drug Enforcement Administration (DEA). An area of 2.5 acres (1 hectare) may yield roughly 17.6–33 lb (8–15 kg) of raw opium.

After harvesting, the wet resin must be dried for several days. It will then be wrapped and stored. If dried correctly, it can be stored for an indefinite period. The DEA has reports of opium that has been stored for 10 years without deteriorating.

Raw opium may be smoked, but it is usually "cooked" first, a process in which the raw opium is boiled in water. The opium dissolves and impurities such as twigs and dirt are removed by straining. This leaves a clear, brown liquid called "liquid opium," which is then re-heated until the water evaporates and all that remains is a thick paste. The paste is then sun-dried to the proper consistency for smoking or eating.

Both raw and cooked opium contain alkaloids. These alkaloids can be extracted from the opium to produce opium derivatives for legal pharmaceuticals or for illegal consumption, such as morphine and heroin. The morphine alkaloid content, which ranges from 8% to 12%, determines the quality of the opium.

Morphine is extracted first, and the resulting product can then be converted into heroin. Addicts generally do not use morphine base because it is not readily water soluble, thus not easily absorbed by the body. Further purification is required to produce a more pure product, morphine hydrochloride. This more refined morphine is commonly pressed into a 2 x 4 x 5 in (5 x 10 x 2 cm) block (also called a "brick") weighing approximately 3 lb (1.3 kg). It takes approximately 28.7 lb (13 kg) of opium to produce one of these morphine blocks.

Morphine can then be converted into heroin base and, finally, into heroin. Because of the odor of the chemicals used, heroin conversion labs may be located in rural areas. In the first step of this process, morphine is converted into a tan-colored heroin base that is approximately 70% pure heroin. In step two, this base can then be converted into smokable heroin (also known as heroin no. 3) or injectible heroin (also known as heroin no. 4).

INGESTION METHODS

Opium and synthetic narcotics can be processed such that they can be swallowed or eaten, drank in a variety of mixtures, smoked, injected, inhaled, or absorbed. Poppy farmers may even experience some effects of opium by walking through their fields after tapping the seed pods. Traditionally, however, opium is taken orally or smoked. Opium is sometimes flavored with spices to disguise its bitter taste, or mixed with wine, sugar, and/or honey; sugar or tobacco is sometimes mixed with opium for smoking. Opium ingestion is rare in the United States and other developed countries today.

THERAPEUTIC USE

Therapeutic uses of opium have been known for centuries. Ancient Assyrian medical writings mentioned poppy juice. Ancient Greek physicians knew the medicinal effects of poppies as did Hippocrates, the "father of medicine" (460–377 B.C.), and Hua To, Chinese surgeon of the Three Kingdoms (A.D. 220–264). In ancient Rome, opium was used both as a religious drug and as a poison to commit suicides or murders. Hannibal allegedly committed suicide by taking opium and Nero's mother poisoned a stepson with opium to assure Nero's ascendance to power. In more recent times, opium use was widespread in the United States and Britain during the nineteenth century. Opium and its derivatives were used as a treatment for almost every ailment, as well as by addicts, and by artists seeking recreation and enhanced creativity.

Several powerful and important modern medicines are derived from opium or are synthetic or semi-synthetic narcotics with opiate-like effects. Many of these medicines are primarily used to control pain but are also used to control coughs and diarrhea, and as anesthesia.

USAGE TRENDS

Even though the developed world's appetite for smoking or eating opium is not large, it still exists. The DEA estimates that the U.S. market for cooked opium, consumed by opium smokers, is still as much as 2.2 tons (2 metric tons) annually. Much of this market is apparently among Laotian Hmong and Mien refugees who have settled in Northern California, Minnesota, and Wisconsin.

In the United States and other developed countries, illicit opium derivatives such as heroin or licit synthetic opioids such as Vicodin have generally replaced the use of smoked or eaten opium. According to Drug Abuse Warning Network (DAWN) data provided by the Substance Abuse and Mental Health Services Administration (SAMHSA), there were more than 82,000 emergency department admissions for narcotic analgesics/narcotic analgesic combinations in 2000. Only 167 of these visits were for opium and opium combinations.

Prescription opioids are often the drugs of choice for physicians and other health care professionals who become substance abusers. Their jobs often grant them easy access to pharmaceuticals, and these prescription drugs provide standardized doses without the dangers encountered in obtaining street drugs. These users frequently favor Demerol, Dilaudid, methadone, and morphine.

Opium use in developing nations

In some developing countries, particularly around the poppy fields themselves, opium is used for its medicinal and recreational effects. Opium smoking and/or eating is still a problem in rural areas where the poppies are cultivated. By some estimates, perhaps as much as 25% of the opium produced in Southeast Asia is consumed by opium poppy farmers.

Poppy farmers commonly smoke opium to fight hunger, cold, and chronic pain. Opium also retains a variety of other uses in developing countries. For example, Afghan carpet weavers eat opium to ease pain and to work longer hours. Opium is also used in some developing areas as a form of childcare to keep children quiet while parents work or to soothe their fussiness. It also serves as a treatment for diarrhea. Indeed, the widespread practice of using opium to treat diarrhea and malaria has been noted as an important factor in its rapid and early establishment throughout India, western China, and Southeast Asia, where these ailments were common. Additionally, opium has been believed in various places and points in history to have aphrodisiac (sexually enhancing) properties.

Opium also has a history of use with animals. For example, trainers have used opium balls in domesticating and training elephants. Increasing an elephant's opium allowance has also been used to control them during *musth* when a rutting, testosterone-driven male elephant might otherwise go on a rampage. For centuries, horses have also been given opium to prepare them for long journeys or military patrols.

MENTAL AND PHYSIOLOGICAL EFFECTS

Opium has been used for centuries for its analgesic (pain-relieving) properties. The opium derivative morphine has long been considered the standard narcotic to which all pain-relieving drugs are compared. These narcotics act on the central nervous system, relieving pain by interrupting pain messages in the brain or spinal cord. Opiates bind to special receptor sites in different parts of the brain and body that are active in transmitting pain signals.

Opium derivatives also have antitussive effects, meaning they suppress the cough reflex. Because of this effect, codeine is a frequently used ingredient in cough syrups. Opiates also slow digestion by slowing messages to the smooth muscles and reducing intestinal secretions. This effect makes them useful in treating diarrhea, but may also lead to constipation, a common problem for those who abuse opium. Additionally, users' heart rate, blood pressure, and respiration slow.

Other central nervous effects of opium and its derivatives include drowsiness, sedation, nausea, weakness, faintness, agitation, restlessness, nervousness, and decreased sex drive. Users may become very sleepy. In some rare cases, effects may include delirium and insomnia. Long-term narcotic use can lead to addiction, depression, difficulty sleeping or concentrating, agitation, tremors, seizures, and an increased sensitivity to pain. An extremely dangerous effect of these drugs is their depressive effect on the respiratory system, which may lead to unconsciousness, coma, and sometimes a rapid death. Users may also experience mood changes, euphoria, dysphoria (feeling unwell or unhappy), mental cloudiness, disorientation, or hallucinations.

These potential effects are impacted by such factors as circumstances of use (e.g., medical use supervised by medical professionals versus abuse), dosage, and route of administration. In general, effects increase as drug potency increases. The onset of these effects ranges from an immediate response to the drug to the user experiencing the impact 30–60 minutes later. The duration of their effects lasts from three to seven hours.

All opium derivatives are addictive and have the potential to be abused. For abusers, these substances produce a strong dependence, a complex concept. In simple terms, long-term opiate use changes the workings of nerve cells in the brain. These cells come to need the drug. The body needs the drug or it will experience effects from the drug's withdrawal. However, many myths surround opiate withdrawal. While it has been described as tortuous (a perspective often perpetuated by the media), other reports equate it to a severe case of the flu. Common withdrawal symptoms include cramps, a runny nose, chills, and muscle aches that are generally over in 24–48 hours.

Tolerance also develops with continued use, meaning that larger doses are needed to achieve the same psychoactive effect. Dosage, route of administration, and medical versus nonmedical use also play a role here. For example, abusers develop a psychological dependence on the drug. They develop a craving for the drug once it is removed. However, this craving does not generally develop among patients taking opioids for relief of severe pain. Pain patients do not continue to seek the drug to satisfy the cravings experienced by abusers. However, like abusers, pain patients do build up a tolerance to the drug. Also, like abusers, they may experience symptoms of physical withdrawal when they stop using the drug.

Harmful side effects

When using opium and its derivatives, the most obvious risk is coma or death from respiratory failure.

Medical professionals are well aware of the potential side effects of opiates and administer them according to strict guidelines. However, overdoses and negative side effects also may occur when taking prescribed drugs; prescription drugs may be diverted from medical use to abuse. Strong painkillers such as Vicodin and OxyContin are likely candidates for abuse. However, for users of street drugs, risks may be especially pronounced.

One group at risk for experiencing unwanted side effects from any drug use are pregnant women. Opioids cross the placenta and some are excreted in breast milk. Some types of prescription opioids may be used during pregnancy on a short-term basis under the direction of a medical professional. Ultimately though, pregnant women should always be guided by the advice of their physicians.

Patients who experience severe pain, either chronically from an illness or short-term from an injury or surgery, are another group with a special interest in the side effects of narcotics. One medical controversy revolves around the extent to which physicians should use powerful narcotics to relieve a patient's suffering. The fear that patients would become addicted (opiophobia) led to cases of doctors under-prescribing pain medication. Research has shown, however, that these fears are largely unfounded. Doctors have also been accused of over-prescribing these medications, leading to additional fears among physicians that legal consequences could result if they liberally prescribe opiate derivatives for patients in severe pain. An unfortunate result was that some patients were not prescribed the strong medicines necessary to alleviate their pain. This controversy led to guidelines from the federal Agency for Health Care Policy and Research addressing pain treatments. Additionally, research is underway seeking compounds that will result in effective pain-relief with smaller doses or no euphoric high.

REACTIONS WITH OTHER DRUGS OR SUBSTANCES

Drug mixing, taking two or more drugs in combination, may alleviate or intensify the effects. Opiates' pain-relieving effects may be intensified by the use of other drugs called nonsteroidal anti-inflammatory drugs (NSAIDs). Such use should be monitored by medical professionals to guard against stomach bleeding or organ damage.

When opium is abused, it may be combined with other licit or illicit drugs. In these cases, opium may be mixed with tobacco or other vegetable matter for smoking, a mixture called madak (or madhak). An A-bomb is a marijuana cigarette that contains heroin or opium, while Buddha is a strong form of marijuana spiked with opium. Opium may also be mixed with hashish in a concoction called black Russian or black hash.

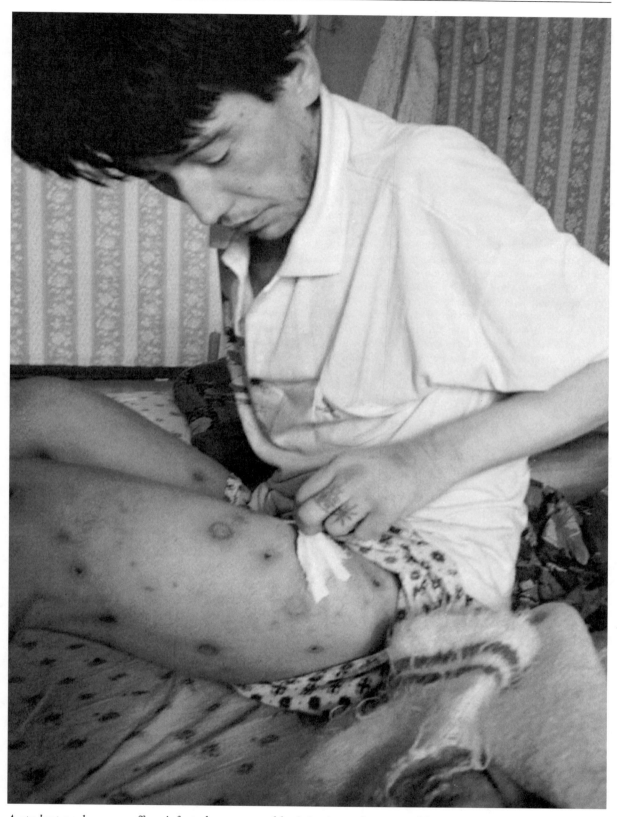

A student peels gauze off an infected sore caused by injecting opium up to 10 times a day. Photo by David Brauchli, AP/World Wide Photos. Reproduced by permission.

HISTORY NOTES

Britain and China fought two wars (1839–42 and 1856–60) over opium trading rights that have come to be known as the Opium Wars. During the 1700s, the British established a lucrative monopoly over the opium trade. This trade continued even after Chinese emperor Kia King's 1799 ban on opium. The First Opium War erupted when the Chinese government attempted to suppress the opium trade through drastic prohibitions. Imperial Chinese commissioner Lin Tse-Hsu seized or destroyed huge amounts of opium, including stocks owned by British traders. The result was a Chinese payment of an indemnity of more than 21 million silver dollars and Hong Kong being ceded to Britain under the Treaty of Nanking. Hong Kong quickly became a center of the growing opium trade around which a substantial shipping business evolved. Tensions remained high between the countries. The Second Opium War (also known as the Arrow War, or the Anglo-French War in China) broke out after a British-flagged ship, the Arrow, was impounded by China. France joined Britain in this effort after the murder of a French missionary. China was again defeated, resulting in another large indemnity and the legalization of opium under the Treaty of Tientsin.

Flavoring substances can also be added to opium, including spices, sugar, and/or honey to disguise its bitter taste. It is also mixed into opium wine mixtures, some of which are called Yen Shee Suey. Dross, the residue remaining in the pipe after prepared opium has been smoked, may be mixed with raw opium. Re-using this dross is a cost-cutting measure in opium production.

TREATMENT AND REHABILITATION

An assortment of treatments for opiate drug abusers are tailored to the needs of each user, including behavioral interventions such as counseling, psychotherapy, family therapy, and the use of support groups, treatment with medications, or some combination of both of these approaches. Research has even looked at acupuncture as part of treatment programs. Programs vary greatly in length and may include outpatient and/or inpatient treatments.

Medically assisted narcotic treatment programs use medications that suppress withdrawal symptoms and drug cravings while the person undergoes behavioral therapy and/or receives other health-related services.

These maintenance therapies supply regular doses of a drug that keeps the addict from experiencing withdrawal symptoms, drug cravings, or highs. Methadone and LAAM (levo-alpha-acetyl-methadol) are medications often used in these programs.

Heroin abusers comprise the vast majority of those in treatment for opiate abuse. According to the SAMHSA's Treatment Episode Data Set (TEDS), only 1% of admissions for addiction treatment recorded in 1999 were related to opiates other than heroin. However, the number of these admissions that was for opium itself cannot be determined from the available data because opium is categorized with all other drugs with morphine-like effects. Methadone was part of the treatment plan for 22% of those admitted.

Treatment programs are also needed to address the concerns of opiate users in developing countries. For example, some Afghan refugee camps have found a need to treat refugees for opium addiction. These refugees include laborers and those dealing with the pain of war wounds. In such situations, treatment options may include alternative medication and education.

PERSONAL AND SOCIAL CONSEQUENCES

Opium and its derivatives are addictive substances. In the developing countries where poppies are cultivated and opium is produced, peasants make more producing opium than they could make cultivating legitimate crops. The trade-offs they face include the personal consequences of addiction, the ethnic tensions fueled by the drug trade, the empowerment of drug lords, and corrupt politics, among others.

Poppy cultivation and opium processing also have consequences for the environment. Waste from morphine extraction can cause environmental damage when dumped by processors. In addition to water pollution from this chemical dumping, other environmental concerns include the deforestation that may occur when clearing land for poppy cultivation, soil erosion, and dangers to wildlife in the area where these chemicals are dumped.

LEGAL CONSEQUENCES

Opium poppies are grown and opium legally produced on government-regulated farms in a handful of countries including India, Turkey, and Tasmania in Australia. For most legal commercial production, alkaloids are extracted through a process of milling the "poppy straw." Rather than going through the entire opium-producing stage, the dried pods (the "poppy straw") are processed to obtain morphine, codeine, and thebaine and the seeds are sold as well. Unlike traditional illicit opium production, this process may be done with mechanized agricultural equipment.

One major benefit of this extract is for legitimate medicinal use. The DEA estimates that more than 500 tons (455,000 kg) of opium or its equivalent in poppy straw are annually imported into the United States for this purpose. The poppy also has other legitimate uses. For example, mature poppy seeds are used in the food industry such as in cake and bread decorations, and added to some dishes for crunchiness or flavor. (Alkaloids are only found in the ripening pod; mature pods cease to manufacture alkaloids.) Poppy seed can be pressed into cooking oil. Poppy seed oil is also legitimately used in artists' oil paints and in manufacturing perfumes. Throughout history, opium has also sometimes been used in religious rituals.

The possession of opium poppies was outlawed in the United States in 1942 by the Opium Poppy Control Act. Growing opium poppies is illegal in most countries. However, a number of areas around the world are infamous for their poppy cultivation. The countries of Laos, Burma, and Thailand comprise the Southeast Asian poppy growing area known as the Golden Triangle. The DEA estimates that Southeast Asian poppy fields produced nearly 3 million lb (1.4 million kg) of opium during 2000. Opium poppies are also illegally cultivated in Southwest Asia across a swatch known as the Golden Crescent, an area cutting across Pakistan, Iran, and Afghanistan. According to the U.N. Economic and Social Council Commission on Narcotic Drugs, illicit opium production is also reported in varying amounts in Armenia, Belarus, Colombia, Egypt, Guatemala, India, Italy, Japan, Kyrgyzstan, Latvia, Lebanon, Lithuania, Mexico, Peru, Portugal, Spain, Turkey, Uzbekistan, and Venezuela.

The U.N. Office for Drug Control and Crime Prevention (UNODCCP) reports that Afghanistan had emerged as the leading single source of illicit opium worldwide by 2000. In that year, Afghanistan produced as much as eight million lb (3.6 million kg) of opium, accounting for 70% of the world's illicit opium and 80% of the heroin reaching Europe. Afghan's Taliban rulers implemented a ban on opium poppy cultivation in 2001 and indications are that only 165,000 lb (75,000 kg) of opium were produced in Afghanistan that year. However, the UNODCCP reports that cultivation resumed after the fall of the Taliban due both to lawlessness and to farmers seeking to survive an ongoing drought. The main routes for smuggling Afghan opium to Europe and, in some cases, on to the United States are through Tajikistan, central Asia, and Eastern Europe; through Iran and Turkey to the Balkans; and through Pakistan.

In 2000, 430,000 lb (195,000 kg) of illegal opium were seized worldwide. The majority of these seizures (80%) were made by Iran, which seized approximately 364,000 lb (165,000 kg) of opium during that year.

Countries with the largest opium seizures in Southeast Asia tended to be those with the largest production.

Efforts to curb poppy cultivation have involved a variety of strategies including drug enforcement, the implementation of various legal frameworks, promoting alternative crops and sources of income, eradication efforts that use pesticides to kill plants, and economic interventions such as setting up rural credit systems. Some approaches focus on reducing drug demand and establishing rehabilitation, prevention, and/or drug abuse programs. In addition to reducing trafficking in drugs, some efforts focus on reducing the sale or trafficking of the chemicals used in the refinement process.

The U.N. Commission on Narcotic Drugs recommends that drug strategies also address money laundering, advising agencies to develop knowledge in this arena from experts such as the Turkish International Academy against Drugs and Organized Crime (TADOC). Other recommended training involves identifying drug couriers, establishing regional information exchanges on drug traffickers and current methods of operation, and training and equipping investigators to target major crime figures and financiers. Other recommendations emphasize government cooperation in information exchange, law enforcement efforts, and efforts to curb money laundering. Such cooperation would avoid duplication of effort and maximize resources. They also encourage governments to use the media in supporting their initiatives. The commission also encourages forward-looking drug strategies that look toward future trends and seek ways to interrupt smugglers' use of technology, with special attention given to sea routes and cargo containers.

Each of these strategies faces a number of challenges. Basic supply-and-demand economics impact drug prices. Opium prices fluctuate depending on a number of factors, including the production cycle, weather conditions that help or hinder poppy output, the availability of chemicals required to process the opium, the quality of the drug, and the local supply of opium and heroin. Opium prices saw large declines after the September 11, 2001, terrorist attacks but had recovered by March 2002, according to the U.N. Commission on Narcotic Drugs.

Opium traders buy the raw opium from farmers. In Southeast Asia, the price for raw opium in 1999–2000 ranged from $150 to $350 per kilogram. The price is marked up as the opium goes through each stage of processing and refinement. For example, the DEA reports that cooked opium is usually marked up approximately 20%. The price is then marked up again as the opium is refined into morphine base, morphine, heroin base, and heroin.

Opium production requires little infrastructure. Efforts to encourage alternative crops commonly find inadequate market infrastructures and transportation systems for handling legitimate crops. Targeting the chemicals necessary for processing the opium can be problematic in that many of the chemicals also have legitimate uses. The opium trade may be one element in on going ethnic conflicts. Additionally, when opium supplies are interrupted in one country, another source tends to take its place. In the late 1970s, the controversial defoliant Agent Orange was used to eliminate Mexican poppy fields. Golden Crescent opium production rapidly increased in response to the decreased Mexican supply.

The 1961 U.N. Single Convention on Drugs called for the eradication of opium in 25 years. A 1998 U.N. General Assembly Special Session called for eradication in 10 years. Instead of leading to the elimination of opium, some observers have argued that such goals are unattainable and sap ever-increasing amounts of resources. Many of these observers argue that the real keys to drug control lie in solving the economic and social problems that underlie drug production such as poverty, inequality, and political turmoil. Some observers contend that answers lie in decriminalization or legalization and a return to the view that addicts should be treated as if they are ill rather than lawbreakers. Other observers suggest that such stringent goals as those put forth by the U.N. are imperative in effectively waging any war on drugs.

Drug control efforts have often attempted to reduce both supply and demand. Strategies have included combinations of a range of legal and economic penalties, technologies, treatments, and educational and prevention efforts. The idea that currently illegal drugs should be legalized, or decriminalized, is also hotly debated. In brief, advocates of legalization or decriminalization contend that low rates of drug interdiction and high rates of use and drug-related crime mean that drug control efforts are not working. Their arguments include assumptions that drug prices would decrease; drug-related crime and corruption would decline, thereby freeing law enforcement resources for other needs; quality could be controlled; revenue would be produced for the government; and drug use would not increase significantly. Opponents of legalization argue that the behavioral, criminal, social, and public health problems that would arise would be considerable. They also point to high rates of legal alcohol and tobacco use as examples of what would happen to use rates if many currently illegal drugs were made legal. They cite evidence including the low rate of opium use in the United States today compared to the widespread use at the turn of the twentieth century in support of this last point.

Legal history

As medical understanding of addiction grew in the late 1800s, so too did the calls for reform of patent medicines and drug use in the United States. Many commentators have also connected the development of U.S. drug laws with growing racial fears. Concerns were raised that opium smoking was spreading beyond Chinese immigrants to the wider population and that blacks and Mexicans were unable to handle the growing drug use among those populations. News stories alleged the seduction of white women in Chinese opium dens and attributed a range of antisocial behaviors to minority users of illegal drugs. This began the current stigmatization of drug abusers as being outside mainstream society and as criminals rather than ill persons.

In 1909, Congressional legislation stopped the importation of smokable opium or opium derivatives except for medicinal purposes. The Harrison Narcotics Act of 1914 placed further controls on narcotics by addressing drug content, prescriptive, manufacturing, distribution, record-keeping, and taxation requirements. Under this act, only those licensed to do so could possess these drugs and they could only be prescribed for legitimate medical purposes, not for addict maintenance. A 1919 Supreme Court ruling upheld this position, consequently leading to strong narcotics regulations and ultimately to the current war on drugs.

After federal bans on opium, black markets developed to supply the demand. World War II temporarily interrupted opium smuggling routes. After the war, smuggling resumed with the U.S. government becoming involved in struggles in Southeast Asia that are sometimes blamed for fostering opium production and the heroin trade.

The development of synthetic narcotics was also encouraged by war needs. However, drug control efforts were somewhat haphazard. Although as of 1946 the Federal Bureau of Narcotics (FBN) oversaw potentially addictive synthetic narcotics, non-narcotics drugs and drug abuse were not adequately controlled. The Controlled Substances Act (CSA), Title II of the Comprehensive Drug Abuse Prevention and Control Act of 1970 attempted to fill this void. It established regulations, including controls on narcotics, which covered a range of drug control activities. The CSA schedule still includes regulations covering opium in the United States.

Federal guidelines, regulations, and penalties

In the United States, the CSA classifies drugs into schedules according to their medical use, potential for abuse, and ability to produce dependence. The CSA places opium derivatives under different schedules. Opium, morphine, and methadone are Schedule II drugs. Schedule II drugs have high abuse potential, some accepted medical use in the United States, and a likelihood of severe psychological or physical dependence if abused. Federal trafficking penalties for a first offense of 2.2 lb (1 kg) or more of a Schedule II substance is 10 years to life (20, if a death is involved) and fines of up to four million dollars for individuals and 10 million dollars for organizations. A second offense carries a minimum 20-year sentence and fines not to exceed eight and 20 million dollars.

Codeine is a Schedule III drug. These drugs have less potential for abuse than Schedule I or II drugs, an accepted medical use in the United States, and the likelihood of moderate or low physical dependence if abused. Federal trafficking penalties for a first offense of a Schedule III substance is not more than five years and fines of up to $250,000 for individuals and one million dollars for organizations. A second offense carries a maximum of 30 years to life if a death is involved and fines up to two and 10 million dollars.

Talwin, another opium derivative, is a Schedule IV narcotic. Schedule IV drugs have less potential for abuse than Schedule III drugs, an accepted medical use in the United States, and the likelihood of limited physical or psychological dependence if abused. Federal trafficking penalties for a first offense of a Schedule III substance is not more than three years and fines of up to $250,000 for individuals and one million dollars for organizations. A second offense carries a maximum of 30 years to life if a death is involved and fines up to two and 10 million dollars.

Non-prescription cough medicines with codeine are Schedule V drugs, which have a low potential for abuse compared to Schedule IV drugs, an accepted medical use in the United States, and the likelihood of limited physical or psychological dependence if abused. Federal trafficking penalties for a first offense of a Schedule V substance is not more than one year and fines of up to $100,000 for individuals and $250,000 for organizations. A second offense carries a maximum of 30 years to life if a death is involved and fines up to two and 10 million dollars.

See also Codeine; Heroin; Morphine; Oxycodone

RESOURCES

Books

Berlin, Laini, ed. *Physician's Drug Handbook*. 8th ed. Springhouse, PA: Springhouse Corp., 1999.

Booth, Martin. *Opium: A History*. New York: St. Martin's Press, 1998.

Courtwright, David T. *Dark Paradise: A History of Opiate Addiction in America*. Cambridge, MA: Harvard University Press, 2001.

Courtwright, David T. *Forces of Habit*. Cambridge, MA: Harvard University Press, 2001.

Inciardi, James A. *The War on Drugs III: The Continuing Saga of the Mysteries and Miseries of Intoxication, Addiction, Crime, and Public Policy*. Boston: Allyn and Bacon, 2001.

Musto, David F. *The American Disease: Origins of Narcotic Control*. New York: Oxford University Press, 1999.

Periodicals

Baldauf, Scott. "Afghan Weavers Unravel a Trade Tradition: Opium Use." *Christian Science Monitor Electronic Edition* (March 28, 2001). <http://www.csmonitor.com/durable/2001/03/28/fp7s2-csm.shtml>.

Food and Drug Administration. "The Story of the Laws Behind the Labels: Part I. The 1906 Food and Drugs Act." *FDA Consumer* (June 1981). <http://www.cfsan.fda.gov/~lrd/history1.html>.

Other

"Beyond the ABCs: Opioids and Pregnancy." Alberta Alcohol and Drug Abuse Commission. 2002 (July 8, 2002). <http://corp.aadac.com/drugs/beyond/opioidspreg.asp>.

Emergency Department Trends from the Drug Abuse Warning Network, Preliminary Estimates January-June 2001, with Revised Estimates 1994-2000. DAWN Series D-20, DHHS Publication No. (SMA) 02-3634. Rockville, MD: Substance Abuse and Mental Health Services Administration (SAMHSA), 2002. <http://www.samhsa.gov/oas/dawn/TrndED/2001/Text/TrndEDtxt.PDF>.

Illicit Drug Traffic and Supply: World Situation with Regard to Illicit Drug Trafficking and Action Taken by Subsidiary Bodies of the Commission on Narcotic Drugs United Nations Economic and Social Council, Commission on Narcotic Drugs, 45th Session, Vienna, 11-15 March, 2002. <http://www.odccp.org/pdf/document_2001-12-21_2.pdf>.

Opium Poppy Cultivation and Heroin Processing in Southeast Asia. U.S. Drug Enforcement Administration, DEA 20026, March 2001. <http://www.usdoj.gov/dea/pubs/intel/20026/20026.html>.

"Opium Throughout History." *The Opium Kings*. PBS Frontline. <http://www.pbs.org/wgbh/pages/frontline/shows/heroin/etc/history.html>.

The Price Dynamics of Southeast Asian Heroin. U.S. Drug Enforcement Administration, Intelligence Brief, February 2001. <http://www.usdoj.gov/dea/pubs/intel/01004-intelbrief.pdf>.

Treatment Episode Data Set (TEDS): 1994-1999. National Admissions to Substance Abuse Treatment Services. DASIS Series S-14, DHHS Publication No. (SMA) 01-3550. Rockville, MD: Substance Abuse and Mental Health Services Administration (SAMHSA), 2001. <http://www.samhsa.gov/oas/teds/99TEDS/99Teds.pdf>.

Organizations

Drug Enforcement Administration (DEA), 2401 Jefferson Davis Highway, Alexandria, VA, USA, 22301, (800) 882-9539, <http://www.usdoj.gov/dea/index.htm>.

National Institute on Drug Abuse (NIDA), National Institutes of Health, 6001 Executive Boulevard, Room 5213, Bethesda, MD, USA, 20892-9561, (301) 443-1124, (888) 644-6432, Information@lists.nida.nih.gov, <http://www.nida.nih.gov/>.

Office of National Drug Control Policy (ONDCP); Drug Policy Information Clearinghouse, P.O. Box 6000, Rockville, MD, USA, 20849-6000, (301) 519-5212, (800) 666-3332, ondcp@ncjrs.org, <http://www.whitehousedrugpolicy.gov/>.

United Nations Office for Drug Control and Crime Prevention (UNODCCP); Vienna International Centre, P.O. Box 500, Vienna, Austria, A-1400, 43 1 26060 0, 43 1 26060 5866, odccp@odccp.org, <http://www.undcp.org/>.

Kathy S. Stolley, Ph.D.

OXYCODONE

OFFICIAL NAMES: Endocet, Endocodone, Endodan, M-Oxy, OxyContin, OxyFast, OxyIR, Percocet, Percodan, Percodan-Demi, Percolone, Roxicet, Roxicodone, Roxilox, Roxiprin, Tylox
STREET NAMES: Hillbilly heroin, poor man's heroin, oxy, oxies, oxycotton, OCs, killers, oxycons, percs (or perks), pink spoons.
DRUG CLASSIFICATIONS: Schedule II, narcotic analgesic

OVERVIEW

Oxycodone is a semi-synthetic prescription drug with pain-relieving properties similar to those of morphine and codeine. Although commonly known as an opioid analgesic, it is also known as a narcotic analgesic. The drug's ability to relieve moderate to severe pain makes it a good choice for the treatment of many painful conditions, including back pain and headache as well as pain due to cancer and some dental procedures.

Oxycodone is derived from thebaine, one of more than 20 components known as alkaloids (including morphine and codeine) found in opium. In addition to being a primary component of oxycodone, thebaine also is a main ingredient of hydrocodone and hydromorphone, two other prescription painkillers.

History

Long before thebaine was identified and synthesized from opium poppies for use as a pain killer, ancient peoples were using opium to induce euphoria and even to stimulate creativity.

Historically, opium was an important crop as far back as 3400 B.C., when it was referred to as Hul Gil, or the joy plant. The milky liquid from the poppy seeds was dried to produce the powerful opium powder. As a commodity, the opium trade flourished in Egypt during the reigns of Thutmose IV, Akhenton, and the boy king Tutankhamen.

The first medicinal use of opium is credited to Hippocrates, the Greek physician known as the "father of medicine." In addition to using opium to relieve pain, Hippocrates advocated its use for treating internal diseases and some so-called women's diseases. Later, the famous physician Paracelsus mixed opium with citrus juice and gold essence and prescribed the compound for use as a pain remedy he called laudenum. In the late 1600s, the English apothecary (the equivalent of today's pharmacist) Thomas Sydenham introduced his own laudenum compound by mixing opium with sherry wine and herbs. The resulting medication, in the form of pills, was used to treat a variety of painful conditions.

Oxycodone was first developed in Germany in 1916 and marketed under the brand name Eukodal. The first documented medical reports of striking "euphoric highs" in patients taking the drug surfaced in the 1920s. Those reports also included warnings about the apparent habit-forming nature of the drug. In the United States, oxycodone was approved by the Food and Drug Administration (FDA) in 1976. Various formulations followed, including drugs that combined oxycodone with either aspirin or acetaminophen.

Evidence suggests that oxycodone has the ability to lock onto a special cell receptor found primarily in the brain, spinal cord, and intestines. When the drug connects to the receptors in the spinal cord, it causes the nerves that are sending pain signals to be temporarily blocked. Similarly, when the drug connects to the receptors in the brain, it causes an overall sense of well-being and relaxation. However, when the drug connects to the receptors in the intestines, the result is often constipation.

Opioids are praised by pain experts for their effectiveness in treating chronic pain because the drugs directly affect the way the body perceives pain. When properly administered in adequate, appropriate doses, opioids such as oxycodone can allow people with chronic pain from arthritis, back problems, cancer, and severe pain syndromes to lead more normal lives.

Pain experts have learned that patients who take opioid drugs for long periods of time will build up a physical tolerance and may need higher and higher dosages to achieve adequate pain relief. Unfortunately, physical dependence is sometimes confused with addiction, and patients may be denied appropriate medication by a doctor who cannot tell the difference between physical dependence and psychological addiction. One way to look at it, according to some pain experts, is that the drugs should be used when they improve a person's functioning (i.e., allow for better overall functioning than what they could achieve without medication).

When drugs interfere with patients' functioning rather than help them cope with daily activities in the face of severe pain, the line between physical dependence and addiction may have been crossed. According to the Center for Substance Abuse Treatment (CSAT), addiction "is characterized by the repeated, compulsive use of a substance despite adverse social, psychological, and/or physical consequences."

That fear of giving pain medication because patients might become addicted, what some experts refer to as *opiophobia,* is unjustified in most cases in which pain medications are needed for proper treatment. Research sponsored by the National Institute on Drug Abuse suggests that most patients will not become addicted when taking opioids. When used properly, the drugs can be tapered or decreased slowly as pain improves. This careful weaning from the drug eliminates the physical dependence and avoids the withdrawal problems that would occur if the person "went cold turkey" and stopped taking the drug too suddenly.

Surprisingly, studies show pain caused by cancer or other terminal disease is often undertreated. Even though the World Health Organization has shown that more than 90% of such pain can be effectively controlled with good pain management, patients who need relief the most are often among those least likely to receive it. In a 1998 study published in the *Journal of*

KEY TERMS

ANALGESIC: A type of drug that alleviates pain without loss of consciousness.

NARCOTIC: A natural or synthetic drug that has properties similar to opium or opium derivatives.

OPIATE: Drug derived directly from opium and used in its natural state, without chemical modification. Opiates include morphine, codeine, thebaine, noscapine, and papaverine.

PHYSICAL DEPENDENCE: A condition that may occur after prolonged use of an opiate, but differing from addiction because the user is dependent on the drug for pain relief, rather than emotional or psychological relief.

WITHDRAWAL: A group of symptoms that may occur from suddenly stopping the use of a substance such as alcohol or other drugs after chronic or prolonged ingestion.

the American Medical Association, researchers found that 26% of elderly cancer patients living in a nursing home who experienced daily pain did not receive a painkiller. People older than age 85 were more likely than those in other age groups to receive no pain medication at all. The oldest patients were also less likely than those ages 65 to 74 to receive strong pain medications such as opioids, despite the fact that they experienced pain daily.

One additional reason some physicians may knowingly undertreat pain is fear of being prosecuted for over-prescribing certain drugs. In one survey conducted in the early 1990s, more than half of physicians admitted to reducing the dose of opioids they prescribe or switching a patient to a non-opioid pain drug out of concern they might be investigated or even fined by their state medical board for over-prescribing.

For years the leading drug used to treat chronic pain was short-acting opioids. However, in 1995 a new long-acting form of oxycodone became available. The drug, known as OxyContin, has quickly become the preferred medication for chronic back pain and cancer pain, among other conditions, because it has fewer side effects and lasts longer than other similar painkillers.

OxyContin's sustained release activity means that a steady stream of medication is released into the bloodstream over a 12-hour period. This allows users to sleep through the night without waking to take more pain pills. It also means there is little or no breakthrough pain, as often occurs with shorter-acting pain medications, because the relief lasts until the next dose is taken.

LAW AND ORDER

In February 2002, a Florida physician was convicted of manslaughter for prescribing OxyContin to four patients who died after overdosing on the powerful drug. He is believed to be the first doctor ever convicted in the death of patients whose deaths were related to Oxycontin use.

During the trial, it was revealed that the physician prescribed more OxyContin than any other doctor in the state of Florida. Prosecutors in the case accused the physician of running an illegal "pill mill" in which Oxy-Contin prescriptions were given to anyone, including known drug dealers, who paid an office visit fee.

In addition to the manslaughter counts, the physician was also convicted of one count of racketeering and five counts of unlawful delivery of a controlled substance. Although the problem is not unique to Florida, another doctor in that state was scheduled to face trial in 2002 for the death of a 21-year-old patient who died of an OxyContin overdose. Prosecutors were seeking the death penalty in that case.

While many doctors and patients consider OxyContin a wonder drug, it has become a controversial and highly abused substance in many parts of the United States that previously had experienced little or no drug problems. Some have gone so far as to call it "pharmaceutical heroin." Within just a few years of its introduction, OxyContin became the source of many news stories as a large number of people, from celebrities to housewives, developed an OxyContin habit. Physicians and health care providers in some affected areas found themselves unprepared for the speed with which an epidemic of OxyContin abuse developed in their communities. The problem is so bad that pharmacies in some areas have chosen not to even stock the drug anymore for safety reasons, and the Drug Enforcement Administration (DEA) created a special national strategy for dealing with the OxyContin problem.

Although abuse of prescription painkillers is nothing new, OxyContin distinguishes itself by being more powerful than other prescription painkillers. OxyContin contains between 10 and 160 mg of oxycodone, whereas other oxycodone-containing drugs such as Tylox contain only 5 mg. The higher dose of oxycodone makes OxyContin attractive to abusers who crush the pills and either snort or inject the oxycodone for a powerful high.

This controversy has created difficulties for patients who rely on OxyContin for pain relief and for the doctors who prescribe it.

Selling OxyContin prescriptions has become big business. According to a report from the Center for Substance Abuse Treatment (CSAT), one 40-mg pill costs about $4 by prescription, but the same pill can go for $20 to $40 on the street, depending on the area of the country. This led to some people in economically depressed areas selling their legitimate prescriptions for profit. In West Virginia, OxyContin earned the nicknames "hillbilly heroin" and "poor man's heroin," as abuse of the drug—and crime related to its use—increased rapidly among residents of Appalachia, historically one of the poorest areas of the country.

Robberies and prescription forging, as well as the activities of unscrupulous doctors seeking to make big profits, also contributed substantially to the problem of OxyContin abuse. From early 2000 through the summer of 2001, at least 700 thefts from pharmacies involving OxyContin were reported, according to the DEA's Office of Diversion Control. States with the highest rates of OxyContin-related theft included Pennsylvania, Florida, Ohio, and Kentucky. Other states that reported a high number of OxyContin crimes included Maine, Massachusetts, Virginia, and California.

CHEMICAL/ORGANIC COMPOSITION

Oxycodone is available alone or in combination with either acetaminophen or aspirin. Its chemical structure is most closely related to codeine, but it has strong painkilling effects equal to those of morphine.

Types of prescription oxycodone

Oral preparations of oxycodone include immediate-release pills, controlled-release pills, and a liquid solution. The immediate-release pills, as their name implies, get the drug into the bloodstream faster than other formulations. Within about 15 minutes of taking immediate-release oxycodone, the drug's analgesic effects take hold. Pain is lessened and the user experiences a feeling of drowsiness and/or well-being.

The controlled-release formulations, on the other hand, prolong the release of oxycodone from the tablet for several hours. These pills have a special protective outer coating that makes them harder to digest, so that the oxycodone inside can be released slowly over a period of about 12 hours. That means the pills are capable of providing relief that lasts twice as long, allowing users to obtain the same effect they would get from taking an immediate-release tablet once every six hours.

For patients with severe pain, one additional advantage of newer controlled-release formulations such as

OxyContin is that they contain a much larger amount of oxycodone than the other prescription painkillers that contain some oxycodone.

Oxycodone with aspirin

Like oxycodone, oxycodone with aspirin is used to treat moderate to severe pain. The aspirin provides additional pain relief and anti-inflammatory properties not found in oxycodone alone. For some types of pain, these medications may be a better choice than oxycodone alone, particularly if pain is accompanied by significant inflammation, swelling, and stiffness. The aspirin component also may be especially beneficial if pain is accompanied by fever.

Pain relief usually begins within 30 minutes of taking oral oxycodone with aspirin. The drug achieves its peak effect within about 90 minutes and lasts for three to four hours.

Oxycodone with acetaminophen

Like oxycodone with aspirin, oxycodone with acetaminophen combines a powerful pain reliever with an additional pain reliever and a fever-reducer. However, unlike aspirin, it does not have anti-inflammatory properties, so it may not be the best medication if a patient's pain is accompanied by inflammation, swelling, and stiffness.

Pain relief usually begins within 30 minutes of taking oxycodone with acetaminophen. The drug achieves its peak effect within about 90 minutes and lasts three to four hours.

INGESTION METHODS

Most of the oxycodone drugs—which include the drug alone or in combination with aspirin or acetaminophen—are available in tablet form. For patients who have trouble swallowing or who cannot take the tablet form for other reasons, the drug is available in a highly concentrated flavored liquid solution. The appropriate dose of the liquid is measured into a dropper either by a nurse or by the patient. Often, the liquid may be added to semi-soft foods such as applesauce or pudding to help disguise its bitter taste. Those who use liquid formulations of oxycodone should be aware that some of them may contain alcohol.

The growing problem of OxyContin abuse has revealed a new and highly dangerous ingestion method. Abusers of the drug crush, chew, or break the pills apart to remove the outer coating. With normal use, the coating serves the purpose of allowing the oxycodone inside the pills to be released slowly over 12 hours. By removing it, abusers can snort the oxycodone powder, or dilute it and inject it, which produces a fast and potentially deadly high.

THERAPEUTIC USE

The primary therapeutic use of oxycodone is to relieve moderate to severe pain. However, the drug also is used before or during dental extractions and other surgery both to relieve pain and to improve the effectiveness of certain anesthesia drugs.

Chronic back pain is a common reason many people use oxycodone or other opioids. The drugs can provide enough relief so that people with unbearable back pain can work and carry on with other daily activities. People may also use the drugs to obtain relief from chronic pain syndromes. Although the term is vague, chronic pain syndrome can refer to any muscle, joint, or body pain that is debilitating to the patient, and is long-lasting or recurs frequently. One example of a patient who would fit into this category is someone who had a serious car or motorcycle accident that left him or her with chronic pain for months or years after the incident. Another example might be a woman who has experienced years of chronic pelvic pain whose cause is not known. For most of these patients, oxycodone is not used on a daily or even a weekly basis. Rather, a prescription is written with instructions to use oxycodone on an as-needed basis, and patients only take the pills when the pain becomes intolerable or interferes with their daily lives.

Another therapeutic use of oxycodone is to relieve the pain of chronic moderate to severe osteoarthritis, arthritis that results from degeneration of cartilage and/or bone in a joint. In a study of patients who had been experiencing osteoarthritis pain for at least one year, controlled-release oxycodone was more effective than a placebo in relieving the pain. The researchers suggested in their report that although opioid analgesics are strong medicines, they might be worthwhile for patients with osteoarthritis who do not get adequate pain relief from other types of pain medication.

Oxycodone also can be helpful to people with diabetes or AIDS who have a painful condition known as peripheral neuropathy. The condition causes burning pain and tingling in the hands, feet, and toes. Over time, the pain worsens and can lead to difficulty sleeping, walking, and performing other normal daily activities.

The decision to give oxycodone or one of the combination drugs consisting of oxycodone and acetaminophen or oxycodone and aspirin may be based on a number of factors. If a person has significant inflammation in addition to pain, for example, an acetaminophen-oxycodone combination drug such as Endocet, Percocet, Roxicet, Roxilox, or Tylox may be the best option. If fever is present in addition to pain, an aspirin-oxycodone combination drug such as Percodan, Percodan-Demi, or Roxiprin may be the most effective treatment. If chronic, uncontrolled pain is the main problem, however, a long-acting oxycodone drug such as OxyContin that controls pain effectively for 12-hour periods may be best. Doctors who treat cancer patients say that Oxy-Contin is one of the most powerful treatments available to relieve patients of treating crippling pain, and unlike morphine, OxyContin does not cause frightening side effects, such as hallucinations, in long-term users.

USAGE TRENDS

Scope and severity

National surveys have shown that abuse of prescription drugs is on the rise in the United States. Compared with the 1980s, when fewer than 500,000 people took a prescription drug for a nonmedical reason each year, the number of people who engaged in this behavior increased 181% from 1990 to 1998 for pain relievers alone.

In a Consensus Development Conference statement published in late 1997, the National Institutes of Health (NIH) estimated that approximately 600,000 people in the United States are opiate-dependent, meaning they use an opiate drug daily or on a frequent basis.

The DEA says oxycodone and hydrocodone are among the most abused of the prescription painkillers. An increasing number of people who abuse these drugs are requiring medical attention because of side effects, overdose, and other issues that arise when the drugs are used for reasons other than their intended purpose. Statistics compiled by the Drug Abuse Warning Network (DAWN) indicate that oxycodone-related visits to hospital emergency departments are increasing steadily. In 2000, the number of such visits was 10,825 per year, more than double the 5,211 visits reported just two years earlier.

The number of prescriptions written for oxycodone combination drugs increased slightly during the period from 1996–2000. However, the DEA's Diversion Control Program found that the number of prescriptions written for oxycodone-only drugs such as OxyContin was 14 times higher during the same time period.

According to a national study undertaken by the DEA, 803 deaths in 31 states in 2000 and 2001 were related to use of oxycodone and another 179 deaths were likely related to oxycodone. Of the 803 total deaths related to the drug, 117 were linked specifically to OxyContin. The study was undertaken in the form of letters sent to 775 medical examiners (MEs). The MEs were asked to supply autopsy reports, blood, and drug test results, and to investigate reports on all deaths caused by or associated with use of oxycodone.

Age, ethnic, and gender trends

NIDA data from 1999 show an estimated four million Americans over age 12 were using prescription pain relievers, sedatives, and stimulants for nonmedical reasons. Nearly 50% of those were first-time users. For the most part, young people appear to be the leading new and first-time users, according to data from the National Household Survey on Drug Abuse (1999). The most dramatic increase in new users of prescription drugs for nonmedical reasons occurred among 12- to 25-year-olds. The same data show that nonmedical use of two pain relievers—oxycodone with aspirin (Percodan) and hydrocodone (Vicodin)—is increasing among college students.

NIDA statistics also indicate that adolescent girls are abusing prescriptions more than ever before and are engaging in illicit drug use to a greater extent than their male peers. Opioids are the prescription drugs most likely to be abused by young people, followed by central nervous system depressants such as Valium and Xanax, and stimulants such as Ritalin.

Among adults, some studies suggest that women are more likely than men to be prescribed the more highly abused drugs, including painkillers and anti-anxiety medications. In fact, some studies have shown that women may be as much as 48% more likely than men to be given these drugs. The studies also indicate, according to NIDA, that women and men who use prescription opioids run an equal risk of becoming addicted. Women run a much higher risk than men of becoming addicted to other drugs, though, particularly sedatives, anti-anxiety medications, and hypnotic drugs such as sleeping pills.

Pain is a common problem in the elderly, and many elderly people are prescribed painkillers. A report from the American Geriatrics Society found that about one-fourth to one-half of all elderly people not living in nursing homes report pain-related problems, and one in five people over age 65 take painkillers one or more times each week. As many as three in five elderly people have taken prescription pain medication for more than six months. In nursing homes or other care facilities, as many as 80% of elderly patients report some type of pain.

Misuse of prescription drugs, including painkillers, is common among elderly people. However, unlike with younger people, when elderly people misuse or abuse prescriptions it is more likely to be accidental or unintentional. Since the body's ability to metabolize, or break down, many medications decreases with age, elderly people usually are prescribed lower doses of potent drugs than younger persons are.

Another group that is potentially at increased risk for abuse of painkillers is doctors, nurses, pharmacists, anesthesiologists, dentists, veterinarians, and others who work in health care. It may be easier for people working in environments where drugs are kept or dispensed to either steal pills or forge prescriptions for themselves or others.

People who abuse prescription drugs may escape detection for years because they have learned how to "beat the system" and obtain prescriptions by visiting different doctors and claiming a different ailment at each place. In addition, some doctors may have trouble saying no to patients asking for prescription pain medication for fear that the patients may truly be in pain. Meanwhile, others simply do not realize they are being tricked by patients with a serious drug problem. The Substance Abuse and Mental Health Services Administration (SAMSHA) began a major training program in 2000 to help doctors, nurses, and others spot signs of drug abuse in patients. If they know how to recognize the signs, health professionals can then talk to patients about the problem and refer them for appropriate treatment.

MENTAL EFFECTS

Because oxycodone may cause drowsiness and/or dizziness, people taking oxycodone-containing drugs should use caution when driving, operating machinery, or performing any other type of work that requires being alert and responsive. For the most part, the effect of oxycodone on mood is a mellow one. Most people feel an improved sense of well-being while taking the drug. In contrast, when people stop taking oxycodone suddenly, they may notice significant shifts in their moods and experience anxiety, restlessness, and insomnia.

Some researchers believe the mood-elevating properties of oxycodone make it a reasonable treatment for depression in certain individuals, although that use of the drug is not yet common. The most likely to benefit from this type of therapy are people with major depression whose illness has not been successfully controlled with standard antidepressant medications. Careful, close monitoring is essential since, unlike antidepressant drugs, oxycodone does cause side effects and poses a risk of addiction.

PHYSIOLOGICAL EFFECTS

Opioid analgesics such as oxycodone act directly on the central nervous system by stimulating opioid receptors in the brain. This action affects how the pain is perceived and can alter the user's emotional response to the pain.

Oxycodone is absorbed by the liver, skeletal muscles, intestinal tract, spleen, lungs, and central nervous system. The drug is broken down in the liver and passes out of the body via the kidney into urine.

Oxycodone's effects on the central nervous system produce pain relief, euphoria, and slowed breathing. It also decreases the activity of the intestinal tract, often leading to constipation. To combat this, patients are advised to drink six to eight full glasses of water per day and increase the amount of dietary fiber they eat.

Other side effects of oxycodone can include: nausea, dizziness, vomiting, itchy skin, weakness, and headache. Oxycodone should not be given to patients

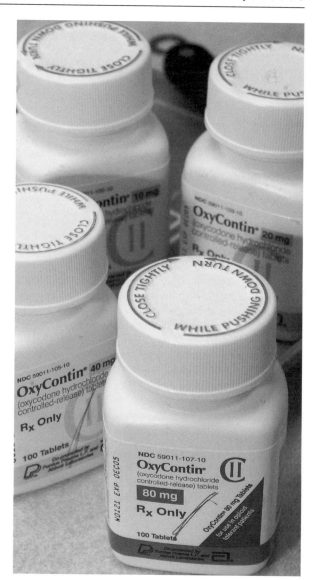

Bottle of OxyContin, a narcotic pain medication.

Photo by Lawrence Jackson, AP/ World Wide Photos. Reproduced by permission.

who have significant breathing problems such as asthma, emphysema, or chronic lung disease, or patients with intestinal abnormalities or blockages.

Harmful side effects

Taking more than the recommended dose of oxycodone can lead to serious health problems including convulsions, coma, or even death.

The Food and Drug Administration (FDA) has placed oxycodone in pregnancy category B because although some studies in animals show an increase in birth defects and other problems, there is no evidence

IN THE NEWS

In just a few short years after it was introduced, OxyContin became the best-selling narcotic in the United States. As of 2001, the drug's manufacturer, Purdue Pharma, was earning an estimated $1 billion a year from sales of OxyContin alone. But as quickly as the drug became popular for legitimate use as a highly effective painkiller, its popularity surged among drug abusers.

Ironically, OxyContin, which was approved by the FDA in 1995, was originally thought to pose a low risk of abuse because of its controlled-release design. The protective outer coating slows digestion of the pill and allows a large dose of oxycodone to be released in small amounts over 12 hours. However, abusers quickly discovered that by crushing or chewing the pills, they could release the oxycodone and snort the powder or mix it with water and inject it for a fast high. This method proved especially powerful when the drug was combined with alcohol or other drugs—a practice known in street terms as "pharming."

The street value of OxyContin appears to be enormous. While other painkillers such as Vicodin, Percodan, and Percocet sell for about $6 to $8 apiece on the street, OxyContin may sell for as much as $20 to $40 for just one 40-mg pill to more than $100 for one 160-mg pill.

OxyContin's street value and appeal to drug abusers has led to a rise in a phenomenon known as doctor shopping, in which people visit multiple doctors and attempt to acquire prescriptions for their own use or to sell for profit.

Some pharmacies have refused to stock OxyContin, fearing robberies and attacks on their employees. Scattered reports have even suggested that patients with legal prescriptions keep their use of the drug secret for fear they might become targets of abusers trying to steal their pills. A few hospitals have limited OxyContin use to cancer patients only, leading some health officials to fear that patients who need the drug may not be able to get it. As of 2001, at least seven states had tried to make it more difficult for patients on Medicaid, the national health insurance program for the poor, to obtain OxyContin prescriptions. In December 2001, Purdue Pharma announced it was working on a new chemical design of OxyContin that would not produce the highs that cause people to become addicted.

---

that taking oxycodone when pregnant causes birth defects in people. However, it is possible for the infants of mothers who took the drug during pregnancy to be born with addiction and withdrawal symptoms, as well as breathing difficulties resulting from the drug's effect of slowing down respiration. The *Physician's Desk Reference* advises that oxycodone only be given to pregnant women if the benefits significantly outweigh potential risks to both the mother and her fetus.

Similarly, caution is advised for women who are breastfeeding, as oxycodone may pass through the breast milk in large enough quantities to cause addiction, withdrawal, and breathing problems in a nursing infant. Women should be sure to tell their doctors they are breastfeeding if they are in need of a strong prescription pain medication such as oxycodone.

Oxycodone also should be used cautiously by people who have a head injury or have abnormally increased pressure in the brain, or by people who have had convulsions or seizures.

People with the following medical conditions also should avoid taking oxycodone or any oxycodone-combination drug:

- kidney disease
- liver disease
- underactive thyroid (hypothyroidism)
- enlarged prostate
- Addison's disease (a disease of the adrenal glands)
- colitis
- gallbladder disease or gallstones

Long-term health effects

The greatest long-term effect on health from oxycodone is addiction. NIDA warns that people who are addicted are at increased risk of overdose and death.

Oxycodone can be addictive when taken in dosages higher than those prescribed by a doctor or when taken for nonmedical purposes (i.e., recreational drug use). For these reasons, people with a prior history of other drug abuse may be advised not to take oxycodone.

REACTIONS WITH OTHER DRUGS OR SUBSTANCES

Oxycodone is a strong prescription analgesic and, as such, it is not advisable to take oxycodone in combination with any other pain medications, including common over-the-counter pain relievers like Tylenol or Advil. If oxycodone taken as prescribed does not relieve the pain adequately, the patient's doctor can adjust the dose or substitute a stronger drug.

Because oxycodone may intensify the effects of other drugs that cause drowsiness, it should not be taken with antidepressants, antihistamines, anti-anxiety drugs, seizure medications, sedatives, sleeping pills, or muscle relaxants, except under the supervision of a doctor. Patients who may be prescribed oxycodone should tell their doctor if they are taking any of these medications.

Similarly, alcohol should be avoided when taking oxycodone. It, too, increases feelings of drowsiness and can cause dizziness when combined with oxycodone. Avoiding alcohol is especially important when taking pain-relievers containing oxycodone and acetaminophen, as studies have shown that liver damage can occur when even relatively small amounts of alcohol are combined with acetaminophen. A current or past history of alcohol or drug abuse should be carefully considered before oxycodone is prescribed.

When taking an acetaminophen-containing oxycodone drug, it is also important to pay attention to the acetaminophen content in other medications, such as over-the-counter cough or cold remedies. The maximum daily recommended amount of acetaminophen for the average adult should not exceed 4 g per day or 4,000 mg per day.

TREATMENT AND REHABILITATION

Addiction to prescription painkillers is a major reason people are admitted to drug rehabilitation centers. In the early part of the twentieth century, however, treatment for addiction to opiates was actually self-administered. Private doctors would prescribe narcotics for opiate addicts, but that practice was soon outlawed, and local governments and communities established formal morphine clinics. By the 1920s, these clinics too were closed and opiate addicts were jailed or treated, usually unsuccessfully, in public health hospitals.

In the 1960s, the emergence of a new drug lifestyle among young people led to increases in opiate addiction as well as deaths from overdose. This growing problem resulted in researchers looking for newer, more effective approaches to treating opiate dependence.

There is some evidence that addiction behaviors may be genetic; in other words, some people who take prescription pain medication may become addicted because of an inherited tendency. However, genetic predisposition is likely to be only partially to blame. Environmental factors, underlying mental illness, and history of known addictions to alcohol or drugs are other factors that contribute to compulsive or addictive drug use.

When a person stops taking, or sharply reduces, the daily amount of oxycodone, severe withdrawal symptoms may occur. These symptoms are similar to those seen in people experiencing morphine withdrawal. To avoid this problem, pain experts slowly reduce the amount of drug the person takes each day.

Withdrawal symptoms can be quite uncomfortable when they do occur, but they are not life-threatening. Typical withdrawal symptoms may begin with yawning, restlessness, insomnia, goose flesh (commonly called goose bumps), and anxiety. Within a few hours symptoms worsen, and may include stomach pain, diarrhea, nausea, vomiting, muscle aches and pain, fevers, sweating, and runny nose and eyes. Symptoms usually begin within six to eight hours of the last dose of short-acting oxycodone, and 24 to 48 hours after the last dose of long-acting oxycodone (such as OxyContin).

One of two common treatment approaches is to combat withdrawal symptoms by treating them with appropriate medications. A drug commonly used in withdrawal treatment is clonidine, a medication most often used to lower blood pressure. For people going through withdrawal, clonidine may help lessen some symptoms. A variety of other drugs also may be used to deal with symptom-specific complaints. Examples include ibuprofen for headaches, muscle, joint, or bone pain, and mild tranquilizers to combat anxiety and/or insomnia.

Withdrawal may also be treated by replacing the drug of abuse with methadone, a long-acting opiate that does not usually produce the heightened sense of well-being characteristic of a drug high. Methadone is typically given every four to six hours under close supervision. The patient's reactions are monitored and the dosages of methadone are slowly decreased until withdrawal symptoms disappear. Methadone withdrawal usually takes about three weeks. Most methadone withdrawals are conducted in hospitals or residential facilities on an in-patient basis, rather than in methadone maintenance programs, which are outpatient programs in which patients who are unwilling to stop using opiates receive methadone as a legal, long-term substitute.

Some experts recommend a newer option for withdrawal known as rapid opiate detoxification (ROD). This method is typically carried out in a hospital or private treatment facility, and as its name implies, it is faster than some of the more conventional methods. In some cases, withdrawal treatment with ROD can be completed in just a few days. Compared with conventional withdrawal treatment, ROD also has been found to cause less physical discomfort. Even more recently, some researchers have investigated an even faster method called ultra-rapid opiate detoxification (UROD), in which the patient goes through withdrawal while asleep under anesthesia. The entire process takes four to seven hours.

Patients undergoing ROD or UROD are given clonidine plus a drug called naltrexone, which blocks opiate receptors and makes withdrawal signs and symptoms occur more rapidly. This method is still considered experimental.

PERSONAL AND SOCIAL CONSEQUENCES

The majority of people who use narcotic pain relievers do so safely and appropriately without becoming addicted. Despite widely held assumptions that increased prescribing of these drugs will lead to increased abuse, recent studies suggest this is not the case.

Patients with chronic pain or who suffer from pain syndromes are sometimes labeled as "weak" or "dependent" because they need prescription pain medication on a daily or as-needed basis. Unfortunately, such labeling might make people who truly need strong prescription pain relief too ashamed or embarrassed to ask for it.

People who do become addicted to oxycodone or other opiates face many personal and social obstacles, including difficulty obtaining or maintaining a steady job. As a result, addicts who do not get the help they need to stop using prescription drugs may end up having to rely on public assistance.

Since the early 1990s the prevalence of human immunodeficiency virus (HIV), hepatitis B and C viruses, and tuberculosis among people who inject opiate drugs has increased dramatically. The annual number of opiate-related emergency room visits has increased dramatically and the number of people who die each year as a result of abusing opiates has nearly doubled in recent years, further underscoring the human, economic, and societal costs of opiate addiction.

LEGAL CONSEQUENCES

Dependence on opiates has long been associated with increased crime and illegal activities. According to data presented at a National Institutes of Health conference in 1997, more than one-quarter of the inmates in state and federal prisons in 1993 were incarcerated for drug-related offenses. Among federal prison inmates, the largest group were those serving drug-related sentences.

In a survey of opiate-dependent people, stealing was the most common illegal activity associated with trying to obtain more of the drug. In addition to improving health and preventing future health problems, one of the goals of treating people addicted to opiates such as oxycodone is to reduce the amount of associated crime and its impact on society.

Federal guidelines, regulations, and penalties

Oxycodone is a Schedule II controlled substance, which is subject to the Controlled Substances Act (CSA) of 1970. The CSA was enacted to control and limit use and distribution of drugs that have a high potential for abuse, including oxycodone, codeine, and morphine.

Listing a drug as a controlled substance is not intended to interfere with the way doctors practice medicine or the availability of that drug for patients who may need it for legitimate medical reasons.

The DEA is considered the "watchdog" in charge of enforcing the CSA, but its authority over doctors and how they prescribe controlled substances for medical purposes is limited. This arrangement is intended to protect doctors—such as those who treat patients with terminal cancer—who might come under suspicion for frequently prescribing large quantities of controlled substances. Doctors who prescribe any drug listed as a controlled substance must be registered with the DEA for tracking and monitoring purposes. Hospitals and pharmacies also must register with the DEA. By registering, the doctor, pharmacy, or hospital is given a number that must be used each time a controlled substance is ordered. Any individual or facility that has been issued a DEA registration number is legally obligated to keep detailed records regarding how, when, and to whom the drug was dispensed.

For the most part, the DEA is on the lookout for doctors who are prescribing controlled substances illegally to people who have no medical need for them. Pharmacists and manufacturers of controlled substances are also monitored for suspected abuse of the CSA. Anyone who dispenses controlled substances and is found to be in violation of the CSA faces fines, imprisonment, or both.

Some states have enacted their own laws regarding controlled substances, and have placed legal limits on dosages and the total number of pills that can be prescribed within a specific time period. Some doctors argue that this type of regulation requires patients who take large quantities of pain medication to obtain more frequent prescriptions, thus putting patients at risk of having refills delayed and or encountering problems with their insurance company.

See also Cocaine; Heroin; Morphine; Opium

RESOURCES

Books

Booth, Martin. *Opium: A History.* New York: St. Martin's Press, 1996.

Periodicals

Armengol, Robert. "Other Victims of OxyContin Abuse." *Courier Times* (Bucks County, Pa.) August 5, 2001.

Chernin, Tammy. "Painkillers and Pill Popping." *Drug Topics* (August 6, 2001).

Kalb, Claudia. "Playing With Painkillers." *Newsweek* (April 9, 2001).

Other

Congressional Testimony. Statement of Asa Hutchinson, Administrator, Drug Enforcement Administration before the House Committee on Appropriations. December 11, 2001. <http://www.usdoj.gov/dea/pubs/testimony.htm>.

Neer, Katherine. "How OxyContin Works." *Marshall Brain's How Stuff Works.* 2002. (April 18, 2002). <http://www.howstuffworks.com/OxyContin.htm>.

U.S. Food and Drug Administration. Center for Drug Evaluation and Research. "OxyContin: Questions and Answers." <http://www.fda.gov/cder/drug/infopage/OxyContin/OxyContin-qa.htm>.

Organizations

National Clearinghouse for Alcohol and Drug Information (NCADI), P.O. Box 2345, Rockville, MD, USA, 20847-2345, (800) 729-6686, webmaster@health.org, <http://www.health.org>.

National Drug Intelligence Center (NDIC), 319 Washington Street, 5th Floor, Johnstown, PA, USA, 15901-1622, (814) 532-4601, (814) 532-4690, cmbwebmgr@ndic.osis.gov, <http://www.usdoj.gov/ndic/>.

National Institute on Drug Abuse (NIDA), National Institutes of Health, 6001 Executive Boulevard, Room 5213, Bethesda, MD, USA, 20892-9561, (301) 443-1124, (888) 644-6432, information@lists.nida.nih.gov, <http://www.nida.nih.gov>.

Substance Abuse and Mental Health Services Administration (SAMHSA)/Center for Substance Abuse Treatment (CSAT), 5600 Fishers Lane, Rockville, MD, USA, 20857, (301) 443-8956, info@samhsa.gov, <http://www.samhsa.gov>.

Laura A. McKeown

PCP (PHENCYCLIDINE)

OFFICIAL NAMES: Phencyclidine, PCP, phencyclidine hydrochloride, phenyl cyclohexyl piperidine, Sernylan, Sernyl
STREET NAMES: AD, amoeba, angel, angel dust, angel hair, angel mist, angel poke, animal crackers, animal trank, animal tranquilizer, aurora borealis, bad pizza, belladonna, blud madman, boat, busy bee, butt naked, Cadillac, cheap cocaine, cristal, cliffhanger, Columbo, cozmo's, crazy coke, crazy Eddie, crazy edge, crystal, cystal T, cycline, cyclones, Detroit pink, devil's dust, dipper, do it Jack, drink, dummy dust, dummy mist, dust, dust of angels, dusted parsley, elephant, elephant tranquilizer, embalming fluid, energizer, erth, fake STP, flakes, fresh, good, goon, goon dust, gorilla tab, gorilla biscuits, green leaves, green tea, greens, guerilla, HCP, heaven and hell, herms, Hinkley, hog, horse tracks, horse tranquilizer, illy, jet, jet fuel, K, kaps, K-blast, killer, kools, krystal, KW, LBJ, leaky bolla, leaky leak, lemon 714, lethal weapon, little ones, live ones, log, loveboat, madman, mad dog, magic, magic dust, mauve, mean green, milk, mint leaf, mintweed, monkey dust, monkey tranquilizer, more, mumm dust, new acid, new magic, niebla, OPP, orange crystal, ozone, paz, peace pill, PeaCe pill, peep, Peter Pan, pig killer, pit, puffy, purple, purple rain, rocket fuel, scaffle, scuffle, sheets, Shermans, sherms, smoking, snorts, soma, special LA coke, spores, squeeze, STP, super, superacid, super kools, surfer, synthetic cocaine, synthetic THT, taking a cruise, TCP, t-buzz, tac, tic tac, tic, tish, titch, trank, t-tabs, TTi, TT2, TT3, wet, white horizon, wobble weed, wolf, worm, yellow fever
DRUG CLASSIFICATIONS: Schedule II, hallucinogen

OVERVIEW

Phencyclidine, commonly known as PCP, is a difficult drug to categorize. The United States Drug Enforcement Administration (DEA) categorizes it as a hallucinogen, like LSD, because it can make people see, hear, or sense things that are not there. Scientists categorized PCP as a dissociative anesthetic because it has a profound numbing effect and makes people feel like they are somehow separated from their bodies.

In fact, PCP was first developed as an anesthetic for use during surgical procedures, but side effects led to its falling out of favor for this purpose in the 1960s. It was used as an animal anesthetic in veterinary medicine for a few years, but as people on the street began to abuse the drug more and more, all legal manufacture of PCP stopped in 1978.

The effects of taking PCP are unique. At lower doses, the drug causes stimulation; while at higher doses, it tends to have a depressant effect. Most people find a PCP high to be disturbing because of the sense of separation from the body it produces. In fact, taking PCP results in the same type of experiences that sensory deprivation does, such as altered awareness of the boundaries of the body and dissociation from body parts. This strange sensation makes many people panic. Such people have been known to seriously harm themselves and others.

People on PCP have impaired judgment similar to that which is produced by drinking too much alcohol. The drug can also numb the body so much that people are virtually impervious to pain. The resulting combination can be deadly. People on PCP may do crazy things, like jump into frigid water or set themselves on fire, and not feel the pain that it produces until severe injury or death results.

A PCP high can be so unpleasant that many people will not knowingly take the drug more than once. However, PCP is quite easy and cheap to produce. As a result,

PCP is very often sold on the street disguised as another drug, from marijuana to LSD to mescaline.

PCP acts on several chemicals in the brain, called neurotransmitters, including dopamine, norepinephrine, serotonin, NMDA, and GABA. Recently, studies in animals have suggested that taking PCP results in brain changes that are associated with the mental disorder schizophrenia. People with schizophrenia have many of the same symptoms as people taking PCP, including paranoia, hallucinations, delusions, disordered thinking, and disrupted speech.

PCP is very similar to another drug that was also initially developed as an anesthetic, ketamine. Both these drugs have experienced a recent increase in their popularity as drugs of abuse, particularly among those who attend clubs and all-night dance parties called raves.

CHEMICAL/ORGANIC COMPOSITION

PCP is a completely artificial substance. That is, it is not derived from anything in nature; it is made purely from industrial chemicals. In fact, police are often tipped off to the presence of an illegal PCP laboratory when neighbors complain of terrible chemical smells or when careless criminals create chemical fires and explosions.

In its pure form, PCP is a white crystalline powder that easily dissolves in water to produce a clear liquid. Often, street PCP is contaminated with chemical impurities, which can change a white powder or clear liquid to tan or brown and change the consistency from powder to sludge. Purity of street PCP can range from 5% to 100%, but 100% pure PCP is considered to be extremely rare on the street. A common contaminant in PCP is a chemically related drug called PCC, which releases cyanide when burned. It does not produce enough cyanide to cause symptoms with one use, but use over time can lead to brain cell and nerve damage.

Street PCP is often contaminated with other chemicals because its easy and cheap manufacture makes it attractive to drug producers without a chemical background. These amateur drug makers do not know how to purify their final product or perform proper experiments to test for purity.

PCP is easy and cheap to manufacture but not very popular, so it is often sold as another drug. Most often, it is sold on the street as THC, the active ingredient in marijuana. In fact, real THC is almost impossible to obtain on the street. PCP might also be sprayed or sprinkled on oregano, parsley, or another herb and sold as marijuana. Alternatively, lower quality marijuana might be laced with PCP to make it seem more potent. Other drugs that PCP is sold as include LSD, cannabinol, mescaline, psilocybin, amphetamine, methamphetamine, peyote, cocaine, Hawaiian woodrose, and other psychedelics. In

KEY TERMS

AFTERSHOCK: Similar to a flashback with LSD, this is the reoccurrence of symptoms associated with taking PCP days, weeks, or months after taking the drug. This happens because PCP is stored in fatty cells in the body.

BUMMER TRIP: Another term for a bad trip, this refers to negative experiences while taking a drug.

DEPERSONALIZATION: A feeling of detachment from one's own mind and body. People experiencing depersonalization might feel they are watching themselves from a distance.

DISSOCIATIVE: A drug action that makes people feel cut off from themselves, their bodies, and reality.

DUSTED: Being intoxicated on PCP.

DUSTER: Someone who regularly takes PCP.

DUSTING: Adding PCP to another drug.

PCP ORGANIC MENTAL DISORDER: A condition similar to schizophrenia that can occur as a result of taking PCP and last for weeks, months, or even a year. It is characterized by confusion, disordered thinking, paranoia, and speech problems.

SCHIZOPHRENIA: A medical condition that falls under the category of psychotic disorders. People with schizophrenia suffer from a variety of symptoms, including confusion, disordered thinking, paranoia, hallucinations, emotional numbness, and speech problems.

one study, only 3% of analyzed street drugs containing PCP were sold as PCP.

PCP is very often mixed with other drugs to produce special highs. PCP mixed with crack is known as wack, space base, beam me up Scottie, clicker, dusty roads, DOA, missile basing, mist, space cadet, space dust, tragic magic, and wickey. PCP mixed with marijuana is known as supergrass, killer weed, super weed, dusters, crystal supergrass, killer joints, ace, bohd, chips, frios, lovelies, peace weed, stick, yerba mala, and zoom. PCP combined with heroin is known as oil or polvo.

Other combinations include PCP with LSD, (black acid), cocaine, methamphetamine, amphetamine, and MDMA (ecstasy). PCP may also be combined with more than one drug at a time.

There are several drugs that are chemically similar to PCP, which are often sold on the street as PCP or other drugs. These include PCPy, TCP, and PCE. Given the makeshift ways in which illegal PCP is manufactured, probably many people who think they are producing and

???? FACT OR FICTION

Are violence and PCP related?

Street rumors and the popular media have spread stories about PCP 'freaks' who have seemingly superhuman strength and are monstrously violent. But does PCP really cause bizarre, violent behavior?

The first major media coverage of PCP started around mid to late 70s, just a few years after the drug hit the street. The stories covered by the media focused on the fact that PCP reduces or even eliminates people's ability to feel pain, which can make them appear to have superhuman strength, and can sometimes unleash extreme agitation or hostility during a bad trip. Stories covered by the media at this time included those of people high on PCP gouging their own eyes out, drowning in a swimming pool or shower stall, burning to death in a fire, cutting off various body parts, and violently attacking innocent people.

The truth is that PCP can, in rare cases, unleash violent behavior in someone who is panicked and having a bad trip. Such a reaction is most likely to happen in people who have never taken the drug before and/or who did not know they were taking PCP. Also, a certain subset of PCP users, angry adolescent males from poor, violent inner city ghettos, are probably prone to violence without any help from PCP. On the other hand, violent behavior among many regular PCP users is actually *lower* than that of the general population. In fact, when regular PCP users were asked about the connection between PCP and violence, they were surprised that any such connection had ever been suggested.

In summary, while PCP has been known in rare, sensationalized cases to make people do bizarre or terrible things, not everyone who takes it turns to violence.

---

selling PCP are actually producing one of these similar drugs. They are classified as Schedule I hallucinogens by the DEA, which is the same category as LSD.

INGESTION METHODS

PCP is found in liquid, powder, and tablet format. It can be smoked, snorted, swallowed, or injected.

Most often, PCP is smoked in either a pipe or cigarette. To do so, users apply the drug to a leafy material, such as parsley, oregano, mint, tobacco, or marijuana, then roll it or place it in a pipe to smoke. Commercial cigarettes are also sometimes dipped in a PCP solution and smoked. PCP smoke is very hot, so users often prefer mixing PCP with mentholated cigarettes or mint to cool the smoke and help prevent mouth and tongue irritation.

Snorting is the second most common way of taking PCP, although it is a distant second choice after smoking the drug. People who snort PCP inhale the powder into their nose through a straw or similar device in much the same way cocaine is snorted.

Most often, people who take PCP by mouth take the drug in the form of tablets. These tablets might be dyed any color.

In rare cases, PCP is injected. This is an especially dangerous way of taking the drug because, in the case of accidental overdose, there is no easy way of removing the drug from the body. Also, people who smoke PCP will often pass out before they overdose, while people who snort or eat the drug often vomit after taking very high doses. Injecting the drug offers neither of these built-in safeguards.

No matter how PCP is ingested, it is very difficult to determine how much of the drug is being taken because people who produce PCP are usually quite careless and do not know how to distribute PCP evenly. Two PCP cigarettes from the same batch might deliver as little as 1 mg or as much as 100 mg of PCP. Street PCP in powder, liquid, or tablet form also varies widely in terms of both potency and purity.

When PCP is smoked, the effects start within a few minutes, peak within a half hour, and wear off after about four to six hours. When eaten, it takes longer for the effects to start, but they last somewhat longer. It generally takes about 24 hours for someone who has taken PCP to feel completely normal again.

THERAPEUTIC USE

PCP was originally developed as an anesthetic to be used in surgery and obstetrics. However, the drug stopped being used for this purpose in the 1960s because it can produce disturbing side effects. Since then, PCP has had no recognized therapeutic use in humans. However, new research suggests that giving PCP to people right after a heart attack or stroke might help protect their brains from permanent damage. This intriguing possibility was still under investigation in 2002. Researchers are looking for a drug that can protect the brain like PCP does without causing the disturbing mental effects.

PCP is currently being studied in animals because it appears to produce changes in the brain that are associated with schizophrenia. People taking PCP often experience effects that are very similar to the symptoms of schizophrenia, including disordered thinking, hallucinations, paranoia, and disrupted speech. Research into the effects of PCP on animal brains may help scientists better understand what is wrong with the brains of people with schizophrenia and lead to the development of better treatments.

USAGE TRENDS

After using PCP once, most people will not use it again. However, a few people (called 'dusters') do use it regularly and consistently. The drug is addictive, and many users say that the only reason they continue taking the drug is because they are addicted. Others use it because it gives them a sense of peace and/or strength. It also numbs physical and emotional pain.

Chronic PCP users often go on PCP "runs" or "sprees," where they use the drug for two to three days straight, during which time they may eat and sleep very little. Afterwards, they sleep for an extended period of time and wake feeling disoriented and depressed.

People who take PCP often combine it with other drugs, including cocaine, LSD, MDMA (ecstasy), methamphetamine, amphetamine, marijuana, and crack. Another common practice is to take a type of tranquilizer called a benzodiazepine to come down off PCP when the party is over. These practices of combining PCP with other drugs is particularly common among young people who attend dance clubs and raves.

Scope and severity

The first reports of illicit use of PCP occurred in the Haight-Ashbury district of San Francisco in 1967 during the Summer of Love. People who took the drug in these early days did so in tablet form and called it the peace pill because it created feeling of peacefulness. Soon, however, as more and more people started having negative experiences on PCP, it became clear how inappropriate that name was.

By the summer of 1968, PCP use dropped off dramatically in Haight-Ashbury, but it started to increase in other parts of the United States, mainly urban centers like Miami, Washington D.C., and New York. Once again, stories of bad trips began to follow the drug, and experienced drug takers began avoiding it.

PCP reemerged in early 1970s as a liquid, crystalline powder, and tablet. At this point, drug manufacturers started selling it as other drugs because the negative associations with PCP made it hard to sell. In addition to sensational stories of nightmarish, violent reactions to the drug, it developed a negative reputation as an animal tranquilizer. As a result, PCP commonly was sold as THC, the active ingredient in marijuana. It was also sold as cannabinol, mescaline, psilocybin, LSD, amphetamine, cocaine, Hawaiian woodrose, and other psychedelics. Low-quality marijuana was laced with

PCP to make it seem more potent. Regular cooking herbs like parsley were laced with PCP and sold as marijuana. Some people also took PCP knowing that it was PCP, despite increasing sensational stories (some of which were passed on by the mainstream media) about its ill effects. Those who took the drug developed reputations for being daring.

Since the 1970s, the popularity of PCP has had a waxing and waning course with the occasional "mini-epidemic." According to the DEA, the drug regained some popularity in the mid-1970s and early 1980s because it is very cheap and powerful, but its use was soon eclipsed by that of crack and cocaine in the mid-1980s. Since the 1990s, PCP has increased in popularity as one of the club drugs people take at dance clubs and raves. It remains widely available, particularly in major U.S. urban centers. The drug is rarely seen outside of North America.

The Monitoring the Future Study (MTF) is a survey performed every year since 1975 by the University of Michigan Institute for Social Research on nearly 17,000 American high school students about their drug use. It is funded by the National Institute on Drug Abuse (NIDA). According to the MTF, PCP use has declined steadily since 1979 among high school seniors. In 1979, 7% reported using PCP in the previous year, compared to only 2.3% in 1997. A low point for its use was 1990, when only 1.2% of high school seniors said they had used the drug in the past year.

The 1998 report of the American Poison Control Center documents 372 PCP exposures and two PCP-related deaths.

Most manufacture of PCP is controlled by Los Angeles street gangs, and most users also take other drugs.

Age, ethnic, and gender trends

PCP is a drug that is preferred by young people living in large cities. It is popular among Hispanic and African Americans, but Caucasians use it too. Most users are males aged 20 to 29, but there is also considerable use of PCP among teenagers.

The National Household Survey on Drug Abuse (NHSDA) tracks drug, alcohol, and tobacco use in a sample of 13,000 Americans aged 12 and over. According to the 1997 NHSDA survey, 3% of Americans over 12 had ever used PCP. Most of those who reported ever having used PCP were aged 26 and older (3.3%). However, the highest proportion of people who reported use of PCP in the past year were aged 12 to 17 (0.5%).

The 1997 NHSDA also found that twice as many men use PCP than women and that it is more often used in the Western portion of the country and least used in the South. In 1997, 3.4% of Caucasians, 2.1% of Hispanics, and 1.7% of African Americans reported ever taking PCP. In this same year, hospital admissions for PCP use were about equally distributed among Caucasians, Hispanics, and African Americans.

Since the mid-1990s, PCP has gained popularity among teens as a drug to take while attending dance clubs and raves.

MENTAL EFFECTS

As with most mind-altering drugs, the effects of PCP vary considerably from person to person and are strongly influenced by the user's mood and mental status, the setting in which it is taken, and the dose used.

In general, PCP tends to be stimulating at low doses and depressing at higher doses. Its primary action is dissociative. That means it makes the mind feel separated from the body, which can be very scary for some people. Distortions in perceptions of bodily feelings can make people panic. People taking PCP often feel that they "lose track" of their bodies or believe that their own limbs do not belong to them. They feel physically and emotionally numb, which can lead to bizarre behavior. The numbness also makes some people think they have superhuman strength, since they do not feel pain, which can lead to dangerous behavior. People have described the feeling of being on PCP as being similar to the dream state experienced during a high fever. Many people consider this to be an unpleasant feeling.

At low to moderate doses (1–5 mg), PCP can produce the following mental effects:

- changes in body awareness/altered body image

- dreamy, floating state

- drunkenness similar to that experienced with alcohol

- anxiety/hostility/agitation, especially in people who did not know they were taking PCP

- lack of coordination

- disorganized thoughts

- depersonalization, or feeling detached from one's own mind and body

- feelings of unreality

- altered sensory perception

- emotional instability

- sense of time slowing

- feeling of numb relaxation and sociability or anxiety and paranoia

- feeling of detachment, distance, estrangement from surroundings

At higher doses (5–15 mg), PCP can produce these additional effects:

- illusions

- hallucinations

- delusions

- mental turmoil

- garbled, sparse speech

- disorientation

- loss of memory

- talkativeness

- increased agitation

- loss of sense of personal identity

- excitement

- image distortion

- euphoria

- religious thoughts

- pleasant feelings of strength and intoxication

- sense of invulnerability or super strength

- amnesia

- acute anxiety with a feeling of impending doom

- paranoia

- violent hostility

- extreme passivity that can turn to violence if confronted or threatened

At very high doses (over 15 mg), PCP produces a schizophrenia-like reaction or hallucinations of a persecutory nature (e.g., voices saying that they are out to kill the user).

PHYSIOLOGICAL EFFECTS

In low doses (1–5 mg), PCP revs the body up, causing increased heart rate, breathing rate, and blood pressure. The individual will also experience profuse sweating and flushing.

At moderate to high doses (5–15 mg), PCP starts to have a depressant effect and causes a host of other side effects, including a drop in blood pressure (although some people experience a blood pressure surge), a drop in pulse rate, and a drop in breathing rate (shallow breathing). In

PCP being packaged for delivery. Custom Medical Stock Photo, Inc. Reproduced by permission.

addition, PCP abusers may experience nausea/vomiting, drooling (enough to affect breathing), increased bronchial secretions, wheezing, or bronchial spasms.

Several muscle problems may occur at higher doses. Examples include involuntary tremors, writhing, shivering, and jerky movements; catatonia, a zombie-like state characterized by changes in muscle tone and bizarre posturing; muscle rigidity and immobility; and loss of balance and dizziness. Many PCP abusers will notice an anesthetic effect resulting in increased pain threshold or numbness.

Visual impairments such as blurred vision, blank stare, involuntary flicking of the eyeballs, or tearing are common at higher doses. Fever, sense of extreme heat, and urinary retention may also occur.

At very high doses (over 15 mg), PCP produces some dangerous physical effects, including coma, convulsions, seizures, and an extremely high fever (up to 108°F), which can cause liver, kidney, or brain damage. Very high or low blood pressure and irregular heartbeats also pose a threat to the abuser.

Harmful side effects

Probably the most dangerous effects that PCP has are the feelings of separation from the body and super-human strength combined with impaired judgment a lack of ability to feel pain. Together, these effects can make people do extremely dangerous things. When peo-

ple also experience agitation, anxiety, and paranoia while on PCP, they become an even greater risk to themselves and others.

People on PCP have been known to:

- drown in pools or shower stalls

- run around naked in very cold weather

- mutilate themselves or others

- commit or attempt suicide

Another important risk of taking PCP is the likelihood of having a "bad trip." A bad PCP trip includes extreme panic, paranoia, delirium, and dissociation from reality and even one's own body. Even one bad trip can produce lasting emotional or psychological trauma. Anyone can have a bad trip on PCP at any time, but it is most likely to happen to people who did not know they were taking PCP or who took a very impure form of the drug or a very high dose. A person who had a bad trip in the past is at increased risk of having a second one.

Some people who take PCP experience symptoms very similar to those seen in people with schizophrenia, including delusions, paranoia, memory problems, confusion, disordered thinking, and impaired speech. This is called PCP organic mental disorder. Such schizophrenia-like episodes usually last several days, but they may last weeks or months after taking the drug only once. Such a reaction is most common in chronic users, but it can

HISTORY NOTES

History of PCP development and use

PCP was first developed in 1926 as an anesthetic to be used in surgery. Early on, the drug showed promise because it appeared to produces anesthesia without depressing breathing or heart rates. Still, lingering questions about safety and effectiveness meant it was largely ignored until 1957.

In 1958 the Parke-Davis pharmaceutical company synthesized and patented PCP and tested it further on animals. Studies revealed that moderate doses had a stimulant effect and higher doses had depressant effect. After some further testing on humans, Parke-Davis began selling the drug as a general anesthetic called Sernyl.

Once Sernyl started to be used as an anesthetic, problems with the drug arose. People waking up from Sernyl sometimes had very disturbing side effects that included horrible nightmares, delusions, hallucinations, agitation, delirium, disorientation, and difficulty speaking. Because of these side effects, PCP use in humans ceased in 1965. Instead, it was sold as a veterinary anesthetic under the brand name Sernylan.

PCP was withdrawn completely from the market in 1978 because more and more people were abusing it illegally on the street. As street use of the drug increased, so did the disturbing stories of the bizarre and dangerous behavior PCP can provoke. Since 1978, there has been no legal therapeutic use of PCP.

---

happen in a seemingly well-adjusted person who takes the drug only once.

PCP is an addictive drug, both mentally and physically. This means that regular users can find it difficult to stop taking the drug. Physical symptoms of withdrawal from PCP include depression, anxiety, belligerence, tremor, cold sweats, stomach upset, and numbed emotions.

Regular PCP use results in tolerance, which means that more and more of the drug is needed to produce the same effects. Higher and higher doses combine with the widely variable potency of street PCP to create a recipe for overdose. A PCP overdose is a life-threatening situation, especially if the drug was taken with another drug. Signs that someone is overdosing on PCP include bizarre, violent, self-destructive behavior, extreme phys-

ical and psychological distress, coma, seizures, convulsions, respiratory depression, and cardiac problems.

Deaths from an overdose of PCP are usually caused by respiratory arrest, but death can also result from seizures, cardiovascular collapse, and extremely high fever, which leads to kidney, liver, and brain damage. High doses of PCP also result in extremely high blood pressure, which may cause a stroke.

People who overdose on PCP may fall into a deep coma, slowly come out of it, and then continue to have signs of mild to moderate PCP intoxication that last two to six weeks. This is one of the longest-lasting toxic reactions produced by drugs of abuse.

In adolescents, taking PCP regularly may interfere with the hormones involved in normal growth, development, and learning.

Long-term health effects

Regular users of PCP have reported the following long-term effects, which have been known to last a year or more after stopping the drug:

- memory loss (especially recent memory)

- difficulties with speech and thinking

- depression/suicidal thoughts

- anxiety

- loss of appetite/weight loss

- constipation

- mood disorders

PCP can cause extremely high blood pressure combined with blood vessel contractions. This can increase the risk of stroke. One study suggests that chronic PCP use leads to brain damage, evidenced by memory gaps, disorientation, visual disturbances, and difficulty with speech, which might be due to mini-strokes caused by the effects of PCP.

PCP can cause long-lasting numbness of body parts, including the lungs, if the drug is smoked. This numbness can make people unaware they are damaging their lungs. Normally, irritation in the throat and lungs due to pollution, smoke, and other irritants causes coughing, which removes particles and germs. Regular PCP users are less likely to have this coughing reaction. It is not known whether PCP users are at greater risk of lung disease.

Even one dose of PCP can lead to "aftershocks," which are similar to the flashbacks experienced by some LSD users. Aftershocks are a re-experiencing of some or all of the effects of PCP intoxication, and can occur weeks, or months after the drug was taken. They have a physical, not psychological, cause. PCP stays in the parts of the body high in fat or oil, like the brain, liver, and fat cells. Stress, exercise, fatigue, or taking certain drugs can release PCP from these fat stores and cause a reaction.

When PCP is taken by pregnant women, it crosses the placenta to reach the baby's blood stream. There have been a few reports of women who took PCP while pregnant who gave birth to babies with deformities. However, it is not clear if these deformities were due to taking the drug. Newborns whose mothers took PCP while they were in the womb sometimes experience symptoms of withdrawal, including jitteriness, irritability, increased muscle tone, and decreased fetal growth. PCP also passes into the breast milk when taken by lactating mothers.

REACTIONS WITH OTHER DRUGS OR SUBSTANCES

PCP is very often used in combination with other drugs, both legal and illegal. Used together, the effects of both drugs are heightened. In particular, PCP has a very sedative effect when used with other sedatives, including alcohol, tranquilizers, anticonvulsants, and nitrous oxide (laughing gas). Because PCP and sedating drugs interact to produce a very sedative effect, it is easy to overdose when taking such combinations. Signs of an overdose include convulsions, coma, seizures, and respiratory arrest.

One study suggests PCP interacts with the active ingredient in marijuana, called THC, to increase the concentrations of PCP in the body. That means that when PCP is taken with marijuana, the effects of the PCP are amplified.

TREATMENT AND REHABILITATION

People taking PCP might require medical care for one of four reasons: to bring them down during a bad trip, to stop them from harming themselves or others while high, to receive emergency treatment for an overdose, or to help addicts stop taking the drug.

Treating people who are having a bad trip on PCP and/or panicking to the point that they are a danger to themselves or others is challenging. They usually cannot be "talked down" as people on LSD can. Trying to talk to someone on PCP often only increases his or her agitation.

The best way to calm down people on PCP is to put them in a dark, quiet environment with as little stimulation as possible. Such people must be watched at all times because they may suddenly become violent or suicidal. When this does not work, hospital staff may give them a mild tranquilizer.

A PCP overdose can lead to death if not adequately treated, so people who overdose on PCP should immedi-

ately be taken to the emergency department of the nearest hospital. There, the medical staff will treat overdose victims with drugs that counteract the individual symptoms they are experiencing. For instance, blood-pressure-lowering drugs are given for high blood pressure, fever reducers for a high fever, and antipsychotic drugs for schizophrenia-like reactions. They may also use drugs and other treatments that help hasten the release of PCP from the body. In severe cases, people who overdose might need life-support equipment to keep them alive until the drug passes out of their bodies.

Fortunately, many people find a PCP high to be unpleasant, so addiction to this drug is not a widespread problem. However, there are a few people who take the drug regularly and become addicted. An addicted person who suddenly stops taking PCP experiences a host of symptoms, including depression, anxiety, belligerence, and numbed emotions. As a result, inpatient drug rehabilitation programs are often not helpful because PCP addicts do not function well in the very confrontational environment of such programs. They are more likely to be successful in 12-step programs, where participants are nonjudgmental and supportive.

The physical effects of withdrawal from PCP include anxiety, tremor, gastrointestinal upset, and cold sweats. To a certain degree, these symptoms can be controlled with medication.

PERSONAL AND SOCIAL CONSEQUENCES

There is no question that taking PCP can sometimes make people act irrationally. These actions range from the relatively harmless, such as disrobing in public places, to extreme violence to themselves and others.

Chronic PCP users report all kinds of social problems. The behavioral and emotional changes that occur often lead to social withdrawal and isolation, divorce, and disassociation from family and friends. PCP abuse impairs the user's ability to think rationally, which often results in job loss. As a result of the physical and social consequences, depression often develops.

PCP use is particularly harmful for adolescents, in whom drug use disrupts their relationships with peers, parents, teachers, and police. It also disrupts the normal maturation process and accentuates the normal social challenges of growing up. Taking PCP can inhibit the development of a healthy sense of awareness and identity.

Chronic PCP users have been likened to children with learning disabilities because of their emotional instability, social incompetence, impulsiveness, and poor attention span.

LEGAL CONSEQUENCES

PCP is considered by the U.S. federal government to be a Schedule II hallucinogen drug under the Controlled Substances Act (CSA). That means it is believed to have a high abuse potential but can be used legally under certain, very restricted, medical settings. In the United Kingdom, PCP is a Class A drug under the Misuse of Drugs Act, which means it is not legally available for medical use, and it is illegal to possess or supply.

Legal history

PCP was first listed by the U.S. federal government as a Schedule III substance in the 1960s. That meant it was legal for use in certain medical settings. However, it was changed to a Schedule II drug in 1978 because of reports of considerable abuse of the drug on the street.

Federal guidelines, regulations, and penalties

As a Schedule II hallucinogen, someone found with PCP faces stiff penalties. For a first offense, penalties in the United States range from five to 40 years in prison and fines of up to four million dollars for an individual. Repeat offenders face a prison sentence of 20 years to life and fines of up to eight million dollars.

In the United Kingdom, maximum penalties for supplying PCP are life imprisonment and a fine. Possession of the drug carries penalties of up to seven years in prison and a fine.

See also Designer drugs; Ketamine; LSD

RESOURCES

Books

Belenko, Steven R., ed. *Drugs and Drug Policy in America: A Documentary History.* Westport: Greenwood Press, 2000.

Bray, Robert M., and Mary E. Marsden, eds. *Drug Use in Metropolitan America.* Thousand Oaks: Sage Publications Inc., 1999.

Clouet, Doris H., ed. *Phencyclidine: An Update.* Rockville: National Institute on Drug Abuse, 1986.

Snyder, Solomon H., ed., and Marilyn Carroll. *PCP: The Dangerous Angel (Encyclopedia of Psychoactive Drugs, Series 1).* Broomall: Chelsea House Publishers, 1991.

Weil, Andrew, and Winnifred Rosen. *From Chocolate to Morphine: Everything you Need to Know about Mind-Altering Drugs.* Boston: Houghton Mifflin Company, 1993.

Periodicals

Miller, Norman S., Mark S. Gold, and Robert Millman. "PCP: A Dangerous Drug." *American Family Physician* 38, no. 3 (September 1988): 215-218.

U.S. Department of Health and Human Services. "Hallucinogenic and Dissociative Drugs." *National Institute on Drug Abuse Research Report Series* (March 2001).

Other

Graham, Steve. "Toxicity, Phencyclidine." *EMedicine Journal* 2, no. 6 (June 2001). [Cited February 27, 2002]. <http://www.emedicine.com/emerg/topic420.htm>.

Monitoring the Future Study (MTF). *Monitoring the Future Study home page.* [Cited February 27, 2002]. <http://www.monitoringthefuture.org>.

National Institute on Drug Abuse. "PCP (Phencyclidine)." October 29, 2001. *InfoFax.* [Cited February 27, 2002]. <http://165.112.78.61/Infofax/pcp.htmll>.

"PCP (Phencyclidine)." *Drugscope.* [Cited February 27, 2002]. <http://www.drugscope.org.uk/druginfo/drugsearch/ds_results.asp?file=\wip\11\1\1\pcp.html>.

Perry, Paul. "Phencyclidine Intoxication." Updated January 27, 2000. *University of Iowa Health Care Virtual Hospital.* [Cited February 27, 2002]. <http://www.vh.org/Providers/Conferences/CPS/29.html>.

U.S. Department of Justice Drug Enforcement Administration. "Phencyclidine (PCP)." *Drugs of Concern* [Cited March 26, 2002]. <http://www.dea.gov/concern/pcp.htm>.

U.S. Department of Justice Drug Enforcement Administration. "Phencyclidine (PCP) and Related Drugs." *Drugs of Abuse* [Cited March 26, 2002.] <http://www.dea.gov/concern/abuse/chap5/pcp.htm>.

U.S. Department of Justice Drug Enforcement Administration. "PCP (phencyclidine)." (Updated September 2001) *Drug Intelligence Brief: Club Drugs: An Update.* [Cited March 26, 2002]. <http://www.dea.gov/pubs/intel/01026/index.html>.

Organizations

National Institute on Drug Abuse (NIDA), National Institutes of Health, 6001 Executive Boulevard, Room 5213, Bethesda, MD, USA, 20892-9561, (301) 443-1124, (888) 644-6432, information@lists.nida.nih.gov, <http://www.drugabuse.gov/Infofax/marijuana.html>.

Alison Farah Palkhivala, BA

PMA AND PMMA

OFFICIAL NAMES: Paramethoxyamphetamine (PMA), four-methoxyamphetamine (4-MA), paramethoxymethamphetamine (PMMA)
STREET NAMES: Death, Mitsubishi double-stack, chicken yellow, chicken powder
DRUG CLASSIFICATIONS: Schedule I, hallucinogen

OVERVIEW

PMA (paramethoxyamphetamine) is a synthetic hallucinogen. It has psychoactive effects similar to methylenedioxymethamphetamine (MDMA, or ecstasy), another Schedule I hallucinogen. Schedule I controlled substances are defined as having a high potential for abuse, no accepted medical use in the United States, and a lack of accepted safety for use under medical supervision. PMA is far more potentially lethal than ecstasy. PMA is most often ingested by drug users who think they are taking ecstasy, and find out too late that they have really ingested PMA, or "death." Overdose victims suffer an extreme rise in body temperature that shuts down the internal organs, causes convulsions, and often death. Relative to ecstasy, very small quantities of PMA are required for an overdose to occur.

PMMA is an illicit chemical compound that is a structural hybrid of PMA. PMMA and PMA are almost identical compounds. PMMA may also be marketed as ecstasy tablets. In humans PMMA has no known distinction from PMA in physiological effects. For the purpose of this informational entry, PMA and PMMA will be considered alike.

Club drugs and raves

Both PMA and ecstasy are hallucinogens. The word hallucinogen is derived from the Latin word *allucinari* which means "to dream, to wander in mind." Hallucinogens are drugs that produce distortions of reality. Hallucinogens like ecstasy allegedly have euphoric, hallucinogenic, stimulant, and empathogenic effects. Ecstasy also reportedly suppresses the desire to eat, drink, or sleep.

This makes it possible for users to remain physically active for extended periods of time. Because of these properties, drugs like ecstasy have become popular at dance clubs and raves.

Raves are all night parties often characterized by loud, rapid music, pyrotechnics, and smoke generators. Rave parties and clubs started to appear in most metropolitan areas of the United States by the early 1990s. Attendance at raves can range from 30 people in a small club to 10,000 people in an open field or football stadium. Many ravers use designer drugs like ecstasy for the euphoric and hallucinogenic effects, and to enable them to dance continuously all night. Raves may even last up to two to three days. Ravers often dance with glow-in-the-dark accessories to enhance their drug-induced visual stimulation. They may use legal substances like Vicks nasal inhalers and Vicks VapoRub to increase the effects of the illicit drugs they use. Because of their popularity at raves and dance clubs, hallucinogens such as ecstasy and PMA are also referred to as club drugs.

PMA toxicity

PMA and ecstasy are both amphetamine-derived, clandestinely manufactured designer drugs produced for

KEY TERMS

CLUB DRUGS: Mostly synthetic, illicit substances found at raves and nightclubs. This group includes LSD, ecstasy, GHB, Rohypnol, ketamine, and methamphetamine.

DESIGNER DRUGS: Drugs that are produced in an illegal laboratory that are chemically similar to a pharmaceutical drug.

EMPATHOGEN: Any substance that produces feelings of sympathy, closeness, acceptance, and peace with surrounding individuals.

the illicit drug market. While PMA does have similar and milder hallucinogenic effects than ecstasy, it is considerably more toxic, dangerous, and potentially lethal. Ecstasy use results in an intense high relatively quickly. The effects of PMA are milder and take a much longer time to develop. When users do not obtain their usual quick and intense high, they assume they have taken weak ecstasy and ingest more pills, resulting in an overdose of PMA. Often within a matter of hours PMA earns its nickname of "death." The drug user's body temperature rises rapidly to as high as 115°F (46°C), via a process that is quickly irreversible, even when the individual is hospitalized. Brain seizures, convulsions, breakdown of internal organs, coma, and death often occur. Taking PMA in combination with other drugs, alcohol, or caffeine may promote this process. PMA has been responsible for many deaths in the United States and other countries.

PMA on the ecstasy market

PMA was first clandestinely produced by a Canadian lab in 1973. Subsequently it appeared in illicit drug circulation in the United States. In 1973, PMA was suspected to be the cause of three deaths, and determined to be the cause of two deaths in the United States. The same year, PMA was also the cause of eight deaths in Canada. Due to its high toxicity and weak euphoric effects, PMA quickly went out of vogue and stopped being circulated. No deaths were associated with PMA in the United States or Canada from the year 1974 to 2000. In 1994 PMA appeared in isolated drug communities in Australia, where it was falsely sold as ecstasy and held responsible for 12 deaths. In mid-2000 PMA came back onto the Canadian and United States black market disguised as ecstasy, and caused more deaths. During the same time period, PMA also showed up in Europe, mainly in Austria, Denmark, and Germany, where it also caused numerous deaths. In all cases the PMA was sold as ecstasy, and the victims of PMA poisoning all believed they were ingesting ecstasy, unaware of the PMA present in their pills.

Since PMA is less expensive to obtain than ecstasy, manufacturers may "cut" ecstasy pills with PMA, or replace ecstasy entirely. The manufacturer then sells the altered pills as ecstasy to individual drug dealers who are usually unaware of the PMA content of their merchandise. PMA can easily be passed off as ecstasy on the drug market due to its similar stimulant and hallucinogenic effects, and its identical appearance to ecstasy pills in size, color, and black market logos. Most of the pills that caused death in the United States carried the Mitsubishi logo, but PMA is present in some pills with other logos as well. Since the ecstasy dealers themselves are often unaware of PMA in their stock, using a "trusted source" of ecstasy pills is not a safeguard against PMA poisoning. This substitution of PMA in ecstasy tablets is an added danger for club drug users, and is causing alarm both within and outside of the United States.

CHEMICAL/ORGANIC COMPOSITION

PMA, its structural hybrid PMMA, and ecstasy are amphetamine derivatives. PMA and PMMA are structurally similar to methamphetamine but have effects more similar to ecstasy. PMMA and PMA only differ by the presence or absence respectively of one methyl group (CH_3). There is no known distinction between the effects of PMA and PMMA in human beings. Of the two, PMA is the hybrid mainly found in the postmortem blood samples of overdose victims. PMA may be sold in pills mixed with other drugs such as ecstasy or in pure preparations. Some of the PMA pills that caused death contained no ecstasy at all. However, the pills on the black market lacking ecstasy are identical in appearance to ecstasy pills in size, color, and logos. The presence or absence of ecstasy in a pill can be tested for with a Marquis reagent testing kit sold over the Internet. In the presence of ecstasy the kit produces a dark blue color. PMA produces no color reaction with the kit. PMA tablets may or may not also contain ecstasy, so a positive result for ecstasy with the kit is not a safeguard against PMA poisoning. Only a chemist with sophisticated testing equipment can determine if a pill does contain PMA.

INGESTION METHODS

PMA is a beige, white, yellow, or pink powder. The most common form of PMA is a pill or capsule disguised as ecstasy and taken orally. PMA may also be used in loose powder form, although this is uncommon. PMA powder is injected or inhaled for an accelerated physiological response. Since PMA is primarily consumed unknowingly by people believing they are taking ecstasy, it may be ingested by any route used for ecstasy consumption. In addition to those routes mentioned, ecstasy pills containing PMA can also be inserted rectally or dissolved in beverages and drunk.

THERAPEUTIC USE

There are no legitimate medical uses for PMA.

USAGE TRENDS

PMA is sold misrepresented as ecstasy, and is only inadvertently used by people who think they are ingesting ecstasy. PMA is not intentionally used as a recreational drug. Because of this circumstance, the trends of PMA abuse run parallel with the trends of ecstasy abuse.

Scope and severity

Reports from the Office of National Drug Control Policy show that club drugs are increasingly available and that their use is on the rise. The most widely available club drug is ecstasy. Over one million ecstasy tablets were seized by the Drug Enforcement Agency (DEA) in 1999, whereas in the year 2000 the DEA seized more than three million ecstasy tablets. The number of arrests made by the DEA for ecstasy violations grew from 681 arrests in 1999, to 1,456 arrests in the year 2000. The United States Customs Service seized 3.5 million ecstasy tablets in the year 1999, which grew to 9.3 million ecstasy tablets seized by Customs in 2000. The number of times ecstasy was mentioned in hospital emergency department reports sent to the Drug Abuse Warning Network (DAWN) increased from 253 in 1994, to 4,511 in the year 2000. The statistics show that increasingly more people are abusing these designer drugs. In response to the ecstasy epidemic, the Federal Sentencing Guidelines for ecstasy abuse were changed. In November 2001, the guidelines for selling large amounts of PMA or ecstasy were brought in parallel with the sentencing for the sale of cocaine.

Age, ethnic, and gender trends

In the 2001 Annual Report on the State of the Drugs Problem in the European Union (EMCDDA), amphetamines and ecstasy were listed as the second most commonly abused drugs in Europe. The report stated that within groups of students from Europe and the United States aged 15–16 years, the United States, Ireland, and the Netherlands had the highest percentage of students who had used ecstasy. The 1999 European School Survey Project on Alcohol and other Drugs (ESPAD) studied a larger number of European countries than the 2001 report by the EMCDDA. The ESPAD report showed that along with those countries mentioned by the EMCDDA, the Czech Republic, Latvia, Lithuania, and Slovenia also had a high percentage of students aged 15–16 years who had used ecstasy. In the 2001 report by the National Drug Monitor of the Netherlands, the average age of ecstasy users was 25 years old. However, 1.9% of 12-year-olds in the Netherlands had used ecstasy.

Ecstasy sellers. From the year 2000 to the year 2002, ecstasy seller populations in the United States expanded at multiple levels. Seller ethnic groups and age groups have broadened to include new categories. Ecstasy sales and raves have extended to new cities across the country. Young adults between the ages of 18–30 are the predominant sellers of ecstasy at the street-level. Adolescent street-level sellers are also common. Ecstasy sales mostly take place in central cities and suburbs. Street-level sellers tend to be independent and mostly target raves, nightclubs, college campuses, and private parties. Other common sales settings include inside cars, private homes, schools, streets, shopping malls, and the Internet. Organized ecstasy sales are mostly seen in nightclubs where the "house dealers" supply the club patrons. Prices in the United States usually range from $20 to $30 a pill. Prices as high as $40 a pill are reported in New York City. Ecstasy sellers tend to use ecstasy themselves.

Typically, street-level ecstasy sellers are not involved in other crimes or violence. However, this is not always the case. In Los Angeles, California, ecstasy sellers tend to be associated with organized crime. Sellers are associated with violent crimes in Baltimore, Maryland, and prostitution in Birmingham, Alabama. Other crimes associated with ecstasy in various cities include drug-assisted rape and gang-related activity. Ecstasy dispersal commonly involves hand-to-hand sales through acquaintance networks, and delivery services may even be employed. According to law enforcement sources, other drugs sold by ecstasy sellers include other club drugs such as gamma hydroxybutyrate (GHB) and ketamine, as well as lysergic acid diethylamide (LSD), heroin, powder and crack cocaine, marijuana, methamphetamine, and diverted prescription drugs.

Ecstasy users. Ecstasy users tend to be between 13–30 years of age. In a 2002 report by the National Criminal Justice Reference Service (NCJRS), 23.8% of eighth graders, 41.4% of tenth graders, and 61.5% of twelfth graders surveyed in the year 2001 reported that ecstasy was easy to obtain. Due to its accessibility, adolescent use of ecstasy is on the rise across the country. Furthermore, in Honolulu, Hawaii, an emerging group of ecstasy users in treatment are preadolescent. Ecstasy users tend to be evenly split between genders, and are of Caucasian ethnicity and middle class financial status. Ethnographic sources indicate that not only are the users predominantly white, but that whites are overrepresented compared with the general population in their cities. However, ecstasy use is expanding to non-white and Hispanic populations across the United States. The use of ecstasy by those of African-American descent has dramatically increased in the Southeast of the United States. Ecstasy users tend to reside in both central cities and suburbs.

The context in which ecstasy is used tends to follow the same context as the settings for the sale of ecstasy.

???? FACT OR FICTION

Ravers often wear baby pacifiers around their necks as pendants. **Fact**—Along with excessive jaw muscle tension, ecstasy can cause users to involuntarily grind their teeth. Ravers often chew on baby pacifiers or lollipops to alleviate this side effect of ecstasy usage.

Club drugs such as ecstasy and LSD have gained popularity primarily due to the false perception that they are not as harmful as mainstream drugs such as cocaine or heroin. **Fact**—All of these drugs are dangerous at any dose, and potentially fatal upon overdose. Some club drugs are associated with drug-assisted rape. Development of psychological dependence to these drugs is common. All club drugs have adverse long-term effects on the brain.

Some ecstasy users take breaks from physical activity and use cold showers to minimize the dangers of elevated body temperatures. Drug users have tried to safeguard against PMA-induced body temperature elevations in this manner. **Fact**—Highly elevated body temperature due to PMA poisoning does not respond to these approaches.

The Marquis reagent testing kit can be used to test if a pill contains ecstasy or PMA. **Fact**—The kit produces a dark blue-purple color in the presence of ecstasy and no color change in response to PMA. However some pills containing PMA also contain ecstasy, so a positive result for ecstasy does not mean the pill is free of PMA.

The most frequent places of estasy use are raves, nightclubs, college campuses, private parties, and private residences. Streets, shopping malls, inside cars, and schools are also common. The predominant route of administration of ecstasy across the country is pills taken orally. However, in parts of the United States, there is an increase in users snorting or injecting ecstasy. In some areas ecstasy is commonly used in mixed beverages.

MENTAL EFFECTS

PMA and ecstasy are pharmacologically similar, producing their effects through very similar or identical mechanisms. While little research has been done on the mental effects of PMA, they are thought to be very similar to those of ecstasy. Studies done by the National Institute of Mental Health (NIMH) in the year 2001 assessed the effects of ecstasy on the human brain. It was discovered that recreational ecstasy use damages the nerve cells, or neurons, that employ the neurotransmitters serotonin, dopamine, and acetylcholine to send information to other neurons of the brain. The use of ecstasy causes an increase in brain serotonin concentrations that deliver the "desirable" effects of ecstasy on the user. The same increase in brain serotonin concentrations also permanently damages the neurons making serotonin. The damage of these neurons eventually leads to a decrease in the level of serotonin present in the brain, resulting in many long-term complications.

Ecstasy or PMA users risk enduring brain damage similar to that found in many neurological diseases. Neuron damage may cause undesirable mental effects including depression, anxiety, loss of memory, learning deficits, difficulty solving simple problems, lack of self-control, sleep disorders, sexual dysfunction, and neuropsychiatric disorders. When a toxin such as ecstasy or PMA is ingested, neuron death occurs immediately upon exposure to the drug. However, the functional aspects of the brain damage may not show up until months or years later. Panic attacks may occur even after months of abstinence from ecstasy usage. Also, recurring paranoia, hallucinations, flashbacks, and psychotic episodes have been caused by ecstasy usage long after the actual time frame in which ecstasy was consumed. Chronic users of PMA or ecstasy may develop a psychological dependence to these drugs.

PHYSIOLOGICAL EFFECTS

Harmful side effects

Ingesting less than 50 mg of PMA without other drugs, alcohol, or caffeine induces mild symptoms of ecstasy ingestion. These symptoms include heightened visual stimulation along with erratic eye movements, an increase in heart rate and blood pressure, motion sickness, muscle spasms, rapid and difficult breathing, and an increase in body temperature. This dose may also cause mild euphoric, hallucinogenic, stimulant, and empathogenic effects. Less than 50 mg of PMA ingested in the presence of other drugs, alcohol, or caffeine may have a more intense effect, along with greatly increased toxicity. The dose of PMA by itself may not be lethal, but becomes lethal in the presence of other drugs.

PMA doses of 50 mg or greater are potentially lethal, especially in the presence of other drugs, both illicit and prescription, alcohol, or caffeine. High doses may cause heart palpitations or heart failure, kidney failure, an extreme rise in body temperature up to 115°F (46°C) that causes multiorgan failure, difficulty breathing, vomiting, brain seizures, delirium and hallucinations, sudden collapse, convulsions, coma, and death. Most people assume their symptoms come from ecstasy poisoning, which can be life-threatening. However, PMA is a far more toxic drug than ecstasy and

PMA has a much higher rate of lethal complications than ecstasy. PMA toxicity is suspected whenever a user has severe or atypical reactions to the ecstasy pills ingested, and is confirmed through urine drug screens. PMA may also cause low blood sugar, a unique effect not seen with ecstasy.

The main negative effects of ecstasy are related to hyperthermia (highly elevated body temperature). Ecstasy users attempt to use adequate hydration, rest periods, and cold showers as a means to safeguard against hyperthermia after ecstasy ingestion. However, when hyperthermia is a result of PMA, these precautions are not effective. PMA is metabolized by the enzyme cytochrome P450–2D6. This enzyme is genetically polymorphic, which means that different people have different functioning levels of the enzyme in their bodies. People who are slow metabolizers due to low enzyme levels have higher concentrations of PMA in their blood after ingestion because they do not metabolize the drug as quickly. Slow metabolizers are at a higher risk for PMA poisoning than individuals with higher levels of enzyme.

Long-term health effects

PMA and ecstasy are pharmacologically comparable, producing their effects on the body through highly similar or identical bodily systems. While little research has been done on the long-term effects of PMA on humans, they are presumed to be very similar to the effects of ecstasy. The long-term effects of ecstasy are continuing to be assessed. Studies done by NIMH in the year 2001 directly measured the effects of ecstasy on the human brain. The research indicated that recreational ecstasy use mainly damages the neurons making serotonin, leading to an overall reduction of serotonin in the brain. Ecstasy users may develop permanent brain damage of the same nature found in many neurological diseases.

Long-term health effects may include depression, anxiety, loss of memory, learning deficits, deficits of logical reasoning, sleep disorders, sexual dysfunction, and multiple neuropsychiatric disorders. Ecstasy causes the damage immediately, but the long term effects may not be seen until much later. According to the Centre for Addiction and Mental Health of Canada, there are other long-term physical problems that arise long after ecstasy usage is over. These problems may or may not also occur during ecstasy usage. They include periodic muscle spasms in the jaw, neck, and lower back, low blood pressure, poor control by the autonomic nervous system of heart rate and blood pressure, changes in blood flow to the brain, and persistent problems with involuntary tooth grinding. Chronic users of PMA or ecstasy may develop a tolerance to the drug, and require increasingly higher doses to obtain the same high. While psychological dependence may develop, physical dependence is not known to develop to these drugs.

REACTIONS WITH OTHER DRUGS OR SUBSTANCES

PMA in ecstasy tablets

PMA is not deliberately used recreationally in its pure form. PMA is sold on the illicit drug market being portrayed as ecstasy tablets. Pure PMA tablets may be sold as ecstasy, but frequently PMA is found in combination with ecstasy. Because PMA can be present in ecstasy pills, it may be used along with any drug normally consumed in combination with ecstasy pills. Ecstasy is frequently used in combination with other club drugs such as LSD, psilocybin mushrooms, GHB, ketamine, and nitrous oxide. Ecstasy is also used with marijuana, methamphetamine, heroin, powder cocaine, diverted prescription depressants, and Viagra. If PMA is ingested in the presence of these other illicit drugs, prescription drugs, alcohol, or caffeine, its toxicity is greatly increased. Lethal repercussions of PMA usage are even more likely in the presence of these other substances. Small doses of PMA that are not normally lethal become lethal in the presence of many other drugs.

An example of PMA toxicity in the presence of other drugs is a victim who died in the late 1990s after ingesting what she believed to be an ecstasy tablet. Toxicological analysis of her blood postmortem revealed elevated but not lethal levels of PMA and therapeutic levels of the prescription drug fluoxetine (Prozac). Ecstasy was not detected in her blood samples. Drug users often abuse fluoxetine to enhance the euphoric and energizing effects of ecstasy. This patient died from cerebral hemorrhage despite the low levels of PMA she had ingested. It is thought that the fluoxetine used all the enzyme normally responsible for metabolizing PMA, hence its unusual toxicity. The fluoxetine may also have had some other reaction with PMA to enhance its toxicity and produce the fatality.

Cocaine, amphetamine, methamphetamine, alcohol, and cannabinoids have already been suspected as aggravating the deadly effects of PMA. As with all drugs, the potency and quality of PMA pills may deviate substantially from one batch to another. Different pills may contain varying amounts of the drug. The clandestine labs that manufacture these illicit drugs are often very dirty, and the pills they generate may contain many dangerous contaminates in addition to PMA.

TREATMENT AND REHABILITATION

There is no official treatment and rehabilitation program solely for PMA abuse because PMA is primarily consumed inadvertently instead of, or in combination with, ecstasy. Because of the large population of ecstasy users in the United States, however, there are treatment centers available for rehabilitation from ecstasy usage.

While ecstasy-like drug users are not known to develop physical addictions, psychological addictions are common. Narconon is an organization widely used by many types of drug addicts in the United States. Narconon is just one of many organizations that offer programs of treatment for overcoming ecstasy addiction. Recovery programs for ecstasy-like drugs work with the psychological nature of the addiction. In addition to organizations with recovery programs, self-help books, and peer support groups are also available.

PERSONAL AND SOCIAL CONSEQUENCES

Ecstasy and PMA users are most often teenagers who consume the drugs in social settings. Studies show that people who use ecstasy tend to be attracted to techno-style rave music. Raves are a major source of illicit ecstasy distribution to the public and may be one of the main sources of the ecstasy "epidemic." Club drug usage has been mostly responsible for the growing popularity of raves in the United States and other countries. Raves have had a large impact on society by providing an organized location for group usage of illicit drugs. Because PMA is only present as an adulterant in ecstasy pills, the social consequences of PMA usage go along with those of ecstasy usage. However, the individual consequences of PMA contamination of ecstasy pills may be far graver.

Social consequences of club drug use

Individuals who choose to experiment with club drugs are often having difficulty coping with life situations, anger, depression, or low self esteem, previous to drug usage. The negative feelings associated with these problems often causes individuals to seek an escape or relief from their troubles. Drug usage supplies an escape route by allowing the users to forget their worries and experience positive sensations in replacement. In addition, club drug use is associated with an increase in sexual activity. Individuals in a drug-induced state may engage in sexual activities they would otherwise avoid. Individuals who use ecstasy, for instance, also risk acquiring permanent brain damage and the onset of neurological or neuropsychiatric disorders, such as parkinsonism. Neuropsychiatric problems that may be associated with past ecstasy use include psychotic episodes, panic attacks, hallucinations, paranoia, and flashbacks.

Personal consequences of PMA

The addition of PMA to the already serious ecstasy situation is alarming. Unknowing ecstasy or PMA users may find themselves in an uncontrollable physical state of hyperthermia, experience convulsions, coma, and death. The covert, silent, but deadly presence of PMA within the ecstasy community results in an additional cause of concern. Ecstasy alone has caused untimely deaths in the past, but with the emergence of PMA the death rate is steadily increasing.

LEGAL CONSEQUENCES

All of the club drugs including PMA and ecstasy have been scheduled under the Controlled Substances Act (CSA), Title II of the Comprehensive Drug Abuse Prevention and Control Act of 1970. PMA has been listed as a Schedule I drug since 1973. Ecstasy has been listed as a Schedule I drug since 1988. Schedule I Controlled Substances are defined as having a high potential for abuse, no accepted medical use in the United States, and a lack of accepted safety for use under medical supervision. However, PMA is produced legally in the United States for limited commercial applications and a small quantity is allocated for Schedule I drug research.

Federal guidelines, regulations, and penalties

PMA is considered an ecstasy-like substance and is regulated under the Ecstasy Anti-Proliferation Act of 2000. The act increased the federal sentencing guidelines for the manufacture, import, export, and trafficking of ecstasy and ecstasy-like substances. This act placed the severity of the penalties for ecstasy and PMA use to greater than that for powder cocaine. It lengthens federal sentences for trafficking 800 pills (approximately 200 g) of ecstasy or PMA from 15 months to five years, an increase of 300%. The act increases the penalization for trafficking 8,000 pills by nearly 200%, from 41 months to 10 years. These extensions were constructed in response to a skyrocketing increase in ecstasy abuse and trafficking compared with previous years.

The ecstasy epidemic, its potential for causing permanent brain damage, and the deaths associated with ecstasy usage led to the passage of the Ecstasy Prevention Act of 2001. The Ecstasy Prevention Act of 2001 built on the Ecstasy Anti-Proliferation Act of 2000 by allotting funding for the education of law enforcement officials and the public, and for medical research done by the National Institute on Drug Abuse (NIDA). In 2001, the average sentence for ecstasy-related crimes rose from 25 months to 60 months. The number of pills triggering a five-year sentence decreased from 11,428 pills to 800 pills.

According to the NCJRS, many communities and law enforcement agencies are forming new anti-rave ordinances to try to decrease the use of club drugs. They are appointing juvenile curfews, ordaining licensing requirements for large public gatherings, and exacting compliance to existing fire codes and laws relating to health, safety, and alcohol use. Another enactment that has impacted ecstasy and PMA substance abuse is the Drug Induced Rape Prevention Act of 1996. Although ecstasy usually is not associated with violent crimes, it has been mentioned by law enforcement agencies as connected to drug-induced rape in certain areas of the country. The purpose of the Drug Induced Rape Prevention Act of 1996 is to confront drug-facilitated crimes of violence, including sexual assaults. The act creates penalties specifically for the use of controlled substances such as ecstasy or PMA with the intent to commit a violent crime.

International penalties

In the United Kingdom, PMA is classified as a Class A Controlled Substance, the most dangerous class of drugs. Offenses involving drugs from Class A obtain the highest penalties. Unlawful possession of Class A drugs under summary conviction can be penalized with up to a six-month prison sentence and a 5,000-pound ($7,350) fine. On indictment the penalty may reach a seven-year prison sentence and an unlimited fine. Class A drug trafficking upon indictment carries a maximum penalty of a lifetime prison sentence. The Powers of Criminal Courts Act of 2000 created a minimum prison sentence of seven years for a third-time offense in the trafficking of Class A drugs such as ecstasy or PMA.

In Canada, there is no accepted medical use for PMA, and it is classified by the Food and Drugs Act as a restricted material. Illicit possession of this drug for a first-time offender carries a penalty of $1,000 in fines and up to a six-month prison sentence. Succeeding offenses are given double the fine and sentence. Conviction by indictment can secure a fine of $5,000 and a three-year prison sentence. PMA drug trafficking and possession of PMA for trafficking purposes may confer a prison sentence of up to 10 years.

Germany is one of the world's largest suppliers of club drugs. Under the German Narcotics Act of 1981, PMA is classified as a Schedule I controlled substance, the most dangerous category of classification. Schedule I drugs in Germany are defined as illicit narcotics with-out medical benefit. Under German law, the type and classification of the narcotic in question does not influence the penalty for possession of the drug. Drug offenses involving PMA may elicit a penalty anywhere from a fine only to a 15-year prison sentence.

See also Designer drugs; Ecstasy (MDMA); Methamphetamine

RESOURCES

Other

Drug Enforcement Agency. PMA Drug Intelligence Brief. *The Hallucinogen PMA, Dancing with Death.* <http://www.usdoj. gov/dea/pubs/intel.htm>.

National Criminal Justice Reference Service. *In the Spotlight, Club Drugs.* <http://www.ncjrs.org/club_drugs/club_drugs.html>.

Organizations

Narconon International, (323) 962-2404, rehab@narconon.org, <http://www.narconon.org>.

National Drug Intelligence Center (NDIC), 319 Washington Street, 5th Fl., Johnstown, PA, USA, 15901-1622, (814) 532-4601, (814) 532-4690, cmbwebmgr@ndic.osis.gov, <http://www.usdoj.gov/ndic/>.

National Institute on Drug Abuse (NIDA), National Institutes of Health, 6001 Executive Boulevard, Room 5213, Bethesda, MD, USA, 20892-9561, (301) 443-1124, (888) 644-6432, information@lists.nida.nih.gov, <http://www.nida.nih.gov>.

National Institutes of Mental Health (NIMH) Public Inquiries, 6001 Executive Boulevard, Room 8184 MSC 9663, Bethesda, MD, USA, 20892-9663, (301) 443-4513, (301) 443-4299, nimhinfo@nih.gov, <http://www.nimh.nih.gov/>.

Substance Abuse and Mental Health Services Administration (SAMHSA)/Center for Substance Abuse Treatment (CSAT), 5600 Fishers Lane, Rockville, MD, USA, 20857, (301) 443-8956, info@samhsa.gov, <http://www.samhsa.gov>.

Maria Basile-Folkerts

PSILOCYBIN

OFFICIAL NAMES: Psilocybin, *Psilocybe* mushrooms
STREET NAMES: Magic mushrooms, shrooms, boomers, caps, cubes (*Psilocybe cubensis*), fungus, liberty caps, Mexican mushrooms, mushies, mushrooms, psychedelic mushrooms, psilocydes, purple passion, sillies, silly putty, simple Simon
DRUG CLASSIFICATIONS: Schedule I, hallucinogen

OVERVIEW

For thousands of years, Native Americans in Central and South America have used *Psilocybe* (mushrooms producing psilocybin—pronounced sill-o-sigh-bin) in rare religious rites and ceremonies. The Aztec word for these hallucinogen-producing mushrooms is *teonanacatl*, which roughly translates as "flesh of god." The shaman (medicine man or woman) and a select group of participants using the mushrooms believed they received special power to talk to the gods, to divine the future, to cure the sick, and to speak with the dead. In 2002, Native Americans in Central, South, and North America still practiced their religious traditions by legally using *Psilocybe* mushrooms.

In the 16th century, when the Spanish conquered the Aztecs, the Spanish tried to eradicate the use of the "magic or Mexican mushroom." The effort was unsuccessful, but in the process, the priests were able to document the traditions, uses, and history associated with the mushroom. Ingesting these mushrooms at that time was largely confined to the Native American population.

Most people in Europe and in the United States were not aware of *Psilocybe* mushrooms until 1957.

That year, R. Gordon Wasson, an enthnomycologist, published an article about *Psilocybe* mushrooms in *Life* magazine. This article brought the mushrooms to the attention of the general public for the first time. As a result of the article, thousands of people flocked to Mexico in search of the mind-altering mushroom. About that same time, the psychoactive chemical psilocybin was isolated and synthesized by Swiss chemist Albert Hofmann, who also discovered LSD (lysergic acid diethylamide).

For about a decade, psilocybin was legal and available in mushroom, powder, or pill form. It was used by psychologists to treat psychological problems and was also studied as a treatment for reforming criminals. By 1968, clinical tests were showing few positive, conclusive results and abuse of the mushroom in the United States was escalating. As a result of these findings, the government made possesion of psilocybin illegal.

As the *Psilocybe* mushroom gained popularity, so did knowledge about its native growth. Prior to the 1950s these mushrooms were only known to grow in Mexico and a few select places. It was soon discovered that *Psilocybe* mushrooms grow around the world. Many of them grow naturally in the United States, especially in the Pacific Northwest and southern states. This makes enforcing the law difficult.

While psilocybin use slowed in the 1980s, its renewed popularity since the mid-1990s is causing concern. In 2002, *Psilocybe* mushrooms are becoming more common at raves, college campuses, and clubs in the United States and several other countries. *Psilocybe* mushrooms are advertised as a "natural" hallucinogen that is safer and gentler than LSD.

CHEMICAL/ORGANIC COMPOSITION

Psilocybin is a naturally occurring hallucinogen. It exerts neurotoxic effects similar to LSD and has a chemical structure similar to the neurotransmitter serotonin in the human brain. Psilocybin is found as an indole alkaloid (nitrogen-containing organic base) in the fungal (Protista) kingdom. Often it is accompanied by the related alkaloids, psilocin, baeocystin, and norbaeocystin.

Mushrooms that contain psilocybin are of the genus *Psilocybe* and belong to the Basidiomycetes class. Over 90 *Psilocybe* species are psychoactive, and they grow naturally around the world. Psilocybin (phosphorylated 4-hydroxydimethyltryptamine) usually accounts for 0.03 to 1.3% of the total weight of the mushroom, though potency can vary greatly.

Psilocybin can be isolated and crystallized or synthesized to nearly 100% purity. Research indicates that *Psilocybe* mushrooms produce a bitter alkaloid as an insecticide to protect itself from predators. In humans, psilocybin is a neurotoxin that can cause hallucinations.

TYPES OF PSILOCYBIN

Psilocybin powder

Psilocybin powder is the most potent form of this hallucinogenic alkaloid. It was isolated in 1958 and can be synthesized to nearly 100% purity. The human body is very sensitive to this neurotoxin and just 0.01 g of psilocybin powder contains the equivalent psilocybin found in 30 fresh *Psilocybe* mushrooms.

For a decade after its isolation, psilocybin, mainly in the form of pills, was readily available in the United States as a pharmacological drug. It was prescribed for psychological therapy. In 1968, psilocybin was made illegal, as few positive conclusions could be drawn about its benefits. Also, it had a high incidence of abuse. Psilocybin powder is usually swallowed, injected intravenously, or sniffed. Due to its high potency, it carries a high risk of overdose. Psilocybin powder or pills are expensive and difficult to produce and therefore difficult to obtain on the street. Studies indicate that when psilocybin is sold on the street, it is usually LSD, PCP (phencyclidine), or both.

Psilocybin liquid

Psilocybin liquid comes from pulverized *Psilocybe* mushrooms. Archeologists in Central and South America have discovered stones, paintings, and slender tubes depicting the practice of extracting and ingesting the liquid. These paintings date back to A.D. 1. This potent liquid, free from the bulky plant material, is then either swallowed or inserted rectally as an enema. Psilocybin liquid is still consumed by both methods by Mexican

 **KEY TERMS**

ALKALOID: Any organic agent isolated from plants that contains nitrogen and reacts with an acid to form a salt.

ENEMA: This is the injection of fluid into the rectum. Native Americans have used this method to ingest psilocybin.

ETHNOMYCOLOGIST: A person who studies the cultural uses of mushrooms.

FLASHBACK: The re-experiencing of a drug high without actually taking the drug. A flashback is usually limited to visual hallucinations and disturbances and can occur weeks, months, or years after taking the drug.

PARANOIA: The presence of delusions of a persacutory nature, involving be hunted or harmed by another person.

PSILOCYBE: A genus of mushroom which produces the bitter-tasting indole alkaloid psilocybin that causes hallucinations and other side effects. Sometimes *Psilocybe* mushrooms are referred to as psilocybin mushrooms.

PSYCHOSIS: A severe mental disorder characterized by the loss of the ability to distinguish what is objectively real from what is imaginary, frequently including hallucinations.

SEROTONIN: An important neurotransmitter in the brain that regulates mood, appetite, sensory perception and other central nervous system functions.

SYNESTHESIA: A chemical "cross-wiring" of the brain circuits often due to the use of hallucinogens that results in colors being felt or heard and sound being tasted or seen.

TOLERANCE: A condition in which higher and higher doses of a drug are needed to produce the original effect or high experienced.

natives as part of their religious rites. Due to its potency and especially if it is used rectally, liquid psilocybin carries a high risk of overdose.

Soaking *Psilocybe* mushrooms in water makes a much less potent psilocybin liquid. This liquid is often drunk as a tea. *Psilocybe* mushrooms and the liquid are illegal to possess in the United States.

Psilocybin mushrooms

The most common way to access psilocybin is by eating *Psilocybe* mushrooms. Fresh *Psilocybe* mushrooms contain 0.03 to 1.3% psilocybin by weight. Dried mushrooms, which can shrink by 90–95%, contain about ten times the amount of psilocybin per weight after the

Drugs and Controlled Substances: Information for Students

```
?????
```
FACT OR FICTION

If it is natural then it is safe—true or false?

A growing number of young people 18–25 years old are seeking a "natural" hallucinogenic experience by eating *Psilocybe* mushrooms. Some believe that if the whole plant is eaten, the naturally occurring psilocybin will produce a "safe" experience.

Is the psilocybin in the mushrooms "natural?"

Maybe or maybe not. Studies done in California, where over 300 street samples of "psilocybin mushrooms" were bought and analyzed revealed that 85% of the mushrooms were not *Psilocybe* (the species that produces psilocybin). Instead, the majority were grocery store mushrooms injected with LSD, PCP, or both. It should be noted that LSD is 100 times as potent as psilocybin and has much more intense, long-lasting, and serious effects. LSD and PCP are both manmade.

What if the user is able to get real "shrooms," "mushies," or "sillies" as they are often called? Just what is this "naturally" occurring hallucinogen?

Psilocybin is a neurotoxin that targets the central nervous system and serotonin receptors in the brain when it is ingested. It is believed that the mushroom produces this bitter toxin as an insecticide to protect itself from predators.

As abuse of these mushrooms increases worldwide, more data is available on the serious side effects. In a 2000 Swiss Toxicological Information Center (STIC) study, researchers examined 161 acute *Psilocybe* mushroom exposures in which people intentionally ate "magic mushrooms." The median age of the person seeking medical attention was 20 years (range 14–56). According to the researchers, "Reasons for hospitalization were marked hallucinations, hyperexcitability, panic attacks, coma, and convulsions." As "good trips" turn "bad" and euphoria turns to fear and panic, there is no antidote or antitoxin that can make it go away. Thirty-one percent of the people in this study experienced panic attacks severe enough to seek medical attention.

Yes, psilocybin is just as "natural" as strychnine (used as rat poison and found naturally in the seed of the nux vomica tree) and cyanide (used as an insecticide and found naturally in the fruit seeds)—but just because it is "natural" doesn't mean it is safe.

---

water is removed. The most commonly cultivated or natively collected species are *Panaeolus subbalteatus* and *tropicalis*, *Psilocybe baeocystis*, *caerulescens*, *cubensis*, *cyanescens*, *mexicana*, *pelliculosa*, *semilanceata*, *stuntzii*, and *Copelandia cyanescens* and *cambodgeniensis*. The amount of psilocybin in mushrooms varies considerably. Even in controlled laboratory conditions the psilocybin content can vary up to four times from mushroom to mushroom. In nature, mushrooms of the same species and in the same location can contain up to ten times the amount of psilocybin from the highest content to the lowest.

While *Psilocybe* mushrooms rarely cause death, except in small children, the greatest risk for those who pick their own mushrooms is accidentally ingesting non-*Psilocybe* poisonous mushrooms. Because mushrooms in one stage of growth can look like mature mushrooms of the desired species, amateurs may pick toxic mushrooms. For users who choose to buy prepicked mushrooms, studies indicate that common grocery store mushrooms are often injected with the much more potent LSD or other drugs and passed off as *Psilocybes*. The mushrooms are then frozen as a black mass so that their true identity is hidden. *Psilocybe* mushrooms, which are illegal to possess in the United States, are either eaten whole or ground up into a powder and swallowed.

INGESTION METHODS

The amount of psilocybin consumed and the way it is ingested greatly determines the effect it will have on the brain and the body. Since psilocybin is a neurotoxin, the more that is consumed and the faster it reaches the brain, the greater the chance of adverse reactions or overdose.

Mouth and stomach

By far, the most common way to ingest psilocybin is by eating *Psilocybe* mushrooms. Mushroom eaters generally consider 1–5 g of dried mushrooms or 10–15 g of fresh mushrooms a moderate dose. While some absorption of psilocybin begins in the mouth, the majority of this neurotoxin passes through into the blood stream via the small intestines. The small intestines, having the surface area of a football field, are well suited for absorbing both nutrients and toxins. However, before the psilocybin reaches the small intestines, it must cross the barrier of the stomach. Since psilocybin is a base and the stomach secretes an acid, the absorption rate is greatly slowed. Within a few minutes it is common to feel nausea and many "eaters" of mushrooms vomit. After the psilocybin passes through the stomach and the small intestines, it reaches the blood. Once there, it must pass through the liver before it can get to its intended site—

the brain. All of this results in the blood levels of psilocybin gradually increasing over a 30-minute to two-hour time period.

Initially, the user notices a feeling of anxiety or anticipation. As the feeling intensifies, emotions may fluctuate rapidly and tension is released by crying and laughing. Perception of space and time are blurred, and visual images or "hallucinations" often appear. The primary effect lasts four to six hours. Many people find it difficult to sleep and notice that the altered sense of reality persists for an additional two to six hours.

Because the psilocybin alkaloid in the mushrooms is so bitter, many users try to mask the flavor by adding spices, orange juice, chocolate or other strong-flavored foods. Some "eaters" put the mushrooms on pizza or inside omelettes or soup. Finally, some bypass the mushroom flesh altogether by making mushroom tea. After soaking the mushrooms in hot water for about five minutes, they discard the mushrooms and drink the liquid. This results in less psilocybin being ingested, but what is swallowed is more quickly absorbed.

Religious customs using the *Psilocybe* mushrooms are still practiced by Native Americans in Mexico, the United States, and other places around the world. However, the practice is generally reserved for rare and sacred rituals.

Injecting

Injecting *Psilocybe* mushroom juice intravenously is not common but it is reported. Most psilocybin users are seeking a "natural" experience and use of needles is not considered natural. Intravenous injection is the fastest means of getting psilocybin to the brain. In less than 16 seconds, the psilocybin is mixed with the blood, taken to the lungs, returned to the heart, and delivered to the brain. As the natural barriers and buffers of the stomach, small intestine, and liver are bypassed, the chances of overdose and adverse side effects such as coma, convulsions, and kidney failure, are greatly increased. It is even more rare for users to inject psilocybin powder, as this drug is difficult to obtain on the street. Supposed psilocybin powder bought on the street is almost always LSD, PCP, or both.

Enema

Injecting psilocybin liquid rectally by means of an enema is second only to intravenous injection for having the drug reach the brain quickly. This area of the body has a significant surface area for absorption. This method reduces nausea and vomiting associated with eating mushrooms. There is no stomach acid to slow the absorption of the psilocybin base. Also, the liver is bypassed as the drug is absorbed into the blood. This method of using psilocybin is uncommon in non-Native American cultures because most users of psilocybin are

interested in a "natural" experience and enema administration is not considered "natural" to most users.

Archeological evidence of psilocybin liquid via enemas dates back to A.D. 1 and some tribes still practice this method today. In ancient times, a hollow bone or tube was inserted deep into the rectum. Then an animal bladder filled with the psilocybin liquid was attached to the end of the tube. The liquid was then squirted deep into the rectum and lower intestine. Because so many natural barriers are bypassed by this method, the user is at great risk for overdose, serious side effects, or death.

Smoking and snorting

There are some reports that psilocybin is smoked or snorted but very little information is available. This is not a very common means of ingesting psilocybin.

THERAPEUTIC USE

Psilocybin is an illegal drug with no accepted therapeutic uses. Before 1968, psilocybin was readily available in natural and synthetic forms in the United States. For over a decade, the drug was used in numerous tests to see if it had therapeutic value. One study was done from 1961–63. Timothy Leary and Ralph Metzner attempted to reform criminals at the Massachusetts Correctional Institute in Concord. The inmates were given two high doses of psilocybin over six weeks, along with several sessions of therapy. It was hoped that in the drug-induced state, inmates would confront their inclinations, gain new personal insights, and choose to leave the life of crime. The real test came when the inmates were released from prison. In the final analysis, the psilocybin-subjected inmates had the same rate of return to prison as the inmates who were not part of the study. In addition, they had more parole violations than the general parolees. In numerous other studies, psilocybin was employed to help people with mental and emotional illnesses. Because psilocybin causes shifts in perception and loosens emotions and thoughts, this drug was used to treat neurotic and psychosomatic disorders.

Numerous studies in the 1960s failed to demonstrate that psilocybin has positive and long-lasting benefits for patients. Abuse of psilocybin by the general population was on the rise. In 1968, psilocybin was made illegal. In 2002, there were psilocybin studies underway to see if the drug can be useful in treating obsessive-compulsive disorder or if it can be used as a truth serum. As there is a worldwide trend for increased use of *Psilocybe* mushrooms, especially among young adults, several studies are underway in Germany and Switzerland to better understand the effects of psilocybin on the mind and body.

Psilocybe mushrooms are still used by Mexican natives in divinatory psychotherapy, which is therapy that focuses on mental and emotional problems. Manuals written in the 1600s detail the use of *Psilocybe* mushrooms by native shamans for curing virtually every physical ailment. There is no scientific evidence supporting the effectiveness of this ancient religious tradition in curing disease.

USAGE TRENDS

Prior to 1957, mainstream Americans had rarely, if ever, heard of psilocybin mushrooms. It was only after pioneering ethnomycologist R. Gordon Wasson published his personal account that people began to take an interest in this mind-altering hallucinogen. His story detailed his experience of eating psilocybin mushrooms during a religious rite with Mexican natives in the Sierra Mazateca. Wasson's publicity took place at a time when the "flower children" and drug culture of the 1960s was just beginning to take root. Thousands of people, ranging from scientists to thrill seekers and hippies, went to Mexico in search of the "magic mushroom." These non-natives did not respect the mushrooms as being sacred. Also, at that time, people did not realize that psilocybin mushrooms grow natively around the world.

Abuse of the psilocybin mushroom continued and clinical studies were finding little evidence that psilocybin mushrooms have medical uses. This trend of increasing "recreational" use of psilocybin was similar to the pattern of drug use in America. In 1962, fewer than 2% of the United States population had tried an illicit drug. By 1979, 65% of high school seniors and 70% of young adults had tried an illicit drug.

In 1968, psilocybin was made illegal. In 1970, in response to the epidemic proportions of drug use, the Comprehensive Drug Abuse Prevention and Control Act was passed. The Controlled Substances Act (CSA) created a schedule for drugs based on their medical uses and the probability of abuse. At that time, psilocybin was placed in the most restrictive category as a Schedule I hallucinogen.

The passing of the Beat Generation of the 1950s and the hippies in the 1960s combined with new findings about the toxicity of psilocybin caused the trend of *Psilocybe* mushroom use to stabilize and then subside by the 1980s and early 1990s. However, in the mid-1990s, there was a noticeable resurgence in psilocybin mushroom consumption. This is fueled in part by a social trend among young adults to try to recreate the 1960s. In 2002, psilocybin mushrooms are becoming more common at raves, parties, and on college campuses.

Scope and severity

According to the National Household Survey on Drug Abuse (NHSDA), *Psilocybe* mushroom use is on the rise. In 1997, 10.2 million Americans had tried psilocybin. A study funded by the National Institute on Drug Abuse (NIDA) reported that even though reported psilocybin use is rising, it might still be significantly underreported. One reason for this is that surveys often ask students if they use "psilocybin," which is a scientific term, instead employing slang terms such as "shrooms" or "mushrooms." The study indicated that the underreporting is not a case of students trying to conceal drug use as much as students not understanding the scientific terms in the survey. NHSDA showed that psilocybin use rose most dramatically among the 18–25 year olds. In 1997, 7.9% of this population surveyed reported using these mushrooms. Just a year later the figure jumped to 10.9%. This agrees with the U.S. Drug Enforcement Administration's (DEA) reports that psilocybin mushrooms are increasingly found on college campuses, in raves, and in clubs. The Community Epidemiology Work Group (CEWG), which follows drug abuse trends in 21 major metropolitan areas, indicates that psilocybin mushrooms are available in Boston, Baltimore, Minneapolis/St. Paul, and Seattle.

Access to *Psilocybe* mushrooms is increasing. They grow naturally in the Gulf States and the Pacific Northwest. In other areas across the United States, the mushrooms are cultivated in laboratories or in homes with kits purchased over the Internet. Psilocybin mushrooms in the United States often sell for $20–40 per one-eighth ounce.

Around the world there is a marked and renewed interest in psilocybin. Mushrooms are regaining the popularity they experienced in the 1960s and 1970s. Germany, Poland, Switzerland, and Scandinavia also report increased psilocybin use. In Canada, according to the 1999 Ontario Student Drug Use Survey, psilocybin use has increased significantly from 1997 to 1999. In Great Britain, 785 second-year medical students were surveyed. Seven percent of those surveyed reported using psilocybin. Combining this with other studies, researchers concluded that psilocybin use is increasing among the general university population as well.

In Japan, however, due to a loophole in the law, psilocybin mushrooms can be sold as long as they are not designated for human consumption. They are sold as "aroma pads" or for "decorative uses" and then openly eaten, especially among the college-aged people. Due to this popular trend, the Ministry of Health, Welfare, and Labor is considering making the mushrooms illegal.

Age, ethnic, and gender trends

According to the NHSDA, 18–25 year olds are the fastest growing group of psilocybin mushroom consumers. In one year, from 1997 to 1998, the number of lifetime users (the number of people who have ever used psilocybin in their lifetime) jumped up 38%. The younger age group of 12–17-year-olds remained the stable at 2.6% of the population. The age group of 26–34

These Psilocybe semilanceata *mushrooms are native to Britain and contain hallucinogenic compounds.* Photo by *Vaughan Fleming, Photo Researchers, Inc./Science Photo Library. Reproduced by permission.*

indicated a slowing as the figure dropped from 7.9% to 7.1%. However, there was another sharp rise in the 35 and older population.

A 1999 NIDA-funded research project at John Hopkins University estimated that 14% of U.S. residents had an opportunity to try hallucinogens, including psilocybin. The vast majority of those who used the drug transitioned from first opportunity to first use within one year. The study indicates that the probability of making this transition is increasing, especially for hallucinogens. This study indicates that the age of first use is directly related to the age of first opportunity.

Race and ethnicity is a factor in hallucinogen use. This is especially apparent in 18–25-year-olds, a category in which whites were more than 10 times as likely to report lifetime hallucinogen use as blacks. In this same age group, Hispanic use of hallucinogens was also greater than that of blacks. This relationship exists for all age groups surveyed except in the two older age groups (26–34 and 35 and older). In this case, there was no difference in reported lifetime use between Hispanics and blacks.

In the adult age groups, males were twice as likely as females to report lifetime and past-year use of hallucinogens. In the age group of 12–17, there was no significant gender difference. The 1999 NIDA-funded research project at John Hopkins University indicated that males have more opportunities to try hallucinogens, but were not more likely than females to progress to actual use once the opportunity presented itself. Research done by the National Poison Control Center determined that women in its survey at raves in the United Kingdom reported a higher consumption of psilocybin than men.

There is no single predictor of psilocybin use. Since the mid-1990s, psilocybin mushrooms have gained broader acceptance as a "natural" hallucinogen. Young people, especially the rave crowd, misinterpret a "naturally" occurring drug as a "safe" drug. Many are unaware of the adverse side effects that can come from an overdose, repeated use, or even a single exposure. The more a person views a drug as socially acceptable or safe, the more likely that person is to use the drug. Additionally, availability greatly affects a person's decision to use. Psilocybin is now easily accessible for 18–25-year-olds who attend colleges and rave clubs. Generally, psilocybin is not the first drug that is tried by a person. Usually, alcohol, tobacco, and marijuana, which are more readily available and more socially acceptable, are tried first as "gateway drugs." Finally, family and friends can influence a person's decision to use psilocybin. According to the National Poison Control Center, psilocybin was accessed through friends more than any other source.

???? FACT OR FICTION

Some *Psilocybe* mushroom eaters, in an effort to avoid LSD and PCP tainted varieties sold on the street, try to pick their own mushrooms. In theory, this should be easy to do. *Psilocybe* (species containing psilocybin) mushrooms grow naturally around the world and in the United States particularly in the Pacific Northwest and southeastern states. Mushroom hunters often seek out cow pastures, riverbanks, pine forests, and wood chips in search of over 90 known species of *Psilocybe* mushrooms. The problem, though, is that it is very difficult to tell the difference between *Psilocybe* and other poisonous mushrooms. *Psilocybe* and poisonous look-alikes can grow side by side.

According to the U.S. Food and Drug Administration Center for Food Safety and Applied Nutrition Foodborne Pathogenic Microorganisms and Natural Toxins Handbook, "Mushroom poisonings are almost always caused by ingestion of wild mushrooms that have been collected by non-specialists (although specialists have also been poisoned)." That parenthetical quote should alert all would-be collectors that properly identifying mushrooms is a difficult task.

Many poisonous species can be nearly indistinguishable from edible species, especially during particular stages of development. Positive mushroom identification is so difficult that professionals collect several types of data before making a determination. While collecting, different species are kept separate, often with wax paper. A written notation is made of the names of nearby trees; whether the mushroom was growing as a cluster or singly; the color of the cap, spores, gills, and stalk as this may change after picking; any peculiar taste, odor, or reaction to bruising. Experts also try to collect the mushrooms at all stages of growth. Once at the lab, the spores are examined under a microscope for size, shape, and color. The cap, stem, and gills are then measured and the color is noted. Even then, experts can not always make a positive identification.

MENTAL EFFECTS

Small doses of psilocybin mushrooms cause the user to feel relaxed. Moderate doses, which are generally 1–5 g of dried mushrooms or 10–15 g of fresh mushrooms, first cause of a feeling of tingling throughout the body, followed by a feeling of anxiety, anticipation, or alarm. It takes 30–60 minutes for the psilocybin to begin to take effect. As the effect of the drug heightens, users will experience mood swings from depression to joy and from euphoria (a feeling of well being) to fear. Perception of time, space, and the user's own body is altered. Time usually seems to slow down. However, sometimes users believe time is standing still, winding backwards, or freezing in place. As hallucinations take on a visual form, users can feel as though the walls are breathing. Small and previously insignificant details can take on a new and profound meaning. Colors can take on brilliant and dazzling shapes such as tunnels/funnels, spirals, lattices/honeycombs, and cobwebs. Synesthesia or "cross-wiring" of the brain's chemical circuitry can cause sound to be felt or seen and colors to be heard or tasted. Boundaries are often distorted and suddenly one's hand may seem like it is several yards away, or shriveled, or shrunken to the size of an infant's hand.

It can be a short step from intrigue to panic. Psilocybin users can have "bad trips" where they may believe they are sinking into the floor or they are being suffocated or harmed by others. The primary effects of psilocybin last four to six hours. For an additional two to four hours many users find it difficult to sleep and continue to experience an altered reality. It is common within the next few days to experience mood swings. Also, due to the intense nature of the experience, it is common to have recurring thoughts or feelings for several days or weeks.

Though psilocybin is known as a "natural" hallucinogen and has a reputation of being gentler than LSD, it is still known to cause panic attacks, "bad trips," and to precipitate mental illness in some people. In 1998, a study at the Psychiatric University Hospital in Zurich, Switzerland, demonstrated that psilocybin produces a psychosis-like syndrome in healthy humans that is similar to early schizophrenia. The study showed that psilocybin-induced psychosis was due to serotonin-2A receptor activation and was not dependent on dopamine stimulation.

PHYSIOLOGICAL EFFECTS

Psilocybin is a neurotoxin that bears close resemblance to the human brain neurotransmitter serotonin. Psilocybin is a specific central nervous system (CNS) serotonin (5-HT) receptor activator. It causes disruption in the normal serotonin levels in the brain. This disruption causes dilated pupils, a feeling of numbness throughout the body, nausea, blurred vision, exaggerated reflexes, tremors, loss of appetite, sleeplessness, and hallucinations. It also causes an increase in body temperature, blood pressure, and heart rate. A large amount of psilocybin, or psilocybin ingested by people with sensitivities to the drug, or by small children, can cause seizures, coma, and death. Ingesting psilocybin also interferes with the transmission and processing of external stimuli. The most common reasons for people who have ingested psilocybin to go to the hospital are hallucinations, hyperexcitability, panic attacks, coma, and convulsions.

Psilocybin is not considered to be addictive. However, there is a high risk of tolerance that leads to increased doses. Tolerance occurs when a person repeatedly uses psilocybin in a short period of time. The user's body will change the way it processes the drug. To recapture the effect from an earlier use, the person experiencing tolerance would have to use increasing amounts of the drug. Using psilocybin more often and in larger quantities increases the chances of experiencing serious side effects requiring medical attention.

Psilocybin is activated in the body by first being converted to psilocin by the enzyme alkaline phosphatase. Psilocin is then metabolized and inactivated by monoamine oxidase to form 4-hydroxyindole-3-acetic acid. This is then excreted in the urine.

Harmful side effects

The most common harmful side effect from ingesting psilocybin mushrooms is a panic attack caused by a "bad trip." A "bad trip" is often described as terrifying hallucinations, unwanted thoughts, frightening visions, serious distress, and paranoia. Some reported "bad trips" include hallucinations of skin turned to liquid, worms crawling inside the users body, sinking into the ground, or being suffocated by someone. In a 2000 study that examined 161 acute psilocybin mushrooms exposures reported to the Swiss Toxicological Information Center (STIC), 31% of the users were admitted to the hospital for panic attacks. The loss of self-control, aggressive response to others, and general psychosis generally lasts fewer than 24 hours, though long-term side effects are possible. Panic attacks and "bad trips" are not preventable or predicable, and often happen to users who have experienced "good trips" in the past.

Other reasons listed for hospitalization of *Psilocybe* mushroom users are hallucinations, hyperexcitability, tachycardia (excessively rapid heart rate), incontinence of urine, coma, and convulsions. Severe complications arise when users mix psilocybin with other drugs such as alcohol, opioids, or LSD. The International Programme on Chemical Safety Poisons Information Monograph (INCHEM) on fungi reports that some people are allergic to psilocybin mushrooms with fatal results. Others accidentally ingest poisonous mushrooms, which results in serious adverse side effects or death. Users who have ingested mushrooms several days consecutively or who are sensitive to other naturally occurring substances in the mushrooms such as phenylethylamine can experience serious heart problems.

Overdoses of psilocybin may cause intense side effects that require medical attention. Overdoses can happen easily because there are over a dozen common species of *Psilocybe* mushrooms, and one mushroom of one species can have the equivalent potency of 20 mush-

rooms of another strain. Also, because LSD is usually cheaper than *Psilocybe* mushrooms, grocery store mushrooms are often injected with LSD and then sold as *Psilocybe* mushrooms. As LSD is 100 times more potent than psilocybin, this greatly increases the chances of an overdose.

When unsuspecting individuals accidentally ingest psilocybin mushrooms, it is common for them to conclude that they are going insane because of the hallucinations and psychosis that occurs.

The effect of psilocybin on pregnant women is not known yet. In studies of LSD, which has a similar structure to psilocybin, it has been shown that large doses can cause spontaneous abortion. Studies also indicated increased risk for birth defects, such as malformed limbs, heart defects, and eye lens defects associated with LSD use during pregnancy. Central and South American natives have used psilocybin for thousands of years, but generally this was done during rare religious rituals and usually women and children did not partake. Therefore, this history offers little insight to the effects of psilocybin during pregnancy.

Long-term health effects

Ingesting *Psilocybe* mushrooms has been known to precipitate long-term mental illness including paranoia, depression, and psychosis. It is uncertain as to whether the user would have eventually developed these conditions in the absence of psilocybin. However, there does appear to be an increased risk of developing chronic mental problems after the use of psilocybin if the user has a family history of mental illness.

Another long-term side effect is called flashbacks. Flashbacks are recurrences of the drug's effects when the drug is not being used. Sometimes several months after last use, persons who ingested *Psilocybe* mushrooms will unexpectedly experience hallucinations or mood swings. Often flashbacks occur when the past user is tired, anxious, uses another drug, or moves from a lighted environment into a dark one. Over 15% of people who use psilocybin experience this delayed effect. Users unaware of this side effect have sometimes sought medical attention fearing they were going insane.

Long term and sometimes lethal side effects also come in the form of self-inflicted injuries due to poor judgement while under the influence of psilocybin. As sensitivity to pain is decreased, the users may not know they are hurting themselves until later. In other instances, the users can overestimate their abilities and attempt something like trying to jump from extreme heights or walk on water. Occasionally, users under the influence of psilocybin become distressed to the point of committing suicide.

REACTIONS WITH OTHER DRUGS OR SUBSTANCES

Combining psilocybin with other drugs greatly increases the risk of having adverse side effects requiring medical treatment. Sometimes drugs are unintentionally combined. This happens to people who are taking monoamine oxidase inhibitors (MAOIs) which are commonly found in some antidepressants. Combining MAOIs and psilocybin can dramatically increase the effect of the psilocybin. On the other hand, users often purposely combine psilocybin with other drugs. Combining psilocybin with MDMA (methylenedioxymethamphetamine, commonly known as ecstasy) is known as a "hippy flip" or "MX-missile." This combination greatly intensifies the effects of psilocybin and likewise greatly increases the chances of serious side effects.

In a 2000 study which examined 161 acute psilocybin mushrooms exposures reported to the Swiss Toxicological Information Center (STIC), researchers noted that severe complications from psilocybin use were most likely to occur when it was combined with other drugs such as opioids, alcohol, or LSD. Some of the severe complications listed in the study were coma and convulsions.

TREATMENT AND REHABILITATION

While there is no antidote or antitoxin available to halt a panic attack brought on by ingesting psilocybin, the trauma can be minimized by placing the patient in a room with dim lights, giving reassuring encouragement to the patient, and using sedatives. According to the International Programme on Chemical Safety (INCHEM) poisons information monograph on fungi, in the case of psilocybin poisoning (whether intentional or not) the hospitalized patient may be given diazepam. Diazepam is also recommended if the patient develops psilocybin-induced seizures. The INCHEM report indicates that most psilocybin-induced side effects are short (less than 24 hours) and uncomplicated. The main threat to the patient and to the hospital staff is violent and uncontrolled behavior.

Psilocybin is not physically addictive. This drug is rarely the only drug of use by people seeking rehabilitation. So admissions into rehabilitation centers remains low for psilocybin. A 1999 study in Russia involving 180 young patients who used psilocybin mushrooms reported that they also used other "natural" drugs such as amanita and datura. In the treatment program, patients were educated about the toxic basis of these drugs. Likewise, a 1999 NIDA-funded study research indicated that rehabilitation programs for young people should include information on the function and toxicity of the drugs, self-control training, and methods for managing anger and impulsiveness.

A popular program for treatment and rehabilitation of psilocybin and other drug use is Narcotics Anonymous (NA). This is a 12-step program that includes admitting there is a problem, seeking help, making amends, and helping others. There are no dues or fees and meetings are held in virtually all major cities in the United States and in 113 countries. In keeping with the explosion of drug use in the United States since the early 1960s, NA's registered groups have gone from 200 in 1978 to over 19,000 in 2001.

PERSONAL AND SOCIAL CONSEQUENCES

One of the most significant personal consequences of psilocybin use is self-inflicted injury. During an euphoric or "good trip" users can overestimate their abilities and use poor judgement. There are reports of users trying to drive a car, standing in front of a moving vehicle, trying to walk on water, or jumping out of high places. Such feats have resulted in life-long injuries and in some cases, death.

On the other end of the spectrum, harm is done to others when users experience fear and panic attacks from "bad trips" or frightful visions. Users have been known to attack their family, friends, or medical staff while under the delusion that such ones were trying to harm them. Though the effects of psilocybin rarely persist after 24 hours, the results of poor judgement can last a lifetime. Also, people convicted of psilocybin possession can be disqualified from obtaining federal college grants and loans.

According to the 1999 Ontario Student Drug Use Survey, researchers note that substance abuse disorders account for the most prevalent mental health conditions in young people. As the abusing population increases, so will future clinical needs of this population. Psilocybin use can precipitate long-term mental illness.

LEGAL CONSEQUENCES

Under the Controlled Substance Act, psilocybin is a Schedule I drug. This means that psilocybin has a high potential for abuse, has no accepted medical use in the United States, and lacks acceptance as being safe for use under medical supervision. Schedule I drugs are subject to the tightest controls. While *Psilocybe* mushrooms are not specifically listed in the federal law, the two primary psychoactive chemicals, psilocybin and psilocin, are listed. Because the substances are illegal to possess, so are the fresh and dried mushrooms. Cultures at the mycelium stage when psilocybin becomes present and cultures at the mushroom stage are also illegal. Because spores do not contain psilocybin, they are legal according to federal law. However, at least one state, California, has passed a law making spores illegal to possess.

Legal history

For thousands of years Native Americans in Central and South America have used *Psilocybe* mushrooms in rare and sacred religious rites and ceremonies. Today, natives in these countries and in the United States use psilocybin legally in practicing their religion. Non-native Americans were not aware of the hallucinogenic effect of *Psilocybe* mushrooms until 1957, even though they grow naturally in many parts of the country. But in 1957, a researcher published his personal experience of eating *Psilocybe* mushrooms during a religious rite in Mexico. His favorable account was printed in the popular *Life* magazine. This account brought a great deal of interest to the *Psilocybe* mushrooms.

Though there was virtually no scientific research done on the drug's side effects prior to the magazine's story, over the next decade thousands of Americans and Europeans were willing to experiment with mushrooms. Scientists, psychologists, and researchers also started experimenting with synthetic psilocybin and *Psilocybe* mushrooms. As use of psilocybin increased, scientists began to see that the drug had few probable medical uses and had a high potential for abuse.

Psilocybin was legal in the United States for about a decade, but in 1968 it was made illegal. In 1970, in response to the epidemic proportions of drug use, the Comprehensive Drug Abuse Prevention and Control Act was passed. The Controlled Substances Act (CSA) listed psilocybin as a Schedule I hallucinogen, which is the most restricted drug category.

In 2002, psilocybin is once again gaining popularity. It is found at raves, on college campuses, and in clubs. *Psilocybe* mushroom seizures at raves are becoming more common. In the past, policing efforts were more difficult because if mushrooms were ground to a powder it was difficult to identify them as *Psilocybe* mushrooms. A new DNA test for mushrooms has helped solve this problem. Also, *Psilocybe* mushrooms are fairly easy to cultivate. In 1999, Orange County, California law enforcement officers seized *Psilocybe* mushrooms valued at one million dollars from a college student's apartment. As the spores are not illegal except in a few states such as California, they are fairly easy to access. But once the spores become mycelium or mushrooms, they are illegal to possess. This little window of "legal" status makes law enforcement more difficult.

The United Nations standard on psilocybin allows for possession of fresh mushrooms, but not dried mushrooms. Most countries that are members of the United Nations follow this standard. However, Japan allows dried mushrooms to be sold legally.

Federal guidelines, regulations, and penalties

The Anti-Drug Abuse Act of 1986 and 1988 set forth federal mandatory minimum sentencing guidelines. According to the Federal Trafficking Penalties, first offense penalties for anyone who manufactures, dispenses, distributes, or possesses psilocybin is imprisonment for up to 20 years. If a death or serious injury is involved there is a mandatory minimum sentence of not less than 20 years, but not to exceed a life sentence. Individuals can also be fined up to one million dollars. In the case of a second offense, offenders can receive up to a 30-year prison sentence. If a death or serious injury is involved, there is a mandatory minimum life sentence. Individuals can also be fined up to two million dollars.

RESOURCES

Books

Friedman, David P., and Sue Rusche. *False Messengers, How Addictive Drugs Change the Brain.* Harwood Academic Publisher, 1999.

Mendelson, Jack, and Nancy Mello. *The Encyclopedia of Psychoactive Drugs: Mushrooms—Psychedelic Fungi.* Chelsea House Publishers, 1986.

Phillips, Jane Ellen. *LSD, PCP, & Other Hallucinogens.* Chelsea House Publishers, 2000.

Other

Emedicine Journal. June 5, 2001, Volume 2, Number 6. *Toxicity, Mushrooms.* <http://www.emedicine.com/emerg/topic874.htm>.

International Programme on Chemical Safety Poisons Information Monograph. G027 Fungi. *Psilocybe and Others.* <http://www.inchem.org/documents/pims/fungi/pimg027.htm>.

National Household Survey on Drug Abuse. Table 40A and Table 40B. *Percentages Reporting Lifetime Use.* <http://www.health.org/govstudy/bkd332/NHSDA98SummTbl-45.htm>.

Natural History. *Anatomy of a Ritual.* <http://web3.infotrac.gale-group.com/itw/infomark/92/3222221/48912538w3/purl=rcl_STO_0.htm>.

U.S. Food & Drug Administration Center for Food Safety & Applied Nutrition Foodborne Pathogenic Microorganisms and Natural Toxins Handbook. Chapter 40. *Psilocybin Poisoning.* <http://vm.cfsan.fda.gov/~mow/chap40.html>.

Organizations

Narcotics Anonymous (NA), P.O. Box 9999, Van Nuys, CA, USA, 91409, (818) 773-9999, (818) 700-0700, <http://www.na.org.>.

Patty Jo Sawvel

ROHYPNOL

OFFICIAL NAMES: Flunitrazepam, Rohypnol
STREET NAMES: Circles, forget-me pill, la rocha, lunch money, Mexican Valium, mind erasers, R-2, rib, ro, roofies, roche, roaches, roachies, roapies, rophies, rophy, rope, ruffies, ruffles, shays, stupefi, wolfies
DRUG CLASSIFICATIONS: Schedule IV, hypnotic, sedative

OVERVIEW

Many people in the United States have heard of Rohypnol (flunitrazepam), otherwise known as "the date rape drug," as a result of news reports about its abuse. Rohypnol is neither actually on the market nor approved for medical use in the United States. However, it is legal and available by prescription in other parts of the world, including Mexico, South America, Asia, and Europe, where it is one of the most widely used benzodiazepine drugs. Like other benzodiazepines, it is a "downer," meaning it acts as a sedative and has a depressant effect on the body's central nervous system (CNS). Other common benzodiazepine drugs include Valium, Xanax, and Halcyon.

Benzodiazepines were first developed and marketed in the 1960s and touted as safer alternatives to barbiturates. They also were thought to be less addictive than barbiturates. Of all controlled substances for which prescriptions are written, benzodiazepines account for about 30%. One of the main uses of prescription Rohypnol is to reduce anxiety and insomnia and induce sleep. As a sedative, Rohypnol is reportedly about 10 times more powerful than Valium.

History

Rohypnol was first developed in the 1970s by the pharmaceutical firm of Hoffmann-La Roche. It was first sold in Switzerland in 1975 as a sleeping aid for the treatment of insomnia. It is also given as a sedative prior to administering anesthesia for certain surgeries, including heart surgery performed on infants. Over time, the drug has come to be used by doctors in a total of 64 countries.

Not long after it was introduced in Europe in the 1970s, reports began surfacing that Rohypnol was being abused as a recreational or "party" drug, often in combination with alcohol and/or other drugs.

Although benzodiazepines were originally believed to have fewer harmful side effects than barbiturates, scientists and others who study these drugs now say benzodiazepines actually share many of the same undesirable side effects of barbiturates and are every bit as dangerous in certain circumstances.

Despite being legally unavailable in the United States, Rohypnol distribution and abuse began to rise sharply in the early to mid-1990s, particularly among young people in high school and college. It became a well-known drug of abuse at dance clubs, fraternity parties and large all-night dance parties called "raves." In fact, some DEA officials compared the popularity of Rohypnol among teenagers in the 1990s to the popularity of Quaaludes among young people in the 1970s and 1980s. Data from the Drug Abuse Warning Network (DAWN) indicates that at least 80% of hospital emergency department admissions involving Rohypnol and other so-called "club drugs" involve people ages 25 and under.

In 1997, Rohypnol was banned in the United States. It is illegal to import it from other countries, and individuals who are found to be in possession of it are subject to significant prison sentences. Prior to the ban, one study found that Rohypnol was second only to Valium as the most common drug declared at U.S. border crossings in Texas. According to the study, an average of 11,000 Valium pills and about 4,000 Rohypnol pills were being declared each day by people—many of them returning Americans—crossing into the United States from Mexico. At that time, it was legal for travelers to bring a three-month supply of Rohypnol into the country for personal use. Since then—even with the ban—the drug has become more widespread throughout the United States.

While the ban on importing Rohypnol prevented people from simply traveling across the border to Mexico—where it is available in pharmacies—and bringing the drug back, it resulted in increased smuggling of Rohypnol. The U.S. Drug Enforcement Administration (DEA) routinely stops shipments of the drug and has prevented large quantities of it from being smuggled over the border in cars and other vehicles. Law enforcement officials in Florida routinely seize packages of Rohypnol that are shipped via overnight mail from Mexico and Central America. Often, the pills may be disguised to look like vitamins or cold medicine.

In addition to rophies or roofies, Rohypnol is known by a multitude of other street names, including roach or roche, a direct reference to Hoffmann-La Roche, the pharmaceutical company that manufactures the drug. In some circles, being under the influence of Rohypnol is referred to as being "roached out." Another street name that is sometimes used is R-2, a reference to the pills themselves, which are imprinted with a "1" or "2" inside a circle to identify whether they are a 1-milligram or 2-milligram dose. Other names may include roachies, La Rocha, rope, rib, and ruffies.

Like other club drugs—including ecstasy (MDMA), ketamine, GHB (gamma-hydroxy butyrate), methamphetamine, and LSD (d-lysergic acid diethylamide)—Rohypnol is easily accessible and relatively inexpensive. Often, users who intentionally take the drugs to get high at rave parties or elsewhere may not even know what they have taken or been given, which can make it difficult for medical professionals to treat them if they overdose or have a reaction.

Wrongly, many young people apparently believe Rohypnol is harmless because it is legal in other countries and has a confirmed medical use. Many also apparently believe that it is not addictive. In fact, the drug can become physically addictive within about 10 days of continuous use. Once someone has started using it regularly, it is often difficult to stop without experiencing withdrawal symptoms, including headaches, muscle pain, restlessness, and confusion. Even worse, stopping

KEY TERMS

AMNESIA: Loss of memory. Rohypnol users may forget events that occurred for up to eight hours immediately after taking the drug.

BENZODIAZEPINES: A class of drugs developed in the 1960s as a safer alternative to barbiturates. Most frequently used as sleeping pills or anti-anxiety drugs.

CLUB DRUGS: Mostly synthetic, illicit substances found at raves and nightclubs. This group includes LSD, ecstasy, GHB, Rohypnol, ketamine, and methamphetamine.

DATE RAPE: A sexual assault crime in which victims know the attackers and are drugged or otherwise coerced into a sexual situation against their will or without their knowledge.

RAVE: An all-night dance party that includes loud, pulsing "house" music and flashing lights. Many participants take hallucinogenic and other mind-altering drugs.

the drug suddenly after taking it for a long period of time can have severe health consequences, including seizures, coma, and even death. As a result, experts say regular users must taper off the drug slowly, as they would from any drug on which they have become dependent.

Another misconception about Rohypnol that some young people have is that it cannot be detected on routine urinalysis. The National Clearinghouse for Alcohol and Drug Information says while many young people think they can take Rohypnol and drive home from a club or rave and avoid being arrested for driving under the influence (DUI), the truth is that drug tests for Rohypnol are available and are in use in some states. In Florida, for example, Rohypnol testing is used as part of DUI checks when a driver appears impaired but the breath test indicates relatively low levels of alcohol. Rohypnol stays within detectable levels in urine for up to 72 hours. Researchers are working on newer tests that may be able to detect Rohypnol as long as one week after ingestion.

At some rave parties where Rohypnol and other club drugs are commonly found, people selling the drug try to convince potential buyers that the drugs are no more harmful than vitamins or energy drinks. They also may suggest that the effects of the drugs can be "danced off" or "sweated off" during the night-long party. None of these statements are true.

One consequence of the recreational use of Rohypnol has been an increase in the number of date or acquaintance rapes reported to have involved the drug.

???? FACT OR FICTION

Many teenagers seem to believe that club drugs such as Rohypnol, GHB, and ecstasy are harmless. The National Institute on Drug Abuse (NIDA) is so alarmed by the lack of recognition of the serious dangers of these drugs that they have increased their funding for club drug research by 40%, raising the total amount of committed research dollars to $54 million. They have also created a website devoted to reliable, science-based information on club drugs: www.clubdrugs.org.

In addition, NIDA and four national organizations—the American Academy of Child and Adolescent Psychiatry, the Community Anti-Drug Coalitions of America, Join Together, and National Families in Action—launched a multi-media public education campaign targeted at teens, young adults, parents, educators, and others to spread the message that club drugs are not harmless "fun drugs." The campaign includes postcards and brochures containing information about how club drugs are used and their various slang names. The information is posted on college campuses, in bookstores, at coffee bars, and other places where young people hang out.

Another aspect of educating people about club drugs is getting them to recognize warning signs that someone close to them may be using Rohypnol or other club drugs.

Warning signs can include:

• problems remembering things they have said or done

• loss of coordination, dizziness, or fainting

• abnormal confusion

• sleep problems

• chills or sweating

• slurred speech

NIDA's research has found that in addition to the known side effects of many club drugs, other serious health problems can result from chronic recreational use of these drugs. These problems include hallucinations, paranoia, and depression.

This has earned Rohypnol its most common nickname: the date rape drug. On college campuses, women are warned not to leave their drinks unattended or accept a drink from someone they do not know. Because Rohypnol is colorless and odorless, it can be used to "spike" just about any beverage. When placed in an alcohlic beverage, Rohypnol increases the effects of the alcohol and the rate at which the person will start to feel "drunk."

While not every person who consumes Rohypnol will have the same reaction, most will seem drunk and may even appear to be having a good time. This situation, unfortunately, makes it difficult for others to realize what is happening and to intervene in situations where Rohypnol has been used on an unsuspecting person. Experts say one warning sign that Rohypnol may have been used is when someone appears extremely drunk after consuming only a small amount of alcohol.

Although date rape involving Rohypnol or other drugs can happen to just about anyone, efforts have been targeted at educating young women because statistics show they are at highest risk. According to the U.S. Department of Justice, more than half of all rape and sexual assault victims in 1998 were females younger than age 25. In addition, alcohol or drug use immediately before a sexual assault has been reported by more than 40% of adolescent victims and their attackers.

Hoffmann-La Roche, Inc., the manufacturer of Rohypnol, has taken steps to stop individuals from using it to drug victims. The most significant of these has been changing the pills so that a bright blue color is released when Rohypnol is dissolved in beverages. The newer tablets also dissolve more slowly—taking an average of 40 minutes to dissolve completely—making it more difficult to "spike" a drink quickly. It is important to remember, however, that illegally manufactured Rohypnol is colorless and does not produce any strong taste or odor when dissolved in a drink. These counterfeit pills also do not release the bright blue dye. Therefore, people should not assume that they will automatically be able to detect Rohypnol.

In addition to adding the blue coloring to their legally manufactured pills, Hoffmann-La Roche also created an ad campaign to increase public awareness about Rohypnol among high school and college students, who are among the most vulnerable to voluntary or involuntary Rohypnol use.

Another serious concern is that young drug users may not be able to distinguish Rohypnol from other potentially harmful drugs. The DEA has received reports of benzodiazepines other than Rohypnol being passed off by drug dealers as Rohypnol pills. One such substitute Rivotril, a benzodiazepine sold in Mexico for the treatment of epilepsy. In the United States, this drug is known as Klonopin (clonazepam).

CHEMICAL/ORGANIC COMPOSITION

Rohypnol is a benzodiazepine with properties similar to those of Valium and Xanax. Its main function is to depress the central nervous system. It is manufactured in 1 mg doses. The 2 mg dose that was once available has been discontinued by the manufacturer. However, law enforcement officials in the United States and other countries say counterfeit 2-mg pills are being discovered.

INGESTION METHODS

Rohypnol is available in pills that are slightly smaller than an aspirin and may or may not be sealed in the manufacturer's plastic bubble pack, making them look like any over-the-counter medication.

The pills are easily crushed and are sometimes both odorless and colorless—although, again, legally manufactured Rohypnol now turns blue when dissolved in beverages. Although the powder does have a slightly bitter taste, illegally manufactured Rohypnol is often easily disguised when dissolved in alcohol or flavored beverages. The drug's effects typically begin within 30 minutes and peak at two hours after ingestion. A single dose can produce effects on the user that last for eight hours or more.

While swallowing the pills or dissolving them in liquid are the most common ways to take Rohypnol, reports suggest some abusers crush the pills and snort the powder much as they would cocaine. The White House's Office of National Drug Control Policy (ONDCP) also indicates there is evidence that some abusers are injecting powdered Rohypnol with hypodermic needles, possibly as a cheap substitute for heroin.

THERAPEUTIC USE

Originally, Rohypnol was developed as a sleeping pill. It has been used successfully for that purpose in many countries outside the United States (It is the most frequently prescribed sleeping pill in Europe.) When used as prescribed, it is an effective short-term therapy for severe sleep disorders. Studies show that Rohypnol increases the total amount of time spent sleeping and lessens the difference between the amount of time spent in bed and the amount of time asleep. Both factors are significant to people who suffer from severe sleep problems that leave them sleep-deprived and anxious. Therapeutic doses of Rohypnol vary from 0.5 mg to 1 mg.

Because it lowers blood pressure, thus reducing bleeding, Rohypnol also is given prior to some surgeries. In addition, it is useful as a muscle relaxant and to control painful muscle spasms.

In typical use, a 2-mg dose of Rohypnol induces sleep within about 15 minutes and allows the user to sleep uninterrupted for at least six to eight hours. Taking higher doses is not recommended. A 4-mg dose, for example, can cause a coma in the same short period of time.

Japanese researchers have reported that adding Rohypnol to an existing drug therapy regimen helps correct severe sleep disturbances in children with epilepsy. Also, fewer seizures were reported when Rohypnol was used along with epilepsy therapy. The study appeared in the medical journal *Brain Development* in 1995.

USAGE TRENDS

Scope and severity

Government trend-watchers say Rohypnol is south Florida's fastest-growing drug problem. High school students who use the drug with alcohol or cocaine make up the greatest proportion of Florida's Rohypnol abusers.

In some areas of the country, such as Texas, Rohypnol abuse and illegal sales and distribution of the drug has become prevalent among gang members.

Some heroin addicts use Rohypnol to intensify the heroin high. Officials say this may be particularly true of users of low-quality heroin. Cocaine addicts may use Rohypnol to mellow cocaine's high and to ease themselves "down" from a crack or cocaine binge. Some drug abusers call Rohypnol "landing gear," when it is used in this manner.

Young people who attend rave parties often take amphetamines ("uppers") to keep themselves awake throughout the night. Similarly, some also will take Rohypnol to ease the effects of the amphetamine use. Others reportedly down Rohypnol as a cure for hangovers.

Compared with other club drugs such as methamphetamine, LSD, GHB, MDMA, and ketamine, the use of Rohypnol is relatively low. Still, U.S. officials say the Rohypnol trend does not show signs of decreasing. In addition, women who have been given Rohypnol in a date-rape setting often do not report the rape or the drug use, so it is impossible to estimate the true extent of Rohypnol use. Even if the rape is reported, they may not have knowledge of the drug that was used on them.

Age, ethnic, and gender trends

Intentional Rohypnol abuse appears to be most prevalent among teenagers and college students, some of whom use the drug recreationally to intensify the effects of alcohol. When Rohypnol is used in this way, it is often referred to as an "alcohol extender." The White House's ONDCP says another common way in which some club-goers use Rohypnol is in combination with methamphetamine. In some areas of the country, the combination is known as a "club mix."

Disturbingly, there are reports of schoolchildren as young as eight to 10 years old abusing Rohypnol, primarily because it is cheap and relatively easy to obtain. Children who use the drug most often dissolve it in soft drinks for a faster effect. Many of them are obtaining the drug from peers their own age. According to the ONDCP, some established drug dealers seek out school-aged children to sell Rohypnol pills. The dealer sells the pills to the child at a "wholesale" price of about $1 apiece. The child then sells the tablets to friends for $2 to $3 apiece. By targeting children in this way, drug dealers not only make money, but they broaden the potential market for other drugs such as marijuana and cocaine later on. They also increase the chance that the juvenile who is able to make fast money from selling Rohypnol will be willing to continue to sell that drug or other drugs for years to their classmates.

A national survey conducted in 1999 found that 0.5% of eighth graders and 1% of tenth and twelfth graders report ever using Rohypnol. The survey, known as "Monitoring the Future," is conducted by the University of Michigan Institute for Social Research.

Another trend that has emerged is the intentional use of Rohypnol by depressed young women. In a study published in 2000 in the *Journal of Pediatric and Adolescent Gynecology,* it was reported that some of these women are using Rohypnol to cope with negative feelings and low self-esteem. A survey of more than 800 sexually active women between the ages of 14 to 26 found that 2% had used Rohypnol in the past and 5% indicated they would use it in the future. Compared with those who indicated they had not or would not use Rohypnol, potential users were three times more likely to be depressed, two times more likely to have low self-esteem, and six times more likely to be unable to "just say no." Such women also were more likely to have had sex before age 15 and to have had multiple sex partners at a young age. The researchers theorized that the powerful euphoric and "drunken" feelings produced by Rohypnol counteract the depression the women are feeling. However, public health officials say the use of Rohypnol also significantly increases a young woman's risk of getting pregnant and/or catching a sexually transmitted disease due to the loss of inhibition and control that occurs after taking the drug.

MENTAL EFFECTS

Rohypnol can cause amnesia—the person under its influence can remember little that happened in the hours after they ingested Rohypnol. When taken in combination with alcohol or other drugs such as cocaine or hero-in, the amnesia will be more severe, and some users describe total "blackouts" from which they do not awaken until the next day.

When the drug leaves the body, the most severe symptoms of Rohypnol intoxication will subside, but many people continue to feel drowsy, confused, and dizzy for hours and even days afterward. Memories of the previous eight hours are usually hazy and may seem like a dream that is being remembered. Victims of date rate involving Rohypnol have reported disturbing memories of feeling paralyzed, powerless, and unable to resist. Some also reported a feeling of separation from their bodies. These hazy recollections can cause a great deal of mental stress and fear.

Chronic users will eventually develop physical and psychological dependence on Rohypnol. Often, chronic users may want to stop using the drug but are unable to stop on their own due to the strong physical need that has developed for the drug. The psychological dependence may lead them to believe they cannot cope with things in their life without using the drug, or that they cannot relax without taking it. This dependence, when it occurs at a young age, can set the stage for a lifetime of drug-seeking behaviors.

PHYSIOLOGICAL EFFECTS

Like other sedative/hypnotic drugs, Rohypnol produces a drowsy, relaxed feeling similar to being drunk. Muscles feel relaxed and speech may be slurred. Blood pressure can drop dangerously low. The effects of Rohypnol may last anywhere from two to eight hours, depending on the person taking it and the dosage they are taking. Some people report experiencing the physical effects for up to 12 hours or even longer. The drug may also cause insomnia when taken at high doses or when taken chronically by abusers who have become physically dependent.

Some effects that Rohypnol can produce include:

- fearlessness/loss of inhibitions

- impaired judgment

- impaired coordination

- confusion/disorientation

- nausea

- dizziness

- unsteady walk

The day after taking Rohypnol, many people report what feels like the worst hangover they have ever had. This feeling may last anywhere from 24 to 48 hours.

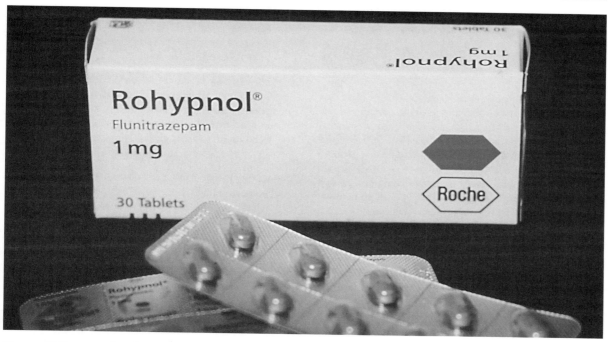

Box and blister packs of Rohypnol tranquilizer pills; each pill contains one milligram of flunitrazepam, which can render the consumer sleepy and suggestible. Photo Researchers, Inc. Reproduced by permission.

This sensation is one reason many people who have been victims of Rohypnol-assisted assaults do not immediately realize what has happened. Instead, they may simply assume they drank too much the previous night, even though they may not remember drinking particularly heavily.

Although the drug acts as a depressant in most people, it may cause aggression and excitability in others. In one Swedish study published in the *Journal of the American Academy of Psychiatry Law,* nearly all teenage juvenile offenders who frequently abused Rohypnol had committed serious violent crimes, including impulsive violence. They reported increased feelings of power and self-esteem, reduced fear and insecurity, and an increased sense that "everything was possible" when taking Rohypnol.

Harmful side effects

In addition to memory loss, confusion, dizziness, and sleepiness, Rohypnol also causes a decrease in blood pressure; stomach and intestinal upset; and urinary retention.

A person who has overdosed on Rohypnol needs immediate medical attention, usually in a hospital emergency department. If the person is conscious, they may be induced to vomit or they may be given gastric lavage, otherwise known as "having your stomach pumped." Doctors also may give the person activated charcoal, which can reduce the amount of Rohypnol that is still being absorbed by the person's body. Depending on symptoms, doctors also may need to monitor the person's breathing and heart rate. In some cases, doctors also will administer another drug, called flumazenil, which can successfully reverse the adverse effects of Rohypnol on the central nervous system.

Rohypnol overdose alone is unlikely to be lethal, but the risk of coma and death increase significantly when Rohypnol is combined with alcohol or other drugs.

The number of hospital emergency department visits involving Rohypnol increased from just 13 cases in 1994 to a high of 624 cases in 1998, according to the DAWN. A disproportionately high percentage of these Rohypnol-related visits—more than 50%—involved Hispanic individuals. Also, many of these visits involved other drugs, with cocaine being the most frequent drug used in combination with Rohypnol.

Long-term health effects

Even when taken at recommended dosages, Rohypnol can cause dependence and addiction among frequent users. Some people addicted to Rohypnol experience seizures when they attempt withdrawal from the drug. The U.S. Department of Justice says such seizures may occur among chronic users after as little as one week without Rohypnol.

IN THE NEWS

Rohypnol is one of at least 20 drugs that law enforcement officials say are used in committing sexual assaults. A study published in the *Journal of Analytical Toxicology* in 1999 found that of nearly 1,200 samples collected from victims of alleged sexual assault, more than one-third were positive for alcohol and a significant percentage were positive for benzodiazepines, which include Rohypnol. Because of the close association between alcohol and Rohypnol in relation to sexual assault crimes, it is important for anyone who frequents bars or parties where drinking occurs to take steps to protect themselves from being victimized.

Some things people can do to protect themselves include:

- Drink only from tamper-proof bottles or cans and insist on opening them yourself.

- Be particularly cautious about drinking out of wide-mouthed cups and wine glasses.

- If you do have a mixed drink or other beverage that is not in a can or tamper-proof bottle that you have

opened yourself, insist on personally watching while the drink is mixed or prepared. Do not accept a cup of punch, for example, that you did not see being poured into the cup.

- Do not ask another person to watch your drink while you dance, go to the rest room, or make a phone call. Even if the person watching your drink is trustworthy and known to you, he or she could become distracted, giving someone an opportunity to tamper with an unattended drink.

- Avoid group drinking or drinking games in which you can quickly become intoxicated and not realize what you are being given to drink.

Party-goers should remember that even though legal Rohypnol pills will emit a blue color when dissolved in liquid, the blue is not as noticeable when the pill is put in a dark ale, fruit punch, cola, or other colored beverage. It will, however, make the drink turn slightly cloudy. If it looks suspicious, the best advice is not to drink it.

In 2002, a company called DrinkSafe Technology announced they had invented a coaster that can be used to test whether a drink has been drugged. If Rohypnol, GHB, or ketamine has been added, the coaster will change color when a drop of the tampered drink is placed on it.

Long-term users may also experience headache, muscle pain, extreme anxiety, tension, confusion, irritability, and restlessness when they stop taking Rohypnol. Symptoms can also progress to more severe problems, such as numbness and tingling of the arms and legs, loss of identity, hallucinations, delirium, convulsions, shock and heart failure.

People who have been taking more than 6 mg of Rohypnol per day for a month or longer will experience the most severe symptoms when the drug is stopped. Fortunately, unlike barbiturates, large doses of benzodiazepines such as Rohypnol are rarely fatal, except when taken in combination with alcohol and/or other drugs.

REACTIONS WITH OTHER DRUGS OR SUBSTANCES

Combining Rohypnol with other substances makes the physical reactions and sensations longer and more intense. In the United States, the most frequent combined use of Rohypnol is with alcohol. This combination can produce dizziness and feelings of disorientation within as little as 10 minutes. It may also cause the

person to feel extremely cold or extremely hot, as well as feeling nauseous.

Some individuals experience a type of paralysis after taking a combination of Rohypnol and another substance. They will have difficulty speaking and moving on their own and will often then pass out. When they awaken, they will have little memory of anything that happened prior to consuming a Rohypnol-laced drink or other Rohypnol combination, such as Rohypnol and methamphetamine.

Although most people who consume Rohypnol in alcohol recover without serious physical consequences, there have been reports of deaths related to the drug. In those cases, death often resulted from breathing difficulties or the inhalation of vomit in a person who has passed out and is unconscious.

Some individuals take Rohypnol with heroin to enhance the high. This may be particularly true for users of low-quality heroin, according to The National Clearinghouse for Alcohol and Drug Information. Users of cocaine and crack cocaine may snort crushed Rohypnol or take Rohypnol pills after using cocaine to ease some of the negative side effects.

TREATMENT AND REHABILITATION

People who have become physically addicted to Rohypnol should not try to stop taking the drug on their own. Rather, they need qualified medical help to wean themselves from the drug.

Stopping the drug abruptly may include the following:

- severe anxiety
- confusion
- irritability
- headache
- muscle aches
- restlessness
- intense dreaming
- increased sensitivity to light and sound
- grand mal seizures (rare)

These symptoms will peak after about three to five days of not taking the drug.

Withdrawal from benzodiazapines such as Rohypnol is similar to withdrawal from alcohol, and is typically more unpleasant and longer lasting than withdrawal from narcotic drugs. Rohypnol withdrawal frequently requires hospitalization. A medical withdrawal treatment that is sometimes used for people with Rohypnol addiction is phenobarbital, a drug that is more commonly used to treat epilepsy. One approach is to substitute 30 mg of phenobarbital for each 1 mg of Rohypnol the person has been taking each day. The dose is then reduced each subsequent day until withdrawal symptoms are eliminated. An essential element of Rohypnol withdrawal is tapering the dose gradually to avoid causing too many unpleasant side effects.

Since many abusers of Rohypnol take the drug with alcohol, there may be two addictions present, and therefore, the addicted person should be referred for treatment for both the drug and alcohol dependence. In these patients, additional drugs must be given to alleviate alcohol withdrawal, which can include rising pulse and blood pressure, tremors, and profuse sweating.

Approximately 50% of all people entering treatment for cocaine abuse or addiction to painkillers also report abusing a benzodiazepine. As with Rohypnol users with a simultaneous alcohol addiction, those with an addiction to other drugs in addition to Rohypnol must undergo a more complex withdrawal treatment than those who are addicted to Rohypnol alone.

PERSONAL AND SOCIAL CONSEQUENCES

Rohypnol has increasingly been linked to incidents of date rape and rape by strangers who drug unsuspecting women by slipping the pill into their drink in a bar or other social setting. Rohypnol is appealing to rapists because it acts so rapidly and often causes a loss of will and an inability of victims to fight back.

Rape is devastating to women and affects all aspects of their lives, including their future relationships. It is estimated that approximately one in four women will be raped in their lifetimes. In addition, approximately 75% of all rapes that occur are date or acquaintance rapes in which women report knowing their attacker well or at least being familiar with them. Many times, the rapist is someone with whom the woman is romantically involved or has been involved with in the past, but the sex is not consensual. The best defense against drug-induced date rape is to become educated about which drugs are used to commit sexual assaults and how to recognize and avoid them.

Many young women who go to dance clubs or parties where they know the people around them may feel the environment is safe and conclude that if someone did try to drug them, someone nearby would surely notice and try to intervene in the situation before anything bad happened.

Yet, a person who has ingested Rohypnol often simply appears drunk or "out of it." Even well-intentioned friends may not realize what is going on and will be reluctant to do anything. Experts in rape prevention say one thing these young women can do is have a prearranged plan with their friends when going out to a club, fraternity party, or even a party at someone's home. This plan should include checking in with each other periodically during the evening. (If someone is suspected of being under the influence of Rohypnol or has taken it voluntarily, they should never be left alone. It takes at least eight hours for the most severe effects of the drug to wear off.)

LEGAL CONSEQUENCES

People found to be in possession of Rohypnol, regardless of the quantity involved, are subject to a maximum sentence of three years in prison. People found to be importing or exporting Rohypnol, regardless of the quantity involved, are subject to a maximum sentence of 20 years. However, if death or bodily injury results, the minimum sentence is 20 years and the maximum sentence is life in prison. If the defendant has a prior felony conviction, the minimum sentence is 30 years in prison.

Law enforcement officials have improved their ability to detect the drug due to more sophisticated tests. Rohypnol remains detectable in urine for up to 72 hours.

The drug's manufacturer, Hoffmann-La Roche maintains a free, 24-hour phone line providing information on Rohypnol and offers free comprehensive testing for the drug to hospital emergency departments, law enforcement officials, and rape crisis centers.

The DEA has documented approximately 4,500 federal, state, and local law enforcement investigations involving the distribution or possession of Rohypnol within the United States since 1985. The cases are spread across 38 states. However, at least two-thirds of those cases are in Florida and Texas, according to testimony given before Congress in 1999 by Terrance Woodworth, Deputy Director of the DEA's Office of Diversional Control. Since 1994, at least nine people have been convicted of sexual assault in five state court cases in which there was evidence that Rohypnol was used to incapacitate the victim. The DEA is aware of 17 other sexual assault cases that took place between 1994 to 1998 in which there is evidence to suggest Rohypnol was used.

Legal history

According to published reports, Rohypnol was first used to commit date rape in 1993. In 1996, President Clinton signed the Drug-Induced Rape Prevention and Punishment Act. This legislation provides for prison sentences of up to 20 years for anyone possessing a controlled substance with the intent to commit a violent crime, including rape, by secretly drugging someone else.

Advocates for rape victims in England and Australia have called for a ban on Rohypnol similar to the one in the United States, but officials there have yet to outlaw the drug. Officials in Germany took an aggressive step toward restricting the illegal use of Rohypnol by removing the 2-mg dose from the market and allowing only hospitals to use doses over 1 mg. Independently, Hoffmann-La Roche discontinued production of the 2-mg tablet worldwide. The company also reduced the number of legal distributors of the drug in Mexico from 200 to 16.

Federal guidelines, regulations, and penalties

The DEA temporarily classified Rohypnol as a Schedule IV drug in the mid-1980s because there was no evidence at that time of abuse or widespread distribution of the drug in the United States. However, because of an increase in use among young people across the country in the 1990s, and because of its mind-altering and potentially addictive properties, the DEA began considering re-classifying Rohypnol as a Schedule I drug. This would put it in the same restrictive class as heroin and LSD. Drugs in Schedule I have a high potential for abuse and are considered unsafe for use according to the standards set by medical professionals. Reclassification to Schedule I status also would be an indication that the medical community can find no evidence that Rohypnol

has a valid medical purpose or benefit. The World Health Organization (WHO) also recognized the potential dangers of Rohypnol, and in 1995 they reclassified Rohypnol as a Schedule III drug, making it the first benzodiazepine to be so tightly controlled.

As of 2002, the DEA had not finalized the decision to reclassify Rohypnol, and it remained a Schedule IV drug. Independent of the DEA's actions, however, several states—including Florida, Idaho, Minnesota, New Mexico, North Dakota, Oklahoma, and Pennsylvania—have placed Rohypnol under Schedule I control.

See also Benzodiazepine; Cocaine; Ecstasy (MDMA); Heroin; Ketamine; LSD; Marijuana; Methaqualone; Methamphetamine

RESOURCES

Books

Lindquist, Scott. *Alcohol and Drugs: The Essential Guide for Girls and Women.* Naperville, IL: Sourcebook, Inc., 2000.

Lindquist, Scott. *The Date Rape Prevention Book: The Essential Guide for Girls and Women.* Naperville, IL: Sourcebook, Inc., 2000.

Perkins, Scott W. *Drug Identification: Designer and Club Drugs Quick Reference Guide.* Cincinnati, OH: Thompson Learning, 2000.

Periodicals

Anglin, D. "Flunitrazepam and Its Involvement in Date or Acquaintance Rape." *Academic Emergency Medicine* 4 (April 1997): 323-26.

Schwartz, R., R. Milteer, and M. LeBeau. "Drug Facilitated Sexual Assault ('Date Rape')." *Southern Medical Journal* 93, no. 6 (June 2000): 558-61.

Walling, A. "Helping Patients Recognize and Avoid 'Date Rape' Drugs." *American Family Physician* 62, no. 2 (December 2000).

Other

Everitt, M., and L. White. "Adolescent Update: Drugs and Date Rape." American College of Emergency Physicians, 2002. <http://www.acep.org/1,2830.0.html>.

Fact Sheet on Rohypnol. The National Clearinghouse for Alcohol and Drug Information, June 1998. <http://www.health.org/nongovpubs/ondcp-rohypnol/>.

Organizations

Control Policy (ONDCP); Drug Policy Information Clearinghouse, P.O. Box 6000, Rockville, MD, USA, 20849-6000, (301) 519-5212, (800) 666-3332, ONDCP@ncjrs.org, <http://www.whitehousedrugpolicy.gov>.

National Institute on Drug Abuse (NIDA), National Institutes of Health, 6001 Executive Boulevard, Room 5213, Bethesda, MD, USA, 20892-9561, (301) 443-1124, (888) 644-6432, information@lists.nida.nih.gov, <http://www.nida.nih.gov>.

Laura A. McKeown

SALVIA DIVINORUM

OVERVIEW

Salvia divinorum is an herb of the mint family indigenous to the highlands of the Sierra Mazateca of Oaxaca, Mexico. The plant grows about 24–36 in (61–91 cm) in height, with leaves about 6 in (15 cm) long. For centuries, the leaves of the plant have been used by the natives of that region as a hallucinogen in rituals of divination and healing. It is one of several hallucinogenic plants which have been used for these purposes. Other plants are peyote *(peyotl)*, psilocybin mushrooms *(teonanactl)*, and morning glory *(ololiuqui)*.

Reports of the use of psychotropic plants in Mexico date back to the Spanish invasion in the sixteenth century. Following the Spanish conquest, ritual practices involving these plants were banned throughout most of Mexico by the Catholic clergy, who were following the dictates of the Inquisition. However, knowledge of the plants and the traditions connected with them persisted among isolated groups in central Mexico. In the 1930s, expeditions to Oaxaca by Richard Schultes and others studied the hallucinogenic plants and the associated rituals, which had continued among the Mazatec Indians of northeastern region of the state. One such plant was *Salvia divinorum*. Around 1960, R. Gordon Wasson and Albert Hoffman brought samples of the plant to the United States, where it was identified as a new species of *Salvia* (sage).

When used by Mazatec shamans for divination or healing, the foliage of *Salvia divinorum* is collected as needed. Only the leaves are used. They are squeezed, crushed, or ground, and brewed as a tea of extremely bitter taste. A dose of four or five pairs of fresh or dried

OFFICIAL NAMES: *Salvia divinorum* (Epling and Jativa-M.), salvinorin A, divinorin A
STREET NAMES: Hierba Maria (the Virgin Mary's herb), ska Maria Pastora (the leaves of Mary, the shepherdess), semilla de la Virgen (the Virgin's seed), salvia, diviner's sage
DRUG CLASSIFICATIONS: Not scheduled, hallucinogen

leaves is used to restore regularity to elimination, relieve headaches, and function as a tonic for generalized weakness, aches, and pains. The herb is deemed a cure for swollen belly, an illness known as *panzon de barrego,* which is believed to be due to a sorcerer's curse. In doses of 20–60 leaves, the plant causes the user to experience hallucinations.

Shamans make use of *Salvia divinorum* to induce hallucinatory experiences for several purposes. When someone suffers from an unknown illness, the plant may be used as an aid in diagnosis. A shamanic healer, known in Spanish as a *curandero*, ascends a mountain where the plants grow to obtain some leaves. Before harvesting the plant, he kneels in prayer. Then, returning to the patient, the *curandero* prepares a dose of 50 leaves. If the patient suffers from alcoholism, the dose is doubled. They go to a quiet place, along with one other person, who serves as a helper. The patient drinks an elixir of water in which the leaves have been squeezed. In 15 minutes, intoxication sets in and the patient enters a trance. During the trance, he speaks out, and it is believed that his words describe the true nature of his illness. Afterward the patient throws off his clothes, as if to free himself, and then goes to sleep. The next morning, the *curandero*

KEY TERMS

HALLUCINATION: The experience of seeing, feeling, hearing, smelling, or tasting something that is not really there.

PSYCHOSIS: A severe mental disorder characterized by the loss of the ability to distinguish what is objectively real from what is imaginary, frequently including hallucinations.

PSYCHOTROPIC: A substance that affects a person's ability to distinguish reality from the imaginary.

RECEPTOR: A specialized part of a nerve cell that recognizes neurotransmitters and communicates with other nerve cells.

SEROTONIN: An important neurotransmitter in the brain that regulates mood, appetite, sensory perception, and other central nervous system functions.

SHAMAN: A religious leader of a tribe who performs rituals of magic, divination, and healing, and acts as an intermediary between ordinary reality and the spirit world; a medicine man.

bathes the patient. It is believed that as a result of this treatment, the patient is cured.

Another use of the hallucinatory experience is to help the victim of a crime find the perpetrator. For example, if a robbery has occurred, the *curandero* listens while another person ingests the plant. It is believed that the intoxicated person will divine the nature of the deed that was done. Shamans also use *Salvia divinorum* to find lost animals and objects. After taking a dose under the supervision of a *curandero*, the person who has lost something goes to sleep in the presence of one other person, who stays awake. The sleeper speaks in his sleep, while the other listens. It is believed that the sleeper will tell the other one the location of the lost item. The next day they go to find it.

Practices such as these also occur among other indigenous peoples of this region, and other hallucinogenic plants are also used in these ways.

The Mazatec *curanderos* believe that the hallucinogenic trance induced by *Salvia divinorum* allows them to travel to heaven and learn from God or the Saints. For this purpose, the herb is used to train new *curanderos*. Because *Salvia* is considered a weaker hallucinogen than morning glory seeds or mushrooms, it is usually the first of these three hallucinogens to be employed in the training program.

Originally, *Salvia divinorum* grew naturally only in the remote mountainous regions the Sierra Mazateca. However, the Mazatec shamans transferred the plant to lower elevations near their villages, where it has continued to grow in cultivated plots and in the wild. After *Salvia divinorum* was brought to the United States, it was first grown in university greenhouses for research. In recent years it has been cultivated in California and Hawaii by persons interested in its effects. There have also been reports that the plant has been spotted growing in the wild in California.

The psychotropic effects of *Salvia divinorum* have generated interest among psychopharmacologists and other scientists. Chemical analysis of the plant has succeeded in identifying the active substance, which is now known as salvinorin A. Research on animals and human volunteers indicates that the psychoactive effects of salvinorin A are comparable to those of mescaline. As little as 200–500 mcg of salvinorin A will reliably produce hallucinations in people, when the crystallized substance is vaporized over a flame and inhaled. On the basis of effective dose, salvinorin A is the most potent natural hallucinogen known. The leaves have been determined to contain 1–4 mg of salvinorin A per gram of dry weight.

At the present time, *Salvia divinorum* is a legal plant in the United States, and no federal laws apply to its possession or use. It is grown for sale by cultivators in Mexico, Hawaii, and California. In recent years, Salvia has gained some popularity as a legal psychedelic drug. A wide range of people has used the plant for recreation, as an aid in meditation, or for herbal healing. As information about *Salvia* has spread on the Internet, the notoriety of the plant has increased. The psychedelic potential of salvinorin A has become the subject of numerous websites and chat rooms.

The leaves and other components of *Salvia divinorum* are available for sale on the Internet. Users may obtain fresh or dried leaves, an extract of the leaves in alcohol and water, or an extra-strength leaf product fortified with the extract. Pure crystallized salvinorin A, which is sold for use in scientific experiments, may also be obtained. Prices currently range from around $100 per 1 oz (28 g) for the leaves to $20 per mg for purified crystals of salvinorin A.

Although most hallucinogenic drugs are believed to induce their effects by acting on the serotonin receptors of nerve cells in the brain, *Salvia divinorum* does not act in this way. At present, the mechanism of the hallucinogenic activity of the plant is completely unknown. Salvinorin A has been tested on more than 40 different receptors in the brain and other tissues, including serotonin receptors. So far, no activity has been detected on any of these receptors.

The Drug Enforcement Administration (DEA) is currently aware of *Salvia divinorum,* and the agency is monitoring the plant's increasing availability and use. The agency states, "There has been a growing interest among young adults and adolescents to re-discover ethnobotanical plants" that can induce hallucinations or "mystical" experiences. The agency explains, "*Salvia* is being smoked to induce hallucinations" that are similar to those caused by tetrahydrocannabinol (THC). The DEA states that it has no plan to classify *Salvia divinorum* as a controlled substance at the present time.

CHEMICAL/ORGANIC COMPOSITION

The active principle of *Salvia divinorum*, salvinorin A, is derived from the leaves of the plant. Chemically, salvinorin A is a neoclerodane diterpene, one of a group of nitrogen-containing terpene compounds that have psychotropic properties. Two other such compounds are tetrahydrocannabinol and absinthe. Purified salvinorin A can be obtained from an ether extract of the leaves, which is then concentrated by chromatography and repeated crystallization.

INGESTION METHODS

Salvinorin A is destroyed in the gastrointestinal tract, and therefore is almost completely inactive if swallowed. For that reason, *Salvia divinorum* is usually consumed in some manner other than by eating it, in order to allow absorption of the intact compound.

Among the Mazatec Indians, it is the practice to chew four or five fresh leaves thoroughly, while retaining them in the mouth, in the manner of chewing a cud of tobacco or coca leaves. After many minutes of mastication, the leaves are swallowed. Chewing the leaves as a cud permits absorption of salvinorin A through the mucous membranes of the mouth. This method is reported to induce long-lasting visions. However, Daniel Siebert, who has studied *Salvia divinorum* and has become one of the plant's popularizers in the United States, has remarked that chewing the leaves can be an arduous task, since it takes time to achieve the effect and the taste is extremely bitter.

Alternatively, the fresh leaves can be squeezed and the juices drunk. The amount of salvinorin A ingested by this method depends on the length of time the user holds the juices in his mouth. Most often when the juices are drunk, the effect is mild, since the substance remains in contact with oral tissues for only a short time. If the juice is kept in the mouth as long as possible, the effect will be stronger.

A third method utilizes fresh leaves, which are crushed and soaked in water to make an extract. A tea prepared from four or five fresh leaves is reported to act as a tonic. A tea made from 20–60 leaves will induce hallucinations.

The leaves may also be dried and smoked like a marijuana joint. Five or six deep puffs are reported to produce an effect similar to marijuana and last one or two hours.

The most efficacious means of ingesting salvinorin A is to vaporize the crystalline form and inhale. A dose of 200–500 mcg produces intense hallucinations.

In an experimental investigation in 20 human volunteers, Siebert studied the effects of salvinorin A administered through different routes of ingestion. The subjects reported no perceptible effects when 10 mg was encapsulated and swallowed. In contrast, when 2 mg was prepared as an alcohol extract, which was sprayed on the subjects' oral tissues, the subjects noted some effects, but the activity of the extract was inconsistent. However, when 200–500 mcg of crystallized salvinorin A were vaporized by heat and inhaled through a tube, hallucinatory effects were consistently experienced, with an intensity similar to those induced by fresh leaves.

THERAPEUTIC USE

There are no recognized therapeutic uses of *Salvia divinorum*. However, tribal shamans in Oaxaca, Mexico have used the plant to restore regularity of elimination, relieve headache, and function as a tonic for generalized weakness, aches, and pains.

Karl Hanes, Ph.D., a cognitive-behavioral therapist in Australia, has described one case of a 26-year-old woman who had been moderately depressed without remission since adolescence. After six months of cognitive-behavioral therapy, she was only slightly improved. Previous treatment with the antidepressant sertraline for three months had produced no benefit. Despite being cautioned against its use, the woman experienced relief of her symptoms after smoking leaves of *Salvia divinorum*. She continued to ingest the herb, chewing two to three leaves as a cud for 15–30 minutes three times a week. While consuming the herb in this way, she remained in remission for at least six months.

Siebert claims that *Salvia divinorum* has healing properties, and cites its use in one case of depression that was reported on the Internet. In the 1960s, however, there were many claims that the leading hallucinogen of that era, LSD, also provided in a self-healing experience. There were attempts to study LSD when used as an adjunct to psychotherapy. The claims for LSD, however, did not pass the test of time. There is no recognized therapeutic role for LSD today. Statements by Siebert and others appear to make a similar case for *Salvia divinorum*. It remains to be seen whether such assertions are proven true.

IN THE NEWS

The use of hallucinogens in the United States appears to be on the rise.

Hallucinogen use first became widespread in the 1960s, especially on college campuses. Promoted by Timothy Leary, a psychology instructor at Harvard, LSD and other drugs were hailed as the source of psychic awakening, happiness, fulfillment, creativity, and other good things. As the decade passed, it became clear that bliss could not be attained simply by dropping acid, and many people experienced negative effects resulting from habitual drug use. The use of hallucinogens decreased and reached its lowest level in the mid-1980s.

Since the beginning of the 1990s, however, hallucinogen use has steadily increased. The Drug Enforcement Agency (DEA) states on its website, "There has been a growing interest among young adults and adolescents to re-discover ethnobotanical plants" that can induce hallucinations or "mystical" experiences. The number of new hallucinogen users among those aged 12–25 doubled from about 12 per 1,000 in 1990 to about 24 per 1,000 in 1997. In the year 2000, there were about one million users of hallucinogens in the United States.

The interest in *Salvia divinorum* is being driven largely by the fact that it is a legal hallucinogenic substance. However, for several reasons, *Salvia* is not considered a substance with a high potential for abuse. The taste of the leaves is extremely bitter, and it is necessary to chew many leaves for many minutes to achieve the desired effect. Moreover, hallucinations induced by the herb are often found to be unpleasant, and many users do not seek to repeat the experience. These properties would probably discourage many potential users. While the DEA notes on its website, "Salvia is being smoked to induce hallucinations" that are similar to those caused by tetrahydrocannabinol (THC), the agency has no plans at the present time to declare the herb a controlled substance.

USAGE TRENDS

Scope and severity

Salvia divinorum is a newcomer to the drug scene in the United States. In the middle of the last century, specimens of the plant were brought to the United States from Mexico by botanists and pharmacologists, who studied the plant because of its hallucinogenic properties and the associated traditions of shamanic use. Knowledge of *Salvia divinorum* remained mostly confined within these academic and scientific circles until recent years. Toward the end of the twentieth century, however, information about *Salvia* became more widely known, and people interested in experiencing of the hallucinogenic herb's effects transplanted it from academic sites to homes and greenhouses throughout California and other parts of the country.

Salvia divinorum is currently being used as a legal hallucinogen. While the users are still relatively few, the number of persons consuming the plant may be growing. Several developments in the last year or two suggest that *Salvia* use has begun to spread more rapidly. Growers of the herb in Mexico, California, and Hawaii have been selling their produce for personal consumption on the Internet. A Texas company recently tried to market *Salvia divinorum* at a trade show for tobacco and head shop supplies in Las Vegas.

Details, a trendy publication for young men, ran a feature on the plant in December 1999, titling the article "The New Ecstasy: It's not illegal." In the summer of 2001, information about *Salvia divinorum* and its increasing use was reported by the *New York Times*, the *Los Angeles Times*, the Associated Press, and other news organizations. In April 2002, a story appeared on the ABC News website. *Salvia divinorum* has spread to other parts of the world as well. In 2000, live specimens of the plant were discovered by Swiss authorities growing in a large illegal hemp farm in that country. Subsequently, the Swiss found the plant growing in several horticultural greenhouses.

Despite its current vogue, the availability of *Salvia divinorum* in the United States has not aroused great alarm among law enforcement agencies. At the present time, federal officials have not received any reports of emergency room visits or health problems resulting from its use. Moreover, in 2001, the federal Center for Substance Abuse Treatment reported that there was no information that use of *Salvia* was increasing. Although they are collecting information on the use of the plant, the federal agencies are not intending to take any action in regard to it.

For several reasons, *Salvia divinorum* is not considered a substance with a high potential for abuse. The taste of the leaves is extremely bitter, and it is necessary to chew many leaves for many minutes to achieve the desired effect. These properties would probably discourage many potential users. One supplier of the herb in the United States explained that *Salvia divinorum* does not act like a party drug that causes users to become expansive and sociable. In contrast, the *Salvia* experience is directed inward, and users tend to withdraw into themselves. The effects of a *Salvia* experience are often profound or bizarre, but not much fun. He reports that only 10% of first-time purchasers place a second order for the plant. The peculiar, introspective nature of the hallucinogenic experience induced by *Salvia divinorum* suggests that it is unlikely that the plant or its active substance, salvinorin A, will become popular.

Age, ethnic, and gender trends

No statistical information about the use of *Salvia divinorum* exists. As of 2002, use of the plant is so uncommon that reliable estimates cannot be made. Nevertheless, *Salvia divinorum* is a hallucinogen, and the appeal of the plant seems motivated by the same kinds of interests as that of other hallucinogens. If it does become more popular and widely consumed, the pattern of its usage may be analogous to that of other hallucinogenic drugs.

The National Household Survey on Drug Abuse (NHSDA), which is conducted by the Substance Abuse and Mental Health Services Administration (SAMHSA), provides statistical data on illegal drug use in the United States. For the purpose of the survey, hallucinogenic drugs were defined to include lysergic acid diethylamide (LSD), phencyclidine (PCP), psilocybin, peyote, and ecstasy.

As estimated in the NHSDA, about one million Americans were current users of hallucinogenic drugs in the year 2000. This number comprised 0.4% of the U.S. population age 12 or older. Users of hallucinogens tended to be younger than users of most other illicit drugs. Hallucinogen use is most common among young adults. About half of all illicit drug users were under the age of 26, as opposed to 83% of all hallucinogen users. Moreover, about 15% of people aged 18–34 report having used hallucinogens at least once during their lifetime. This rate is twice the frequency of adolescents in the 12–17 age group or people older than 34.

Gender and ethnic data from the study show disproportionate distributions. Adult males are twice as likely as adult females to have used hallucinogens. Furthermore, whites use these drugs more frequently than Hispanics, who use them more frequently than blacks.

Use of hallucinogens may be increasing. The number of persons who used hallucinogens for the first time at least once hallucinogen in 1999 was 1.4 million, the largest number ever. Rates of first hallucinogen use have risen steadily since the 1990, and by 1999, these rates had more than doubled. Moreover, the rate of first use is rising most quickly among the youngest group surveyed, adolescents aged 12–17.

MENTAL EFFECTS

The hallucinatory experience induced by *Salvia divinorum* has been described by users as unique and more intense than that of other hallucinogens, which often simply distort perceptions rather than cause true hallucinations. Salvia, however, dramatically alters consciousness, producing all-encompassing hallucinations and a complete loss of contact with reality. Users often report that the experience is not entirely pleasant. One person said it was like calling in some kind of presence. The intense effects last from several minutes to an hour or more. Experienced users caution others that the herb should not be taken while alone.

Several graphic descriptions of the *Salvia* experience were provided by L. J. Valdes, an ethnopharmacologist who visited the Mazatecs in 1983. The scientist recorded his personal experience of two hallucinogenic trips induced by the plant, which he ingested under the guidance of a *curandero*. Before his first experience, Valdes drank a liquid prepared by crushing 20 leaves in water. About 45 minutes later, he felt himself rushing through black space past brightly colored objects. Approaching one of them, he saw a Mazatec village, as viewed from above. The houses of the village were flanked by pillars of Kaleidoscopic color.

On a second occasion, the scientist drank a liquid prepared from 50 leaves at about 9 p.m. one evening. Within an hour, he experienced visions of elaborate scenes. Shapes appeared and grew into the forms of plants and flowers. This was followed by a vision of a flaming cross that began to emit light. Humanoid figures appeared in clothes covered with gold. A church appeared around the figures, and they began to pray before a jeweled cross that changed into a sword. The images then began to change rapidly. Visions of animals, plants, and people flew by. Valdes' last visions were of a castle, which then changed into a Byzantine church, along with a procession of hooded monks who were marching around it.

Valdes emphasized that one should consume the plant in a dark, quiet environment. This is essential if visions are to occur, since light and noise interfere with the effects. The hallucinations that develop include visual, auditory, and tactile sensations. Sensations of floating, spinning, twisting, flying through space, and bodily lightness or heaviness may be experienced. An audiotape recording made during Valdes' second experience revealed that the scientist slurred his speech and spoke in unusual patterns. Although the hallucinations were most intense at about an hour after taking the drug, a few hours later, Valdes again hallucinated an elaborate vision of himself in broad meadow, where he talked to a man in a white robe, and also touched the figure and held onto him. He continued to experience visions intermittently for about four hours until he went to sleep.

The effects of *Salvia* are extremely variable and depend on the dose and the environment in which the plant is consumed. Visions of people, objects, and places occur frequently. There have been reports of out-of-body experiences, loss of the sense of one's body and one's identity, being in several locations at once, becoming one with objects, and visiting places from the past. A common experience is the feeling that one has become a two-

Daniel Siebert, an amateur botanist, poses with Salvia divinorum *plants outside his Malibu, California, home.* Photo by Nick Ut, AP/World Wide Photos. Reproduced by permission.

dimensional surface or membrane, which is being pulled or twisted. Users may also laugh uncontrollably.

Salvia users in the United States have reported that smoking the leaves or chewing them in a cud induces an experience that can be more intense than one from LSD, but much shorter in duration. While an "acid trip" can last for many hours, the *Salvia* experience usually goes on for about an hour, peaking around 20 minutes after consumption.

When salvinorin A is consumed, a dose of 200–500 mcg will induce an elaborate hallucinatory experience lasting one-half to two hours. Doses greater than 500 mcg may cause the subject to lose awareness of surroundings and become delirious. The effect can be frightening. Users may be disoriented, babble incoherently, and stagger about. Accidental injuries may occur. Since so little salvinorin A is needed for an overdose, it would be easy for an inexperienced user to ingest more than intended. For this reason, it would be foolhardy for most users to try to obtain and consume pure crystals of this substance.

Adverse reactions affecting the user's mental state have been associated with hallucinogenic drugs, and it is likely that *Salvia divinorum* could produce similar reactions. Since few scientific studies of the effects of *Salvia* on human beings have been reported, there is very little known about adverse effect related to this herb. Howev-

er, anecdotal reports by users of the plant have described episodes of uncoordinated, purposeless movement, which may have the potential for causing injuries; Siebert has described the delirious state that can result from a large dose of salvinorin A.

Acute adverse mental effects that have been associated with other hallucinogens include anxiety states, panic reactions, paranoid ideation, confusion, and delirium. Longer-lasting adverse mental effects have included a variety of persistent disorders of mood, anxiety, and perception. In some cases, prolonged hallucinatory states and other forms of loss of contact with reality have resulted. These long-term adverse mental effects have been classified in the *Diagnostic and Statistical Manual of the American Psychiatric Association (DSM-IV)* as hallucinogen-induced mood disorder, hallucinogen-induced anxiety disorder, hallucinogen persisting perception disorder, and hallucinogen-induced psychotic disorders.

A striking form of persistent mental effect of hallucinogen use is called the flashback. This disorder is properly called hallucinogen persisting perception disorder. In a flashback experience, the drug-induced state is re-experienced, along with the perceptual distortions and loss of contact with reality. These episodes occur during the weeks or months following the initial experience. They may occur spontaneously, in response to stressful situations, or during a later instance of drug use. Flashbacks have also been reported to occur as an adverse effect of antidepressant drug treatment. Although they have been widely reported, flashbacks are rare; few hallucinogen users actually have such experiences.

PHYSIOLOGICAL EFFECTS

The actions of *Salvia divinorum* on the physiology of the body have not been studied as of 2002 and are thus unknown. However, other hallucinogenic substances have substantial effects on the autonomic nervous system, the part of the nervous system that governs bodily functions. These effects may include dilation of the pupils, blurred vision, tremors, uncoordination, elevated heart rate, heart palpitations, elevated body temperature, and sweating.

Pharmacological studies of the effects of salvinorin A on mice have shown that the substance acts similarly to mescaline. The animals cease to scamper about as usual. While they appear sedated, the effect is not true sedation, since they are easily stimulated to move by a noise or light touch. The mice also maintain their righting reflex.

In the laboratory, receptor studies have shown no significant activity at more than 40 receptor sites on nerve cells and other tissues, including the monoamine receptors usually involved in producing the effects of hallucinogenic substances. Thus the mechanism of hallucinogenic activity of *Salvia divinorum* remains unknown.

Harmful side effects

Neither animal nor human toxicity studies of *Salvia divinorum* have been done. Very little scientific data exist in regard to adverse effects of the substance on the functioning of the human body. However, hallucinogens have been associated with harmful mental effects.

Long-term health effects

As of 2002, no scientific data exist on the long-term effects of *Salvia divinorum* on human health. Other hallucinogenic substances have been associated with long-term adverse mental effects.

REACTIONS WITH OTHER DRUGS OR SUBSTANCES

There is no scientific data on the interactions of *Salvia divinorum* with medicines or other illicit substances. Reports of the use of *Salvia divinorum* indicate that this substance is usually consumed without other drugs.

TREATMENT AND REHABILITATION

Acute mental reactions to *Salvia divinorum* may require treatment. Panic reactions, confusion, delirium, and other acute adverse mental effects are usually managed by means of the reassuring presence of a counselor who has knowledge of the drug's effects. In addition to "talking the person down," a counselor can observe the user and prevent any injurious behavior until the effects of the drug have worn off. Among the Mazatec Indians, the *curandero* functions in this manner, by preparing the initiate and guiding him or her through the experience. Since the effects of *Salvia divinorum* are short-lived, lasting less than two hours, the presence of a reassuring counselor should almost always be sufficient.

In rare cases, it may happen that a user develops extremely intense anxiety or loses contact with reality and becomes acutely psychotic. Such conditions might require pharmacological intervention. For severe anxiety or panic, a tranquilizer, such as lorazepam, may be administered. For a psychotic state, an antipsychotic drug, such as haloperidol or chlorpromazine, may be given. If a user becomes extremely agitated, both a tranquilizer and antipsychotic agent can be administered together. The combination of lorazepam and haloperidol is often used by emergency room personnel to calm agitated or belligerent patients. Administration of medicines should only be done by qualified practitioners.

HISTORY NOTES

The Mazatec Indians of Oaxaca, Mexico have used hallucinogenic plants for hundreds of years. Peyote *(peyotl)*, psilocybin mushrooms *(teonanactl)*, morning glory seeds *(ololiuqui)*, and *Salvia divinorum* (hierba Maria, ska Maria Pastora) have been used in religious ceremonies of divination and healing.

Beginning in the middle of the last century, specimens of the plant were brought to the United States from Mexico by botanists and ethnopharmacologists, who were studying the plant because of its hallucinogenic properties and the associated traditions of ritual use.

If someone suffers from an unknown illness, a *curandero* (ritual healer) will use *Salvia divinorum* for the purposes of diagnosis and treatment. The patient, the *curandero*, and an aide go to a quiet place. The patient drinks an elixir of water in which *Salvia* leaves have been squeezed. In 15 minutes, he enters a trance, during which he speaks out, describing the true nature of his illness. After the effects of the drug have worn off, the patient throws off his clothes, as if to free himself. The next morning, the *curandero* bathes the patient. It is believed that, as a result of this experience, the patient is cured.

The Mazatec *curanderos* also believe that the hallucinogenic trance induced by *Salvia divinorum* allows them to travel to heaven and learn from God or the Saints. For this purpose, the herb is used to instruct new *curanderos*. *Salvia* is considered a weaker hallucinogen than morning glory seeds or psilocybin mushrooms, and for that reason, it is usually the first of the three hallucinogenic plants given to the neophyte as part his training.

It is not known whether the use of *Salvia divinorum* is associated with long-lasting adverse mental effects in some users. However, such disorders have resulted from the use of other hallucinogenic substances, and it would be reasonable to expect that long-term mental disorders could also develop in certain individuals as a consequence of *Salvia* consumption.

Such disorders are described in the *Diagnostic and Statistical Manual of the American Psychiatric Association (DSM-IV)*. They include hallucinogen persisting perception disorder, hallucinogen-induced anxiety disorder, hallucinogen-induced mood disorder, and hallucinogen-induced psychotic disorders. These mental disorders may necessitate treatment by qualified mental health practitioners.

Hallucinogen persisting perception disorder is commonly called the flashback. While flashbacks are brief, usually lasting only a few seconds, these experiences often cause considerable anxiety and distress, due to the sudden, unanticipated onset of the episodes and the inability of the sufferer to control their occurrence. Psychotherapy is often sufficient treatment for anxiety and distress associated with flashbacks. Occasionally treatment with a long-acting tranquilizer, such as clonazepam, may be required. Anticonvulsant drugs, such as valproic acid and carbamazepine, have also been used to control flashbacks. However, antipsychotic drugs have been reported to exacerbate flashbacks and should not be prescribed.

With time flashbacks usually become shorter, less intense, and less frequently. Most subside eventually with or without treatment. About half of those experiencing flashbacks cease having such experiences within five years.

Hallucinogen-induced anxiety disorder and hallucinogen-induced mood disorder may also be adequately treated by psychotherapy. When necessary, pharmacotherapy may be employed as an adjunct to such treatment.

Hallucinogen-induced psychotic disorder is a continuing loss of contact with reality long after the hallucinogenic drug has been eliminated from the body. It is uncertain whether hallucinogen use can actually cause a persisting psychotic illness *de novo*, or whether it simply precipitates the onset of a psychosis in a person who would have developed such a condition in any case. Psychotic episodes in reaction to hallucinogens tend to occur in individuals who had previously been functioning poorly.

A continuing psychosis triggered by hallucinogen use should be treated in the same manner as any other ongoing psychotic disorder. Hospitalization may be required to stabilize the patient's condition, to initiate treatment, or to prevent injury to the patient or others. Long-term use of antipsychotic medications may be necessary, as well as continuing involvement in programs of mental health treatment and rehabilitation.

Long-term use of hallucinogenic drugs has been associated in some individuals with changes in personality and withdrawal from social relationships. Both psychotherapy and pharmacological treatment may be necessary to help some chronic users reintegrate into society and resume normal functioning. In addition to medical treatment, participation in self-help groups can be effective. Twelve-step programs such as Narcotics Anonymous and reality-oriented groups such as Smart Recovery may be particularly helpful in allowing a user to limit

or completely give up the use of illicit drugs and begin to participate in society.

PERSONAL AND SOCIAL CONSEQUENCES

As it only recently became widely known in the United States, *Salvia divinorum* has had limited use. There have been no reports of hospital or emergency room treatment of users for adverse reactions. Negative personal or social consequences of its use have so far gone undetected. Nevertheless, if use of *Salvia* becomes more widespread, these facts may change.

It is worthwhile to recall that the use of hallucinogens in the United States has had marked social and personal consequences in the past. In the 1960s, hallucinogen use became widespread, especially on college campuses. Promoted by Timothy Leary, a psychology instructor at Harvard, and others, LSD was hailed as the source of psychic awakening, happiness, fulfillment, creativity, and other good things. Other hallucinogens such as peyote and mescaline were also employed in the service of attaining allegedly greater insight and understanding. However, Leary lost his position at Harvard, and other frequent voyagers on "acid trips" found that their supposedly expanded awareness and understanding did not translate into greater success in the everyday world.

"Turn on, tune in, drop out" became the mantra of those who preferred the reality found through hallucinogen use to that of participation in ordinary social life. A subculture of users emerged. Terms such as hippie, flower child, acid head, and others came to describe those mostly young people who withdrew from mainstream society. Centers of the subculture arose in East and West Coast cities. Many of these youths joined protest movements, such as those in support of civil rights and against the Vietnam War.

Eventually, a number of negative repercussions of this social ferment became evident. Hospitals and emergency rooms began reporting adverse reactions to hallucinogen use. Accounts of users becoming permanently psychotic or suicidal were publicized and sometimes sensationalized in the press. In certain individuals, repeated use of hallucinogenic drugs resulted in changes in personality. Some developed a passive, noncompetitive attitude and withdrew from participation in various aspects of society. Such behavior was often associated with involvement in the subculture, in which values and behavior differed from the social norm and drug use was common. Many users began to abuse other drugs besides hallucinogens, including marijuana, hashish, methamphetamine, and heroin. Young people without means of support wandered on the streets of New York, Chicago, San Francisco, and other cities. Some went through periods of poverty and even starvation. Some became victims of crime. Others became criminals themselves. Parents feared that those of their children who had become involved in the subculture would remain permanently dysfunctional and fail to obtain education and gainful employment.

Although many young people who joined the hallucinogen subculture went on to hold jobs, marry, create families, and be responsible adults, there is little doubt that many young people were harmed and their lives permanently set back. In consequence, LSD was classified as a Schedule I substance, and its possession and distribution were made crimes. The National Institute of Drug Abuse (NIDA) was created to promote scientific research into drug abuse and addiction.

In the decades following the 1960s, the use of hallucinogens subsided. The American economy went through difficult times, and the concerns of youth turned away from protest and toward finding good jobs and achieving financial stability. In the 1990s, however, there were signs that interest in hallucinogens may have emerged again. The National Household Survey on Drug Abuse has indicated that usage of hallucinogens is again on the rise.

It is too soon to know whether *Salvia divinorum* will play a role in a new wave of hallucinogen abuse. That this will not be the case is suggested by reports by Siebert and others that the effects of the substance are often unpleasant and users do not seek to repeat the experience. Still it is useful to recall the upheavals that once took place, in order that knowledge of the past may help to prevent the repetition of it.

LEGAL CONSEQUENCES

Salvia divinorum is presently a legal substance. The DEA has not placed *Salvia* on its list of controlled substances. Various forms of the substance are available for purchase, and users may grow their own plants. If the use of *Salvia* becomes more widespread or if negative consequences of its use appear, this situation may change.

See also LSD; Mescaline; Psilocybin

RESOURCES

Books

Pechnick, R. N., and J. T. Unger. "Hallucinogens." In *Substance Abuse: A Comprehensive Textbook*. 3rd ed. Baltimore: Williams & Wilkins, 1997.

Periodicals

Jones, R. L. "New Cautions Over a Plant With a Buzz." *New York Times* 9 July 2001, late edition—final.

Siebert, D. J. "*Salvia divinorum* and Salvinorin A: New Pharmacologic Findings." *Journal of Ethnopharmacology* 43 (1994): 53–56.

Valdes, L. J., III. "*Salvia divinorum* and the Unique Diterpene Hallucinogen, Salvinorin (Divinorin) A." *Journal of Psychoactive Drugs* 26 (1994): 277–283.

Other

Diversion Control Program, Drug Enforcement Administration, U.S. Department of Justice. "Salvia Divinorum, ska Maria Pastora, Salvia (Salvinorin A, Divinorin A)." <http://www.deadiversion.usdoj.gov/drugs_concern/salvia_d/summary.htm>.

Siebert, D. J. "Salvinorin A: Notes of Caution." <http://www.sagewisdom.org/caution.html>.

Substance Abuse and Mental Health Services Administration. *2000 National Household Survey on Drug Abuse*. <http://www.health.org/govstudy/nhsda2000>.

Organizations

National Clearinghouse for Alcohol and Drug Information (NCADI), P.O. Box 2345, Rockville, MD, USA, 20847-2345, (800) 729-6686, webmaster@health.org, <http://www.health.org>.

National Drug Intelligence Center (NDIC), 319 Washington Street, 5th Floor, Johnstown, PA, USA, 15901-1622, (814) 532-4601, (814) 532-4690, cmbwebmgr@ndic.osis.gov, <http://www.usdoj.gov/ndic/>.

National Institute on Drug Abuse (NIDA), National Institutes of Health, 6001 Executive Boulevard, Room 5213, Bethesda, MD, USA, 20892-9561, (301) 443-1124, (888) 644-6432, information@lists.nida.nih.gov, <http://www.nida.nih.gov>.

Substance Abuse and Mental Health Services Administration (SAMHSA)/Center for Substance Abuse Treatment (CSAT), 5600 Fishers Lane, Rockville, MD, USA, 20857, (301) 443-8956, info@samhsa.gov, <http://www.samhsa.gov>.

Richard M. Kapit, M.D.

STEROIDS

OFFICIAL NAMES: Anabolic-androgenic steroids, ergogenic drugs
STREET NAMES: Rhoids, juice, gear, stuff, junk, and ragers, D-bol or D-ball (Dianabol); Depo-T (Depo-Testosterone); test or t (testosterone); Andro (androstenedione); Deca or Deca-D (Deca-Durabolin)
DRUG CLASSIFICATIONS: Schedule III, hallucinogen

OVERVIEW

Anabolic steroids is the familiar term for the synthetic versions of the male sex hormone testosterone. One of the body's many chemical messengers, testosterone promotes the growth of skeletal muscle and the development of male sexual characteristics in puberty, such as enlargement of the penis, growth of facial and pubic hair, a deepening voice, and greater muscular development in boys. The average adult male naturally produces less than 10 milligrams (mg) of testosterone each day. In contrast, the average steroid user takes more than 100 mg daily. The proper term for these compounds is anabolic-androgenic steroids (AAS) because they have bodybuilding (anabolic) effects as well as masculinizing (androgenic) effects. Commonly referred to as steroids, AAS should not be confused with a different group of steroids called corticosteroids. Corticosteroids such as prednisone and cortisone are used to treat illnesses such as rheumatoid arthritis, asthma, and inflammatory diseases.

AASs are used nonmedically to improve athletic performance, physical appearance, and fighting ability. AAS-using bodybuilders believe that AASs enhance their physical strength, boost their confidence and assertiveness, and improve feelings of sexuality. Teens who use AAS tend to use them to improve their physical appearance, and are more likely to use other drugs, tobacco, or alcohol. Three types of nonmedical AAS users have been identified. The first group are athletes who desire to win at any cost, often believing that their competitors are also using AASs. The second group are often bodybuilders or aspiring models whose aim is to create a beautiful body. They display their bodies to obtain financial rewards and respect. The third group use AASs to become more intimidating and to improve their fighting ability. These may include body or prison guards, police, or gang members whose survival depends on their readiness to fight.

History

The first synthetic versions of testosterone were created by European researchers soon after 1935, the year testosterone was first isolated in laboratories. Intended for medical reasons, AASs were devised to help people rebuild body tissue lost through disease. In fact, after World War II ended in 1945, AASs were given to many starving concentration camp survivors to help them add skeletal muscle and gain body weight. Overall, the medical use of AASs has been rare. For example, in the 1960s AASs were used to treat the reduced height (also called short stature) that occurs in a condition called Turner syndrome. Then human growth hormone became available and replaced the use of AASs for this condition. The primary medical use of AASs has been to treat hypogonadism, a condition in which the testes do not produce sufficient testosterone.

While bodybuilders and weightlifters may have started using AASs in the 1940s, Olympic athlete usage began in the 1950s. Until the 1970s, when drug testing technology advances could detect AASs in the urine, their usage went undetected. In 1975 AASs were added to the International Olympic Committee's list of banned substances. However, testing was spotty. For example, at some of the 1984 Olympic sporting events, unplanned detection tests were given to athletes. The results? About half the tested athletes had taken steroids. International awareness of steroid abuse increased in 1988 when Canadian sprinter Ben Johnson tested positive for AASs in the Seoul Olympic games and had to forfeit his gold medal to the second-place finisher, American Carl Lewis. Also that year, a survey showed that 6.6% of American male high school seniors had tried AASs. These two events jumpstarted efforts to include AASs in the Schedule III of Controlled Substances Act, which occurred in 1991. Today the use among teenagers does not appear to be decreasing. Also, because the testing of athletes for AAS use varies widely among countries and competitive events, many athletes continue to take AASs without detection.

Scientists have developed hundreds of different AASs, which require a prescription to be used legally in the United States. Those obtained illegally are smuggled in from other countries, diverted from U.S. pharmacies, or synthesized in illegitimate laboratories. Most illicit AASs are sold at gyms, during competitive events, or through illegal mail operations. It is estimated that illegal steroid sales top more than $500 million each year.

In addition, dietary supplements that have steroidal properties can be purchased legally; common ones are dehydroeiandrosteroine (DHEA) and androstenedione. As of 2002, the effects of these dietary supplements are being researched for possible inclusion as an banned substance.

CHEMICAL/ORGANIC COMPOSITION

Testosterone contains 19 carbon atoms in a four-ring structure, with each numbered from one to 19. Modifications in the carbon atoms creates the hundreds of synthetic AASs that exist today. For example, many common synthetic forms of testosterone have alterations on their seventeenth carbon. AASs created in pill form have an added alkyl group, which is a chain of carbon and hydrogen atoms. These 17-alkylated AAS compounds are more toxic to the liver and more likely to cause cholesterol abnormalities. Common 17-aldylated AASs include Dianabol, Android, and Winstrol. When the addition to the seventeenth carbon is an ester, which is an acidic chain of carbon and hydrogen, the synthetic form is an injectable form that is less toxic on the liver and cholesterol levels. Depo-Testosterone is an example of the injectable testosterone ester. AAS abusers also use veterinary products, such as Finajet and Equipoise, that have been devised for animal usage.

KEY TERMS

ANABOLIC EFFECTS: A drug-induced growth or thickening of the body's nonreproductive tract tissues, such as muscle, bones, larynx, and vocal cords, and a decrease in body fat.

ANDROGENIC EFFECTS: A drug's effects on the growth of the male reproductive tract and the development of male secondary sexual characteristics.

HDL: The type of cholesterol called high-density lipoprotein, which transfers excess cholesterol to the liver for removal.

LDL: The predominant type of blood cholesterol called low-density lipoprotein, which transports cholesterol throughout the body.

LEAN BODY MASS: The portion of the body, such as muscle and organs, that is devoid of fat and bone.

TESTOSTERONE: A hormone produced in higher amounts in males that is responsible for male characteristics such as muscle-building, maintaining sexual organs, and causing hair growth and a deepening voice during puberty.

Why were all these derivatives of testosterone initially developed? Researchers had several goals. They sought to make derivatives that were oral medications, that prolonged its biologic activity, and that are more anabolic (particularly, muscle-building) and less androgenic (masculine characteristics) than the parent testosterone. Unfortunately many of the illegal steroids are manufactured under unsupervised conditions, and may be contaminated, or contain unexpected or fake ingredients. A European study analyzed 40 AASs obtained on the illegal market and found over one-third did not contain ingredients indicated on the label. One report estimates that one-third to one-half of the illegal steroids that teens buy are fake.

INGESTION METHODS

Steroids are taken orally, by injection, through skin patches, or as gels or creams rubbed on the skin. Injections are taken in the large muscle groups such as buttocks, thigh, or shoulder; or under the skin. The doses taken are often 10 to 100 times higher than the doses prescribed for medical conditions.

Steroid abusers often "stack," "cycle," and "pyramid." Stacking is the term used when different AASs are

LAW AND ORDER

The vast majority of AASs are coming in from outside the United States, by mail through illegal Internet sites. Prosecution in the United States is hampered since these sites are located in foreign countries. Smuggling of anabolic steroids across borders is a second source, with the Mexican border the site of many seizures. Steps being taken to curb these illegal entries include a ban on AASs in any amounts that cross the border. To combat the illegal shipment of AASs, Customs in 2000 reportedly confiscated approximately 10,000 packages, a rate similar to 1999.

Another issue is the dietary supplements commonly referred to as prohormones, which are touted as muscle builders and available legally at health food stores. In 1998 during the homerun race between baseball stars Mark McGuire and Sammy Sosa these supplements were propelled into the media spotlight. Mark McGuire announced he was quitting his use of the most popular prohormone, androstenedione (or "andro") to help boost his performance. DHEA is another popular one. Now under scrutiny by the DEA, FDA, and Federal Trade Commission, these prohormones are intermediates in the synthesis of testosterone, and can be converted to testosterone and other hormones in the body.

Banned substances must meet several criteria for anabolic steroids set up in the 1991 Controlled Substances Act. These dietary supplements have met all the criteria but one: whether or not they build muscle. A variety of current studies are underway, particularly to determine if these supplements convert to sufficient testosterone to stimulate muscle growth. If research shows this to be true, the DEA is expected to add them to the list of banned substances, since substantial quantities would likely produce the same side effects as AASs.

combined, such as taking two or more different anabolic steroids; or mixing oral, injectable, and even veterinary products, because of the belief that different steroids produce a greater effect than each drug individually. Cycling is six to 12 weeks on the drug followed by the same time period off. Pyramid doses are often used, which is when the dosage of the drugs is increased during the first half of the cycle and then slowly decreased the second half. Abusers believe pyramiding gives the body time to adjust to the high doses. No scientific research exists that backs the perceived benefits of stacking, cycling, or pyramiding.

The most common illegal AASs include: boldenone (Equipoise), ethlestrenol (Maxibolin), fluxoymesterone (Halotestin), methandriol, methandrostenolone (Dianabol), methyltestosterone, nandrolone (Durabolin, DecaDurabolin), oxandrolone (Anavar), oxymetholone (Anadrol), stanozolol (Winstrol), testosterone, and trenbolone (Finajet).

THERAPEUTIC USE

Physicians most commonly prescribe AASs for hypogonadism or testosterone deficiency, a condition where boys and men produce deficient levels of testosterone. AAS has also been prescribed to treat body-wasting diseases such as advanced human immunodeficiency virus (HIV) infection, when the loss of lean body mass is common. Additionally, men with the advanced disease often have low testosterone levels. Studies have shown that HIV patients given AASs experience significant increases in muscle and lean body mass, as well as improved quality of life, appearance, and well-being. AASs also increase muscle in other muscle-wasting conditions, such as chronic obstructive pulmonary disease (COPD), severe burn injuries, alcoholic hepatitis, and most recently in patients with chronic renal failure. The loss of lean body mass is associated with a higher death rate in many of these conditions. Also, AASs have been medically used in bone marrow failure syndromes, in a rare skin condition called hereditary angioedema, and certain forms of anemia and impotence. In women, AASs have been used in advanced breast cancer, endometriosis, a condition of abnormal uterine tissue growth, and have been combined with female hormones to treat menopausal symptoms. While all these uses are uncommon, AASs do provide a valuable treatment option.

Use of AASs as a therapy for cardiovascular disease, particularly to increase skeletal muscle strength in patients who have congestive heart failure, a condition in which fluid congestion occurs as a result of heart failure, is also being studied. AASs have been proposed for treatment in the cachexia, or wasting that accompanies certain cancers, as well.

USAGE TRENDS

Scope and severity

AAS usage has increased substantially over the past decade. In the United States, the typical AAS user is male, but usage is growing among females. Although adults make up a majority of AAS users, the estimated use among teens ranges from 2.5% up to 6%, depending on the study and age group. According to the 2001 National Institute on Drug Abuses' Monitoring the Future study, which tracks drug use and attitudes in adolescents, an estimated 2.8% of eighth, 3.5% of tenth graders and 3.7% of twelfth graders have taken AASs at least once in their lives. This represents a significant 1.2% increase for seniors, and a plateau for tenth graders. Lifetime usage for eighth graders had decreased slightly compared to the prior year (3% in 2000). Not surprisingly, recent use also increased for seniors. Seniors' use of AASs during the prior year had increased from 1.7% in 2000 to 2.4% in 2001. Other surveys of middle school students and college students in the United States and among Canadian middle and high school students found overall prevalence rates of 2.7% to 2.8%. Higher figures are often found in youth participating in sports. Obtaining anabolic steroids is not difficult. Almost half (44%) of twelfth grade students reported that it is "fairly easy" or "very easy" to get steroids. In an 1992 investigation by *U.S. News and World Report*, over half of teen AAS users said they were influenced to use the drugs by reading muscle magazines. Four of 10 were influenced because they thought famous athletes were taking them.

It is known that adult bodybuilders and weightlifters are big users of AASs. Less data exists on the extent of steroid abuse among adults, however, the percentage of adults who have tried AASs appears to be lower than adolescents. In a 2000 Monitoring the Future study that surveyed Americans aged 19–40, 1.4% of young adults (ages 19–28) surveyed reported using steroids at least one time during their lives, and 0.4% reported past year usage. Still AAS use is fairly common in society. About 19% of 19–22 year-olds reported having a friend who was a current AAS user. In addition, experts think the usage figures for both teens and adults are probably considerably higher, because many people hide AAS use.

Age, ethnic, and gender trends

Use in adolescents. Teenage males are most likely to use anabolic steroids; about three times as many male teens use anabolic steroids compared to female teens. The average age of starting AASs is 14, which alarms the medical community because of the stunting of height that can occur. One leading AAS researcher, who bases his estimates on regional and national data, believes that 4–6% of high school boys have taken steroids, and 1–2% of high school girls. This means at least a half million American teenagers have used AASs. Among high school seniors surveyed in 2000, 2.5% of males reported steroid use in the past year compared to 0.9% of females. For tenth graders it was 3.7% of males compared to 0.8% of females. A 1998 Pennsylvania State University study found 175,000 high school girls nationwide had taken steroids at least once in their lifetime. According to the study, more than half have tried AASs before age 16, but some start as young as age 10. In the United States, these adolescents are more likely to use other illicit drugs (particularly

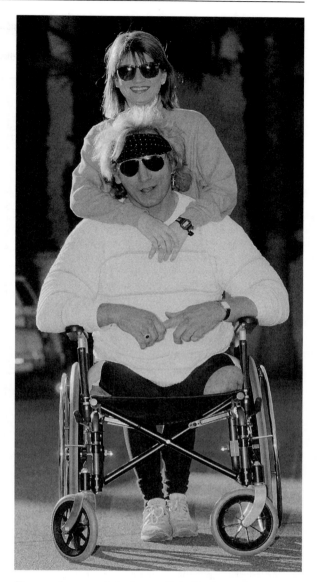

Former heavyweight boxer Bob Hazleton is now a double amputee due to many years of steroid use.

Photo by Michael Brennan/CORBIS. Reproduced by permission.

cocaine, amphetamines, and heroin), as well as alcohol and tobacco.

Student athletes are more likely than non-athletes to use AASs. Football players, wrestlers, weightlifters, and bodybuilders have significantly higher usage rates than students not engaged in these activities. In one 1999 study of 873 Indiana high school football players 6.3% were current or former AAS users, with the average age at first use being 14 years. Fifteen percent had begun taking AASs before age 10. Almost half the respondents said they could easily obtain steroids and

IN THE NEWS

Some experts believe illegal AAS usage is linked with a body image disorder called muscle dysmorphia. Affecting mostly males, people with muscle dysmorphia feel ashamed of looking too small when they're actually big. For this reason, it is often referred to as "reverse anorexia" because it is the opposite of the mostly female disease of anorexia nervosa, in which patients believe they are always too fat, sometimes despite extreme weight loss.

According to Dr. Arnold Andersen, M.D. of the University of Iowa, seven out of 10 males are dissatisfied with their bodies. Half of those want to bulk up, while the other half want to lose weight. Another indicator that men are increasingly concerned about their body image is the dramatic increase in cosmetic surgery. In 1992, men underwent 6,000 liposuction procedures to surgically remove excess fat; five years later that figure has jumped to 24,000. Other cosmetic procedures are also becoming popular. "There's penis enlarging or widening, hair transplants, cheek lifts, and pectoral and calf implants," says Roberto Olivardia, co-author of *The Adonis Complex: The Secret Crisis of Male Body Obsession*, a book that describes men's increasing preoccupation with body image, weightlifting compulsions, and steroid abuse. Olivardia estimates that one in five body builders and weightlifters may have some form of muscle dysmorphia.

A Canadian study that examined body image among 139 male bodybuilders found the bodybuilders reported significantly greater body dissatisfaction with a high drive for bulk and thinness. They also reported higher perfectionism, lower self-esteem, greater maturity fears, and more eating disorders than nonusing bodybuilders. As might be expected, the use of AASs higher among people with muscle dysmorphia. Olivardia surveyed 26 bodybuilders with the condition and found almost half used AASs.

---

listed athletes, physicians, and coaches as sources. Usage was higher in the South and Midwest than the West and Northeast.

Fewer studies outside the United States are available, but prevalence rates in countries such as Canada, Australia, Great Britain, and Sweden appear to be similar. Primary users in other countries are also male adolescents. One Swedish study showed a higher usage (3.7% prevalence) among 16 year-olds than 17 year-olds (2.8%). These male users tended to strength train but also exhibited self-esteem or school achievement problems and used tobacco, alcohol, and other drugs, such as

narcotics. Usage among female adolescents in Sweden was nil. Among 13,355 Australian high school students, 3.2% of males and 1.2% of females reported using AASs sometime in their lives. In other countries, such as South Africa, prevalence appears to be less.

Use in adults and ethnic use. Usage among professional athletes is also high, although exact figures are not known. Fifteen U.S. powerlifters who competed internationally participated in a survey that involved an anonymous questionnaire. Of these 15, 10 reported using AASs and five admitted they avoided detection during the International Olympic Committee's doping control procedures. In a 2000 study, 25 of 75 women athletes from Boston gyms reported current or previous use of AASs, and also reported using many other performance-enhancing drugs.

One interesting finding in women users is the history of rape. One 1999 study of 75 female weightlifters found nine women began or greatly increased weight lifting activities after being raped as a teenager or adult. Five began abusing anabolic steroids and two others began to use another illegal substance called clenbuterol to gain muscle mass after their rape.

Little data exists on ethnic breakdown of AAS usage in teens and adults. In one study, African American and Hispanic girls were less likely than Caucasians to diet and exercise, but were more likely to report behaviors aimed at weight gain.

MENTAL EFFECTS

AASs typically do not have any immediate psychological effect, but men and women often experience both negative and positive effects. Psychological effects reported by over half of users in one study included a mild state of mania and increased irritability. Probably the most significant behavioral effect is increased aggressive behavior, which was reported by 40% of those surveyed. Steroid users have reported aggressive acts, such as fighting, using force, and armed robbery, while others have committed property crimes, such as stealing, damaging property, or breaking into houses or buildings. "Roid rage" is a slang term for describing the aggressive feelings and behaviors from AAS use. What is uncertain is whether the steroids' direct effects on the brain triggered the aggression or whether the perceived link between steroids and aggression is an excuse to commit the acts. To test this, four studies have been conducted that compared high steroid doses or placebo to reported behavioral symptoms. Three of the four studies showed high steroid doses produced greater feelings of irritability and aggression than placebo. Some researchers believe many, but not all, anabolic steroids increase irritability and aggression.

Tolerance, needing more of a drug to get the same effect, was first demonstrated in AAS use among animals in the 1950s. In two 2000 studies, 12% to 18% of AAS users reported tolerance. Other behavioral effects reported are euphoria, increased energy, sexual arousal, mood swings, distractibility, forgetfulness, and confusion. A minority of volunteers that were given high steroid doses developed extreme behavioral symptoms that affected their jobs and personal lives. There are also the following reported behavior effects when steroid use is stopped: depression, mood swings, fatigue, restlessness, loss of appetite, and reduced sex drive. Overall, the prevalence of extreme cases of violence and behavioral disorders is small, but incidents may be underreported.

In a 2000 study of female athletes from gymnasiums, 40% reported symptoms of depression during withdrawal from AASs. Another finding was both AAS-using and nonusing women reported several unusual psychiatric syndromes, such as eating disorders, nontraditional gender roles, and chronic preoccupation with their physiques.

PHYSIOLOGICAL EFFECTS

Oral AASs are rapidly absorbed and result in an increased AAS concentration in the bloodstream within a few hours, although it is several days before the AAS completely passes through the system. Intravenous AAS solutions are absorbed more slowly. Athletes who use large doses of AASs and strength train do get larger and stronger muscles. One study involving 21 male weight trainers showed greater strength and body weight and increased muscle girth when compared to the group without AAS. Another study showed the trunk and legs of 16 bodybuilders on AASs experienced the most significant increase. While the composition of the muscle fibers does not differ, it appears that AAS users form new and larger muscle fibers. The increase in lean body mass and body weight continues for at least a short time after AAS use stops. However, AAS use is linked to a number of adverse side effects, which range from acne to life-threatening heart attacks and liver cancer. While most side effects, are reversible when the user stops taking the drug, some are permanent. Certain side effects occur due to some of the testosterone being chemically changed in the body to the female hormone estrogen. This leads to higher than normal estrogen levels—and potential side effects.

Harmful side effects

Hormonal effects. Steroid use alters the normal production of hormones, raising the blood levels to many times the amount naturally produced. This change in the body's hormonal balance can cause both reversible and irreversible effects in many parts of the body. Males can experience enlarged prostate glands, which makes urination difficult. A shrinking in testes (called testicular atro-

phy), lowered sperm production, and sterility has resulted from AAS use. In a 2001 study by J. Torres-Calleja published in *Life Sciences*, eight of 15 bodybuilders using AAS had below-normal sperm counts, and three had no sperm. The average sperm counts for the control group, 15 bodybuilders not on AAS, were within normal limits. Luckily, these changes are reversible, although one case of prostate cancer has been reported. Irreversible changes in males include breast enlargement, called gynecomastia, painful breast lumps, and baldness. In one study of male bodybuilders, more than half experienced testicular atrophy and gynecomastia. In fact, the number one visit to physicians for AAS users is gynecomastia. In severe cases, AAS users with enlarged breasts resort to surgical treatment that involves liposuction, a cosmetic surgery in which excess fatty tissue is removed. However, this is not without risks. A review of 20 patients surgically treated for AAS-induced gynecomastia showed six had complications or recurrence of the gynecomastia.

Children or adolescents taking AASs before or during puberty can seriously stunt their height. The artificially high sex hormone levels found in AASs can initiate the characteristics of male puberty. Normally, rising levels of testosterone trigger bone growth, but when hormones reach certain levels they signal a halt in bone growth. The high levels in AAS use can prematurely end the growth of the long bones, which results in shorter adult heights than would normally occur.

In women who take AASs, the surge in male hormones exerts a profound effect on a delicate hormonal balance. Due to the higher testosterone levels from AAS use, breast size and body fat decrease, skin becomes coarse, voice deepens, and the clitoris enlarges. Menstrual periods become irregular and sterility may result. Also, women may develop excessive hair growth on the chest and face but lose scalp hair. As steroid use continues, some of these effects may be permanent. For both sexes, increases and decreases in sex drive have both been reported.

Cardiovascular and liver effects. Steroid use has been linked to cardiovascular diseases (CVD), including heart attacks and strokes in athletes younger than 30. Although studies are required to determine how much of this is due to a genetic propensity for CVD, changes in cholesterol levels of AAS users have been noted. One study that analyzed the blood of AAS-using bodybuilders found high calcium and cholesterol levels in a significant number of them. Research has been published that shows AASs, particularly the oral or 17-alkylated compounds, decrease the level of high-density lipoprotein (HDL), which is referred to as the good cholesterol because it is thought to protect against heart disease. Some research has also shown increased levels of low-density lipoproteins (LDL) or bad cholesterol. Studies are mixed as to whether the lowered HDL level from AAS use leads to CVD.

Steroid use (percentage) among 8th, 10th, and 12th graders, 1997-2001															
	8th graders					10th graders					12th graders				
	1997	1998	1999	2000	2001	1997	1998	1999	2000	2001	1997	1998	1999	2000	2001
Lifetime	1.8	2.3	2.7	3.0	2.8	2.0	2.0	2.7	3.5	3.5	2.4	2.7	2.9	2.5	3.7
Annual	1.0	1.2	1.7	1.7	1.6	1.2	1.2	0.7	2.2	2.1	1.4	1.7	1.8	1.7	2.4
30-day	0.5	0.5	0.7	0.8	0.7	0.7	0.6	0.9	1.0	0.9	1.0	1.1	0.9	0.8	1.3

Lifetime = at least once during a respondent's lifetime.
Annual = at least once during the year preceding the response to the survey.
30-day = at least once during the month preceding the response to the survey.
SOURCE: 2001 Monitoring the Future Study (MTF). The MTF survey is conducted by the University of Michigan's Institute for Social Research and is funded by the National Institute on Drug Abuse, National Institutes of Health.
http://www.nida.nih.gov/Infofax/HSYouthtrends.html

Chart by Argosy.

Additionally, AAS users experience lower triglyceride levels than non-users. High triglyceride levels are also associated with heart disease. Low HDL levels and high LDL levels increase the risk of atherosclerosis, the condition where fatty substances are deposited on the inner walls of arteries. The disruption in blood flow can cause a stroke when blood is prevented from reaching the brain, or a heart attack when blood does not reach the heart muscle. Cholesterol levels return to normal when AAS use stops. The potential development of blood clots also increases with AAS use, which can disrupt blood flow. The changes in cholesterol levels appear to return to the person's baseline levels after AAS discontinuation.

Another possible adverse effect is an increase in blood pressure, which also returns to normal when AAS use stops. Some studies also show that those taking AASs can develop an enlarged heart. One 2001 study reported that 10 bodybuilders on AAS had larger left heart ventricles, the heart's primary pumping chamber, compared to 10 bodybuilders who were not taking AASs. It does appear that enlarged ventricles also routinely occur in AAS-free athletes who intensively resistance-train as part of the body's physiological response to weight lifting. Anabolic steroid use probably accelerates the process. As of early 2002, studies do not show evidence that this leads to heart problems.

As mentioned, the 17-alkylated AASs are more toxic to the liver than the other forms. With AAS use, the liver releases higher levels of some enzymes into the bloodstream. However, some researchers have found that all bodybuilders, both those taking and not taking AASs, experience higher enzyme levels due to the muscle damage that occurs in the sport. Bilirubin, the substance that causes the yellow skin and eyes, called jaundice, is also increased, and has been reported in users. A 2000 study by Yesalis showed that up to 17% of patients treated med-

ically with 17-alkylated AASs developed jaundice. Jaundice usually disappears after anabolic steroids are discontinued. AAS use has been linked with a rare condition called peliosis hepatis, in which little sacs of blood form in the liver. Lastly, liver tumors may occur in 1–3% of patients or users who have taken high doses of 17-alkylated AAS for more than two years. Other rare liver tumors have occurred with other types of AASs. Although more than half of the tumors disappeared with AAS stoppage, others were cancerous and/or resulted in death.

Other effects. The most common skin side effect with steroid use is acne, which is reversible, and occurred in 48% of AAS users in one study. Cysts, and oily hair and skin have also been reported. Other possible effects include small increases in the number of red blood cells, and a worsening of pre-existing conditions such as sleep apnea, a condition where people stop breathing during sleep; and muscle twitches called tics.

People who inject AASs are at higher risk for infections because of nonsterile injection techniques or sharing contaminated needles. In the United States, half of AAS users administer their compounds by needle and one-fourth of adolescent AAS users share needles, placing them at high risk. Products manufactured illegally may also have been prepared with nonsterile methods, which increase the potential of developing viral infections such as HIV, and hepatitis B or C. Bacterial infections can result at injection sites or in the body as infective endocarditis, a bacterial illness that causes a serious inflammation of the inner lining of the heart.

Long-term health effects

Overall, the incidence of life-threatening effects appears to be low, but this may be due to a failure to recognize and report negative effects. Most data on the long-term effects of AAS come from individual case studies rather than formal larger studies. Problems that may persist after usage stops in men are breast development (gyneocomastia) and male-pattern baldness. The situation for women is more serious. The side effects of excessive body hair, skin coarsening, male pattern baldness, and voice deepening are often irreversible. As mentioned, the stunting of normal growth in young AAS users may be permanent.

Increased mortality among AAS users is another possibility. In 2000 a study was published that analyzed 62 male high-ranking competitive powerlifters in Finland who were strongly suspected to have used AASs for several years. Following them for 12 years, nearly 13% had died compared to 3.1% in a control population of powerlifters. Suicide and heart attacks were the most common reasons. The Finnish authors identified three significant issues as causing early disease or death: negative effects on the cardiovascular system, effects on mental health, and a possible increase in the incidence of tumors. Probable causes were AAS use and other concurrent drug use. In fact, another study named the use of AASs with other drugs as a probable cause of increased death rates. Animal studies also demonstrate higher mortality. One study exposed laboratory mice to steroid doses comparable to human AAS doses for one-fifth of their life span. The result was a higher death rate among those given the highest dose than those given a low dose or no steroids. The average life span of the mice receiving the low dose was also shorter than the AAS-free group.

REACTIONS WITH OTHER DRUGS OR SUBSTANCES

As previously discussed, users often combine different AASs, sometimes over a dozen drugs, to achieve what they perceive as a more optimal effect. It is common for AAS users to take other drugs for several reasons: to increase body-building effects, to avoid detection by urine testing, or to manage unpleasant side effects. For example, research by Dr. Harrison Pope and other Harvard Medical School colleagues found that 9% of 227 men admitted for opioid treatment reported AAS use. Most had started opioid drugs to counteract steroid-induced insomnia and irritability or depression. Many said they were introduced to opiods through their steroid dealers and through the bodybuilding subculture. Other examples of drugs taken concurrently with AASs include estrogen blockers such as tamoxifen or clomiphene to prevent breast development; water pills (diuretics) to eliminate water so muscles look more defined; and human chorionic gonadotropin (HCG) to prevent testes shrinkage. HCG is an injectable, nonsteroidal hormone that stimulates the testicles to produce more testosterone. Another nonsteroidal hormone, human growth hormone, is taken to increase muscle and

body size. Other illegal drugs include thyroid hormones, amphetamines, gamma-hydroxybutyrate, clenbuterol, and Nubain. All these carry potentially serious side effects.

TREATMENT AND REHABILITATION

Studies on AAS treatment are lacking, but most experts believe a standard substance abuse treatment model works with AAS treatment. Current knowledge is

---

Physical and Psychological Effects of Steroids

Positive Physical Effects	
Increased leanness/muscle definition	23 – 92 %
Increased muscularity/bigger	21 – 84 %
Increased strength	20 – 80 %
"Harder"	7 – 28 %
Increased weight	6 – 24 %
Negative Physical Effects	
Voice change	14 – 56 %
Acne	12 – 48 %
Clitoromegally	12 – 48 %
Increased facial hair	10 – 40 %
Fluid retention	5 – 20 %
Acute renal failure	3 – 12 %
Chronic fatigue	2 – 8 %
Galactorrhea	1 – 4 %
Insomnia	1 – 4 %
Muscle aches after stopping steroids	1 – 4 %
Psychological Effects	
Hypomania	14 – 56 %
Increased irritability	13 – 52 %
Depression after stopping steroids	10 – 40 %
Increased aggressivity	10 – 40 %
Labile mood	6 – 24 %
Increased libido	6 – 24 %

SOURCE: Amanda Gruber, MD Harvard Medical School, 617-855-3705, ajangle@mail.int.isr.com

Chart by Argosy.

---

based on feedback from a few physicians who have worked with patients undergoing anabolic steroid withdrawal. Supportive therapy, in which patients are educated about what they will experience during withdrawal, is helpful in some cases. Medications or hospitalization may be necessary if symptoms are severe or prolonged. Medications used have included antidepressants for depression, analgesics for pain, and other medications that help restore the hormonal system after AAS use. Behavioral therapies are sometimes used.

PERSONAL AND SOCIAL CONSEQUENCES

While AASs typically do not have any immediate effect, users often experience both negative and positive effects. People on steroids can experience personality and mood changes. Wide mood swings can occur, and users can suddenly become angry and bad-tempered. Withdrawal from steroids can be difficult. Significant depression often begins when AAS use is stopped. Dr. Roberto Olivardia, a psychologist at McLean Hospital, finds men often experience very severe depression within months of AAS stoppage. They are often emotionally numb, and operate in a zombie-like state, which often leads to a continued steroid use. Backing this observation are studies indicating between 14% and 57% of non-medical AAS users develop depression. The depression can become severe enough that suicidal thoughts occur, with the suicide risk highest during withdrawal. Other reported side effects during withdrawal include fatigue, loss of appetite, difficulty sleeping, decreased sex drive, headaches, and muscle aches.

Another difficulty of AAS use is the expense. Anabolic steroids are not cheap. One teen's combination of four steroids for one "stack," consisting of two injectables and two pills, cost $800.

As mentioned above, a serious consequence among children or teens who use AAS is a stunting of growth, and never reaching their intended height. Because small doses of steroids can stunt height, physicians seldom prescribe AASs for young people.

How the AAS user is perceived

Most people believe AAS users take them because they want to improve their physical appearance. In fact, teens surveyed named this for a primary reason, as opposed to improving sport performance. One study found AAS users tend to have more narcissistic personalities traits, defined as excessive admiration of oneself, and have less empathy. It is unclear whether these traits contribute to starting AASs or result from the use of steroids. Adolescents are less likely than they were a decade ago to disapprove of short-term steroid use or to view it as a great risk. In the 2001 Monitoring the Future survey, 60% saw it as a great risk compared to 70% in

surveys in the 1990s. Likewise, the number of adolescents who disapproved of using AAS once or twice had decreased from 90% in the early 1990s to 85%.

Perhaps more than other drugs, AAS users often hide use from their peers. "For many anabolic steroid users it can be a very isolating experience because they don't want anyone to know," says Dr. Olivardia. "They want to project the illusion that their body was produced by diet and hard work alone." Others will only disclose usage with close friends because of the element of shame that accompanies AAS use.

LEGAL CONSEQUENCES

Legal history

Although AASs were first developed in the mid to late 1930s for medical use, it was not until 1991 that AASs were added by federal law to the list of Schedule III of the Controlled Substances Act (CSA). In the mid-1980s media reports of the increasing use of AASs in sports and a "silent epidemic " in high schools came to the attention of the U.S. government and Congress. Between 1988 and 1990, Congressional hearings were held, and consequently AASs were added to Schedule III, the same legal class as amphetamines, methamphetamines, opium, and morphine. Before that, federal regulation for AASs came under the jurisdiction of the Food and Drug Administration. In fact, trafficking of anabolic steroids was already illegal before they became classified as controlled substances. The CSA defines AASs as any drug or hormonal substance chemically and pharmacologically related to testosterone (other than estrogens, progestins, and corticosteroids) that promotes muscle growth. Schedule III controlled substances have recognized value as prescribed medications but carry the potential for abuse that may lead to either low or moderate physical dependence or high psychological dependence. In 1994, another act called the Dietary Supplement Health and Education Act was passed. This opened the door for dietary supplements with steroidal properties to be easily purchased over the counter.

Federal and state guidelines and penalties

Simple possession of AASs is a federal offense punishable by up to one year in prison and/or a minimum fine of $1,000. If the person has a previous conviction for certain offenses, the penalty is imprisonment of at least 15 days up to two years and a minimum fine of $2,500. Selling or possessing AASs with intent to sell is a federal felony. The first time someone is caught making or distributing steroids the penalty is up to five years in prison and/or a $250,000 fine. If caught a second time, prison time can be increased to 10 years. During 1989 and 1990, many states reclassified AASs to become controlled substances under state law. A 1991 survey of state legislation found that approximately 22 states had tightened their AAS laws. Because state laws differ, however, a wide range of penalties exist.

People who receive AASs by mail order can also be arrested. Federal law enforcement authorities monitor both international and domestic mail and can open suspicious packages. The Customs Mail Division inspects packages from outside the United States, and the Postal Inspector inspects domestic parcels. The huge volume of mail makes it difficult, but these agencies monitor and try to intercept parcels from addresses known to be connected with steroids.

In the United Kingdom, AASs and other performance-enhancing drugs were added to the Misuse of Drugs Act (MDA) in 1996.

See also Creatine

RESOURCES

Books

Carson, Judy. *Steroid Drug Dangers.* Berkeley Hieghts, NJ: Enslow Publishers, Inc., 1999.

Pope, H., et al. *The Adonis Complex: The Secret Crisis of Male Body Obsession.* New York: The Free Press, 2000.

U. S. National Institutes of Health. National Institute on Drug Abuse. *Anabolic Steroid Abuse Research Report.* Washington, DC: U.S. Department of Health and Human Services, April 2000.

Periodicals

"NIDA Initiative Targets Increasing Teen Use of Anabolic Steroids." *NIDA Notes* 15, no. 3 (July 2000).

Other

Collins, Rick. "Anabolic Steroids, Bodybuilding and the Law." <http://www.steoidlaw.com>.

"Steroids (Anabolic-Androgenic)." NIDA Infofax. February 2, 2001 (July 8, 2002). <www.drugabuse.gov/ infofax/steroids.html>.

SteroidAbuse.org: A Service of the National Institute of Drug Abuse. <http://www.steroidabuse.org>.

Organizations

National Clearinghouse for Alcohol and Drug Information (NCADI), (800) 729-6686, webmaster@health.org, <http://www.health.org>.

National Institute on Drug Abuse (NIDA), National Institutes of Health, 6001 Executive Boulevard, Room 5213, Bethesda, MD, USA, 20892-9561, (301) 443-1124, (888) 644-6432, information@lists.nida.hih.gov, <http://www.drugabuse.gov>.

U.S. Drug Enforcement Administration, 2401 Jefferson Davis Highway, Alexandria, VA, USA, 22301, (800) 882-9539, <http://www.dea.gov>.

Linda S. Richards, MS, RD, CHES

TRANQUILIZERS

OFFICIAL NAMES: Major tranquilizers
(neuroleptics/antipsychotics): Chlorpromazine (Thorazine);
chlorprothixene (Taractan); clozaril (Clozapine); fluphenazine
(Permitil, Prolixin); haloperidol (Haldol); loxapine (Daxolin,
Loxitane); mesoridazine (Serentil); molindone (Lidone,
Moban); olanzapine (Zyprexa); perphenazine (Trilafon);
pimozide (Orap); quetiapine (Seroquel); risperidone
(Risperdal); thioridazine (Mellaril); thiothixene (Navane); triflu-
operazine (Stelazine); trifuluopromazine (Vesprin); ziprasidone
(Geodon).
STREET NAMES: Major tranquilizers: antipsychotics, neuroleptics.
DRUG CLASSIFICATIONS: Major tranquilizers: Not sched-
uled
OFFICIAL NAMES: Minor tranquilizers (sedative-hyp-
notics/anxiolytics)/Benzodiazepines: Alprazolam (Xanax);
chlordiazepoxide (Librium, Novopoxide); clonazepam
(Klonopin); clorazepate (Azene, Tranxene); diazepam (Valium);
estazolam (ProSom); flunitrazepam (Rohypnol/illegal in the
United States); flurazepam (Dalmane); halazepam (Paxipam);
lorazepam (Ativan); midazolam (Versed); oxazepam (Serax);
prazepam (Centrax); quazepam (Doral); temazepam (Restoril);
triazolam (Halcion)
STREET NAMES: Minor tranquilizers: (benzodiazepines:
BZDs, tranks, downers, benzos, goofballs, happy pills, sedative-hypnotics, anxiolytics); (barbiturates: Amys, barbs, blues,
downers, yellow jackets, rainbows, red devils); (nonbarbiturate
sedative-hypnotics: ludes, Sopors)
DRUG CLASSIFICATIONS: Benzodiazepines: Schedule IV,
depressants
OFFICIAL NAMES: Minor tranquilizers (sedative-hyp-
notics/anxiolytics)/Nonbenzodiazepines: Zaleplon (Sonata);
zolpidem (Ambien); Buspirone (BuSpar)
DRUG CLASSIFICATIONS: Nonbenzodiadepine hypnotics:
Zaleplon (Sonata); zolpidem (Ambien), Schedule IV, depressants; Buspirone (Buspar): Not scheduled

OFFICIAL NAMES: Minor tranquilizers (sedative-hyp-
notics/anxiolytics)/ Barbiturates: Amobarbital (Amytal);
butabarbital (Butisol); butalbital (Fiorinal, Sedapap); mephobarbital (Mebaral); methohexital (Brevital); pentobarbital
(Nembutal); phenobarbital (Luminal); secobarbital (Seconal)
DRUG CLASSIFICATIONS: Barbiturates: Amobarbital
(Amytal); butabarbital (Butisol); pentobarbital (Nembutal); secobarbital (Seconal), Schedule II, narcotic analgesics; mepho-
barbital (Mebaral); methohexital (Brevital); phenobarbital
(Luminal), Schedule IV, narcotic analgesics
OFFICIAL NAMES: Minor tranquilizers/Nonbarbiturate
sedative-hypnotics: Chloral hydrate (Aquachloral Supprettes,
Noctec, Somnos); ethchlorvynol (Placidyl); glutethimide (Dori-
den); meprobamate (Miltown, Equanil); methaqualone
(Quaalude); methyprylon (Noludar)
DRUG CLASSIFICATIONS: Nonbarbiturate sedative-hyp-
notics: Chloral hydrate (Noctec, Somnos), ethchlorvynol
(Placidyl), Schedule IV, depressants; glutethimide (Doriden),
Schedule II, depressant; meprobamate (Miltown, Equanil),
Schedule IV, depressant; methaqualone (Quaalude); methypry-
lon (Noludar), Schedule I, depressant

OVERVIEW

Tranquilizers are agents that suppress or inhibit
some aspects of central nervous system (CNS) activity—the brain, spinal cord, and the nerves from both—
and are thus referred to as CNS depressants. Used primarily to treat insomnia as well as a wide variety of
anxiety disorders, tranquilizers are among the most com-

monly prescribed—and abused—psychiatric medications in the United States. According to Food and Drug Administration (FDA) estimates, over 60 million people receive prescriptions for tranquilizers every year.

As a group, tranquilizers act mostly on the brain by affecting the neurotransmitter gamma-aminobutyric acid (GABA). Neurotransmitters are brain chemicals that facilitate communication between brain cells (neurons). Although the various classes of CNS depressants work in different ways, ultimately it is through their ability to increase GABA activity (thereby decreasing brain activity) that they produce a drowsy or calming effect that is beneficial to those suffering from anxiety or sleep disorders.

Although a wide variety of substances can have tranquilizing effects, historically, the term "major tranquilizer" was applied to the category of drugs used to treat severe mental illnesses such as schizophrenia. This term, however, arose from the inaccurate belief that the major positive action of the earliest drugs used to treat this illness was sedating and that these drugs were on a continuum with other, less powerful, antianxiety drugs.

However, these drugs are now more commonly—and more accurately—called neuroleptics or antipsychotics. As opposed to medications prescribed for sedation, the neuroleptics often produce signs of neurological dysfunction, such as extrapyrimidal effects (involuntary movements such as Parkinson-like tremors and other abnormal movements). The term "antipsychotics" is sometimes used because these drugs are generally used to treat symptoms of paranoia, psychosis, or serious distortions in the perception of reality, such as hallucinations or delusions. The neuroleptics are not typically drugs of abuse.

The term "minor tranquilizer" (which has been replaced by the more precise terms "sedative-hypnotic" or "anxiolytic") refers to drugs used to treat conditions such as insomnia and anxiety. Because they reduce anxiety and produce pleasantly sedating or "tranquilizing" effects, these drugs are more subject to abuse than the neuroleptics.

History

Since antiquity, people of virtually every culture have used chemical substances to induce sleep, relieve stress, alleviate anxiety, and manage the crippling symptoms of severe mental illness. Although clinical descriptions of psychotic patients—especially schizophrenics—date back to at least 1400 B.C., prior to 1950, effective drugs for the treatment of psychotic patients were virtually nonexistent.

Reserpine, an alkaloid, and the active ingredient of *Rauwolfia serpentina*, the Indian snakeroot, was the basis of the first major tranquilizer. Reserpine was used in the treatment of snake bites, high blood pressure, and

KEY TERMS

ANESTHETIC: An agent that causes loss of sensation or consciousness.

ANXIOLYTIC: A drug that decreases anxiety.

HYPNOTIC: A drug that induces sleep by depressing the central nervous system.

OPIOID: A drug, hormone, or other chemical substance having sedative or narcotic effects similar to those containing opium or its derivatives; a natural brain opiate.

PSYCHOTHERAPEUTICS: Drugs that have an effect on brain function; often used to treat psychiatric disorders

SEDATIVE: A drug that decreases CNS activity; a calming agent.

anxiety. *Rauwolfia* was long used in India for the treatment of mental illness (especially paranoia and schizophrenia) and known to medicine men and locals as the "insanity herb." And although the plant was well known in India—Ghandi sometimes sipped tea made from its leaves—Westerners paid little attention to it until an Indian physician wrote an article about it in 1943.

After a U.S. physician named Wilkins demonstrated the positive effects of reserpine in 1952, the drug gained instant notoriety. Reserpine rapidly replaced induced insulin shock therapy (injecting patients with insulin until their blood sugar levels fall so low that the they become comatose), electroconvulsive (ECT) therapy (inducing seizures by passing an electric current through the brain), and lobotomy (making an incision in the lobe of the brain) as treatments for certain types of mental illness. Moreover, knowledge about the chemistry of this natural plant stimulated the synthesis of other similar alkaloids that were later used as major tranquilizers.

The advent of neuroleptics is sometimes identified as a turning point in the practice of psychiatry because it made possible for the first time the treatment and control of mentally ill people outside an institutional setting. In most developed countries, a large percentage of the people suffering, or in remission, from psychosis are treated in the community. This community-based treatment depends almost entirely on dosing with neuroleptics.

However, since their discovery, the use of neuroleptics has fueled an ongoing debate within the mainstream psychiatric community. This discussion arises primarily as a result of the serious nature and unpredictability of side effects associated with these drugs.

The first sedative-hypnotic, or minor tranquilizer, bromide, originated in the 1860s. Bromides are long-acting sedatives that were rarely used past the turn of the nineteenth century; however, bromide can still be found in Bromo Seltzer. The bromides are gastric irritants with a narrow safety margin and may cause a chronic toxicity known as bromism.

Barbiturates (a class of drugs with more effective sedative-hypnotic effects) replaced bromides in 1903. Depending on the dose, frequency, and duration of use, however, tolerance, physical dependence, and psychological dependence on barbiturates can occur relatively rapidly. With the development of tolerance, the margin of safety between the effective dose and the lethal dose becomes very narrow. That is, in order to obtain the same level of intoxication, the tolerant abuser may raise his or her dose to a level that can produce coma and death.

Major tranquilizers (neuroleptics/antipsychotics)

The most frequently cited possible cause of mental illnesses is an abnormal hyperactivity of the dopamine neurotransmitter system in the brain. Neuroleptics inhibit dopamine nerve transmission in the frontal lobes and in the limbic system—the emotion-regulating brain structures. Inhibiting this portion of the brain causes diffuse CNS depression and disrupts an individual's behavior entirely—reducing psychotic thoughts, perceptions, and agitation.

Neuroleptics are used primarily in managing the symptoms of schizophrenia, although they are also used to treat a variety of conditions, including autism, attention deficit hyperactivity disorder (ADHD), bipolar disorder, and even to alleviate severe pain.

Neuroleptics are sometimes placed into two categories, typical and atypical. The typical neuroleptics are those that were marketed before 1990. The atypical or "new generation" neuroleptics work on different neurotransmitters than the older medications. The most common typical or conventional neuroleptic drugs include:

- haloperidol (Haldol)

- thiothixene (Navane)

- trifluoperazine (Stelazine)

- mesoridazine (Serentil)

- thioridazine (Mellaril)

- chlorpromazine (Thorazine)

This list ranks the neuroleptics in increasing order of causing sedation and in decreasing order of causing abnormal involuntary muscle movements and potency. All are equally effective in treating the symptoms of schizophrenia.

The atypical neuroleptics—or "new generation" neuroleptics—cause fewer adverse side effects, are more effective in managing the symptoms of schizophrenia, and are effective for the treatment of bipolar disorder with or without psychosis. However, these drugs are cost more than the older medications. The five approved in the United States as of 2002 are:

- clozaril (Clozapine)

- olanzapine (Zyprexa)

- quetiapine (Seroquel)

- risperidone (Risperdal)

- ziprasidone (Geodon)

The atypical neuroleptics also cause less sedation than the low-potency older neuroleptics such as chlorpromazine (Thorazine) and thioridazine (Mellaril), and fewer movement disorders than the older high-potency neuroleptics fluphenazine (Permitil, Prolixin) and haloperidol (Haldol). Although they often improve the symptoms of psychosis more effectively than the older drugs, the atypical neuroleptics are not without adverse side effects.

Clozaril (Clozapine), for example, can cause agranulocytosis (a potentially lethal suppression of white blood cells by the bone marrow). Parkinsonian symptoms and weight gain occur with risperidone (Risperdal) and olanzapine (Zyprexa). In addition, quetiapine (Seroquel) has been associated with an increased incidence of cataracts.

As researchers have pointed out, well-controlled, rigorous studies of the neuroleptics have been rare. One analysis of seven studies showed improvement of behavioral symptoms in 59% of patients, but there was also improvement in 41% of those taking placebo (sugar pill). Patients with psychosis but without signs of movement disorder are often started on 0.5–1 mg of haloperidol (Haldol), with a subsequent increase in the dosage, trading off between adverse side effects and benefits.

Minor tranquilizers (sedative-hypnotics/anxiolytics)

Like the neuroleptics, all of the commonly used minor tranquilizers—with the possible exception of buspirone (BuSpar)—are CNS depressants. Unlike the neuroleptics, however, these drugs are called sedative-hypnotics because they produce relaxation (sedation) at lower doses and sleep (hypnosis) and eventually coma at higher ones. The anxiolytic (antianxiety) effect is merely an early stage of CNS depression.

The sedative-hypnotics, which include all prescription sleep medications and nearly all antianxiety medications, are sometimes prescribed for other conditions, such as preventing or alleviating epileptic seizures. Benzodiazepines are the most commonly prescribed forms of all the major and minor tranquilizers and among the most abused. Unlike most other classes of drugs of abuse, however, CNS depressants such as the barbiturates or the BZDs are rarely manufactured in clandestine laboratories. Instead, legal pharmaceutical products are usually diverted to the black market.

Several motivating factors are involved in sedative-hypnotic misuse and abuse. Abusers may seek to

• sleep

• relieve stress

• feel euphoria or pleasurable sensations

• escape/avoidance—unpleasant sensations, tension, fear, or anxiety

• enhance effects of other narcotic drugs or alcohol

• offset effects of stimulant drugs

Benzodiazepines. The first benzodiazepine—chlordiazepoxide (Librium)—was developed as an antianxiety agent in 1957. BZDs largely replaced the barbiturates because they were safer, since the margin between the therapeutic and toxic level is wider than the barbiturates. In addition, the BZDs were also found to be less-sedating alternatives for treating anxiety and effective for sleep problems, muscle strains, and seizures. Quickly rising in popularity, in the 1970s, diazepam (Valium) was the most widely prescribed drug in North America; in 1986, alprazolam (Xanax) moved to the top of the list. As of 2001, alprazolam (Xanax) was the most widely prescribed BZD in the United States.

Although the BZDs are CNS depressants, they differ from other depressant drugs in that they target specific receptors in the limbic region of the brain instead of depressing activity throughout the entire CNS. Thus, these drugs, if taken as indicated, produce their intended effects without many of the side effects—such as impaired thinking and judgment, and serious respiratory depression—linked to, for example, the neuroleptics.

Most of the minor tranquilizers in the BZD exhibit similar clinical effects; they differ primarily in their duration of action and in the dosage required to achieve the same effect. The BZDs are classified as short- (triazolam [Halcion]), intermediate- (alprazolam [Xanax] and lorazepam [Ativan]), and long-acting (chlordiazepoxide [Librium] and diazepam [Valium]). Of the various BZDs available in the United States in 2002, those primarily prescribed as anxiolytics and hypnotics include the intermediate- and long-acting variety.

Benzodiazepines are highly lipid (fat) soluble—they are stored in body fat and may be toxic if taken in large amounts. They also easily cross the blood-brain barrier and rapidly travel into the CNS. Tolerance builds rapidly to the sedative and the euphoric effects of the

 # IN THE NEWS

Although most people use prescription medications responsibly, the nonmedical use of prescription drugs is a serious public health concern in the United States. According to the 2000 National Household Survey on Drug Abuse, an estimated 14 million Americans were current illicit drug users—6.3% of the population 12 years old and older. Although marijuana was the most commonly used illicit drug (used by 76% of current illicit drug users), about 41% of current illicit drug users in 2000 (an estimated 5.7 million Americans) used illicit drugs other than, or in addition to, marijuana and hashish.

Of the 5.7 million users of illicit drugs other than marijuana, 3.8 million used psychotherapeutic drugs nonmedically. Psychotherapeutics include pain relievers (2.8 million users), tranquilizers (1 million users), stimulants (0.8 million users), and sedatives (0.2 million users).

BZDS, sometimes within a few days. In contrast, tolerance to the antianxiety and antipanic effects of these drugs is almost nonexistent.

Although the BZDs have minimal depressant effects on respiration, when combined with other CNS depressants (alcohol, opioids), BZDs can cause fatal respiratory suppression. However, most non-BZD sedatives may also cause death by suppression of breathing and heart failure if taken in sufficient quantity. Benzodiazepines can also cause some degree of memory loss called anterograde amnesia—a form of amnesia that involves the formation of memories after a specific event; a person with anterograde amnesia cannot remember information presented to them after ingesting the BZD, a process similar to an alcohol black-out.

Withdrawal from sedative-hypnotics may be accompanied by a delirium that can be life threatening. In severe withdrawal, seizures, visual, tactile, or auditory hallucinations may occur.

Nonbenzodiazepine sedative-hypnotics. The non-BZD hypnotic zolpidem (Ambien) is a newer sleeping agent that is thought to work on more specific subdivisions of the GABA receptor complex than, for example, some of the older benzodiazepine agents. It is indicated for short-term insomnia and is generally limited to seven to 10 days of use.

Zaleplon (Sonata), as of 2002, was the newest sleep medication on the market. Like zolpidem, it also acts on a subdivision of GABA receptors. It has a very short half-life of approximately one hour. (The half-life is the time it takes for the body to metabolize half the substance taken in.) Therefore, it usually produces no effects the next day, such as sedation or memory impairment.

Both zolpidem and zaleplon have a rapid onset of action and are useful in both initiating and maintaining sleep, as well as in decreasing the number of awakenings per night. These drugs also have been shown to lack withdrawal effects and do not demonstrate rebound insomnia. Another benefit of these two non-BZD sedative-hypnotics over the BZDs is the minimal effect on sleep stages. It does not alter the physiologic sleep architecture, providing a more natural sleep. Both hypnotics have a lower tolerance and abuse potential than the BZDs.

Nonbenzodiazepine anxiolytic. Busprione (BuSpar) is the first in a class of drugs that specifically work as anxiolytics. In addition to exerting no sedative effect, this medication poses few of the disadvantages associated with the benzodiazepines—such as physical or psychological dependency—and does not significantly interact with most other compounds.

Barbiturates. Barbiturates—which produce a wide spectrum of CNS depression, from mild sedation to coma—have been used as sedatives, hypnotics, anesthetics, and anticonvulsants since they were first introduced for medical use in the early 1900s.

As a class, the barbiturates are very similar; all are fat soluble. Once barbiturates reach the bloodstream, they distribute throughout the body and affect all body tissues. Barbiturates depress the activity of muscle tissues, including the heart, and have a great impact on the respiratory system.

The barbiturates are classified according to how quickly they produce an effect and how long those effects last: ultrashort-, short-, intermediate-, and long-acting. The ultrashort-acting barbiturates produce anesthesia within about one minute after intravenous (IV) administration. When administered orally, these drugs begin acting within 15–40 minutes and maintain their effects for up to six hours.

Long-acting barbiturates include phenobarbital (Luminal) and mephobarbital (Mebaral). These drugs, which take effect in about one hour and last for about 12 hours, are used primarily for daytime sedation and the treatment of seizure disorders or mild anxiety. Generally, these are not drugs of abuse; rather the short- and intermediate-acting barbiturates—such as amobarbital (Amytal), pentobarbital (Nembutal), and secobarbital (Seconal)—are among those most commonly abused.

Depending on dosage, barbiturates may act as either sedatives or as hypnotics. Subjectively, the effects of barbiturates are very similar to those of alcohol. Like alcohol intoxication, a barbiturate state of intoxication involves slurred speech and unsteady gait. Also, both substances can cause a hangover; the barbiturate hangover is caused by traces of unmetabolized drug remaining in the bloodstream when the medication is discontinued.

Tolerance to many of the effects of barbiturates develops rapidly, but it is a characteristic of this class of drugs that tolerance to the effects does not develop uniformly. Tolerance builds to the euphoric effects but not to the lethal dose; euphoric doses come closer and closer to the lethal dose.

Barbiturate overdose is a factor in nearly one-third of all reported drug-related deaths in the United States. These deaths include suicides and accidental drug poisonings. Accidental deaths sometimes occur when a user takes one dose, becomes confused, and unintentionally takes additional or larger doses. In the case of barbiturates, there is a narrow margin between the amount that induces sleep and the amount that kills.

Barbiturate withdrawal time is related to whether the drug is short or long-lasting. Symptoms accompanying withdrawal include apprehension, weakness, tremors, anorexia, muscle twitches, and possible delirium. However, barbiturate withdrawal is seldom symptom-free and can be more difficult than heroin withdrawal.

Although many individuals have taken barbiturates therapeutically without harmful effects, concern about the degree of drowsiness produced in routine dosage, the potential for addiction, and the growing numbers of fatalities associated with the barbiturates led to the development of alternative medications such as the benzodiazepines. As of 2001, barbiturates comprised only about 20% of all depressant prescriptions written in the United States.

Nonbarbiturate sedative-hypnotics. Nonbarbiturate sedative-hypnotics are drugs with chemical or physiological properties similar to barbiturates and are considered barbiturate-like substances. These drugs include:

- chloral hydrate (Noctec, Somnos)

- ethchlorvynol (Placidyl)

- glutethimide (Doriden)

- meprobamate (Miltown, Equanil)

- methaqualone (Quaalude)

- methyprylon (Noludar)

Due to their high potential for abuse, most barbiturate-like substances have been replaced by newer, safer agents—such as the BZDs and non-BZD sedative-hypnotics—that exert a sedative-hypnotic effect.

Chloral hydrate (Noctec, Somnos) is metabolized into trichloroethanol, which in turn produces sleep and anesthesia. Chloral hydrate was used in the "Mickey

Finn," an anesthetic cocktail used to lure sailors to the Orient in the 1800s. It has a rapid onset, short duration, and few cardiovascular or respiratory effects. Its side effects include an unpleasant taste, gastric irritation, nausea, vomiting, lightheadedness, and nightmares. It has a low margin of safety.

Ethchlorvynol (Placidyl) is an alcohol derivative indicated for short-term (up to one week) therapy in the management of insomnia. The hypnotic dose induces sleep within 15–60 minutes and usually lasts for about five hours. Prolonged use of ethchlorvynol may result in tolerance and physical and psychological dependence. Abrupt discontinuation may result in withdrawal symptoms. The main adverse effects associated with ethchlorvynol are dizziness, gastrointestinal distress, blurred vision, nausea and vomiting, and mild hangover. Ethchlorvynol also has a narrow margin of safety in comparison to other sedative-hypnotic agents. In 1999, the manufacturer, Abbott Laboratories, notified Placidyl prescribers that the drug would be discontinued.

Glutethimide (Doriden), a highly lipid-soluble drug classified as a sedative-hypnotic, was introduced in 1954 as a safe barbiturate substitute. However, its addiction potential and the severity of withdrawal symptoms were similar to those of barbiturates. In 1991, glutethimide was classified as a Schedule II controlled substance in response to an upsurge in the prevalence of diversion, abuse, and overdose deaths. The drug is illegal in the United States and in several other countries. It is classified as a sedative-hypnotic.

Meprobamate (Miltown, Equanil) was introduced in the 1950s. It had the effect of relieving anxiety without producing sleep. However, regular use produced psychological and physical dependence.

Methaqualone (Quaalude, Sopor) is a nonbarbiturate hypnotic that is said to give a heroin-like high without drowsiness. When it was first introduced as a prescription drug to treat anxiety and insomnia in 1965, it already had a reputation as a drug of abuse in other countries. It was banned in the United States in 1984 due to the high incidence of its abuse. Despite its nickname "the love drug," it diminishes sexual performance.

By 1972, "luding out"—taking methaqualone with wine—was popular on college campuses. Excessive use of the drug leads to tolerance, dependence, and withdrawal symptoms similar to those of barbiturates. Overdose by methaqualone is more difficult to treat than barbiturate overdose, and deaths have frequently occurred. In the United States, the marketing of methaqualone pharmaceutical products was discontinued in 1984, and the drug became a Schedule I controlled substance. However, some level of occasional abuse has continued.

Methyprylon (Nodular) was introduced as a sedative and hypnotic in 1955. Its effects are nearly identical to the barbiturate secobarbital (Seconal); it acts by raising the threshold of arousal centers in the CNS. However, overdose produces shock, low blood pressure, and water in the lungs more often than respiratory depression.

Antihistamines. Because of their sedating effects, antihistamines are sometimes used to treat insomnia. These drugs include diphenhydramine (Benadryl), an over-the-counter medication, and the prescription drugs hydroxizine (Atarax, Vistaril) and promethazine (Phenergan). Tylenol PM and many similar agents combine a pain medication with an antihistamine.

Beta-blockers. Beta-blocking agents (including atenolol [Tenormin] and metoprol [Lopressor]) are a class of drugs that block substances such as adrenaline (epinephrine), a key agent in the autonomic (involuntary) nervous system and in the activation of heart muscle.

Beta-blockers relieve stress on the heart by slowing the heart beat and reducing blood vessel contraction in the heart, brain, and throughout the body. Generally, these drugs are used to treat abnormal heart rhythms, chest pain, high blood pressure, and certain types of tremors (familial or hereditary essential tremors).

In addition to these uses, beta-blockers are sometimes used to treat a variety of physical symptoms associated with anxiety and tension. The ability of these drugs to relieve anxiety led to their nonmedical use by, for example, students prior to exams, competitors, and performers before going on stage. Beta-blockers are sometimes called "the musician's underground drug."

Herbs and supplements. Increasingly, people with sleep difficulties have been turning to herbal remedies instead of sedative-hypnotic drugs such as the BZDs. Melatonin (5-methoxy-N-acetyltryptamine), a hormone released from the pineal gland (a small pine-cone shaped structure in the brain) is essential in regulating circadian rhythms (approximately 24-hour intervals). In mammals, the melatonin rhythm is generated by an internal circadian clock in the hypothalamus region of the brain that is linked to the light/dark cycle of the 24-hour day.

Melatonin production decreases with advancing age, and in a small number of insomniacs, true melatonin deficiency occurs. Whether melatonin is effective for those who are not melatonin-deficient is not known, and research does not support the indiscriminate use of this supplement.

Valerian root (*Valerian officinalis)* has also been a popular sleep aid. It is believed to work by stimulating the release of the neurotransmitter GABA. Several trials have shown a 400 mg dose to significantly reduce sleep latency (the time it takes to fall asleep) and improve subjective sleep quality. Some commercial preparations of valerian root also contain hops (*Flores humuli*) as a synergistic ingredient.

???? FACT OR FICTION

According to some researchers, most often, behavioral "problems" in elderly patients with dementia are not directly caused by cognitive decline, but instead may arise as a result of many other factors, such as health, medication, and physical and social environment. Coexisting illnesses, impaired vision or hearing, mood-altering medications, understimulation or overstimulation, lack of familiarity with the environment, and lack of meaningful activities and social relationships may cause a wide variety of responses in individuals with dementia—including wandering, anxiety, paranoia, difficulty with personal care, incontinence, sleep problems, and aggression. However this "problem" behavior is often an attempt to communicate by patients who are losing language and reasoning skills. Researchers maintain that instead of prescribing dangerous neuroleptics, many nonpharmacologic strategies may be used for managing behavioral disturbances in the elderly.

Other supplements having milder effects on sleep include kava, scullcap, chamomile, passion flower, lemon balm, and lavender.

Antidepressants. Although not specifically indicated to treat insomnia, antidepressant compounds are often used for their sedating properties, particularly when coexisting depression or anxiety are present. Newer antidepressants that often help with insomnia include trazodone (Desyrel); nefazodone (Serzone); mirtazapine (Remeron); amytriptyline (Elavil); trimipramine (Surmontil); and doxepin (Sinequan).

Illicit sedative-hypnotic drugs

A number of street drugs have tranquilizing effects and are often associated with sexual assaults in the United States. These so-called "date-rape drugs" include:

- Flunitrazepam (Rohypnol), also known as roofies, is a benzodiazepine with physiological effects similar to diazepam (Valium), although it is about 10 times more potent. The drug produces sedative-hypnotic effects that include muscle relaxation and amnesia; it can also produce physical and psychological dependence. It is illegal and not approved for use in the United States.

- Gamma-hydroxybutyrate (GHB), also called liquid ecstasy, is a clear, odorless, and tasteless liquid whose sedative-hypnotic effects are intensified by alcohol. It has been poured into the drink of an unsuspecting person and used as a "date rape" drug and in "rave" dance clubs and bars. The drug is used illicitly for its sedative and euphoric effects, and it is also claimed to promote muscle development. In 2000, the FDA classified it as a Schedule I controlled substance.

- Ketamine hydrochloride (Ketalar) is primarily used as an animal tranquilizer. When humans use the drug in a nonmedical setting, ketamine can cause hallucinations, amnesia, and dissociation. It is often used with other drugs such as ecstasy, heroin, or cocaine. Due to widespread abuse by young people, the DEA classified this drug as a Schedule III controlled substance in 1999.

CHEMICAL/ORGANIC COMPOSITION

All of the neuroleptics are consumed in their pure form and are rarely abused. Most of the sedative-hypnotics of abuse are diverted from legitimate sources and remain in their pure form. However, occasionally powdered forms of illegal drugs (such as ketamine hydrochloride), which are often manufactured in clandestine laboratories, are mixed with tobacco, marijuana, or other drugs.

INGESTION METHODS

Tranquilizers are usually swallowed as a capsule or tablet but may be injected into the bloodstream or muscle (intramuscularly) as a solution as well. Some are available in rectal suppositories and sublingual (under the tongue) forms. Illicit tranquilizers are also snorted or taken with other drugs, alcohol, or tobacco.

THERAPEUTIC USE

Although the major and minor tranquilizers are used for their ability to depress CNS activity, these classes of drugs are used to manage a variety of specific symptoms and conditions.

Major tranquilizers

Initially, the neuroleptics were used to manage severe anxiety, agitation, and aggression in individuals with severe mental illness such as schizophrenia, a psychotic illness characterized by delusions, hallucinations, and disorganized, illogical thinking. The first neuroleptic used in schizophrenia was chlorpromazine (Thorazine) in 1952. Additional neuroleptics were later developed to treat a variety of other disorders and conditions in children and adults, including autism, attention-deficit hyperactivity disorder (ADHD), bipolar disorder, and Tourette's syndrome. Occasionally, these drugs are also used to manage severe pain.

Minor tranquilizers

BZDs such as chlordiazepoxide (Librium) or diazepam (Valium) may be prescribed to treat anxiety, seizures, acute stress reactions, and panic attacks, or to alleviate the side effects of drug or alcohol withdrawal. Those BZDs with a more sedating effect, such as estazolam (ProSom) or triazolam (Halcion), may be prescribed for short-term treatment of sleep disorders. However, the newer generation of non-BZD agents—zolpidem (Ambien) and (Sonata)—are less potentially addictive hypnotic drugs than the BZDs.

In addition to treating anxiety and insomnia, intravenous BZDs are used as a sedating agent in outpatient surgical procedures. The most commonly used BZD for this indication is the short-acting agent midazolam (Versed). There is a lower potential for respiratory suppression with midazolam than with the barbiturates.

Barbiturates such as mephobarbital (Mebaral) and pentobarbital (Nembutal), although not prescribed as often as the BZDs, may be used to treat anxiety, tension, and sleep disorders. Veterinarians also use pentobarbital (Nembutal) for anesthesia and euthanasia. In some states, a form of barbiturate is used to execute criminals by lethal injection.

The rapid-acting barbiturates, such as methohexital (Brevital), are used as intravenous anesthetics/induction agents. Advantages are rapid anesthesia and short duration of action. A disadvantage is respiratory suppression with higher doses.

Buspirone (BuSpar) is specifically formulated to reduce the symptoms of anxiety but takes two to four weeks to take effect. Adverse reactions include agitation, nausea, and dizziness.

USAGE TRENDS

The Food and Drug Administration (FDA) estimates that over 60 million people receive prescriptions for tranquilizers every year. In the 1980s, the focus of psychiatric care was on depression and its treatment; in the 1990s, the focus turned to the early identification, diagnosis, and treatment of anxiety disorders. This shift in focus resulted in a corresponding shift in drug usage patterns.

In targeting those suffering from anxiety, pharmaceutical companies generated greater consumer demand for their drugs. Prescriptions for one class of these drugs, the BZDs, already are estimated at nearly 100 million a year in the United States, at a cost of about $500 million. Some estimates place the total cost at $800 million or more.

Scope and severity

Since the early 1960s, the BZDs have accounted for more than half the total world sales of tranquilizers. As of 2002, the BZDs were the most commonly prescribed class of tranquilizers in the United States. According to FDA data, however, there has been a dramatic decline in the use of minor tranquilizers and other antianxiety drugs since 1975, when prescriptions peaked at 103 million. An American Psychiatric Association task force report estimates that annual prescriptions for BZDs have leveled off since the mid-1980s to about 61 million.

Age, ethnic, and gender trends

Although many Americans abuse prescription drugs, certain usage trends can be seen among adolescents, young adults, older adults, and women. National Household Survey on Drug Abuse (2000) statistics indicate that the sharpest increases in new users of prescription drugs for nonmedical purposes occurred in 12–17 and 18–25 year-olds. Among 12–14 year-olds, psychiatric medications (including sedative-hypnotics) and narcotics (opioids) were reportedly the two main classes of drugs used.

The 1999 Monitoring the Future Survey of eighth, tenth, and twelfth graders nationwide showed that general declines in the use of barbiturates, sedative-hypnotics, and opioids other than heroin in the 1980s leveled off in the early 1990s, with modest increases again in the mid-1990s.

According to a number of national surveys, men and women have roughly similar rates of nonmedical use of prescription drugs, with the exception of 12–17 year-olds. In this age group, young women are more likely than young men to use psychiatric drugs nonmedically. Also, among men and women who use either a sedative, antianxiety drug, or hypnotic, women are almost twice as likely to become addicted.

Studies indicate that women who were abused as girls, or who saw their mothers abused by a male partner, are more likely, as adults, to use tranquilizers and also illegal drugs. Also, women who are abused by their partners use more tranquilizers—as well as more alcohol—than other women. Other frequent tranquilizer users are those with only an elementary school education; those in the lowest income group; and those who do not work outside the home (including housewives, students, the disabled, and the retired).

In terms of approved medical use, the neuroleptics are often prescribed for children with autism, attention-deficit hyperactivity disorder (ADHD), and Tourette's syndrome. In addition, the popularity of the newer atypical neuroleptics for childhood bipolar disorder is growing rapidly, and sometimes these drugs are the only treatment offered. The neuroleptics are also commonly prescribed for the elderly in nursing homes or other institutional settings.

MENTAL EFFECTS

The most significant beneficial mental effects of the major and minor tranquilizers include:

- anxiety reduction

- mild euphoria

- panic reduction

PHYSIOLOGICAL EFFECTS

Beneficial physiological effects of the major and minor tranquilizers include:

- anesthesia

- anticonvulsant effects

- blood vessel dilation

- decreased contractability of the heart

- decreased hyperactivity, impulsivity, and aggression

- muscle relaxation

- pain relief

- reduced muscle spasms

- relaxation

- sedation

- slowed heart rate

Harmful side effects

At high doses, both the major and minor tranquilizers are severely toxic and may cause coma, respiratory arrest, convulsions, acute renal failure, speech impairment, or death. However, at therapeutic doses, the neuroleptics have been associated with more severe, long-term side effects than the sedative-hypnotics.

Major tranquilizers. Although long-term studies are few, the adverse side effects of the atypical neuroleptics are thought to be less severe than the typical agents. However, adverse side effects have been reported with all neuroleptics. These side effects include:

- agitation and confusion

- cardiac symptoms (such as irregularities in cardiac rhythm)

- dyskinesias (involuntary movements) of the face and tongue

- extrapyramidal symptoms (tremor, slowing down of the movements, muscle stiffening)

- moderate respiratory depression with increased bronchial secretions

- postural hypotension (drop in blood pressure upon standing up)

- sedation

- weight gain

Minor tranquilizers. Some of the most commonly reported adverse effects of the sedative-hypnotics, particularly when used long-term, include:

- blurred and double vision

- compromised mechanical performance (such as automobile driving)

- depression

- dizziness

- hallucinations

- hostility

- impaired mental alertness, thinking, and memory

- paradoxical reactions (acute agitation, confusion, disorientation, anxiety, and aggression), especially in children, adults with brain disease, and the elderly

- rebound anxiety or insomnia (continued use eventually causes an increase of the very symptoms that the drug is supposed to ameliorate)

Regular use of the sedative-hypnotics may result in tolerance—the need for increasing doses to achieve the same effect. Within two to four weeks, tolerance can develop to the sedative effect of minor tranquilizers taken at night for sleep. Thus, these drugs are not usually used prescribed for more than a few days at a time.

The risk of drug dependence increases if sedative-hypnotics are taken regularly for more than a few months, although problems have been reported within shorter periods. The onset and severity of withdrawal differ between the BZDs that are rapidly eliminated from the body (such as triazolam [Halcion]) and those that are slowly eliminated (such as diazepam [Valium]). In the drugs that are rapidly eliminated, symptoms appear within a few hours after stopping treatment of the drug and may be more severe. In drugs that are eliminated slowly, symptoms usually take several days to appear. The frequency and severity of the withdrawal symptoms—which include gastrointestinal problems, loss of appetite, sleep disturbances, sweating, trembling, weakness, anxiety, and changes in perception (such as increased sensitivity to light, sound, and smells), depends on the dosage, duration of use, and whether usage ceases abruptly or tapers gradually.

Obvious withdrawal symptoms typically last two to four weeks; however, the more subtle symptoms may last for months.

Although the barbiturates do not directly cause CNS damage, some individuals with asthma may have a hypersensitive reaction to these drugs. Many individuals who are prescribed barbiturates develop an extreme sensitivity to sunlight known as photosensitivity. In addition, physical dependence on barbiturates can be one of the most dangerous of all drug dependencies; growing tolerance can lead to chronic use close to a lethal level, and abrupt withdrawal can cause symptoms severe enough to lead to death.

Long-term health effects

Both the neuroleptics and the sedative-hypnotics may cause severe, long-term adverse health effects, depending on the dosage and how long the drugs are in use.

Major tranquilizers. Long-term, the most serious side effect of neuroleptics is tardive dyskinesia (TD), a movement disorder that can affect any of the voluntary muscles. The disorder, which strikes usually after six months to two years of treatment, occurs in about 20% to 35% of patients treated with neuroleptics. This incurable condition is most severe in young men and most common in elderly women. Tardive dyskinesia affects the muscles of the mouth and face and causes lip smacking, teeth grinding, rolling or protrusion of the tongue, tics, and diaphragmatic (chest and abdominal) movements that may impair breathing.

All of the major tranquilizers have been implicated in the development of neuroleptic malignant syndrome, a life-threatening disorder that affects multiple organ systems and may result in death in up to 20% of individuals, especially if the symptoms (including extreme muscle rigidity, rapid heart rate, fever, high blood pressure, incontinence, delirium, stupor, coma) are not recognized immediately. The neuroleptics also have the potential to cause brain damage as a result of impairment to the frontal lobes and limbic system. Typical changes are apathy, loss of memory and concentration, and loss of deeper feelings and tenderness.

Minor tranquilizers. There have been very few studies to measure the long-term impact of regular sedative-hypnotic use on overall mental function. Thus, it is impossible to determine how long it is safe for an individual to continue to take BZDs, or at what dosage, before cognitive ability begins to deteriorate. Some researchers have indicated, however, that like alcohol, the minor tranquilizers, when used long-term, may cause brain shrinkage. There is evidence to show that taking a low dose for a short time has little effect, whereas a high intake is almost always certainly harmful.

Tranquilizer overdose, particularly with BZDs, has become increasingly common since the 1960s. Although the sedative-hypnotics are usually safe even when an overdose is taken, they can be fatal in combination with alcohol and other CNS depressants. In addition, the drugs used in suicide attempts—most drug-related suicide attempts are made by women under 30—are those most widely prescribed and available.

REACTIONS WITH OTHER DRUGS OR SUBSTANCES

The major and minor tranquilizers, as CNS depressants, should be used with other medications only under a physician's supervision. Typically, they should not be combined with any other medication or substance that causes CNS depression, including prescription pain medications, some over-the-counter cold and allergy medications, or alcohol. Using CNS depressants with these substances—particularly alcohol—potentiates (amplifies) their effects and can slow breathing, or slow both the heart and respiration, and possibly lead to death from overdose or from driving under the influence. A large percentage of drug-related emergency room visits involve minor tranquilizers.

Although primary abuse of the BZDs is well documented, abuse of these drugs usually occurs as part of a pattern of multiple drug abuse. Heroin or cocaine abusers, for example, use BZDs with other depressants to intensify their "high" or alter the side effects associated with overstimulation or narcotic withdrawal.

TREATMENT AND REHABILITATION

Anyone taking BZDs daily for six to eight weeks may develop dependence and suffer from withdrawal symptoms. Although treatment strategies are usually tailored to the severity of symptoms—a high-dose withdrawal (usually at doses greater than the therapeutic for longer than one month); or low-dose withdrawal (therapeutic doses for more than a few months)—the most effective way to treat dependence is a very gradual tapering (gradual dose reduction) of the drug. If an individual abruptly stops taking the drug, the brain, having become accustomed to sedated activity, can race out of control. This can lead to seizures and other serious or life-threatening consequences. Close monitoring by a qualified physician is critical to the safe use of, and withdrawal from, the sedative-hypnotics. Inpatient or outpatient counseling is also helpful during the detoxification/withdrawal process.

Patients are typically withdrawn from high-dose sedative-hypnotics by gradually reducing the substance of dependence, substituting a longer-acting BZD, which is later tapered, or substituting the barbiturate phenobarbital (Luminal) and subsequently tapering. The chosen method depends on the substance of abuse. Gradual dose reduction is used in a medical setting and requires that the patient use no other drugs of abuse and adhere strictly to the dosing regimen. Substituting a long-acting BZD with subsequent taper is often used to treat BZD withdrawal or mixed BZD-alcohol withdrawal. Substituting phenobarbital may be used for withdrawal from BZDs or other sedative-hypnotics or in patients with multiple drug dependence.

Most individuals who are tapered and withdrawn from therapeutic (low) doses of BZDs experience mild to no withdrawal symptoms that gradually subside and disappear within a few days to a few weeks. For those individuals who experience continued symptoms, a slow, gradual taper from the original BZD dose usually minimizes these symptoms.

PERSONAL AND SOCIAL CONSEQUENCES

The personal cost of dependence on prescription sedative-hypnotics is high. Aside from the short- or long-term health effects, physical or psychological dependence may lead to family discord, job loss, birth defects in infants born to addicted mothers, and even criminal behavior and incarceration in individuals who purchase these drugs illicitly.

Although not often considered, the social cost of prescribing neuroleptics to some groups of people may be enormous. Recent research suggests that an older person living in a nursing home receives four times as many prescription drugs as an older person in their own home. Thus, some healthcare professionals are concerned that the neuroleptics are often overprescribed in the elderly—especially those living in nursing homes and long-term treatment facilities. Critics argue that these medications are often routinely used to suppress emotions and render elderly patients passive and docile, thus easing the workload of caregivers, rather than alleviating the symptoms of dementia.

Some maintain that rather than treating a disease or condition, neuroleptics often create another disease. Although these drugs eliminate or reduce the intensity of psychotic experiences such as delusions and hallucinations, the adverse side effects that may actually worsen the symptoms of dementia.

Dealing with the "problem" behavior of children with autism or ADHD by prescribing neuroleptics, according to some, has much in common with the treatment of the elderly. Although stimulants like methylphenidate (Ritalin) have been reportedly prescribed to large numbers of children and received much media attention, other psychotropic (mind-altering) drugs, such as the neuroleptics, are also prescribed. However, there

has been virtually no testing of these drugs conducted on children, and the long-term effects are unknown.

LEGAL CONSEQUENCES

Legal history

Although some sedative-hypnotics such as the non-barbiturates glutethimide (Doriden) and methaqualone (Quaalude) were once legally prescribed drugs, these substances were banned from use in the United States because of their potential for addiction and abuse. Some sedative-hypnotics such as flunitrazepam (Rohypnol) are illegal in the United States but are legal in Europe and Latin America.

Federal guidelines, regulations, and penalties

The major and minor tranquilizers are legal as manufactured and prescribed and are classified as Schedule II, III, or IV controlled substances under the federal Controlled Substances Act (CSA). However, manufacturing, distributing, and selling these drugs without a prescription are subject to federal and state penalties. The CSA dictates penalties of up to 15 years imprisonment and fines up to $25,000 for unlawful distribution or possession of a controlled substance.

See also Antidepressants; Barbiturates; Benzodiazepines; GHB; Herbal drugs; Ketamine; Melatonin; Methaqualone; Rohypnol

RESOURCES

Books

Bloomfield, Harold. *Healing Anxiety With Herbs.* New York: HarperCollins, 1998.

Breggin, Peter R. and David Cohen. *Your Drug May Be Your Problem: How and Why to Stop Taking Psychiatric Medications.* Reading, MA: Perseus Books, 1999.

Gorman, Jack M. *The Essential Guide to Psychotropic Drugs.* New York: St. Martin's Press, 1998.

Keltner, Norman L. and David G. Folks. *Psychotropic Drugs.* Philadelphia: Mosby, 2001.

Parker, Jim. *The Benzodiazepine Blues: Living With (and Without) Minor Tranquilizers.* Tempe, AZ: Do It Now Foundation, 2000.

Periodicals

Garfinkel D., N. Zisapel, J. Wainstein, et al. "Facilitation of Benzodiazepine Discontinuation by Melatonin. A New Clinical Approach." *Archives of Internal Medicine* 159, no. 20 (November 1999): 2456-60.

Longo, L.P. "Addiction: Part I. Benzodiazepines: Side Effects, Abuse Risk, and Alternatives." *American Family Physician* 61 (April 1, 2000): 2121-2128.

U.S. National Institute on Drug Abuse Research Report, NIH Pub. # 01-4881. April 2001.

Zito, Julie Magno et al. "Trends in the Prescribing of Psychotropic Medications to Preschoolers." *Journal of the American Medical Association* 283 (February 23, 2000): 1025-1030.

Organizations

National Clearinghouse for Alcohol and Drug Information (NCADI), P.O. Box 2345, Rockville, USA, (800) 729-6686.

National Council on Alcohol and Drug Dependence, 12 West 21st Street, New York, NY, USA, 10010, (800) 622-2255 or (800) 475-4673, <http://ncadd.org>.

National Institute on Drug Abuse (NIDA), National Institutes of Health, 6001 Executive Boulevard, Room 5213, Bethesda, MD, USA, 20892-9561, (301) 443-1124, (888) 644-6432, information @lists.nida.nih.gov, <http://www.drugabuse.gov>.

Substance Abuse and Mental Health Services Administration (SAMSHA)/Center for Substance Abuse Treatment (CSAT), 5600 Fishers Lane, Rockville, MD, USA, 20857, (301) 443-8956, info@samsha.gov, <http://www.samhsa.gov>.

Genevieve T. Slomski, Ph.D.

2C-B (Nexus)

OFFICIAL NAMES: 4-bromo-2,5-dimethoxyphenethylamine (2C-B)
STREET NAMES: Nexus, bromo, afterburner bromo, utopia, Venus, spectrum, BDMPEA, toonies, MFT, erox, cloud nine zenith
DRUG CLASSIFICATIONS: Schedule I, hallucinogen

OVERVIEW

2C-B is a relatively new drug to emerge on the club or rave scene. According to the Drug Enforcement Administration (DEA), there is a significant rise in usage in the United States over the past several years. The drug is already popular in the Netherlands, where much of the supply comes from, as well as Germany, Switzerland, and South Africa.

Known popularly as Nexus, 2C-B is a hallucinogen that was legal in the United States until 1995, when it was classified as a Schedule I drug under the U.S. Controlled Substances Act (CSA). Other Schedule I drugs include opium, heroin, and cocaine. It is a synthetic substance, meaning it is manufactured from chemicals and does not occur naturally. Since 2000, large quantities of the drug have been seized by local police and federal agents in Las Vegas, Chicago, Kansas City, South Dakota, Virginia, and Maine, indicating a nationwide distribution network.

The effects of 2C-B are unpredictable and can be radically violent. It is a hallucinogen that produces euphoria and heightened sensual awareness, including vision, hearing, smell, and touch. Low doses of 4–6 mg make the user become passive and relaxed. High doses of 20–30 mg can cause extreme hallucinations and morbid delusions. The effects usually last from four to eight hours, although they can last for up to 12 hours.

The drug can produce profound distortions in the way a person perceives reality. People under the influence of 2C-B see images, hear sounds, and feel sensations that are not real. It can also produce sudden and intense emotional swings. The drug works by disrupting the normal functions of the serotonin system. Serotonin is a substance widely distributed in nerve cells and acts as a neurotransmitter in the brain.

The chemical properties of 2C-B most closely resemble those of mescaline, and 2C-B is 10 times more powerful than another popular club drug, MDMA (ecstasy). It is considered both a hallucinogen and an entactogen, a term that means "touching within." The visual effects, including hallucinations, can be more intense than those produced by LSD or "magic mushrooms" (psilocybin), both powerful and potentially deadly drugs in their own right.

History

Dr. Alexander Shulgin, an American chemist and pharmacologist, first produced 2C-B in 1974. Shulgin has discovered or synthesized more than 150 drugs, most of them hallucinogens. Shulgin has drawn the displeasure of U.S. law enforcement agencies for publishing the chemical formulas for all of his drug discoveries. He has also written of his personal experiences while using the drugs.

2C-B was introduced to psychotherapists in the United States in the late 1970s. A German pharmaceutical company became the first to manufacture and sell the drug worldwide under the trade name Nexus, and was marketed as a treatment for impotency and frigidity. Several other foreign pharmaceutical companies followed suit, marketing the drug under the brand names of Eros and Performax. By 1993, the United States had become the largest market for 2C-B, which was sold without the need for a prescription.

The drug caught the attention of U.S. drug authorities and the American public in December 1993 when *Newsweek* reported it had become one of the most popular drugs at all-night raves and dance clubs frequented by teenagers and young adults. Since it did not require a prescription, the drug was sold in adult book and video stores, drug paraphernalia stores called "head" shops, bars, and nightclubs. It was sold in yellow, unmarked capsules for $17–$25 each. Users could also buy 10 capsules in matchbox-like packages that included instructions for use.

Although it was not yet a controlled substance, DEA agents closed 2C-B manufacturing laboratories in California in 1986 and 1994 and in Arizona in 1992. On June 5, 1995, the drug was placed on Schedule I of the CSA. The drug's effects are similar to other Schedule I hallucinogens; it has a high potential for abuse, and has no accepted medical uses. 2C-B is banned or controlled in Great Britain, Canada, France, Japan, the Netherlands, Germany, Sweden, and South Africa.

2C-B hit the Netherlands at about the same time it found its way into the U.S. drug scene. It was not covered under the Dutch Opium Act, under which drugs are deemed illegal. Tablets of the drug were manufactured by a Dutch firm and were available without a prescription at so-called "smart-drug" shops. The abuse of 2C-B skyrocketed in a short time. The drug was finally scheduled on the list of illegal drugs in mid-1997, and production in the Netherlands all but ceased. Since then, use has dropped substantially and the tablets are difficult to find, according to a 1999 article in the *Journal of Analytical Toxicology*.

When the Netherlands banned 2C-B, two offshoots of the drug, para-methylthioamphetamine and 4-ethylthio-2,5-dimethoxyphenethylamine (2C-T), were introduced. Since they are not specifically named in the Dutch Opium Act, they are not banned. These offshoots have not been reported to be used in the United States.

CHEMICAL/ORGANIC COMPOSITION

2C-B is a synthetically produced hallucinogen that is most closely related to mescaline. It acts primarily on the central serotonin receptors of the brain. Serotonin is a chemical derived from the amino acid tryptophan, and widely distributed in tissues. It acts as a neurotransmitter, constricts blood vessels at injury sites, and may affect emotional states. 2C-B works by interfering with serotonin in the brain.

 **KEY TERMS**

AMPHETAMINES: A class of drugs frequently abused as a stimulant. Used medically to treat narcolepsy (a condition characterized by brief attacks of deep sleep) and as an appetite suppressant.

GHB (GAMMA HYDROXYBUTYRATE): Originally sold in health food stores as a growth hormone, a liquid nervous depressant touted for its ecstasy-like qualities. Banned by the FDA in 1990, the respiratory depression it can cause makes it among the most dangerous club drugs in circulation.

HALLUCINOGENS: A group of drugs that induces sensory distortions and hallucinations.

KETAMINE: An anesthetic abused for its mind-altering effects that is popular as an illicit club drug. It is sometimes used to facilitate sexual assault, or date rape.

LSD (D-LYSERGIC ACID DIETHYLAMIDE): A powerful chemical compound renowned for its hallucinogenic properties.

MDMA (3,4-METHYLENEDIOXYMETHAMPHETAMINE): Known as ecstasy, E and X, MDMA is the most popular of the "club drugs," a synthetic stimulant with mild hallucinogenic properties.

MESCALINE: A hallucinatory drug that is the chief acting agent found in mescal buttons of the peyote plant.

NEUROTRANSMITTER: Chemical in the brain that transmits messages between neurons, or nerve cells.

SEROTONIN: An important neurotransmitter in the brain that regulates mood, appetite, sensory perception, and other central nervous system functions.

TRYPTOPHAN: An amino acid that is widely distributed in proteins.

INGESTION METHODS

2C-B is taken orally and is generally available in pill, capsule, or powder form. The powdered form is usually mixed with a drink, although it is sometimes inhaled through the nose. Users report its effects are more intense when snorted. It is less commonly found as a sugar cube or a liquid, and placed in drinks. It is sometimes combined with MDMA (ecstasy) and called a "party pack" or with LSD and referred to as a "banana split." The average dose of 2C-B sold on the street is 10–25 mg and costs $10–$30 each. The pills can be off-white with brown specks; small, off-white, thick pills stamped with a bull head logo; pink, red, or purple pills; and clear, yellow, or gray and blue capsules.

LAW AND ORDER

2C-B became illegal in the United States in 1995 when the DEA placed it on Schedule I of the Controlled Substances Act. In 1977, Great Britain became the first country to ban the drug. In the late 1990s, 2C-B was banned or placed under strict control in France, Japan, Canada, the Netherlands, Germany, Australia, South Africa, and Sweden.

THERAPEUTIC USE

In the 1970s, 2C-B was used in patients by a small number of psychotherapists in the United States. These therapists reported the drug created a warm, empathetic bond between them and their patients. The therapists also said the drug helped break down a patient's ego defenses and inner resistances, allowing the patient to get in touch with suppressed emotions and repressed memories. However, medical usage was limited and had all but disappeared by the time 2C-B was made a Schedule I substance in 1995. Today, 2C-B is not recognized by most in the medical community as having any therapeutic usefulness.

In the past several years, a few medical researchers have stated they believe some hallucinogens may have valid medical uses, particularly in psychiatry. Also, studies are underway in Baltimore and New Mexico on the possible uses of hallucinogens to treat drug and alcohol addictions. The U.S. Food and Drug Administration (FDA) has approved the studies. Recent advances in science have created opportunities for using hallucinogens as tools in learning how the brain functions.

USAGE TRENDS

Based on the amount of 2C-B seized in drug raids, use of the drug appears be on the increase in the United States. Teenagers and young adults who frequent raves are the most common users. The rise in 2C-B use has coincided with the increasing popularity of raves, which cater to those under age 21. It is often sold as MDMA or used in conjunction with other so-called club drugs.

Drug treatment programs across the United States that specialize in treating substance abusers under 18 years old were surveyed about their current population of patients. The survey found their clients use a variety of drugs, although alcohol, marijuana, and hallucinogens were the most frequently abused substances. For most youths in treatment, hallucinogen consumption is part of an extensive drug use history. Counselors rarely see adolescents who abuse only hallucinogens. Anecdotal reports from some counselors indicate as many as 80% of clients have used hallucinogens. Others report diagnosing as many as three or four cases per week of adolescents with hallucinogen-related perceptual disorders. The reports attribute the perception disorders to the number of "trips," including consecutive multiple doses, that teenagers often take.

Renewed interest in hallucinogens coincides with a perception of reduced risk and greater peer support for use, the Monitoring the Future (MTF) studies show. In 1991, 90% of high school seniors reported that they disapproved of hallucinogen use even once or twice. That number had dropped to 83% in 1994 and to 80% in 1996.

Scope and severity

It is difficult to track the scope and severity of 2C-B use in the United States for the following reasons:

- The drug has only been illegal since 1995, when it was classified as a Schedule I drug under the CSA.

- Few state and federal agencies track 2C-B use specifically, usually lumping it in with either club drugs or hallucinogens.

- The drug is often sold and used in combination with other drugs such as LSD, MDMA, ketamine, and methamphetamines. Also, it is often sold as MDMA, especially at raves.

- Standard drug tests, including urinalysis, do not currently detect the presence of 2C-B.

Some conclusions can be drawn based on existing data from state and federal agencies involved in drug control and treatment. The distribution of 2C-B has been sporadic since it became scheduled in 1995, according to a 2001 report by the National Drug Intelligence Center (NDIC). Beginning in 1991, though, seizures of large quantities of 2C-B have increased. In the 2001 report, the NDIC warned local law enforcement agencies they should consider 2C-B an emerging drug threat.

Local police agencies and federal drug enforcement officials began noticing a sharp increase in 2C-B seizures and arrests beginning in December 1999 when the drug surfaced in Virginia. Police in Las Vegas first came across 2C-B in May 2000 when they discovered it was being sold in nightclubs as MDMA. By May 2001, Las Vegas police undercover agents had purchased 1,900 tablets of 2C-B, many of which came from southern California. At about the same time, police were making arrests for possession of 2C-B in Sioux Falls, South Dakota; Maine; and Chicago. Within a few months, arrests were made in Kansas, Missouri, and Pennsylvania. By 2002, the drug was reported nationwide, and drug officials said they did not expect to see a reversal of this trend in the near future.

The 2001 NDIC report stated that the use of 2C-B is likely to increase due to its marketing as MDMA and the rapidly increasing demand for synthetic club drugs at raves and dance clubs.

Age, ethnic, and gender trends

Monitoring the Future study. The Monitoring the Future (MTF) study does not specifically track 2C-B use. However, some insight can be gained by looking at the statistics for two categories that are tracked: hallucinogens and MDMA (ecstasy). These categories are important because 2C-B is a hallucinogen, and 2C-B users often take the drug in combination with or as a replacement for MDMA.

Student use of MDMA increased in 2001 from the previous four years, according to the study of eighth-, tenth-, and twelfth-grade students across the United States. Among eighth graders, 5.2% reported in 2001 that they had used MDMA at least once in their lives. This compared to 4.3% in 2000 and 3.2% in 1997. The rate among tenth graders was 8% in 2001, compared to 7.3% in 2000 and 5.7% in 1997. The rate among high school seniors was 11.7% in 2001, up from 11% in 2000 and 6.9% in 1997.

Use of hallucinogens decreased in 2001 from the previous four years. In 2001, 4% of eighth-grade students reported they had used a hallucinogen sometime in their life. This compared to 4.6% in 2000 and 5.4% in 1997. Among tenth graders, the rate was 7.8% in 2001, 8.9% in 2000, and 10.5% in 1997. Students in the twelfth grade had rates of 12.8% in 2001, 13% in 2000, and 15.1% in 1997.

National Household Study on Drug Abuse. The National Household Survey on Drug Abuse (NHSDA) found that hallucinogen use is on the rise among the general U.S. population, especially among people under age 26. In 1999, the survey found 1.4 million Americans were new users of hallucinogens, the highest number since 1965. The survey found 669,000 new users were youths ages 12–17, 604,000 ages 18–25, and only 127,000 were age 26 and over. In 2000, 83% of hallucinogen users were under age 26, according to the survey.

In the 2000 survey, 19.3% of respondents between the ages of 18–25, and 5.8% between the ages of 12–17 reported using a hallucinogen at least once. As is true for the MTF survey data, NHSDA data indicate that much of this increase has been among whites and Hispanics. The greatest concentration of reported lifetime use is found among two groups: white youths ages 18–25 (19%) and Hispanics ages 18–25 (9%).

The survey also identified hallucinogen users today as mainstream college students. Private and public cam-

The rise in 2C-B use has coincided with the increasing popularity of raves. Photo by Lawrence Manning/CORBIS. Reproduced by permission.

puses are equally likely to report hallucinogen use, while religious schools are most likely to report little or no use. Larger campuses and institutions in urban areas report the widest range of hallucinogen use. This is likely because of greater student accessibility to the off-campus urban rave and club scene near larger schools.

Based on these and other studies, a profile emerges of the typical 2C-B user: usually white but sometimes Hispanic, medium to high family income levels, 18–26 years old, from an urban area, regularly attends all-night dance parties or raves. Use of hallucinogens was higher among males than females, especially those in the 18–25

HISTORY NOTES

Dr. Alexander Shulgin, an American chemist and pharmacologist, first produced 2C-B in 1974. It was introduced to therapists in the United States in the late 1970s. A German pharmaceutical company became the first to manufacture and sell the drug worldwide under the trade name Nexus. The company marketed Nexus as a treatment for impotency and frigidity. Several other foreign pharmaceutical companies followed suit, marketing the drug under the brand names of Eros and Performax. By 1993, the United States had become the largest market for 2C-B, which was being sold without the need for a prescription. Around the same time, researchers studying the emerging music and dance phenomena known as "raves" found 2C-B played a significant part in these activities. It was listed as a Schedule I drug by the DEA in 1995.

age group. A user of 2C-B is also very likely to abuse other drugs.

MENTAL EFFECTS

2C-B is capable of producing a number of varying effects based on dose. A few milligrams of increase in dose can produce a tremendous difference in the effect. Doses as low as 4 mg can make users become passive and relaxed. Users report the effects are similar to those of ecstasy. At slightly higher doses of 8–10 mg, the drug's stimulating effects are increased and a completely intoxicated state is produced. Mild hallucinations may also be experienced. High doses of 20–30 mg produce overt and vivid hallucinations. Doses higher than 30 mg can produce paranoia, extremely frightening hallucinations, and morbid delusions.

The visual effects of 2C-B can be much more intense than those produced by LSD or psychedelic mushrooms. Music can heighten the visual effects of the drug. Moving objects leave "trails" behind them, and colors may appear from nowhere. Surfaces may appear covered with geometric patterns and may seem to be moving.

The effects of 2C-B can last for up to 12 hours, depending on dose. They usually start 20–90 minutes after ingestion and last for three to four hours before starting to decrease. It usually takes two hours to come down from the drug, and the aftereffect can last for four hours.

PHYSIOLOGICAL EFFECTS

There is little information about the toxicity of 2C-B as there are only a limited number of studies done on the drug. However, some conclusions can be draw about its physiological effects based on studies of drugs that are chemically similar to 2C-B. The drug binds to serotonin receptors in the brain, which is why it has hallucinogenic properties. Serotonin is a neurotransmitter or "messenger" substance that carries information through the peripheral and central nervous systems.

2C-B does not have the same chemical properties as amphetamines, so it does not seem to deplete the serotonin levels in the brain. This means it probably does not damage nerves as amphetamines do. Since 2C-B chemically resembles mescaline, it is likely to increase the heart rate, elevate blood pressure, and raise body temperature. In some people, 2C-B can cause nausea, vomiting, trembling, chills, and nervousness.

The drug is extremely dose-sensitive and even a small increase in dose (a few milligrams) can produce radically different, unpredictable, and potentially violent effects. The most noticeable physical effects are anxiety, muscle clenching, poor coordination, shaking, dilated pupils, and increased blood pressure and heart rate.

2C-B differs in several ways from other commonly abused drugs such as heroin or cocaine. Although their reality-distorting effects may make them attractive and reinforce repeated usage, 2C-B is not physiologically addictive in the same way that opiates or even sedatives are. That means once tolerance is established, 2C-B does not produce long-term physiological craving after its effects have worn off. They also differ in the duration of drug action. Unlike the effects of cocaine, which last for only minutes, and those of heroin, which last for a couple hours, the active effects of 2C-B can continue for up to 12 hours. Only methamphetamine can produce a similar long-lasting effect from a single ingestion.

Harmful side effects

Side effects can vary but the most common is gastrointestinal distress such as nausea, vomiting, cramps, and diarrhea. There have also been reports of allergic reactions, in which the symptoms include red, itchy, watery eyes, runny or stuffy nose, fever, coughing, and sneezing. Harmful mental effects include agitation, anxiety, difficulty in concentrating, and frightening thoughts and visions long after use has stopped. It has also been known to trigger latent psychological and mental problems.

Some users also report episodes of hallucinogen-persisting perception disorder (HPPD), commonly known as flashbacks. These episodes are spontaneous and repeated, and sometimes involve continuous recurrences of some of the sensory distortions experienced

PHOTO GALLERY

Adderall®, 5 mg (amphetamine aspartate, amphetamine sulfate, dextroamphetamine saccharate, dextroamphetamine sulfate).
(Copyright Micromedex. Reproduced by permission.)

Adipex-P®, 37.5 mg capsule (phentermine hydrochloride).
(Copyright Micromedex. Reproduced by permission.)

Adipex-P®, 37.5 mg tablet (phentermine hydrochloride).
(Copyright Micromedex. Reproduced by permission.)

Anadrol-50®, 50 mg (oxymetholone). Front (left) and back views.
(Copyright Micromedex. Reproduced by permission.)

Ativan®, 0.5 mg (lorazepam). Front (left) and back views.
(Copyright Micromedex. Reproduced by permission.)

Darvocet-N® 100, 100 mg/650 mg (propoxyphene napsylate, acetaminophen).
(Copyright Micromedex. Reproduced by permission.)

Demerol®, 100 mg (meperidine hydrochloride). Front (left) and back views.
(Copyright Micromedex. Reproduced by permission.)

Dexedrine®, 5 mg (dextroamphetamine sulfate).
(Copyright Micromedex. Reproduced by permission.)

Dilaudid®, 4 mg (hydromorphone hydrochloride). Front (left) and back views.
(Copyright, Micromedex. Reproduced by permission.)

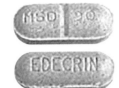

Edecrin®, 50 mg (ethacrynic acid). Front (top) and back views.
(Copyright Micromedex. Reproduced by permission.)

Lasix®, 20 mg (furosemide).
(Copyright Micromedex. Reproduced by permission.)

Lasix®, 40 mg (furosemide). Front (left) and back views.
(Copyright Micromedex. Reproduced by permission.)

Lortab®, 10 mg/500 mg (hydrocodone bitartrate, acetaminophen).
(Copyright Micromedex. eproduced by permission.)

Lortab®, 2.5 mg/ 500 mg (hydrocodone bitartrate, acetaminophen).
(Copyright Micromedex. Reproduced by permission.)

Marinol®, 5 mg (dronabinol).
(Copyright Micromedex. Reproduced by permission.)

Marinol®, 10 mg (dronabinol).
(Copyright Micromedex. Reproduced by permission.)

Meridia®, 10 mg (sibutramine hydrochloride monohydrate).
(Copyright Micromedex. Reproduced by permission.)

*Meridia®, 15 mg
(sibutramine
hydrochloride
monohydrate).*
*(Copyright Micromedex.
Reproduced by permission.)*

*Methylphenidate
hydrochloride
generic, 36 mg.*
*(Copyright Micromedex.
Reproduced by permission.)*

*Methylphenidate
hydrochloride
generic, 54 mg.*
*(Copyright Micromedex.
Reproduced by permission.)*

*MS Contin®, 15 mg
(morphine sulfate).
Front (left) and
back views.*
*(Copyright Micromedex.
Reproduced by permission.)*

*MS Contin®, 100 mg
(morphine sulfate).
Front (left) and
back views.*
*(Copyright Micromedex.
Reproduced by permission.)*

*Paxil®, 40 mg
(paroxetine
hydrochloride).
Front (top)
and back views.*
*(Copyright Micromedex.
Reproduced by permission.)*

*Percocet®,
7.5 mg/325 mg
(oxycodone,
acetaminophen).*
*(Copyright Micromedex.
Reproduced by permission.)*

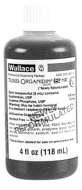

*Percodan®, 4.5 mg/
0.38 mg/325 mg
(oxycodone,
oxycodone
terephthalate, aspirin).*
*(Copyright Micromedex.
Reproduced by permission.)*

*Ritalin®, 20 mg
(methylphenidate
hydrochloride).*
*(Copyright Micromedex.
Reproduced by permission.)*

*Tussi-Organidin-S NR®,
100 mg/10/mg/5 ml
(guaifenesin,
codeine phosphate).*
*(Copyright Micromedex.
Reproduced by permission.)*

Tylenol® with Codeine No. 3, 30 mg (acetaminophen, codeine phosphate). Front (left) and back views.
(Copyright Micromedex. Reproduced by permission.)

Tylenol® with Codeine No. 4, 60 mg (acetaminophen, codeine phosphate). Front (left) and back views.
(Copyright Micromedex. Reproduced by permission.)

Valium®, 2 mg (diazepam). Front (left) and back views.
(Copyright Micromedex. Reproduced by permission.)

Valium®, 5 mg (diazepam). Front (left) and back views.
(Copyright Micromedex. Reproduced by permission.)

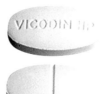

Vicodin HP®, 10 mg/660 mg (hydrocodone bitartrate, acetaminophen). Front (top) and back views.
(Copyright Micromedex. Reproduced by permission.)

Vicodin ES®, 7.5 mg/750 mg (hydrocodone bitartrate, acetaminophen). Front (top) and back views.
(Copyright Micromedex. Reproduced by permission.)

Xanax®, 2 mg (alprazolam). Front (left) and back views.
(Copyright Micromedex. Reproduced by permission.)

Xanax®, 0.5 mg (alprazolam).
(Copyright Micromedex. Reproduced by permission.)

Xenical®, 120 mg (orlistat).
(Copyright Micromedex. Reproduced by permission.)

while on the drug. The experiences may include halluci-nations, but usually consist of visual disturbances such as seeing false motion at the edges of the field of vision, bright white or color flashes, and halos or trails around or behind moving objects.

Typically, HPPD is persistent and may remain unchanged for years after a person has stopped using the drug. Because HPPD symptoms are easily mistaken for those of other neurological disorders such as stroke or brain tumors, it is often difficult to diagnose. There is no established treatment for HPPD, although some antide-pressant drugs may reduce the symptoms. Psychothera-py also is sometimes helpful.

Flashbacks may occur days, months, or years after using the drug, and may include seeing intense colors and other hallucinations. They can be sparked by the use of another drug, stress, fatigue, or physical exercise. The flashbacks can range from mild to intense and include feelings of anxiety. They can last several minutes.

Using 2C-B when a person is sick, depressed, emo-tionally upset, or angry increases the risk of having a bad experience. Persons with psychiatric disorders, epileptic disorders, and blood circulation problems also run an increased risk of having adverse reactions to the drug. Since 2C-B is a hallucinogenic, it impairs mental func-tions, greatly increasing the risk of accidents. Persons on 2C-B should not drive, operate machinery, or engage in other potentially dangerous activities.

Bad trips. While using 2C-B, or "tripping," the per-son can have strong feelings of anxiety or fear. The hal-lucinatory effects can be unpleasant and disturbing. They can also be so intense that the person feels they are los-ing control or going crazy. When negative feelings dom-inate the experience, it is commonly called a "bad trip." The reasons for these frightening experiences are not known. They are particularly common among first-time users.

Having a bad trip can cause the user to panic, which can lead to dangerous behavior. Paranoia and feelings of superiority sometimes develop. When a bad experience occurs, the user needs to be reassured or calmed until the immediate effects have passed, which can be eight hours or longer, depending on the dose.

To help a person who is having a bad trip, make sure the user and those around him or her are safe; move and speak to the person in a calm and confident manner; call the individual by name and remind the person who he or she is, if needed; do not leave the person alone. Medical attention and physical restraint are sometimes required if the user becomes violent. The negative feelings usually leave when the drug wears off.

Long-term health effects

There have been no specific studies into the long-term health effects of using 2C-B. However, experience from other drugs such as MDMA, LSD, and mescaline suggest that regular use can leave the user feeling fatigued, disoriented, and anxious. Users may also expe-rience depression, psychotic syndromes, visual illusions, panic attacks, and depersonalization. Women who are pregnant or breastfeeding should not take the drug, as there is the possibility it could damage the fetus or infant.

REACTIONS WITH OTHER DRUGS OR SUBSTANCES

Since 2C-B is relatively new and not yet widespread to the club or rave scene, little is known about its effects when taken with other drugs. 2C-B is often used in com-bination with other illicit drugs, particularly ampheta-mines, MDMA (ecstasy), and other so-called club drugs, including ketamine, GHB, and methamphetamine. It is often said by users that 2C-B heightens or increases the effects of other drugs. When taken with ecstasy, it is said by users to intensify feelings of exhilaration through the entire length of intoxication. Feelings of nausea and anx-iety are likely to intensify when combined with ecstasy. Using an illicit drug itself can be dangerous and using it with one or more other illicit substances only increases the dangers. Alcohol can increase the effects of 2C-B, which also increases the risks for harm.

2C-B should not be taken by persons who use a spe-cific category of antidepressants called monoamine oxi-dase (MAO) inhibitors. These include phenelzine (Nardil), isocarboxazid (Marplan), tranylcypromine (Parnate), and moclobemide (Aurorix, Manerix). It also should not be used by diabetics.

TREATMENT AND REHABILITATION

2C-B is not physiologically addictive. However, chronic users can become psychologically dependent on 2C-B. The treatment regimen for chronic users of 2C-B is the same as for other hallucinogens. A combination of therapy methods is often used, including individual counseling, group therapy, and medication. Treatment is usually more effective if it is tailored to an individual's needs and other circumstances.

PERSONAL AND SOCIAL CONSEQUENCES

Studies and surveys in the United States, Canada, and Great Britain show that people who use any type of illicit drug generally tend to do worse in school and are more likely to drop out. These people in turn, are more likely to end up in low-paying jobs or become part of the welfare system. A number of studies show that people who abuse drugs are much more prone to illness, particularly viruses and other infections.

Hallucinogens powerfully affect the brain, distorting the way a person's five senses work and changing the impressions of time and space. People who use these drugs often may have a hard time concentrating, communicating, or telling the difference between reality and illusion. 2C-B can disrupt a person's ability to think, communicate, and act rationally or even to recognize reality. There is medical evidence that heavy use of hallucinogens can impair a user's memory and concentration.

Users of 2C-B will develop a tolerance over time. If they increase the dose, they face greater risk of having a bad trip or disturbing flashbacks. A large number of users of 2C-B also do other drugs, which increases their risks for physical and psychological problems.

People who become terrified of losing their minds or dying while on 2C-B should seek professional help. In extreme cases, when users become agitated, hurt themselves, or become suicidal, sedation and hospitalization may be required.

Students who are convicted of using or possessing 2C-B can be denied federal scholarships and loan guarantees, which may affect their ability to get a college education. In 2001, about 14,000 high school graduates were denied federal aid, at least temporarily, because of prior drug convictions.

LEGAL CONSEQUENCES

A person convicted of possessing a Schedule I drug such as 2C-B can get a sentence ranging from no jail time to life imprisonment, and a fine of $5,000 to $1 million.

In Wisconsin, a first-time conviction in a state court for possession of 2C-B can result in a sentence of up to a year in prison and a fine of up to $5,000. A person convicted of sale or possession for sale of 2C-B can get a prison sentence of up to 30 years and a fine of up to $1 million. If the sale is to a minor, sentencing can be doubled at the discretion of the court. In neighboring Illinois, possession of 2C-B is a Class 4 felony, and conviction brings a prison sentence of from one to three years and a fine of up to $25,000. Conviction in a South Dakota state court of possession or sale of a small amount of 2C-B carries a minimum sentence of a year in prison and a fine of up to $10,000. Sale or distribution to a minor carries a minimum prison term of five years.

California's Proposition 36

In 2000, California voters approved a ballot measure that allows state courts to sentence first- and second-time drug use offenders to rehabilitative treatment rather than jail or prison. The measure, Proposition 36 (Prop. 36), also known as the Substance Abuse and Crime Prevention Act, took effect July 1, 2001. As of March 1, 2002, more than 15,000 persons had been referred to treatment under Prop. 36. The law mandates probation and drug abuse treatment for offenders instead of jail time. Persons sentenced under Prop. 36 are required to spend up to a year in a state-approved treatment regimen. Treatment can include outpatient care, inpatient treatment at a halfway house, and drug education and prevention classes.

The philosophy behind the law is two-fold. First, it frees up jail and prison space for persons convicted of violent offenses. Second, it mandates treatment and education that a drug user may not get in jail. Prop. 36's overall goal is to reduce repeat drug use and lower crime rates. Drug policy officials say it is too early to determine if the California program is successful in achieving either of these goals. A similar measure, Proposition 200, was approved by voters in Arizona in 1996.

In California, the state Drug Policy Alliance issued a report in 2002 that stated the program appears to be effective in meeting its goals. However, it listed several areas of concern. These included a lack of diversity in treatment options, a lack of state licensing regulations for halfway houses, and a high rate of drug offenders failing to appear for treatment in several counties, where the failure to appear rate was close to 50%.

Federal guidelines, regulations, and penalties

The federal government and state governments use schedules as a way of classifying controlled substances such as 2C-B and other hallucinogens. A drug is placed on a particular schedule based on how safe it is, its potential for medical use, and its potential for abuse. A drug's schedule plays a primary role in determining penalties for illegal possession or sale of the drug.

Drugs are placed in Schedule I because they have a high potential for abuse, have no current accepted medical use, and because the drug is unsafe even under medical supervision. Besides 2C-B, other Schedule I drugs include heroin, marijuana, and LSD.

2C-B is a Schedule I substance and thereby falls under the penalties associated with that group of drugs. Persons convicted of first-time possession of 2C-B in a federal court face up to a year in prison and a mandatory fine of at least $1,000 up to a maximum of $100,000. A first-time conviction for the sale or possession for sale of 2C-B by a federal court carries a prison sentence of up to 20 years and a fine of up to $1 million.

International penalties

In Canada, 2C-B is a scheduled drug under the Controlled Drugs and Substances Act. If convicted of possession of 2C-B, the maximum penalty is three years in jail and up to a $1,000 fine for a first offense. A conviction for sale of 2C-B carries a maximum penalty of 10 years in prison.

Great Britain regulates 2C-B under the Medicines Act. A conviction for possession of the drug carries an average sentence of two years and two months in prison and a fine of about $185. The maximum sentence is seven years in prison and an unlimited fine. The maximum penalty for selling 2C-B is life in prison and an unlimited fine.

In Australia, 2C-B is regulated by each state. In the state of Queensland, the penalty for possession of any illegal drug is one year in prison and a fine of $3,000, according to the Australian Drug Foundation. The trafficking or sale of 2C-B in Queensland carries a maximum sentence of 25 years in prison and a fine of up to $250,000.

Japan's Health and Welfare Ministry ruled the drug had no legitimate medical uses and banned it in 1998 under the Narcotics Control Law. The maximum penalty for a conviction of possessing or using 2C-B is seven years in prison. The drug had been marketed in Japan and sold over the Internet under the name Performax. In 2000, the World Health Organization (WHO) classified it as a Schedule II drug under the 1971 Convention on Psychotropic Substances. In a recent report, WHO said 2C-B is likely to be abused enough as to constitute a "substantial" public health and social problem, warranting its placement under international control. The WHO report had no recommendations for penalties or treatment for abusers.

See also Club drugs; Ecstasy (MDMA); GHB; Ketamine; Methamphetamine

RESOURCES

Books

Barter, James. *Hallucinogens (Drug Education Library)*. San Diego: Lucent Books, 2001.

Knowles, Cynthia R. *Up All Night: A Closer Look at Club Drugs and Rave Culture*. North Springfield, VT: Red House Press, 2001.

Periodicals

De Boer, D., et al. "More Data About the New Psychoactive Drug 2C-B." *Journal of Analytical Toxicology* (May-June 1999): 227- 228.

"The Death of the Party." *FDA Consumer* (March 2000): 14.

Grinspoon, Lester, and Rick Doblin. "Psychedelics as Catalysts of Insight-oriented Psychotherapy." *Social Research* (Fall 2001): 677-698.

Kintz, P. "Interpreting the Results of Medico-Legal Analyses in Cases of Substance Abuse." *Journal of Toxicology: Clinical Toxicology* (March 2000): 197.

Kowalski, Kathiann M. "What Hallucinogens Can Do to Your Brain." *Current Health* 2 (April 2000): 6.

Makenzie, Dana. "Secrets of an Acid Head (Research on Hallucinogenic Drugs)." *New Scientist* (June 23, 2001): 26.

Organizations

National Institute on Drug Abuse (NIDA), National Institutes of Health, 6001 Executive Boulevard, Room 5213, Bethesda, MD, USA, 20892-9561, (301) 443-1124, (888) 644-6432, information@lists.nida.nih.gov, <http://www.drugabuse.gov>.

Ken R. Wells

GLOSSARY

A

Acetylcholine: A type of neurotransmitter. The pleasurable effects of nicotine are a direct result of nicotine binding to acetylcholine receptors in the brain.

Active ingredient: The chemical or substance in a compound known or believed to have a therapeutic effect.

Addiction: Physical dependence on a drug characterized by tolerance and withdrawal.

Adverse event: Term used to denote a side effect, or negative health consequence, reported after taking a certain substance. The event may or may not be linked to the substance.

Aftershock: Similar to a flashback with LSD, this is the reoccurrence of symptoms associated with taking PCP days, weeks, or months after taking the drug. This happens because PCP is stored in fatty cells in the body.

Alcoholism: A disease that results in chronic alcohol abuse. Alcoholism can cause early death from diseases of the brain, liver, and heart.

Alkaloid: Any organic agent isolated from plants that contains nitrogen and reacts with an acid to form a salt.

Amino acids: Organic molecules that make up proteins. The human body requires 20 amino acids to function properly. Essential amino acids are supplied by food and non-essential amino acids (including creatine) are produced within the body.

Amnesia: Loss of memory. Rohypnol users may forget events that occurred for up to eight hours immediately after taking the drug.

Amphetamine psychosis: A delusional state of mind caused by severe amphetamine abuse. Paranoia, hallucinations, and unfounded feelings of persecution are common features.

Amphetamines: A class of drugs frequently abused as a stimulant. Used medically to treat narcolepsy (a condition characterized by brief attacks of deep sleep) and as an appetite suppressant.

Anabolic effects: A drug-induced growth or thickening of the body's nonreproductive tract tissues, such as muscle, bones, larynx, and vocal cords, and a decrease in body fat.

Anaerobic exercise: Exercise that isn't fueled by oxygen intake (as aerobic exercise is). Anaerobic exercise is defined by short, vigorous, and frequent muscle contractions, and includes activities like sprinting and weight lifting.

Analgesic: A type of drug that alleviates pain without loss of consciousness.

Analog: Different form of a chemical or drug structurally related to the parent chemical or drug.

Androgenic effects: A drug's effects on the growth of the male reproductive tract and the development of male secondary sexual characteristics

Anesthetic: An agent that produces a loss of sensation or consciousness.

Angina pectoris: A disease marked by spasmodic attacks of intense, suffocating chest pain due to insufficient blood flow to the heart.

Anorectics: Diet pills developed to replace amphetamines.

Anorexia: An eating disorder characterized by a refusal to maintain body weight at a minimal normal weight for age and height, an intense fear of gaining weight, and a distorted sense of self-image.

Antagonist: A drug that counteracts or blocks the effects of another drug.

Anthelminthic drugs: Drugs that rid the lower intestinal tract of parasitic worms.

Anticonvulsants: Drugs that relieve or prevent seizures.

Antioxidant: A substance that prevents oxidation and protects cells from free radicals. Free radicals are molecules that contain an odd number of electrons. They can cause tissue death and damage.

Antispasmodic: A substance or drug that relieves muscle spasms and/or cramps.

Anxiety disorders: A group of mental disorders or conditions characterized in part by chronic feelings of fear, excessive and obsessive worrying, restlessness, and panic attacks. Anxiety disorders include panic disorder, agoraphobia, obsessive-compulsive disorder, post-traumatic stress disorder, and others.

Anxiolytic: A drug that decreases anxiety.

Aphasia: Partial or total loss of the ability to explain ideas or understand spoken or written language, resulting from damage to the brain caused by injury or disease.

Aphrodisiac: A substance or drug that increases sexual desire.

Ataxia: Loss of control of muscle coordination.

Atherosclerosis: A cardiovascular condition that causes arteries to narrow, or clog, with plaque build-up from excess blood cholesterol.

Attention deficit hyperactivity disorder (ADHD): A mental disorder characterized by persistent impulsive behavior, difficulty concentrating, and hyperactivity that causes lowered social, academic, or occupational functioning.

Ayahuasca: An intoxicating beverage made from *Banisteriopsis caapi* plants, which contain DMT.

B

Bad trip: A negative LSD experience characterized by anxiety, panic, and despair, which can be extremely traumatic.

Bagging: Breathing mind-altering fumes from a substance sprayed or placed inside a plastic or paper bag, with the bag held tightly around the mouth.

Barbiturates: Highly habit-forming (addictive) sedative drugs chemically based on barbituric acid. Barbiturates are central nervous system depressants.

Benzodiazepines: A class of drugs developed in the 1960s as a safer alternative to barbiturates. Most frequently used as sleeping pills or antianxiety drugs.

Bhang: The mildest form of cannabis, used in India.

Body mass index (BMI): A measurement of body fat based on a person's height and weight.

Bromide: A sedative compound made from the chemical element bromine.

Bronchitis: An acute inflammation of the bronchial tubes in the lungs.

Bulimia: An eating disorder characterized by binge eating and then excessive behavior (such as vomiting, laxative or diuretic abuse, or exercising excessively) to rid the body of the food eaten.

Bummer trip: Another term for a bad trip, this refers to negative experiences while taking a drug.

Buprenorphine: (Also known as Temgesic and Subutex.) New substances that have proven to reduce cravings associated with heroin withdrawal. May also be helpful in treating cocaine addiction.

C

Candy flipping: The practice of combining ecstasy with LSD, which is popular among young people who attend raves and dance clubs.

Cannabinoid: One of the approximately 60 chemical compounds found in *Cannabis sativa*.

Cannabis: Refers to all plant and/or drug forms of the Indian hemp plant, *Cannabis sativa*.

Carbon monoxide (CO): A gaseous byproduct of incomplete burning of tobacco. It replaces necessary oxygen being carried by the hemoglobin in the blood and is thought to contribute to the development of cardiovascular disease.

Carcinogens: Substances or agents that cause cancer.

Cardiopulmonary resuscitation: A procedure designed to restore normal breathing after the heart stops. It includes clearing air passages to the lungs, mouth-to-mouth artificial respiration, and heart massage by exerting pressure on the chest.

Cardiovascular system: The body system composed of the heart and blood vessels.

Cataplexy: An abrupt, total loss of muscle control spurred by an emotional event. Cataplexy frequently occurs along with narcolepsy.

Central nervous system (CNS): The part of the nervous system consisting of the brain and spinal cord to which sensory and motor information is transmitted, coordinating activity of the entire nervous system.

Cerebellum: A large part of the brain that controls muscle coordination and balance.

Cerebral cortex: The surface layer of gray matter in the front part of the brain that coordinates the senses and motor functions.

Charas: Concentrated cannabis resin, similar to hashish.

Chloral hydrate: A colorless compound used as a sedative.

Chronic obstructive pulmonary disease (COPD): A general term to describe airflow obstruction due to emphysema and chronic bronchitis.

Cirrhosis: A chronic liver disease that is caused by alcohol abuse, toxins, nutritional deficiency, or infection. A main symptom of cirrhosis is portal hypertension.

Clandestine laboratory: An illegal laboratory used to make designer drugs.

Clinical trial: A scientific experiment that tests the effect of a drug in humans.

Club drugs: Mostly synthetic, illicit substances found at raves and nightclubs. This group includes LSD, ecstasy, GHB, Rohypnol, ketamine, and methamphetamine.

Coca paste: An impure free-base cocaine made from coca leaves. It is used mainly in South America. Coca paste is smoked and is highly addictive.

Cocaethylene: A substance formed by the body when cocaine and alcohol are consumed together. Cocaethylene increases the chances of serious adverse reaction or sudden death from cocaine.

Cocaine bugs: Hallucinations that feel like bugs crawling under the skin, occurring in heavy or binge users of cocaine. This sensation can be so intense that users will scratch their skin or use a knife to attempt to remove the bugs.

Cocaine psychosis: A mental illness characterized by paranoia, disorientation, and severe depression. It is often the result of long-term cocaine abuse.

Coma: An abnormal state of depressed responsiveness with absence of response to stimuli.

Coming down: The experience of a drug wearing off.

Compensatory smoking: A practice by which smokers puff harder, deeper, and more frequently to obtain desired amounts of nicotine from fewer cigarettes or from low-nicotine cigarettes. Smokers may also hold the smoke in the lungs longer before exhaling and smoke the cigarette further down.

Congestive heart failure: A potentially fatal condition in which the heart loses its ability to pump an adequate volume of blood. As blood flow slows, fluid builds up in tissues throughout the body.

Cotinine: A breakdown product of nicotine that stays much longer in the blood than nicotine, and so can be used as a measurement of nicotine exposure, ETS exposure, or even nonsmoking compliance.

Crack cocaine: A highly addictive free-base cocaine that is smoked. Crack is made by combining powder cocaine and sodium bicarbonate.

Craving: A powerful, often uncontrollable desire.

Crystal meth (methamphetamine): A central nervous system stimulant that has emerged as a readily available alternative to MDMA at clubs and raves. Also known as "speed."

Cyanide: Any of several chemical compounds that acts on the respiratory system and can quickly cause death.

D

Date rape: A sexual assault crime in which victims know the attackers and are drugged or otherwise coerced into a sexual situation against their will or without their knowledge.

Decoction: A tea or soup made from boiling herbs in water.

Delusions: False beliefs.

Dementia: A type of disease characterized by progressive loss of memory, learning, and thinking ability.

Dependence: A psychological compulsion to use a drug that is not linked to physical addiction.

Depersonalization: A feeling of detachment from one's own body. People experiencing depersonalization might feel they are watching themselves from a distance.

Depression: A feeling of sadness and helplessness with little drive for communication or socialization with others.

Designer drugs: Drugs that are produced in an illegal laboratory and are chemically similar to a pharmaceutical drug.

Detox: An abbreviation for detoxification, it refers to ridding the body of the toxic effects of regular, excessive alcohol consumption. During detox, alcoholics often experience severe withdrawal symptoms including acute cravings for alcohol, delirium tremens, and convulsions.

Dietary supplement: A substance sold and marketed under the protection of the DSHEA. These substances are available without a prescription and are not subject to rigorous clinical testing.

Dietary Supplement Health and Education Act (DSHEA): Passed in 1994, this law allows manufacturers to sell dietary and nutritional supplements without federal regulation. According to this act, supplements can be regulated only after they are proven to be harmful to users.

Dissociative: A drug action that makes people feel cut off from themselves, their bodies, and reality.

Dissociative anesthetic: An anesthetic that produces an unresponsive state by chemically muting the ability of N-methyl-D-aspartate (NMDA) receptors in the brain to process signals.

Distillation: A heat-dependent process used to produce alcoholic beverages, such as whiskey, rum, and vodka. In this process, a fermented mash (of grains, vegetables, or fruits) is heated in a boiler, causing the alcohol to evaporate. The alcohol vapors are then collected and cooled in a condenser to produce the beverage.

Doctor shopping: A practice in which an individual continually switches physicians so that he or she can get enough of a prescription drug to feed an addiction. This practice makes it difficult for physicians to track whether the patient has already been prescribed the same drug by another physician.

Dopamine: Neurotransmitter associated with the regulation of movement, emotional response, pleasure, and pain.

Drop: A common term used to describe the taking of LSD, as in "dropping acid."

Dross: The residue remaining in the pipe after prepared opium has been smoked.

Drug Abuse Resistance Education (D.A.R.E.): A substance abuse education and prevention program.

DUI: Driving under the influence of alcohol.

Dusted: Being intoxicated on PCP.

Duster: Someone who regularly takes PCP.

Dusting: Adding PCP to another drug.

DXM (dextromethorphan): Easily synthesized dissociative psychedelic found in some cough medicines, used illicitly for its numbing and hallucinogenic properties.

E

Ecstasy: The street name for MDMA, an illegal club drug that is mildly hallucinogenic.

Edema: Water retention in the tissues that causes swelling.

Electrolyte: The salts that the body requires in its fluids to function properly. They can conduct electricity, and therefore are essential in nerve, muscle, and heart function.

Electrolyte imbalance: Improper proportions of acids, bases, salts, and fluids in the body. Electrolytes include the salts sodium, potassium, magnesium, chloride chlorine.

Empathogen: Any substance that produces feelings of sympathy, closeness, acceptance, and peace with surrounding individuals.

Empathy: A feeling on connectedness and understanding with another person or people.

Emphysema: An irreversible, smoking-related disease in which damage of the tiny air sacs (alveoli) in the lung results in air being trapped and a reduced exchange of gases. The result is shortness of breath, wheezing, coughing, and difficulty breathing.

Endocrine system: Organ system that produces hormones.

Endogenous: Produced within the body.

Endogenous opioids: Naturally occurring opioids in the body; includes three classes of neurotransmitters—the endorphins, enkephalins, and dynorphins.

Endorphins: Naturally produced chemicals in the brain that create feelings of happiness, euphoria, serenity, and fearlessness.

Enema: The injection of fluid into the rectum. Native Americans have used this method to ingest psilocybin.

Entheogen: A term from the Greek meaning "God-facilitating substance." Some scholars prefer this term to hallucinogen when applied to plants such as the peyote cactus that are used in religious practices.

Environmental tobacco smoke (ETS): Also called passive or second-hand smoke, ETS is the combination of the smoke from smoldering tobacco together with exhaled smoke and is responsible for extensive health problems in smokers and nonsmokers alike.

Ergogenic: Something that increases work output.

Ergot: A fungus that grows on grains, particularly rye, that contains lysergic acid, a chemical used to make LSD.

Esophagus: The tube in the throat that carries food to the stomach.

Ethnomycologist: A person who studies the cultural uses of mushrooms.

Ethyl alcohol: C_2H_5OH; also called grain alcohol or ethanol. This is the only type of alcohol that is safe to drink. Other alcohols like methyl alcohol and isopropyl alcohol are highly toxic and poisonous.

Euphoria: An exaggerated feeling of well being.

Exogenous: Produced by a source outside of the body.

F

Fetal alcohol syndrome: A pattern of birth defects, and learning and behavioral problems affecting individuals whose mothers consumed alcohol during pregnancy.

Flashback: The re-experiencing of a drug high without actually taking the drug. A flashback is usually limited to visual hallucinations and disturbances and can occur weeks, months, or years after taking the drug.

Flavonoids: Chemical compounds found in many herbal drugs. Flavonoids may help fight off infections and clear the body of harmful free radical molecules.

Fluntrazepam (Rohypnol): An overseas prescription sleeping aid that, in lower doses, gives users a feeling similar to alcohol intoxication; also used as a date rape drug.

Food and Drug Administration (FDA): The federal agency responsible for reviewing and regulating drugs and supplements.

Free base: The form of cocaine that can be smoked. There are three free-base forms of cocaine: coca paste made from processed coca leaves; crack (which is made with powder cocaine and sodium bicarbonate); and "free base" (which is made with powder cocaine, ammonia, and ether. This form is rarely used since crack was discovered). All free base is highly addictive.

G

Ganja: A moderately potent form of Indian cannabis, marked by a greater THC content than bhang.

GHB (gamma hydroxybutyrate): Originally sold in health food stores as a growth hormone, a liquid nervous depressant touted for its ecstasy-like qualities. Banned by the FDA in 1990, the respiratory depression it can cause makes it among the most dangerous club drugs in circulation.

Glaucoma: A disease of the eye that can lead to blindness.

H

Half-life: The amount of time it takes for one half of a substance to be broken down or excreted. Nicotine has a short half-life; therefore, frequent tobacco intake is required to maintain desired nicotine levels in the blood.

Hallucination: The experience of seeing, feeling, hearing, smelling, or tasting something that is not really there.

Hallucinogens: A group of drugs that induces sensory distortions and hallucinations.

Hashish: Concentrated cannabis resin, similar to charas.

Hashish oil: The most potent form of cannabis resin, extracted by chemical solvent.

HDL: The type of cholesterol called high-density lipoprotein, which transfers excess cholesterol to the liver for removal.

Hemp: Cannabis plants that are grown for fiber; in nineteenth-century medicine, also referred to cannabis used medicinally.

Herb: Any plant used as a medicine, seasoning, or food: mint, thyme, basil, St. John's wort, and sage are herbs.

Hit: A common term for a dose of LSD.

Hormone: Substance secreted by a gland into the bloodstream and carried to another part of the body, where it causes a physiological change.

HPPD: Short for "hallucinogen persisting perception disorder," which is the medical term for flashbacks.

Huffing: Breathing mind-altering fumes from a cloth that has been soaked in a volatile substance and stuffed into the mouth.

Hypersensitivity: An exaggerated response to a given stimulus.

Hypertension: Long-term elevation of blood pressure; defined by two readings, systolic and diastolic blood pressure, respectively, that are above the normal of 140 and 90 mm Hg. Hypertension risks damage to the blood vessels, and complications, including stroke, heart attack, and kidney failure.

Hypnotic: A drug that induces sleep by depressing the central nervous system.

Hypoxia: A condition in which too little oxygen reaches body tissues.

I

Impotence: The inability to achieve or maintain an erection.

Inborn error of metabolism: An inherited genetic defect present from birth that causes a deficiency in the body's essential enzymes and impairs metabolism.

Inhalants: Legal household, industrial, medical, and office products that are volatile (vaporize or evaporate easily), producing chemical vapors. Abusers inhale concentrated amounts of these vapors, by various means, to alter their consciousness.

Intravenous drug: Any drug that is injected via a needle into the bloodstream.

Intubation: Putting a plastic tube into the lungs through the nose and throat to allow artificial respiration in a person unable to breathe independently.

J

Jet lag: Condition caused by traveling over several time zones in a short period of time.

K

Ketamine: An anesthetic abused for its mind-altering effects that is popular as an illicit club drug. It is sometimes used to facilitate sexual assault, or date rape.

L

LAAM (levo-alpha-acetylmethadol): Like methadone, LAAM is a synthetic opiate used to treat heroin addiction, blunting withdrawal for up to 72 hours.

LDL: The predominant type of blood cholesterol called low-density lipoprotein, which transports cholesterol throughout the body.

Lean body mass: The portion of the body such as muscle and organs that is devoid of fat and bone.

Lipids: A group of organic compounds consisting of fats and other substances.

LSD (d-lysergic acid diethylamide): A powerful chemical compound renowned for its hallucinogenic properties.

Lysergic acid: A naturally occurring chemical that is used to make LSD.

M

Marijuana: The dried leaves and flowers of female *Cannabis sativa* plants.

Master Settlement Agreement (MSA): A 1998 agreement between the States' Attorneys General and the tobacco industry. Tobacco companies agreed to several changes in advertising and promotion in exchange for protection from further lawsuits. Companies also agreed to pay billions of dollars over 25 years to reimburse states for the cost of treating smoking-related illnesses.

MDMA (3,4-methylenedioxymethamphetamine): Known as ecstasy, E and X, MDMA is the most popular of the "club drugs," a synthetic stimulant with mild hallucinogenic properties.

Medulla: The lower portion of the brain stem.

Mescaline: A hallucinatory drug that is the chief active agent found in mescal buttons of the peyote plant.

Metabolism: The body's ability to break down and process substances taken into the body.

Methadone (methadone hydrochloride): Like LAAM, a synthetic opiate used to treat heroin addiction. Methadone is non-intoxicating and blunts symptoms of withdrawal.

Methamphetamine (crystal): An amine derivative of amphetamine, used in the form of its crystalline hydrochloride as a central nervous system stimulant. It is often illicitly produced in secret labs.

Methylphenidate (Ritalin): A stimulant drug choice for the treatment of attention deficit hyperactivity disorder (ADHD).

Morphine: The primary alkaloid chemical in opium, used as a drug to treat severe acute and chronic pain.

N

Naloxone: A short-acting narcotic antagonist that binds to opiate receptors and blocks them. Used to treat opiate overdose.

Naltrexone: A long-lasting narcotic antagonist that blocks opiate receptors. Used to treat heroin addiction.

Narcolepsy: A rare, chronic sleep disorder characterized by constant daytime fatigue and sudden attacks of sleep.

Narcotic: A natural or synthetic drug that has properties similar to opium or opium derivatives.

Neurons: Nerve cells found throughout the central nervous system. Neurons release neurotransmitters.

Neuropathic: Relating to a disease of the nerves.

Neurotransmitter: A substance released by one nerve cell that activates or inhibits a neighboring nerve cell.

Nicotine: An alkaloid derived from the tobacco plant that is responsible for smoking's addictive effects; it is toxic at high doses but can be effective as a medicine at lower doses.

Nitric oxide: NO; a potentially toxic gas found both in the atmosphere and in the body in small amounts. In the body, nitric oxide helps to move oxygen to the tissues and transmit nerve impulses.

Nitroglycerine: A heavy, oily, explosive liquid used medicinally in tiny amounts to dilate blood vessels in treating angina pectoris.

NMDA receptor antagonist: A class of anesthetics that block particular neurotransmitters located in the brain's cerebral cortex and hippocampus—regions responsible for memory, language, and motor control.

Noradrenaline: Chemical produced by the nervous system.

O

Opiate: A drug originating in the opium poppy, such as codeine and morphine.

Opioid: A drug, hormone, or other chemical substance having sedative or narcotic effects similar to those containing opium or its derivatives; a natural brain opiate.

Opioid receptors: A class of proteins on the surface of cells that bind with opioids, either endogenous or drugs. An opioid either activates (agonist) or prevents activation by another opioid (antagonist).

Opiophobia: The fear of patients becoming addicted to their narcotic pain medication.

Osteoporosis: A loss in total bone density that can be the result of a chronic calcium deficiency, early menopause, certain endocrine diseases, advanced age, endocrine diseases, certain medications, or other risk factors.

Overdose: The result of ingesting too much of a substance such as a drug either in one dose or over the course of time. Symptoms of drug overdose vary with the type of drug taken, and may include severe drowsiness or unconsciousness.

P

Pancreatitis: Inflammation of the pancreas, an essential part of both the endocrine and the digestive systems. The pancreas secretes juices that aid in digestion, and a number of hormones (including insulin).

Panic attacks: Sudden, repeated, paralyzing bouts of extreme fear and anxiety.

Paranoia: The presence of delusions of a persacutory nature, involving be hunted or harmed by another person.

Patent medicines: Medical remedies of doubtful value commonly sold in the 1800s and 1900s. Many patent medicines were herb-based, although they were often laced with alcohol, narcotics, and other drugs.

PCC (1-piperidinocyclohexanecarbonitrile): An unstable byproduct common to PCP's illicit manufacture; when smoked, PCC releases hydrogen cyanide that is inhaled by the user.

PCP (phencyclidine): Also known as angel dust, a powerful and toxic synthetic chemical developed in home laboratories.

PCP organic mental disorder: A condition similar to schizophrenia that can occur as a result of taking PCP and last for weeks, months, or even a year. It is characterized by confusion, disordered thinking, paranoia, and speech problems.

Pelvic toning exercises: Exercises that focus on tightening the muscles of the pelvic floor to relieve urinary stress incontinence. Also known as Kegel or PC muscle exercises.

Peyote: A hallucinogenic cactus, usually *L. williamsii* from which mescaline is derived.

Phobia: The irrational fear of a specific object or situation that limits normal functioning.

Physical dependence: A condition that may occur after prolonged use of an opiate, but differing from addiction because the user is dependent on the drug for pain relief, rather than emotional or psychological relief.

Placebo effect: A psychological phenomenon noted by researchers in which patients who receive a phony medication feel better and report improvements in subjective symptoms such as pain or depression.

PMA (paramethoxyamphetamine): Highly toxic hallucinogenic compound linked to sudden collapse and seizures, structurally similar to MDMA and occasionally substituted as such.

Podarea: Raised, segmented cushion-part of the peyote cactus.

Polydrug use: Use of more than one drug.

Post-traumatic stress disorder: A mental disorder that can occur in those who have experienced a life threatening-situation. PTSD is characterized by nightmares and flashbacks, among other symptoms.

Powder cocaine (cocaine hydrochloride): A psychoactive substance derived from coca leaves. Powder cocaine is either snorted into the nose or mixed with water and injected into the veins. It is addictive when snorted and more so if injected.

Precursors: A substance or compound from which another substance is synthesized, or made.

Proof: A measure of the strength of an alcoholic beverage. The proof of an alcoholic beverage is twice the amount of its alcohol content. For example, 100 proof whiskey is 50% alcohol.

Psilocybe: A genus of mushroom that produces the bitter-tasting indole alkaloid psilocybin that causes hallucinations and other side effects. Sometimes *Psilocybe* mushrooms are referred to as psilocybin mushrooms.

Psychedelic: A term given to hallucinogenic drugs, like LSD, which implies that these drugs have the ability to access as-yet untapped potential of the mind.

Psychosis: A severe mental disorder characterized by the loss of the ability to distinguish what is objectively real from what is imaginary, frequently including hallucinations.

Psychotherapeutic drugs: Drugs used to relieve the symptoms of mental illness, such as depression, anxiety, and psychosis.

Psychotherapeutics: Drugs that have an effect on brain function; often used to treat psychiatric disorders

Psychotherapy: The non-drug treatment of psychological disorders. It can be in the form of behavioral therapy (where the person is gradually exposed to their fears) or cognitive therapy (where people learn to control their unrealistic or negative thinking).

Psychotropic: A substance that affects a person's ability to distinguish reality from the imaginary.

R

Rave: An all-night dance party that includes loud, pulsing "house" music and flashing lights. Many participants take hallucinogenic and other mind-altering drugs.

Rebound: Also known as discontinuation symptoms, these occur when the benzodiazepines are withdrawn. These symptoms are an aspect of withdrawal in which the patient develops anxiety, insomnia, or other serious emotional reactions that are more intense than before treatment with the drug was begun.

Receptor: A specialized part of a nerve cell that recognizes neurotransmitters and communicates with other nerve cells.

Recreational use: The casual and infrequent use of a drug or substance, often in social situations, for its pleasurable effects.

Relapse: Term used in substance abuse treatment and recovery that refers to an addict's return to substance use following a period of abstinence or sobriety.

Respiratory depression: The slowing of a person's breathing rate. Severe respiratory depression can cause a person to go into a coma or even stop breathing.

Reuptake: The process by which a nerve cell reabsorbs the chemical it had used to send a message to another nerve cell.

Rohypnol (fluntrazepam): An overseas prescription sleeping aid that, in lower doses, gives users a feeling similar to alcohol intoxication; also used as a date rape drug.

Rush: A surge of pleasure that rapidly follows administration of a drug.

S

Schizophrenia: A medical condition that falls under the category of psychotic disorders. People with schizophrenia suffer from a variety of symptoms, including confusion, disordered thinking, paranoia, hallucinations, emotional numbness, and speech problems.

Seasonal affective disorder (SAD): Type of depression that occurs during the fall and winter months.

Sedative: A drug that decreases CNS activity; a calming agent.

Seizures (epileptic fits): Bursts of abnormal electrical activity in the brain causing episodic symptoms, including coma or reduced level of awareness, flailing movements of arms and legs, and loss of control of bowels and bladder. Prolonged, untreated seizures may cause brain damage or even death.

Serotonin: An important neurotransmitter in the brain that regulates mood, appetite, sensory perception, and other central nervous system functions.

Shaman: A religious leader of a tribe who performs rituals of magic, divination, and healing, and acts as an intermediary between ordinary reality and the spirit world; a medicine man.

Smoker's cough: Recurring cough experienced by smokers because damaged tiny hair-like structures (cilia) in airways cannot move mucus and debris up and out efficiently.

Sniffing or snorting: Inhaling intoxicating vapors, through the nose, from a volatile substance such as an anesthetic gas, industrial or household solvent, art supply, or aerosol propellant.

Snuff: A preparation of DMT-containing plants, which is smoked; also traditionally called cohoba, parica, and yopo.

Speedball: Also called "dynamite" or "whiz-bang," a speedball is a combination of cocaine or methampetamine (stimulants) and heroin (a depressant). This combination increases the chances of serious adverse reactions and can be more toxic than either drug alone.

Stress: A disturbance in the body's physiological equibrium, resulting from psychological or physical forces on a person.

Styptic: The contraction of a blood vessel or the containment of a hemorrhage.

Sudden sniffing death (SSD) syndrome: Fatal cardiac arrest that results, under certain conditions, after someone deeply inhales a volatile chemical for its intoxicating effects. Death occurs within minutes.

Sympathomimetic: A medication similar to amphetamine, but is less powerful and has less potential for addiction than amphetamine.

Synapse: The gap between communicating nerve cells.

Synergy: The effect from a combination of drugs which is greater than the addition of its individual effects.

Synesthesia: A chemical "cross-wiring" of the brain circuits often due to the use of hallucinogens that results in colors being felt or heard and sound being tasted or seen.

Synthetic opioid: An opioid drug produced from chemicals that are created in a laboratory.

T

Talk down: The process in which someone helps a person on drugs reconnect with reality by talking in soothing tones and helping distinguish reality from fantasy.

Tar/TPM: Total particulate matter. An all-purpose term for particle-phase constituents of tobacco smoke, many of which are carcinogenic (cancer-causing) or otherwise toxic.

Testosterone: A hormone produced in higher amounts in males that is responsible for male characteristics such as muscle-building, maintaining sexual organs, and causing hair growth and a deepening voice during puberty.

Tetrahydrocannabinols (THC): A group of cannabinoid compounds thought to cause most of the psychoactive reactions to marijuana use.

Thalamus: The central area of the brain below the cerebral lobes that relays messages from the spine to the forebrain.

Tic: A repetitive, involuntary spasm that increases in severity when it is purposefully surpressed. Tics may be motor (such as muscle contractions or eye blinking) or vocal.

Tincture: An extract of an herb made by soaking it in glycerine, alcohol, or vinegar for several weeks, then straining the liquid.

Tolerance: A condition in which higher and higher doses of a drug are needed to produce the original effect or high experienced.

Tourette's syndrome: A chronic disorder involving multiple motor and/or vocal tics that cause distress or significant impairment in social, occupational, or other important areas of functioning.

Trichomes: Tuft of hairs in the center of the peyote cactus.

Trip: A common term for a drug experience.

Tryptophan: An amino acid that is widely distributed in proteins.

2C-B (Nexus): A synthetic hallucinogenic gaining wider illicit use as a stronger but shorter-lasting alternative to MDMA.

U

U.S. Pharmacopeia (USP): A non-profit organization that provides standards for prescription and over-the-counter drugs, nutritional and dietary supplements, and health care products. USP publishes its standards in the *United States Pharmacopeia and the National Formulary (USP-NF)*, which are officially recognized by the U.S. Food and Drug Administration (FDA). USP also has a dietary supplement verification program (DSVP).

Urinary incontinence: Inability to retain urine in the bladder until the person chooses to empty it.

W

Withdrawal: A group of symptoms that may occur from suddenly stopping the use of a substance such as alcohol or other drugs after chronic or prolonged ingestion.

CONTROLLED SUBSTANCES ACT APPENDIX

In an effort to enact an organized drug regulatory strategy, the Controlled Substances Act, Title II of the Comprehensive Drug Abuse Prevention and Control Act, was enacted by the U.S. Congress in 1970. This act replaced the Harrison Narcotic Act of 1914 and has been amended considerably since its inception. Both the legal and illicit distribution and manufacture of narcotics, stimulants, depressants, hallucinogens, and anabolic steroids are regulated by the CSA. As proscribed by the CSA, these substances are categorized into five schedules according to their potential for abuse and their medicinal value. As in other federal regulations, the act allows for changes in which substances can be added, decontrolled, removed, or transferred.

The process by which a drug is scheduled lies in the hands of the Drug Enforcement Administration, the Department of Health and Human Services, and/or by petition from an interested party that would be subsequently reviewed by the DEA. As a part of the review, the DEA requests health information from the HHS, which itself collects information from the Food and Drug Administration, the National Institute on Drug Abuse, and often, the scientific community at large in order to report a final recommendation to the DEA. The FDA is compelled to refer the drug to DEA for scheduling should it discover that the drug has abuse potential. The FDA offers a recommendation to the DEA, and the DEA invariably accepts the recommendation and schedules the drug accordingly.

If the FDA recommends not to schedule a drug, then the DEA is powerless to schedule the drug on its own. This occurred in the case of the synthetic opioid tramadol (Ultram), which has a very low abuse potential. The administrator of the DEA then compiles all available data in addition to the HHS recommendation and makes a final decision as to the control of the substance and its appropriate schedule. Power lies with the administrator to emergency schedule drugs that are analogs of currently controlled substances until Congress can pass a related amendment. Once scheduled, the handling of such controlled substances is closely supervised by the DEA through a manufacturer, and distributor/practitioner registration process.

The scheduled listings are updated and reviewed annually and are currently described by the following parameters: actual or relative potential for abuse; scientific evidence of its pharmacological effect, if known; state of current scientific knowledge regarding the drug or other substance; history and current pattern of abuse; scope, duration, and significance of abuse; risk to the public health; psychic or physiological dependence liability; and whether or not the substance is an immediate precursor of a substance already controlled under this subchapter.

Drugs included in Schedule I are those deemed to have a significant potential for abuse with psychological or physical dependence liability. These drugs have no recognized medical use and cannot be prescribed by a physician despite what state laws allow. Federal law always supersedes state laws. This comes into play in states that in the past several years have enacted medical marijuana statutes. According to federal law, there is no such thing as medical marijuana, and any doctor who prescribes it commits a felony under the CSA. Physicians and scientists are required to receive special permission from the FDA or DEA in order to conduct or participate in research protocols involving Schedule I substances. One such study is that involving marijuana for the treatment of wasting syndrome in AIDS patients. Some examples of Schedule I drugs are heroin, marijuana, LSD, peyote,

Controlled Substances Act Appendix

Federal Drug Trafficking Penalties*

Drug/Schedule	Quantity	Penalties	Quantity	Penalties
Cocaine (Schedule I)	500–4999 gms	**First Offense:** Not less than 5 years, and not more than 40 yrs. If death or serious injury, not less than 20 or more than life. Fine of not more than $2 million if an individual, $5 million if not an individual. **Second Offense:** Not less than 10 yrs, and not more than life. If death or serious injury, life imprisonment. Fine of not more than $4 million if an individual, $10 million if not an individual.	5 kgs or more	**First Offense:** Not less than 10 years and not more than life. If death or serious injury, not less than 20 or more than life. Fine of not more than $4 million if an individual, $10 million if not an individual. **Second Offense:** Not less than 20 yrs, and not more than life. If death or serious injury, life imprisonment. Fine of not more than $8 million if an individual, $20 million if not an individual. **2 or More Prior Offenses:** Life imprisonment
Cocaine Base (Schedule I)	5–49 gms mixture		50 gms or more mixture	
Fentanyl (Schedule I)	40–399 gms mixture		400 gms or more mixture	
Fentanyl Analogue (Schedule I)	10–99 gms mixture		100 gms or more mixture	
Heroin (Schedule I)	100–999 gms mixture		1 kg or more mixture	
LSD (Schedule I)	1–9 gms mixture		10 gms or more mixture	
Methamphetamine (Schedule II)	5–49 gms pure or 50–499 gms mixture		50 gms or more pure or 500 gms or more mixture	
PCP (Schedule I)	10–99 gms pure or 100–999 gms mixture		100 gm or more pure or 1kg or more mixture	

Penalties		
Other Schedule I and II drugs	Any amount	**First Offense:** Not more than 20 yrs. If death or serious injury, not less than 20 yrs, or more than life. Fine $1 million if an individual, $5 million if not an individual. **Second Offense:** Not more than 30 yrs. If death or serious injury, not less than life. Fine $2 million if an individual, $10 million if not an individual.
Flunitrazepam (Schedule IV)	1 gms	
Other Schedule III drugs	Any amount	**First Offense:** Not more than 5 years. Fine not more than $250,000 if an individual, $1 million if not an individual. **Second Offense:** Not more than 10 yrs. Fine not more than $500,000 if an individual, $2 million if not an individual.
Flunitrazepam (Schedule IV)	30 or more mgs	
All other Schedule IV drugs	Any amount	**First Offense:** Not more than 3 years. Fine not more than $250,000 if an individual, $1 million if not an individual. **Second Offense:** Not more than 6 yrs. Fine not more than $500,000 if an individual, $2 million if not an individual.
Flunitrazepam (Schedule IV)	Less than 30 mgs	
All Schedule V drugs	Any amount	**First Offense:** Not more than 1 yr. Fine not more than $100,000 if an individual, $250,000 if not an individual. **Second Offense:** Not more than 2 yrs. Fine not more than $200,000 if an individual, $500,000 if not an individual.

*Does not include marijuana, hashish, or hash oil
SOURCE Drug Enforcement Agency. <www.dea.gov>

mescaline, psilocybin, tetrahydrocannabinols, ketobemidone, levomoramide, racemoramide, benrylmorphine, dihydromorphine, nicocodeine, and nicomorphine.

Schedule II drugs are determined to have a high potential for abuse with psychological or physical dependence liability. In this category, the drug or other substance has a currently accepted medical use as disease treatment in the United States or a currently accepted medical use with severe restrictions. This category contains most of the opioid analgesics used in the treatment of pain and is regulated through rules such as single-fill prescriptions. This is the most tightly regulated category of drugs approved for medical use. Some examples of Schedule II controlled narcotic substances are opium, morphine, hydromorphone (Dilaudid), methadone (Dolophine), pantopon, meperidine (Demerol), cocaine, oxycodone (Percodan), Anileridine (Leritine), and oxymorphone (Numorphan). Also in Schedule II are amphetamine (Benzedrine, Dexedrine), methamphetamine (Desoxyn), phenmetrazine (Preludin), methylphenidate (Ritalin), amobarbital, pentobarbital, secobarbital, methaqualone, etorphine hydrochloride, diphenoxylate, and phencyclidine.

Substances categorized as Schedule III have a less significant abuse potential than those in Schedules I and II; however, abuse of these drugs may lead to moderate or low physical dependence or high psychological dependence. These substances include compounds containing limited quantities of certain narcotic drugs, and non-narcotic drugs such as derivatives of barbituric acid except those that are listed in another schedule, glutethimide (Doriden), methyprylon (Nodular), chlorhexadol, sulfondiethyl-methane, sulfomethane, nalorphine, benzphetamine, chlorphentermine, clortermine, mazindol, phendimetrazine, and paregoric. Other drugs in this category include codeine and hydrocodone (Vicodin).

The drugs in Schedule IV have a relatively low abuse potential and risk for psychological or physical dependence relative to those listed in Schedule III and include such drugs as barbital, phenobarbital, methylphenobarbital, chloral betaine (Beta Chlor), chloral hydrate, ethchlorvynol (Placidyl), ethinamate (Valmid), meprobamate (Equanil, Miltown), paraldehyde, methohexital, fenfluramine, diethyipropion, phentermine, chlordiazepoxide (Librium), diazepam (Valium), oxazepam (Serax), clorazepate (Tranxene), flurazepam (Dalmane), clonazepam (Clonopin), prazepam (Verstran), lorazepam (Ativan), mebutamate, and dextropropoxyphene (Darvon).

Drugs in Schedule V are generally reserved for antitussive and antidiarrheal purposes with the least potential for abuse of the scheduled substances.

Penalties for possession, manufacture, and distribution vary widely under the CSA (see federal trafficking penalty chart). Penalties for violations involving Schedule I and II drugs naturally are more severe than other classifications. At the U.S. Attorney's (federal prosecutor) discretion, lesser federal charges of simple possession can be brought in extenuating circumstances. Beginning in July 2000, federal financial aid applications require that students certify they have not been convicted of any drug-related offense to qualify for support. If convicted, the student loses eligibility for federal financial aid for a minimum of one year. The evolution of the CSA is one that involves many informed parties and is subject to dynamic growth and change as we learn more about the potential dangers and benefits of emerging and existing substances.

Ronald J. Brogan
New York City Bureau Chief, D.A.R.E America

Federal Marijuana Trafficking Penalties

Drug	Quantity	1st Offense	2nd Offense
Marijuana	1,000 kg or more mixture; or 1,000 or more plants	Not less than 10 years, not more than life. If death or serious injury, not less than 20 years, not more than life. Fine not more than $4 million if an individual, $10 million if other than an individual	Not less than 20 years, not more than life. If death or serious injury, mandatory life. Fine not more than $8 million if an individual, $20 million if other than an individual
Marijuana	100 kg to 999 kg mixture; or 100 to 999 plants	Not less than 5 years, not more than 40 years. If death or serious injury, not less than 20 years, not more than life. Fine not more than $2 million if an individual, $5 million if other than an individual	Not less than 10 years, not more than life. If death or serious injury, mandatory life. Fine not more than $4 million if an individual, $10 million if other than an individual
Marijuana	10 kg or more hashish; 50 to 99 kg mixture; 1 kg or more hashish oil; 50 to 99 plants	Not more than 20 years. If death or serious injury, not less than 20 years, not more than life. Fine $1 million if an individual, $5 million if other than an individual	Not more than 30 years. If death or serious injury, mandatory life. Fine $2 million if an individual, $10 million if other than an individual
Marijuana	1 to 49 plants; less than 50 kg mixture	Not more than 5 years. Fine not more than $250,000, $1 million if other than an individual	Not more than 10 years. Fine not more than $500,000, $2 million if other than an individual
Hashish	10 kg or less		
Hashish Oil	1 kg or less		

SOURCE: Drug Enforcement Agency. <www.dea.gov>

VARIANT NAME INDEX

Barr (codeine cough syrup) *see* **Codeine**
Base *see* **Cocaine**
BD *see* **GBL**
BDMPEA *see* **2C-B**
Bean *see* **Ecstasy**
Beans *see* **Dextroamphetamine**
Beedies *see* **Nicotine**
Belladonna *see* **PCP (phencyclidine)**
Bendroflumethiazide *see* **Diuretics**
Bennies *see* **Dextroamphetamine**
Bens *see* **Amphetamines**
Benylin Adult Formula Cough Syrup *see* **Dextro-methorphan**
Benylin Expectorant *see* **Dextromethorphan**
Benylin Pediatric Cough Suppressant *see* **Dextromethorphan**
Benz *see* **Amphetamines**
Benzedrine *see* **Amphetamines**
Benzos *see* **Benzodiazepine**
Benzphetamine *see* **Diet pills**
Benzthiazide *see* **Diuretics**
Benzylpiperazine *see* **Benzylpiperazine/Trifluoro-methylphenylpiperazine**
Bernice *see* **Cocaine**
Bhang *see* **Marijuana**
Bidis *see* **Nicotine**
Big chief *see* **Mescaline**
Big d *see* **Hydromorphone**
Big O *see* **Opium**
Black *see* **Opium**
Black and white *see* **Amphetamines**
Black beauties *see* **Dextroamphetamine**
Black bombers *see* **Amphetamines**
Black Cadillacs *see* **Amphetamines**
Black dex *see* **Amphetamines**
Black mollies *see* **Amphetamines**
Black pill *see* **Opium**
Black stuff *see* **Opium**
Black tar *see* **Heroin**
Blackbirds *see* **Amphetamines**
Blacks *see* **Amphetamines**
Blanche *see* **Marijuana**
Blind squid *see* **Ketamine**
BLO *see* **GBL**
Block *see* **Opium**
Block busters *see* **Barbiturates**
Blotter *see* **LSD (lysergic acid diethylamide)**
Blow *see* **Cocaine; GBL**
Blud madman *see* **PCP (phencyclidine)**
Blue boys *see* **Amphetamines**
Blue devils *see* **Barbiturates**
Blue heavens *see* **Barbiturates**
Blue mollies *see* **Amphetamines**
Blue moon *see* **GBL**
Blue nitro *see* **GBL; GHB**
Blue nitro vitality *see* **GBL**
Blues *see* **Barbiturates**
Boat *see* **PCP (phencyclidine)**
Body bag *see* **Heroin**

Bolt *see* **Inhalants**
Bontril *see* **Diet pills**
Boo *see* **Marijuana**
Boom *see* **Marijuana**
Boomers *see* **LSD (lysergic acid diethylamide); Psilocybin**
Booze *see* **Alcohol**
Boppers *see* **Inhalants**
Botanicals *see* **Herbal drugs**
Boy *see* **Heroin**
Brain pills *see* **Amphetamines**
Brain ticklers *see* **Amphetamines**
Brevital *see* **Barbiturates**
Bromo *see* **2C-B**
Brownies *see* **Amphetamines**
Browns *see* **Amphetamines**
Bubalbital *see* **Barbiturates**
Bullet *see* **Inhalants**
Bullet bolt *see* **Inhalants**
Bumblebees *see* **Amphetamines**
Bumetanide *see* **Diuretics**
Bupropion *see* **Antidepressants**
Bush *see* **Marijuana**
Bushman's tea *see* **Catha edulis**
Businessman's LSD *see* **Dimethyltryptamine (DMT)**
Businessman's special *see* **Dimethyltryptamine (DMT)**
Businessman's trip *see* **Dimethyltryptamine (DMT)**
Buspirone *see* **Tranquilizers**
Busy bee *see* **PCP (phencyclidine)**
Butabarbital *see* **Barbiturates**
Butane *see* **Inhalants**
Butisol *see* **Barbiturates**
Butt naked *see* **PCP (phencyclidine)**
Buttons *see* **Mescaline; Methaqualone**
Butyrolactone gamma *see* **GBL**
Buzz bomb *see* **Inhalants**
BZP *see* **Benzylpiperazine/Trifluoromethylphenyl-piperazine**

C

"C" *see* **Cocaine**
Cactus buttons *see* **Mescaline**
Cactus head *see* **Mescaline**
Cadillac *see* **PCP (phencyclidine)**
Cap *see* **Heroin**
Caps *see* **Psilocybin**
Cat valium *see* **Ketamine**
Cat woman *see* **Heroin**
Celexa *see* **Antidepressants**
Centrax *see* **Benzodiazepine**
Chafta *see* **Catha edulis**
Chalk *see* **Methamphetamine**
Chandoo/chandu *see* **Opium**
Charas *see* **Marijuana**
Chat *see* **Catha edulis**
Cheap cocaine *see* **PCP (phencyclidine)**
Cheer *see* **LSD (lysergic acid diethylamide)**
Cheracol-D *see* **Dextromethorphan**

Cherry meth *see GHB*
Chew *see Nicotine*
Chewing tobacco *see Nicotine*
Chicken powder *see Amphetamines*
Chicken yellow *see PMA and PMMA*
Chief *see Mescaline*
China girl *see Fentanyl*
China town *see Fentanyl*
China white *see Fentanyl; Heroin*
Chinese molasses *see Opium*
Chinese tobacco *see Opium*
Chiva *see Heroin*
Chloral hydrate *see Tranquilizers*
Chlorazepate *see Benzodiazepine*
Chlordiazepoxide *see Benzodiazepine*
Chlorofluorocarbons *see Inhalants*
Chloroform *see Inhalants*
Chlorothiazide *see Diuretics*
Chlorpromazine *see Tranquilizers*
Chlorprothixene *see Tranquilizers*
Chlorthalidone *see Diuretics*
Christmas trees *see Barbiturates*
Chronic *see Marijuana*
Ciat *see Catha edulis*
Cid *see LSD (lysergic acid diethylamide)*
Cigarettes *see Nicotine*
Cigars *see Nicotine*
Circles *see Rohypnol*
Citalopram *see Antidepressants*
Clarity *see Ecstasy*
Cliffhanger *see PCP (phencyclidine)*
Climax *see Inhalants*
Clomipramine Anafranil *see Antidepressants*
Clonazepam *see Benzodiazepine*
Clorazepate *see Benzodiazepine*
Clove cigarettes *see Nicotine*
Clozapine *see Tranquilizers*
Clozaril *see Tranquilizers*
Co-pilot *see Amphetamines*
Coasts-to-coasts *see Amphetamines*
Codeine phosphate *see Codeine*
Codeine sulfate *see Codeine*
Coke *see Cocaine*
Columbo *see PCP (phencyclidine)*
Concerta *see Methylphenidate*
Coties *see Codeine*
Cough syrup *see Codeine*
Cough-X *see Dextromethorphan*
Cozmo's *see PCP (phencyclidine)*
Crack cocaine *see Cocaine*
Crafta *see Catha edulis*
Crank *see Methamphetamine*
Crazy coke *see PCP (phencyclidine)*
Crazy Eddie *see PCP (phencyclidine)*
Crazy edge *see PCP (phencyclidine)*
Creatine monohydrate *see Creatine*
Creatine phosphate *see Creatine*
Creeper *see Heroin*
Creo-Terpin *see Dextromethorphan*

Crisscross *see Amphetamines*
Cristal *see PCP (phencyclidine)*
Cross tops *see Amphetamines*
Crystal *see PCP (phencyclidine)*
Cubes *see Psilocybin*
Cycline *see PCP (phencyclidine)*
Cyclones *see PCP (phencyclidine)*
Cystal T *see PCP (phencyclidine)*

D

D's *see Hydromorphone*
D-amphetamine *see Dextroamphetamine*
D-ball *see Steroids*
D-bol *see Steroids*
Dagga *see Marijuana*
Dalmane *see Benzodiazepine*
Dance fever *see Fentanyl*
Date rape *see Benzodiazepine*
Daxolin *see Tranquilizers*
Death *see PMA and PMMA*
Deca *see Steroids*
Deca-D *see Steroids*
Delantz *see Hydromorphone*
Delats *see Hydromorphone*
Delaud *see Hydromorphone*
Delsym Cough Formula *see Dextromethorphan*
Demerol *see Meperidine*
Depo-T *see Steroids*
Depo-Testosterone *see Steroids*
Desert tea *see Ephedra*
Desipramine *see Antidepressants*
Desoxybufotenine *see Dimethyltryptamine (DMT)*
Desyrel *see Antidepressants*
DET *see Dimethyltryptamine (DMT)*
Detroit pink *see PCP (phencyclidine)*
Devil's dandruff *see Cocaine*
Devil's dust *see PCP (phencyclidine)*
Dex *see Dextromethorphan*
Dexedrine *see Dextroamphetamine*
Dexfenluramine *see Diet pills*
Dexies *see Dextroamphetamine*
Dextroamphetamine sulfate *see Dextroamphetamine*
Diabe-TUSS DM Syrup *see Dextromethorphan*
Diacetylmorphine *see Heroin*
Diamonds *see Amphetamines*
Dianabol *see Steroids*
Diazepam *see Benzodiazepine*
Dichlorphenamide *see Diuretics*
Didrex *see Diet pills*
Diesel *see Heroin*
Dietary supplements *see Herbal drugs*
Diethylpropion *see Diet pills*
Dihydro-2(3H)-furanone *see GBL*
Dilaudid *see Hydromorphone*
Dilaudid-Hp *see Hydromorphone*
Dillies *see Hydromorphone*
Dipper *see PCP (phencyclidine)*
Disco biscuits *see Ecstasy; Methaqualone*

Discorama *see* **Inhalants**
Divinorin A *see* **Salvia divinorum**
Djimma *see* **Catha edulis**
DMT *see* **Dimethyltryptamine**
Do it Jack *see* **PCP (phencyclidine)**
Dollies *see* **Methadone**
Dolophine *see* **Methadone**
Dominoes *see* **Amphetamines**
Dope *see* **Heroin; Marijuana**
Dopium *see* **Opium**
Doral *see* **Benzodiazepine**
Doriden *see* **Tranquilizers**
Dors and fours *see* **Codeine**
Dorzolamide *see* **Diuretics**
Doses *see* **LSD (lysergic acid diethylamide)**
Dot *see* **LSD (lysergic acid diethylamide)**
Double cross *see* **Amphetamines**
Dover's deck *see* **Opium**
Dover's powder *see* **Opium**
Down (codeine cough syrup) *see* **Codeine**
Downers *see* **Barbiturates; Benzodiazepine**
Doxepin *see* **Antidepressants**
Dragon *see* **Heroin**
Dragon fire *see* **Heroin**
Dream *see* **Cocaine**
Dream gun *see* **Opium**
Dream stick *see* **Opium**
Dreams *see* **Opium**
Drink *see* **PCP (phencyclidine)**
Drivers *see* **Amphetamines**
Drug store heroin *see* **Hydromorphone**
Dummy dust *see* **PCP (phencyclidine)**
Dummy mist *see* **PCP (phencyclidine)**
Duragesic *see* **Fentanyl**
Duramorph *see* **Morphine**
Duratuss DM *see* **Dextromethorphan**
Dust *see* **Cocaine; PCP (phencyclidine)**
Dust of angels *see* **PCP (phencyclidine)**
Dusted parsley *see* **PCP (phencyclidine)**
DXM *see* **Dextromethorphan**

E

E *see* **Ecstasy**
Easing powder *see* **Opium**
Easy lay *see* **GHB**
Echinacea *see* **Herbal drugs**
Echinacea purpurea see **Herbal drugs**
Effexor *see* **Antidepressants**
Elavil *see* **Antidepressants**
Elephant *see* **PCP (phencyclidine)**
Elephant tranquilizer *see* **PCP (phencyclidine)**
Embalming fluid *see* **PCP (phencyclidine)**
Endocet *see* **Oxycodone**
Endocodone *see* **Oxycodone**
Endodan *see* **Oxycodone**
Energizer *see* **PCP (phencyclidine)**
Energy drink *see* **GHB**
Ephedrine *see* **Ephedra**

Ephedrine alkaloids *see* **Ephedra**
Epling *see* **Salvia divinorum**
Equanil *see* **Tranquilizers**
Ergogenic aid *see* **Creatine**
Ergogenic drugs *see* **Steroids**
Erox *see* **2C-B**
Erth *see* **PCP (phencyclidine)**
Estazolam *see* **Benzodiazepine**
Ethacrynic acid *see* **Diuretics**
Ethanol *see* **Alcohol**
Ethchlorvynol *see* **Tranquilizers**
Ether *see* **Inhalants**
Ethyl alcohol *see* **Alcohol**
European ephedra *see* **Ephedra**
Everclear *see* **GHB**
Eye openers *see* **Amphetamines**

F

Fake STP *see* **PCP (phencyclidine)**
Fastin *see* **Diet pills**
Fenesin DM *see* **Dextromethorphan**
Fenfluramine *see* **Diet pills**
Fi-do-nie *see* **Opium**
Fioricet *see* **Barbiturates**
Firewater *see* **GBL; GHB**
5-dimethoxyphenethylamine *see* **2C-B**
5-methoxy-N-acetyltryptamine *see* **Melatonin**
Fives *see* **Amphetamines**
Fizzies *see* **Methadone**
Flakes *see* **Cocaine; PCP (phencyclidine)**
Florinal *see* **Barbiturates**
Flower of paradise *see* **Catha edulis**
Flumethiazide *see* **Diuretics**
Flunitrazepam *see* **Rohypnol**
Fluoxetine Prozac *see* **Antidepressants**
Fluphenazine *see* **Tranquilizers**
Flurazepam *see* **Benzodiazepine**
Footballs *see* **Amphetamines**
Forget-me pill *see* **Rohypnol**
45-minute psychosis *see* **Dimethyltryptamine (DMT)**
Forwards *see* **Amphetamines**
4 butanediol *see* **GBL**
4-butanolide *see* **GBL**
4-diazacyclohexane dihydrochloride *see* **Benzyl-piperazine/Trifluoromethylphenylpiperazine**
4-hydroxy butyrate *see* **GHB**
Four-methoxyamphetamine (4-MA) *see* **PMA and PMMA**
4-Methylenedioxymethamphetamine *see* **Ecstasy**
French blues *see* **Amphetamines**
Fresh *see* **PCP (phencyclidine)**
Friend *see* **Fentanyl**
Fungus *see* **Psilocybin**
Furosemide *see* **Diuretics**

G

G *see* **GHB**

G-juice *see GHB*
G3 *see GBL*
Gamma butyrolactone *see GBL*
Gamma G *see GBL*
Gamma hydrate *see GHB*
Gamma hydroxybutyric acid *see GHB*
Gamma-hydroxybutyrate *see GHB*
Gamma-hydroxybutyrate sodium *see GHB*
Gamma-oh *see GHB*
Gangster *see Marijuana*
Ganja *see Marijuana*
Gar-Pure *see Herbal drugs*
Garlic *see Herbal drugs*
Garlix *see Herbal drugs*
Gear *see Steroids*
Gee *see Opium*
Genex *see GBL*
Genx *see GBL*
Georgia home boy *see GHB*
GG-DM SR *see Dextromethorphan*
GH revitalizer *see GBL*
GH-gold *see GBL*
GHG *see GBL*
Ginkgo biloba see Herbal drugs
Ginseng *see Herbal drugs*
Glutethimide *see Tranquilizers*
Glycerin *see Diuretics*
Glycotuss-DM *see Dextromethorphan*
Go *see Amphetamines*
Go pills *see Dextroamphetamine*
Goatweed *see Herbal drugs*
God's medicine *see Opium*
Gondola *see Opium*
Good *see PCP (phencyclidine)*
Goodfellas *see Fentanyl*
Goof balls *see Barbiturates; Benzodiazepine*
Goon *see PCP (phencyclidine)*
Goon dust *see PCP (phencyclidine)*
Goop *see GHB*
Goric *see Opium*
Gorilla biscuits *see PCP (phencyclidine)*
Gorilla tab *see PCP (phencyclidine)*
Grain alcohol *see Alcohol*
Grass *see Marijuana*
Great bear *see Fentanyl*
Great tobacco *see Opium*
Green *see Ketamine*
Green leaves *see PCP (phencyclidine)*
Green tea *see PCP (phencyclidine)*
Greenies *see Amphetamines*
Greens *see PCP (phencyclidine)*
Grievous bodily harm *see GHB*
Growth hormone booster *see GHB*
Guaibid DM *see Dextromethorphan*
Guaifenex DM *see Dextromethorphan*
Guerilla *see PCP (phencyclidine)*
Gum *see Opium*
Guma *see Opium*

H

H *see Heroin*
Halazepam *see Benzodiazepine*
Halcion *see Benzodiazepine*
Haldol *see Tranquilizers*
Haloperidol *see Tranquilizers*
Halothane *see Inhalants*
Halotussin DM *see Dextromethorphan*
Hardhay *see Herbal drugs*
Hardware *see Inhalants*
Hash *see Marijuana*
Hash oil *see Marijuana*
Hashish *see Marijuana*
Hashish oil *see Marijuana*
Hat man *see Heroin*
Hawk *see LSD (lysergic acid diethylamide)*
HCP *see PCP (phencyclidine)*
He-man *see Fentanyl*
Head drugs *see Amphetamines*
Heart-on *see Inhalants*
Hearts *see Amphetamines*
Heaven and hell *see PCP (phencyclidine)*
Heavenly blues *see Benzodiazepine*
Herb *see Marijuana*
Herms *see PCP (phencyclidine)*
Heron *see Heroin*
Hierba Maria (the Virgin Mary's herb) *see* **Salvia divinorum**
High-tech *see Amyl nitrite*
Highball *see Inhalants*
Hillbilly heroin *see Oxycodone*
Hinkley *see PCP (phencyclidine)*
Hippie crack *see Inhalants*
Hits *see LSD (lysergic acid diethylamide)*
Hog *see PCP (phencyclidine)*
Hold DM *see Dextromethorphan*
Honey oil *see Inhalants; Ketamine*
Hooch *see Alcohol*
Hop/hops *see Opium*
Horse *see Heroin*
Horse heads *see Amphetamines*
Horse tracks *see PCP (phencyclidine)*
Horse tranquilizer *see PCP (phencyclidine)*
Huff *see Inhalants*
Hug drug *see Ecstasy*
Humibid DM *see Dextromethorphan*
Hydrochlorothiazide (HCT) *see Diuretics*
Hydroflumethiazide *see Diuretics*
Hydrostat *see Hydromorphone*
Hypericum perforatum see Antidepressants; Herbal drugs

I

Ice *see Amphetamines; Methamphetamine*
Ikwa *see Catha edulis*
Illy *see PCP (phencyclidine)*
Imipramine *see Antidepressants*

Insom-X *see GBL; GHB*
Invigorate *see GBL; GHB*
Ionamin *see Diet pills*
Iophen DM NR *see Dextromethorphan*
Ischott *see Catha edulis*
Isobutyl nitrite *see Inhalants*
Isocarboxazid Marplan *see Antidepressants*
Isosorbide *see Diuretics*
Iubulu *see Catha edulis*

J

Jackpot *see Fentanyl*
Jativa-M. *see Salvia divinorum*
Jelly baby *see Amphetamines*
Jet *see Ketamine; PCP (phencyclidine)*
Jet fuel *see PCP (phencyclidine)*
Jolt *see GBL*
Joy plant *see Opium*
Jugs *see Amphetamines*
Juice *see Alcohol; Steroids*
Junk *see Steroids*

K

K *see Ketamine; PCP (phencyclidine)*
K-blast *see PCP (phencyclidine)*
Kaad *see Catha edulis*
Kadian *see Morphine*
Kafta *see Catha edulis*
Kaps *see PCP (phencyclidine)*
Karo (codeine cough syrup) *see Codeine*
Kat *see Catha edulis*
Kef *see Marijuana*
Ket *see Ketamine*
Ketaject *see Ketamine*
Ketalar *see Ketamine*
Ketamine hydrochloride *see Ketamine*
Ketaset *see Ketamine*
Khat *see Catha edulis*
Kick *see Inhalants*
Kief *see Marijuana*
Kif *see Marijuana*
Killer *see PCP (phencyclidine)*
Killers *see Oxycodone*
King ivory *see Fentanyl*
King kong *see Heroin*
Kit-Kat *see Ketamine*
Kix *see Amyl nitrite*
Klamath weed *see Herbal drugs*
Klonopin *see Benzodiazepine*
Kools *see PCP (phencyclidine)*
Kreteks *see Nicotine*
Krystal *see PCP (phencyclidine)*
KW *see PCP (phencyclidine)*

L

L *see LSD (lysergic acid diethylamide)*

La rocha *see Rohypnol*
La salade *see Catha edulis*
LA turnarounds *see Dextroamphetamine*
Lady *see Heroin*
Lady K *see Ketamine*
Laevoamphetamine *see Amphetamines*
Laudanum *see Opium*
Laughing gas *see Nitrous oxide*
LBJ *see PCP (phencyclidine)*
Leaky bolla *see PCP (phencyclidine)*
Leaky leak *see PCP (phencyclidine)*
Lean (codeine cough syrup) *see Codeine*
Leapers *see Amphetamines*
Legal E *see Benzylpiperazine/Trifluoromethylphenyl-piperazine*
Legal steroid *see Creatine*
Legal X *see Benzylpiperazine/Trifluoromethylphenyl-piperazine*
Lemon 714 *see PCP (phencyclidine)*
Lemon fX drops *see GHB*
Lethal weapon *see PCP (phencyclidine)*
Liberty caps *see Psilocybin*
Librium *see Benzodiazepine*
Lid poppers *see Amphetamines*
Lid proppers *see Amphetamines*
Lidone *see Tranquilizers*
Lightning *see Amphetamines*
Lightning bolt *see Inhalants*
Lightning flash *see LSD (lysergic acid diethylamide)*
Liquid acid *see LSD (lysergic acid diethylamide)*
Liquid E *see GHB*
Liquid ecstasy *see GHB*
Liquid gold *see Amyl nitrite; GBL*
Liquid X *see GHB*
Liruti *see Catha edulis*
Liss *see Catha edulis*
Little d *see Hydromorphone*
Little ones *see PCP (phencyclidine)*
Live ones *see PCP (phencyclidine)*
Locker room *see Amyl nitrite*
Log *see PCP (phencyclidine)*
Longevity *see GBL; GHB*
Lorazepam *see Benzodiazepine*
Lords *see Hydromorphone*
Lotusate *see Barbiturates*
Loveboat *see PCP (phencyclidine)*
Lover's speed *see Ecstasy*
Loxapine *see Tranquilizers*
Loxitane *see Tranquilizers*
LSD25 *see LSD (lysergic acid diethylamide)*
Ludes *see Methaqualone*
Ludiomil *see Antidepressants*
Luminal *see Barbiturates*
Lunch money *see Rohypnol*

M

M *see Ecstasy; Morphine*
M-Oxy *see Oxycodone*

Ma huang *see* **Ephedra**
Mac *see* **Heroin**
Mad dog *see* **PCP (phencyclidine)**
Madman *see* **PCP (phencyclidine)**
Magic *see* **Heroin; PCP (phencyclidine)**
Magic dust *see* **PCP (phencyclidine)**
Magic mushrooms *see* **Psilocybin**
Mahuang *see* **Ephedra**
Mairongi *see* **Catha edulis**
Mandies *see* **Methaqualone**
Mandoma *see* **Catha edulis**
Mandrakes *see* **Methaqualone**
Mandrax *see* **Methaqualone**
Mannitol *see* **Diuretics**
Manteca *see* **Heroin**
Maonj *see* **Catha edulis**
MAP *see* **Amphetamines; Methamphetamine**
Maprotiline *see* **Antidepressants**
Marihuana *see* **Marijuana**
Marongi *see* **Catha edulis**
Mary Jane *see* **Marijuana**
Masbukinja *see* **Catha edulis**
Mauve *see* **PCP (phencyclidine)**
Mazanor *see* **Diet pills**
Mazindol *see* **Diet pills**
Mbugula mabwe *see* **Catha edulis**
MDMA *see* **Ecstasy**
Mean green *see* **PCP (phencyclidine)**
Mebaral *see* **Barbiturates**
Medical anesthetic gases *see* **Inhalants**
Medusa *see* **Inhalants**
Mellaril *see* **Antidepressants**
Mellaril *see* **Tranquilizers**
Melliquid *see* **Melatonin**
Mellow tonin *see* **Melatonin**
Meperidine hydrochloride *see* **Meperidine**
Mephobarbital *see* **Barbiturates**
Meprobamate *see* **Tranquilizers**
Mesc *see* **Mescaline**
Mescal *see* **Mescaline**
Mesoridazine *see* **Tranquilizers**
Metadate *see* **Methylphenidate**
Meth *see* **Methamphetamine**
Methohexital *see* **Barbiturates**
Methyclothiazide *see* **Diuretics**
Methylin *see* **Methylphenidate**
Methylmorphine *see* **Codeine**
Methyprylon *see* **Tranquilizers**
Metolazone *see* **Diuretics**
Mexican *see* **Benzodiazepine**
Mexican brown *see* **Fentanyl**
Mexican mushrooms *see* **Psilocybin**
Mexican reds *see* **Barbiturates**
Mexican Valium *see* **Rohypnol**
Mezc *see* **Mescaline**
MFT *see* **2C-B**
Mhulu *see* **Catha edulis**
Microdot *see* **LSD (lysergic acid diethylamide)**
Midnight oil *see* **Opium**

Milk *see* **PCP (phencyclidine)**
Miltown *see* **Tranquilizers**
Mind erasers *see* **Rohypnol**
Minibennies *see* **Amphetamines**
Mint leaf *see* **PCP (phencyclidine)**
Mintweed *see* **PCP (phencyclidine)**
Miraa *see* **Catha edulis**
Mirtazapine *see* **Antidepressants**
Miss Emma *see* **Morphine**
Mitsubishi double-stack *see* **PMA and PMMA**
Miungi *see* **Catha edulis**
Mlonge *see* **Catha edulis**
Moban *see* **Tranquilizers**
Mogadon *see* **Benzodiazepine**
Molindone *see* **Tranquilizers**
Monkey *see* **Heroin; Morphine**
Monkey dust *see* **PCP (phencyclidine)**
Monkey tranquilizer *see* **PCP (phencyclidine)**
Moon *see* **Mescaline**
Moon gas *see* **Inhalants**
More *see* **PCP (phencyclidine)**
Mormon tea *see* **Ephedra**
Morning shot *see* **Amphetamines**
Morph *see* **Morphine**
Morphine hydrochloride *see* **Morphine**
Morphine sulfate *see* **Morphine**
MS Contin *see* **Morphine**
Msabukinga *see* **Catha edulis**
Msekera *see* **Catha edulis**
MSIR *see* **Morphine**
Msuruti *see* **Catha edulis**
Msuvuti *see* **Catha edulis**
Mucobid DM *see* **Dextromethorphan**
Mud *see* **Heroin**
Muholo *see* **Catha edulis**
Muhulu *see* **Catha edulis**
Muirungi *see* **Catha edulis**
Mulungi *see* **Catha edulis**
Mumm dust *see* **PCP (phencyclidine)**
Muraa *see* **Catha edulis**
Murder 8 *see* **Fentanyl**
Muscle candy *see* **Creatine**
Mushies *see* **Psilocybin**
Mushrooms *see* **Psilocybin**
Musitate *see* **Catha edulis**
Mutsawari *see* **Catha edulis**
Mwandama *see* **Catha edulis**
Mzengo *see* **Catha edulis**

N

N-dimethyltryptamine *see* **Dimethyltryptamine (DMT)**
N-force *see* **GBL**
N₂O *see* **Nitrous oxide**
Naldecon DX Liquigel *see* **Dextromethorphan**
Nangungwe *see* **Catha edulis**
Nardil *see* **Antidepressants**
Natural supplements *see* **Herbal drugs**
Nature's Quaalude *see* **GHB**

Navane *see Tranquilizers*
Nefazodone *see Antidepressants*
Nembutal *see Barbiturates*
Neuroleptics *see Tranquilizers*
New acid *see PCP (phencyclidine)*
New magic *see PCP (phencyclidine)*
Nexus *see 2C-B*
Nickel *see Marijuana*
Niebla *see PCP (phencyclidine)*
Nigerine *see Dimethyltryptamine (DMT)*
Nitrazepam *see Benzodiazepine*
Nitrous *see Nitrous oxide*
Noctec *see Tranquilizers*
Norfranil *see Antidepressants*
Norpramin *see Antidepressants*
Nortriptyline *see Antidepressants*
Nose candy *see Cocaine*
Novoflupam *see Benzodiazepine*
Novopoxide *see Benzodiazepine*
Nugget *see Amphetamines*
Nutraceuticals *see Herbal drugs*

O

O *see Opium*
O.P. *see Opium*
Oby-trim *see Diet pills*
OCs *see Oxycodone*
Oil *see Marijuana*
Ol meraa *see Catha edulis*
Ol nerra *see Catha edulis*
Olanzapine *see Tranquilizers*
Old man *see Marijuana*
Ope *see Opium*
OPP *see PCP (phencyclidine)*
Oralet *see Fentanyl*
Oramorph SR *see Morphine*
Orange crystal *see PCP (phencyclidine)*
Orange fX rush *see GHB*
Oranges *see Amphetamines*
Orap *see Tranquilizers*
Organic solvents *see Inhalants*
Orlistat *see Diet pills*
Oxazepam *see Benzodiazepine*
Oxies *see Oxycodone*
Oxy *see Oxycodone*
Oxy-sleep *see GHB*
Oxycons *see Oxycodone*
OxyContin *see Oxycodone*
Oxycotton *see Oxycodone*
OxyFast *see Oxycodone*
OxyIR *see Oxycodone*
Oz *see Inhalants*
Ozone *see PCP (phencyclidine)*

P

P-dope *see Fentanyl*
P-funk *see Fentanyl*

Pakistani ephedra *see Ephedra*
Pamelor *see Antidepressants*
Panax ginseng see Herbal drugs
Paper mushrooms *see LSD (lysergic acid diethylamide)*
Paramethoxyamphetamine *see PMA and PMMA*
Paramethoxymethamphetamine *see PMA and PMMA*
Paregoric *see Opium*
Parnate *see Antidepressants*
Paroxetine *see Antidepressants*
Paxil *see Antidepressants*
Paxipam *see Benzodiazepine*
Paz *see PCP (phencyclidine)*
Peace pill *see PCP (phencyclidine)*
Peaches *see Amphetamines*
Pearls *see Inhalants*
Peep *see PCP (phencyclidine)*
Pen yan *see Opium*
Pentobarbital *see Barbiturates*
Pentothal *see Barbiturates*
Pep pills *see Amphetamines*
Percocet *see Oxycodone*
Percodan *see Oxycodone*
Percodan-Demi *see Oxycodone*
Percolone *see Oxycodone*
Percs (or perks) *see Oxycodone*
Permitil *see Tranquilizers*
Perphenazine *see Tranquilizers*
Persian white *see Fentanyl*
Pertussin CS Children's Strength *see Dextromethorphan*
Pertussin DM Extra Strength *see Dextromethorphan*
Peruvian marching powder *see Cocaine*
Peter Pan *see PCP (phencyclidine)*
Pethidine *see Meperidine*
Peyote *see Mescaline*
Phendimetrazine *see Diet pills*
Phenelzine *see Antidepressants*
Phenobarbital *see Barbiturates*
Phentermine *see Diet pills*
Phenyl cyclohexyl piperidine *see PCP (phencyclidine)*
Phytopharmaceuticals *see Herbal drugs*
Pig killer *see PCP (phencyclidine)*
Pimozide *see Tranquilizers*
Pin gon *see Opium*
Pin yen *see Opium*
Pink hearts *see Amphetamines*
Pinks *see Barbiturates*
Piperazine *see Benzylpiperazine/Trifluromethylphenylpiperazine*
Pipes *see Nicotine*
Pit *see PCP (phencyclidine)*
Pixies *see Amphetamines*
Placidyl *see Tranquilizers*
Plegine *see Diet pills*
Poison *see Fentanyl*
Polythiazide *see Diuretics*
Pondimin *see Diet pills*
Poor man's heroin *see GHB; Oxycodone*
Poor man's pot *see Inhalants*

Poppers *see Amyl nitrite*
Pot *see Marijuana*
Powder *see Cocaine*
Powder cocaine *see Cocaine*
Pox *see Opium*
Prazepam *see Benzodiazepine*
Prelu-2 *see Diet pills*
Prolixin *see Tranquilizers*
ProSom *see Benzodiazepine*
Protriptyline *see Antidepressants*
Pseudoephedrine *see Ephedra*
Psilocybe mushrooms *see Psilocybin*
Psilocydes *see Psilocybin*
Psychedelic mushrooms *see Psilocybin*
Puffy *see PCP (phencyclidine)*
Pure raine *see GBL*
Purple *see PCP (phencyclidine)*
Purple passion *see Psilocybin*
Purple rain *see PCP (phencyclidine)*

Q

Qat *see Catha edulis*
Quaaludes *see Methaqualone*
Quads *see Methaqualone*
Quat *see Catha edulis*
Quay *see Methaqualone*
Quazepam *see Benzodiazepine*
Quetiapine *see Tranquilizers*
Quick *see Ketamine*
Quicksilver *see Inhalants*
Quinethazone *see Diuretics*

R

R-2 *see Rohypnol*
Ragers *see Steroids*
Rainbows *see Barbiturates; LSD (lysergic acid diethylamide)*
Ram *see Amyl nitrite*
Rave *see Amyl nitrite*
Reactive *see GBL*
Red birds *see Barbiturates*
Red devils *see Barbiturates*
Reds *see Barbiturates*
Redux *see Diet pills*
Reefer *see Marijuana*
Refrigerant gases *see Inhalants*
Regenerize *see GBL*
Rejoov *see GBL*
Rejuv+nite *see GBL*
Remedy GH *see GBL*
Remeron *see Antidepressants*
Remforce *see GBL; GHB*
Renewtrient *see GBL*
Respa-DM *see Dextromethorphan*
Restoril *see Benzodiazepine*
Revivarant *see GBL; GHB*
Revivarant G *see GBL*

Rhoids *see Steroids*
Rhythm *see Amphetamines*
Rib *see Rohypnol*
Rippers *see Amphetamines*
Risperdal *see Tranquilizers*
Risperidone *see Tranquilizers*
Ritalin *see Methylphenidate*
Ro *see Rohypnol*
Roach *see Benzodiazepine*
Roaches *see Rohypnol*
Roachies *see Rohypnol*
Road dope *see Amphetamines*
Roapies *see Rohypnol*
Robitussin Maximum Strength Cough Suppressant *see Dextromethorphan*
Robitussin Pediatric Cough Suppressant *see Dextromethorphan*
Robo *see Dextromethorphan*
Roboing *see Dextromethorphan*
Roche *see Rohypnol*
Rock *see Cocaine*
Rocket fuel *see PCP (phencyclidine)*
Roll *see Ecstasy*
Roofies *see Rohypnol*
Rope *see Rohypnol*
Rophies *see Rohypnol*
Rophy *see Rohypnol*
Rosa *see Amphetamines*
Roses *see Amphetamines*
Roxanol *see Morphine*
Roxicet *see Oxycodone*
Roxicodone *see Oxycodone*
Roxilox *see Oxycodone*
Roxiprin *see Oxycodone*
Ruffies *see Rohypnol*
Ruffles *see Rohypnol*
Rush *see Amyl nitrite; Inhalants*
Rush snappers *see Inhalants*

S

Safe Tussin 30 *see Dextromethorphan*
Salahin *see Catha edulis*
Salty dog *see GHB*
Salty water *see GHB*
Salvia *see Salvia divinorum*
Salvinorin A *see Salvia divinorum*
Sanorex *see Diet pills*
Satan's secret *see Inhalants*
Sauce *see Alcohol*
Saw palmetto *see Herbal drugs*
Scaffle *see PCP (phencyclidine)*
Schoolboy *see Codeine*
Scooby snacks *see Ecstasy*
Scoop *see GHB*
Scot-Tussin DM *see Dextromethorphan*
Scuffle *see PCP (phencyclidine)*
Secobarbital *see Barbiturates*
Seconal *see Barbiturates*

Sedative-hypnotics *see Tranquilizers*

Semilla de la Virgen (the Virgin's seed) *see **Salvia divinorum***

Sensi *see Marijuana*

Serax *see Benzodiazepine*

Serenoa repens *see Herbal drugs*

Serentil *see Tranquilizers*

Seri *see **Catha edulis***

Sernyl *see PCP (phencyclidine)*

Sernylan *see PCP (phencyclidine)*

Seroquel *see Tranquilizers*

Sertraline *see Antidepressants*

Serzone *see Antidepressants*

714s *see Methaqualone*

Shake *see Heroin*

Shays *see Rohypnol*

Sheets *see PCP (phencyclidine)*

Shepherdess *see **Salvia divinorum***

Shermans *see PCP (phencyclidine)*

Sherms *see PCP (phencyclidine)*

Shoot the breeze *see Inhalants*

Shrooms *see Psilocybin*

Sibutramine *see Diet pills*

Sillies *see Psilocybin*

Silly putty *see Psilocybin*

Sinequan *see Antidepressants*

Sinsemilla *see Marijuana*

Ska Maria Pastora (the leaves of Mary) *see **Salvia divinorum***

Skee *see Opium*

Skittles *see Dextromethorphan*

Skunk *see Marijuana*

Slag *see Heroin*

Smack *see Heroin*

Smilies *see LSD (lysergic acid diethylamide)*

Smoke *see Marijuana*

Smoking *see PCP (phencyclidine)*

Snap *see Amphetamines*

Snappers *see Amyl nitrite*

Sniff *see Inhalants*

Snorts *see PCP (phencyclidine)*

Snotballs *see Inhalants*

Snow *see Cocaine*

Snow pallets *see Amphetamines*

Soap *see GHB*

Sodium oxybate *see GBL; GHB*

Sodium oxybutyrate *see GHB*

Soma *see PCP (phencyclidine)*

Somali tea *see **Catha edulis***

Somatomax *see GHB*

Somnol *see Benzodiazepine*

Somnos *see Tranquilizers*

Sonata *see Tranquilizers*

Sopors *see Methaqualone*

Sparkle plenty *see Amphetamines*

Sparklers *see Amphetamines*

Special K *see Ketamine*

Special LA coke *see PCP (phencyclidine)*

Spectrum *see 2C-B*

Speed *see Amphetamines; Dextroamphetamine; Methamphetamine*

Spironolactone *see Diuretics*

Spit *see Nicotine*

Spit tobacco *see Nicotine*

Spivias *see Amphetamines*

Splash *see Amphetamines*

Splivins *see Amphetamines*

Spoon *see Heroin*

Spores *see PCP (phencyclidine)*

Spray *see Inhalants*

Squeeze *see PCP (phencyclidine)*

St. John's wort *see Antidepressants; Herbal drugs*

Stardust *see Cocaine*

Stars *see LSD (lysergic acid diethylamide)*

Stelazine *see Tranquilizers*

STP *see PCP (phencyclidine)*

Stuff *see Heroin; Steroids*

Stupefi *see Rohypnol*

Stupefy *see Benzodiazepine*

Sublimaze *see Fentanyl*

Substance *see Benzylpiperazine/Trifluoromethylphenylpiperazine*

Sucol B *see GBL*

Sucrets 4-Hour Cough Suppressant *see Dextromethorphan*

Sufenta *see Fentanyl*

Sugar *see Cocaine; LSD (lysergic acid diethylamide)*

Super *see PCP (phencyclidine)*

Super acid *see Ketamine*

Super kools *see PCP (phencyclidine)*

Superacid *see PCP (phencyclidine)*

Surfer *see PCP (phencyclidine)*

Surital *see Barbiturates*

Surmontil *see Antidepressants*

Sweeties *see Amphetamines*

Sweets *see Amphetamines*

Synthetic cocaine *see PCP (phencyclidine)*

Synthetic heroin *see Fentanyl*

Synthetic THT *see PCP (phencyclidine)*

T

T *see Steroids*

T-buzz *see PCP (phencyclidine)*

T-tabs *see PCP (phencyclidine)*

T-threes *see Codeine*

T-Tusin DM *see Dextromethorphan*

Tabs *see LSD (lysergic acid diethylamide)*

Tac *see PCP (phencyclidine)*

Taking a cruise *see PCP (phencyclidine)*

Talbutal *see Barbiturates*

Tammy *see Heroin*

Tango & Cash *see Fentanyl*

Tar *see Heroin; Marijuana*

Taractan *see Tranquilizers*

TCP *see PCP (phencyclidine)*

Temazepam *see Benzodiazepine*

Tens *see Amphetamines*

Tenuate *see Diet pills*
Tenuate dospan *see Diet pills*
Tepanil *see Diet pills*
Test *see Steroids*
Testosterone *see Steroids*
Tetrahydro-2-furanone *see GBL*
Tetramethylene glycol *see GBL*
Texas shoe-shine *see Inhalants*
TFMPP *see Benzylpiperazine/Trifluromethylphenyl-piperazine*
Thiamylal *see Barbiturates*
Thiopental *see Barbiturates*
Thioridazine *see Antidepressants; Tranquilizers*
Thiothixene *see Tranquilizers*
Thorazine *see Tranquilizers*
3-(2-dimethylaminoethyl)-indole *see Dimethyl-tryptamine (DMT)*
Thrust *see Amyl nitrite; Inhalants*
Thrusters *see Amphetamines*
Thunder *see GBL*
Tic *see PCP (phencyclidine)*
Tic tac *see PCP (phencyclidine)*
Tipton weed *see Herbal drugs*
Tish *see PCP (phencyclidine)*
Titch *see PCP (phencyclidine)*
TNT *see Fentanyl; Heroin*
Tobacco *see Nicotine*
Tofranil *see Antidepressants*
Tohai *see Catha edulis*
Tohat *see Catha edulis*
Toilet water *see Inhalants*
Tolly *see Inhalants*
Toluene *see Inhalants*
Toncho *see Inhalants*
Toonies *see 2C-B*
Topi *see Mescaline*
Torsemide *see Diuretics*
Touro DM *see Dextromethorphan*
Toxy *see Opium*
Toys *see Opium*
Trank *see PCP (phencyclidine)*
Tranks *see Benzodiazepine*
Tranxene *see Benzodiazepine*
Tranylcypromine *see Antidepressants*
Trazodone *see Antidepressants*
Treat *see Heroin*
Triamterene *see Diuretics*
Triazolam *see Benzodiazepine*
Trichlormethiazide *see Diuretics*
Trifluoperazine *see Tranquilizers*
Trifluoromethylphenylpiperazine *see Benzylpiperazine/Trifluoromethylphenylpiperazine*
Trifuluopromazine *see Tranquilizers*
Trilafon *see Tranquilizers*
Trimipramine *see Antidepressants*
Tripper *see LSD (lysergic acid diethylamide)*
Trips *see LSD (lysergic acid diethylamide)*
Trocal *see Dextromethorphan*
Truck drivers *see Amphetamines*

Tsad *see Catha edulis*
Tschad *see Catha edulis*
Tschat *see Catha edulis*
Tshut *see Catha edulis*
TT2 *see PCP (phencyclidine)*
TT3 *see PCP (phencyclidine)*
TTi *see PCP (phencyclidine)*
Tuinal *see Barbiturates*
Tumayot *see Catha edulis*
Turnabout *see Amphetamines*
Tuss-DM *see Dextromethorphan*
Tussi-Organidin DM NR *see Dextromethorphan*
2(3H)-furanone dihydro *see GBL*
Tylox *see Oxycodone*

U

Uppers *see Amphetamines; Dextroamphetamine*
Uppies *see Amphetamines*
Utopia *see 2C-B*

V

Valium *see Benzodiazepine*
Valo *see Benzodiazepine*
Venlafaxine *see Antidepressants*
Venus *see 2C-B*
Verve *see GBL*
Vesprin *see Tranquilizers*
Vicks 44 Cough Relief *see Dextromethorphan*
Vita-G *see GHB*
Vitamin D *see Dextromethorphan*
Vitamin K *see Ketamine*
Vitamin R *see Methylphenidate*
Vivactil *see Antidepressants*
Vivol *see Benzodiazepine*
Volatile solvents *see Inhalants*

W

Waifo *see Catha edulis*
Wake ups *see Amphetamines*
Warfi *see Catha edulis*
Water *see GHB*
Wellbutrin *see Antidepressants*
West Coast turnarounds *see Dextroamphetamine*
Wet *see PCP (phencyclidine)*
When-shee *see Opium*
Whip-its *see Nitrous oxide*
Whippets *see Nitrous oxide*
Whippets or whippits *see Inhalants*
White horizon *see PCP (phencyclidine)*
White skull *see Heroin*
Wobble weed *see PCP (phencyclidine)*
Wolf *see PCP (phencyclidine)*
Wolfies *see GHB*
Worm *see PCP (phencyclidine)*

X

X *see Ecstasy*
X-Trozine *see Diet pills*
Xanax *see Benzodiazepine*
Xenical *see Diet pills*
XTC *see Ecstasy*
Xyrem *see GBL*

Y

Yellow jackets *see Barbiturates*

Yellow sunshines *see LSD (lysergic acid diethylamide)*

Z

Zaleplon *see Tranquilizers*
Ze *see Opium*
Zen *see LSD (lysergic acid diethylamide)*
Zip *see Methamphetamine*
Ziprasidone *see Tranquilizers*
Zoloft *see Antidepressants*
Zolpidem *see Tranquilizers*

INDEX

Page numbers in **boldface** indicate main topical essays. Page numbers in *italic* indicate illustrations.

Index

Index

W

Z

DATE DUE

April 27, 2009			

FOLLETT